Fodor's 94
Caribbean

Fodor's Travel Publications, Inc.
New York • Toronto • London • Sydney • Auckland

Fodor's Caribbean

Editor: Caroline Haberfeld
Editorial Contributors: Pamela Acheson, Suzanne DeGalan, Harriet Edleson, Nigel Fisher, Jane Hershey, Amy Hunter, Joan Iaconetti, Karl Luntta, Sue McManus, Denise Nolty, Carolyn Price, Marcy Pritchard, Laurie Senz, Jordan Simon, Heidi Waldrop, Simon Worrall
Creative Director: Fabrizio La Rocca
Cartographer: David Lindroth
Illustrator: Karl Tanner
Cover Photograph: Melanie Carr/Viesti Associates

Design: Vignelli Associates

Special Sales

Contents

Contents

Maps and Plans

Foreword

We would like to thank the Caribbean Tourism Association, all the island tourist boards, and the people at American Airlines, British West Indies Airlines, and Leeward Island Air Transport for their help and support.

While every care has been taken to assure the accuracy of the information in this guide, the passage of time will always bring change, and consequently, the publisher cannot accept responsibility for errors that may occur.

All prices and opening times quoted here are based on information supplied to us at press time. Hours and admission fees may change, however, and the prudent traveler will avoid inconvenience by calling ahead.

Fodor's wants to hear about your travel experiences, both pleasant and unpleasant. When a hotel or restaurant fails to live up to its billing, let us know and we will investigate the complaint and revise our entries where the facts warrant it.

Send your letters to the editors of Fodor's Travel Publications, 201 E. 50th Street, New York, NY 10022.

Highlights'94 and Fodor'sChoice

Highlights '94

A decade ago some Caribbean islands gave more emphasis to tourism than others. St. Maarten and the Virgin Islands actively sought tourists, while St. Lucia relied on its banana crop and Guadeloupe on sugarcane for revenue. Now, however, the scramble for tourists and the dollars that they bring is fast becoming the primary focus of all the Caribbean islands.

While the competition for tourists hasn't led to lower prices—in fact some governments have been increasing tourist taxes to pay for advertising costs—it has created more options for the traveler. New hotels open all the time, while old ones are renovated, and transportation to and from the islands is a main focus.

Interisland air transportation, as well as service to and from the Caribbean, is expanding. **American Airlines** now covers most of the islands with either direct flights from the mainland or with connecting flights through San Juan on its subsidiary, American Eagle. **ALM,** the Antillian airline is also becoming a major carrier to many of the islands, with departures from Atlanta and Miami as well as interisland flights. Improvements are underway on the departure area of the **Barbados Airport,** and the customs area of the **Las America International Airport** in the Dominican Republic has undergone changes aimed at keeping baggage and taxi hustlers at bay.

Those who cruise to the Caribbean will appreciate the new **cruise-ship terminal** in Guadaloupe's Pointe-à-Pitre, with its complex of 80 shops, three restaurants, and a hotel. Martinique also has a new **berthing facility** within a 10-minute walk to downtown Fort-de-France.

After a headlong entry into the race for tourism development, some islands are having to rethink their strategy. On **Aruba,** several hotels, including the Ramada Renaissance and Plantation Bay, remain half-built and awaiting financing. The glut of hotel and time-share properties here has inspired the government to place a five-year moratorium on hotel development. The **Cayman Islands** have followed a similar route and have an indefinite ban on hotel construction. Development of new resorts has exceeded the increase in tourism to the **Dominican Republic,** and the new competition among hotels has made the island a place for bargain holidays.

Despite the restrictions on these islands, hotel and resort development continues throughout the Caribbean. These days the trend is to create **all-inclusive properties.** In fact, some hotels that used to be on various meal plans are now changing over to the all-inclusive way of doing things. It definitely has its advantages: No fighting over where to go for dinner, no worries about how many activities you can afford, and perhaps the biggest plus, no need to carry a wallet for the entire trip. The drawbacks are that you'll probably end up seeing less of the island and sticking more to your particular resort. New all-inclusive resorts include **The Liberty Club** and the **Grenadian Hotel** in Grenada and **Couples Negril** in Jamaica. In Barbados, all-inclusive **Sandals** is replacing the former Cunard Paradise Village & Beach Club. Opening in time for the 1993–94 season, this couples-oriented resort encompasses 20 acres of landscaped terraced gardens and a half-mile of beach. Facilities will include a restaurant and bars, two freshwater pools, five tennis courts with tournament-style seating, and a fitness center. Several other resorts on Barbados have become all-inclusive, among them the **Almond Beach Club, Heywoods,** and **Rockley Resort and Beach Club.**

Puerto Rico's **El Conquistador** will be the first new resort on the island since 1970, and the only $200-million resort opening this year in the Western Hemisphere! Thirty-one miles from San Juan, in Las Croabas, the 926-room resort is perched on a cliff between the Atlantic Ocean and the Caribbean Sea. Not only will El Conquistador have two 18-hole golf courses, it will also have 16 restaurants and lounges, five swimming pools, a marina, conference facilities, and a water-sports center.

Development of other new tourist attractions is also going strong. In **Antigua** a government sponsored multimedia center has opened at Dows Hill, offering visitors a colorful overview of Antiguan history and culture. **Bonaire** is developing its ecotourism by promoting bird-watching, hiking, and biking in Washington-Slagbaai National Park. A new seafront development in **Montserrat** will include an esplanade, shops, and an arts-and-crafts center.

Golfers will be pleased to hear that construction in underway on the premier 18-hole courses for Aruba and Grand Cayman. The course in Aruba, slated to open this fall, is part of the **Tierra del Sol** recreation complex, which also includes a health club, swimming pools, and eight tennis courts. **The Links** on Grand Cayman is part of the 280-acre Safehaven development on the island's west coast. Nine holes were open at press time, with the rest of the course scheduled for completion in December.

Fodor's Choice

No two people will agree on what makes a perfect vacation, but it's fun and helpful to know what others think. We hope you'll have the chance to experience some of Fodor's Choices yourself while visiting the Caribbean. For detailed information about each entry, refer to the appropriate chapter in this guidebook.

Scenic Views

Dows Hill Interpretation Centre, Antigua

Appleton Express train ride out of Montego Bay into the Jamaica mountains

Grand Etang National Park, Grenada

El Yunque Rain Forest, Puerto Rico

Brimstone Hill, St. Kitts

The Pitons (Petit and Gros), St. Lucia

Mountain Top, St. Thomas

Beaches

Shoal Bay, Anguilla

Palm Beach, Aruba

Seven Mile Beach, Grand Cayman

Negril, Jamaica

Anse du Gouverneur, St. Barts

Magens Bay, St. Thomas, U.S. Virgin Islands

Trunk Bay, St. John, U.S. Virgin Islands

Diving/Snorkeling

Reefs around Bonaire

Virgin Gorda, British Virgin Islands

Cayman Islands (especially Sting Ray City)

Southern Coast of Curaçao

Scott's Head, Dominica

Saba's pinnacles

St. Vincent

Reefs around Speyside, Tobago

Turks and Caicos Islands' reefs

Buck Island Reef, St. Croix, U.S. Virgin Islands

Golf

Britannia Golf Course, Grand Cayman (played with a Jack Nicklaus-designed ball that goes half the normal distance)

Tryall Golf, Tennis and Beach Club, Jamaica

Four Seasons, Nevis (Robert Trent Jones II's latest masterpiece in green)

Hyatt Dorado Beach, Puerto Rico

Mount Irvine, Tobago

Mahogany Run, St. Thomas, U.S. Virgin Islands

Fishing

The waters around

Caicos Island

Little Cayman

Port Antonio, Jamaica

Puerto Rico

Turks and Caicos Islands

U.S. Virgin Islands

Parks and Gardens

Andromeda Gardens, Barbados

Washington/Slagbaai National Park, Bonaire

Christoffel Park, Curaçao

Morne Trois Pitons National Park, Dominica

Parc Naturel, Basse-Terre, Guadeloupe

Las Cabezas de San Juan Nature Reserve, Puerto Rico

National Parks Service–protected land, St. John, U.S. Virgin Islands

Shopping

Oranjestad, Aruba

Willemstad, Curaçao

George Town, Grand Cayman

St. George's, Grenada (if just for those incredible spices)

Old San Juan, Puerto Rico

Philipsburg, St. Maarten, and Marigot, St. Martin

Charlotte Amalie, St. Thomas, U.S. Virgin Islands

Casinos

The Royal Cabana, Aruba

Sonesta Beach Hotel and Casino, Curaçao

Hyatt Regency/Cerromar Beach, Puerto Rico

Nightlife and Bars

Silver's Nightclub, Ramada Treasure Island Resort, Grand Cayman

Disco at Hedonism II, Jamaica

Coco Lobo, Martinique

Condado Beach Hotel, Puerto Rico

Le Club disco, St. Maarten

Mas Camp Pub, Trinidad

Piccola Marina Cafe, St. Thomas, U.S. Virgin Islands

Hotels

Four Seasona Resort, Nevis (*Very Expensive*)

Carl Gustaf, St. Barthélemy (*Very Expensive*)

Habitation Lagrange, Martinique (*Very Expensive*)

Malliouhana, Anguilla (*Very Expensive*)

Sandy Lane Hotel and Golf Club, Barbados (*Very Expensive*)

Sappire Beach, St. Thomas, U.S. Virgin Islands (*Very Expensive*)

Secret Harbour, Grenada (*Very Expensive*)

Half Moon Club, Jamaica (*Very Expensive*)

Anse Chastanet Hotel, St. Lucia (*Expensive*)

Arnos Vale, Tobago (*Expensive*)

Crane Beach Hotel, Barbados (*Expensive*)

Gran Bahía, Dominican Republic (*Expensive*)

Siboney Beach Club, Antigua (*Expensive*)

La Belle Creole, St. Martin (*Expensive*)

Restaurants

Alizéa, St. Martin (*Very Expensive*)

Malliouhana, Anguilla (*Very Expensive*)

Ramiro's, Puerto Rico (*Very Expensive*)

Sandy Bay, Barbados (*Expensive*)

Bistro Le Clochard, Curaçao (*Expensive*)

Château de Feuilles, Guadeloupe (*Expensive*)

Chez Mathilde, Aruba (*Expensive*)

Lafayette, Martinique (*Expensive*)

Lantana's, Grand Cayman (*Expensive*)

La Perouche, Antigua (*Expensive*)

Canboulay, Grenada (*Moderate*)

Ile de France, Barbados (*Moderate*)

Mango's, Anguilla (*Moderate*)

Richard's Waterfront Dining, Bonaire (*Moderate*)

Getaways

Jumby Bay, Long Island, off Antigua

Peter Island Resort and Yacht Harbour, British Virgin Islands

Mustique, The Grenadines (where you can rent Princess Margaret's house)

Southern Cross Club and Pirate's Point Resort, Little Cayman

PSV Resort, Petit St. Vincent

The Golden Lemon, Dieppe Bay, St. Kitts

Rawlins Plantation, St. Kitts

The Caribbean

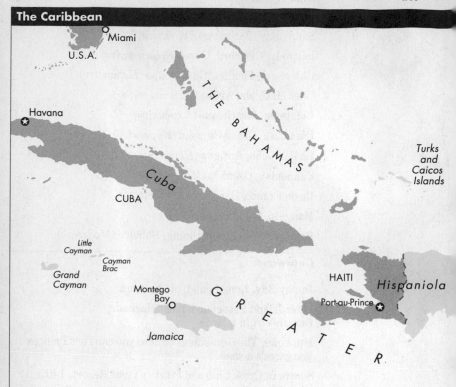

Miami

U.S.A.

THE BAHAMAS

Turks
and
Caicos
Islands

Havana

Cuba

CUBA

*Little
Cayman*

*Cayman
Brac*

*Grand
Cayman*

Montego
Bay

G R E A T E R

HAITI

Hispaniola

Port-au-Prince

Jamaica

Caribbean

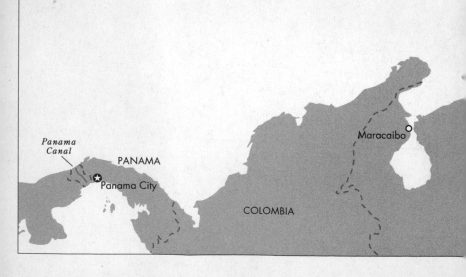

*Panama
Canal*

PANAMA

Panama City

Maracaibo

COLOMBIA

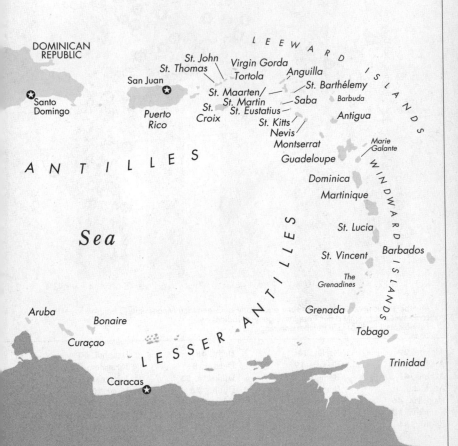

0   200 miles
0   300 km

N

ATLANTIC   OCEAN

DOMINICAN
REPUBLIC

L E E W A R D

St. John
St. Thomas   Virgin Gorda   Anguilla
San Juan   Tortola   *I S L A N D S*
                                                        St. Barthélemy
Santo   St. Maarten/
Domingo   St. Martin   Saba   *Barbuda*
                        St.   St. Eustatius
Puerto   Croix   Antigua
Rico   St. Kitts
                  Nevis
                  Montserrat   Marie
                                            Galante
A N T I L L E S   Guadeloupe

                              Dominica   *W I N D W A R D*

Sea   Martinique

                              St. Lucia

                          St. Vincent   Barbados

                              The
                          Grenadines   *I S L A N D S*

Aruba   Grenada
        Bonaire   Tobago
Curaçao   *L E S S E R   A N T I L L E S*
                                                Trinidad

Caracas

VENEZUELA

World Time Zones

International Date Line

MONDAY / SUNDAY

+12 +13   -9

-10

-11   -10

+11

+12

-4

-3

25

3

7

4   -7

5   -8   8   9   13 14 15

6   10   17 16
                  11   -3:30
                 18
        12   -4

            19   22

         -5   -4   -3

         20

                        23

      21   24   -3

+11   +12 -   -11   -10   -9   -8   -7   -6   -5   -4   -3   -2

Numbers below vertical bands relate each zone to Greenwich Mean Time (0 hrs.).
Local times frequently differ from these general indications,
as indicated by light-face numbers on map.

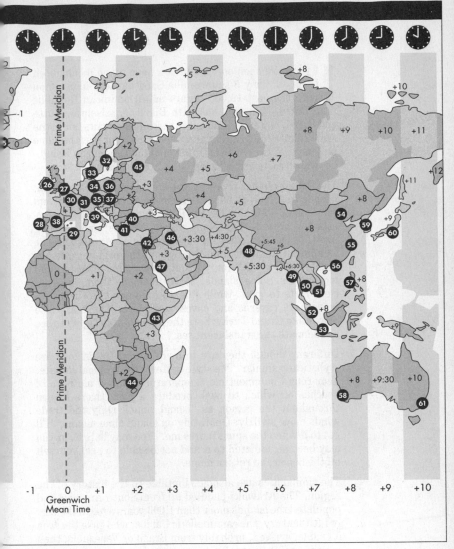

Mecca, **47**	Ottawa, **14**	San Francisco, **5**
Mexico City, **12**	Paris, **30**	Santiago, **21**
Miami, **18**	Perth, **58**	Seoul, **59**
Montréal, **15**	Reykjavík, **25**	Shanghai, **55**
Moscow, **45**	Rio de Janeiro, **23**	Singapore, **52**
Nairobi, **43**	Rome, **39**	Stockholm, **32**
New Orleans, **11**	Saigon (Ho Chi Minh	Sydney, **61**
New York City, **16**	City), **51**	Tokyo, **60**

Toronto, **13**
Vancouver, **4**
Vienna, **35**
Warsaw, **36**
Washington, D.C., **17**
Yangon, **49**
Zürich, **31**

Introduction

If you have seen one island you have by no means seen them all. Tiny 5-square-mile Saba has less in common with the vast 19,000-square-mile Dominican Republic than Butte, Montana, has with Biloxi, Mississippi. Butte and Biloxi, however different in terrain and traits, sit in the same country and the citizenry speak more or less the same language. Saba, which is Dutch, and the Dominican Republic, whose roots are in Spain, simply sit in the same sea.

The Caribbean has towering volcanic islands, such as Saba; islands with forests, such as Dominica and Guadeloupe; and some islands, notably Puerto Rico, that boast both rain forests and deserts. Glittering discos, casinos, and dazzling nightlife can be found on such islands as Aruba and the Dominican Republic, and throughout the region there are isolated cays with only sand, sea, sun, lizards, and mosquitoes. Some islands, St. Kitts among them, have ancient forts to view, while Puerto Rico and the Caicos Islands have caverns and caves to explore. There are also places like Grand Turk where the only notable sights to see are beneath the translucent sea.

Different though they are in many ways, the islands are stylistically similar. The style-setter is the tropical climate. Year-round summertime temperatures and a plethora of beaches on which to bask produce a pace that's known throughout the region as "island time." Only the trade winds move swiftly. Operating on island time means, "I'll get to it when the spirit moves me." You may hate it, or you may become addicted to it and not be able to peel yourself off the beach and return home.

The similarities are also attributable to the history of the region. The Arawaks paddled up from South America and populated the islands more than 1,000 years ago. In the early 14th century, the cannibalistic Caribs, who gave the area its name, arrived, probably from Brazil or Venezuela, then polished off the peaceful Arawaks and managed, for a time at least, to scare the living daylights out of the Europeans who sailed through in search of gold. (The original name of the Caribs was Galibi, a word the Spanish corrupted to *Canibal*—the origin of the word "cannibal.") Christopher Columbus made four voyages through the region between 1492 and 1504, christening the islands while dodging the Carib arrows. He landed on or sailed past all of the Greater Antilles and virtually all of the eastern Caribbean islands.

From the 16th century until the early 19th century, the Dutch, Danes, Swedes, English, French, Irish, and Spanish fought bitterly for control of the islands. Some islands have almost as many battle sites as sand flies. Having gained control of the islands and annihilated the Caribs, the Europeans established vast sugar plantations and brought in Africans to work the fields. With the abolition of slavery in the mid-19th century, Asians were imported as indentured laborers. Today, the Caribbean population is a rich gumbo of numerous nationalities, including Americans and Canadians who have retired to and invested in the islands.

It must be remembered that the Caribbean, like the European continent, is made up of individual countries, replete with customs, immigration officials, and, in some instances, political difficulties. Most of the islands/nations have opted for independence; others retain their ties to the mother country. They are developing nations, and many have severe economic and unemployment problems.

Virtually all of the islands depend upon tourism, which is an industry that moves on island time. Human nature being what it is, many islanders are resentful of their dependency on tourist dollars. Like as not, the person who serves you has stood in a long line, vying with other anxious applicants for the few available jobs. After serving your meals and cleaning your luxurious room, he or she returns to a tiny shack knowing full well that in less than a week you will have shelled out more than an islander makes in a month. If you encounter fewer smiling faces than you anticipated, consider chalking it up to your perceived great wealth and life of leisure.

Mother Nature has endowed most of these islands with the proverbial sun-kissed beaches, swaying palms, and year-round summer. These pleasures notwithstanding, there are some who deem it overrated. They object to encountering resentment when all they seek is a pleasant vacation for which they have paid dearly. Some feel rather keenly that they'd always like hot water—or at least *some* water—when they turn on the shower; in even the most luxurious resorts there are times when things simply don't work, and that's a fact of Caribbean life. And other visitors simply have no patience with island time.

On the other hand, there are those who travel to the Caribbean year after year. Some return to the same familiar hotel on the same familiar beach on the same familiar island, while the more adventurous try to sample as much as this smorgasbord has to offer.

Defining the Caribbean

The Caribbean Sea, an area of more than a million square miles, stretches south of Florida down to the coast of Venezuela. In the northern Caribbean are the **Greater Antilles**—the islands closest to the United States—composed of Cuba, Jamaica, Haiti, the Dominican Republic, and Puerto Rico. (Due to the political unrest in Haiti and Cuba, they are not included in this book.) The Cayman Islands lie south of Cuba. The Lesser Antilles—greater in number but smaller in size than the Greater Antilles—are divided into three groups: the Leewards and the Windwards in the eastern Caribbean, and the islands in the southern Caribbean. The eastern Caribbean islands, from the Virgin Islands in the north all the way south to Grenada, form an arc between the Atlantic Ocean and the Caribbean Sea. Islands in the Leeward chain in order of appearance are the U.S. and British Virgin Islands, Anguilla, St. Martin/St. Maarten, St. Barthélemy, Saba, St. Eustatius, St. Kitts, Nevis, Antigua, Barbuda, Montserrat, Guadeloupe, and Dominica; the Windwards are composed of Martinique, St. Lucia, St. Vincent and the Grenadines, and Grenada. Barbados is just east of this group. In the southern Caribbean, off the coast of Venezuela, Trinidad and Tobago are anchored in the east, while Aruba, Bonaire, and Curaçao (known as the ABC Islands) bathe in the western waters. The Turks and Caicos Islands, which lie in the Atlantic Ocean between Florida and the north coast of Hispaniola (Haiti and the Dominican Republic), are part of the Bahamas but are included in this book because of their proximity to and affinity with the Caribbean islands.

When to Go?

"The Season" in the Caribbean traditionally coincides with winter in North America—that is, roughly, from mid-December till mid-April. But, contrary to common North American belief, the islands are not completely deserted during the summer. That's the time when the islanders themselves and many Europeans travel in the region. While the climate varies less than 10° between summer and winter, many hotels slash prices 30% or more in the summer. And Mother Nature is at her glamorous best then, with brilliant flamboyant trees, as well as other spectacular tropical plants that bloom from summer till fall.

You will find it easier to rent a car and to make hotel and restaurant reservations in summer; easier, that is, if the facilities are open. Many hotels and restaurants close during August and September or have limited facilities; some are also closed in October. They close to renovate, to rest . . . and to wait out the season for hurricanes and tropical depressions, which are most likely to occur between June and October. Storms, such as Hurricane Gilbert in 1988 and the even nastier Hugo in 1989, can wreak great havoc.

Finding Your Own Place in the Sun

The glory of the Caribbean, aside from the guaranteed qualities of warm sun and warm sea, is that no one island is exactly like another, so that they cater to a variety of tastes. Below is a list of the Caribbean islands broken down by their specialties. Consult the Island-Finder chart on the following pages to help you choose your destination.

Luxury Resorts A wealth of posh resorts await those who seek comfort in the lap of luxury. **Anguilla,** rapidly becoming one of the Caribbean's most popular destinations, has the dazzling Malliouhana and the Moroccan-style Cap Juluca. **Antigua's** elegant Curtain Bluff has a long list of well-heeled repeat guests. Four Seasons' new resort on **Nevis** combines European elegance, state-of-the-art sports facilities, and Caribbean casualness. On **Jamaica** there's the well-established Half Moon Club, Montego Bay. On French **St. Martin,** La Samanna is a favorite hideaway of the rich and not-so-famous, and La Belle Creole is a re-creation of a Mediterranean village, replete with a village square and opulent villas. For the ultimate in luxurious privacy, the **British Virgin Islands** has the Peter Island Resort and Yacht Club on its own 1,300-acre private island. Sapore di Mare and Le Toiny on **St. Barts** draw worldly personalities to its intimate setting. And Caneel Bay resort on **St. John, U.S. Virgin Islands,** has seven beaches and takes up 170 acres adjacent to the Virgin Islands National Park.

Casinos and Nightlife You can flirt with Lady Luck until the wee small hours in the dazzling casinos of Santo Domingo, **Dominican Republic;** San Juan, **Puerto Rico; St. Maarten;** and **Curaçao. Aruba** is loaded with lively night places, and San Juan's glittering floor shows are legendary. The merengue, born in the **Dominican Republic,** is exuberantly danced everywhere on the island. Both **Guadeloupe** and **Martinique** claim to have begun the beguine, and on both islands it is danced with great gusto, although the *zouk* (all-night revelry) is now the rage.

Getting Away from It All If you're looking to back out of the fast lane, you can park at one of the secluded, Spartan mountain lodges on **Dominica,** which is one of the friendliest islands in the Caribbean. Or opt for the quiet grandeur of a renovated sugar plantation on **Nevis,** where you can feast in an elegant dining room or enjoy a barbecue on the beach. Tranquil **Anguilla,** with soft white beaches nudged by incredibly clear water, offers posh resorts as well as small, inexpensive, locally owned lodgings. From the low-key **Turks and Caicos Islands,** which lie in stunning blue-green waters, you can boat to more than a score of isolated cays where the term "low-key" sounds too fast-paced. **St. Kitts** is another peaceful green oasis, with lovely beaches and upscale, "great house" ac-

	Cost of Island	Number of rooms	Nonstop flights	Cruise ship port	U.S. dollars accepted	Historic sites	Natural beauty	Lush	Arid	Mountainous	Rain forest	Beautiful beaches	Good roads
Anguilla	$$$	863			•				•			•	
Antigua	$$$$	2752	•	•	•	•	•		•			•	
Aruba	$$	5459	•	•	•				•			•	•
Barbados	$$	6650	•	•	•	•						•	
Bonaire	$$	714	•		•							•	
British Virgin Islands	$$$	1163		•	•	•	•	•	•	•	•	•	
Cayman Islands	$$$$	2573	•	•	•				•			•	•
Curaçao	$$	2159	•	•	•	•						•	
Dominica	$	547					•	•		•	•		
Dominican Republic	$	22555	•			•		•				•	
The Grenadines	$	400					•	•		•		•	
Grenada	$$$	1118		•	•	•	•	•		•		•	
Guadelope	$$	7016		•			•	•		•		•	
Jamaica	$$$	17337		•			•	•		•		•	
Martinique	$$$	5802		•			•	•		•		•	
Montserrat	$$	233			•		•	•		•	•		
Nevis	$$$	363			•	•				•		•	
Puerto Rico	$	8500	•	•	•	•	•			•	•	•	
Saba	$	100			•					•	•		
St. Barthélemy	$$$$	1130				•				•		•	•
St. Eustatius	$	102			•	•					•		
St. Kitts	$$	705			•		•	•		•	•	•	•
St. Lucia	$$	2464	•				•	•		•	•		
St. Martin/St. Maarten	$$$	3400			•							•	•
St. Vincent	$$	700			•	•	•	•		•		•	
Trinidad	$	1300	•								•		
Tobago	$$	1000							•			•	
Turks and Caicos	$$$	1004	•		•				•			•	
U.S. Virgin Islands:													
St. Croix	$$	1000		•	•	•				•	•		
St. John	$$	500			•		•	•		•		•	
St. Thomas	$$	2419	•	•	•					•		•	•

	Public transportation	Fine dining	Local cuisine	Shopping	Music	Casinos	Nightlife	Diving and Snorkeling	Sailing	Golfing	Hiking	Ecotourism	Villa rentals	All-inclusives	Campgrounds	Luxury resorts	Secluded getaway	Good for families	Romantic hideaway	
		•	•	•	•			•								•	•		•	
		•	•	•			•	•	•	•				•		•		•		
	•	•	•	•	•	•	•	•		•				•		•		•		
	•	•			•		•			•				•		•		•		
								•	•		•	•								
	•	•	•	•	•	•	•	•	•		•	•	•	•		•	•	•		
		•		•			•	•			•			•		•		•		
	•	•	•	•		•	•	•	•		•	•				•		•		
	•							•			•	•					•			
			•			•	•			•			•				•		
	•							•	•		•	•				•	•	•	•	
		•	•			•	•			•	•		•		•	•	•		
		•	•			•	•	•		•	•		•						
	•		•		•		•	•	•		•		•	•		•		•	•	
			•				•	•			•		•						
	•	•	•					•	•		•	•	•				•	•		
		•			•			•	•	•						•			•	
	•	•	•	•		•	•	•	•		•			•		•		•		
							•				•		•				•			
		•	•	•				•					•			•			•	
							•				•					•			
		•	•	•	•	•	•	•	•	•	•			•		•	•	•	•	
	•							•		•		•		•		•	•	•	•	
	•	•	•	•			•	•		•			•	•		•		•		
	•		•					•		•	•					•	•	•	•	
	•				•												•			
							•	•		•	•	•	•			•	•		•	
			•					•		•	•					•				
	•							•				•			•			•	•	
	•	•	•	•				•					•			•				

commodations in the bargain. **St. Lucia** offers a plethora of places, from the simple to the simply elegant, for "liming" (we call it "hanging out"), the favorite local pastime. On tiny **Saba** there is little to do but tuck into a small guest house, admire the lush beauty of the island, and chat with the friendly Sabans. Nearby **St. Eustatius** is another friendly, laid-back island, as is **Montserrat. The Grenadines** offers three tiny, private-island luxury resorts: Young Island, Palm Island, and Petit St. Vincent.

Foreign Culture **Trinidad** moves with the rhythm of calypso and is the

African stomping ground of a flatout, freewheeling Carnival that rivals the pre-Lenten celebrations in Rio and New Orleans. The Trinidadians, whose African heritage has been augmented by many Asian races, have built up one of the most prosperous commercial centers in the Caribbean. Politically volatile Haiti is not included in this book, but exotic and unique Haitian artwork is prominently displayed throughout the Caribbean.

British **St. Kitts** is known as the Mother Colony of the West Indies; it was from here that British colonists were dispatched in the 17th century to settle Antigua, Barbuda, Tortola, and Montserrat. If you're a history buff, you won't want to miss Nelson's Dockyard at **Antigua's** English Harbour or the hunkering fortress of Brimstone Hill on St. Kitts. Sports fans who understand the intricacies of cricket can watch matches between **Nevis** and St. Kitts teams. And the waters around Antigua and the **British Virgin Islands** are a mecca for serious sailors. **Barbados,** with its lovely tradewinds, has cricket, horseracing at Garrison Savannah, and rugby. A British colony from 1627, the island gained independence in 1966.

Dutch **Saba, St. Eustatius, St. Maarten, Bonaire,** and **Curaçao** all fly the Dutch flag, but there the similarity ends. Saba is a tiny volcanic island known for its beauty, its friendly inhabitants, and its gingerbread-trimmed houses. Curaçao's colorful waterfront shops and restaurants are reminiscent of Amsterdam. Quiet St. Eustatius—affectionately called Statia—has well-preserved historical sites and is famed for being the first foreign nation to salute the new American flag in 1776. The main streets of Philipsburg, the capital of St. Maarten, are lined with colorful Dutch colonial buildings replete with fretwork and verandas. Bonaire is best known for its excellent scuba diving.

French **Martinique, Guadeloupe, St. Martin,** and **St. Barthélemy** (often called St. Barts or St. Barths) compose the French West Indies. The language, the currency, the cuisine (the most imaginative in the Caribbean), the culture, and the style are *très* French. St. Barts is the quietest, Martinique the liveliest, St. Martin the friendliest, and Guadeloupe the lushest. And as an extra added attraction, you can wing over from Guadeloupe to see what life is like on the nearby islands of Les Saintes, Marie Galante, and Désirade.

Spanish In the **Dominican Republic,** which occupies the eastern two-thirds of the island of Hispaniola, the language and culture are decidedly Spanish. The Colonial Zone of Santo Domingo is site of the oldest city in the Western Hemisphere, and its restored buildings reflect the 15th-century Columbus period. One also gets a sense of the past in **Puerto Rico's** Old San Juan, with its narrow cobblestone streets and filigreed iron balconies.

The Beauties of Nature **Dominica,** laced with rivers and streams, is a ruggedly beautiful island with arguably the lushest, most untamed vegetation in the Caribbean. **Puerto Rico's** luxuriant 28,000-acre El Yunque is the only rain forest in the U.S. forestry system. Little **Saba** is awash with giant vegetation, and the island's Mt. Scenery is justly named. **Guadeloupe's** 74,000-square-mile Natural Park boasts dramatic waterfalls, cool pools, and miles of hiking trails. Majestic Mt. Pelée, a not entirely dormant volcano, towers over **Martinique's** rain forest; on **St. Eustatius,** adventurers can crawl down into a jungle cradled within a volcanic crater; and on **St. Lucia** you can drive right through a volcano.

The Lure of History **Antigua's** well-preserved Nelson's Dockyard is a must for history aficionados. The ancient colonial zones of both Santo Domingo, **Dominican Republic,** and Old San Juan, **Puerto Rico,** should also be high on your "history" list. The Historical Society in **St. Eustatius** (Statia) publishes an excellent walking tour of sites to be seen. Brimstone Hill on **St. Kitts** is a well-maintained fortress with several museums full of military memorabilia. **Nevis** has many sugar mills restored as comfortable hotels. Port Royal, outside Kingston, **Jamaica,** was a pirates' stronghold until an earthquake shook things up in 1692.

Cuisine The cuisine on **Martinique** and **Guadeloupe** is a marvelous marriage of Creole cooking and classic French dishes; you'll find much of the same on the other French islands of **St. Martin** and **St. Barts.** You'll also find a fine selection of French wines in the French West Indies. **Grenada,** the spice island, has an abundance of seafood available and an incredible variety of vegetables.

Music Calypso was born in **Trinidad; Jamaica** is the home of reggae; the **Dominican Republic** gave the world the merengue; and both **Martinique** and **Guadeloupe** claim to be the cradle of the beguine. The music of **Barbados** ranges from the Crop-Over Festival (mid-July–early August) to the hottest jazz. Steel drums, limbo dancers, and jump-ups are ubiquitous in the Caribbean. Jump-up? Simple. You hear the music, jump up, and begin to dance.

Diving Jacques Cousteau named Pigeon Island, off the west coast of **Guadeloupe,** one of the 10 best dive sites in the world. The Wall off Grand Turk in the **Turks and Caicos Islands** is a sheer drop of 7,000 feet and has long been known by scuba divers. The eruption of Mt. Pelée at 8 AM on May 8, 1902, on

Martinique resulted in the sinking of several ships. **St. Eustatius** boasts an undersea "supermarket" of ships, as well as entire 18th-century warehouses, somewhat the worse for wear, below the surface of Oranjestad Bay. The waters surrounding all three of the **Cayman Islands** are acclaimed by experts, who make similar pilgrimages to **Bonaire**'s 86 spectacular sites.

Boating **Guadeloupe**'s Port de Plaisance and the marinas on Tortola in the **British Virgin Islands, St. Vincent and the Grenadines,** and St. Thomas in the U.S. **Virgin Islands** are the starting points for some of the Caribbean's finest sailing. Yachtsmen also favor the waters around **Antigua** and put in regularly at Nelson's Dockyard, which hosts a colorful regatta in late April or early May.

Golfing According to those who have played it, the course at Casa de Campo in the **Dominican Republic** is one of the best in the Caribbean. The newest contender is the challenging (and breathtaking) course at the Four Seasons Resort on **Nevis.** Golfers on St. Thomas, **U.S. Virgin Islands,** play the spectacular Mahogany Run. There are superb courses in **Puerto Rico,** including four shared by the Hyatt Dorado Beach and the Hyatt Regency Cerromar Beach. **Jamaica** has nine courses, with Tryall west of Montego Bay rated among the top.

Day Trips There are many day trips from St. Martin/St. Maarten. **Saba** is just 28 miles away; **St. Eustatius** is another 17 miles south; and **Anguilla,** the new "in" place in the Caribbean, is less than an hour's boat ride away from St. Martin/St. Maarten. **Nevis** is a mere 2 miles south of **St. Kitts,** while **Dominica** sits about halfway between **Martinique** and **Guadeloupe. Barbuda,** 30 miles from **Antigua,** is noted for hunting and diving. **Les Saintes, Désirade,** and **Marie Galante** are easily accessible from Guadeloupe. Islands like these are small enough to explore in a day, and so seductive that you'll probably insist upon returning.

Water Sports

Sunbathing

Before abandoning yourself to the pleasures of the tropics, you would be well advised to take precautions against the ravages of its equatorial sun. Be sure to use a sunscreen with a high sun-protection factor, or SPF (an SPF of under 15 offers little protection); if you're engaging in water sports, be sure the sunscreen is waterproof. At this latitude, the safest hours for sunbathing are 4–6 PM, but even during these hours it is wise to limit exposure during your first few days to short intervals of 15–20 minutes. Keep your system plied with fruit juices and water; avoid coffee, tea, and alcohol, which have a dehydrating effect.

Touring the island in an open Jeep or dangling an arm out of a car window can also expose you to sunburn, so be sure to use sunscreen. If you have permed or color-treated hair, you may wish to use a sun-protective gel to keep it from becoming brittle; if you have a bald head, apply sunscreen. While snorkeling, *always* wear a T-shirt and apply sunscreen to protect the top and backs of your thighs from "duck burn."

Swimming

Any resort you visit is likely to offer a variety of swimming experiences, depending on which side of the island you choose.

The calm, leeward Caribbean side of most islands has the safest and most popular beaches for swimming. There are no big waves, there is little undertow, and the saltwater—which buoys the swimmer or snorkeler—makes staying afloat almost effortless.

The windward, or Atlantic, side of the islands, however, is a different story: Even strong, experienced swimmers should exercise caution here. The ocean waves are tremendously powerful and can be rough to the point of being dangerous; unseen currents, strong undertows, and uneven, rocky bottoms may scuttle the novice. Some beaches post signs or flags daily to alert swimmers to the water conditions. Pay attention to them! Where there are no flags, limit your water sports to wading and sunbathing.

Swimmers on these islands must also be aware of underwater rocks, reefs, shells, and sea urchins—small, spike-covered creatures whose spines, while not fatal, can cause very painful punctures if you step on them, even through snorkel fins. Moray eels, which are harmless unless provoked, almost never leave the crevices they live in. But don't *ever* poke at one, or even point closely at them—they're lightningfast and may mistake your finger for a predator. It's possible to receive a minor cut while swimming and not feel it until you're out of the water, so make a habit of checking yourself over after leaving the beach. If you do get a small cut from a broken glass or shell, clean it immediately with soap and water.

Nike, Inc. manufactures an athletic shoe for wear in water sports. The Aqua Sock, a lightweight slip-on shoe with a waffle rubber outsole and Spandex mesh upper, offers protection from rocky beaches and underwater hazards such as coral and broken shells, and cushions the foot against the impact of windsurfing. It floats, is unaffected by salt and chlorine, and dries quickly.

How much truth is there to the old saw that you should wait an hour after eating before going for a swim? According to Mark Pitman, MD, Director of Sports Medicine at the Hospital for Joint Diseases in New York City, blood travels from the muscles to the intestines after a meal to absorb the digesting food. This leaves the muscles "cold" and more likely to cramp. It is safe to float or dogpaddle after a light lunch, but save the Olympic lap-swimming for later.

Never dive, particularly from a boat or cliff, without checking the depth of the water and the bottom conditions. And even when the Caribbean is mirror-calm, never run blindly into the water, even if the beach is familiar. Changes in the tide can turn what was a sandy bottom yesterday into a collection of broken shells today.

Few beaches or pools in the Caribbean—even those at the best hotels—are protected by lifeguards, so you and your children swim at your own risk.

Sharks More than a decade after the release of the film *Jaws*, shark phobia endures. Sharks *are* among the fish that populate Caribbean waters; they can swim in water as shallow as three feet and are attracted by the splashing of swimmers. But there are only about a dozen shark attacks reported each year worldwide, and most of these take place off the coasts of California and Florida. You are unlikely to see a shark while swimming or diving in the Caribbean, especially if you spot dolphins nearby. The dolphin is a natural enemy of the shark, and will attack its most vulnerable points—the gills and the tip of the nose—so sharks steer clear of them.

Snorkeling

Snorkeling requires no special skills, and most hotels that rent equipment have a staff member or, at the very least, a booklet offering instruction in snorkeling basics.

As with any water sport, it's never a good idea to snorkel alone, especially if you're out of shape. You don't have to be a great swimmer to snorkel, but occasionally currents come up that require stamina. The four dimensions as we know them seem altered underwater. Time seems to slow and stand still, so wear a water-resistant watch and let someone on land know when to expect you back. Your sense of direction may also fail you when you're submerged. Many a vacationer has ended up half a mile or more from shore—which isn't a disaster unless you're already tired, chilly, and it's starting to get dark.

Remember that taking souvenirs—shells, pieces of coral, interesting rocks—is forbidden. Many reefs are legally protected marine parks, where removal of living shells is prohibited because it upsets the ecology. Because it is impossible to tell a living shell from a dead one, the wisest course is simply not to remove any. Needless to say, underwater is also not the place to discard your cigarette packs, gum wrappers, or any other litter.

Good snorkel equipment isn't cheap, and you may not like the sport once you've tried it, so get some experience with rented equipment, which is always inexpensive, before investing in quality mask, fins, and snorkel. The best prices for gear, as you might imagine, are not to be found at seaside resorts.

Scuba Diving

Diving is America's fastest-growing sport. While scuba (which stands for *s*elf-*c*ontained *u*nderwater *b*reathing *ap*paratus) looks and is surprisingly simple, *phone your physician before your vacation and make sure that you have no condition that should prevent you from diving!* Possibilities include common colds and other nasal infections, which can be worsened by diving, and ear infections, which can be worsened and cause underwater vertigo as well. Asthmatics can usually dive safely but must have their doctor's okay. A full checkup is an excellent idea, especially if you're over 30. Since it can be dangerous to travel on a plane after diving, you should schedule both your diving courses and travel plans accordingly.

At depths of below 30 feet, all sorts of physiological and chemical changes take place in the body in response to an increase in water pressure, so learning to dive with a reputable instructor is a must. Nitrogen, for example, which ordinarily escapes from the body through respiration, forms bubbles in the diver's bloodstream. If the diver resurfaces at a rate of more than one foot per second, these nitrogen bubbles may accumulate; the severe joint pains caused by this process are known as "the bends." If the nitrogen bubbles travel to your heart or brain, the result can be fatal.

In addition to training you how to resurface slowly enough, a qualified instructor can teach you to read "dive tables," the charts that calculate how long you can safely stay at certain depths.

The ideal way to learn this sport is to take a resort course once you've arrived at your Caribbean destination. The course will usually consist of two to three hours of instruction on land, with time spent in a swimming pool or waist-deep water to get used to the mouthpiece and hose (known as the regulator) and the mask. A shallow 20-foot dive from a boat or beach, supervised by the instructor, follows.

Successful completion of this introductory course may prompt you to earn a certification card—often called a C-card—from one of the major accredited diving organizations: NAUI (National Association of Underwater Instructors), CMAS (Confederation Mondiale des Activités Subaquatiques, which translates into World Underwater Federation), NASE (National Association of Scuba Educators), or PADI (Professional Association of Diving Instructors). PADI offers a free list of training facilities; write

PADI for information (1251 E. Dyer Rd., #100, Santa Ana, CA 92705).

A certification course will keep you very busy and pleasantly tired for most of your vacation. If your travel plans include a great deal of sightseeing as well, you'll have little time left to relax. You may wish to complete the classroom instruction and basic skills training at your hometown YMCA, for example, then do your five required open-water dives on vacation.

Unfortunately, there are a few disreputable individuals who may try to assure you that they can teach you everything you need to know about diving even though they aren't certified instructors. DON'T BELIEVE IT! Reputable diving shops proudly display their association with the organizations mentioned above. If you have any doubt, ask to see evidence of accreditation. Legitimate instructors will happily show you their credentials and will insist on seeing *your* C-card before a dive.

Keep in mind that your presence can easily damage the delicate underwater ecology. By standing on the bottom you can break fragile coral that took centuries to grow. Many reefs are legally protected marine parks; spearfishing or taking living shells and coral is rude and destructive, and often strictly prohibited. When in doubt, remember the diver's caveat: "Take only pictures, leave only bubbles."

Snuba

Not quite ready for scuba diving? Not to worry. For those kept from diving by poor health or claustrophobia, there is snuba, a combination of snorkeling and scuba diving. The snuba system consists of an inflatable raft that supports a tank of compressed air and a 20-foot air hose for one or two persons. The raft not only warns boats of your presence, but also provides a convenient resting place when you're tired. (There is even a clear window in the raft so you can still have an underwater view while taking a break.) The rental cost is approximately $45 an hour, and it takes only about an hour to become a certified snuba user.

Caribbean snuba outlets include **Pineapple Beach Club Resort,** Antigua (tel. 809/463–2006), and **SNUBA of St. John,** U.S. Virgin Islands (tel. 809/776–6922). At press time several additional Caribbean islands were slated to get snuba equipment. Check with your travel agent or the tourism board of the island you plan to visit for availability and information.

Waterskiing

Some large hotels have their own waterskiing concessions, with special boats, equipment, and instructors. Many beaches (especially those in Barbados), however, are patrolled by private individuals who own boats and several sizes of skis; they will offer their services through a hotel or directly to vacationers, or can be hailed like taxis. Ask your hotel staff or other guests about their experiences with these entrepreneurs. Be *sure* they provide life vests and at least two people in the boat: one to drive and one to watch the skier at all times.

Windsurfing

Windsurfing is as strenuous as it is exciting, so it may not be the sport to try on your first day out, unless you're already in excellent shape. As with most water sports, it is essential to windsurf with someone else around who can watch you and go for help if necessary.

Always wear a life vest and preferably a diveskin to protect your own skin from the sun. Avoid suntan oil that could make your feet slippery and interfere with your ability to stand on the board. Nike, Inc. makes athletic shoes specifically for water sports (*see* Swimming, *above*).

Sailing

Whether you charter a yacht with crew or captain a boat yourself, the waters of the Caribbean—especially those around the Virgin Islands and the Grenadines—are excellent for sailing, and the many secluded bays and inlets provide ideal spots to drop anchor and picnic or explore. Like hotel rates, charter prices are lower during the off-season.

The Sailing School (tel. 800/447–4700), sponsored by the National Sailing Industry Association, can provide you with information about sailing schools in resort areas throughout the world.

St. Thomas, U.S. Virgin Islands, and Tortola and Virgin Gorda in the British Virgin Islands do most of the charter and marina business. In St. Thomas, contact the **Virgin Island Charter Yacht League** (tel. 809/774–3944). In Tortola, **The Moorings** (tel. 809/494–2332) and **North South Yacht Vacations** (tel. 809/494–0096). The cost of chartering a yacht varies widely, depending on the number of passengers, the season, and the length of the cruise. Contact the charter companies for exact rates.

Sailing out of St. Vincent to Grenada is also recommended, and many charters are available. From Guadeloupe, you can sail to Dominica and Antigua and anchor at the isles of Marie Galante and Les Saintes.

1 Essential Information

Before You Go

Government Tourist Offices

Each island has a U.S.–based tourist board, listed with its name and address under Important Addresses in the individual island chapters that follow; they're good sources of general information, up-to-date calendars of events, and listings of hotels, restaurants, sights, and shops. The **Caribbean Tourism Organization** (20 E. 46th St., New York, NY 10017–2452, tel. 212/682–0435) is another resource, especially for information on the islands that don't have tourist offices in the United States.

The Department of State's **Citizens Emergency Center** issues Consular Information Sheets, which cover crime, security, and health risks as well as embassy locations, entry requirements, currency regulations, and other routine matters. (Travel Warnings, which counsel travelers to avoid a country entirely, are issued in extreme cases.) For the latest travel advisories, stop in at any passport office, consulate, or embassy; call the interactive hotline (tel. 202/647–5225); or, with your PC's modem, tap into the Bureau of Consular Affairs' computer bulletin board (tel. 202/647–9225).

Tours and Packages

Should you buy your travel arrangements to the Caribbean packaged or do it yourself? There are advantages either way. Buying packaged arrangements, saves you money, particularly if you can find a program that includes exactly the features you want. You also get a pretty good idea of what your trip will cost from the outset. For most destinations, you have two options: fully escorted tours and independent packages. Since most travelers to the Caribbean visit one island and stay at one resort, there is little need for escorted tours. (Cruises fill the gap here; *see* Cruises, *below*.) There is a wide variety of independent packages for every budget and taste, whether you want golf, tennis, water sports, activities for kids, hiking, or culture, as well as a number of special-interest programs. Travel agents are your best source of recommendations. They will have the largest selection, and the cost to you is the same as buying direct. Whatever program you ultimately choose, be sure to find out exactly what is included: taxes, tips, transfers, meals, baggage handling, ground transportation, entertainment, excursions, sports or recreation (and rental equipment for any sport you plan to pursue). Ask about the level of hotel used, its location, the size of its rooms, the kind of beds, and its amenities, such as pool, room service, or programs for children, if they're important to you. One other important point: If the beach is the centerpiece of your vacation, ask exactly where your hotel is located with respect to the nearest one—the words "beach nearby" can have a disturbing number of meanings.

Find out the operator's cancellation penalties. Nearly everyone charges them, and the only way to avoid them is to buy trip-cancellation insurance (*see* Insurance, *below*). Also ask about the single supplement, a surcharge assessed to solo travelers. Some operators do not make you pay it if you agree to be matched up with a roommate of the same sex, even if one is not found by departure time. Remember that a program that has features you won't use, whether for rental sporting equipment or discounted museum admissions, may not be the most cost-wise choice for you. Note that when pricing different packages, it sometimes pays to purchase the same arrangements separately, as when a rock-bottom promotional airfare is being offered. Base your choice on what's available at your budget for the destinations you want to visit.

Independent Packages Independent packages are offered by airlines, tour operators who may also do escorted programs, and any number of other companies from large, established firms to small, new entrepreneurs.

One excellent source is **Tour-Scan, Inc.** (Box 2367, Darien, CT 06820, tel. 203/655–8019 or 800/962–2080), a one-stop travel shop that sells, direct to the public, more than 15,000 Caribbean packages, from the least to the most expensive, for all kinds of interests, most containing hotel and airfare along with transfers and various activities. Attesting that his staff checks out each resort personally, President Arthur Mehmel promises savings of "up to several hundred dollars" and says it makes the Caribbean affordable, even islands with a reputation for being pricey. The $4 you pay for the catalogue listing all the offerings is refundable if you book, which entails no fee.

Airline packages almost always include round-trip airfare, accommodations, and transfers. Contact **American Airlines Fly AAway Vacations** (tel. 800/321–2121), **Cayman Airtours** (tel. 800/247–2966), **Continental Airlines' Grand Destinations** (tel. 800/634–5555), and **Delta Dream Vacations** (tel. 800/872–7786). Independent packages are also available from **American Express Vacations** (300 Pinnacle Way, Norcross, GA 30093, tel. 800/241–1700); **Horizon Tours** (1010 Vermont Ave., NW, Suite 202, Washington, DC 20005, tel. 202/393–8390 or 800/395–0025) with over 50 different programs; **GWV International** (300 First Ave., Needham, MA 02194, tel. 617/449–5460 or 800/225–5498); and **Cavalcade Tours** (465 Smith St., Farmingdale, NY 11735, tel. 800/284–0044 from the eastern U.S. or 800/284–0077 in the West). **Club Med** (tel. 800/258–2633) has numerous all-inclusive resorts throughout the region.

Such programs come in a wide range of prices based on levels of luxury and options—in addition to hotel and airfare, sightseeing, car rental, transfers, admission to local attractions, and other extras.

Special-Interest Travel Golf, tennis, and sailing vacations are available throughout the Caribbean. In addition, many more specialized programs are available. Some require a certain amount of expertise, but most are for the average traveler with an interest and are usually hosted by experts in the subject matter. When the program is escorted, it enjoys the advantages and disadvantages of all escorted programs; because your fellow travelers are apt to be passionate or knowledgeable about the subject, they can prove as enjoyable a part of your travel experience as the destination itself. The price range is wide, but the cost is usually higher—sometimes a lot higher—than for ordinary escorted tours and packages, because of the expert guiding and special activities.

Clothing Optional **Caribbean Islands Travel Service** (7145 Deer Valley Rd., Highland, MD 20777, tel. 301/854–2110 or 800/476–5849) offers a package to a clothing-optional resort on St. Martin.

Diving **Sea Safaris** (3770 Highland Ave., Suite 102, Manhattan Beach, CA 90266 tel. 415/441–1106 or 800/326–7491) has scuba-diving packages to the Caymans, Bonaire, St. Lucia, Turks and Caicos, and Curaçao.

Environmental and Natural History Programs **Questers Worldwide Nature Tours** (257 Park Ave. S, New York, NY 10010, tel. 212/673–3120) focuses in the Caribbean on Trinidad and Tobago, exploring rain forests, beaches and swamps in the company of an experienced environmentalist. **Caribbean Islands Travel Service** (*see above*) will arrange custom nature tours for bird-watching and visits to rain forests. The **Smithsonian National Associate Program** (1100 Jefferson Dr. SW, Room 3045, Washington, DC 20560, tel. 202/357–4700) offers natural-history programs and cruises in the Caribbean. Smithsonian membership ($22 annually) is required.

Singles **Gramercy's SingleWorld** (401 Theodore Fremd Ave., Rye, NY 10580, tel. 914/967–3334 or 800/223–6490) offers separate singles-only cruise programs for those 20–33 and for those 29–49 as well as another with no age restrictions.

Tips for British Travelers

Tourist Information Contact the **Caribbean Tourism Organization** (Vigilant House, 120 Wilton Rd., London SW1V 1JZ, tel. 071/233–8382).

Passports and Visas See the Before You Go section in each island chapter for specific passport and visa requirements. Some islands require passports; others do not but may require a British Visitor's passport.

How to Apply Applications for new and renewal passports are available from main post offices as well as at the six passport offices, located in Belfast, Glasgow, Liverpool, London, Newport, and Peterborough. You may apply in person at all passport offices, or by mail to all except the London office; Londoners should mail applications to the Glasgow office (3 Northgate, 96 Milton St., Cowcaddens, Glasgow G4 0BT, tel. 041/332–0271). For your first passport, you must submit the completed form plus the original of your birth or adoption certificate; two recent, identical photographs measuring 45 millimeters by 35 millimeters; and, if you're a married or divorced woman, the original of your marriage certificate or divorce documents. The form and one of the photographs must be countersigned by a Commonwealth citizen who has known you personally for at least two years and is a minister, judge, doctor, lawyer, teacher, civil servant, member of parliament, police officer, or person of similar standing. For a renewal passport, you may submit the renewal application along with your old passport and new photos; the application and photographs must be countersigned as above only if your appearance has changed so much that you no longer look like the same person. The fee is £18 for a 32-page passport, £27 for a 48-page document. If applying by mail, send a postal order or check made out to "Passport Office," crossed "Account Payee," and with your name and address written on the back; if applying in person, you must pay cash or support the check with a bank card. Children under 16 may travel on a parent's passport when accompanying them. All passports are valid for 10 years. Allow a month for processing.

A British Visitor's Passport can include both partners of a married couple. You must apply in person at a main post office and present your uncanceled British passport (or the original of your birth or adoption certificate, an uncanceled British visitor's passport, a U.K. passport in which you were included as a child, your naturalization certificate, or your pension book or card, plus your NHS medical card, driver's license, valid check or credit card, your child-benefit book, or a recent gas, phone, or electricity bill). In addition, you need two recent, identical photographs 35 millimeters by 45 millimeters and the fee (£12, or £18 if your spouse is included on the document). A British visitor's passport is valid for one year and will be issued on the same day that you apply.

Customs Exact customs regulations vary slightly from island to island, but in general, from countries outside the EC, you may bring home duty-free 200 cigarettes, 100 cigarillos, 50 cigars or 250 grams of tobacco; 1 liter of spirits or 2 liters of fortified or sparkling wine; 2 liters of still table wine; 60 milliliters of perfume; 250 milliliters of toilet water; plus £36 worth of other goods, including gifts and souvenirs.

For further information or a copy of "A Guide for Travellers," which details standard customs procedures as well as what you may bring into the United Kingdom from abroad, contact HM Customs and Excise (New King's Beam House, 22 Upper Ground, London SE1 9PJ, tel. 071/620–1313).

Insurance Most tour operators, travel agents, and insurance agents sell specialized policies covering accident, medical expenses, personal liability, trip cancellation, and loss or theft of personal property. Some policies include coverage for delayed departure and legal expenses, winter sports, accidents, or motoring abroad. You can also purchase an annual travel-insurance policy valid for every trip you make during the year in which it's purchased (usually only trips of less than 90 days). Before you leave, make sure you will be covered if you have a preexisting medical condition or are pregnant; your insurers may not pay for routine or continuing treatment, or may require a note from your doctor certifying your fitness to travel.

For advice by phone or a free booklet, "Holiday Insurance," that sets out what to expect from a holiday-insurance policy and gives price guidelines, contact the Association of British Insurers (51 Gresham St., London EC2V 7HQ, tel. 071/600–3333; 30 Gordon St., Glasgow G1 3PU, tel. 041/226–3905; Scottish Provincial Bldg., Donegall Sq. W, Belfast BT1 6JE, tel. 0232/249176; call for other locations).

Tour Operators Packages to the Caribbean are available from **Caribbean Connection** (Concorde House, Forest St., Chester CH1 1QR, tel. 0244/341131), with a 100-page catalogue devoted to Caribbean holidays; **Caribtours** (161 Fulham Rd., London SW3 6SN, tel. 071/581–3517), another Caribbean specialist; **Kuoni Travel** (Kuoni House, Dorking, Surrey RH5 4AZ, tel. 0306/742222); and **Tradewinds Faraway Holidays** (Station House, 81/83 Fulham High St., London SW6 3JP, tel. 071/731–8000).

Airlines and **British Airways** and **British West Indian Airways** are the only
Airfares airlines with direct flights from London to the Caribbean. It is

always worth checking the small ads in *Time Out* magazine or the Sunday papers for cheaper charter flights.

Travelers with Disabilities Main information sources include the **Royal Association for Disability and Rehabilitation** (RADAR, 25 Mortimer St., London W1N 8AB, tel. 071/637–5400), which publishes travel information for the disabled in Britain, and **Mobility International** (228 Borough High St., London SE1 1JX, tel. 071/403–5688), the headquarters of an international membership organization that serves as a clearinghouse of travel information for people with disabilities.

Festivals and Seasonal Events

Regardless of when Carnival season starts on each island, it always means days and nights of continuous partying. There's a celebration going on from January through August, it's just a matter of being on the right island!

Curaçao's Carnival season, which lasts from late January to early February, is the first to hit the Caribbean; it features music, dance, and a costumed parade. **Guadaloupe's** Carnival, also in January, begins on a Sunday late in the month and continues until Lent, finishing with a parade of floats and costumes on "Mardi Gras" and a huge bash on Ash Wednesday.

February brings a flood of Carnival events including those on **Bonaire, Martinique, Puerto Rico, St. Lucia, St. Maarten,** and **Trinidad and Tobago,** all of which combine feasting, dancing, music, and parades. **Martinique,** one of the biggest and best celebrations, offers six weeks of *zouks* (all-night revelries). During Carnival on **Trinidad and Tobago,** adults and children alike are swept up in the excitement of Playing Mas'—the state of surrendering completely to the rapture of fantastic spectacle, parades, music, and dancing. For those who feel the urge, places in a genuine "mas' band" can be purchased (long in advance) for fees that vary according to the prestige of the group and the intricacy of the costumes.

Spring brings only the **Cayman Islands'** Carnival, which begins on Grand Cayman in May. In July, the season reaches **Saba** and the **Dominican Republic,** whose popular 10-day Merengue Festival features entertainment from outdoor bands and orchestras and the best cuisine from local hotel chefs. **Anguilla's** Carnival begins in early August with street dancing, calypso competitions, the Carnival Queen Coronation, and sumptuous beach barbecues. The **Turks and Caicos** islands finish the string of festivals during the last days of the month.

There are many other festivals each year around the islands that celebrate their rich local cultures. Barbados' **Holetown Festival** commemorates the first settlement of Barbados on February 17, 1627, with a week of fairs, street markets, and revelry. The Historical and Cultural Foundations organize the **St. Martin Food Festival** in May. During the **Tobago Heritage Festival** in July, each village on Trinidad and Tobago mounts a different show or festivity. Beginning in July and continuing through August, Barbados celebrates the **Crop-Over Festival,** a month-long cheer for the end of the sugarcane harvest. Calypsonians battle for the coveted Calypso Monarch award, and Bajan cooking abounds at the massive "Bridgetown Market" street fair. The **Hatillo Festival of the Masks,** held in December in Puerto Rico, is a carnival featuring folk music and dancing, as well as parades in which islanders don brightly colored masks and costumes.

Swimming, splashing, and snorkling aren't the only things going on in these gorgeous green and blue waters. Sportsmen, tourists and islanders travel throughout the Caribbean to watch the many Regattas. Grenada's **New Year Fiesta Yacht Race** in late January is highlighted by the"Around Grenada" sailing contest. Antigua's **Sailing Week** in April brings together more than 300 yachts from around the world. The British Virgin Islands' **Spring Regatta, The Curacao Regatta, The Grenada Easter Regatta,** and the U.S. Virgin Islands' **International Rolex Cup Regatta** take palce in April. Boat racing is the national sport in Anguilla, and the most important competitions take place on **Anguilla Day,** May 30. Just about every type of competition that can be held on or in water constitutes the week-long "Aqua Action" Festival held in St. Lucia at the end of June. Canoe racing, Sunfish sailing, windsurfing, sportfishing, waterskiing, and a nonmariners race are some of the main attractions. The U.S. and British Virgin Islands share the **Hook In & Hold On Boardsailing Regatta** in June and July. Grenada's annual **Carriacou Regatta,** which takes place on this island some 16 miles to the north, brings a week of racing and partying at the end of July. Martinique hosts the **Tour des Yoles Rondes** point-to-point yawl race in early August, and the annual **Sailing Regatta** in Bonaire takes place in October. The **Route du Rosé,** a transatlantic regatta of tall ships that set sail from St-Tropez in early November, is welcomed to St. Barts in December with a round of festivities.

Music lovers should also take note of several annual events. In January, St. Barthélemy is host to an international collection of soloists and musicians as part of the **Annual St. Barts Music Festival. The Barbados Caribbean Jazz Festival** in Bridgetown features performances of original compositions and traditional jazz for three days at the end of May. At the end of June, the **Aruba Jazz and Latin Music Festival** is held in Oranjestad, offering well-know entertainers performing Latin, pop, jazz, and salsa music at Mansur stadium. And the **August Reggae Sunsplash International Music Festival** is getting hotter every year, as the best, brightest, and newest of the reggae stars gather to perform in open-air concerts in MoBay on Jamaica.

When to Go

The Caribbean "season" has traditionally been a winter one, usually extending from December 15 to April 14. The winter months are the most fashionable, the most expensive, and the most popular, and most hotels are heavily booked. You have to make your reservations at least two or three months in advance for the very best places. Hotel prices are at their highest in winter; the 20%–50% drop in rates for "summer" (after April 15) is one of the chief advantages of off-season travel. Cruise prices also rise and fall with the seasons. Saving money isn't the only reason to visit the Caribbean during the off-season. Temperatures in summer are virtually the same as in winter. Some restaurants close and many hotels offer limited facilities, but reservations are easy to get, even at top establishments, and you'll have the beaches virtually to yourselves. Singles in search of partners should visit during the high season, or choose a resort with a high year-round occupancy rate.

The flamboyant flowering trees are at their height in summer, and so are most of the flowers and shrubs of the West Indies. The water is clearer for snorkeling and smoother in May, June, and July for sailing in the Virgin Islands and the Grenadines.

Climate The Caribbean climate approaches the ideal of perpetual June. Average year-round temperature for the region is 78°F–85°F. The extremes of temperature are 65°F low, 95°F high, but as everyone knows, it's the humidity, not the heat, that makes you suffer, especially when the two go hand in hand. You can count on downtown shopping areas being hot at midday any time of the year, but air-conditioning provides some respite. Stay near beaches, where water and trade winds can keep you cool, and shop early or late in the day.

High places can be cool, particularly when the Christmas winds hit Caribbean peaks (they come in late November and last through January). Since most Caribbean islands are mountainous (notable exceptions being the Caymans, Aruba, Bonaire, and Curaçao), the altitude always offers an escape from the latitude. Kingston (Jamaica), Port-of-Spain (Trinidad), and Fort-de-France (Martinique) swelter in summer; climb 1,000 feet or so and everything is fine.

Hurricanes occasionally sweep through the Caribbean, and officials on many islands are not well equipped to warn locals, much less tourists. Check the news daily and keep abreast of brewing tropical storms by reading stateside papers if you can get them. The rainy season, usually in fall, consists mostly of brief showers interspersed with sunshine. You can watch the clouds come over, feel the rain, and remain on your lounge chair for the sun to dry you off. A spell of overcast days is "unusual," as everyone will tell you.

Generally speaking, there's more planned entertainment in winter. The peak of local excitement on many islands, most notably Trinidad, St. Vincent, and the French West Indies, is Carnival. (*see* Festivals and Seasonal Events, *above*).

For More Information For current weather conditions for cities in the United States and abroad, plus the local time and helpful travel tips, call the **Weather Channel Connection** (tel. 900/WEATHER; 95¢ per minute) from a touch-tone phone.

What to Pack

Pack light because baggage carts are scarce at airports and luggage restrictions are tight.

Clothing Dress on the islands is light and casual. Bring loose-fitting clothes made of natural fabrics to see you through days of heat and high humidity. Take a coverup for the beaches, not only to protect you from the sun, but also to wear to and from your hotel room. Bathing suits and immodest attire are frowned upon off the beach on many islands. A sun hat is advisable, but you don't have to pack one, since inexpensive straw hats are available everywhere. For shopping and sightseeing, bring walking shorts, jeans, T-shirts, long-sleeve cotton shirts, slacks, and sundresses. You'll need a sweater in the many glacially air-conditioned hotels and restaurants, for protection from the trade winds, and at higher altitudes. Evenings are casual; jacket and tie are rarely required except in the fancier casinos.

Adapters, The general rule in the Caribbean is 110 and 120 volts AC, and
Converters, the outlets take the same two-prong plugs found in the United
Transformers States, but there are a number of exceptions. To be sure, check with your hotel when making reservations.

You may need an adapter plug, plus a converter, which reduces the voltage entering the appliance from 220 to 110 volts. There are converters for high-wattage appliances (such as hair dryers), low-wattage items (such as electric toothbrushes and razors), and combination models. Hotels sometimes have outlets marked "For Shavers Only" near the sink; these are 110-volt outlets for low-wattage appliances; don't use them for a high-wattage appliance. If you're traveling with a laptop computer, especially an older one, you may need a transformer—a type of converter used with electronic-circuitry products. Newer laptop computers are auto-sensing, operating equally well on 110 and 220 volts (so you need only the appropriate adapter plug). When in doubt, consult your appliance's owner's manual or the manufacturer. Or get a copy of the free brochure "Foreign Electricity is No Deep Dark Secret," published by adapter-converter manufacturer Franzus (Murtha Industrial Park, Box 142, Beacon Falls, CT 06403, tel. 203/723–6664; send a stamped, self-addressed envelope when ordering).

Miscellaneous Bring a spare pair of eyeglasses and sunglasses, and if you have a health problem that may require you to purchase a prescription drug, have your doctor write a prescription using its generic name, since nomenclature varies from island to island. Better still, take enough to last the duration of the trip: Although you can probably find what you need in the pharmacies, you may need a local doctor's prescription. You'll want an umbrella during the rainy season; leave the plastic or nylon raincoats at home, since they're extremely uncomfortable in hot, humid weather. Bring suntan lotion and film from home; they're much more expensive on the islands. You'll need insect repellent, too, especially if you plan to walk through rain forests or visit during the rainy season. Don't forget to pack a list of the addresses of offices that supply refunds for lost or stolen traveler's checks.

Luggage Free baggage allowances on an airline depend on the airline,
Regulations the route, and the class of your ticket. In general, on domestic flights and on international flights between the United States and foreign destinations, you are entitled to check two bags— neither exceeding 62 inches, or 158 centimeters (length + width + height), or weighing more than 70 pounds (32 kilograms). A third piece may be brought aboard as a carryon; its total dimensions are generally limited to less than 45 inches (114 centimeters), so it will fit easily under the seat in front of you or in the overhead compartment. There are variations, so ask in advance. The only rule, a Federal Aviation Administration safety regulation that pertains to carry-on baggage on U.S. airlines, requires only that carryons be properly stowed and allows the airline to limit allowances and tailor them to different aircraft and operational conditions. Charges for excess, oversize, or overweight pieces vary, so inquire before you pack.

If you are flying between two foreign destinations, note that baggage allowances may be determined not by the piece method but by the weight method, which generally allows 88 pounds (40 kilograms) of luggage in first class, 66 pounds (30 kilograms) in business class, and 44 pounds (20 kilograms) in economy. If your flight between two cities abroad *connects* with your transatlantic or transpacific flight, the piece method still applies.

Safeguarding Your Luggage
Before leaving home, itemize your bags' contents and their worth; this list will help you estimate the extent of your loss if your bags go astray. To minimize that risk, tag them inside and out with your name, address, and phone number. (If you use your home address, cover it so that potential thieves can't see it.) At check-in, make sure that the tag attached by baggage handlers bears the correct three-letter code for your destination. If your bags do not arrive with you, or if you detect damage, do not leave the airport until you've filed a written report with the airline.

Taking Money Abroad

Traveler's checks and all major U.S. credit cards are accepted in the Caribbean. Although large hotels, restaurants, and department stores accept credit cards readily, some smaller restaurants and shops operate on a cash-only basis. U.S. dollars are also accepted on most islands; paying in dollars may even allow you to bargain for a lower price.

Traveler's Checks
Although you will want plenty of cash when visiting small cities or rural areas, traveler's checks are usually preferable. The most widely recognized are **American Express, Barclay's, Thomas Cook,** and those issued by major commercial banks such as **Citibank** and **Bank of America.** American Express also issues **Traveler's Cheques for Two,** which can be signed and used by you or your traveling companion. Some checks are free; usually the issuing company or the bank at which you make your purchase charges 1% of the checks' face value as a fee. Be sure to buy a few checks in small denominations to cash toward the end of your trip, when you don't want to be left with more foreign currency than you can spend. Always record the numbers of checks as you spend them, and keep this list separate from the checks.

You can also buy traveler's checks in the currency of some of the islands, a good idea if the dollar is dropping in relation to the local currency. The value of some currencies changes with great frequency and very radically; some are subject to inflation, others to devaluation, while still others float with the U.S. dollar. Banks and government-approved exchange houses give the best rates; hotels will also change currency, but generally at lower rates. Remember to take the addresses of offices in the islands where you can get refunds for lost or stolen traveler's checks.

Currency Exchange
Banks and bank-operated exchange booths at airports are usually the best places to change money. Hotels, stores, and privately run exchange firms typically offer less favorable rates.

Before your trip, pay attention to how the dollar is doing vis-à-vis your destination's currency. If the dollar is losing strength, try to pay as many travel bills as possible in advance, especially the big ones. If it is getting stronger, pay for costly items overseas, and use your credit card whenever possible—you'll come out ahead, whether the exchange rate at which your purchase is calculated is the one in effect the day the vendor's bank abroad processes the charge, or the one prevailing on the day the charge company's service center processes it at home.

To avoid lines at airport currency-exchange booths, arrive in a foreign country with a small amount of the local currency already in your pocket—a so-called tip pack. **Thomas Cook Currency Services** (630 5th Ave., New York, NY 10111, tel. 212/757–6915) supplies foreign currency by mail.

Getting Money from Home

Cash Machines
Automated-teller machines (ATMs) are proliferating; many are tied to international networks such as **Cirrus** and **Plus,** both of which have expanded their service in the Caribbean. You can use your bank card at ATMs away from home to withdraw money from your checking account and get cash advances on a credit-card account (providing your card has been programmed with a personal identification number, or PIN). Check in advance on limits on withdrawals and cash advances within specified periods. Ask whether your bank-card or credit-card PIN number will need to be reprogrammed for use in the area you'll be visiting—a possibility if the number has more than four digits. Remember that finance charges apply on credit-card cash advances from ATMs as well as on those from tellers. And note that, although transaction fees for ATM withdrawals abroad will probably be higher than fees for withdrawals at home, Cirrus and Plus exchange rates tend to be good. Be sure to plan ahead: Obtain ATM locations and the names of affiliated cash-machine networks before departure. For specific foreign Cirrus locations, call 800/4–CIRRUS; for foreign Plus locations, consult the Plus directory at your local bank.

American Express Cardholder Services
The company's **Express Cash** system lets you withdraw cash and/or traveler's checks from a worldwide network of 57,000 American Express dispensers and participating bank ATMs. You must *enroll first* (call 800/CASH–NOW for a form and allow two weeks for processing). Withdrawals are charged not to your card but to a designated bank account. You can withdraw up to $1,000 per seven-day period on the basic card, more if your card is gold or platinum. There is a 2% fee (minimum $2.50, maximum $10) for each cash transaction, and a 1% fee for traveler's checks (except for the platinum card), which are available only from American Express dispensers.

At AmEx offices, cardholders can also cash personal checks for up to $1,000 in any seven-day period in United States territory (21 days abroad); of this, $200 can be in cash, more if available, with the balance paid in traveler's checks, for which all but platinum cardholders pay a 1% fee. Higher limits apply to the gold and platinum cards.

Wiring Money
You don't have to be a cardholder to send or receive an **American Express MoneyGram** for up to $10,000. To send one, go to an American Express MoneyGram agent, pay up to $1,000 with a credit card and anything over that in cash, and phone a transaction reference number to your intended recipient, who needs only present identification and the reference number to the nearest MoneyGram agent to pick up the cash. There are MoneyGram agents in more than 60 countries (call 800/543–

4080 for locations). Fees range from 5% to 10%, depending on the amount and how you pay. You can't use American Express, which is really a convenience card—only Discover, Master-Card, and Visa credit cards.

You can also use **Western Union.** To wire money, take either cash or a check to the nearest office. (Or you can order money sent by phone, using a credit card.) Money sent from the United States or Canada will be available for pickup at agent locations in the Caribbean within minutes, and fees are roughly 5%–10%. (Note that once the money is in the system it can be picked up at *any* location. You don't have to miss your train waiting for it to arrive in City A, because if there's an agent in City B, where you're headed, you can pick it up there, too.) There are approximately 20,000 agents worldwide (call 800/325–6000 for locations).

Passports and Visas

If your passport is lost or stolen abroad, report it immediately to the nearest embassy or consulate and to the local police. If you can provide the consular officer with the information contained in the passport, they will usually be able to issue you a new passport. For this reason, it is a good idea to keep a copy of the data page of your passport in a separate place, or to leave the passport number, date, and place of issuance with a relative or friend at home.

U.S. Citizens You can pick up new and renewal application forms at any of the 13 U.S. Passport Agency offices and at some post offices and courthouses. Although passports are usually mailed within two weeks of your application's receipt, it's best to allow three weeks for delivery in low season, five weeks or more from April through summer. Call the Department of State Office of Passport Services' information line (1425 K St. NW, Washington, DC 20522, tel. 202/647–0518) for details.

Canadian Citizens Application forms are available at 23 regional passport offices as well as post offices and travel agencies. Whether applying for a first or subsequent passport, you must apply in person. Children under 16 may be included on a parent's passport but must have their own passport to travel alone. Passports are valid for five years and are usually mailed within two weeks of an application's receipt. For more information in English or French, call the passport office (tel. 514/283–2152).

Customs and Duties

U.S. Customs Provided you've been out of the country for at least 48 hours and haven't already used the exemption, or any part of it, in the past 30 days, you may bring $600 worth of goods home duty-free from *most* Caribbean countries. This amount—more generous than the $400 duty-free exemption allowed on return from almost everywhere else—applies to two dozen Caribbean Basin Initiative beneficiary countries. If you're returning from the U.S. Virgin Islands, the duty-free allowance is even higher—$1,200. A flat 10% duty applies to the next $1,000 of goods; above that, the rate varies with the merchandise. These exemptions may be pooled among family members, regardless of age, so that one may bring in more if another brings in less. If the 48-hour or 30-day limits apply, your duty-free allowance drops to $25, which may *not* be pooled.

Some wrinkles to the above: If you are visiting more than one island, say the U.S. Virgins and the Dominican Republic (a beneficiary country), you may bring in a total of $1,200 duty-free, of which no more than $600 may be from the Dominican Republic. If you visit a beneficiary country and an excluded one, such as Martinique, you may bring in a total of $600 goods duty-free, of which no more than $400 may be from Martinique.

In addition, the Generalized System of Preferences, aimed at helping developing countries improve their economies through trade, exempts certain items from the same beneficiary countries from duty entirely, meaning that they do not count toward the duty-free total at all. At press time, however, the future of GSP beyond its July 4, 1994, expiration date was unknown.

Travelers 21 or older may bring back two liters of alcohol duty-free from most Caribbean countries, provided the beverage laws of the state through which they reenter the U.S. allow it. (This is again more generous than the usual limit, which is one liter.) In the case of the U.S. Virgin Islands, five liters are allowed. If you are visiting a beneficiary country and an excluded one, no more than one of the two liters allowed may be from the excluded country; if you are visiting the U.S. Virgin Islands and a beneficiary country, no more than two liters of the five allowed may be from the beneficiary country.

Regardless of age, you may bring 100 non-Cuban cigars and 200 cigarettes back to the U.S. From the U.S. Virgin Islands, 1,000 cigarettes are allowed, but only 200 of them may have been acquired elsewhere.

Gifts under $50 may be mailed duty-free to stateside friends and relatives, with a limit of one package per day per addressee (do not send alcohol or tobacco products, nor perfume valued at more than $5). These gifts do not count as part of your exemption, although if you bring them home with you, they do. Mark the package "Unsolicited Gift" and include the nature of the gift and its retail value.

The free brochure "Know Before You Go" lists all Caribbean Basin Initiative beneficiary countries, and details what you may and may not bring back to this country, rates of duty, and other pointers; to obtain it, contact the U.S. Customs Service (Box 7407, Washington, DC 20044, tel. 202/927–6724). A copy of "GSP and the Traveler" is available from the same source.

Canadian Customs Once per calendar year, when you've been out of Canada for at least seven days, you may bring in $300 worth of goods duty-free. If you've been away less than seven days but more than 48 hours, the duty-free exemption drops to $100 but can be claimed any number of times (as can a $20 duty-free exemption for absences of 24 hours or more). You cannot combine the yearly and 48-hour exemptions, use the $300 exemption only partially (to save the balance for a later trip), or pool exemptions with family members. Goods claimed under the $300 exemption may follow you by mail; those claimed under the lesser exemptions must accompany you on your return.

Alcohol and tobacco products may be included in the yearly and 48-hour exemptions but not in the 24-hour exemption. If you meet the age requirements of the province through which you reenter Canada, you may bring in, duty-free, 1.14 liters (40 imperial ounces) of wine or liquor *or* two dozen 12-ounce cans or bottles of beer or ale. If you are 16 or older, you may bring in, duty-free, 200 cigarettes, 50 cigars or cigarillos, and 400 tobacco sticks or 400 grams of manufactured tobacco. Alcohol and tobacco must accompany you on your return.

Gifts may be mailed to friends in Canada duty-free. These do not count as part of your exemption. Each gift may be worth up to $60—label the package "Unsolicited Gift—Value under $60." There are no limits on the number of gifts that may be sent per day or per addressee, but you can't mail alcohol or tobacco.

For more information, including details of duties on items that exceed your duty-free limit, ask the Revenue Canada Customs and Excise Department (Connaught Bldg., MacKenzie Ave., Ottawa, Ont., K1A OL5, tel. 613/957–0275) for a copy of the free brochure "I Declare/Je Déclare."

Traveling with Cameras, Camcorders, and Laptops

About Film and Cameras
If your camera is new or if you haven't used it for a while, shoot and develop a few rolls of film before leaving home. Pack some lens tissue and an extra battery for your built-in light meter, and invest in an inexpensive skylight filter, to both protect your lens and provide some definition in hazy shots. Store film in a cool, dry place—never in the car's glove compartment or on the shelf under the rear window.

Films above ISO 400 are more sensitive to damage from airport security X-rays than others; very high speed films, ISO 1,000 and above, are exceedingly vulnerable. To protect your film, don't put it in checked luggage; carry it with you in a plastic bag and ask for a hand inspection. Such requests are honored at U.S. airports, but may not be by the inspector abroad. Don't depend on a lead-lined bag to protect film in checked luggage—the airline may very well turn up the dosage of radiation to see what you've got in there. Airport metal detectors do not harm film, although you'll set off the alarm if you walk through one with a roll in your pocket. Call the Kodak Information Center (tel. 800/242–2424) for details.

About Camcorders
Before your trip, put new or long-unused camcorders through their paces, and practice panning and zooming. Invest in a skylight filter to protect the lens, and check the lithium battery that lights up the LCD (liquid crystal display) modes. As for the rechargeable nickel-cadmium batteries that are the camera's power source, take along an extra pair, so while you're using your camcorder you'll have one battery ready and another recharging. Most newer camcorders are equipped with the battery (which generally slides or clicks onto the camera body) and, to recharge it, with what's known as a universal or worldwide AC adapter charger (or multivoltage converter) that can be used whether the voltage is 110 or 220. All that's needed is the appropriate plug.

About Videotape
Unlike still-camera film, videotape is not damaged by X-rays. However, it may well be harmed by the magnetic field of a walk-through metal detector. Airport security personnel may want you to turn the camcorder on to prove that that's what it

Scuba divers take note: PADI recommends that you not scuba dive and fly within a 24-hour period.

Finding a Doctor   **The International Association for Medical Assistance to Travellers** (IAMAT, 417 Center St., Lewiston, NY 14092, tel. 716/754–4883; 40 Regal Rd., Guelph, Ont. N1K 1B5; 57 Voirets, 1212 Grand-Lancy, Geneva, Switzerland) publishes a worldwide directory of English-speaking physicians whose qualifications meet IAMAT standards and who have agreed to treat members for a set fee. Membership is free.

Assistance   Pretrip medical referrals, emergency evacuation or repatria-
Companies   tion, 24-hour telephone hot lines for medical consultation, dispatch of medical personnel, relay of medical records, up-front cash for emergencies, and other personal and legal assistance are among the services provided by several membership organizations specializing in medical assistance to travelers. Among them are **International SOS Assistance** (Box 11568, Philadelphia, PA 19116, tel. 215/244–1500 or 800/523–8930; Box 466, Pl. Bonaventure, Montréal, Qué., H5A 1C1, tel. 514/874–7674 or 800/363–0263), **Near Services** (450 Prairie Ave., Suite 101, Calumet City, IL 60409, tel. 708/868–6700 or 800/654–6700), and **Travel Assistance International** (1133 15th St. NW, Suite 400, Washington, DC 20005, tel. 202/331–1609 or 800/821–2828), part of Europ Assistance Worldwide Services, Inc. Because these companies will also sell you death-and-dismemberment, trip-cancellation, and other insurance coverage, there is some overlap with the travel-insurance policies discussed below, which may include the services of an assistance company among the insurance options or reimburse travelers for such services without providing them.

Insurance

Most tour operators, travel agents, and insurance agents sell specialized health-and-accident, flight, trip-cancellation, and luggage insurance as well as comprehensive policies with some or all of these features. But before you make any purchase, review your existing health and homeowner policies to find out whether they cover expenses incurred while travelling.

Health-and-Accident   Supplemental health-and-accident insurance for travelers is
Insurance   usually a part of comprehensive policies. Specific policy provisions vary, but they tend to address three general areas, beginning with reimbursement for medical expenses caused by illness or an accident during a trip. Such policies may reimburse anywhere from $1,000 to $150,000 worth of medical expenses; dental benefits may also be included. A second common feature is the personal-accident, or death-and-dismemberment, provision, which pays a lump sum to your beneficiaries if you die or to you if you lose one or both limbs or your eyesight. This is similar to the flight insurance described below, although it is not necessarily limited to accidents involving airplanes or even other "common carriers" (buses, trains, and ships) and can be in effect 24 hours a day. The lump sum awarded can range from $15,000 to $500,000. A third area generally addressed by these policies is medical assistance (referrals, evacuation, or repatriation and other services). Some policies reimburse travelers for the cost of such services; others may automatically enroll you as a member of a particular medical-assistance company.

is, so make sure the battery is charged when you get to
port. Note that while most Caribbean islands operate
National Television System Committee video st
(NTSC), like the United States and Canada, Guadelou
Martinique use a different technology known as Seca
that reason, you will not be able to view your tapes throu
local TV set or view movies bought there in your home
(Blank tapes bought in the Caribbean can be used for
camcorder taping, however—although you'll probab
they cost more in the islands and wish you'd brought a
quate supply along.)

About Laptops Security X-rays do not harm hard-disk or floppy-disk st
Most airlines allow you to use your laptop aloft but reque
you turn it off during takeoff and landing so as not to int
with navigation equipment. Make sure the battery is cl
when you arrive at the airport, because you may be as
turn on the computer at security checkpoints to prove th
what it appears to be. If you're a heavy computer user, co
traveling with a backup battery. For international trave
ister your laptop with U.S. Customs as you leave the co
providing it's manufactured abroad (U.S.-origin items
be registered at U.S. Customs); when you do so, you'll
certificate, good for as long as you own the item, cont
your name and address, a description of the laptop, and it
al number, that will quash any questions that may arise o
return. If your laptop is U.S.-made, call the consulate
country you'll be visiting to find out whether it should be
tered with customs in that country upon arrival. Some t
ers do this as a matter of course and ask customs officers to
a document that specifies the total configuration of the sys
computer and peripherals, and its value. In addition, b
leaving home, find out about repair facilities at your des
tion, and don't forget any transformer or adapter plug you
need (*see* What to Pack, *above*).

Staying Healthy

Few real hazards threaten the health of a visitor to the Ca
bean. The small lizards that seem to have overrun the islar
are harmless, and poisonous snakes are hard to find, althou
you should exercise caution while bird-watching in Trinida
The worst problem may well be a tiny sand fly known as the "r
see'um," which tends to appear after a rain, near wet o
swampy ground, and around sunset. If you feel particularly
vulnerable to insect bites, bring along a good repellent.

The worst problem tends to be sunburn or sunstroke. Even
people who are not normally bothered by strong sun should
head into this area with a long-sleeve shirt, a hat, and long
pants or a beach wrap. These are essential for a day on a boat
but are also advisable for midday at the beach and whenever
you go out sightseeing. Also carry some sun-block lotion for
nose, ears, and other sensitive areas such as eyelids, ankles,
etc. Limit your sun time for the first few days until you become
used to the heat. And be sure to drink enough liquids.

Since health standards vary from island to island, inquire on local conditions before you go. No special shots are required for
most destinations; where they are, we have made note of it.

Flight Insurance This insurance, often bought as a last-minute impulse at the airport, pays a lump sum to a beneficiary when a plane crashes and the insured dies (and sometimes to a surviving passenger who loses eyesight or a limb); thus it supplements the airlines' own coverage as described in the limits-of-liability paragraphs on your ticket (up to $75,000 on international flights, $20,000 on domestic ones—and that is generally subject to litigation). Charging an airline ticket to a major credit card often automatically signs you up for flight insurance; in this case, the coverage may also embrace travel by bus, train, and ship.

Baggage Insurance In the event of loss, damage, or theft on international flights, airlines limit their liability to $20 per kilogram for checked baggage (roughly about $640 per 70-pound bag) and $400 per passenger for unchecked baggage. On domestic flights, the ceiling is $1,250 per passenger. Excess-valuation insurance can be bought directly from the airline at check-in but leaves your bags vulnerable on the ground.

Trip Insurance There are two sides to this coin. **Trip-cancellation-and-interruption insurance** protects you in the event you are unable to undertake or finish your trip. **Default** or **bankruptcy insurance** protects you against a supplier's failure to deliver. Consider the former if your airline ticket, cruise, or package tour does not allow changes or cancellations. The amount of coverage to buy should equal the cost of your trip should you, a traveling companion, or a family member get sick, forcing you to stay home, plus the nondiscounted one-way airline ticket you would need to buy if you had to return home early. Read the fine print carefully; pay attention to sections defining "family member" and "preexisting medical conditions." A characteristic quirk of default policies is that they often do not cover default by travel agencies or default by a tour operator, airline, or cruise line if you bought your tour and the coverage directly from the firm in question. To reduce your need for default insurance, give preference to tours packaged by members of the United States Tour Operators Association (USTOA), which maintains a fund to reimburse clients in the event of member defaults. Even better, pay for travel arrangements with a major credit card, so you can refuse to pay the bill if services have not been rendered—and let the card company fight your battles.

Comprehensive Policies Companies supplying comprehensive policies with some or all of the above features include **Access America, Inc.**, underwritten by BCS Insurance Company (Box 11188, Richmond, VA 23230, tel. 800/284–8300); **Carefree Travel Insurance,** underwritten by The Hartford (Box 310, 120 Mineola Blvd., Mineola, NY 11501, tel. 516/294–0220 or 800/323–3149); **Tele-Trip** (Mutual of Omaha Plaza, Box 31762, Omaha, NE 68131, tel. 800/228–9792), a subsidiary of Mutual of Omaha; **The Travelers Companies** (1 Tower Sq., Hartford, CT 06183, tel. 203/277–0111 or 800/243–3174); **Travel Guard International,** underwritten by Transamerica Occidental Life Companies (1145 Clark St., Stevens Point, WI 54481, tel. 715/345–0505 or 800/782–5151); and **Wallach and Company, Inc.** (107 W. Federal St., Box 480, Middleburg, VA 22117, tel. 703/687–3166 or 800/237–6615), underwritten by Lloyds, London. These companies may also offer the above types of insurance separately.

Student and Youth Travel

The Caribbean is not as far out of a student's budget as you might expect. All but the toniest islands such as St. Barthélemy have fine camping facilities, inexpensive guest houses, or small no-frills hotels. You're most likely to meet students from other countries in the French and Dutch West Indies, where many go on holiday or sabbatical. Puerto Rico, Jamaica, Grenada, and Dominica, among others, have large resident international student populations at their universities.

Travel Agencies The foremost U.S. student travel agency is **Council Travel,** a subsidiary of the nonprofit Council on International Educational Exchange. It specializes in low-cost travel arrangements, is the exclusive U.S. agent for several discount cards, and, with its sister CIEE subsidiary, **Council Charter,** is a source of airfare bargains. The Council Charter brochure and CIEE's twice-yearly *Student Travels* magazine, which details its programs, are available at the Council Travel office at CIEE headquarters (205 E. 42nd Street, New York, NY 10017, tel. 212/661–1450) and at 37 branches in college towns nationwide (free in person, $1 by mail). The **Educational Travel Center** (ETC, 438 N. Francis St., Madison, WI 53703, tel. 608/256–5551) also offers low-cost rail passes, domestic and international airline tickets (mostly for flights departing from Chicago), and other budgetwise travel arrangements. Other travel agencies catering to students include **Travel Management International** (TMI, 18 Prescott St., Suite 4, Cambridge, MA 02138, tel. 617/661–8187) and **Travel Cuts** (187 College St., Toronto, Ont. M5T 1P7, tel. 416/979–2406).

Discount Cards For discounts on transportation and on museum and attractions admissions, buy the **International Student Identity Card** (ISIC) if you're a bona fide student, or the **International Youth Card** (IYC) if you're under 26. In the United States, the ISIC and IYC cards cost $15 each and include basic travel accident and sickness coverage. Apply to **CIEE** (*see* address *above*, tel. 212/661–1414; the application is in *Student Travels*). In Canada, the cards are available for $15 each from **Travel Cuts** (*see above*). In the United Kingdom, they cost £5 and £4, respectively, at student unions and student travel companies, including Council Travel's London office (28A Poland St., London W1V 3DB, tel. 071/437–7767).

Traveling with Children

The Caribbean islands and their resorts are increasingly sensitive to the needs of families. Children's programs are part of all major new developments. Baby food is easy to find, but outside major hotels you may not find such items as high chairs and cribs. Another thing to consider is whether or not English is spoken widely; the language barrier can be frustrating for children.

Getting There All children, including infants, must have a passport for foreign travel.

Airfares What you will pay for your children's tickets depends on your starting and ending points. In some cases, the fare for infants under 2 not occupying a seat is 10% of the accompanying adult's fare, and children ages 2–11 pay half to two-thirds of the adult fare. In other instances, children under 2 not occupying a seat travel free, and older children currently travel on the "lowest applicable" adult fare, as on flights within the United States. Other routes have still other rules, so check ahead.

Safety Seats The FAA recommends the use of safety seats aloft and details approved models in the free leaflet **"Child/Infant Safety Seats Recommended for Use in Aircraft"** (available from the Federal Aviation Administration, APA–200, 800 Independence Ave. SW, Washington, DC 20591, tel. 202/267–3479). Airline policy varies. U.S. carriers must allow FAA-approved models, but because these seats are strapped into a regular passenger seat, they may require that parents buy a ticket even for an infant under 2 who would otherwise ride free. Foreign carriers may not allow infant seats, may charge the child's rather than the infant's fare for their use, or may require you to hold your baby during takeoff and landing, thus defeating the seat's purpose.

Facilities Aloft Airlines do provide other facilities and services for children, such as children's meals and freestanding bassinets (to those sitting in seats on the bulkhead, where there's enough legroom to accommodate them). Make your request when reserving. The annual February/March issue of *Family Travel Times* gives details of the children's services of dozens of airlines (*see below*). "Kids and Teens in Flight" (free from the U.S. Department of Transportation, tel. 202/366–2220) offers tips for children flying alone.

Tour Operators **GrandTravel** (6900 Wisconsin Ave., Suite 706, Chevy Chase, MD 20815, tel. 301/986–0790 or 800/247–7651) offers international and domestic tours for grandparents traveling with their grandchildren. The catalogue, as charmingly written and illustrated as a children's book, positively invites armchair traveling with lap-sitters aboard. **Rascals in Paradise** (650 5th St., Suite 505, San Francisco, CA 94107, tel. 415/978–9800 or 800/872–7225) specializes in programs for families.

Accommodations Children are welcome except in the most exclusive resorts; *Hotels* many hotels allow children under 12 or 16 to stay free in their parents' room (be sure to find out the cut-off age when booking). In addition, several hotel chains have developed children's programs that free parents to explore or relax, and many hotels and resorts arrange for baby-sitting. The following brief list is representative of the kinds of services and activities offered by some of the major chains and resorts.

In **Aruba, Aruba Sonesta Hotel, Beach Club & Casino** (tel. 800/766–3782) operates a complimentary "Just Us Kids" program for children ages 5–12. The daily, year-round program features field trips to local Aruban attractions, sports and games, arts-and-crafts classes, and special bonfire nights. Baby-sitting services are also offered.

In **Puerto Rico,** the **Hyatt Regency Cerromar Beach** and the **Hyatt Dorado Beach** operate a camp (tel. 800/233–1234) for children ages 5–12 all summer, at Christmastime, and at Easter. One of the camp's main attractions is a meandering, free-form freshwater pool with waterfalls, bridges, and a 187-foot water slide. The camp's staff includes bilingual college-age counselors. The cost at both hotels is $25 per child per day. The **El San Juan** (tel. 800/468–2818) in Puerto Rico has a program for children in the same age group that features swimnastics, treasure hunts, beach walks, exercise classes, tennis, and an always-open games room.

SuperClubs Boscobel Beach (tel. 800/858–8009) in **Jamaica** is an all-inclusive resort that specializes in families. Seven-night packages are in the $1,000-per-person range, and two children under 14 are allowed to stay free if they occupy the same room as their parents. A small army of SuperNannies is on hand to take charge. The activities are scheduled in half-hour periods so children can drop in and out. For younger children there are morning "Mousercises," a petting zoo, shell hunts, and crafts classes; for teens, "Coke-tail" parties at a disco and "No-Talent" shows.

Casa de Campo (tel. 800/223–6620) in the **Dominican Republic** has a summer and holiday camp that children can attend on a day-by-day basis. The program includes lessons in sailing, tennis, golf, painting, and pottery as well as donkey polo and softball and soccer games. "Campers" are divided into two groups: ages 7–10 and 11–13.

On **St. Thomas** in the U.S. Virgin Islands the **Stouffer Grand Beach Resort** (tel. 800/233–4935) has half-day and full-day programs for children ages 3–12. In addition to supervising volleyball matches, arts-and-crafts classes, water games, and iguana hunts, the staff arranges outings to the Coral World Marine Life Park and Observatory.

Club Med (tel. 800/CLUB–MED) has Mini Club programs for children as well as a regular roster of activities at resorts in the **Dominican Republic** and **St. Lucia.** Designed for children ages 2–11 and scheduled from 9 AM to 9 PM, the fully supervised Mini Club activities include tennis, waterskiing, sailing, scuba experience in a pool, costume parties, painting and pottery classes, and circus workshops.

Four Seasons (tel. 800/332–3442) on **Nevis** has a complete program for children age 2 and above, with story-telling, crafts, and supervised beach sports.

Villa Rentals   Villa rentals are abundant, often economical, and great for families; island tourist boards can usually refer you to the appropriate realtors. When you book these, be sure to ask about the availability of baby-sitters, housekeepers, and medical facilities. (*See* Staying in the Caribbean, *below.*)

Publications   **Family Travel Times,** published 10 times a year by Travel With
Newsletter   Your Children (TWYCH, 45 W. 18th St., 7th Floor Tower, New York, NY 10011, tel. 212/206–0688; annual subscription $55), covers destinations, types of vacations, and modes of travel; an airline issue comes out every other year (the last one, February/March 1993, is sold to nonsubscribers for $10). On Wednesday, the staff answers subscribers' questions on specific destinations.

Books   *Great Vacations with Your Kids,* by Dorothy Jordan and Marjorie Cohen ($13; Penguin USA, 120 Woodbine St., Bergenfield, NJ 07621, tel. 800/253–6476), and *Traveling with Children—And Enjoying It,* by Arlene K. Butler ($11.95 plus $3 shipping per book; Globe Pequot Press, Box 833, Old Saybrook, CT 06475, tel. 800/243–0495 or 800/962–0973 in CT), both helps you plan your trip with children, from toddlers to teens. Also from Globe Pequot is *Recommended Family Resorts in the United States, Canada, and the Caribbean,* by Jane Wilford with Janet Tice ($12.95), which describes 100 resorts

at length and includes a "Children's World" section describing
activities and facilities as part of each entry.

Hints for Travelers with Disabilities

The Caribbean has not progressed as far as other areas of the
world in terms of accommodating travelers with disabilities,
and very few attractions and sights are equipped with ramps,
elevators, or wheelchair-accessible rest rooms. However, major new properties are beginning to do their planning with the
needs of travelers with mobility problems and hearing and visual impairments in mind. Wherever possible in our lodging listings, we indicate if special facilities are available.

Accommodations A number of cruise ships, such as the *QE II* and the Norwegian
Cruise Line's *Seaward*, have recently adapted some of their
cabins to meet the needs of passengers with disabilities. To
make sure that a given establishment provides adequate access, ask about specific facilities when making a reservation or
consider booking through a travel agent who specializes in
travel for the disabled (*see below*).

Divi Hotels (tel. 800/367–3484), which has six properties in the
Caribbean, runs one of the best dive programs for the disabled
at its resort in **Bonaire**. The facility is equipped with ramps;
guest rooms and bathrooms can accommodate wheelchairs; and
the staff is specially trained to assist divers with disabilities.

Travel Agencies **Tomorrow's Level of Care** (TLC, Box 470299, Brooklyn, NY
and Tour Operators 11247, tel. 718/756–0794 or 800/932–2012) was started by two
Barbadian nurses who develop unique vacation programs tai-
lored to travelers with mobility problems and their families.
They can arrange everything from accommodations to entire
packages.**Directions Unlimited** (720 N. Bedford Rd., Bedford
Hills, NY 10507, tel. 914/241–1700), a travel agency, has expertise in tours and cruises for the disabled; **Evergreen Travel Service** (4114 198th St. SW, Suite 13, Lynnwood, WA 98036, tel.
206/776–1184 or 800/435–2288), which operates Wings on
Wheels Tours for those in wheelchairs, White Cane Tours for
the blind, and tours for the deaf and makes group and independent arrangements for travelers with any disability. **Flying
Wheels Travel** (143 W. Bridge St., Box 382, Owatonna, MN
55060, tel. 800/535–6790 or 800/722–9351 in MN), a tour operator and travel agency, arranges international tours, cruises,
and independent travel itineraries for people with mobility disabilities. **Nautilus,** at the same address as TIDE (*see below*),
packages tours for the disabled internationally.

Information Several organizations provide travel information for people
Sources with disabilities, usually for a membership fee, and some pub-
lish newsletters and bulletins. Among them are the **Information Center for Individuals with Disabilities** (Fort Point Pl., 27-
43 Wormwood St., Boston, MA 02210, tel. 617/727–5540 or 800/
462–5015 in MA between 11 and 4, or leave message; TDD/TTY
tel. 617/345–9743); **Mobility International USA** (Box 3551,
Eugene, OR 97403, voice and TDD tel. 503/343–1284), the U.S.
branch of an international organization based in Britain and
present in 30 countries. **MossRehab Hospital Travel Information Service** (1200 W. Tabor Rd., Philadelphia, PA 19141, tel.
215/456–9603, TDD tel. 215/456–9602);The **Society for the Ad-
vancement of Travel for the Handicapped** (SATH, 347 5th Ave.,
Suite 610, New York, NY 10016, tel. 212/447–7284, fax 212/

725–8253); the **Travel Industry and Disabled Exchange** (TIDE, 5435 Donna Ave., Tarzana, CA 91356, tel. 818/368–5648); and **Travelin' Talk** (Box 3534, Clarksville, TN 37043, tel. 615/552–6670).

Publications In addition to the fact sheets, newsletters, and books mentioned above are several free publications available from the Consumer Information Center (Pueblo, CO 81009): "New Horizons for the Air Traveler with a Disability," a U.S. Department of Transportation booklet describing changes resulting from the 1986 Air Carrier Access Act and those still to come from the 1990 Americans with Disabilities Act (include Department 608Y in the address), and the Airport Operators Council's *Access Travel: Airports* (Dept. 5804), which describes facilities and services for the disabled at more than 500 airports worldwide.

Twin Peaks Press (Box 129, Vancouver, WA 98666, tel. 206/694–2462 or 800/637–2256) publishes the *Directory of Travel Agencies for the Disabled* ($19.95), listing more than 370 agencies worldwide; *Travel for the Disabled* ($19.95), listing some 500 access guides and accessible places worldwide; the *Directory of Accessible Van Rentals* ($9.95) for campers and RV travelers worldwide; and *Wheelchair Vagabond* ($14.95), a collection of personal travel tips. Add $2 per book for shipping.

Hints for Older Travelers

Special facilities, rates, and package deals for older travelers are rare. When planning your trip, be sure to inquire about everything from senior-citizen discounts to available medical facilities. Focus on your vacation needs: Are you interested in sightseeing, activities, golf, ecotourism, the beach? Accessibility is an important consideration. When booking, inquire whether you can easily get to the things that you enjoy. The more remote islands have fewer options and amenities.

Organizations The **American Association of Retired Persons** (AARP, 601 E St. NW, Washington, DC 20049, tel. 202/434–2277) provides independent travelers the Purchase Privilege Program, which offers discounts on hotels, car rentals, and sightseeing. AARP also arranges group tours, cruises, and apartment living through AARP Travel Experience from American Express (400 Pinnacle Way, Suite 450, Norcross, GA 30071, tel. 800/927–0111); these can be booked through travel agents, except for the cruises, which must be booked directly (tel. 800/745–4567). AARP membership is open to those 50 and over; annual dues are $8 per person or couple.

Two other membership organizations offer discounts on lodgings, car rentals, and other travel products, along with such nontravel perks as magazines and newsletters. The **National Council of Senior Citizens** (1331 F St. NW, Washington, DC 20004, tel. 202/347–8800) is a nonprofit advocacy group with some 5,000 local clubs across the United States; membership costs $12 per person or couple annually. **Mature Outlook** (6001 N. Clark St., Chicago, IL 60660, tel. 800/336–6330), a Sears Roebuck & Co. subsidiary with 800,000 members, charges $9.95 for an annual membership.

Note: When using any senior-citizen identification card for reduced hotel rates, mention it when booking, not when checking out. At restaurants, show your card before you're seated; discounts may be limited to certain menus, days, or hours. If you are renting a car, ask about promotional rates that might improve on your senior-citizen discount.

Educational Travel **Elderhostel** (75 Federal St., 3rd floor, Boston, MA 02110, tel. 617/426–7788) is a nonprofit organization that has inexpensive study programs for people 60 and older. Programs take place at more than 1,800 educational institutions in the United States, Canada, and 45 countries overseas, and courses cover everything from marine science to Greek myths and cowboy poetry. Participants generally attend lectures in the morning and spend the afternoon sightseeing or on field trips; they live in dorms on the host campuses. Unique home-stay programs are offered in a few countries. Fees for the two- to three-week international trips—including room, board, tuition, and transportation from the United States—range from $1,800 to $4,500.

Tour Operators **Saga International Holidays** (222 Berkeley St., Boston, MA 02116, tel. 800/343–0273), which specializes in group travel for people over 60, offers a selection of variously priced tours and cruises covering five continents. If you want to take your grandchildren, look into GrandTravel (*see* Traveling with Children, *above*).

Further Reading

Caribbean Style (Crown Publishers) is a coffee-table book with magnificent photographs of the interiors and exteriors of homes and buildings in the Caribbean. The collection runs the gamut from splendid plantations to ramshackle shanties.

Don't Stop the Carnival, by Herman Wouk, is a hilarious novel about a New York press agent who left his old life behind and bought a resort hotel in the Caribbean. The novel is slightly dated, but the vicissitudes of the hero are acknowledged by everyone who has ever tried to run a hotel in the islands. It is a marvelous romp through the region.

Short stories—some dark, some full of laughs—about life in the southern Caribbean made *Easy in the Islands* by Bob Schacochis a National Book Award winner. Schacochis's ear for local patois and eye for the absurd make this book required reading.

If you want to familiarize yourself with the sights, smells, and sounds of the West Indies, pick up Jamaica Kincaid's *Annie John*, a richly textured, coming-of-age novel about a girl growing up on the island of Antigua. *At The Bottom Of The River*, also by Kincaid, is a collection of short stories that depicts the mysteries and manners of a world replete with merengue music, bay rum, and blooming red hibiscus in the dreams and reminiscences of a young adult.

Omeros is Nobel Prize–winning Trinidadian poet Derek Walcott's imaginative Caribbean retelling of the *Odyssey*.

Michelle Cliff is the author of *The Land of Look Behind*, and, most recently, *No Telephone to Heaven*, a structurally daring, often violent novel set in Jamaica—a landscape of wild bamboo and jasmine, populated by refugees moving through the outskirts of Kingston.

Anthony C. Winkler's novels, *The Great Yacht Race*, *The Lunatic*, and *The Painted Canoe*, provide scathingly witty glimpses into Jamaica's class structure.

Another notable chronicle of Caribbean life and customs is the provocative *Wide Sargasso Sea*, by Jean Rhys. Published in 1968, the novel has an imaginative construction that still entices the reader into a world of exotic, haunting beauty that Rhys herself encountered growing up on the Windward Islands of the West Indies.

James Michener's islands saga, titled *Caribbean*, was published in 1989. Michener headquartered himself in Coral Gables, Florida, to facilitate his 10 extensive research expeditions through the Caribbean region, and he has publicly expressed both the dramatic assets and liabilities inherent in a culture so rich in diversity.

If you're interested in probing this very issue more deeply, head for V. S. Naipaul. *Guerrillas*, *The Loss of El Dorado*, and *The Enigma of Arrival* all examine the multicultural origins of Caribbean society, and the complexities of colonization, enslavement, and economic dispossession.

Staying in the Caribbean

Dining

For the longest time, cuisine in the Caribbean was thought to be the weakest part of many an island vacation. In recent years, however, island visitors have come to realize that most of what they had been eating and complaining about was not Caribbean at all—just poorly prepared Continental fare garnished with a papaya slice or banana leaf.

The cuisine of the islands is difficult to pin down because of the region's history as a colonial battleground and ethnic melting pot. The gracefully sauced French presentations of Martinique, for example, are far removed from the hearty Spanish casseroles of Puerto Rico, and even further removed from the pungent curries of Trinidad.

The one quality that best defines Caribbean-style cooking has to be its essential spiciness. While reminiscent of Tex-Mex and Cajun, Caribbean cuisine is more varied and more subtle than its love of peppers implies. There is also the seafood that is unique to and abundant in the region. Caribbean lobster, closer in comparison to crawfish than to Maine lobster, have no claws and tend to be much tougher than the New England variety.

Another local favorite is conch, biologically quite close to land-loving escargots. Conch chowder, conch fritters, conch salad, conch cocktail—no island menu would be complete without at least a half-dozen conch dishes.

For many vacationers, much of the Caribbean experience has to do with the consumption of frothy blended fruit drinks, whose main and potent ingredient is Caribbean rum. Whether you are staying in a superdeluxe resort or a small, locally operated guest house, you will find that rum flows as freely as water.

After each restaurant review, we have indicated only whe reservations are necessary or suggested. Since dining is usu ly casual throughout the region, we have mentioned attire only when formal attire is needed.

Lodging

Plan ahead and reserve a room well before you travel to the Caribbean. If you have reservations but expect to arrive later than 5 or 6 PM, advise the hotel, inn, or guest house in advance. Unless so advised, some places will not hold your reservations after 6 PM. Also, be sure to find out what the rate quoted includes— use of sports facilities and equipment, airport transfers, and the like—and whether it operates on the European Plan (EP, with no meals), Continental Plan (CP, with Continental breakfast), Breakfast Plan (BP, with full not breakfast), Modified American Plan (MAP, with two meals), or Full American Plan (FAP, with three meals), or is All-inclusive (with three meals, all facilities, and drinks unless otherwise noted). At the end of each renew, we have used the meal plans that the hotel offers. Not all plans are offered all-year round. Be sure to bring your deposit receipt with you in case any questions arise when you arrive at your hotel.

A Full American Plan may be ideal for travelers on a budget who don't want to worry about additional expenses; but travelers who enjoy a different dining experience each night will prefer to book rooms on a European Plan. Since many hotels insist on a Modified American Plan, particularly during the high season, find out whether you can exchange dinners for lunch.

Decide whether you want a hotel on the leeward side of the island (with calm water, good for snorkeling) or the windward (with waves, for good surfing). Decide, too, whether you want to pay the extra price for a room overlooking the ocean or pool. Also find out how close the property is to a beach; at some hotels you can walk barefoot from your room onto the sand; others are across a road or a 10-minute drive away.

Nighttime entertainment is alfresco in the Caribbean, so if you go to sleep early or are a light sleeper, ask for a room that doesn't overlook the dance floor.

Air-conditioning is not a necessity on all islands, most of which are cooled by trade winds; but an air conditioner can be a plus if you enjoy an afternoon snooze. Breezes are stronger in second-floor rooms, particularly corner rooms, which enjoy cross ventilation. If you like to sleep without air-conditioning, make sure that windows are openable and equipped with screens.

Given the vast differences in standards and accommodations in the various islands covered in this book, it would be impossible (and misleading) to establish uniform categories such as deluxe, first class, and so forth. Instead, we have used categories to indicate price rather than quality. Prices are intended as a guideline only. The larger resort hotels with the greater number of facilities will, naturally, be more expensive, but the Caribbean is full of smaller places that make up in charm, individuality, and price for what they lack in activities—and the activity is generally available on a pay-per-use basis everywhere.

Apartment and Villa Rentals If you want a home base that's roomy enough for a family and comes with cooking facilities, a furnished rental may be the solution. It's generally cost-wise, too, although not always— some rentals are luxury properties (economical only when your party is large). Home-exchange directories do list rentals—often second homes owned by prospective house swappers—and there are services that can not only look for a house or apartment for you (even a castle if that's your fancy) but also handle the paperwork. Some send an illustrated catalogue and others send photographs of specific properties, sometimes at a charge; up-front registration fees may apply.

Among the companies with properties in the Caribbean are **At Home Abroad** (405 E. 56th St., Suite 6H, New York, NY 10022, tel. 212/421–9165); **Interhome Inc.** (124 Little Falls Rd., Fairfield, NJ 07004, tel. 201/882–6864), active in Europe almost exclusively, with a few U.S. properties; **Overseas Connection** (31 N. Harbor Dr., Sag Harbor, NY 11963, tel. 516/725–9308); **Rent a Home International** (7200 34th Ave. NW, Seattle, WA 98117, tel. 206/789–9377 or 800/488–7368); **Vacation Home Rentals Worldwide** (235 Kensington Ave., Norwood, NJ 07648, tel. 201/767–9393 or 800/633–3284); **Villa Leisure** (Box 209, Westport, CT 06881, tel. 407/624–9000 or 800/526–4244), which specializes in the Caribbean; **Villas and Apartments Abroad** (420 Madison Ave., Suite 1105, New York, NY 10017, tel. 212/759–1025 or 800/433–3020); and **Villas International** (605 Market St., Suite 510, San Francisco, CA 94105, tel. 415/281–0910 or 800/221–2260). **Hideaways International** (15 Goldsmith St., Box 1270, Littleton, MA 01460, tel. 508/486–8955 or 800/843–4433), with properties in the Caribbean, functions as a travel club. Membership ($79 yearly per person or family at the same address) includes two annual guides plus quarterly newsletters; rentals are arranged directly between members, not by the club staff.

Home Exchange This is obviously an inexpensive solution to the lodging problem, because house-swapping means living rent-free. You find a house, apartment, or other vacation property to exchange for your own by becoming a member of a home-exchange organization, which then sends you its annual directories listing available exchanges and includes your own listing in at least one of them. Arrangements for the actual exchange are made by the two parties to it, not by the organization. Principal clearinghouses include **Intervac U.S./International Home Exchange** (Box 590504, San Francisco, CA 94159, tel. 415/435–3497), the oldest, with thousands of foreign and domestic homes for exchange in its three annual directories; membership is $62, or $72 if you want to receive the directories but remain unlisted. The **Vacation Exchange Club** (Box 650, Key West, FL 33041, tel. 800/638–3841), also with thousands of foreign and domestic listings, publishes four annual directories plus updates; the $50 membership includes your listing in one book. **Loan-a-Home** (2 Park La., Apt. 6E, Mount Vernon, NY 10552, tel. 914/664–7640) specializes in long-term exchanges; there is no charge to list your home, but the directories cost $35 or $45 depending on the number you receive.

Credit Cards

The following credit card abbreviations have been used: AE, American Express; D, Discover Card; DC, Diners Club; MC, MasterCard; V, Visa. It's a good idea to call ahead to check current credit card policies.

Cruises

Cruising the Caribbean is perhaps the most relaxed and convenient way to tour this beautiful part of the world. A cruise offers all the benefits of island-hopping without the inconvenience. For example, a cruise passenger packs and unpacks only once and is not bound by flight schedules, tour-bus schedules, and "nonschedules" of fellow travelers.

Cruise ships usually call at several Caribbean ports on a single voyage. Thus, a cruise passenger experiences and savors the mix of nationalities and cultures of the Caribbean, as well as the variety of sightseeing opportunities, the geographic and topographic characteristics, and the ambience of each of the islands. A cruise passenger tries out each island on his or her cruise itinerary and has the opportunity to select favorites for in-depth discovery on a later visit.

As a vacation, a cruise offers total peace of mind. All important decisions are made long before boarding the ship. The itinerary is set in advance, and the costs are known ahead of time and are all-inclusive, with no additional charge for meals, accommodations, entertainment, or recreational activities. (Only tips, shore excursions, and shopping are extra.) A cruise ship is a floating Caribbean resort. For details beyond the basics, given below, see *Fodor's Cruises and Ports of Call 1994.*

Fly-and-Cruise

Several cruise lines offer attractive fly-and-cruise options, which give passengers the option of flying first to a warm-weather port like Aruba or San Juan and boarding the ship there. The airfare is built into the rate, so the cost of the total package is usually higher than the cost of cruise-only packages that cover comparable distances at sea. In most cases, however, the airfare for air/cruise packages is lower than round-trip airfare to the ship's pier.

When to Go

Cruise ships sail the Caribbean year-round—the waters are almost always calm, and the prevailing breezes keep temperatures fairly steady. Tropical storms are most likely September through November, but modern navigational equipment warns ships well in advance of impending foul weather, and, when necessary, cruise lines vary their itineraries to avoid storms.

Cruises are in high demand—and therefore also higher priced—during the standard vacation times in midsummer to early fall and around Easter. Some very good bargains are usually available during the immediate post-vacation periods such as fall to mid-December, early spring, and the first few weeks after the Christmas and New Year's holidays. Christmas sailings are usually quite full and are priced at a premium.

Choosing a Cabin

Write to the cruise line or ask your travel agent for a ship's plan. This elaborate layout, with cabins numbered, will show you all facilities available on all decks (usually, the higher the deck, the higher the prices). Outside cabins have dramatic portholes or picture-windows that contribute to the romance of cruising, and, though usually sealed shut, most provide expansive sea views. Some windows overlook a public promenade, probably less desirable. Inside cabins are less expensive, but check the plan—you don't want to be over the kitchen, near the engine room, or next to the elevators. Then check on the facilities offered. Those prone to motion sickness would do best in a cabin at midship, on one of the middle decks. The higher you go, the more motion you'll experience.

Tipping

Although some ships have no-tipping policies, tipping is a major expense on most Caribbean ships. The ship's service personnel depend on tips for their livelihood, and you may feel extreme pressure to help them out. There is no hard-and-fast rule about who gets what, but if you think of services rendered on board as you would at resort hotels, bars, and restaurants, you'll come close. It is customary to tip the cabin steward, the dining-room waiter, the maître d', the wine steward, and the bartender. Gratuities are usually given the night before the voyage ends.

Shore Excursions

Tour options, which typically cost $20–$140 per port, are heavily promoted during shore-excursion talks a day or two prior to reaching your post. Better deals are often had by choosing a tour offered by one of the local vendors or renting a car yourself. However, it's always riskier to explore on your own than to leave your one day at port in the hands of the cruise line (*see* Guided Tours and Getting Around sections of the individual island chapters).

Cruise Lines

To find out which ships are sailing where and when they depart, contact the **Caribbean Tourism Organization** (20 E. 46th St., 4th floor, New York, NY 10017, tel. 212/682–0435). The CTO carries up-to-date information about cruise lines that sail to its member nations. Full-service and cruise-only travel agencies are also a good source; they stock brochures and catalogues issued by most of the major lines and have the latest information about prices, departure dates, and itineraries. The **Cruise Lines International Association** (CLIA) publishes a useful pamphlet entitled "Cruising Answers to Your Questions"; to order a copy send a self-addressed business-size envelope with 52¢ postage to CLIA (500 5th Ave., Suite 1407, New York, NY 10110).

The following chart gives the names and ports of call of a sampling of cruise ships that sail in the Caribbean. A complete list of cruise lines that operate in the Caribbean appears below.

American Canadian Caribbean Line (Box 368, Warren, RI 02885, tel. 401/247–0955 in Rhode Island or 800/556–7450).
Carnival Cruise Lines (3655 N.W. 87th Ave., Miami, FL 33178, tel. 800/327–9501).
Celebrity Cruises (5200 Blue Lagoon Dr., Miami, FL 33126, tel. 800/437–3111).

Clipper Cruise Line (7711 Bonhomme Ave., St. Louis, MO 63105, tel. 800/325–0010).

Club Med (40 W. 57th St., New York, NY 10019, tel. 800/ CLUB–MED).

Commodore Cruise Line (800 Douglas Rd., Suite 700, Coral Gables, FL 33134, tel. 800/237–5361).

Costa Cruises (World Trade Center, 80 S.W. 8th St., Miami, FL 33130, tel. 800/462–6782).

Crown Cruise Line (Box 3000, 2790 N. Federal Hwy., Boca Raton, FL 33431, tel. 800/841–7447).

Crystal Cruises (2121 Ave. of the Stars, Los Angeles, CA 90067, tel. 800/446–6645).

Cunard (555 5th Ave., New York, NY 10017, tel. 800/221–4770).

Dolphin/Majesty Cruise Lines (901 South American Way, Miami, FL 33132, tel. 800/222–1003).

Fantasy Cruise Lines (5200 Blue Lagoon Dr., Miami, FL 33126, tel. 800/437–3111).

Holland America Line (300 Elliott Ave. W, Seattle, WA 98119, tel. 800/426–0327).

Norwegian Cruise Line (95 Merrick Way, Coral Gables, FL 33134, tel. 305/447–9660 or 800/327–7030).

Ocean Cruises (1510 S.E. 17th St., Fort Lauderdale, FL 33316, tel. 800/556–8850).

Premier Cruise Lines (Box 517, Cape Canaveral, FL 32920, tel. 800/327–7113).

Princess Cruises (10100 Santa Monica Blvd., Los Angeles, CA 90067, tel. 310/553–1770).

Regency Cruises (260 Madison Ave., New York, NY 10016, tel. 212/972–4499 or 800/388–5500).

Renaissance Cruises (1800 Eller Dr., Suite 300, Box 350307, Fort Lauderdale, FL 33335, tel. 800/525–2450).

Royal Caribbean Cruise Line (1050 Caribbean Way, Miami, FL 33132, tel. 800/327–6700).

Royal Cruise Line (1 Maritime Plaza, San Francisco, CA 94111, tel. 415/956–7200).

Royal Viking Line (Kloster Cruise Limited, 95 Merrick Way, Coral Gables, FL 33134, tel. 800/422–8000).

Seabourn Cruise Line (55 Francisco St., San Francisco, CA 94133, tel. 800/351–9595).

Seawind Cruise Line (1750 Coral Way, Miami, FL 33145, tel. 800/258–8006).

Sun Line Cruises (1 Rockefeller Plaza, Suite 315, New York, NY 10020, tel. 800/872–6400).

Windstar Cruises (300 Elliott Ave. W, Seattle, WA 98119, tel. 800/258–7245).

Caribbean Cruises

Class/Ship	Number of passengers	Length (days)	Alternate lengths (segments) available	Departs from	Anguilla	Antigua	Aruba	Barbados	Bonaire	BVI	Cayman Islands
CELEBRITY CRUISES											
Horizon and Zenith	1374	7		San Juan		●		●		●	
Meridian	1006	7	6, 10, 11	NY, San Juan			●	●	●		
COMMODORE CRUISE LINE											
Caribe I	875	7		Miami						●	
COSTA CRUISES											
CostaAllegra	800	7		San Juan				●			
CostaClassica–Romantica	1300	7		Miami		●				●	●
CUNARD LINE											
Countess	791	7	14	San Juan		●		●	●		
Cunard Crown Dynasty	800	7	7	Ft. Lauderdale							●
Queen Elizabeth II	1800	5	15	New York			●				
Sagafjord	618	14		Ft. Lauderdale	●	●	●			●	
Vistafjord	749	11	14	Ft. Lauderdale	●	●	●			●	
DIAMOND CRUISES											
Radison Diamond	354	7		San Juan						●	
FANTASY CRUISES											
Amerikanis	617	7		San Juan		●		●			
HOLLAND AMERICA LINE											
Nieuw Amsterdam	1214	7		Tampa							●
Noordam	1214	10		Ft. Laud., N. Orleans			●				●
Rotterdam	1114	10		Ft. Lauderdale			●				●
Westerdam	1500	7		Ft. Lauderdale						●	●
NORWEGIAN CRUISE LINE											
Dreamward	800	7		NY/Ft. Lauderdale							●
Norway	2044	7		Miami							
Seaward	1798	7		Miami							●
Windward	800	7		San Juan		●	●	●			
PRINCESS CRUISES											
Crown Princess	1562	7		Ft. Lauderdale				●			●
Regal Princess	1590	7		Ft. Lauderdale				●		●	●
Royal Princess	1200	7	10	Ft. Laud., San Juan							●
Star Princess	1470	7	10	San Juan				●			
REGENCY CRUISES											
Regent Sea	729	7		Tampa							●
ROYAL CARIBBEAN CRUISE LINE											
Maj.–Sov. of the Seas	2278	7		Miami							●
Monarch of the Seas	2354	7		San Juan		●		●			
Nordic Prince	1012	7	8, 10	NY, Miami, San Juan							
Song of America	1402	7		San Juan							

Curaçao	Dominica	Dominican Rep.	Grenada	Guadeloupe	Jamaica	Martinique	Montserrat	Nevis	Puerto Rico	Saba	St. Barthelemy	St. Eustatius	St. Kitts	St. Lucia	St. Martin	St. Vincent & the Grenadines	Trinidad/Tobago	Turks & Caicos	USVI	Bahamas	Bermuda	Mexico
					●	●			●					●					●	●	●	●
			●		●	●			●					●	●				●			
		●			●				●										●	●		
		●												●	●				●			
					●				●					●	●							●
			●	●		●							●	●	●				●			
	●			●					●										●	●		●
						●								●					●			
●			●	●		●					●			●					●			●
●			●	●	●	●		●					●	●	●				●			●
									●													●
●			●	●					●					●	●				●			
					●														●			●
					●				●										●	●		●
					●																	●
●					●														●	●		●
					●				●										●	●	●	
					●				●						●				●	●		
					●				●												●	●
●						●			●						●				●			
					●	●					●				●				●	●		●
					●	●			●						●				●	●		●
●			●			●			●						●				●			●
						●			●						●	●			●	●		●
					●																	●
					●				●										●	●		●
						●									●				●			
	●			●					●				●		●			●	●		●	
●																			●			

2 Anguilla

Updated by
Jordan Simon

At first glance, Anguilla's (pronounced an-GWIL-lah) charms may be difficult to detect. It is not a particularly pretty island. There are no lush rain forests or majestic mountains. The highest point on the island rises a dizzying 213 feet above sea level. It's a dry limestone isle with a thin covering of soil over the rock and has neither streams nor rivers, only saline ponds used for salt production. And there isn't a whole lot to do here. You won't find glittering casinos, dance-till-dawn discos, knock-your-socks-off nightclubs, world-famous historic sites, or duty-free shops stuffed with irresistible buys. Nevertheless, this long, skinny, eel-shape island just 20 minutes from the bustle of St. Martin-St. Maarten's resorts and casinos has debuted and become a very popular, and so far unspoiled, princess at the Caribbean ball.

Anguilla's beauty is apt to be found in its 30 beaches surrounded by crystal-clear waters and coral reefs. Peace, quiet, and pampering account for the island's growing popularity among travelers searching for a Caribbean getaway. You can swim, do some diving, practice your backhand, catch up on your reading, compare the relative merits of the beaches, or just find one that suits you and sink down on it to worship the sun. Times are slowly changing, however, and there are now six traffic lights on the island instead of the solitary traffic signal five years ago.

This is the most northerly of the Leeward Islands, lying between the Caribbean Sea and the Atlantic Ocean. Stretching from northeast to southwest, it's about 16 miles long and only 3 miles across at its widest point. The keen eye of Christopher Columbus seems not to have spotted this island. *Anguilla* means "eel" in Italian, but the Spanish *anguila* or French *anguille* (both of which also mean "eel") may have been the original name. New archaeological evidence shows that the island was inhabited as many as 2,000 years ago by Indians who named the island Malliouhana, a more mellifluous title that's been adopted by some of the island's shops and resorts.

In 1631, the Dutch built a fort here and maintained it for several years, but no one has been able to locate it today. English settlers from St. Kitts colonized the island in 1650. And, despite a brief period of independence with St. Kitts-Nevis in the 1960s, Anguilla has remained a British colony ever since the 17th century.

There were the obligatory Caribbean battles between the English and the French, and in 1688 the island was attacked by a party of "wild Irishmen," some of whom settled on the island. But Anguilla's primary discontent was over its status vis-à-vis the other British colonies, particularly St. Kitts. In the 18th century, Anguilla, as part of the Leeward Islands, was administered by British officials in Antigua. In 1816, Britain split the Leeward Islands into two groups, one of them composed of Anguilla, St. Kitts, Nevis, and the British Virgin Islands and administered by a magistrate in St. Kitts. For more than 150 years thereafter various island units and federations were formed and disbanded, with Anguilla all the while simmering over its subordinate status and enforced union with St. Kitts. Anguillans twice petitioned for direct rule from Britain, and twice were ignored. In 1967, when St. Kitts, Nevis, and Anguilla became an Associated State, the mouse roared, kicked St. Kitts policemen off the island, held a self-rule referendum,

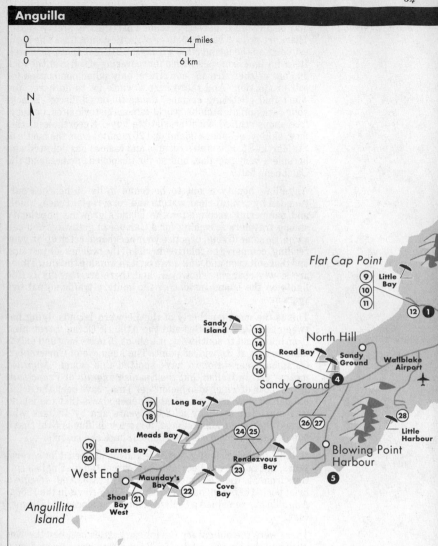

Anguilla

0 ——————— 4 miles
0 ——————— 6 km

N

Flat Cap Point

Little Bay — 9 10 11 12 1

Sandy Island — 13 14 15 16
Road Bay
North Hill
Sandy Ground
Wallblake Airport
Sandy Ground — 4

Long Bay — 17 18

Meads Bay

26 27
24 25

Barnes Bay — 19 20

West End

Maunday's Bay
Shoal Bay West — 21 22
Cove Bay
Rendezvous Bay — 23

Anguillita Island

Little Harbour — 28

Blowing Point Harbour
5

Exploring
Blowing Point Harbour, **5**
The Fountain, **2**
Sandy Ground, **4**
Sandy Hill Bay, **3**
Wallblake House, **1**

Dining
Aquarium, **26**
Coccoloba Plantation, **19**
Cross Roads, **9**
Hibernia, **6**
Johnno's, **14**

La Fontana, **8**
Lucy's Harbour View Restaurant, **27**
Malliouhana, **18**
Mango's, **20**
The Palm Court, **28**

Paradise Cafe, **21**
Pepper Pot, **10**
Pimm's, **22**
Riviera Bar & Restaurant, **13**
Roy's, **12**
Smuggler's Grill, **29**

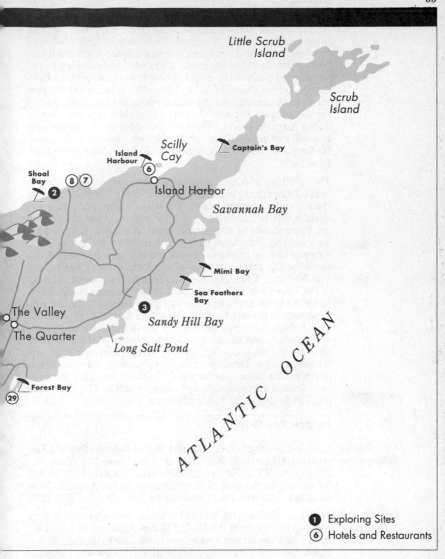

Little Scrub
Island

Scrub
Island

Captain's Bay

Scilly
Cay

Island
Harbour

6

Shoal
Bay

8 **7**

2

Island Harbor

Savannah Bay

Mimi Bay

Sea Feathers
Bay

The Valley

3

Sandy Hill Bay

The Quarter

Long Salt Pond

ATLANTIC OCEAN

Forest Bay

29

1 Exploring Sites
6 Hotels and Restaurants

Lodging
Anguilla Great
House, **24**
Cap Juluca, **22**
Casablanca Resort, **23**
Cinnamon Reef Beach
Club, **28**
Coccoloba
Plantation, **19**

Fountain Beach, **8**
Inter-Island Hotel, **11**
La Sirena, **17**
Malliouhana, **18**
The Mariners, **15**
Rendezvous Bay
Hotel, **25**
Shoal Bay Villas, **7**
Sydan's, **16**

and for two years conducted its own affairs. In 1968, a senior British official arrived and remained for a year working with the Anguilla Council. A second referendum in 1969 confirmed the desire of the Anguillans to remain apart from St. Kitts-Nevis, and the following month a British "peacekeeping force" parachuted down to the island, where it was greeted with flowers, fluttering Union Jacks, and friendly smiles. When the paratroopers were not working on their tans, they helped a team of royal engineers improve the port and build roads and schools. Today Anguilla elects a House of Assembly and its own leader to handle internal affairs, while a British governor is responsible for public service, the police, and judiciary and external affairs.

The territory of Anguilla includes a few islets or cays, such as Scrub Island to the east, Dog Island, Prickly Pear Cays, Sandy Island, and Sombrero Island. The island's population numbers about 8,000, predominantly of African descent but also including descendants of Europeans, especially Irish. Historically, because the limestone land was hardly fit for agriculture, Anguillans have had to seek work on neighboring islands. Until recently, the primary means of employment were fishing and boat building. Today, tourism has become the growth industry of the island's stable economy. But the government is determined to keep Anguilla's tourism growing at a slow and cautious pace to protect the island's natural resources and beauty. New hotels, scattered throughout the islands, are being kept small, select, and casino-free, and promotion of the island emphasizes its high-quality service, serene surroundings, and friendly people. However, times are changing. Two new hotels added nearly 200 rooms for the 1993 season, bringing the number of island accommodations to more than 900. There are even plans to design an 18-hole golf course.

Before You Go

Tourist Information
Contact the very helpful **Anguilla Tourist Information and Reservation Office** (c/o Medhurst & Associates, 271 Main St., Northport, NY 11768, tel. 212/869-0402, 516/261-1234, or 800/553-4939). In the United Kingdom, contact the **Anguilla Tourist Office** (3 Epirus Rd., London SW6 7UJ, tel. 071/937-7725).

Arriving and Departing
By Plane
American Airlines (tel. 800/433-7300) is the major airline with nonstop flights from the United States to its hub in San Juan, from which the airline's **American Eagle** flies twice daily to Anguilla, the first flight connecting with East Coast and Canadian flights, the second with those from the Midwest and West. **Windward Islands Airways** (Winair) (tel. 809/775-0183) wings in daily from St. Thomas and four times a day from St. Maarten's Juliana Airport. **Air BVI** (tel. 809/774-6500) flies in five times daily from St. Thomas and from San Juan three times a week, and **LIAT** (tel. 809/465-2286) comes in from St. Kitts and Antigua. **Air Anguilla** (tel. 809/497-2643) has regularly scheduled daily flights from St. Thomas, St. Maarten, San Juan, and Tortola. It also provides air-taxi service on request from neighboring islands, as does **Tyden Air** (tel. 809/497-2719).

From the Airport
At **Wallblake Airport** you'll find taxis lined up to meet the planes. A trip from the airport to Sandy Ground will cost about $7. Fares, which are government-regulated, should be listed in

brochures the drivers carry. If you are traveling in a group, the fares apply to the first two people; each additional passenger adds $2 to the total.

By Boat   There are ferry-boat journeys across the water from Marigot on St. Martin several times a day between 8 AM and 5:30 PM to Blowing Point on Anguilla. You pay the $9 one-way fare on board, plus a 15F ($3) departure tax before boarding. Don't buy a round-trip ticket because it restricts you to the boat on which you bought the ticket. The trip can be bouncy, but it takes only 15–20 minutes, so even if you suffer from motion sickness, you may not need medication. Check the schedules for the return ferries. The last hourly ferry departs Anguilla at 5 PM. The next ferry is at 6:15, and a late ferry departs at 10:15 PM. There is a $2 departure tax. An information booth outside the customs shed in Blowing Point, Anguilla, is usually open daily from 8:30 AM to 5 PM, but sometimes the attendant wanders off.

From the Docks   Taxis are always waiting to pick passengers up at the Blowing Point landing. It costs $12 to get to the Malliouhana Hotel and $15 to the most distant point, the Cap Juluca Hotel. Rates are fixed by the government and quoted in the local paper *What We Do in Anguilla*. The taxi driver should have a list of these fares.

Passports and Visas   U.S. and Canadian citizens need proof of identity. A passport is preferred (even one that's expired, but not more than five years ago). A photo ID, along with a birth certificate (original with raised seal), a voter registration card, or a driver's license is also acceptable. Visitor's passes are valid for stays of up to three months. British citizens must have a passport. All visitors must also have a return or ongoing ticket.

Language   English, with a West Indian lilt, is spoken on Anguilla.

Precautions   The manchineel tree, which resembles an apple tree, shades many beaches. The tree bears poisonous fruit, and the sap from the tree causes painful blisters, so avoid sitting beneath the tree because even dew or raindrops falling from the leaves can blister your skin.

Be *sure* to take along a can of insect repellent—mosquitoes are all over the place.

Anguilla is a quiet, relatively safe island, but there's no point in tempting fate by leaving your valuables unattended in your hotel room or on the beach.

Staying in Anguilla

Important Addresses   **Tourist Information:** The **Anguilla Tourist Office** (The Social Security Building, The Valley, tel. 809/497–2759) is open weekdays 8–noon and 1–4.

Emergencies   **Police** and **Fire:** 809/497–2333; **Hospital:** There is a 24-hour emergency room at the **Cottage Hospital** (The Valley, tel. 809/497–2551). By 1994, the new Princess Alexandra Hospital in Stoney Ground, under construction at press time, may have supplanted it. **Ambulance:** 809/497–2551; **Pharmacies:** The **Government Pharmacy** (The Valley, tel. 809/497–2551) is located in the Cottage Hospital. The **Paramount Pharmacy** (Waterswamp, tel. 809/497–2366) is open Monday–Saturday 8:30 AM–8:30 PM and has a 24-hour emergency service.

Currency Legal tender here is the Eastern Caribbean dollar (E.C.), but U.S. dollars are widely accepted. (You'll usually get change in E.C. dollars.) The E.C. is fairly stable relative to the U.S. dollar, hovering between E.C.$2.60 and $2.70 to U.S.$1. Credit cards are not widely accepted, but some places accept personal and traveler's checks. Be sure to carry lots of small bills; change for a $20 bill is often difficult to obtain.

Taxes and Service Charges The government imposes an 8% tax on accommodations. The departure tax is $7 at the airport, $2 by boat.

A 10% service charge is added to all hotel bills and most restaurant bills. If you're not certain about the restaurant service charge, ask. If you are particularly pleased with the service, you can certainly leave a little extra. Tip taxi drivers 10% of the fare.

Guided Tours A round-the-island tour by taxi will take about 2½ hours and will cost $40 for one or two people, $5 for each additional passenger.

Bennie's Tours (Blowing Point, tel. 809/497–2788), and **Malliouhana Travel and Tours** (The Valley, tel. 809/497–2431) put together personalized package tours on and around the island.

Getting Around
Taxis Taxi rates are regulated by the government and there are fixed fares from point to point. Posted rates are for one to two people; each additional person pays $2. The fare from the airport and from Blowing Point Landing ranges from $10 to $15.

Rental Cars This is your best bet for maximum mobility if you're comfortable driving on the left. For the most part, Anguilla's roads are narrow, paved two-laners, and some of the ritziest hotels are reachable only on ghastly dirt roads. Watch out for the four-legged critters that amble across the road and observe the 30 mph speed limit. To rent a car you'll need a valid driver's license and a local license, which can be obtained for $6 at any of the car rental agencies. Among the agencies are **Avis** (tel. 809/497–6221 or 800/331–2112), **Budget** (tel. 809/497–2217 or 800/527–0700), **Connors (National)** (tel. 809/497–6433 or 800/328–4567), and **Island Car Rental** (tel. 809/497–2723). Count on $35 to $45 per day's rental, plus insurance. Motorcycles and scooters are available for about $30 per day from **R & M Cycle** (tel. 809/497–2430).

Telephones and Mail To call Anguilla from the United States, dial area code 809 + 497 + the local four-digit number. International direct-dial is available on the island. **Cable & Wireless** (Wallblake Rd., tel. 809/497–3100) is open weekdays 8–6, Saturday 9–1, Sunday and holidays 10–2. A pay phone is accessible 24 hours a day for credit card and collect calls. To make a local call on the island, dial the four-digit number. Inside the departure lounge at the Blowing Point Ferry and at the airport, there is an AT&T USADIRECT access telephone for collect or credit card calls to the United States.

Airmail letters to the United States cost E.C.60¢; postcards, E.C.25¢.

Opening and Closing Times Banks are open Monday–Thursday 8–1, Friday 8–1 and 3–5. Shopping hours are variable. No two shops seem to have the same hours. Your best bet is to call the shop you're interested in, or ask at the tourist office for opening and closing times.

Exploring Anguilla

Numbers in the margin correspond to points of interest on the Anguilla map.

If you have not collected maps and brochures from the tourist booths either at the airport or on the boat ferry, then make the Tourist Office in The Valley your first stop on the island. Here you can pick up a large, colorful map of the island with splashy pictures of Anguilla's beaches. The island is sprinkled with salt ponds and small villages, the most important of which is The Valley, where administrative offices, banks, a few boutiques, guest houses, eateries, and markets are located. But there is little to see in Anguilla except for the beaches and the resorts. Take a look at the island's historic house, and then go beach-combing.

① **Wallblake House** is a plantation house that was built around 1787 by Will Blake (Wallblake is probably a corruption of his name). Legends of murders, invasions by the French in 1796, and high living surround the house. Now owned and actively used by the Catholic Church, the plantation has spacious rooms, some with tray ceilings edged with handsome carving. The long, narrow pantry with red and black baked brick tiles is now being converted to a kitchen. On the grounds there is an ancient vaulted stone cistern and an outbuilding called the Bakery (which wasn't used for breadmaking but for baking turkeys and hams). The oven measures 12 feet across and rises 3 feet up through a stepped chimney. *Cross Roads, The Valley. Call Father John, tel. 809/497-2405, to make an appointment to tour the plantation.*

If you follow the road west toward the Cottage Hospital, you'll come to a dirt road that leads to **Crocus Bay** and several strips of white-sand beaches.

② Four miles northeast of The Valley on the main road, as you approach the coast at **Shoal Bay,** you'll pass near **The Fountain,** where Arawak petroglyphs have been discovered. Presently closed to the public, the area is being researched by the Anguilla Archaeological and Historical Society. The AAHS (tel. 809/497-2767) plans to open a museum in the former Customs House in The Valley.

Two miles farther east, the fishing village of **Island Harbour** nestles in its sheltered cove.

Follow rutted dirt roads from Island Harbour to the easternmost tip of the island. On the way to the aptly named **Scrub Island** and **Little Scrub Island** off the eastern tip of Anguilla, you'll pass Captain's Bay, with its isolated beach, on the north coast.

③ You can also choose to bypass the east end of the island because there isn't much to see there. From Island Harbour, a paved road leads south, skirts Savannah Bay on the southeast coast, and continues to **Sandy Hill Bay.** If you're an aficionado of ruined forts, there's one here you may want to explore.

Four miles down the coast, beyond the Long Salt Pond, is **Forest Bay,** a fit place for scuba diving. South of Forest Bay lies **Little Harbour,** with a lovely horseshoe-shape bay and the splendid **Cinnamon Reef Beach Club.**

From Little Harbour, follow the paved road past Wallblake Airport, just outside The Valley, and turn left on the main **4** road. In 4 miles you'll come to **Sandy Ground,** one of the most active and most developed of the island's beaches. It is home to the **Mariners Hotel, Tamariain Watersports,** a dive shop, a commercial pier, and several small guest houses and restaurants. The *Shauna* departs from here for Sandy Island 2 miles offshore.

5 On the south coast is **Blowing Point Harbour,** where you'll have docked if you arrived by ferry from Marigot in St. Martin.

Time Out If you plan to picnic (on the beach or in your room), try the **Fat Cat** (George Hill, tel. 809/497–2307) for escargots to go, as well as takeout quiche, soups, chili, chicken, and conch dishes. **Amy's Bakery** (Blowing Point, tel. 809/497–6775) turns out homemade pies, cakes, tarts, cookies, and breads.

The main paved road travels more or less down the center of the island, which at this west end is quite narrow. Teeth-jarring dirt roads lead to the coasts, the beaches, and some of the best resorts on the island.

On the south coast, west of Blowing Point, is the crescent-shape home of **Rendezvous Bay,** the island's first hotel, built in 1959. The white sand drifts down the coastline to **Cove Bay,** a pretty coconut palm–fringed beach.

Maunday's Bay, on the extreme southwest coast, is the home of **Cap Juluca,** a stunning resort that looks as if it were plucked out of Marrakech.

On the opposite side of the island is **Coccoloba Plantation,** one of the largest resorts on the island, overlooking the white sands of **Barnes Bay.** A five-minute walk from Barnes Bay is **Meads Bay,** and **Long Bay** is farther to the north.

Beaches

The island's big attractions are its beaches. All are free to the public and all are white sand. Nude bathing is a no-no but is nevertheless not uncommon. Most of the island's beaches are on coral reefs that are great for snorkeling.

One of the prettiest beaches in the Caribbean, **Shoal Bay** is a 2-mile L-shape beach of talcum-powder-soft white sand. There are beach chairs, umbrellas, a backdrop of sea-grape and coconut trees, and for seafood and tropical drinks there's Trader Vic's, Uncle Ernie, and the Round Rock. Souvenir shops for T-shirts, suntan lotion, and the like abound. Head to Shoal Bay for good snorkeling in the offshore coral reefs, and visit the water-sports center to arrange diving, sailing, and fishing trips.

Island Harbor, another busy beach, is shaded by coconut trees and lined with colorful fishing boats. Depart from here for **Scilly Cay,** a three-minute motorboat ride away. You can get snorkeling equipment on the ferrying motorboat, but at times the waters are too rough to see much. On Scilly Cay there is a beach bar that serves drinks and grilled lobster and seafood.

The reward for traveling along an inhospitable dirt road via four-wheel drive is complete isolation at **Captain's Bay** on the northeastern end of the island. The surf slaps the sands with a vengeance and the undertow is quite strong here. Wading is the safest water sport.

Mimi Bay is a difficult-to-reach, isolated, half-mile beach east of Sea Feathers. But the trip is worth it. When the surf is not too rough, the barrier reef makes for great snorkeling.

Also not far from Sea Feathers is **Sandy Hill,** a base for fishermen. Here you can buy fresh fish and lobster right off the boats and snorkel in the warm waters. Don't plan to sunbathe—the beach is quite narrow here.

Rendezvous Bay is 1½ miles of pearl-white sand. Here the water is calm, and there's a great view of St. Martin. The Anguilla Great House's open-air beach bar is handy for snacks and Happy Jacks (rum punches).

The good news and the bad news about **Cove Bay** is the same—it's virtually deserted. There are no restaurants or bars, just calm waters, coconut trees, and soft sand that stretches down to Maunday's Bay.

One of the most popular beaches, wide, mile-long **Maunday's Bay** is known for good swimming and snorkeling. Rent watersport gear at Tropical Watersports. Try Pimm's at Cap Juluca for fine food and drink (*see* Dining, *below*).

Adjacent to Maunday's Bay, **Shoal Bay West** is a pleasant beach with a backdrop of the white stucco buildings of Cove Castles, a set of futuristic villas where Chuck Norris has a home, set apart by its pink-colored stone. The snorkeling is best in the area of the Oasis restaurant. Comb this beach for lovely conch shells as well.

Barnes Bay is a superb spot for windsurfing and snorkeling. The elegant Coccoloba Plantation perches above and offers a poolside bar. In high season this beach can get a bit crowded with day-trippers from St. Martin.

The clear blue waters of **Road Bay** beach are usually dotted with yachts. The Mariners Hotel, several restaurants (*see* Lodging, *below*), a water-sports center, and lots of windsurfing and waterskiing activity make this an active commercial area. It's a typical Caribbean scene daily, as fishermen set out in their boats and goats ramble the littoral at will. The snorkeling is not very good here, but do visit this bay for its glorious sunsets.

Sandy Island, nestled in coral reefs about 2 miles offshore from Road Bay, is a tiny speck of sand and sea, equipped with a beach boutique, beach bar and restaurant, and free use of snorkeling gear and underwater cameras. The *Shauna* (tel. 809/497–6395 or 809/497–6845) will ferry you there from Sandy Ground.

At **Little Bay** sheer cliffs embroidered with agave and creeping vines plummet to a small gray sand beach, usually accessible only by water (it's a favored spot for snorkeling and night dives). But virtually assured of total privacy, the hale and hearty can clamber down a rope to explore the caves and surrounding reef.

Sports and the Outdoors

Bicycling There are plenty of flat stretches, making wheeling pretty easy. Bikes can be rented at **Boothes** (tel. 809/497–2075).

Boating Sunfish and Hobie Cats are available at **Tropical Watersports** (tel. 809/497–6666 or 809/497–6779). *Sundancer*, a 30-foot powerboat, is available for charters at **Tamariain Watersports** (tel. 809/497–2020). Sailboats and speedboats can be rented at **Sandy Island Enterprises** (tel. 809/497–6395).

Deep-Sea Fishing Albacore, dolphin, and kingfish are among the sea creatures angled after off Anguilla's shores. Trips can be arranged through **Tropical Watersports**. Fishing tackle, diving gear, and other sports equipment are available at the **Tackle Box Sports Center** (tel. 809/497–2896).

Fitness Lest you go flabby lolling around on the beach, you'll find exercise equipment, aerobics, and martial arts instruction at **Highway Gym** (George Hill Rd., tel. 809/497–2363).

Jogging There are miles and miles of broad, flat beaches. Just pick one out and jog away.

Tennis For professional instruction, contact the Peter Burwash International pro at **Coccoloba** (tel. 809/497–6871), where there are two lighted courts. There are two courts at the **Carimar Beach Club** (tel. 809/497–6881), three championship courts at **Malliouhana** (tel. 809/497–6111), two Deco Turf tournament courts at **Cinnamon Reef** (tel. 809/497–2727), and two courts at **Fountain Beach and Tennis Club** (tel. 809/497–6395). Tennis is also available at **Cap Juluca** (tel. 809/497–6666), **Cove Castles** (tel. 809/497–6801), **Mariners** (tel. 809/497–2671), **Masara** (tel. 809/497–3200), **Rendezvous Bay** (tel. 809/497–6549), **Pelicans** (tel. 809/497–6593), **Sea Grapes** (tel. 809/497–6433), and **Spindrift Apts.** (tel. 809/497–4164).

Sea Excursions Picnic, swimming, and diving excursions to Prickly Pear, Sandy Island, and Scilly Cay are available through **Sandy Island Enterprises** (tel. 809/497–6395), **Enchanted Island Cruises** (tel. 809/497–3111), **Suntastic Cruises** (tel. 809/497–3400), and **Tropical Watersports** (tel. 809/497–6666 or 809/497–6779).

Water Sports The major resorts offer complimentary Windsurfers, paddleboats, and waterskis to their guests. If your hotel has no water-sports facilities, you can get in gear at **Tropical Watersports** (tel. 809/497–6666 or 809/497–6779) or **Tamariain Watersports** (tel. 809/497–2020). Tamariain Watersports also has PADI instructors, short resort courses, and more than a dozen dive sites.

Shopping

Shopping tips are readily available in the informative free publications *Anguilla Life* and *What We Do in Anguilla*, but you have to be a really dedicated shopper to peel yourself off the beach and poke around in Anguilla's few shops.

Clothing Head for **La Romana** (Mead's Bay, tel. 809/497–6181), cloned from the St. Martin and St. Barts boutiques; **Whispers** (Cap Juluca, tel. 809/497–6666); and **Sunshine Shop** (South Hill, tel. 809/497–6964) for island cotton *pareos* (Polynesian-style wraps), silk-screened items, cotton resort wear, and hand-painted wood items from Haiti. **La Sirena Boutique** (Meads

Bay, tel. 809/467–6827) offers a colorful range of dresses, slacks, belts, and other accessories. **Beach Stuff** (Back St., South Hill, tel. 809/497–6814) has a fun collection of sportswear. **The Valley Gap** (Shoal Bay Beach, tel. 809/497–2754) has local crafts, T-shirts, and swimwear. **Vanhelle Boutique** (Sandy Ground, tel. 809/497–2965) carries gift items, as well as Brazilian swimsuits for men and women. **Java Wraps** (George Hill Rd., tel. 809/497–5497) carries superb batikwear.

Native crafts The **Anguilla Arts and Crafts Center** (The Valley, tel. 809/497–2200) has a wide selection of island crafts. **Alicea's Place** (The Quarter, tel. 809/497–3540) has some locally made ceramics and pottery. The **Scruples Gift Shop** (Social Security Bldg., tel. 809/497–2800) has shells, handmade baskets, wood dolls, hand-crocheted mats, lace tablecloths, and bedspreads. **Devonish Art Gallery** (The Valley, tel. 809/497–2949) displays the ceramics and sculpture of Courtney Devonish, as well as works by other prominent local artists. **Cheddie's Carving Shop** (The Cove, tel. 809/497–6027), just down the road from Coccoloba Plantation, showcases Cheddie's own work, wonderfully textured, fanciful creatures fashioned from driftwood. Even the whimsically carved desk and balustrade in his studio testify to his vivid imagination. Many artists hold open studios; the tourism board can provide brochures.

Dining

Anguilla's eateries range from the exotic to down-home seaside shacks. Casual chic prevails; a jacket (no tie) is usually required in high season at the top resorts. Call ahead—in the winter to make a reservation, and in the summer to see if the place you've chosen is open. Most restaurants not affiliated with a hotel tack on an additional 5% to the service charge if you pay by credit card.

Highly recommended restaurants are indicated by a star ★.

Category	Cost*
Very Expensive	over $45
Expensive	$35–$45
Moderate	$25–$35
Inexpensive	under $25

per person, excluding drinks, service, and sales tax (8%)

★ **Malliouhana.** Sparkling crystal, fine china, romantic lighting, and sterling-silver domed platters make even a lowly hamburger seem elegant. Michel Rostang, who received two Michelin stars for his Paris boîte, created the menu and is still the consulting chef. Not surprisingly, the cuisine is haute French. You might begin with a sublime melting foie gras in red wine jelly or warm stewed lobster with pumpkin and green salad, then segue into sea bass with fennel and dill zabaglione or Bresse chicken breasts stuffed with asparagus. Don't pass up desserts, especially the roast pear in Sauternes with walnut brioche and cinnamon ice cream. The wine cellar contains about 25,000 bottles. A sumptuous, memorable evening in all respects. During high season the restaurant is reserved for guests. *Meads Bay, tel. 809/497–2731. Reservations imperative. No credit cards. Very Expensive.*

Pimm's. You expect Rudolph Valentino to sweep in beneath the domes, arches, and billowing canvas of this Arabian Nights tent. With its location at the end of a half-moon bay and recent expansion, this restaurant offers diners a magnificent setting with water lapping the steps that lead up to the clay-tiled floor. The new Anguillan chef has added a Creole flair to the fine if traditional Continental fare. *Cap Juluca, Maunday's Bay, tel. 809/497–6666. Reservations required. AE, MC, V. Expensive–Very Expensive.*

Coccoloba Plantation. Dining here is either indoors or on a lovely terrace overlooking the sea. Your choices might include red pepper and orange soup perfumed with cardamom, lobster cassoulet in vermouth saffron cream, and duck magret in plum and Beaumes des Venise sauce. At $30 the three-course table d'hôte is a steal. Lunch is a poolside buffet of salads, burgers, fish, cold meats, and homemade desserts. *Barnes Bay, tel. 8098/497–6871. Reservations required in high season. AE, D, MC, V. Expensive.*

★ **Hibernia.** Hibernia, set in unspoiled Island Harbour, in an absolutely delightful seaside cottage with wood beams, bamboo furniture, raspberry latticework, and East Indian paintings, boasts the island's most creative, assured menu. Unorthodox yet delectable pairings include fricassee of lobster in mustard cinnamon sauce and breast of chicken cooked with honey and mild chiles. To start, the house smoked fish is a must. You can conclude your meal with a Cuban cigar, a vintage port, or an aged armagnac, providing a sense of Caribbean high life a generation ago. *Island Harbour, tel. 809/497–4290. Reservations suggested. AE, D, MC, V. Closed Mon. Expensive.*

★ **The Palm Court.** This stylish eatery in the Cinnamon Reef Beach Club has a long palm-lined corridor with red terra-cotta tile floors, Haitian furniture, local murals, and huge arched picture windows fronting the Caribbean. Frenchman Didier Rochat and Anguillan Vernon Hughes collaborate on an exciting nouvelle Caribbean cuisine, their strengths complementing each other beautifully. Vernon contributes his knowledge of local foods and culinary traditions, while Didier provides a classic French gloss. Signature dishes you might select include chargrilled tuna with cinnamon tomato confit and swordfish steak in passion fruit salsa. The mango puffs in caramel sauce are justly famous. *Cinammon Beach Club, Little Harbour, tel. 809/497–2727. Reservations advised. AE, MC, V. Expensive.*

Paradise Cafe. The twinkling music of wind chimes and seductive aromas from the kitchen waft through this brightly decorated, open-air restaurant. Chef Michael Marciezyk also grafts Oriental influences—Thai, Indonesian, Mandarin—onto traditional French methods of preparation. Among the standouts are West Indian bouillabaisse, rack of lamb chinois (black bean sauce), and rockfish filet flash fried in peanut oil with sake, hoisin, and tamarind sauce. *Shoal Bay West, tel. 809/497–6010. Reservations suggested. AE, MC, V. Closed Mon. Expensive.*

La Fontana. Set back from the beach, this small restaurant has an ambitious northern Italian menu, deftly seasoned with island touches by the Rastafarian chef. You can select from a range of pastas for your *primi piatti*, including fettucini al limone and rasta pasta (usually tossed with crayfish and radicchio). For the main course, there is a wide selection, from chicken to T-bone steak and duck to fish. *Fountain Beach Ho-*

tel, Shoal Bay, tel. 809/497–3491. Reservations accepted. No credit cards. Moderate.

★ **Lucy's Harbour View Restaurant.** Passing through a swinging wood gate, you'll step up to a terrace restaurant with a splendid sea view. The specialty is "Lucy's delicious whole red snapper," but there is a wide selection here, including several curried and Creole dishes, such as conch and goat. Be sure to try Lucy's sautéed potatoes. Live music Wednesday and Friday. *South Hill, tel. 809/497–6253. Reservations accepted. No credit cards. Closed Sun. Moderate.*

Mango's. Husband-and-wife team Bob and Melinda Blanchard sold their hugely successful operation last year, but the new owners have retained much of the staff and Melinda's most popular inventions, including pumpkin shrimp bisque and sesame swordfish with ginger-mango sauce. Try one of the unusual pizza combinations for lunch. *Barnes Bay, tel. 809/497–6479. Reservations suggested in high season. MC, V. Usually closed on Tues. Moderate.*

Riviera Bar & Restaurant. This is a beachside bistro serving French and Creole specialties with an Oriental accent. A four-course lobster meal is featured, and the fish soup à la Provençale is highly recommended. Sushi, sashimi, and oysters sautéed in soy sauce and sake are also among the eclectic offerings. There's a very happy Happy Hour from 6 to 7 daily. Live entertainment is featured frequently in season. *Sandy Ground, tel. 809/497–2833. Reservations accepted. AE, V. Moderate.*

Smuggler's Grill. Somewhat out of the way on Forest Bay, this romantic nautically themed restaurant offers 10 different preparations of lobster at very competitive prices, in addition to the usual bistro fare. Animated energetic Marysa is a fresh wind blown in direct from Paris. *Forest Bay, tel. 809/497–3728. AE, MC, V. Closed Sun. Moderate.*

★ **Aquarium.** An upstairs terrace, the Aquarium is all gussied up with gingerbread trim, bright blue walls, and red cloths. The lunch menu lists sandwiches and burgers. Stewed lobster, curried chicken, barbecued chicken, and mutton stew are offered at night. This is a popular spot with locals. *South Hill, tel. 809/ 497–2720. Reservations accepted. No credit cards. Closed Sun. Inexpensive.*

Cross Roads. Millie Philip's roadside bar features hearty breakfasts and, at lunch, seafood salads, fish, and chicken. Hearty fare at low prices. *Wallblake, The Valley, tel. 809/497–2581. Reservations accepted. No credit cards. Inexpensive.*

Johnno's. This is *the* place to be on Sunday afternoons for barbecue and music by the island band Dumpa and the AnVibes, but grilled or barbecued lobster, chicken, and fish are good anytime. This is a classic Caribbean beach bar, attracting a funky eclectic mix, from locals to movie stars. *Sandy Ground, tel. 809/497–2728. No credit cards. Inexpensive.*

Pepper Pot. Cora Richardson's small eatery in the center of town offers *roti* aficionados their favorite dish, made of boneless chicken, *tanias* (poi), celery, pepper, onion, garlic, and local peas, all wrapped in a crepe and panfried. A full meal in itself, it sells for E.C.$5. Dumpling dinners, lobster, whelk, and conch are also good choices. *The Valley, tel. 809/497–2328. Reservations accepted. No credit cards. Inexpensive.*

★ **Roy's.** The dainty pink-and-white–covered deck belies the rowdy reputation of Roy and Mandy Bosson's pub, an Anguillan mainstay. One of the island's best buys, it features Roy's fish-and-chips, cold English beer, pork fricassee, and a wonderful chocolate rum cake. Sunday lunch special is roast beef and Yorkshire pudding. A faithful clientele gathers in the lively bar. *Crocus Bay, tel. 809/497–2470. Reservations accepted. No credit cards. Closed Mon. and Sat. lunch. Inexpensive.*

Lodging

Anguilla has a wide range of accommodations. There are grand and glorious resorts; apartments and villas from the deluxe to the simple; and small locally owned guest houses where you can get a real taste of life on Anguilla. Each property has carved out its own distinctive niche. When you call to reserve a room in a resort, be sure to inquire about special packages. Meal plans are available, but the particulars vary from resort to resort.

Highly recommended lodgings are indicated by a star ★.

Category	Cost*
Very Expensive	over $375
Expensive	$250–$375
Moderate	$150–$250
Inexpensive	under $150

* *All prices are for a standard double room for two, excluding 8% tax and a 10% service charge.*

Hotels
★ **Cap Juluca.** Once you get past the potholed road leading to this luxurious, whitewashed Moorish resort with its domes, arches, low walls, and private courtyards, you'll be rewarded with a pampering touch. Situated on 179 acres, the 18 sparkling-white, two-story villas line the mile-long beach of powdery sand. Six of the villas have such luxe touches as huge marble baths and sunken double tubs in walled gardens, private pools, rooftop solariums with refrigerators and built-in barbecues, and Continental breakfast brought to your terrace. Ceiling fans whir over spacious rooms and suites with king-size platform beds. (All rooms are also fully air-conditioned.) Prices are high: For the suites with their private plunge pool, count on $1,500 a day; even the standard room, with shower only, is $390. Around the main pool are palm-shaded areas and a terrace dining room for breakfast and lunch. Dinner is at Pimms, set at the edge of the bay and resembling a sultan's pavilion. Cap Juluca's obvious likeness to harem-style living is the epitome of glitz, luring a youthful but oh so well-heeled crowd. *Box 240, Maunday's Bay, tel. 809/497–6666/6779 or 800/235–3505. 56 1-bedroom suites, 36 junior suites, 7 deluxe rooms. Facilities: 3 restaurants, bar, boutique, room service, laundry service, library, VCRs and cassettes for rent, pool, 3 tennis courts, water-sports and fitness centers. AE. CP, MAP. Closed Sept.– mid-Oct. Very Expensive.*

Coccoloba Plantation. The reception area in the main house is an enormous room with soaring ceiling, sofas upholstered in vivid fabrics, and handsome artwork. Guests stay in oceanfront villas, done in orange or magenta, each with a step-up bedroom, oversize marble bath, and gingerbread-trim patio. All rooms and suites are air-conditioned, with ceiling fans, glass-top coffee tables, personal safe-deposit box, built-in hair dryer, amenity packages, and onetime complimentary fully stocked refrigerator and minibar. Most bathrooms have showers only. Complimentary early-morning coffee and afternoon tea are served. The tennis program is directed by a professional from Peter Burwash International. A tennis package is one of several special packages available, but prices tend to be on the high side, especially considering the dire need for refurbishment. *Box 332, Barnes Bay, tel. 809/497–6871 or 800/351–5656; in Canada, 800/468–0023. 51 units. Facilities: restaurant, 2 bars, library, concierge, boutique, 2 tennis courts, 2 pools, Jacuzzi, TV/reading room, sauna, massage, exercise rooms, water sports available. AE, DC, MC, V. EP, MAP. Very Expensive.*

★ **Malliouhana.** Brick steps lead to a broad, airy reception area with high ceilings, splashing fountain, and Haitian artwork. Accommodations range from deluxe double rooms to superdeluxe suites. All are stunning, with miles of white tile, king-size platform beds or canopied king-size or twin beds, balconies, Haitian prints, minibars, oversize tubs in marble baths, and ceiling fans (as well as air-conditioning). The hotel sits on a bluff overlooking the beach and a secluded cove. The resort also provides excursions to Sandy Island, which is excellent for snorkeling. It is necessary to reserve rooms well in advance: Malliouhana is Anguilla's most sophisticated resort. *Box 173, Meads Bay, tel. 809/497–6111 or 212/696–1323. 20 rooms, 2 2-bedroom suites, 14 1-bedroom suites, 14 junior suites. Facilities: restaurant, bar, boutique, beauty salon, concierge, 3 pools, 4 lighted tennis courts, Nautilus-equipped exercise room, massage room, water-sports center. No credit cards. EP, MAP. Very Expensive.*

Casablanca Resort. This new coral-and-lime Moorish fantasia is the largest resort on Anguilla. Five splashing fountains lead to the reception area, intricate tracery embellishes the ceilings, authentic Moroccan mosaics and carvings adorn the walls. The rooms are done up in bold-patterned pastels, with Moroccan throw rugs for effect. TV, VCR, radio, safe, minibar, air-conditioning, and ceiling fan are standard throughout. Yet this is the closest thing to motel-style accommodations on Anguilla, sure to be wildly popular with affluent tour groups. On another, more developed island Casablanca might not seem so garnish. A great deal of effort and planning clearly went into this impressive property, but it's all a bit much for poor little Anguilla. *Box 444, Rendezvous Bay West, tel. 809/496–6999 or 800/231–1945. 76 rooms and suites. Facilities: 3 restaurants, bar, pool, 2 lit tennis courts, boutique, library, billiard room, jewelry store, sundry shop, piano bar, health club, 9-hole golf course (slated for completion late 1993), water-sports center. AE, D, MC, V. EP. Expensive.*

★ **Cinnamon Reef Beach Club.** Low-key luxury sets the tone in these recently redecorated villas with vast expanses of terracotta tile, polished wood, and handsome upholstered bamboo furniture. Each villa is split-level, with living room, raised bedroom, dressing room, sunken shower, patio, and hammock. Each has a built-in hair dryer and minibar. Most of the villas are beachfront; five are tucked up on a bluff. This is a fun, friendly place with a gracious staff and lots of repeat guests who revel in the seclusion and civility. The small, tame beach is good for children, but the sea is often too calm for invigorating swims. A calypso combo plays nightly, and the Friday-night barbecue is an island favorite. Meal plans and packages are available. *Box 141, Little Harbour, tel. 809/497–2727 or 800/ 223–1108; in Canada, 416/485–8724. 14 studios, 8 1-bedroom suites. Facilities: restaurant, lounge, pool, 2 tennis courts, room service, turndown and laundry service, all water sports. AE, MC, V. EP, MAP. Expensive.*

Anguilla Great House. These five one-story gleaming white West Indian bungalows, set around the lovely curve of Rendez-vous Bay, feature chaise longues on verandas with vine-covered trellises and gingerbread trim. You expect to see white-clad croquet players strolling the immaculately manicured lawns. The spacious accommodations all feature mahogany furnishings, hand-embroidered linens, and huge tile showers. Plans are afoot to expand the property and to improve the beautifully situated restaurant, which even the friendly Anguillan owner admits is mediocre. *Box 157, Rendezvous Bay, tel. 809/497–6061 or 800/223–0079. 10 1-bedroom suites with kitchenettes, 5 studios. Facilities: restaurant, pool, gallery/boutique, gym. AE. EP, MAP. Moderate–Expensive.*

Fountain Beach. The owning family is of Italian descent, and it shows in this delightful Mediterranean-style property. The rooms come with a fully equipped kitchen, a large bathroom with an open sunken shower (the studio also has a deep tub) and a view of the sea. Furnishings are in rattan and colorfully painted wicker, with Haitian art decorating the walls. Forty additional units, some with plunge pool, are planned over the next few years. *Shoal Bay, tel. 809/497–3491. 8 1-bedroom suites, 2 junior suites. Facilities: restaurant, 2 pools, 2 tennis courts. AE, MC, V. EP, MAP. Moderate–Expensive.*

The Mariners. This is Anguilla's first all-inclusive resort, though EP is just as popular with the honeymooners and businesspeople on retreat who make up much of the clientele. Accommodations vary considerably, ranging from deluxe two-bedroom, two-bath cottages with full kitchens to small rooms with twin beds, minibars, and shower baths. Charter the Mariner's Boston whaler for picnics, snorkeling, and fishing trips. The Thursday-night barbecue and Saturday West Indian night in the beachfront restaurant are popular island events. Unlike the other top Anguillan resorts, The Mariners is very West Indian in style and ambience; that means 19th-century gingerbread cottages and the standard muted pastel decor and service that, while friendly, seems laid back verging on lackadaisical. But once you get used to it, there's tremendous charm to a staff that hasn't been thoroughly schooled. *Box 139, Sandy Ground, tel. 809/497–2671, 809/497–2815 or 800/223–0079; in NY, 212/545–7688. 25 1-bedroom suites, 25 studios. Facilities: 2 restaurants, 2 bars, jacuzzi, laundry service, boutique, pool, lighted tennis court, water-sports center. AE, MC, V. EP, MAP, FAP, All-inclusive (drinks not included). Moderate–Expensive.*

Shoal Bay Villas. On 2 splendid miles of sand, these fan-cooled units, hidden within just barely contained gardens, feature modern Italian furnishings and kitchens. Reefside Beach Bar and open-air restaurant is a pleasant spot for breakfast, lunch, and dinner. All water sports can be arranged. Children are not allowed during the winter. *Box 61, Shoal Bay, tel. 809/497– 2051 or 800/722–7045; 212/535–9530 in NY; 416/283–2621 in Canada. 3 2-bedroom villas, 5 1-bedroom villas, 5 studios. Facilities: restaurant, bar. AE, MC, V. EP, BP, MAP. Moderate–Expensive.*

★ **La Sirena.** Overlooking Meads Bay—and a 2-minute walk by a path—La Sirena offers the best value on Anguilla. After taking over in 1988, Rolf and Viviane Masshardt, who are from Switzerland, have made this into an extremely comfortable, personable, and well-run hotel. Upstairs are two small restaurants open to the sea breezes, one serving Swiss cuisine, the other, of all things, Southwestern fare. The key to the hotel's success is the personal service offered by the owner-managers. La Sirena does not have the chic elegance of Malliouhana, but you can stay here for three weeks for the price of one at Malliouhana. *Box 200, The Valley, tel. 809/497–6827 or 800/ 331–9358. 20 rooms, 7 one-bedroom suites. Facilities: 2 pools, 2 restaurants, bar, car rental, picnic and snorkeling equipment. No credit cards. EP. Moderate.*

Rendezvous Bay Hotel. Anguilla's first hotel sits amid 60 acres of coconut groves and fine white sand. The water here is as clear as Perrier. The main building is low and rose-colored, with a broad front patio, tile floors, and wicker chairs. The rooms are clean, simple, and very quaint with one double and one single bed; a private shower bath; and Haitian art, bamboo, and wicker everywhere. New two-story villas along the broad beach are spacious, decorated in muted earth tones, with modern furnishings and some with kitchenettes. On the other side of the main house are more new villa units, which are stepped back from a secluded beach area. Rooms in these new units are designed so that they may be joined together to form suites for families or two or more couples. *Box 31, Rendezvous Bay, tel. 809/497–6549; in the United States, 201/738–0246 or 800/274– 4893; in Canada, 800/468–0023. 20 rooms, 26 1-bedroom suites. Facilities: restaurant, lounge, game and TV room, 2 tennis courts, water-sports center. No credit cards. EP. Inexpensive– Moderate.*

Inter-Island Hotel. The West Indian cottage is modestly furnished (no air-conditioning) with wicker and rattan, and the hotel has some rooms with balconies. Most rooms have refrigerators and cramped shower baths that define the term "water closet." There are also two small one-bedroom apartments, each with a separate entrance on the ground floor. A homey dining room serves hearty breakfasts and fine West Indian dinners. *Box 194, The Valley, tel. 809/497–6259 or 800/223–9815; in Canada, 800/468–0023. 10 rooms, 2 1-bedroom apartments. Facilities: restaurant, bar, TV lounge, transportation to beach ½ mi away. AE, D, MC, V. EP. Inexpensive.*

★ **Sydan's.** Just across the street from all the activity on Road Bay, these very pleasant, clean efficiencies contain comfortable furnishings, kitchenette, and shower bath. A tremendous bargain. *Sandy Ground, tel. 809/497–3180. 6 studios. Facilities: gift shop. AE, MC, V. EP. Inexpensive.*

Villa and Apartment Rentals
The Tourist Office has a complete listing of vacation rentals. You can also contact **Sunshine Villas** (Box 142, Blowing Point, tel. 809/497–6149) or **Property Real Estate Management Services** (Box 256, George Hill, tel. 809/497–2596), which represents more moderate choices. Housekeeping accommodations are plentiful and well organized. The following are a selection:

★ **Cove Castles Villa Resort.** This is a sumptuously decorated, well-equipped, and very private compound along the beach of Shoal Bay West. The buildings are futuristic in design but Portofino in feel, a series of lunar modules poised to take flight, and the interiors are very elegant. *Shoal Bay West, Box 248,*

*tel. 809/497–6809 or 800/348–4716; in Canada, 800/468–0023. 4
3-bedroom villas, 8 2-bedroom villas. Facilities: restaurant,
boutique, tennis court. No credit cards. Very Expensive.*

Sea Grape Beach Club. Also on Meads Bay, these luxurious
2,000-square-foot two-bedroom condos are laid out on five levels. Each unit features acres of glass affording spectacular
views, enormous closets, three baths, king-size beds, elegant
furnishings, and spacious, very private decks. *Box 65, The Valley, tel. 809/497–6433, 809/497–6541, or 800/223–9815. 10 condos. Facilities: restaurant, bar, 2 tennis courts, satellite TV,
water-sports center. No credit cards. Very Expensive.*

Easy Corner Villas. These one-, two-, and three-bedroom
apartments with kitchens are furnished right down to microwaves. Only three of the units are air-conditioned; all have only
shower baths. No. 10 is a deluxe two-bedroom villa. Not located
on the beach but on a bluff overlooking Road Bay, this is a good
buy for families. *Box 65, South Hill, tel. 809/497–6433, 809/
497–6541, or 800/223–8815. 17 units. AE, MC, V. Moderate.*

Rainbow Reef. David and Charlotte Berglund's secluded units
are set on three dramatic seaside acres. A gazebo, with beach
furniture and barbecue facilities, perches right over the beach.
Each self-contained villa has two bedrooms, fully equipped
kitchen, spacious dining and living area, and a large gallery
overlooking the sea. *Box 130, Sea Feather Bay, tel. 809/497–
2817 or 708/325–2299. 14 units. No credit cards. Moderate.*

★ **Skiffles Villas.** These self-catering villas, perched on a hill overlooking Road Bay, are usually booked a year in advance. The
one-, two-, and three-bedroom apartments have fully equipped
kitchens, floor-to-ceiling windows, and pleasant porches. *Box
82, Lower South Hill, tel. 809/497–6619, 219/642–4855, or 219/
642–4445. 5 units. Facilities: pool. No credit cards. Moderate.*

Nightlife

The **Mayoumba Folkloric Group** performs song-and-dance skits
depicting Antillean and Caribbean culture, replete with African drums and a string band. They entertain every Thursday
night at **La Sirena** (The Valley, tel. 809/497–6827). Be on the
lookout for Bankie Banx, Anguilla's own reggae superstar. He
has his own group called New Generations. Other local groups
include Keith Gumbs and The Mellow Tones; Spracka;
Megaforce; Sleepy and the All-Stars, a string-and-scratch
band; Joe and the Invaders; and Dumpa and the AnVibes. Steel
Vibrations, a pan band, often entertains at barbecues and West
Indian evenings. Most of the major hotels feature some kind of
live entertainment in season. A Calypso combo plays most
nights at **Cinnamon Reef Beach Club** (Little Harbour, tel. 809/
497–2850). The **Mariners** (Sandy Ground, tel. 809/497–2671)
has regularly scheduled Thursday night barbecues and Saturday night West Indian parties, both with live entertainment by
local groups. During high season, **Pimm's** (Cap Juluca, tel. 809/
497–6666) has live music during dinner. Things are pretty loose
and lively at **Johnno's** beach bar (tel. 809/497–2728) in Sandy
Ground, which has alfresco dancing on weekends. The **Red
Dragon Disco** (South Hill, tel. 809/497–2687) is a hot spot on
weekends after midnight. The **Coconut Paradise** restaurant
(Island Harbour, tel. 809/497–4150) has nightly entertainment
ranging from disco to limbo. For soft dance music after a meal,
go to **Lucy's Palm Palm** (tel. 809/497–2253) at Sandy Ground.

There is usually a live band on Tuesday and Friday evenings. Sunday is the big night in restaurants. In addition to the above, **Uncle Ernie's** (Shoal Bay, no tel.), **Round Rock** (Shoal Bay, tel. 809/497–2076), and **Smitty's** (Island Harbour, tel. 809/497–4300) swing all day and well into the night.

3 Antigua

Updated by
Simon Worrall

One could spend an entire year—and a leap year, at that—exploring Antigua's (*An-TEE-ga*) beaches; the island has 366 of them, many with snow-white sand. All the beaches are public, and many are backed by lavish resorts offering sailing, diving, windsurfing, and snorkeling.

Antigua, the largest of the British Leeward Islands, is an island with a strong sense of national identity and rich, historic inheritance. Its cricketers, like the legendary Viv Richards, arguably the greatest batsmen the game has ever seen, are famous throughout the Caribbean. Its people are known for their sharp, commerical spirit; their wit; and, unfortunately at the government level, their corruption.

In the colonial era, Antigua was the headquarters of Lord Horatio Nelson's fleet. From here, Nelson sailed out to do battle with the French and strictly enforce the British Navigation Act. Since this act prohibited trade with the newly independent "Americans" and Nelson enforced it to the letter, he was not particularly popular with the plantation owners of Antigua, who depended on that trade. Indeed, he was shunned by island society and spent most of his time aboard his ship, HMS *Boreus*.

English Harbour, in the southeast of the island, is steeped in the history of that time. At its center is Nelson's Dockyard. It is Antigua's answer to Williamsburg, Virginia—a carefully restored gem of British Georgian architecture that still powerfully evokes a now-vanished era and the world-famous admiral who served here. With its coves and bays, it is like a tropical version of Cornwall, England. Accommodations are generally in smaller, inn-type hotels. For Anglophiles and those interested in history, English Harbour, and the surrounding villages and historic sites, will be immensely rewarding.

For those who want beaches; nightlife; and larger, resort-type accommodations, Dickenson Bay, at the northwestern end of the island, is the place to head. It is around Dickenson Bay that a lively, Florida-style tourist trade has grown up, centered on the bustling capital, St. John's. At St. John's you will be able to parasail and waterski, bounce across the azure water on an inflatable rubber banana, lie in a Jacuzzi, or sip piña coladas at a swim-up bar.

The least developed part of the island is in the southwest, in the shadow of Antigua's highest mountain, Boggy Peak. At beaches like Fry's Bay and Darkwood Beach, visitors will find long, unspoiled beaches. At Fry's Beach, on weekends, Antiguan families come to picnic under the tamarind tree–lined beaches and swim in the ocean.

The original inhabitants of Antigua were a people called the Siboney. They lived here as early as 4,000 years ago and disappeared mysteriously, leaving the island unpopulated for about 1,000 years. When Columbus happened on the 108-square-mile island in 1493, the Arawaks had set up housekeeping. The English took up residence 139 years later in 1632. Then a sequence of bloody battles involving the Caribs, the Dutch, the French, and the English began. Slaves had been imported from Africa to work the sugar plantations by the time the French ceded the island to the English in 1667. On November 1, 1981, Antigua, with its sister island Barbuda (30 miles to the north), achieved full independence.

Antigua (and Barbuda)

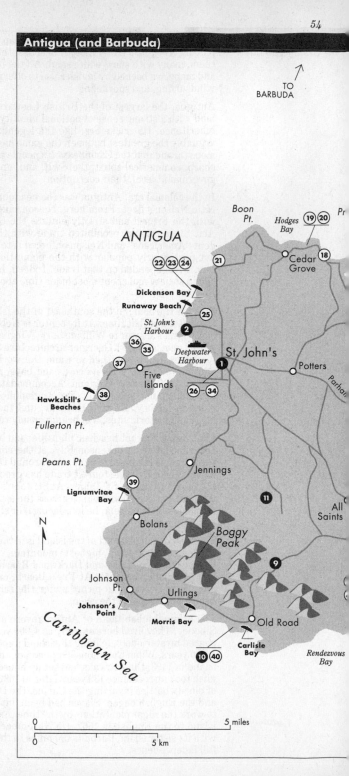

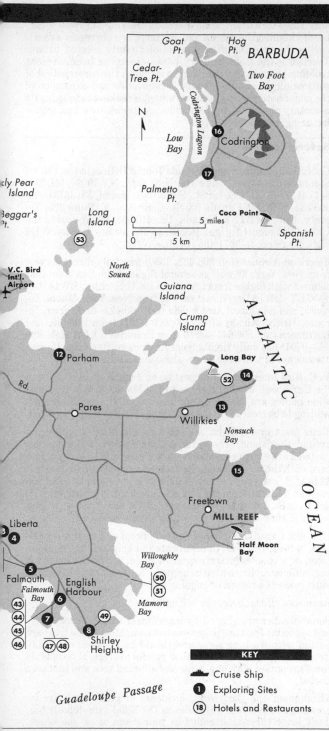

KEY

🚢 Cruise Ship

1 Exploring Sites

18 Hotels and Restaurants

The combined population of the two islands is about 90,000, only 1,200 of whom live on Barbuda. Having survived a battered childhood, Antigua and Barbuda are currently experiencing the growing pains typical of a newly created nation. Tourism is the main industry here—there has been a recent building boom in tourism properties, with the construction of condominiums and the extensive renovation and expansion of the major hotels—and the government is seeking to broaden its monetary resources by reintroducing agriculture and manufacturing into the economy.

Before You Go

Tourist Information
Contact the **Antigua and Barbuda Tourist Offices** in the United States (610 5th Ave., Suite 311, New York, NY 10020, tel. 212/541–4117, or 121 S.E. 1st St., Suite 1001, Miami, FL 33131, tel. 305/381–6762), in Canada (60 St. Clair Ave. E, Suite 205, Toronto, Ont. M4T 1N5, Canada, tel. 416/961–3085), and in the United Kingdom (Antigua House, 15 Thayer St., London W1M 5LD, England, tel. 071/486–7073).

Arriving and Departing
By Plane
American Airlines (tel. 800/433–7300) has daily direct service from New York, as well as several flights from San Juan that connect with flights from more than 100 U.S. cities. **BWIA** (tel. 800/JET–BWIA) has direct service from New York, Miami, Toronto, and San Juan; **Air Canada** (tel. 800/422–6232) from Toronto, **British Airways** (tel. 800/247–9297) from London, and **Lufthansa** (tel. 800/645–3880) from Frankfurt. **LIAT** (tel. 809/462–0701) has daily flights from Antigua to Barbuda, 15 minutes away, as well as to down-island destinations.

V. C. Bird International Airport is, on a much smaller scale, to the Caribbean what O'Hare is to the Midwest. When several wide-bodies are sitting on the runway at the same time, all waiting to be cleared for takeoff, things can get a bit congested.

From the Airport
Taxis meet every flight, and drivers will offer to guide you around the island. The taxis are unmetered, but rates are posted at the airport and drivers are required to carry a rate card with them. The fixed rate from the airport to St. John's is $8 in U.S. currency (although drivers often *quote* Eastern Caribbean dollars); from the airport to English Harbour, $18.75; and from St. John's to the Dockyard, $33 round-trip, with "reasonable" time allocated for waiting while you wander.

Passports and Visas
U.S. and Canadian citizens need only proof of identity. A passport is best, but a birth certificate (an original, not a photocopy) or a voter registration card will do. A driver's license is *not* sufficient. British citizens need a passport. All visitors must present a return or ongoing ticket.

Language
Antigua's official language is English.

Precautions
Some beaches are shaded by manchineel trees, whose leaves and applelike fruit are poisonous to touch. Most of the trees are posted with warning signs and should be avoided; even raindrops falling from them can cause painful blisters. If you should come in contact with one, rinse the affected area and contact a doctor.

Throughout the Caribbean, incidents of petty theft are increasing. Leave your valuables in the hotel safe-deposit box; don't leave them unattended in your room or on the beach.

Also, the streets of St. John's are fairly deserted at night, so it's not a good idea to wander out alone.

Staying in Antigua

Important Addresses

Tourist Information: The **Antigua and Barbuda Department of Tourism** (Thames and Long Sts., St. John's, tel. 809/462–0480) is open Monday–Thursday 8–4:30, Friday 8–3. There is also a tourist-information desk at the airport, just beyond the immigration checkpoint. The tourist office gives limited information. You may have more success with the **Antigua Hotels Association** (Long St., St. John's, tel. 809/462–3702), which also provides assistance.

Emergencies

Police (tel. 809/462–0125), **Fire** (tel. 809/462–0044), and **Ambulance** (tel. 809/462–0251). **Hospital:** There is a 24-hour emergency room at the 210-bed **Holberton Hospital** (Hospital Rd., St. John's, tel. 809/462–0251/2/3). **Pharmacies: Joseph's Pharmacy** (Redcliffe St., St. John's, tel. 809/462–1025) and **Health Pharmacy** (Redcliffe St., St. John's, tel. 809/462–1255).

Currency

Local currency is the Eastern Caribbean dollar (E.C.$), which is tied to the U.S. dollar and fluctuates only slightly. At hotels, the rate is E.C.$2.60 to U.S.$1; at banks, it's about E.C.$2.70. American dollars are readily accepted, although you will usually receive change in E.C. dollars. Be sure you understand which currency is being used, since most places quote prices in E.C. dollars. Most hotels, restaurants, and duty-free shops take major credit cards, and all accept traveler's checks. It's a good idea to inquire at the Tourist Office or your hotel about current credit-card policy. Note: Prices quoted are in U.S. dollars unless indicated otherwise.

Taxes and Service Charges

Hotels collect a 7% government room tax. The departure tax is $10.

Hotels add a 10% service charge to your bill. In restaurants, a 10% service charge is usually added to your bill. Taxi drivers expect a 10% tip.

Guided Tours

All **taxi** drivers double as guides, and you can arrange an island tour with one for about $20 an hour. The most reliable and informed driver/guides are at **Capital Car Rental** (High St., St. John's, tel. 809/462–0863). A four-hour island tour costs $70. These prices are sometimes negotiable.

Bryson's Travel (St. John's, tel. 809/462–0223) offers personalized tours of the island, as well as cruises and deep-sea fishing trips. **Alexander, Parrish Ltd.** (St. John's, tel. 809/462–0387) specializes in island tours and can also arrange overnight stays. **Antours** (St. John's, tel. 809/462–4788) gives half- and full-day tours of the island. Antours is also the **American Express** representative on the island.

Until **Tropikelly** (tel. 809/461–0383) came along, it was hard to get into the bush in Antigua. There were no marked trails or walking paths, and roads were poor. Then Kelly Scales, a native Antiguan, and her husband, Patrick, put together their four-wheel drive operation. For $55 per person you will get an insider's guide to Antigua—deserted plantation houses, rainforest trails and ruined sugar mills and forts, as well as drinks and a picnic lunch. One highlight is the luxuriant tropical forest around the island's highest point, Boggy Peak.

Getting Around
Buses You'll see the East and West Bus Stations in St. John's, but don't expect to see many buses. Bus schedules here epitomize what is called "island time," which is to say they roll when the spirit (infrequently) moves them.

Taxis If you're uncomfortable about driving on the left, a taxi is your best bet. Taxis are unmetered, but rates are fixed from here to there and drivers are required to carry a rate card at all times.

Rental Cars To rent a car, you'll need a valid driver's license and a temporary permit ($12), which is available through the rental agent. Rentals average about $50, in season, per day, with unlimited mileage. Most agencies provide both automatic and stick shift and both right- and left-hand-drive vehicles. If you plan on driving, be careful! Not only is driving on the left, but Antiguan roads are generally unmarked and full of potholes.

Jeeps are also available from most of the rental agencies. Among the agencies are **Budget** (St. John's, tel. 809/462–3009 or 800/527–0700), **National** (St. John's, tel. 809/462–2113 or 800/468–0008), **Carib Car Rentals** (St. John's, tel. 809/462–2062), and **Avis** (at the airport or the St. James's Club, tel. 809/462–2840).

Telephones and Mail To call Antigua from the United States, dial 1, then area code 809, then the local seven-digit number (and cross your fingers for luck). Many numbers are restricted from receiving incoming international calls. In addition, the telephone system is primitive, and even local connections crackle. Few hotels have direct-dial telephones, but connections are easily made through the switchboard. Recently introduced is the phone card, to be used in new public telephones, that permits the placing of local and overseas telephone calls. You may purchase the phone card from most hotels or from a post office.

To place a call to the United States, dial 1, the appropriate area code, and the seven-digit number. AT&T's USADIRECT is available only from a few designated telephones, such as those at the airport departure lounge, the cruise terminal at St. John's, the English Harbour Marina, the Pineapple Beach Club, and the Sugar Mill Hotel. To place an interisland call, dial the local seven-digit number.

In an emergency, you can make calls from Cable & Wireless (WI) Ltd. (42–44 St. Mary's St., St. John's, tel. 809/462–9840, and Nelson's Dockyard, English Harbour, tel. 809/463–1517).

Airmail letters to North America cost E.C.60¢; postcards, E.C.40¢. The post office is at the foot of High Street in St. John's.

Opening and Closing Times In general, shops are open Monday–Saturday 8:30–noon and 1–4. Some close at noon on Thursday and Saturday. Duty-free shops that cater to tourists often have flexible hours. Banks are open Monday–Wednesday 8–2, Thursday 8–1, Friday 8–1 and 3–5.

Exploring Antigua

Numbers in the margin correspond to points of interest on the Antigua (and Barbuda) map.

St. John's The capital city of **St. John's,** home to some 40,000 people
❶ (nearly half the island's population), lies at sea level on the

northwest coast of the island. The city has seen better days, but it is in the midst of a face-lift, and there are some notable sights.

All major hotels provide free maps and island brochures or if you happen to be in St. John's, stop in at the Tourist Bureau, at the corner of Long and Thames streets.

Cross Long Street and walk one block to Church Street. The **Museum of Antigua and Barbuda** is a "hands-on history" opportunity. Signs say Please Touch, with the hope of welcoming both citizens and visitors into Antigua's past. Exhibits interpret the history of the nation from its geological birth to political independence in 1981. There are fossil and coral remains from some 34 million years ago, a life-size Arawak house, models of a sugar plantation, a wattle-and-daub house, and a minishop with handicrafts, books, historical prints, and paintings. The colonial building that houses the museum is the former courthouse, which dates from 1750. *Church and Market Sts., tel. 809/463–1060 or 809/462–3946. Admission free. Open weekdays 8:30–4, Sat. 10–1.*

Walk two blocks east on Church Street to **St. John's Cathedral.** The Anglican church sits on a hilltop, surrounded by its churchyard. At the south gate, there are figures of St. John the Baptist and St. John the Divine, said to have been taken from one of Napoleon's ships and brought to Antigua. The original church on this site was built in 1681 and replaced by a stone building in 1745. An earthquake destroyed that church in 1843, and the present building dates from 1845. With an eye to future earthquakes, the parishioners had the interior completely encased in pitch pine, hoping to forestall heavy damage. The church was elevated to the status of cathedral in 1848. *Between Long and Newcastle Sts., tel. 809/461–0082. Admission free.*

Recross Long Street, walk one block, and turn left on High Street. At the end of High Street, you'll see the **Cenotaph,** which honors Antiguans who lost their lives in World Wars I and II.

Trek seven blocks to the **Westerby Memorial,** which was erected in 1888 in memory of the Moravian bishop George Westerby. One block south of the memorial is **Heritage Quay,** a new multi-million-dollar complex, which opened some of its 40 shops in summer 1988. The complex, when completed, will include a 28-unit condominium/hotel, casino, supper club, 200-seat theater, shopping arcade, and food court. Now that the 500-foot pier and 200-foot causeway are completed, cruise-ship passengers can disembark in the middle of Heritage Quay.

Redcliffe Quay, just south of Heritage Quay, is an attractive waterfront marketplace with more of an upscale feel to its shops, restaurants, and boutiques. This is the shopping area favored by both residents and return guests. Goods here are not duty-free as they are at Heritage Quay, but prices are just as good, and the charm of the restored buildings around small courtyards is far greater. There are also cafés where you can sit and ponder the scene of two centuries ago. On this site, slaves were held captive prior to being sold.

Time Out   At **Hemingway's** (Jardine Court, tel. 809/462–2763), a historic, clapboard house in the center of St. John's, you can sit on the upstairs verandah and drink local juices like papaya and mango or have breakfast and watch the bustling life of the streets below.

At the far south end of town, where Market Street forks into Valley Road and All Saints Road, a whole lot of haggling goes on every Friday and Saturday during the day, when locals jam the public **marketplace** to buy and sell fruits, vegetables, fish, and spices. Be sure to ask before you aim a camera and expect the subject of your shot to ask for a tip.

Elsewhere on the Island After touring Fort James, we will divide the island into two more tours. First, we'll take in English Harbour and Nelson's Dockyard on the south coast, returning to St. John's along the Caribbean (western) coast. Then we'll travel to the eastern side of the island for sights ranging from historical churches to Devil's Bridge.

It's a good idea to wear a swimsuit under your clothes while you're sightseeing—one of the sights to strike your fancy may be an enticing, secluded beach. Be sure to bring your camera along. There are some picture-perfect spots around the island.

Fort James ❷ Follow Fort Road northwest out of town. In 2 miles, you'll come to **Fort James,** named after King James II. The fort was constructed between 1704 and 1739 as a lookout point for the city and St. John's Harbour. The ramparts overlooking the small islands in the bay are in ruins, but 10 cannons still point out to sea. If you continue on this road, you'll come to Dickenson Bay, with its string of smart, expensive resorts.

English Harbour ❸ Take All Saints Road south out of St. John's. Eight miles out of town—almost to the south coast—is **Liberta,** one of the first settlements founded by freed slaves. East of the village, on ❹ Monk's Hill, is the site of **Fort George,** built from 1689 to 1720. The fort wouldn't be of much help to anybody these days, but among the ruins, you can make out the sites for its 32 cannons, its water cisterns, the base of the old flagstaff, and some of the original buildings.

❺ **Falmouth,** 1½ miles farther south, sits on a lovely bay, backed by former sugar plantations and sugar mills. **St. Paul's Church** was rebuilt on the site of a church once used by troops during the Nelson period.

❻ **English Harbour** lies on the coast, just south of Falmouth. This is the most famous of Antigua's attractions. In 1671, the governor of the Leeward Islands wrote to the Council for Foreign Plantations in London pointing out the advantages of this landlocked harbor, and by 1704, English Harbour was in regular use as a garrisoned station.

In 1784, 26-year-old Horatio Nelson sailed in on HMS *Boreas* to serve as captain and second in command of the Leeward Island Station; he made frequent stops there for a period of three years. Under his command was the captain of HMS *Pegasus*, Prince William Henry, Duke of Clarence, who was to ascend the throne of England as William IV. The prince was Nelson's close friend and acted as best man when Nelson married the young widow Fannie Nisbet on Nevis in 1787.

The Royal Navy abandoned the station in 1889, and it fell into a state of decay. The Society of the Friends of English Harbour began restoring it in 1951, and on Dockyard Day, November 14, ❼ 1961, **Nelson's Dockyard** was opened with much fanfare.

Nelson's Dockyard is to the Caribbean very much what Williamsburg, Virginia, is to the United States. Within the compound there are crafts shops, hotels, and restaurants. It is a hub for oceangoing yachts and serves as headquarters for the annual Sailing Week Regatta. A lively community of mariners keeps the area active in season. Visitors who do not want to spend their entire vacation on the beach should make this their base. One of the Dockyard's former storehouses is now the beautifully restored and very British **Copper and Lumber Store Hotel.** Another fine hostelry, the **Admiral's Inn,** started out as a pitch-and-tar store, built of bricks that had been used as ballast in British ships.

The **Admiral's House Museum** has several rooms displaying ship models, a model of English Harbour, silver trophies, maps, prints, and Nelson's very own telescope and tea caddy. *English Harbour, tel. 809/463–1053 or 809/463–1379. Admission: $1.60 per person. Open daily 8–6.*

On a ridge overlooking the dockyard is **Clarence House** (tel. 809/463–1026), built in 1787 and once the home of the duke of Clarence. Princess Margaret and Lord Snowdon spent part of their honeymoon here in 1960, and Queen Elizabeth and Prince Philip have dined here. It is now used by the governor-general; visits are possible when he is not in residence. Slip a tip to the caretaker, who will give you a fascinating tour; the place is worth a visit.

⑧ As you leave the dockyard, turn right at the crossroads in English Harbour and drive to **Shirley Heights** for a spectacular view of English Harbour. The heights are named for Sir Thomas Shirley, the governor who fortified the harbor in 1787.

Not far from Shirley Heights is the brand-new **Dows Hill Interpretation Center.** Viewing platforms afford excellent views of the whole English Harbour area, but the highlight of the center is the multimedia presentation. Visitors sit in a darkened room and watch as different displays, incorporating lifelike figures and colorful tableaus, are illuminated. A commentary, synchronized TV displays, and music combine to give a cheery, if rather bland, portrait of the island's history and culture from Amerindian times to the present. *Admission: E.C.$15. Open daily 9–5.*

Time Out   Cool off with the yachting crowd on the terrace of the **Admiral's Inn** (English Harbour, tel. 809/463–1027), where the deeply tanned crews can keep an eye on their multimillion-dollar babies offshore, and on each other. The people-watching is first-rate, and so are the banana daiquiris (with or without Antiguan rum).

Drive back up to Liberta. Four and a half miles north of town, opposite the Catholic church, turn left and head southwest on **⑨** **Fig Tree Drive.** (Forget about plucking figs; *fig* is the Antiguan word for banana.) This drive takes you through the rain forest, which is rich in mangoes, pineapples, and banana trees. This is also the hilliest part of the island—**Boggy Peak,** to the west, is the highest point, rising to 1,319 feet. Fig Tree Drive runs into **⑩** Old Road, which leads down to **Curtain Bluff,** an unforgettable sight. On this peninsula, between Carlisle Bay and Morris Bay, the Atlantic Ocean meets the Caribbean Sea, resulting in wonderful color contrasts in the water.

From here, the main road sweeps along the southwest coast, where there are lovely beaches and spectacular views. The road then veers off to the northeast and goes through the villages of Bolans and Jennings.

⓫ From Jennings, a road turns right to the **Megaliths of Green-castle Hill,** an arduous climb away (you'll have to walk the last 500 yards). Some say the megaliths were set up by humans for the worship of the sun and moon; others believe they are nothing more than unusual geological formations.

The East End   St. John's is 6 miles northeast of Jennings. To explore the other half of the island, take Parham Road east out of St. John's. Three and a half miles to the east, you'll see on your left the now-defunct sugar refinery. Drive 2 miles farther and turn left on the side road that leads 1¼ miles to the settlement of
⓬ **Parham. St. Peter's Church,** built in 1840 by Thomas Weekes, an English architect, is an octagonal Italianate building whose facade was once richly decorated with stucco, though it suffered considerable damage during the earthquake of 1843.

Backtrack and continue east on Parham Road for about ¾ mile, to a fork in the road. One branch veers to the right in a southeasterly direction toward Half Moon Bay, and the other continues toward the northeast coast. The latter route runs through
⓭ the villages of Pares and Willikies to **Indian Town,** a national park, where archaeological digs have revealed evidence of Carib occupation.

⓮ Less than a mile farther along the coast is **Devil's Bridge,** a natural formation sculpted by the crashing breakers of the Atlantic at Indian Creek. The bluffs took their name from the slaves who committed suicide there in the 18th century because they believed they had the devil in them. Surf gushes out through blowholes that were carved by the breakers.

Backtrack again to Parham Road and take the fork that runs southeast. You'll travel 9 miles to Half Moon Bay. Just before the coast are the village of **Freetown** and the **Mill Reef area,** where many pre-Columbian discoveries have been made.

⓯ **Harmony Hall,** northeast of Freetown, is an interesting art gallery. A sister to the Jamaican gallery near Ocho Rios, Harmony Hall is built on the foundation of a 17th-century sugar-plantation great house. Artist Graham Davis and Peter and Annabella Proudlock, who founded the Jamaican gallery, teamed up with local entrepreneur Geoffrey Pidduck to create an Antiguan art gallery specializing in high-quality West Indian art. A large gallery is used for one-man shows, and another exhibition hall displays watercolors. A small bar and an outside restaurant under the trees are open in season. *Brown's Mill Bay, tel. 809/463–2057. Open daily 10–6.*

Barbuda   Thirty miles due north of Antigua is Barbuda—all 62 square
⓰ miles of it. Almost all the island's 1,200 people live in **Codrington.** Barbuda's 8-mile **Coco Point Beach** lures beachcombers, and the island is ringed by wrecks and reef, which makes it a great draw for divers and snorkelers.

⓱ The sole historic ruin here is **Martello Tower,** which is believed to have been a lighthouse built by the Spaniards before the English occupied the island. LIAT (*see* Before You Go, *above*) has regularly scheduled daily flights from Antigua; air and boat charters are also available (contact the Tourist Board).

Beaches

All of Antigua's beaches are public, and many are dotted with resorts that provide water-sports equipment rentals and a place to grab a cool drink. Sunbathing topless or in the buff is strictly illegal; however, on the small private beach at Hawksbill Beach Club, allover tans are possible.

Antigua **Dickenson Bay** has a lengthy stretch of powder-soft white sand and a host of hotels (the Siboney, Sandals, Antigua Beach Village, and Halcyon Cove) that cater to water-sports enthusiasts.

The white sand of **Runaway Beach** is home to the Barrymore Beach Hotel and the Runaway Beach Hotel, so things can get crowded. Refresh yourself with hot dogs and beer at the Barrymore's Satay Hut.

Five Islands has four secluded beaches of fine tan sand and coral reefs for snorkeling. The Hawksbill Hotel is nearby.

Lignumvitae Bay, south of the Jolly Beach Hotel on the west coast, is a beautiful beach at the edge of a saltwater swamp that is currently being dredged for a condominium-and-marina complex.

Johnson's Point is a deliciously deserted beach of bleached white sand on the southwest coast.

A large coconut grove adds to the tropical beauty of **Carlisle Bay,** a long snow-white beach over which the estimable Curtain Bluff resort sits. Standing on the bluff of this peninsula, you can see the almost blinding blue waters of the Atlantic Ocean drifting into the Caribbean Sea.

Half Moon Bay (home of Half Moon Bay Hotel) is a ¾-mile crescent of sand, a prime area for snorkeling and windsurfing. The hotel will let you borrow gear with a refundable deposit.

Long Bay, on the far eastern coast, has coral reefs in water so shallow that you can actually walk out to them. Here is a lovely beach, as well as the Long Bay Hotel and the rambling Pineapple Beach Club.

Barbuda **Coco Point,** on Barbuda, is an uncrowded 8-mile stretch of white sand. Barbuda is great for scuba diving, with dozens of shipwrecks off reefs that encircle the island.

Sports and the Outdoors

Almost all the resort hotels can come up with fins and masks, Windsurfers, Sunfish, glass-bottom boats, catamarans, and other water-related gear (*see* Lodging, *below*).

Bicycling Try **Sun Cycles** (tel. 809/461–0324) for short- or long-term leases.

Boating **Wadadli Watersports** (tel. 809/462–2890) rents catamarans and other crafts. **Shorty's** at Dickenson Bay has some of the best water sports on the island, if a somewhat hectic pace (tel. 809/462–2393). **Nicholson Yacht Charters** (tel. 800/662–6066) are the real professionals. A long-established island family, they can charter you anything from a 20-foot ketch to a giant schooner for $10,000 per week.

Fitness Center The **Benair Fitness Club** (Country Club Rd., Hodges Bay, tel. 809/462–1540) has fitness equipment, Jacuzzi, aerobic classes, and a juice bar.

Golf There is an 18-hole course at **Cedar Valley Golf Club** (tel. 809/462–0161), and a nine-hole course at **Half Moon Bay Hotel** (tel. 809/460–4300).

Horseback Riding First-rate Texas quarter horses and former racehorses are found at the **St. James Stables,** attached to the St. James's Club (tel. 809/463–1430 or 809/463–1113).

Sailing The **Antigua School of Sailing** (tel. 809/462–2026) offers short resort courses.

Scuba Diving With all the wrecks and reefs, there are lots of undersea sights to see. Contact **Dive Antigua** (tel. 809/462–0256) or **Aquanaut Dive Center** (Halcyon Cove Hotel, tel. 809/462–3483), which offers certification courses and day and night dives from three separate locations: the St. James's Club (tel. 809/460–5000), Galleon Beach Club (tel. 809/460–1024), and the Royal Antiguan (tel. 809/462–3733). Dive packages are offered by the **Runaway Beach Club** (tel. 809/462–2626). If you are in the English Harbour area, Captain A. G. Fincham, a British ex-merchant seaman and proprietor of **Dockyard Divers** (tel. 809/464–8591, fax 809/460–1179), one of the oldest established outfits on the island, offers diving and snorkeling trips, PADI courses, and dive packages with accommodations.

Sea Excursions The 50-foot catamaran *Cariba* offers full-day sails (10–4) with lunch or half-day sails (9:30–12:30 or 1:30–4:30) that include an on-board picnic. There are swim and snorkel stops on all trips, but the *Cariba* also has underwater viewing windows for those who prefer to stay dry. **Wadadli Watersports** (tel. 809/462–2890) makes trips to Bird Island and Barbuda that include soft drinks and barbecue on the beach. The *Jolly Roger* (tel. 809/462–2064) has a "fun cruise," complete with "pirate" crew, limbo dancing, plank walking, and other pranks. *Paradise I* (tel. 809/462–4158) is a 45-foot Beneteau yacht that offers lunch or sunset cruises. The *Falcon* (tel. 809/462–4792) is a catamaran schooner that cruises to Bird Island and Barbuda for snorkeling and barbecue; it also makes sunset cruises.

Tennis The **Temo Sports Complex** (Falmouth Bay, tel. 809/463–1781) has floodlit courts, glass-backed squash courts, showers, a sports shop, and snack bars. There are also seven courts at the **St. James's Club** (five are lighted for night play), five courts at the **Half Moon Club,** four Har-Tru and one grass court at **Curtain Bluff.**

Waterskiing Rentals are available at **Wadadli Watersports** (tel. 809/462–2890).

Windsurfing The **High Wind Centre** at the Lord Nelson Hotel is *the* spot for serious board sailors, run by expert Patrick Scales (tel. 809/462–3094). Rentals are also available at **Wadadli Watersports** (tel. 809/462–2890) and **Hodges Bay Club** (tel. 809/462–2300); most major hotels offer boardsailing equipment.

Spectator Sports For information about sports events, contact **Antigua Sports and Games** (tel. 809/462–1925).

Cricket Practically the only thing most Americans know about this game is that there's something called a sticky wicket. Here, as in Britain and all the West Indies, the game is a national passion. Youngsters play on makeshift pitches, which apparently are comparable to sandlots, and international matches are fought out in the stadium on Independence Avenue, St. John's.

Shopping

Antigua's duty-free shops are at Heritage Quay and are the reason so many cruise ships call here. Bargains can be found in perfumes, liqueurs and liquor (including, of course, Antiguan rum), jewelry, china, and crystal. As for local items, look for straw hats, baskets, batik, pottery, and hand-printed cotton clothing.

Shopping Areas The 30-odd boutiques, plus restaurants and nightclub, at **Redcliffe Quay** are generally interesting and upscale, all housed in a restored "barracoon," once a slave-holding compound and auction site. The newer **Heritage Quay** (also in St. John's) has some 35 shops that cater primarily to the cruise-ship crowd that docks almost at its doorstep. The main tourist shops in St. John's are along **St. Mary's, High,** and **Long streets.**

Good Buys **Specialty Shoppe** (St. Mary's St., tel. 809/462-1198), **The Scent**
China and Crystal **Shop** (High St., tel. 809/462-0303), and **Norma's Duty-Free Shop** (Heritage Quay Shopping Center and Halcyon Cove Hotel, tel. 809/462-0172) have wares that make impressive presents. **Little Switzerland** (Heritage Quay, tel. 809/462-3108) houses pricey buys in a luxurious, and air-conditioned, setting.

Jewelry Hans Smit is **The Goldsmitty** (Redcliffe Quay, tel. 809/462-4601), a European-trained expert goldsmith who turns gold, black coral, and precious and semiprecious stones into one-of-a-kind works of art that adorn the wrists and necks of the rich and famous. (Be aware that environmental groups discourage tourists from purchasing corals that are designated as endangered species because the reefs are often harvested carelessly.) **Colombian Emeralds** (Heritage Quay, tel. 809/462-2086) is the largest retailer of Colombian emeralds in the world. Jewelry bargains are also at **Norma's Duty-Free Shop** (Heritage Quay Shopping Center and the Halcyon Cove Hotel, tel. 809/462-0172).

Liquor and **The Warehouse** (St. Mary's St., tel. 809/462-0495) and **Manuel**
Liqueurs **Diaz Liquor Store** (Long and Market Sts., tel. 809/462-0440) should whet your appetite. Cuban cigars are found at **The Cigar Shop** (Heritage Quay, tel. 890/462-2677), but can't be brought legally back to the United States.

Native Crafts **Base,** in Redcliffe Quay (tel. 809/462-0920), is the brainchild of English designer Steven Giles and his stripey, cotton and lycra beachwear is now all the rage on the island. Janie Easton designs many of the original finds in her two **Galley Boutiques** (the main shop in a historic building in English Harbour, tel. 809/462-1525; another at the upscale **St. James's Club,** tel. 809/463-1333) with pizzazz and reasonable prices. Trinidadian Natalie White sells her sculptured cushions and wall hangings, all hand-painted on silk, and signed, from her home-studio (tel. 809/463-2519), but she is expanding to a larger **Craft Originals Studio** on the Coast Road. Artist-filmmaker Nick Maley, with his wife, Gloria, have turned the **Island Arts Galleries** (three locations: their home-studio, Alton Place, on Sandy Lane, behind the Hodges Bay Club, tel. 809/461-3332; Heritage Quay, tel. 809/462-2787; and the St. James's Club, tel. 809/463-1113) into

a melting pot for Caribbean artists, with prices ranging from
$10 to $15,000. **Harmony Hall** (at Brown's Bay Mill, near Freetown, tel. 809/460–4120) is the Antiguan sister to the original
Jamaica location. In addition to "Annabella Boxes," books, and
cards, there is pottery and ceramic pieces, carved wooden fantasy birds, and an ever-changing roster of exhibits. The **CoCo
Shop** (St. Mary's St., tel. 809/462–1128) is a favorite haunt for
Sea Island cotton designs, Daks clothing, and Liberty of London fabrics, along with the shop's own designs for the country-
club set. **Karibbean Kids** (Redcliffe Quay, tel. 809/462–4566)
has great gifts for youngsters. **A Thousand Flowers** (Redcliffe
Quay, tel. 809/462–4264) sells items made of natural fibers and
is also the place for Java wraps. A "must" buy at the **Map Shop**
(St. Mary's St., tel. 809/462–3993) for those interested in Antiguan life, is the paperback *To Shoot Hard Labour (The Life and
Times of Samuel Smith, an Antiguan Workingman);* it costs
$12 you won't regret spending. Also check out any of the books
of Jamaica Kincaid, whose works on her native Antigua have
won international, albeit controversial, acclaim.

Perfume **CoCo Shop** (St. Mary's St., tel. 809/462–1128), **The Scent Shop**
(High St., tel. 809/462–0303). In Heritage Quay, two shops, **La
Parfumerie** (tel. 809/462–2601) and **Little Switzerland** (tel. 809/
462–3108), have extensive selections of European scents for
men and women.

Dining

The focus, naturally, is on fresh-caught fish and lobster, but
Antigua offers sophisticated Continental and American dining
as well. Because of the island's British heritage, Antiguans
tend to dress more formally for dinner than is the custom on
many of the other Caribbean islands. A few places, which will
be noted, require both jacket and tie.

Most menu prices are listed in E.C. dollars; some are listed in
both E.C. and U.S. dollars. Be sure to ask if credit cards are
accepted and in which currency the prices are quoted. Prices
below are in U.S. dollars. Dinner reservations are needed during high season.

Highly recommended restaurants are indicated by a star ★.

Category	Cost*
Very Expensive	over $45
Expensive	$25–$45
Moderate	$15–$25
Inexpensive	under $15

per person, excluding drinks, service, and sales tax (7%)

★ **Jumby Bay.** A private 300-acre island resort, just a 15-minute
launch ride from Antigua's shores, accepts a limited number of
outside guests for lunch or dinner when advance reservations
are made. For a set price of $55 (plus government 10% service
tax), guests board the noon boat for a nonstop buffet at the resort, after several sips of Woody's (the infamous bar director's)
famed fruit punches. For the food, the price is outrageous,
while the setting looking out through the coconut palms onto

the beach and turquoise Caribbean Sea is priceless. The management will also give an informal tour of their special island on request. A dinner reservation means catching the 6 or 7 PM launch and, for $85, a choice of five entrées. While the menu changes nightly, a few of the favored dishes are sautéed breast of chicken filled with wild mushrooms, Mediterranean seafood terrine with sprinkled saffron, and soufflé of scallops with basil puree. *Long Island, tel. 809/462–6000. No outside dinner reservations Wed. or Sun. nights. AE, MC, V. Closed Sept. and Oct. Very Expensive.*

★ **Le Bistro.** This elegant creation of Raffaele and Philippa Esposito, offers two sittings for dinner in season (7–7:30 or 9–9:30). Sip one of the wines from the extensive wine cellar, then move on to tables tucked inside this renovated country house with beamed ceiling, crisp linen, and crystal. An extensive menu offers some 18 main dishes, including fresh grilled local fish, diced lobster with fresh vegetables in a tarragon sauce, imported Dover sole, salmon garnished with caviar, prime rib of beef, roast Long Island duck, and roast quail in a passion-fruit sauce. Desserts are divine, and don't miss the limoncella, a tangy lemon liqueur that the owner imports from his native Capri and serves with delicious espresso coffee. *Hodges Bay, tel. 809/462–3881. AE, DC, MC, V. Closed Mon. and early May–early Aug. Very Expensive.*

Cacubi Room. Candlelight and crisp white napery enhance the elegant mood in the Blue Waters Hotel's air-conditioned restaurant. For openers, try the homemade liver pâté marinated in brandy and flavored with herbs. The chef's special creation is Flying Fish Cavalier (two fillets cooked in white wine and herbs, served in a cream sauce flavored with Cavalier rum and sprinkled with butter-fried coconut). This restaurant is famed for its flambéed desserts—try the pineapple flambé or crepes Suzette. Liqueurs and cigars are brought to your table after your meal. *Blue Waters Hotel, Boon Pt., tel. 809/462–0290. Reservations suggested. Jackets required. AE, MC, V. Expensive.*

Clouds. The elegantly decorated terrace sits high on a hill, overlooking Halcyon Cove and Dickenson Bay. The chef turns out such starters as melon glazed with ginger and honey, accompanied by grape and red-wine sorbet. Soups include chilled zucchini and carrot. Among the entrées are pan-fried medallions of venison, noisettes of lamb, and breast of chicken filled with duck and pistachio-nut mousse, accompanied by herb butter and avocado. For dessert, try the fresh strawberry parfait. *Halcyon Cove Beach Resort, tel. 809/462–0256. Reservations required. Jacket and tie required. AE, MC, V. Closed Sun. Expensive.*

Colombo's. The Sardinians who run this restaurant make every effort to please, and the result is a little bit of Italy in Antigua. On a small bay in English Harbour, with views of palm trees and historic cannons, the restaurant's dining room has timbered, white-painted ceilings, a stone floor, and hanging flags. The full Italian menu includes homemade pastas, veal scallopine, tournedos, and lobster Mornay. On Wednesday nights a reggae band entertains. *Galleon Beach Club, English Harbour, tel. 809/460–1452. Reservations suggested. AE, MC, V. Closed Sept. Expensive.*

★ **La Perouche.** David Wallach, the chef at this fine, gourmet restaurant, is only 28, but his résumé is long—training at the Culinary Institute of America and a spell at L'Esperance in France (among others), before he decided to come to Antigua and help

Mona Frisell, an aristocratic-looking Swede, turn La Perouche into one of the best restaurants on the island. Among the feats of culinary magic he performs nightly is the *escalar*, a rare deep-sea fish from Ecuador with a mild, slightly lemony taste, served in a polenta and lobster bordelaise sauce. An avocado mousse with sweet potato wafers arranged like petals around the wooden serving bowl is typical of the restaurant's determination to please the eye as well as the taste buds. The fruit plate—rock-fig bananas, black pineapple, fresh kidney mango, and passion fruit arranged around a hub of Antiguan golden apple—is a work of art. The plant-filled patio itself is a pleasure, with pretty green-and-white trim, crystal glasses, and a profusion of painted wooden parrots that hang everywhere —hence, the restaurant's name. *English Harbour, tel. 809/460-3040. Dinner only. AE, MC, V. Closed Sundays and Sept. Expensive.*

★ **The Wardroom Restaurant.** On the ground-floor of the beautifully restored Copper and Lumber Store, around a charming central courtyard hung with bougainvillea, this restaurant, with its massive brick walls, stained beams, and views of the floodlit battlements of English Harbour, breathes the atmosphere of Olde England in the Caribbean. The menu is international, mixing dishes like West African peanut soup with lobster in puff-pastry, a good selection of local fish dishes, and even lamb cutlets. It has been greatly improved under new (Scottish) management. *Nelson's Dockyard, tel. 809/460-1058. Reservations advised. Moderate-Expensive.*

★ **Admiral's Inn.** Known as the Ad to yachtsmen around the world, this historic inn, in the heart of English Harbour, is a must for Anglophiles and mariners. At the bar inside, you can sit and soak up the centuries under dark, timbered wood (the bar top even has the names of sailors from Nelson's fleet carved into it), but most guests tend to sit on the terrace under shady Australian pines to enjoy the splendid views of the harbor complex and Clarence House opposite. Specialties include curried conch, fresh snapper with equally fresh limes, or Lobster Thermidor. The pumpkin soup is not to be missed. *Nelson's Dockyard, tel. 809/460-1027. Reservations required. AE, MC, V. Moderate.*

Alberto's. Owners Alberto and Vanessa Ravanello, who once held sway at the Yacht Club, now wow the English Harbour crowd with local seafood with an Italian accent. Try eggplant parmigiana, veal pizzaiola, linguini with clams, fresh langouste, or Alberto's creation for the evening. *Red Hill, near the St. James's Club, tel. 809/460-3007 or via VHF 68. Reservations required. AE, DC, MC, V. Closed Mon. in season; Mon. and Tues. off-season. Dinner only. Moderate.*

★ **Coconut Grove.** There are few more pleasant places to eat in Antigua than the waterfront restaurant at the Siboney Beach Club. With the coconut palms growing up through the roof and the waves lapping on the white coral sand a few feet away, you feel as though you are in the South Seas. Service is friendly and attentive, and the English-born owner is a charming hostess. The Trinidad-born chef makes good use of local produce, though the menu is mainstream European. Start with a chilled gazpacho or the superb terrine of broccoli with lobster. Follow this with lamb, steak, or fish. The fish is especially good, with sauces that complement the flavor of the marlin, kingfish, or snapper. Lobsters are available for the asking. Vegetarian dishes and low-cholesterol recipes are also offered. *Box 1760,*

Dickenson Bay, tel. 809/462–1538, fax 809/461–4555. Reservations suggested in peak season. MC, V. Moderate.

Lemon Tree. This air-conditioned, art-deco restaurant, on the second floor of a historic building in the old part of St. John's, is a smart, up-beat eating place, popular with cruise-ship guests. Live music is offered every night, varying from soft classical piano to funky reggae. The owner Janet Ferraro, a voluminous local lady with close-cropped hair and a winning smile, fills the place with her *bon viveur* presence. The menu is eclectic, mixing minipizzas and ribs with beef Wellington, Cornish hen, lobster, vegetarian crepes, a very spicy Cajun garlic shrimp, and pasta dishes. For those who like Mexican food, the Lemon Tree offers unbeatable burritos, as well as chili, nachos, and fajitas. *Long and Church Sts., St. John's, tel. 809/462–1689. AE, DC, MC, V. Open 10 AM–11 PM. Moderate.*

Lobster Pot. This bistro-style restaurant has improved considerably since being taken over by ex-British Airways steward, Tony Sayers. Even with a fishing boat in the center of it, the large stone-flagged dining room, with its spirelike timbered roof supported on stone columns, is airy and open to the sea breeze (the best seats are in the gallery right on the water). The diverse menu includes coconut-milk curry; baked breast of chicken stuffed with goat's cheese, broccoli, and sun-dried tomatoes; and good local seafood (lobster, mahi-mahi, and red snapper). For Anglophiles, there is bread-and-butter pudding and, for children, hamburgers and 4-oz. steaks. *Runaway Bay, tel. 809/462–2855. Reservations advised. D, MC, V. Moderate.*

Shirley Heights Lookout. This restaurant is in part of an 18th-century fortification, and the view of English Harbour below is breathtaking. A breezy pub downstairs opens onto the lookout point and upstairs, there's a cozy, windowed room with hardwood floors and beamed ceilings. Pub offerings include burgers, sandwiches, and barbecue, while the upstairs room serves the likes of pumpkin soup and lobster in lime sauce. The best time to come is on Sunday after 3 PM, when crowds troop up the hill for the barbecue livened by a steel-band island music from 3 to 6 and reggae music from 6 to 9. *Shirley Heights, tel. 809/463–1785. Reservations required in season. AE, MC, V. Moderate.*

The Dolphin. The honey-colored hurricane shutters; rattan chairs from Dominica; and Madras cotton tablecloths, handsewn by the redoubtable Mrs. Murphy (the owner's mother who runs the guest house opposite) make this small restaurant in a suburb of St. John's worth the $4 cab fare to get there. The menu is traditional Caribbean, with dishes like saltfish and ducana; shrimp in a freshly grated ginger and garlic sauce; *orpionos*, a delicious Puerto Rican specialty of diced vegetables sautéed in hot seasoning, dipped in batter, deep-fried, and served with a creole sauce. The young Antiguan owner and his Toronto-born wife make pleasant hosts, and Mrs. Murphy's coconut meringue pie is to die for. On Saturday evenings there is live jazz. *All Saint's Rd., St. John's, tel. 809/462–1183. MC, V. Inexpensive–Moderate.*

Redcliffe Tavern. If you're in St. John's for shopping, stop by at this uniquely decorated restaurant in the old section of Redcliffe Quay. The aged brick, and white-and-black painted woodwork of this former colonial warehouse give it a lot of charm. But what really makes the decor special is the antique water-pumping equipment, still bearing the original maker's crests from England. Salvaged from all over the island by the owners and given a coat of fresh, white paint, these beautiful old machines, with their flywheels and pistons, have been imaginatively integrated into the restaurant's structure (one supports the buffet bar, for instance). The menu has an especially good selection of local fishes like wahoo, marlin, shark, and mahi-mahi. Other specialties include mango-stuffed chicken breast and curry sauce, beer-battered flying fish from Trinidad, and Guyanese shrimp. *Redcliffe Quay, St. John's, tel. 809/ 461–4557. AE, MC, V. Inexpensive–Moderate.*

Calypso. This cheerful outdoor spot has, since opening in the fall of 1992, become a favorite with St. John's professional set. At lunchtime it is packed with smartly dressed lawyers and government functionaries smoking cigars and flirting over traditional Caribbean food. Tables are arranged under green umbrellas on a sunny patio dominated by the remains of a brick kiln. Specials change every day, but generally include stewed lamb, grilled lobster, and baked chicken served with fungi, a pastelike vegetable dish made of cornmeal and okra, rice, and dumplings. *Redcliffe St., St. John's, tel. 809/462–1965. No credit cards. Inexpensive–Moderate.*

Brother B's. It's impossible to miss this funky restaurant in the appropriately named Soul Alley, with its yellow-painted wooden fence and hand-painted boards advertising its fare. If you want to try such local specialties as pepperpot and *fungi; pelleau,* a seasoned rice dish with chicken, meat and peas; saltfish and *ducana,* a dumplinglike mixture of grated sweet potato and coconut, wrapped in a banana leaf; or bull's foot soup, a Caribbean variant of a 19th-century dish from Manchester, England, this is the place to do it. The ambience is downbeat, and rather surly waitresses makes Brother B's is as authentically Antiguan as you will find. *Soul Alley, St. John's, tel. 809/462–0616. Also open for breakfast. No credit cards. Inexpensive.*

★ **Home.** It's an interesting idea and deserves to prosper. Carl Thomas returned to his native Montserrat after years in Manhattan, and opened a restaurant in his boyhood home, a '50s bungalow in a quiet suburb of St. John's. He completely refurbished the original house, knocking down walls to create one large, open space; planted an herb and vegetable garden; and hired a Dutch cook. Furnishing is Ikea-style stripped-pine and polished-wood floors with artwork from Africa and the Caribbean (Carl's own watercolors are in the rest room). At press time (admittedly only two weeks after it opened), there were still a few teething troubles. The food, described as "Caribbean haute cuisine," varied greatly in quality—the smoked fish, a specialty of the house, and a delicious bread pudding with whisky sauce were excellent, but one guest had tears streaming down her face after inadvertently swallowing a whole hot pepper—and the interior is so squeaky-clean and new that it lacks atmosphere. Be careful of the "Homewrecker," Carl's own fruit punch; it will knock you off your feet. *Gambles Terrace, St. John's, tel. 809/461–7651. Reservations advised. AE, MC, V. Inexpensive.*

Lodging

Antigua's beaches are decorated with an assortment of resorts, ranging from the spectacular to small and self-catering homes away from home. Those seeking active nightlife and opportunities for meeting other island guests will want to stay in one of the hotels in Dickenson Bay, where properties are close together, which makes for lots of beach action, and St. John's is just a five-minute cab ride away. The resorts scattered elsewhere on the island tend to cater more to honeymooners and to those who seek some seclusion. Increasingly, hotels are offering all-inclusive rates that cover all meals, drinks, and most of their sporting facilities. Though these rates help in budgeting your vacation, they tend to make you the hotel's prisoner. The price categories below reflect the room cost during high season—not the all-inclusive rate, which you will be quoted on making a reservation.

Highly recommended lodgings are indicated by a star ★.

Category	Cost*
Very Expensive	over $350
Expensive	$250–$350
Moderate	$150–$250
Inexpensive	under $150

All prices are for a standard double room for two, excluding 7% tax and a 10% service charge.

Blue Waters Beach Hotel. Luscious lime-colored buildings, set in a tropical garden along two white-sand beaches, draw a European clientele to this casually elegant property, where the staff speaks 10 different languages. Accommodations are in air-conditioned rooms or two- and three-bedroom villas, all of which are beachfront with balconies or patios. *Box 256, St. John's (Boon Pt.), tel. 809/462–0290 or 800/372–1323; in the United Kingdom, 081/367–5175, fax 809/462–0293. 67 rooms. Facilities: 2 restaurants, 2 bars, pool, 1 lighted tennis court, gift shop, water-sports center. AE, MC, V. EP, MAP. Very Expensive.*

★ **Curtain Bluff.** Curtain Bluff is in a league of its own. It could be called Howard Hulford's Dream, after the owner: a tough American who now lives in a gated villa at the top of the property. Like another HH (Howard Hughes), he built a hotel where no one believed one could be built—in this case, on a spectacular bluff bordered on one side by the Atlantic Ocean and on the other by the Caribbean. Beachfront rooms each have their own small balcony, king-size bed, and tiled bathroom. The suites zigzag their way up the bluff on the Atlantic side. The best of them are arguably the finest accommodations on Antigua—huge, split-level apartments, with two large balconies offering spectacular views of the beach below; a large, tastefully decorated living room; and, up a flight of steps, a spacious, cool bedroom with a timbered "tray" ceiling. Food, served in a restaurant surrounded by carefully tended gardens, is prepared by a Swiss chef and served by an army of waiters ready to please. The jacket-and-tie dress code for dinner has recently been relaxed, but except on Sundays, when dinner is served at the beach house to the sounds of a Calypso band, Curtain Bluff is still for the "dressed-for-dinner" set. *Box 288, St. John's, tel. 809/462–8400 or in NY, 212/289–8888, fax 809/462–8409. 62 rooms and suites. Facilities: restaurant, lounge, 4 tennis courts, squash court, fitness center, pro shop, croquet, putting green, water-sports center. AE. Closed mid-May–mid-Oct. All-inclusive. Very Expensive.*

Hawksbill Beach Hotel. The recently refurbished Hawksbill, named after the spectacular rock that juts out of the bay, sprawls over 37 acres of the bucolic Five Islands peninsula. It boasts four beaches of fine, tan sand—one of which permits sunbathing in the buff—that are the hotel's chief benefit. The main building, reception area, and dining room are on a small bluff that commands a sweeping view of the sea and Montserrat beyond, set off by the restored ruins of a sugar mill in the foreground. The best accommodations are in the West Indian Great House, an old, colonial-style building with king-size beds, tile floors, wicker furniture, and kitchenette (the rate is $1,330 per night, albeit for six persons). The deluxe rooms facing the sea have just enough room to walk around the bed, and the bathrooms tend to have sloppy plasterwork. The less-expensive rooms in row buildings face the garden and do not have telephones or TVs. Gentlemen are requested not to wear short sleeves into the dining room after 7 PM. And though children are now more welcome than they used to be ("screamers" not included), Hawksbill is more a place for young couples and singles. Breakfast and the use of most water-sports facilities are complimentary. *Box 108, St. John's, tel. 809/462–0301, in Canada, 416/622–8813, fax 809/462–1515. 75 rooms. Facilities: 2 restaurants, 2 bars, pool, tennis court, boutique, water-sports center. AE, DC, MC, V. BP. Very Expensive.*

Hodges Bay Club. Opposite Prickly Pear Island, on a great snorkeling beach, are Hodges Bay's luxury one- and two-bedroom condominium villas. All villas have fully equipped kitchens, king-size beds, two balconies, and daily maid service. All bedrooms are air-conditioned, and each has a private bath. *Box 1237, St. John's, tel. 809/462–2300 or 800/432–4229; in NY 212/535–9530, fax 809/462–1962. 26 suites. Facilities: restaurant, pool, 2 tennis courts, water-sports center. AE, DC, MC, V. EP. Very Expensive.*

★ **Jumby Bay.** Fifteen minutes by launch from Antigua is this 300-acre private island retreat, with little to distract you but the occasional roar of aircraft landing at the nearby airport. Billing itself as "very exclusive, very private," Jumby Bay is also very expensive. The least that you will pay for a double room in high season is $900 a day, though it includes all meals and drinks, plus some of the sporting facilities. This princely sum will give you a bed, a small sitting area, and a bathroom that has no tub but an oversize shower, bathrobes, and hair dryer. Some bathrooms boast garden showers where the door opens onto a tiny walled-in plant area. More than half these rooms are in cottages scattered over the property, and another dozen are in the Pond Bay House—room number 36 is a choice one. Continental breakfasts are served at the Pond Bay House while for buffet breakfasts guests must trek to the main house. The most desirable rooms (adding another $500 a day to your bill) are in private villas leased back to the hotel—these are spacious with a separate lounge, a kitchen/dining room, two large bedrooms (each with an oversize bathroom), and a shared small swimming pool. Privacy on the island's four beaches and 300 acres of groomed land is ensured by wandering security guards. Lunch is an alfresco buffet; dinner is in the old manor house—a relaxed occasion with the opportunity for alfresco dining. Transportation on the island is by bicycle. The management believes that children under age 8 would not be comfortable here. *Box 243, St. John's, tel. 809/462–6000 or 800/421–9016, fax 809/462–6020. 38 suites. Facilities: 2 restaurants, 3* *bars, tennis, bicycles, sailboats, water-sports center. AE, MC, V. All-inclusive. Very Expensive.*

Pineapple Beach Club (formerly the New Horizons). A broad stone walk leads directly from the reception area to the beach of this all-inclusive (meals, drinks, gratuities, sports, you name it) resort. The fan-cooled beachfront doubles have private terraces and shower baths. There are no phones or TVs. Garden-view rooms are air-conditioned. The pool and the windsurfing school are located on Long Bay's white-sand beach. Live entertainment is offered nightly. Be sure to bring the letter confirming your reservation; sometimes the hotel overbooks and reservation information is lost. *Box 54, St. John's, tel. 809/463–2006 or 800/345–0356, fax 809/465–2452; in Canada, 800/468–0023. 125 rooms. Facilities: restaurant, bar, pool, 4 tennis courts. AE, MC, V. All-inclusive. Very Expensive.*

St. James's Club. The hotel's location, on a 100-acre spit of land that follows the curve of Mamora Bay, is dramatic, and continual refurbishing of the facilities keeps the resort looking smart. The main buildings and its wings, with 85 rooms and 20 one-bedroom suites, sit atop the peninsula. "Premier" rooms, created in 1992, for which you pay 10% more, have *baldachinos* (canopy beds), remote-control TV, and hair dryers. The "villa village," a group of 73 two-bedroom villas that spill down the hillside facing the bay, are connected by cobbled streets. Inside, rattan furniture, pastel fabrics, and rag rugs strewn over tile floors are complemented by the Haitian paintings and lithographs, but the whole thing feels a bit like a suburban development in Los Angeles, with views onto your neighbor's roof. A deli in the complex offers a small selection of imported foods, or guests can take the shuttle bus to one of the three restaurants in the main building. The food is, unfortunately, not as good as it should be, and overall St. James tends to live off its *renommé* (it is affiliated with other like-named resorts in London, Paris, and Los Angeles), rather than what it delivers. That said, the beaches and sports facilities—snorkeling on the nearby Mamora Reef, state-of-the-art tennis courts (and a "clinic" given by Martina Navratilova), and a large children's playground—are superb. Misty, Hi-Fi, Fool, and Poker, the resort's four Texas quarter horses, are good for gallops along the beach or treks through the hills. *Box 63, St. John's, tel. 809/460–5000; in NY, 212/486–2575 or 800/274–0008, fax 809/460–3015. 178 total accommodations. Facilities: 3 restaurants, 5 bars, 24-hour room service; 3 swimming pools, Jacuzzi, minigym, 4 boutiques, beauty salon and masseuse, nightclub, casino, 7 tennis courts (5 hard, 2 omniturf, 5 lighted), water sports and scuba diving, lawn croquet, children's playground, golf at the 18-hole Cedar Valley Gold Club, horseback riding. AE, MC, V. EP, MAP. Very Expensive.*

Galley Bay. Set between what is virtually a private curving beach of white sand and a blue lagoon, this 30-year-old hotel is an all-inclusive quiet retreat—the food is of high caliber, with dinner consisting of a five-course meal under the stars. Beachfront villas have king-size beds, ceiling fans, showers, tiled floors, and floral-tropics coverlets and drapes. Ten of the rooms are designated "executive rooms," located on the quietest section of the beach, and offer slightly more space and a private patio with a hammock to swing in. Rooms in Gauguin Village, a group of small, round thatch-roof Tahitian-style cottages on the lagoon, are furnished with a large bed under a canopy of mosquito netting and a small table for the coffee

machine. Across a connecting patio just large enough for two
deck chairs in another thatch cottage of a similar size is the
bathroom with a shower for two and a dressing table. These
cottages are cutsy romantic for some and confining native huts
for others. *Box 305, St. John's, tel. 809/462–0302, fax 809/462–
4551. 30 rooms. Facilities: restaurant, bar, tennis court, water-sports center. AE, MC, V. All-inclusive. Expensive–Very
Expensive.*

Dickenson Bay Cottages. This small, exclusive, U.K.-managed
development on Marble Hill, overlooking Dickenson Bay,
opened in 1992. The rooms, in two-story, villa-style buildings
set into the hillside, are crisp and elegantly furnished, if just a
little sterile. Downstairs there is a large living-room area and
well-equipped kitchen. The bedroom and bathroom are up a
flight of stairs in a galleried area. Larger units have two bedrooms upstairs and a large verandah overlooking the ocean.
One annoying feature, out of keeping with the price, is the lack
of a cross-breeze, which pretty much obliges you to keep the
air-conditioner on. A beach, shared with Halcyon Cove, is five
minutes' walk away, and the resort has an arrangement for the
use of tennis and water-sports facilities at a 20% reduction.
Several other resorts nearby enable you to move easily between lively entertainment and eating and secluded hillside
tranquility. *Box 1379, St. John's, tel. 809/462–4940, fax 809/
462–4941. 13 rooms. Facilities: pool, cable TV, room service,
telephone with direct U.S. dial. AE, MC, V. All-inclusive. Expensive.*

Halcyon Cove Beach Resort. Days and nights are activity-
packed in this government-owned Dickenson Bay hotel, which
attracts discount tour groups from Europe and America—so
that while you may be paying $350 for your room, your neigh-
bor is paying a third of the price. Accommodations, all with air-
conditioning and private balcony or patio, are scattered around
the courtyard pool or on the beach. A water-sports center offers excursions on a glass-bottom boat and waterskiing, in addition to the other usual water sports. In the evening, you can
go for a spin in the casino or around the dance floor. At press
time, the resort was being considerably expanded, with the addition of 77 new rooms. *Box 251, St. John's, tel. 809/462–0256 or
800/255–5589, fax 809/462–0271. 135 rooms. Facilities: 4 restaurants, 3 bars, room service, pool, 4 lighted tennis courts,
casino, boutiques, water-sports center. AE, DC, MC, V. EP,
MAP. Expensive.*

The Inn at English Harbour. The main part of this small, historic hotel sits atop a hill with stunning views of English Harbour.
The bar, with its green leather chairs, wooden floors, and maritime prints, is one of the most pleasant on the island. Off to the
side of the main house are the hilltop rooms, housed in individual, cottage-style units. Down at the inn's own beach there are
more rooms in two-story, wooden buildings, surrounded by hibiscus and bougainvillea. The superior rooms are slightly larger, but all rooms have phones, wall safes, refrigerators, and
hair dryers and are attractively furnished with wicker furniture and pastel fabrics. Also on the beach is a second bar-res-
taurant that stays open till 6 PM. A shuttle bus runs guests up
and down the hill. The beach, like all those in English Harbour, is
not the best. During high season only MAP bookings are accepted. *Box 187, St. John's, tel. 809/460–1014, fax 809/460–
1603. 28 rooms. Facilities: 2 restaurants, 2 bars, water sports.
AE, MC, V. EP, MAP. Expensive.*

★ **Sandals.** Pool olympics and beach volleyball, aerobics sessions, and evening social events are all organized by a social hostess who will veritably scowl if you don't join in the fun, but you can still enjoy the place if you just want to read and relax. Its appeal is as an all-inclusive couples-only resort. Everything, from the tennis coaching to the pedal boats, the scuba diving to the swim-up pool-bars, discos, and meals, is included in the price. For a little extra, you can even get married in front of a miniature waterfall. Rooms, facing the beach or the garden, are spacious, with four-poster beds, terra-cotta tiled floors, and pastel furnishings. There are also a group of rondevals (circular bungalows) facing the beach. Food (all imported from the U.S.) is served in three restaurants offering Continental, West Indian, and westernized Oriental fare. The whole property, packed though it is in season, is exceptionally well maintained; fixtures and fittings, from the marble-tiled steam rooms in the Fitness Center to the swimming pools and Jacuzzis scattered about the property, are of a uniformly high standard. *Box 147, St. John's, tel. 809/462-0267, fax 809/462-4135. U.S. reservations, tel. 800/SANDALS. Facilities: 3 restaurants, 4 bars, 4 pools, 4 Jacuzzis, health spa, 4 tennis courts, and water sports. AE. All-inclusive. Expensive.*

Trade Winds Hotel. This German-run resort, on the crest of Marble Hill, with spectacular views down to Dickenson Bay and the ocean beyond, should be one of the most popular in Antigua. Attractive Spanish-style villas, built along the edge of the hillside, are of three types: deluxe, double, and studio. The deluxe suites are on the first floor and have a kitchen; large living-room area, furnished with lacquered, bamboo furniture, art posters, a large E-shaped sofa, and a Murphy bed; and a cool, spacious bedroom with white floor-tiles and ceiling fans, connected by a small passageway, off of which is one of the two bathrooms. The double rooms, on the ground floor, open onto a large patio with stunning views right across to Montserrat. But the place lacks character and identity. And though there are Jeeps to shuttle you there and back, it is a nuisance that the beach is nearly a mile away. *Box 1390, St. John's, tel. 809/462-1223, fax 809/462-5007. 30 rooms. Facilities: restaurant, bar, pool, cable TV, room service. AE, MC, V. EP. Expensive.*

★ **Copper and Lumber Store Hotel.** Formerly the supply store for Nelson's Caribbean fleet, this fine example of Georgian British architecture has been beautifully transformed into a quiet, gracious inn. The warm brick; hardwood floors; timbered ceilings; and burgundy leather, button armchairs and sofas give it an Old-World charm unique in the West Indies. The sunny, bougainvillea-hung central courtyard is reminiscent of Italy or Portugal. There are two types of suites: the more expensive Georgian suites, each decorated differently but all with period furnishings, antique washstands, secretaries, and four-poster and canopy beds, and the larger, contemporary suites. Neither of the two types has a full bath—just showers. A shuttle ferry service takes guests to a beach on the other side of English Harbour. If you're an Anglophile, you won't want to go home. *Box 184, St. John's, tel. 809/460-1058, fax 809/460-1529. 14 suites. Facilities: restaurant, pub. AE, MC, V. EP, MAP. Moderate–Expensive.*

Ramada Renaissance Royal Antiguan Resort. This is the second-largest hotel in Antigua and possibly the island's ugliest. It has long, rectangular, blocklike buildings that are shabby and have been weathered by the tropical climate. It was built in

1987 by an Italian firm, but when Ramada took over, in 1990, they recognized the need for a complete overhaul. Perhaps by 1992 it will look a little smarter, but it will always remain large and impersonal, catering to groups and conventions and lacking the Antiguan experience. On the plus side are its numerous facilities: three restaurants (the premier room is La Regence), three bars, a huge ballroom used for meetings and cocktail parties, and a 5,500-square-foot casino with the games (blackjack, roulette, craps, baccarat, and 130 slot machines) played by Atlantic City rules. *Deep Bay, St. John's, tel. 809/462–3733 or 800/228–9898, fax 809/462–3732. 300 air-conditioned rooms. Facilities: 3 restaurants, 3 bars, casino, swimming pool with swim-up bar, full water sports (snorkeling, Sunfish sailing, windsurfing, waterskiing, fishing), a certified dive master, 5 tennis courts, golf arranged at nearby 18-hole Cedar Valley course, a minicrafts market on site. All major credit cards. EP. Moderate–Expensive.*

★ **Siboney Beach Club.** When Tony Johnson arrived in Antigua in the late '50s aboard a yacht, he planned to stay just a few weeks. Instead, he ended up building or refurbishing some of the island's finest resorts, including the Admiral's Inn at English Harbour. Everything he learned was then fed into the conception and planning of his own, all-suites resort. The result is a gem set in a beautiful tropical garden. Each suite has a spacious bedroom, attractive bathroom, a cleverly designed Pullman kitchen that can be screened off behind louvered doors, a living room that is elegantly furnished with a tropical decor, and a patio that is festooned with plants. Great trouble has been taken to ensure that space is maximized and fittings, are of the highest quality. A few yards away is a beach of powdery white-coral sand and one of the best restaurants on the island, The Coconut Grove (*see* Dining, *above*). Here, guests can enjoy a candlelight dinner and entertainment on most nights. The Saturday night special is the Rio Band, the best traditional folk band on the island. The exceptionally friendly staff and Tony's charming, Trinidad-born wife, Ann, ensure that within moments of your arrival, Siboney will become your home away from home in Antigua. *Box 222, St. John's, tel. 809/462–0806 or 800/533–0234, fax 809/462–0806. 12 suites. Facilities: restaurant, bar, pool. AE, MC, V. EP. Moderate–Expensive.*

Yepton Beach Resort. Set on the unattractively named Hog John Bay, on the Five Islands peninsula, this Swiss-designed, all-suites resort still feels, five years after opening, as though it has still not quite hit its stride. Accommodations are in a row of four Mediterranean-style, white-stucco blocks, looking, in one direction, onto the resort's own attractive beach and, in the other, onto a lagoon dotted with pelicans and egrets. Some of the rooms are two-room suites, with a bedroom and large living-room-cum-kitchenette. Others are studios, with a folding Murphy bed and kitchenette. By putting together a double bedroom and a studio, one can also make an apartment that sleeps four. There are two excellent tennis courts, and Lou Belizaire, an operatic Antiguan, works wonders in the kitchen of the on-property restaurant. *Box 1427, St. John's, tel. 809/ 462–2520 or 800/361–4621. Facilities: restaurant, tennis courts, pool, Sunfish sailing, and snorkeling. AE, MC, V. EP, MAP. Moderate–Expensive.*

Club Antigua. Formerly known as the Jolly Beach Resort, this vast, sprawling resort is in one of the least attractive parts of the island. The nearby saltwater lagoon, a mosquito breeding ground, has been dredged to create a vast marina and condominium complex. With 570 rooms, it is the largest resort in the Caribbean and about to get even larger. The rooms themselves are tiny, functional boxes. The clientele is budget, package tourists, many of whom come from Germany (the owner is German). In the dining hall long lines form for meals, and the evening cruise on the resort's reproduction pirate ship is a notorious drinking binge. *Box 744, St. John's, tel. 809/462-0061; in FL, 800/432-6083; in Canada, 800/368-6669, fax 809/462-4900. 500 rooms. Facilities: 3 restaurants, 4 bars, disco, pool, 8 tennis courts, movie room, shops, car-rental desk, watersports center. AE, MC, V. All-inclusive. Moderate.*

★ **Admiral's Inn.** Lovingly restored 30 years ago to its former glory, this 18th-century Georgian inn is the centerpiece of the magnificent Nelson's Dockyard complex. Once the engineers' office and warehouse (the bricks were originally used as ballast for British ships), the Admiral's Inn reverberates with history; whether you're a sailing buff or not, you can't help being drawn into the historic, maritime ambience of the place. The best rooms are upstairs in the main building. They have the original timbered ceilings, complete with iron braces, and massive, white-washed brick walls. Straw mats from Dominica on the floors and views through wispy, Australian pines to the sunny harbor beyond complete the effect. The finest room, 1A, which tends to be booked up months in advance, has a *baldachino* (canopy bed). The rooms in the garden annex are smaller and tend to be a little airless. The best-kept secret here is The Loft, a simple, timbered space upstairs in a separate building that used to be the dockyard's joinery. It has two big bedrooms, an enormous kitchen, and a magnificent view from the timbered living room onto the busy harbor. *Box 713, St. John's, tel. 809/460-1027 or 800/223-5695; in NY, 914/833-3303; in Canada, 416/447-2335; fax 809/460-1534. 14 rooms. Facilities: restaurant, pub. AE, MC, V. EP. Inexpensive.*

★ **The Catamaran Hotel.** Carefully renovated in 1989 to retain its historical ambience, this plantation-style house, with its attractive apricot, white, and black trim and wraparound verandah supported on white, classical-style pediments, sits right on the water at Falmouth Harbour on a beach lined with palm and almond trees. The best rooms are the eight, first-floor suites with a four-poster bed, bath and shower, kitchenette, and private balcony, though none of the rooms has air-conditioning, TV, or telephone. English Harbour is only 2 miles, or US$6 by taxi away, and there is a nearby supermarket to shop for provisions. At Avril's, on the same property, you can eat good à la carte seafood. Rowboats and Sunfishes are available for guests, who can use them to get to an ocean beach at Pigeon Point. For those who want a low-key low-priced tranquil resort, this is excellent value. *Box 958, Falmouth, tel. 809/460-1036, fax 809/460-1506. 16 rooms. Facilities: restaurant, bar, sailing. AE, MC, V. EP. Inexpensive.*

Falmouth Beach Apartments. This is the sister hotel of the famous Admiral's Inn at English Harbour. The best accommodations are in an attractive colonial-style house at the water's edge of its own, small palm-lined beach. The apartments are basically one large room comprising a bedroom-cum-livingroom, a bathroom (shower only), and a kitchenette screened off from the main living area. A door opens directly onto a timbered, wraparound verandah with a view of the water and the mountainous peninsula opposite. Since the beach is very sheltered, it is perfect for toddlers and small children who are learning to swim. There are no air-conditioning, telephones, or TVs. The other rooms are in four modern buildings perched on the hillside. These rooms have a separate kitchen, a bedroom with twin beds, and a bathroom with shower. All apartments have daily maid service. Quiet and simple—a good value. *Box 713, Falmouth Harbour, tel. 809/460–1094 or 800/223–5695, fax 809/460–1534. 28 rooms. Facilities: sailing. AE, MC, V. EP. Inexpensive.*

★ **Lord Nelson Beach Hotel.** This small, weathered resort feels like the sort of places you used to be able to find on the Greek islands 20 years ago—a simple, no-frills, Mom-and-Pop operation, with the son-in-law cutting the grass and Mom in the office at the back. The Fullers, who run it, are expatriate Americans who have been here since 1949. Since they have a vast, extended family of their own, it is a perfect place for children to scamper about and explore. If you don't mind a bit of chipped paint and organized chaos, you'll love it, too (as did Eugene Fodor when he once stayed here). An extensive collection of windsurfing boards, easy access to the water, and a dedicated pro have also made it a mecca for windsurfers. The best rooms are in a two-story, apricot-colored building looking directly onto the property's own horseshoe-shaped beach. Each room is slightly different (one has beautiful tiled floors and an ornately carved bed from Dominica that is so high you almost need to be a pole-vaulter to get into it). The timbered dining room, dominated by a full-size replica of the boat in which Captain Bligh was cast off from the *Bounty*, serves hearty dishes like stuffed pork chops, wahoo, and snapper. Because the resort is fairly isolated (5 miles from St. John's), the price of a meal anywhere else will automatically have EC$20 added to it for the taxi fare there and back. *Box 155, St. John's, tel. 809/462–3094, fax 809/462–0751. Facilities: restaurant, bar, maid service, dive shop, windsurfing. AE, MC, V. EP, MAP, FAP. Inexpensive.*

Murphy's Place. Mrs. Murphy, a hard-working, talkative woman, first started taking guests into her home, a modern bungalow on the outskirts of St. John's, to pay for her children's education. The rooms, in a simple, wooden annex, hung with yellow bella flowers, are either single, with a double bed, shower, and fan, or larger units, with two bedrooms, a large living-room area, and a well-equipped kitchen. The furnishing is simple enough, but Mrs. Murphy sews many of the curtains and bedspreads herself and takes a lot of trouble seeing that everything is shipshape and clean. On a patio festooned with plants she serves afternoon tea for those who want it and a pancake breakfast on Saturday. As a result, the guest book is full of signatures of (mostly young) people from all over the world. At The Dolphin Restaurant, a few yards away, her son serves good, Caribbean food at reasonable prices. Excellent value. *Box 491, St. John's, tel. 809/461–1183. 4 rooms. Facilities: patio. No credit cards. EP. Inexpensive.*

Nightlife

Most of Antigua's evening entertainment centers on the resort hotels, which feature calypso singers, steel bands, limbo dancers, and folkloric groups on a regular basis. Check with the Tourist Board for up-to-date information.

Shirley Heights Lookout (Shirley Heights, tel. 809/463–1785) does Sunday-afternoon barbecues that continue into the night with music and dancing. It's a favorite local spot on Sunday night for residents, visitors, and the ever-changing yachting crowd. (Best gossip on the island!) **Hemingway's** (St. Mary's St., St. John's, tel. 809/462–2783), a restaurant serving West Indian fare, is a popular gathering spot for Yuppie locals.

Casinos There are five hotel casinos open from early evening until 4 AM. The "world's largest slot machine" as well as gaming tables are at the **King's Casino** (tel. 809/462–1727), at Heritage Quay. Slot machines and gaming tables attract gamblers to the **Flamingo** (Michaels Mount, tel. 809/462–1266). The **St. James's Club** (Mamora Bay, tel. 809/463–1113) has a private casino with a European ambience. Ramada has turned the casino at the **Ramada Renaissance Royal Antiguan Resort** (tel. 809/462–3733) into an Atlantic City–style casino.

Discos **Tropix** (Redcliffe Quay, St. John's, tel. 809/462–2317) is very popular. Open Wednesday through Saturday, from 9 PM till whenever, it draws locals, residents, and energetic visitors; An insider's favorite remains **Peter Scott's Cafe** (St. John's, no phone). Owner Scott is his own best entertainment, playing the guitar and mixing songs from reggae to ballads. On Wednesday nights, **Columbo's** (Galleon Beach Club, English Harbour, tel. 809/463–1081) is the place to be for live reggae, and the **Lemon Tree Restaurant** (Long and Church Sts., St. John's, tel. 809/461–2507) swings every night in season until at least 11 PM.

4 Aruba

Updated by
Laurie Senz

Imagine Aruba as one big Love Boat cruise. Most of its 25 hotels sit side by side down one major strip along the southwestern shore, with restaurants, exotic boutiques, fiery floor shows, and glitzy casinos right on their premises. Nearly every night there are organized theme parties, treasure hunts, beachside barbecues, and fish fries with steel bands and limbo dancers. Every Tuesday evening year-round, Arubans celebrate the Bon Bini ("Welcome" in the native Papiamento dialect) with arts and crafts and musical and dancing shows in the courtyard of Oranjestad's Fort Zoutman.

The "A" in the ABC Islands, Aruba is small—only 19.6 miles long and 6 miles across at its widest point, approximately 70 square miles. The national anthem proclaims, "The greatness of our people is their great cordiality," and this is no exaggeration. Once a member of the Netherlands Antilles, Aruba became an independent entity within the Netherlands in 1986, with its own royally appointed governor, a democratic government, and a 21-member elected Parliament. With education, housing, and health care financed by an economy based on tourism, the island's population of 70,000 recognizes visitors as valued guests. Waiters serve you with smiles and solid eye contact, English is spoken everywhere, and hotel-hospitality directors appear delighted to serve your special needs. Good direct air service from the United States makes Aruba an excellent choice for even a short vacation.

Time-sharing units bring back the committed year after year, and the huge high-rise hotel complexes fill their rooms with special package rates. Overbuilding has caused the government to place a five-year moratorium on new hotel construction while unfinished hotel construction waits for refinancing.

The island's distinctive beauty lies in its countryside—an almost extraterrestrial landscape full of rocky deserts, cactus jungles, secluded coves, and aquamarine vistas with crashing waves. With its low humidity and average temperatures of 82°F, Aruba has the climate of a paradise; rain comes mostly during November. Sun, cooling trade winds, friendly and courteous service, modern and efficient amenities, and 10 modern casinos are Aruba's strong suit to fill the 7,156 hotel rooms.

Before You Go

Tourist Information
Contact the **Aruba Tourism Authority**, 1000 Harbor Blvd. (ground level), Weehawken, NJ 07087, tel. 201/330–0800 or 800/TO–ARUBA, fax 201/330–8757; in Miami, 2344 Salezdo St., Miami, FL 33134, tel. 305/567–2720, fax 305/567–2721; in Canada, 86 Bloor St. W, Suite 204, Toronto, Ontario, M5S 1M5, tel. 416/975–1950.

Arriving and Departing
By Plane
Flights leave daily to Aruba from New York area airports and Miami's International airport, with easy connections from most American cities. **Air Aruba** (tel. 800/882–7822), the island's official airline, flies nonstop to Aruba daily from Miami and five days a week from Newark. **American Airlines** (tel. 800/433–7300) offers daily nonstop service from both Miami International and New York's JFK International airports. **ALM** (tel. 800/327–7230), the major airline of the Dutch Caribbean islands, flies five days a week nonstop from Miami to Aruba; two nonstop and two direct flights a week leave out of Atlanta with connecting services (throughfares) to most major U.S. gate-

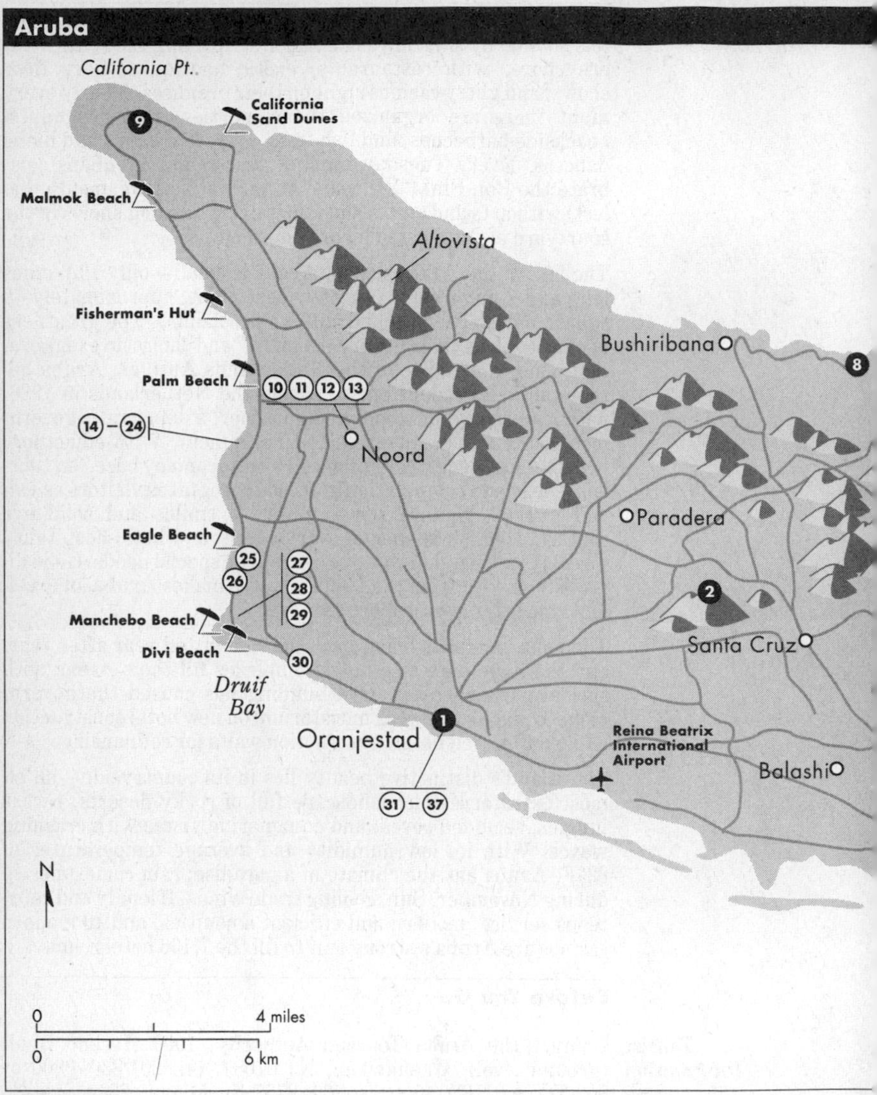

Aruba

California Pt.

California Sand Dunes

⑨

Malmok Beach

Altovista

Fisherman's Hut

Bushiribana ○

⑧

Palm Beach ⑩ ⑪ ⑫ ⑬

⑭ – ㉔

○ Noord

○ Paradera

Eagle Beach ㉕ ㉗
㉖ ㉘
㉙

Manchebo Beach ❷

Divi Beach ㉚ Santa Cruz ○

Druif Bay

Oranjestad ❶

Reina Beatrix International Airport

Balashi ○

㉛ – �37

N

0		4 miles
0		6 km

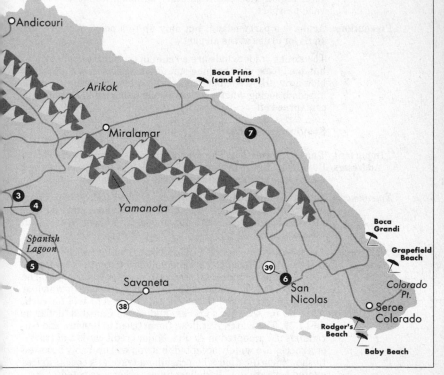

① Exploring Sites

⑩ Hotels and Restaurants

Caribbean Sea

Andicouri

Arikok

Boca Prins
(sand dunes)

Miralamar

⑦

Yamanota

Boca
Grandi

Grapefield
Beach

Colorado
Pt.

③
④

Spanish
Lagoon

⑤

Savaneta

㊳

㊴

⑥ San
Nicolas

Seroe
Colorado

Rodger's
Beach

Baby Beach

Lodging

Americana Aruba
Hotel & Casino, **17**

Aruba Beach Club, **28**

Aruba Concorde, **18**

Aruba Palm Beach
Hotel & Casino, **19**

Aruba Royal
Resort, **23**

Best Western Talk of
the Town Resort, **34**

Bushiri Beach
Resort, **31**

Casa del Mar Beach
Resort, **30**

Divi Aruba Beach
Resort, **27**

Hilton Aruba
Concorde, **18**

Hyatt Regency Aruba
Resort & Casino, **22**

La Cabana All Suite
Beach Resort &
Casino, **25**

La Quinta Beach
Resort, **26**

The Mill Resort, **24**

Playa Linda Beach
Resort, **21**

Radisson Aruba
Caribbean Resort &
Casino, **20**

Sonesta Hotel, Beach
Club & Casino, **37**

Tamarijn Aruba Beach
Resort, **29**

ways tied in with Delta. Air Aruba and ALM also have connecting flights to Caracas, Bonaire, Curaçao, and St. Maarten as well as other Caribbean islands. ALM also offers a "Visit Caribbean Pass" for interisland travel. From Toronto and Montreal, you can fly to Aruba on American Airlines via San Juan. American also has connecting flights from several U.S. cities via San Juan. **VIASA** (tel. 800/327–5454) has Monday and Thursday nonstop flights out of Houston. **AeroPostal** (tel. 800/468–9419) offers nonstop flights from Atlanta four times a week and from Orlando three times a week.

Passports and Visas U.S. and Canadian residents need show proof only of identity—a valid passport, birth certificate, naturalization certificate, green card, valid nonquota immigration visa, or a valid voter registration card. All other nationalities must submit a valid passport.

Precautions Aruba is a party island, but only up to a point. A police dog sniffs for drugs at the airport.

The strong trade winds are a relief in the subtropical climate, but don't hang your bathing suit on a balcony—it will probably blow away. Help Arubans conserve water and energy: Turn off air-conditioning when you leave your room and keep your faucets turned off.

Staying in Aruba

Important Addresses Tourist Information: The **Aruba Tourism Authority** (L. G. Smith Blvd. 172, Box 1019, tel. 297/8–23777) has free brochures and guides who are ready to answer any questions.

Emergencies **Police:** (tel. 100). **Hospital:** Horaceo Oduber (tel. 24300). **Pharmacy:** Botica del Pueblo (tel. 21254). **Ambulance and Fire** (tel. 115). All hotels have house doctors on call 24 hours a day. Call the front desk.

Currency Arubans happily accept U.S. dollars virtually everywhere, so there's no real need to exchange money, except for necessary pocket change (cigarettes, soda machines, or pay phones). The currency used, however, is the Aruban florin (AFl), which at press time exchanged to the U.S. dollar at AFl 1.77 for cash, AFl 1.79 for traveler's checks, and to the Canadian dollar at AFl 1.30. The Dutch Antillean florin (used in Bonaire and Curaçao) is not accepted in Aruba. Major credit cards and traveler's checks are widely accepted, but you will probably be asked to show identification when cashing a traveler's check. Prices quoted here are in U.S. dollars unless otherwise noted.

Taxes and Service Charges Hotels collect a 5% government tax. The departure tax is $10. Hotels add an 11% service charge on rooms and a 15% service charge on food and beverages; restaurants usually add a 15% service charge to your bill.

Guided Tours *Orientation* Most of Aruba's highways are in excellent condition, but guided tours save time and energy. **De Palm Tours** (L. G. Smith Blvd. 142, tel. 297/8–24400 or 297/8–24545; telex 5049 DPALM NA; fax 297/8–23012) has a near monopoly on the Aruban sightseeing business; reservations may be made through its general office or at hotel tour-desk branches. The basic 3½-hour tour hits the high spots of the island. Wear tennis or hiking shoes (there'll be optional climbing) and note that the air-conditioned bus can get cold. The tour, which begins at 9:30 AM, picks you up in your lobby and costs $17.50 per person. De Palm also offers full-day tours of Caracas, Venezuela ($225, passport required) and Curaçao ($185). Prices include round-trip airfare, transfers, sightseeing, lunch, and free time for shopping.

General Travel Bureau (Elleboogstr. 23, tel. 297/8–26609 or 297/8–34717) also offers trips to Caracas on Thursday, Friday, and Monday. The full-day tour ($225) includes round-trip airfare, transfers, a historical sightseeing tour, shopping, and lunch.

Friendly Tours (tel. 297/8–23230) offers guided 3½-hour sight-seeing tours to the island's main sights twice a day ($20).

Special-Interest **Corvalou Tours** (tel. 297/8–21149) offers unusual excursions for specialized interests. The Archaeological/Geological Tour involves a four- to six-hour field trip through Aruba's past, including the huge monoliths and rugged, desolate north coast. Also available are architectural, bird-watching, and botanical tours. The fee for all tours is $40 per person, $70 per couple, with special prices for parties of five or more.

A new way of exploring Aruba is by jeep caravan. **De Palm Tours** (tel. 297/8–24400) offers full-day, on-and-off-the-road tours every Wednesday and Thursday. The $49.50 per person price (four people per jeep) includes a tour guide, lunch, and snorkeling equipment. Bring a bathing suit, lots of sunblock, and a camera.

For a three-in-one tour of prehistoric Indian cultures, volcanic formations, and natural wildlife, contact archaeologist Eppie Boerstra of **Marlin Booster Tracking, Inc.,** at Charlie's Bar (tel. 297/8–45086 or 297/8–41513). The fee for a six-hour tour is $35 per person, including a cold picnic lunch and beverages. Tours can be given in English, Dutch, German, French, and Spanish.

Hikers will enjoy a guided three-hour trip to remote sites of unusual natural beauty, accessible only on foot. The fee is $25 per person, including refreshments and transportation; a minimum of four people is required. Contact **De Palm Tours** (tel. 297/8–24545).

Private Safaris Educational Tours (tel. 297/8–34869) offers adventure safaris by land cruiser into Aruba's interior. The half-day ($30) and full-day ($40) tours explore the island's history, geology, and wildlife.

Landlubbers can now explore an underwater reef teeming with marine life without getting wet. **Atlantis Submarines** (Seaport Village Marina, tel. 297/8–36090) operates a 65-foot, modern, air-conditioned sub that takes 46 passengers 50–90 feet below the surface along Aruba's Barcadera Reef. The 50-minute plunge costs $68 for adults, half price for children. If you are not a scuba diver, the hour in the submarine is the next best thing to being down among the fish and coral.

Boat Cruises If you try a cruise around the island, know that trimarans are much smoother than monohull boats. People with queasy stomachs will be helped by lemon or lime candy, and everyone should avoid going on an empty stomach. The most popular and reputable sailing cruises are offered by **De Palm Tours** (tel. 297/8–24400 or 297/8–24545), **Mi Dushi** (tel. 297/8–26034), **Red Sail Sports** (tel. 297/8–31603), **Pelican Watersports** (tel. 297/8–

24739), **Wave Dancer** (tel. 297/8–25520), and **Topaz** (tel. 297/8–24401).

Moonlight cruises, though stunning, are appreciated most by honeymooners. Prices run about $25 per person. Contact **Red Sail Sports** (tel. 297/8–31603), **Pelican Watersports** (tel. 297/8–24739) or **De Palm Tours** (tel. 297/8–24400). De Palm Tours' three-hour trimaran cruise with an hour's stop for swimming and snorkeling runs daily except Sunday; the cost is $22.50 per person. Four-hour snorkel, sail, and lunch cruises aboard a 53-foot catamaran plus sunset sails and a romantic dinner cruise are among the on-the-water delights offered at prices that range from $27.50 to $49.50 per person. Contact Red Sail Sports.

If you've ever wanted to walk the plank, take a swing from the yardarm, or be a swashbuckler defending his lady, then take a Pirate Cruise aboard the *Topaz*, the original tall ship used in Walt Disney's production *Return to Treasure Island*. The $39.50 cost includes unlimited drinks, a barbecue dinner, and a sunset swim. Runs daily. Call De Palm Tours.

Getting Around
Taxis   A dispatch office is located at Alhambra Bazaar and Casino (tel. 297/8–21604 or 297/8–22116); you can also flag down taxis on the street. Since taxis do not have meters, rates are fixed and should be confirmed before your ride begins. All Aruba's taxi drivers have participated in the government's Tourism Awareness Programs and have received their Tourism Guide Certificate. An hour's tour of the island by taxi will run you about $30, for a maximum of four people per car.

Rental Cars   You'll need a valid U.S. or Canadian driver's license to rent a car, and you must be able to meet the minimum age requirements of each rental service, implemented for insurance reasons. **Budget** (tel. 800/527–0700) requires drivers to be between 25 and 65, **Avis** (tel. 800/331–2112) requires drivers to be between 23 and 70, and **Hertz** (tel. 800/654–3131) requires drivers to be older than 21. Insurance is available starting at $10 per day, and all companies offer unlimited mileage. Local car rental companies generally have lower rates.

Local addresses and phone numbers for the rental agencies are **Avis** (Kolibristraat 14, tel. 297/8–28787; airport tel. 297/8–25496), **Budget Rent-A-Car** (Kolibristraat 1, tel. 297/8–28600; airport tel. 297/8–25423; at Divi resorts tel. 297/8–35000), **Hertz, De Palm Car Rental** (L. G. Smith Blvd. 142, Box 656, tel. 297/8–24545; airport tel. 297/8–24886), **Dollar Rent-a-Car** (Grendeaweg 15, tel. 297/8–22783; airport tel. 297/8–25651; Manchebo tel. 297/8–26696), **National** (Tank Leendert 170, tel. 297/8–21967; airport tel. 297/8–25451; Holiday Inn tel. 297/8–23600), **Thrifty** (airport tel. 297/8–35335), and **Hedwina Car Rental** (airport tel. 297/8–37393; Fortheuvelstraat 32, tel. 297/8–26442).

Motorcycle Rentals   Rates vary according to the make of the vehicle. For Suzuki scooters ($24 day, $132 week), contact **George Cycle Center** (L. G. Smith Blvd. 136, tel. 297/8–25975). Other moped, scooter, and motorcycle rental companies are **Ron's Motorcycle Rental** (Bakval 17A, tel. 297/8–32090), **Nelson Motorcycle Rental** (Gasparito 10A, tel. 297/8–26801), and **Semver Cycle Rental** (Noord 22, tel. 297/8–26851).

Buses For inexpensive trips between the beach hotels and Oranjestad, buses run hourly. One-way fare is 90¢; round-trip fare is $1.50, and exact change is preferred. Contact the Aruba Tourism Authority (tel. 297/8–27089) for a bus schedule or inquire at the front desk of your hotel. A free Shopping Tour Bus (you'll know it by its wild colors) departs every hour beginning at 9:15 AM and ending at 3:15 PM from the Holiday Inn, making stops at all the major hotels on its way toward Oranjestad. Be aware that you'll have to find your own way back to your hotel.

Telephones and Mail To dial direct to Aruba from the United States, dial 011–297–8, followed by the number in Aruba. Local and international calls in Aruba can be made via hotel operators or from the Government Long Distance Telephone Office, SETAR, which is in the Post Office in Oranjestad. When dialing locally in Aruba, simply dial the five-digit number. To reach the United States, dial 001, then the area code and number.

Telegrams and telexes can be sent through SETAR, the Government Telegraph and Radio Office at the Post Office Building in Oranjestad or via your hotel. There is also a SETAR office in front of the Hyatt Regency Hotel, adjacent to the hotel's parking lot (tel. 297/8–37138).

You can send an airmail letter from Aruba to anywhere in the world for AFl 1.00, a postcard for AFl .70.

Opening and Closing Times Shops are generally open between 8 AM and 6 PM, Monday through Saturday. Most stores stay open through the lunch hour, noon–2 PM. Many stores open when cruise ships are in port on Sunday and holidays. Nighttime shopping at the Alahambra Bazaar runs 5 PM–midnight. Bank hours are weekdays from 8 to noon and 1:30 to 4. The Aruba Bank at the airport is open on Saturday from 9 to 4 and on Sunday from 9 to 1.

Exploring Aruba

Numbers in the margin correspond to points of interest on the Aruba map.

Oranjestad Aruba's charming Dutch capital, **Oranjestad,** is best explored
❶ on foot. Take a taxi or bus from your hotel to the **Port of Call Marketplace,** a new shopping mall. After exploring the boutiques and shops, head up L. G. Smith Boulevard to the colorful **Fruit Market,** located along the docks on your right.

Stop in for lunch at the **Bali Floating Restaurant,** where you can enjoy *rijstaffel* (a buffet of Indonesian foods served over rice) or sip a cool drink and watch the fishermen bringing in their catch (*see* Dining, *below*).

Continue walking along the harbor until you come to **Harbourtown Market,** a festive shopping, dining, and entertainment mall. Next door (one block southwest) is **Wilhelmina Park,** a small grove of palm trees and flowers overlooking the sea.

Cross L. G. Smith Boulevard to Oranjestraat and walk one block to **Fort Zoutman,** one of the island's oldest buildings. It was built in 1796 and used as a major fortress in the skirmishes between British and Curaçao troops. The Willem III Tower, named for the Dutch monarch of that time, was added in 1868. The fort's Historical Museum displays centuries' worth of Aruban relics and artifacts in an 18th-century Aruban house.

Oranjestraat, tel. 297/8–26099. Admission: $1. Open weekdays 9–noon and 1–4.

Turn left onto Zoutmanstraat and walk two blocks to the **Archeology Museum,** where there are two rooms of Indian artifacts, farm and domestic utensils, and skeletons. *Zoutmanstr. 1, tel. 297/8–28979. Admission free. Open weekdays 8–noon and 1:30–4:30.*

From here, cross the street to the Protestant Church. You're now on Wilhelminastraat. Walk one block and turn right on Kazernestraat. On your right side is the **Strada Complex I** and on your left, **Strada Complex II.** Both are shopping malls, and both are excellent examples of Dutch Colonial architecture. Behind Strada Complex II is the **Holland Aruba Mall,** a new shopping complex built to resemble a Dutch Colonial village. Upstairs is an international food court.

At the intersection of Kazernestraat and Caya G. F. Betico Croes, turn right. This is Oranjestad's main street. When you come to Hendrikstraat, turn left and continue walking until you come to the **Saint Francis Roman Catholic Church.** Next to the church is the **Numismatic Museum,** displaying coins and paper money from more than 400 countries. *Iraussquilnplein 2-A, tel. 297/8–28831. Admission free. Open weekdays 8:30–noon and 1–4:30 PM.*

Diagonally across from the church is the **Post Office,** where you can buy colorful Aruban stamps. Next door is the SETAR, where you can place overseas phone calls.

Time Out   The motto at **Le Petit Café** (at Mainstreet, corner of Schlepstraat, tel. 297/8–33716) is "Romancing the Stone"—referring to tasty cuisine cooked on hot stones. The low ceiling and hanging plants make this an intimate lunch spot for shoppers. Jumbo shrimps, sandwiches, ice cream, and fresh fruit dishes are light delights. *Open lunch and dinner, Mon.–Sat. Closed Sun.*

The Countryside   The "real Aruba"—what's left of a wild, untamed beauty—can be found only in the countryside. Either rent a car, take a sightseeing tour, or hire a cab for $30 an hour (for up to four people). The main highways are well paved, but on the windward side of the island some roads are still a mixture of compacted dirt and stones. Although a car is fine, a Jeep will allow you to explore the unpaved interior. Traffic is sparse, and you can't get lost. If you do lose your way, just follow the divi-divi trees (because of the direction of the trade winds, the trees are bent toward the leeward side of the island, where all the hotels are).

Few beaches outside the hotel strip have refreshment stands, so take your own food and drink. And one more caution: Note that there are *no* public bathrooms—anywhere—once you leave Oranjestad, except in the infrequent restaurant.

East to San Nicolas   For a shimmering vista of blue-green sea, drive east on L. G. Smith Boulevard toward San Nicolas, on what is known as the Sunrise side of the island. Past the airport, you'll soon see the towering 541-foot peak of **Hooiberg** (Haystack Hill). If you have the energy, climb the 562 steps up to the top for an impressive view of the city.

Turn left where you see the drive-in theater (a popular hangout for Arubans). Drive to the first intersection, turn right, and

❸ follow the curve to the right to **Frenchman's Pass,** a dark, luscious stretch of highway arbored by overhanging trees. Local legend claims the French and native Indians warred here during the 17th century for control of the island. Nearby are the
❹ cement ruins of the **Balashi Gold Mine** (take the dirt road veering to the right)—a lovely place to picnic, listen to the parakeets, and contemplate the towering cacti. A magnificent gnarled divi-divi tree guards the entrance.

Backtrack all the way to the main road, past the drive-in, and
❺ drive through the area called **Spanish Lagoon,** where pirates once hid to repair their ships.

❻ Back on the main highway, pay a visit to **San Nicolas,** Aruba's oldest village. During the heyday of the Exxon refineries, the town was a bustling port; now it's dedicated to tourism, with the main-street promenade full of interesting kiosks. The **China Clipper Bar** on Main Street used to be a famous "whore" bar frequented by sailors docked in port.

Time Out Now an institution, **Charlie's Bar** has been a San Nicolas hangout for more than 50 years. During the oil-refinery days, it was a hopping bar for all kinds of rough-and-scruffs. Now it is owned by the second-generation Charlie, who is eager to promote San Nicolas as a historic town. Tourists flock here, if only to gawk at the unusual decor: license plates, hard hats, baseball pennants, and old credit cards cover and crowd every inch of the walls and ceiling. The specialty is "shrimps—jumbo and dumbo." The bus to San Nicolas stops right at the door. *Zeppenfeldstraat 56, San Nicolas, tel. 297/8-45086. Open Mon.–Sat. noon–10 PM.*

Anyone looking for geological exotica should head for the northern coast, driving northwest from San Nicolas. Stop at
❼ the two old Indian caves **Guadirikiri** and **Fontein.** Both were used by the native Indians centuries ago, but you'll have to decide for yourself whether the "ancient Indian inscriptions" are genuine—rumor has it they were added by a European film company that made a movie here years ago. You may enter the caves, but there are no guides available, and bats are known to make appearances. Wear sneakers and take a flashlight or rent one from the soda vendor who has set up shop here.

❽ A few miles up the coast is the **Natural Bridge,** sculpted out of coral rock by centuries of raging wind and sea. To get to it, you'll have to follow the main road inland and then the signs that lead the way. Nearby is a café overlooking the water and a souvenir shop stuffed with trinkets, T-shirts, and postcards for reasonable prices.

West of Palm Beach Drive or take a taxi west from the hotel strip to Malmok, where Aruba's wealthiest families reside. Open to the public, **Malmok Beach** is considered one of the finest spots for shelling, snorkeling, and windsurfing (*see* Beaches, *below*). Right off the coast here is the wreck of the German ship *Antilla*, which was scuttled in 1940—a favorite haunt for divers. At the very end of the
❾ island stands the **California Lighthouse,** now closed, which is surrounded by huge boulders that look like extraterrestrial monsters; in this stark landscape, you'll feel as though you've just landed on the moon.

What to See and Do with Children

The **Neptalie Henriquez Children's Playground,** on L. G. Smith Boulevard across the street from the Talk of the Town Hotel, is open Friday and Saturday 4–6, Sunday 4–6:30. Admission: AFl 1 or about U.S. 60¢. For parties, call Mrs. Wekker (tel. 297/8–21059).

Off the Beaten Track

Near the Fontein and Guadirikiri caves lies the **Tunnel of Love.** Marco Marlin, a local artist with a quirky sense of humor, will lead you on a 20-minute climb through the heart-shape tunnel past naturally sculpted rocks that look just like the Madonna, Abe Lincoln, and even a jaguar. Depending on your state of mind, the tour and Marco's jokes are either very scary or hysterically funny—and Marco just might call out his bats for you. Afterward, calm your nerves with a beer at his bar without walls. Warning: The actual climb is difficult for anyone not in average physical condition, and it's definitely not recommended for elderly people or young children who lack coordination. The fee is $4 per person; no reservations are necessary.

Beaches

Beaches in Aruba are legendary in the Caribbean: white sand, turquoise waters, and virtually no garbage, for everyone takes the "no littering" sign—"No Tira Sushi"—very seriously, especially with an AFl 500 fine. The influx of tourists in the past decade, however, has crowded the major beaches, which back up to the hotels along the southwestern strip. These beaches are public, and you can make the two-hour hike from the Holiday Inn to the Bushiri Beach Hotel free of charge and without ever leaving sand. If you go strolling during the day, make sure you are well protected from the sun—it scorches fast. Luckily, there's at least one covered bar (and often an ice-cream stand) at virtually every hotel you pass. If you take the stroll at night, you can hotel-hop for dinner, dancing, gambling, and late-night entertainment. On the northern side of the island, heavy trade winds make the waters too choppy for swimming, but the vistas are great and the terrain is wonderfully suited to sunbathing and geological explorations. Among the finer beaches are:

Rodger's Beach. Next to Baby Beach on the eastern tip of the island, this is a beautiful curving stretch of sand only slightly marred by the view of the oil refinery at the far side of the bay.

Baby Beach. On the island's eastern tip, this semicircular beach bordering a bay is as placid as a wading pool and only four to five feet deep—perfect for tots and terrible swimmers. Thatched shaded areas are good for cooling off.

Grapefield Beach. On the north of San Nicolas, this gorgeous beach is perfect for professional windsurfing.

Boca Grandi. Just west of Bachelor's Beach, on the northwest coast (near the Seagrape Grove and the Aruba Golf Club), Boca Grandi is excellent for wave jumping and windsurfing.

Boca Prins. Near the Fontein Cave and Blue Lagoon, this beach is about as large as a Brazilian bikini, but with two rocky cliffs and tumultuously crashing waves, it's as romantic as you get in

Aruba. This is not a swimming beach, however. Boca Prins is famous for its backdrop of enormous vanilla sand dunes. Most folks bring a picnic lunch, a beach blanket, and sturdy sneakers.

Malmok Beach. On the southwestern shore, this lackluster beach borders shallow waters that stretch out 300 yards from shore, making it perfect for beginners learning to windsurf.

Fisherman's Hut. Next to the Holiday Inn, this beach is a windsurfer's haven. Take a picnic lunch (tables are available) and watch the elegant purple, aqua, and orange Windsurfer sails struggle in the wind.

Palm Beach. Once called one of the 10 best beaches in the world by the *Miami Herald*, this is the stretch behind the Americana Aruba, Concorde, Aruba Palm Beach, and Holiday Inn hotels. It's the center of Aruban tourism, offering the best in swimming, sailing, and fishing. During high season, however, it's a sardine can.

Eagle Beach. Across the highway from what is quickly becoming known as Time-Share Lane is Eagle Beach on the southern coast. Not long ago, it was a nearly deserted stretch of pristine sands dotted with the occasional thatched picnic hut. Now that the new time-share resorts are completed, this beach is one of the more hopping on the island.

Manchebo Beach (formerly Punta Brabo Beach). In front of the Manchebo Beach Resort, this impressively wide stretch of white powder is where officials turn a blind eye to those who wish to sunbathe topless. Elsewhere on the island, topless sunbathing is not permitted.

Sports and the Outdoors

Bowling   Opened in 1991, the **Eagle Bowling Palace** (Pos Abou, tel. 297/8–35038) has 12 lanes, a cocktail lounge, and snack bar. The cost is $8.25 a game from 10 AM to 3 PM, $10.25 a game from 3 PM to 2 AM, and $1.20 for shoe rentals. Open 10 AM–2 AM.

Deep-Sea Fishing   With catches ranging from barracuda to kingfish, bonito, and black and yellow tuna, deep-sea fishing is great sport on Aruba, and many charter boats are available. Sail for a half day or a full day. **De Palm Tours** (L. G. Smith Blvd. 142, Box 656, tel. 297/8–24400) can arrange parties for up to six people, in boats that range from 24 to 27 feet. Half-day tours, including all equipment, can be arranged for $220–$250 for up to six people. Private yachts, manned by independent sea captains, can also be arranged. Check with the Aruba Tourism Authority or your hotel. Half-day tours run about $200, full-day about $425. **Pelican Tours** (tel. 297/8–31228 or 297/8–24739) and **Red Sail Sports** (tel. 297/8–31603) also arrange deep-sea fishing charters.

Golf   The **Aruba Golf Club** (Golfweg 82, near San Nicolas, tel. 297/8–42006) features a nine-hole course with 25 sand traps, roaming goats, and lots of cacti. There are 11 Astroturf greens, enabling 18-hole tournaments. The clubhouse contains a bar, storage rooms, workshop, and separate men's and women's locker rooms. The course's official U.S. Golf Association rating is 67; greens fees are $7.50 for 9 holes, $10 for 18 holes. There are no caddies, but golf carts are available. Golfers should also check with the Tourism Authority on the status of the par 72

Robert Trent Jones Jr., 18-hole golf course, which, at press time, was planned for the area known as Arashi.

Horseback Riding One-hour jaunts ($15) arranged through **Rancho El Paso** (Washington 44, tel. 297/8–23310) or **De Palm Tours** (tel. 297/8–24400) will take you through countryside flanked by cacti, divi-divi trees, and aloe vera plants; two-hour trips ($30) also go to the beach. Remember to wear a hat and take lots of suntan lotion.

Land Sailing Carts with a Windsurfer-type sail are rented at **Aruba SailCart** (Bushire 23, tel. 297/8–35133) at $15 (single seater) and $20 (double seater) for 30 minutes of speeding back and forth across a dirt field. The sport is new to Aruba and thrilling for landbound sailors. Anyone can learn the rudiments of driving the cart in just a few minutes. Open 10 AM–7 PM. Food and drinks are served until 10 PM.

Miniature Golf Two elevated 18-hole minigolf courses surrounded by a moat are available at **Joe Mendez Adventure Golf** (Eagle Beach, tel. 297/8–36625). There are also paddle boats and bumper boats, a bar, and a snack stand. Fees are $6 for a round of minigolf, $5 for 30 minutes of paddleboating, and $5 for 10 minutes of bumper boating.

Parasailing Motorboats from Eagle and Palm beaches tow people up and over the water for about 15 minutes and $40.

Snorkeling and Scuba Diving With visibility up to 90 feet, Aruban waters are excellent for snorkeling in shallow waters, and scuba divers will discover exotic marine life and coral. Certified divers can go wall diving, reef diving, or explore wrecks sunk during World War II. The *Antilla* shipwreck—a German freighter sunk off the northwest coast of Aruba near Palm Beach—is a favorite spot with divers and snorkelers.

De Palm Tours (L. G. Smith Blvd. 142, tel. 297/8–24545 or 297/8–24400; telex 5049 DPALM NA; fax 297/8–23012) offers daily snorkeling and scuba-diving trips. However, its rates are the most expensive on the island.

Pelican Watersports (J. G. Emanstraat 1, Oranjestad, tel. 297/8–31228 or 297/8–23600, ext. 329) also offers snorkeling and scuba diving.

Red Sail Sports (L. G. Smith Blvd. 83, tel. 297/8–31603, 297/8–24500, ext. 109, or 800/255–6425) offers scuba packages, resort courses, PADI-certification courses, night diving, and underwater camera rental.

Aruba Pro Dive (Ponton 88, tel. 297/8–25520) offers resort courses, daily one-tank dives, two-tank dives, and night dives. Other reputable dive operators offering daily one- and two-tank dives are **Charlie's Buddies S.E.A. Scuba** (San Nicholas, tel. 297/8–41640 or 800/252–0557), **Mermaid Sports Divers** (Manchebo Beach Resort, tel. 297/8–35546 or 800/223–1108), and **Hallo Aruba Dive Shop** (Talk of the Town Hotel, L. G. Smith Blvd. 2, tel. 297/8–38270).

Windsurfing **Pelican Watersports** (J. G. Emanstraat 1, tel. 297/8–23600) rents equipment and offers instruction with a certified Mistral instructor. Stock boards and custom boards rent for $30 per 2 hours, $55 per day.

Red Sail Sports (L. G. Smith Blvd. 83, tel. 297/8–31603 or 800/ 255–6425) offers two-hour beginner lessons for $44 and advanced lessons for $33 per hour. It also offers Fanatic board and regular windsurfing board rentals by the hour, day, and week.

Windsurfing instruction and board rental are also available through **Carib Asurf** (Manchebo Beach Resort, tel. 297/8– 23444), **Sailboard Vacation** (L. G. Smith Blvd. 462, tel. 297/8– 21072), **Roger's Windsurf Place** (L. G. Smith Blvd. 472, tel. 297/ 8–21918), **Windsurfing Aruba** (Boliviastraat 14, Box 256, tel. 297/8–33472), and **De Palm Tours** (L. G. Smith Blvd. 142, Box 656, tel. 297/8–24545).

Shopping

Caya G. F. Betico Croes—Aruba's chief shopping street— makes for a pleasant diversion from the beach and casino life. *Duty-free* is a magic word here. Major credit cards are welcome virtually everywhere, U.S. dollars are accepted almost as often as local currency, and traveler's checks can be cashed with proof of identity. Shopping malls have arrived in Aruba, so when you finish walking the main street, stop in at a mall to browse through the chic new boutiques.

Aruba's souvenir and crafts stores are full of Dutch porcelains and figurines, as befits the island's Netherlands heritage. Dutch cheese is a good buy (you are allowed to bring up to one pound of hard cheese through U.S. customs), as are hand-embroidered linens and any products made from the native plant aloe vera—sunburn cream, face masks, and skin refresheners. Since there is no sales tax, the price you see on the tag is the price you pay. But one word of warning: Don't pull any bargaining tricks. Arubans consider it rude to haggle.

Crafts   Crafts can be found at several stores. At **Artesania Arubiano** (L. G. Smith Blvd. 142, next to the Aruba Tourism Authority, tel. 297/8–37494) you'll find charming Aruban home-crafted pottery, silkscreened T-shirts and wall hangings, and folklore objects. The **Artistic Boutique** (Caya G. F. Betico Croes 25, tel. 297/8–23142, with branches at the Aruba Concorde, tel. 297/8– 24466, ext. 3508; La Cabana, tel. 297/8–20675; Seaport Village Mall, tel. 297/8–32567; and the Holiday Inn, tel. 297/8–33383) sells Aruban hand-embroidered linens, gold and silver jewelry, Persian carpets and dhurries, porcelain and pottery from Spain, and lots of antiques.

For duty-free perfumes and cosmetics, stop in at **Aruba Trading Company** (Caya G. F. Betico Croes 14, tel. 297/8–22600) whose name is synonymous with old-fashioned reliability. ATC offers internationally known brand names, at discounts, but you have to hunt for them. Perfumes and cosmetics are on the first floor, jewelry on the second. Both men's and women's clothes are sold.

Clothing is also sold at **Wulfsen's** (Caya G. F. Betico Croes 52, tel. 297/8–23823). For 18 years one of the highest-rated stores in the Netherlands Antilles, Wulfsen's offers Italian, French, German, and Dutch fashions for both sexes. The Dutch-line Mexx is a favorite of hip teens; Betty Buckley and Mondo are popular for women.

J. L. Penha & Son's (Caya G. F. Betico Croes 11, tel. 297/8– 24161), another venerated name in Aruban merchandising, also sells clothes and cosmetics and features Boucheron, Lanvin, Dior, and Cartier for women and Givenchy and Pierre Cardin, for men.

For jewelry and watches, stop in at **Gandelman's Jewelers** (Caya G. F. Betico Croes 5-A, tel. 297/8–32121 or 297/8–34433) for Gucci and Swatch watches at reasonable prices, gold bracelets, pink and red coral, and a full line of Gucci accessories, from key chains to handbags. More watches can be found at **Little Switzerland** (Caya G. F. Betico Croes 14, tel. 297/8–21192). The Curaçao-based giant in china, crystal, and fine tableware offers good buys on Omega and Rado watches, Swarovski silver, Baccarat crystal, and Lladro figurines. If you don't see what you want, ask and they'll ship it to you.

Shopping Malls   **Seaport Village Mall** (located on L. G. Smith Blvd., tel. 297/8–23754) is landmarked by the Crystal Casino Tower. This covered mall is located only five minutes away from the cruise terminal. It has more than 85 stores, boutiques, and perfumeries, featuring merchandise to meet every taste and budget. The arcade is lined with tropical plants and caged parrots, and the casino is located just at the top of the escalator.

There are several other shopping malls in Oranjestad, all of which are worth visiting. The **Holland Aruba Mall** (Havenstr. 6, right downtown) houses a collection of smart shops and eateries. Nearby are the **Strada I** and **Strada II,** two small complexes of shops in tall Dutch buildings painted in pastels.

In **Harbourtown** (Swain Wharf), a blue-and-white postmodern version of a seaside village, look for handmade china by Venezuelan artists, discounted perfumes, and embroidered linens from China.

Port of Call Marketplace (L. G. Smith Blvd. 17) features fine jewelry, perfumes, duty-free liquors, batiks, crystal, leather goods, and fashionable clothing.

Dining

Aruba's restaurants serve a cosmopolitan variety of cuisines, although most menus are specifically designed to please American palates—you can get fresh surf and New York turf almost anywhere. Make the effort to try Aruban specialties—*pan bati* is a delicious beaten bread that resembles a pancake, and plantains are similar to cooked bananas.

Dress ranges from casual to elegant, but even the finest restaurants require at the most only a jacket for men and a sundress for women. The air-conditioning does get cold, so don't go barearmed. And anytime you plan to eat in the open air, remember to douse yourself first with insect repellent—the mosquitoes can get unruly, especially in July and August, when the winds drop.

On Sunday, it may be difficult to find a restaurant outside of the hotels that's open for lunch. One of the best bets is the extensive buffet at the Holiday Inn.

For good or for bad, fast food has arrived in Aruba. For those who are homesick, there's McDonald's, Kentucky Fried Chicken, Burger King, and Wendy's. For breakfast and lunch, the restaurants in the hotels tend to be more expensive than the ones in town. Most hotels offer several food plans, which you can purchase either in advance or upon arrival. But before you purchase a Full American Plan (FAP), which includes breakfast, lunch, and dinner, remember that Aruba has numerous excellent and reasonably priced restaurants from which to choose and that eating at different places can be part of the fun of a vacation.

Another option is Aruba's Dine-Around program. Eight restaurants have joined together and agreed to honor the $27.50-per-person coupons used by the plan. You can purchase as many coupons as you like and use them more than once at the same restaurant. Each coupon is good for dinner only and includes either an appetizer or soup, salad, main course, dessert, coffee, taxes, and all gratuities. Best bets are the Buccaneer, Twinklebones, and La Taurina. Coupons must be purchased in the United States. For information call 800/544-0799.

Highly recommended restaurants are indicated by a star ★.

Category	Cost*
Expensive	over $25
Moderate	$15–$25
Inexpensive	under $15

Prices are for a main course only and are per person, excluding drinks, service, and sales tax (15%).

★ **Chez Mathilde.** This elegant restaurant is in a renovated private home, one of the last surviving 19th-century dwellings in Aruba. Though the previous chef and maître d' left to open another restaurant, the new Swiss chef maintains his predecessor's high culinary standards. The French-style menu is constantly being re-created. To the tune of Strauss waltzes, dine on frogs' legs or escargots Dijonaise, or try the *emincée à boeuf*—paper-thin slices of beef spiked with horseradish. The wine list is one of the best on the island. Ask to sit in the Pavilion Room, which has an ecletic mix of turn-of-the-century Italian and French decor. *Havenstraat 23, Oranjestad, tel. 297/8–34968. Reservations required. AE, MC, V. Closed for lunch Sun. Expensive.*

★ **Ruinas del Mar.** Imagine dining on a crescent-shaped marble terrace amid the ruins of an ancient gold mine or inside, with stone pillars flanking your candlelit table and gentle Aruban breezes stirring the placid moat that surrounds your dining oasis. Water tumbling from a small artificial waterfall or reflecting the Aruban stars from placid ponds sets the scene for romance. Located in the new Hyatt Regency, this restaurant is easily the most romantic in Aruba. The menu is limited and a bit eclectic, mixing international appetizers with pasta specialties and grilled fish and beef entrées. In general, the meat dishes are better than the fish, and the mixed grill, with four types of beef, is superb. Save room for the wicked coffee crème brûlée or white chocolate mousse sprinkled with fresh raspberries. Then sip an after-dinner drink and fall in love all over again. *Hyatt Regency Aruba Resort, L. G. Smith Blvd. 85, tel. 297/8–31234. Reservations necessary. AE, DC, MC, V. Expensive.*

Valentino's. The airy, two-level dining room here is inviting, with its rose and sparkling-white color scheme. The tables are placed comfortably far apart, and the service is attentive without being overbearing. The menu is Italian, and the *gamberoni di teresa* (shrimps sautéed in garlic and fresh tomatoes) is a knockout. The atmosphere is festive since the restaurant is popular with celebrating Arubans. You'll find their gaiety infectious. *Caribbean Palm Village, Noord, tel. 297/8–69455. Reservations requested. AE, DC, MC, V. Expensive.*

Bali Floating Restaurant. Floating in its own Oriental houseboat and anchored in Oranjestad's harbor, the Bali has one of the island's best *rijsttafel* dinners (an Indonesian buffet table with 21 different meat, chicken, shrimp, vegetable, fruit, and relish dishes, served over rice). It runs $39 for two people. Bamboo rooftops and Indonesian antiques add to the charm of this popular restaurant. Recently, the owners of the Japanese & Thai Dynasty Restaurant took over the management of the restaurant and have added less-spicy fare. The service is slow, but well meaning. Happy hour 6–8 PM. *L. G. Smith Blvd., Oranjestad, tel. 297/8–22131. AE, MC, V. Moderate.*

★ **Bon Appetit.** With its white tablecloths, clay-potted plants, low lighting, and warm-looking wood beams, this restaurant glows like a beautiful tan—but it's the savory smells that hook you. The international cuisine wins acclaim—*Gourmet* magazine once requested the recipe for *keshi yena*, baked cheese stuffed with meat and condiments. Generous portions of seafood and beef (with Dutch specialties) adorn the plates of this mid-priced restaurant. The kitchen won a Dutch award for being the cleanest in Aruba. The prime ribs of beef will satisfy even the largest appetites. Leave room for the flaming Max dessert, named after owner and charming host Max Croes. *Palm Beach 29, tel. 297/8–25241. Reservations advised. AE, D, DC, MC, V. Moderate.*

Buccaneer Restaurant. Imagine you're in a sunken ship—fish nets and turtle shells hang from the ceiling, and through the portholes you see live sharks, barracudas, and groupers swimming by. That's the Buccaneer, snug in an old stone building flanked by heavy black chains and boasting a fantastic 5,000-gallon saltwater aquarium, plus 12 more porthole-size tanks. The surf-and-turf cuisine is prepared by the chef-owners with European élan, and the tables are always full. Order the fresh catch of the day or more exotic fare, such as shrimps with Pernod; smoked pork cutlets with sausage, sauerkraut, and potatoes; or the turtle steak with a light cream sauce. Go early (around 5:45 PM) to get a booth next to the aquariums. *Gasparito 11-C., Oranjestad, tel. 297/8–26172. AE, MC, V. Closed Sun. Moderate.*

The Old Mill (Die Olde Molen). A gift from the queen of Holland, this real Dutch mill was shipped brick by brick to Aruba in 1920 and reassembled here. The present owner, Bill Waldron, is a native Virginian, but he has maintained the excellence of the international cuisine. For starters, try the seafood crepe Neptune, nestled in a delicate cheese bed. Also excellent is the shrimp with spinach and cream sauce, or the dutch fries—crunchy little nuggets of potato. Order the ice cream with chocolate liqueur and take the bottle home as a souvenir of Aruba's oldest restaurant. A time-sharing condominium complex, including tennis courts, is now being added to the estate. *L. G. Smith Blvd. 330, Palm Beach, tel. 297/8–22060. Reservations required. AE, MC, V. 2 dinner seatings: 6:30 and 9 PM. Moderate.*

Olé. Spain comes alive within the coral stone walls of this romantic restaurant. Waiters and waitresses croon Spanish love songs tableside to the melodic music of a classical guitarist while a strategically lit waterfall tumbles into a moat just outside. The ambience makes up for the limited menu. Order some sangria, share a few *tapas*, and then split a *paella* (chicken, sausage, and seafood in a sauce over saffron rice) for two. Honeymooners will want to request, in advance, the sole table on the private terrace overlooking the waterfall. *Hyatt Regency Aruba Resort, L. G. Smith Blvd. 85, tel. 297/8–31234. Reservations necessary. AE, DC, MC, V. Moderate.*

Papiamento. Longtime restaurateurs Lenie and Eduardo Ellis decided Aruba needed a bistro that was cozy yet elegant, intimate, and always romantic. So they converted their 130-year-old home into an dining spot where guests can dine indoors surrounded by antiques or outdoors on the patio garden beneath ficus and palm trees adorned with lights. The service is impeccable at this family-run establishment. The chef utilizes flavors from both Continental and Caribbean cuisines to produce favorites that include seafood and meat dishes. Try the Dover sole, the Caribbean lobster, shrimps and red snapper cooked tableside on a hot marble stone, or the "claypot" for two—a medley of seafoods prepared in a sealed clay pot. *Washington 61, Noord, tel. 297/8–64544. Reservations advised. AE, MC, V. Dinner only. Moderate.*

Talk of the Town Restaurant. Here you'll find candlelight dining and some of the best steaks in town—the owner comes from a family of Dutch butchers. Located in the Best Western Talk of the Town Resort, between the airport and Oranjestad, this fine restaurant is now a member of the elite honorary restaurant society, Chaine de Rotisseurs. Saturday night is prime-rib-as-much-as-you-can-eat night ($18.95), but seafood specialties are popular, too—such as the crabmeat crepes and the *escargots à la bourguignonne.* For late-night suppers, the poolside grill stays open until 2 AM. *L. G. Smith Blvd. 2, Oranjestad, tel. 297/8–23380. AE, DC, MC, V. Moderate.*

Twinklebone's House of Roastbeef. Prime rib with Yorkshire pudding is the kitchen's pride, but there's a full international menu with dishes named after local friends and residents. The chef is known to leave the stove and sing Aruban tunes with the maître d'. In fact, the owner, hostess, and waiters are all known to break into song and encourage the patrons to sing along. There are two seatings, so be sure to call ahead. *Turibana Plaza, Noord 124, tel. 297/8–69800 or 297/8–26780. Reservations advised. AE, MC, V. Closed Sun. Moderate.*

Boonoonoonoos. The name—say it just as it looks!—means extraordinary, which is a bit of hyperbole for this Austrian-owned Caribbean bistroquet in the heart of town. The decor is simple in bright and pastel colors, but the tasty food, served with hearty portions of peas-and-rice and plantains, makes up for the lack of tablecloths, china, and crystal. It should be avoided when crowded, since the service and the quality of the food deteriorate. The roast chicken Barbados is sweet and tangy, marinated in pineapple and cinnamon and simmered in fruit juices. The Jamaican jerk ribs (a 300-year-old recipe) are tiny but spicy, and the satin-smooth hot pumpkin soup drizzled with cheese and served in a pumpkin shell may as well be dessert. The place is small, and the tables are close together. *Wilhelminastr. 18A, Oranjestad, tel. 297/8–31888. Reservations advised. AE, V. Dinner only. Closed Sun. Inexpensive.*

Brisas del Mar. This is a friendly 10-table place that is popular with tourists because you'll feel as if you're dining in an Aruban home overlooking the sea. The menu features mostly fried fish with Creole sauces of tomatoes and onions. Try the baby-shark steak and the turtle soup. The pan bati is some of the best on the island. The restaurant is useful for lunch when exploring the area, but the food does not justify a taxi ride to reach it—10 miles east of Oranjestad in the town of Savaneta. *Savaneta 22A, tel. 297/8–47718. Reservations suggested. No credit cards. Closed Mon. Inexpensive.*

★ **La Paloma.** "The Dove" has an air of low-key loveliness with no gimmicks, and it's usually packed. The restaurant has its own fishing boat, so the fish is always fresh. There's conch stew with pan bati and fried plantains for exotic tastes. The Caesar salad and minestrone soup are house specialties. This is not the place for a romantic interlude; come for the family atmosphere, American-style Italian food, and reasonable prices. *Noord 39, tel. 297/8–62770. AE, MC, V. Closed Tues. Inexpensive.*

Mi Cushina. The name means "My Kitchen," and the menu lists such Aruban specialties as *sopi di mariscos* (seafood soup) and *kreeft stoba* (lobster stew). The walls are hung with antique farm tools, and there's a small museum devoted to the aloe vera plant. You'll need a car to get here, about a mile from San Nicolas. *Cura Cabai 24, San Nicolas, tel. 297/8–48335. Reservations advised. AE, MC, V. Closed Thurs. Inexpensive.*

New Old Cunucu House. Situated on a small estate in a residential neighborhood three minutes from the high-rise hotels, this 72-year-old Aruban home has been renovated into a seafood and international restaurant of casual élan. Dine on local recipes for red snapper, coconut-fried shrimp, Cornish hen, and New York sirloins, or beef fondue à deux. Private dining rooms hold groups up to 20. An Aruban trio sings and plays background music every Friday, and on Saturday evenings a mariachi band serenades the patrons. Happy hour 5–6 PM. *Palm Beach 150, tel. 297/8–61666. Reservations suggested. AE, DC, MC. Closed Mon. Inexpensive.*

Lodging

Most of the hotels in Aruba are located west of Oranjestad along L. G. Smith Boulevard, and there are several new properties that are scheduled to open for the 1993–1994 winter season. You may want to check with the Aruba Tourism Authority (tel. 201/330–0800 or 800/TO–ARUBA) about the status of these new ones. Most hotels include a host of facilities—drugstores, boutiques, health spas, beauty parlors, casinos, restaurants, pool bars, and gourmet delis. Do not arrive in Aruba without a reservation; many hotels are booked months in advance, especially in the winter season. All hotels offer packages, and these are considerably less expensive than the one-night rate. Hotel restaurants and clubs are open to all guests on the island, so you can visit other properties no matter where you're staying. Most hotels, unless specified, do not include meals in their room rates. The meal plans offered are optional and incur an additional per-day expense. Off-season rates are discounted approximately 40%.

Look for Charlie, the island's coconut expert, who makes the rounds of the hotels demonstrating his special talent: slicing a coconut samurai-style in three seconds without losing a drop of the precious milk.

Highly recommended lodgings are indicated by a star ★.

Category	Cost*
Very Expensive	over $250
Expensive	$180–$250
Moderate	$110–$180
Inexpensive	under $110

All prices are for a standard double room for two, excluding 5% tax and a 10% service charge.

Americana Aruba Hotel & Casino. This established high-rise hotel on Palm Beach underwent a $20 million renovation that was completed in May 1990. The new clover-leaf-shaped pool area has a waterfall and two Jacuzzis in its center. The Jardin Brasilian Lounge features live entertainment nightly, except Sunday, and there is a cabaret show at the Las Palmas nightclub every night except Monday (don't miss it). On Monday guests enjoy a seafood barbecue with limbo-dancing instruction and a live band. The hotel teems with activity from beer-drinking contests to bikini shows around the pool, and a social director cajoles your participation in events. Children are treated to a daily activities program, which is free, as well as a video arcade. White bamboo and bleached-wood furniture are complemented by tropical blue, green, and peach fabrics in the rooms. Cable TV with remote control and hair dryers are added niceties. Rooms on the top floors tend to be nicer than those on the lower floors. Americans and Canadians make up 80% of the clientele. *L. G. Smith Blvd. 83, Palm Beach, tel. 297/8–24500 or 800/447–7462, fax 297/8–23191; in NY, 212/661–4540. 419 rooms. Facilities: 2 restaurants, swimming pool with swim-up bar, TV, 2 lighted tennis courts, tour desk, water-sports concession, children's activities program, weight room/gym, casino, laundry/valet, 2 car rentals, company desks, telex/fax/ typewriters, boutiques, beauty parlor/barbershop. AE, DC, MC, V. EP, MAP, All-inclusive. Very Expensive.*

★ **Hyatt Regency Aruba Resort & Casino.** The center of this $57 million resort is spectacular, with a multilevel pool, two-story waterslide, waterfalls, and a lagoon stocked with tropical fish and black swans. Beyond is a white-sand beach dotted with palms. All the spacious rooms here are the same size, so the view determines their price, for example, $270 for a garden view and $430 for a sea view on the Regency floor. The decor is southwestern, with bleached-wood furniture and luxury appointments. All the air-conditioned rooms feature a digital safe, stocked minibar, remote-control color TV, clock radio, ceiling fan, oversized bathroom, and a tiny balcony that's more for show than use. There's a no-smoking floor. The top floor houses the hedonistic Regency Club rooms, each with two huge his-and-her marble bathrooms loaded with every amenity, plus a private-floor lounge where free breakfast, afternoon tea, and happy hour drinks are served. Camp Hyatt keeps children ages 3–15 busy day and night, so parents can enjoy time alone. Four excellent restaurants are on the premises, among them Olé and Ruinas del Mar, (see Dining, above). Lighted tennis courts; a comprehensive water-sports center, offering scuba diving, sailing cruises, windsurfing, waterskiing, and jetskiing; a sleek health-and-fitness center; and a shopping arcade, plus a host of well-managed services and a fine staff have turned this property into the top luxury resort on the island. *L. G. Smith Blvd. 85, tel. 297/8–31234 or 800/233–1234, fax 297/8–35478. 325 rooms and 25 suites. Facilities: free-form pool with swim-up bar, 4 restaurants, 2 bars, snack bar, casino, fitness center, 2 lighted tennis courts, water-sports center, tour desk, baby-sitting, shops. AE, DC, MC, V. EP, MAP. Very Expensive.*

★ **Divi Aruba Beach Resort.** The motto at this popular low rise, recently taken over by Doral Resorts, remains "barefoot elegance," which means you can streak through the lobby in your bikini. The main section has 90 standard guest rooms, 20 beachfront lanai rooms, and 40 casitas (garden bungalows) that look out onto individual courtyards. A newer section, Divi Dos, contains 49 luxury rooms and 1 bridal suite, all with minirefrigerators and Jacuzzi bathtubs. The recently redecorated rooms are yellow, green, and creamy white and have balconies, cable TV, safe-deposit boxes, and air-conditioning. The Divi Dos section is known as a honeymoon haven: Special packages include champagne breakfast, "just married" signs, photo albums, colorful beach towels, and fruit baskets. Divi Dos's free-form pool includes a small island at the center, accessible by a bridge. A breakfast buffet is served on the Pelican Terrace, just steps away from the sea ($9 plus 15% service). Ask about the various meal plans. Special theme nights include Tuesday's Carnival and Saturday's Beach BBQ Fiesta, with folkloric show and steel band. *L. G. Smith Blvd. 93, Divi Beach, tel. 297/8–23300 or 800/22–DORAL, fax 297/8–34002. 203 rooms. Facilities: 2 restaurants, 2 bars, 2 pools, Jacuzzi, tennis court, shuffleboard, shops, tour desk, water-sports concession, adult activities program, baby-sitting. AE, MC, V. EP, MAP. Expensive–Very Expensive.*

Aruba Royal Resort. This sleek glass-and-granite high-rise time-share property is the first stage of the Aruba Royal Resort, which will eventually include the Ramada Renaissance Resort Aruba and the Casino Royale. Opened in February 1990, the Aruba Royal Club has 50 guest rooms and studio apartments with kitchenettes, 22 one-bedroom parlor suites and 24 one-bedroom beachfront villas. All have minibars, complimentary nightly in-room videos, and balconies. At press time, one restaurant was serving breakfast, lunch, and dinner and offering three themed dinner buffets a week with entertainment. Unfortunately, the service isn't up to much, and there is a marked lack of facilities because of the stalled opening of the adjacent Ramada Renaissance. *L. G. Smith Blvd. 75, tel. 297/8–37000 or 800/223–6510, fax 297/8–39090. 96 rooms. Facilities: beach, pool, Jacuzzi, air-conditioned squash court, water-sports desk, tour desk, sundries shop, car rental, baby-sitting. AE, DC, MC, V. EP. Expensive.*

Casa del Mar Beach Resort. This beachfront, low-rise time-share hotel has combined its facilities with its time-share neighbor, the Aruba Beach Club. As time shares go, Casa Del Mar's completely furnished suites are among the most expensive on the island. Each has a dining table seating six, and the kitchen comes fully stocked. Baby-sitters are on call, and a social hostess provides children's programs. *L. G. Smith Blvd. 53, Punta Brabo Beach, tel. 297/8–27000 or 800/346–7084; in NJ, 201/617–8877, fax 297/8–26557. 107 2-bedroom, 2-bath suites. Facilities: restaurant (2 restaurants and pool bar at sister property), lobby bar, TVs with in-room movie satellite, fitness center, sauna and massage, pool, 2 Jacuzzis, 4 lighted* *tennis courts, children's playground, games room, 2 pools, 2 kiddie pools, baby-sitting, shops. AE, DC, MC, V. EP. Expensive.*

Tamarijn Aruba Beach Resort. A sprawling melange of two-story white stucco buildings with an open-air lobby, two restaurants, and two beachside bars, the Tamarijn boasts a lovely stretch of white-sand beach dotted with tiki huts. The ambience here is casual. A freshwater seaside pool, two lighted tennis courts, and water sports provide active entertainment. All rooms have a beachfront view, a patio or balcony, air-conditioning, cable TV, and safe-deposit boxes. A 1990 redecoration brought these once basic accommodations up to getaway status. Guests can ride to the Alhambra Casino and the Divi Aruba Beach Hotel in free carts, and exchange privileges have been arranged with them, including nightly entertainment. If you're staying for a full week, ask about the meal plan. The poolside bar stays open till 1 AM. *L. G. Smith Blvd. 64, Divi Beach, tel. 297/8–24150 or 800/22–DORAL, fax 297/8–34002. 236 rooms. Facilities: 2 restaurants, 2 bars, pool, tennis courts, 2 Jacuzzis, shops, activities center. AE, MC, V. EP, MAP. Expensive.*

Radisson Aruba Caribbean Resort & Casino. Called La Grande Dame of the Caribbean, this resort, formerly the Golden Tulip, was the first high rise on the island. Liz Taylor used to stay here when she was married to Eddie Fisher, and the queen of Holland still stays in the Royal Suite (available on request), so the staff is used to filling special needs. The turquoise-and-white tiled lobby gives the feeling of an art deco tropical palazzo. The sunny air-conditioned rooms, all with either an ocean or a garden view, are scattered among four buildings. In general, the rooms in the older wings are larger, but even the newest wing has an old look. The hotel simply has not kept up with the other properties on the island and is looking very tired and worn. At press time, the hotel was in the midst of becoming a Radisson property, which should mean a good infusion of funds for renovations. The fitness center near the tennis courts offers a Universal weight system and aerobics classes. Bands play every Saturday night in the blue-and-gold Fandango Nightclub. *L. G. Smith Blvd. 81, Palm Beach, tel. 297/8–33555 or 800/777–1700, fax 297/8–23260. 378 rooms and suites. Facilities: 4 restaurants, 4 bars, nightclub, meeting and banquet rooms, casino, pool, 4 lighted tennis courts, fitness center, tour desk, car rental, baby-sitting, water sports, videogame room, shops, beauty parlor, deli. AE, MC, V. EP, MAP, All-inclusive. Expensive.*

Playa Linda Beach Resort. Designed in a ziggurat of receding balconies, this time-share complex, sheathed in a facade of terra-cotta and cream, sits on one of the most beautiful and enticing sections of Palm Beach. Accommodations are stylishly comfortable, outfitted with private kitchens, verandas, and air-conditioning. Units (all of which are suites) sleep four to six. All three meals are heartily served poolside, overlooking the ocean, at the open-air Linda Vista Restaurant. Water sports and tennis can be arranged. *L. G. Smith Blvd. 87, Palm Beach, tel. 297/8–31000 or 800/346–7084; in NJ, 201/617–8877, fax 297/8–25210. 194 1- and 2-bedroom suites and studio apartments. Facilities: restaurant, bar, activities center, adults' and children's pools, tennis courts, minimarket/gift shop. AE, MC, V. EP, MAP, FAP. Expensive.*

★ **Sonesta Hotel, Beach Club & Casino.** If falling out of bed and
onto a beach isn't important to you, then Sonesta's in-town location is ideal—especially if you like to shop, eat, and gamble.
This new hotel stands out amid the Dutch architecture of
Oranjestad: In the lobby, sleek low couches wrap around pink
stucco pillars while glass elevators rise above the circular deep-
water grotto and motor skiffs board guests headed for the hotel's 40-acre private island. The 300 tropical green-and-pink
guest rooms and suites are spacious and modern, with tiny balconies, cable TV, hair dryers, safe-deposit boxes, and stocked
minibars. The free daily "Just Us Kids" program offers children ages 5 to 12 supervised activities, including kite flying,
bowling, movies, storytelling, and field trips. For adults there
are free casino classes, volleyball, and beach bingo. The neighboring Crystal Casino houses the Caribbean's largest $1 slot
machine. Dancers should head for the Desires Lounge, which
features live entertainment every night except Sunday. The
hotel is popular with businessmen and those who do not wish to
depend on taxis or a rental car every time they leave their hotel.
*L. G. Smith Blvd. 82, tel. 297/8–36000, 800/SONESTA, or 800/
343–7170, fax 297/8–34389. 274 rooms and 25 suites. Facilities:
minispa and fitness center, pool, 40-acre private island with
water-sports center, 3 restaurants, bar, casino, nightclub, 85
shops, children's program, tour desk, beauty salon. AE, DC,
MC, V. EP. Expensive.*

Aruba Concorde. Hilton Hotels recently took over this run-
down 18-story high rise and gutted it completely. At press
time, the renovations were impressive but still under way. The
new slogan promises "In Aruba, some of the hotels have
changed their names. At the Aruba Concorde, we are changing
the hotel." At press time $20 million had been poured into the
rooms, the pool, the lobby, and the casino—all new and all of
which should be open and serving guests by the 1993–1994 season. This comprehensive renovation will make this hotel a serious contender as one of the top resorts in Aruba. *L. G. Smith
Blvd. 77, Palm Beach, tel. 297/8–24466 or 800/445–8667. 500
rooms. Facilities: 5 restaurants, nightclub, casino, 3 cocktail
lounges, pool, children's wading pool, 2 lighted tennis courts,
massage room, games room, car rental, tour desk, water-
sports desk, beach, beach bar, ballroom with meeting and banquet rooms, shops, beauty parlor, deli, children's corner. AE,
DC, MC, V. EP, CP, BP, MAP, FAP. Moderate–Expensive.*

Bushiri Beach Resort. Two long, low buildings—built around a
lush Jacuzzi garden and situated on a wide expanse of beach—
make up this all-inclusive resort, Aruba's first. These buildings
are old and nondescript, and although the rooms were recently
renovated, they remain ordinary. But the Bushiri is a hotel-
training school, a factor that shows in the enthusiastic staff.
The best rooms are in the West Wing; "deluxe" rooms, the largest, have balconies that face the ocean, minifridges, and safe-
deposit boxes. Where this resort shines is in its full daily activities program for adults. Snorkeling (with instruction and
equipment), tennis, sailing, windsurfing, pool volleyball, and
casino gambling classes are among the offerings. Kids are kept
busy with their own day-long supervised program. Three
sightseeing tours around the island, three meals daily, a poolside barbecue, and a midnight buffet, as well as all soft drinks
and alcoholic beverages, are included in the single tab. *L. G.
Smith Blvd. 35, Oranjestad, tel. 297/8–25216, 800/GO–BOUN-*

*TY, or 800/462–6868, fax 297/8–26789. 150 rooms. Facilities: 2
restaurants, pool bar, cocktail lounge, piano bar, pool, satellite TV, 2 tennis courts, nightly entertainment, beach, water-
sports center, drugstore, health club, 3 Jacuzzis, free nightly
shuttle to the Holiday Inn casino. AE, DC, MC, V. All-inclusive. Moderate–Expensive.*

Aruba Beach Club. This attractive low-rise resort on Druif
Beach also doubles as a time share. The open-air lobby leads to
a patio, gardens, and pool, with the beach only a few steps beyond. Action settles around the pool bar, with a clientele that's
mostly American, mostly young-to-middle-aged couples with
children. The pastel rooms are more basic than luxurious, even
though they're refurbished every two years. Each features a
kitchenette and a balcony. Guests may use all the facilities at
the Casa Del Mar resort next door. *L. G. Smith Blvd. 53, Punta
Brabo Beach, tel. 297/8–23000 or 800/346–7084, fax 297/8–
26557. 131 studio and 1-bedroom suites. Facilities: 2 restaurants, cocktail lounge, pool bar, ice-cream parlor, satellite TV,
radio, adults' and children's pools, 2 lighted tennis courts,
children's playground, baby-sitting. AE, MC, V. EP. Moderate.*

Aruba Palm Beach Hotel & Casino. Formerly a Sheraton, this
pink, eight-story Moorish palazzo even has pink-swaddled
palm trees dotting its drive. The lobby, with its impressive
grand piano, is a haze of pink and purple, underlaid with cool
marble. The large backyard sunning grounds are a well-manicured tropical garden, with a fleet of pesky parrots guarding
the entrance. The guest rooms are roomy and cheerful, decorated in either burgundy and mauve or emerald and pink. Each
has a walk-in closet, color cable TV, and a tiny balcony. All
overlook either the ocean, the pool, or the gardens. For a peaceful meal, eat alfresco in the rock-garden setting of the Sea-
watch Restaurant. For live music, try the Players Club lounge,
open nightly until 3 AM. Every Wednesday there's a popular limbo and barbecue party around the pool for $23 per person. *L. G.
Smith Blvd. 79, Palm Beach, tel. 297/8–23900 or 800/428–9933;
in FL, 305/539–9933, fax 297/8–21941. 202 rooms. Facilities: 2
restaurants, pool, coffee shop, disco, TV, shops, casino, 2
lighted tennis courts, water sports, tour desk, beauty salon.
AE, DC, MC, V. EP, MAP. Moderate.*

La Cabana All Suite Beach Resort & Casino. At the top end of
Eagle Beach and across the road from the sand is Aruba's largest time-sharing condominium/hotel complex. The large four-
story building forms a horseshoe around a huge free-form pool
complex with a water slide, poolside bar, outdoor cafe, and water-sports center. The entire complex faces the pristine white
sands of Eagle Beach just across the street. One-third of the
rooms have a full sea view; two-thirds have a partial view. All
rooms—studios or one-bedroom suites—come with a fully
equipped kitchenette, a small balcony, a Jacuzzi, and have both
air-conditioning and ceiling fans. The tropically decorated
suites have interconnecting doors so that three of them may be
linked together. to form two- and three-bedroom units. The
ground-floor living rooms do not offer as much privacy as do the
higher floors' because they look out onto the pool area. Claustrophobic elevators (or stairs) lead to upper floors with plain
open-air corridors. This complete resort has much to offer: a
modern fitness and health center, an ice-cream and expresso
shop, a budget restaurant, a small grocery store, several
shops, and an activities center in the main complex. Shuttle

buses run guests over to the upscale casino, the island's largest, where the hotel has another three restaurants and the *rouge et noir* Tropicana nightclub that features top shows. In addition, comedians perform every weekend. *L. G. Smith Blvd. 250, tel. 297/8–39000 or 800/835–7193; in NY, 212/251–1710, fax 297/8–37208. 440 rooms. Facilities: 5 restaurants, including poolside bar; shops; casino; racquetball, squash, and tennis courts; health and fitness center. AE, DC, MC, V. EP, MAP. Moderate.*

The Mill Resort. Two-story, red-roof buildings flank the open-air common areas of this small condominium hotel, which opened in September 1990. Unlike time-share resorts, this hotel sells each unit to an individual, who then leases the unit back to the resort for use as a hotel room. The decor is soft, country French, with a delicate rose-and-white color scheme, white wicker furniture, and wall-to-wall silver carpeting. The junior suites feature a king-size bed, sitting area, and kitchenette. The studios have a full kitchen, but only a queen-size convertible sofa bed and a tiny bathroom. There's no kitchen in the hedonistic Royal Den, but there's a marble Jacuzzi tub big enough for two. This resort is popular with couples seeking a quiet getaway and with families vacationing with small children. There is no restaurant on the premises, but The Mill Restaurant is next door (*see* Dining, *above*). There are also no bars, no tour desk, and no organized evening activities. The theme here is one of peaceful bliss. Action can be found at the nearby large resorts, and the beach is only a five-minute walk away. *L. G. Smith Blvd. 330, Palm Beach, tel. 297/8–37700, fax 297/8–37271. 99 studio, junior, and Royal Den suites. One- and 2-bedroom suites are available by combining two of the above units. Facilities: pool, kiddie pool, mini food market, baby-sitting, car rental, 2 lighted tennis courts, fitness center, pool snack bar. AE, DC, MC, V. EP, BP. Moderate.*

★ **Best Western Talk of the Town Resort.** Originally a run-down chemical plant, Talk of the Town was transformed by Ike and Grete Cohen into an top-notch budget resort. It gets its name from the excellent on-premises restaurant (*see* Dining, *above*). A huge pool is at the center of this two-story motellike structure, with most of the rooms in the new wing overlooking the charming Spanish-style courtyard. Some accommodations have kitchens and all offer TVs, air-conditioning, and minifridges. There's also a Jacuzzi. Though the resort is on the outskirts of Oranjestad, there is a beach just across the street, where guests have the run of the Surfside Beach Club, complete with pool, two Jacuzzis, snack bar, and a water-sports and dive center. *L. G. Smith Blvd. 2, Oranjestad, tel. 297/8–23380 or 800/233–1108, fax 297/8–32446. 63 rooms. Facilities: 3 restaurants, nightclub, cable TV, facilities exchange with Manchebo Beach Hotel, gift shop, beach club with pool, 2 Jacuzzis, snack bar, water-sports and dive center. AE, MC, V. EP, BP, MAP. Inexpensive.*

La Quinta Beach Resort. Across the road from Eagle Beach is this time-share complex, built in two phases, with 24 units scheduled for construction in 1993. The efficiency and one-bedroom units are small but well designed and stylish, with full cooking facilities, TVs, and hair dryers in the tiled bathrooms. One-, two- and three-bedroom units also have sleep sofas and VCRs. This is a moderately priced hotel with a friendly staff. *Eagle Beach, tel. 297/8–35010 or 800/223–9815, fax 297/8–*

26263. Facilities: bar, 2 pools, cable TV, tennis courts. AE, DC, MC, V. EP. Inexpensive.

Nightlife

Casinos Casinos are all the rage in Aruba. At last count there were 10. The crowds seem to flock to the newest of the new: The Crystal Casino enjoyed the business until the Hyatt Regency's ultramodern gaming room stole the show (the marquee above the bar at this casino opens to reveal a live band). Now both are getting stiff competition from the popular (and new) **Royal Cabana Casino** (L. G. Smith Blvd. 250, tel. 297/8–39000) with its sleek interior, multitheme three-in-one restaurant, and showcase Tropicana nightclub. One place where you'll always find some action is the **Alhambra Casino** (L. G. Smith Blvd. 93, Oranjestad, tel. 297/8–35000), where a "Moorish slave" gives every gambler a hearty handshake upon entering.

There's also action along the Oranjestad "strip" in the casinos at the **Aruba Concorde Hotel** (L. G. Smith Blvd. 77, tel. 297/8–24466) and the **Golden Tulip Caribbean** (L. G. Smith Blvd. 81, tel. 297/8–33555). The **Holiday Inn's** casino (L. G. Smith Blvd. 230, tel. 297/8–23419) is open 19 hours a day, with an adjacent New York–style deli open until 5 AM. The **Americana Aruba Beach Resort & Hotel Casino** (L. G. Smith Blvd. 83, tel. 297/ 8–24500) opens daily at 1 PM for slots, 5 PM for all games. The **Aruba Palm Beach Hotel Casino** (L. G. Smith Blvd. 79, tel. 297/ 8–23900) opens at 10 AM for slots, 6 PM for all games. You can also woo Lady Luck at the Sonesta Hotel's **Crystal Casino** (L. G. Smith Blvd. 82, tel. 297/8–36000), where the action is nonstop from 10 AM to 4 AM for slots; 1 PM to 4 AM for the gaming tables. And there's the new **Hyatt Regency Aruba Resort Casino** (L. G. Smith Blvd. 85, tel. 297/8–31234), a 10,000-square-foot complex with a Carnival-in-Rio theme and live entertainment. Low-key gambling can be found at the new waterside **Harbourtown Casino** (L. G. Smith Blvd. 9, tel. 297/8–35600 or 297/8–32165).

Disco and Dancing Arubans usually start partying late, and action doesn't start till around midnight, mostly on the weekends. The newest in place is **Papas & Beer** (L. G. Smith Blvd. 184, tel. 297/8–60300), whose purple-and-pink neon signs can be seen lighting up the night from as far away as hotel row. Live bands perform nightly, waiters in funky costumes do dance routines under flickering strobe lights, video screens flash, and food and drinks are served almost round-the-clock. Another popular nightclub is **Blue Wave** (Shellstr., tel. 297/8–38856) with live bands on Saturday nights and a "Ladies Night" drawing in the crowds on Thursdays. For a young adult-style "amusement park," stop in at **La Visage** (L. G. Smith Blvd. 152A, tel. 297/8–22397), the disco for the young set, both Arubans and tourists. Jazz lovers will prefer the quiet piano bar atmosphere of **La Nota** (Emmastr. 7, tel. 297/8–32739) which gets lively around 10 PM until close at 2 AM.

Theater **Aladdin Theater** (L. G. Smith Blvd. 93, tel. 297/8–35000). This cabaret theater tucked into the Alhambra Bazaar features a variety of shows, including Broadway musicals.

Tropicana (L. G. Smith Blvd. 250, tel 297/8–39000). Aruba's newest cabaret theater and nightclub, part of the La Cabana All Suite Beach Resort complex, features first-class Las

Vegas–style reviews and modern shows, plus a special revolving comedy series every weekend.

Specialty Theme Nights One of the unique things about Aruba's nightlife is the number of specialty theme nights offered by the hotels: At last count there were more than 30. Each "party" features dinner and entertainment, followed by dancing. For a complete list, contact the Aruba Tourism Authority (tel. 297/8–23777).

An Aruban must is the **Bon Bini Festival,** held every Tuesday evening from 6:30 to 8:30 PM in the outdoor courtyard of the Fort Zoutman Museum. *Bon Bini* is Papiamento for "welcome," and this tourist event is the Aruba Institute of Culture and Education's way of introducing visitors to all things Aruban. Stroll by the stands of Aruban foods, drinks, and crafts, or watch Aruban entertainers perform Antillean music and folkloric dancing. A master of ceremonies explains the history of the dances, instruments, and music. It's a fun event, and a good way to meet other tourists. Look for the clock tower. *Oranjestr., tel. 297/8–22185. Admission: Afl 2. adults, Afl 1. children.*

Weekend evenings are lively all over town, so the theme-night pickings are fewer. The best ones are Divi Divi Beach Resort's **Barefoot Elegance Beach BBQ** (L. G. Smith Blvd. 93, tel. 297/8–23300) on Saturday nights and the Mexican fiesta **Fajitas and 'ritas** (L. G. Smith Blvd. 85, tel. 297/8–31234) held Friday nights at the beachside Palms Restaurant in the Hyatt Regency.

5 Barbados

Updated by
Nigel Fisher

Barbados has a life of its own that goes on after the tourists have packed their sun oils and returned home. Since the government is stable and unemployment is relatively low, the difference between haves and have-nots is less marked—or at least less visible—than on other islands, and visitors are neither fawned upon nor resented for their assumed wealth. Genuinely proud of their country, the quarter million Bajans welcome visitors as privileged guests. Barbados is fine for people who want nothing more than to offer their bodies to the sun; yet the island, unlike many in the Caribbean, is also ideal for travelers who want to discover another life and culture.

Because the beaches of Barbados are open to the public, they lack the privacy that some visitors seek; but the beaches themselves are lovely, and many along the tranquil west coast—in the lee of the northwest trade winds—are backed by first-class resorts. Most of the hotels are situated along the beaches on the southern and southwestern coasts. The British and Canadians often favor the hotels of St. James Parish; Americans (couples more often than singles) tend to prefer the large south-coast resorts.

To the northeast are rolling hills and valleys covered by acres of impenetrable sugarcane. The Atlantic surf pounds the gigantic boulders along the rugged east coast, where the Bajans themselves have their vacation homes. Elsewhere on the island, linked by almost 900 miles of good roads, are historic plantation houses, stalactite-studded caves, a wildlife preserve, and the Andromeda Gardens, one of the most attractive small tropical gardens in the world.

No one is sure whether the name *los Barbados* ("the bearded ones") refers to the beardlike root that hangs from the island's fig trees or to the bearded natives who greeted the Portuguese "discoverer" of the island in 1536. The name Los Barbados was still current almost a century later when the British landed—by accident—in what is now Holetown in St. James Parish. They colonized the island in 1627 and remained until it achieved independence in 1966.

Barbadians retain a British accent. Afternoon tea is habitual at numerous hotels. Cricket is still the national sport, producing some of the world's top cricket players. Polo is played in winter. The British tradition of dressing for dinner is firmly entrenched; a few luxury hotels require tie and jacket at dinner, and in good restaurants most women will consider themselves inappropriately dressed in anything less formal than a sundress. (A daytime stroll in a swimsuit is as inappropriate in Bridgetown as it would be on New York's 5th Avenue.) Yet the island's atmosphere is hardly stuffy. When the boat you ordered for noon doesn't arrive until 12:30, you can expect a cheerful response, "He okay, mon, he just on Caribbean time." Translation: No one, including you, needs to be in a hurry here.

Before You Go

Tourist
Information
Contact the **Barbados Board of Tourism,** 800 2nd Ave., New York, NY 10017, tel. 212/986–6516; or 3440 Wilshire Blvd., Suite 1215, Los Angeles, CA 90010, tel. 213/380–2199. **In Canada:** 5160 Yonge St., Suite 1800, N. York, Ont. M2N–6L9, tel. 416/512–6569; 615 Dorchester, Montreal, Suite 960, Montreal,

P.Q. H3B 1P5, tel. 514/861–0085. **In the United Kingdom:** 263 Tottenham Court Rd., London W1P 9AA, tel. 441/636–9448.

Arriving and Departing By Plane Grantley Adams Airport in Barbados is a Caribbean hub. There are daily flights from New York (via San Juan); however, **American Airlines** (tel. 800/433–7300), and **BWIA** (tel. 800/JET–BWIA) both have nonstop flights from New York. There are direct flights from Miami on BWIA. From Canada, **Air Canada** (tel. 800/776–3000) connects from Montreal through New York or Miami and flies nonstop from Toronto. From London, **British Airways** (tel. 800/247–9297) has nonstop service and BWIA connects through Trinidad.

Flights to St. Vincent, St. Lucia, Trinidad, and other islands are scheduled on LIAT (tel. 809/462–0801) and BWIA; Air St. Vincent/Air Mustique links Barbados with St. Vincent and the Grenadines.

From the Airport Airport taxis are not metered. A large sign at the airport announces the fixed rate to each hotel or area, stated in both Barbados and U.S. dollars (about $20 to the west coast hotels, $13 to the south coast ones). The new highway around Bridgetown saves time and trouble in getting up the western coast.

By Boat A popular cruise port, Barbados has room for eight ships (which is some indication of how crowded the Bridgetown shops can be). Bridgetown Harbour is located on the northwest side of Carlisle Bay, and most cruise ships organize transportation to and from the **Carlisle Bay Centre,** a "hotel without rooms" for passengers on shore excursions. The CBC provides changing facilities, a restaurant, gift shops, and water-sports facilities—including floats, snorkel equipment, Sunfish sailboats, waterskiing, Windsurfers—for a nominal fee.

Passports and Visas U.S. and Canadian citizens need proof of citizenship plus a return or ongoing ticket to enter the country. Acceptable proof of citizenship is a valid passport or an original birth certificate and a photo ID; a voter registration card is not acceptable. British citizens need a valid passport.

Language English is spoken everywhere, sometimes accented with the phrases and lilt of a Bajan dialect.

Precautions Beach vendors of coral jewelry and beachwear will not hesitate to offer you their wares. The degree of persistence varies, and some of their jewelry offerings are good; sharp bargaining is expected on both sides. One hotel's brochure gives sound advice: "Please realize that encouraging the beach musicians means you may find yourself listening to the same three tunes over and over for the duration of your stay."

Water The water on the island, both in hotels and in restaurants, has been treated and is safe to drink.

Insects Insects aren't much of a problem on Barbados, but if you plan to hike or spend time on secluded beaches, it's wise to use insect repellent.

Toxic Tree Little green apples that fall from the large branches of the manchineel tree may look tempting, but they are poisonous to eat and toxic to the touch. Even taking shelter under the tree when it rains can give you blisters. Most manchineels are identified with signs; if you do come in contact with one, go to the nearest hotel and have someone there phone for a physician.

Barbados

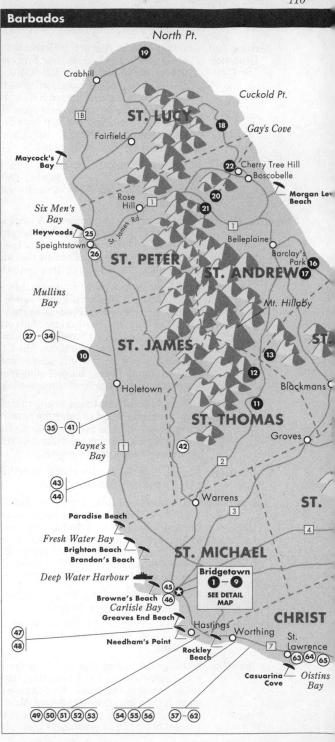

Exploring
Andromeda
Gardens, **15**
Animal Flower Cave, **19**
Barbados Wildlife
Reserve, **20**
Barclay's Park, **16**
Chalky Mount
Potteries, **17**
Codrington Theological
College, **24**
Farley Hill, **21**
Flower Forest, **13**
Folkstone Underwater
Park, **10**
Gun Hill, **14**
Harrison's Cave, **11**
Pie Corner, **18**
Ragged Point
Lighthouse, **23**
St. Nicholas Abbey, **22**
Welchman Hall
Gully, **12**

Dining
Atlantis Hotel, **68**
Bagatelle Great
House, **42**
Brown Sugar, **47**
Carambola, **34**
David's Place, **56**
Fathoms, **40**
Ile de France, **52**
Josef's, **64**
La Cage aux Folles, **36**
La Maison, **32**
Nico's, **35**
Ocean View Hotel, **49**
The Palm Terrace, **30**
Pisces, **63**
Plantation, **58**
Raffles, **31**
Rose and Crown, **43**
Sandy Bay
Restaurant, **38**
The Virginian, **50**
The Waterfront
Cafe, **45**
Witch Doctor, **59**

Lodging
Accra Beach Hotel, **51**
Almond Beach Club, **41**
Atlantis Hotel, **68**
Barbados Beach
Village, **44**
Barbados Hilton
International, **48**
Benston Windsurfing
Club Hotel, **65**
Casuarina Beach
Club, **62**

North Pt.

Cuckold Pt.

Crabhill

ST. LUCY

Fairfield

Gay's Cove

**Maycock's
Bay**

Cherry Tree Hill
Boscobelle

**Morgan Lev
Beach**

Rose
Hill

*Six Men's
Bay*

Heywoods
Speightstown

Belleplaine

Barclay's
Park

ST. PETER

ST. ANDREW

*Mullins
Bay*

Mt. Hillaby

ST. JAMES

Holetown

Blackmans

ST. THOMAS

Groves

*Payne's
Bay*

Warrens

ST.

Paradise Beach

Fresh Water Bay
Brighton Beach
Brandon's Beach

Deep Water Harbour

ST. MICHAEL

Bridgetown
1 – 9
SEE DETAIL
MAP

CHRIST

Browne's Beach
Carlisle Bay
Greaves End Beach

Hastings
Worthing

St.
Lawrence

Needham's Point

**Rockley
Beach**

**Casuarina
Cove**
*Oistins
Bay*

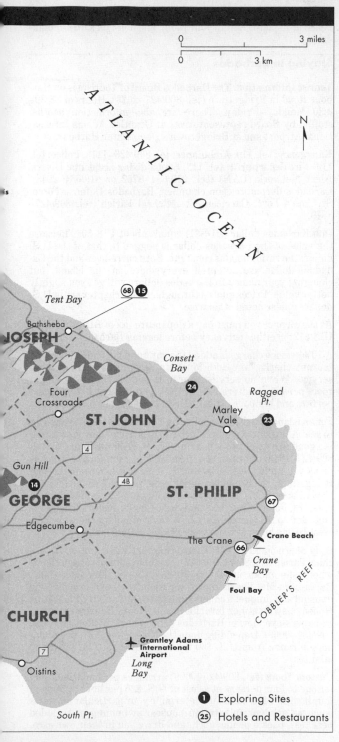

0   3 miles
0   3 km

N

ATLANTIC OCEAN

Tent Bay

68 **15**

Bathsheba

JOSEPH

Consett Bay

24

Ragged Pt.

Four Crossroads

ST. JOHN

Marley Vale

23

4

Gun Hill

4B

14

GEORGE

ST. PHILIP

67

Edgecumbe

The Crane

Crane Beach

66

Crane Bay

Foul Bay

COBBLER'S REEF

CHURCH

Grantley Adams International Airport

Long Bay

7

Oistins

South Pt.

1 Exploring Sites

25 Hotels and Restaurants

Crime Don't invite trouble by leaving valuables unattended on the beach or in plain sight in your room, and don't pick up hitchhikers.

Staying in Barbados

Important Addresses **Tourist Information: The Barbados Board of Tourism** is on Harbour Road in Bridgetown (tel. 809/427–2623). Hours are 8:30–4:30 Monday–Friday. There are also information booths, staffed by Board representatives at Grantley Adams International Airport and at Bridgetown's Deep Water Harbour.

Emergencies **Emergency:** tel. 119. **Ambulance:** tel. 809/426–1113. **Police:** tel. 112. **Fire department:** tel. 113. **Scuba diving accidents:** Divers' Alert Network (DAN) (tel. 919/684–8762 or 919/684–2948). Barbados decompression chamber, Barbados Defense Force, St. Ann's Fort, Garrison, St. Michael Parish (tel. 809/427–8819).

Currency One Barbados dollar (BDS$1) equals about U.S.50¢. Because the value of the Barbados dollar is pegged to that of the U.S. dollar, the ratio remains constant. Both currencies and the Canadian dollar are accepted everywhere on the island, but changing your money to Barbados dollars will get you slightly better value. Prices quoted throughout this chapter are in U.S. dollars unless noted otherwise.

Taxes and Service Charges At the airport you must pay a departure tax of BDS$25 (about U.S.$12) in either currency before leaving Barbados.

A 10% service charge is added to your hotel bill and to most restaurant checks; any additional tip recognizes extraordinary service. When no service charge is added, tip maids $1 per room per day, waiters 10% to 15%, taxi drivers 10%. Airport porters and bellboys expect BDS$2 (U.S.$1) per bag.

Guided Tours For an island of its size (14 miles by 21 miles), Barbados has a lot to see. A bus or taxi tour, which can be arranged by your hotel, is a good way to get your bearings. **L. E. Williams Tour Co.** (tel. 809/427–1043) offers an 80-mile island tour for about $50; a bus picks you up between 8:30 and 9:30 AM and takes you through Bridgetown, the St. James beach area, past the James Flower Cave, Farley Hill, Cherry Tree Hill, Morgan Lewis Mill, the east coast, St. John's Church, Sam Lord's Castle, Oistin's fishing village, and to St. Michael Parish, with drinks along the way and a West Indian lunch at the Atlantis Hotel in Bathsheba.

Sally Shern operates **VIP Tours** (Hillcrest Villa, Upton, St. Michael Parish, tel. 809/429–4617), custom-tailored to each client, whom she picks up in an air-conditioned Mercedes-Benz. Bajan-born Ms. Shern knows her island well and provides the unusual and unique: a champagne lunch at Sunbury Plantation House, a swim at her favorite beach. **Bajan Helicopters** offers an eagle's-eye view of Barbados (The Wharf, Bridgetown, tel. 809/431–0069). Depending upon the time spent aloft, prices per person range from U.S. $60 for 20 minutes to U.S. $90 for 30 minutes.

Custom Tours (tel. 809/425–0099) arranges personalized tours for one to four persons at a cost of U.S. $25 per hour (minimum four hours). Staff members determine your particular interests (such as gardens, plantation houses, swimming at secluded beaches), pack a picnic lunch, and drive you in their own cars.

They offer a familiarization tour for first-time visitors and often can take you to places that aren't normally open to the public. Ask for Margaret Leacock, the owner.

Getting Around   Taxis operate at a fixed rate (BDS$30 for the first hour, less af-
Taxis   ter that); settle the rate before you start off, and be sure you agree on whether it's in U.S. or Barbados dollars. Most drivers will cheerfully narrate a tour, though the noise of the car may make it difficult for you to follow a rambling commentary colored with Bajan inflections.

Buses   Public buses along Highway 1, St. James Road, are cheap (BDS$1.50, exact change appreciated), plentiful, reliable, and usually packed. The buses provide a great opportunity to experience local color, and your fellow passengers will be eager to share their knowledge.

Rental Cars   It's a pleasure to explore Barbados by car, provided you take the time to study a good map and don't mind asking directions frequently. The more remote roads are in good repair, yet few are well lighted at night, and night falls quickly—at about 6 PM. Even in full daylight, the tall sugarcane fields lining a road can create near-zero visibility. Yet local residents are used to pointing travelers in the right direction, and some confused but intelligent drivers have been known to flag a passing taxi and pay to follow it back to a city area. Use caution: Pedestrians are everywhere. And remember, traffic keeps to the left throughout the island.

To rent a car you must have an international driver's license, obtainable at the airport and major car-rental firms for $5 if you have a valid driver's license. More than 40 offices rent minimokes for upwards of $45 a day plus insurance (about $215 a week), usually with a three-day or four-day minimum; cars with automatic shift are $45–$55 a day, or approximately $285 a week. Gas costs just over BDS$1 a liter (about $2 a gallon) and is extra. The speed limit, in keeping with the pace of life, is 37 miles per hour (60 kilometers per hour) in the country, 21 miles per hour in town. Operating a motorbike also requires an international driver's license—and some skill and daring.

The principal car-rental firms are **National** (tel. 809/426–0603), **Dear's Garage** on the south coast (tel. 809/429–9277 or 809/427–7853), **Sunny Isle** in Worthing (tel. 809/428–8009 or 809/428–2965), and **Sunset Crest Rentals** in St. James (tel. 809/432–1482). **P&S Car Rentals** (Spring Garden Hwy., tel. 809/424–2052) offers air-conditioned cars and Jeeps with free customer delivery; it also arranges visitor driving permits.

Telephones   The area code for Barbados is 809. Except for emergency num-
and Mail   bers, all phone numbers have seven digits and begin with 42 or 43.

An airmail letter from Barbados to the United States or Canada costs BDS95¢ per half ounce; an airmail postcard costs BDS65¢. Letters to the United Kingdom are BDS$1.10; postcards are BDS70¢.

Opening and   Stores are open weekdays 8–4, Saturday 8–1. Some supermar-
Closing Times   kets remain open daily 8–6. Banks are open Monday to Thursday 9–3, Friday 9–1 and 3–5.

Exploring Barbados

Numbers in the margin correspond to points of interest on the Bridgetown map.

The island's most popular sights and attractions can be seen comfortably in four or five excursions, each lasting one day or less. The five tours described here begin with Bridgetown and then cover central Barbados, the eastern shore, north-central Barbados, and the south shore. Before you set out in a car, minimoke, or taxi, ask at your hotel or the Board of Tourism for a free copy of the detailed Barbados Holiday Map and check performance or opening times.

Bridgetown **Bridgetown** is a bustling city, complete with rush hours and traffic congestion; you'll avoid hassle by taking the bus or a taxi. Sightseeing will take only an hour or so, and the shopping areas are within walking distance.

In the center of town, overlooking the picturesque harbor known as the Careenage, is **Trafalgar Square,** with its impressive monument to Horatio, Lord Nelson. It predates the Nelson's Column in London's Trafalgar Square by about two decades (and for more than a century Bajans have petitioned to replace it with a statue of a Bajan). Here are also a war memorial and a three-dolphin fountain commemorating the advent of running water in Barbados in 1865.

Bridgetown is a major Caribbean free port. The principal shopping area is **Broad Street,** which leads west from Trafalgar Square past the House of Assembly and Parliament buildings. These Victorian Gothic structures, like so many smaller buildings in Bridgetown, stand beside a growing number of modern office buildings and shops. Small colonial buildings, their balconies trimmed with wrought iron, reward the visitor who has patience and an appreciative eye.

The water that bounds Trafalgar Square is called the **Careenage,** a finger of sea that made early Bridgetown a natural harbor and a gathering place. Here working schooners were careened (turned on their sides) to be scraped of barnacles and repainted. Today the Careenage serves mainly as a berth for fiberglass pleasure yachts.

Although no one has proved it conclusively, George Washington, on his only visit outside the United States, is said to have worshiped at **St. Michael's Cathedral** east of Trafalgar Square. The structure was nearly a century old when he visited in 1751, and it has since been destroyed by hurricanes and rebuilt twice, in 1780 and 1831.

The two bridges over the Careenage are the Chamberlain Bridge and the Charles O'Neal Bridge, both of which lead to Highway 7 and south to the **Fairchild Market.** On Saturdays the activity there and at the **Cheapside Market** (on the north end of Lower Broad Street, across from St. Mary's Church Square) recall the lively days before the coming of the supermarket and the mall, when the outdoor markets of Barbados were the daily heart and soul of shopping and socializing.

About a mile south of Bridgetown on Highway 7, the unusually interesting **Barbados Museum** has artifacts and mementos of military history and everyday life in the 19th century. Here you'll see cane-harvesting implements, lace wedding dresses,

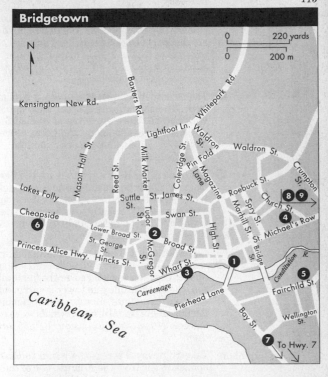

ancient (and frightening) dentistry instruments, and slave sale accounts kept in a spidery copperplate handwriting. Wildlife and natural history exhibits, a well-stocked gift shop, and a good café are also here, in what used to be the military prison. *Hwy. 7, Garrison Savannah, tel. 809/427–0201. Admission: BDS$7. Open Mon.–Sat. 10–6.*

⑧ East of St. Michael's Cathedral, **Queen's Park,** now being restored to its original splendor, is home to one of the largest trees in Barbados: an immense baobab more than 10 centuries

⑨ old. The historic **Queen's Park House,** former home of the commander of the British troops, has been converted into a theater—with an exhibition room on the lower floor—and a restaurant. Queen's Park is a long walk from Trafalgar Square or the museum; you may want to take a taxi. *Open daily 9–5.*

Central Barbados *Numbers in the margin correspond to points of interest on the Barbados map.*

⑩ For nervous swimmers, the most interesting place for getting into the water is the **Folkstone Underwater Park,** north of Holetown. While Folkstone has a land museum of marine life, the real draw is the underwater snorkeling trail around Dottin's Reef, with glass-bottom boats available for use by nonswimmers. A dredge barge sunk in shallow water is the home to myriad fish, and it and the reef are popular with scuba divers. Huge sea fans, soft coral, and the occasional giant turtle are sights to see.

⑪ Highway 2 will take you to **Harrison's Cave.** These pale-gold limestone caverns, complete with subterranean streams and waterfalls, are entirely organic and said to be unique in the Caribbean. Open since 1981, the caves are so extensive that tours are made by electric tram (hard hats are provided, but all that may fall on you is a little dripping water). *Tel. 809/438–6640. Admission: BDS$15 adults, BDS$7.50 children. Reservations recommended. Open daily 9–4.*

⑫ The nearby **Welchman Hall Gully,** a part of the National Trust in St. Thomas, affords another ideal opportunity to commune with nature. Here are acres of labeled flowers and trees, the occasional green monkey, and great peace and quiet. *Tel. 809/438–6671. Admission: BDS$5 adults, BDS$2.50 children. Open daily 9–5.*

⑬ Continue along Highway 2 to reach the **Flower Forest,** 8 acres of fragrant flowering bushes, canna and ginger lilies, and puffball trees. Another hundred species of flora combine with the tranquil views of Mt. Hillaby to induce in visitors what may be a relaxing and very pleasant light-headedness. *Tel. 809/433–8152. Admission: BDS$10. Open daily 9–5.*

Go back toward Bridgetown and take Highway 4 and smaller **⑭** roads to **Gun Hill** for a view so pretty it seems almost unreal: Shades of green and gold cover the fields all the way to the horizon, the picturesque gun tower is surrounded by brilliant flowers, and the white limestone lion behind the garrison is a famous landmark. Military invalids were once sent here to convalesce. *No phone. Admission: BDS$5 adults, BDS$2.50 children.*

The Eastern Shore Take Highway 3 across the island to Bathsheba and the phenomenal view from the **Atlantis,** one of the oldest hotels in Barbados, where you may need help getting up from the table after sampling the lunch buffet.

⑮ In the nearby **Andromeda Gardens** (tel. 809/433–9261), a fascinating small garden set into the cliffs overlooking the sea, are unusual and beautiful plant specimens from around the world, collected by the late horticulturist Iris Bannochie and now administered by the Barbados National Trust. *Tel. 809/433–1524. Admission: BDS$10. Open daily 9–5.*

⑯ North of Bathsheba, **Barclay's Park** offers a similar view and picnic facilities in a wooded seafront area. At the nearby **⑰** **Chalky Mount Potteries,** you'll find craftspersons making and selling their wares.

A drive north to the isolated Morgan Lewis Beach (*see* Beaches, *below*) or to Gay's Cove, which every Bajan calls Cove Bay, **⑱** will put you in reach of the town of **Pie Corner.** Pie Corner is known not for baked goods but for artifacts left by the Caribe and Arawak tribes who once lived here.

⑲ The **Animal Flower Cave** at North Point, reached by Highway 1B, displays small sea anemones, or seaworms, that resemble jewellike flowers as they open their tiny tentacles. For a small fee you can explore inside the cavern and see the waves breaking just outside it. *Tel. 439–8797. Admission: BDS$3 adults, BDS$1.50 children under 12. Open daily 9–5.*

North-Central The attractions of north-central Barbados may well be com-
Barbados bined with the tour of the eastern shore.

⑳ The **Barbados Wildlife Reserve** can be reached on Highway 1 from Speightstown on the west coast. Here are herons, land turtles, a kangaroo, screeching peacocks, innumerable green monkeys and their babies doing all manner of things, geese, brilliantly colored parrots, and a friendly otter. The fauna are not in cages, so step carefully and keep your hands to yourself. The preserve has been much improved in recent years with the addition of a giant walk-in aviary and natural-history exhibits. Terrific photo opportunities are everywhere. *Tel. 809/422–8826. Admission: BDS$10 adults, BDS$5 children under 12 with adult. Open daily 10–5.*

㉑ Just to the south is **Farley Hill,** a national park in northern St. Peter Parish; the rugged landscape explains why they call this the Scotland area. Gardens; lawns; gigantic mahogany, white-wood, and casuarina trees; and an avenue of towering royal palms surround the imposing ruins of a once magnificent plantation great house. Partially rebuilt for the filming of *Island in the Sun,* the structure was later destroyed by fire. *Admission: BDS$2 per car; walkers free. Open daily 8:30–6.*

㉒ **St. Nicholas Abbey** near Cherry Tree Hill, named for a former owner and the oldest (c. 1650) great house in Barbados, is well worth visiting for its stone and wood architecture in the Jaco-bean style. Fascinating home movies, made by the present own-er's father, record scenes of Bajan town and plantation life in the 1920s and 1930s. There are no set showing times; you need only ask to see them. *Tel. 809/422–8725. Admission: $2.50. Open weekdays 10–3:30.*

The South Shore Driving east on Highways 4 and 4B, you'll note the many **chat-tel houses** along the route; the property of tenant farmers, these ever-expandable houses were built to be dismantled and moved when necessary. On the coast, the appropriately named ㉓ **Ragged Point Lighthouse** is where the sun first shines on Barbados and its dramatic Atlantic seascape. About 4 miles to the northwest, in the eastern corner of St. John Parish, the ㉔ coralstone buildings and serenely beautiful grounds of **Cod-rington Theological College,** founded in 1748, stand on a cliff overlooking Consett Bay.

Take the smaller roads southeast to reach **Marriott's Sam Lord's Castle** (*see* Lodging, *below*), the Regency house built by the buccaneer. Most of the rooms are furnished with the fine antiques he is said to have acquired from passing ships (note the mahogany four-poster), but he had to hire Italian artisans to create the elaborate plaster ceilings. The tour is free to guests; others pay a small fee.

Beaches

Barbados is blessed with some of the Caribbean's most beauti-ful beaches, all of them open to the public. (Access to hotel beaches may not always be public, but you can walk onto almost any beach from another one.)

West Coast Beaches The west coast has the stunning coves and white-sand beaches that are dear to postcard publishers—plus calm, clear water for snorkeling, scuba diving, and swimming. The afternoon clouds and sunsets may seem to be right out of a Turner paint-ing; because there is nothing but ocean between Barbados and Africa, the sunsets are rendered even more spectacular by the fine red sand that sometimes blows in from the Sahara.

While beaches here are seldom crowded, the west coast is not the place to find isolation. Owners of private boats stroll by, offering waterskiing, parasailing, and snorkel cruises. There are no concession stands per se, but hotels welcome nonguests for terrace lunches (wear a cover-up). Picnic items and necessities can be bought at the Sunset Crest shopping center in Holetown.

Beaches begin in the north at **Heywoods** (about a mile of sand) and continue almost unbroken to Bridgetown at **Brighton Beach,** a popular spot with locals. There is public access through the Barbados Beach Club and the Barbados Pizza House (both good for casual lunches), south of the Discovery Bay Hotel.

Good spots for swimming include **Paradise Beach,** just off the Cunard Paradise Village & Beach Club; **Brandon's Beach,** a 10-minute walk south; **Browne's Beach,** in Bridgetown; and **Greaves End Beach,** south of Bridgetown at Aquatic Gap, between the Grand Barbados Beach Resort and the Hilton in St. Michael Parish.

The west coast is the area for scuba diving, sailing, and lunch-and-rum cruises on the red-sailed *Jolly Roger* "pirate" party ship (Fun Cruises, tel. 809/436–6424 or 809/429–4545). Somewhat more sedate sea experiences can be had on the *Wind Warrior* (tel. 809/425–5800) and the *Secret Love* (tel. 809/425–5800).

The *Atlantis* **submarine** (tel. 809/436–8929 or 809/436–8932) goes to depths of 150 feet off wrecks and reefs in a Canadian-built 50-foot submarine that seats 28 passengers at a time, each at his or her own porthole. Classical music plays while an oceanography specialist informs. *Cost: $69.50 per person.*

South Coast Beaches The heavily traveled south coast of Christ Church Parish is much more built up than the St. James Parish coast in the west; here you'll find condos, high-rise hotels, many places to eat and shop, and the traffic (including public transportation) that serves them. These busier beaches generally draw a younger, more active crowd. The quality of the beach itself is consistently good, the reef-protected waters safe for swimming and snorkeling.

Needham's Point, with its lighthouse, is one of Barbados's best beaches, crowded with locals on weekends and holidays. Two others are in the St. Lawrence Gap area, near **Casuarina Cove.** The **Barbados Windsurfing Club Hotel** in Maxwell caters specifically to windsurfing aficionados, and most hotels and resorts provide boards or rent them for a nominal fee.

Crane Beach has for years been a popular swimming beach. As you move toward the Atlantic side of the island, the waves roll in bigger and faster; the waves at the nearby Crane Hotel are a favorite with bodysurfers. (But remember that this is the ocean, not the Caribbean, and exercise caution.)

Nearby **Foul Bay** lives up to its name only for sailboats; for swimmers and alfresco lunches, it's lovely.

North Coast Beaches Those who love wild natural beauty will want to head north up the east-coast highway. With secluded beaches and crashing ocean waves on one side, rocky cliffs and verdant landscape on the other, the windward side of Barbados won't disappoint anyone who seeks dramatic views. But be cautioned: Swimming here is treacherous and *not* recommended. The waves are high, the bottom tends to be rocky, and the currents are unpredictable. Limit yourself to enjoying the view and watching the surfers—who have been at it since they were kids.

A worthwhile little-visited beach for the adventurous who don't mind trekking about a mile off the beaten track is **Morgan Lewis Beach,** on the coast east of Morgan Lewis Mill, the oldest intact windmill on the island. Turn east on the small road that goes to the town of Boscobelle (between Cherry Tree Hill and Morgan Lewis Mill), but instead of going to the town, take the even less traveled road (unmarked on most maps; you will have to ask for directions) that goes down the cliff to the beach. What awaits is more than 2 miles of unspoiled, uninhabited white sand and sweeping views of the Atlantic coastline. You may see a few Barbadians swimming, sunning, or fishing, but for the most part you'll have privacy.

Return to your car, cross the island's north point on the secondary roads until you reach the west coast. About a mile west from the end of Highway 1B is **Maycock's Bay,** an isolated area in St. Lucy Parish about 2 miles north of Heywoods, the west coast's northernmost resort complex.

Sports and the Outdoors

Golfing The Royal Westmoreland Golf and Country Club is still in its planning stages and until it is completed, golfers favor the 18 holes at the **Sandy Lane Club** (tel. 809/432–1145), whose dramatic 7th hole is famous both for its elevated tee and its incredible view. There is also a 9-hole course at the **Rockley Resort** (tel. 809/435–7873), and another 9 holes at **Heywoods** (tel. 809/422–4900). All are open (for various fees) to nonguests.

Hiking/Jogging Hilly but not mountainous, the interior of Barbados is ideal for hiking. The **Barbados National Trust** (Belleville, St. Michael, tel. 809/436–9033) sponsors free walks year-round on Sunday, from 6:30 AM to about 9:30 AM and from 3:30 PM to 5:30 PM, as well as special moonlight hikes when the heavens permit. Newspapers announce the time and meeting place (or you can call the Trust).

Less serious (but great fun) is the **Hash House Harriers,** an international running group with relaxed jogging at different points each week. Contact John Carpenter (tel. 809/429–5151 days or 809/429–3818 evenings).

Horseback Riding Reasonable prices ($17–$22) for one-hour trots, including hotel pickup, come from **Valley Hill Stables** (Christ Church, tel. 809/423–6180) and **Ye Old Congo Road Stables** (St. Philip, tel. 809/423–8293), which take riders through sugar plantations. On the west coast, **Brighton Stables** (tel. 809/425–9381) offers sunrise and sunset walks along beaches and palm groves.

Parasailing Parasailing, during which you wear a parachute harness and take off from a raft as you're towed by a speedboat, is available, wind conditions permitting, on the beaches of St. James and Christ Church. Just ask at any hotel, then flag down a speedboat (though it may have found you first).

Sailing and Fishing **Blue Jay Charters** (tel. 809/422–2098) has a 45-foot, fully equipped fishing boat, with a crew that knows the waters where blue marlin, sailfish, barracuda, and kingfish play. Two other choices are **Sailing Charter Tiami Cruises** (tel. 809/425–5800) and *Carie-Dee,* a 36-foot private yacht (tel. 809/422–2319) that takes guests by the day or half day.

Scuba Diving Barbados, with a rich and varied underwater world, is one of the few islands in the Caribbean that offer activity for both divers and nondivers. Many dive shops provide instruction (the three-hour beginner's "resort courses" and the week-long certification courses) followed by a shallow dive, usually on Dottin's Reef. Trained divers can explore reefs, wrecks, and the walls of "blue holes," the huge circular depressions in the ocean floor. Not to be missed by certified, guided divers is the *Stavronikita,* a 368-foot Greek freighter that was deliberately sunk at about 125 feet; hundreds of butterfly fish hang out around its mast, and the thin rays of sunlight that filter down through the water make exploring the huge ship a wonderfully eerie experience.

Dive Barbados (Watersports, Sunset Crest Beach, near Holetown, St. James Parish, tel. 809/432–7090) provides beginner's instruction (resort course) and reef and wreck dives with a friendly, knowledgeable staff. At **The Dive Shop, Ltd.** (Grand Barbados Beach Resort, tel. 809/426–9947), experienced divers can participate in deep dives to old wrecks to look for bottles and other artifacts (and you can usually keep what you find). **Willie's Watersports** (Heywoods Hotel, tel. 809/422–4900, ext. 2831) offers instruction and a range of diving excursions. **Exploresub Barbados** (Divi Southwinds Beach Resort, tel. 809/428–7181) operates a full range of daily dives. **Dive Boat Safari** (Barbados Hilton, tel. 809/427–4350) offers full diving and instruction services.

Snorkeling Snorkeling gear can be rented for a small charge from nearly every hotel.

Squash Squash courts can be reserved at the **Rockley Resort** (tel. 809/435–7880) and **Barbados Squash Club** (Marine House, Christ Church, tel. 809/427–7913).

Submarining Submarines are enormously popular with families and those who enjoy watching fish without getting wet, and the 28-passenger *Atlantis* turns the Caribbean into a giant aquarium. The 45-minute trip takes you as much as 150 feet below the surface for a look at what even sport divers rarely see. The nighttime dives, using high-power searchlights, are spectacular. *Tel. 809/436–8929. Cost: $69.50 adults, $31.50 children 4–12.*

Surfing The best surfing is available on the east coast, and most wave riders congregate at the Soup Bowl, near Bathsheba. An annual international surfing competition is held on Barbados every November.

Tennis Most hotels have tennis courts that can be reserved day and night. Be sure to bring your whites; appropriate dress is expected on the court.

Waterskiing Waterskiing is widely available, often provided along St. James and Christ Church by the private speedboat owners. Inquire at your hotel, which can direct you to the nearest Sunfish sailing and Hobie Cat rentals as well.

Windsurfing Windsurfing boards and equipment are often guest amenities at the larger hotels and can be rented by nonguests. The best place to learn and to practice is on the south coast at the **Barba-**

dos **Windsurfing Club Hotel** (Maxwell, Christ Church Parish, tel. 809/428–9095).

Spectator Sports

Cricket The island is mad for cricket, and you can sample a match at almost any time of year. While the season is June through late December, test matches are played in the first half of the year. The newspapers give the details of time and place.

Horse Racing Horse racing takes place on alternate Saturdays, from January to May and from July to November, at the **Garrison Savannah** in Christ Church, about 3 miles south of Bridgetown. Appropriate dress might be described as "casual elegance." *Tel. 809/ 426–3980. Admission: BDS$10 adults, BDS$5 children under 12.*

Polo Polo, the sport of kings, is played seriously in Barbados. Matches are held at the **Polo Club** in St. James on Wednesday and Saturday from September to March. Hang around the club room after the match. That's where the lies, the legends, and the invitations happen. *Admission: about $2.50.*

Rugby The rough-and-tumble game of rugby is played at the Garrison Savannah; schedules are available from the **Barbados Rugby Club.** Contact Victor Roach (809/435–6543).

Soccer The "football," or soccer, season runs from January through June; game schedules are available from the **Barbados Football Association** (tel. 809/424–4413).

Shopping

Traditionally, Broad Street and its side streets in Bridgetown have been the center for shopping action. Hours are generally weekdays 8–4, Saturday 8–1. Many stores have an in-bound (duty-free) department where you must show your travel tickets or a passport in order to buy duty-free goods.

Recently, several new areas opened their freshly painted doors. The mall-like **Sheraton Centre** (at Sargeant's Village in Christ Church) has toys for tots, togs for teens, and temptations for all. The **Quayside Shopping Center** (at Rockley in Christ Church) is smaller and more select, with frozen yogurt at **Toppings** and handmade articles at **Artworx** in Shop 5, where everything comes from Barbados, Trinidad, St. Lucia, or Guyana.

Best 'N The Bunch is both a wildly colored chattel house at The Chattel House Village (at St. Lawrence Gap) and its own best advertisement. Here the expert jewelry of Bajan David Trottman sells for that rarity—reasonable prices. **Perfections** also has good finds—all from Bajan artists—for men, women, and children, and **Beach Bum** offers teens "barely" bikinis.

Luxury Goods Bridgetown stores have values on fine bone china, crystal, cameras, stereo and video equipment, jewelry, perfumes, and clothing. **Cave Shepherd** and **Harrison's** department stores offer wide selections of goods at many locations and at the airport. **De Lima's** and **Da Costa's Ltd.** stock high-quality imports. Among the specialty stores are **Louis I. Bayley** (gold watches), **J. Baldini** (Brazilian jewelry and Danish silver), and **Correia's** (diamonds, pearls, semiprecious stones). The 20 small shops of **Mall 34** in Bridgetown's central district sell everything from luxury goods to crafts.

Handicrafts Island handicrafts are everywhere: woven mats and place mats, dresses, dolls, handbags, shell jewelry. The **Best of Barbados** shops, at the Sandpiper Inn, Mall 34 in Bridgetown (tel. 809/436–1416), and three other locations, offer the highest-quality artwork and crafts, both "native style" and modern designs. A resident artist, Jill Walker, sells her watercolors and prints here and at **Walker's World** shops near the south shore hotels in St. Lawrence Gap.

At the **Pelican Village Handicrafts Center** on the Princess Alice Highway near the Cheapside Market in Bridgetown, in a cluster of conical shops, you can watch goods and crafts being made before you purchase them. Rugs and mats made from pandanus grass and khuskhus are good buys.

For native Caribbean arts and crafts, including items from Barbados and Haiti, try the Guardhouse Gallery near the Grand Barbados Hotel in St. Michael. A selection of wooden, straw, and ceramic items is available.

Antiques Antiques and fine memorabilia are the stock of **Greenwich House Antiques** (tel. 809/432–1169) in Greenwich Village, Trents Hill, St. James Parish, and at **Antiquaria** (tel. 809/426–0635) on St. Michael's Row next to the Anglican cathedral in Bridgetown.

Chic Shops Hidden in separate corners of Barbados are some very upscale, little-known shops that can hold their own in New York or London. Carol Cadogan's **Cotton Days Designs** at Rose Cottage (Lower Bay St., tel. 809/427–7191) and on the Wharf in Bridgetown sets the international pace with all-cotton, collage creations that have been declared "wearable art." These are fantasy designs, with prices that begin at U.S. $250. Fortunately, she takes credit cards.

Corrie Scott, owner of **Corrie's** (Bay St. in Hastings, tel. 809/427–9184), designs hand-knit cotton sweaters and dresses that begin at U.S. $75; she also carries jewelry by David Trottman, as well as the exotic dress designs of Derek Went.

Another shop worth a visit on the Wharf is **Origins** (tel. 809/436–8522), where original hand-painted and dyed clothing, imported cottons, linens and silks for day and evening, and handmade jewelry and accessories are the order of the day. The hand-painted T-shirts are especially good here.

In St. Michael, stop in at **Petal's** in the Barbados Hilton shopping arcade for fashionable shoes and handbags: Friendly service and good-quality items make this shop special.

Dining

The better hotels and restaurants of Barbados have employed chefs trained in New York and Europe to attract and keep their sophisticated clientele. Gourmet dining here usually means fresh seafood, beef, or veal with finely blended sauces.

The native West Indian cuisine offers an entirely different dining experience. The island's West African heritage brought rice, peas, beans, and okra to its table, the staples that make a perfect base for slowly cooked meat and fish dishes. Many side dishes are cooked in oil (the pumpkin fritters can be addictive). And be cautious at first with the West Indian seasonings; like the sun, they are hotter than you think.

Every menu features dolphin (the fish, not the mammal), king-fish, snapper, and flying fish prepared every way imaginable. Shellfish abound; so does steak. Everywhere for breakfast and dessert you'll find mangoes, soursop, papaya (called pawpaw), and, in season, mammyapples, a basketball-size, thick-skinned fruit with giant seeds.

Cou-cou is a mix of cornmeal and okra with a spicy Creole sauce made from tomatoes, onions, and sweet peppers; steamed fly-ing fish is often served over it. A version served by the Brown Sugar restaurant, called "red herring," is smoked herring and breadfruit in Creole sauce.

Pepperpot stew, a hearty mix of oxtail, beef chunks, and "any other meat you may have," simmered overnight, is flavored with *cassareep*, an ancient preservative and seasoning that gives the stew its dark, rich color.

Christophines and **eddoes** are tasty, potatolike vegetables that are often served with curried shrimp, chicken, or goat.

Buljol is a cold salad of codfish, tomatoes, onions, sweet pep-pers, and celery, marinated and served raw.

Callaloo is a soup made from okra, crabmeat, a spinachlike veg-etable that gives the dish its name, and seasonings.

Among the liquid refreshments of Barbados, in addition to the omnipresent Banks Beer and Mount Gay rum, there are **faler-num,** a liqueur concocted of rum, sugar, lime juice, and almond essence, and **mauby,** a refreshing nonalcoholic beerlike drink made by boiling bitter bark and spices, straining the mixture, and sweetening it.

Barbados's British heritage and large resident population keep the island's dress code modest. While this does not always mean a tie and jacket, jeans, shorts, and beach shirts are frowned upon at dinnertime.

Highly recommended restaurants are indicated by a star ★.

Category	Cost*
Expensive	over $40
Moderate	$25–$40
Inexpensive	under $25

per person, excluding drinks and 5% service charge

Expensive **Bagatelle Great House.** Occupying a converted plantation house in a hilly area, Bagatelle Great House gives diners an im-pression of colonial life. The terrace allows intimate dining at tables for two, while inside the castlelike walls there are much larger round tables. The superb ambience is somewhat more memorable than the expensive Continental dishes. *St. Thomas Parish, tel. 809/421–6767. Reservations necessary. Jacket and tie required. MC, V.*

★ **Carambola.** This romantic al fresco restaurant is set on a cliff overlooking the Caribbean in St. James Parish. Here, by can-dlelight, you can enjoy what is considered some of the best food in Barbados, created by British chef Paul Owens using tradi-tional French recipes. Try the lobster or the more inventive dishes, such as the flying-fish salad and snapper with pimento sauce, or for dessert, the chocolate and lime pie. *Derricks, St. James Parish, tel. 809/432–0832. Reservations required. Dinner only. AE, MC, V.*

La Cage aux Folles. Acclaimed as one of the island's finest restaurants, La Cage aux Folles has moved to a new location, set in the restored Summerland Great House amid 2 acres of tropical gardens, and is lovelier than ever. The exotic five-course menu features international cuisine. Items include fresh fish with orange and Cointreau, sweet-and-sour shrimp, Malaysian satay, and sesame prawn pâté. *Prospect, St. James Parish, tel. 809/424–2424. Reservations necessary. Jacket and tie required. AE, MC, V. Dinner only. Closed Tues.*

The Palm Terrace. Arriving from London's Le Gavroche, the Palm's young British chef applies his talents to combine Barbadian produce with top-quality imports. The result is modern European creations, such as *mille feuille* of home-smoked chicken with tomato, chives, and carrots in a light mustard cream sauce for an appetizer. Home-grown mint accents New Zealand rack of lamb, and panfried crab becomes a stuffing for the breast of chicken entrée. Widely spaced tables, comfortable chairs, and indoor palms swaying under floor-to-ceiling arches create an ambience that is formal, yet relaxed as you dine facing the Caribbean Sea. *Royal Pavilion, Porters, St. James Parish, tel. 809/422–5555. Reservations advised. Dinner only. AE, DC, MC, V.*

★ **Raffles.** Young, international owners have made this one of Barbados's top restaurants. Forty guests can be seated at beautifully decorated tables featuring a tropical safari theme. Main dishes may be shrimp saki, blackened fish, steak served in a wine-and-lime sauce, basil-curry chicken, and sweet-and-sour pork. The desserts are both delicious and decadent. *1st St., Holetown, St. James Parish, tel. 809/432–6557 or 809/432–1280. Reservations necessary. Dinner only. AE, D, DC, MC, V.*

Sandy Bay Restaurant. Located at the renowned Sandy Lane Hotel, this is the perfect place for an elegant meal overlooking one of the best beaches on the island. The hotel's general manager brought British chef Mel Rumbles to the restaurant to create a menu that is both tasty and healthful. Grilled dolphin; lobster; and grilled lamb with honey, thyme, and wild rosemary are among the entrées. The vegetables, including local christophines and the delicate puréed pumpkin soup, are tasty. To ensure that the best produce is used, a van is sent out every morning to scour the island for the freshest vegetables and fish. The chef has also begun cultivating a spice and vegetable garden specifically to meet the hotel's needs. The desserts, created by a French pastry chef, are not to be missed, especially the dark chocolate truffle and the pecan pie with almond sauce. *Sandy Lane Hotel and Golf Club, St. James Parish, tel. 809/432–1311. AE, MC, V.*

Moderate **Brown Sugar.** A special-occasion atmosphere prevails at Brown Sugar, located just behind the Island Inn outside Bridgetown. Dozens of ferns and hanging plants decorate the breezy multilevel restaurant. The extensive and authentic West Indian lunch buffets, served between 11:30 and 2:30 and popular with local businessmen, include cou-cou, pepperpot stew, Creole orange chicken, and such homemade desserts as angelfood chocolate mousse cake and passion fruit and nutmeg ice cream.

Aquatic Gap, St. Michael Parish, tel. 809/426-7684. Reservations recommended. AE, MC.

★ **Fathoms.** Veteran restaurateurs Stephen and Sandra Toppin have opened their newest property seven days a week, for lunch and dinner, with 22 well-dressed tables scattered from the inside dining rooms to the patio's ocean edge. Dinner may bring a grilled lobster, island rabbit, jumbo baked shrimp, or cashew-crusted kingfish. This place is casual by day, candlelit by night. *Payne's Bay, St. James Parish, tel. 809/432-2568. Reservations advised for dinner. AE, MC, V.*

★ **Ile de France.** French owners Martine (from Lyon) and Michel (from Toulouse) Gramaglia have adapted the pool and garden areas of the Windsor Arms Hotel and turned them into an island "in" spot. White latticework opens to the night sounds; soft taped French music plays; and a single, perfect hibiscus dresses each table. Just a few of their specialties: foie gras; tournedos Rossini; lobster-and-crepe flambé; and filet Mignon with a choice of pepper, béarnaise, or champignon sauce. *Windsor Arms Hotel, Hastings, Christ Church Parish, tel. 809/435-6869. Reservations required. No credit cards. Dinner only. Closed Mon.*

Josef's. Swede Nils Ryman created a menu from the unusual combination of Caribbean cooking—blackened fish in which the fish is fried, rolled in Cajun spices, and seared in oil before being slightly baked in the oven—and Scandinavian fare— Toast Skagen made from diced shrimp blended with mayonnaise and fresh dill. Stroll around the garden before moving to the alfresco dining room downstairs or to the simply decorated room upstairs for a table that looks out over the sea. *Waverly House, St. Lawrence Gap, tel. 809/435-6541. Reservations advised. AE, DC, MC, V.*

La Maison. The elegant, colonial-style Balmore House reopened in October 1990 under the ownership of Geoffrey Farmer. The atmosphere is created by English country furnishings and a paneled bar opening onto a seaside terrace for dining. A French chef from the Loire Valley creates seafood specials, including a flying-fish parfait appetizer. Passion-fruit ice cream highlights the dessert menu. Lunch and dinner. *Holetown, St. James Parish, tel. 809/432-1156. Reservations recommended. D, MC, V.*

★ **Ocean View Hotel.** This elegant pink grande dame hotel is dressed in fresh fabrics, with great bunches of equally fresh flowers and sparkling crystal chandeliers. Bajan dishes are featured for lunch and dinner, and the Sunday-only Planter's Luncheon Buffet in the downstairs Club Xanadu (which fronts the beach) offers course after course of traditional dishes. Pianist Jean Emerson plays Hoagy Carmichael tunes and sings in dusky tones. *Hastings, Christ Church Parish, tel. 809/427-7821. Reservations recommended. AE, MC, V.*

Pisces. For Caribbean seafood at the water's edge, this restaurant in lively St. Lawrence Gap specializes in seasonal dishes. Fish is the way to go here—flying fish, dolphin, crab, kingfish, shrimp, prawns, and lobster—prepared any way from charbroiled to sautéed. There are also some chicken and beef dishes. Other items include conch fritters, tropical gazpacho, and seafood terrine with a mango sauce. Enjoy a meal in a contemporary setting filled with hanging tropical plants. *St. Lawrence Gap, Christ Church Parish, tel. 809/435-6564. Reservations recommended. Dinner only during low season. AE, MC, V.*

Plantation. Wednesday's Bajan buffet and Tuesday's entertainment are big attractions here. The Plantation is set in a renovated Barbadian residence surrounded by spacious grounds above the Southwinds Resort; its cuisine combines French and Barbadian influences, and you can eat indoors or on the terrace. *St. Lawrence, Christ Church Parish, tel. 809/428–5048. Reservations suggested. AE, MC, V. Dinner only.*

Rose and Crown. The casual Rose and Crown serves a variety of fresh seafood, but it's the local lobster that's high on diners' lists. Indoors is a paneled bar, outdoors are tables on a wraparound porch. *Prospect, St. James Parish, tel. 809/425–1074. Reservations suggested. AE, MC, V. Dinner served 6–10.*

The Virginian. The locally popular Virginian offers intimate surroundings and some of the island's best dining values. The specialties are seafood, shrimp, and steaks. *Sea View Hotel, Hastings, Christ Church Parish, tel. 809/427–7963, ext. 121. Reservations suggested. AE, MC, V. Dinner only.*

Witch Doctor. The interior of the Witch Doctor is decorated with pseudo-African art that gives a lighthearted carefree atmosphere to this casual hangout across the street from the sea; the menu features traditional Barbadian dishes, European fare, and local seafood. *St. Lawrence Gap, Christ Church Parish, tel. 809/435–6581. Reservations recommended. MC, V. Dinner only.*

Inexpensive **Atlantis Hotel.** While the surroundings may be simple and the rest room could use a coat of paint, the nonstop food and the magnificent ocean view at the Atlantis Hotel in Bathsheba make it a real find. Owner-chef Enid Maxwell serves up an enormous Bajan buffet daily, where you're likely to find pickled souse (marinated pig parts and vegetables), pumpkin fritters, spinach balls, pickled breadfruit, fried "fline" (flying) fish, roast chicken, pepperpot stew, and West Indian–style okra and eggplant. Among the homemade pies are an apple and a dense coconut. *Bathsheba, St. Joseph Parish, tel. 809/433–9445. Reservations suggested. No credit cards.*

★ **David's Place.** Here you'll be served first-rate dishes in a first-rate location—a black-and-white Bajan cottage overlooking St. Lawrence Bay. Specialties include Baxters Road chicken, local flying fish, pepperpot (salt pork, beef, and chicken boiled and bubbling in a spicy cassareep stock), and curried shrimp. Homemade cheesebread is served with all dishes. Desserts might be banana pudding, coconut-cream pie, carrot cake with rum sauce, or cassava pone. *St. Lawrence Main Road, Worthing, Christ Church Parish, tel. 809/435–6550. Reservations preferred. AE, MC, V.*

Nico's. This small second-floor bistro is a cheery, intimate gathering spot for ex-patriates and visitors. An oval bar, surrounded by stools, stands in the middle of the room, with the tables on the perimeter and a few more on the terrace above the street. Come to Nico's for drinks and to socialize, as well as order off the blackboard menu something small like deep-fried Camembert or more substantial, such as seafood thermidor. *Second St., Holetown, tel. 809/432–6386. MC, V. Inexpensive.*

The Waterfront Cafe. Located on the Careenage, a sliver of sea in Bridgetown, this is the perfect place to enjoy a drink, snack, or meal. Locals and tourists gather here for sandwiches, salads, fish, steak-and-kidney pie, and casseroles. The panfried flying-fish sandwich is especially tasty. From the brick and mirrored interior you can gaze through the arched windows, enjoy the cool trade winds and let time pass. *Bridgetown, St. Michael Parish, tel. 809/427–0093. MC, V. Dress: casual. Live jazz Mon.–Sat. Food served 10–10, open until midnight.*

Lodging

The southern and western shores of Barbados are lined with hotels and resorts of every size and price, offering a variety of accommodations from private villas to modest but comfortable rooms in simple inns. At the same time, apartment and home rentals and time-share condominiums have become widely available and are growing increasingly popular among visitors to the island. A few of Barbados's hotels have recently become all-inclusive, though most still offer either EP or MAP meal plans.

Choosing the location of your hotel is important. Hotels to the north of Bridgetown, in the parishes of St. Peter, St. James, and St. Michael, tend to be more self-contained resorts with stretches of empty road between them that discourage strolling to a neighborhood bar or restaurant. Southwest of Bridgetown, in Christ Church Parish, many of the hotels cluster near or along the busy strip known at St. Lawrence Gap, where small restaurants, bars, and nightclubs are close by.

Hotels listed are grouped here by parish, beginning with St. James in the west and St. Peter to the north, then St. Michael, Christ Church, St. Philip, and St. Joseph.

Highly recommended lodgings are indicated by a star ★.

Category	Cost*
Very Expensive	over $350
Expensive	$250–$350
Moderate	$150–$250
Inexpensive	under $150

All prices are for a standard double room, excluding 5% government tax and 10% service charge.

Hotels
St. James Parish

Coral Reef Club. Days here are spent relaxing on the white-sand beach or around the pool, with time taken out for the hotel's superb afternoon tea. The public areas ramble along the beach and face the Caribbean Sea, with small coralstone cottages scattered over the surrounding 12 flower-filled acres. (The cottages farthest from the beach are a bit of a hike to the main house.) The accommodations are spacious, each with air-conditioning and ceiling fans, a small patio terrace, and fresh flowers. The restaurant, under the direction of Bajan chef, Graham Licorish, is noted for its inventive cuisine that combines local cooking with European flair. Most guests are on a MAP plan that includes a complimentary buffet lunch. Another convenience is the free shuttle into Bridgetown. *Porters, St. James Parish, tel. 809/422–2372, fax 809/422–1776. 70 rooms. Facilities: pool, entertainment. AE, MC, V. EP. Very Expensive.*

★ **Glitter Bay.** In the 1930s, Sir Edward Cunard, of the English shipping family, bought this estate, built the main Great House and a beach house similar to his palazzo in Venice, and began hosting famous parties in honor of visiting aristocrats and celebrities, making Glitter Bay synonomous with grandeur. Today, new buildings, angled back from the beach, house 81 one to three-bedroom suites (each with a full kitchen) that have recently been refurbished, and the beach house has been transformed into five garden suites. Manicured landscaped gardens separate the reception area and the large, comfortable tea lounge from the pool; the alfresco dining room where evening entertainment is held; and the half mile of crunchy beach. Glitter Bay is more casual and family oriented than its next-door sister property, the Royal Pavilion, but they share facilities, including complimentary water-sports and dining privileges at either resort. *Porters, St. James Parish, tel. 809/422–4111, fax 809/422–3940. 86 rooms. Facilities: pool, restaurant, water sports, 2 lighted tennis courts, golf course nearby. AE, DC, MC, V. EP, MAP. Very Expensive.*

★ **The Royal Pavilion.** Seventy-two of the 75 rooms here are oceanfront suites; the remaining three are nestled in a garden villa. The ground-floor ocean-front rooms, allow guests simply to step through sliding doors, cross their private patio, and walk onto the sands. Second- and third-floor rooms, however, have the advantage of an elevated view of the sea. Breakfast and lunch are served alfresco along the edge of the beach. Afternoon tea and dinner are in the Palm Terrace (*see* Dining, *above*). The Royal Pavilion attracts the sophisticated guest who wants serenity (children under 12 are discouraged during the winter months), but are welcome to share the facilities of its adjoining sister hotel, the more informal Glitter Bay. *Porters, St. James Parish, tel. 809/422–5555, fax 809/422–3940. 75 rooms. Facilities: 2 restaurants, 2 bars, 2 lighted, artificial-grass tennis courts, supper-club entertainment, water-sports center, golf course nearby. AE, D, DC, MC, V. EP. Very Expensive.*

★ **Sandy Lane Hotel.** The complete renovation of this prestigious hotel has given it good reason to remain the island's most expensive property. If you like low-key luxury set on one of the best beaches in Barbados, Sandy Lane is the place. One choice room is 310, with a large private balcony for breakfast and for watching magnificent sunsets in the evening. It has a huge king-size bed and a vast bathroom, complete with double washbasin, a deep oval tub, and bidet. Afternoon tea, fine dining, and personalized service all add to the charm. The white coral structure, finished with Zandobbio marble throughout and a staircase leading to the beach shaded with mahogany trees, is reminiscent of *The Great Gatsby. Hwy. 1, St. James Parish, tel. 809/432–1311, fax 809/432–2954. 91 doubles, 30 suites. Facilities: free water sports, 18-hole golf course and club, pool, 5 tennis courts (2 floodlit); two oceanfront restaurants, poolside snack bar, 5 bars, live entertainment nightly. AE, DC, MC, V. EP, MAP. Very Expensive.*

Settlers' Beach. The accommodations at Settlers' Beach are two-story, two-bedroom homes with full kitchen and dining room (or one-story villas with atrium), arranged asymmetrically around a large courtyard filled with towering palms and a pool. The property is small, squeezed between newer resorts, and attracts those seeking a quiet vacation. *Hwy. 1, St. James Parish, tel. 809/422–3052, fax 809/422–1937. 22 villas. Facilities: pool, restaurant. AE, MC, V. EP. Very Expensive.*

Coconut Creek Club. A luxury cottage colony, the Coconut Creek Club is set on handsomely landscaped grounds with a small but adequate private beach and a bar pavilion for entertainment and dancing. The atmosphere here is more casual than its sister hotel, the Colony Club. *Reservations: Box 249, Bridgetown; Hwy. 1, St. James Parish, tel. 809/432–0803, fax 809/422–1726. 53 rooms. Facilities: pool, dining room, pub. AE, DC, MC, V. EP, MAP. Expensive.*

Discovery Bay Hotel. The rooms of the quiet, white-columned, recently renovated Discovery Bay Hotel open onto a central lawn and a pool. Some rooms have ocean views. *Hwy. 1, Holetown, St. James Parish, tel. 809/432–1301, fax 809/422–1726. 85 rooms. Facilities: pool, table tennis, terrace restaurant, boutique, water sports. AE, MC, V. EP. Expensive.*

Treasure Beach. Under a new manageress, this compact resort, with small one-bedroom suites, is tightly run. The ground-floor rooms offer little privacy from other guests unless the shutters are closed, so you may wish to be on the second or third floor. Most of the rooms overlook the small garden; a few have sea views. The atmosphere is casual, and the staff is equally so. *Payne's Bay, St. James Parish, tel. 809/432–1346, fax 809/432–1740. 24 one-bedroom, air-conditioned suites; 1 two-bedroom penthouse suite. Facilities: restaurant, pool, water sports. AE, DC, MC, V. EP, MAP. Expensive.*

Almond Beach Club. In this hotel, everything is included in the price of the room—all you want to eat and drink (that includes wine and liquor); water sports; boat trips; tennis; tours of the island; shopping excursions to Bridgetown; accommodations, mostly in one-bedroom suites with balconies; departure transportation to the airport; and service and taxes. The food is excellent, from the breakfast buffet and a four-course lunch to the afternoon tea and pastries and the extensive dinner menu. Menus offer plenty of choice, but if your stay is seven days or more and you want something different, the Almond Beach Club offers a dine-around program—dinner or lunch at a number of area restaurants with round-trip transportation included. The Almond Beach Club has none of the enforced-activity, "whistle-blowing" atmosphere of some all-inclusives. *Vauxhall, St. James, tel. 809/432–7840 or 800/966–4737, fax 407/994–6344. 147 rooms. Facilities: restaurant, 3 pools, snorkeling, fishing, windsurfing, waterskiing, tennis, squash, sauna, fitness center. AE, MC, V. All-inclusive. Moderate–Expensive.*

Barbados Beach Village. Vacationers choose from twin-bedded rooms, studios, apartments, and duplexes at the Barbados Beach Village. The beach has a terrace bar, and the restaurant is seaside. *Hwy. 1, St. James Parish, tel. 809/425–1440, fax 809/424–0996. 88 rooms. Facilities: pool, restaurant, disco nightclub. AE, DC, MC, V. EP. Moderate.*

St. Peter Parish
★

Cobblers Cove Hotel. This all-suite hotel, renovated in 1992, 12 miles up the west coast from Bridgetown, combines comfort and informal elegance. Each luxury suite has a balcony or patio and wet bar. The pink-and-white buildings contrasting with tropical gardens overlooking the sea create a fine retreat that recently joined the Relais et Château marketing group. The atmosphere is casual and smart, with a clublike lounge-library and a bar that becomes the evening gathering spot. *Hwy. 1, St. Peter Parish, tel. 809/422–2291, fax 809/422–1460. 38 suites plus the Camelot Suite, with king-size, four-poster bed; whirlpool bath; private pool; and lounge. Facilities: pool, floodlit tennis court, water sports, child care available, but no children* *under 12 allowed at hotel late Jan.–late March. Closed Sept. AE, MC, V. CP, MAP. Very Expensive.*

Heywoods Barbados. Everything is on a grand scale here: The seven buildings of the Heywoods Barbados, each with its own theme and decor, house hundreds of rooms. The mile-long beach has space for all water sports. Now a Wyndham resort, the property is well laid out to accept large groups. *Hwy. 1, St. Peter Parish, tel. 809/422–4900, fax 809/422–1581. 306 rooms. Facilities: 3 pools, 5 lighted tennis courts, squash courts, 9-hole golf course, restaurants, bars, boutiques, entertainment. AE, DC, MC, V. All-inclusive. Moderate.*

St. Michael Parish   **Grand Barbados Beach Resort.** A mile from Bridgetown on Carlisle Bay, this convenient hotel has pleasant rooms and suites. The white-sand beach is lapped by a surprisingly clear sea, despite the oil refinery close by. The Aquatic Club executive floor has rooms that include a Continental breakfast and secretarial services suitable for business travelers. A 260-foot-long pier for romantic walks, plus live music and a dance floor, enhances a stay here. *Box 639, Bridgetown, St. Michael Parish, tel. 809/426–0890 or 800/223–9815, fax 809/424–0096. 133 rooms. Facilities: beach, pool, exercise room, whirlpool, sauna, shopping arcade, beauty salon/barber shop, 2 restaurants. AE, DC, MC, V. EP. Expensive.*

Barbados Hilton International. This large resort, just five minutes from Bridgetown, is for those who like activity and having plenty of people around. Expect to rub shoulders with delegates attending seminars and conventioneers, and don't be surprised by the strong odor from the nearby oil refinery. Its attractions include an atrium lobby, a man-made beach 1,000 feet wide with full water sports, and lots of shops. All rooms and suites have balconies. *Needham's Point, St. Michael Parish, tel. 809/426–0200, fax 809/436–8646. 185 rooms. Facilities: pool, tennis courts, restaurant, lounge, health club. AE, DC, MC, V. EP. Moderate–Expensive.*

Christ Church   **Divi Southwinds Beach Resort.** In this resort, situated on 20
Parish lush acres, the toss-up is whether to take one of the one-bedroom suites, with a balcony and kitchenette overlooking the gardens and pool, or one of the smaller and older-looking rooms, just steps from the white sandy beach. Though all the rooms are pleasant, the buildings themselves have a barracks ambience. Dining facilities next to the pool have the tour-package feel, with the emphasis on self-service. Guests come here for a rollicking good time that includes making full use of the scuba and water-sports facilities. *St. Lawrence, Christ Church Parish, tel. 800/367–3484, fax 809/428–4674. 166 rooms. Facilities: 2 restaurants, 3 pools, 2 lighted tennis courts, putting green, shopping arcade. AE, DC, MC, V. EP, MAP. Expensive.*

Southern Palms. A plantation-style hotel on a 1,000-foot stretch of pink sand near the Dover Convention Center, Southern Palms is a convenient businessperson's hotel. You may choose from standard bedrooms, deluxe oceanfront suites with kitchenettes, and a four-bedroom penthouse. Each wing of the hotel has its own small pool. *St. Lawrence, Christ Church Parish, tel. 809/428–7171, fax 809/428–7175. 93 rooms. Facilities: 2 pools, duty-free shop, small conference center, miniature-golf course, tennis court, dining room, water sports. AE, D, DC, MC, V. EP. Expensive.*

Casuarina Beach Club. This luxury apartment hotel on 900 feet of pink sand takes its name from the casuarina pines that surround it, and the quiet setting provides a dramatic contrast to that of the platinum-coast resorts. The bar and restaurant are on the beach. A new reception area includes small lounges where guests can get a dose of TV—there aren't any in the bedrooms. Scuba diving, golf, and other activities can be arranged. The Casuarina Beach is popular with those who prefer self-catering holidays in a secluded setting, convenient to nightlife and shopping. *St. Lawrence Gap, Christ Church Parish, tel. 809/428-3600, fax 809/428-1970. 134 rooms. Facilities: pool, tennis courts, squash courts, restaurant, bar, minimarket, duty-free shop. AE, MC, V. EP. Moderate.*

Club Rockley Barbados. At press time, part of these time-share condominiums was being transformed into an all-inclusive resort with air-conditioned one- and two-bedroom accommodations, with a balcony or a patio. On the grounds are a massage center; six swimming pools; five tennis courts; a 9-hole golf course; and squash courts; a free shuttle bus to the beach (five minutes); two dining rooms, one offering buffet dinners and another with an à la carte menu; a disco for late-night revelry; and a children's program. *Christ Church Parish, tel. 809/435-7880, fax 809/435-8015. 288 rooms. AE, DC, MC, V. All-inclusive. Moderate.*

Sandy Beach Hotel. On a wide, sparkling white beach, this comfortable hotel has a popular poolside bar and the Green House Restaurant, which serves a weekly West Indian buffet. All rooms have kitchenettes. Water sports, at extra cost, include scuba-diving certification, deep-sea fishing, harbor cruises, catamaran sailing, and windsurfing. Guests can walk to St. Lawrence Gap for other restaurants and entertainment. *Worthing, Christ Church Parish, tel. 809/435-8000, fax 809/435-8053. 89 units. Facilities: pool, restaurant, bar, entertainment. AE, D, DC, MC, V. EP. Moderate.*

Accra Beach Hotel. A complete renovation of the rooms should inject new life into this utilitarian hotel on the beach. The rooms obliquely face a small lawn area, permitting an angled view of the sea. Dining on the other side of the garden adjacent to the pool provides the focus for guests. *Rockley Beach, Christ Church Parish, tel. 809/427-7866 or 800/223-9815, fax 809/435-6794. 52 rooms. Facilities: dining room, lounge, beach bar, water-sports center. AE, MC, V. EP. Inexpensive.*

Benston Windsurfing Club Hotel. A small hotel that began as a gathering place for windsurfing enthusiasts, the Benston Windsurfing Club is now a complete school and center for the sport. The rooms are spacious and sparsely furnished to accommodate the active and young crowd who choose this bare-bones hotel right on the beach. The bar and restaurant overlook the water. All sports can be arranged, but windsurfing (learning, practicing, and perfecting it) is king. *Maxwell Main Rd., Christ Church Parish, tel. 809/428-9095, fax 809/435-6621. 15 rooms. Facilities: restaurant, bar, entertainment. AE, MC, V. EP. Inexpensive.*

Little Bay Hotel. This small hotel is a find for anyone who wants to go easy on the wallet and yet sleep to the sounds of the sea. Each room has a private balcony, bedroom, small lounge, and kitchenette. Room 100 is a favorite. This year the owner, Charlene Paterson from Toronto, planned to throw away the drab carpets and replace them with a clay-tile floor. There are no TVs in the rooms, but guests can catch up on the news and watch sports in the small lounge next to the popular restaurant, Southern Accents. *St. Lawrence Gap, tel. 809/435–8574, fax 809/435–8586. 10 rooms. Facilities: lounge, bar, restaurant. AE, MC, V. EP. Inexpensive.*

★ **Ocean View.** Possibly the best-kept secret in the Caribbean, the 40 rooms and suites of this individualistic hideaway are home to celebrities on their commute to private villas in Mustique. The rooms vary considerably, and their charm depends on whether you appreciate the eclectic furnishings. Although it lacks modern amenities, bear in mind that this is an old colonial-style building and enjoy it for that. Owner John Chandler places his personal antiques throughout his three-story grande dame nestled against the sea, adds great bouquets of tropical flowers everywhere, and calls it home. In season, the downstairs Xanadu Club presents very good, off-off-Broadway reviews. *Hastings, Christ Church Parish, tel. 809/427–7821, fax 809/427–7826. 40 rooms. Facilities: restaurant and bar, supper club. AE, MC, V. CP. Inexpensive.*

Sichris Hotel. The Sichris is a "discovery," more attractive inside than seen from the road, a comfortable and convenient self-contained resort that can be ideal for businesspeople who need a quiet place in which to work. Just minutes from the city, the air-conditioned one-bedroom suites all have kitchenettes and private balconies or patios. It's a walk of two or three minutes to the beach. *Worthing, Christ Church Parish, tel. 809/435–7930, fax 809/435–8232. 24 rooms. Facilities: pool, restaurant, bar. AE, MC, V. EP. Inexpensive.*

St. Philip Parish **Crane Beach Hotel.** This remote hilltop property on a cliff over-
★ looking the dramatic Atlantic coast remains one of the special places of Barbados. The Crane Beach has suites and one-bedroom apartments in the main building. Room rates vary considerably. Corner suite 1 is one of the nicest, with its two walls of windows and patio terrace. The Roman-style pool with columns separates the main house from the dining room. To reach the beach, you walk down some 200 steps onto a beautiful stretch of sand thumped by waves that are good both for body surfing and swimming. *Crane Bay, St. Philip Parish, tel. 809/423–6220, fax 809/423–5343. 18 rooms. Facilities: pool, restaurant, 2 bars. AE, DC, MC, V. EP, MAP. Expensive.*

Marriott's Sam Lord's Castle. Set on the Atlantic coast about 14 miles east of Bridgetown, Sam Lord's Castle is not a castle with moat and towers but a sprawling great house surrounded by 72 acres of grounds, gardens, and beach. The seven rooms in the main house have canopied beds; downstairs, the public rooms have furniture by Sheraton, Hepplewhite, and Chippendale—unfortunately, for admiring, not for sitting. Additional guest rooms in surrounding cottages have more-conventional hotel furnishings. The beach is a mile long, the Wanderer Restaurant offers Continental cuisine, and there are even a few slot machines, as befits a pirate's lair. *Long Bay, St. Philip Parish, tel. 809/423–7350, fax 809/423–5918. 256 rooms. Facilities: 3 pools, lighted tennis courts, 3 restaurants, entertainment. AE, DC, MC, V. EP, MAP. Moderate.*

St. Joseph Parish **Atlantis Hotel.** The Atlantis provides a warm, pleasant atmosphere in a pastoral location overlooking a majestically rocky Atlantic coast. The hotel is modest, yet the congeniality and the Bajan food more than make up for that. *Bathsheba, St. Joseph Parish, tel. 809/433–9445. 16 rooms. Facilities: dining room. AE. EP. Inexpensive.*

Rental Homes and Apartments Private homes are available for rent south of Bridgetown in the Hastings–Worthing area, along the St. James Parish coast, and in St. Peter Parish. The **Barbados Board of Tourism** (tel. 809/427–2623) has a listing of rental properties and prices.

Villas and private home rentals are also available through Barbados realtors. Among them are **Alleyne, Aguilar & Altman,** Rosebank, St. James (tel. 809/432–0840); **Bajan Services,** St. Peter (tel. 809/422–2618); **Ronald Stoute & Sons Ltd.,** St. Philip (tel. 809/423–6800).

In the United States, contact **At Home Abroad** (tel. 212/421–9165) or Jan Pizzi at **Villa Vacations** (tel. 617/593–8885 or 800/800–5576).

The Arts and Nightlife

The Arts **Barbados Art Council.** The gallery shows drawings, paintings, and other art, with a new show about every two weeks. *2 Pelican Village, Bridgetown, tel. 809/426–4385. Admission free. Open Mon.–Fri. 10–5, Sat. 9–1.*

A selection of private art galleries offers Bajan and West Indian art at collectible prices. **The Studio Art Gallery** (Fairchild St., Bridgetown, tel. 809/427–5463) exhibits local work (particularly that of Rachael Altman) and will frame purchases. The **Queen's Park Gallery** (Queen's Park, Bridgetown, tel. 809/427–2345) is run by the National Culture Foundation and is the island's largest gallery, presenting month-long exhibits. **Artworx** (Shop 5, Quayside Centre, Christ Church Parish, tel. 809/435–8112) is the most recent entry, selling only handmade items, from carved wooden trains, pottery, and ceramic jewelry to watercolors and prints.

Nightlife When the sun goes down, the musicians come out, and folks go limin' in Barbados (anything from hanging out to a chat-up or jump-up). Competitions among reggae groups, steel bands, and calypso singers are major events, and tickets can be hard to come by, but give it a try.

Most of the large resorts have weekend shows aimed at visitors, and there is a selection of dinner shows that are a Barbados-only occasion. The cultural, folklore dinner show **1627 And All That** is held at the Barbados Museum on Thursday and Sunday. There's transportation to and from your hotel, hot hors d'oeuvres, a buffet dinner (with a l-o-n-g line), an open bar, and a good show put on by the Barbados Dance Theatre that combines history and folklore with calypso, limbo, and stilt dancing. *Hwy. 7, Garrison Savannah, tel. 809/435–6900. $41. Reservations recommended. AE, MC, V. Show and dinner, Sun. and Thurs.*

If it's Monday, it must be the **Plantation Tropical Spectacular** at the Plantation and Garden Theatre, with the internationally known Merrymen making the music and dance. It's a high-energy calypso show with fire-eaters, flaming limbo dancers, steel bands, and calypso, preceded by dinner and drinks, for $42 (show and drinks only, $17.50). Wednesday and Friday, the contemporary group Barbados By Night with Spice performs, and Saturday is a complete musical show. *St. Lawrence Rd., Christ Church Parish, tel. 809/428–5048. Reservations recommended. AE, DC, MC, V.*

The Xanadu is a mid-December through April cabaret, and on Thursday and Friday nights, that's the hottest ticket in town. David McCarty, who danced on Broadway and with the New York City Ballet, has joined forces with chanteuse Jean Emerson, and, along with local strutters, they put on the best show in town. Dinner in the upstairs flower-decked dining room is $44 for dinner and show; cabaret admission only, approximately $12.50. *Ocean View Hotel, Hastings, tel. 809/427-7821. Reservations required.*

Island residents have their own favorite night spots that change with the seasons. The most popular one is still **After Dark** (St. Lawrence Gap, Christ Church, tel. 809/435-6547), with the longest bar on the island and a jazz-club annex.

Harbour Lights claims to be the "home of the party animal," and most any night features live music with dancing under the stars. *On the Bay, Marine Villa, Bay St., St. Michael, tel. 809/436-7225.*

Another "in" spot, **Front Line** (Wharf St., tel. 809/429-6160) at the Wharf in Bridgetown, attracts a young crowd for its Reggae music.

Disco moves are made on the floor at the **Hippo Disco** in the Barbados Beach Village Hotel (St. James, tel. 809/425-1440), and above it, where dancers girate until the early hours of the morning.

Another dusky disco, **Club Miliki** (tel. 809/422-4900), takes center stage at the Heywoods Resort in St. Peter. Live music begins at 9 PM Friday and Saturday.

A late-night (after 11) excursion to **Baxter Road** is de rigueur for midnight Bajan street snacks, local rum, great gossip, and good lie-telling. **Enid & Livy's** and **Collins** are just two of the many long-standing favorites. The later, the better.

Bars and Inns Barbados supports the rum industry in more than 1,600 "rum shops," simple bars where men congregate to discuss the world's ills, and in more sophisticated inns, where you'll find world-class rum drinks and the island's renowned Mount Gay and Cockspur rums. The following offer welcoming spirits: **The Ship Inn** (St. Lawrence Gap, Christ Church Parish, tel. 809/435-6961), **The Coach House** (Paynes Bay, St. James Parish, tel. 809/432-1163), and **Harry's Oasis** (St. Lawrence, Christ Church Parish, no phone; **Bert's Bar** at the Abbeville Hotel; (Rockley, Christ Church Parish, tel. 809/435-7924), serves the best daiquiris in town . . . any town. Also try **The Boat Yard** (Bay Street, Bridgetown, tel. 809/436-2622), **The Waterfront Cafe** (Bridgetown, tel. 809/427-0093), **The Warehouse** (Bridgetown, tel. 809/436-2897), and **TGI Boomers** (St. Lawrence Gap, Christ Church Parish, tel. 809/428-8439).

6 Bonaire

Updated by
Laurie Senz

Bonaire is a stark desert island, perfect for the rugged individualist who is turned off by the overcommercialized high life of the other Antillean islands. The island boasts a spectacular array of exotic wildlife—from fish to fowl to flowers—that will keep nature-watchers awestruck for days. It's the kind of place where you'll want to rent a Jeep and go dashing off madly in search of the wild flamingo, the wild iguana, or even the wild yellow-winged parrot named the Bonairian lora.

A mecca for divers, Bonaire offers one of the most unspoiled reef systems in the world. The water is so clear that you can lean over the dock and look the fish straight in the eye.

Kudos for the preservation of the 112-square-mile isle go to the people and government of Bonaire, who in 1970, with the help of the World Wildlife Fund, developed the Bonaire Marine Park—a model of ecological conservation. The underwater park includes, roughly, the entire coastline, from the high-water tidemark to a depth of 200 feet, all of which is protected by strict laws. Because the Bonairians desperately want to keep their paradise intact, any diver with a reckless streak is firmly requested to go elsewhere.

This is not the island for connoisseurs of fine cuisine, shopping maniacs, beachcombers, or those who prefer hobnobbing with society. The island itself may be lacking in splendor, but what lies off its shores keeps divers enthralled. With only 11,000 inhabitants, the island has a feeling of a small community with a gentle pace.

Before You Go

Tourist Information
Contact the **Bonaire Government Tourist** Office (444 Madison Ave., suite 2403, New York, NY 10022, tel. 212/832–0779 or 800/U–BONAIR. In Canada: 512 Duplex Ave., Toronto, Ont. M4R 2E3, tel. 416/484–4864) for advice and information on planning your trip.

Arriving and Departing
By Plane
ALM (tel. 800/327–7230) and **Air Aruba** (tel. 800/882–7822) will get you to Bonaire. ALM has eight direct flights (through Curaçao), two nonstop flights a week from Miami, and five flights a week from Atlanta through Curaçao, with connecting service (throughfares) to most U.S. gateways tied in with Delta and other airlines, making ALM Bonaire's major airline. ALM also flies to Caracas, Aruba, Curaçao, and St. Martin, as well as other Caribbean islands, using Curaçao as its Caribbean hub. Air Aruba flies six days a week from Newark and daily from Miami to Aruba with connecting service to Bonaire. **American Airlines** (tel. 800/433–7300) offers daily flights from New York to Aruba, but you must connect to Bonaire through ALM or Air Aruba. ALM also offers a Visit Caribbean Pass, which allows easy interisland travel.

From the Airport
Bonaire's Flamingo Airport is tiny, but you'll appreciate its welcoming ambience. The customs check is perfunctory if you are arriving from another Dutch isle; otherwise you will have to show proof of citizenship, plus a return or ongoing ticket. Rental cars and taxis are available at the airport, but try to arrange the pickup through your hotel. A taxi will run between $6 and $10 (for up to four people) to most hotels.

Passports and Visas
U.S. and Canadian citizens need offer only proof of identity, so a passport, notarized birth certificate, or voter registration

card will suffice. British subjects may carry a British Visitor's Passport, available from any post office. All other visitors must carry an official passport. In addition, any visitor who steps onto the island must have a return or ongoing ticket and is advised to confirm that reservation 48 hours before departure.

Language The official language is Dutch, but few speak it, and even then only on official occasions. The street language is Papiamento, a mixture of Spanish, Portuguese, Dutch, English, African, and French—full of colorful Bonairian idioms that even Curaçaoans sometimes don't get. You'll light up your waiter's eyes, though, if you can remember to say *Masha danki* (thank you). English is spoken by most people working at the hotels, restaurants, and tourist shops.

Precautions Because of violent trade winds pounding against the rocks, the windward (eastern) side of Bonaire is much too rough for diving. The *Guide to the Bonaire Marine Park* (available at dive shops around the island) specifies the level of diving skill required for 44 sites, and it knows what it's talking about. No matter how beautiful a beach may look, heed all warning signs regarding the rough undertow.

From October through December the mosquitoes in Bonaire are nearly vampiric. Spray your hotel room before you go to bed. Smart, happy people douse themselves, including their arms, legs, and face, with repellent all day long.

Get an orientation on what stings underwater and what doesn't. As the island's joke goes, you won't appreciate Bonaire until you've stepped on a long-spined urchin, but by then, you won't appreciate the joke.

Bonaire used to have a reputation for being the friendliest and safest island in the Caribbean, but lately, even residents are locking their car doors. Don't leave your camera in an open car, and leave your money, credit cards, jewelry, and other valuables in your hotel's safety-deposit box.

Staying in Bonaire

Important Addresses **Tourist Information:** The **Bonaire Tourist Board** (Kaya Simon Bolivar 12, tel. 599/7–8322 or 599/7–8649, fax 599/7–8408).

Emergencies **Police:** For assistance call 7–8000. In an emergency, dial 11. **Ambulance: 14. Hospitals: St. Franciscus Hospital**, Kralendijk (tel. 599/7–8900).

Currency The great thing about Bonaire is that you don't need to convert your American dollars into the local currency, the NAf guilder. U.S. currency and traveler's checks are accepted everywhere, and the difference in exchange rates is negligible. Banks accept U.S. dollar banknotes at the official rate of NAf 1.77 to the U.S. dollar, traveler's checks at NAf 1.79. The rate of exchange at shops and hotels ranges from NAf 1.75 to NAf 1.80. The guilder is divided into 100 cents, and there are coins of 1 cent, 2½, 5, 10, 25, 50, 100, 250, and 500 guilders. Note: Prices quoted here are in U.S. dollars unless indicated otherwise.

Taxes and Service Charges Hotels charge a room tax of $4.10 per person, per night, and many hotels (not all) add a 10% maid service charge to your bill. Most restaurants add a 10% service charge to your bill. There's no sales tax on purchases in Bonaire. Departure tax when going to Curaçao is $5.65. For all other destinations it's $10.

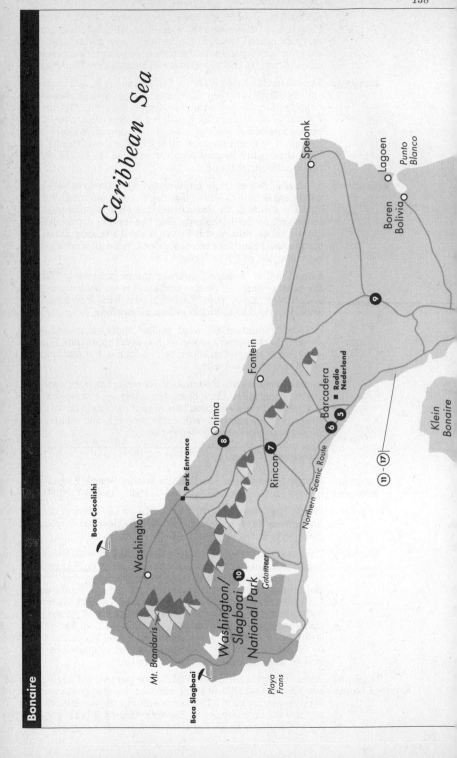

Bonaire

Caribbean Sea

Spelonk

Lagoen

Boren
Bolivia

Punto
Blanco

Klein
Bonaire

Fontein

Onima

Barcadera

Radio
Nederland

Rincon

Northern Scenic Route

Park Entrance

Boca Cocolishi

Washington

Mt. Brandaris

Washington/
Slagbaai
National Park

Cotomeer

Playa
Frans

Boca Slagbaai

138

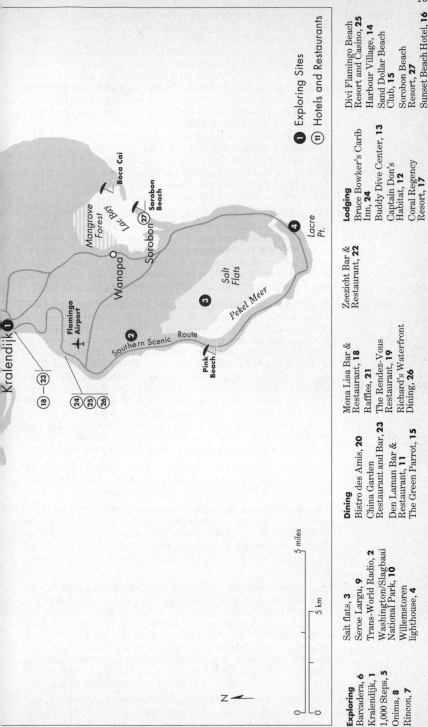

Kralendijk **1**

Flamingo Airport

Wanapa

Mangrove Forest

Lac Bay

Boca Cai

Sorobon Beach

Sorobon

Southern Scenic Route

Salt Flats

Pekel Meer

Pink Beach

Lacre Pt. **4**

3

2

N

0 ——— 5 miles
0 ——— 5 km

1 Exploring Sites

11 Hotels and Restaurants

Exploring
Barcadera, **6**
Kralendijk, **1**
1,000 Steps, **5**
Washington/Slagbaai
National Park, **10**
Onima, **8**
Rincon, **7**

Salt flats, **3**
Seroe Largu, **9**
Trans-World Radio, **2**
Willemstoren
lighthouse, **4**

Dining
Bistro des Amis, **20**
China Garden
Restaurant and Bar, **23**
Den Laman Bar &
Restaurant, **11**
The Green Parrot, **15**

Mona Lisa Bar &
Restaurant, **18**
Raffles, **21**
The Rendez-Vous
Restaurant, **19**
Richard's Waterfront
Dining, **26**

Zeezicht Bar &
Restaurant, **22**

Lodging
Bruce Bowker's Carib
Inn, **24**
Buddy Dive Center, **13**
Captain Don's
Habitat, **12**
Coral Regency
Resort, **17**

Divi Flamingo Beach
Resort and Casino, **25**
Harbour Village, **14**
Sand Dollar Beach
Club, **15**
Sorobon Beach
Resort, **27**
Sunset Beach Hotel, **16**

Guided Tours If you don't like to drive, **Bonaire Sightseeing Tours** (tel. 599/7–8778 or 599/7–8300, ext. 212) will chauffeur you around the island on four different tours: a two-hour Northern Island Tour ($12) that visits the 1,000 steps, Goto Lake, and Rincon, the oldest settlement on the island; a two-hour Southern Island Tour ($12) that covers Akzo Salt Antilles N.V., a modern salt-manufacturing facility where flamingos gather, Lac Bay, and the oldest lighthouse on the island. A half-day tour ($17) visits sites in both the north and south. For $25, you can take a half-day tour of Bonaire's Washington/Slagbaai National Park (entrance fee included), 13,500 acres of majestic scenery, wildlife, unspoiled beaches, and tropical flora. A full-day tour of the park costs $45. Day trips to Curaçao are offered for $125 per person and include round-trip airfare and transfers, an island tour of Curaçao, and lunch. **Ayubi's Tours** (tel. 599/7–5338) also offers several half- and full-day island tours.

Getting Around You can zip about the island in a car or a Suzuki Jeep. Scooters and bicycles, which are also available, are less practical but can be fun, too. Just remember that there are at least 20 miles of unpaved road; the roller-coaster hills at the national park require strong stomachs; and during the rainy season, mud—called Bonairian snow—is unpleasant. All traffic stays to the right and, delightfully, there is yet to be a single traffic light.

Rental Cars **Budget** has cars and Jeeps available from its six locations, but reservations can be made only at the Head Office (tel. 599/7–8300, ext. 225). Pickups are at the airport (tel. 599/7–8315) and at several hotels. It's always a good idea to make advance reservations (fax 599/7–8865 or 599/7–8118; cable BUDGET BON-AIRE; in the U.S., tel. 800/472–3325). Prices range from $28 a day for a Volkswagon to $60 a day for an automatic, air-conditioned four-door sedan. Other agencies are **Avis** (tel. 599/7–5795, fax 599/7–5791; telex 1900 ROCAR), **Dollar Rent-A-Car** (tel. 599/7–5588, at the airport; tel. 599/7–8888; fax 599/7–7788), **Sunray** (tel. 599/7–5230, fax 599/7–4888), and **AB Car Rental** (tel. 599/7–8980 or 599/7–5410, fax 599/7–5034). There is also a new government tax of $2 per day per car rental.

Scooters Two-seater scooters are available from **Bonaire Bicycle & Motorbike Rental** (tel. 599/7–8226) and **S. F. Wave Touch** (tel. 599/7–4246) for about $26 a day and $165 a week.

Bicycles **Bonaire Bicycle & Motorbike Rental** (tel. 599/7–8226) rents bicycles for $15 a day. **Captain Don's Habitat** (tel. 599/7–8290 or 599/7–8913) rents mountain bicycles for $6 per day plus a $250 deposit. **Harbour Village Beach Resort** (tel. 599/7–7500) rents Hybrid bikes for $11 a day to nonhotel guests, but hotel guests get first dibs.

Taxis Taxis are unmetered; they have fixed rates controlled by the government. A trip from the airport to your hotel will cost between $6 to $10 for up to four passengers. A taxi from most hotels into town costs between $4 and $6. Fares increase from 7 PM to midnight by 25% and from midnight to 6 AM by 50%. Taxi drivers are usually knowledgeable enough about the island to conduct half-day tours; they charge about $60 for a northern-route tour and $40 for a southern-route tour. Call **Taxi Central Dispatch** (tel. 599/7–8100 or dial 10), or inquire at your hotel.

Telephones and Mail It's difficult for visitors to Bonaire to get involved in dramatic, heart-wrenching phone conversations or *any* phone discussions requiring a degree of privacy: Only about one-third of the major hotels have phones in their rooms, so calls must be made from hotel front desks or from the central telephone company office in Kralendijk. Telephone connections have improved, but static is still common. To call Bonaire from the United States, dial 011–599–7 + the local four-digit number. When making interisland calls, dial the local four-digit number. Local phone calls cost NAf25¢.

Airmail postage rates to the United States are NAf1.15 for letters and NAf.70 for postcards; to Canada, NAf1.45 for letters and NAf.70 for postcards; to Britain, NAf1.90 for letters and NAf.75 for postcards.

Opening and Closing Times Stores in the Kralendijk area are generally open Monday through Saturday 8–noon and 2–6 PM. On Sundays and holidays, when cruise ships arrive, most shops open for a few extra hours. Most restaurants are open for lunch and dinner, but few not affiliated with hotels are open for breakfast.

Exploring Bonaire

Numbers in the margin correspond to points of interest on the Bonaire map.

Kralendijk
❶ Bonaire's capital city of **Kralendijk** (population: 2,500) is five minutes from the airport and a short walk from the Carib Inn and the Flamingo Beach Resort. There's really not much to explore here, but there are a few sights worth noting in this small, very tidy city.

Kralendijk has one main drag, J. A. Abraham Boulevard, which turns into **Kaya Grandi** in the center of town. Along it are most of the island's major stores, boutiques, restaurants, duty-free shops, and jewelry stores (*see* Shopping, *below*).

Across Kaya Grandi, opposite Spritzer & Fuhrmann Jewelry store, is Kaya L. D. Gerharts, with several small supermarkets, the ALM office, a handful of snack shops, and some of the better restaurants, including Bistro des Amis and The Rendez-Vous (*see* Dining, *below*). Walk down the narrow waterfront avenue called Kaya C. E. B. Hellmund, which leads straight to the **North** and **South piers.** In the center of town, stop in at the new Harborside Mall, which has 13 chic boutiques. Along this route you will see **Fort Oranje,** with cannons pointing to the sea. From December through April, cruise ships, including the *Seabourn Pride* and the *Regent Suns,* dock in the harbor every few days. The *Ocean Breeze* stops at Bonaire year-round. The elegant white structure that looks like a tiny Greek temple is the **Fish Market,** where local fishermen sell their early-morning haul, along with vegetables and fruits.

Elsewhere on the Island Two tours, north and south, are possible of the 24-mile-long island; both will take from a few hours to a full day, depending upon whether you stop to snorkel, swim, dive, or lounge.

South Bonaire The trail south from Kralendijk is chock-full of icons—both natural and man-made—that tell the minisaga of Bonaire. Rent a Jeep (a car will do, but during the rainy months the roads can become muddy, making traction difficult) and head south along the Southern Scenic Route.

The first icon you'll come to is the unexpected symbol of **❷** modernism—the towering 500-foot antennas of **Trans-World Radio,** one of the most powerful stations in Christian broadcasting. From here, evangelical programs and gospel music are transmitted daily in five languages to all of North, South, and Central America, as well as the entire Caribbean.

❸ Keep on cruising past, the salt pans until you come to the **salt flats,** voluptuous white drifts that look something like huge mounds of vanilla ice cream. Harvested twice a year, the "ponds" are owned by the Akzo Salt Antilles N.V. company, which has re-activated the 19th-century salt industry with great success. (One reason for that success is that the ocean on this part of the island is higher than the land—which makes irrigation a snap.) Keep a lookout for the three 30-foot obelisks—white, blue, and red—that were used to guide the trade boats coming to pick up the salt. On this stark landscape, these obelisks look decidedly phallic; today, they are photographed as historical curiosities.

Along the sea just a bit farther south is **Pink Beach,** a half-mile-long stretch of incredibly soft sand that derives its name from the delicate pink hue of the sand at the shoreline (*see* Beaches, *below*).

The gritty history of the salt industry is revealed down the road in **Rode Pan,** the site of two groups of tiny slave huts. During the 19th century, the salt workers, imported slaves from Africa, worked the fields by day, then crawled into these huts at night to sleep. Each Friday afternoon, they walked seven hours to Rincon to weekend with their families, returning each Sunday to the salt pans. In recent years, the government has restored the huts to their original simplicity. Only very small people will be able to go inside, but take a walk around and put your head in for a look.

❹ Continue heading south to **Willemstoren,** Bonaire's first lighthouse, built in 1837 and still in use, but closed to visitors.

Rounding the tip of the island, head north and notice how the waves, driven by the trade winds, play a crashing symphony against the rocks. Locals make a habit of stopping here to collect pieces of driftwood in spectacular shapes. To the north are two more picturesque beaches—**Sorobon Beach** and **Boca Cai** at Lac Bay. The road here winds through otherworldly desert terrain, full of organ-pipe cacti and spiny-trunk mangroves—huge stumps of saltwater trees that rise out of the marshes like witches. At Boca Cai, you'll be impressed by the huge piles of conch shells discarded by local fishermen. (Sift through them; they make great gifts—but pack them carefully.) On Sundays at Cai, live bands play from noon to 4, and there's beer and food available at the local restaurant. When the mosquitoes arrive at dusk, it's time to hightail it home.

North Bonaire The northern tour takes you right into the heart of Bonaire's natural wonders—desert gardens of towering cacti, tiny coastal coves, dramatically shaped coral grottoes, and plenty of fantastic panoramas. A snappy excursion with the requisite photo stops will take about 2½ hours, but if you pack your swimsuit and a hefty picnic basket (forget finding a Burger King), you could spend the entire day exploring this northern sector, including a few hours snorkeling in Washington Park.

Head out from Kralendijk on the Kaya Gobernador N. Debrot until it turns into the Northern Scenic Route, a one-lane, one-way street on the outskirts of town. Fifteen minutes north of **❺** the Sunset Beach Hotel is a site called **1,000 Steps,** a limestone staircase carved right out of the cliff on the left side of the road. If you take the trek down them, you'll discover a great place to snorkel and scuba dive. Actually, you'll only climb 67 steps, but it feels like 1,000 when you walk up them carrying scuba gear.

Following the route northward, look closely for a turnoff marked Vista Al Mar Restaurant. A few yards ahead, you'll discover some stone steps that lead down into a cave full of stalactites and vegetation. Once used to trap goats, this cave, **⑥** called **Barcadera,** is one of the oldest in Bonaire; there's even a tunnel that looks intriguingly spooky.

Note that once you pass the antennas of the Radio Nederland, you cannot turn back to Kralendijk. The road becomes one-way, and you will have to follow the cross-island road to Rincon and return via the main road through the center of the island.

If you continue toward the northern curve of the island, the green storage tanks of the Bonaire Petroleum Corporation become visible. Follow the sign to **Goto Meer,** a popular flamingo **⑦** hangout. The road will loop around and pass through **Rincon,** a well-kept cluster of pastel cottages and century-old buildings that constitute Bonaire's oldest village. Watch your driving—both goats and dogs often sit right in the middle of the main drag.

Rincon was the original Spanish settlement on the island: It became home to the slaves brought from Africa to work on the plantations and salt fields. Superstition and voodoo lore still have a powerful impact here, more so than in Kralendijk, where they work hard at suppressing the old ways. Rincon has a couple of local eateries. **Verona's Bar & Restaurant** (no phone) on Kaya Para Mira, on the road south, has tasty local dishes, but the real temptation is **Prisca's Ice Cream** (tel. 599/7–6334), to be found at her house on Kaya Komkomber.

Pass through Rincon on the road that heads toward Fontein, **⑧** but take the left-hand turn before Fontein to **Onima.** Small signposts direct the way to the **Indian inscriptions** found on a three-foot limestone ledge that juts out like a partially formed cave entrance. Look up to see the red-stained designs and symbols inscribed on the limestone, said to have been the handiwork of the Arawak Indians when they inhabited the island centuries ago.

Backtrack to the main road and continue on to Fontein and then **⑨** to **Seroe Largu,** the highest point on the southern part of the island. During the day, a winding path leads to a magnificent view of Kralendijk's rooftops and the island of Klein Bonaire; at night, the twinkling city lights below make this a romantic stop. If you've got some time, sit on one of the stone benches and watch the friendly turquoise-footed lizards slithering about. They rely on tourists for their main source of crumbs, but if they should happen to ignore you, throw a pebble near them and they'll trot right over.

Washington/ Once a plantation producing divi-divi trees (whose pods were
Slagbaai National used for tanning animal skins), aloe (used for medicinal lo-
Park tions), charcoal, and goats, **Washington/Slagbaai National Park**
⑩ is now a model of conservation, designed to maintain fauna, flora, and geological treasures in their natural state. Visitors may easily tour the 13,500-acre tropical desert terrain along the dirt roads. As befits a wilderness sanctuary, the well-

marked, rugged roads force you to drive slowly enough to appreciate the animal life and the terrain. A four-wheel-drive is a must. (Think twice about coming here if it rained the day before—the mud you may encounter will be more than inconvenient.) If you are planning to hike, bring a picnic lunch, camera, sunscreen, and plenty of water. There are two different routes: The long one, 22 miles (about 2½ hours), is marked by yellow arrows; the short one, 15 miles (about 1½ hours), is marked by green arrows. Goats and donkeys may dart across the road; and if you keep your eyes peeled, you may catch sight of large, camouflaged iguanas in the shrubbery. Some folks even look out for shooting cacti.

Bird-watchers are really in their element here. Right inside the park's gate, flamingos roost on the salt pad known as **Salina Mathijs,** and exotic parakeets dot the foot of **Mt. Brandaris,** Bonaire's highest peak at 784 feet. Some 130 species of colorful birds fly in and out of the shrubbery in the park. Keep your eyes open and your binoculars at hand. (For choice beach sites in the park, *see* Beaches, *below.*) Swimming, snorkeling, and scuba diving are permitted, but visitors are requested not to frighten the animals or remove anything from the grounds. There is absolutely no hunting, fishing, or camping allowed. A useful guidebook to the park is available at the entrance for about $6. *Admission: $3 adults, 50¢ children under 15. The park is open daily 8–5, but you must enter before 3:30.*

What to See and Do with Children

Captain Don's Habitat offers all-inclusive **Family Weeks** in August, with packages that provide a variety of activities, in and out of the water, for both children and adults (*see* Lodging, *below*).

The Sand Dollar Beach Club resort has the daily, year-round **Sand Penny Club** for the children (ages 3–15) of guests. The kids can learn to snorkel and will have a chance to participate in a number of activities and games (*see* Lodging, *below*).

The **Sunset Beach Hotel** and the **Divi Flamingo Beach Resort** also offer family packages and programs for children (*see* Lodging, *below*).

Off the Beaten Track

Bonaire is one of the few places in the world where pink flamingos nest. The spiny-legged creatures—affectionately called "pink clouds"—at first look like swizzlesticks. But they're magnificent birds to observe—and there are about 15,000 of them in Bonaire. The best time to catch them at home is January–June, when they tend to their gray-plumed young. One of their favorite spots is in **Gotomeer,** a saltwater lagoon on the north coast, easily reached by the Northern Scenic Route. Right inside the gate of **Washington/Slagbaai National Park** is another flamingo haunt. And in the south, the birds camp out at the flamingo sanctuary within the salt ponds, site of their largest breeding grounds.

Beaches

Beaches in Bonaire are not the island's strong point. Don't come expecting Aruba-length stretches of glorious white sand. Bonaire's beaches are smaller, and though the water is indeed blue (several shades of it, in fact), the sand is not always white. You can have your pick of beach in Bonaire according to color: pink, black, or white. The best hotel beaches are found at Harbour Village, Sunset Beach, and Sorobon (*see* Lodging, *below*).

Hermit crabs can be found along the shore at **Boca Cocolishi,** a black-sand beach in Washington/Slagbaai Park on the northeast coast. The dark hues of tiny bits of dried coral and shells form the basin and beach, give the sand an unusual look. Located on the windward side of the island, the water is too rough for anything more than wading; however, the spot is perfect for an intimate picnic *à deux*. To get there, take the Northern Scenic Route to the park, then ask for directions at the gate.

Also inside Washington Park is **Boca Slagbaai,** a beach of coral fossils and rocks, with interesting coral gardens that are good for snorkeling just offshore. Bring scuba boots or canvas sandals to walk into the water because the "beach" is rough on bare feet. The gentle surf makes it an ideal place for picnicking or swimming, especially for children.

As the name suggests, the sand at **Pink Beach** boasts a pinkish tint that takes on a magical shimmer in the late-afternoon sun. The water is suitable for swimming, snorkeling, and scuba diving. Take the Southern Scenic Route on the western side of the island, past the Trans-World Radio station, close to the slave huts. A favorite hangout for Bonairians on the weekend, it is virtually deserted during the week.

For uninhibited sun worshipers who'd rather enjoy the rays in the altogether, the private, "clothes-optional" beach, the **Sorobon Beach Resort,** offers calm water, soft clean sand, and delightfully strong tropical breezes. Nonguests are welcome and can purchase a $15 day pass at the entrance gate.

Boca Cai is across Lac Bay, which is an ideal spot for windsurfing.

If you enjoy water sports, find out which beaches are best for a specific sport (*see* Sports and the Outdoors, *below*).

Sports and the Outdoors

Scuba Diving   Bonaire has some of the best reef diving this side of Australia's Great Barrier Reef. The island is unique primarily for its incredible dive sites; it takes only 5–25 minutes to reach your site, the current is usually mild, and while some reefs have very sudden, steep drops, most begin just offshore and slope gently downward at a 45° angle. General visibility runs 60 to 100 feet, except during surges in October and November. An enormous range of coral can be seen, from knobby brain and giant brain coral to elkhorn, staghorn, mountainous star, gorgonian, and black coral. You're also likely to encounter schools of parrotfish, surgeonfish, angelfish, eels, snappers, and groupers. Beach diving is excellent just about everywhere on the leeward side of the island.

The well-policed Bonaire Marine Park, which encompasses the entire coastline around Bonaire and Klein Bonaire, remains an underwater wonder because visitors take the rules here seriously. Do not even think about (1) spearfishing, (2) dropping anchor, or (3) touching, stepping on, or collecting coral. Divers must pay an admission charge of $10, for which they receive a colored plastic tag (to be attached to an item of scuba gear) entitling them to one calendar year of unlimited diving in the Marine Park. The fees are used to maintain the underwater park. Tags are available at all scuba facilities and from the Marine Park headquarters in the Old Fort in Kralendijk (tel. 599/7–8444). To help preserve the reef, all dive operations on Bonaire now offer free bouyancy-control, advanced bouyancy-control, and photographic bouyancy-control classes. Check with any dive shop for the schedule.

There is a hyperbaric decompression chamber located next to the hospital in Kralendijk (tel. 599/7–8187 or 599/7–8900 for emergencies).

Dive Operations Most of the hotels listed in this guide have dive centers. The competition for quality and variety is fierce. Before making a room reservation, inquire about specific dive/room packages that are available. Many of the dive shops also have boutiques where you can purchase T-shirts, color slides showing underwater views, postcards, and tropical jewelry. **Peter Hughes Dive Bonaire** (Divi Flamingo Beach Resort, tel. 599/7–8285 or 800/367–3484), **Sand Dollar Dive and Photo** (Sand Dollar Beach Club, Caya Gob. de Brot 79, tel. 599/7–5252), and **Habitat Dive Center** (Captain Don's Habitat, Kaya Gob. Debrot 103, tel. 599/7–8290 or 800/327–6709) are all PADI five-star dive facilities qualified to offer both PADI and NAUI certification courses. Sand Dollar Dive and Photo is also qualified to certify dive instructors. Other centers include **Bonaire Scuba Center** (Black Durgon Inn; in the U.S., write Box 775, Morgan, NJ 08879, or call 908/566–8866 or 800/526–2370), **Buddy Dive Resort** (Kaya Gob. N., Debrot 85, tel. 599/7–8647), **Dive Inn** (Kaya C.E.B. Hellmund 27, tel. 599/7–8761 and at the Sunset Beach Hotel, tel. 599/7–8448), **Neal Watson's Bonaire Undersea Adventures** (Coral Regency Resort, Kaya Gob. Debrot 90, tel. 599/7–5580 or 800/327–8150), **Great Adventures Bonaire** (Harbour Village Beach Resort, tel. 599/7–7500 or 800/424–0004), and **Bruce Bowker's Carib Inn Dive Center** (Bruce Bowker's Carib Inn, tel. 599/7–8819, fax 599/7–5295).

Americans Jerry Schnabel and Suzi Swygert of **Photo Tours N.V.** (Kaya Grandi 68, tel. 599/7–8060) specialize in teaching and guiding novice-through-professional underwater photographers. They also offer land-excursion tours of Bonaire's birds, wildlife, and vegetation. **Dee Scarr's Touch the Sea** (Box 369, tel. 599/7–8529) is a personalized (two people at a time) diving program that provides interaction with marine life; it is available to certified divers.

Dive Sites The *Guide to the Bonaire Marine Park* lists 44 sites that have been identified and marked by moorings. In the past few years, however, an additional 42 designated mooring and shore diving sites have been added through a conservation program called Sea Tether. Guides associated with the various dive centers can give you more complete directions. The following are a few popular sites to whet your appetite; these and selected other sites are pinpointed on our Bonaire Diving map.

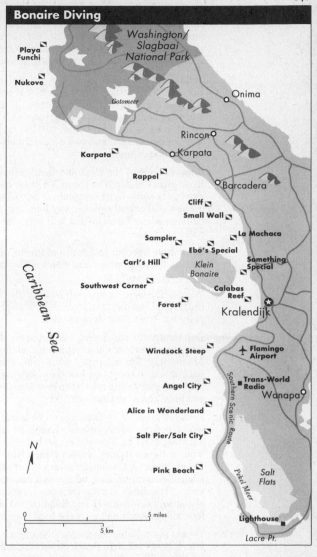

Bonaire Diving

Washington/
Slagbaai
National Park

Playa
Funchi

Nukove

Gotomeer

Onima

Rincon

Karpata

Karpata

Rappel

Barcadera

Cliff

Small Wall

La Machaca

Sampler

Ebo's Special

Carl's Hill

Klein
Bonaire

Something
Special

Southwest Corner

Calabas
Reef

Forest

Kralendijk

Caribbean Sea

Windsock Steep

Flamingo
Airport

Angel City

Trans-World
Radio

Wanapa

Alice in Wonderland

Southern Scenic Route

Salt Pier/Salt City

N

Pink Beach

Pekel Meer

Salt
Flats

0 ——————— 5 miles
0 ——————— 5 km

Lighthouse

Lacre Pt.

Take the track down to the shore just behind Trans-World Radio station; dive in and swim south to **Angel City,** one of the shallowest and most popular sites in a two-reef complex that includes **Alice in Wonderland.** The boulder-size green and tan coral heads are home to black margates, Spanish hogfish, gray snappers, and the large, purple tube sponges.

Calabas Reef, located off the Flamingo Beach Hotel, is the island's most popular dive site. All divers using the hotel's facilities take their warm-up dive here where they can inspect the wreck sunk by Don Stewart for just this purpose. The site is replete with Christmas-tree sponges and fire coral adhering to the ship's hull. Fish life is frenzied, with the occasional octopus putting in an appearance.

You'll need to catch a boat to reach **Forest,** a dive site off the coast of Klein Bonaire, so named for the abundant black-coral forest found there. Responsible for occasional currents, this site gets a lot of fish action, including what's been described as a "friendly" spotted eel that lives in a cave.

Small Wall is one of Bonaire's only complete vertical wall dives. Located off the Black Durgon Inn, it is one of the island's most popular night diving spots. Access is made by boat (Black Durgon guests can access it from shore). The 60-foot wall is frequented by seahorses, squid, turtles, tarpon, and barracudas and has dense hard and soft coral formations; it also allows for excellent snorkeling.

Rappel is one of the most spectacular dives, near the Karpata Ecological Center. The shore is a sheer cliff, and the lush coral growth is home to an unusual variety of marine life, including orange seahorses, squid, spiny lobsters, and a spotted trunk-fish named Sir Timothy that will befriend you for a banana or a piece of cheese.

Something Special, just south of the entrance of the marina, is famous for its garden eels, which slither around the relatively shallow sand terrace.

Windsock Steep, situated in front of the small beach opposite the airport runway, is an excellent first-dive spot and a popular place for snorkeling close to town.

Snorkeling Don't consider snorkeling the cowardly diver's sport; in Bonaire the experience is anything but elementary. For only $8–$11 per day, you can rent a mask, fins, and snorkel at any hotel with a water-sports center (*see* Lodging, *below*). The better spots for snorkeling are on the leeward side of the island, where you have access to the reefs.

Swimming Beaches good for swimming can be found anywhere along the western coast of the island. Excellent sites are **Pink Beach, Sorobon,** and **Cai.** The best resort beaches are found at **Harbour Village Beach Resort, Sunset Beach Hotel,** and **Divi Flamingo Beach Resort & Casino.** Or take a water taxi ($12 round-trip) to **Klein Bonaire,** an islet where you can spend the day playing king of the dune. Except for a few forgotten sneakers, there is absolutely *nothing* on Klein Bonaire, so remember to take some food along. And don't miss the boat back home.

Tennis Tennis is available for free to the guests at the **Sunset Beach Hotel, Divi Flamingo Beach Resort & Casino,** and the **Sand Dollar Beach Club.** Nonguests can play for free during the day at the **Divi Flamingo Beach Resort & Casino** and even take the free tennis clinics on Tuesday and Wednesday mornings (8:30–10 AM). At night, there's a $10 an hour charge. At press time, the Sunset Beach Hotel was considering charging nonguests $10 an hour to use its two courts.

Windsurfing Lac Bay, a protected cove on the east coast, is ideal for windsurfing. Novices will find it especially comforting since there's no way to be blown out to sea. **Windsurfing Bonaire,** known locally as "Jibe City," (fax 599/7–5363; U.S. representative, 800/748–8733) offers courses for beginning to advanced board sailors. Lessons cost $20; board rentals start at $20 an hour; $40 for a half day. There are free regular pickups at all the hotels at 9 AM and 1 PM.

Deep-Sea Fishing **Captain Rich** (tel. 599/7–5421) will take you on his 30-foot twin diesel sport-fishing boat, the *Slamdunk*, to fish for wahoo, marlin, tuna, and sailfish. Rates are $275 for a half day, $375 for a full day (maximum six people). **Piscatur Charters** (tel. 599/7–8774) offers the light-tackle angler reef fishing for jacks, barracudas, and snappers from a 15-foot skiff. Rates are $125 for a half day, $225 for a full day. The 30-foot sport fisher *Piscatur* is available for charter at $275 for a half day, $375 for a full day.

Sailing Cruises The *Samur* (tel. 599/7–5433), the *Oscarina* (tel. 599/7–8290 or 599/7–8819), and the *Woodwind* (tel. 599/7–8285) offer a variety of cruises for snorkeling, picnicking, and watching the sunset. A private day's cruise on the sailboat *Oscarina* (tel. 599/7–8290) is $350 for a party of four. Glass-bottom boat trips are offered on the *Bonaire Dream.* The 1½-hour trip costs $15 for adults, $7.50 for children, and leaves daily, except Sundays, from the Harbour Village Marina.

Shopping

You can get to know all the shops in Bonaire in a matter of a few hours, but sometimes there's no better way to enjoy some time out of the sun and sea than to go shopping, particularly if your companion is a dive fanatic and you're not. Almost all the shops are situated on the Kaya Grandi or in adjacent streets and tiny malls. There are several snazzy boutiques worth a browse. One word of caution: Buy as many flamingo T-shirts as you want, but don't take home anything made of goatskin or tortoiseshell; they are not allowed into the United States.

Clothing **Benetton** (19 Kaya Grandi, tel. 599/7–5107) has added Bonaire to its list of franchises in the Caribbean and makes the claim that prices here are 20% less than in New York. At **Caro's Boutique** (34 Kaya Grandi, tel. 599/7–8308) men can find designs by LaCoste and Guy LaRoche.

One shop that's sure to inspire a purchase is the **Ki Bo Ke Pakus,** or **What Do You Want?** (Flamingo Beach Hotel, tel. 599/7–8239), with an exquisite line of batiks, material for dashikis, island-made jewelry, and chic designer swimsuits and beach cover-ups.

Perfume and Cosmetics **D'Orsy's** (Harborside Mall, tel. 599/7–5288) sells name-brand, duty-free perfumes and makeup from Lancôme, Clinique, Estee Lauder, Chanel, Nina Ricci, and Ralph Lauren, to name a few.

Souvenirs and Crafts The hippest boutique in Bonaire is **Birds of Paradise** (Bonaire Shopping Gallery, 36 Kaya Grandi, tel. 599/7–8998), with merchandise ranging from wooden fish earrings and other desert-chic jewelry to Esprit sportswear and stylish swimsuits. **Kibrahacha Souvenir and Gifts** (Bonaire Shopping Gallery, 33 Kaya Grandi, tel. 599/7–8434) features wall hangings, exotic shells and driftwood, embroidered dresses, Dutch curios, and black coral (conservation groups advise against buying coral products). **Home Collection Shop** (Bonaire Shopping Gallery, 36-A Kaya Grandi, tel. 599/7–8460) specializes in decorations for the home, including locally made *chibichibi* (sugar birds), tile paintings, Dutch souvenirs, and unusual stuffed fish and cloth parrots. **Littman Gifts** (35 Kaya Grandi, tel. 599/7–8091) is the place for gourmet foods—mouth-watering Dutch cheeses, rye breads, Dutch and American chocolates, and fine wines. Batik cloth by the yard, European costume jewelry, T-shirts, framed underwater pictures, wooden divers, and glass flamingos are also sold. **Caribbean Arts and Crafts** (38-A Kaya Grandi, tel. 599/7–5051) is a welcome newcomer to Bonaire's shopping scene. Here you'll find Mexican onyx, papier-mâché clowns, woven wall tapestries, painted wooden fish and parrots, straw carrying bags, and hand-blown glass vases. **Things Bonaire** (Sunset Beach Hotel, Kaya Grandi 38C, tel. 599/7–8423) offers T-shirts, shorts, colorful earrings, batik dresses, souvenirs, and guidebooks. A government-funded crafts center, **Fundashon Arte Industri Bonairiano** (J. A. Abraham Blvd., Kralendijk, next to the post office, no phone), offers locally made necklaces of coral in a variety of colors, hand-painted shirts and dresses, and the "fresh craft of the day."

Dining

Gourmets have not been sneaking off to Bonaire for five-star cuisine, but with a healthy variety of dining experiences, visitors should not go home hungry. Dress on the island is casual but conservative.

Highly recommended restaurants are indicated by a star ★.

Category	Cost*
Expensive	over $20
Moderate	$12–$20
Inexpensive	under $12

Per person, excluding drinks and service. There is no sales tax.

Raffles. In one of the oldest two-story houses on Bonaire, this air-conditioned oasis of green and white is a find for seekers of a romantic tête-à-tête. Inside, soft jazz plays in the background, tables are intimate and candlelit, and the service is unobtrusive. More casual, café-style dining can be found outside on the terrace, where you can watch the strolling passersby. Dutch-born owners Astrid and Peter Lensvelt have put together an international menu with an emphasis on British, Caribbean, and Continental cuisines. There's an à la carte menu and three fixed-priced complete dinners. The Aruban chef makes sauces and desserts that are out of this world. Excellent beginners include the seven-seafood soup and fish pâté. Order the Seafood Platter Caribe (lobstertail, shrimp, scallops, and a fillet of grouper) or the salmon cascade. Save room for a mango parfait, dark and white chocolate mousse, or homemade fruit sherbets. Look for the landmark red British phone box that sits outside the door. *Kaya C.E.B. Helmund 5, tel. 599/7–8617. Reservations suggested. AE, MC, V. Dinner only. Closed Mon. Expensive.*

Bistro des Amis. Expensive but worth every guilder. The Bistro's creative French menu and the sensual Folies Bergère ambience have both been designed by owner Lucille Martyn. Try to get this engaging Dutch woman to talk about her specialties, then savor the Dutch chef's unforgettable red-pepper soup, duck with orange sauce, carpaccio, and red snapper steamed in fish stock. Or just have a drink around the mahogany bar. *1*

Kaya L. D. Gerharts, tel. 599/7-8003. Reservations required.
AE, MC, V. Dinner only. Closed Sun. Expensive–Moderate.

Den Laman Bar & Restaurant. A 6,000-foot aquarium provides
the backdrop to this nautically decorated, sea-breeze-cooled
restaurant. Eat indoors next to the glass-enclosed "ocean
show" (request a table in advance) or outdoors on the noisier
patio overlooking the sea. Pick a fresh Caribbean lobster from
the lobster tank, or choose red snapper Creole, which is a
hands-down winner. *77 Gob. Debrot, next to the Sunset Beach
Hotel, tel. 599/7-8599. Reservations advised. AE, MC, V. Dinner only. Closed Tues. Moderate.*

★ **The Rendez-Vous Restaurant.** From the terrace of this bistro-
like café, watch the world of Bonaire go by as you fill up on
warm bread, hearty soups, seafood, steaks, and vegetarian
specialties. Or munch on light pastries accompanied by steamy
espresso. Those in the know swear the Rendez-Vous is the place
to go to recover from disco-burnout. *3 Kaya L. D. Gerharts, tel.
599/7-8454. AE. Dinner only. Closed Tues. Moderate.*

★ **Richard's Waterfront Dining.** Located on the airport side of
Kralendijk and next door to a seafood stand, Richard's specializes in grilled seafood dishes. Chef Bonito caters to an American palate, serving up flavorful, not spicy, dishes. Owner
Richard Beady, who is from Boston, personally checks on every
table. His alfresco eatery on the water is casually romantic and
has become the most recommended restaurant on the island—a
reputation that's well deserved. Although the menu is limited,
the food is consistently excellent. Among the best dishes are
conch *alajillo* (fillet of conch with garlic and butter), shrimp
primavera, and grilled wahoo. Start with the fish soup, a tasty
broth with chunks of the catch of the day. A new pier lets you
arrive by boat. The Sunset Happy Hour is popular with locals
in the know. *60 J. A. Abraham Blvd., a few houses away from
the Carib Inn, tel. 599/7-5263. Reservations advised. AE, MC,
V. Dinner only. Closed Mon. Moderate.*

The Green Parrot. This family-run restaurant, on the dock of
the Sand Dollar Beach Club, features the biggest hamburgers
and the best strawberry margaritas on the island. Try the onion string appetizer, which consists of onion rings shaped into a
small bread loaf. Bagels with cream cheese, char-grilled
steaks, Creole fish, and barbecue chicken and ribs are also
served. This is where you'll find both the American expatriates
and visiting tourists hanging out. It's also a good place for
viewing the setting sun. *Sand Dollar Beach Club, tel. 599/7-
5454. Reservations suggested in high season. AE, MC, V. Inexpensive–Moderate.*

Zeezicht Bar & Restaurant. Zeezicht (pronounced *zay-zeekt*
and meaning sea view) is one of the better restaurants open for
both breakfast and lunch in town. At lunch you'll get basic
American fare with an Antillean touch, such as fish omelet.
Dinner is either on the terrace overlooking the harbor or upstairs inside a romantic, air-conditioned enclave that's popular
with couples and honeymooners. Locals are dedicated to this
hangout, especially for the ceviche, conch sandwiches, local
snails in hot sauce, and the Zeezicht special soup with conch,
fish, shrimps, and oysters. After dessert, stop in the garden to
see the monkey and parrots. *10 Kaya Corsow, across from
Karel's Beach Bar, tel. 599/7-8434. AE, MC, V. Inexpensive–
Moderate.*

China Garden Restaurant and Bar. Despite its name, this place
has an everything-you-could-ever-want menu, from American

sandwiches to shark's-fin soup, steaks, lobster, even omelets. But Cantonese dishes are still the specialty. Try the goat Chinese-style, anything in black-bean sauce, or one of the sweet-and-sour dishes. Lots of locals turn up between 5 and 7 PM to have a drink and watch the latest in sports on the bar's cable TV. At press time, the sleazy decor was scheduled for a change. *47 Kaya Grandi, tel. 599/7–8480. Reservations suggested in season. AE, DC, MC, V. Closed Tues. Inexpensive.*

Mona Lisa Bar & Restaurant. This restaurant offers authentic Dutch fare, along with a few Indonesian dishes, at unbeatable prices. Its most famous plate is the pork tenderloin *sate* drizzled with a special peanut-butter sauce. Somehow, Mona Lisa has become renowned for fresh vegetables, though God knows where they come from, since nearly everything in Bonaire has to be imported. This is a late-night hangout for local schmoozing and light snacks, which are served until about 2 AM. *15 Kaya Grandi, tel. 599/7–8718. Closed Sun. MC, V. Inexpensive.*

Lodging

Hotels on Bonaire, with the exception of Harbour Village, cater primarily to avid divers who spend their days under water and come up for air only for evening festivities. Hence, hotel facilities tend to be modest with small swimming pools and limited service. Groomed sandy beaches are not a requisite for a hotel, but an efficient dive shop is. Many resort accommodations have fully equipped kitchens. Although the larger hotels offer a variety of meal plans, most are on the European Plan. As a general rule, hotel restaurants can be significantly more expensive than restaurants in town.

Highly recommended lodgings are indicated by a star ★.

Category	Cost*
Very Expensive	over $225
Expensive	$140–$225
Moderate	$100–$140
Inexpensive	under $100

* *All prices are for a standard double room for two in high season, excluding a $4.10 per person, per night government room tax and a 10% service charge.*

Hotels
★

Harbour Village. This is the resort for divers who want the best of both an upscale resort and a dive vacation. Set on a point of land jutting into the Caribbean, this resort first opened in January 1990 under the Sonesta name, but is now managed by the South American family who built it. Wide walkways bordered by lush foliage and blooming tropical flowers separate eight low-rise, southwestern-style buildings, with Moorish arches, red barrel-tile roofs, and an adobe color scheme. The palm tree–lined beach is wide and inviting. While not as impressive as the grounds or building exteriors, the rooms and suites are done in dusty rose and aqua and have French doors leading to a terrace or patio (except for second-story courtyard rooms), white tile floors, and pale wood furniture. Rooms are similar in decor, with price categories determined by the view—garden courtyard, marina, or ocean. Each room has a hair dryer, cable TV, amenity package, and direct-dial telephone. There is a full-service dive shop and a water-sports concession that offers sailing, windsurfing, deep-sea fishing, kayaking, and powerboat rentals. A new fitness center offers an air-conditioned state-of-the-art workout. Harbour Village appeals to those who like the quiet life. It's also the only resort on Bonaire to offer room service. The restaurant, which overlooks the pool, serves full American buffet breakfasts, international *à la carte* lunches, and gourmet, fixed-price, multicourse dinners. The dockside bar closes at 8 PM. The hotel has a large marina in front with 72 slips. *Box 312, tel. 599/7–7500 or 800/424–0004, fax 599/7–7507. 64 rooms, 8 oceanfront suites, 30 condominium units. Facilities: 2 restaurants, 2 bars/lounges, dive center, dive lockers at beach, fitness center, meeting room, water-sports center, pool, bicycles, baby-sitting, marina, gift shop. AE, DC, MC, V. EP, BP, MAP, FAP. Very Expensive.*

★ **Captain Don's Habitat.** With its recent expansion and massive renovation, the Habitat can no longer pass itself off as a mere guest house for divers, once a sort of extended home of Captain Don Stewart, the island's wildest sharpshooting personality. Stewart's Curaçaon partners have poured money into this resort, adding a set of upscale rooms (Junior suites) and then a long row of private villas (the Hamlet section) that rank among the island's best: all with ocean-view verandas, full kitchens, and spacious, stylish arrangements. The rooms in the original 11 cottages are spacious but in need of renovation (which is scheduled to be completed by 1994). The atmosphere at the Habitat is laid back and easygoing, with the emphasis on the staff's personal warmth rather than on spick-and-span efficiency. The beachfront property units are spaced widely apart, and the grounds have been landscaped with rocks and cacti. Be sure to meet Captain Don, who shows up twice a week just to say hello; shoot the breeze; and tell his incredible tales, most of which are actually true. In August, the resort hosts two all-inclusive family weeks with day-long fun and educational activities for children. A full dive center with seven boats, complete with a resident photo pro, rounds out the picture. *Kaya Gob. Debrot 103, Box 88, tel. 599/7–8290. U.S. representative: Habitat North American, tel. 800/327–6709, fax 599/7–8240. 11 cottages, 11 villas, 16 rooms. Facilities: 2 bars, restaurant, gift shop, pool, cruises, baby-sitting, laundry facilities, bicycles, dive center, photo labs. AE, DC, MC, V. EP, BP, MAP, FAP. Expensive.*

Coral Regency Resort. You'll find the Coral Regency along the coastal strip where most of Bonaire's resort hotels are found. The 10 coral-pink, two-story buildings, composed of 32 studios and one- and two-bedroom suites, are situated in a quadrangle around a small pool where guests sunbathe—there's no beach for lounging. As a result, for privacy, the rooms on the second floor are more desirable than those on the first. The studio apartments have a small but complete kitchen, while the suites have a spacious living room with overhead fan, a large balcony looking out to sea (wonderful for morning breakfasts), and a fully equipped kitchen—including microwave and blender. The air-conditioned bedrooms are compact, with little space left over after the huge king-size bed or two twins, but the marble-tiled bathrooms are large. Paul's Oceanfront Bar & Restaurant and the dive shop, a Neal Watson Undersea Adventures affiliate, add to the offerings. This time-share hotel is geared to quiet divers and nondivers in search of upscale, modern accommodations, who are traveling with their children or who prefer the option of cooking their own meals. More villa units are planned, but these will be in a separate enclave and several hundred yards from the waterfront. *Kaya Gob, Debrot 90, Box 380, tel. 599/7–5580, fax 599/7–5680; in the U.S., tel. 800/327– 8150. 32 suites. Facilities: bar, restaurant, pool, dive center, direct-dial phones, cable TV. AE, DC, MC, V. CP, BP, MAP, FAP. Expensive.*

★ **Sand Dollar Beach Club.** These spacious apartments combine a European design with a tropical rattan decor. Each has a full kitchen, a large bathroom, a couch that turns into a queen-size bed, and a private patio or terrace that looks out to the sea and the low silhouette of Klein Bonaire. Some units also have telephones. This American enclave is for serious divers and their families. There's daily maid service, and the maids will even do your laundry for $4 a load. There's an on-premise PADI five-star dive center, a limited activities club for children and two lighted tennis courts. There is a beach, but it's minuscule and disappears at high tide. The resort's waterfront Green Parrot restaurant serves breakfast, lunch, and dinner, and there's a grocery store for those who like to cook. *Kaya Grandi, tel. 599/ 7–8738, fax 599/7–8760; in the U.S., tel. 800/766–6016 or 617/ 821–1012. 77 studio, 1-, 2-, and 3-bedroom units and 8 2-bedroom town houses. Facilities: restaurant, bar, dive center, photo lab, pool, 2 lighted tennis courts, outdoor showers, cable TV, strip shopping center, grocery/convenience store. AE, DC, MC, V. EP, BP, MAP, FAP. Expensive.*

Sorobon Beach Resort. Here's the perfect place for acting out all your *Swept Away* fantasies. The Sorobon is an intimate cluster of cottages on a private sandy beach at Lac Bay, on the southeast shore. This delightfully unpretentious and small resort is for "naturalists" who take its clothing-optional motto literally. Guests are a fair mix of Europeans and Americans. New Agers will like the natural look of the Scandinavian wood furniture. The chalets are arranged in a "V" shape so as to give the resort more openness and access to the beach. Each chalet consists of two small one-bedroom units, each with simple furnishings, an older-style kitchen, and a shower-only bath. In keeping with the get-away-from-it-all concept, there's no air-conditioning, TV, or telephone. A daily shuttle will take you to town. Relax sitting around full-moon bonfires, playing ping-pong, or enjoying a shiatsu massage all right on the beach. The heady windsurfing in Lac Bay, a result of the unbeatable combo of shallow bay and strong trade winds, draws raves. Restaurant, bar, volleyball, nature-oriented book and video library, even a telescope to view the stunning night skies are all for the asking. But act blasé when the manager arrives wrapped in a towel. *Box 14, tel. 599/7–8080, fax 599/7–5363. 25 cottages. Facilities: kitchenettes, restaurant, bar, library, center. AE, MC, V. EP. Expensive.*

Divi Flamingo Beach Resort and Casino. The Divi Flamingo is the closest thing you'll find to a small village on Bonaire—a plantation-style resort that will serve your every need. No matter which hotel you're staying at, reserve a table at the Chibi Chibi Restaurant, where you can hear ocean waves pounding beneath the floorboards. The resort consists of the hotel and the Club Flamingo studio apartments, which have the newest and nicest rooms. This is the oldest hotel on the island—a former internment camp for German POWs during

World War II. Though plans still call for sorely needed renovations, even those that have been "renovated" still cry out for new furnishings and another coat of fresh paint. Even though the resort is definitely showing signs of age, because of its dive facility and upbeat activities programs it still receives a fair share of repeat guests. The dive facility, called Dive Bonaire, was founded by world-class expert Peter Hughes and features some of the best photo labs in the Caribbean. Several rooms are accessible to the handicapped, and the dive operation even has specially trained masters who teach scuba diving to handicapped individuals and dive with them. The on-premise tennis pro offers free clinics every Tuesday and Wednesday mornings, there's a daily activities program, live bands perform several nights a week, and the island's only casino—billed as the world's only barefoot gaming center—is here as well. The all-inclusive package offers great value for the price. *J. A. Abraham Blvd., tel. 599/7–8285. U.S. representative: Divi Hotels, tel. 800/367–3484, fax 599/7–8238. 105 rooms, 40 time-share units. Facilities: casino, 2 restaurants, 2 pools, 2 dive shops, jewelry store, lighted tennis court, 3 bars, 2 car-rental desks, tour desk, Jacuzzi, boutique. AE, D, MC, V. EP, MAP, All-inclusive. Expensive–Moderate.*

Sunset Beach Hotel. In 1990 a group of businessmen purchased this hotel (then called the Bonaire Beach Hotel) and began renovations. New beds were brought in, walls were painted, wood floors were polished, and new drapes were ordered. Each room got a digital safety vault, direct-dial telephone, remote-control color TV, minirefrigerator, and coffee maker. Age, however, has its drawbacks, and here the drawback is the location of the original buildings: They are all set back from the shore, giving even the best rooms only garden views. And in spite of the new amenities, the old-looking rooms and bathrooms lack brightness and appeal. Still, the 12 acres encompass one of the island's better hotel beaches (in contrast to the swimming pool, which is tiny), a miniature golf course, a water-sports concession that offers more than any other on the island, and a romantic thatch-roof restaurant overlooking the sea. Unfortunately, the food is not the island's best, and although the service is superfriendly, it is not always efficient. Divers come for the complete on-premise scuba center, Dive Inn, which has three dive boats. Nondivers can rent Sunfish, Windsurfers, and snorkeling gear, or go parasailing or boogie boarding. The Bonairian Theme night, with native buffet, folkloric dance show, steel band, and dancing waitresses, costs $20 per person. *Kaya Gob. Debrot 75, Box 333, tel. 599/7–8448. U.S./Canada rep: 800/333–1212, 800/344–4439 or 800/223–9815, fax 599/7–8118. 142 rooms, 3 1-bedroom suites. Facilities: alfresco restaurant, bar/lounge, beach, dive center, water-sports center, water taxi to Klein Bonaire, miniature golf, shuffleboard, 2 lighted tennis courts, billiards, ping-pong, tour desk, gift shop, car rental. AE, MC, V. EP, MAP. Moderate.*

★ **Bruce Bowker's Carib Inn.** Sixteen years ago, American diver Bruce Bowker started his small diving lodge out of a private home, continually adding on and refurbishing the air-conditioned inn. New rattan furnishings, completely renovated kitchens, and a family-style atmosphere have turned this inn into one of the island's best bets, albeit one that gets booked far in advance by repeat guests. Bowker knows everybody by name and loves to fill special requests. The two units with no kitchen have a refrigerator and electric kettle, but for more involved dining, you'll have to leave the premises—there's no restaurant. (Richard's Waterfront Restaurant is right next door.) Those who prefer to cook can shop for supplies at the grocery store just across the street. Nervous virgin divers will enjoy Bowker's small scuba classes (one or two people); PADI certification is available. *Box 68, tel. 599/7–8819. U.S. rep: ITR, tel. 800/223–9815 or 212/545–8649, fax 599/7–599/7–5295. 9 units. Facilities: pool, scuba classes, dive center, retail dive store, cable TV. AE, MC, V. EP. Inexpensive.*

Buddy Dive Center. Europeans who tend to eschew luxury and require only basic amenities with matching rates enjoy this growing complex situated on the beach. In keeping with its no-frills style, the five units on the ground level have no air-conditioning and no TV, while the five second-floor units have air-conditioning. All these original 10 "apartments" are tiny but clean, with a kitchenette, tile floors, twin beds, a sleep sofa, and a shower-only bathroom. In January 1993, the first of two new buildings housing more upscale, spacious, and air-conditioned two- and three-bedroom apartments opened. A dive operation and pool is also on the premises. *Kaya Gob. Debrot, Box 231, tel 599/7–8065 or 800/359–0747, fax 599/7–2647. 10 apartments and 15 2- and 3-bedroom condominium units. Facilities: pool with bar, dive shop. AE, MC, V. EP. Inexpensive.*

Home and Apartment Rentals The **Bonaire Government Tourist Office** (tel. 800/U–BONAIR) can help you locate suitable guest houses and smaller rental apartments in Bonaire. Rental apartments are also available through **Bonaire Sunset Villas** (tel. 800/223–9815, fax 599/7–8118), **Sunset Oceanfront Apartments** (tel. 800/223–9815, fax 599/7–8865), **Club Laman Caribe** (fax 599/7–7741), or **Black Durgon Inn Properties** (tel. 800/526–2370).

The Arts and Nightlife

The Arts Slide shows of underwater scenes keep both divers and non-divers fascinated in the evenings. The best is Dee Scarr, a dive guide whose show "Touch the Sea" is presented Monday night at 8:45, from the beginning of November to the end of June, at **Captain Don's Habitat** (tel. 599/7–8290). Check with the Habitat for other shows throughout the week. **Sunset Beach Hotel** (tel. 599/7–8448) offers a free one-hour slide show every Wednesday evening at 7. **Flamingo Beach Resort** (tel. 599/7–8285) offers a free underwater video, "Discover the Caribbean," on Sunday night at 7 PM.

The best singer on the island is guitarist **Cai-Cai Cecelia,** who performs with his duo Monday night at the **Flamingo Beach Resort,** Wednesday night at **Sunset Beach Hotel,** and Thursday night at **Captain Don's Habitat.** He sings his own compositions, as well as Harry Belafonte classics. A local duo also sings and plays music every Thursday night at the **Divi Flamingo Beach Resort.** The Kunuku Band plays every Friday and Sunday for Happy Hour at **Captain Don's Habitat.** The M & M Duo also entertains three nights a week at the Chibi Chibi restaurant at the **Divi Flamingo Beach Resort & Casino.**

Nightlife Most divers are exhausted after they finish their third, fourth, or fifth dive of the day, which probably explains why there's only one disco in Bonaire. Nevertheless, **E Wowo** (Kralendijk, at the corner of Kaya Grandi and Kaya L. D. Gerharts, no phone) is usually packed in high season, so get there early. The name E Wowo means "eye" in Papiamento, illustrated with two flashing op-art eyes on the wall. Recorded music is loud, and the large circular bar seats a lot of action. The entrance fee varies according to the season.

For late-night conversations, **The Rendez-Vous Restaurant** (Kaya L. D. Gerharts 3, tel. 599/7–8454) is open late, with light pastries and espresso, as are the **Mona Lisa Bar & Restaurant** (Kaya Grandi 15, tel. 599/7–8718) and **Raffles** (*see* Dining, *above*).

The popular bar **Karel's** (tel. 599/7–8434), on the waterfront across from the Zeezicht Restaurant, sits on stilts above the sea and is *the* place for mingling with islanders, dive pros, and tourists. Closed Monday.

Friday and Saturday nights are party time, when Bonairians gather along the main street of Kralendijk to dance to informal bands that set up on the sidewalk.

The island has only one casino, the **Flamingo Beach Hotel Casino,** which opens at 8 PM, and is closed on Sunday.

7 The British Virgin Islands

Tortola, Virgin Gorda, and Outlying Islands

Updated by
Jordan Simon

Serene, seductive, and spectacularly beautiful even by Caribbean standards, the British Virgin Islands are happily free of the runaway development that has detracted from the charm of so many West Indian islands. The pleasures to be found here are of the understated sort—sailing around the multitude of tiny, nearby islands; diving to the wreck of the RMS *Rhone*, sunk off Salt Island in 1867; exploring the twisting passages and sunlit grottoes of Virgin Gorda's famed Baths; and settling down on some breeze-swept terrace to admire the sunset.

One reason the B.V.I. have retained this sense of blissful simplicity is their strict building codes. No building can rise higher than the surrounding palms—two stories is the limit. The lack of direct air flights from the mainland United States also helps the British islands retain the endearing qualities of yesteryear's Caribbean. One first has to get to Puerto Rico, 60 miles to the west, or to nearby St. Thomas in the United States Virgin Islands and catch a small plane to the little airports on Beef Island/Tortola and Virgin Gorda. Many of the travelers who return year after year prefer arriving by water, either aboard their own ketches and yawls or on one of the convenient ferryboats that cross the turquoise waters between St. Thomas and Tortola.

Sailing has always been a popular activity in the B.V.I. The first arrivals here were a romantic seafaring tribe, the Siboney Indians. Christopher Columbus was the first European to visit, during his second voyage to the New World, in 1493. The redoubtable "Admiral of the Ocean Seas," impressed by the number of islands dotting the horizon, named them *Las Once Mil Virgines* (The 11,000 Virgins) in honor of the 11,000 virgin-companions of Saint Ursula, martyred in the fourth century. Columbus's arithmetic might have been weaker than his navigational skills, or else he was given to exaggeration; there are, in fact, just over 50 islands in the archipelago. Tortola, about 10 square miles, is the largest, and Virgin Gorda, with 8 square miles, ranks second. Scattered around them are the islands of Jost Van Dyke; Great Camanoe; Norman; Peter; Salt; Cooper; Dead Chest; the low-lying, coral Anegada; and others.

In the ensuing years, the Spaniards passed through these waters seeking gold, and, finding none, they quickly moved on to the richer pastures of Mexico. The next seafarers to arrive were a number of pirates who found the islands' hidden coves and treacherous reefs an ideal base from which to prey on passing galleons crammed with Mexican and Peruvian gold, silver, and spices. Among the most notorious of these predatory men were Blackbeard Teach; Bluebeard; Captain Kidd; and Sir Francis Drake, who lent his name to the channel that sweeps through the two main clusters of the B.V.I.

In the 17th century, these colorful cutthroats were replaced by the Dutch. The Dutch, in turn, were soon sent packing by the British, who retained control of the islands for nearly three centuries. The British established a plantation economy, and for the next 150 years they developed the sugar industry. African slaves were brought in to work the cane fields while the plantation owners and their families reaped the benefits. When slavery was abolished in 1838, the plantation economy quickly faltered, and the majority of the white population returned to Europe.

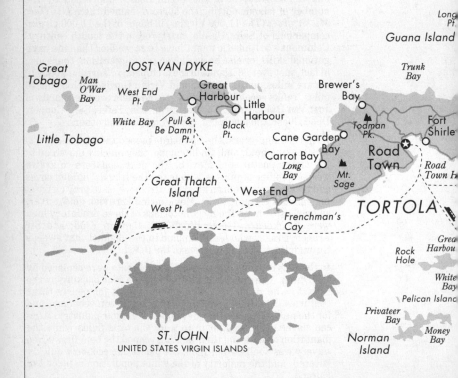

ATLANTIC

Long Pt.

Guana Island

Great Tobago

Man O'War Bay

JOST VAN DYKE

West End Pt.

Great Harbour

White Bay

Pull & Be Damn Pt.

Little Harbour

Black Pt.

Brewer's Bay

Trunk Bay

Fort Shirle

Little Tobago

Cane Garden Bay

Carrot Bay

Todman Pk.

Road Town

Long Bay

Mt. Sage

Road Town H

Great Thatch Island

West Pt.

West End

Frenchman's Cay

TORTOLA

Grea Harbou

Rock Hole

White Bay

Pelican Island

Privateer Bay

ST. JOHN
UNITED STATES VIRGIN ISLANDS

Norman Island

Money Bay

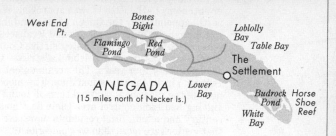

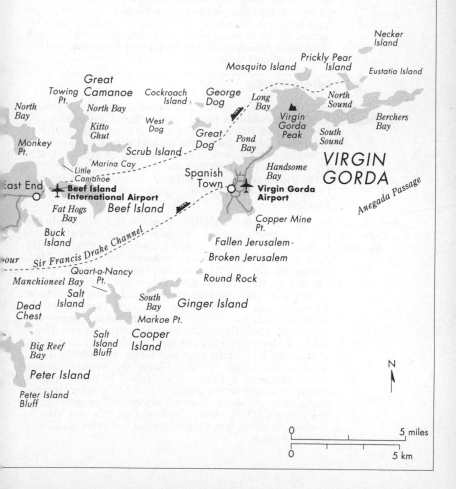

West End
Pt.

Bones
Bight

Flamingo
Pond

Red
Pond

Loblolly
Bay

Table Bay

The
Settlement

ANEGADA
(15 miles north of Necker Is.)

Lower
Bay

Budrock
Pond

Horse
Shoe
Reef

White
Bay

O C E A N

Necker
Island

Prickly Pear
Island

Mosquito Island

Eustatia Island

Great
Camanoe

Towing
Pt.

Cockroach
Island

George
Dog

Long
Bay

North
Sound

North
Bay

North Bay

West
Dog

Great
Dog

Virgin
Gorda
Peak

South
Sound

Berchers
Bay

Monkey
Pt.

Kitto
Ghut

Scrub Island

Pond
Bay

VIRGIN
GORDA

Marina Cay

Little
Camanoe

Handsome
Bay

Anegada Passage

Spanish
Town

East End

Beef Island
International Airport

Virgin Gorda
Airport

Fat Hogs
Bay

Beef Island

Copper Mine
Pt.

Buck
Island

Fallen Jerusalem

Sir Francis Drake Channel

Broken Jerusalem

our

Quart-a-Nancy
Pt.

Round Rock

Manchioneel Bay

Salt
Island

South
Bay

Ginger Island

Dead
Chest

Markoe Pt.

Big Reef
Bay

Salt
Island
Bluff

Cooper
Island

Peter Island

N

Peter Island
Bluff

0					5 miles

0			5 km

The islands dozed, a forgotten corner of the British empire, until the early 1960s. In 1966, a new constitution, granting greater autonomy to the islands, was approved. While the governor is still appointed by the Queen of England, his limited powers concentrate on external affairs and local security. Other matters are administered by the Legislative Council, consisting of representatives from nine island districts. General elections are held every four years. The arrangement seems to suit the British Virgin Islanders just fine: The mood is serene, with none of the occasional political turmoil found on other islands. Having had tacit control over their destinies for more than a century and a half, local residents now have no reason to feel that visitors are more than welcome guests.

The 1960s also saw the arrival of a few profit-seeking souls, notably Laurance Rockefeller and American-expatriate Charlie Cary, who became convinced that the islands' balmy weather, powder-soft beaches, and splendid sailing would make them an ideal holiday destination. Attempts at building a small tourist industry began in 1965, when Rockefeller set about creating the Little Dix resort on Virgin Gorda. A few years later, Cary and his wife, Ginny, established The Moorings marina complex on Tortola, and sailing in the area burgeoned. Today the majority of jobs on the islands are tourism-related. British Virgin Islanders love their unspoiled tropical home and are determined to maintain its easygoing charms, for both themselves and the travelers who are their guests.

Before You Go

Tourist Information Information about the B.V.I. is available through the **British Virgin Islands Tourist Board** (370 Lexington Ave., Suite 416, New York, NY 10017, tel. 212/696–0400 or 800/835–8530) or at the **British Virgin Islands Information Office** in San Francisco (1686 Union St., Suite 305, San Francisco, CA 94123, tel. 415/775–0344; in CA, tel. 800/922–4873; nationwide, tel. 800/232–7770). British travelers can write or visit the **BVI Information Office** (110 St. Martin's Lane, London WC2N 4DY, tel. 071/2404259).

Arriving and Departing By Plane No nonstop service is available from the United States to the B.V.I.; connections are usually made through San Juan, Puerto Rico, or St. Thomas, U.S.V.I. Airlines serving both San Juan and St. Thomas include **American** (tel. 800/433–7300), **Continental** (tel. 800/231–0856), and **Delta** (tel. 800/323–2323). **Key Airlines** (tel. 800/786–2386) flies to and from St. Thomas from major cities through its Savannah, Georgia hub on Thursdays and Sundays. From San Juan, carriers include **American Eagle** (tel. 800/433–7300), and **Sunaire Express** (809/495–2480), which fly to both Beef Island/Tortola and Virgin Gorda. Airlines flying to those same two destinations from St. Thomas are Sunaire Express and **Virgin Air** (809/495–1735); American Eagle flies to Virgin Gorda only. Sunaire Express also flies between St. Croix and Beef Island/Tortola. Regularly scheduled service between the B.V.I. and most other Caribbean islands is provided by **Leeward Islands Air Transport (LIAT)** (tel. 809/495–1187). Many Caribbean islands can also be reached via **Gorda Aero Service** (Tortola, tel. 809/495–2271), a charter service.

By Boat Various ferries connect St. Thomas, U.S.V.I., with Tortola and Virgin Gorda. **Native Son, Inc.** (tel. 809/495–4617), operates three ferries (*Native Son, Oriole,* or *Voyager Eagle*), and offers service between St. Thomas and Tortola (West End and Road Town) daily and between St. Thomas and Spanish Town, Virgin Gorda, on Wednesday and Sunday. **Smiths Ferry Services** (tel. 809/494–4430 or 809/494–2355) carries passengers between downtown St. Thomas and Road Town and West End on Monday through Saturday, offers daily service between Red Hook on St. Thomas and Tortola's West End, and travels between St. Thomas and Spanish Town on Sunday. **Inter-Island Boat Services'** Sundance II (tel. 809/776–6597) connects St. John and West End on Tortola daily.

Passports and Visas Upon entering the B.V.I., U.S. and Canadian citizens are required to present some proof of citizenship, if not a passport then a birth certificate or voter-registration card with a driver's license or photo ID.

Language British English, with a West Indian inflection, is the language spoken.

Precautions Although there are generally no perils from drinking the water in these islands it is a good idea to ask if the water is potable when you check in to your hotel. Insects, notably mosquitoes, are not usually a problem in these breeze-blessed isles, but it is always a good idea to bring some repellent along. Animals in the B.V.I. are not dangerous but they can be road hazards, if shy ones. Give goats, sheep, horses, and cows the right of way.

Beware of the little varmints called "no-see 'ums." They're for real and are especially pesky at twilight near the water. So if you're going for an evening stroll on the beach, apply some type of repellent liberally. No-see 'um bites itch worse than mosquito bites and take a lot longer to go away. Prevention is the best cure, but witch hazel (or a dab of gin or vodka) offers *some* relief if they get you.

Further Reading Vernon Pickering's *Concise History of the British Virgin Islands* is a wordy but worthy guide to the events and personalities that shaped the region. Pickering also produces the *Official Tourist Handbook* for the B.V.I.

For linguists, *What a Pistarckle!* by Lito Valls gives the origins of the many expressions you'll be hearing, and historians will enjoy *Eyewitness Accounts of Slavery in the Danish West Indies* by Isidor Paiewonsky and *Conquest of Eden* by Michael Paiewonsky. For sailors, Simon Scott has written a *Cruising Guide to the Virgin Islands*.

On the B.V.I., the *Island Sun* and *The BVI Beacon* are the best local papers for everything from entertainment listings to local gossip. The *Welcome Tourist Guide* is comprehensive and available free at airports and larger hotels.

Staying in the British Virgin Islands

Important Addresses On Tortola there is a **B.V.I. Tourist Board Office** at the center of Road Town near the ferry dock, just south of Wickham's Cay I (Box 134, Road Town, Tortola, tel. 809/494–3134). For all kinds of useful information about these islands, including rates and phone numbers, get a free copy of *The Welcome Tourist Guide*, available at hotels and other places.

Emergencies   Dial 999 for a medical emergency. On Tortola there is **Peebles Hospital** in Road Town (tel. 809/494–3497). Pharmacies in Road Town include **J. R. O'Neal Drug Store** (tel. 809/494–2292) and **Lagoon Plaza Drug Store** (tel. 809/494–2498).

Currency   British though they are, the B.V.I. have the U.S. dollar as the standard currency.

Taxes and Service Charges   Hotels collect a 7% accommodations tax, which they will add to your bill along with a 10% service charge. Restaurants may put a similar service charge on the bill, or they may leave it up to you. For those leaving the B.V.I. by air, the departure tax is $5; by sea it is $4.

Guided Tours   If you'd like to do some chauffeured sightseeing on Tortola, get in touch with the **B.V.I. Taxi Association** (three-person minimum, tel. 809/494–2875, 809/494–2322, or 809/495–2378), **Style's Taxi Service** (tel. 809/494–2260 during the day or 809/494–3341 at night), or **Travel Plan Tours** (tel. 809/494–2872). **Scato's Bus Service** (tel. 809/494–2365), in Road Town, provides public transportation, special tours with group rates, and beach outings. Guided tours on Virgin Gorda can be arranged through **Andy's Taxi and Jeep Rental** (tel. 809/495–5252) or **Mahogany Rentals and Island Tours** (tel. 809/495–5469).

Getting Around   **Speedy's Fantasy** (tel. 809/495–5240) makes the run between
Boat   Road Town, Tortola, Spanish Town and Virgin Gorda daily. Running daily between Virgin Gorda's North Sound (Bitter End Yacht Club) and Beef Island, Tortola are **North Sound Express** (tel. 809/494–2746) boats. There are also daily boats between Tortola's CSY Dock just east of Road Town and Peter Island. **Jost Van Dyke Ferry Service** (tel. 809/495–2775) makes the Jost Van Dyke–Tortola run daily via the **When** ferry, and the *Reel World* ferry (tel. 809/495–9277) also makes daily trips between Jost Van Dyke and Tortola.

Cars   Driving on Tortola and Virgin Gorda is not for the timid. Roller-coaster roads with breathtaking ascents and descents and tight turns that give new meaning to the term "hair-pin curves" are the norm. It's a challenge well worth trying, however; the ever-changing views of land, sea, and neighboring islands are among the most spectacular in the Caribbean. Most people will strongly recommend renting a four-wheel drive vehicle. Driving is *à l'Anglais*, on the left side of the road. It's easy to become accustomed to it if you drive slowly, think before you make a turn, and pay attention when driving in and out of the occasional traffic circle, locally called a "roundabout." Speed limits are 30–40 mph outside town and 10–15 mph in residential areas. A valid B.V.I. driver's license is required and can be obtained for $10 at car rental agencies. You must be at least 25 and have a valid driver's license from another country to obtain one.

On Tortola, car rentals are available from **AVIS** (tel. 809/494–3322), **Budget** (tel. 809/494–2639), **Hertz** (tel. 809/495–4405), and **National** (tel. 809/494–3197). On Virgin Gorda, try **Mahogany Rentals** (tel. 809/495–5469) or **Andy's Taxi and Jeep Rental** (tel. 809/495–5252).

Taxis   Your hotel staff will be happy to summon a taxi for you. On Tortola, there is a B.V.I. Taxi Association stand in Road Town near the ferry dock (tel. 809/494–3456) and Wickhams Cay I (tel. 809/494–2322) and one on Beef Island, at the airport (tel. 809/

495–2466). You can also usually find a taxi at the Sopers Hole ferry dock, West End, where ferries from St. Thomas arrive. On Virgin Gorda, Mahogany or Andy's (*see above*) also provide taxi service.

Buses For information about rates and schedules on Tortola, call **Scato's Bus Service** (tel. 809/494–2365).

Mopeds and Scooters and bicycles can be rented on Tortola from **Hero's Bi-**
Bicycles **cycle Rental** (tel. 809/494–3536). On Virgin Gorda, **Honda Scooter Rental** (tel. 809/495–5212) rents mopeds.

Telephones and The area code for the B.V.I. is 809. To call anywhere in the
Mail B.V.I. once you've arrived, dial only the last five digits: Instead of dialing 494–1234, just dial 4–1234. A local call from a public pay phone costs 25¢. Pay phones are frequently on the blink, but using them is often easier with a **Caribbean Phone Card**, available in $5, $10, and $20 denominations. The cards are sold at most major hotels and many stores and can be used all over the Caribbean. For credit-card or collect long-distance calls to the United States, look for special U.S.A. Direct phones that are linked to an ATT operator, or dial 111 from a pay phone and charge the call to your Master Charge or Visa. U.S.A. Direct and pay phones can be found at most hotels and in towns.

There are post offices in Road Town on Tortola and in Spanish Town on Virgin Gorda. Postage for a first-class letter to the United States is 35¢ and for a postcard 20¢. (It might be noted that postal efficiency is not first class in the B.V.I.) For a small fee, **Rush It** in Road Town (809/494–4421) or Spanishtown (809/495–5821) offers most U.S. mail and UPS services via St. Thomas the next day.

Opening and Stores are generally open from 9 to 5 Monday through Satur-
Closing Times day. Bank hours are Monday through Thursday 9–2:30 and Friday 9–2:30 and 4:30–6.

Exploring Tortola

Numbers in the margin correspond to points of interest on the Tortola map.

The drives on Tortola are dramatic, with dizzying roller-coaster dips and climbs and glorious views. Leave plenty of time to negotiate the hilly roads and drink in the irresistible vistas at nearly every hairpin turn. Distractions are the real danger here, from the glittering mosaic of azure sea, white skies, and emerald islets to the ambling cattle and grazing goats roadside.

Before setting out on your tour of Tortola, you may want to devote an hour or so to strolling down Main Street and along the
❶ waterfront in **Road Town,** the laid-back island capital. A good place to start is at the General Post Office facing **Sir Olva Georges Square,** across from the ferry dock and customs office. (Locals don't use street names much because they *know* where everything is, so if you ask directions, ask how to get to such-and-such restaurant or store, rather than how to find the street.) The hands of the clock atop this building permanently point to 10 minutes to 5, rather appropriate in this drowsy town, where time does seem to be standing still.

The eastern side of Sir Olva Georges Square is open to the harbor, and a handful of elderly Tortolans can generally be found sitting under the square's shade trees enjoying the breeze that

Tortola

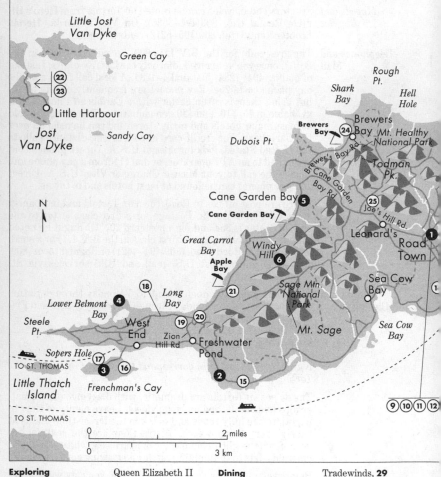

ATLANTIC OCEAN

Little Jost
Van Dyke

Green Cay

22
23

Little Harbour

Jost
Van Dyke

Sandy Cay

Rough
Pt.

Shark
Bay

Hell
Hole

Dubois Pt.

Brewers
Bay 24 Brewers Bay

Mt. Healthy
National Park

Brewer's Bay Rd

B. Cane Garden Bay Rd

Todman
Pk.

Cane Garden Bay 5

Cane Garden Bay

25

Joe's Hill Rd.

Leonard's

Road
Town

1

Great Carrot
Bay

Apple
Bay

Windy
Hill 6

21

Sage Mtn.
National
Park

Sea Cow
Bay

18 Long
Bay

Lower Belmont
Bay 4

Steele
Pt.

West
End

19 20

Zion
Hill Rd

Mt. Sage

Sea Cow
Bay

Freshwater
Pond

Sopers Hole 17

TO ST. THOMAS

3 16

Little Thatch
Island

Frenchman's Cay

2

15

9 10 11 12

TO ST. THOMAS

N

0 ──────────── 2 miles
0 ──────────── 3 km

Exploring
Beef Island, **7**
Belmont Point, **4**
Callwood Distillery, **6**
Cane Garden Bay, **5**
Fort Recovery, **2**
Frenchman's Cay, **3**

Queen Elizabeth II
Bridge, **8**
Road Town, **1**

Dining
The Apple, **20**
Brandywine Bay, **28**
The Fishtrap, **9**
Pusser's Landing, **17**
Skyworld, **25**
Spaghetti Junction, **10**
Sugar Mill, **20**

Tradewinds, **29**
The Upstairs, **14**
Virgin Queen, **13**

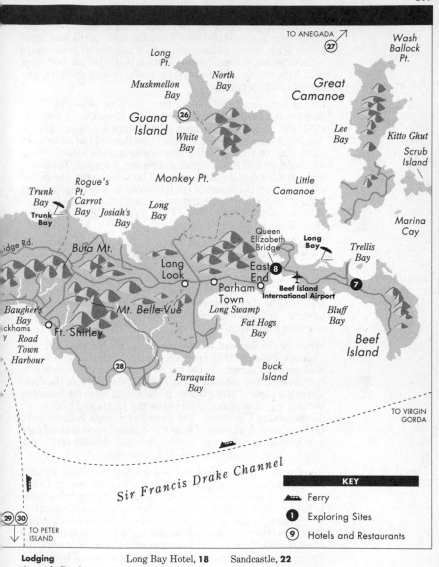

sweeps in from the water here. The General Post Office and government offices occupy two other sides of the square, and small shops line the third side. From the front of the post office follow Main Street to the right past a number of small shops housed in traditional pastel-painted West Indian buildings with high-pitched, corrugated tin roofs, bright shutters, and delicate fretwork trim.

On the left, about half a block from the post office, you'll encounter the **British Virgin Islands Folk Museum.** Founded in 1983, the museum has a large collection of artifacts from the Arawak Indians, some of the early settlers of the islands. Of particular interest are the triangular stones called *zemis*, which depict the Arawak gods Julihu and Yuccahu. The museum also has a display of a number of bottles, bowls, and plates salvaged from the wreck of the RMS *Rhone*, a British mail ship sunk off Salt Island in a hurricane in 1867. *Main St., no phone. Admission free. Open Mon., Tues., Thurs., Fri. 10–4; Sat. 10–1, though hours may vary.*

From Main Street, turn right onto Challwell Street, cross Waterfront Drive, and proceed a few hundred yards to **Wickham's Cay** to admire the boats moored at **Village Cay Marina.** Enjoy a broad view of the wide harbor, home of countless sailing vessels and yachts and a base of the well-known yacht-chartering enterprise The Moorings. You'll find a **B.V.I. Tourist Board** office to serve you right here as well as banks, a post office, and more stores and boutiques.

When you've finished wandering about Wickham's Cay, take Fishlock Road up to the courthouse, and make a right to get back on Main Street. At the police station, turn left onto Station Avenue and follow it to the **J. R. O'Neal Botanic Gardens.** These 2.8 acres of lush gardens include hothouses for ferns and orchids, gardens of medicinal herbs and plants and plants that bloom around Christmas, and plants and trees indigenous to the seashore. A number of flower shows and special events are held here during the year. *Station Ave., tel. 809/494–4557. Admission free. Open Mon.–Sat. 8–4, Sun. noon–5.*

Retrace your steps to Sir Olva Georges Square to pick up your car. From Road Town, head southwest along Waterfront Drive. Follow the coastline for 5 miles or so of the easiest driving in the B.V.I.: no hills; little traffic; lots of curves to keep things interesting; and the lovely, island-studded channel on your left. At Sea Cows Bay the road bends inland just a bit to pass through a small residential area, but it soon rejoins the water's edge. Sir Francis Drake Channel provides a kaleidoscope of turquoise, jade green, and morning-glory blue on your left, and further entertainment is provided by pelicans diving for their supper.

The next development you come to is **Nanny Cay.** Jutting out into the channel, this villagelike complex, with brightly painted buildings trimmed with lacy wood gingerbread, also contains a marina that can accommodate more than 200 yachts. A bar and restaurant, Peg Leg's Landing, offers a good place to stop for a soft drink and a view.

From Nanny Cay the route continues westward as St. John, the smallest of the three main U.S.V.I., comes into view across the channel. The road curves into **West End** past the ruins of the ❷ 17th-century Dutch **Fort Recovery,** a historic fort 30 feet in diameter, on the grounds of Fort Recovery Villas. There are no guided tours, but the public is welcome to stop by. The road ends at **Sopers Hole.** The waterfront here is dominated by the boat terminal and customs office that service the St. Thomas/ St. John/Tortola ferries. Turn around and head back, taking your very first right over a bridge, following signs to ➌ **Frenchman's Cay** and bear right on the other side of the bridge. There's a marina and a captivating complex of pastel-hued West Indian–style buildings with shady second-floor balconies, colonnaded arcades, shuttered windows, and gingerbread trim that showcase art galleries, boutiques, and restaurants.

Retrace your route out of West End, turn left, and head across the island on Zion Hill Road, a steep byway that rises and then drops precipitously to the other side of the island. Follow the road to the end and then turn left, drive up a steep hill, and be prepared for a dazzling view of **Long Bay,** a mile-long stretch of ➍ white sand secured on the west end by **Belmont Point,** a sugarloaf promontory that has been described as "a giant, green gumdrop." On this stretch of beach are the Long Bay Hotel, one of Tortola's more appealing resorts, and one of the island's two pitch-and-putt golf courses (Prospect Reef has the other). The large island visible in the distance is Jost Van Dyke. Follow North Coast Road northeast for about five minutes to **Capoon's Bay.**

Continue on to **Apple Bay** and the **Sugar Mill Hotel.** You'll want to inspect the 350-year-old mill that now serves as the hotel's main dining room and owners Jeff and Jinx Morgan's superb collection of Haitian primitive art. With any luck you'll meet the Morgans, a delightful couple with a seemingly inexhaustible repertoire of island stories.

Time Out **The Islands** (tel. 809/495–4355), the beachside bar and restaurant at the Sugar Mill, is a perfect spot to take a break for lunch. Salads and imaginative sandwiches (how about grilled peanut butter, bacon, and banana?) are served by an attentive staff.

Back in the car, follow the North Coast Road over **Windy Hill,** a gripping climb that affords splendid vistas of the sea and sky. ➎ You'll descend to sea level at **Cane Garden Bay:** Its crystalline water and silky stretch of sand make this enticing beach one of Tortola's most popular getaways. Its existence is no secret, however, and it can get crowded, though never uncomfortably so.

➏ And, for a *taste* of old-time Tortola, pop into the **Callwood Distillery** (Cane Garden Bay, no phone). A tropical version of moonshine bubbles away here most days. If you purchase some of this potent brew, it will almost certainly be presented in an old gin or vodka bottle. Now, *that's* recycling.

Go up Cane Garden Bay Road, bearing right, and follow the mountainous Ridge Road eastward. The views from this twisting road are breathtaking; the dizzying turn-offs that lead to tranquil bays like **Trunk, Carrot** and **Josiah's** would make a Grand Prix racer blanch. To return to Road Town, take Joe's Hill Road, the first right after the sign to Skyworld. Follow this right and bear left (and down) when you come to the "Y." Whoever is driving may gasp at how steeply the road drops, but passengers will be "oohing" and "aahing" at the spectacular, airplanelike view of Road Town and the harbor.

If you want to keep exploring, continue along Ridge Road, which ultimately winds up at East End, the sleepy village that **(7)** is the entryway to **Beef Island,** and the Beef Island Internation-**(8)** al Airport. The narrow **Queen Elizabeth II Bridge** connects Tortola and Beef Island, and you'll have to pay a toll to cross (50¢ for passenger cars, $1 for vans and trucks). It's worth it if only for the sight of the tolltaker extending a tin can attached to the end of a board through your car window to collect the fee. If you like interesting seashells, **Long Bay** on Beef Island has them for the picking.

From East End, proceed southwest on Blackburn Highway to Sir Francis Drake Highway, then west along the coast back to Road Town.

Exploring Virgin Gorda

Numbers in the margin correspond to points of interest on the Virgin Gorda map.

Virgin Gorda's main settlement, located on the island's south-**(1)** ern wing, is **Spanish Town,** a peaceful village so tiny that it barely qualifies as a town at all. Also known as The Valley, Spanish Town is home to a marina, a small cluster of shops, a couple of car-rental agencies, and the ferry slip. At the **Virgin Gorda Yacht Harbour** you can enjoy a stroll along the dock front or do a little browsing in the shops there.

Having rented a vehicle (you'll find a four-wheel drive the most satisfactory for negotiating some of the rougher terrain; remember that many of the roads are unmarked, so be prepared to stop and ask for directions), turn right from the marina parking lot onto Lee Road and head through the more populated, flat countryside of the south for about 15 minutes. Continue past the Fischer's Cove Beach Hotel on your right and look for **(2)** signs for **The Baths,** Virgin Gorda's most celebrated site. Giant boulders, brought to the surface eons ago by a vast volcanic eruption, are scattered about the beach and in the water. They are the size of small houses and form remarkable grottos. Climb between these rocks to swim in the many pools. Early morning and late afternoon are the best times to visit, since The Baths and the beach here are usually crowded with daytrippers visiting from Tortola.

Time Out There is a small bar called **Mad Dog's** (tel. 809/495–5830) set up at the top of the hill where you may want to pause for a cool drink and a sandwich after making the climb back to the parking area. Piña coladas are its specialty.

If it's privacy you crave, follow the shore north for a few hundred yards to reach several other quieter bays—Spring, The Crawl, Little Trunk, and Valley Trunk—or head south to Devil's Bay. These beaches have the same giant boulders as those found at The Baths.

Back in the car, retrace your route along Lee Road until you reach the southern edge of Spanish Town. Take a right onto Millionaire Road and proceed to a T-intersection, then make another right and follow Copper Mine Road, part of it unpaved, **(3)** to **Copper Mine Point.** Here you will discover a tall, stone chimney silhouetted against the sky and a small stone structure overlooking the sea. These are the ruins of a copper mine established here 400 years ago and worked first by the Spanish, then by English miners until the early 20th century. This is one of the few places in the B.V.I. where you won't see islands along the horizon.

Pass through town and continue north to **Savannah Bay** and **Pond Bay,** two pristine stretches of sand that mark the thin neck of land connecting Virgin Gorda's southern extension to the larger northern half. The view from this scenic elbow, **❹** called **Black Rock,** is of the Sir Francis Drake Channel to the northeast and the Caribbean Sea to the southwest. The road forks as it goes uphill. The unpaved left prong winds past the Mango Bay Club resort (and not much else) to Long Bay and not quite to Mountain Point. To continue exploring, take the road on the right, which winds uphill and looks down on beautiful South Sound. You'll notice nary a dwelling or sign of mundane civilization up here, only a green mountain slope on your left and a spectacular view down to South Sound on the right. From here, too, you can also look back and get a wonderful, living sense of Virgin Gorda's stringy, crooked shape: Back there, looking flat and almost like a separate island, is the Valley, which you've just left. Because of this shape, Virgin Gorda is one of those places where you can get a bird's-eye (or map's-eye) view of things from right inside your car.

You'll see a small sign on the left for the trail up to the 265-acre **❺** **Virgin Gorda Peak** National Park and the island's summit at 1,359 feet. It's about a 15-minute hike up to a small clearing, where you can climb a ladder to the platform of a wood observation tower. If you're keen for some woodsy exercise or just want to stretch your legs, go for it. The view at the top is dazzling if somewhat tree-obstructed. A bit farther on, the road forks again. The right fork leads to **Gun Creek,** where launches pick up passengers for the Bitter End, Biras Creek, and Drake's Anchorage, three of Virgin Gorda's most appealing hostelries.

The left fork will bring you to **Leverick Bay.** There is a resort here, with a cozy beach and marina, a restaurant, a cluster of shops, and some luxurious hillside villas to rent, all a little like a tucked-away tropical suburb.

Time Out Stop by **Pusser's Beach Bar** for a snack and browse in the nearby stores before your return trip to your vacation headquarters.

Low-gear your way up one of the narrow hillside roads (you're not on a driveway, it only seems that way) to one of those topmost Leverick dwellings, where you can park for a moment. Out to the left, across Blunder Bay, you'll see **Mosquito Island,** home of Drake's Anchorage Resort; the hunk of land straight ahead is **Prickly Pear,** which has been named a national park to protect it from development. At the neck of land to your right, across from Gun Creek, is **Biras Creek Hotel,** and around the bend to the north of that you'll see the Danish-roof buildings of the **Bitter End Yacht Club and Marina.** Between the Bitter End **❻** and Prickly Pear you should be able to make out **Saba Rock,** home of one of the Caribbean's best-known diving entrepreneurs, Bert Kilbride—a colorful character who knows where all the wrecks are and who is recognized and commissioned by the Queen of England as Honorary Keeper of the Wrecks.

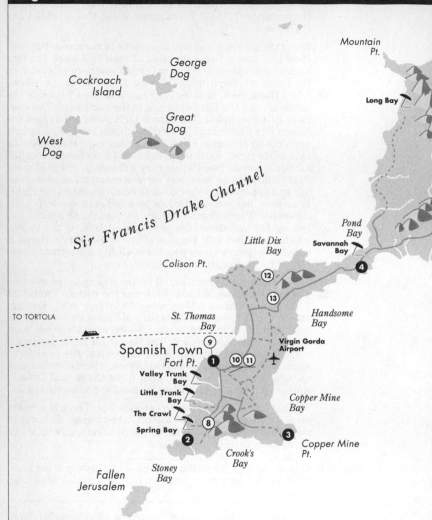

Mountain Pt.

George Dog

Cockroach Island

Long Bay

Great Dog

West Dog

Sir Francis Drake Channel

Pond Bay

Little Dix Bay

Savannah Bay **4**

Colison Pt.

Handsome Bay

TO TORTOLA

St. Thomas Bay

Spanish Town **9**

Fort Pt.

1

Virgin Gorda Airport

10 **11**

Valley Trunk Bay

Little Trunk Bay

The Crawl

Copper Mine Bay

Spring Bay

8

2

3

Copper Mine Pt.

Crook's Bay

Stoney Bay

Fallen Jerusalem

12

13

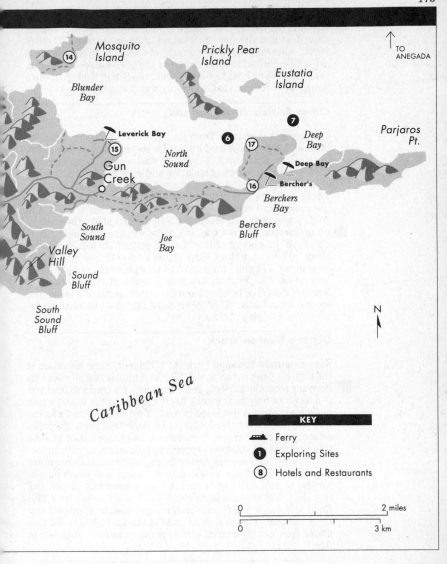

TO
ANEGADA

Mosquito
Island

Prickly Pear
Island

Eustatia
Island

Blunder
Bay

Parjaros
Pt.

14

Leverick Bay

15

Deep
Bay

7

6 **17**

Deep Bay

North
Sound

Gun
Creek

16 Bercher's

Berchers
Bay

Berchers
Bluff

South
Sound

Joe
Bay

Valley
Hill

Sound
Bluff

South
Sound
Bluff

N

Caribbean Sea

KEY
Ferry
1 Exploring Sites
8 Hotels and Restaurants

0   2 miles
0   3 km

That magical color change in the sea near Prickly Pear reveals
❼ **Eustatia Sound** and its extensive, reef. Beyond that are Horseshoe Reef and the flat coral island of Anegada some 20 miles
north, where most of those wrecks *are* and where bare-boaters
are not permitted to sail because of the perilous reefs. But you
can easily take a boat to Biras Creek, the Bitter End or Drake's
Anchorage. In fact, that's the only way you can get there.

Other British Virgin Islands

Just across the channel from Road Town on Tortola is **Peter Island,** an 1,800-acre island known for its resort. **Jost Van Dyke,**
the sizable island north of Tortola's western tip, is a good choice
for travelers in search of isolation and good hiking trails; it has
several hostelries and a campground, but only two small settlements, few cars, and small generators for electricity. Guests of
the resort on **Guana Island** also enjoy the nature trails and
wildlife sanctuary on this private island just above the eastern
tip of Tortola. **Marina Cay** is a snug six-acre islet near Great
Camanoe, just north of Beef Island, east of Tortola. **Anegada,**
about 20 miles north of Virgin Gorda's North Sound, is a flat
mass of coral 11 miles long and 3 miles wide with a population of
only about 250. Visitors are chiefly scuba divers, snorkelers,
lovers of deserted beaches, and fishermen, some of whom come
for the bonefishing here. (For more information on these islands, *see* Lodging, *below*.)

Off the Beaten Track

Sage Mountain National Park. At 1,716 feet, Sage Mountain is
the highest peak in the B.V.I. The best unobstructed views up
here are from the parking area, from which a trail will lead you
in a loop not only to the peak itself but also to the island's rain
forest, sometimes shrouded in mist. Most of the island's forest
was cut down over the centuries to clear land for sugarcane,
cotton, and other crops; pastureland; and timber. But in 1964
this park was established to preserve the remaining rain forest.
Up here you can see mahogany trees, white cedars, mountain
guavas, elephant-ear vines, mamey trees, and giant bullet-
woods, to say nothing of such birds as mountain doves and
thrushes. Take a taxi from Road Town or drive up Joe's Hill
Road and make a left onto Ridge Road toward Chalwell and
Doty villages. The road dead-ends at the park. *Ridge Rd., no
phone (contact the tourist office for information). Admission
free.*

Beaches

Beaches here are less developed than, say, on St. Thomas or St.
Croix. You'll also find fewer people. Try to get out on a boat at
least one day during your stay in these islands, whether a dive-
snorkeling boat or a day-trip sailing vessel. It's sometimes the
best way to get to the most virgin Virgin beaches (some have no
road access).

Tortola Tortola's north side has a number of postcard-perfect, palm-
fringed white-sand beaches that curl luxuriantly around turquoise bays and coves. Nearly all are accessible by car (preferably with 4-wheel drive), albeit down bumpy roads that

corkscrew precipitously. Facilities tend toward the basic, but you can usually find a humble beach bar with rest rooms.

If you want to surf, **Apple Bay** (Capoon's Bay) is the spot. Sebastian's, the very casual hotel here, caters especially to those in search of the perfect wave. Good waves are never a sure thing, but January and February are usually high times here. **Josiah's Bay** is another favored place to hang-10.

The water at **Brewers Bay** is good for either snorkeling (calm) or surfing (swells). There's a campground here, but in the summer you'll find almost nobody around. The beach and its old sugar mill and rum-distillery ruins are just north of Cane Garden Bay (up and over a steep hill), just past Luck Hill.

Cane Garden Bay rivals St. Thomas's Magens Bay in beauty, but is Tortola's most popular beach (it's the closest beach to Road Town—one steep up- and downhill drive) and one of the B.V.I.'s best-known anchorages. It's a grand beach for jogging if you can resist staying out of that translucent water. You can rent sailboards and such, and for noshing or sipping you have a choice of going to Stanley's Welcome Bar; Rhymer's The Wedding; or Quito's Gazebo, where local recording star Quito Rhymer sings island ballads four nights a week. For true romance, nothing beats an evening of stargazing from the bow of a boat, listening to Quito's love songs drift across the bay.

Long Bay on Beef Island offers scenery that draws superlatives and is visited only by a knowledgeable few. The view of Little Camanoe and Great Camanoe islands is appealing, and if you walk around the bend to the right, you can see little Marina Cay and Scrub Island. Take the Queen Elizabeth II Bridge to Beef Island and watch for a small dirt turnoff on the left before the airport. Drive across that dried-up marsh flat—there really is a beach (with interesting seashells) on the other side.

After bouncing your way to beautiful **Smuggler's Cove** (Lower Belmont Bay), you'll really feel as if you've found a hidden paradise (although don't expect to be alone on weekends). Have a beer or a toasted cheese sandwich, the only items on the menu, at the *extremely casual* snack bar. There is a fine view of the island of Jost Van Dyke, and the snorkeling is good.

About the only thing you'll find moving at **Trunk Bay** is the surf. It's directly north of Road Town, midway between Cane Garden Bay and Beef Island, and you'll have to hike down a *ghut* (gully) from the high Ridge Road.

Virgin Gorda The best beaches are most easily reached by water, although they are accessible on foot, usually after a moderately strenuous hike of 10 to 15 minutes. But your persistence is amply rewarded.

Anybody going to Virgin Gorda must experience swimming or snorkeling among its unique boulder formations. But why go to **The Baths,** which is usually crowded, when you can catch some rays just north at **Spring Bay** beach, which is a gem, and, a little farther north, at **The Crawl?** Both are easily reached from The Baths on foot or by swimming.

Leverick Bay is a small, busy beach-cum-marina that fronts a resort restaurant and pool. Don't come here to be alone or to jog. But if you want a lively little place and a break from the island's noble quiet, take the road north and turn left before

Gun Creek. The view of Prickly Pear Island is an added plus, and there's a dive facility right here to motor you out to beautiful Eustatia Reef just across North Sound.

It's worth going out to **Long Bay** (near Virgin Gorda's northern tip, past the Diamond Beach Club) for the snorkeling (Little Dix Bay resort has outings here). Going north from Spanish Town, go left at the fork near Pond Bay. Part of the route there is dirt road.

The North Shore has many nice beaches. From Biras Creek or Bitter End you can walk to **Bercher's** and **Deep Bay** beach. Two of the prettiest beaches in North Sound are accessible only by boat: Mosquito Island's **Hay Point Beach** and Prickley Pear's **Vixen Point Beach.**

Savannah Bay is a lovely long stretch of white sand, and though it may not always be deserted, it seems wonderfully private for a beach just north of Spanish Town (on the north side of where the island narrows, at Black Rock). From town it's about 30 minutes on foot.

Other Islands Beaches on other islands, reachable only by boat, include Jost Van Dyke's **Great Harbour** and **White Bay; Marina Cay;** Peter Island's **Big Reef Bay, White Bay,** and **Dead Man's Bay;** Mosquito Island's **Limetree Beach, Long Beach,** and **Honeymoon Beach;** and Cooper Island's **Manchioneel Bay.** Farther off, and reachable by plane as well as boat, is beach-ringed, reef-laced **Anegada.**

Sports and the Outdoors

Horseback Riding On Tortola, equestrians should get in touch with **Shadow Stables** (tel. 809/494–2262).

Sailboarding One of the best spots for sailboarding is at Trellis Bay on Beef Island. **Boardsailing B.V.I.** (Trellis Bay, Beef Island, tel. 809/495–2447) has rentals, private lessons, and group rates. On Virgin Gorda, **The Nick Trotter Sailing School** (Bitter End Yacht Club, North Sound, tel. 800/872–2392) has beginner and advanced courses.

Sailing/Boating The B.V.I. offer some of the finest sailing waters in the world, with hundreds of boats available for charter—with or without crew—as well as numerous opportunities for day-sails. For help in chartering a boat and crew for an extended trip, contact **Virgin Island Sailing** (Box 146, Road Town, Tortola, B.V.I., tel. 800/233–7936), a top brokerage house. For sailors interested in renting a bare boat, contact **The Moorings** (1305 U.S. 19 S, Suite 402, Clearwater, FL 34624, tel. 800/535–7289). Based in Road Town, it is the largest operator in the islands and offers day sails as well as longer trips.

Scuba Diving and Snorkeling The famed wreck of the R.M.S. *Rhone*, off Salt Island, is reason enough to dive during your B.V.I. stay. For snorkelers, perhaps the most popular spot is at the famed Baths on Virgin Gorda. Dive and snorkel sites also abound near the smaller islands of Norman, Peter, Cooper, Ginger, the Dogs, and Jost Van Dyke; the North Sound area of Virgin Gorda; Brewer's Bay and Frenchman's Cay on Tortola; and the wreck-strewn waters off Anegada. In addition to renting equipment, many of the dive operators here also offer instruction, hotel/dive packages, and snorkeling excursions. On Tortola, contact **Baskin-in-the-**

Sun (Box 108, Road Harbour, tel. 809/494–2858 or 800/233–7938) or **Underwater Safaris Ltd.** (Box 139, Road Town, tel. 809/494–3235 or 800/537–7032). **Dive BVI** (VG Yacht Harbour, tel. 809/495–5513 or 800/848–7078) has locations on Virgin Gorda and Peter Island.

Sportfishing A number of companies can transport and outfit you for fishing. On Tortola try **Charter Fishing Virgin Islands** (Prospect Reef, tel. 809/494–3311). On Virgin Gorda contact **Dale "Blondie" Wheatley** (809/495–7248), who operates the 38-foot Batram *Classic* out of Biras Creek.

Tennis Several resorts on Tortola have tennis courts for guests' use. Nonguests may use courts at **Prospect Reef** (Road Town, tel. 809/494–3311) and at Peter Island Resort and Yacht Harbour (a 20-minute ferry ride from Road Town). On Virgin Gorda, nonguests can use the courts at **Biras Creek** (tel. 809/494–3555).

Shopping

The British Virgins are not known as a shopping haven, but what is there is select and sophisticated. Don't be put off by an informal shop entrance. Some of the best finds in the B.V.I. lie behind a shopworn door.

Shopping Districts Most of the shops and boutiques on Tortola are clustered on and off Road Town's **Main Street** and at **Wickhams Cay** shopping area adjacent to the Marina. There is also an ever-growing group of art, jewelry, clothing, and souvenir stores at **Sopers Hole** on Tortola's West End. On Tortola's resort-crested sister isles most boutiques are located within the individual hotel complexes. One of the best is the one in **Little Dix Bay** on Virgin Gorda. Other properties on the same island—**Biras Creek,** the **Bitter End,** and **Leverick Bay**—have small but equally select boutiques, and there's a more than respectable and diverse scattering of shops in the minimall adjacent to the bustling yacht harbor in Spanish Town.

Specialty Stores
Art and Antiques **Antiquities and Presents Unlimited** (Waterfront Dr., Road Town, tel. 809/495–2439) has a small but excellent collection of 18th- and 19th-century furniture, wall hangings, rugs, and pottery from Africa, Asia, and South America, as well as some B.V.I. pottery. **Artica** (Soper's Hole Marina, tel. 809/494–6000) offers an appealing selection of paintings, sculptures, handcrafted jewelry, and one-of-a-kind art objects. **Collector's Corner** (Columbus Centre, Wickham's Cay, tel. 809/494–3550) carries antique maps; watercolors by local artists; gold and silver jewelry; coral; and larimar, a pale blue Caribbean gemstone. **The Courtyard Gallery** (Main St., Road Town, no phone) shows its exclusive Carinia Collection, delicate crushed-coral sculptures created on the premises and depicting darting hummingbirds, angelfish, nesting pelicans, and flowers. The place to find model ships, coffee-table books on the Caribbean, and prints of Caribbean maps and scenes is at **Islands Treasures** (Soper's Hole Marina, tel. 809/495–4787). **Caribbean Fine Arts Ltd.** (Main St., Road Town, tel. 809/494–4240) has a wide range of Caribbean art, including original watercolors, oils, and acrylics, as well as signed prints, limited-edition serigraphs, and turn-of-the-century sepia photographs. **Sunny Caribbee Skyworld Boutique and Art Gallery** (Skyworld Restaurant, Ridge Rd., tel. 809/494–3567) has one of the largest displays of

paintings in the Caribbean; the collection is hung in the restaurant's dining room and is heavy on Haitian primitive. It also sells its own line of spices, soaps, and sun-protection creams.

Clothing **Bonker's Gallery** (Main St., Road Town, tel. 809/494–2535) carries trendy resortwear for women, including cotton and washable-silk tops and bottoms and cover-ups. There is also a small collection of pants and shirts for men.
Sea Urchin (Columbus Centre, Road Town, tel. 809/494–2044; Soper's Hole Marina, tel. 809/495–4850) has a good selection of island-living designs: print shirts and shorts, slinky swimsuits, sandals, and T-shirts.

Food and Drink **The Ample Hamper** (Village Cay Marina, Wickham's Cay, tel. 809/494–2494; Soper's Hole Marina, tel. 809/495–4684), and **The Gourmet Galley** (Wickham's Cay II, Road Town, tel. 809/ 494–6999) offer fine selections of wines, cheeses, fresh fruits and vegetables, and canned goods from the United Kingdom and the United States and provide full provisioning for yachtspeople and villa renters. At the Bitter End, **Bitter End's Emporium** (North Sound, tel. 809/494–2745), resort is the place to look for such edible treats as local fruits, bakery goods, and cheeses. **The Wine Cellar** (Spanish Town, tel. 809/495– 5250) offers cheeses and fresh-baked breads in addition to a full selection of liquor and wines.

Gifts **J. R. O'Neal, Ltd.** (Main St., Road Town, tel. 809/494–2292) carries fine crystal, Royal Worcester china, a wonderful selection of hand-painted Italian dishes, hand-blown Mexican glassware, ceramic housewares from Spain, and woven rugs and tablecloths from India. A remarkable array of gift items, from wearable artwork and hand-painted jewelry to watercolors and batik fabric can be found at **Pink Pineapple** (Prospect Reef Hotel, tel. 809/494–3311).
The Pusser's Company Store (Main St. and Waterfront Rd., Road Town, tel. 809/494–2467; Soper's Hole Marina, tel. 809/ 495–4603) features nautical memorabilia, ship models, marine paintings, an entire line of clothes and gift items bearing the Pusser's logo, and handsome decorator bottles of Pusser's rum.
The Sunny Caribbee Herb and Spice Company (Main St., Road Town, tel. 809/494–2178), located in a brightly painted West Indian house, packages its own herbs, teas, coffees, herb vinegars, hot sauces, natural soaps, skin and suntan lotions, Caribbean art, and hand-painted decorative accessories. A small branch of this store is located at the Skyworld Restaurant (*see above*). **Turtle Dove Boutique** (Flemming St., Road Town, tel. 809/494–3611) is among the best in the B.V.I. for French perfume, international swimwear, and silk dresses, as well as gifts and accessories for the home.

Jewelry **Felix Gold and Silver Ltd.** (Main St., tel. 809/494–2406) handcrafts exceptionally fine jewelry in their on-site workshop. Choose from island or nautical themes or have something custom made (in most cases, they'll make it for you within 24 hours!). **Flaxcraft Jewellers** (Main St., Road Town, tel. 809/494– 2892) carries fine gold and silver jewelry; many of the pieces are one-of-a-kind creations incorporating shells and fragments of coral. **Samarkand** (Main St., Road Town, tel. 809/494–6415) features handmade gold and silver pendants, earrings, bracelets, and pins.

Local Crafts **Caribbean Handprints** (Main St., Road Town, tel. 809/494–3717) creates silkscreened fabric and sells it by the yard and fashioned into dresses, shirts, pants, bathrobes, beach cover-ups, and beach bags. **Virgin Gorda Craft Shop** (Virgin Gorda Yacht Harbour, no phone) features the work of island artisans and carries West Indian jewelry and crafts styled in straw, shells, and other local materials. It also stocks clothing and paintings by Caribbean artists.

Textiles **Zenaida** (Cutlass House, Wickham's Cay, Road Town, tel. 809/494–2113) displays the fabric finds of Argentinian Vivian Jenik Helm, who travels through South America, Africa, and India in search of batiks, hand-painted and hand-blocked fabrics, and interesting weaves that can be made into pareos or wall hangings. The shop also offers a selection of unusual bags, belts, sarongs, scarves, and ethnic jewelry.

Dining

The most popular choices in B.V.I. restaurants are seafood dishes. You'll find a greater range of eateries on Tortola than on more remote Virgin Gorda and the other islands, where most hotels offer a meal plan. On both islands, the way to dress is casual but neat.

Highly recommended restaurants are indicated by a star ★.

Category	Cost*
Very Expensive	over $35
Expensive	$25–$35
Moderate	$15–$25
Inexpensive	under $15

per person for three courses, excluding drinks and service; there is no sales tax in the B.V.I.

Tortola **Tradewinds.** Catch the Peter Island ferry for a 25-minute ride
★ to this elegant restaurant on Peter Island and dine and dance under the stars. The excellent new menu (which is no longer prix-fixe) offers five different entrées that change daily. These Continental selections are prepared with a Caribbean flair and include grilled yellowfin tuna with tomato and pineapple salsa and veal with avocado and mushrooms, as well as local lobster. The desserts are prepared daily; indulge in the piña colada cheesecake or the Grand Marnier souffle. *Peter Island, tel. 809/494–2561. Reservations essential. Dress: casual elegant (no shorts or jeans; collared shirts for men). AE, MC, V. Closed Monday. Very Expensive.*

★ **Brandywine Bay.** For the best in romantic dining, don't miss this hillside gem, where candlelit alfresco tables have a sweeping view of neighboring islands. Italian owner/chef Davide Pugliese prepares food the Tuscan way—lots of fresh ingredients, herbs, and grilled dishes. The remarkable menu, which hostess Cele Pugliese describes tableside, can include homemade mozzarella, grilled portobello mushrooms, petite pizzas, grilled local wahoo, grilled veal chop with ricotta and sun-dried tomatoes, and irresistible desserts. *Sir Francis Drake Hwy., east of Road Town, tel. 809/495–2301. Reservations advised. AE, MC, V. Closed for lunch; closed Sun. Expensive.*

★ **Skyworld.** You'll want to arrive early for dinner at this mountaintop aerie; the sunset views are breathtaking. Watch the western horizon go ablaze with color, then settle back in the casually elegant dining room to feast on chef George Petcoff's delectable offerings. Try the veal in lemon caper sauce, the local swordfish with sun-dried–tomato pesto, or the passion fruit sorbet. This is also a special place for lunch. Not only are the sandwiches on homebaked bread delicious, but both the restaurant and the observation tower above offer the B.V.I.'s highest (and absolutely spectacular) 360-degree view of numerous islands and cays. Even St. Croix and Anegada (both 20 miles away) can be seen on a clear day. *Ridge Rd., tel. 809/494–3567. Reservations advised. AE, MC, V. Expensive.*

Sugar Mill Restaurant. This restaurant's candles gleam and the background music is (blessedly) restrained in this well-known restaurant. Ranking among America's top food writers, owners Jeff and Jinx Morgan do not disappoint with well-prepared selections that may include smoked duck breast with honey-lemon glaze, herbed prawns with drawn butter, or His Majesty's West Indian Regimental beef curry. *Apple Bay, tel. 809/495–4355. Reservations advised. AE, MC, V. Expensive.*

The Upstairs. Ask for a window table here and you'll be bathed in gentle tropical breezes as you gaze out at the stars. Excellent service and excellent food are hallmarks of this elegant and well-established restaurant overlooking a small marina. House specialties include a delicious lobster au gratin appetizer, grilled local fish, steak with port and peaches, roast duck, and key lime pie. *On Prospect Reef Hotel grounds (turn left just after the entrance), Road Town, tel. 809/494–2228. Reservations accepted. AE, MC, V. Closed for lunch. Expensive.*

★ **Pusser's Landing.** Yachters flock to the new two-story home of this popular waterfront restaurant. Downstairs, belly up to the large, comfortable mahogany bar or choose a waterside table for drinks, sandwiches, or a light dinner. Head upstairs for quieter alfresco dining and a delightfully eclectic menu that includes homemade black bean soup, freshly grilled local fish, pasta, and such pub favorites as "bubble and squeak" (mashed potatoes with sauteed onions). The air-conditioned Dinner Theater, with its 15-foot screen, features prix-fixe, three-course meal and shows movie combos and sports events. *Sopers Hole, tel. 809/495–4554. AE, MC, V. Moderate–Expensive.*

The Apple. This small, inviting restaurant is located in a small West Indian house not far from the cooling breezes of Little Apple Bay. Soft candlelight complements local seafood dishes, such as fish steamed in lime butter and conch or whelks in garlic sauce. *Little Apple Bay, tel. 809/495–4437. Reservations accepted. No credit cards. Moderate.*

The Fishtrap. Dine alfresco at this new restaurant, which serves grilled local fish, steaks, and chicken. Friday and Saturday there's a barbecue with a terrific salad bar and Sunday prime rib is featured. *Columbus Centre, Wickham's Cay, Road Town, tel. 809/494–2636. AE, MC, V. Closed for Sunday lunch. Moderate.*

Spaghetti Junction. This funky spot is popular with the boating crowd. Nightly specials complement the tasty and traditional Italian menu (veal or chicken parmigiana, pastas, etc.), and sun-dried tomato in the Caesar salad is a nice twist. Check out the gorilla in the rest room. *Waterfront Dr., Road Town, tel. 809/494–4880. No credit cards. Closed lunch, holidays, and all of September. Moderate.*

★ **Virgin Queen.** The sailing and rugby crowd and locals gather here to play darts, drink beer, and eat Queen's Pizza (some say it's the best pizza in the Caribbean) or some of the excellent West Indian and English fare. A delicious menu includes saltfish, barbecued ribs with beans and rice, bangers and mash, shepherd's pie, and chili. *Fleming St., Road Town, tel. 809/494–2310. No reservations. No credit cards. Closed Sun. Moderate.*

Virgin Gorda **Biras Creek.** You come by boat (provided free) to this serene
★ and elegant restaurant. Candlelit tables are set on a turretlike stonework terrace with the wild Caribbean on one side and calm North Sound on the other. The menu for the four-course prix fixe dinner changes nightly and always includes a choice of four entrées. The meals are among the best in the B.V.I., and there is an excellent wine list. *North Sound, tel. 809/494– 3555 or 809/495–4356. Reservations advised. Dress: neat but casual (no shorts at dinner). AE, MC, V. Very Expensive.*

Olde Yard Inn. Civilized and charming, the dining room here is suffused with gentle classical melodies and the scent of herbs. A cedar roof covers the breezy, open-air room decorated with old-style Caribbean charm. The French-accented cuisine includes seafood in puff pastry, chicken breast in a rum cream sauce, grilled local fish and steaks. *The Valley, north of the marina, tel. 809/495–5544. Reservations advised. AE, MC, V. Expensive.*

★ **The Bath and Turtle.** This informal patio tavern with its friendly staff is a popular spot to sit back and relax. Burgers, well-stuffed sandwiches, pizzas, pasta dishes, and daily specials round out the casual menu. Live entertainment performs on Wednesday and Sunday nights. *Virgin Gorda Yacht Harbour, tel. 809/495–5239. Reservations accepted. MC, V. Moderate.*

The Crab Hole. This homey hangout, serving Creole specialties like callaloo soup, saltfish, and curried chicken roti, rocks with live bands and a mostly local crowd on Saturdays. *The Valley, tel. 809/495–5307. Reservations accepted. No credit cards. Inexpensive–Moderate.*

Lodging

The number of rooms available in the B.V.I. is small compared with other destinations in the Caribbean; what is available is also often in great demand, and the prices are not low. The top-of-the-line resorts here are among the most expensive in the Caribbean and are sometimes difficult to book even off-season. Even the more moderately priced hotels command top dollar during the season; off-season, however, they are legitimate bargains at about half the price. In addition, many of the hotels offer rates that include all three meals.

Highly recommended lodgings are indicated by a star ★.

Category	Cost*
Very Expensive	over $275
Expensive	$180–$275

Moderate	$130–$180
Inexpensive	under $130

All prices are for a standard double room in high season, excluding 7% hotel tax and 10% service charge.

Tortola **Long Bay Hotel.** Set on a mile-long arc of white sand, this hotel
★ offers a wide variety of accommodations, including 32 deluxe
beachfront rooms, with two queen beds or one king-size four-
poster bed, marble-top wet bars, and showers with Italian
tiles. There are also smaller beach cabanas, 10 rustic, tropical
hideaways set on stilts at the water's edge. Hillside choices all
have balconies with lovely views and range from small but adequate rooms to studios with a comfortable seating area, to
roomy one- and two-bedroom villas. The Beach restaurant offers all-day dining, and the Garden Restaurant serves prix-fixe
three-course dinners in a romantic, candlelit setting. *Box 433,
Road Town, tel. 809/495–4252 or 800/729–9599, fax 809/495–
4677. 62 rooms. Facilities: 2 restaurants, 2 bars, beach, pool,
pitch-and-putt golf, small tennis court, commissary. AE, MC,
V. EP, MAP. Expensive.*

Frenchman's Cay. This well-maintained resort consists of one-
and two-bedroom villas that overlook Sir Francis Drake Channel. Each unit includes a full kitchen, dining area, and sitting
room—ideal for families or couples. Rooms are done in neutral
colors, with cream-color curtains and bedspreads and tile
floors. Ceiling fans and pleasant breezes keep the rooms cool.
There is a pool and a small man-made beach that is sandy to the
water's edge but rocky offshore. It's not good for wading without shoes but does offer good snorkeling. The alfresco bar and
dining room are breeze-swept and inviting. *Box 1054, West
End, tel. 809/495–4844, fax 809/495–5046. 9 units. Facilities:
restaurant, bar, tennis court, beach, pool, water sports. AE,
D, MC, V. EP. Expensive.*

Sugar Mill Hotel. The hosts at this small, out-of-the-way hotel
are Jeff and Jinx Morgan who opened it almost two decades ago
after becoming well established travel and food writers. The
reception area, bar, and restaurant are located in the ruins of a
centuries-old sugar mill and are decorated with bright Haitian
artwork. Simple guest houses are scattered on the hillside, and
the rooms are furnished in soft pastels and rattan. (Light sleep-
ers may be disturbed by the roosters, who start crowing long
before dawn.) There's a circular swimming pool set into the
hillside and a tiny beach where lunch is served on a shady terrace. The restaurant here is well known on the island. (*see* Dining, *above*). *Box 425, Road Town, tel. 809/495–4355, fax 809/
495–4696. 20 rooms. Facilities: restaurant, 2 bars, beach, pool,
water sports. AE, MC, V. EP, MAP. Expensive.*

★ **Prospect Reef Resort.** This appealing, sprawling resort is near
town and overlooks Sir Francis Drake Channel. There are 11
different housing units spread over 7 acres, and all are near the
beach. All the rooms have a balcony, patio, or both, and may
face either the water or the hotel's gardens. Decor varies
throughout the rooms, with furnishings done in rattan or natural wood, and color schemes range from cool blue to bright tropical prints. The suites are two-story units with small
courtyards, and many rooms have kitchenettes. In addition to
the hotel's Junior Olympic-size swimming pool and diving pool,
Prospect Reef features a saltwater pool sectioned off from the
sea with large rocks and a narrow, man-made beach. The resort

also boasts its own harbor with sailboats available for day trips or longer excursions. *Box 104, Road Town, tel. 809/494–3311, fax 809/494–5595. 131 rooms. Facilities: beach, 2 restaurants, beachside snackbar, bars, 3 pools (2 freshwater: 1 Junior Olympic-size, 1 for diving), children's splash pool, 6 tennis courts, pitch-and-put golf, water sports, unisex hair salon, shopping arcade, conference center. AE, MC, V. EP. Moderate–Expensive.*

Fort Recovery. Built around the remnants of a Dutch fort, this appealing group of one- to four-bedroom bungalows stretches along a small beach facing Sir Francis Drake Channel. All units have patios, kitchens, and equally excellent views. The grounds are bright with tropical flowers. *Box 239, Road Town, tel. 809/495–4467, fax 809/495–4036. 10 units. Facilities: beach, commissary selling basic food supplies and frozen homemade entrées. AE, MC, V. EP. Moderate.*

Moorings-Mariner Inn. Headquarters for the Moorings Charter operation and popular with yachting folk who find its full-service facilities convenient and the companionship of fellow "boaties" congenial, this is also a good choice for those who want to be within easy walking distance of town. The atmosphere is a combination of laid-back and lively and the rooms, including four full-size suites, are large and comfortable. The rooms' pale-peach decor is picked up in the peach tiles on the floors, and bright, tropical-print bedspreads and curtains add color. All rooms have a small kitchenette (with sink, refrigerator, and two-burner stove) and a balcony. Most rooms face the water except for eight, which overlook the pool or the tennis court. *Box 139, Road Town, tel. 809/494–2331, fax 809/494–2226. 40 rooms. Facilities: restaurant, bar, pool, tennis court, volleyball court, dive shop, gourmet shop. AE, MC, V. EP. Moderate.*

Sebastian's on the Beach. The beach is the main attraction here; the surfing on Little Apple Bay is considered among the best in the B.V.I. "Hang-10" types dote on Sebastian's casual atmosphere and the wide range of water sports available. The rooms are divided among three buildings, only one of which is on the beach—this is also the only building that has balconies in each room. The appealing on-site restaurant overlooks the water and offers a pleasing variety of choices for lunch and dinner. *Box 441, Road Town, tel. 809/495–4212, fax 809/495–4466. 26 rooms. Facilities: restaurant, bar, beach, water sports, commissary. AE. EP. Moderate.*

Treasure Isle Hotel. Recently purchased by The Moorings, this hillside hotel, painted in bright shades of lemon, violet, and mango pink, is one of the prettiest properties on the island. The air-conditioned rooms are spacious and accented with fabrics sporting prints in the manner of Matisse. Set on a hillside overlooking the harbor, Treasure Isle makes a handy base for in-town shopping and visits to nearby marinas. Open to the breezes and the heady aroma of tropical flowers, the Spy Glass Bar with its comfortable lounges is the perfect place to relax and look out at a stunning view of the harbor and islands in the distance. There is daily transportation to Cane Garden Bay and Brewers Bay. *Box 68, Road Town, tel. 809/494–2501, fax 809/494–2507. 40 rooms. Facilities: restaurant, 2 bars, pool, water sports. AE, MC, V. EP. Moderate.*

Campgrounds **Brewers Bay Campground.** Both prepared and bare sites are located on Brewers Bay, one of Tortola's prime snorkeling spots.

Check out the ruins of the distillery that gave the bay its name. *Box 185, Road Town, tel. 809/494–3463. Facilities: beach, bar, restaurant, commissary, water sports, baby-sitters available.*

Virgin Gorda **Biras Creek Hotel.** This enchanting 150-acre hideaway is so se-
★ cluded that the only way to reach it is by launch. The hilltop open-air bar and restaurant area is made perfectly of stone-work and offers stunning views of North Sound. Each guest cottage is a suite, with bedroom, bath, and living room. Per-haps its loveliest feature is the sensuous open-air walled show-er in each bathroom. Tucked away in the greenery are gardens and a salt-pond sanctuary. Guests can explore the grounds on foot or on bicycles provided by the hotel. There's a pool set right at the edge of the sea; tennis courts are lighted for night play; sailing, boardsailing, and snorkeling equipment is avail-able. Guests are pampered here. The atmosphere is one of casu-al elegance, and the restaurant is one of the best in the B.V.I. *Box 54, North Sound, tel. 809/494–3555, fax 809/494–3557. 34 rooms. Facilities: restaurant, bar, 2 beaches, tennis courts, marina, pool, water sports, hiking and biking trails. AE, MC, V. FAP. Very Expensive.*

★ **Bitter End Yacht Club and Marina.** Stretching along the coast-line of North Sound, the BEYC enjoys panoramic views of the Sound, Leverick Bay, and nearby islands. Accommodations range from hillside or beachfront villas and chalets to live-aboard yachts, all of which include the basics, but are refresh-ingly nofrills. What's most inviting about this propery, howev-er, is the friendly, unpretentious welcome the resort extends to all its guests. The resort organizes daily snorkeling and div-ing trips to nearby reefs, windsurfing lessons, and excursions to local attractions, but the BEYC is most touted for its Nick Trotter Sailing School. Regarded as the best sailing instruction in the Caribbean, the school helps both seasoned salts and be-ginners to sharpen their nautical skills. When the sun goes down, the festivities continue at either the elegant Carvery, where themed buffets are served on special occasions, or at the Clubhouse, an open-air restaurant overlooking the Sound. The hotel's character is one of the liveliest and most convivial in the B.V.I. *Box 46, North Sound, tel. 809/494–2746, fax 809/494–3557. 100 rooms. Facilities: 2 restaurants, bar, beach, marina, pool. AE, MC, V. FAP. Very Expensive.*

★ **Little Dix Bay.** The luxury resort that first set the standards for understated elegance in the B.V.I. is still going strong. In-dividual cottages, each with its own hammock-hung terrace or balcony, are comfortably spaced throughout the manicured grounds. The reef-protected beach is long and silken; the can-dlelight dining in an open peak-roof pavilion is a memorable ex-perience. Tennis, sailing, snorkeling, water-skiing, and bicycling, are included in the rate. Popular with honeymooners and older couples who have apparently been coming back for years, Little Dix may leave the single traveler feeling slightly left out occasionally. Nonetheless, the accommodations are su-perb, the service is thoughtful and attentive, and the setting is unforgettable. *Box 70, tel. 809/495–5555, fax 809/495–5661. 102 rooms. Facilities: restaurant, 2 bars, beach, water sports, marina, 7 tennis courts, boutique. AE, MC, V. EP, MAP, FAP. Very Expensive.*

Guavaberry Spring Bay Vacation Homes. These unusual hexag-onal cottages are perched on stilts, and you'll feel as if you are in a tree house, with chirping birds and branches swaying in the breezes. These one- and two-bedroom units are situated on a hill, a short walk down to a tamarind-shaded beach and not far from the mammoth boulders and cool basins of the famed Baths. *Box 20, Virgin Gorda, tel. 809/495–5227, fax 809/495–7367. 16 units. Facilities: commissary, beach. No credit cards. EP. Moderate.*

Leverick Bay Resort. This small hotel offers 16 hillside rooms, decorated in pastels and with original artwork. All rooms have refrigerators, balconies, and lovely views of North Sound. Four two-bedroom condos are also available. A Spanish Colonial–style main building houses a restaurant operated by Pusser's of Tortola. A dive operation, a crafts shop, commissary, coin-operated laundry, and beauty salon are also on-site. *Box 63, tel. 809/495–7421, fax 809/495–7367. 20 rooms. Facilities: restaurant, bar, beach, marina, pool, shopping arcade, water sports. AE, D, MC, V. EP. Moderate.*

Olde Yard Inn. Owners Charlie Williams and Carol Kaufman have cultivated a refreshingly unique atmosphere at this quiet retreat just outside Spanish Town. Classical music plays in the small bar; a large and varied collection of books lines the walls of the octagonal library cottage. The restaurant's French-accented menu is lovingly prepared and served with style in the high-ceiling dining rooms. The cedar-paneled guest rooms are cozy and simply furnished. Though the hotel is not on the beach (Savannah Bay and Pond Bay are only a 20-minute walk away) and has no pool, it does have a loyal group of repeat guests. You may want to request one of the air-conditioned rooms; the hotel's location in the Valley means trade winds are less noticeable here. *Box 26, Spanish Town, tel. 809/495–5544, fax 809/495–5986. 14 rooms. Facilities: restaurant, bar, library, horseback riding. AE, MC, V. EP, MAP. Moderate.*

The Wheelhouse. This hotel is easy on the pocketbook for those seeking a no-frills vacation headquarters. The cinder-block building has rooms that are air-conditioned but small, and the restaurant and bar can get noisy. It is conveniently close to the Virgin Gorda marina and shopping center. *Box 66, tel. 809/495–5230. 12 rooms. Facilities: restaurant, bar. AE, MC, V. CP. Inexpensive.*

Anegada **Anegada Reef Hotel.** It is away from it all in every sense of the phrase, because it is the only hotel on Anegada, and the island itself is off the beaten path. Snorkeling and diving are as good here as anywhere in the islands. Bonefishing in the flats is a favorite activity, and deep-sea fishing trips can be arranged. If you favor water-oriented activities, this is the spot for you. *Anegada, tel. 809/495–8002, fax 809/495–9362. 16 rooms. Facilities: restaurant, bar, beach, gift shop, water sports. FAP. Expensive.*

Guana Island **Guana Island Club.** Fifteen guest rooms are spread among seven separate houses scattered along the hillside. The houses are decorated in Caribbean style, with rattan furniture and ceiling fans, and each has its own porch. *Box 32, Road Town, Tortola, tel. 809/494–2354, fax 914/967–8048. 15 rooms. Facilities: restaurant, wildlife sanctuary, tennis, croquet, hiking trails, water sports. FAP. Very Expensive.*

Jost Van Dyke **Sandcastle.** This small hotel at White Bay has four beach cottages. *6501 Red Hook Plaza, Suite 201, St. Thomas, U.S.V.I. 00802–1306, tel. 809/775–5262, fax 809/775–3590. Facilities: restaurant, bar. MC, V. FAP. Very Expensive.*

Rudy's Mariner Inn. Located at Great Harbour, this hostelry has three rooms with kitchenettes and dining areas. *Great Harbour, Jost Van Dyke, tel. 809/495–9282. Facilities: restaurant, beach bar. No credit cards. EP. Expensive.*

Mosquito Island **Drake's Anchorage.** Manager Albert Wheatley ensures that this small, secluded getaway offers true privacy and the pampering of the more elegant resorts without the formality. Changing for dinner here means switching from a bathing suit to comfortable cottons. The three West Indian–style, waterfront bungalows contain 10 comfortably furnished rooms, including two suites. (There are also two fully equipped villas for rent.) There is a highly regarded restaurant, hiking trails, water-sports facilities, and four delightful beaches with hammocks here and there—a truly peaceful, rejuvenating experience. *Box 2510, North Sound, Virgin Gorda, tel. 809/ 494–2254 or 800/624–6651, fax 809/494–2254. Facilities: restaurant, bar, 4 beaches, water sports, hiking trails, gift shop. AE, MC, V. FAP. Very Expensive.*

Peter Island **Peter Island Resort and Yacht Harbour.** This resort is close to
★ the last word in luxury in all the Caribbean. General Manager Jamie Holmes has made sure that every imaginable living, dining, and recreational amenity is available, including a gourmet restaurant, stunning freshwater pool, and tennis courts complete with a resident pro. There are also small sailboats, Sunfishes, kyacks, mountain bicycles, windsurfers, Hobie Cats, a 20-station fitness trail, an exercise room, 10 miles of walking trails, a dive shop, and a masseuse. The 50 guest rooms, tucked among beds of radiant tropical flowers, are located either on the beach or near the pool. *Box 211, Road Town, Tortola, tel. 809/494–2561 or 800/346–4451, fax 809/494–2313. 50 rooms, 4 villas. Facilities: 2 restaurants, bar, 5 beaches, marina (limited services), pool, tennis, five-star PADI dive facility. AE, MC, V. EP, MAP, FAP. Very Expensive.*

Nightlife

On Tortola, live bands play at **Pusser's Landing** (Sophers Hole, tel. 809/494–4554) Thursday through Sunday, the **Jolly Rodger** (West End, tel. 809/495–4559) Friday and Saturday, **Sebastian's** (Apple Bay, tel. 809/495–4214) Saturday and Sunday, and **Bomba's Shack** (Apple Bay, tel. 809/495–4148) on Sunday, Wednesday, and every full moon. At **Quito's Gazebo** (Cane Garden Bay, tel. 809/495–4837), B.V.I. recording star Quito Rymer sings island ballads. **Stanley's Welcome Bar** (Cane Garden Bay, tel. 809/495–4520) gets rowdy when crews stop by to party. On Virgin Gorda, **Andy's Chateau de Pirate** (Fischer's Cove Beach Hotel, The Valley, tel. 809/495–5252) has live music and dancing on the weekends. One of the busiest nocturnal spots in the B.V.I. is little Jost Van Dyke. Check out **Rudy's Mariner Rendezvous** (tel. 809/495–9282), **Foxy's Tamarind** (tel. 809/495–9258), and **Sydney's Peace and Love** (tel. 809/495–9271).

8 Cayman Islands

Updated by
Joan Iaconetti

The venerable old *Saturday Evening Post* dubbed them "the islands that time forgot." But the past decade has changed all that: The Cayman Islands, a British Crown colony that includes Grand Cayman, Cayman Brac, and Little Cayman, are now one of the Caribbean's hottest destinations.

Why do metropolis-weary visitors trek 480 miles south of Miami, filling the hotels and condominiums that line famed Seven Mile Beach, even during the traditionally slow summer season? Their dollars certainly go further in other Caribbean destinations, for in Grand Cayman—which positively reeks of suburban prosperity, bulging as it does with some 544 offshore banks located in George Town, the capital—the U.S. dollar is worth 80 Cayman cents, and the cost of living is 20% higher than in the United States.

Effective advertising accounts for some visitors, but the secret is word-of-mouth testimonials. The Cayman Islanders—the population is 27,000, almost all of it residents of Grand Cayman—are renowned for the courteous and civil manners befitting their British heritage. If they sometimes appear to be slightly aloof, the truth is, their attitude is born of innate shyness. Visitors will find no hasslers or panhandlers and no need to look apprehensively over their shoulder on dark evenings, for the colony is virtually crime-free. Add to that permanent political and economic stability, and you have a fairly rosy picture.

The Caymans fully deserve their reputation as a paradise for divers: Translucent waters and a colorful variety of marine life are protected by the government, which has created a marine parks system in all three islands.

Columbus is said to have sighted the islands in 1503, but he didn't stop off to explore. He did note that the surrounding sea was alive with turtles, so the islands were named Las Tortugas. The name was later changed to Cayman.

The islands stayed largely uninhabited until the late 1600s, when Britain took over the Cayman Islands and Jamaica from Spain under the Treaty of Madrid. Cayman attracted a mixed bag of settlers, pirates, refugees from the Spanish Inquisition, shipwrecked sailors, and deserters from Oliver Cromwell's army in Jamaica. Today's Caymanians are the descendants of those nationalities.

The caves and coves of the islands—still fascinating to explore—were a perfect hideout for pirates like Blackbeard and Sir Henry Morgan, who plundered Spanish galleons hauling riches from the New World of South America to Spain. Many a ship also fell afoul of the reefs surrounding the islands, often with the help of the Caymanians, who lured the vessels to shore with beacon fires. Some of the old pioneer homes on the islands were made from the remains of those galleons.

The legend of the Wreck of the Ten Sails was to have a lasting effect on the Caymanians. In 1788, a convoy of 10 Jamaican ships bound for England foundered on the reefs, but the islanders managed to rescue everyone. Royalty was purportedly aboard, and a grateful George III decreed that Caymanians should forever be exempt from conscription and never have to pay taxes.

The Cayman Islands are still a British colony. A governor appoints three official members to the Legislative Assembly and has to accept the advice of the Executive Council in all matters except foreign affairs, defense, internal security, and civil service appointments.

Before You Go

Tourist Information For the latest information on activities and lodging, write or call any of the following offices of the **Cayman Islands Department of Tourism:** 6100 Waterford Bldg., 6100 Blue Lagoon Dr., Suite 150, Miami, FL 33126–2085, tel. 305/266–2300; 2 Memorial City Plaza, 820 Gessner, Suite 170, Houston, TX 77024, tel. 713/461–1317; 420 Lexington Ave., Suite 2733, New York, NY 10170, tel. 212/682–5582; 9525 West Bryn Mawr Ave., Suite 160, Rosemont, IL 60018, tel. 708/678–6446; 3440 Wilshire Blvd., Suite 1202, Los Angeles, CA 90010, tel. 213/738–1968; 234 Eglinton Ave. E., Suite 306, Toronto, Ont. M4P 1K5, tel. 416/485–1550; Trevor House, 100 Brompton Rd., Knightsbridge, London SW3 1EX, tel. 071/581–9960.

Arriving and Departing By Plane Grand Cayman is serviced by **Northwest** (tel. 800/447–4747), **Cayman Airways** (tel. 800/422–9626), **American Airlines** (tel. 800/433–7300), and **United** (tel. 800/241–6522) from Miami. Cayman Airways flies nonstop from Miami daily and has nonstop service from Houston Thursday, Saturday, and Monday. Regular service on Cayman Airways is also scheduled from Tampa and Atlanta. **Cayman Airtours** (tel. 800/247–2966) offers package deals. Cayman Airways also operates flights to Cayman Brac every day except Tuesday and to Little Cayman daily except Tuesday. Flights land at Owen Roberts Airport, Gerrard Smith Airport, or Edward Bodden Airport.

Upon arrival, some hotels offer free pickup at the airport. Taxi service and car rentals are also available.

Passports and Visas American and Canadian citizens do not have to carry passports, but they must show some proof of citizenship, such as a birth certificate or voter registration card, plus a return ticket. British and Commonwealth subjects do not need a visa but must carry a passport. Visitors to the islands cannot be employed without a work permit.

Language English is spoken everywhere; all local publications are in English as well.

Precautions Locals make a constant effort to conserve fresh water, so don't waste a precious commodity.

Penalties for drug importation and possession of controlled substances include large fines and prison terms.

Theft is uncommon, but be smart: Lock up your room and car and secure valuables as you would at home. Outdoors, marauding blackbirds called "ching chings" have been known to carry off jewelry if it is left out in the open.

Staying in the Cayman Islands

Important Addresses **Tourist Information:** The main office of the **Department of Tourism** is located in the Harbour Center (N. Church St., tel. 809/949–0623). Information booths are in the George Town Craft Market, on Cardinal Avenue, open when cruise ships are in

Grand Cayman

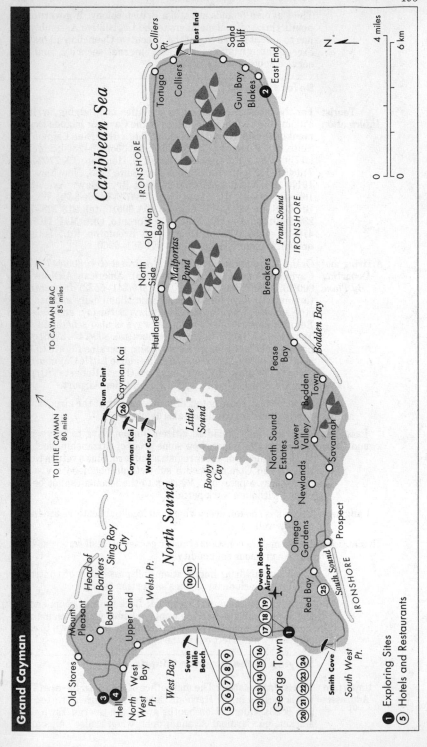

Caribbean Sea

North Sound

TO CAYMAN BRAC 85 miles

TO LITTLE CAYMAN 80 miles

Rum Point

Cayman Kai (26)

Water Cay

Little Sound

Booby Cay

Colliers Pt.

East End

Sand Bluff

Colliers

Tortuga

Gun Bay

Blakes

East End (2)

Old Man Bay

North Side

Hutland

Malportas Pond

IRONSHORE

Breakers

Frank Sound

IRONSHORE

Bodden Bay

Pease Bay

Bodden Town

Savannah

Lower Valley

Newlands

North Sound Estates

Omega Gardens

Prospect

South Sound (25)

Red Bay

IRONSHORE

Owen Roberts Airport

George Town (1)

(17)(18)(19)

(10)(11)

Welsh Pt.

Upper Land

Seven Mile Beach

(5)(6)(7)(8)(9)

(12)(13)(14)(15)(16)

(20)(21)(22)(23)(24)

Smith Cove

South West Pt.

Sting Ray City

Head of Barkers

Batabano

Mount Pleasant

Old Stores

Hell (4)

(3)

North West Pt.

West Bay

West Bay Pt.

(1) Exploring Sites

(5) Hotels and Restaurants

N

0   4 miles

0   6 km

191

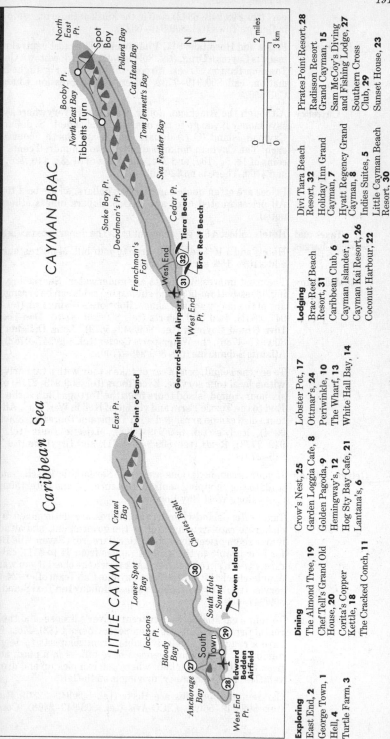

Cayman Brac and Little Cayman

Exploring
East End, **2**
George Town, **1**
Hell, **4**
Turtle Farm, **3**

Dining
The Almond Tree, **19**
Chef Tell's Grand Old House, **20**
Corita's Copper Kettle, **18**
The Cracked Conch, **11**
Crow's Nest, **25**
Garden Loggia Cafe, **8**
Golden Pagoda, **9**
Hemingway's, **12**
Hog Sty Bay Cafe, **21**
Lantana's, **6**
Lobster Pot, **17**
Ottmar's, **24**
Periwinkle, **10**
The Wharf, **13**
White Hall Bay, **14**

Lodging
Brac Reef Beach Resort, **31**
Caribbean Club, **6**
Cayman Islander, **16**
Cayman Kai Resort, **26**
Coconut Harbour, **22**
Divi Tiara Beach Resort, **32**
Holiday Inn Grand Cayman, **7**
Hyatt Regency Grand Cayman, **8**
Indies Suites, **5**
Little Cayman Beach Resort, **30**
Pirates Point Resort, **28**
Radisson Resort, Grand Cayman, **15**
Sam McCoy's Diving and Fishing Lodge, **27**
Southern Cross Club, **29**
Sunset House, **23**

port (tel. 809/949–8342), and in the kiosk at the cruise ship dock in George Town (tel. 809/949–0623).

Emergencies **Police and Hospitals:** 911. **Pharmacies:** The most central pharmacy is **Cayman Drug,** (tel. 809/949–2597) in downtown George Town on Panton Street. **Airport Information:** For flight information, call 809/949–7733. **Divers' Recompression Chamber:** Call 555.

Currency Although the American dollar is accepted everywhere, you'll save money if you go to the bank and exchange U.S. dollars for Cayman Island (C.I.) dollars, which are worth about $1.25 each. The Cayman dollar is divided into a hundred cents with coins of 1¢, 5¢, 10¢, and 25¢, and notes of $1, $5, $10, $25, $50, and $100. There is no $20 bill.

Prices are often quoted in Cayman dollars, so it's best to ask. All prices quoted here are in U.S. dollars unless otherwise noted.

Taxes and Hotels collect a 6% government tax. The departure tax is $10.
Service Charges Hotels add a 10% service charge to your bill. Many restaurants add a 10%–15% service charge.

Guided Tours The most impressive sights are underwater. Snorkeling, diving, glass-bottom-boat and submarine rides can be arranged at any of the major aquatic shops: **Bob Soto's Diving Ltd.** (tel. 809/947–4631), **Red Sail Sports** (tel. 809/949–8745), **Don Foster's Dive Grand Cayman** (tel. 809/949–5679), **Aqua Delights** (tel. 809/947–4786), the **Watersports Center** (tel. 809/947–0762), and **Atlantis Submarine** (tel. 809/949–7700).

To see the island, rent a car or take a tour with a taxi driver or with a local tour service. **Evco Tours** (tel. 809/949–2118) offers six-hour, round-island tours from the Tortuga Club at the East End to the Turtle Farm and village of Hell in West Bay. All-day tours also can be arranged with **Tropicana Tours** (tel. 809/949–0944), **Rudy's** (tel. 809/949–3208), **Majestic Tours** (tel. 809/949–7773), **Reids** (tel. 809/949–6531), and **GreyLine** (tel. 809/949–2791).

Getting Around If your accommodations are along Seven Mile Beach, you can walk to the shopping centers, restaurants, and entertainment spots along West Bay Road.

Taxis Taxis offer islandwide service. Fares are determined by an elaborate rate structure set by the government, and although it may seem pricey for a short ride (fare from Seven Mile Beach for four people to the airport ranges from $7 to $11), cabbies rarely try to rip off tourists. Ask to see the chart if you want to double-check the quoted fare. **Cayman Cab Team** offers 24-hour service (tel. 809/947–0859), as does **Holiday Inn Taxi Stand** (tel. 809/947–4491).

Rental Cars To rent a car, bring your current driver's license and the car-rental firm will issue you a temporary permit ($3). Most firms have a range of models available, from compacts to Jeeps to minibuses. The major agencies have offices in a plaza across from the airport terminal, where you can pick up and drop off vehicles. Just remember, driving is on the left.

Car-rental companies are **Hertz** (tel. 809/949–2280), **Budget** (tel. 809/949–5605), **CICO-Avis** (tel. 809/949–2468), **Coconut** (tel. 809/949–4037), **Dollar** (tel. 809/949–2981), **Payless** (tel. 809/949–7074), and **National** (tel. 809/949–4790).

For mopeds, motorbikes, and bicycles: **Caribbean Motors** (tel. 809/949–4051 or 809/947–4466), **Cayman Cycle** (tel. 809/947–4020), **Honda** (tel. 809/947–4466), and **Soto Scooters** (tel. 809/947–4652).

Telephones and Mail For international dialing to Cayman, the area code is 809. To call outside, dial 0+1+ area code and number. You can call anywhere, anytime through the Cable and Wireless system and local operators. To make local calls, dial the seven-digit number.

Beautiful stamps and first-day covers are available at the main post office in downtown George Town weekdays from 8:30 to 4 and from the Philatelic office in West Shore Plaza, weekdays from 8:30 to 3:30. Sending a postcard to the United States, Canada, the Caribbean, or Central America costs C.I. 10¢. An airmail letter is C.I. 25¢ per half ounce. To Europe and South America, the rates are C.I. 15¢ for a postcard and C.I. 50¢ per half ounce for airmail letters.

Opening and Closing Times Banking hours are generally Monday–Thursday 9–2:30 and Friday 9–1 and 2:30–4:30. Shops are open Monday–Friday 9–5, and on Saturday in George Town from 10 to 2; in outer shopping plazas, from 10 to 5. Shops are usually closed on Sunday except in hotels.

Exploring the Cayman Islands

Numbers in the margin correspond to points of interest on the Grand Cayman and Cayman Brac and Little Cayman maps.

George Town
❶
Begin exploring **George Town** at the **National Museum** on Harbour Drive, slightly south of the Cruise Ship Dock Gazebo. Small but fascinating, the museum has excellent displays and videos illustrating the history of Cayman plant, animal, human, and geological life. *Harbour Drive, tel. 809/949–8368. Admission: C.I.$5. Open Mon.–Sat. 9:30–4:30.*

Along the waterfront, heading along North Church Street toward town, notice part of the original wall of the old Fort George, which is being restored. Across the street is the Wholesome Bakery and Cafe, which adds the homey smell of baking bread to the sea breezes off George Town Harbour. Try one of its delicious meat patties.

Turn left onto **Fort Street,** a main shopping street where you'll find the People's Boutique and a whole row of jewelry shops featuring black coral products—Bernard Passman, Finiterre, Smith's, and the Jewellery Factory.

At the end of the block is the heart of downtown George Town. At the corner of Fort Street and **Edward Street,** notice the small clock tower dedicated to Britain's King George V and the huge fig tree, manicured into an umbrella shape. The Cayman Islands **Legislative Assembly Building** is next door to the 1919 **Peace Memorial Building.**

Turning right on Edward Street, you'll find the charming **Library,** built in 1939; it has English novels, current newspapers from the United States, and a small reference section. It's worth a visit just for the Old World atmosphere. Across the street is the new **Court House.** Down the next block, a stroller enters the "financial district," where banks from all over the world have offices.

Straight ahead is the **General Post Office,** also built in 1939, with its strands of decorative colored lights and some 2,000 private mailboxes on the outside. (Mail is not delivered on the island.) Behind the post office is **Elizabethan Square,** a new shopping and office complex on **Shedden Road** that houses various food, clothing, and souvenir establishments. The courtyard has a pleasant garden and fountain as well as outdoor tables at La Fontaine, a German restaurant.

Exiting Elizabethan Square onto Shedden Road and walking past Anderson Square and Caymania Freeport, turn right back onto Edward Street, then left at the Royal Bank of Canada onto **Cardinal Avenue.** This is the main shopping area. On the right is the chic Kirk Freeport Plaza, known for its fine jewelry, plus duty-free bargains in china, crystal, Gucci items, perfumes, and fine cosmetics.

Turn left on **Harbour Drive** and make your way back to Shedden Road, passing the English Shoppe, a souvenir outlet that looks more as if it belongs on Shaftesbury Avenue in London than in the West Indies, and the Cayside Galleries, with its maritime antiques and cameras.

Walking back into town on Harbour Drive, you can enjoy a leisurely stroll along a waterfront sidewalk. A new public park with a circular gazebo is where visitors from the cruise ships disembark, but the park offers no shade from the sun.

Across the street is a pleasant church, the **Elmslie Memorial United.** Its vaulted ceiling with wood arches and a sedate nave reflects the quietly religious nature of island residents.

The **Treasure Museum,** located on West Bay Road in front of the Hyatt Hotel, is a real find. Dioramas show how Caymanians became seafarers, boat builders, and turtle breeders. An animated figure of Blackbeard the Pirate spins salty tales about the pirates and buccaneers who "worked" the Caribbean. Since the museum is owned by a professional treasure-salvaging firm, it's not surprising that there are a lot of artifacts from shipwrecks. There is even a gold bar that visitors can lift to appreciate its weight. *West Bay Rd., tel. 809/947–5033. Admission: C.I.$5. Open Mon.–Sat. 9–4:30 but hours can change; phone to check.*

The Outer Districts   Venturing away from the Seven Mile Beach strip, travelers will encounter the more down-home character of the islands. Heading out on South Church Street, you can see some of the old houses, which feature elaborate Victorian gingerbread on modest frame homes. Heading east in a district called **Pantonville,** after the Pantons who live there, there are three pretty cottages with lacy woodwork. Then at **South Sound** you see larger residences, some with fine detail and gracious verandas.

In the Savannah district, **Pedro's Castle,** built in 1780, lays claim to being the oldest structure on the island. Formerly a restaurant, it was purchased by the government in late 1991 for restoration as a historic landmark. At **Bodden Town,** you'll find an old cemetery on the shore side of the road. Graves with A-frame structures are said to contain the remains of pirates, but, in fact, they may be those of early settlers. A curio shop serves as the entrance to what's called the **Pirate's Caves,** and you'll pass a minizoo en route to these partially underground caves. The natural formations are interesting, but the place is more hokey than spooky.

Time Out | The large and airy **Lighthouse Club** (Breakers, tel. 809/947–2047) has booth seating around spectacular waterfront windows. Under new ownership, it now offers seafood and Italian cuisine.

② The village of **East End** is the first recorded settlement on the island. Its major claim to fame these days is that it's where renowned local musician called the "Violin Man," aka Radley Gourzong and His Happy Boys, lives and occasionally performs his distinctive form of music (more akin to Louisiana's backwater zydeco than reggae). It's also the site of a number of shipwrecks and **Morritt's Tortuga Club** (55 time-share units), whose guests include avid divers and windsurfers.

③ At the other end of the island is the **West Bay** community, whose main attraction is the **Turtle Farm**. The farm, which was started about 25 years ago, is the most popular attraction on the island today, with some 70,000 visitors a year. There are turtles of all ages, from day-old hatchlings to huge 600-pounders that can live to be 100 years old. The Turtle Farm was set up both as a conservation and a commercial enterprise; it releases about 5% of its stock back out to sea every year, harvests turtles for local restaurants, and exports the by-products. (Note: U.S. citizens cannot take home any turtle products because of a U.S. regulation banning their import.) In the adjoining café, you can sample turtle soup or turtle sandwiches while looking over an exhibit about turtles. *West Bay Rd., tel. 809/949–3893. Admission: $5 adults, $2.50 children 6–12. Open daily 9–5.*

④ The other area of West Bay that is of brief interest is the tiny village of **Hell**, which is little more than a patch of incredibly jagged rock formations called ironshore. The big attraction here is a small post office, which does a land-office business selling stamps and postmarking cards from Hell, and lots of T-shirt and souvenir shops. Almost unbelievably, a nearby nightclub, called the Club Inferno, is run by the McDoom family.

Cayman Brac

Brac, the Gaelic word for "bluff," aptly identifies this island's most distinctive feature, a rugged limestone cliff that runs down the center of the island's 12-mile length. At the eastern end, the bluff soars to 140 feet—rather dramatic for the Caribbean. Cayman Brac lies 89 miles east of Grand Cayman via Cayman Airways. It's a spelunker's paradise: you can explore the island's half-dozen large caves, some of which are still used for hurricane protection, via moped or taxi. Wear sneakers for this, not flip-flops; some of the paths to the caves are steep and rocky. Only 1,700 people live on this island, in communities such as Watering Place and Halfway Ground. The variety of flora includes unusual orchids, mangoes, and papaya, and the Cayman Brac parrot lives among the Brac's bird population. Parts of the island are unpopulated, so visitors can explore truly isolated areas both inland and along the shore.

Two hotels catering to divers, the Tiara Beach and the Brac Reef Beach Resort, are located on sandy beaches in a lagoon on the southwest coast. Swimming is possible, but the bottom is much rockier than on Seven Mile Beach.

Little Cayman

Only 7 miles away from Cayman Brac is Little Cayman Island, which boasts a population of only two dozen on its 12 square miles. This tiny place really is paradise for those intent on getting away from crowds—it has only two small shops and a jeep-rental office in the "plaza" by the airstrip, with a few private phones and one pay phone on the entire island. It does have ample accommodations for visitors, however, in five small lodges—the Southern Cross Club, Sam McCoy's Diving and Fishing Lodge, the Village Inn, the Little Cayman Beach Resort, and Pirate's Point. In addition to privacy, the real attractions of Little Cayman are diving in spectacular Bloody Bay, off the north coast, and fishing, which includes angling for tarpon and bonefish.

And if Little Cayman ever gets too busy, there is one final retreat—**Owen Island,** which is just 200 yards offshore. Accessible by rowboat, it has a blue lagoon and a sandy beach. Take your own picnic if you plan to spend the day.

What to See and Do with Children

Don't miss the one-hour **Atlantis Submarine** (tel. 809/949–7700) ride, which takes 48 passengers, a driver, and a guide down along the Cayman Wall to depths of 150 feet. This $2.8 million submarine has entertained hundreds of thousands of passengers, has all sorts of safety features, including a constantly circling surface monitor boat, and is air-conditioned. Through its large windows, you can see huge barrel sponges, corals of extraterrestriallike configurations, strange eels, and schools of beautiful and beastly fish. Night dives are quite dramatic because the artificial lights of the ship make the colors more vivid than they are in daytime excursions.

Turtle Farm (*see* Exploring the Cayman Islands, *above*).

Older children can also enjoy many of the water sports and beach games available. Only the Hyatt Hotel has a (seasonal) children's program. Other hotels politely say that they do not organize children's activities; be prepared to do so yourself.

Off the Beaten Track

Two architectural curiosities are worth a look if you are driving around. One is the little pink-and-white house on West Bay Road just past the cemetery. This 100-year-old cottage is made of mahogany and ironwood. Another odd residence is the conch house, near the power plant. This house was covered with conch shells years ago, but a recent renovation has added modern skylights and a garish satellite dish in the front yard.

Carey Cayman Coral (no phone) is a workshop out in South Sound run by Carey Hurlstone. Carey, a gentle bear of a man with tattoos covering his skin, professes he was a biker with the Hell's Angels before coming home to Cayman to work as a craftsman. He also carves glass. Carey's workmanship is superb, and his prices are quite reasonable for the quality.

Beaches

Grand Cayman You may read or hear about the "dozens of beaches" of these islands, but that's more exaggeration than reality. Grand Cayman's west coast, the most developed area of the entire colony, is where you'll find its famous **Seven Mile Beach** (actually 5½ miles long) and its expanses of powdery white sand. The beach is litter-free and sans peddlers, so you can relax in an unspoiled, hassle-free (if somewhat crowded) atmosphere. This is also Grand Cayman's busiest vacation center, and most of the island's accommodations, restaurants, and shopping centers are on this strip. The seaside bar and pool at the Holiday Inn are "party central" to repeat visitors on the island. You'll find headquarters for the island's aquatic activities here are scattered along the strip (*see* Sports and the Outdoors, *below*).

Grand Cayman has several smaller beaches that may better be called coves, including **Smith Cove,** off South Church Street, south of the Grand Old House—a popular bathing spot with residents on weekends .

The best snorkeling locations are off **the ironshore** (coral ledge area) south of **George Town** on Grand Cayman's west coast and in the reef-protected shallows of the island's north and south coasts, where coral and fish life are much more varied and abundant.

Other good beaches include **East End,** at Colliers, by Morritt's Tortuga Club, which can be lovely if it's kept clean of seaweed tossed ashore by trade winds. Seldom discovered by visitors unless they're staying out there are the beautiful beach areas of **Cayman Kai, Rum Point,** and, even more isolated and unspoiled, **Water Cay.** These are favored hideaways for residents and popular Sunday picnic spots.

Cayman Brac Both **Tiara Beach** and **Brac Reef Beach** resorts have fine small beaches, better for sunning than for snorkeling. Excellent snorkeling can be found immediately offshore of the now-defunct **Buccaneer's Inn** on the north coast.

Little Cayman The beaches **Point o' Sand,** on the eastern tip, and **Owen Island,** off the south coast, are exquisite isolated patches of powder that are great for sunbathing and worth every effort to reach by car, bike, or boat.

Sports and the Outdoors

Deep-Sea Fishing If you enjoy action fishing, Cayman waters have plenty to offer—blue and white marlin, yellowfin tuna, sailfish, dolphin, and wahoo. Bonefish and tarpon are also plentiful off Little Cayman. Some 25 boats are available for charter. Since 1984 a Million Dollar Month fishing tournament has been held in June, and registered anglers can win cash prizes by landing record-breaking catches. Each of the five tournaments has its own rules, records, and entrance fees. For information and applications, write Million Dollar Month Committee (Box 878, Grand Cayman, Cayman Islands, B.W.I.).

Diving To say that the Cayman Islands are a scuba diver's paradise is not overstating the case. Jacques Cousteau called Bloody Bay (off Little Cayman) one of the world's top dives. Pristine water (often exceeding 100-foot visibility), breathtaking coral formations, and plentiful and exotic marine life await divers. A host of top-notch dive operations offer a variety of services, instruction, and equipment. Predictably, however, most of Grand Cayman's dive boats tend to be full all year. Still, Sting Ray City is an absolute must, and the sister islands are far less crowded.

Divers are required to be certified and possess a "C" card or take a short resort or full certification course. A certification course, including classroom, pool, and boat sessions as well as checkout dives, takes five or six days and costs $300–$350. A resort course usually lasts a day and costs about $75–$90. It introduces the novice to the sport and teaches the rudimentary skills needed to make a shallow, instructor-monitored dive.

All dive operations on Cayman are more than competent; among them are **Bob Soto's** (tel. 809/947–4631 or 800/262–7686), **Don Foster's** (tel. 809/949–5679), **Red Sail Sports** (tel. 809/949–8745 or 800/255–6425), **Quabbin Dives** (tel. 809/949–5597), and **Sunset Divers** (tel. 809/949–7111 or 800/854–4767). Request full information on all operators from the Department of Tourism (*see* Before You Go, *above*).

On Cayman Brac, **Brac Aquatics** (tel. 809/858–7429 or 809/858–7323) and **Divi Tiara** (tel. 809/948–7553) offer scuba and snorkeling. On Little Cayman, each hotel has its own instructors.

Most operations can rent all diving gear, including equipment for underwater photography; Don Foster's, Fisheye Photographic, and Sunset U/W Photo have facilities for film processing and underwater photo courses.

Fitness A **Nautilus Fitness Center** (tel. 809/949–5132), with machines, weights, sauna, and whirlpool, is in operation on Crewe Road, in the Crighton Building just across from the airport. Daily membership is $10; weekly, $25. **Fitness Connection** (tel. 809/949–8485) offers aerobics classes, private instruction, and fitness counseling at three locations in George Town.

Golf The **Grand Cayman–Britannia** golf course, next to the Hyatt Regency, was designed by Jack Nicklaus. The course is really three in one—a nine-hole championship course, an 18-hole executive course, and a Cayman course, played with a Cayman ball that goes about half the distance of a regulation ball. Greens fees range from $25 to $50.

The first 9 holes of "The Links," the Cayman's first 18-hole championship course, should be playable by May 1993, with completion by the end of the year.

Tennis Most hotels and condo complexes have tennis courts for guests.

Water Sports Waterskiing, windsurfing, Hobie Cats, and jet skis are available at many of the aquatic shops along Seven Mile Beach (*see* Diving, *above*).

Shopping

If your motto is "Born to Shop," then Grand Cayman has two money-saving attributes—duty-free merchandise and the absence of a sales tax. Prices on imported merchandise—English china, Swiss watches, French perfumes, and Japanese cameras and electronic goods—are relatively cheaper than elsewhere. Expensive jewelry is another good buy, and the selection is vast—including authentic sunken treasure and ancient coins made into jewelry. If you've been postponing buying such luxury goods, you might consider this opportunity.

Good Buys
Black Coral

Black coral products are popular and exquisite choices; however, environmental groups discourage tourists from purchasing any coral that is designated as endangered species because the reefs are not always harvested carefully. If you feel differently, there are a number of local craftsmen who create original designs and finish their own work. Among those who have retail outlets in downtown George Town are **Coral Art Collections by Mitzi** (tel. 809/949–5086), in the Old Fort building on North Church Street; **Bernard Passman** (tel. 809/949–0123), whose creations won the approval of the English royal family, on Fort Street; and **Black Coral Jewelry and Other Fine Gems** (tel. 809/949–7156), whose creators, Richard and Rafaela Barile, have attracted lots of celebrities to their shop on Harbour Drive.

Arts and Crafts

Debbie van der Bol runs an arts and crafts shop called **Pure Art** (tel. 809/949–4433) on South Church Street and at the Hyatt Regency Hotel (tel. 809/347–5633). She features watercolors, woodcarvings, and lacemaking by local artists, as well as her own sketches and cards.

The **Heritage Crafts Shop** (tel. 809/949–7093), near the harbor in George Town, sells local crafts and gifts. The new **West Shore Shopping Center** on Seven Mile Beach near the Radisson offers good-quality island art, beachwear, ice cream, and more. Original prints, paintings, and sculpture with a tropical theme are found at **Cayman Fine Art** (tel. 809/949–8007). The **Oasis Boutique** (tel. 809/947–4444) at the Holiday Inn has a superior selection of contemporary, unique art pieces: jewelry, gifts, carvings, and clothing. T-shirt shops abound all over town.

Dining

Grand Cayman's restaurants satisfy every palate and pocketbook. Gourmet Continental cuisine is available to the high rollers; ethnic food can be had at moderate prices. West Indian fare in dining spots serving locals is the best in taste and value.

Seafood, not surprisingly, appears on most restaurant menus. Fish—including grouper, snapper, dolphin, tuna, wahoo, and marlin—is served either simply or Cayman style, with peppers, onions, and tomatoes. Conch, the meat of a large pink mollusk, is ubiquitous in stews and chowders and as fritters or panfried ("cracked"). Caribbean lobster is available but is often quite expensive, and other shellfish are in short supply in local waters. The only traditional culinary treat of the islands is turtle soup, stew, or steak, but only a few restaurants carry it these days.

Dining out on Grand Cayman can be expensive, so replenish your billfold because some places do not accept plastic. Prices are quoted in Cayman dollars.

All the restaurants reviewed below are located on Grand Cayman. Highly recommended restaurants are indicated by a star ★.

Category	Cost*
Expensive	over $30
Moderate	$20–$30
Inexpensive	under $20

per person, excluding drinks and service

★ **Chef Tell's Grand Old House.** TV celebrity chef Tell Erhardt has been running this popular establishment since 1986. His menu features Continental entrées and a few local specialties. Among the spicier appetizer choices is grouper Beignete, marinated and deep-fried grouper served with curry sauce and minted yogurt. On the bland side is Lobster Chef Fred's Way, dipped in egg batter and sautéed with shallots, mushrooms, and white wine. The back-porch dining room, with its Victorian trim and ceiling fans, is the liveliest and best spot for dining. The excellent service adds to this gracious dining experience. *S. Church St., tel. 809/949–9333. Reservations necessary for dinner, suggested for lunch. AE, MC, V. Closed for lunch weekends. Expensive.*

Garden Loggia Cafe. The Hyatt's indoor-outdoor café opens onto the most beautifully landscaped garden courtyard on the island. The Caribbean decor includes pastel colors, ceiling fans, and marble-top tables. The menu combines European and Caribbean tastes. The Friday-night seafood buffet and sumptuous Sunday champagne brunch feature everything from roast suckling pig, king crab, and lobster to waffles and custom-made omelets. Live music is featured at breakfast and dinner every day except Sunday. *Hyatt Regency Grand Cayman, West Bay Rd., tel. 809/949–1234. Reservations necessary. AE, MC, V. Expensive.*

★ **Hemingway's.** Located right on Seven Mile Beach, this classy restaurant features open-air dining with a sea view and breezes. Nouvelle Caribbean and seafood dishes include conch and turtle steak prepared in coconut milk and green bananas or beer-batter coconut shrimp. For a tropical drink, try the Seven Mile Meltdown, with dark rum, peach schnapps, pineapple juice, and fresh coconut. There is superb service and Caribbean decor. Buffet dinner is served on the *Spirit of Ppalu*, a glass-bottom catamaran. *Hyatt/Britannia Beach Club, West Bay Rd., tel. 809/949–1234. Reservations accepted. AE, MC, V. Expensive.*

★ **Lantana's.** Alfred Schrock, longtime chef at the top-rated Wharf Restaurant, now serves his own excellent southwestern cuisine at lunch and dinner. The decor is as tasteful and imaginatively authentic as the food: Enjoy blackened Canadian salmon with banana fritters, sweet-and-sour salsa, and cilantro pasta or Cayman conch fritters with ancho chile mayonnaise and cilantro pesto. *Caribbean Club, West Bay Rd., tel. 809/947–5595. Reservations necessary. AE, MC, V. Expensive.*

Lobster Pot. The second-floor terrace of this cozy restaurant overlooks the bay downtown, so the sunsets are an extra attraction. Its menu features both Continental dishes and such Caribbean specialties as conch chowder, turtle soup, steak, seafood curry, and, of course, lobster. This place is popular, so the constant turnover makes the atmosphere feel rushed. If you can't make dinner, drop by the pub and have a frozen banana daiquiri. *N. Church St., tel. 809/949–2736. Reservations recommended. MC, V. Expensive.*

Ottmar's. Dress is "smart casual" in this quietly elegant restaurant, styled after a West Indian great house. Jade carpeting, peach walls, linen, and glass chandeliers create an attractive setting for the excellent service. The Mesquite-grilled entrées, seafood, and French cuisine are no less exciting. Start the meal with drinks on a garden terrace. *In the Transnational Conference Center, West Bay Rd., tel. 809/941–5879 and 809/947–5882. Reservations required. Dinner only; closed Sun. AE, MC, V. Expensive.*

Periwinkle. This Italian restaurant, decorated in soothing pink and gray, is quiet and romantic. The menu features such Italian fare as seafood lasagna and chicken cacciatore, and grouper Cayman-style. During summer months, a grill is set up on the patio to charcoal dishes like fresh swordfish. *West Bay Rd., tel. 809/947–5181. Reservations accepted. AE, MC, V. Expensive.*

The Wharf. Stylishly decorated in blue and white, The Wharf looks onto a veranda and the nearby sea. On the menu are such Caribbean specialties as turtle steak, conch chowder, and sea scallops Provençal. Daily specials include seafood paella and soft-shell and stone crabs. Live music entertains diners. The Ports of Call bar is a perfect spot from which to watch the sun set. *West Bay Rd., tel. 809/949–2231. MC, V. Expensive.*

The Almond Tree. Looking for authentic island atmosphere in modern Grand Cayman? This eatery combines architecture from the South Seas isle of Yap, decorated with bones, skulls, and bric-a-brac from Africa, South America, and the Pacific. Sample good-value seafood entrées, including environmentally correct turtle steak, with "All-U-Can-Eat" entrées for C.I.$11 on Wednesday and Friday. *North Church St., tel. 809/459–2893. Dinner reservations recommended. AE, MC, V. Closed Tues. Moderate–Expensive.*

The Cracked Conch. This popular seafood restaurant has the ambience of a crowded fish house. Specialties include conch fritters, conch chowder, spicy Cayman-style snapper, and three types of turtle steak. The Key lime pie is divine. Take-out service is available. The bar has live entertainment and is a local hangout. *Selkirk's Plaza, West Bay Rd., tel. 809/947–5217. Reservations suggested in winter. AE, MC, V. Moderate.*

★ **Crow's Nest.** With the ocean right in its backyard, this secluded small restaurant is a great spot for snorkeling as well as lunching. One drawback: Insect repellent is required for patio dining in the evening. The gourmet shrimp and conch dishes are excellent, as is the dessert of raisins and rum cake. *South Sound, tel. 809/949–9366. Reservations required. MC, V. Closed Sun. Moderate.*

Golden Pagoda. The oldest Chinese restaurant in the Caymans features Hakka-style cooking. Among its specialties are Mahlah chicken, butterfly shrimp, and chicken in black-bean sauce. Takeout is available. *West Bay Rd., tel. 809/949–5475. Reservations accepted. Dress: no shorts at dinner. AE, MC, V. Moderate.*

Hog Sty Bay Cafe. Lots of socializing goes on in the casual atmosphere of this new English-style cafe on the harbor in George Town. A simple menu of sandwiches, hamburgers, and Caribbean dishes will satisfy you for lunch and dinner. Come and watch the sun set from the seaside patio or for the weekday happy hour. *N. Church St., tel. 809/949–6163. AE, MC, V. Closed lunch Sat. Moderate.*

White Hall Bay. Formerly the Cook Rum, the White Hall Bay has moved across the street to a restored waterfront

Caymanian house, but hasn't lost any of its casual ambience and charm. The hearty West Indian menu includes turtle stew, salt beef and beans, and pepperpot stew. Follow up with dessert specials, such as yam cake and coconut cream pie. *N. Church St., tel. 809/949–8670. AE, D, MC, V. Moderate.*

Corita's Copper Kettle. Here is a tidy downtown diner featuring Jamaican breakfasts and such native specialties as conch and lobster burgers. The fare is tasty and plain. *Edward St., tel. 809/949–2696.* A second location (in Dolphin Center, tel. 809/ 949–7078) opened in 1990. *No reservations. No credit cards. Inexpensive.*

Lodging

The success of the Cayman Islands as a resort destination means visitors should book ahead for holidays, especially at Christmastime. During the summer season, it is possible to find suitable lodging even on short notice. If you choose to stay in a condominium, you can book on a daily basis and stay any length of time. While about a third of the visitors come for the diving, a growing number are young honeymooners. There are few accommodations in the economy range, so guests must be prepared for resort prices. Most of the larger hotels along Seven Mile Beach don't offer meal plans. The smaller properties that are more remote from the restaurants usually offer MAP or FAP. Cayman Islands Hotel Reservations: 800/327–8777.

Highly recommended lodgings are indicated by a star ★.

Category	Cost*
Very Expensive	over $240
Expensive	$200–$240
Moderate	$160–$200
Inexpensive	under $160

*All prices are for a standard double room for two, excluding 6% tax and a 10% service charge.

Hotels
Grand Cayman
★

Caribbean Club. Eighteen one- and two-bedroom villas (six located on the beach) make up this quiet island getaway. All units were renovated in 1990. They are individually decorated and contain full kitchens, living and dining rooms, patios, and a bathroom for every bedroom. Secluded and luxurious. *Box 504, Grand Cayman, tel. 809/947–4099 or 800/327–8777, fax 809/ 947–4443. 18 villas. Facilities: tennis courts, water-sports center, restaurant (open for lunch and dinner), bar. AE, MC, V. EP. Very Expensive.*

★ **Hyatt Regency Grand Cayman.** Painted sky-blue and white and set amid gorgeous grounds, the Hyatt is adjacent to the only golf course on Grand Cayman. The rooms are exquisite, each with a marble entrance, oversize bathtub, bar, French doors, and a veranda. The Hyatt's beach club offers every water sport imaginable. Regency Club accommodations include complimentary Continental breakfast, early-evening hors d'oeuvres, and 24-hour concierge service. *Box 1698, Grand Cayman, tel. 809/949–1234 or 800/553–1300. 236 rooms; 43 rooms in Regency Club; 1-, 2-, and 3-bedroom Britannia villas. Facilities: pool, golf course, tennis courts, full-service water-sports center, 3* *restaurants, conference rooms. AE, MC, V. EP. Very Expensive.*

Indies Suites. Cayman's first and only all-suite hotel is attractive, comfortable, and across the road from the beach. One- or two-bedroom suites are done in cream and burnt orange, with contemporary wood furniture. Each has a fully equipped modern kitchen, living/dining rooms (with sleeper sofas), terraces, and storerooms for dive gear. Free Continental breakfast daily and entertainment in the lushly landscaped courtyard twice a week are nice extras. *Box 2070 GT, Seven Mile Beach, Grand Cayman, tel. 809/947–5025 or 800/654–3130, fax 809/947–5024. 40 suites. Facilities: water-sports shop, pool, poolside bar, TV. AE, MC, V. CP. Very Expensive.*

Radisson Resort Grand Cayman. This is a five-story luxury property on Seven Mile Beach, just a half-mile from George Town. Designed in colonial style with arched doorways, the hotel's airy, pale yellow and marble lobby opens onto a plant-filled courtyard. Families like the adjoining large, air-conditioned rooms, done in bright tropical colors; all have balconies facing either the ocean or a garden court. There is an inviting beach bar near the pool, an on-site dive shop (with every imaginable water sport), and a lively nightclub that entertains six nights a week. *Box 30371, Grand Cayman, tel. 809/949–0088 or 800/ 333–3333, fax 809/949–0288. 315 rooms. Facilities: restaurant, bar, pool, nightclub, Jacuzzi, water sports through Don Foster's Watersports. AE, DC, MC, V. EP. Very Expensive.*

★ **Coconut Harbour.** There's only one drawback to this serious diver's retreat: It's located near a field of oil storage tanks. This delightful resort has a dive shop, waterfront thatch-roof bar, and an informal restaurant. There's excellent diving offshore at Waldo's Reef, which is known for its population of tame marine life. *Box 2086, Grand Cayman, tel. 809/949–7468 or 800/552– 6281, fax 809/949–7117. 35 rooms, all with kitchens. Facilities: bar/grill, dive shop. AE, MC, V. CP. Expensive.*

Holiday Inn Grand Cayman. This hotel, home of the Coconuts Comedy Club, was the pioneer resort establishment on the beach, and it's still loose and fun. The property is cheerfully glitzy yet unpretentious, a sprawling modern hotel with bright tropical colors in the spacious public rooms. The guest rooms are standard Holiday Inn: large and comfortable, if not luxurious, with pool or ocean views. The huge breakfast buffet is a good value and don't miss the "Barefoot Man," who performs nightly outside on the patio. *Box 904, Grand Cayman, tel. 809/ 947–4444 or 800/421–9999. 215 rooms. Facilities: restaurant, 3 bars, water-sports center. AE, D, MC, V. EP. Expensive.*

Cayman Kai Resort. Nestled next to a coconut grove, each sea lodge features a full kitchen, dining and living areas, and two screened-in porches overlooking the ocean. *Box 1112, North Side, tel. 809/947–9055 or for reservations, 800/223–5427. 26 sea lodges, 1 villa. Facilities: restaurant, 2 bars, tennis court, diving, fishing and water-sports shop. AE, MC, V. EP. Moderate.*

★ **Sunset House.** Low-key and laid-back describe this resort on the ironshore south of George Town. A well-run dive operation, congenial staff, popular bar, and excellent seafood restaurant, "Seaharvest," make this resort a favorite with divers. The relaxed atmosphere on the deck in the evening makes it a great place for meeting people. *Box 479, S. Church St., tel. 809/949– 7111 or 800/854–4767, fax 809/949–7101. 57 rooms, 2 suites. Fa-*

*cilities: restaurant, bar, dive shop, fishing and sailing char-
ters. AE, D, MC, V. EP. Moderate.*

Cayman Islander. New management has done a lot for this simple, casual hotel across the road from Seven Mile Beach. The
small, but pleasant pool area has been refurbished, as have the
67 rooms. Although the rooms aren't fancy, they're comfortable and more than adequate with new air-conditioning and
brighter decor. Some have been turned into efficiencies with
microwaves and refrigerators. A complete dive shop is on the
premises. This hotel is a good value. *Box 30081, Seven Mile
Beach, Grand Cayman, tel. 809/949–0990 or 800/327–8777, fax
809/949–7896. 67 rooms and 3 suites. Facilities: dive shop,
pool, satellite TV. AE, MC, V. EP. Inexpensive–Moderate.*

Cayman Brac **Brac Reef Beach Resort.** Designed, built, and owned by
Bracker Linton Tibbets, the resort lures divers and vacationers who come to savor the special ambience of this tiny island.
Just-renovated good-quality accommodations, a pool, a beach,
snorkeling, and the waterside two-story covered deck are additional reasons to stay here. *Box 56, Cayman Brac, tel. 809/948–
7323, 800/327–3835, in FL, 800/233–8880. 40 rooms. Facilities:
restaurant, 2 bars, pool, Jacuzzi, beach, dive shop. AE, MC, V.
EP, MAP, FAP. Moderate.*

Divi Tiara Beach Resort. This resort is dedicated to divers; it
has an excellent brand-new diving facility complemented by the
DIVI chain's standards: tile floors, rattan furniture, louvered
windows, balconies, and ocean views. *Box 238, Cayman Brac,
tel. 809/948–7553; in the U.S., 800/FOR–DIVI. 70 rooms. Facilities: restaurant, bar, pool, Jacuzzi, tennis, dive operation,
water-sports center, fishing. AE, MC, V. EP. Moderate.*

Little Cayman **Pirates Point Resort.** Opened by Texan Gladys Howard, this
comfortably informal beach resort has added four more large
rooms to its six octagonal units just a few minutes from the airstrip. The voluble Ms. Howard leads nature walks and is a cordon bleu chef. "Relaxing" rates include meals only; all-inclusive
rates include mouth-watering meals, wine, dives, fishing, and
picnics on uninhabited Owen Island. *Little Cayman, tel. 809/
948–4210 or 800/654–7537, fax 809/948–4610. 10 rooms. Facilities: diving, fishing, restaurant. No credit cards. FAP. Moderate–Expensive.*

Sam McCoy's Diving and Fishing Lodge. Staying at this remote
getaway is rather like being a welcome houseguest of Sam and
his family. Very reasonable rates and the owner's infectious
good nature are the hallmarks of this small and simple locally
run diving/fishing resort. There is superb diving and snorkeling right offshore. In late 1991, Sam opened a new beach bar a
few minutes away overlooking Bloody Bay. Totally secluded, it
offers outdoor dancing and light snacks. Meals at the lodge are
included in the rates. *Little Cayman, tel. 809/948–4526 or 800/
626–0496, fax 809/949–6821. 6 rooms. No credit cards. FAP.
Moderate.*

Southern Cross Club. Three family-style meals a day are included in the rates at this relaxing retreat that caters to fishermen and divers. The rooms are mostly white and furnished
with wicker. Excellent diving and bonefishing. *Little Cayman,
tel. 809/948–3255; in the U.S., 317/636–9501. 10 rooms. Facilities: diving, fishing, bird-watching in sanctuary. No credit
cards. FAP. Moderate.*

Little Cayman Beach Resort. This two-story property, on the
south side of the island, opened in early 1993. Considerably less

rustic than other Little Cayman resorts, the 32 oceanfront rooms have modern furnishings in pastel tropical colors and double hammocks to relax in. For the more active there are paddleboats and windsurfers in addition to the pool and Jacuzzi. *Little Cayman, tel. 809/948–4533 or 800/327–3835, 809/948–4507. 32 rooms. Facilities: dive shop, pool, Jacuzzi, bar/restaurant, dive packages available. AE, MC, V. MAP, FAP, All-inclusive. Inexpensive.*

Condominiums and Villas The **Cayman Islands Department of Tourism** provides a complete list of condominiums and small rental apartments in the Moderate to Inexpensive range. Rates are higher during the winter season, so check before you book. **Cayman Villas** (Box 681, Grand Cayman, tel. 809/947–4144) can help you locate a rental house or cottage. **Reef House Ltd. Property Management** (Box 1540, Grand Cayman, tel. 809/949–7093) also rents villas, houses, and apartments on all three islands.

Nightlife

Each of the island hot spots attracts a different clientele. The **Holiday Inn** (tel. 809/947–4444) offers something for everyone: A live local band for dancing plays outdoors around the pool six nights a week. **Coconuts** (tel. 809/947–5757), the Caymans' original Comedy Club, features young American stand-up comedians who entertain year-round. The crowd gathers poolside at the Holiday Inn (tel. 809/947–4444), where the "Barefoot Man" sings and plays. The dance floor is always crowded, and it's also a great spot to people-watch. **Silver's Nightclub** (tel. 809/949–7777), at the Ramada Treasure Island Resort, is a spacious, tiered club that is usually filled to capacity. A lively house band plays Monday–Saturday nights. The **BWI High Energy Club** (tel. 809/949–0088), at the Radisson Resort Grand Cayman, offers recorded music and dancing six nights a week. Also at the Radisson, "The Comedy Zone" features stand-up comedians from the United States Saturdays 8:30–10 PM for $16.

Island Rock Nightclub (Falls Shopping Center, tel. 809/947–5366), a new disco and bar, features live bands some nights.

For current entertainment, look at the freebie magazine, *What's Hot*, which gives listings of music, movies, theater, and other entertainment possibilities.

9 Curaçao

Updated by
Laurie Senz

Thirty-five miles north of Venezuela and 42 miles east of Aruba is Curaçao, the largest of the islands in the Netherlands Antilles. The sun smiles down on Curaçao, but it never gets stiflingly hot: The gentle trade winds refresh. Water sports attract enthusiasts from all over the world, and some of the best reef diving is here. Though the island claims 38 beaches, Curaçao does not have long stretches of sand or enchanting scenery. The island is dominated by an arid countryside, rocky coves, and a sprawling capital situated around a natural harbor. Until recently, the island's economy was not based on tourism but on oil refining and catering to offshore corporations seeking tax hedges. Although tourism has become a major economic force in the past five years, the atmosphere on the island remains low key—a big appeal to visitors seeking an alternative to the commercialism found on many of the other Caribbean islands.

As seen from the Otrabanda of Willemstad by the first-time visitor, Curaçao's "face" will be a surprise—spiffy rows of pastel-colored town houses that look as though they were transplanted from Holland. Although the gabled roofs and red tiles show a Dutch influence, the absurdly gay colors of the facades, as novelist Christopher Isherwood once described them, are peculiar to Curaçao. It is said that the first governor of Curaçao developed a terrible allergy to the color white (it gave him migraines), so all the houses were painted in colors. The dollhouse look of the architecture makes a cheerful contrast to the stark cacti and the austere shrubbery dotting the countryside.

The history books still cannot agree on who discovered Curaçao—one school of thought believes it was Alonzo de Ojeda, another says it was Amerigo Vespucci—but they seem to agree that it was around 1499. The first Spanish settlers arrived in 1527. In 1634, the Dutch came via the Netherlands West India Company. They promptly shipped off the Spaniards and the few remaining Indians—survivors of the battles for ownership of the island, famine, and disease—to Venezuela. Eight years later, Peter Stuyvesant ruled as governor until he left for New York around 1645. Twelve Jewish families arrived from Amsterdam in 1651 and built a synagogue; today, it is the oldest synagogue still in use in the Western Hemisphere. Over the years, the city built massive fortresses to defend itself against French and British invasions—many of those ramparts now house unusual restaurants and hotels. The Dutch claim to Curaçao was finally recognized in 1815 by the Treaty of Paris. In 1954, Curaçao became an autonomous part of the Kingdom of the Netherlands, with an elected parliament and island council. It is ruled by a governor appointed by the queen.

Today Curaçao's population is derived from more than 50 nationalities blending together in an exuberant mix of Latin and African roots. The island is known for its religious tolerance, and tourists are warmly welcomed. In the past few years, millions of dollars have been poured into restoring the old colonial landmarks and upgrading and modernizing hotels. The International Trade Center, a major convention hall that opened in 1989, has helped attract business to the island, as has the opening of the new 248-room Sonesta Beach Hotel & Casino.

Curaçao

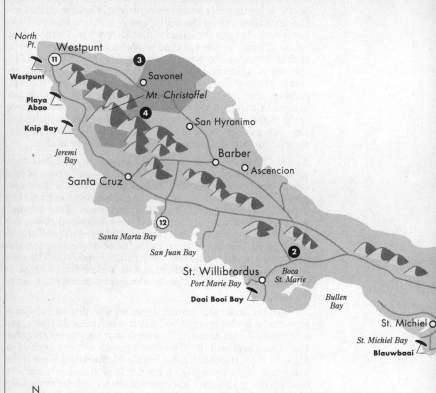

North
Pt.   **Westpunt**
⑪   ③
Westpunt   ○ *Savonet*
Playa   *Mt. Christoffel*
Abao   ④
Knip Bay   ○ *San Hyronimo*

Jeremi
Bay   **Barber**
   ○ ○ *Ascencion*
Santa Cruz ○

⑫

Santa Marta Bay
San Juan Bay   ②
St. Willibrordus   *Boca*
Port Marie Bay   *St. Marie*
Daai Booi Bay   *Bullen*
   Bay
   St. Michiel ○
   St. Michiel Bay
   Blauwbaai

N

0 _____ 10 miles
0 _____ 15 km

Exploring
Arawak Clay
Products, **8**
Boca Tabla, **3**
Caracas Bay, **10**
Christoffel Park, **4**

Curaçao
Seaquarium, **5**
Curaçao Underwater
Marine Park, **6**
Hato Caves, **9**
Landhuis
Brievengat, **7**
Landhuis Jan Kock, **2**
Willemstad, **1**

Dining
Belle Terrace, **21**
Bistro Le Clochard, **16**
Bon Appetit, **25**
Cozzoli's Pizza, **22**
De Taveerne, **19**
El Marinero, **24**
Fort Nassau
Restaurant, **20**
Fort
Waarzaamreid, **18**

Garuda Indonesian
Restaurant, **14**
Golden Star
Restaurant, **30**
Guacamaya
Steakhouse, **26**
Jaanchi Christiaan's
Restaurant, **11**
L'Alouette, **31**
Rijstaffel Indonesia
Restaurant, **29**

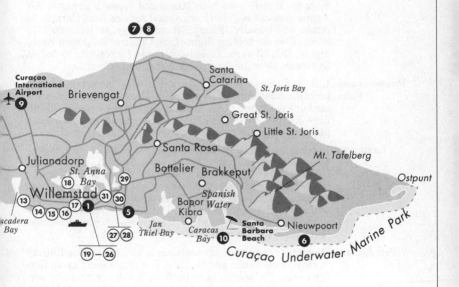

Caribbean Sea

Curaçao International Airport ✈ **9**

Brievengat

Santa Catarina

St. Joris Bay

Great St. Joris

Little St. Joris

Santa Rosa

Bottelier   Brakkeput

Mt. Tafelberg

Ostpunt

Julianadorp

St. Anna Bay

18

Willemstad

29

31 **30**

17 **1**

13

14 **15** **16**

scadera Bay

5

27 **28**

19 — 26

Bapor Kibra

Spanish Water

Jan Thiel Bay   *Caracas Bay* **10**

Santa Barbara Beach

Nieuwpoort

6

Curaçao Underwater Marine Park

7 **8**

Lodging

Avila Beach Hotel, **20**

Coral Cliff Resort and Beach Club, **12**

Curaçao Caribbean Hotel and Casino, **14**

Holiday Beach Hotel and Casino, **15**

Lions Dive Hotel & Marina, **28**

Otrabanda Hotel & Casino, **17**

Princess Beach Hotel and Casino, **27**

Sonesta Beach Hotel & Casino, **13**

Van Der Valk Plaza Hotel and Casino, **23**

Before You Go

Tourist Information   Contact the **Curaçao Tourist Office** (400 Madison Ave., New York, NY 10017, tel. 212/751–8266 or 800/332–8266 and at 330 Biscayne Blvd., Suite 330, Miami, FL 33132, tel. 305/374–5811) for information.

Arriving and Departing
By Plane   **ALM** (tel. 800/327–7230) has four nonstop and 10 direct flights a week from Miami and four direct flights a week from Atlanta. For Atlanta departures, ALM has connecting services (throughfares) to most U.S. gateways with Delta. This arrangement makes ALM Curaçao's major carrier. ALM uses Curaçao as its hub to fly to Aruba, Bonaire, Caracas, Trinidad, Puerto Rico, and St. Maarten. ALM also offers a Visit Caribbean Pass, allowing easy interisland travel. **Air Aruba** (tel. 800/882–7822) has direct flights to Curaçao (flights make brief stops in Aruba) from both Miami and Newark airports. Air Aruba also has regularly scheduled service from Curaçao to Aruba and Bonaire. Every Saturday, **Key Air** (tel. 800/786–2386) offers connecting flights from Chicago, Baltimore/Washington, DC, Newark, Philadelphia, and Boston into its hub in Savannah, Georgia, for a nonstop flight into Curaçao.

Passports and Visas   U.S. and Canadian citizens traveling to Curaçao need only proof of citizenship and a valid photo ID. A voter's registration card or a notarized birth certificate (not a photocopy) will suffice—a driver's license will *not*. British citizens must produce a passport. All visitors must show an ongoing or return ticket.

Language   Dutch is the official language, but the vernacular is Papiamento—a mixture of Dutch, Portuguese, Spanish, and English. Developed during the 18th century by Africans, Papiamento evolved in Curaçao as the mode of communication between landowners and their slaves. These days, however, English, as well as Spanish, and, of course, Dutch, are studied by schoolchildren. Anyone involved with tourism—shopkeepers, restaurateurs, and museum guides—speaks English.

Precautions   Mosquitoes on Curaçao do not seem as vicious and bloodthirsty as they do on Aruba and Bonaire, but that doesn't mean they don't exist. To be safe, keep perfume to the minimum, be prepared to use insect repellent before dining alfresco, and spray your hotel room at night—especially if you've opened a window.

If you plan to go into the water, beware of long-spined sea urchins, which can cause pain and discomfort if you come in contact with them.

Do not eat any of the little green applelike fruits of the manchineel tree: They're poisonous. In fact, steer clear of the trees altogether; raindrops or dewdrops dripping off the leaves can blister your skin. If contact does occur, rinse the affected area with water and, in extreme cases, get medical attention. Usually, the burning sensation won't last longer than two hours.

Staying in Curaçao

Important Addresses   **Tourist Information:** The **Curaçao Tourism Development Foundation** has three offices on the island, where multilingual guides are ready to answer questions. You can also pick up maps, brochures, and a copy of *Curaçao Holiday*. The main office is located in Willemstad at Pietermaai No. 19 (tel. 599/9-616000); other offices are in the Waterfort Arches (tel. 599/9-613397), next to the Van Der Valk Plaza Hotel, and at the airport (tel. 599/9-686789).

Emergencies **Police** or **Fire:** tel. 114. The **Main Police Station** number is 599/9-611000. **Hospitals:** For medical emergencies, call **St. Elisabeth's Hospital** (tel. 599/9-624900) or an ambulance (tel. 112). **Pharmacies: Botica Popular** (Madurostraat 15, tel. 599/9-611269). Or ask at your hotel for the nearest one.

Currency U.S. dollars—in cash or traveler's checks—are accepted nearly everywhere, so there's no need to worry about exchanging money. However, you may need small change for pay phones, cigarettes, or soda machines. The currency in the Netherlands Antilles is the guilder, or florin, as it is also called, indicated by an fl. or NAf. on price tags. The U.S. dollar is considered very stable; the official rate of exchange at press time was NAf 1.79 to U.S. $1. Note: Prices quoted here are in U.S. dollars unless indicated otherwise.

Taxes and Service Charges Hotels collect a 7% government tax and add a 12% service charge to the bill; restaurants add 10%–15%.

The airport departure tax is U.S. $10 ($5.65 for Bonaire).

Guided Tours You don't really need a guide to show you downtown Willemstad—it's an easy taxi or bus ride from most major hotels and small enough for a self-conducted walking tour (follow the one outlined in the free tourist booklet *Curaçao Holiday*). To see the rest of the island, however, a guided tour can save you time and energy, though it is easy to cover the island yourself in a rented car. Most hotels have tour desks where arrangements can be made with reputable tour operators. For very personal, amiable service, try **Casper Tours** (tel. 599/9-653010 or 599/9-616789). For $25 per person, you'll be escorted around the island in an air-conditioned van, with stops at the Juliana Bridge, the salt lakes, Knip Bay for a swim, the grotto at Boca Tabla, and lunch at Jaanchi Christiaan's, which is famous for its native cuisine. **Taber Tours** (tel. 599/9-376637) offers a 3½-hour city and country tour ($10) that includes visits to the Curaçao Liqueur Factory, the Curaçao Museum, and the Bloempot shopping center. A full-day tour includes a visit to the Seaquarium and a snorkel trip; it costs $25 per person. Tabor Tours also offers a two-hour sunset cruise ($29.50 for adults and $20 for children) with a feast of French bread, cheese, and wine. A day trip to Aruba or Bonaire is also available.

Getting Around Taxis Taxi drivers have an official tariff chart, with fares from the airport vicinity running about $11 to Willemstad and $10 to Piscadera Bay. Taxis tend to be moderately priced, but since there are no meters, you should confirm the fare with the driver before departure. There is an additional 25% surcharge after 11 PM. Taxis are readily available at hotels; in other cases, call Central Dispatch at tel. 599/9-616711.

Rental Cars You can rent a car from **Budget** (tel. 599/9-683420), **Avis** (tel. 599/9-681163), or **National Car Rental** (tel. 599/9-683489) at the airport or have it delivered free to your hotel. A typical rate is about $46 a day for a Toyota Starlet to about $73 for a four-door sedan. The least expensive car-rental companies at press time were **Love Car Rental** (tel. 599/9-690444) and **Dollar** (tel. 599/9-690262). Their prices range from $33 for a Starlet to $50 for a four-door sedan. Off-season prices are about $25 a day. If you're planning to do country driving or rough it through Christoffel Park, a Jeep is best. All you'll need is a valid U.S. or Canadian driver's license.

Telephones and Mail Phone service through the hotel operators in Curaçao is slow, but direct-dial service, both on-island and to the United States, is fast and clear. Hotel operators will put the call through for you, but if you make a collect call, do check immediately afterward that the hotel does not charge you as well. To call Curaçao direct, dial 011–599–9 plus the number in Curaçao. To place a local call on the island, dial the six-digit local number. An airmail letter to anywhere in the world costs NAf 1.25, a postcard NAf .70.

Opening and Closing Times Most shops are open Monday–Saturday 8–noon and 2–6. Banks are open weekdays 8:00–3:30.

Exploring Curaçao

Numbers in the margin correspond to points of interest on the Curaçao map.

Willemstad ① The capital city, **Willemstad,** is a favorite cruise stop for two reasons: The shopping is considered among the best in the Caribbean, and a quick tour of most of the downtown sights can be managed within a six-block radius. Santa Anna Bay slices the city down the middle: On one side is the Punda, and on the other is the Otrabanda (literally, the "other side"). Think of the Punda as the side for tourists, crammed with shops, restaurants, monuments, and markets. Otrabanda is less touristy, with lots of narrow winding streets full of private homes notable for their picturesque gables and Dutch-influenced designs.

There are three ways to make the crossing from one side to the other: (1) drive or take a taxi over the Juliana Bridge, (2) traverse the Queen Emma Pontoon Bridge on foot, or (3) ride the free ferry, which runs when the bridge is open for passing ships. All the major hotels outside of town offer free shuttle service to town. Shuttles coming from the Otrabanda side leave you at Rif Fort. From there it's a short walk north to the foot of the Pontoon Bridge. Shuttles coming from the Punda side leave you near the main entrance to Fort Amsterdam.

Our walking tour of Willemstad starts at the **Queen Emma Bridge,** affectionately called the Lady by the natives. During the hurricane season in 1988, the 700-foot floating bridge practically floated right out to sea; it was later taken down for major reconstruction. If you're standing on the Otrabanda side, take a few moments to scan Curaçao's multicolored "face" on the other side of Santa Anna Bay. If you wait long enough, the bridge will swing open (at least 30 times a day) to let the seagoing ships pass through. The original bridge, built in 1888, was the brainchild of the American consul Leonard Burlington Smith, who made a mint off the tolls he charged for the bridge. Initially, the charge was 2¢ per person for those wearing shoes, free to those crossing barefoot. Today it's free to everyone.

Take a breather at the peak of the bridge and look north to the 1,625-foot-long **Queen Juliana Bridge,** completed in 1974 and standing 200 feet above water. That's the bridge you drive over to cross to the other side of the city, and although the route is time consuming (and more expensive if you're going by taxi), the view from this bridge is worth it. At every hour of the day, the sun casts a different tint over the city, creating an ever-changing panorama; the nighttime view, rivaling Rio's, is breathtaking.

When you cross the Pontoon Bridge and arrive on the Punda side, turn left and walk down the waterfront, along **Handel-skade.** You'll soon pass the ferry landing. Now take a close look at the buildings you've seen only from afar; the original red tiles of the roofs came from Europe and arrived on trade ships as ballast.

Walk down to the corner and turn right at the customs building onto Sha Caprileskade. This is the bustling **floating market,** where each morning dozens of Venezuelan schooners arrive laden with tropical fruits and vegetables. Fresh mangoes, papayas, and exotic vegetables vie for space with freshly caught fish and herbs and spices. It's probably too much to ask a tourist to arrive by 6:30 AM when the buying is best, but there's plenty of action to see throughout the afternoon. Any produce bought here, however, should be thoroughly washed before eating.

When the sun is beating down, the **Reading Corner** in the Maduro and Curiel's Bank building (right in front of the floating market) will feel like an oasis. It's an open-air reading room, where you can sit and catch up on the latest newspapers from the United States, Venezuela, and Holland.

Keep walking down Sha Caprileskade. Head toward the Wilhelmina Drawbridge, which connects Punda with the once-flourishing district of **Scharloo,** where the early Jewish merchants first built stately homes. Scharloo is now a red-light district.

If you continue straight ahead, Sha Caprileskade becomes De Ruyterkade. Soon you'll come to the post office, which will be on your left. Behind it is the **Old Market** (Marche). Here you'll find local women preparing hearty Antillean lunches. For $4–$6 you can enjoy such Curaçaon specialties as *funchi* (cornbread), *kesi yena* (Gouda cheese stuffed with meat), goat stew, fried fish, peas and rice, and fried plantains. After lunch, return to the intersection of De Ruyterkade and Columbusstraat and turn left.

Walk up Columbusstraat to the **Mikveh Israel-Emmanuel Synagogue,** founded in 1651 and the oldest temple still in use in the Western Hemisphere. One of the most important sights in Curaçao, it draws 20,000 visitors a year. Enter through the gates around the corner on Hanchi Snoa and ask the front office to direct you to the guide on duty. A unique feature is the brilliant white sand covering the synagogue floor, a remembrance of Moses leading his people through the desert; the Hebrew letters on the four pillars signify the names of the Four Daughters of Israel: Eve, Sarah, Rachel, and Esther. A fascinating museum (tel. 599/9–611633) in the back displays Jewish antiques (including a set of circumcision instruments) and artifacts from Jewish families collected from all over the world. The gift shop near the gate has excellent postcards and commemorative medallions. *Hanchi Di Snoa 29, tel. 599/9–611067. Open weekdays 9–11:45 and 2:30–5. English and Hebrew services conducted by an American rabbi are held Fri. at 6:30 PM and on Sat. at 10 AM. Jacket and tie required.*

Continue down Columbusstraat and cross Wilhelminaplein (Wilhelmina Park). Now you will be in front of the courthouse, with its stately balustrade, and the impressive Georgian facade of the Bank of Boston. The statue keeping watch over the park is of Queen Wilhelmina, a deceased popular monarch of the Netherlands, who gave up her throne to her daughter Juliana after her Golden Jubilee in 1948. Cut back across the park and turn left at Breedestraat, where you can browse at two of the best jewelry shops in the Caribbean: **Spritzer & Fuhrmann** and **Gandleman's Jewelers.** Take Breedestraat down to the Pontoon Bridge, then turn left at the waterfront. At the foot of the bridge are the mustard-colored walls of **Fort Amsterdam.** Take a few steps through the archway and enter another century. The entire structure dates from the 1700s, when it was actually the center of the city and the most important fort on the island. Now it houses the governor's residence, the Fort Church, the ministry, and several other government offices. Next door is the **Plaza Piar,** dedicated to Manuel Piar, a native Curaçaoan who fought for the independence of Venezuela under the liberator Simon Bolívar. On the other side of the plaza is the **Waterfort,** a bastion dating from 1634. The original cannons are still positioned in the battlements. The foundation, however, now forms the walls of the Van Der Valk Plaza Hotel. Following the sidewalk around the Plaza, you'll discover one of the most delightful shopping areas on the island, newly built under the **Waterfort arches** (*see* Shopping, *below,* for details).

Western Side The road through the village of Soto that leads to the northwest tip of the island winds through landscape that Georgia O'Keefe might have painted—towering cacti, flamboyant dried shrubbery, and aluminum-roof houses. Throughout this *cunucu,* or countryside, you'll see native fishermen hauling in their nets, women pounding cornmeal, and an occasional donkey blocking traffic. Landhouses, large estate houses from centuries past, dot the countryside, though most are closed to the public. Their facades, though, can often be glimpsed from the highway. For a splendid view, and some unusual island tales of ghosts, follow Wespunt Highway to the intersection at Cunucu Abao, then veer left onto Weg Naar San Willibrordo until you come to

❷ **Landhuis Jan Kock** (tel. 599/9–648087), located across from the salt pans. Since the hours are irregular, be sure to call ahead to arrange a tour of this reputedly haunted mid-17th-century house or stop by on Sunday mornings, when the proprietor opens her small restaurant behind her home and serves delicious Dutch pancakes.

Continuing north on this road, you'll come to the village of Soto. From here the road leads to the northwest tip of the island, where it becomes Wespunt Highway again and heads

❸ south to **Boca Tabla,** where the sea has carved a magnificent grotto. Safely tucked in the back, you can watch and listen to the waves crashing ferociously against the rocks. A short dis-

❹ tance farther is **Christoffel Park,** a fantastic 4,450-acre garden and wildlife preserve with the towering Mt. Christoffel at its center. Open to the public since 1978, the park consists of three former plantations with individual trails that take about one to 1½ hours each to traverse. You may drive your own car (heavy-treaded wheels) or rent a Jeep with an accompanying guide ($15). Start out early (by 10 AM the park starts to feel like a sauna), and if you're going solo, first study the *Excursion Guide to Christoffel Park* (sold at the front desk), which outlines the various routes and identifies the flora and fauna found here. No matter what route you take, you'll be treated to interesting views of hilly fields full of prickly-pear cacti, divi-divi trees, bushy-haired palms, and exotic flowers that bloom unpredictably after April showers. There are also caves and ancient Indian drawings. For the strong of heart: Walk through the bat caves on the Savonet route (marked in blue); you'll hear bat wings rustling in the corners and see a few scary but nonpoisonous scorpion spiders scuttling over the walls. Make sure you're wearing the proper shoes; the ground is covered with *guano* (bird and bat droppings) that almost seems alive because of the millions of harmless mites. It's not all a shop of horrors, though—if you make it to the last chamber, you may see a magnificent white-faced barn owl that nests in the cave fissures.

As you drive through the park, keep a lookout for tiny deer, goats, and other small wildlife that might suddenly dart in front of your car. The snakes you could encounter—the whipsnake and the minute silver snake—are not poisonous. Whitetail hawks may be seen on the green route, white orchids and crownlike passion flowers on the yellow route.

Climbing up the 1,239-foot Mt. Christoffel on foot is an exhilarating experience and a definite challenge to anyone who hasn't grown up scaling the Alps. The guidebook claims the round-trip will take you one hour, and Curaçaoan adolescent boys do make a sport of racing up and down, but it took this writer 2½ sweaty hours to make it back to camp. And the last few feet are deadly. The view from the peak, however, *is* thrilling—a panorama of the island, including Santa Marta Bay and the tabletop mountain of St. Hironimus. On a clear day, you can even see the mountain ranges of Venezuela, Bonaire, and Aruba. *Savonet, tel. 599/9–640363. Admission: $5 adults, $3 children 6–15. Open Mon.–Sat. 8–5, Sun. 6–3.*

Eastern Side To explore the eastern side of the island, take the coastal road —Martin Luther King Blvd.—out from Willemstad past the zoo and botanical gardens (neither is exceptional) about 2 miles to Bapor Kibra. There you'll find the Seaquarium and the Underwater Park.

❺ The **Curaçao Seaquarium** is *the* place to see the island's underwater treasures without getting your feet wet. In fact, it's the world's only public aquarium where sea creatures are raised and cultivated totally by natural methods. You can spend several hours here, mesmerized by the 46 freshwater tanks full of more than 400 varieties of exotic fish and vegetation found in the waters around Curaçao, including sharks, lobsters, turtles, corals, and sponges. Look out for the over five-foot-long mascot, Herbie the lugubrious jewfish. Four sea lions from Uruguay are the most recent pride of the aquarium. If you get hungry, stop at the excellent Italian restaurant or the steak house–cum–Mexican eatery. There are also glass-bottom boat tours and a viewing platform overlooking the wreck of the steamship *S.S. Oranje Nassau*, which sank in 1906 and now sits in 10 feet of water. A nearby 495-yard man-made beach of white sand is well suited to novice swimmers and children, and bathroom and shower facilities are available. A souvenir shop sells some of the best postcards and coral jewelry on the island. *Tel. 599/9–616666. Admission: $6 adults, $3 children. Open daily 9 AM–10 PM.*

⑥ Curaçao Underwater Marine Park (tel. 599/9–618131) consists of about 12½ miles of untouched coral reefs that have been granted the status of national park. Mooring buoys have been placed at the most interesting dive sites on the reef to provide safe anchoring and to prevent damage to the reef. The park stretches along the south shore from the Princess Beach Hotel in Willemstad to the eastern tip of the island.

⑦ Landhuis Brievengat (tel. 599/9–378344) is a 10-minute drive northeast of Willemstad, near the Centro Deportivo sports stadium. On the last Sunday of the month (from 10 AM to 3 PM), this old estate holds an open house with crafts demonstrations and folkloric shows. You can see the original kitchen still intact, the 18-inch-thick walls, fine antiques, and the watchtowers, once used for lovers' trysts. The restaurant, which is open only on Wednesday, serves a fine *rijsttafel* (Indonesian smorgasbord). Every Friday night a party is held on the wide wraparound terrace, with two bands and plenty to drink.

⑧ Opposite the Industry Park at Brievengat, is **Arawak Clay Products,** which has a factory showroom of native-made crafts. You can purchase a variety of tiles, plates, pots, and tiny replicas of landhouses. Tour operators usually include a stop here. *Tel. 599/9–377658. Open Mon.–Sat. 7:30–5.*

Head northwest toward the airport to the island's newest attraction, **Hato Caves.** Hour-long guided tours wind down into **⑨** the various chambers to the water pools; voodoo chamber; wishing well; fruit bats' sleeping quarters; and Curaçao Falls, where a stream of silver joins with a stream of gold and is guarded by a limestone "dragon" perched nearby. Hidden lights illuminate the limestone formations and gravel walkways. One of the better Caribbean caves open to the public. *Tel. 599/9–680378. Admission: $4.25 adults, $2.75 children. Open Tues.–Sun. 10 AM–5 PM. Closed Mon.*

Wind southward past Spanish Water, where you'll pass several private yacht clubs that attract sports anglers from all over the world for international tournaments. And make a stop at **Santa Barbara Beach,** especially on Sundays, when the atmosphere **⑩** approaches party time (*see* Beaches, *above*). **Caracas Bay,** off Bapor Kibra, is a popular dive site, with a sunken ship so close to the surface that even snorkelers can balance their flippers on the helm.

Curaçao for Free

Located on Salina Arriba, in the Landhouse Cholobo, the **Senior Liqueur Factory** (tel. 599/9–613526) distills and distributes the original Curaçao liqueur. Don't expect to find a massive factory—it's just a small showroom in the open-air foyer of a beautiful 17th-century landhouse. There are no guides, but you can read the story of the distillation process on posters, and you'll be graciously offered samples in various flavors. If you're interested in buying—the orange-flavored chocolate liqueur is fantastic over ice cream—you can choose from a complete selection, which is bottled in a variety of fascinating shapes, including Dutch ceramic houses.

The **Amstel Brewery Tours** (tel. 599/9–612944) offer insights into the world's only beer made from distilled seawater. Free tours (followed by all-you-can-drink beer tastings) are held every Tuesday and Thursday mornings at 10 AM. *Closed June 15–Aug. 6.*

What to See and Do with Children

The new **Sonesta Beach Hotel** works hard to provide a variety of free supervised activities for children—crafts, volleyball, water sports, and other group games. If you are staying elsewhere, talk to the activities director or hostess of your hotel for suggestions; they're usually very creative and may even plan a party for your child's birthday if other children are available.

Next to the water plant on the Otrabanda side of town is **Coney Island,** a festive fair that will thrill both children and adults. Among the many rides are a Ferris wheel, a merry-go-round, and a swinging pirate boat. A band plays at night. *Tel. 599/9–62380. Open one or two weekends a month, Fri.–Sun. 5–midnight.*

Sports programs for youngsters can be found at **Chirino** (12 Orionweg, tel. 599/9–613346), a sports and recreation center. It also offers classes called *arte infantil*, where children sing, dance, act, and play. Also available is a fully equipped gym for adults, complete with aerobics classes, fitness training, jazz dancing, massage, and sauna.

Off the Beaten Track

Beth Haim, the oldest Jewish burial ground still in use in the Western Hemisphere, is a wonderful offbeat stop. Consecrated before 1659, it has more than 2,500 graves on 3 acres, and grand history can be read from the inscriptions on the magnificently carved tombstones.

Beaches

Curaçao has some 38 beaches, but unfortunately, many are extremely rocky and litter-strewn. The best way to find "your" beach is to rent a Jeep, motorscooter, or heavy-treaded car. Ask your hotel to pack a picnic basket for you and go exploring. Getting lost and ending up in some undiscovered cove is half the fun. Curaçao doesn't have Aruba's long, powdery stretches of sand; instead, you'll discover the joy of inlets: tiny bay openings to the sea marked by craggy cliffs, exotic trees, and scads of interesting pebbles. Imagine a beach that's just big enough for your party of four—or a party of just two. Beware of thorns and keep an eye out for flying fish. They propel their tails through the water until they reach a speed of 44 mph, then spread their fins and soar.

Hotels with the best beach properties include the new **Sonesta Beach Hotel** (impressively long), the **Princess Beach** (impressively sensuous), and the **Coral Cliff Resort** (impressively deserted). No matter which hotel you're staying at, beach hopping to other hotels can be fun. Nonguests are supposed to pay the hotels a beach fee, but often there is no one to collect.

One of the largest, more spectacular beaches on Curaçao is **Blauwbaai** (Blue Bay). There's plenty of white sand and lots of shady places, showers, and changing facilities, but since it's a private beach, you'll pay an entrance fee of about $2.50 per car. Take the road that leads past the Holiday Beach Hotel and the

Curaçao Caribbean north toward Julianadorp. At the end of the stretch of straight road, a sign will instruct you to bear left for Blauwbaai and the fishing village of St. Michiel. The latter is a good place for diving.

Starting from the church of St. Willibrordus, signs will direct you to **Daai Booi Bay,** a sandy shore dotted with thatched shelters. The road to this public beach is a small paved highway flanked on either side by thick lush trees and huge organpipe cacti. The beach is curved, with shrubbery rooted into the side of the rocky cliffs—a great place for swimming.

Knip Bay has two parts: Big (Groot) Knip and Little (Kleine) Knip. Only Little Knip is shaded with trees, but these are manchineels, so steer clear of them. Also beware of cutting your feet on beer bottle caps. Both have alluring white sand, but only Big Knip has changing facilities. Big Knip also has several tiki huts for shade and calm turquoise waters that are perfect for swimming and lounging. The protected cove, flanked by sheer cliffs, is usually a blast on Sundays, when there is live music. To get there, take the road to the Knip Landhouse, then turn right. Signs will direct you. In between the big and the little bay is a superb scenic route.

Playa Abao boasts crystal-clear turquoise water and a small beach. Sunday afternoons are crowded and festive. Amenities include a snack center and public toilets. It is located northwest of Knip Bay.

Westpunt, on the northwest tip of the island, is shady in the morning. It doesn't have much sand, but you can sit on a shaded rock ledge. On Sunday, watch the divers jump from the high cliff. The bay view is worth the trip. For lunch, stop at Jaanchi Christiaan's nearby (*see* Dining, *below*).

Santa Barbara, a popular family beach on the eastern tip, has changing facilities and a snack bar but charges a small fee, usually around $3.35 per car.

Sports and the Outdoors

Golf   Visitors are welcome to play golf at the **Curaçao Golf and Squash Club** (tel. 599/9–373590) in Emmastad. The nine-hole course offers a challenge because of the stiff trade winds and the sand greens. *Open 8–12:30.*

Horseback Riding   **Ashari's Ranch** (tel. 599/9–686254) is the only stable to offer romps to the beach ($15 an hour). **Joe Pineda** (tel. 599/9–681181) offers mountain trail rides at his ranch for $15 an hour. Dressage riding can be found only at **Société Hippique Curaçao** (tel. 599/9–379160).

Jogging   The **Rif Recreation Area,** locally known as the *corredor*, stretches from the water plant at Mundo Nobo to the Curaçao Caribbean Hotel along the sea. It consists of more than 1.2 miles of palm-lined beachfront, a wading pond, and a jogging track with an artificial surface, as well as a big playground. There is good security and street lighting along the entire length of the beachfront.

Tennis   Most hotels (including Sonesta Beach, Curaçao Caribbean, Las Palmas, Princess Beach, and Holiday Beach) offer well-paved courts, illuminated for day and night games.

Water Sports   Curaçao has facilities for all kinds of water sports, thanks to the government-sponsored **Curaçao Underwater Marine Park** (tel. 599/9–618131), which includes almost a third of the island's southern diving waters. Scuba divers and snorkelers can enjoy more than 12½ miles of protected reefs and shores, with normal visibility from 60 to 80 feet (up to 150 feet on good days). With water temperatures ranging from 75° to 82°F, wet suits are generally unnecessary. No coral collecting, spearfishing, or littering is allowed. An exciting wreck to explore is the SS *Oranje Nassau*, which ran aground over 80 years ago and now hosts hundreds of exotic fish and unusually shaped coral.

Most hotels either offer their own program of water sports or will be happy to make arrangements for you. An introductory scuba resort course usually runs about $50–$65.

Underwater Curaçao (tel. 599/9–618131) offers complete vacation/dive packages in conjunction with the Lions Dive Hotel & Marina. Its fully stocked dive shop, located between the Lions Dive Hotel and the Curaçao Seaquarium, offers equipment for both sale and rental. Personal instruction and group lessons are conducted on state-of-the art dive boats personally designed by "Dutch" Schrier. One dive will run you $33; dive-only packages are available. Take a dive/snorkeling trip on the *Coral Sea*, a 40-foot twin diesel yacht-style dive boat. Landlubbers can see beneath the sea aboard *The Coral View*, a monohull flat-top glass-bottom boat that makes four excursions a day.

Seascape (tel. 599/9–625000, ext. 177), at the Curaçao Caribbean Hotel, specializes in snorkeling and scuba-diving trips to reefs and underwater wrecks in every type of water vehicle—from pedal boats and water scooters to waterskis and windsurf boards. A six-dive package costs $155 and includes unlimited beach diving plus one free night dive. Snorkeling gear costs about $5 an hour or $10 a day to rent. Die-hard fishermen with companions who prefer to suntan will enjoy the day trip to Little Curaçao, the "clothes optional" island between Curaçao and Bonaire, where the fish are reputed to be lively: Plan on $25 per person. Deep-sea fishing for a maximum of six people can also be arranged; it costs $300 for a half day, $500 for a full day.

Peter Hughes Diving (tel. 599/9–614944, ext. 5047) at the Princess Beach Hotel rents equipment and conducts diving and snorkeling trips. Also available is a cabin cruiser for half-day ($200) or full-day ($500) deep-sea fishing excursions.

For windsurfing, check out the **Curaçao High Wind Center** (Princess Beach Hotel, tel. 599/9–614944). Lessons cost $20 an hour.

Coral Cliff Diving (tel. 599/9–642822) offers scuba certification courses ($320), a one-week windsurfing school ($170), a one-week basic sailing course ($255), and a full schedule of dive and snorkeling trips to Curaçao's southwest coast. It also rents pedal boats, Hobie Cats, and underwater cameras.

Spectator Sports   The graceful Windsurfers, bobbing sailboats, and commercial ships passing through the harbor make an ongoing sport spectacle in Curaçao. Soccer matches and baseball games, from March through October, are held in the modern and comfortable **Centro Deportivo** stadium, located about 10 minutes from town at Bonamweg 49. *Tel. 599/9–376620. Open daily 9:30–12:30 and 3–6.*

Shopping

Curaçao has long enjoyed the reputation of having some of the best shops in the Caribbean, but don't expect posh Madison Avenue boutiques. With a few exceptions (such as Benetton, which recently moved into the Caribbean with a vengeance), the quality of women's fashions here lies along the lines of sales racks.

If you're looking for bargains on Swiss watches, cameras, crystal, or electronic equipment, do some comparison shopping back home and come armed with a list of prices.

Shopping Areas Most of the shops are concentrated in one place—**Punda**—in downtown Willemstad, within about a six-block area. The main shopping streets are **Heerenstraat, Breedestraat,** and **Madurostraat. Heerenstraat** and **Gomezplein** are pedestrian malls, closed to traffic, and their roadbeds have been raised to sidewalk level and covered with pink inlaid tiles.

The hippest shopping area lies under the **Waterfort arches,** along with a variety of restaurants and bars. Our two favorite shops under the arches are **Bamali** (tel. 599/9–612258), which sells Indonesian batik clothing, leather bags, and charming handcrafts, and **The African Queen** (tel. 599/9–612682), an exotic bazaar of fine African jewelry, batik clothes, and Kenyan handbags handmade of coconut husk and sisal.

Good Buys The leading jewelers in the Netherlands Antilles, **Spritzer &**
Jewelery/Watches **Fuhrmann** (Gomezplein 1, tel. 599/9–612600) carries gold jewelry, watches, French crystal, diamonds, emeralds, and china.

La Zahav N.V. (Curaçao International Airport, tel. 599/9–689594) is one of the best places to buy gold jewelry—with or without diamonds, rubies, and emeralds—at true discount prices. The shop is located in the airport transit hall, just at the top of the staircase.

Large Stores **Julius L. Penha & Sons** (Heerenstraat 1, tel. 599/9–612266), in front of the Pontoon Bridge, sells French perfumes, Hummel figurines, linen from Madeira, delftware, and handbags from Argentina, Italy, and Spain. The store also has an extensive cosmetics counter. **Boolchand's** (Heerenstraat 4B, tel. 599/9–616233) handles an interesting variety of merchandise behind a facade of red-and-white checked tiles. Stock up here on French perfumes, British cashmere sweaters, Italian silk ties, Dutch dolls, Swiss watches, and Japanese cameras.

Clothing **Benetton** (Madurostraat 4, tel. 599/9–614619) has winter stock in July and summer stock in December; both stocks are 20% off the retail price. **Crazy Look** (Madurostraat 6, tel. 599/9–611440) has French, Italian, and Dutch fashions with a hip Eurotrash look, as well as trendy sweat shirts and baggy pants. **Boutique Liska** (Schottegatweg Oost 191-A, tel. 599/9–613111) is where local residents shop for smart women's fashions. **Boutique Aquarius** (Breedestraat 9, tel. 599/9–612618) sells Fendi merchandise for 25% less than in the United States. Fendi fanatics can stock up on belts, shoes, pocketbooks, wallets, and even watches.

Delicacies **Toko Zuikertuintje** (Zuikertuintjeweg, tel. 599/9–370188), a supermarket built on the original 17th-century Zuikertuintje Landhuis, is where most of the local elite shop. Enjoy the free tea and coffee while you stock up on all sorts of European and Dutch delicacies. Shopping here for a picnic is a treat in itself.

Linens **New Amsterdam** (Gomezplein 14, tel. 599/9–613823) is the place to price hand-embroidered tablecloths, napkins, and pillow-cases.

Local Crafts Native crafts and curios are on hand at **Fundason Obra di Man** (Bargestraat 57, tel. 599/9–612413). Particularly impressive are the posters of Curaçao's architecture. **Black Coral** (Princess Beach Hotel, tel. 599/9–614944) is owned by Dutch-born artisan Bert Knubben, one of Curaçao's true characters. For the past 30 years, he's been designing and sculpting the most exciting black-coral jewelry in the Caribbean—and even dives for it himself, with special permission from the government. Dolphin pendants and twiglike earrings finished in 14-karat gold are excellent buys. Call before you drop by.

Dining

Restaurateurs in Curaçao believe in whetting appetites with a variety of cuisines and intriguing ambience: Dine under the boughs of magnificent old trees, in the romantic gloom of wine cellars in renovated landhouses, or on the ramparts of 18th-century forts. Curaçaoans partake of some of the best Indonesian food in the Caribbean, and they also find it hard to resist the French, Swiss, Dutch, and Swedish delights. Dress in restaurants is almost always casual, but if you feel like putting on your finery, there will always be a place for you. Do take a wrap or a light sweater with you—for some reason, most restaurants have their air conditioners going full blast.

Highly recommended restaurants are indicated by a star ★.

Category	Cost*
Expensive	over $25
Moderate	$15–$25
Inexpensive	under $15

**per person, excluding drinks and service*

L'Alouette. This newcomer deserves to succeed for its innovative cuisine. Maria Eugenia Saban is an inspired amateur chef who has turned professional. She creates enticing appetizers, such as spinach *feuillantine* (puffed pastry filled with spinach and sautéed in shallot butter and then topped with oysters in a champagne sauce) and squids Alouette, which are filled with gorganzola and grilled in olive oil. The main courses change monthly, but you may expect such pleasures as three minitenderloins each served with a different sauce, or something more simple, such as lamb chops grilled to perfection. Leave room for the lemon-lime tarts or the Grand Marnier soufflé. Ricardo plays the genial host in the small, spartanly furnished dining room and is able to suggest very reasonably priced wines. The hard-to-find location of L'Alouette is its drawback. The restaurant is in a small house down a side road at the back of a Burger King in Salinja, a commercial suburb of Willemstad. *Orionweg 12, tel. 599/9–618222. Reservations suggested. AE, DC, MC, V. Closed Sun. Expensive.*

★ **Bistro Le Clochard.** The charming Dutch couple who own this harborside restaurant laugh now about the 1988 hurricane that blew out the big picture windows and sent ocean trout swimming through the dining area. A romantic gem, the bistro is built into the 18th-century Rif Fort and is suffused with the cool, dark atmosphere of ages past. The use of fresh ingredients in the consistently well-prepared French and Swiss dishes makes dining here a dream, though a pricey one. Try the fresh-fish platters or the tender veal in mushroom sauce. Savor the fondue and let yourself get carried away by the unusual setting; just save room for the chocolate mousse. *On the Otrabanda Rif Fort, tel. 599/9–625666. Reservations required. AE, DC, MC, V. Closed Sat. for lunch and Sun. off-season. Expensive.*

★ **De Taveerne.** From the intricate detail of its centuries-old antiques to its impressive Continental menu, this restaurant is one of the most elegant, romantic spots on the island. Dining is in the whitewashed wine cellar of this magnificent renovated country estate, built in the 1800s by an exiled Venezuelan revolutionary. The best appetizer is the slices of tangy, smoked dorado. The young Dutch chef, Hennie, also excels in grilled lobster and works wonders with veal. For dessert, there's the absolutely unforgettable broiled pears, topped with vanilla ice cream and drenched with Curaçao chocolate liqueur. For the Dutch, hearty eaters always, this restaurant is a favorite. *LandhuisGroot Davelaar, on Silena, near the Promenade Shopping Center, tel. 599/9–370669. Reservations required. AE, DC, MC, V. Closed Sun. Expensive.*

Fort Nassau Restaurant. This is *the* place from which to witness the twinkling magic of Curaçao at night. High on a hilltop overlooking Willemstad, the restaurant is built into an 18th-century fort and gives a 360-degree view of the city's rooftops. Go for a drink in the breezy, couple-filled Battery Terrace bar or dine in air-conditioned civility in front of the huge bay windows. The view is superb. In the air-conditioned restaurant with wide bay windows, the menu is diverse, from duck with a molasses sauce to lightly broiled fish, but the price that you pay is more for the views and ambience than for innovative cuisine. You may prefer just to go before or after dinner to check out the action in the Infinity Club downstairs, one of the sexiest, plushest discos we've ever seen. *Near Juliana Bridge, tel. 599/9–613086. Reservations required. AE, DC, MC, V. Expensive.*

Belle Terrace. Tucked into the quaint Avila Beach Hotel, this seaside restaurant sits right underneath the boughs of an ancient tree. Each night it features a different specialty, from such Curaçao dishes as *keshi yena* to *sopito* (fish and coconut soup) to salted boiled breast of duck and filet Mignon. In between stops at the creative salad bar, watch the fish jumping out of the sea—they fly up to 20 feet. *Avila Beach Hotel, Penstraat 130–134, tel. 599/9–614377. Dinner only. Reservations required. AE, DC, MC, V. Moderate.*

★ **El Marinero.** This restaurant is a favorite of the island's governor and with good reason. The setting is lighthearted nautical, with in white sailor suits and the bow of a boat jutting out of one wall, the waiters dressed in white sailor suits, and the owner, Luis Chavarria, dressed as the captain. Service is both friendly and efficient, and the food is excellent. The chef whips up one superb seafood dish after another, including such delicacies as shellfish soup, ceviche, paella, and conch. The sea bass Creole-style is delicious, as is the garlic lobster. Diners with a hearty appetite are likely to add up a large tab. *Schottegatweg Noord 87-B, tel. 599/9–379833. Reservations suggested. AE, DC, MC, V. Moderate.*

Fort Waarzaamreid. High on a hill overlooking Willemstad and the harbor, this fort was captured by Captain Bligh of HMS *Bounty* two centuries ago. Now it is controlled by an Irishman, Tom Farrel, who operates an open-air restaurant and bar in the evening. The atmosphere is informal, and the food is primarily barbecued seafood and steaks decorated with your own makings from a salad bar. You will be equally well greeted if you go just for cocktails and snacks—and the sunsets are magnificent. *Seru Domi, Willemstad, tel. 599/9–623633. Located off the main highway on the Otrabanda side of the suspension bridge. Dinner only AE, V. Moderate.*

Garuda Indonesian Restaurant. The special *rijsttafel* (Indonesian smorgasbord) features 19 trays of traditional vegetable, chicken, meat, fish, and shrimp dishes, each with its own sauce. The ocean breezes, bamboo and rattan decor, and Far Eastern music add to the feeling of being a guest in a foreign land. Save room for a dessert of *spekkok*, a multilayered pastry with nuts that will melt in your mouth. *Curaçao Caribbean Hotel, tel. 599/9–626519. Open Tues.–Fri. lunch and dinner, Sat. and Sun. dinner only. Reservations recommended. AE, DC, MC, V. Moderate.*

Guacamaya Steakhouse. The portions here are hearty, the chef knows what *rare* means, and there's even a small selection of seafood to satisfy the noncarnivore in the crowd. A large papier-mâché parrot sits on a brass perch, waiters stroll by in Bermuda shorts and safari hats, and the drink of the house—a guacamaya—is a tall iced concoction the color of foliage. Try the chateaubriand or the tenderloin medallions. There's also steak tartare and a mixed skewer of chicken, pork, and beef kebabs. *Schottegatweg-West 365, tel. 599/9–689208. Reservations required. AE, DC, MC, V. Closed Mon. Moderate.*

Rijstaffel Indonesia Restaurant. No steaks or chops here, just one dish after another of exotic delicacies that make up the traditional Indonesian banquet called rijsttafel. Choose from 16 to 25 traditional dishes that are set buffet-style around you. Lesser appetites will enjoy the lighter meals, such as the fried noodles, fresh jumbo shrimps in garlic, or combination meatand-fish platters. Desserts are nearly mystical; a "ladies only" ice cream comes with a red rose. The coconut ice cream comes packed in a coconut shell you can take home. The walls are stocked with beautiful Indonesian puppets ($25–$40) that will make stunning gifts. *Mercurriusstraat 13–15, Salinja, tel. 599/9–612999. Open Mon.–Sat. for lunch and dinner, Sun. for dinner only. Reservations required. AE, DC, MC, V. Moderate.*

Bon Appetit. This popular breakfast spot is in the heart of the shopping district. The fare is reasonably priced, the portions are large, and the service is friendly and pleasant. Think of this as a Dutch diner, good for breakfast and lunch, less so for dinner. Try the Dutch pancakes with pineapple. *Hanchi di Snoa 4, tel. 599/9–616916. AE, DC, MC, V. Closed Sun. Inexpensive.*

Cozzoli's Pizza. Fast, cheap, hearty New York–style pizzas oven-baked, just like they make them in Brooklyn, are offered here. Pig out on calzones, sausage rolls, and lasagna. It is right in the middle of downtown Willemstad. *Breedestraat 2, tel. 599/ 9–617184. No credit cards. Inexpensive.*

★ **Golden Star Restaurant.** This place looks and feels more like a friendly roadside diner than a full-fledged restaurant, but the native food here is among the best in town. Owner Marie Burke turns out such Antillean specialties as *bestia chiki* (goat stew), shrimp Creole, and delicately seasoned grilled conch, all served with generous heaps of rice, fried plantains, and avocado. Steaks and chops can be had for the asking. *Socratestraat 2, tel. 599/9–654795. AE, DC, MC, V. Inexpensive.*

Jaanchi Christiaan's Restaurant. Tour buses stop regularly at this open-air restaurant for lunch and for weird-sounding but mouth-watering native dishes. The main-course specialty is a hefty platter of fresh-caught fish, potatoes, and vegetables. Curaçaoans joke that Jaanchi's "iguana soup is so strong it could resurrect the dead"—truth is, it tastes just like chicken soup, only better. But Jaanchi, Jr., says if you want iguana, you must order in advance "because we have to go out and catch them." He's not kidding. *Westpunt 15, tel. 599/9–640126. AE, DC, MC, V. Inexpensive.*

Lodging

Hotels in Curaçao all have their pluses and minuses. If you're a business traveler, you'll appreciate the modest Van Der Valk Plaza, with easy access to the city center, but you'll have a long trek to the beach. The sophisticated Avila Beach Hotel, now that it has added new rooms, offers modern or traditional rooms, a reasonable beach, and close proximity to town. Guests at the Sonesta Beach, Curaçao Caribbean, Princess Beach Hotel, Las Palmas, and Holiday Beach hotels enjoy their own beaches, but they're a 10-minute drive from town. The Curaçao Caribbean and the Sonesta Beach Hotel are across the road from the International Trade Center. Most hotels offer free shuttle bus services to the downtown area. They also either include breakfast or offer a large buffet breakfast at a reasonable price. Full American Plans are not popular because of the abundance of good restaurants in all price ranges.

Highly recommended lodgings are indicated by a star ★.

Category	Cost*
Expensive	over $160
Moderate	$110–$160
Inexpensive	under $110

All prices are for a standard double room for two and include tax and service charges.

Hotels **Curaçao Caribbean Hotel and Casino.** Formerly a Hilton, this hotel has a small, V-shape beach leading into a cove enclosed by a semicircular pier, where plans are in the works for a bar serving refreshments and snacks. The beach can become crowded, but there is a lounging area above it that is perfect for sunbathing. It's a 10-minute drive by car from the center of town. The five-story complex is self-contained, with one of the best organized activities program on the island, including rum-swizzle parties, volleyball, T-shirt painting contests, Papiamento lessons, walking tours, and special theme nights for dinner and dancing. Water sports include everything imaginable. And the row of boutiques means you never have to leave the premises to shop. Guest rooms on the first four floors are rundown and old looking in spite of the new burgundy rugs and a minor facelift. The top floor, dedicated to business guests, has its own reception area, breakfast area, and fax and computer capabilities. It's the only floor that was completely renovated, and the only one that will please discriminating guests. All the hotel rooms have small balconies, but only half face the sea. Plans are in progress to extend the hotel's beach area, build new townhouse time-sharing units, and open a formal dining room called Coco's. Across the street is the new International Trade Center. Special dive and honeymoon packages are available. *Box 2133, Piscadera Bay, Willemstad, tel. 599/9–625000 or 800/ 344–1212, fax 599/9–625846. 200 rooms. Facilities: 3 restaurants, 24-hour coffee shop, 2 bars, pool, casino, beauty salon, barbershop, lighted tennis courts, health spa, boutiques, drugstore, secretarial services, telex, fax, meeting and convention rooms. AE, D, DC, MC, V. EP, MAP. Expensive.*

★ **Princess Beach Hotel and Casino.** The beach, lined with palm trees and one of the most beautiful in Curaçao, is located right in front of the underwater park. The rooms are huge, most with breathtaking ocean or garden views. The garden-view rooms were renovated in 1987 and are the more spacious of the two. However, the sea-view rooms are new—they were built in 1989—and are much more tropical, modern, and upscale. All rooms include a hair dryer, an amenity package, air-conditioning, color cable TV, and either a balcony or a patio. The pathway to guest rooms is through lush, tropical grounds full of chirping birds. The new freshwater pool has the added bonus of a staff to offer drinks to guests as they paddle about on floats. The casino is one of the more exciting ones in Curaçao. This is a high-energy place, with lively happy hours, popular theme buffet dinners, and a slew of sports activities to keep guests busy. New, luxury one-bedroom suites are in the planning, but these are off to the side and should not interfere with the day-to-day functioning of the hotel. Also under construction are a new restaurant and a much-needed second swimming pool. The **Curaçao High Wind Center** is on the premises. *M. L. King Blvd. 8, tel. 599/9–614944 or 800/327–3286, fax 599/9–614131. 202 rooms. Facilities: restaurant, pool with bar, boutiques, drugstore, dive shop, tour desk, car- and scooter-rental agent, casino, beauty salon, baby-sitting services, disabled facilities and rooms. AE, DC, MC, V. EP, BP, MAP, FAP. Expensive.*

★ **Sonesta Beach Hotel & Casino.** Curaçao's newest resort, just across the street from the International Trade Center, has its own long slice of beautiful beach. The sprawling, burnished gold-colored low rise, built to blend in with the surrounding Dutch Colonial–style architecture had just opened at press time and looked as if it will live up to its expected reputation– that it will be the island's top luxury resort. The air-conditioned accommodations feature a muted tropical pastel color scheme, TVs, minibars, tiled showers and baths, and either a terrace or a balcony. Two children under age 12 stay free when sharing the room with their parents. The free daily "Just Us Kids" program offers supervised activities for children ages 5 to 12. *Box 6003, Piscadera Bay, tel. 599/9–368800 or 800/ SONESTA, fax 599/9–627502. 214 rooms, 34 suites. Facilities: 3 restaurants, 2 bars, casino, watersports and dive center, freeform swimming pool with swim-up bar, children's wading pool, 2 lighted tennis courts, health club, shopping arcade, 2* *whirlpools, baby-sitting service, children's program. AE, DC, MC, V. EP. Expensive.*

★ **Avila Beach Hotel.** The royal family of Holland and its ministers stay at this 200-year-old mansion for three good reasons: the privacy, the personalized service, and the austere elegance. Americans used to luxurious resorts will find the air-conditioned rooms rather plain and old-fashioned, but the double quarter-moon-shape beach is enchanting. The original guest rooms are charming, but basic looking, with hardwood or tile floors and small baths with showers only. Most guests will prefer the newer *La Belle Alliance* section, on its own beach adjacent to the main property. The Mediterranean-style yellow-and-gold low-rise buildings feature Moorish arches, Dutch red-gabled roofs, and lighted walkways. Sold as condominium units and leased back to the hotel as guest accommodations, these 45 rooms and 18 one- and two-bedroom apartments all have either balconies or patios with sea views. Half the rooms are equipped with kitchenettes. While these rooms may have less charm than the old, their larger size and modern amenities make them the more desirable—and more expensive. The hotel has a unique outdoor dining area shaded by the leafy, intertwining boughs of an enormous tree. The Danish chefs, who specialize in a Viking pot, local dishes, and weekly smorgasbord, also smoke their own fish and bake their own bread. Classical concerts performed by the owner, a recorded artist, take place once a month on Sunday mornings. Recent renovations include a new coffee shop with an open-air sea view, a tennis court, and a conference room. *Box 791, Penstraat 130134, Willemstad, tel. 599/9–614377 or 800/448–8355, fax 599/9–611493. 95 rooms. Facilities: restaurant, coffee shop, tennis court, bar, baby-sitting service, cable TV, conference room, shuttle bus to city center. AE, DC, MC, V. EP. Moderate.*

Holiday Beach Hotel and Casino. This ex–Holiday Inn is a four-story, 26-year-old U-shape building around a pool area. Over the past four years, the rooms have been completely renovated and refurnished in a beige, emerald, and rose color scheme, with bleached wood and rattan furniture, TVs, showers and baths, and balconies. Half the rooms face the car park; most of the others face the pool area, and only a few have sea views. The air-conditioned lobby is spacious to permit the assembly of tour groups, and the island's largest casino is off to the lobby's left. A beachside alfresco restaurant features a well-stocked, all-you-can-eat breakfast buffet. In the evening, international dishes and island specialties are served in addition to several weekly theme-buffet dinners, one of the best being the festive Caribbean Buffet with entertainment provided by fire-eaters, limbo dancers, and a steel band. The hotel's outstanding feature is its crescent beach, quite large for Curaçao and dotted with palm trees. There's also a water-sports concession and a tiki-hut beach bar. Guests are encouraged to join the daily volleyball game, sign up for the free Curaçao Museum tour (*see* Arts and Nightlife, *below*), or hop the free shuttle into town. The lobby bar happy hour is one of the most popular on the island. While this hotel is an older property, the completed renovation, along with the friendly service, make it a good choice for people seeking good value on a middle-of-the-road budget. *Box 2178, Otrabanda, Pater Euwensweg, Willemstad, tel. 599/9–625400, fax 599/9–624397. 197 rooms; 2 suites. Facilities: playground, 2 tennis courts, beauty shop, boutique, drugstore,* *gift shop, car-rental agent, baby-sitting service, casino. AE, DC, MC, V. EP. Moderate.*

Coral Cliff Resort and Beach Club. Seclusion and rustic simplicity are everything here. A 45-minute ride from the center of Willemstad, the grounds boast a beach so enticing that it even attracts native islanders seeking a weekend retreat. (The beach is open to the public for a $5 admission charge.) The caged iguanas near the restaurant are the only ones you will see in captivity on the island, and you're apt to find low-flying parakeets alighting on your dinner table. This resort exudes a European atmosphere and is very popular with Dutch tourists. Americans used to luxurious or amenity-laden resorts will find the rooms stark and in sore need of modernizing. However, all are air-conditioned, have spectacular views of the sea, and are equipped with an old but functional kitchenette. The hotel recently installed a children's playground, a tennis court, and slot machines in the bar. All guests receive complimentary airport transfers. *Box 3782, Santa Marta Bay, tel. 599/9–641820 or 800/344–1212, fax 599/9–641781. 35 rooms. Facilities: pool, restaurant, bar, car-rental agent, marina, water-sports center, and PADI 4-star dive shop. AE, DC, MC, V. EP, BP, MAP, FAP. Inexpensive.*

Lions Dive Hotel & Marina. This recent addition to the Curaçao vacation scene is a hop, skip, and plunge away from the Seaquarium. The pink-and-green caravansary is set next to a quarter mile of private beach. The rooms are airy, modern, and light filled, with tile floors, large bathrooms, and lots of windows. A pair of French doors leads out to a spacious balcony or terrace, and every room has a view of the sea. The Sunday-night happy hour is especially festive, with a local merengue band playing poolside. By midnight, however, the only sound to be heard is the whir of your room's air conditioner. Pluses include a young, attractive staff who are eager to please and a scuba center that's top-notch. Dive packages are offered with Underwater Curaçao, and most, if not all, of the guests are dive enthusiasts. *Bapor Kibra, Curaçao, tel. 599/9–618100, fax 599/ 9–618200. 72 air-conditioned rooms with color TV. Facilities: Antillean restaurant, terrace bar, pool, scuba-diving center with 2 dive boats, each with a 25-passenger capacity, water-sports concession, video-rental shop. AE, DC, MC, V. CP. Inexpensive.*

Otrabanda Hotel & Casino. New in 1991, this city hotel is across the harbor from downtown Willemstad. The management appears more interested in keeping the locals gambling in the ground-floor casino than in attracting visitors to the small but clean and simple rooms. However, for watching the budget, it is a hotel to keep in mind, with double rooms at $105 during high season. *Breedestradt (O), Otrabanda, tel. 599/9–627400, fax 599/9–627299. 45 rooms. Facilities: casino, coffee shop, restaurant, bar. AE, V. CP. Inexpensive.*

Van Der Valk Plaza Hotel and Casino. "Please don't touch the passing ships" is the slogan of the Van Der Valk Plaza, the only hotel in the world with marine-collision insurance. The ships do come close to the island's first high-rise hotel, which is built right into the massive walls of a 17th-century fort at the entrance of Willemstad's harbor. At the Plaza, you give up beachfront (you have beach privileges at major hotels, however) for walking access to the city's center—consequently, it's a business traveler's oasis, complete with secretarial service, fax and telex machines, and typing and translation services. The ramparts rising from the sea offer a fantastic evening view of the twinkling lights of the city. The hotel is owned by the Van Der Valk company, a Dutch family-run concern that owns more than 50 hotels in Europe. A new, enlarged casino has been completed, and the lobby has been smartened. On the second floor a coffee shop has opened for light refreshments with a view of the ships weighing anchor in the harbor. Long-range plans include building a beach nearby and renovating the rooms, which are sorely lacking in style and decor. Currently, the Plaza's restaurant offers some of the best values in town. Stop in for dinner—the lunch service is abysmally slow. One hundred and thirty-five of the rooms are in the tower, many with a sea view and some with balconies. All rooms have color cable TV, air-conditioning, and a minifridge. *Box 229, Plaza Piar, Willemstad, tel. 599/9–612500, fax 599/9–616543. 254 rooms. Facilities: restaurant, coffee shop, casino, room service, 3 bars, dive shop, drugstore, gift shop, car-rental agent, tour desk, pool. Baby-sitter and house physician on call. AE, DC, MC, V. CP. Inexpensive.*

Home and Apartment Rentals
There are many rentals available on the island. Your best bet is to contact the **Curaçao Tourist Board** (Box 3266, Curaçao, Netherlands Antilles) at least two months before you plan to go; it will send you a list of available properties.

The Arts and Nightlife

The Arts
The Curaçao Museum, housed in a century-old former plantation house, is filled with artifacts, paintings, and antique furnishings that trace the island's history. *Across from the Holiday Beach Hotel, off Pater Euwensweg, tel. 599/9–623777. Admission: $1.50. Open Tues.–Fri. 9–noon and 2–5, Sat. 10–4.*

Gallery 86 (tel. 599/9–613417), in the Bloksteeg (Punda) opposite the Bank of the Netherlands Antilles, features the works of local artists and occasionally those of South Americans and Africans.

Nightlife
The once-a-month open house at Landhuis Brievengat (*see* Exploring, Curaçao, Eastern Side, *above*) is a great way to meet interesting locals—it usually offers a folkloric show, snacks, and local handicrafts. Every Friday night the landhouse holds a big party with two bands. The Sonesta Beach, Van Der Valk Plaza, Curaçao Caribbean, Holiday Beach, Las Palmas, and the Princess Beach hotels all have casinos that are open 1 PM–4 AM.

Blue Note Jazz Cafe (Schout bij N. Doormanweg 37, tel. 599/9–370685) has reopened under new management but still remains a singles bar–cum–Dutch pub that fills up fast. There's likely to be more TV-watching than dancing. There is live jazz on Wednesday and Friday 8:30 PM–1 AM and Sunday noon–5 PM.

The Pub (Salina 144A, tel. 599/9–612190) is a crowded, energetic dancing and drinking club. It's the place for the loud, the hip, the young, and the wanna-bes checking on the latest Curaçao fads and fancies. The dress is casual to funky, so leave your heels at home. Open Friday 8–4, Saturday 9–4, Monday–Thursday and Sunday 9–3.

Infinity (tel. 599/9–613450), a tiny club underneath the Fort Nassau Restaurant, is a romantic disco, with semicircular alcoves, plush couches, curtains made of strings of lights, and a teeny dance floor. This upscale evening spot, with its waterfall wall, doesn't get busy until the clock strikes the bewitching hour. Friday and Saturday 9–3, Monday–Thursday and Sunday 9–1.

Rum Runner (Otrobanda Waterfront, DeRouvilleweg 9, tel. 599/9–623038) is another casual hot spot. This well-lit indoor/ outdoor bar and eatery serves up tapas in an atmosphere that's reminiscent of a college fraternity hall. There's music nightly. The crowd stays until about midnight, after which the majority switch to **Facade, The Pub,** or **L'Aristocrat.**

Considered the most colorful disco in town, **Facade** (Lindbergweg 32, Salina, tel. 599/9–614640) is about as hip as Curaçao gets. It's dark and cool, with huge bamboo chairs for lounging. The men cruise and the women are dressed to kill. There are two disco floors with flashing lights and an intense aural assault. It's packed on Thursday, Friday, and Saturday nights from 10 PM to 4 AM. Closed Tuesday.

L'Aristocrat (Lindbergweg-Salina, tel. 599/9–614353) attracts the more mature crowd seeking late-night pleasures, and on Saturday night, the line to get in stretches down the block. Inside, the trendy clientele gyrates to a heavy beat while silent large-screen TVs flash sensual images. The place to see and be seen. There's a $9 cover charge, and it's open Friday and Saturday 10 PM to 4 AM; closed Monday.

10 Dominica

Updated by
Nigel Fisher

The national motto emblazoned on the coat of arms of the Commonwealth of Dominica reads *"Après Bondi, c'est la ter."* It is a French-Creole phrase meaning "After God, it is the land." On this unspoiled isle, the land is indeed the main attraction . . . it turns and twists, towers to mountain crests, then tumbles to falls and valleys. It is a land that the Smithsonian Institution called a giant plant laboratory, unchanged for 10,000 years. Indeed, after a heavy rain you half expect to see things grow before your very eyes; the island is a virtual rainbow in entirely green hues.

The grandeur of Dominica (pronounced *dom-in-EE-ka*) is not man-made. This untamed, ruggedly beautiful land, located in the eastern Caribbean between Guadeloupe to the north and Martinique to the south, is a 305-square-mile nature retreat; 29 miles long and 15 miles wide, the island is dominated by some of the highest elevations in the Caribbean and is laced with 365 rivers, "one for every day of the year." Much of the interior is covered by a luxuriant rain forest, a wild place where you almost expect Tarzan to swing howling by on a vine. Straight out of Conan Doyle's *Lost World*, everything here is larger than life, from the towering tree ferns to the enormous insects. This exotic spot is home to such unusual critters as the Sisserou (or Imperial) parrot and the red-necked (or Jacquot) parrot, neither of which can be found anywhere else in the world.

Dominica is home, too, to the last remnants of the Carib Indians, whose ancestors came paddling up from South America more than a thousand years ago. The fierce, cannibalistic Caribs kept Christopher Columbus at bay when he came to call during his second voyage to the New World. Columbus turned up at the island on Sunday, November 3, 1493. In between Carib arrows he hastily christened it Dominica (Sunday Island), and then sailed on.

For almost two centuries the British and French tried unsuccessfully to subdue the Caribs, and in 1748 they agreed to let the Caribs keep the island. However, French and English planters, unable to resist the lure of the fertile land, began to fight one another for squatter's rights. The Caribs had named their island *waitukubuli* ("tall is her body"), but it was *Dominica* that remained in history. In 1805, the English paid a "ransom" of £12,000 to the French, and Dominica became a British possession. In 1967, the British colony became self-governing, and on November 3, 1978, Dominica became a fully independent republic, officially called the Commonwealth of Dominica. Despite (or perhaps because of) its ferocious past, Dominica today is a quiet, peaceful place. There are about 82,000 people living on the island, and they are some of the friendliest people in all of the Caribbean.

Before You Go

Tourist
Information

Contact the **Caribbean Tourism Organization**, 20 E. 46th St., New York, NY 10017, tel. 212/682–0435. In the United Kingdom, contact the **Dominica Tourist Office** (1 Collingham Gardens, London SW5 0HW, tel. 071/835–1937 or 071/370–5194). You can write to the **Dominica Division of Tourism** (Box 73, Roseau, Dominica, WI, tel. 809/448–2186 or 809/448–2351; telex 8642, fax 809/448–5840), but allow

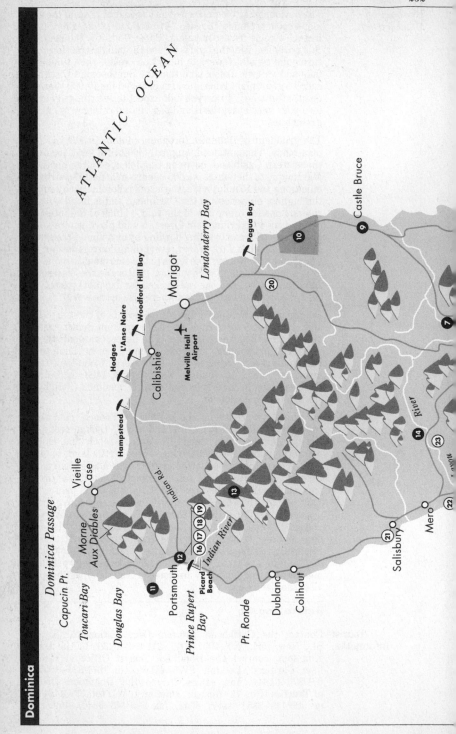

Dominica

ATLANTIC OCEAN

Castle Bruce

10

Pagua Bay

9

20

Londonderry Bay

Marigot

Woodford Hill Bay

L'Anse Noire

Hodges

Melville Hall Airport

Calibishie

Hampstead

Vieille Case

7

Morne Aux Diables

14

River

23

Indian Rd.

13

Portsmouth

Prince Rupert Bay

16 **17** **18** **19**

12

Picard Beach Indian River

11

Douglas Bay

Toucari Bay

Capucin Pt.

Dominica Passage

Pt. Ronde

Dublanc

Colihaut

21

Salisbury

22

Mero

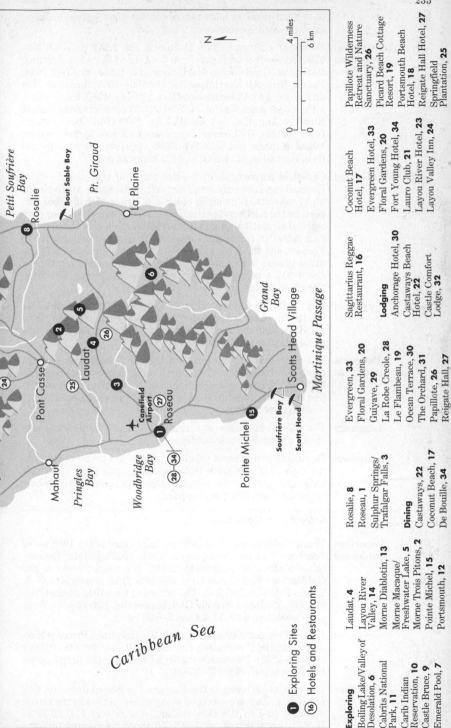

233

Caribbean Sea

Pringles Bay

Woodbridge Bay

Petit Soufrière Bay

Rosalie

Bout Sable Bay

Mahaut

Pont Casse

Canefield Airport

Roseau

Laudat

La Plaine

Pt. Giraud

Pointe Michel

Scotts Head Village

Grand Bay

Soufrière Bay

Scotts Head

Martinique Passage

N

0   4 miles

0   6 km

Exploring
Boiling Lake/Valley of Desolation, **6**
Cabrits National Park, **11**
Carib Indian Reservation, **10**
Castle Bruce, **9**
Emerald Pool, **7**

Laudat, **4**
Layou River Valley, **14**
Morne Diablotin, **13**
Morne Macaque/ Freshwater Lake, **5**
Morne Trois Pitons, **2**
Pointe Michel, **15**
Portsmouth, **12**

Rosalie, **8**
Roseau, **1**
Sulphur Springs/ Trafalgar Falls, **3**

Dining
Castaways, **22**
Coconut Beach, **17**
De Bouille, **34**

Evergreen, **33**
Floral Gardens, **20**
Guiyave, **29**
La Robe Creole, **28**
Le Flambeau, **19**
Ocean Terrace, **30**
The Orchard, **31**
Papillote, **26**
Reigate Hall, **27**

Sagittarius Reggae Restaurant, **16**

Lodging
Anchorage Hotel, **30**
Castaways Beach Hotel, **22**
Castle Comfort Lodge, **32**

Coconut Beach Hotel, **17**
Evergreen Hotel, **33**
Floral Gardens, **20**
Fort Young Hotel, **34**
Lauro Club, **21**
Layou River Hotel, **23**
Layou Valley Inn, **24**

Papillote Wilderness Retreat and Nature Sanctuary, **26**
Picard Beach Cottage Resort, **19**
Portsmouth Beach Hotel, **18**
Reigate Hall Hotel, **27**
Springfield Plantation, **25**

5840), but allow at least two weeks for your letter to arrive, since the mail is notoriously slow.

Arriving and Departing By Plane No major airlines fly into Dominica, but **LIAT** (tel. 809/462–0700) connects with flights from the United States on Antigua, Barbados, Guadeloupe, Martinique, St. Lucia, and San Juan, Puerto Rico. **Air Martinique** (tel. 809/449–1060) flies from Fort de France, and **Air Guadeloupe** (tel. 809/449–1060) from Pointe-à-Pitre. **Air Anguilla** (tel. 809/497–2643) connects from Puerto Rico via Anguilla, and **Air BVI** (tel. 809/774–6500) connects from Tortola, BVI, three days a week. A new airline, **Nature Island Express** (tel. 809/449–2309), provides service to and from Barbados, St. Lucia, and St. Maarten daily.

From the Airport **Canefield Airport** (about 3 miles north of the capital city of Roseau) can take only small aircraft, with lights available for night takeoffs. Dominica's older and larger **Melville Hall Airport**, on the northeast (Atlantic) coast, can manage larger commercial aircraft; although it is an interesting ride through the rain forest in the island's interior, it is a 90-minute drive to Roseau, and the fare is about U.S.$50 for a private taxi. The usual system is a co-op cab, where all seats must be taken for about $17 a person, as opposed to the $8-per-car fare from Canefield to Roseau.

By Boat **The Caribbean Express** (Fort-de-France, Martinique, tel. 596/60–12–38) has scheduled twice-weekly departures from Guadeloupe in the north to Martinique in the south, with stops at Les Saintes and Dominica.

Passports and Visas The only entry requirements for U.S. or Canadian citizens are proof of citizenship, such as a birth certificate or voter registration card bearing a photograph, and an ongoing or return airline ticket. British citizens are required to have passports, but visas are not necessary.

Language The official language is English, but most Dominicans also speak a French-Creole patois.

Precautions Be sure to bring insect repellent. If you are prone to car sickness, you will also want to bring along some pills. The roads twist and turn dramatically, and the (expert) local drivers barrel across them at a dizzying pace.

Staying in Dominica

Important Addresses **Tourist Information:** Contact the main office of the **Division of Tourism,** National Development Corp. (Bath Estate, Roseau, tel. 809/448–2186 or 809/448–2351). The tourist desks at the **Old Market Plaza** (Roseau, tel. 809/448–2186) is open Mon. 8–5, Tues.–Fri. 8–4, Sat. 9–1. The offices at **Canefield Airport** (tel. 809/449–1242) and **Melville Hall Airport** (tel. 809/445–7051) are open weekdays 6:15–11 AM and 2–5:30 PM.

Emergencies **Police, Fire, and Ambulance:** Call 999. **Hospitals: Princess Margaret Hospital** (Federation Dr., Goodwill, tel. 809/448–2231 or 809/448–2233). **Pharmacies: Jolly's Pharmacy** (33 King George St., Roseau, tel. 809/448–3388).

Currency The official currency is the Eastern Caribbean dollar (E.C.), but U.S. dollars are accepted everywhere. At banks the rate is officially tied to the U.S. dollar, at a rate of E.C.$2.70 to U.S.$1. Local prices, especially in shops frequented by tourists, are often quoted in both currencies, so be sure to ask. Prices quoted here are in U.S. dollars unless noted otherwise.

Taxes and Service Charges Hotels collect a 5% government tax; restaurants a 3% tax. The departure tax is $8 or E.C.$20. A security service charge tax of $2 or E.C.$5 is also imposed.

Most hotels and restaurants add a 10% service charge to your bill. Taxi drivers appreciate a 10% tip.

Guided Tours A wide variety of hiking and photo safari tours are conducted by **Dominica Tours** (tel. 809/448–2638) in sturdy four-wheel-drive vehicles. Prices range from $25 to $75 per person, depending upon the length of the trip and whether picnics and rum punches are included. There are also boat tours that include snorkeling, swimming, and rum or fruit drinks.

Rainbow Rover Tours (tel. 809/448–8650) are conducted in air-conditioned Land Rovers. Tours take in the island for a half or full day at a per-person cost of $30–$50, which includes food and drink. **Ken's Hinterland Adventure Tours** (tel. 809/448–4850) provides tours in vans with knowledgeable guides and can design expeditions to fit your needs.

Any taxi driver will be happy to offer his services as a guide at the cost of $18 an hour, with tip extra. It's a good idea to get a recommendation from your hotel manager or the Dominica Tourist Board (*see* Tourist Information, *above*) before selecting a guide and driver.

Getting Around **Rental Cars** If it doesn't bother you to drive on the left on potholed mountainous roads with hairpin curves, rent a car and strike out on your own. Daily car-rental rates begin at $35 (weekly about $190), plus collision damage at $6 a day, and personal accident insurance at $2 a day, and you'll have to put down a deposit and purchase a visitor's driving permit for E.C.$20. You can rent a car from **Wide Range Car Rentals** (79 Bath Rd., Roseau, tel. 809/448–2198), **Valley Rent-A-Car** (Goodwill Rd., Roseau, tel. 809/448–3233), **Anselm's Car Rental** (3 Great Marlborough, Roseau, tel. 809/448–2730), or **S.T.L. Rent-A-Car** (Goodwill Rd., Roseau, tel. 809/448–2340 or 809/448–4525); **Budget Rent-A-Car** (Canefield Industrial Estate, Canefield, tel. 809/449–2080) offers daily rates, three-day specials, and weekly and monthly rates.

Telephones and Mail To call Dominica from the United States, dial area code 809 and the local access code, 44. On the island, you need to dial only the five-digit number. Direct telephone, telegraph, telefax, teletype, and telex services are via **Cable & Wireless (West Indies) Ltd.** All pay phones are equipped for local and overseas dialing.

First-class (airmail) letters to the United States and Canada cost E.C.60¢; postcards cost E.C.35¢.

Opening and Closing Times Business hours are weekdays 8–1 and 2–4, Saturday 8–1. Banks are open Monday–Thursday 8–1, Friday 8–1 and 3–5.

Exploring Dominica

Numbers in the margin correspond to points of interest on the Dominica map.

Given the small size of this almond-shape island, virtually any destination is within reach on any easy day trip. The amount of time you spend hiking, mountain climbing, bird-watching, or just enjoying the scenery will determine how much you can see during one round-the-island trip. The highways ringing the island's perimeter have been upgraded in recent years, making many sights and towns easier to reach when driving on your own. However, when heading toward some of the more remote destinations, it is advisable to hire a car and driver or to take an escorted tour (*see* Guided Tours, *above*).

Roseau   All the hotels and virtually all the island's population are on the leeward, or Caribbean, side of the island. Twenty thousand or so inhabitants reside in **Roseau,** a town on the flat delta of the Roseau River. Stop first in the Tourist Office in the **Old Market Plaza.** Then stroll through the center of town, where crafts shops and tiny cafés are tucked into old buildings made of wood, stone, and concrete. On Victoria Street is the **Fort Young Hotel,** which was originally built as a fort in the 18th century. Directly across the street is the **State House;** the **Public Library** and the **old Court House** are both nearby.

The National Park Office, fittingly located in the 40-acre Botanical Gardens in Roseau, can provide tour guides and a wealth of printed information. *Tel. 809/448-2401, ext. 417. Open Mon. 8–1 and 2–5, Tues.–Fri. 8–1 and 2–4.*

Head north to Woodbridge Bay Harbour and stroll along the harbor, where you can watch bananas, citrus, and spices being loaded onto ships.

Time Out   Sit in the garden of the late Jean Rhys, the Dominican-born novelist who won Britain's Royal Literary Award. It's now been turned into a garden bistro, the **World of Food** (Queen Mary St. and Field's La., tel. 809/448–6125). If you've never read Rhys, stop off at **Paperbacks** (6 Cork St., tel. 809/448–2370) and purchase her *Wide Sargasso Sea* or any of her other many books.

Elsewhere on   **Morne Trois Pitons** is a blue-green hill of three peaks, the high-
the Island   est of which is 4,403 feet. The mountain is usually veiled in swirling mists and clouds, and the 16,000-acre national park over which it looms is awash with cool mountain lakes, waterfalls, and rushing rivers. Ferns grow 30 feet tall, and wild orchids sprout from trees. Sunlight leaks through green canopies, and a gentle mist rises over the jungle floor.

The road from the capital to the Morne Trois Pitons National Park runs through the **Roseau River Valley.** About 5 miles out of Roseau, a side road branches, one direction leading to Wotten Waven, the other to **Sulphur Springs** (visible evidence of the island's volcanic origins) and the spectacular triple **Trafalgar Falls,** dropping 200 feet into a warm rock-strewn pool that's ideal for bathing.

The village of **Laudat** (about 7 miles from Roseau) is a good starting point for a venture into the park. Two miles northeast of Laudat, at the base of **Morne Macaque** (3,500 feet), you'll find **Freshwater Lake,** and farther on, **Boeri Lake,** with a fringe of greenery and purple hyacinths floating on the water.

From Freshwater Lake there are several sights to be seen, but the hiking trails are not for the faint of heart. **Boiling Lake** and the **Valley of Desolation** are reached by a rugged, all-day, 6-mile ramble, and you should go only with an experienced guide. There are *very* hot springs here that shift direction from time to time under an outer crust. Even experienced guides keep small groups of hikers (six to eight maximum) under their eye at all times (*see* Sports and the Outdoors, *below*).

Boiling Lake, the world's second-largest boiling lake, is like a caldron of gurgling gray-blue water. It is 70 yards wide, and the temperature of the water ranges from 180 to 197°F. Its depth is unknown. It is believed that the lake is not a volcanic crater but a flooded fumarole—a crack through which gases escape from the molten lava below. This is a serious expedition for serious hikers. You must be in excellent condition and bring your own drinking water.

The Valley of Desolation lies below Boiling Lake, and it lives up to its name. Harsh sulfuric fumes have destroyed virtually all the vegetation in what was once a lush forested area. Hikers in the Valley of Desolation are advised to stay on the trail to avoid breaking through the crust that covers the hot lava below.

7 You'll have to backtrack to Roseau and head north toward Pont Casse to reach **Emerald Pool,** 3½ miles northeast of Pont Casse. It's a 10-minute walk along the road that leads to Castle Bruce. Lookout points along the trail provide sweeping views of the windward (Atlantic) coast and the forested interior. Emerald Pool is a swirling, fern-bedecked basin into which a 50-foot waterfall splashes.

A good map and steady nerves are necessary for driving along the rugged, ragged windward coast. A few miles east of Pont Casse there is a fork in the road where a right turn will take you to the southeast coast and a left, to the northeast coast.

8 The south-coast road goes to **Rosalie,** where there is a river for swimming, a black-sand beach, an old aqueduct, and a waterwheel. There is also a waterfall that dashes down a cliff into the ocean. A hike leads to **Petite Soufrière.**

9 The northerly road leads to the little fishing village of **Castle Bruce.** On the beach here you can watch dugout canoes being made from the trunks of gommier trees using traditional Carib methods (after the tree is cut it gets stretched). About 6 miles **10** north of Castle Bruce lies the **Carib Indian Reservation,** which was established in 1903 and covers 3,700 acres. Don't expect a lot in the way of ancient culture and costume. The folks who gave the Caribbean its name live pretty much like other West Indians, as fishermen and farmers. However, they have maintained their traditional skills at woodcarving, basket weaving, and canoe building. Their wares are displayed and sold in little thatch-top huts lining the road. The reservation's Roman Catholic church at Salibia has an altar that was once a canoe. Another point of interest on the reservation is **L'Escalier Tête Chien** ("trail of the snake staircase" in Creole patois)—a hardened lava flow that juts down to the ocean.

The Atlantic here is particularly fierce and roily, the shore marked with countless coves and inlets. The Carib still tell wondrous colorful legends of the island's origins: La Roche Pagua, they say, is home to a fragrant white flower; bathe in its petals and your loved one will obey your every command. By night, Londonderry Islets metamorphose into grand canoes to take the spirits of the dead out to sea.

Time Out Stop for an hour or an overnight at the **Carib Territory Guesthouse** (tel. 809/445–7256), a very basic and fascinating wayside Carib house owned by Charles and Margaret Williams, who live on the premises with their children. There are some 10 bedrooms here for the adventurous traveler, lunch and a cold drink, or a good choice of Carib crafts. You can call Williams in advance and schedule a half-day or full-day walk with him through the territory.

Continuing north from the reservation, you'll go past lovely **Pagua Bay,** with its beach of dark sand. A bit farther along, near Melville Hall Airport, is **Marigot,** the largest (population: 5,000) settlement on the east coast. On the northeast coast, steep cliffs rise out of the Atlantic, which flings its frothy waters over dramatic reefs, and rivers crash through forests of mangroves and fields of coconut. The beaches at **Woodford Hill, Hampstead, Anse Noir,** and **Hodges** are excellent for snorkeling and scuba diving, though all this wind-tossed beauty can be dangerous to swimmers, since there are strong underwater currents as well as whipped-cream waves. From this vantage point you can see the French island of Marie Galante in the distance.

Time Out Take a break from the sun and sea and stop by the **Almond Beach Restaurant & Bar** (tel. 809/445–7783) in Calibishie for some local sustenance. Try the callaloo soup, lobster, or octopus. There is a great selection of fresh local fruit juices, including guava, passion fruit, tangerine, soursop, and papaya, as well as bewitching rums steeped for more than two months in various herbs and spices. Try the *pweve* (patois for pepper), the aniselike *nanie,* or *lapsenth,* a violet-scented pick-me-up and digestive. The delightful owners, Mr. and Mrs. Joseph, are experts in local culture and custom and will arrange a traditional bélé dance on a little stage in the restaurant for groups.

The road continues through banana plantations to Portsmouth, but a side road leads up to the village of **Vieille Case** and **Capucion Pointe,** at the northernmost tip of the island. **Morne Aux Diables** soars 2,826 feet over this area, and slopes down to **Toucari Bay** and **Douglas Bay** on the west coast, where there are spectacular dark-sand beaches.

⓫ Just 2 miles south of Douglas Bay, the 250-acre **Cabrits National Park** is surrounded on three sides by the Caribbean Sea. Local historian Lennox Honychurch has restored **Fort Shirley,** a military complex built between 1770 and 1815. Some of the buildings have been restored, and there is a small museum in the park. The park is connected to the mainland by a freshwater swamp, verdant with ferns, grasses, and trees, where you can see a variety of migrant birds.

A new cruise-ship pier development with both berthing and passenger facilities is open at the port of Cabrits, below Fort Shirley. Present plans are to host only one ship at a time, which will make this a desirable stop on cruise itineraries.

Time Out The bar in the **Purple Turtle Guest House** (Portsmouth, tel. 809/ 445–5296) is a fine place for a rum punch before or after a tour of Portsmouth, especially at sunset.

⑫ **Portsmouth,** 2 miles south of Cabrits, is a peaceful little town with a population of about 5,000. **Prince Rupert Bay,** site of a naval battle in 1782 between the French and the English, is far and away the island's most beautiful harbor. There are more than 2 miles of sandy beaches fringed with coconut trees and most of the island's beachfront hotels. The **Indian River** flows to the sea from here, and a canoe ride takes you through an exotic rain forest thick with mangrove swamps. Board a row boat (not power) for total tranquillity, to be able to hear fish jumping and exotic birds calling. The guides here are notoriously overeager: Choose carefully or ask your hotel to recommend someone.

Just south of Indian River is **Pointe Ronde,** the starting point
⑬ for an expedition to **Morne Diablotin,** at 4,747 feet the island's highest summit. This is not an expedition you should attempt alone; the uninhabited interior is an almost impenetrable primeval forest. You'll need a good guide (*see* Sports and the Outdoors, *below*), sturdy shoes, a warm sweater, and firm resolve.

The west-coast road dips down through the little villages of **Dublanc** (with a side road off to the Syndicate Estate), **Colihaut,** and **Salisbury** before reaching the mouth of the Layou
⑭ River. The **Layou River valley** is rich with bananas, cacao, citrus fruits, and coconuts. The remains of Hillsborough Estate, once a rum-producing plantation, are here. The river is the island's longest and largest, with deep gorges, quiet pools and beaches, waterfalls and rapids—a great place for a full day's outing of swimming and shooting the rapids, or just sunning and picnicking. However, plans are under way to build a large hotel and conference center, the Shangri-la, which will probably disturb the peace in the area.

The road at the bend near Dublanc that leads to the Syndicate Estate also leads to the 200-acre site of the new **Project Sisserou.** This protected site has been set aside with the help of some 6,000 schoolchildren, each of whom donated 25¢ for the land where the endangered Sisserou parrot (found only in Dominica) flies free. At last estimate, there were only about 60 of these shy and beautiful birds, covered in rich green feathers with a mauve front.

Just south of Roseau the road forks, with a treacherous prong leading east to **Grand Bay,** where bay leaves are grown and distilled. If you continue due south from Roseau you'll go through
⑮ **Pointe Michel,** settled decades ago by Martinicans who fled the catastrophic eruption of Mont Pelée. The stretch all the way from Roseau to Scotts Head at the southernmost tip of the island has excellent beaches for scuba diving and snorkeling.

Beaches

Don't come to Dominica in search of powdery white-sand beaches. The travel-poster beaches do exist on the northeast coast, but this is still an almost totally undeveloped area. The beaches that most visitors see are of dark sand, evidence of the island's volcanic origins. The best beaches are found at the mouths of rivers and in protected bays. Scuba diving, snorkeling, and windsurfing are all excellent here.

Layou River has the best river swimming on the island, and its banks are great for sunbathing.

Picard Beach, on the northwest coast, is the island's best beach. Great for windsurfing and snorkeling, it's a 2-mile stretch of brown sand fringed with coconut trees. The Picard Beach Cottage Resort, Portsmouth Beach, and Coconut Beach hotels are along this beach.

Pagua Bay, a quiet, secluded beach of dark sand, is on the Atlantic coast.

Woodford Hill Bay, Hampstead, L'Anse Noir, and **Hodges,** all on the northeast coast, are excellent beaches for snorkeling and scuba diving.

In the southeast, near La Plaine, **Bout Sable Bay** is not much good for swimming, but the surroundings are stirringly elemental: towering red cliffs challenge the rollicking Atlantic.

The beaches south of Roseau to **Scotts Head** at the southernmost tip of the island are good for scuba diving and snorkeling because of the dramatic underwater walls and sudden drops.

The scuba diving is excellent at **Soufrière Bay,** a sandy beach south of Roseau. Volcanic vents puff steam into the sea; the experience has been described as "swimming in champagne."

Sports and the Outdoors

Boating Motorboat and sailing trips can be arranged through **Dominica Tours** (tel. 809/448–2638) and the **Castaways Hotel** (tel. 809/449–6245).

Hiking Trails range from the easygoing to the arduous. For the former, all you'll need are sturdy, rubber-soled shoes and an adventurous spirit.

For the hike to Boiling Lake or the climb up Morne Diablotin you will need hiking boots, a guide, and water. Guides will charge about $30–$35 per person and can be contacted through the Tourist Office or the Forestry Division (tel. 809/448–2401 or 809/448–2638).

Scuba Diving *Skin Diver* magazine recently ranked Dominica among the top five Caribbean dive destinations. **Dive Dominica** (Castle Comfort, tel. 809/448–2188, fax 809/448–6088), with three boats, is one of the oldest dive shops in Dominica, run by owners Derek and Ginette Perryman, NAUI-approved instructors. They offer snorkeling and resort dives for beginners and, for the advanced set, dives on drop-offs, walls, and pinnacles—by day or night. The owners of the **Dominica Dive Resorts, Waitukubuli** (there are two: one at the Anchorage Hotel, tel. 809/448–2638, the other at the Portsmouth Beach Hotel, tel. 809/445–5142) are PADI-certified and offer both resort courses and full certification. **The Castaways Hotel,** only 11 miles from Roseau, has diving at its new water-sports center (tel. 809/449–6244 or 809/449–6245). The going rate at all of the above is about $65 for a two-tank dive or $90 for a resort course with two open-water dives.

Snorkeling Major island operators rent equipment: **Anchorage Hotel** (tel. 809/448–2638), **Castaways Hotel** (tel. 809/449–6244 or 809/449–6245), **Coconut Beach Hotel** (tel. 809/445–5393), **Portsmouth Beach Hotel** (tel. 809/551–4255), **Sunshine Village** (tel. 809/445–5066), and **Picard Beach Cottage Resort** (tel. 809/445–5131).

Swimming   River swimming is extremely popular on Dominica, and the best river to jump into is the Layou River (*see* Exploring Dominica, *above*). Also see Beaches, above, for our pick of the best beaches to swim, snorkel, or surf at.

Windsurfing   Contact either **Anchorage Hotel, Picard Beach Cottage Resort,** or **Castaways Hotel** (*see* Snorkeling, *above*).

Shopping

Gift Ideas   The distinctive handicrafts of the Carib Indians include traditional baskets made of dyed larouma reeds and waterproofed with tightly woven balizier leaves. These crafts are sold on the reservation, as well as in Roseau's shops. Dominica is also noted for its spices, hot peppers, bay rum, and coconut-oil soap; its vetiver-grass mats are sold all over the world.

One of the nicest buys here (or anywhere) is a "then-and-now" book of photography and prose, *Views in the Island of Dominica, 1849*, that shows 1849 Dominica in sepia prints and again some 100 years later in color. Try the Aquarela Gallery on King George V Street.

Good gifts are stylized candles from **Starbrite Industries** (Canefield Industrial Site, tel. 809/449–1006) that come in the shape of the Dominican parrot, cupids, and trees, as well as more traditional shapes. Open weekdays 8–1 and 2–4. **The Old Mill Culture Centre and Historic Site** on Canefield Road presents exhibits on the historical, cultural, and political development of Dominica. In addition, the center exhibits and sells wood carvings by a master carver, Louis Desire, and those of his students—all lovingly carved from Dominican woods. Open weekdays 9–1 and 2–4. There are excellent gift shops at both Papillote (magnificent carvings) and Floral Gardens (domestic goods and crafts). (*See* Lodging, *below*.)

Stop in at **Caribana Handcrafts** (31 Cork St., Roseau, tel. 809/448–2761) or **Tropicrafts** (41 Queen Mary St., Roseau, tel. 809/448–2747), where you'll find soaps, spices, and stacks of handmade hats, baskets, and woven straw mats.

Siblings **Arnold** and **Roberta Toulon** hand-paint T-shirts at their studio-home (54 Queen Mary St., tel. 809/448–3740) that sell so well, stock is always limited. They will, however, make up a special order within two days. Arnold's canvases of fine art are also on display.

Dining

The fertile Dominican soil produces a cornucopia of fresh vegetables, and chefs here utilize them to great advantage, most often with a Creole flair. There are sweet green bananas, kushkush yams, breadfruit, and dasheen (a tuber similar to the potato called taro elsewhere)—these and other staples are known as ground provisions. You'll find fresh fish on virtually every menu, as well as "mountain chicken"—a euphemism for a large frog called *crapaud*. Two rare delicacies for the intrepid diner are *manicou* (a small opossum) and the tender, gamey *agouti* (a large, indigenous rodent)—both are best smoked or stewed.

Dominica is far from the chic, fashion world. Clothes here are practical—for dinner it's shirt and trousers for men and modest dresses for women.

Highly recommended restaurants are indicated by a star ★.

Category	Cost*
Expensive	over $35
Moderate	$15–$35
Inexpensive	under $15

*per person, excluding drinks, service, and 3% sales taxes

★ **La Robe Creole.** A cozy place with wood rafters, ladderback chairs, and colorful Madras cloths, this restaurant has an eclectic à la carte listing. A specialty is callaloo and crab soup, made with dasheen and coconut. You can also have crepes of lobster and conch, charcoal-grilled fish and meats, barbecued chicken, and salads. The downstairs take-out annex, The Mouse Hole, is an inexpensive place to stock up for your picnic. *3 Victoria St., Roseau, tel. 809/448–2896. Reservations advised. AE. Closed Sun. Expensive.*

★ **Reigate Hall.** In this stylish restaurant an old-fashioned waterwheel turns while you dine. While some new, health-oriented dishes have been added, favored specialties remain mountain chicken in champagne sauce and coq au vin. *Reigate Hall Hotel, Roseau, tel. 809/448–4031. Reservations recommended. AE, MC, V. Expensive.*

De Bouille. The attractive dining room at the Fort Young Hotel—with its stone walls and wood-raftered ceiling—is usually filled with the businesspeople who frequent the hotel. The upscale restaurant has an Indian chef, who adds a touch of his homeland cuisine to international and Dominican specialties. The menu includes callaloo and pumpkin soup, grilled lobster, steak, curried chicken, and mountain chicken. *Fort Young Hotel, Roseau, tel. 809/448–5000. Reservations recommended. AE, MC, V. Moderate.*

★ **Evergreen.** This large, airy dining room, which opens onto a small terrace overlooking the sea, has a slightly European feel. Decorated with antiques, marble-tiled floors, and the paintings and wood carvings of local artist Carl Winston—and replete with classical background music—it is a peaceful place in which to enjoy a meal. Dinner includes an interesting choice of soup and salad; entrées of chicken, fish, and beef are served with local fruits and vegetables, such as kushkush and plantains. Homemade desserts include fresh fruit, cake, and ice cream. *Evergreen Hotel, Roseau, tel. 809/448–3288. Reservations recommended. AE, V, MC. Moderate.*

★ **Floral Gardens.** You feel as if you're eating in a private home at this warm-welcoming restaurant. The food is delectable; it's the perfect spot to sample local specialties, such as crapaud and agouti. *Floral Gardens Hotel, Concord, tel. 809/445–7636. AE, MC, V. Moderate.*

Guiyave. Have a drink at the second-floor bar and then repair to the table-filled balcony for dining. Spareribs, lobster, rabbit, and mountain chicken are offered, along with homemade beef or chicken patties, spicy *rotis* (Caribbean burritos), and a variety of light snacks and sandwiches. This restaurant is noted for its fresh tropical fruit juices (a local cherry, guava, passion fruit, and barbadine) and its homemade pies, tarts, and cakes. *15 Cork St., Roseau, tel. 809/448–2930. No credit cards. No dinner. Moderate.*

Le Flambeau. This open-air beach restaurant at the Picard Beach Cottage Resort serves an American-style breakfast of pancakes and French toast that will keep you from being homesick. Lunch and dinner entrées are not memorable, but leave room for the homemade ice cream—peanut, coconut, or mixed berry. *Picard Beach Cottage Resort, Portsmouth, tel. 809/445–5131. AE, D, MC, V. Moderate.*

Ocean Terrace. As the name suggests, this eatery in the Anchorage Hotel is on a terrace overlooking the ocean. Grilled lamb chops with mint jelly, Creole-style fish court bouillon, and chilled lobster in a chives-vinaigrette marinade are among the à la carte specialties. There is live Caribbean entertainment on Thursday nights. *Anchorage Hotel, Roseau, tel. 809/448–2638. Reservations recommended. AE, D, MC, V. Moderate.*

The Orchard. You can dine indoors in a spacious, unadorned dining room or in a pleasant covered courtyard surrounded by latticework. Chef Joan Cools-Lartique offers Creole-style coconut shrimp, lobster, black pudding, mountain chicken, and callaloo soup with crabmeat, among other delicacies, on a changing menu. Sandwiches are also on the menu. *31 King George V St., Roseau, tel. 809/448–3051. AE, D, MC, V. Moderate.*

Papillote. This open-air restaurant, with trellises of woven orchids and ferns, and popular with birds, butterflies, and tour groups, seems hacked from the undergrowth. Try the bracing callaloo soup, the knockout rum punches and, if they're on the menu, the succulent *souk* (tiny, delicate river shrimp). *Papillote Wilderness Retreat, tel. 809/448–2287. AE, D, MC, V. Moderate.*

★ **Castaways.** The hotel's guests often lunch or dine here, but it's the Sunday brunch (which starts at 11 AM and goes to 6 PM) that's the real draw. The grill is fired up, and fresh fish, steak, chicken, and lobster are tossed on the fire. Side dishes of fresh fruits and vegetables, along with hot breads, round out the beach party. *Castaways Hotel, Mero, tel. 809/449–6244 or 809/449–6245. AE, MC, V. Inexpensive.*

Coconut Beach. This casual, low-key beachfront restaurant and bar is popular with both visiting yacht owners (moorings are available) and anyone interested in an afternoon on a stretch of white-sand beach. Fresh tropical drinks and local seafood dishes are the specialty here; sandwiches and *rotis* are also served. *Coconut Beach Hotel, Portsmouth, tel. 809/445–5393. AE, D, MC, V. Inexpensive.*

Sagittarius Reggae Restaurant. This funky place, plastered with astrological paraphernalia, serves johnnycakes that have Egg McMuffins beat by a country mile and sublime fresh fruit juices. Weekends it's transformed into a hopping club that blasts reggae and soca. *Portsmouth, no tel. No credit cards. Inexpensive.*

Lodging

Hotels on Dominica range from spartan to rural chic, but even in the swankier places informality is the rule. There are only 430 rooms on the entire island, but an additional 80 or so are planned for the near future. All the beachfront hotels but one are in the Portsmouth area, the one exception being the Castaways on Mero Beach outside Roseau. Roseau's seaside facilities have a splendid view of the Caribbean but are beachless. There are also a few exceptional nature retreats perched in the rain forest. A variety of meal plans exist. Since restaurant options are limited in Dominica, especially for dinner, you may wish to choose an MAP plan in your vacation package. It's a good idea to check current credit-card policy. As befits "The Nature Isle," whose beauties aren't seasonal, most rates remain year-round, though a few hotels are catching on.

Highly recommended lodgings are indicated by a star ★.

Category	Cost*
Expensive	over $100
Moderate	$65–$100
Inexpensive	under $65

All prices are for a standard double room for two, excluding 5% tax, 3% sales tax, and a 10%–15% service charge.

Hotels　**Castaways Beach Hotel.** This hotel is popular with young people, mostly because of its young and energetic manager, Linda Harris. The island's first resort hotel, it's located in Mero, 11 miles north of Roseau, on a mile-long, dappled gray beach. The rooms have double beds and balconies overlooking tropical gardens and come with or without air-conditioning. The furnishings are a bit worn, but promises have been made to remedy this situation in the near future. The sunsets, however, remain spectacular. The restaurant serves French-Creole cuisine, island music plays most nights in the beach bar, and an all-day Sunday brunch/beach barbecue has a loyal following. *Box 5, Roseau, tel. 809/449–6245 or 800/626–0581, fax 809/449–6246. 27 rooms. Facilities: beach, restaurant, 2 bars, tennis court, water-sports center, scuba, dive packages offered. AE, MC, V. EP, MAP. Expensive.*

★　**Fort Young Hotel.** This hotel reopened in the summer of 1989 following a total renovation. Now Dominican paintings and prints from the late 1700s meld with the massive stone walls of the 18th century, when this was Dominica's main fort. Set on a cliff in Roseau, it's a good location for business travelers who also appreciate the chance to dip into the swimming pool adjacent to the bar and restaurant. The rooms are standard, but most have a small private balcony. Be sure to ask for a room facing the sea and away from the road. Plans are to add 30 more rooms. *Box 519, Roseau, tel. 809/448–5000, fax 809/448–5006. 33 air-conditioned rooms with telephone and TV. Facilities: pool, entertainment, conference room, bar, disco, and restaurant. AE, MC, V. EP. Expensive.*

★　**Lauro Club.** On a small but clean ribbon of sand, this sleek and stunning development boasts simple but attractive units furnished in refreshingly bold colors, each with a kitchenette, a living room, and a terrace bigger than most hotel rooms. Private and very charming. *Box 483, Roseau, tel. 809/449–6602, fax 809/449–6603. 10 units. Facilities: restaurant, bar, pool. AE, MC, V. EP. Expensive.*

Picard Beach Cottage Resort. This resort comprises eight beachside wood cottages built in 18th-century West Indian style on the site of an old coconut plantation. There's both beach and pool (next door at the Portsmouth Beach Hotel) here, below the peaks of Morne Diablotin, on the northwest coast. *Box 34, Roseau, tel. 809/445–5131; in the U.S., 800/424–5500, fax 809/445–5599. 8 individual cottages with bedroom, bath, sitting/dining area, kitchen, and veranda. Facilities: beach, pool, dive center with scuba, snorkeling, and windsurfing, bar, and restaurant. AE, MC, V. EP. Expensive.*

★ **Reigate Hall Hotel.** Perched high on a steep cliff above Roseau, this is a stunning stone-and-wood facility. The suite has a magnificent carved-wood four-poster bed, bar, and Jacuzzi. It also has the dubious distinction of being the most expensive accommodation on the island (other rooms are cheaper). All rooms have air-conditioning, private balconies, embroidered bedspreads on double or twin beds, and bidets. Rooms 17 and 18 are the nicest, with balcony views of the sea. *Reigate, tel. 809/ 448–4031; in the U.S., 800/223–9815; in Canada, 800/468– 0023, fax 809/448–4034. 17 rooms. Facilities: restaurant, 2 bars, pool, lighted tennis court, sauna, clock radios. AE, MC, V. EP, MAP. Moderate–Expensive.*

Anchorage Hotel. A two-story, galleried section of this hotel has spacious, air-conditioned rooms, each with a double and a twin bed, and a private balcony overlooking the sea. Smaller rooms are located by the swimming pool. The hotel is headquarters for Dominica Tours (*see* Guided Tours, *above*), but is generally devoid of personality. *Box 34, Roseau, tel. 809/448– 2638, fax 809/448–5680. 36 rooms. Facilities: restaurant, bar, pool, squash court, yacht mooring. AE, D, MC, V. EP. Moderate.*

Coconut Beach Hotel. The sprawling acreage of this informal hotel curves around its beachside location, on the north coast. It's casual and comfortable, if basic. Apartments and beachfront bungalows have double rooms that are cooled by air-conditioning or fans. *Box 37, Roseau, tel. 809/445–5393, fax 809/445–5693. 13 rooms. Facilities: beach, restaurant, bar, snorkeling, yacht moorings. AE, D, MC, V. EP, MAP. Moderate.*

★ **Evergreen Hotel.** A small gem perched on the Caribbean Sea, 2 miles from downtown Roseau, Mena Winston's hotel has air-conditioned rooms with simple, traditional furnishings. Some rooms have private terraces and others have cable TV. Rooms on the upper (main) floor are brighter and therefore preferable. Winston and her family turn out fine local fare in the high-ceilinged dining room that opens onto a small terrace, where there is now a small pool and snack bar. Six more guest rooms should be ready by the 1994 season. *Box 309, Roseau, tel. 809/ 448–3288, fax 809/448–6800. 10 rooms. Facilities: restaurant, lounge. AE, MC, V. MAP. Moderate.*

Springfield Plantation. This former plantation home, complete with sweeping veranda, has been enlarged and furnished in colonial style, including some four-poster beds. The setting (6 miles from Roseau) is some 1,200 feet above sea level in jungle-covered hills, with river bathing nearby. The compound includes hotel rooms as well as apartments and cottages, both with kitchens. Since it has become affiliated with the Archibald Tropical Research Center of Clemson University, South Carolina, it has lost some of the loving care given to it by its previous owners. The lounge and dining areas look slightly shabby. It is no longer quite the special place that it once was. *Box 456, Roseau, tel. 809/449–1401, fax 809/449–2160. 7 rooms. Facilities: restaurant, 2 bars. AE, D, MC, V. EP, MAP. Moderate.*

Layou River Hotel. This is a rambling estate property focused around the turbulent beauty of the Layou River, which rushes through a mountain funnel. Forty rooms, with modest bathrooms, decorated in muted pastels (most with telephones) are scattered throughout a chalet-style main house and hexagonal-shaped two-story buildings. An Olympic-size swimming pool with adjacent bar dominates the back lawn, and thick jungle foliage contrasts with the modern architecture. At press time, a Chinese company was planning to build a 200-room hotel and convention center, the Shangri-la, across the road and to incorporate the Layou River Hotel into the complex. *Box 8, Roseau, tel. 809/449–6281, fax 809/449–6793. 40 air-conditioned rooms. Facilities: restaurant, bar, pool, conference rooms. AE, D, MC, V. EP. Inexpensive–Moderate.*

Papillote Wilderness Retreat and Nature Sanctuary. This inn is in the rain forest, only a short hike from the 200-foot Trafalgar Falls. The setting is spectacular, and Florida-born Anne Jean-Baptiste, who has lived on Dominica for more than 25 years, can provide helpful tips about nature walks, tours, and other adventures in the area. Her botanical garden has a mind-boggling assortment of exotic plants and flowers, which she'll graciously use to brew you a soothing herbal infusion—bergamot to combat insomnia or l'oiselles for colds. The inn is small, homey, and comfortable and has a loyal following of nature lovers. A hot tub bubbles right next to the restaurant; geese and guinea fowl ramble the grounds; and surreal stone animals crop up everywhere. This place is truly a magical retreat. *Box 67, Roseau, tel. 809/448–2287, fax 809/448–2286. 10 rooms. Facilities: restaurant, bar, gift shop, nature tours. AE, DC, MC, V. EP. Inexpensive–Moderate.*

Portsmouth Beach Hotel. Many of the hotel's rooms are used by students from the nearby American medical school, so things get a bit noisy here, but it *is* right on the beach. (The architecture has been accurately called "prisonlike.") Rooms beginning with the number 9 are the closest to the sea. This hotel is a companion to the Anchorage Hotel in Roseau, and it's possible to arrange north–south stays. *Box 34, Roseau, tel. 809/445–5142, fax 809/445–5599. 97 rooms. Facilities: beach, restaurant, bar. AE, D, V. EP. Inexpensive–Moderate.*

Guest Houses/ Lodges
★

Castle Comfort Lodge. In 1988, owner Dorothy Perryman's son Derek and his wife, Ginette, returned to Dominica to help run this lodge and on-the-premises dive shop, Dive Dominica that, with three boats, has made this hotel the preferred choice for many divers. The lodge has been enlarged and redecorated. All rooms are bright and cheerful; some have balconies, others have cable TV. Although the hotel caters to divers with attractive packages, nondivers will enjoy it as well. The Perrymans can arrange various adventures and scenic tours and their enthusiasm for the island carries over to their guests. *Box 63, Roseau, tel. 809/448–2188, fax 809/448–6088. 10 rooms. Facilities: restaurant, dive shop. AE, MC, V. EP. Moderate.*

Floral Gardens. This 15-room motel is situated on the edge of the rain forest reserve on the windward side of the island. This location affords access to unlimited activities: excellent river bathing, bird-watching, hiking, and relaxing on nearby beaches. Although Roseau is an hour away, the property is only 10 minutes from the Melville Hall Airport and 15 minutes from the white-sand beach of Woodford Hill. This is one of Dominica's most congenial spots, thanks to owner O. J.

Seraphin, the former interim prime minister, who oversaw the island's stormy passage to independence. *Concord, tel. 809/ 445-7636, fax 809/445-7636. 15 rooms. Facilities: restaurant, gift shop. AE, MC, V. EP. Inexpensive.*

★ **Layou Valley Inn.** Tasteful and splendid is this house that Tamara Holmes and her late husband built in the foothills of the National Preserve, under the peaks of Morne Trois Pitons. She's a Russian who once translated for NASA but now devotes her talents to the kitchen. Mme. Holmes sums up this hideaway best: "My sheets are percale and my food is French." The rooms are simple and clean, and the sunken lounge and glass-fronted dining area are comfortable, attractive areas to relax in with other guests. *Box 196, Roseau, tel. 809/449-6203, fax 809/448- 5212. 10 rooms. Facilities: restaurant, bar, swimming in mountain rivers, guided climbs to the Boiling Lake at extra cost. AE, MC, V. EP. Inexpensive.*

Nightlife

Discos If you're not too exhausted from mountain climbing, swimming, and the like, you can join the locals on weekends at **The Warehouse** (tel. 809/449-1303), outside Roseau toward the airport, or the **Night Box** (Goodwill Road, no tel.), which attracts a rowdier clientele.

Nightclubs When the moon comes up, most visitors go down to the dining room in their resident hotel for the music or chat offered there, which is always liveliest on weekends. Newly reopened Ft. Young has upscale entertainment, as do many of the better hotels—the Castaways, Anchorage, and Reigate Hall in particular.

The **Shipwreck,** in the Canefield Industrial area (tel. 809/449-1059), has live reggae and taped music on weekends, and a Sunday bash that starts at noon and continues into the night.

The best insider's spot is definitely **Wykie's La Tropical** (51 Old St., Roseau, tel. 809/448-8015). This classic Caribbean hole-in-the-wall is a gathering spot for the island's movers and shakers, especially during Friday's "Happy Hours" from 5 to 7, when they nibble on stewed chicken or black pudding, then stay on for a local calypso band or Jing-Ping—a group playing local music on the accordion, quage (a kind of washboard instrument), drums, and a boom boom (a percussive instrument). Another resident favorite is **Lenville** (tel. 809/446-6598), a very basic rum shop with barbecued chicken and dancing in the village of Coulivistrie.

11 Dominican Republic

Updated by
Nigel Fisher

Sprawling over two-thirds of the island of Hispaniola, the Dominican Republic is the spot where European settlement of the Western Hemisphere really began. Santo Domingo, its capital, is the oldest continuously inhabited city in this half of the globe, and history buffs who visit have difficulty tearing themselves away from the many sites that boast of antiquity in the city's 16th-century Colonial Zone. Sun-seekers head for the beach resorts of Puerto Plata, Samaná, and La Romana; at Punta Cana, beachcombers tan on the Caribbean's longest stretch of white-sand beach. The highest peak in the West Indies is here: Pico Duarte (10,128 feet) lures hikers to the central mountain range, and ancient sunken galleons and coral reefs divert divers and snorkelers.

Columbus happened upon this island on December 5, 1492, and on Christmas Eve his ship, the *Santa María*, was wrecked on the Atlantic shore. He named it *La Isla Española* ("the Spanish island"), established a small colony, and sailed back to Spain on the *Pinta*. A year later, he returned, only to find that the Spanish colony had been destroyed by the Taino Indians, the island's original inhabitants. But Columbus established another colony nearby, leaving his brother Bartholomew in charge. Santo Domingo, which is located on the south coast where the Río Ozama spills into the Caribbean Sea, was founded in 1496 by Bartholomew Columbus and Nicolás de Ovando, and during the first half of the 16th century became the bustling hub of Spanish commerce and culture in the New World.

Hispaniola (a derivation of *La Isla Española*) has had an unusually chaotic history, replete with bloody revolutions, military coups, yellow-fever epidemics, invasions, and bankruptcy. In the 17th century, the western third of the island was ceded to France; a slave revolt in 1804 resulted in the establishment there of the first black republic, Haiti. Dominicans and Haitians battled for control of the island on and off throughout the 19th century. The Dominicans declared themselves independent from Haiti in 1844 and from Spain in 1865. The country was, however, bankrupt by the turn of the century. The United States helped to administer the island's finances, and eventually U.S. Marines occupied the country from 1916 to 1924, until a new Dominican constitution was signed. Rafael Trujillo ruled the Dominican Republic with an iron fist from 1930 until his assassination in 1961. A short-lived democracy was overthrown soon thereafter, followed by another occupation by the U.S. Marines in 1965. The country has been relatively stable since the early 1970s, and administrations have been staunch supporters of the United States.

American influence looms large in Dominican life. If Dominicans do not actually have relatives living in the United States, they know someone who does; and many speak at least rudimentary English. Still, it is a Latin country, and the Hispanic flavor contrasts sharply with the culture of the British, French, and Dutch islands in the Caribbean. The Dominican Republic also reflects racial mixtures.

Dominican towns and cities are generally not quaint, neat, or particularly pretty. Poverty is everywhere, but the country is also alive and chaotic, sometimes frenzied, sometimes laidback. Its tourist zones are as varied as they come—from extravagant Casa de Campo and the manicured hotels of Playa Dorada to the neglected streets of Jarabacoa in its gorgeous

Dominican Republic

Cofresí Beach
Luperón Beach
Montecristi
35
36 — 48
49 50
Playa Dorada
Cabar Beach
Puerto Plata 31
33
Sosúa
32
51
Guayubin
Dajabón
La Unión International Airport
Santiago de los Caballeros
Moca
30
San Francisco de Macorís
52
Jarabacoa
HAITI
29
Bánica
San Juan
Lago Enriquillo
Neiba
Azua
Duvergé
Bani
Bahia de Ocoa
Pedernales
Barahona
HISPANIOLA
Oviedo
Isla Beata
Cabo Beata

Exploring
Altos de Chavón, **28**
La Vega Vieja, **30**
Mt. Isabel de Torres, **32**
Parque de los Tres Ojos, **26**
Pico Duarte, **29**
Puerto Plata, **31**

Samaná, **34**
San Pedro de Macorís, **27**
Sosúa, **33**

Dining
Alcázar, **53**
Amazonia, **75**
Antoine's, **54**
Café del Sol, **72**

Café St. Michel, **61**
Cafemba, **48**
Castillo del Rio, **73**
De Armando, **44**
El Caserio, **63**
El Castillo del Mar, **60**
Flamingo's, **36**
Fonda de la Atarazana, **57**

Jimmy's, **45**
La Bahía, **59**
Lina, **55**
Lucky Seven, **58**
Mesón de la Cava, **56**
Porto Dorado, **37**
Roma II, **46**
Vesuvio, **62**
Villa Casita, **74**

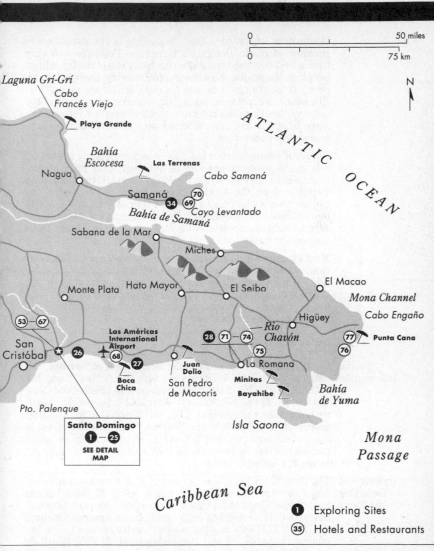

0 ____ 50 miles
0 ____ 75 km

N

Laguna Grí-Grí

Cabo Francés Viejo

Playa Grande

ATLANTIC OCEAN

Bahía Escocesa

Las Terrenas

Nagua

Cabo Samaná

Samaná 34 69 70

Bahía de Samaná Cayo Levantado

Sabana de la Mar

Miches

Monte Plata Hato Mayor

El Seibo

El Macao

Mona Channel

Cabo Engaño

53 — 67

Higüey

San Cristóbal

26

Las Américas International Airport

28 71 74

Río Chavón

77 **Punta Cana**

75

76

68

27

Boca Chica

Juan Dolio

San Pedro de Macorís

La Romana

Minitas

Bayahibe

Bahía de Yuma

Pto. Palenque

Santo Domingo
1 — 25
SEE DETAIL MAP

Isla Saona

Mona Passage

Caribbean Sea

1 Exploring Sites

35 Hotels and Restaurants

Lodging

Bahía Beach, **69**

Bávaro Beach Resort, **76**

Boca Chica Resort, **68**

Caribbean Village Club and Resort, **42**

Casa de Campo, **71**

Club Mediterranée, **77**

Dorado Naco and Playa Naco, **36**

Gran Hotel Lina and Casino, **55**

Heavens, **48**

Hostal Palacio Nicolás de Ovando, **66**

Hostal Jimessón, **38**

Hotel Cofresi, **35**

Hotel El Embajador and Casino, **65**

Hotel V Centenario, **67**

Hotel Gran Bahía, **70**

Hotel Hogar, **52**

Hotel Montemar, **43**

Hotel Santo Domingo, **53**

Jack Tar Village, **39**

Jaragua Resort Hotel, Casino and European Spa, **64**

Paradise Beach Resort and Club, **37**

Playa Chiquita, **49**

Playa Dorada Beach Resort, **40**

Puerto Plata Beach Resort and Casino, **41**

Punta Goleta Beach Resort, **51**

Sand Castle, **50**

Santo Domingo Sheraton Hotel and Casino, **54**

mountain setting and the world-weary beauty of the Samaná peninsula.

Dominicans love music—there is dancing in the streets every summer at Santo Domingo's Merengue Festival—and they have a well-deserved reputation for being one of the friendliest people in the region. This is a tropical country; there is less urgency to get things done and tempers don't flare up quickly. Blackouts, for instance, are a daily occurrence in much of the country, but this does not cause much discomfort for visitors, since hotels in the most affected area—Puerto Plata—have emergency generators.

In recent years, tourism has played an increasingly important role in the government's scheme of things. Like Puerto Rico, its cousin to the east across the Mona Channel, the Dominican Republic used the 500th anniversary of its "discovery" by Christopher Columbus to give the tourist industry a much-needed boost. Nonetheless, the government bureaucracies are slow to help the traveler with other than rudimentary maps and basic information.

Most vacations on the island are one- to two-week packages arranged through tour operators working with airlines and hotels. Hotel prices are among the least expensive in the Caribbean, and, even with a large number of four- and five-star hotels already in operation and more under construction, prices are likely to stay low.

Before You Go

Tourist Information   Contact the **Dominican Republic Department of Tourism,** Dominican Consulate, 1 Times Sq., 11th floor, New York, NY 10036, tel. 212/768–2480; 2355 Sanzedo Ave., Suite 305, Coral Gables, FL 33134, tel. 305/444–4592; 1464 Crescent St., Montreal, Quebec, Canada H3A 2B6, tel. 514/933–6126. The best source of information is the **Tourism Promotional Council** in Santo Domingo (tel. 800/752–1151), which will advise on all tourist matter. Be prepared to wait at least two weeks to get requested material sent to you.

Arriving and Departing
By Plane   The Dominican Republic has two major international airports: Las Américas International Airport, about 20 miles outside Santo Domingo, and La Unión International Airport, about 25 miles east of Puerto Plata on the north coast. **American Airlines** (tel. 800/433–7300), has the most extensive service to the Dominican Republic. It and **Dominicana** (tel. 212/765–7310) fly nonstop from New York to Santo Domingo; American, **Continental** (tel. 800/231–0856), and Dominicana fly nonstop from New York to Puerto Plata; American and Dominicana fly nonstop from Miami to Santo Domingo; and American and Dominicana fly nonstop from Miami to Puerto Plata. Continental has connecting service from Puerto Plata to Santo Domingo; American offers connections to both Santo Domingo and Puerto Plata from San Juan, Puerto Rico; and American Eagle has two flights a day from San Juan to La Romana.

Several regional carriers serve neighboring islands. **ALM** (tel. 800/327–7230) connects Santo Domingo to St. Maarten and Curaçao. There is also limited domestic service available from La Herrera Airport in Santo Domingo to smaller airfields in La

Romana, Samaná, and Santiago. A new airport is planned for Barahona.

Long-needed expansions and rehauls continue at both Las Américas and La Unión. The old terminal at Las Américas suffered a major fire; consequently, the newly completed terminal, although quite pleasant, is now congested with the overflow. Overworked customs and immigration officials are often less than courteous, and luggage theft is rife. Try to travel with carry-on luggage, and keep a sharp eye on it. Be prepared for a daunting experience as you leave customs. However, some order is being imposed—taxis now line up and, for the most part, charge the official established rates. If you have arranged for a hotel transfer, a representative should be waiting for you in the immigration hall.

From the Airport   Taxis are available at the airport, and the 25-minute ride into Santo Domingo averages R.D.$250 (about U.S. $21). Taxi fares from the Puerto Plata airport average R.D.$200.

Passports   U.S. and Canadian citizens must have either a valid passport or
and Visas   proof of citizenship, such as an original (not photocopied) birth certificate, and a Tourist Card. Legal residents of the United States must have an Alien Registration Card (green card), a valid passport, and a Tourist Card. British citizens need only a valid passport; no entry visa is required. The requisite Tourist Card costs $10, and you should be sure to purchase it at the airline counter when you check in, and then fill it out on the plane. You can purchase the card on arrival at the airport, but you'll encounter long lines. Keep the bottom half of the card in a safe place because you'll need to present it to immigration authorities when you leave. There is also a U.S.$10 departure tax (payable only in U.S. dollars).

Language   Before you travel to the Dominican Republic, you should know at least a smattering of Spanish. Unlike throughout the rest of the Caribbean, there is little effort to learn English. Guides at major tourist attractions and front-desk personnel in the major hotels speak a fascinating form of English, though they often have trouble understanding tourists. The people who serve you in the hotel coffee shop are usually speechless when English is spoken to them, as are people you meet in the streets of Santo Domingo. Traffic signs and restaurant menus, except at popular tourist establishments, are in Spanish. Using smiles and gestures will help, but a nodding acquaintance with the language or a phrase book is more useful.

Precautions   Beware of the *buscones* at the airports. They offer to assist you, and do so by relieving you of your luggage and disappearing with it. Also avoid the black marketers, who will offer you a tempting rate of exchange for your U.S. dollars. If the police catch you changing money on the street, they'll haul you off to jail (the *calabozo*). Also, buy amber only from reputable shops. The attractively priced piece offered by the street vendor is more than likely plastic. Guard your wallet or pocketbook in Santo Domingo, especially around the Malecón (waterfront boulevard), which seems to teem with pickpockets.

Staying in the Dominican Republic

Important   **Tourist Information:** There is the **Secretary of Tourism,** in
Addresses   Santo Domingo in a complex of government offices at the corner

of Av. Mexico and 30 de Maizo (Officinas Guberbamentales Building D, tel. 809/689–3655, fax 809/682–3806). Unless you are seeking special assistance, it is not worth making the trek here for the limited material offered to tourists. The tourist office is in Puerto Plata (Playa Long Beach, tel. 809/586–3676). Both offices are open weekdays 9–2:30, but the Puerta Plata office often opens late and closes early.

Emergencies **Police:** In Santo Domingo, call 711; in Puerto Plata, call 586–2804; in Sosúa, call 571–2233. However, do not expect too much from the police, aside from a bit of a hassle and some paperwork that they will consider the end of the matter. In general, the police and government bureaucrats take a hostile approach to visitors.

Hospitals: Santo Domingo emergency rooms that are open 24 hours are **Centro Médico Universidad Central del Este** (UCE) (Av. Máximo Gómez 68, tel. 809/682–1220), **Clínica Abreu** (Calle Beller 42, tel. 809/688–4411), and **Clínica Gómez Patino** (Av. Independencia 701, tel. 809/685–9131 or 685–9141). In Puerto Plata, you can go to **Clínica Dr. Brugal** (Calle José del Carmen Ariza 15, tel. 809/586–2519). In Sosúa, try the **Centro Médico Sosúa** (Av. Martinez, tel. 809/571–2305).

Pharmacies: The following pharmacies are open 24 hours a day: in Santo Domingo, **San Judas Tadeo** (Av. Independencia 57, tel. 809/689–2851 or 809/685–8165); in Puerto Plata, **Farmacia Deleyte** (Av. John F. Kennedy 89, tel. 809/571–2515); in Sosúa, **San Rafael** (Carretera Cabarete Km. 1, tel. 809/571–0777).

Currency The coin of the realm is the Dominican peso, which is divided into 100 centavos. It is written R.D.$, and fluctuates relative to the U.S. dollar. At press time, U.S.$1 was equivalent to R.D.$12.30. Always make certain you know in which currency any transaction is taking place (any confusion will probably not be to your advantage). There is a growing black market for hard currency, so be wary of offers to exchange U.S. dollars at a rate more favorable than the official one.

Taxes and Service Charges Hotels and restaurants add a 21% government tax (which includes a 10% service charge) to your bill. U.S. visitors must buy a $10 tourist card before entering the Dominican Republic. All foreign visitors must pay a $10 departure tax. Both must be paid in U.S. dollars.

Although hotels add the 10% service charge, it is customary to leave a dollar per day for the hotel maid. At restaurants and nightclubs you may want to leave an additional 5%–10% tip for a job well done. Taxi drivers expect a 10% tip. Skycaps and hotel porters expect at least five pesos per bag.

Guided Tours **Prieto Tours** (tel. 809/685–0102 or 809/688–5715) operates Gray Line of the Dominican Republic. It offers half-day bus tours of Santo Domingo, nightclub tours, beach tours, tours to Cibao Valley and the Amber Coast, and a variety of other tours.

Turinter (tel. 809/685–4020) tours include dinner and a show or casino visit, a full-day tour of Samaná, as well as specialty tours (museum, shopping, fishing).

Apolo Tours (tel. 809/586–5329) offers a full-day tour of Playa Grande and tours to Santiago (including a casino tour) and Sosúa. It will also arrange transfers between your hotel and the airport, day sightseeing tours, and custom and small-group tours along the north coast, which include stops along the way for swimming and an overnight stay at La Samaná.

Getting Around Taxis, which are government regulated, line up outside hotels
Taxis and restaurants. The taxis are unmetered, and the minimum fare within Santo Domingo is about R.D.$50, but you can bargain for less if you order a taxi away from the major hotels. Hiring a taxi by the hour and with any number of stops is R.D.$125 per hour with a minimum of two hours. Be sure to establish the time that you start; drivers like to advance the time a little. Just be certain it is clearly understood in advance which currency is to be used in the agreed-upon fare. Taxis can also drive you to destinations outside the city. Rates are posted in hotels and at the airport. Sample fares are R.D.$930 to La Romana and R.D.$1,830 to Puerta Plata. Round-trips are considerably less than twice the one-way fare. **Taxi la Paloma** (tel. 809/562–3460), **Taxi Raffi** (tel. 809/689–5468), and **Centro Taxi** (tel. 809/687–6128) will transport you.

In a separate category are radio taxis, which are convenient if you'd like to schedule a pickup, and academic if you don't speak Spanish. The fare is negotiated over the phone when you make the appointment. The most reliable company is **Apolo Taxi** (tel. 809/541–9595).

Avoid unmarked street taxis—there have been numerous incidents of assaults and robberies, particularly in Santo Domingo.

Buses *Públicos* are small blue-and-white or blue-and-red cars that run regular routes, stopping to let passengers on and off. The fare is two pesos. Competing with the públicos are the *conchos* or *colectivos* (privately owned buses), whose drivers tool around the major thoroughfares, leaning out of the window or jumping out to try to persuade passengers to climb aboard. It's a colorful, if cramped, way to get around town. The fare is about one peso. Privately owned air-conditioned buses make regular runs to Santiago, Puerto Plata, and other destinations. Avoid night travel because the country's roads are full of potholes. You should make reservations by calling **Metro Buses** (Av. Winston Churchill, tel. 809/566–6590, 809/566–6587, or 809/566–7126 in Santo Domingo; 809/586–6063 in Puerto Plata; 809/583–9111 in Santiago; and 809/584–2259 in Nagua) or **Caribe Tours** (Av. 27 de Febrero at Leopoldo Navarro, tel. 809/687–3171). One-way bus fare from Santo Domingo to Puerto Plata is R.D.$70.

Motorbike Taxis Known as *motoconchos*, these bikes are a popular and inexpensive way to get around such tourist areas as Puerto Plata, Sosúa, and Jarabacoa. Bikes can be flagged down both on the road and in town; rates vary from 3 to 20 pesos, depending upon distance.

Rental Cars You'll need a valid driver's license from your own country and a major credit card and/or cash deposit. Cars can be rented at the airports and at many hotels. Among the known names are **Avis** (tel. 809/532–2969), **Budget** (tel. 809/562–6812), **Hertz** (tel. 809/688–2277), and **National** (tel. 809/562–1444). Rates average U.S.$70 and up per day, depending upon the make and size of the car. Driving is on the right. Many Dominicans drive recklessly, often taking their half of the road out of the middle, but they will flash their headlights to warn against highway patrols.

If for some unavoidable reason you must drive on the narrow, unlighted mountain roads at night, exercise extreme caution. Many local cars are without headlights or taillights, bicyclists do not have lights, and cows stand by the side of the road. Traffic and directional signs are less than adequate, and unseen potholes can easily break a car's axle. The 80-kph (50-mph) speed limit is strictly enforced. Finally, keep in mind that gas stations are few and far between in some of the remote regions. Police supplement their income by stopping drivers on various pretexts and expecting a "gift." Locals give R.D.$20 or R.D.$40.

Plane If you lack the time to travel overland, you can charter a small plane for trips around the island and to neighboring countries, and for surprisingly inexpensive rates. Contact Jimmy or Irene Butler at **Air Taxi** (Núñez de Cáceres 2, Santo Domingo, tel. 809/541–5333 or 809/541–7366).

Telephones and Mail To call the Dominican Republic from the United States, dial area code 809 and the local number. Connections are clear and easy to make. Trying to place calls from the Dominican Republic, however, is another matter. The system is, to put it kindly, archaic. However, there is direct-dial service to the United States; dial 1, followed by area code and number.

Airmail postage to North America for a letter or postcard costs R.D.$2; to Europe, R.D.$4, and may take up to three weeks to reach the destination.

Opening and Closing Times Regular office hours are weekdays 8–noon and 2–5, Saturday 8–noon. Government offices are open weekdays 7:30–2:30. Banking hours are weekdays 8:30–4:30.

Exploring the Dominican Republic

Numbers in the margin correspond to points of interest on the Santo Domingo map.

Santo Domingo We'll begin our tour where Spanish civilization in the New World began, in the 12-block area of **Santo Domingo** called the Colonial Zone. This historical area is now a bustling, noisy district with narrow cobbled streets, shops, restaurants, residents, and traffic jams. Ironically, all the noise and congestion make it somehow easier to imagine this old city as it was when it was yet a colony—when the likes of Columbus, Cortés, Ponce de León, and pirates sailed in and out and colonists were settling themselves in the New World. Tourist brochures boast that "history comes alive here"—a surprisingly truthful statement.

A quick taxi tour of the old section takes about an hour, but if you're interested in history, you'll want to spend a day or two exploring the many old "firsts," and you'll want to do it in the most comfortable shoes you own. Be aware that wearing shorts, miniskirts, and halters in churches is considered inappropriate. (Note: Hours and admission charges are erratic; check with the Tourist Office for up-to-date information.)

One of the first things you'll see as you approach the Colonial Zone is a statue, only slightly smaller than the Colossus of Rhodes, staring out over the Caribbean Sea. It is **Montesina,** the Spanish priest who came to the Dominican Republic in the 16th century to appeal for human rights for Indians.

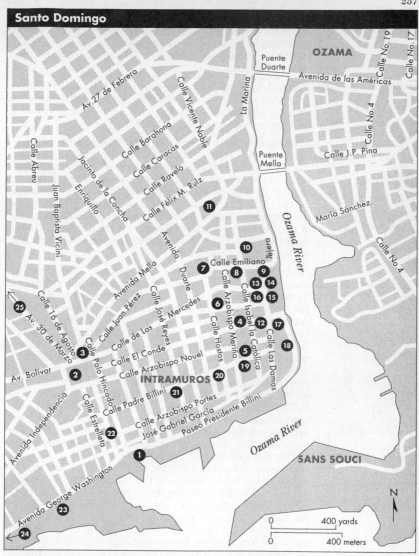

Santo Domingo

Alcázar de Colón, **9**
Calle Las Damas, **12**
Capilla de los
Remedios, **14**
Casa de Bastidas, **17**
Casa de Tostado, **19**
Casa del Cordón, **8**
Catedral Santa María
la Menor, **5**

Concepción Fortress, **3**
Hospital de San Nicolás
de Bari, **6**
Hostal Palacio Nicolás
de Ovando, **15**
Iglesia y Convento
Domínico, **20**
Jardín Botánico
Nacional Dr. Rafael M.
Moscoso, **25**
La Atarazana, **10**

La Iglesia de Regina
Angelorum, **21**
Malecón, **23**
Montesina, **1**
Museo de las Casas
Reales, **13**
National Pantheon, **16**
Parque Colón, **4**
Parque Indepen-
dencia, **2**

Plaza de la Cultura, **24**
Puerta de la
Misericordia, **22**
San Francisco
Monastery, **7**
Santa Bárbara
Church, **11**
Torre del
Homenaje, **18**

② **Parque Independencia,** on the far western border of the Colonial Zone, is a big city park dominated by the marble and concrete **Altar de la Patria.** The impressive mausoleum was built in 1976 to honor the founding fathers of the country (Duarte, Sánchez, and Mella).

③ To your left as you leave the square, the **Concepción Fortress,** within the old city walls, was the northwest defense post of the colony. *Calle Palo Hincado at Calle Isidro Duarte, no phone. Admission free. Open Tues.–Sun. 9–6.*

From Independence Square, walk eight blocks east on Calle El **④** Conde and you'll come to **Parque Colón.** The huge statue of Columbus dates from 1897 and is the work of French sculptor Gilbert. On the west side of the square is the old **Town Hall** and on the east, the **Palacio de Borgella,** residence of the governor during the Haitian occupation of 1822–44 and presently the seat of the Permanent Dominican Commission for the **Fifth Centennial of the Discovery and Evangelization of the Americas.** Gallery spaces house architectural and archaeological exhibits pertaining to the Fifth Centennial.

Towering over the south side of the square is the coral lime-**⑤** stone facade of the **Catedral Santa María la Menor, Primada de América,** the first cathedral in America. Spanish workmen began building the cathedral in 1514 but left off construction to search for gold in Mexico. The church was finally finished in 1540. Its facade is composed of architectural elements from the late-Gothic to the Plateresque style. Inside, the high altar is made of beaten silver, and in the Treasury there is a magnificent collection of gold and silver. Some of its 14 lateral chapels serve as mausoleums for noted Dominicans, including Archbishop Meriño, who was once president of the Dominican Republic. Of interest is the Chapel of Our Lady of Antigua, which was reconsecrated by John Paul II in 1984. In the nave are four baroque columns, carved to resemble royal palms, which for more than four centuries guarded the magnificent bronze and marble sarcophagus containing (say Dominican historians) the remains of Christopher Columbus. (Cuba and Spain also lay claims to the famed remains.) The sarcophagus has recently been moved to the Columbus Memorial Lighthouse (*see* Off the Beaten Track, *below*)—only the latest in the Great Navigator's posthumous journeys. When Columbus died in Spain in 1506, his last wish was to be buried in Santo Domingo, and, when the cathedral was finished, his remains were deposited there. After the French occupation of 1795, the Spaniards, determined to keep Columbus on Spanish soil, supposedly moved the remains to Cuba. Later, both Spain and Cuba got hold of exhumed corpses that they claimed were the remains of somebody named Columbus. Cuban and Spanish historians say it was Christopher; Dominican authorities say that it was Christopher's grandson Luís and that Christopher's remains rest in Santo Domingo. *Calle Arzobispo Meriño, tel. 809/689–1920. Admission free. Open Mon.–Sat. 9–4; Sun. masses begin at 6 AM.*

When you leave the cathedral, turn right, walk to Columbus Square, and turn left on Calle El Conde. Walk one more block and turn right on Calle Hostos and continue for two more **⑥** blocks. You'll see the ruins of the **Hospital de San Nicolás de Bari,** the first hospital in the New World, which was built in

1503 by Nicolás de Ovando. *Calle Hostos, between Calle de Las Mercedes and Calle Luperon, no phone.*

Continue along Calle Hostos, crossing Calle Emiliano Tejera, up the hill, and about mid-block on your left you'll see the majestic ruins of the **San Francisco Monastery.** (If you look toward the horizon, you will see the impressive Columbus Lighthouse.) Constructed between 1512 and 1544, the monastery contained the church, chapel, and convent of the Franciscan order. Sir Francis Drake's demolition squad significantly damaged the building in 1586, and in 1673 an earthquake nearly finished the job, but when it's floodlit at night, the old monastery is indeed a dramatic sight. Plans are in the works to begin holding occasional cultural events here.

Walk east for two blocks along Calle Emiliano Tejera. Opposite the Telecom building on Calle Isabel la Católica, the **Casa del Cordón** is recognizable by the sash of the Franciscan order carved in stone over the arched entrance. This house, built in 1503, is the Western Hemisphere's oldest surviving stone house. Columbus's son Diego Colón, viceroy of the colony, and his wife lived here until the Alcázar was finished. It was in this house, too, that Sir Francis Drake was paid a ransom to prevent him from totally destroying the city. The house is now home to the Banco Popular. *Corner of Calle Emiliano Tejera and Calle Isabel la Católica, no phone. Admission free. Open weekdays 8:30–4:30.*

To reach the **Alcázar de Colón,** walk one block east along Calle Emiliano Tejera. You'll come across the imposing castle, with its balustrade and double row of arches. The Renaissance structure has strong Moorish, Gothic, and Isabelline influences. The castle of Don Diego Colón, built in 1514, was painstakingly reconstructed and restored in 1957. Forty-inch-thick coral limestone walls were patched and shored with blocks from the original quarry. There are 22 rooms, furnished in a style to which the viceroy of the island would have been accustomed—right down to the dishes and the viceregal shaving mug. Many of the period paintings, statues, tapestries, and furnishings were donated by the University of Madrid. *Just off Calle Emiliano Tejera at the foot of Calle Las Damas, tel. 809/ 687–5361. Admission: R.D.$10. Open Mon. and Wed.–Fri. 9–5, Sat. 9–4, Sun. 9–1. Closed Tues.*

Across from the Alcázar, **La Atarazana** (the Royal Mooring Docks) was once the colonial commercial district, where naval supplies were stored. There are eight restored buildings, the oldest of which dates from 1507. It now houses crafts shops, restaurants, and art galleries.

Time Out If your walking tour leads you to La Atarazana by midday, join the Reserve Bank and Telecom staff at the **Café Montesinos** (Calle La Atarazana 23) for a typical Dominican noonday meal. For R.D.$40 the hearty specials may include fish or beef in a succulent Creole sauce and a tasty bean soup with plantains. If you happen to be in that area in the late afternoon, stop in for a pizza and a drink at **Drake's Pub** (Calle La Atarazana 25). There's a fine view of the Alcázar from here, and the place fills up with congenial locals and foreigners.

To reach the **Santa Bárbara Church,** go back to Calle Isabel la Católica, turn right, and walk several blocks. This combination church and fortress, the only one of its kind in Santo Domingo, was completed in 1562. *Av. Mella, between Calle Isabel la Católica and Calle Arzobispo Meriño, no phone. Admission free. Open weekdays 8–noon. Sun. masses begin at 6 AM.*

⑫ Retrace your steps to Calle Isabel la Católica, turn left on Calle de Las Mercedes, and walk one block right to **Calle Las Damas,** where you'll make a right turn to the New World's oldest street. The "Street of the Ladies" was named after the elegant ladies of the court who, in the Spanish tradition, promenaded in the evening.

On your left you'll see a sundial dating from 1753 and the **Casa de los Jesuitas,** which houses a fine research library for colonial history as well as the Institute for Hispanic Culture. *Admission free. Open weekdays 8–4:30.*

⑬ Across the street is the **Museo de las Casas Reales** (Museum of the Royal Houses). The collections in the museum are displayed in two early 16th-century palaces that have been altered many times over the years. Exhibits cover everything from antique coins to replicas of the *Niña,* the *Pinta,* and the *Santa María.* There are statue and cartography galleries, coats of armor and coats of arms, coaches and a royal court room, gilded furnishings, and Indian artifacts. The first room of the former Governor's Residence has a wall-size map marking the routes sailed by Columbus's ships on expeditions beginning in 1492. If you like museums, you may have a hard time taking leave of this one. *Calle Las Damas, corner Calle Mercedes, tel. 809/682–4202. Admission: R.D.$10. Open Tues.–Sat. 9–4:45, Sun. 10–1.*

⑭ Across the street is the **Capilla de los Remedios** (Chapel of Our Lady of Remedies), which was originally built as a private chapel for the family of Francisco de Dávila. Early colonists worshiped here as well before the completion of the cathedral. Its architectural details, particularly the lateral arches, are evocative of the Castilian-Romanesque style. *Calle Las Damas, at the foot of Calle Mercedes, no phone. Admission free. Open Mon.–Sat. 9–6; Sun. masses begin at 6 AM.*

⑮ Just south of the chapel on Calle Las Damas, the **Hostal Palacio Nicolás de Ovando** (*see* Lodging, *below*), now a highly praised hotel, was once the residence of Nicolás de Ovando, one of the principal organizers of the colonial city.

⑯ Across the street from the hotel looms the massive **National Pantheon.** The building, which dates from 1714, was once a Jesuit monastery and later a theater. Trujillo had it restored in 1955 with an eye toward being buried there. (He is buried instead at Père Lachaise in Paris.) An allegorical mural of his assassination is painted on the ceiling above the altar, where an eternal flame burns. The impressive chandelier was a gift from Spain's Generalissimo Franco. *Calle Las Damas, near the corner of Calle Mercedes, no phone. Admission free. Open Mon.–Sat. 10–5.*

Continue south on Calle Las Damas and cross Calle El Conde. ⑰ Look on your left for the **Casa de Bastidas,** where there is a lovely inner courtyard with tropical plants and temporary exhibit galleries. *Calle Las Damas, just off Calle El Conde, no phone. Admission free. Open Tues.–Sun. 9–5.*

⑱ You won't have any trouble spotting the **Torre del Homenaje** (Tower of Homage) in the Fort Ozama. The fort sprawls two blocks south of the Casa de Bastidas, with a brooding crenellated tower that still guards the Ozama River. The fort and its tower were built in 1503 to protect the eastern border of the city. The sinister tower was the last home of many a condemned prisoner. *On Paseo Presidente Bellini, overlooking Río Ozama, no phone. Admission: R.D.$10. Open Tues.–Sun. 8–7.*

When you leave the fortress, turn left off Calle Las Damas onto ⑲ Calle Padre Bellini. A two-block walk will bring you to **Casa de Tostado.** The house was built in the first decade of the 16th century and was the residence of writer Don Francisco Tostado. Its twin Gothic windows are the only ones that are still in existence in the New World. It now houses the **Museo de la Familia Dominicana** (Museum of the Dominican Family), which features exhibits on the well-heeled Dominican family in the 19th century. *Calle Padre Bellini, near Calle Arzobispo Meriño, tel. 809/689–5057. Admission: R.D.$10. Open Thurs.–Tues. 9–2.*

Walk two blocks west on Calle Padre Bellini to the corner of Avenida Duarte. The graceful building with the rose window is ⑳ the **Iglesia y Convento Domínico** (Dominican Church and Convent), founded in 1510. In 1538, Pope Paul III visited here and was so impressed with the lectures on theology that he granted the church and convent the title of university, making it the oldest institution of higher learning in the New World. *Calle Padre Bellini and Av. Duarte, tel. 809/682–3780. Admission free. Open Tues.–Sun. 9–6.*

Continue west on Calle Padre Bellini for two blocks, and at the ㉑ corner of Calle José Reyes you'll see another lovely church, **La Iglesia de Regina Angelorum** (Church of Regina Angelorum), which dates from 1537. The church was damaged during the Haitian regime, from 1822 to 1844, but you can still appreciate its Baroque dome, Gothic arches, and traceries. *Corner of Calle Padre Bellini and Calle José Reyes, tel. 809/682–2783. Admission free. Open Mon.–Sat. 9–6.*

Walk four blocks west on Calle Padre Bellini, turn left on Calle ㉒ Palo Hincado, and keep going straight till you reach the **Puerta de la Misericordia** (Gate of Mercy), part of the old wall of Santo Domingo. It was here on the plaza, on February 27, 1844, that Ramón Mata Mella, one of the country's founding fathers, fired the shot that began the struggle for independence from Haiti.

Parque Independencia separates the old city from the new. Avenidas 30 de Marzo, Bolívar, and Independencia traverse the park and mingle with avenues named for George Washington, John F. Kennedy, and Abraham Lincoln. Modern Santo Domingo is a sprawling, noisy city with a population of close to 2 million.

Avenida George Washington, which features tall palms and Las Vegas–style tourist hotels, breezes along the Caribbean Sea. ㉓ The Parque Litoral de Sur, better known as the **Malecón,** borders the avenue from the colonial city to the Hotel Santo Domingo, a distance of about 3 miles. The seaside park, with its cafés and places to relax, is a popular spot, but beware of pickpockets.

Time Out Before leaving the seafront, check out the **Bar Bleu** (Av. George Washington 503, tel. 809/686–2629). Locals come here to watch TV *béisbol* (baseball), the ocean, and one another. There's a happy hour from 5 to 8, when jazz is played.

Avenida Máximo Gómez comes down from the north. Take a right turn on it, cross Avenida Bolívar, and you'll come to the landscaped lawns, modern sculptures, and sleek buildings of the **Plaza de la Cultura.** Among the buildings are the **National Theater** (tel. 809/687–3191), which stages performances in Spanish; the **National Library**, in which the written word is Spanish; and museums and art galleries, whose notations are also in Spanish. The following museums on the plaza are open Tuesday–Saturday from 10 to 5, and admission to each is R.D.$10: The **Museum of Dominican Man** (tel. 809/687–3622) traces the migrations of Indians from South America through the Caribbean islands. The **Museum of Natural History** (tel. 809/689–0106) examines the flora and fauna of the island. In the **Gallery of Modern Art** (tel. 809/682–8260), the works of 20th-century Dominican and foreign artists are displayed.

㉕ North of town in the Arroyo Hondo district is the **Jardín Botánico Nacional Dr. Rafael M. Moscoso** (Dr. Rafael M. Moscoso National Botanical Gardens), the largest garden in the Caribbean. Its 445 acres include a Japanese Garden, a Great Ravine, a glen, a gorgeous display of orchids, and an enormous floral clock. You can tour the gardens by train, boat, or horse-drawn carriage. *Arroyo Hondo, no phone. Admission: R.D.$2. Open daily 10–6.*

In the 320-acre **Parque Zoológico Nacional** (National Zoological Park), not far from the Botanical Gardens, animals roam free in natural habitats. There is an African plain, a children's zoo, and what the zoo claims is the world's largest bird cage. *Av. Máximo Gómez at Av. de los Proceres, tel. 809/562–2080. Admission: R.D.$10. Open daily 10–6.*

The **Acuario Nacional** (National Aquarium)—whose construction was a controversial public expenditure during a time of crisis—is the largest aquarium in the Caribbean, with an impressive collection of tropical fish and dolphins. *In the Sans Souci district on the Avenida de las Americas. Admission: R.D.$10. Open daily 10–6.*

La Romana *Numbers in the margin correspond to points of interest on the Dominican Republic map.*

Head east on Las Américas Highway toward La Romana, about a two-hour drive along the southeast coast. All along the highway to Romana are small resort-hotel complexes where you can find refreshments or stay overnight. About 1½ miles outside the capital, you'll come to the **Parque de los Tres Ojos** (Park of the Three Eyes). The "eyes" are cool blue pools peering out of deep limestone caves, and it's actually a four-eyed park. If you've a mind to, you can look into the eyes more closely by climbing down into the caves.

About 20 minutes east of the city is **Boca Chica Beach,** popular because of its proximity to the capital. Another 45 minutes or so farther east is the city of **San Pedro de Macorís,** where the national sport and the national drink are both well represented. Some of the country's best béisbol games are played in **Tetelo**

Vargas Stadium, which you can see off the highway to your left.
The **Macorís Rum distillery** is on the eastern edge of the city.

The two big businesses around La Romana used to be cattle and
sugarcane. That was before Gulf & Western created (and sub-
sequently sold) the **Casa de Campo** resort, which is a very big
business, indeed, and **Altos de Chavón,** a re-creation of a 16th-
century village and art colony on the resort grounds.

Casa de Campo means "house in the country," and, yes, you
could call it that. This particular "house" is a resort that
sprawls over 7,000 acres, accommodates some 3,000 guests,
and offers two public golf courses (one of them, a teeth-clencher
called Teeth of the Dog, has seven holes that skirt the sea), 16
tennis courts, horseback riding, polo, archery, trap shooting,
and every imaginable water sport. Oscar de la Renta designed
much of the resort and has a boutique in Altos de Chavón. He
also owns a villa at Casa de Campo.

㉘ **Altos de Chavón** sits on a bluff overlooking the Rio Chavón,
about 3 miles east of the main facility of Casa de Campo. You
can drive there easily enough, or you can take one of the free
shuttle buses from the resort. In this re-creation of a medieval
Spanish village there are cobblestone streets lined with lan-
terns, wrought-iron balconies, and courtyards swathed with
bougainvillea. More than a museum piece, this village is a place
where artists live, work, and play. There is an art school, affiliated with New York's Parsons School of Design; a disco; an archaeological museum; five restaurants; and a 5,000-seat
outdoor amphitheater (used about four times a year) where
Frank Sinatra and Julio Iglesias have entertained. The focal
point of the village is **Iglesia St. Stanislaus,** which is named after the patron saint of Poland in tribute to the Polish Pope John
Paul II, who visited the Dominican Republic in 1979 and left
some of the ashes of St. Stanislaus behind.

The Cibao Valley The road to the north coast cuts through the lush banana plantations, rice and tobacco fields, and Royal Poinciana trees of the
Cibao Valley. All along the road there are stands where, for a
few centavos, you can buy ripe pineapples, mangoes, avocados,
chicharrones (either fried pork rinds or chicken pieces), and
㉙ fresh fruit drinks. To the west is **Pico Duarte,** at 10,128 feet the
highest peak in the West Indies.

In the heart of the Cibao is La Vega. Founded in 1495 by Columbus, it is the site of one of the oldest settlements in the New
World. The inquisitive will find the tour of the ruins of the origi-
㉚ nal settlement, **La Vega Vieja** (The Old La Vega), a rewarding
experience. About 3 miles north of La Vega is **Santo Cerro**
(Holy Mount), site of a miraculous apparition of the Virgin and
therefore many local pilgrimages. The **Convent of La Merced** is
located there, and the views of the Cibao Valley are breathtaking.

About 144 kilometers (90 miles) north of the capital, you'll come
to the industrial city of **Santiago de los Caballeros,** where a massive monument honoring the Restoration of the Republic
guards the entrance to the city. Many past presidents were
born in Santiago, and it is currently a center for processing tobacco leaf. Cuban cigar-making skills are found here, and a tour
of **La Aurora Tabacalera** (tel. 809/582–1131) gives the visitor an
appreciation of this art.

The Amber Coast   The Autopista Duarte ultimately leads (in three to four hours from Santo Domingo) to the Amber Coast, so called because of its large, rich, and unique deposits of amber. The coastal area around Puerto Plata is a region of splashy resorts. The north coast boasts more than 70 miles of beaches with condominiums and villas going up fast.

㉛ Puerto Plata, although now quiet and almost sleepy, was a dynamic city in its heyday. Visitors can get a feeling for this past in the magnificent Victorian **Glorieta** (Gazebo) in the central **Parque Independencia.** Next to the park, the recently refurbished **Catedral de San Felipe** recalls a simpler, colonial past. On Puerto Plata's own Malecón, the **Fortaleza de San Felipe** protected the city from many a pirate attack and was later used as a political prison. The fort is most dramatic at night.

Puerto Plata is also the home of the **Museum of Dominican Amber,** a lovely galleried mansion and one of several tenants in the Tourist Bazaar. The museum displays and sells the Dominican Republic's national stone. Semiprecious, translucent amber is actually fossilized pine resin that dates back about 50 million years, give or take a few millennia. The north coast of the Dominican Republic has the largest deposits of amber in the world (the only other deposits are found in Germany and the U.S.S.R.), and jewelry crafted from the stone is the best-selling item on the island. *Calle Duarte 61, tel. 809/586-2848. Admission: R.D.$10. Open Mon.–Sat. 9–5.*

Southwest of Puerto Plata, you can take a cable car (when it is
㉜ working) to the top of **Mt. Isabel de Torres,** which soars 2,600 feet above sea level. On the mountain there is a botanical garden, a huge statue of Christ, and a spectacular view. The cable was first laid in 1754, although rest assured that it's been replaced since then. Lines can be long, and once on top of the mountain you will wonder if it was worth the time. Don't eat at the restaurant at the top—the food is awful. *The cable car operates Tues., Thurs., Fri., Sat., and Sun. 8–6. Round-trip is R.D.$20.*

Take the Autopista east from Puerto Plata about 15 miles to
㉝ Sosúa, a small community settled during World War II by 600 Austrian and German Jews. After the war, many of them returned to Europe or went to the United States, and most of those who remained married Dominicans. Only a few Jewish families reside in the community today, and there is only one small, one-room synagogue. The flavor of the town is decidedly Spanish. There are numerous hotels, condominiums, and apartments in Sosúa. (The roads off the Autopista, incidentally, are horribly punctured with potholes.)

Sosúa has become one of the most frequently visited tourist destinations in the country, favored by French Canadians and Europeans. Hotels and condos are going up at breakneck speed. It actually consists of two communities, **El Batey** and **Los Charamicos,** which are separated by a cove and one of the island's prettiest beaches. The sand is soft and white, the water gin-clear and calm. The walkway above the beach is packed with tents filled with souvenirs, pizzas, and even clothing for sale—a jarring note in this otherwise idyllic setting.

Time Out   **The Albatros** (Calle Pedro Clisante, tel. 809/571-2325), in the center of Sosúa, is a hot spot for tacos, hamburgers, and a rum punch or two. It also serves as an impromptu library filled with an eclectic collection of paperbacks that are ideal for beach reading.

Continue east on the Autopista past **Playa Grande.** The powdery white beach remains miraculously undisturbed and unspoiled by development.

The Autopista rolls along eastward and rides out onto a ❸❹ "thumb" of the island, where you'll find **Samaná.** Back in 1824, a sailing vessel called the *Turtle Dove,* carrying several hundred escaped American slaves from the Freeman Sisters' underground railway, was blown ashore in Samaná. The escapees settled and prospered, and today their descendants number several thousand. The churches here are Protestant; the worshipers live in villages called Bethesda, Northeast, and Philadelphia; and the language spoken is an odd 19th-century form of English.

About 3,000 humpback whales winter off the coast of Samaná from December to March. Plans are under way for organizing major whale-watching expeditions, such as those out of Massachusetts, that will boost the region's economy without scaring away the world's largest mammals.

In the meantime, sport fishing at Samaná is considered to be among the best in the world. A beautiful bay and beach round out Samaná's attractions. Tourism is finding its way here. The most deluxe resort is the Gran Bahai, which just opened. Other resort hotels are in the planning stages.

Dominican Republic for Free

Concerts. The quadrangle of Santo Domingo's Plaza de la Cultura is the site of occasional classical music concerts that you can hear for a song. There are also open-air concerts along the Malecón. Check with local newspapers, your hotel, or the Tourist Office for dates and programs.

Colonial Zone. Many of the ancient buildings have no admission charge, notably the Catedral Santa María la Menor, the Tower of Homage, the San Francisco Monastery, and the Casa del Cordón (*see* Exploring the Dominican Republic, *above*).

Parque de los Tres Ojos. The Park of the Three Eyes, 10 minutes east of Santo Domingo, is free (*see* Exploring the Dominican Republic, *above*).

What to See and Do with Children

Acuario Nacional (*see* Exploring the Dominican Republic, *above*).

Jardín Botánica Nacional Dr. Rafael M. Moscoso (*see* Exploring the Dominican Republic, *above*).

Parque Zoológico Nacional (*see* Exploring the Dominican Republic, *above*).

Parque de los Tres Ojos (*see* Exploring the Dominican Republic, *above*).

Parque Quisqueya. Santo Domingo's amusement park has a merry-go-round, swings, seesaws, and other playground attractions. *Av. Bolívar and Av. Tiradentes, tel. 809/682–9191. Admission: R.D.$10. Open Thurs.–Sun. 10–10.*

Off the Beaten Track

The Dominican Republic offers vastly different microclimates in an area that is twice the size of Massachusetts.

Laguna Grí-Grí is a swampland smack out of the Louisiana bayou country, with the added attraction of a cool blue grotto that almost outdoes the Blue Grotto of Capri. Since Laguna Grí-Grí is only about 90 minutes west of Puerto Plata, in Río San Juan, you can board a boat for a peaceful trip through the swamps and into the grotto. Contact the Tourist Office for arrangements.

Nature lovers should consider a trip to **Jarabacoa,** in the mountainous region known rather wistfully as the Dominican Alps. There is little to do in the town itself but eat and rest up for excursions on foot, horseback, or by motorbike taxi to the surrounding waterfalls and forests—quite incongruous in such a tropical country. Accommodations in the area are rustic but comfortable.

Less accessible and vastly different is the largest lake in the Antilles, **Lago Enriquillo,** near the Haitian border. The salt lake is also the lowest point in the Antilles: 114-feet below sea level. The lake encircles wild, arid, and thorny islands that serve as sanctuary to such exotic birds and reptiles as the flamingo, the iguana, and the caiman—the indigenous crocodile.

Just off the east coast of Hispaniola lies **Isla Saona,** now a national park inhabited by sea turtles, pigeons, and other wildlife. Caves on the island were once used by Indians. The beaches are beautiful, and legend has it that Columbus once strayed ashore here.

Just east of colonial Santo Domingo, across the Ozama River, in the San Souci district, is the **Columbus Memorial Lighthouse** (Av. España, no phone). This lighthouse monument and museum complex dedicated to the Great Navigator was completed in 1992, its inauguration set to coincide with the 500th anniversary of Christopher Columbus's landing on the island. Along with its showpiece laser-powered lighthouse, the complex holds the tomb of Columbus (recently moved there after 400 years in the Catedral Santa María la Menor) and will eventually house six museums featuring exhibits related to Columbus and early exploration of the New World (one museum will focus on the long, rocky, and often controversial history of the Lighthouse Memorial itself). *Open Tues.–Sun. 9–4.*

Las Terrenas, on the north coast of the Samaná peninsula, is only barely known to North American tourists. Meanwhile, French Canadians and Europeans, especially Germans, have begun making the long trek to this remote stretch of nearly deserted but beautiful beaches. The place is a sort of latter-day hippie haven that also attracts surfboarders and windsurfers. There are several modest restaurants, the best of which is **Boca Fina** (no phone) for fresh seafood, and a dusty main street in the town of Las Terrenas, a small airfield and the **Portillo Beach Club** (tel. 809/688–5785) at Portillo, and several congenial hotels right on the beach at Punta Bonita. If you're seeking tranquillity and are happy just hanging out drinking beer and soaking up sun, this is the place for you. You can also hire a motorbike taxi or bicycle to explore the rest of the peninsula. Las Terrenas is 4½ hours from Santo Domingo by bus. The road from Samaná, even though it is longer and not paved, is a lot less strenuous than coming over the hills from Sanchez.

Beaches

The Dominican Republic has more than 1,000 miles of beaches, including the Caribbean's longest strip of white sand—Punta Cana. Many beaches are accessible to the public and may tempt you to stop for a swim. Be careful: Some have dangerously strong currents.

Boca Chica is the beach closest to Santo Domingo (2 miles east of Las Américas Airport, 21 miles from the capital), and it's crowded with city folks on weekends. Five years ago, this beach was virtually a four-lane highway of fine white sand. "Progress" has since cluttered it with plastic beach tables, chaise longues, pizza stands, and beach cottages for rent. But the sand is still fine, and you can walk far out into clear blue water, which is protected by natural coral reefs that help keep the big fish at bay.

About 20 minutes east of Boca Chica is another beach of fine white sand, **Juan Dolio.** The Villas del Mar Hotel and Punta Garza Beach Club are on this beach.

Moving counterclockwise around the island, you'll come to the La Romana area, with its miniature **Minitas** beach and lagoon, and the long white-sand, palm-lined crescent of **Bayahibe** beach, which is accessible only by boat. La Romana is the home of the 7,000-acre Casa de Campo resort (*see* Lodging, *below*), so you're not likely to find any private place in the sun here.

The gem of the Caribbean, **Punta Cana** is a 20-mile strand of pearl-white sand shaded by trees and coconut palms. Located on the easternmost coast, it is the home of Club Med, the new Melia Punta Cana, and the Bavaro Beach Resort (*see* Lodging, *below*).

Las Terrenas, on the north coast of the Samaná peninsula, looks like something from *Robinson Crusoe:* Tall palms list toward the sea, away from the mountains; the beach is narrow but sandy, and best of all, there is nothing man-made in sight—just vivid blues, greens, and yellows. Two adjacent hotels are right on the beach at nearby Punta Bonita (*see* Lodging, *below*).

Playa Grande, on the north coast, is a long stretch of powdery sand that is slated for development. At present, it's undisturbed, but you'd better hurry if you want to enjoy it in solitude.

Farther west is the lovely beach at **Sosúa,** where calm waters gently lap at long stretches of soft white sand. Unfortunately the backdrop here is a string of tents, with hawkers pushing cheap souvenirs. You can, however, get snacks and rent watersports equipment from the vendors.

The ideal wind and surf conditions of **Cabarete Beach,** also on the north coast, have made it an integral part of the international windsurfing circuit.

On the north Amber Coast, **Puerto Plata** is situated in a developed and still-developing area that is about to outdo San Juan's famed Condado strip. The beaches are of soft écru or white sand, with lots of reefs for snorkeling. The Atlantic waters are great for windsurfing, waterskiing, and fishing expeditions.

About an hour west of Puerto Plata lies **Luperón Beach,** a wide white-sand beach fit for snorkeling, windsurfing, and scuba diving. The Luperón Beach Resort is handy for rentals and refreshments.

Sports and the Outdoors

Although there is hardly a shortage of outdoor activities here, the resorts have virtually cornered the market on sports, including every conceivable water sport. In some cases, facilities may be available only to guests. You can check with the Tourist Office for more details. Listed below is a mere smattering of the island's athletic options:

Archery Robin Hood never had it so good. Bows and arrows can be rented at **Club Med** (Punta Cana, tel. 809/567–5228) and **Bávaro Beach Resort** (Punta Cana, tel. 809/682–2162).

Bicycling Pedaling is easy on pancake-flat beaches, but there are also steep hills in the Dominican Republic. Bikes are available at **Villas Doradas** (Playa Dorada, Puerto Plata, tel. 809/586–3000), **Dorado Naco** (Dorado Beach, tel. 809/586–2019), **Jack Tar Village** (Puerto Plata, tel. 809/586–3800), and **Cofresi Beach Hotel** (Puerto Plata, tel. 809/586–2898).

Boating Hobie Cats and pedal boats are available at **Heavens** (Playa Dorada, tel. 809/586–5250). Check also at **Casa de Campo** (La Romana, tel. 809/682–2111) and **Club Med** (Punta Cana, tel. 809/567–5228).

Deep-Sea Fishing Marlin and wahoo are among the fish that folks angle for here. Arrangements can be made through **Casa de Campo** (La Romana, tel. 809/682–2111) or **Actividas Acuaticás** (Playa Dorada, tel. 809/506–3988). Fishing is best between January and June.

Golf **Casa de Campo** has two 18-hole Pete Dye courses and a third for the private use of villa owners. Two new 18-hole courses are planned for the **Punta Cana Beach Resort** and the **Bávaro Beach.** The Playa Dorada hotels have their own 18-hole Robert Trent Jones–designed course; there is also a 9-hole course nearby at the **Costambar.** Guests in Santo Domingo hotels are usually allowed to use the 18-hole course at the **Santo Domingo Country Club** on weekdays—*after* members have teed off. There is a 9-hole course outside of town, at Lomas Lindas. A new Pete Dye course is under construction outside Santo Domingo.

Horseback Riding **Casa de Campo** (La Romana) has a dude ranch on its premises, saddled with 2,000 horses.

Polo You can arrange for lessons at **Casa de Campo** (La Romana).

Sailing Sailboats are available at **Club Med** (Punta Cana) and **Casa de Campo** (La Romana).

Scuba Diving and Snorkeling Ancient sunken galleons, undersea gardens, and offshore reefs are the lures here. For equipment and trips, contact **Mundo Submarino** (Santo Domingo, tel. 809/566–0344). A new Diving Instructors World Association (DIWA) scuba-certification school has been opened at the **Demar Beach Club** in Boca Chica, outside the capital, offering three-day and one-week programs.

Tennis There must be a million nets laced around the island, and most of them can be found at the large resorts (*see* Lodging, *below*).

Windsurfing Between June and October, **Cabarete Beach** offers what many consider to be optimal windsurfing conditions: wind speeds at 20–25 knots and 3- to 15-foot waves. The Professional Boardsurfers Association has included Cabarete Beach in its international windsurfing slalom competition. But the novice is also welcome to learn and train on modified boards stabilized by flotation devices. **CaribBIC Windsurfing Center**, on Caberete Beach (tel. 800/635–1155 or 800/243–9675), offers accommodations, equipment, training, and professional coaching.

Spectator Sports The dogs make tracks every Monday, Wednesday, Friday, and
Greyhound Races Sunday at **Canódromo El Coco.** *Av. Monumental, La Yuca— about 15 min north of the capital, tel. 809/560–6968 or 560– 8342. Admission: R.D.$1–R.D.$4. Races Mon.–Fri. 7:30 PM, Sun. and holidays 4 PM.*

Horse Racing There are races year-round at the **Hipódromo Perla Antillana.** *Av. San Cristóbal, Santo Domingo, tel. 809/565–2353. Admission free. Post time: Tues., Thurs., Sat. 3 PM.*

Polo The ponies pound down the field at **Sierra Prieta** (Santo Domingo) and at **Casa de Campo** (La Romana). The season runs from October through May. For information about polo games, call 809/565–6880.

Shopping

The hot ticket in the Dominican Republic is amber jewelry. This island has the world's largest deposits of amber, and the prices here for the translucent, semiprecious stone are unmatched anywhere. The stones, which range in color from pale lemon to dark brown, are actually petrified resin from coniferous trees that disappeared from Earth about 50 million years ago. The most valuable stones are those in which tiny insects or small leaves are embedded. (Don't knock it till you've seen it.)

The Dominican Republic is the homeland of designer Oscar de la Renta, and you may want to stop at some of the chic shops that carry his creations. In the crafts department, hand-carved wood rocking chairs are big sellers, and they are sold unassembled and boxed for easy transport. Look also for the delicate ceramic lime figurines that symbolize the Dominican culture.

Bargaining is both a game and a social activity in the Dominican Republic, especially with street vendors and at the stalls in El Mercado Modelo. Vendors are disappointed and perplexed if you don't haggle. They also tend to be tenacious, so unless you really have an eye on buying, don't even stop to look—you may get stuck buying a souvenir just to get rid of an annoying vendor.

Shopping Districts **El Mercado Modelo** in Santo Domingo is a covered market in the Colonial Zone bordering Calle Mella. The restored buildings of **La Atarazana** (across from the Alcázar in the Colonial Zone) are filled with shops, art galleries, restaurants, and bars. The main shopping streets in the Colonial Zone are **Calle El Conde,** which has been transformed into an exclusively pedestrian thoroughfare, and **Calle Duarte.** (Some of the best shops on Calle Duarte are north of the Colonial Zone, between Calle Mella and Av. Las Américas). **Plaza Criolla** (corner of Av. 27 de Febrero and Av. Anacaona) is filled with shops that sell everything from scents to nonsense. Duty-free shops selling liquors, cameras, and the like are at the **Centro de los Héroes** (Av. George Washington), the **Embajador Hotel, Santo Domingo Sheraton,** and at **Las Américas Airport.**

In Puerto Plata, the seven showrooms of the **Tourist Bazaar** (Calle Duarte 61) are in a wonderful old galleried mansion with a patio bar. Another cluster of shops is at the **Plaza Shopping Center** (Calle Duarte at Av. 30 de Marzo). A popular shopping street for jewelry and local souveniers is **Calle Beller.**

In **Altos de Chavón,** art galleries and shops are grouped around the main square.

Good Buys **Ambar Tres** (La Atarazana 3, Colonial Zone, Santo Domingo,
Amber/Jewelry tel. 809/688–0474) carries a wide selection of the Dominican product.

Dominican Art Galleries in Santo Domingo are **Arawak Gallery** (Av. Pasteur 104, tel. 809/685–1661) and **Galería de Arte Nader** (La Atarazana 9, Colonial Zone, tel. 809/688–0969). **Novo Atarazana** (Atarazana 21, tel. 809/689–0582) has a varied assortment of artifacts made by locals.

Macaluso's (Calle Duarte 32, and in Plaza Turisol, tel. 809/586–3433) and **The Collector's Corner Gallery and Gift Shop** (Plaza Shopping Center, Calle Duarte at Av. 30 de Marzo, no phone) are the better-known galleries in Puerto Plata.

Check out the Dominican fashions at **Jenny Polanco's** boutiques in the Santo Domingo Sheraton (tel. 809/221–6666, ext. 2270) and the Paradise Beach Resort in Playa Dorado (tel. 809/586–3663, ext. 314).

Mink One does not necessarily think mink (or fox) in the tropics, but the Dominican Republic has the largest mink and fox factory in the Western Hemisphere. **Mink America** furnishes lavish collections not only to New York's Seventh Avenue but also to the individual buyer. Whether made to order or prêt-à-porter, the merchandise is tax- and duty-free and therefore an attractive buy at almost half the price (Puerto Plata Free Zone, showroom and factory by appointment. Tel. 809/586–4396. AE, MC, V).

Wood Crafts Visit the stalls of **El Mercado Modelo** in the Colonial Zone and **El Conde Gift Shop** (Calle El Conde 153, tel. 809/682–5909), both in Santo Domingo.

In Puerto Plata, browse and shop at **Macaluso's** (Calle Duarte 32, tel. 809/586–3433) and at the **Collector's Corner Gallery and Gift Shop** (Plaza Shopping Center, no phone). In Santiago, try **Artesanía Lime** (Autopista Duarte, Km 21–2, Santiago, tel. 809/582–3754).

Dining

Dining out is a favorite form of entertainment for Dominicans, and they tend to dress up for the occasion. Most restaurants begin serving dinner around 6 PM, but the locals don't generally turn up until 9 or 10. There are French, Italian, and Chinese restaurants, as well as those serving traditional Dominican fare.

Some favorite local dishes you should sample are paella, *sancocho* (a thick stew usually made with five different meats, though sometimes as many as seven), *arroz con pollo* (rice with chicken), *plátanos* (plantains) in all their tasty varieties, and *tortilla de jamón* (spicy ham omelet). Country snacks include *chicharrones* (fried pork rinds) and *galletas* (flat biscuit crackers). Many a meal is topped off with *majarete*, a tasty cornmeal custard. Presidente, Bohemia, and Quisqueya are the local beers, Bermúdez and Brugal the local rums. Wine is on the expensive side because it has to be imported.

Highly recommended restaurants are indicated by a star ★.

Category	Cost*
Expensive	over $30
Moderate	$20–$30
Inexpensive	under $20

per person, excluding drinks, service, and sales tax (6%)

La Romana **Castillo del Rio.** "The chef is crazy tonight," the headwaiter
★ gave by way of explanation for the long wait before the lobster salad with a vinaigrette sauce arrived. Another waiter in the far corner of the room mopped his brow with a napkin. But when the creations of chef Philippe Mongereau arrive, delays and amateur service are forgiven, if not forgotten. Even so, the maigret of duck could have had a slightly lighter sauce. However, one comes here primarily for the ambience of dining in the cellars of the "castle" above the Rio Chavón. *Altos de Chavón, tel. 809/523–3333, ext. 2345. Jacket and reservations required. AE, DC, MC, V. Expensive.*

Café del Sol. This is an outdoor café in a 16th-century village setting. You can sample pizza and assorted light dishes while enjoying the view of the distant mountain range. *Altos de Chavón, tel. 809/523–3333, ext. 2346. No reservations. AE, DC, MC, V. Moderate.*

Villa Casita. This small and intimate restaurant serves creative Dominican cooking amid candles and muted lights. Start with octopus vinaigrette, spinach crepes, or pasta with anchovies and clams before feasting on sea bass or local lobster. Meat eaters fare slightly less well with steak or—the better choice— veal rollatine. Piano music accompanies your dinner, and the polished wood bar is a relaxing place for cognac and coffee. *Francisco Richer 71, La Romana, tel. 809/556–2808. Reservations accepted. Dress: smart casual. AE, MC, V. Moderate.*

Amazonia. The *filet de tigre* (fillet of tiger) listed on the menu at this exotic restaurant in the back woods 10 miles from Casa de Campo is actually flank steak from a steer. The real roaring tiger is in a cage, along with other carnivorous animals, in the garden. It is for the novel setting, a minizoo with colorful birds, reptiles, and animals, rather than for the very average food, that this restaurant could be on your itinerary. *10 mi north of La Romana on the road to Punta Cana, tel. 809/526–3337. No reservations. No credit cards. Inexpensive–Moderate.*

Puerto Plata **De Armando.** Here on the north coast, a restaurant in a pretty blue-and-white house dishes up steak, seafood, and Continental dishes, all served to the tune of a guitar trio. Although this spot ranks as one of the area's best, it's also the most expensive.

*Av. Mota 23, at Av. Separación, tel. 809/586–3418. Reserva-
tions required. MC, V. Expensive.*

Flamingo's. You can dine either indoors in a stately room or
outside on the balcony overlooking the pool. In any case, you
can feast on fettuccine al pesto, lobster fricassee in sherry
sauce, and medallions of beef with béarnaise sauce. *Dorado
Naco hotel, tel. 809/586–2019. Reservations suggested. AE,
DC, MC, V. Expensive.*

Cafemba. The view of Fort San Felipe and the sunset over the
mountain of Isabel de Torres set the scene for this refined dining room. Start with the carpaccio or the clams oreganata that
comes with a Creole sauce. Follow this with grilled medallions
of beef, chicken, or veal, each with its own sauce—red wine,
pomodoro, and hollandaise—or the fillet of sea bass. Desserts
are freshly made pastries chosen from a trolley. Service is
slightly strained, with waiters wearing white gloves, but the
attention is there. *Bayside Hill Resort, Costambar, tel. 809/
566–9206. Dinner only. AE, DC, MC, V. Moderate.*

★ **Jimmy's.** Within this old Victorian house you'll be served chateaubriand, filet Mignon, and a variety of creatures from the
sea. Be sure to top it all off with something flambéed. *Calle
Beller 72, tel. 809/586–4325. Jacket and reservations recommended. AE, MC, V. Moderate.*

Porto Dorado. Local fish and other fruits of the sea are served
alfresco in a breezy, tropical setting. If the conch fritters are on
the menu for the day, order a tasty batch. This place is billed as
the only seafood restaurant in the Dominican Republic that is
on the sea, a claim that seems to hold true. *Eurotel Playa
Dorada, tel. 809/586–3663. No reservations. AE, MC, V. Moderate.*

Roma II. This is just an open-sided stand with a metal roof, but
the pizzas, cooked in a wood-burning oven, are some of the best
you'll ever eat. The pizza dough and pasta are made fresh daily.
Other specialties include *spaghetti con pulpo* (octopus), *filete
chito* (steak with garlic), and a host of other pastas and special
sauces. *Corner Calle E. Prudhomme and Calle Beller, tel. 809/
586–3904. No reservations. No credit cards. Inexpensive.*

Santo Domingo
Continental

Alcázar. Oscar de la Renta designed this elegant Moorish setting. Start with lobster bisque, followed by sea bass with
★ crabmeat au gratin or filet Mignon with béarnaise sauce. A
lunch buffet is served each day, with Dominican food on Monday, Mexican food on Tuesday, Chinese on Wednesday, Italian
on Thursday, and so forth. *Hotel Santo Domingo, tel. 809/532–
1511. Jacket and reservations required. AE, DC, MC, V. Very
Expensive.*

Antoine's. In this *très intime* eatery, hotel guests rub shoulders
with well-heeled Dominicans, with whom the restaurant is
popular. Starters include black-bean soup, and among the main
dishes on the extensive menu are lobster thermidor and imperial stew, made with lobster, shrimp, and scallops. There are no
fewer than 20 dessert offerings. *Santo Domingo Sheraton Hotel, Av. George Washington, tel. 809/686–6666. Jacket and reservations required. AE, DC, MC, V. Expensive.*

★ **Lina.** Lina was the personal chef of Trujillo, and she taught her
secret recipes to the chefs of this stylish contemporary restaurant. Paella is the best-known specialty, but other offerings include steak au poivre and a casserole of mixed seafood flavored
with Pernod. *Gran Hotel Lina, Av. Máximo Gómez at Av. 27 de*

Febrero, tel. 809/686–5000. Jacket and reservations required. AE, DC, MC, V. Expensive.

Mesón de la Cava. The capital's most unusual restaurant is more than 50 feet below ground in a natural cave complete with stalagmites and stalactites. Guests clamber down a circular staircase ducking rock protrusions to dine on prime filet with Dijon flambé, tournedos Roquefort, and excellent seafood dishes. Live music and dancing nightly until 1 AM. *Av. Mirador del Sur, tel. 809/533–2818. Jacket and reservations required. AE, DC, MC, V. Expensive.*

Fonda de la Atarazana. This patio restaurant in the Colonial Zone is especially romantic at night, when music and dancing are added. Try the kingfish, shrimp, or *chicharrones de pollo* (bits of fried Dominican chicken). *La Atarazana 5, tel. 809/689–2900. AE, MC, V. Moderate.*

Lucky Seven. Baseball is the big deal here. Owner Evelio Oliva has two satellite dishes, and telecasts of six major-league games go on at once. Incidentally, there's also steak, chicken, and seafood to satisfy pre- or postgame appetites. *Casimiro de Moya and Av. Pasteur, tel. 809/682–7588. No reservations. No credit cards. Moderate.*

Dominican **El Castillo del Mar.** Another seafood restaurant on the Malecón, this one has an open-air setting by the sea. Start with fish soup, then feast on lobster thermidor or sea bass smothered in onions, tomatoes, peas, and basil. *Av. George Washington 2, tel. 809/688–4047. No reservations. MC, V. Inexpensive.*

★ **La Bahía.** This is an unpretentious spot where the catch of the day is tops. Conch appears in a variety of dishes. For starters, try the *sopa palúdica*, a thick soup made with fish, shrimp, and lobster, served with tangy garlic bread. Then move on to kingfish in coconut sauce or *espaguettis a la canona* (spaghetti heaped with seafood). *Av. George Washington 1, tel. 809/682–4022. No reservations. AE, MC, V. Inexpensive.*

French **Café St. Michel.** The cream of pumpkin soup and steak tartare
★ should clue you in to why this popular restaurant has won many gastronomical awards. Desserts include a prize-winning chocolate torte and spectacular soufflés. *Av. Lope de Vega 24, tel. 809/562–4141. Jacket and reservations suggested. AE, MC, V. Moderate.*

Italian **Vesuvio.** Capital-city denizens flock to this superb Italian res-
★ taurant, where everything on the lengthy menu is either freshly caught, homemade, or homegrown. Part of the restaurant's appeal is the gay, social ambience of Dominican families relishing their meal. Start with antipasti, then try the seafood platter, *calamares al vino blanco* (squid in white-wine sauce) or *scaloppina al tarragon* (veal with tarragon). (**Vesuvio II** is at Av. Tiradentes 17, tel. 809/562–6090.) *Av. George Washington 521, tel. 809/689–2141. No reservations. Jacket required. DC, MC, V. Expensive.*

Spanish **El Caserio.** An extensive menu lists such specialties as paella
★ Valenciana, seafood zarzuela, bluefish with anchovies, and leg of lamb Segovia. For dessert, swallow your diet and order chocolate cake Caserio. Adjacent to the formal dining room is **La Taverna,** with a bistro-type atmosphere that offers an appetite-whetting range of *tapas* (appetizers). *Av. George Washington 459, tel. 809/685–3392. Jacket and reservations required. AE, DC, MC, V. Expensive.*

Lodging

Your options here vary from the New World's first hotel to some of the world's newest and poshest resorts. An ambitious development plan continues, especially on the north coast. The Dominican Republic has the largest hotel inventory in the Caribbean. Puerto Plata alone features 6,000 rooms and hosts 200,000 tourists a year. There are already so many adjoining resorts that when you go out for a stroll you have to flag landmarks to find your way back to the one where your luggage is. Be sure to inquire about special packages when you call to reserve; arranging your room as a package through a tour operator will cost considerably less.

Hotels in Santo Domingo base their tariffs on the EP and maintain the same room rates through the year. In contrast, resorts have high winter and low summer rates, with the low rate reducing the room prices by as much as 50%. All-inclusive properties are concentrated especially along the north coast. Those that aren't all-inclusive offer EP or MAP. Our prices, in U.S. dollars, are based on a double room during the high season.

Highly recommended lodgings are indicated by a star ★.

Category	Cost*
Very Expensive	over $150
Expensive	$100–$150
Moderate	$75–$100
Inexpensive	under $75

All prices are for a standard double room for two, excluding 21% tax.

Boca Chica **Boca Chica Resort.** This all-inclusive resort is half an hour east of Santo Domingo and just a few minutes from Las Américas Airport and the exclusive Santo Domingo Yacht Club. Air-conditioned rooms are furnished in rattan with dark woods. *Boca Chica Beach, tel. 809/523–4455 or 800/828–8895, fax 809/523–4438. 209 rooms. Facilities: 3 restaurants, 2 bars, terrace, grill, cable TV, tennis, scuba diving, archery, bicycling, horseback riding, snorkeling, sailing, windsurfing, excursions to Catalina Island, transportation to Santo Domingo casinos. AE, MC, V. All-inclusive. Expensive.*

The Amber Coast **Caribbean Village Club and Resort.** Formerly called the Playa Dorado Princess, this is a luxurious resort with accommodations in 44 two-story pastel-colored villas. Rooms are air-conditioned, with remote-control cable TVs and minibars. The free-form pool has a swim-up terrace, and there's free shuttle service to the beach, or you can make the 10-minute hike. On the beach is the hotel's La Tortuga, a snack bar, and the watersports facilities. Nightly entertainment and dancing take place in the patio lounge and lobby bar. *Playa Dorada, tel. 809/586–25350 or 800/852–4523, fax 809/320–5386. 310 rooms, 26 suites. Facilities: 2 restaurants, 3 bars/lounges, pool, 7 lighted tennis courts, health club, gym, spa, Jacuzzi, golf. AE, MC, V. CP, MAP. Expensive.*
Dorado Naco and Playa Naco. These two sister hotels make up a sprawling complex of 700 rooms, the largest in Playa Dorada.

Dorado Naco, the elder of the two, shows its age. The design is a cluster of air-conditioned villas with spacious carpeted one- and two-bedroom apartments. The living and dining area has a sofa bed, cable TV, two phones, dining table that seats four, and a counter bar. Each apartment has a large patio or terrace surrounded by tropical flowers and plants. The more expensive rooms have views of the pool, surrounded by restaurants. The new Playa Naco, with 234 rooms, abuts the beach, although the main lobby and standard hotel rooms, overlooking the pool and tennis courts, are a four-minute walk from the sands. The more expensive accommodations are the one- and two-bedroom units in the two-story buildings that follow the path to the beach. A fault found with most of Playa Dorado's hotels—the Playa Naco lacks character, but perhaps it's the newness. The Dorado's aggressive activities program arranges beach barbecues, bonfires, and the like. The big draw, however, is the 18-hole Robert Trent–designed golf course. *Box 162, Playa Dorada, Dorado Naco: tel. 809/586–2019, fax 809/320–3608. Playa Naco: tel. 809/320–6226, fax 809/320–6225. U.S. reservations for both, tel. 800/322–2388. 700 rooms. Facilities: pool, restaurant, 3 bars, coffee shop, games room, minimarket, bicycle rental, horseback riding, tennis, golf, disco, pub, Jacuzzi, beach club, convention center, water-sports center. AE, DC, MC, V. EP, MAP, FAP. Expensive.*

Jack Tar Village. At this link in the all-inclusive chain of JTVs, everything, including drinks and golf greens fees, is included in the cost of your accommodations. The activities program is varied, enhanced by nightly entertainment and all manner of enjoyable pursuits. Accommodations are in Spanish-style villas set back from the beach in a large landscaped garden. There is free transportation to town, but the all-inclusive deal will probably keep you on the premises. *Box 368, Playa Dorada, tel. 809/586–3800 or 800/999–9182, fax 809/320–4161. 240 rooms. Facilities: 2 pools, 3 restaurants, 5 bars, casino, disco, golf, horseback riding, day and night tennis, water-sports center. AE, MC, V. All-inclusive. Expensive.*

Playa Dorada Beach Resort. This beach resort is known for its lively nightlife. It's set on a mile-long white-sand beach, and there are a variety of social and sports programs. The grounds are beautifully landscaped, and the pool, with swim-up bar, is just a few steps from the beach. Air-conditioned rooms come with cable TVs and either two double or one king-size bed. As one of the older hotels in the complex, its rectangular layout appears dated and lacks an upbeat spirit found in the newer hotels. However, it's still one of the few hotels that's right on the beach. *Box 272, Puerta Plata, tel. 809/586–3988 or 800/423–6902, fax 809/320–1190. 252 rooms, 1 suite. Facilities: pool, 4 restaurants, 2 bars, disco, casino, ice-cream parlor, golf, tennis courts, horseback riding, bikes, jogging trail, water-sports center. AE, DC, MC, V. EP. Expensive.*

★ **Paradise Beach Resort and Club.** Of the 12 hotels in the Playa Dorado complex, this hotel, formerly the Eurotel Playa Dorado, stands out on two counts. It is one of the four that fronts the beach and perhaps is the only one that has any individuality of design. Its cluster of low-rise buildings with white-tile roofs and latticed balconies and windows follow the winding paths through palms, birds-of-paradise, and hibiscus, from the reception area down to the beach. Bold, imaginative designs contrast with a carefully chosen palette of pastel greens and blues. Standard rooms have one double or two twin beds; some of the one-bedroom apartments have kitchens. In the center of the resort is the free-form pool, with a water channel that winds its way from the pool to the beach. There guests can dine in open-air restaurants or take advantage of the water-sports facilities. *Box 337, Playa Dorada, tel. 809/586–3663 or 800/752–0836, fax 809/320–4858. 216 rooms, 186 suites. Facilities: 3 restaurants, 3 bars, 2 lighted tennis courts, golf, horseback riding, water-sports clinic, bicycles, scooters. AE, DC, MC, V. All-inclusive. Expensive.*

★ **Puerto Plata Beach Resort and Casino.** This is a 7-acre village with cobblestone pathways, colorful gardens, and suites in 23 two- and three-story buildings. An activities center sets up water-sports clinics, rents bicycles, and so forth. The resort also caters to the little ones, with children's games and enclosures for them at the shallow end of the pool. Bogart's is the glitzy disco. Ylang-Ylang, named after the evening flower that blooms here, is a highly rated gourmet restaurant and catering service. The Neptune restaurant across the road on the beach is good for seafood. This resort is just outside of town and a ways from Playa Dorada, which will be an added attraction to some. *Box 600, Av. Malecón, Puerto Plata, tel. 809/586–4243 or 800/223–9815, fax 809/586–4377. 216 suites. Facilities: pool, 4 restaurants, bar, outdoor Jacuzzi, horseback riding, 3 lighted tennis courts, water-sports center. AE, MC, V. EP, MAP. Expensive.*

★ **Sand Castle.** The name says it all. This resort is a fantasy of curves, balconies, and balustrades set high above coral cliffs. Royal palms rise majestically from the beachside gardens. Rooms are simple and comfortable—extremely beige. Your stay here will be made more enjoyable if you have a room with a view, especially of the small curving beach down below. Though the hotel is by itself on a peninsula, lots of organized activities and the nearby village of Sosúa keep guests busy. *Puerto Chiquito, Sosúa, tel. 809/571–2420 or 800/445–5963, fax 809/571–2000. 240 air-conditioned rooms. Facilities: 4 restaurants, 5 bars, 2 pools, Jacuzzi, cable TV, shopping, disco, convention center, beach house, horseback riding, bicycling, snorkeling, deep-sea fishing, scuba diving, water-skiing, parasailing. AE, MC, V. EP, MAP. Expensive.*

Heavens. The accent at this compact all-inclusive property is on fun and active playtime. From exercise to merengue lessons, Heavens caters to the young (not the young at heart), and children are welcome, too. Outside guests may use the facilities with a daily ($45) pass. The decor is composed of stylized palms in rattan, cloth, and metal, and the health-conscious Rainbow Restaurant is the only Dominican eatery to offer a separate smoking section. Locals frequent the high-tech Andromeda disco, but ask for a room away from it—things can get noisy. This is one of Playa Dorado's smaller resorts with buildings vying with each other for space and a pool area crowded with chaise longues. *Box 576, Playa Dorada, Puerta Plata, tel. 809/586–5250 or 800/835–7697, fax 809/320–4733. 150 rooms and suites. Facilities: pool, 2 restaurants, disco, bar, cable TV, horseback riding, water aerobics, windsurfing, sailing, snorkeling and scuba, merengue lessons. AE, MC, V. All-inclusive. Moderate.*

Hotel Cofresi. The rooms here are simply furnished with twin beds, but the setting is breathtaking. The all-inclusive resort is built on the reefs along the Atlantic, which spritzes its waters into the peaceful man-made lagoon and pools along the beach.

There are jogging and exercise trails, paddleboats for the lagoon, scuba-diving clinics, and evening entertainment, including a disco. The cost covers drinks and all. *Box 327, Costambar, tel. 809/586–2898, fax 809/586–8064. 145 rooms, 5 suites. Facilities: 2 restaurants, 3 bars, disco, nightclub, 2 pools (1 saltwater), bicycling, horseback riding, paddleboats, tennis, water-sports center. AE, MC, V. EP, FAP. Moderate.*

★ **Playa Chiquita.** In this new Sosúa resort you register in a broad breezeway that leads past the free-form pool right to the small private beach. The all-suite, air-conditioned complex has contemporary tropical decor, with terra-cotta floors, cable TVs, double or king-size beds, wet bar, kitchenettes, and patios or balconies. A sun deck overlooks the ocean. The pool has a swim-up bar for adult guests and a shallow section for children. Plans are to have doubled the number of rooms by the end of 1993, but construction may continue into 1994. In the meantime, a new casino has opened. *Sosúa, tel. 809/689–6191 or 800/922–4272, fax 809/571–2460. 90 rooms. Facilities: restaurant, coffee shop, pool, gift shop, horseback riding, casino, water sports. MC, V. EP, MAP. Moderate.*

Punta Goleta Beach Resort. This bare-bones resort is set on 100 tropical acres across the road from the Cabarete beach, where wind-surfing is the big deal. All the hotel's rooms are air-conditioned, and most have terraces or patios with gingerbread trim. There is a lot of activity here, such as volleyball in the pool or on the beach, frog and crab racing, board games, merengue lessons, disco, and boating on the lagoon. *Box 318, Cabarete, tel. 809/571–0700, fax 809/571–0707. 126 rooms and 10 villas. Facilities: 2 restaurants, 4 bars, disco, jogging track, pool, lagoon, horseback riding, golf, tennis, water-sports center. AE, DC, MC, V. All-inclusive. Moderate.*

★ **Hostal Jimessón.** One of the few hotels in downtown Puerto Plata, the Jimessón is a gingerbread, century-old clapboard house right out of New Orleans. There are rocking chairs on the front porch, and the parlor houses a veritable museum of antique grandfather clocks, Victrolas, and mahogany and wicker furniture. Other superb, homey touches include a live parrot, hanging plants, and the owners' genuine hospitality. The drawback is that the guest rooms are actually in the newer concrete addition at the back and have nothing more than a bed and table cooled by air-conditioning and a basic bathroom. *Calle John F. Kennedy 41, Puerto Plata, tel. 809/586–5131, fax 809/586–6313. 22 air-conditioned rooms. Facilities: bar, cable TV. AE, MC, V. EP. Inexpensive.*

Hotel Montemar. Located on the Malecón, between Puerto Plata and Playa Dorada, this is a good choice for a cost-conscious holiday. All rooms have an ocean view. Superior rooms are air-conditioned, but small standard rooms are not. There is a daily schedule of activities and transportation to the beaches at Playa Dorada. It's a fine, inexpensive alternative to Playa Dorada. *Box 382, Puerto Plata, tel. 809/586–2800 or 800/332–4872, fax 809/586–2009. 95 rooms. Facilities: restaurant, coffee shop, bar, 2 tennis courts, beach club, golf, horseback riding. AE, MC, V. EP, MAP, FAP. Inexpensive.*

Jarabacoa **Hotel Hogar.** Tasty home-cooked meals and a very friendly
★ staff add to the charm of this simple establishment right in the middle of town (only a block from the bus station). Look for the huge Montecarlo cigarette sign hanging out front. The rooms are spartan but serviceable and come with their own mosquito

netting. *Calle Mella 34, Jarabacoa, tel. 809/574–2739. 9 rooms. Facilities: restaurant. No credit cards. CP. Inexpensive.*

La Romana **Casa de Campo.** This luxury resort is—in a word—awesome. It
★ occupies 7,000 landscaped acres along the edge of the Caribbean. Much of the resort was designed by Oscar de la Renta, who owns a villa here and has a boutique in Altos de Chavón, the recreated village and art colony on the property (*see* Exploring the Dominican Republic, *above*). There are 350 casitas, casita suites; and one-, two-, and three-bedroom golf and tennis villas, plus 150 condominium apartments. There is a ranch with 2,000 horses, three polo fields, and two 18-hole Pete Dye golf courses. Minibuses provide free transportation around the resort, but you can also rent electric carts, scooters, and bicycles. The advantage of staying here is that American Eagle flies in twice a day from San Juan to the La Romana airstrip. The disadvantage is that there are few attractions in the vicinity of the hotel other than the hotel's own campus. *Box 140, La Romana, tel. 809/523–3333 or 800/223–6620, fax 809/523–8548. 740 rooms. Facilities: 9 restaurants, 8 bars, 13 pools, 13 tennis courts (6 lighted), fitness center, Jacuzzi, sauna, polo fields, ranch, 2 18-hole golf courses, boutiques, marina, airstrip. AE, DC, MC, V. EP, MAP. Very Expensive.*

Punta Cana **Bávaro Beach Resort.** More than 20 miles of the Caribbean's best beach are to be found in front of this four-star luxury resort. The rooms are in five low-rise buildings by the beach or overlooking the gardens. Each room is air-conditioned and has a private balcony or terrace and refrigerator. A social director coordinates a wide variety of daily activities, but it is a very impersonal hotel. *Higüey, tel. 809/682–2162 or 800/336–6612, fax 809/682–2169. 1,001 rooms. Facilities: 3 restaurants, 3 bars, 2 pools, cable TV, archery, bicycles, horseback riding, tennis, disco, water sports. AE, MC, V. MAP. Expensive.*

Club Mediterranée. Everything but hard liquor is included in the price you pay for a stay in this 70-acre facility on the Punta Cana beach. Its air-conditioned, double-occupancy rooms are in three-story beach and coconut-grove lodgings, with twin beds and showers. There's a disco on the beach, plus the whole spectrum of Club Med activities, from archery to yoga. *Punta Cana, tel. 809/687–2767 or 800-CLUBMED; in NY, 212/750–1670, fax 809/565–2558. 332 rooms. Facilities: 2 restaurants, bar, disco, pool, 14 tennis courts (6 lighted), golf driving range and putting green, archery, bocce ball, volleyball, boat rides, soccer, ping-pong, aerobics classes, water-sports center. AE, MC, V. All-inclusive (drinks not included). Moderate.*

Samaná **Hotel Gran Bahía.** This new luxury resort is built at the water's edge in an area yet to be spoiled with overdevelopment. The modern Colonial Victorian allows for verandas and balconies looking out over the pool and the sea beyond. Breakfast on your room's private terrace is a treat, especially with the superb views. The large guest rooms are furnished with cheerful floral prints, tiled floors, and pastel watercolor paintings. Dining alfresco is pleasant, though you would be wise to stay with the fresh seafood rather than the meat dishes. *Box 2024, Santo Domingo, tel. 809/538–3111 or 800/372–1323, fax 809/538–2764. 98 rooms. Facilities: 2 restaurants, pool, 2 tennis courts, gym, archery, and whale watching arranged. AE, MC, V. CP, MAP. Very Expensive.*

Bahía Beach. On a cliff above the beach in one of the best game-fishing areas of the Caribbean, the Bahía offers air-conditioned rooms with ocean view on the mainland, plus fan-cooled cottages on Cayo Levantado, a nearby island. This is a favorite with young Dominicans. *Samaná Bay, tel. 809/583–3111. 85 rooms in the main hotel, 29 on the island. Facilities: restaurant, bar, pool, 2 tennis courts, disco, water sports. AE, MC, V. All-inclusive. Inexpensive.*

Santo Domingo **Jaragua Resort Hotel, Casino and European Spa.** This ultra-modern complex is set on 14 acres of gardens, waterfalls, and fountains. Top-name entertainers are booked into the 800-seat nightclub, master chefs from four countries tend to the cuisine, and a staff doctor supervises the diet program in the spa. The resort was featured on "Lifestyles of the Rich and Famous." Air-conditioned accommodations are in Garden or Tower rooms, and all have 3 phones, 21-channel satellite TVs, mini-bars, and hair dryers. Rooms facing the pool and the Caribbean, such as No. 821 with a king-size bed, are the nicest. Twelve cabanas surround the Olympic-size free-form pool, and the casino covers 20,000 square feet. *Av. George Washington 367, Santo Domingo, tel. 809/221–2222 or 800/331–3542, fax 809/686–0528. 337 rooms, 18 suites. Facilities: casino, pool, 6 restaurants, 5 bars, 4 tennis courts (1 lighted), golf (at the Santo Domingo Country Club), and European spa with exercise/diet programs, saunas, Jacuzzis, whirlpool. AE, MC, V. EP. Very Expensive.*

Hotel V Centenario. Santo Domingo's newest five-star hotel opened in late 1992 on the Malecón, a block away from the Sheraton. At press time, the paucity of guests and the newness of the hotel made the atmosphere appear cold and impersonal, but this may change. Certainly the marble floors and pillars give the hotel a crisp freshness. The rooms are furnished in the ubiquitous Caribbean pastels, but come with up-to-date features, including an electronic safe. Guests can try their luck at the casino or take time out and relax in the lounge bar area with subdued lighting and enticing easy chairs. A casual coffee shop looks out over the Caribbean, and the pool shares a terrace with a bar and alfresco seafood restaurant. *Av. George Washington 218, Santo Domingo, tel. 809/221–0000, fax 809/221–2020. 167 rooms, 33 suites. Facilities: 3 restaurants, 2 bars, pool, shops, casino. 1 tennis and 2 squash courts, sauna, gym, parking. AE, MC, V. EP. Expensive.*

★ **Hotel Santo Domingo.** This complex actually consists of two different hotels: **Hotel Hispaniola** and **Hotel Santo Domingo.** Catering to a younger crowd, the Hispaniola has 165 rooms, with an active pool, a modern disco favored by *capitaleños*, and a recently refurbished casino. There are two restaurants here, Las Cañas and La Pizetta, as well as the Hispaniola Bar, which has a small dance area. The bar is very dark; very intimate; and very, very red. Guest rooms are best characterized by their worn and stained carpets. In short, they are in desperate need of refurbishing. In a dramatic juxtaposition is the Hotel Santo Domingo. This is the epitome of an haute hotel. Oscar de la Renta designed the interiors: with the black- and red-lacquered accents of hall lamps, conch-shell mirrors, bold colors, and handcrafted Dominican furniture. The rooms have balconies and cable TVs, and most have double beds. Located on 14 delicately manicured acres overlooking the Caribbean, the hotel caters to the executive. Many VIPs check into the Premier

Club for the extra perks. No-smoking rooms are available, as are conference rooms. The newly renovated Caonabo Room transcends the postmodern. The elegant Alcázar features excellent Continental dining in de la Renta's romantic Moorish rendition. Dimly lit, Las Palmas is a local favorite for music and dancing. The hotels are at the Western edge of the Malecón— often more convenient for businessmen who want to be close to the new commercial section of town than for tourists who prefer being closer to the historic area. *Av. Independencia and Abraham Lincoln. Box 2112, Santo Domingo, tel. 809/535–1511 or 800/223–6620, fax 809/535–4050. 220 rooms. Facilities: 3 restaurants, 2 bars, pool, sun deck, sauna, 3 lighted tennis courts, conference rooms, and helipad. AE, MC, V. EP. Expensive.*

★ **Santo Domingo Sheraton Hotel and Casino.** This 11-story, modern, air-conditioned hotel is on Avenida George Washington, next to the Jaragua, and many of the rooms have balconies overlooking the sea. Most of the rooms have a minibar, and all have a color TV with English-language movies. Service is disorganized, but the staff tries to be helpful. On the second floor next to the terrace and swimming pool is a popular coffee shop. *Box 1493, Santo Domingo, tel. 809/686–6666 or 800/325–3535, fax 809/687–8150. 260 rooms. Facilities: casino, pool, Antoine's restaurant, bar, disco, 2 lighted tennis courts, beauty salon, shops, saunas, health club, facilities for the disabled. AE, DC, MC, V. EP. Expensive.*

Hotel El Embajador and Casino. The rooms in this air-conditioned hotel are spacious, with carpeting, twin or king-size beds, radios, cable TVs, and balconies with either a mountain or an ocean view (choose the latter). An executive concierge floor is good for business travelers. The pool is a popular weekend gathering place for resident foreigners. *Av. Sarasota 65, Santo Domingo, tel. 809/221–2131 or 800/457–0067, fax 809/532–4494. 304 rooms, 12 suites. Facilities: casino, pool, free transport to beach, 4 tennis courts, 2 restaurants, 2 bars, shopping arcade, facilities for the disabled. AE, DC, MC, V. EP. Moderate.*

Gran Hotel Lina and Casino. This balconied hotel, on Avenida Máximo Gómez near the Plaza de la Cultura, has a staid but secure ambience. The rooms are air-conditioned, spacious, and carpeted, with double beds, minifridges, huge marble baths, and cable TVs. The staff is friendly and helpful. *Box 1915, Santo Domingo, tel. 809/686–5000 or 800/942–2461, fax 809/686–5521. 205 rooms, 15 suites. Facilities: casino, Spanish restaurant, piano bar, nightclub, coffee shop, health club, 2 tennis courts, pool facilities for the disabled. AE, DC, MC, V. EP. Inexpensive.*

★ **Hostal Palacio Nicolás de Ovando.** The oldest hotel in the New World, and one of the few in the Colonial Zone, was home to the first governor in the early 1500s. The decor is Spanish, with carved mahogany doors, beamed ceilings, tapestries, arched colonnades, and three courtyards with splashing fountains. The rooms have views of the port, the pool, or the Colonial Zone. Dominican specialties are served in the restaurant. This is Santo Domingo's only hotel with the charm of antiquity. Its disadvantage is its location. At nighttime, the area can be deserted and unpleasant for walking alone. *Calle Las Damas 44, Apdo. 89-2, Santo Domingo, tel. 809/687–3101, fax 809/686–5170. 55 air-conditioned rooms. Facilities: restaurant, bar, TV, pool. AE, MC, V. EP. Inexpensive.*

The Arts and Nightlife

Get a copy of the magazine *Vacation Guide* and the newspaper *Touring*, both of which are available free at the Tourist Office and at hotels, to find out what's happening around the island. Also look in the *Santo Domingo News* and the *Puerto Plata News* for listings of events. The monthly *Dominican Fiesta!* also provides up-to-date information.

Casinos   Most of the casinos are concentrated in the larger hotels of Santo Domingo, but there are others here and there, and all offer blackjack, craps, and roulette. Casinos are open daily 3 PM–4 AM. You must be 18 to enter, and jackets are required. In Santo Domingo, the most popular casinos are in the **Dominican Concorde** (Calle Anacaona, tel. 809/562–8222), the **Jaragua** (Av. Independencia, tel. 809/686–2222), the **Embajador** (Av. Sarasota, tel. 809/533–2131), the **Gran Hotel Lina** (Av. Máximo Gómez, tel. 809/689–5185), the **Naco Hotel** (Av. Tiradentes 22, tel. 809/562–3100), and the **San Géronimo** (Av. Independencia 1067, tel. 809/533–8181).

You'll soon discover that there is no such thing as last call in the Dominican Republic. Customers usually decide when closing time will be.

Cafés   **Café Atlantico** (Prolongación Mexico 152 at Abraham Lincoln, tel. 809/565–1840) is responsible for bringing Happy Hour and Tex-Mex cooking to the Dominican Republic. (Its sister restaurant of the same name is a hot spot in Washington, D.C.) It has been attracting well-to-do Dominicans and an international crowd for more than six years. Usually young, very lively, and very friendly, the late-afternoon Yuppie crowd comes for the music, the food, the exotic drinks, and the energetic atmosphere. You may even find owner-host Gustavo spinning your favorite record.

The wine and cheese bar **Exquesito** (Av. Tiradentes 8, tel. 809/541–0233) is in an odd setting that mixes traditional Dominican decor with deconstructivist provincial Italian. The fare includes French cheeses, Italian antipasti, and a local version of the deli. Talk, relax, and try the fondue.

A recent annex to the Café St. Michel, the **Grand Café** (Av. Lope de Vega 26, tel. 809/562–4141) attracts a relaxed local crowd. You can escape the music by going upstairs to the Tree House. The menu is informal and generally light, but try the Creole oxtail *fradiabolo* served with crabmeat patties.

Music and Dance   An active and frenzied young crowd dances to new wave; house; and, of course, merengue at **Alexander's** club (Av. Pasteur 23, tel. 809/685–9728). An institution, it is open till all hours.

The neon palm tree outside **Bella Blue** (Av. George Washington 165, tel. 809/689–2911) is a noticeable night beacon for a fun time. The crowd at this Malecón dance club is definitely over 21, and no jeans are allowed.

A favorite of locals for live music featuring local merengue bands, **Las Palmas** (Hotel Santo Domingo, Av. Independencia at Abraham Lincoln, tel. 809/535–1511) has a happy hour from 6 to 8 PM. The newest sensation is **Guacara Taina** (tel. 809/530–2666), a cultural center/disco set in a cave, hosting folkloric dances during the day and transforming into the city's hottest night spot in the late evening.

An aptly named club, **Tops** (Plaza Naco Hotel, Av. Tiradentes, tel. 809/541–6226) offers excellent views of the city. Located on the 12th floor of the hotel, it features a variety of special events, from lingerie fashion shows to the latest bands.

Also on the Malecón, **La Regine** (Av. George Washington 557, no phone) plays a variety of music and sometimes features local bands.

When all the partying is over and the *nuit blanche* is coming to an end, capitaleños will guide you to **La Aurora** (Av. Hermanos Deligne, no phone), a pediatric clinic turned lush after-hours supper club. Savor typical dishes, even sancocho, at four in the morning. Here you'll see not only partygoers but also the musicians who entertained them. It's a spot of preference for Santo Domingo's hottest music band, 4:40.

12 Grenada

Updated by
Carolyn Price

Grenada, a tiny island only 21 miles long and 12 miles wide, is bordered by dozens of beaches and secluded coves; crisscrossed by nature trails; and filled with spice plantations, tropical forests, and select hotels clinging to hillsides overlooking the sea.

Known as the Isle of Spice, Grenada is a major producer of nutmeg, cinnamon, mace, cocoa, and many other common household spices. The pungent aroma of spices fills the air at the outdoor markets, where they're sold from large burlap bags; in the restaurants, where chefs believe in using them liberally; and in the pubs, where cinnamon and nutmeg are sprinkled on the rum punches. If the Irish hadn't beaten them to the name, Grenadians might have called their land the Emerald Isle, for the lush pine forests and the thick brush on the hillsides give it a great, green beauty that few Caribbean islands duplicate.

Located in the Eastern Caribbean 90 miles north of Trinidad, Grenada is the most southerly of the Windward Islands. It is a nation composed of three inhabited islands and a few uninhabited islets: Grenada island is the largest, with 120 square miles and about 86,000 people; Carriacou, 16 miles north of Grenada, is 13 square miles and has a population of about 5,000; and Petit Martinique, 5 miles northeast of Carriacou, has 486 acres and a population of 700. Although Carriacou and Petit Martinique are popular for day trips and fishing and snorkeling excursions, most of the tourist action is on Grenada. Here, too, you will find the nation's capital, St. George's, and its largest harbor, St. George's Harbour.

Until 1983 when the United States/Eastern Caribbean invasion of Grenada catapulted this tiny nation into the forefront of international news, it was a relatively obscure island providing a quiet hideaway for those who love fishing, snorkeling, or simply lazing in the sun.

Today Grenada is back to normal, a safe and secure vacation spot with enough good shopping, restaurants, and pubs to make it a regular port of call for major cruise lines, and plenty of beaches and coves for those who want to scuba dive, snorkel, or just sit and stare at the waves.

Although Grenada's tourism industry is undergoing an expansion, it is a controlled expansion, counterbalanced by the island's West Indian flavor. No building can stand taller than a coconut palm, and new construction on the beaches must be at least 165 feet from the high-water mark. The hotels, resorts, and restaurants remain small and are mostly family-owned by people who get to know their guests and pride themselves on giving personalized service. They're typical of the islanders as a whole—friendly and hospitable.

Grenada was sighted by Columbus in 1498. Although he never stepped foot on the island, he nevertheless named it Concepción. Throughout the 17th century it was the scene of bloody battles between the indigenous Carib Indians and the French. The French finally captured the island in 1650 and lost it in 1762 to the British. This was the beginning of the seesaw of power between the two nations that became a familiar tale on many of the Windward Islands.

In 1967 Grenada became part of the British Commonwealth; seven years later it was granted total independence. The New Jewel Movement (NJM) seized power in 1979, formed the People's Revolutionary Government, and named as prime minister Maurice Bishop, who established controversial ties with Cuba. Bishop's prime ministry lasted until 1983, when a coup d'état led to his execution, along with that of many of his supporters. Bernard Coard, NJM deputy prime minister, and Army Commander Hudson Austin took over the government. U.S. troops invaded the island on October 25, 1983, and evacuated the American students who were attending St. George's University Medical School. Coard and Austin were arrested, and resistance to the invasion was quickly put down. Since then, the annual number of U.S. residents alone traveling to this splendid isle has almost tripled.

Herbert A. Blaize was elected prime minister in December 1984. With $57.2 million in U.S. aid, his government began reorganizing Grenada's economy, focusing on agriculture, light manufacturing, and tourism. The country started to rebuild roads, and a new telephone system, with direct-dial from the United States, replaced the outdated one. Point Salines International Airport opened in 1984, enabling jets to land on the island and allowing night landings, both firsts for Grenada.

Construction has been completed on Camerhogne Park, a recreation center at Grand Anse Bay, where many of the hotels and resorts are located. The park, designed primarily for the use of visiting cruise-ship passengers and resident Grenadians, has picnic tables, locker and shower facilities, food concessions, and a jetty for water taxis.

The most recent election of Nicholas Braithwaite as prime minister, which took place in March 1990, brought more peaceful progress to this island-nation with a stable and U.S.-friendly government.

Before You Go

Tourist Information Contact the **Grenada Tourist Office:** in the United States (820 2nd Ave., Suite 900D, New York, NY 10017, tel. 212/687–9554 or 800/927–9554; fax 212/573–9731); in Canada (Suite 820, 439 University Ave., Toronto, Ontario M5G 1Y8, tel. 416/595–1339; fax 416/595–8278); or in Britain (1 Collingham Gardens, Earl's Court, London SW5 0HW, tel. 071/370–5164 or 071/370–5165; fax 071/370–7040).

Arriving and Departing
By Plane **BWIA** (tel. 800/JET–BWIA) flies from Miami, Toronto, and London to Grenada. **American Airlines** (tel. 800/334–7400) has daily flights during high season from major U.S. and Canadian cities via their San Juan hub; **Air Canada** (tel. 800/776–3000) flies from Toronto to Barbados, where **LIAT** (Leeward Islands Air Transport, tel. 809/440–2796 or 809/440–2797) connects with flights to Grenada. LIAT has scheduled service between Barbados, Grenada, and Carriacou and also serves Trinidad and Venezuela.

From the Airport Taxis and minivans are available at the airport to take you to your hotel. Rates to St. George's and the hotels of Grand Anse and L'Anse aux Epines are about $10–$13. In Eastern Caribbean currency, this amounts to about E.C.$25–E.C.$35. A charge of E.C.$10 is tacked on to any ride taken after 6 PM.

Passports and Visas Passports are not required of U.S., Canadian, and British citizens, provided they have two proofs of citizenship (one with photo) and a return air ticket. A passport, even an expired one,

Grenada (and Carriacou)

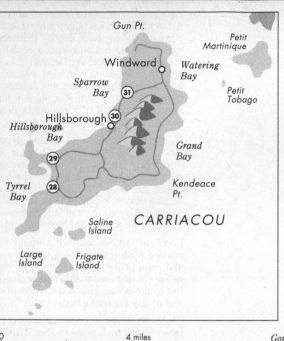

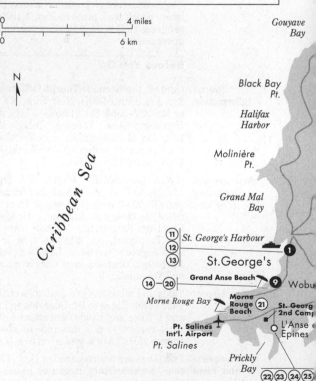

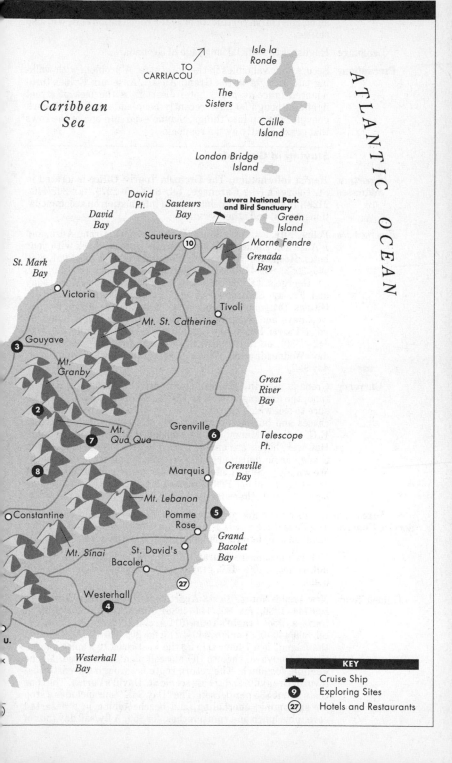

TO
CARRIACOU

Isle la
Ronde

The
Sisters

Caille
Island

London Bridge
Island

*Caribbean
Sea*

ATLANTIC OCEAN

David
Pt.

David
Bay

*Sauteurs
Bay*

**Levera National Park
and Bird Sanctuary**

Green
Island

Sauteurs

(10)

Morne Fendre

*Grenada
Bay*

*St. Mark
Bay*

Victoria

Tivoli

Mt. St. Catherine

(3) Gouyave

*Mt.
Granby*

*Great
River
Bay*

(2)

Grenville (6)

(7)

*Mt.
Qua Qua*

Telescope
Pt.

(8)

Marquis

*Grenville
Bay*

Constantine

Mt. Lebanon

Pomme
Rose

(5)

*Grand
Bacolet
Bay*

Mt. Sinai

St. David's

Bacolet

(27)

Westerhall

(4)

U.

*Westerhall
Bay*

KEY	
⛴	Cruise Ship
(9)	Exploring Sites
(27)	Hotels and Restaurants

is the best proof of citizenship; a driver's license with photo *and* an original birth certificate or voter registration card will also suffice.

Language   English is the official language of Grenada.

Precautions   Secure your valuables in the hotel safe. A problem with walking late at night in the Grand Anse/L'Anse aux Epines (pronounced *lance-au-peen*) hotel districts is the lack of street lights (although 50 have recently been added). It's still dark enough to bump into things, maybe even into one of the cows that graze silently by the roadside.

Staying in Grenada

Important   **Tourist Information:** The **Grenada Tourist Office** is located in
Addresses   St. George's (the Carenage, tel. 809/440–2279, fax 809/440–2123). It has maps, brochures, and information on accommodations, tours, and other services.

Emergencies   **Police, Fire,** and **Ambulance:** In St. George's, Grand Anse, and L'Anse aux Epines, call 911. For other areas, check with your hotel. **Hospitals: St. George's Hospital** (tel. 809/440–2051; 809/440–2052; 809/440–2053). **Pharmacies: Gitten's** (Halifax St., St. George's, tel. 809/440–2165) is open Monday–Wednesday and Friday–Saturday 8–5 and Thursday 8–noon and 1–5. **Gittens Drugmart** (Grand Anse, tel. 809/444–4954) is open weekdays and Saturday 9–8, Sunday and public holidays 9–noon. **Parris' Pharmacy Ltd.** (Victoria St., Grenville, tel. 809/442–7330), on the windward side of the island, is open Monday–Wednesday and Friday 9–4:30, Thursday 9–1, and Saturday 9–7.

Currency   Grenada uses the Eastern Caribbean (E.C.) dollar. At press time, the exchange rate was E.C.$2.67 in banks to U.S.$1. Be sure to ask which currency is referred to when you make purchases and business transactions; prices are often quoted in E.C. dollars. Money can be exchanged at any bank or hotel. However, hotels are unable by law to give foreign currency in change or on departure. U.S. currency and traveler's checks are widely accepted. Most hotels and major restaurants accept credit cards. *Note:* Prices quoted here are in U.S. dollars unless indicated otherwise.

Taxes and   Hotels add an 8% government tax; restaurants add a 10% tax.
Service Charges   The departure tax is E.C. $35 for adults and E.C.$17.50 for children ages 5 to 12. Children under 5 are exempt.

Hotels and some restaurants add a 10% service charge to your bill. If not, a 10%–15% gratuity should be added for a job well done.

Guided Tours   **New Trends Tours** (Siesta Apartment Hotel, Grand Anse, tel. 809/444–1236, fax 809/444–4836) offers a wide selection of tours, as does **Arnold's Tours** (611 Archibald Ave., St. George's, tel. 809/440–0531 or 809/440–2213, fax 809/440–4118). "Around the Island" is a 7-hour trip up the west coast to a spice plantation at Gouyave, then to the Mascoll plantation house, Morne Fendue, for lunch. The return route is through the east-coast town of Grenville and across scenic St. David's Parish. The tour costs about $35 per person. The "Day Sail" tour includes a stop for swimming, snorkeling, and beachcombing in a deserted cove, plus lunch and rum punches, for $50. A fly/sail day tour of the Grenadines includes air transportation from Grenada to Union Island, a sail on an 80-foot island schooner, a gourmet lunch, and snorkeling for about $180 per person.

A number of car-rental agencies and tour operators in St. George's offer standard tours such as the "Royal Drive," which includes the town of St. George's; scenic Westerhall Point, across the island on the Atlantic; a small fishing village; a sugar-processing factory; and Grand Anse Beach. Agencies that offer such tours include **Otways Tours** (the Carenage, tel. 809/440–2558, 809/440–2423, fax 809/440–4179) and, in Grand Anse, **Carib Tours,** just south of the shopping center (tel. 809/444–4363 or 809/444–4364, fax 809/444–4560.).

Getting Around Minivans ply the winding road between St. George's and Grand
Buses Anse Beach, where many of the hotels are located. Hail one anywhere along the way, pay E.C.$1, and hold on to your hat. They are available from about 6 to 8 daily except Sundays and public holidays. By minivan, you can get anywhere on the island for E.C.$1–E.C.$6—a bargain by any standard—but be prepared for packed vehicles, unpredictable schedules, and some hair-raising maneuvers on mountainous roads and by-ways.

Taxis Taxis are plentiful and rates are posted at the hotels and at the pier on the Carenage in St. George's. The trip from the airport to Grand Anse is E.C.$25, and from the airport to St. George's, E.C.$30. A charge of E.C.$10 is added to all fares for rides taken after 6 PM. Cabs are plentiful at all hotels, at the pier, and near the Tourist Office on the Carenage.

Rental Cars To rent a car, you will need a valid driver's license, with which you may obtain a local permit at a cost of E.C.$30. Driving is on the left. Rental cars cost about $45 a day or $250 a week with unlimited mileage. A Jeep and automatic drive run about $50 a day, and $275 a week. Gas costs about $2.25 per gallon. Your hotel can arrange a rental for you. Car-rental agencies in St. George's are numerous. **David's** (tel. 809/440–2399, 809/440–3038, or 809/444–4310) maintains four offices: Point Salines International Airport, the Ramada Renaissance Hotel, Archibold Avenue in St. George's, and South Wind Cottages in Grand Anse. **Avis** at Spice Isle Rental (tel. 809/440–3936 or 809/440–2624; after hours: 809/444–4563) is on Paddock and Lagoon roads in St. George's. Look for **McIntyre Bros. Ltd.** (tel. 809/440–2044 or 809/440–2901; after hours: 809/440–4053) on Lagoon Road in the capital.

Telephones Telephone service on the island has much improved in the last
and Mail few years. Grenada can be dialed directly from the United States and Canada. The area code is 809. Long-distance calls from Grenada can now be dialed directly as well.

Airmail rates for letters to the United States and Canada are E.C. 75¢ for a half-ounce letter and E.C. 35¢ for a postcard.

Opening and Store hours are generally from 8–noon and 1–4 weekdays; 8–
Closing Times noon, Saturday; they are closed Sunday. Banks are open 8–noon Monday–Thursday; 8–noon and 2:30–5 PM on Friday.

Exploring Grenada

Numbers in the margin correspond to points of interest on the Grenada (and Carriacou) map.

St. George's Grenada's capital city and major port is one of the most picturesque and truly West Indian towns in the Caribbean. Pastel warehouses cling to the curving shore along the horseshoe-shape Carenage, the harborside thoroughfare; rainbow-colored houses rise above it and disappear into the green hills.

❶ A walking tour of **St. George's** can be made in about two hours, particularly with the help of the Department of Tourism's free brochure, *Historical Walking Tour of St. George's*, which directs you to 21 points of historical interest. Pick it up.

Start on the **Carenage,** a walkway along St. George's Harbour and the town's main thoroughfare. Ocean liners dock at the pier at the eastern end, and the **Delicious Landing** restaurant (tel. 809/440–3948), with outdoor tables, is at the western end. In between are the **public library,** a number of small **shops,** the **Grenada Tourist Office,** and two more good restaurants, **Rudolf's** and the **Nutmeg** (*see* Dining, *below*), boasting a huge open window that provides a great view of the harbor.

You can reach the **Grenada National Museum** by walking along the west end of the Carenage and taking Young Street west to Monckton Street. The museum has a small, interesting collection of ancient and colonial artifacts and recent political memorabilia. *Young and Monckton Sts., tel. 809/440–3725. Admission: $1 adults, 25¢ children under 18. Open weekdays 9–4:30; Sat. 10–1:30.*

Walk west along Young Street, turn left on Cross Street, and you'll reach the **Esplanade,** the thoroughfare that runs along the ocean side of town. At the intersection of Cross Street and the Esplanade is the **Yellow Poui Art Gallery** (tel. 809/440–3878), which keeps irregular hours (tourist brochures put it this way: "Open by appointment or by chance"). The studio displays art from Grenada, Jamaica, Trinidad, and Guyana and canvases by British, German, and French artists now living here. On the nearby Esplanade you'll find a row of tiny shops that sell such treats as guava jelly and coconut fudge. *Shopping hours: weekdays 9:15–12:15 and 1:15–3:15, Sat. 9:15–12:15; closed Sun. Appointments may be scheduled after hours.*

Take the Esplanade north to Granby Street and turn right. Granby Street will take you to **Market Square,** which comes alive every Saturday morning from 8 to noon with vendors selling baskets and fresh produce, including tropical fruit you can eat on the spot. Don't miss it!

Walk back on Granby Street to Halifax Street and turn left. At the intersection of Halifax and Church streets is **St. Andrew's Presbyterian Church,** built in 1830. Follow Church Street east to Gore Street, to **St. George's Anglican Church,** built in 1828. It's lined with plaques representing Grenada in the 18th and 19th centuries. Continue up Church Street to the **York House,** built around 1800. Now home to the Senate and Supreme Court, it's open to the public for unstructured visits. Go back to Market Hill and turn left to reach **St. George's Methodist Church,** built in 1820, on Green Street near Tyrrel Street.

Take Tyrrel Street east to the corner of Park Lane to see the **Marryshow House.** Built in 1917, it combines Victorian and West Indian architecture. The Marryshow also houses the **Marryshow Folk Theatre,** Grenada's first cultural center. Plays, West Indian dance and music, and poetry readings are presented here on occasion. *Tyrrel St., near Bain Alley, tel.*

809/440–2451. Admission free. Open weekdays 8:30–4:30, Sat. 9–1.

Head back west on Tyrrel Street and turn left onto Church Street. **Fort George** is at the southern tip of Church Street. The fort, rising above the point that separates the harbor from the ocean, was built by the French in 1705. The inner courtyard now houses the police headquarters. *Church St., no phone. Outer courtyard open to the public. Admission free. Open daily during daylight hours.*

The fastest way from the Carenage to the Esplanade is through the **Sendall Tunnel,** slightly north of Fort George. Take it if you're too tired to walk up the steep hill.

The West Coast The coast road north from St. George's winds past soaring mountains and valleys covered with banana and breadfruit trees, palms, bamboo, and tropical flowers. You can drive to **②** **Concord Falls,** about 8 miles north of St. George's, and then hike 2 miles to the main falls, and another hour to a second, spectacular waterfall. Use the small changing room at the main falls to don your bathing suit. During the dry months when the currents aren't too strong, you can take a dip under the cascades. About 15 minutes farther north is the town of **Gouyave,** center of the nutmeg industry.

③ **Dougaldston Estate,** near the entrance to the town, has a spice factory where you can see cocoa, nutmeg, mace, cloves, cinnamon, and other spices in their natural state, laid out on giant trays to dry in the sun. Old women walk barefoot through the spices, shuffling them so they dry evenly. *Gouyave, no phone. Admission free. Open weekdays 9–4.*

Time Out For lunch take the short drive to Betty Mascoll's old plantation house, **Morne Fendue** (St. Patrick's Parish, tel. 809/440–9330). The large, two-story house was built by Mrs. Mascoll's father in 1912 of hand-chiseled, colored stones mortared with lime and molasses. Outside, poinsettias grow in profusion; inside, amid Victorian antiques and dainty lace curtains, Mrs. Mascoll serves superb West Indian cuisine (sample the callaloo soup) and the best rum punch on an island that has distilled the drink into an art form.

The East Coast Start your tour at **Westerhall,** a residential area about 5 miles **④** southeast of St. George's, known for its beautiful villas, gardens, and panoramic views. From here, take a dirt road north **⑤** to **Grand Bacolet Bay,** a jagged peninsula on the Atlantic where the surf pounds against deserted beaches. Some miles north **⑥** is **Grenville,** the island's second-largest city. From here you can watch schooners set sail for the outer islands. As in St. George's, Saturday is market day, and the town fills with local people doing their shopping for the week. Cooking enthusiasts may want to see the town's spice-processing factory, which is open to the public.

If you take the interior route back to St. George's, you'll get a full sense of the lush, mountainous nature of the island. There is only one paved road that cuts across the island. Leaving Grenville and heading for St. George's, you'll wind upward through the rain forest until you're surrounded by mist, then you'll descend onto the sunny hillsides. In the middle of the is- **⑦** land is **Grand Etang National Park.** The lake, in the crater of an extinct volcano here, is a 13-acre glasslike expanse of cobalt-blue water. The area is a bird sanctuary and forest reserve, where you can go fishing and hiking. *Main interior road, halfway between Grenville and St. George's, tel. 809/442–7425. Open weekdays 8–4.*

8 Another place to visit is **Annandale Falls and Visitors' Centre,** where a mountain stream cascades 50 feet into a pool surrounded by such exotic tropical flora as liana vines and elephant ears. This is a good swimming and picnic spot. *Main interior road, 15 min east of St. George's, tel. 809/440–2452. Open daily 9–5.*

Grand Anse and the South End Most of the island's hotels and its nightlife are in Grand Anse or the adjacent community of L'Anse aux Epines, which means Cove of Pines. Here you will find one of the two campuses of **9** **St. George's University Medical School.** Chez Josephine, its unofficial beachfront cafeteria, serves drinks and light snacks.

The second campus is in **True Blue,** a residential area near L'Anse aux Epines. To reach it, take Grand Anse Road south toward the airport and turn left just before you reach the airport. Although the road is unnamed, it is the only one off Grand Anse Road.

The **Grand Anse Shopping Centre** has a supermarket/liquor store, a clothing store, shoe store, a fast-food joint, and several small gift shops with good-quality souvenirs and such luxury items as English china and Swedish crystal (*see* Shopping, *below*). Prices are competitive with duty-free shops elsewhere in the Caribbean.

Grenada's Grenadines **Carriacou, Petit Martinique,** and a handful of uninhabited specks that comprise the nation of Grenada are north of Grenada island and part of the Grenadines, a chain of 32 tiny islands and cays.

Carriacou is a little island (13 square miles) with a lot of punch. A hideaway with "over a hundred rum shops and only one gasoline station," this place moves the fastest Manhattan metabolism down several notches and exudes the kind of ebullient spirit and goodwill you'd hoped for in a Caribbean retreat but proved to be a travel brochure's illusion. Don't come here if you don't want peace, if you do want luxurious amenities, or if you would suffer coldly a parrot on your breakfast table.

Carriacou's colonial history parallels Grenada's; its tiny size has restricted its political role to a minor part in the area's history. A chain of hills cuts a wide swath through its center, from Gun Point in the north to Tyrrel Bay in the south. LIAT has seven daily flights (flying time approximately 20 minutes) to and from Grenada island, and schooners leave from St. George's Harbour twice a week. Hillsborough is the main town. In August, the Carriacou Regatta attracts yachts and sailing vessels from throughout the Caribbean.

The only museum in the Eastern Caribbean that is owned by the people, not the government, is the **Carriacou Museum,** located in Hillsborough behind Gramma's Bakery. This operation, housed in an old cotton ginnery, displays unearthed Amerindian, European, and African artifacts and features a gift shop loaded with locally made wares.

Five miles northeast of Carriacou is Petit Martinique, the smallest of Grenada's inhabited islands. Like Carriacou and Grenada, Petit Martinique was settled by the French.

Grenada for Free

A good way to spend an afternoon without spending money is to watch fishing boats of all sizes and descriptions pull in and out of St. George's Harbour. On Tuesday afternoons you can watch the boats being loaded with crates and bags of fruit and vegetables bound for Trinidad. It's also fun to roam through the Saturday markets in St. George's and Grenville, which are ablaze with color and humming with activity. Farm women sitting under umbrellas sell bananas, papayas, oranges, yams, plantains, exotic roots and vegetables, and fresh spices; ask the women for their permission before grabbing a photo opportunity. At the nearby fish market, just a short stroll down the Esplanade, you can see the day's catch on display. Bird- or butterfly-watchers can view a multitude of species at Levera Beach or La Sagesse Nature Center.

Beaches

Grenada has some 30 miles of coastline, 65 bays, and 45 white-sand beaches, many with secluded little coves. All the beaches are public and within an easy cab ride of St. George's. Most are located on the Caribbean, south of St. George's in the Grand Anse and L'Anse aux Epines areas, where most of the hotels are clustered. Virtually every hotel, apartment complex, and residential area has its own beach or tiny cove.

The loveliest and most popular beach is **Grand Anse,** about a 10-minute taxi ride from St. George's. It's a gleaming, 2-mile curve of sand and clear, gentle surf. At its southern end is a palm-covered point; to the north you can see the narrow mouth of St. George's Harbour and the pastel houses with fish-scale-tile rooftops on the hillsides above it. The sunset is particularly beautiful at Grand Anse—enjoy it over cocktails at Spice Island Inn, where tables line the beach.

Morne Rouge Beach is on the Caribbean side, about 1 mile south of Grand Anse Bay and 3 miles south of St. George's Harbour. The beach forms a ½-mile-long crescent and has a gentle surf excellent for swimming. A small café serves light meals during the day. In the evening, there's the disco, Fantazia 2001 (*see* Nightlife, *below*).

Levera National Park and Bird Sanctuary is at the northern tip of the island where the Caribbean meets the Atlantic. The first of the Grenadines is visible in the distance. The surf is rougher here than on the Caribbean beaches, but it is great for body surfing or watching the waves roll in. In 1991, this area, with its thick mangroves for food and protection, became an official sanctuary for nesting seabirds and seldom-seen tropical parrots. There are some fine Arawak ruins and pertroglyphs to be seen as well.

Sports and the Outdoors

Bicycling   Level ground is about as common here as are reindeer, but that doesn't stop the aerobically primed. What's more, 15-speed mountain bikes are available for a much more reasonable rate than a 4WD; you can find them at **Ride Grenada** (L'Anse aux Epine, tel. 809/444–1157).

Fishing Deep-sea fishing around Grenada is excellent, with marlin, sailfish, tuna, yellowfin, and dolphin topping the list of good catches. The annual **Game Fishing Tournament** is held in late January. Half-day and full-day excursions are available, plus tours to Sandy Island, Carriacou, and the Grenadines. Your hotel can help you charter a fishing boat.

Golf The Grenada Golf Club in Grand Anse (tel. 809/444–4128) has an 18-hole golf course that charges $16 for greens fees; your hotel will make arrangements for you.

Sailing, Diving, **The Moorings** (tel. 800/535–7289 in the United States; 800/633–
and Snorkeling 7348 in Canada) has taken over Secret Harbour on the southeast shore, added some of its finest charter yachts, and combined Shore 'n' Sail programs developed by America's cup racer Steve Colgate for beginning and experienced sailors.

You can rent 32- to 45-foot yachts, with or without crew, from **Go Vacations** at the Spice Island Marine Services (tel. 809/444–4924; from the United States, 800/387–3998). Diving in this area is excellent, with visibility as much as 200 feet. Hundreds of varieties of fish and more than 40 species of coral await underwater explorers. The best snorkeling is found around Carriacou's offshore islands. A superb spot for scuba diving is at the site of the largest shipwreck in the Caribbean, the *Bianca C*, a cruise ship that caught fire and sank in 1961. It settled in waters more than 100 feet deep and is now home to giant turtles, spotted eagle rays with 15-foot wingspans, and a 350-pound grouper that lives in the ship's smokestack.

Dive Grenada at Grand Anse Beach (Ramada Renaissance, tel. 809/444–4371 or 809/444–4372, ext. 638, fax 809/444–4800) offers a variety of scuba courses, as well as certification for novices. It also takes expert divers to the reefs and shipwrecks.

Swimming Take your pick from Grenada's 45 beaches and secluded coves, but don't miss Grand Anse Beach.

Other Water Sports The major hotels on Grand Anse Beach have water-sports centers where you can rent small sailboats, Windsurfers, and Sunfish equipment. The centers are located in front of the hotels. Your hotel can make arrangements for you, or you can call one of the major hotels for information.

Tennis Several hotels have tennis courts that are free to their guests, including **Calabash** (tel. 809/444–4234), **Secret Harbour** (tel. 809/444–4548), **Coyaba** (tel. 809/444–4129), **Spice Island Inn** (tel. 809/444–4258), **Ramada Renaissance** (tel. 809/444–4371), **Coral Cove** (809/444–4217), and **Twelve Degrees North** (tel. 809/444–4580). If there are no courts where you're staying, you can play at some private clubs on the island. Your hotel desk clerk can contact them for you.

Shopping

The best souvenirs in Grenada are little spice baskets filled with cinnamon, nutmeg, mace, bay leaf, vanilla, and ginger. You can find them in practically every shop. Vendors who stroll the beach in Grand Anse also sell spice baskets as well as fabric dolls, T-shirts, hats, fans, visors woven from green palm, and

black-coral jewelry. (Be aware that environmental groups discourage tourists from buying coral that is designated as endangered species because the reefs are not always harvested
carefully.) Shops are open weekdays 8–4. Many are closed
noon–1. Saturday hours are 8–noon. Shops are generally
closed Sunday, but some make exceptions when cruise ships
are in port.

Good Buys **The Yellow Poui Art Gallery** (Cross Street, tel. 809/440–3001)
St. George's offers the most serious art finds, with canvases from Grenada,
Jamaica, Guyana, and Trinidad and offerings by overseas artists who have settled here. Prices range from $2 to $2,000 in
this excellent creation by James and Corry Rudin. In a less serious mood, **Gifts Remembered** (Cross St., tel. 809/440–2482)
has prints of island scenes, books, and handmade necklaces for
a pittance. **Spice Island Perfumes** on the Carenage (tel. 809/
440–2006) is a treasure trove of local perfumes, body oils, natural extracts of spices and herbs, shampoos, suntan oils and lotions, teas, and spices. **Bon Voyage,** also on the Carenage (tel.
809/440–4217), carries batiks. **Tikal** (Young St., tel. 809/440–
2310) is pricey but worth it for exquisite handicrafts and fashions, both local and imported.

Grand Anse In Grand Anse, the **Grand Anse Shopping Complex** houses **The
Gift Shop,** an outlet for such luxury items as watches, leather
goods, fine jewelry, imported crystal and china, and framed
prints, all at competitive prices, and **Imagine,** which specializes
in island handicrafts, including batik fabrics. The complex also
has a clothing boutique for children and adults, with sportswear, novelty T-shirts, bathing suits, and some English wool
sweaters; a record shop; and a shoe store.

At press time, the new **Le Marquis Shopping Center** had just
opened its doors: a doctor's office, several boutiques, a fast-
food canteen, and a hair salon will soon be in full swing.

Heading toward the village of St. Paul's, the **Comahogne Gallery** on the main road is the studio-home of sculptor John
Pivott.

Carriacou In L'Esterre on Carriacou, hand-painted signs announce,
"This way to the great artist," **Canute Calliste.** If you get lost,
one of his many (more than 20) grandchildren will lead the way.
Works by Calliste are also available at the Carriacou Museum,
as are the creations of Frankie Francis.

Dining

Unlike most Caribbean islands, which have a scarcity of fresh
produce, Grenada has everything from cabbages and tomatoes
to bananas, mangoes, papaya (called pawpaw), plantains, mel-
ons, callaloo (similar to spinach), breadfruits, oranges, tanger-
ines, limes, christophines (similar to squash), and avocados—
the list is endless. In addition, fresh seafood of all kinds, including lobster and oyster, is also plentiful. Conch, known here as
lambi, is very popular and appears on most menus in some
form, but usually as a stew. Be sure to try one of the exotic ice
creams made from avocado or nutmeg. Almost all the Grenadian restaurants serve local dishes, which are varied enough to
be continually interesting.

Rum punches are served everywhere, but no two places make
them exactly alike. The local beer, Carib, is also very popular.

Highly recommended restaurants are indicated by a star ★.

Category	Cost*
Expensive	over $40
Moderate	$20–$40
Inexpensive	under $20

per person, excluding drinks, service, and sales tax (10%)

Grenada **The Calabash.** The open-air restaurant here is small and pretty, surrounded by palms and tropical flowers. There is a fixed-price dinner and menu each evening that may include fillet of kingfish duglere with roast potatoes, mixed vegetables, and fried plaintains or chicken with ginger and chive sauce, accompanied by a salad and cauliflower in mustard sauce. Cheese and biscuits with coffee, tea, or cocoa top off the meal. *L'Anse aux Epines, tel. 809/444–4234. Reservations suggested. AE, MC, V. Expensive.*

★ **La Belle Creole.** This restaurant is celebrated for its creative nouvelle West Indian cuisine and wraparound hilltop view of St. George's. The lunch and dinner menus are always changing, but if you're lucky, there will be an appetizer made from Grenadian caviar (roe of the white sea urchin), soursop mousse, or lobster-egg flan. Entrées may be stuffed baked rainbow runner, Creole saffron pork chops, or lobster à la Creole. The Sunday barbecue features many of the delicate dishes and live entertainment. It is worth noting that the graciousness with which you are served at this restaurant would impress even the most jaded traveler. *Blue Horizons Cottage Hotel, Morne Rouge, St. George's, tel. 809/444–4316. Reservations required for nonhotel guests. AE, MC, V. Expensive.*

Red Crab. This is a favorite meeting and eating spot (especially on Saturday nights) where guests dine in a relaxed pub or outside under trees and stars, although the food itself is not exemplary and remains overpriced. The accent is on fresh seafood, local lobster in particular, but the spicy chicken and grilled meats are worth a try. Hot garlic bread comes with all orders. *L'Anse aux Epines (near the Calabash Hotel), tel. 809/444–4424. AE, MC, V. Expensive.*

★ **Spice Island Inn.** The dining room, open on three sides, is just a few steps from the beach. (Guests at the hotel can opt to eat on their patios.) Whatever ambience you choose, Spice Island can be relied on for impeccable service. The Wednesday-night Grenadian buffet is exceptional and a great way to sample the various types of local seafood and salads. Retire to the dining area's adjacent bar for an after-dinner drink without giving up the sound of surf or views of the horizon. *Grand Anse, tel. 809/444–4258 or 444–4423. Reservations required late Dec.–mid-Apr. AE, D, MC, V. Expensive.*

★ **Betty Mascoll's Great House.** Although it's a one-hour drive from St. George's, this restaurant is definitely worth the trip. The owner, Mrs. Mascoll, serves only lunch—and what a lunch! The buffet usually includes her legendary pepperpot, a stew of pork, oxtail, and other meats, rumored to have been bubbling for years. The rum punches, fragrant with fresh nutmeg, are truly intoxicating. *St. Patrick's Parish, near Sauteurs, tel. 809/440–9330. Reservations required. No credit cards. Moderate.*

The Boatyard. Smack in the middle of a marina, this restaurant is a lively place, filled with embassy personnel and expatriates. Lunches include burgers, fish and chips, and deep-fried shrimp. Dinner features club steaks, lobster, and different types of meat and seafood brochettes. In season (late Dec.–mid-Apr.) there's a steel band on Saturday night, jazz on Sunday, and disco music on Friday night. *L'Anse aux Epines, tel. 809/444–4662. MC, V. Moderate.*

★ **Canboulay.** Two Trinidadians, Erik and Gina-Lee Johnson, designed this recent culinary addition that now outranks its predecessors at the well-established hotels. The founding, and most charming couple present the best food with the most subtle and sophisticated use of local produce on the island. Menus change every few months, so, sad to say, the tomato fettucini topped with garlic and lemon-flavored fish sauce may not be featured when you arrive at this pink-washed converted residence, trimmed in bright green and cobalt blue. The good news: Something as good or better will be. Consider fresh tuna with a tangy citrus pepper sauce or seasoned shrimp rolled in coconut and a light beer batter, then fried and served with a boost of sweet pineapple relish. Desserts here will inspire the most flaccid taste buds; the Alamanda Ice is a flower-shaped cookie filled with vanilla ice cream and passion fruit, all of which wades delicately in guava, carambola, and cherry coulis. (One note of caution: Opt for sorbet over salad for your intermediate course since greens in Grenada still appear to be pushing middle age.) *Morne Rouge, St. George's, tel. 809/444–4401. Reservations suggested. Dress: casual to elegant. AE, D, MC, V. Open for lunch and dinner weekdays, dinner only Sat., closed Sun. Moderate.*

The Nutmeg. Fresh seafood is the specialty of this second-floor restaurant that has a great view of the harbor. Try the grilled turtle steaks, lobsters, or shrimp. *The Carenage, St. George's, tel. 809/440–2539. Dress: informal. AE, D, MC, V. Moderate.*

Rudolf's. This informal, publike place offers fine West Indian fare. Skip the attempts at haute cuisine "Viennoise" or "Parisienne," and enjoy the crab back, lambi, and delectable nutmeg ice cream. This is *the* place for eavesdropping on local gossip. Even for Grenada the rum punches are lethal. *The Carenage, St. George's, tel. 809/440–2241. Closed Sun. No credit cards. Moderate.*

Cot Bam. Wedged between the Coyaba Hotel and the Medical School on Grand Anse beach, this bar/restaurant/night spot with a tin roof and bamboo railings is a place to kick back and enjoy. Order a chicken *roti* (curried meat, potatoes, and beans wrapped in a giant tortilla) served with coleslaw for E.C.$6 and a Carib beer, and you're set for the evening. It's within walking distance of all the Grand Anse hotels; the staff is a delight; and you can hop over in your shorts after a long day at the beach to dance or socialize with abandon. *Grand Anse, tel. 809/444–2050. Open Sun.–Thurs. 10 AM–midnight, Fri.–Sat. 10 AM–3 AM. AE. Inexpensive.*

★ **Mama's.** This restaurant is more like a diner, West Indian style and very charming. One of Mama's daughters will set generous helpings of local specialties before you—probably some roast turtle, lobster salad, christophine salad, cabbage salad, or fried plantain, as well as such exotica as armadillo, opossum, and sea urchin. Menus don't list prices, but the broad buffet offerings are available at a fixed E.C.$45 per person. Request the iguana in advance. You will not leave hungry. *Lagoon Rd., St.*

George's, tel. 809/440–1459. Reservations required. No credit cards. Inexpensive.

Carriacou **Barba's Oyster Shell.** This place is elemental, but it is the only one that offers Carriacou's rare and succulent mangrove oysters. *Tyrrel Bay, Carriacou, tel. 809/443–7454. No credit cards. Inexpensive.*

Scrapers. Good things are happening at Tyrrel Bay. Scrapers serves up lobster, conch, and an assortment of fresh catches, along with an artless spirit and decor seasoned with occasional calypsonian serenades (owner Steven Gay "Scraper" is a pro). Order a rum punch and exercise your right to do nothing. *Tyrrel Bay, Carriacou, tel. 809/443–7403. AE, D, MC, V. Inexpensive.*

Lodging

Grenada's accommodations range from simply furnished kitchenette suites to suites representing Caribbean-style elegance. There are no pretentious hotels—Grenada is a simple place, and its hotels have been furnished in "casual tropical" decor. Most of the hotels are owned and operated by Grenadians; those that aren't are usually run by British or American expatriates who thrive on the simplicity of Grenadian life. The hotels tend to be small (10 to 20 rooms in most cases), but they exude a sense of intimacy, with friendly managers or owners.

For confirmation on reservations at any of the 24 members of the **Grenada Hotel Association,** call, in the United States or Canada, 800/223–9815; in New York State, 212/545–8469.

Most posted daily room rates at Grenadian hotels are quoted in U.S. currency and represent the room rate only, without meals. Visitors can often opt for CP or MAP, depending on the season. The plans specified in individual listings, below, apply year-round unless otherwise noted. Prices for the summer are discounted by 20% to 40%.

Highly recommended lodgings are indicated by a star ★.

Category	Cost*
Very Expensive	over $200
Expensive	$150–$200
Moderate	$100–$150
Inexpensive	under $100

**All prices are for a standard double room for two during high season, excluding 8% tax and a 10% service charge.*

Hotels **The Calabash.** This all-suite hotel is set on a wide green lawn
Grenada overlooking a curved beach, a yacht harbor, and charter-boat anchorage in Prickly Bay, L'Anse aux Epines. The deluxe suites have their own private swimming pool. You'll have to live with the noise generated by the nearby Point Salines Airport: Early-morning flights can bounce you out of bed. *Box 382, St. George's, tel. 809/444–4334, fax 809/444–4804. 28 suites. Facilities: restaurant, beach bar, pool, water-sports center, tennis. AE, MC, V. BP, MAP; off season, BP and MAP. Very Expensive.*

★ **Secret Harbour.** The Moorings (which specializes in sailing vacations) has taken over this deluxe resort, and it's an ideal match. The hotel has oversize rooms tucked into Mediterranean-style villas on a bluff overlooking Mt. Hartman Bay. Casual elegance and understated luxury define this delightful property, the island's most romantic. Outside, yachts dock at the door (all with professional crew), ready for a day at sea, or, if you opt for the hotel's Club Mariner plans, four nights ashore and three cruising the offshore islands. Secret Harbour may not lie on Grand Anse beach, but its tropical gardens, marina, and windward position (this side of the island receives less rainfall than does the west coast) boost its desirability quotient to the top. *Box 11, St. George's, tel. 809/444–4439 or 800/334–2435, and outside continental U.S. 813/538–8760, fax 809/444–4819. 20 rooms. Facilities: restaurant, lounge, tennis, beach with bar, pool, sailboats (day sailers, bareboat to crewed). AE, DC, MC, V. EP, MAP. Very Expensive.*

★ **Spice Island Inn.** The suites here are sumptuous, each with a supersize interior whirlpool and/or a spa-Jacuzzi or a 16- by 20-foot private swimming pool inside a walled garden. There are over 1,600 feet of sprawling beach (literally at your doorstep if you're in one of the beachfront cottages) with sea-grape, almond, and palm trees for shade and small tables for afternoon tea. The rooms are well decorated in soft pastels, with telephones, minibars, and minirefrigerators. The luxurious bathrooms are the size of a small parking garage: The showers measure almost 16 square feet, and adjacent whirlpool tubs (with skylight overhead) in the beachfront cottages are capable of submerging a family of four. Climb out and dry off with a 3 by 5½-foot terry-cloth bath sheet. It would be a mistake to bid automatically for a beachfront cottage when the private pool suites are so desirable; some are spanking new, and they all front finely manicured courtyards. You'll still be very near the sea, with your views enhanced by lush green vines of golden-yellow, trumpet-shaped allamanda or hibiscus spiraling up the garden trellises. *Box 6, Grand Anse, St. George's, tel. 809/444–4258 or 800/223–9815, fax 809/444–4807. 39 whirlpool suites and 17 private pool suites. Facilities: tennis courts, watersports center, restaurant, lounge, boutique, fitness center, entertainment most nights, 18-hole golf course nearby. AE, MC, V. MAP. Very Expensive.*

Coyaba. *Coyaba* means "heaven" in the Arawak Indian language. All the rooms at this beachfront hotel have patios, satellite TVs, radios, telephones, and hair dryers, but you probably won't spend much time there: Coyaba's indoor and outdoor sports facilities are extensive. In addition, some of the best restaurants and night spots are within walking distance or a quick cab ride away. *Box 336, Grand Anse, St. George's, tel. 809/444–4129 or 800/223–9815, fax 809/444–4808. 40 double rooms. Facilities: pool with swim-up bar, tennis courts, water-sports center, restaurant, bar, lounge. AE, D, DC, MC, V. EP, CP, BP, MAP, FAP. Expensive.*

Ramada Renaissance Hotel. Since Ramada took over this resort, it has spent $15 million on renovation. Directly across from the Grand Anse shopping center, the hotel is the island's largest, but "unit" aptly describes its accommodations: They still suffer from an American motel decor. The ceilings are low, the rooms less spacious than competing resorts', and the interior spaces tend to be dark. Still all rooms have king-size or extra-large beds and satellite TVs, and the Ramada is also the hub of a Grand Anse night out—sooner or later everyone seems to end up here for drinks. *Box 441, Grand Anse, St. George's, tel. 809/444–4371, fax 809/444–4800. 184 doubles, 2 luxury suites. Facilities: 2 restaurants, lounge, pool, tennis, barber shop/beauty salon, 2 gift shops, hair dryers in rooms. AE, DC, MC, V. EP, MAP. Expensive.*

★ **Blue Horizons Cottage Hotel.** This comfortable hotel appointed in handsome mahogany furnishings is a very good value; it is set among the palms around a large, sunny lawn and swimming pool on 6½ acres. Grand Anse Beach is a six-minute walk down the hill, where the sister hotel, the Spice Island Inn, sprawls along 1,600 feet of beach. Water sports are free for guests at either hotel. Guests may eat at either property, and evening entertainment alternates between the two. *Box 41, Grand Anse, St. George's, tel. 809/444–4316, 809/444–4592 or 800/223–9815 in the U.S., fax 809/444–2815. 32 suites with terraces. Facilities: restaurant, 2 bars, lounge, pool. AE, MC, V. EP, CP, MAP. Moderate.*

The Flamboyant Hotel and Cottages. The charming Lawrence Lambert, managing director of the fifth largest hotel in Grenada, may just convince you that crab racing is the greatest diplomatic strategy since the creation of the United Nations. Once a week, you'll discover a wildly diverse score of jovial citizens—Italian, German, American, British, Grenadian, or Dutch—hunkering down on the terrace of the Flamboyant's Beachside restaurant as they urge their chosen sidestepping Secretariat to the finish line. You may think it's corny, but the most bah-humbug characters get sucked into the heat of competition. The rooms at the Flamboyant are simply furnished—there's nothing lavish here in appointments or amenities—but the views from every unit are quite impressive. The hotel's prime hillside site overlooking Grand Anse Beach, a mere 10-minute drive from downtown St. George's, along with the benefits of its new, energetic management, guarantee a pleasurable stay. *Box 214, St. George's, tel. 809/444–4247, fax 809/444–1234. 38 units include 16 doubles, 20 suites (with kitchenettes), and 2 cottages. Facilities: freshwater swimming pool, bar, restaurant, satellite TV, free snorkeling equipment. AE, D, MC, V. EP, BP, MAP. Inexpensive.*

La Sagesse Nature Center. Set on a bay 10 miles from Point Salines Airport, the center has a guest house with basic but spacious rooms. There are an old sugar mill and rum distillery at the entrance. Mangroves, a salt-pond bird sanctuary, and hiking trails provide a peaceful, unspoiled setting. La Sagesse is a best bet for nature lovers or for those who don't fancy a rousing night life. Though it's away from St. George's and Grand Anse, breakfast, lunch, and dinner are available here, and most of the rooms have small kitchens. Mike Meranski, the American owner/manager, cheerfully runs guests into town for grocery supplies and shopping when he takes his daughter to school. Of course he's cheerful—he lives on a secluded beach in a paradisiacal setting. *Box 44, St. David's, tel. 809/444–6458, fax 809/444–6458. 4 double rooms. Facilities: restaurant, bar, beach, satellite TV. MC, V. EP. Inexpensive.*

Carriacou **Cassada Bay Resort.** This resort doesn't just offer a breathtaking panorama of the ocean, you have the use of a private island for snorkeling and windsurfing, and some of the finest lemonade this side of the equator. Cabins here, on the south side of Carriacou, shimmy down the side of a hilltop overlooking the sea and offer an unadorned, but peaceful, sea-sprayed hideaway. *Carriacou, tel. 809/443-7494, fax 809/443-7672. 20 doubles. Facilities: restaurant, bar, water-sports center. AE, DC, MC, V. EP, CP, MAP. Moderate.*

Silver Beach Resort. This 18-room hotel is tucked away on stretches of pristine beach on Carriacou, Grenada's sister isle. Totally refurbished, all rooms have private patios and ocean views. An owner-managed hotel, it has the biggest scuba facilities in the Grenadines and, incidentally, is the best place on the island for a hearty, early-morning breakfast in its open-air restaurant by the water. *Silver Beach, Carriacou, tel. 809/443-7337, fax 809/443-7165. 12 doubles (2 with kitchenettes) and 6 cottages. Facilities: snorkeling, windsurfing, spearfishing, day trip to offshore islets, boutique, gift shop, floating dock, complimentary moorings, docking facilities, complimentary showers and garbage disposal for yachts, complete scuba certification course, in-house bus, complimentary transfers, car rental. AE, MC, V. EP, CP, MAP. Inexpensive–Moderate.*

Apartment Hotels These fully equipped units often represent a great Inexpensive–Moderate alternative, especially for families. Contact the Tourist Office for additional listings.

Twelve Degrees North is top of the line (and most expensive), with eight one- and two-bedroom apartments, maid service (which includes cooking your breakfast and lunch), private beach, pool, and tennis. A minimum stay of one week is required during high season, and children under 12 are not allowed. *Box 241, Lance aux Epines, St. George's, tel. 809/444-4580, fax 809/444-4580. AE, V.*

Wave Crest Holiday Apartments. Joyce Dabrieo runs a tight ship. She lives here with her husband (owner-managed properties make all the difference in the world) and takes great pains to keep all 20 fully furnished and sunny rooms spotless and well maintained. Wave Crest, an excellent value, is a five minutes' walk to Grand Anse beach. *Box 278, St. George's, tel. 809/444-4116, fax 809/444-4847. 14 1-bedroom apartments, 2 2-bedroom apartments, 4 double rooms. AE, D, MC, V.*

Villa and Private-Home Rentals Several local agencies handle rentals of villas and private homes: The most reliable is **Grenada Property Management** (Melville St., St. George's, tel. 809/440-1896). In-season rates range from about $600 a week for a two-bedroom home with a pool to about $3,500 for a six-bedroom home on the beach.

Nightlife

Grenada's nightlife centers on the hotel lounges and bars. During winter, many of the hotel lounges have steel, reggae, and pop bands in the evenings. **Spice Island Inn, The Calabash, Coyaba,** and the **Ramada Renaissance** are among the most lively (*see* Lodging, *above*). Check with your hotel or the Tourist Information Office to find out where various bands are performing on a given night.

Fantazia 2001 (Gem Apartments premises, Morne Beach, tel. 809/444-4224) is a popular disco on Morne Rouge Beach where soca, reggae, and cadance are local steps, in addition to international tapes. There is a small cover charge on Friday and Saturday nights. **Le Sucrier** (Grand Anse, tel. 800/444-1068) has reopened in the Sugar Mill on Wednesday, Thursday, Friday, and Saturday from 9 PM to 3 AM, with live jazz on Thursday and "oldies" night on Wednesday. Friday night only is "the" night at the **Boatyard Restaurant and Bar,** (Lance aux Epines beach in the Marina, tel. 809/444–4662), from 11 PM till sunup, with international discs spun by a smooth-talkin' local DJ. Check out **Cot Bam** (tel. 809/444–2050) on Grand Anse Beach for a night of dancing, dining, and socializing. The place is open until 3 AM on Friday and Saturday, and it definitely hits the spot for visitors who want something simple, lively, and friendly for little money. Don't forget the **Beachside Terrace** (St. George's, tel. 809/444–4247) at the Flamboyant Hotel in Grand Anse. Crab racing on Monday nights, a live steel band on Wednesdays, and a beach barbecue with calypso music on Friday evenings draw an international set who savor a casual, unpretentious environment.

Brave the twin otter to Carriacou (you may note the solo pilot becoming deeply immersed in a Sidney Sheldon novel), then buy yourself a drink at the **Hillsborough Bar** (Carriacou, tel. 809/443–7932). The bar is a small, white, flat-topped structure on the main street of the island's seat of government—a town populated by no more than about 600 citizens—and one Edward Primus owns the place. Rum flows freely.

13 Guadeloupe

Updated by
Nigel Fisher

It's a steamy hot Saturday in mid-August. There may be a tropical depression brewing somewhere to the west. It's that time of year. But the mood in Pointe-à-Pitre, Guadeloupe's commercial center, is anything but depressing. Amid music and laughter, women adorned with gold jewelry and the traditional madras and foulard parade through the streets. Balanced on their heads are huge baskets decorated with miniature kitchen utensils and filled with mangoes, papayas, breadfruits, christophines, and other island edibles. The procession wends its way to the Cathédrale de St-Pierre et St-Paul, where a high mass is celebrated. A five-hour feast with music, song, and dance will follow.

The *Fête des Cuisinières* (Cooks' Festival) takes place annually in honor of St. Laurent, patron saint of cooks. The parading *cuisinières* are the island's women chefs, an honored group. This festival gives you a tempting glimpse of one of Guadeloupe's stellar attractions—its cuisine. The island's more than 200 restaurants serve some of the best food in all the Caribbean.

But there is more here than meets the palate. Night owls and nature enthusiasts, hikers and bikers, scuba divers, sailors, mountain climbers, beachcombers, and hammock potatoes all can indulge themselves in Guadeloupe. Driving around the island is the best way to fully appreciate its diversity.

Sugar, not tourism, is Guadeloupe's primary source of income. As a result, the island's attractions are less commercialized than are those of neighboring isles. However, Guadeloupe is eager to pull in a larger share of the tourist trade, and each year more field workers opt for jobs in resorts and restaurants. Currently, about 10% of the work force is engaged in the tourist trade, compared with the situation in St. Maarten, where the whole island is sold to tourists. At harvesttime in late January, the fields teem with workers cutting the sugarcane, and the roads are clogged with trucks taking the cane to distilleries. French is the official language here. But even if your tongue twirls easily around a few French phrases, you will sometimes receive a bewildered response. The Guadeloupeans' Creole patois greatly affects their French pronunciation. However, their friendliness allows for repeated attempts at communication, so eventually you'll be understood. If not, don't despair—most hotels and many of the restaurants have some English-speaking staff.

Guadeloupe looks like a giant butterfly resting on the sea between Antigua and Dominica. Its two wings—Basse-Terre and Grande-Terre—are the two largest islands in the 659-square-mile Guadeloupe archipelago, which includes the little islands of Marie-Galante, La Désirade, and Les Saintes, as well as French St. Martin and St. Barthélemy to the north. Mountainous 312-square-mile Basse-Terre (lowland) lies on the leeward side, where the winds are "lower." Smaller, flatter Grande-Terre (218 square miles) gets the "bigger" winds on its windward side. The Rivière Salée, a four-mile seawater channel flowing between the Caribbean and the Atlantic, forms the "spine" of the butterfly. A drawbridge over the channel connects the two islands.

If you're seeking resort hotels, casinos, and white sandy beaches, your target is Grande-Terre. By contrast, Basse-

Terre's Natural Park, laced with mountain trails and washed by waterfalls and rivers, is a 74,100-acre haven for hikers, nature lovers, and anyone yearning to peer into the steaming crater of an active volcano. If you want to get away from it all, head for the islands of Les Saintes, La Désirade, and Marie-Galante.

Christopher Columbus "discovered" Guadeloupe on November 4, 1493, when he landed at Ste-Marie on the southern shore of Basse-Terre and named the island Santa Marie de Guadeloupe de Estremadura. The Carib inhabitants, who had already polished off the peaceful Arawaks, had no intention of relinquishing the land they called *Karukera* (Island of Beautiful Waters). The Spaniards gave up on the island in 1604. In 1635, the French laid claim to it. They ran the Caribs off, brought in African slaves to work their sugar plantations, and in 1674 Guadeloupe was annexed by France. The British also had designs on the island, and they gained control of it from 1759 until 1763, when they relinquished it in exchange for all French rights to Canada. During the French Revolution battles broke out between royalists and revolutionaries on the island. In 1794, Britain responded to the call from Guadeloupe royalists to come to their aid, and that same year France dispatched Victor Hugues to sort things out. (In virtually every town and village you'll run across a "Victor Hugues" street, boulevard, or park.) After his troops banished the British, Hugues issued a decree abolishing slavery and guillotined recalcitrant planters. The ones who managed to keep their heads fled to Louisiana or hid in the hills of Grande-Terre, where their descendants now live. Hugues was soon relieved of his command, slavery was reestablished by Napoleon, and the French and English continued to battle over the island. The 1815 Treaty of Paris restored Guadeloupe to France, and in 1848, due largely to the efforts of Alsatian Victor Schoelcher, slavery was permanently abolished. The island has been a full-fledged *département* of France since 1946, and in 1974 it was elevated to a *région*, administered by a prefect appointed from Paris by the Minister of the Interior.

Before You Go

Tourist Information For information contact the **French West Indies Tourist Board** by calling France-on-Call at 900/990–0040 (50¢ per minute) or write to the **French Government Tourist Office**, 610 5th Ave., New York, NY 10020; 9454 Wilshire Blvd., Beverly Hills, CA 90212; 645 N. Michigan Ave., Chicago, IL 60611; 2305 Cedar Spring Rd., Dallas TX 75201. In Canada contact the French Government Tourist Office, 1981 McGill College Ave., Suite 490, Montreal, P.Q. H3A 2W9, tel. 514/288–4264 or 1 Dundas St. W, Suite 2405, Toronto, Ont. M5G 1Z3, tel. 416/593–4723 or 800/361–9099. In the United Kingdom the tourist office can be reached at 178 Piccadilly, London, United Kingdom W1V 0AL, tel. 071/499–6911.

Arriving and Departing
By Plane **American Airlines** (tel. 800/433–7300) is usually the most convenient, with year-round daily flights from more than 100 U.S. cities direct to San Juan and nonstop connections to Guadeloupe via American Eagle. **Minerve Airlines** (tel. 800/765–6065), a French charter carrier, has flights Friday–Sunday from New York during the December–March peak season. **Air Canada** (tel. 800/422–6232) flies direct from Montreal and Toronto. **Air France** (tel. 800/237–2747) flies nonstop from Par-

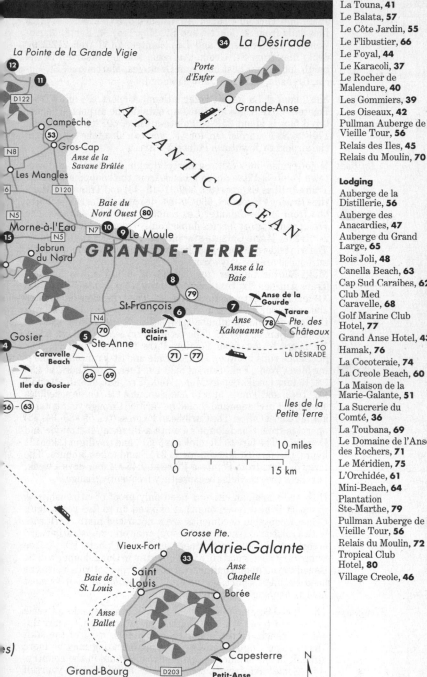

La Touna, **41**
Le Balata, **57**
Le Côte Jardin, **55**
Le Flibustier, **66**
Le Foyal, **44**
Le Karacoli, **37**
Le Rocher de
Malendure, **40**
Les Gommiers, **39**
Les Oiseaux, **42**
Pullman Auberge de la
Vieille Tour, **56**
Relais des Iles, **45**
Relais du Moulin, **70**

Lodging
Auberge de la
Distillerie, **56**
Auberge des
Anacardies, **47**
Auberge du Grand
Large, **65**
Bois Joli, **48**
Canella Beach, **63**
Cap Sud Caraïbes, **62**
Club Med
Caravelle, **68**
Golf Marine Club
Hotel, **77**
Grand Anse Hotel, **43**
Hamak, **76**
La Cocoteraie, **74**
La Creole Beach, **60**
La Maison de la
Marie-Galante, **51**
La Sucrerie du
Comté, **36**
La Toubana, **69**
Le Domaine de l'Anse
des Rochers, **71**
Le Méridien, **75**
L'Orchidée, **61**
Mini-Beach, **64**
Plantation
Ste-Marthe, **79**
Pullman Auberge de la
Vieille Tour, **56**
Relais du Moulin, **72**
Tropical Club
Hotel, **80**
Village Creole, **46**

is and Fort-de-France, and has direct service from Miami, San Juan, and Port-au-Prince. **Air Guadeloupe** (tel. 599/5–44212) flies daily from St. Martin and St. Maarten, St. Barts, Marie-Galante, La Désirade, and Les Saintes. **LIAT** (tel. 212/269–6925) flies from St. Croix, Antigua, and St. Maarten in the north and is your best bet from Dominica, Martinique, St. Lucia, Grenada, Barbados, and Trinidad.

From the Airport You'll land at La Raizet International Airport, 2½ miles from Pointe-à-Pitre. Cabs are lined up outside the airport. The metered fare is about 35F to Pointe-à-Pitre, 60F to Gosier, and 170F to St-François. Or, for 5F, you can also take a bus from the airport to downtown Pointe-à-Pitre.

By Boat Major cruise lines call regularly, docking at berths in downtown Pointe-à-Pitre about a block from the shopping district. **Trans Antilles Express** (tel. 590/91–13–43) and **Transport Maritime Brudey Frères** (tel. 590/90–04–48) provide ferry service to and from Marie-Galante, Les Saintes, and La Désirade. The *Jetcat* and *Madras* ferries depart daily from the pier at Pointe-à-Pitre for Marie Galante starting at 8 AM (check the schedule). The trip takes one hour, and the fare is 160F round-trip. Recently introduced are one-day excursions from St-François operated by **Multi Marine Charter** (tel. 590/83–32–67). For Les Saintes, Trans Antilles Express connects daily from Pointe-à-Pitre at 8 AM and from Terre-de-Haut at 4 PM. The trip takes 60 minutes and costs 160F round-trip. The *Princess Caroline* leaves Trois Rivières for the 30-minute trip to Les Saintes Mon.–Sat. at 8:30 AM, Sun. at 7:30 AM. The return ferry leaves at 3 PM. Allow 1½ hours to get from Pointe-à-Pitre to Trois Rivières. The *Socimade* runs between La Désirade and St-François, departing Mon., Wed., Fri.–Sun. at 8:30 AM, Tues. 3 PM, Thurs. at 4:30 PM. Return ferries depart Mon., Wed., Fri., Sat. at 6:15 AM and 4 PM, Tues. and Thurs. at 6:15 AM, Sun. at 4 PM. These schedules are subject to change and should be verified through your hotel or at the Tourist Office. The **Caribbean Express** (tel. 590/83–04–43) operates from Guadeloupe's Pointe-à-Pitre to Martinique and Dominica. The fare to Dominica is 305F, and the flight takes 2½ hours; the fare to Martinique is 315F and takes 5 hours. The ferry departs from Pointe-à-Pitre at 7:45 AM four days a week, but check the schedules because they frequently change.

Passports and Visas U.S. and Canadian citizens need only proof of citizenship. A passport is best (even one that expired up to five years ago). Other acceptable documents are a notarized birth certificate with a raised seal (not a photocopy) or a voter registration card accompanied by a government-authorized photo ID. A free temporary visa, good only for your stay in Guadeloupe, will be issued to you upon your arrival at the airport. British citizens need a valid passport, but no visa. In addition, all visitors must hold an ongoing or return ticket.

Language The official language is French. Everyone also speaks a Creole patois, which you won't be able to understand even if you're fluent in French. In the major tourist hotels, most of the staff knows some English. However, communicating may be more difficult in the smaller hotels and restaurants in the countryside. Some taxi drivers speak a little English. Arm yourself with a phrase book, a dictionary, patience, and a sense of humor.

Precautions Put your valuables in the hotel safe. Don't leave them unattended in your room or on the beach. Keep an eye out for motorcyclists riding double. They sometimes play the notorious game of veering close to the sidewalk and snatching shoulder bags. It isn't a good idea to walk around Pointe-à-Pitre at night because it's almost deserted after dark. If you rent a car, always lock it with luggage and valuables stashed out of sight.

The rough Atlantic waters off the northeast coast of Grande-Terre are dangerous for swimming.

Ask permission before taking a picture of an islander, and don't be surprised if the answer is a firm "No." Guadeloupeans are also deeply religious and traditional. Don't offend them by wearing short shorts or swimwear off the beach.

Staying in Guadeloupe

Important Addresses **Tourist Information:** The **Office Departmental du Tourism** has offices in Pointe-à-Pitre (23 rue Delgrès, corner rue Schoelcher, tel. 590/82–09–30), in Basse-Terre (Maison du Port, tel. 590/81–24–83), and in St-François (Ave. de l'Europe, tel. 590/88–48–74). All offices are open weekdays 8–5, Saturday 8–noon. A tourist information booth is at the airport.

Emergencies **Police:** In Pointe-à-Pitre (tel. 590/17 or 590/82–00–17), in Basse-Terre (tel. 590/81–11–55). **Fire:** In Pointe-à-Pitre (tel. 590/18 or 590/82–00–28), in Basse-Terre (tel. 590/81–19–22). **SOS Ambulance:** Tel. 590/82–89–33. **Hospitals:** There is a 24-hour emergency room at the main hospital, **Centre Hopitalier de Pointe-à-Pitre** (Abymes, tel. 590/82–98–80 or 590/82–88–88). There are 23 clinics and five hospitals located around the island. The Tourist Office or your hotel can assist you in locating an English-speaking doctor. **Pharmacies:** Pharmacies alternate in staying open around the clock. The Tourist Office or your hotel can help you locate the one that's on duty.

Currency Legal tender is the French franc, which comprises 100 centimes. At press time, U.S.$1 bought 5.00F and £1 bought 8.50F, but currencies fluctuate daily. Check the current rate of exchange. Some places accept U.S. dollars, but it's best to change your money into the local currency. Credit cards are accepted in most major hotels, restaurants, and shops, less so in smaller places and in the countryside. Prices are quoted here in U.S. dollars unless otherwise noted.

Taxes and Service Charges A *taxe de séjour* varies from hotel to hotel but never exceeds $1.50 per person, per day.

Most hotel prices include a 10%–15% service charge; if not—it will be added to your bill.

Restaurants are legally required to include 15% in the menu price. No additional gratuity is necessary. Tip skycaps and porters about 5F. Many cab drivers own their own cabs and don't expect a tip. You won't have any trouble ascertaining if a 10% tip is expected.

Guided Tours There are set fares for taxi tours to various points on the island. The Tourist Office or your hotel can arrange for an English-speaking taxi driver and even organize a small group for you to share the cost of the tour.

George-Marie Gabrielle (Pointe-à-Pitre, tel. 590/82–05–38) and **Petrelluzzi Travel** (Pointe-à-Pitre, tel. 590/82–82–30) both offer half- and full-day excursions around the island. A modern bus with an English-speaking guide will pick you up at your hotel.

At Raizet Airport, helicopter tours can be arranged through **Caraibe Air Tourisme** (tel. 590/91–61–24) and **Safari Tours** (tel. 590/84–06–74).

Organization des Guides de Montagne de la Caraibe, O.G.M.C., (Maison Forestière, Matouba, tel. 590/80–05–79) provides guides for hiking tours in the mountains.

Getting Around
Taxis Fares are regulated by the government and posted at the airport, at taxi stands, and at major hotels. During the day you'll pay about 35F from the airport to Pointe-à-Pitre, about 60F to Gosier, and about 170F to St-François. Between 9 PM and 7 AM, fares increase 40%. If your French is in working order, you can contact radio cabs at 590/82–15–09, 590/83–64–27, and 590/84–37–65.

Buses Modern public buses run from 5:30 AM to 7:30 PM. They stop along the road at bus stops and shelters marked *arrêtbus*, but you can also flag one down along the route.

Vespas or Bikes If you opt to tour the island by bike, you won't be alone. Biking is a major sport here (*see* Sports and the Outdoors, *below*, for rental information).

Vespas can be rented at **Vespa Sun** (Pointe-à-Pitre, tel. 590/82–17–80), **Location de Motos** (Meridien Hotel, St-François, tel. 590/88–51–00), and **Dingo Location Scooter** (Gosier, tel. 590/90–97–01).

Rental Cars Your valid driver's license will suffice for up to 20 days, after which you'll need an international driver's permit. Guadeloupe has 1,225 miles of excellent roads (marked as in Europe), and driving around Grande-Terre is relatively easy. On Basse-Terre it will take more effort to navigate the hairpin bends that twist through the mountains and around the eastern shore. Guadeloupeans are skillful drivers, but they do like to drive fast. Cars can be rented at **Avis** (tel. 590/82–33–47 or 800/331–1212), **Budget** (tel. 590/82–95–58 or 800/527–0700), **Hertz** (tel. 590/82–00–14 or 800/654–3131), and **National-Europcar** (tel. 590/82–50–51 or 800/468–0008). There are rental offices at the airport as well as at the major resort areas. Car rentals cost a bit more on Guadeloupe than on the other islands. Count on about $60 a day for a small rental car.

Telephones and Mail To call from the United States, dial 011 + 590 + the local six-digit number. (To call person-to-person, dial 01–590.) It is not possible to place collect or credit card calls to the United States from Guadeloupe. Coin-operated phones are rare but can be found in restaurants and cafés. If you need to make many calls outside of your hotel, purchase a *Telecarte* at the post office or other outlets marked *Telecarte en Vente Ici*. Telecartes look like credit cards and are used in special booths marked "Telecom." Local and international calls made with the cards are cheaper than operator-assisted calls.

To call the United States from Guadeloupe, dial 19 + 1 + the area code and phone number. To dial locally in Guadeloupe, simply dial the six-digit phone number.

Postcards to the United States cost 3.50F; letters up to 20 grams, 4.40F. Stamps can be purchased at the post office, *café-tabacs*, hotel newsstands, or souvenir shops. Postcards and letters to the United Kingdom cost 3.40F.

Opening and Closing Times Banks are open weekdays 8–noon and 2–4. Credit Agricole, Banque Populaire, and Société Générale de Banque aux Antilles have branches that are open Saturday. During the summer most banks are open 8–3. Banks close at noon the day before a legal holiday that falls during the week. As a rule, shops are open weekdays 8 or 8:30–noon and 2:30–6, but hours are flexible when cruise ships are in town.

Exploring Guadeloupe

Numbers in the margin correspond to points of interest on the Guadeloupe map.

Pointe-à-Pitre **Pointe-à-Pitre** is a city of some 100,000 people in the extreme ➊ southwest of Grande-Terre. It lies almost on the "backbone" of the butterfly, near the bridge that crosses the Salée River. In this bustling, noisy city, with its narrow streets, honking horns, and traffic jams, there is a faster pulse than in many other Caribbean capitals, though at night the city streets are deserted.

Life has not been easy for Pointe-à-Pitre. The city has suffered severe damage over the years as a result of earthquakes, fires, and hurricanes. The most recent damage was done in 1979 by Hurricane Frederick, in 1980 by Hurricane David, and in 1989 by Hurricane Hugo. Standing on boulevarde Frébault, you can see on one side the remaining French colonial structures and on the other the modern city. However, downtown is rejuvenating itself while maintaining its old charm. The recent completion of the Centre St-John Perse has transformed old warehouses into a new cruise-terminal complex comprising a hotel (the Hotel St-John), three restaurants, space for 80 shops, and the headquarters for Guadeloupe's Port Authority.

Stop at the Office of Tourism, in Place de la Victoire across from the quays where the cruise ships dock, to pick up maps and brochures. *Bonjour, Guadeloupe*, the free visitors' guide, is very useful. Outside the tourist office stalls take over the sidewalk, selling everything from clothes to kitchen utensils. Across the road alongside the harbor, a gaggle of colorfully dressed women sells fruits and vegetables.

When you leave the office, turn left, walk one block along rue Schoelcher, and turn right on rue Achille René-Boisneuf. Two more blocks will bring you to the **Musée St-John Perse.** The restored colonial house is dedicated to the Guadeloupean poet who won the 1960 Nobel Prize in Literature. (Nearby, at No. 54, rue René-Boisneuf, a plaque marks his birthplace.) The museum contains a complete collection of his poetry, as well as some of his personal effects. There are also works written about him and various mementos, documents, and photographs. *Corner rues Noizières and Achille René-Boisneuf, tel. 590/90–01–92. Admission: 10F. Open Mon.–Fri. 8–12:30 and 2:30–5:30, Sat. 8–12:30.*

Rues Noizières, Frébault, and Schoelcher are Pointe-à-Pitre's main shopping streets. In sharp contrast to the duty-free shops is the bustling **Marketplace,** which you'll find by backtracking one block from the museum and turning right on rue Frébault. Located between rues St-John Perse, Frébault, Schoelcher, and Peynier, the market is a cacophonous and colorful place where housewives bargain for papayas, breadfruits, christophines, tomatoes, and a vivid assortment of other produce.

Take a left at the corner of rues Schoelcher and Peynier. The **Musée Schoelcher** honors the memory of Victor Schoelcher, the 19th-century Alsatian abolitionist who fought slavery in the French West Indies. The museum contains many of his personal effects, and the exhibits trace his life and work. *24 rue Peynier, tel. 590/82–08–04. Admission: 5F. Open weekdays 9–noon and 2:30–5:30.*

Walk back along rue Peynier past the market for three blocks. You'll come to **Place de la Victoire,** surrounded by wood buildings with balconies and shutters. Many sidewalk cafés have opened up on this revitalized square, making it a good place for lunch or light refreshments. The square was named in honor of Victor Hugues's 1794 victory over the British. The sandbox trees in the park are said to have been planted by Hugues the day after the victory. During the French Revolution, Hugues's guillotine in this square lopped off the heads of many a white aristocrat. Today the large palm-shaded park is a popular gathering place. The Tourist Office is at the harbor end of the square.

Rue Duplessis runs between the southern edge of the park and La Darse, the head of the harbor, where fishing boats dock and fast motorboats depart for the choppy ride to Marie-Galante and Les Saintes.

Rue Bebian is the western border of the square. Walk north along it (away from the harbor) and turn left on rue Alexandre Isaac. You'll see the imposing **Cathedral of St. Peter and St. Paul,** which dates from 1847. Mother Nature's rampages have wreaked havoc on the church, and it is now reinforced with iron ribs. Hurricane Hugo took out many of the upper windows and shutters, but the lovely stained-glass windows survived intact.

Grande-Terre This round-trip tour of **Grande-Terre** will cover about 85 miles. Drive south out of Pointe-à-Pitre on Route N4 (named the "Riviera Road" in honor of the man-made beaches and resort hotels of Bas-du-Fort). The road goes past the marina, which is always crowded with yachts and cabin cruisers. The numerous boutiques and restaurants surrounding the marina make it popular in the evening.

② The road turns east and heads along the coast. In 2 miles you'll sight **Fort Fleur d'Epée,** an 18th-century fortress that hunkers on a hillside behind a deep moat. This was the scene of hard-fought battles between the French and the English. You can explore the well-preserved dungeons and battlements, and on a clear day take in a sweeping view of Iles des Saintes and Marie-Galante.

③ The **Guadeloupe Aquarium** is just past the fort off the main highway. This aquarium, the Caribbean's largest and most modern, also ranks third in all of France. *Place Créole (just off Rte. N4), tel. 590/90–92–38. Admission: 15F adults, 10F children. Open weekdays 8:30–12:30 and 2:30–5:30, Sat. 8:30–5:30.*

❹ Gosier, a major tourist center 2 miles farther east, is a busy place indeed, with big hotels and tiny inns, cafés, discos, shops, and a long stretch of sand. The Creole Beach, the Auberge de la Vieille Tour, and the Canella Beach are among the hotels here, as well as a casino.

Breeze along the coast through the little hamlet of St-Felix and **❺** on to **Ste-Anne,** about 8 miles east of Gosier. Only ruined sugar mills remain from the days in the early 18th century when this village was a major sugar-exporting center. Sand has replaced sugar as the town's most valuable asset. The soft white-sand beaches here are among the best in Guadeloupe. The Club Med Caravelle occupies a secluded spot on the Caravelle Beach to the west of town, and there are several small Relais Creoles with their "feet in the sand." The hotel La Toubana sits on a bluff with its bungalows tumbling down to the beach, and the Relais du Moulin occupies one of the old sugar mills. On a more spiritual note, you'll pass Ste-Anne's lovely cemetery with stark-white above-ground tombs.

Don't fret about leaving the beaches of Ste-Anne behind you as you head eastward. The entire south coast of Grande-Terre is scalloped with white-sand beaches. Eight miles along, just be-
❻ fore coming to the blue-roof houses of **St-François,** you'll come to the Raisins-Clairs beach, another beauty.

St-François was once a simple little village primarily involved with fishing and tomatoes. The fish and tomatoes are still here, but so are some of the island's ritziest hotels. This is the home of the Hamak and Le Méridien's new extension, La Cocoteraie, two very plush properties. Avenue de l'Europe runs between the well-groomed 18-hole Robert Trent Jones municipal golf course and the man-made marina. On the marina side, a string of shops, hotels, and restaurants caters to tourists. Just inland is the new 120-room Plantation Ste-Marthe hotel, and just to the south is the new 360-room Domaines de l'Anse des Rochers.

❼ To reach **Pointe des Châteaux,** take the narrow road east from St-François and drive 8 miles out onto the rugged promontory that is the easternmost point on the island. The Atlantic and the Caribbean waters join here and crash against huge rocks, carving them into castlelike shapes. The jagged, majestic cliffs are reminiscent of the headlands of Brittany. The only human contribution to this dramatic scene is a white cross high on a hill above the tumultuous waters. From this point there are spectacular views of the south and east coasts of Guadeloupe and the distant cliffs of La Désirade.

Time Out   **Paillote** (no phone) is a tiny roadside stand right on the *pointe* where you can get libations and light bites.

About 2 miles from the farthest point, a rugged dirt road crunches off to the north and leads to the nudist beach Pointe Tarare.

A mile closer to St-François is another beach, Anse de la Gourde, where at least half of a bikini is kept on. The half-mile stretch of coarse white sand and reef-protected waters makes it a choice beach and, off the car park, is **La Langouste** (tel. 590/88–52–19), a popular lunch spot on the weekends.

Take Route N5 north from St-François for a drive through fragrant silvery-green seas of sugarcane. About 4 miles beyond

⑧ St-François you'll see **Zévalos,** a handsome colonial mansion that was once the manor house of the island's largest sugar plantation.

⑨ Four miles northwest you'll come to **Le Moule,** a port city of about 17,000 people. This busy city was once the capital of Guadeloupe. It was bombarded by the British in 1794 and 1809 and by a hurricane in 1928. Canopies of flamboyants hang over narrow streets where colorful vegetable and fish markets do a brisk business. Small buildings are of weathered wood with shutters, balconies, and bright awnings. The town hall, with graceful balustrades, and a small 19th-century neoclassical church are on the main square. Le Moule also has a beautiful crescent-shape beach. A mile to the east is an excellent beach protected by a reef, making it perfect for windsurfing; boards may be rented from the Tropical Club Hotel (tel. 590/93–97–97).

North of Le Moule archaeologists have uncovered the remains
⑩ of Arawak and Carib settlements. The **Edgar-Clerc Archaeological Museum,** 3 miles out of Le Moule in the direction of Campêche, contains Amerindian artifacts from the personal collection of this well-known archaeologist and historian. There are several rooms with displays pertaining to the Carib and Arawak civilizations. *La Rosette, tel. 590/23–57–43. Admission free. Open Mon., Wed.–Fri., and Sun. 9:30–12:30 and 2:30–5:30; Sat. 9:30–5:30.*

From Le Moule you can turn west on Route D101 to return to Pointe-à-Pitre or continue northwest to see the rugged north coast.

To reach the coast, drive 8 miles northwest along Route D120 to Campêche, going through Gros-Cap.

Time Out | **Château de Feuilles** (tel. 590/22–19–10), between Le Moule and Campêche (nearer Gros-Cap), is an absolutely superb place for a long, lingering lunch. A mini-estate, the château has style and excellent cuisine. Bring your swimming togs and use the pool while lunch is being prepared (*see* Dining, *below*).

At 1½ miles beyond Campêche, turn north on Route D122.
⑪ **Porte d'Enfer** (Gate of Hell) marks a dramatic point on the coast where two jagged cliffs are stormed by the wild Atlantic waters. One legend has it that a Madame Coco strolled out across the waves carrying a parasol and vanished without a trace.

⑫ Four miles from Porte d'Enfer, **La Pointe de la Grande Vigie** is the northernmost tip of the island. Park your car and walk along the paths that lead right out to the edge. There is a splendid view of the Porte d'Enfer from here, and on a clear day you can see Antigua 35 miles away.

⑬ **Anse-Bertrand,** the northernmost village in Guadeloupe, lies 4 miles south of La Pointe de la Grande Vigie along a gravel road. Drive carefully. En route to Anse-Bertrand you'll pass another good beach, Anse Laborde. The area around Anse-Bertrand was the last refuge of the Caribs. Most of the excitement these days takes place in the St-Jacques Hippodrome, where horse races and cockfights are held.

⑭ Route N6 will take you 5 miles south to **Port-Louis,** a fishing village of about 7,000. As you come in from the north, look for the

turnoff to the Souffleur beach, once one of the island's prettiest, which, though, has become a little shabby. The sand is
fringed by flamboyant trees whose brilliant orange-red flowers
bloom during the summer and early fall. The beach is crowded
on weekends, but during the week it's blissfully quiet. The sunsets here are something to write home about.

Time Out **Poisson d'Or** is a rustic seaside restaurant that features spicy
Creole dishes. *Rue Sadi Carnot, Port-Louis, tel. 590/84–90–
22. No credit cards.*

From Port-Louis the road leads 5 miles south through mangrove swamps to Petit Canal, where it turns inland. Three
miles east of Petit Canal, turn right on the main road. Head 6
⑮ miles south to **Morne-à-l'Eau,** an agricultural city of about
16,000 people. Morne-à-l'Eau's unusual amphitheater-shape
cemetery is the scene of a moving (and photogenic) candlelight
service on All Saints' Day. Take Route N5 out of town along
gently undulating hills past fields of sugarcane and dairy
farms.

Just south of Morne-à-l'Eau are the villages of **Jabrun du Sud**
and **Jabrun du Nord,** which are inhabited by the descendants of
the "Blancs Matignon," the whites who hid in the hills and valleys of the Grands Fonds after the abolition of slavery in 1848.

Continue on Route N5 to Pointe-à-Pitre.

Basse-Terre: There is high adventure on the butterfly's west wing, which
The Southern Half swirls with mountain trails and lakes, waterfalls, and hot
springs. Basse-Terre is the home of the Old Lady, as the Soufrière volcano is called locally, as well as of the capital, also
called Basse-Terre.

Guadeloupe's de rigueur tour takes you through the 74,100-
acre **Parc Naturel,** a sizable chunk of Basse-Terre. (The park's
administrative headquarters is in Basse-Terre, tel. 590/80–24–
25.) Before going, pick up a *Guide to the Natural Park* from the
Tourist Office, which rates the hiking trails according to difficulty.

The Route de la Traversée (La Traversée) is a good paved road
that runs east–west, cutting a 16-mile-long swath through the
park to the west-coast village of Mahaut. La Traversée divides
Basse-Terre into two almost equal sections. The majority of
mountain trails falls into the southern half. Allow a full day for
this excursion. Wear rubber-soled shoes, and take along both
swimsuit and sweater, and perhaps food for a picnic.

Begin your tour by heading west from Pointe-à-Pitre on Route
N1, crossing the Rivière Salée on the Pont de la Gabare drawbridge. At the Destrelan traffic circle turn left and drive 6
miles south through sweet-scented fields of sugarcane to the
Route de la Traversée (aka D23), where you'll turn west.

As soon as you cross the bridge you'll begin to see the riches
produced by Basse-Terre's fertile volcanic soil and heavier
rainfall. La Traversée is lined with masses of thick tree-ferns,
shrubs, flowers, tall trees, and green plantains that stand like
soldiers in a row.

Five miles from where you turned off Route N1 you'll come to a
junction. Turn left and go a little over a mile south to **Vernou.**
Traipsing along a path that leads beyond the village through

⑯ the lush forest you'll come to the pretty waterfall at **Saut de la Lézarde,** the first of many you'll see.

⑰ Back on La Traversée, 3 miles farther, you'll come to the next one, **Cascade aux Ecrevisses.** Park your car and walk along the marked trail that leads to a splendid waterfall dashing down into the Corossol River (a fit place for a dip). Walk carefully—the rocks along the trail can be slippery.

⑱ Two miles farther along La Traversée you'll come to the **Parc Tropical de Bras-David,** where you can park and explore various nature trails. The **Maison de la Forêt** (admission free, open daily 9–5) has a variety of displays that describe (for those who can read French) the flora, fauna, and topography of the Natural Park. There are picnic tables where you can enjoy your lunch in tropical splendor.

⑲ Two and a half miles more will bring you to the two mountains known as **Les Mamelles**—Mamelle de Petit-Bourg at 2,350 feet and Mamelle de Pigeon at 2,500 feet. (*Mamelle* means "breast," and when you see the mountains you'll understand why they are so named.) There is a spectacular view from the pass that runs between the Mamelles to the south and a lesser mountain to the north. From this point, trails ranging from easy to arduous lace up into the surrounding mountains. There's a glorious view from the lookout point 1,969 feet up the Mamelle de Pigeon. If you're a climber, you'll want to spend several hours exploring this area.

⑳ You don't have to be much of a hiker to climb the stone steps leading from the road to the **Zoological Park and Botanical Gardens.** Titi the Raccoon is the mascot of the Natural Park. There are also cockatoos, iguanas, and turtles. A snack bar is open for lunch daily except Monday. *La Traversée, tel. 590/98–83–52. Admission: 20F adults, 10F children. Open daily 9–5.*

On the winding 4-mile descent from the mountains to **Mahaut** you'll see patches of the blue Caribbean through the green trees. In the village of Mahaut turn left on Route N2 for the drive south along the coast. In less than a mile you'll come to **Malendure.** The big attraction here is offshore on **Pigeon Island.** Club Nautilus and Chez Guy, both on the Malendure Beach, conduct diving trips, and the glass-bottom *Aquarium* and *Nautilus* make daily snorkeling trips to this spectacular site.

Time Out   While there are a couple of café/bars on Malendure Beach, the restaurant for lunch is **Le Rocher de Malendure** (tel. 590/98–70–84). Perched on a bluff overlooking Pigeon Island, the open-air restaurant is a gem, with dining on a series of terraces affording marvelous views. The owner can also arrange deep-sea fishing expeditions.

㉑
㉒ From Malendure continue through neighboring **Bouillante,** where hot springs burst up through the earth, and **Vieux-Habitants,** one of the oldest settlements on the island. Pause to see the restored church, which dates from 1650, before driving 8 miles south to the capital city.

㉓ **Basse-Terre,** the capital and administrative center, is an active city of about 15,000 people. Founded in 1640, it has had even more difficulties than Pointe-à-Pitre. The capital has endured not only foreign attacks and hurricanes but sputtering threats from La Soufrière as well. More than once it has been evacuated when the volcano began to hiss and fume. The last major eruption was in the 16th century. But the volcano seemed active enough to warrant the evacuation of more than 70,000 people in 1975.

The centers of activity are the port and the market, both of which you'll pass along boulevard Général de Gaulle. The 17th-century **Fort St. Charles** at the extreme south end of town, and the **Cathedral of Our Lady of Guadeloupe** to the north, across the Rivière aux Herbes, are worth a short visit. Drive along boulevard Felix Eboue to see the colonial buildings that house government offices. Follow the boulevard to the **Jardin Pichon** to see its beautiful gardens. Stop off at **Champ d'Arbaud,** an Old World square surrounded by colonial buildings. Continue along the boulevard to the **Botanical Gardens**. A steep, narrow road ② leads 4 miles up to the suburb of **St-Claude,** on the slopes of La Soufrière. In St-Claude there are picnic tables and good views of the volcano. You can also get a closer look at the volcano by driving up to the Savane à Mulets. From there leave your car and hike the strenuous two-hour climb (with an experienced guide) to the summit at 4,813 feet, the highest point in the Lesser Antilles. Water boils out of the eastern slope of the volcano and spills into the Carbet Falls.

② Drive 2 miles farther north from St-Claude to visit **Matouba,** a village settled by East Indians whose descendants still practice ancient rites including animal sacrifice. If you've an idle 10 hours or so, take off from Matouba for a 19-mile hike on a marked trail through the Monts Caraibes to the east coast.

Descend and continue east on Route N1 for 4 miles to **Gourbeyre.** ② Visit **Etang As de Pique.** Reaching this lake, located 2,454 feet above the town, is another challenge for hikers, but you can also reach it in an hour by car via paved Palmetto Road. The 5-acre lake, formed by a lava flow, is shaped like an *as de pique* (ace of spades).

From Gourbeyre you have the option of continuing east along Route N1 or backtracking to the outskirts of Basse-Terre and taking the roller-coaster Route D6 along the coast. Either route will take you through lush greenery to **Trois-Rivières.**

② Not far from the ferry landing for Les Saintes, the **Parc Archéologique des Roches Gravées** contains a collection of pre-Columbian rock engravings. Pick up an information sheet at the park's entrance. Displays interpret the figures of folk and fauna depicted on the petroglyphs. The park is set in a lovely botanical garden that is off the beaten track for many tourists, so it remains a haven of tranquillity. *Trois-Rivières, no phone. Admission: 4F. Open daily 9–5.*

Continue through banana fields and the village of Bananier for 5 miles to reach the village of **St-Sauveur,** gateway to the mag-② nificent **Chutes du Carbet** (Carbet Falls). Three of the chutes, which drop from 65 feet, 360 feet, and 410 feet, can be reached by following the narrow, steep, and spiraling Habituée Road for 5 miles up past the **Grand Etang** (Great Pond). At the end of the road you'll have to proceed on foot. Well-marked but slippery trails lead to viewing points of the chutes.

Time Out   You can have a hearty lunch of Creole chicken, curried goat, or crayfish at **Chez Dollin-Le Crepuscule** (Habituée Village, tel.

590/86–34–56) before or after viewing the falls. There's also a four-course menu.

Continue along Route N1 for 3 miles toward **Capesterre-Belle-Eau.** You'll cross the Carbet River and come to **Dumanoir Alley,** lined with century-old royal palms.

Three miles farther along, through fields of pineapples, bananas, and sugarcane, you'll arrive at **Ste-Marie,** where Columbus landed in 1493. In the town there is a monument to the Great Discoverer.

Seventeen miles farther north you'll return to Pointe-à-Pitre.

Iles des Saintes This eight-island archipelago, usually referred to as **Les Saintes,** dots the waters off the south coast of Guadeloupe. The islands are Terre-de-Haut, Terre-de-Bas, Ilet à Cabrit, Grand Ilet, La Redonde, La Coche, Le Pâté, and Les Augustins. Columbus discovered the islands on November 4, 1493, and christened them Los Santos in honor of All Saints' Day.

Of the islands, only Terre-de-Haut and Terre-de-Bas are inhabited, with a combined population of 3,260. Les Saintois, as the islanders are called, are fair-haired, blue-eyed descendants of Breton and Norman sailors. Fishing is the main source of income for les Saintois, and the shores are lined with their fishing boats and *filets bleus* (blue nets dotted with burnt-orange buoys). The fishermen wear hats called *salakos,* which look like inverted saucers or coolie hats. They are patterned after a hat said to have been brought here by a seafarer from China or Indonesia.

With 5 square miles and a population of about 1,500, Terre-de-Haut is the largest island and the most developed for tourism. Its big city is Bourg, which boasts one street and a few bistros, cafés, and shops. Clutching the hillside are trim white houses with bright red or blue doors, balconies, and gingerbread frills.

Arrival on Terre-de-Haut is an exhilarating affair, whether by land or sea. Air Guadeloupe has regularly scheduled flights, and your whole life may flash before your eyes as you soar down to the tiny airstrip. However, the flight is mercifully brief and you may prefer it to the choppy 35-minute ferry crossing from Trois-Rivières or the 60-minute ride from Pointe-à-Pitre. Ferries leave Trois-Rivières at about 8:30 AM (7:30 AM on Sunday) and return about 3 PM. From Pointe-à-Pitre the usual departure time is 8 AM, with return at 4 PM. The round-trip fare is 160F. Check with the Tourist Office for up-to-date ferry schedules.

Terre-de-Haut's ragged coastline is scalloped with lovely coves and beaches, including the nudist beach at Anse Crawen. The beautiful bay, complete with sugarloaf, has been called a mini Rio. This is a quiet, peaceful getaway, but it may not remain unspoiled. At present, tourism accounts for 20%–30% of the economy. Although government plans call for a total of only 250 hotel rooms, the tourist-related industries are making a major pitch for tourists.

There are three paved roads on the island, but don't even think about driving here. The roads are ghastly, and backing up is a minor art form choreographed on those frequent occasions when two vehicles meet on one of the steep, narrow roads. There are four minibuses that transport passengers from the airstrip and the wharf and double as tour buses. However, the island is so small you can get around by walking. It's a mere five-minute stroll from the airstrip and ferry dock to downtown Bourg.

32 **Fort Napoléon** is a relic from the period when the French fortified these islands against the Caribs and the English, but nobody has ever fired a shot at or from it. The nearby museum contains a collection of 250 modern paintings. You can also visit the well-preserved barracks, prison cells, and museum and admire the surrounding botanical gardens. From the fort you can see Fort Josephine across the channel on the Ilet à Cabrit. *Bourg, no phone. Admission: 10F. Open daily 9–noon.*

For such a tiny place, Terre-de-Haut offers a variety of hotels and restaurants. For details, *see* Dining and Lodging, *below.* Also, new to Terre-de-Haut is the **Centre Nautique des Saintes** (Plage de la Coline, tel. 590/99–54–25) should you wish to scuba dive off the islands.

Marie-Galante The ferry to this flat island departs from Pointe-à-Pitre at 8 AM,
33 2 PM, and 5 PM with returns at 6 AM, 9 AM, and 3:45 PM. (Schedules often change, especially on the weekends, so check them at the tourist office or the harbor offices.) The round trip costs 160F. You'll put in at Grand Bourg, its major city, with a population of about 8,000. A plane will land you 2 miles from Grand Bourg. If your French or phrase book are good enough, you can negotiate a price with the taxi drivers for touring the island.

Covering about 60 square miles, Marie-Galante is the largest of Guadeloupe's islands. It is dotted with ruined 19th-century sugar mills, and sugar is still one of its major products (the others are cotton and rum). One of the last refuges of the Caribs when they were driven from the mainland by the French, the island is a favorite retreat of Guadeloupeans who come on weekends to enjoy the beach at Petit-Anse.

Columbus sighted the island on November 3, 1493, the day before he landed at Ste-Marie on Basse-Terre. He named it for his flagship, the *Maria Galanda*, and sailed on.

There are several places near the ferry landing where you can get an inexpensive meal of seafood and Creole sauce. If you want to stay over, you can choose from Le Salut, in St-Louis (15 rooms, tel. 590/97–02–67), Auberge de l'Arbre à Pain (7 rooms, tel. 590/97–73–69) or Auberge de Soledad (18 rooms, tel. 590/97–75–44) in Grand Bourg, or Hotel Hajo (6 rooms, tel. 590/97–32–76) in Capesterre. An entertainment complex in Grand Bourg El Rancho has a 400-seat movie theater, restaurant, terrace grill, snack bar, disco, and a few double rooms.

La Désirade According to legend, this island is the "desired land" of Colum-
34 bus's second voyage. He spotted it on November 3, 1493. The 8-square-mile island, 5 miles east of St-François, was for many years a leper colony. The main settlement is Grande-Anse, where there is a pretty church and a hotel called La Guitoune. Nothing fancy, but the restaurant serves excellent seafood. Most of the 1,600 inhabitants are fishermen.

There are good beaches here, notably Souffleur and Baie Mahault, and there's little to do but loll around on them. The island is virtually unspoiled by tourism and is likely to remain so, at least for the foreseeable future.

Three or four minibuses meet the flights and ferries, and you can negotiate with one of them to give you a tour. Ferries depart from St-François Monday, Wednesday, Friday through Sunday 8:30; Tuesday and Thursday 4:30. The return ferry departs (at varying hours) afternoons daily except Tuesday and Thursday. However, be sure to check schedules.

Beaches

Generally Guadeloupe's beaches, all free and open to the public, have no facilities. For a small fee, hotels allow nonguests to use changing facilities, towels, and beach chairs. You'll find long stretches of white sand on Grande-Terre. On the south coast of Basse-Terre the beaches are gray volcanic sand, and on the northwest coast the color is golden-tan. There are several nudist beaches (noted below), and topless bathing is prevalent at the resort hotels. Note that the Atlantic waters on the northeast coast of Grande-Terre are too rough for swimming.

Ilet du Gosier is a little speck off the shore of Gosier where you can bathe in the buff. Make arrangements for water-sports rentals and boat trips to the island through the Creole Beach Hotel in Gosier (tel. 590/84–26–26). Take along a picnic for an all-day outing. *Beach closed weekends.*

Some of the island's best beaches of soft white sand lie on the coast of Grande-Terre from Ste-Anne to Pointe des Châteaux.

One of the longest and prettiest stretches is just outside the town of Ste-Anne at **Caravelle Beach,** though there are rather dilapidated shacks and cafés scattered about the area. Protected by reefs, the beach makes a fine place for snorkeling. At the hotel La Toubana (tel. 590/88–25–78) in the hills above, you can rent fins and masks, as well as canoes and Windsurfers. Club Med, with its staggering array of activities, occupies one end of this beach.

Just outside of St-François is **Raisin-Clairs,** home of the Le Méridien (tel. 590/88–51–00), which rents Windsurfers, water skis, and sailboats.

Between St-François and Pointe des Châteaux, **Anse de la Gourde** is a beautiful stretch of sand that becomes very popular on weekends. A restaurant and snack bar are at the entrance to the beach.

Tarare is a secluded strip just before the tip of Pointe des Châteaux; many bathe naked there. There is a small bar/café located where you park the car, a four-minute walk from the beach.

Located just outside of Deshaies on the northwest coast of Basse-Terre, **La Grande Anse** is a secluded beach of soft beige sand sheltered by palms. There's a large parking area but no facilities other than the Karacoli restaurant, which sits with its "feet in the water," ready to serve you rum punch and Creole dishes.

All along the western shore of Basse Terre you'll see signposts to small beaches. The sand starts turning gray as you reach Pigeon Island, and, as you work your way farther south, the sand becomes volcanic black.

From **Malendure** beach, on the west coast of Basse-Terre, Pigeon Island lies just offshore. Jacques Cousteau called it one of the 10 best diving places in the world. The Nautilus Club (tel. 590/98–85–89) and Chez Guy (tel. 590/98–81–72) at Malendure are two of the island's top scuba operations. There are also glass-bottom boat trips for those who prefer keeping their heads above water.

Souffleur, on the west coast of Grande-Terre, on the north side of Port-Louis, has brilliant flamboyant trees that bloom in the summer. There are no facilities on the beach, but you can buy the makings of a picnic from nearby shops. Be sure to stick around long enough for a super sunset.

Place Crawen, Les Saintes' quiet, secluded beach for skinny-dipping, is a half mile of white sand on Terre-de-Haut. Facilities are within a five-minute walk at Bois Joli hotel (tel. 590/99–50–38).

Petit-Anse, on Marie-Galante, is a long gold-sand beach crowded with locals on weekends. During the week it's quiet, and there are no facilities other than the little seafood restaurant, La Touloulou.

Sports and the Outdoors

Bicycling
The relatively flat terrain of Grande-Terre makes for easy wheeling. See Christian Rolle at **Veló-Vert** (Pointe-à-Pitre, tel. 590/83–15–74) to rent bikes and maps that cover a 270-mile tour. **Le Relais du Moulin** (near Ste-Anne, tel. 590/88–23–96) offers bike tours. You can also rent bikes at **Cyclo-Tours** (Gosier, tel. 590/84–11–34), **Le Flamboyant** (St-François, tel. 590/84–45–51), and **Rent-a-Bike** (Meridien Hotel, St-François, tel. 590/84–51–00). Mountain bikes with 18 speeds, to manage all kinds of terrain, are available from **VTT Evasion** (Ste-Rose, tel. 590/28–85–60). For planned excursions, contact the **Velo Club V.C.G.F.** (801 Residence du Port, Pointe-à-Pitre, tel. 590/91–60–31). For information about cycling tours from the United States to Guadeloupe, contact **Country Cycling Tours** (140 W. 83rd St., New York, NY 10024, tel. 212/874–5151).

Boating
If you plan to sail these waters, you should be aware that the winds and currents of Guadeloupe tend to be strong. There are excellent, well-equipped marinas in Pointe-à-Pitre, Bas-du-Fort, Deshaies, St-François, and Gourbeyre. Bare-boat or crewed yachts can be rented in Bas-du-Fort at **Locaraibes** (tel. 590/90–82–80), **Vacances Yachting Antilles** (tel. 590/90–82–95), and **Soleil et Voile** (tel. 590/90–81–81). All beachfront hotels rent Hobie Cats, Sunfish, pedal boats, motorboats, and water skis.

Deep-Sea Fishing
Half- and full-day trips in search of bonito, dolphin, captain-fish, barracuda, kingfish, and tuna can be arranged through **Fishing Club Antilles** (Route de Briloton, Bouillante, tel. 590/98–78–10), **Le Rocher de Malendure** (Pigeon, Bouillante, tel. 590/98–73–25), and **Caraibe Peche** (Marina, Bas-du-Fort, tel. 590/90–97–51). Count on about 3,500F for a half day's boat charter and 4,500F for a full day.

Fitness
The **PLM-Azur Marissol** (Bas-du-Fort, tel. 590/90–84–44) offers gym facilities for calisthenics, stretching, water exercises in pool or sea, yoga, and beauty care. **Viva Forme** (Gosier, tel.

590/90–98–74) has equipment for muscle toning as well as two squash courts.

Flying Popular with the Europeans are ULMs (Ultra Lègér Motorisé). These extremely lightweight seaplanes soar along the coast at approximately 100 feet. Try one at **Holywind** (Residence Canella Beach, Pointe de la Verdure, Gosier, tel. 590/90–44–84). The cost is 170F for 10 minutes.

Golf **Golf Municipal Saint-François** (St-François, tel. 590/88–41–87) has an 18-hole Robert Trent Jones course, an English-speaking pro, a clubhouse, a pro shop, and electric carts for rental. Expect to pay 250F for a day's greens fees.

Hiking Basse-Terre's Natural Park is laced with fascinating trails, many of which should be attempted only with an experienced guide. Trips for up to 12 people are arranged by **Organisation des Guides de Montagne de la Caraibe (O.G.M.C.)** (Maison Forestière, Matouba, tel. 590/80–05–79) or **Association des Amies de Parc Naturel** (BP 256 Basse Terre 97100, tel. 590/81–45–43 in Basse Terre or 590/82–88–16 in Pointe-à-Pitre).

Horseback Riding Beach rides, picnics, and lessons are available through **Le Criolo** (St-Felix, Gosier, tel. 590/84–38–90) and **Le Relais du Moulin** (Châteaubrun, between Ste-Anne and St-François, tel. 590/88–23–96).

Scuba Diving The main diving area is the Cousteau Underwater Park off Pigeon Island (west coast of Basse-Terre). Guides and instructors here are certified under the French CMAS rather than PADI or NAUI. To explore the wrecks and reefs, contact **Nautilus Club** (Bouillante, tel. 590/98–85–69) or **Chez Guy** (Bouillante, tel. 590/98–81–72). Both of these outfits arrange dives elsewhere around Guadeloupe. Chez Guy also arranges weekly packages that include accommodations in bungalows. On the Isle des Saintes, the new **Centre Nautique des Saintes** (Plage de la Coline, Terre de Haut, tel. 590/99–54–25) will arrange dives.

Sea Excursions and Snorkeling Most hotels rent snorkeling gear and post information about excursions. The *Papyrus* (Marina Bas-du-Fort, tel. 590/90–92–98) is a glass-bottom catamaran that offers full-day outings replete with rum, dances, and games, as well as moonlight sails. Glass-bottom boats also make snorkeling excursions to Pigeon Island (*see* Scuba Diving, *above*). The sailing school **Evasion Marine** (locations in St-François and Bas-du-Fort, tel. 590/84–46–67) offers excursions on board the *Ginn Fizz*, the *Ketch*, or the *Sloop*.

Tennis Courts are located at the following hotels: **Arawak** (2 courts), **Auberge de la Vieille Tour** (1 court), **Caravelle/Club Med** (6 courts), **La Creole Beach** (2 courts), **Golf Marine Club** (2 courts), **Hamak** (1 court), **Les Marines de St-François** (2 courts), **Le Méridien** (2 courts), **Novotel Fleur d'Epée** (2 courts), **PLM-Azur Marissol** (2 courts), **Relais du Moulin** (1 court), **Residence Karukera** (1 court), **Salako** (2 courts), and **Toubana** (1 court). Games can also be arranged through the **St-François Tennis Club** (tel. 590/88–41–87).

Windsurfing Immensely popular here, windsurfing rentals and lessons are available at all beachfront hotels. Windsurfing buffs congregate at the UCPA hotel club (tel. 590/88–54–84) in St-François. You can also rent a *planche-à-voile* (Windsurfer) at **Holywind** (Residence Canella Beach, Pointe de la Verdure, Gosier, tel. 590/90–44–84) and at the **Tropical Club Hotel** (Le Moule, tel.

590/93–97–97). There are constant Atlantic trade winds at Le Moule.

Shopping

If shopping is your goal and you're headed for a French island, head for Martinique—the selection is larger and the language is less of a barrier. But shopping in Pointe-à-Pitre can be fun at the street stalls around the harbor quay, in front of the tourist office, and at the market. Moreover, numerous small boutiques, offering unique designs, have opened in town. The more touristy shops are down at the Jean-Perse cruise terminal, where a new attractive mall is home to two dozen shops. Get an early start, because it gets very hot and sticky around midday.

Many stores offer a 20% discount on luxury items purchased with traveler's checks or, in some cases, major credit cards. You can find good buys on anything French—perfumes, crystal, china, cosmetics, fashions, scarves. As for local handcrafted items, you'll see a lot of junk, but you can also find island dolls dressed in madras, finely woven straw baskets and hats, salako hats made of split bamboo, madras table linens, and wood carvings. And, of course, the favorite Guadeloupean souvenir—rum.

Shopping Areas In Pointe-à-Pitre the main shopping streets are **rue Schoelcher, rue de Nozières,** and **rue Frébault.** Bas-du-Fort's two shopping districts are the **Mammouth Shopping Center** and the **Marina,** where there are 20 or so boutiques and several restaurants. In **St-François** there are also several shops surrounding the marina. Many of the resorts have fashion boutiques. There are also a number of duty-free shops at Raizet Airport.

Good Buys For Baccarat, Lalique, Porcelaine de Paris, Limoges, and other *China, Crystal,* upscale tableware, check **Selection** (rue Schoelcher, Pointe-à-*and Silver* Pitre, no phone), **A la Pensée** (44 rue Frébault, Pointe-à-Pitre, tel. 590/82–10–47), and **Rosebleu** (5 rue Frébault, Pointe-à-Pitre, tel. 590/82–93–44). A new boutique, **Long Courrier** (18 rue Schoelcher, Pointe-à-Pitre, tel. 590/82–04–89), has the latest designs in leather bags and belts.

Cosmetics Guadeloupe's exclusive purveyor of Orlane, Stendhal, and *and Lingerie* Germaine Monteil is **Vendome** (8–10 rue Frébault, Pointe-à-Pitre, tel. 590/83–42–84). Tickle someone's fancy with the delicate, fanciful, and very French lingerie found at **Soph't** (41, Immeuble Lesseps, Centre Daint-John Perse, Pointe-a-Pitre, tel. 590/83–07–73).

Native Crafts **Tim Tim** (16 rue Henri IV, tel. 590/83–48–71) is an upscale nostalgia shop with elegant (and expensive) antiques ranging from Creole furniture to maps. For dolls, straw hats, baskets, and madras table linens, try **Au Caraibe** (4 rue Frébault, Pointe-à-Pitre, no phone). Anthuriums and other plants that pass muster at U.S. customs are packaged at **Casafleurs** (42 rue René-Boisneuf, tel. 590/82–31–23, and Raizet Airport, tel. 590/82–33–34) and **Floral Antilles** (80 rue Schoelcher, tel. 590/82–18–63, and Raizet Airport, tel. 590/82–97–65). **Mariposa,** (13 Galerie du Port, St-François, tel. 590/88–69–38) offers a collection of local crafts, and **L'Imagerie Créole** (Bas-du-Fort, tel. 590/90–87–28) also carries native-art antiques. For imaginative art, visit the **Centre d'Art Haitien** (Rue Delgres, Pointe-à-

Pitre, tel. 590/82–54–46 and at 65 Montauban, Gosier, tel. 590/84–04–84).

Perfumes Sweet buys can be found at **Phoenicia** (3 locations in Pointe-à-Pitre: 93 rue de Nozières, tel. 590/82–17–66; 8 rue Frébault, tel. 590/83–50–36; and 121 rue Frébault, tel. 590/82–25–75), **Au Bonheur des Dames** (49 rue Frébault, Pointe-à-Pitre, tel. 590/82–00–30), and **L'Artisan Parfumeur** (rue Schoelcher, Pointe-à-Pitre, no phone).

Rum and Tobacco **Delice Shop** (45 rue Achille René-Boisneuf, Pointe-à-Pitre, tel. 590/82–98–24), **Ets Azincourt** (13 rue Henry IV, Pointe-à-Pitre, tel. 590/82–21–02), and **Comptoir sous Douane** (Raizet Airport, tel. 590/82–22–76) have good choices of island rum as well as tobacco.

Dining

The food here is superb. Many of Guadeloupe's restaurants feature seafood (shellfish is a great favorite), often flavored with rich herbs and spices à la Creole. Favorite appetizers are *accras* (codfish fritters), *boudin* (highly seasoned pork sausage), and *crabes farcis* (stuffed land crabs). Christophine is a vegetable pear (plantain is considered a vegetable banana—served as a side dish) prepared in a variety of ways. *Blaff* is a spicy fish stew. Lobster, turtle steak, and *lambi* (conch) are often among the main dishes, and homemade coconut ice cream is a typical dessert. The island boasts 200 restaurants, including those serving classic French, Italian, African, Indian, Vietnamese, and South American fare. The local libation of choice is the *'ti punch* (little "poonch," as it is pronounced)—a heady concoction of rum, lime juice, and sugarcane syrup. The innocent-sounding little punch packs a powerful wallop.

Highly recommended restaurants are indicated by a star ★.

Category	Cost*
Expensive	over $35
Moderate	$25–$35
Inexpensive	under $25

per person, excluding drinks

Grande-Terre **Auberge de St-François.** Claude Simon's country home is set in
★ an orchard, and his tables are set with Royal Doulton china and fine crystal. Dining is indoors or on one of the flower-filled patios, with a superb view of Marie-Galante and Pointe des Châteaux. The house specialty is crayfish prepared in several different ways. Also try brochette of smoked shark with a pepper sauce or conch. A *menu touriste* (for 160F) of three courses, each with a choice of three dishes, makes an affordable alternative to the à la carte offering. M. Simon has also developed a superior wine cellar to complement his cuisine. *St-François, tel. 590/88–51–71. Reservations advised. MC, V. Closed Sun. Expensive.*

★ **Château de Feuilles.** This restaurant is worth a special trip for lunch. You will savor no finer luncheon than in this relaxed, stylish country setting, hosted by Martine and Jean-Pierre Dubost. Take a dip in the pool or stroll around the 2-acre farm of this country home while waiting for your lunch. For an aperitif, about 20 different punch concoctions are made with different juices and flavors—sample all if you dare. The changing menu may include goose *rillettes* (pâté), breaded conch, tuna carpaccio (with olive and lemon), swordfish with sorrel, or the deep-sea fish *capitan* grilled with lime and green pepper. For dessert, try the pineapple flan. The estate is 15 kilometers (9 miles) from Le Moule on the Campêche road, between Gros-Cap and Campêche. *Campêche, tel. 590/22–30–30. Reservations advised. V. No dinner. Closed Mon. Expensive.*

Le Côte Jardin. The marina between Bas-du-Fort and Pointe-à-Pitre is a lively evening venue with a dozen restaurants, bar lounges, and shops around the quay. Diners may take their pick from pizzas to hamburgers. Try something more formal with a view of the harbor at La Plantation (tel. 590/90–84–83), or try creative cuisine at Le Côte Jardin. This intimate restaurant filled with plants offers haute French Creole dishes that range from the safe—lamb Provençal and baked red snapper—to the more exotic, such as escargots de la mer with garlic butter. *La Marina, tel. 590/90–91–28. Reservations advised. AE, MC, V. Expensive.*

La Canne à Sucre. A favorite over the years for its innovative Creole cuisine, La Canne à Sucre has the reputation for being the best restaurant in Pointe-à-Pitre. The restaurant moved from its gingerbread house to a new complex adjacent to the cruise-ship terminal. It's a commanding position at the corner of the quay, and the views from the upstairs dining room are wide-sweeping—as are the prices. Though he no longer has the patent on innovative cuisine in Guadeloupe, Gerard Virginius still masterminds the creative recipes coming from the kitchen. There are two dining rooms, with separate menus and separate prices. Fare at the main-floor Brasserie ranges from crayfish salad with smoked ham to a puff pastry of skate with a saffron sauce. Dining upstairs is more elaborate and twice as expensive, with *foie gras frais de canard au vieux rhum* (fresh duck liver in old rum) or *papillotte de perroquet* (red parrot baked in a paper bag and served with basil sauce). *Quai No. 1, Port Autonome, Point-à-Pitre, tel. 590/82–10–19. Reservations suggested. Jacket required upstairs. Restaurant closed Sun. and Sat. lunch. Dinner only at Brasserie; closed Sun. AE, V. Expensive.*

★ **La Louisiane.** The owner, chef Daniel Hogon, hails from the Carlton in Cannes and, along with his charming wife, Muriel, offers such traditional favorites as duck-liver confit with raspberry vinaigrette or smoked fish as starters; then crayfish with cassis or roast rack of lamb; and, for dessert, a *miroir aux framboises*. The dozen tables of this small restaurant are on a terrace decorated with paintings and hanging flower-filled pots. Since the restaurant is on the road to Ste-Marthe, about 2 miles from St-François, M. Hogon will send a car for you on request. *St-François, tel. 590/88–44–34. Reservations suggested. MC, V. Closed Mon. Expensive.*

★ **Le Balata.** This commanding restaurant sits high on a bluff above the main Gosier Bas-du-Fort highway (the entrance road is off the highway at the Elf gas station traveling from Gosier in the direction of Fort-de-France). Pierre and Marie Cecillon present classic Lyonnaise cuisine with Creole touches. Begin with shellfish in a cucumber sauce or homemade foie gras, then contemplate the catch of the day with parsley butter. A special businessman's lunch is available at 110F, including wine. For the surroundings, choose a table by the window (reserve early), and enjoy the magnificent view of Fort Fleur d'Epée. *Route de Labrousse, Gosier, tel. 590/90–88–25. AE, DC, V. Closed Sat. lunch, Sun., and Aug. Expensive.*

★ **Pullman Auberge de la Vieille Tour.** Gilles Ballereau's superb cuisine is artistically presented in a stylish, air-conditioned room with intimate lighting. The large windows afford a splendid view of Ilet du Gosier; be sure to request a window table when you make your reservations. The highlights of the menu include fresh duck foie gras, sliced pork fillet in saffron sauce, and salmon and dorado with banana butter. The *menu dégustation* for 220F is the best opportunity to test Ballerau's skills. There is an extensive (and expensive) wine list. Robert Sarkis's band plays cool jazz Wednesday–Saturday evenings. *Gosier, tel. 590/84–23–23. Reservations advised. AE, DC, MC, V. No lunch. Expensive.*

Jardin Gourmand. The Ecotel Hotel's dining room is a training ground for student cooks, waiters, and waitresses. The menu changes with the visiting French master chefs and apprentices, but usually includes red snapper and lobster prepared in various ways. Exotic Creole courses are sometimes offered: Try gratinéed octopus with a pink sauce or shark in coconut milk. For dessert the delicious frozen nougat with banana is a good choice. Gourmet galas are prepared twice a month by visiting chefs for about $36 per person. *Ecotel, Montauban, Gosier, tel. 590/84–15–66. Reservations suggested. Jacket required. AE, DC, MC, V. No lunch. Moderate–Expensive.*

Le Flibustier. This rustic hilltop farmhouse is a favorite with staffers from neighboring Club Med. A complete dinner of mixed salad, grilled lobster, coconut ice cream, petit punch, and half a pitcher of wine is $46, or you can order à la carte off the blackboard menu. It's a lively, fun place that warms up after 8 PM. *La Colline, Fonds Thézan (between Ste-Anne and St-Felix), tel. 590/88–23–36. No credit cards. Closed Mon., no lunch Sun. Moderate–Expensive.*

Les Oiseaux. Claudette and Arthur Rolle's menu includes *filet en croûte* with red-wine sauce, as well as such unusual dishes as *marmite de Robinson*, a fish fondue with dorado, king-fish, tuna, shrimp, and local vegetables. Shellfish aficionados should try *cigale de mer*, which is sea cricket, a member of the shrimp family. The stone house of Les Oiseaux, on the coast road south of St-François, has a small pool good for a refreshing dip. *Anse des Rochers, tel. 590/88–56–92. Reservations essential. MC, V. Closed Thurs., Sun. dinner. Moderate–Expensive.*

★ **Relais du Moulin.** The restaurant of this inn overlooks a restored windmill. Inside, nouvelle cuisine includes the house specialty: grouper and lobster served with Creole sauce or stuffed with fresh homemade pâté. Crème caramel in coconut sauce is among the sumptuous desserts. Recently introduced is a *menu dégustation* for 199F that offers seven courses so you can sample Creole cooking. By day, sunlight floods through large windows; by night, candles flicker on crisp white cloths. *Châteaubrun (between Ste-Anne and St-François), tel. 590/ 88–13–78. Reservations advised. AE, DC, MC, V. Moderate– Expensive.*

La Grande Pizzeria. Open late and very popular, this seaside spot serves pizza; pasta; salads; and some Milanese, Bolognese, and other Italian seafood specialties. *Bas-du-Fort, tel. 590/90– 82–64. Moderate.*

★ **La Maison de la Marie-Galante.** Around Place de la Victoire there are several sidewalk cafés, but if you are looking for a more sophisticated lunch without paying the exorbitant prices of Canne à Sucre, this restaurant will fit the bill. You can choose to eat either on the patio or inside, which is pristinely decorated with a mural and white tablecloths over peach linens. The menu ranges from roast pork or onion quiche to more creative dishes, such as poached fish with a puree of aubergine. *16 bis Place de la Victoire, Point-à-Pitre, tel. 590/90–10–41. No credit cards. Open lunch and dinner. Moderate.*

La Mouette. Tables in a gazebo and in the front yard set the tone for barefoot and bathing-suit lunching here. Grilled lobster, curried goat, ragouts, accras, and stuffed or roasted trunkfish are on the menu. *Pointe des Châteaux, tel. 590/88–43–53. No credit cards. Closed Tues. and Sun. dinner. Moderate.*

★ **Chez Violetta-La Creole.** Head of Guadeloupe's association of cuisinières (lady chefs), award-winning Violetta Chaville presents an à la carte menu of traditional Creole dishes. You'll be served by waitresses in madras and foulard garb. The restaurant is popular with American visitors in part because it is neat and smart with its checkered tablecloths. *Eastern outskirts of Gosier Village, tel. 590/84–10–34. No credit cards. Moderate-Inexpensive.*

Folie Plage. North of Anse-Bertrand, this lively spot is especially popular with families on weekends. In addition to the reliable Creole food of Prudence Marcelin, there is a children's wading pool, a boutique, and a disco on weekends. Superb court bouillon and imaginative curried dishes are among the specialties. *Anse Laborde, tel. 590/22–11–17. Reservations suggested. No credit cards. Inexpensive.*

L'Amour en Fleurs. Close to Club Med (and very popular with its guests), this is an unpretentious little roadhouse, where the award-winning Madame Tresor Amanthe prepares spicy *blaffs* (fish stews) and a tasty blend of conch, octopus, rice and beans, and court bouillon. Don't miss the homemade coconut ice cream. *Ste-Anne, tel. 590/88–23–72. No credit cards. Inexpensive.*

Basse-Terre **La Touna.** If you can't get a table at Le Rocher de Malendure, try the casual La Touna, down the shore toward Pigeon. Waves wash the edge of this open-fronted restaurant, where the fresh fare includes home-smoked local fish that the owner has personally caught. Sauces are Creole or French—your choice. *Pigeon, Bouillante, tel. 590/78–70–10. MC, V. Lunch only. Closed Thurs. Moderate.*

★ **Le Rocher de Malendure.** The setting on a bluff above Malendure Bay overlooking Pigeon Island makes this restaurant worth a special trip for lunch. The tiered terrace is decked with flowers, and the best choices of the menu are the fresh fish, but there are also meat selections as veal in raspberry vinaigrette and tournedos in three sauces. The owners, M. and Mme. Lesueur, also have five bungalows for rent at very reasonable prices and can arrange deep-sea fishing trips. Even if you do not want a large lunch, stop here for a drink and, perhaps, a plate of accras, if only to enjoy the hospitality of Mme. Lespeur, who usually tends the bar. *Malendure Beach, Bouillante, tel. 590/98–70–84. Reservations suggested on weekends. DC, MC, V. Lunch daily, dinner Fri., Sat. Moderate.*

★ **Chez Clara.** This restaurant is popular and crowded even in the off-season. Clara Laseur and her mother turn out Creole dishes with daily specials listed on the blackboard. Clara (whose English is excellent) gave up a jazz-dancing career in Paris to run her family's seaside restaurant. She takes the orders, and the place is often so crowded with her friends and fans that you may have to wait at the new hexagonal bar before being seated at a table with smart white wicker chairs. The food is worth the wait, however. *Ste-Rose, tel. 590/28–72–99. Reservations advised. MC, V. Closed Wed., Sun. dinner, Oct. Moderate–Inexpensive.*

Le Karacoli. Lucienne Salcede's rustic seaside restaurant is well established and well regarded. The restaurant has its feet firmly planted in the sands of Grande-Anse, a great place for a swim. Creole boudin is a hot item here, as are accras. Other offerings include coquilles Karacoli, court bouillon, fried chicken, and turtle ragout. For dessert, try the banana flambé. *Grande-Anse, north of Deshaies, tel. 590/28–41–17. MC, V. No dinner Sat.–Thurs.; closed Fri. Moderate–Inexpensive.*

Chez Jacky. Jacqueline Cabrion serves Creole and African dishes in her cheerful seaside restaurant. Creole boudin is featured, as are lobster (grilled, vinaigrette, or fricassee), fried crayfish, and ragout of lamb. There's also a wide selection of omelets, sandwiches, and salads. For dessert, try peach melba or banana flambé. *Anse Guyonneau, Pte. Noire, tel. 590/98–06–98. AE, MC, V. Closed Sun. dinner. Inexpensive.*

Les Gommiers. Lovely peacock chairs grace the bar of this stylish restaurant. The changing menu may list beef tongue in mango sauce, lobster in sauce piquante, fillet beef Roquefort, escallopes of veal, and grilled entrecote. Banana split and profiteroles are on the dessert list. Light lunches include salade Niçoise. *Rue Baudot, Pte. Noire, tel. 590/98–01–79. MC, V. Closed Mon., Wed. dinner. Inexpensive.*

Iles des Saintes, Terre-de-Haut **Le Foyal.** This delightful seaside terrace restaurant serves a sophisticated mélange of Creole and Continental dishes. Begin
★ with a warm crepe filled with lobster, conch, octopus, and fish; crabe farci; or a *rillette* of smoked fish. A house specialty is an assiette of smoked fish served cold; another is stuffed fish fillet served in a white-wine sauce. A special plate for children under 10 is also offered. *Anse Mirre, tel. 590/99–50–92. No credit cards. Moderate–Inexpensive.*

★ **Relais des Iles.** Select your lobster from the *vivier* (tank) and enjoy the splendid view from this hilltop eatery while your meal is expertly prepared by Bernard Mathieu. Imaginative things are done with local vegetables. For dessert, try the melt-in-your-mouth chocolate mousse. Choose your spirits from an excellent wine list. *Rte. de Pompierre, tel. 590/99–53–04. Reservations suggested in high season. No credit cards. Moderate–Inexpensive.*

Lodging

Gosier and Bas-du-Fort have been the main venues for resort hotels, but the areas around Ste-Anne and especially St-François also have their fair share of resorts. Indeed, a number of new hotels have opened along St-Francois's marina, including Le Méridien's deluxe extension, La Cocoteraie. To the south at Anse des Rochers is a new 360-room hotel, and inland, toward Le Moule, the new Plantation Ste-Marthe has a nine-hole golf course under development. Basse Terre still only has the large Fort Royal Touring Hotel that attracts families from

France on package tours. However, some small hotels have opened: La Sucrerie du Comté (tel. 590/28–60–17), with 26 rooms; Les Villas de Petit Anse (tel. 590/98–80–28), with 10 bungalows; and Domaine de Malendure in Bouillante (tel. 590/28–60–17), geared to divers, with 44 rooms. The Hotel Lagrange at Bouillante, with approximately 75 rooms to be built in 1993–94 will incorporate the existing Domaine de Petit Anse. There are also small hotels on Iles des Saintes and Marie-Galante. Guadeloupe doesn't have the selection of elegant, tasteful hotels found on other islands, but you can opt for a splashy hotel with a full complement of resort activities or head for a small inn called a Relais Creole. But if French is not your forte, you'll fare better in the large hotels. Most hotels include buffet breakfast in their rates. Prices decline 25% to 40% in the off-season.

Highly recommended lodgings are indicated by a star ★.

Category	Cost*
Very Expensive	over $300
Expensive	$225–$300
Moderate	$150–$225
Inexpensive	under $150

All prices are for a standard double room for two, excluding a taxe de séjour, *which varies from hotel to hotel, and a 10%–15% service charge.*

La Cocoteraie. This annex to Le Méridien serves as an enclave for guests who are willing to pay almost $600 for the privilege of privacy while having access to all of its parent facilities (*see below*). La Cocoteraie comprises 52 suites, each with a view of the sea, a private balcony, a round tub and separate shower in the bathroom, a restaurant exclusively for its clientele, tennis courts, and a very small beach area at the entrance to a marina. The management caters to the French bourgeois—the booking office is in Paris—and expresses little interest in attracting English-speaking guests. *Avenue de l'Europe, St-François 97118, tel. 590/88–79–81 or 800/543–4300, fax 590/88–78–33. 52 suites. Facilities: restaurant, pool, tennis courts; access to Meridien's facilities. AE, DC, MC, V. CP. Very Expensive.*

Hamak. Five landscaped acres, a private white-sand beach, and attentive service once made this the smartest place on Guadeloupe. Golfers are delighted that Guadeloupe's municipal golf course is across the street, and gardeners appreciate the hotel's array of flowers and shrubs. One-bedroom suites are in bungalows; each unit has a living room, a small bedroom, a kitchenette, a private rear patio with outdoor freshwater shower, and a front terrace with a hammock. All are air-conditioned, with twin beds, hair dryers, and international direct-dial phones. TVs and videos are available. The hotel shows its age in the patched-up plastering and dated amenities. Considering the high price for a seaside bungalow, the rooms are pitifully small and poorly furnished, the bathrooms are no more than closets, and the beach is tiny and crowded. *St-François 97118, tel. 590/88–59–99 or 800/633–7411, fax 590/88–41–92. 56 units. Facilities: restaurant, 2 bars, lighted tennis court, water-sports center. AE, DC, MC, V. BP. Very Expensive.*

La Creole Beach. Set in 10 acres of tropical greenery, this three-star hotel boasts two beaches and spacious rooms. All rooms have individually controlled air conditioners, TVs, VCRs, radios, international direct-dial phones, and sliding glass doors that open onto a balcony. Water activities include boat excursions to Ilet du Gosier. La Creole Beach was extensively refurbished and in 1992 added a 63-room extension. The mazelike corridors and pathways can be somewhat confusing. *Box 19, Gosier 97190, tel. 590/90–46–46 or 800/755–9313, fax 590/90–46–96. 221 rooms. Facilities: restaurant, bar, pool, 2 lighted tennis courts, car-rental desk, boat excursions, water-sports center. AE, DC, MC, V. CP. Expensive.*

★ **Pullman Auberge de la Vieille Tour.** Recently acquired by the PLM hotel group, the hotel has doubled its room capacity by adding an arc-shape row of town-house units. La Vieille Tour is no longer an auberge but a large chain hotel. The personal flavor and individual service have gone; nevertheless, the hotel still has a desirable location three blocks from the Gosier center. The main building occupies the hilltop on a four-acre estate. Steep steps go down to the pool and beach. The older rooms are in the main building, and another series of rooms are in a long building facing Ilet du Gosier. These older rooms tend to be rather small and dully furnished, though this may be forgiven if your room has a view out to sea. The new rooms in the town houses on the other side of the pool are larger and have cheerful contemporary furnishings. In high season, breakfast, lunch, and barbecues are served in the terrace restaurant at the pool level. Robert Zarkis's orchestra plays nightly in the formal dining room. Water-sports equipment is available for guests at the sister hotel, Callinago-PLM Azur. *Montauban Gosier 97190, tel. 590/84–23–23 or 800/223–9862, fax 590/84–33–43. 160 rooms. Facilities: 2 restaurants, bar, boutiques, 2 lighted tennis courts, pool. AE, DC, MC, V. BP. Expensive.*

Club Med Caravelle. Occupying 50 secluded acres at the western end of a magnificent white-sand beach, this version of the well-known villages has air-conditioned twin-bed rooms, some with balconies. Activities include a French-English language lab, yoga, volleyball, calisthenics, and water sports. This property has never been the smartest of Club Med's villages, but it draws a fun-loving younger crowd, most of whom are from France, and serves as the home port for Club Med's sailing cruises. *Ste-Anne 97180, tel. 590/88–21–00 or 800/258–2633, fax 590/88–06–06. 275 rooms. Facilities: restaurant, pub, boutiques, 6 lighted tennis courts (with pro), pool, water-sports center. AE. All-inclusive (drinks not included). Moderate–Expensive.*

La Toubana. Red-roof bungalows are sprinkled on a hilltop overlooking the Caravelle Peninsula, arguably the best beach on the island. The bungalows are air-conditioned, and all rooms have private bath, phone, and an ocean view. Seven suites have kitchenettes and private terraced gardens. The pool is rather small. There's evening entertainment at the French-Creole restaurant, including a piano bar. Pets are welcome. Despite the renovations made after Hurricane Hugo, La Toubana requires more work and maintenance. *Box 63, Ste-Anne 97180, tel. 590/88–25–78 or 800/223–9815, fax 590/88–38–90. 45 rooms, 12 suites. Facilities: restaurant, bar, pool, tennis court, water-sports center. AE, DC, V. CP. Moderate–Expensive.*

Le Méridien. This hotel is recommended for those who want to pack as much activity as possible into a vacation. The 150-acre resort puts out its own *A to Z Leisure Guide* and broadcasts from Radio Méridien to let you know about resort activities. The activities director organizes everything from bocci to book lending. The hotel's beach hut is a busy place even off-season (partly because the Air France crews use the hotel). The spacious, breezy lobby is filled with Haitian artwork and fresh flowers. Standard rooms are rather modest, and wear and tear has taken its toll, but all are air-conditioned with double or twin beds, radios, direct-dial phones, and balconies, about half of which face the sea. *St-François 97118, tel. 590/88–51–00 or 800/543–4300, fax 590/88–40–71. 265 rooms, 10 suites. Facilities: 4 restaurants, 2 bars, disco, boutiques, pool, 2 lighted tennis courts, bike rental, car-rental desk, water-sports center. AE, DC, MC, V. CP. Moderate–Expensive.*

Plantation Ste-Marthe. This new hotel, on 15 acres, is a few miles inland from the coast, though the ocean may be seen from the first- and second-floor guest rooms. In four three-story Creole-style buildings, the guest rooms, most of which are standard doubles, open onto terraces that overlook the large pool and a nine-hole golf course (to be completed in 1994). In addition, 34 duplex suites have loft-style bedrooms looking down upon the salon. Bathrooms, with separate toilets, are cheerfully patterned with red-and-blue tiles. The furniture throughout the hotel combines a modern rendering of period French with cane-pattern work, the result of which is smart and clean. The main reception house is large and grand enough to process incentive groups, accommodate several conference rooms, and serve those in need of a refreshing drink at the bar. A separate building, with its own kitchens, has a grand dining hall for as many as 500 guests. Next to the large free-form pool is the main restaurant, with indoor and terrace dining. The chef, due to arrive after press time, is from Paris, where his last position was at Taillevent. Dining should be a pleasure. *Saint-François 97110, tel. 590/88–72–46 or 800/333–1970, fax 590/88–72–47. 96 rooms and 24 duplexes. Facilities: restaurant, 4 lighted tennis courts, 9-hole golf course under construction, conference rooms. AE, DC, MC, V. EP. Moderate–Expensive.*

Canella Beach. One of the latest additions to the Gosier hotels is this 150-room resort built to resemble a Creole village. Guests have a choice of one-level and duplex studios and junior and duplex suites. Each has its own terrace or balcony with a small kitchenette. Guests are assigned their own direct telephone line, making the hotel desirable for businessmen and anyone planning to send or receive faxes. Water sports are complimentary, and there is a beach bar for refreshments. Set back from the beach is the swimming pool and tennis courts. If you are not fluent in French, a definite plus to this resort is that the staff, inspired by Jean-Pierre Reuff, the general manager, is enthusiastic and enjoys speaking English. The other strong plus is the Verandah restaurant, which offers dining indoors with air-conditioning or outdoors cooled by the sea breezes. The menu offers a choice between Creole and French dishes; for a light meal or an appetizer, the salad with warm goat cheese is excellent. *Pointe de la Verdure, 97190 Gosier, tel. 590/90–44–00 or 800/233–9815, fax 590/90–44–44; 212/545–8469 in NY, 150 rooms. Facilities: restaurant, pool, tennis courts, water sports, excursions arranged to nearby islands. AE, DC, MC, V. EP. Moderate.*

Cap Sud Caraibes. This is a tiny Relais Creole on a country road
between Gosier and Ste-Anne, just a five-minute walk from a
quiet beach. English is not the first language here, but every
attempt is made to make you feel at home. Individually decorated rooms are air-conditioned, and each has a balcony and an
enormous bath. There's a big kitchen that guests are welcome
to share. *Gosier 97190, tel. 590/85–96–02, fax 590/85–80–39. 12
rooms. Facilities: transfer from airport to hotel, bar, dry-
cleaning and laundry facilities, snorkeling equipment. AE,
MC, V. CP. Moderate.*

Golf Marine Club Hotel. Within the new area of shops and restaurants, this small hotel offers a more moderately priced alternative to Hamak and Le Méridien. But the hotel's name
overpromises: It is not a club—the municipal golf course is
across the street—and it has neither marina nor beach. Guests
must walk two blocks to the nearest public beach. The rooms,
however, are clean, pristine, and softly furnished in light blues.
Each has a balcony, but those facing the street tend to be
noisy—reserve one looking onto the gardens. A third of the
rooms are called mezzanine suites. These have loft bedrooms
and a roll-out couch in the lounge. The space is pleasant for two
people, and a small family can squeeze in. The patio terrace facing the small pool serves breakfast, lunch, and dinner in a relaxed, informal setting. *Avenue de l'Europe, B.P. 204, St-
François 97118, tel. 590/88–60–60, fax 590/88–74–67. 52
rooms, 24 suites. Facilities: restaurant, pool. AE, DC, MC, V.
CP. Moderate.*

Le Domaine de l'Anse des Rochers. This new 27-acre complex is
on the coast a few miles from St.-François. Guests can choose
rooms in Creole-style buildings or the 34 "villas" that climb the
rise behind the hotel. All rooms have red-tile floors, rich rus-
set-patterned bedspeads, and functional bathrooms. A formal
restaurant offers à la carte dining, and the terrace bar offers
casual drinks. On most evenings, guests dine on the "theme
buffet dinner" at the Blan Mange restaurant in a separate
building where performers entertain on the large piazza in
front. Across the piazza is the open-sided disco for late-night
revelry. The complex is large enough so the trek to the man-
made beach at one end can prompt you to use the car. And
though Anse des Rochers may not have the best beach on the
island, it does boast the largest swimming pool. Dramatically
set, the pool creates the effect of water cascading into the sea.
Your travel agent should be able to obtain discounted rates for
you, which can make this hotel very reasonable. *Anse des
Rochers, St-François 97118, tel. 590/93–90–00, fax 590/93–91–
00. 360 rooms. Facilities: 2 restaurants, beach snack bar, pool,
2 lighted tennis courts, archery, conference rooms. AE, DC,
MC, V. EP. Moderate.*

L'Orchidée. For the businessperson who does not need resort
facilities or a beach, a new, smart hotel has opened in the center
of Gosier. Its studios have a small kitchenette, a balcony, a direct-dial telephone, and air-conditioning. On the ground floor
an eatery makes morning coffee and croissants convenient. The
manageress/owner, Mme. Karine Chenaf, speaks English and
can help you arrange your day. *32, blvd. Général de Gaulle,
Gosier 97130, tel. 590/84–54–20, fax 590/84–54–90. 20 rooms.
MC, V. EP. Moderate.*

★ **Relais du Moulin.** A restored windmill serves as the reception
room for this Relais Creole tucked in Châteaubrun, near Ste-
Anne. A spiral staircase leads up to a TV/reading room from

which there is a splendid view. Accommodations are in air-conditioned bungalows; the rooms are immaculate and tiny, with twin beds, small terraces, and kitchenettes. The hotel is on a small hill, and there is usually a pleasant cooling breeze. The beach is a 10-minute hike away. Guests are advised to have their own rental car. Horseback riding can be arranged, and bikes are available. The owner-manager speaks English. *Châteaubrun, Ste-Anne 97180, tel. 590/88–23–96 or 800/223–9815, fax 590/88–03–92. 40 rooms. Facilities: restaurant, bar, pool, tennis court, archery. AE, MC, V. CP. Moderate.*

Tropical Club Hotel. At this hotel, on the northeastern coast of Grand-Terre, you'll get the best of both worlds: Constant cooling trade winds from the Atlantic make for great windsurfing and a reef about 100 yards offshore creates gentle waves that wash up on a dark, golden beach making it perfect for swimming. In from the beach is an almond-shaped pool, adjacent to an open-sided dining room for French and Creole fare. The guest rooms are in three buildings on a rise at the back of the main hotel building. Each room has a double bed, TV, air-conditioning, a fan, and two bunk beds in the entrance annex that are ideal for children. The bathroom has a shower only and the toilet is in a separate area. Every room has a private balcony with a small kitchenette, table and chairs, and a view of the sea; better views are from the rooms on the top (third) floor. *Le Moule, 97160, tel. 590/93–97–97, fax 590/93–97–00. 72 rooms. Facilities: restaurant, bar, pool, windsurfing, petanque, gym, boutique, and 3 floodlit tennis courts nearby. AE, MC, V. CP. Moderate.*

★ **Auberge de la Distillerie.** This is an excellent choice for those who want to be close to the Natural Park and its hiking trails. The small country inn has air-conditioned studios with phones (you'll have to share a bath) and a TV lounge. There's also a rustic wood chalet that sleeps two to four people. Boat trips are arranged on the Lezarde River, in which you can also swim. Pets are welcome. *Vernou 97170, Petit-Bourg, tel. 590/94–25–91 or 800/223–9815, fax 590/94–11–91. 7 studios, 1 chalet. Facilities: restaurant, bar, piano bar. AE, V. CP. Inexpensive.*

Auberge du Grand Large. This casual family-style inn on the grand Ste-Anne beach has bungalows on the beach or tucked in a garden. All are air-conditioned with private baths. The restaurant serves Creole specialties. Pets are welcome. *Ste-Anne 97180, tel. 590/88–20–06, fax 590/88–16–69. 10 rooms. Facilities: restaurant, bar. AE, MC. EP. Inexpensive.*

Grand Anse Hotel. Located near the ferry landing from which you leave for Les Saintes, this Relais Creole offers air-conditioned bungalows with shower baths, phones, and little balconies. The view of the mountains is spectacular. It's less than a mile from a black-sand beach, and water sports can be arranged. A good choice for nature lovers. *Trois-Rivières 97114, tel. 590/92–92–21 fax 590/92–93–69. 16 bungalows. Facilities: restaurant, bar. V. CP. Inexpensive.*

La Maison de la Marie-Galante. New in 1990, this hotel in the heart of Pointe-à-Pitre facing Place de la Victoire has small, neat rooms. Most have twin beds and few furnishings; the toilet is separate from the small private bathroom, which has a shower but no tub. The staff speaks English and is wonderfully helpful. The current prices make this hotel a tremendous value if you wish to stay in town. *16 bis Place de la Victoire, Pointe-à-Pitre 97110, tel. 590/90–10–41, fax 590/90–22–75. 9 rooms. Facilities: restaurant. No credit cards. CP. Inexpensive.*

La Sucrerie du Comté. Pristine white bungalows dot this former sugar plantation to offer clean, simple air-conditioned accommodations at reasonable prices. Though the rooms are small, the pool in the center court, the alfresco restaurant, and the bar lounge are large, pleasant gathering spots. In the evening, the enthusiastic young French owner, M. Girard Jean-Luc, will have you speaking French in no time as you try the home-made fruit punches lined up in great jars on the bar. Although the hotel is a mile inland from the sea, there are numerous small beaches close by. To find the hotel, look for a left turn off the main road just after Ste-Rose. Once at its gates, you'll recognize the hotel by the ancient remains of a sugar factory and a rusted, twisted steam train that looks like a modern-art sculpture—adding a sense of history to this friendly and informal place. *Comté de Lohéac, Sainte-Rose 97115, tel. 590/28–60–17, fax 590/28–65–63. 26 rooms. Facilities: restaurant, bar, pool, 1 tennis court. MC, V. CP. Inexpensive.*

Mini-Beach. This small hotel, at the northern end of Ste-Anne's beach, has recently been spruced. Now, a comfortable open-front lounge and dining area with wicker chairs, hanging plants, and an open-hearth kitchen add to the relaxed atmosphere. Six simply furnished rooms with private bath can be found in the main house. Three bungalows are scattered around: one at the water's edge, another on the beach, and the third in the gardens. Like the rooms in the main house, these bungalows are very simply furnished, but are more than adequate for a beachcombing life. *BP 77, Sainte-Anne 97180, tel. 590/88–21–13, fax 590/88–19–29. 9 rooms. Facilities: restaurant, pool table. MC, V. CP. Inexpensive.*

Iles des Saintes

Village Creole. Baths by Courreges, dishwashers, freezers, satellite TV/videos, and international direct-dial phones are among the amenities in this apartment hotel. Ghyslain Laps, the English-speaking owner, will help you whip up meals in the kitchen. If you'd prefer not to cook, he can provide you with a cook and housekeeper for an extra charge. A sailboat is available for excursions to Marie-Galante and Dominica. *Pte. Coquelet 97137, Terre-de-Haut, tel. 590/99–53–83 (telex 919671), fax 590/99–55–55. 22 duplexes. Facilities: airport shuttle service, daily maid service, safe deposit, business center, scooter and boat rentals, water-sports center. MC, V. EP. Moderate–Inexpensive.*

★ **Auberge des Anacardies.** Trimmed with trellises, topped by dormers, and formerly owned by the mayor, this inn offers air-conditioned, twin-bed rooms with phones and baths. Casement windows open to a splendid view of the gardens, the hills, and the bay. Furnishings are an odd assortment of antiques. This hostelry has the island's only swimming pool, and the new owners, Jean-Paul Coles and Didier Spindler, have installed a sauna alongside. A new bungalow has also been built next to the main house. Steak au poivre, grilled lobster, and steaks are among the restaurant's offerings. The hotel's private boat will take guests on excursions around the islands. *La Savane 97137, Terre-de-Haut, Les Saintes, tel. 590/99–50–99, fax 590/99–54–51. 11 rooms. Facilities: restaurant, bar, pool. AE, MC, V. CP. Inexpensive.*

★ **Bois Joli.** In high season, you'll need to reserve a room here three months in advance. Facing the "Sugarloaf" on the island's beautiful bay, the hotel consists of modern rooms in bungalows, 14 of which are air-conditioned. Private baths were recently added to every room. The more modern and fresher rooms are in the recently added, fully equipped bungalows. The hotel restaurant serves wonderful clams in Creole sauce on a terrace that overlooks the sea. Water sports can be arranged, and the Anse Crawen nudist beach is a five-minute walk away. Pets are allowed. *Terre-de-Haut 97137, tel. 590/99–52–53 or 800/223–9815, fax 590/99–55–05. 26 rooms. Facilities: restaurant, 2 bars, pool, airport transfers. MC, V. CP. Inexpensive.*

Home and Apartment Rental For information about villas, apartments, and private rooms in modest houses, contact **Gîtes de France** (tel. 590/82–09–30). For additional information about apartment-style accommodations, contact the **ANTRE Association** (tel. 590/88–53–09).

The Arts and Nightlife

Cole Porter notwithstanding, Guadeloupeans maintain that the beguine began here (the Martinicans make the same claim for their island). Discos come, discos go, and the current music craze is "zouk," but the beat of the beguine remains steady. Many of the resort hotels feature dinner dancing, as well as entertainment by steel bands and folkloric groups.

Casinos There are two casinos on the island. Neither has one-armed bandits, but both have American-style roulette, blackjack, and chemin de fer. The legal age is 21. Admission is $10, and you'll need a photo ID. Tie and jacket are not required, but "proper attire" means no shorts. The **Casino de Gosier les Bains** (Gosier, tel. 590/84–18–33) has a bar, restaurant, and nightclub, and is open Monday–Saturday 9 PM–dawn. The **Casino de St-François** (Marina, St-François, tel. 590/84–41–40) has a snack bar and nightclub and is open Tuesday–Sunday 9 PM–3 AM.

Discos A mixed crowd of locals and tourists frequents the discos. Night owls should note that carousing is not cheap. Most discos charge an admission of at least $8, which includes one drink. Drinks cost about $5 each. Some of the enduring hot spots are **Le Foufou** (Hotel Frankel, Bas-du-Fort, tel. 590/84–35–59), the very Parisian **Elysée Matignon** (Rte. des Hôtels, Bas-du-Fort, tel. 590/90–89–05), **Ti Raccoon** (Creole Beach Hotel, Pointe de la Verdure, tel. 590/84–26–26), **Le Caraibe** (Salako, Gosier, tel. 590/84–22–22), **New Land** (Rte. Riviera, Gosier, tel. 590/84–37–91), the **Bet-a-Feu** (Le Méridien, St-François, tel. 590/88–51–00), and the down-home **Neptune disco** (Quartier Cayenne, St-François, tel. 590/88–48–65) on weekends.

Bars and Nightclubs If discos are not your dish, tune in to the **Auberge de la Vieille Tour** (Gosier, tel. 590/84–23–23), where Robert Zarkis's orchestra plays for touch-dancing—is never passé here. **La Toubana** (Ste-Anne, tel. 590/88–25–78) offers a popular piano bar; there's nightly entertainment at the **Lele Bar** (Le Méridien, St-François, tel. 590/88–51–00); and an orchestra plays dance music at the **Marissol PLM Azur** (Bas-du-Fort, tel. 590/90–84–44). **Le Jardin Brésilien** (Marina, Bas-du-Fort, tel. 590/90–99–31) has light music in a relaxed setting on the waterfront.

14 Jamaica

*Updated by
Jordan Simon*

The third-largest island in the Caribbean (after Cuba and Puerto Rico), the English-speaking nation of Jamaica enjoys a considerable self-sufficiency based on tourism, agriculture, and mining. Its physical attractions include jungle mountaintops, clear waterfalls, and unforgettable beaches, yet the country's greatest resource may be the Jamaicans themselves. Although 95% of the population trace their bloodlines to Africa, their national origins lie in Great Britain, the Middle East, India, China, Germany, Portugal, South America, and many of the other islands in the Caribbean. Their cultural life is a wealthy one; the music, art, and cuisine of Jamaica are vibrant, with a spirit easy to sense but as hard to describe as the rhythms of reggae or a flourish of the streetwise patois.

Jamaica is unusual in that in addition to such pleasure capitals of the north coast as Montego Bay and Ocho Rios, it has a real capital in Kingston. For all its congestion and for all the disparity between city life and the bikinis and parasails to the north, Kingston is the true heart and head of the island. This is the place where politics, literature, music, and art wrestle for acceptance in the largest English-speaking city south of Miami, its actual population of nearly 1 million bolstered by the emotional membership of virtually all Jamaicans.

The first people known to have reached Jamaica were the Arawaks, gentle Indians who paddled their canoes from the Orinoco region of South America about a thousand years after the death of Christ. Then, in 1494, Christopher Columbus stepped ashore at what is now called Discovery Bay. Having spent four centuries on the island, the Arawaks had little notion that his feet on their sand would mean their extinction within 50 years.

What is now St. Ann's Bay was established as New Seville in 1509 and served as the Spanish capital until local government crossed the island to Santiago de la Vega (now Spanish Town). The Spaniards were never impressed with Jamaica; their searches found no precious metals, and they let the island fester in poverty for 161 years. When 5,000 British soldiers and sailors appeared in Kingston Harbor in 1655, the Spaniards did not put up a fight.

The arrival of the English, and the three centuries of rule that followed, provided Jamaica with the surprisingly genteel underpinnings of its present life—and the rousing pirate tradition fueled by rum that enlivened a long period of Caribbean history. The British buccaneer Henry Morgan counted Jamaica's governor as one of his closest friends and enjoyed the protection of His Majesty's government no matter what he chose to plunder. Port Royal, once said to be the "wickedest city of Christendom," grew up on a spit of land across from present-day Kingston precisely because it served so many interests. Morgan and his brigands were delighted to have such a haven, and the people of Jamaica profited by being able to buy pirate booty at Port Royal at terrific bargains.

Morgan enjoyed a prosperous life; he was knighted and made lieutenant governor of Jamaica before the age of 30, and, like every good bureaucrat, he died in bed and was given a state funeral. Port Royal fared less well. On June 7, 1692, an earthquake tilted two-thirds of the city into the sea, the tidal wave that followed the last tremors washed away millions in pirate treasure, and Port Royal simply disappeared. In recent years

Jamaica

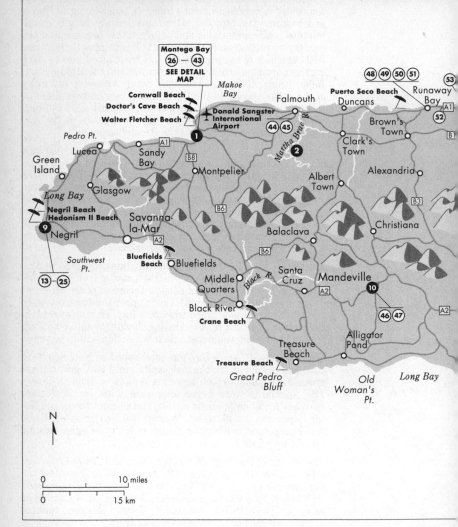

Montego Bay
(26) — (43)
SEE DETAIL
MAP

Mahoe Bay

Cornwall Beach
Doctor's Cave Beach
Walter Fletcher Beach

Falmouth

Puerto Seco Beach

(48) (49) (50) (51)

(53) Runaway Bay

Duncans

Donald Sangster International Airport

(44) (45)

Brown's Town

(52) A1

B

Pedro Pt.

Lucea

A1

Sandy Bay

B8

Montpelier

Martha Brae R.

(2)

Clark's Town

Green Island

Glasgow

Albert Town

Alexandria

Long Bay

Negril Beach
Hedonism II Beach

Savanna-la-Mar

B6

B3

Christiana

(9) Negril

A2

Balaclava

B6

Mandeville

Southwest Pt.

(13) — (25)

Bluefields Beach

Bluefields

Black R.

Middle Quarters

Santa Cruz

A2

(10)

A2

Black River

Crane Beach

(46) (47)

Alligator Pond

Treasure Beach

Treasure Beach

Great Pedro Bluff

Old Woman's Pt.

Long Bay

N

0 ——— 10 miles
0 ——— 15 km

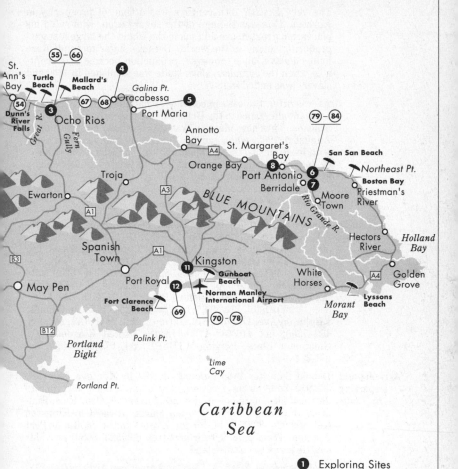

1 Exploring Sites

13 Hotels and Restaurants

divers have turned up some of the treasure, but most of it still lies in the depths, adding an exotic quality to the water sports pursued along Kingston's reefs.

The very British 18th century was a time of prosperity in Jamaica. This was the age of the sugar baron, who ruled his plantation great house and made the island the largest sugar-producing colony in the world. Because sugar fortunes were built on slave labor, however, production became less profitable when the Jamaican slave trade was abolished in 1807 and slavery was ended in 1838.

As was often the case in colonies, a national identity came to supplant allegiance to the British in the hearts and minds of Jamaicans. This new identity was given official recognition on August 6, 1962, when Jamaica became an independent nation with loose ties to the Commonwealth. The island today has a democratic form of government led by a prime minister and by a cabinet of fellow ministers.

Before You Go

Tourist Information
Contact the **Jamaica Tourist Board,** 866 2nd Ave., New York, NY 10017, tel. 212/688–7650 or 800/223–5225, fax 212/759–5012; 36 S. Wabash Ave., Suite 1210, Chicago, IL 60603, tel. 312/346–1546, fax 312/346–1667; 1320 S. Dixie Hwy., Coral Gables, FL 33146, tel. 305/665–0557, fax 305/666–7239; 8214 Westchester, Suite 500, Dallas, TX 75225, tel. 214/361–8778, fax 214/361–7049; 3440 Wilshire Blvd., Suite 1207, Los Angeles, CA 90010, tel. 213/384–1123, fax 213/384–1123. **In Canada:** 1 Eglinton Ave. E, Suite 616, Toronto, Ont. M4P 3A1, tel. 416/482–7850, fax 416/482–1730. **In the United Kingdom:** 111 Gloucester Place, London W1H3PH, tel. 071/224–0505, fax 071/224–0551.

Arriving and Departing
By Plane
Donald Sangster International Airport in Montego Bay (tel. 809/952–3009) is the most efficient point of entry for visitors destined for Montego Bay, Round Hill-Tryall, Ocho Rios, Runaway Bay, and Negril. **Norman Manley Airport** in Kingston (tel. 809/924–8024) is better for visitors to the capital or Port Antonio. **Trans Jamaica Airlines** (tel. 809/923–8680) provides shuttle services on the island.

Air Jamaica (tel. 800/523–5585) and **American Airlines** (tel. 212/619–6991 or 800/433–7300) fly nonstop from New York; Air Jamaica also comes in from Miami, and **BWIA** (tel. 800/JET-BWIA) from San Juan. **Continental** (tel. 800/231–0856) flies in daily from Newark, **Northwest Airlines** (tel. 212/563–7200 or 800/447–4747) flies in daily to Montego Bay from Minneapolis and Tampa, and **Aeroflot** (tel. 809/929–2251) flies in from Havana. Air Jamaica provides the most frequent service from U.S. cities, flying from Philadelphia, Atlanta, New York, Baltimore, and Miami. **Air Canada** (tel. 800/776–3000) offers service from Toronto and Montreal in conjunction with Air Jamaica, and both **British Airways** (tel. 800/247–9297) and Air Jamaica connect the island with London.

Passports and Visas
Passports are not required of visitors from the United States or Canada, but every visitor must have proof of citizenship, such as a birth certificate or a voter registration card (a driver's license is *not* enough). British visitors need passports but not visas. Each visitor must possess a return or ongoing ticket.

Declaration forms are distributed in flight in order to keep customs formalities to a minimum.

Language The official language of Jamaica is English. Islanders usually speak a patois among themselves, and they may use it when they don't want you to understand something.

Precautions Do not let the beauty of Jamaica cause you to relax the caution and good sense you would use in your own hometown. Never leave money or other valuables in your hotel room; use the safe-deposit boxes that most establishments make available. Carry your funds in traveler's checks, not cash, and keep a record of the check numbers in a secure place. Never leave a rental car unlocked, and never leave valuables even in a locked car. Finally, resist the call of the wild when it presents itself as a scruffy-looking native offering to show you the "real" Jamaica. Jamaica *on* the beaten path is wonderful enough; don't take chances by wandering far from it. And ignore his efforts, however persistent, to sell you a ganja joint.

Staying in Jamaica

Important **Tourist Information:** The main office of the **Jamaica Tourist**
Addresses **Board** is in Kingston (Tourism Centre Bldg., New Kingston Box 360, Kingston 5, tel. 809/929–9200). There are also JTB desks at both Montego Bay and Kingston airports and JTB offices in all resort areas.

Emergencies **Police, Fire, and Ambulance:** Police and Air-Rescue is 119; fire department and ambulance is 110. **Hospitals: University Hospital** at Mona in Kingston (tel. 809/927–1620), **Cornwall Regional Hospital** (Mt. Salem, in Montego Bay, tel. 809/952–5100), **Port Antonio General Hospital** (Naylor's Hill in Port Antonio, tel. 809/993–2646), and **St. Ann's Bay Hospital** (near Ocho Rios, tel. 809/972–2272). **Pharmacies: Pegasus Hotel** in Kingston (tel. 809/926–3690), **McKenzie's Drug Store** (16 Strand St. in Montego Bay, tel. 809/952–2467), and **Great House Pharmacy** (Brown's Plaza in Ocho Rios, tel. 809/974–2352).

Currency The Jamaican government abolished the fixed rate of exchange for the Jamaican dollar, allowing it to be traded publicly and subject to market fluctuations. At press time the Jamaican dollar was worth about J$22 to US$1. Currency can be exchanged at airport bank counters, exchange bureaus, or commercial banks. Prices quoted below are in U.S. dollars unless otherwise noted.

Taxes and Hotels collect a 5% government tax on room occupancy. The de-
Service Charges parture tax is approximately $10.

Most hotels and restaurants add a 10% service charge to your bill. Otherwise, tips may average 15%–20%.

Guided Tours Half-day tours are offered by a variety of operators in the important areas of Jamaica. The best Great Houses tours include Rose Hall, Greenwood, and Devon House. Plantations to tour are Prospect and Brimmer's Hall. The Appleton Estate Express Tour uses a diesel railcar to visit villages, plantations, and a rum distillery. The increasingly popular waterside folklore feasts are offered on the Dunn's, Great, and White rivers. The significant city tours are those in Kingston, Montego Bay, and Ocho Rios. Quality tour operators include **Martin's Tours** (tel. 809/922–5246), **Tropical Tours** (tel. 809/952–1110),

Greenlight Tours (tel. 809/952–4490), Estate Tours Services (tel. 809/974–2058), and Jamaica Tours (tel. 809/952–8074). The highlight of the Hilton High Day Tour (tel. 809/952–3343), which has been dubbed "Up, Up, and Buffet," is a Meet the People, experience Jamaican food, and learn some of its history day, all on a private estate ($55, including transportation). Helitours Jamaica Ltd. offers a way to see Jamaica from the air, with helicopter tours ranging from 10 minutes to an hour aloft at prices that vary accordingly ($50–$250). Contact the Ocho Rios office (tel. 809/974–2265). South Coast Safaris Ltd. has guided boat excursions up the Black River for some 10 miles (round-trip), into the mangroves and marshlands, aboard the 25-passenger *Safari Queen* and 25-passenger *Safari Princess* (tel. 809/962–0220 or 809/965–2513).

Getting Around
Taxis Some but not all of Jamaica's taxis are metered. If you accept a driver's offer of his services as a tour guide, be sure to agree on a price *before* the vehicle is put into gear. All licensed taxis display red Public Passenger Vehicle (PPV) plates, as well as regular license plates. Cabs can be summoned by telephone or flagged down on the street. Taxi rates are per car, not per passenger, and 25% is added to the metered rate between midnight and 5 AM. Licensed minivans are also available and bear the red PPV plates.

Rental Cars Jamaica has dozens of car-rental companies throughout the island. Because rentals can be difficult to arrange once you've arrived, you *must* make reservations and send a deposit before your trip. (Cars are scarce, and without either a confirmation number or a receipt you may have to walk.) Best bets are: Avis (tel. 800/331–1212), Dollar (tel. 800/800–4000), Hertz (tel. 800/654–3131), National (tel. 800/227–3876). In Jamaica, try the branch offices in your resort area: United Car Rentals (tel. 809/952–3077), or Jamaica Car Rental (tel. 809/924–8217). You must be at least 21 years old to rent a car, and you must have a valid driver's license (from any country). You may be required to post a security of several hundred dollars before taking possession of your car; ask about it when you make the reservation.

Traffic keeps to the left in Jamaica, and those who are unfamiliar with driving on the left will find that it takes some getting used to. Be cautious until you are comfortable with it.

Trains The diesel train run by the Jamaica Railway Corporation (tel. 809/922–6620) between Kingston and Montego Bay reveals virtually every type of scenery Jamaica has to offer in a trip of nearly five hours. At press time operation was temporarily suspended.

Buses Buses are the mode of transportation Jamaicans use most, and consequently some buses are very crowded and slow. Yet the service is quite good between Kingston and Montego Bay and between other significant destinations. Schedule or route information is available at bus stops or from the bus driver.

Cycles The front desks of most major hotels can arrange the rental of bicycles, mopeds, and motorcycles. Daily rates run from about $45 for a moped to $70 for a Honda 550. Deposits of $100–$300 or more are required.

Telephones and Mail The area code for all Jamaica is 809. Direct telephone, telegraph, telefax, and telex services are available.

At press time, airmail postage from Jamaica to the United States or Canada was J$1.10 for letters, J$.90 for postcards. Local mail cost J$.50.

Opening and Closing Times Normal business hours for stores are weekdays 8–4, Saturday 8–1. Banking hours are generally Monday–Thursday 9–2, Friday 9–noon, 2:30–5.

Exploring Jamaica

Numbers in the margin correspond to points of interest on the Jamaica map.

Montego Bay
❶ The number and variety of its attractions make **Montego Bay,** on the island's northwest corner, the logical place to begin an exploration of Jamaica. Confronting the string of high-rise developments that crowd the water's edge, you may find it hard to believe that little of what is now Montego Bay (the locals call it MoBay) existed before the turn of the century. Today many explorations of Montego Bay are conducted from a reclining chair on Doctor's Cave Beach, with a table nearby to hold frothy drinks.

Rose Hall Great House, perhaps the greatest in the West Indies in the 1700s, enjoys its popularity less for its architecture than for the legend surrounding its second mistress, Annie Palmer, who was credited with murdering three husbands and a plantation overseer who was her lover. The story is told in two novels sold everywhere in Jamaica: *The White Witch of Rose Hall* and *Jamaica White.* The great house is east of Montego Bay, just across the highway from the Rose Hall resorts. *Tel. 809/953–2323. Admission: $10 adults, $6 children. Open daily 9:30–6.*

Greenwood Great House, 15 miles east of Montego Bay, has no spooky legend to titillate visitors, but it's much better than Rose Hall at evoking the atmosphere of life on a sugar plantation. The Barrett family, from which the English poet Elizabeth Barrett Browning was descended, once owned all the land from Rose Hall to Falmouth, and the family built several great houses on it. The poet's father, Edward Moulton Barrett ("the Tyrant of Wimpole Street"), was born at Cinnamon Hill, currently the private estate of country singer Johnny Cash. Highlights of Greenwood include oil paintings of the Barretts, china made especially for the family by Wedgwood, a library filled with rare books printed as early as 1697, fine antique furniture, and a collection of exotic musical instruments. *Tel. 809/953–1077. Admission: $8. Open daily 9–6.*

❷ One of the most popular excursions in Jamaica is rafting on the **Martha Brae River.** The gentle waterway takes its name from that of an Arawak Indian who killed herself because she refused to reveal the whereabouts of a local gold mine to the Spanish. According to legend, she finally agreed to take them there and, on reaching the river, used magic to change its course and drowned herself along with the greedy Spaniards. Her *duppy* (ghost) is said to guard the mine's entrance to this day. Bookings are made through hotel tour desks. The trip is $32 per raft (two per raft) for the 1½-hour river run, about 28 miles from most hotels in Montego Bay. There are gift shops, a bar/restaurant, and swimming pool at the top of the river where you purchase tickets. To make arrangements call 809/952–0889.

The **Appleton Estate Express** (tel. 809/952–3692 or 809/952–6606), an air-conditioned diesel railcar, takes you through the lush hills and countryside around Montego Bay. You'll get a look at Jamaican villages, plantations growing banana and coconut, coffee groves, and the facility that turns out Appleton Rum. The full-day excursion leaves from the Appleton Estate station Tuesday–Friday at 8:50 AM and returns at 4:30 PM. The $60 fare includes transfers to and from your hotel, Continental breakfast prior to departure from the station, buffet lunch, and open bar.

There is also **Mountain Valley Rafting** on the river Lethe, approximately 12 miles (about 30 minutes) southwest of Montego Bay. The trip is $32 per raft (two per raft), lasting an hour or so through unspoilled hillside country. Bookings are made through hotel tour desks or by calling 809/952–0527.

An Evening on the Great River is a must for tour groups, yet fun nonetheless. The adventure includes a boat ride up the torchlit river, a full Jamaican dinner, a native folklore show, and dancing to a reggae band. *Tel. 809/952–5047. $55 per person with hotel pickup and return; $50 if you arrive via your own transport. Sun., Tues., and Thurs.*

Ocho Rios
❸
Perhaps more than anywhere else in Jamaica, **Ocho Rios**—67 miles east of Montego Bay—presents a striking contrast of natural beauty and recreational development. The Jamaicans can fill the place by themselves, especially on a busy market day, when cars and buses from the countryside clog the heavily traveled coastal road that links Port Antonio with Montego Bay. Add a tour bus or three and the entire passenger list from a cruise ship, and you may find yourself mired in a considerable traffic jam.

Time Out
Double V Jerk Centre (109 Main St., tel. 809/974–2084) is a good place to park yourself for frosty Red Stripe beer and fiery jerk pork or chicken. Lively at lunch (when you can tour the minizoo and botanical gardens), it also rocks at night with an informal disco.

Yet a visit to Ocho Rios is worthwhile, if only to enjoy its two chief attractions—Dunn's River Falls and Prospect Plantation. A few steps away from the main road in Ocho Rios await some of the most charming inns and oceanfront restaurants in the Caribbean. Lying on the sand of what will seem to be your private cove or swinging gently in a hammock with a tropical drink in your hand, you'll soon forget the traffic that's only a brief stroll away.

The dispute continues as to the origin of the name *Ocho Rios.* Some claim it's Spanish for "eight rivers"; others maintain that the name is a corruption of *chorreras,* which describes a seemingly endless series of cascades that sparkle from the limestone rocks along this stretch of coast. For as long as anyone can remember, Jamaicans have favored Ocho Rios as their own escape from the heat and the crowds of Kingston.

Dunn's River Falls (tel. 809/974–2857) is an eye-catching sight: 600 feet of cold, clear mountain water splashing over a series of stone steps to the warm Caribbean. The best way to enjoy the falls is to climb the slippery steps. Don a swimsuit, take the hand of the person ahead of you, and trust that the chain of hands and bodies leads to an experienced guide. Those who lead the climbs are personable fellows who reel off bits of local lore while telling you where to stop. *Admission: $1.50 adults, 75¢ children.*

Prospect Plantation Tour (tel. 809/974–2058) is the best of several offerings that delve into the island's former agricultural lifestyle. It's not just for specialists; virtually everyone enjoys the beautiful views over the White River Gorge and the tour by jitney (a canopied open-air cart pulled by a tractor) through a plantation with exotic fruits and tropical trees planted over the years by such celebrities as Winston Churchill and Charlie Chaplin. Horseback riding over 1,000 acres is available. *Admission: about $10.*

The only major historic site in Ocho Rios is **The Old Fort,** built in 1777 as a defense against invaders from the sea. The original "defenders" spent much of their time sacking and plundering as far afield as St. Augustine, Florida, and sharing their bounty with the local plantation owners who financed their missions. Fifteen miles west is Discovery Bay, site of Columbus's landing. A small museum of artifacts is scheduled to open in 1994 as part of the ongoing Columbus Park development.

Other excursions of note are the one to Runaway Bay's Green Grotto Caves (and a boat ride on an underground lake), a ramble through the Shaw Park Botanical Gardens, and a drive through Fern Gully, a natural canopy of vegetation filtered by sunlight (Jamaica has the world's largest number of fern species, over 350).

❹ Two area residences are of more than passing interest. **Golden Eye,** just east of Ocho Rios on the main coast road, was used in wintertime by Ian Fleming, the creator of James Bond, from 1946 until his death in 1964. Since then Golden Eye has served as home to reggae legend Bob Marley and to the founder of Island Records, Chris Blackwell. Today it can be seen only by those who can afford to rent it from the record company. It's an airy complex of deep-blue buildings, walls and bookcases bursting with Bond memorabilia, and a private cove reached by stone steps that would have delighted 007 (provided the Martini would not be badly shaken during the descent).

❺ **Firefly,** about 20 miles east of Ocho Rios in Port Maria, was once Sir Noël Coward's vacation residence and is now preserved in all its hilltop wonder by the National Trust of Jamaica. Coward used to entertain jet-setters and royalty in the surprisingly Spartan digs in an Eden-like setting. The Jamaicans who give impromptu tours of Firefly, for a cost of $1.75, used to work for Sir Noël, and they show a moving reverence for his simple grave on the grounds. Further information on Ocho Rios is available from the Ocho Rios JTB Office (tel. 809/974–2570).

Port Antonio Every visitor's presence in **Port Antonio** pays homage to the
❻ beginnings of Jamaican tourism. Early in the century the first tourists arrived here on the island's northeast tip, 133 miles east of Montego Bay, drawn by the exoticism of the island's banana trade and seeking a respite from the New York winters. The original posters of the shipping lines make Port Antonio appear as foreign as the moon, yet in time it became the tropical darling of a fast-moving crowd and counted Clara Bow, Bette Davis, Ginger Rogers, Rudyard Kipling, J. P. Morgan, and

William Randolph Hearst among its admirers. Its most passionate devotee was the actor Errol Flynn, whose spirit still seems to haunt the docks, devouring raw dolphin and swigging gin at 10 AM. Flynn's widow, Patrice Wymore Flynn, owns a boutique in the Palace Hotel and operates a working cattle farm.

Although the action has moved elsewhere, the area can still weave a spell. Robin Moore wrote *The French Connection* here, and Broadway's tall and talented Tommy Tune found inspiration for the musical *Nine* while being pampered at Trident.

With the help of recent renovations, a stroll through the town suggests a step into the past. A couple of miles north of Port Antonio's main street, **Queen Street** in the residential Titchfield area offers fine Georgian architecture. **DeMontevin Lodge** (21 Fort George St., on Titchfield Hill, tel. 809/993–2604), owned by the Mullings family (the late Gladys Mullings was Errol Flynn's cook), and the nearby **Musgrave Street** (the Craft Market is here) are in the traditional sea-captain style that one finds along coasts as far away as New England.

The town's best-known landmark is **Folly,** on the way to Trident, a Roman-style villa in ruins on the eastern edge of East Harbor. The creation of a Connecticut millionaire in 1905, the manse was made almost entirely of concrete. Unfortunately, the cement was mixed with seawater, and it began to crumble as it dried. According to local lore, the millionaire's bride took one look at her shattered dream, burst into tears, and fled forever. Little more than the marble floor remains today.

Time Out   **Navy Island Resort and Marina** is the 64-acre island made famous by Errol Flynn when he bought it. The present operator welcomes visitors, who catch the private launch to his restaurant for lunch (or dinner, by prior reservation: tel. 809/993–2667). Lunch can be as simple as a thick pepperpot soup and grilled fish with lime; dinner can be a five-course spectacular.

7 Rafting on the **Rio Grande River** (yes, Jamaica has a Rio Grande, too) is a must. This is the granddaddy of the river-rafting attractions, an 8-mile-long, swift green waterway from Berrydale to Rafter's Rest. Here the river flows into the Caribbean at St. Margaret's Bay. The trip of about three hours is made on bamboo rafts pushed along by a raftsman who is likely to be a character. You can pack a picnic lunch and eat it on the raft or along the riverbank; wherever you lunch, a vendor of Red Stripe beer will appear at your elbow. A restaurant, bar, and souvenir shops are at Rafter's Rest (tel. 809/993–2778). About $42 per two-person raft.

8 Another interesting excursion takes you to **Somerset Falls,** a special sun-dappled spot crawling with flowering vines, where you can climb the 400 feet with some assistance from a concrete staircase. A brief raft ride takes you part of the way. **Athenry Gardens** (tel. 809/993–3740), a 16-acre tropical wonderland, and **Nonsuch Cave** are some 6 miles northeast of Port Antonio in the village of Nonsuch. The cave's underground beauty has been made accessible by concrete walkways, railed stairways, and careful lighting.

A short drive east from Port Antonio deposits you at **Boston Bay,** which is popular with swimmers and has been enshrined by lovers of jerk pork. The spicy barbecue was originated by the Arawaks and perfected by runaway slaves called the Maroons. Eating almost nothing but wild hog preserved over smoking coals enabled the Maroons to survive years of fierce guerrilla warfare with the English.

For as long as anyone can remember, Port Antonio has been a center for some of the finest deep-sea fishing in the Caribbean. Dolphins (the delectable fish, not the lovable mammal) are the likely catch here, along with tuna, kingfish, and wahoo. In October the week-long Blue Marlin Tournament attracts anglers from around the world. By the time enough beer has been consumed, it's a bit like the running of the bulls at Pamplona, except that fish stories carry the day. Further information on Port Antonio is available from the Port Antonio JTB Office (tel. 809/993–3051).

Crystal Springs, about 18 miles west of Port Antonio, has more than 15,000 orchids, and hummingbirds dart among the blossoms, landing on visitors' outstretched hands. Hiking and camping are available here.

Negril Situated 52 miles southwest of Montego Bay on the winding
9 coast road, **Negril** is no longer Jamaica's best-kept secret. In fact, it has begun to shed some of its bohemian, ramshackle atmosphere for the attractions and activities traditionally associated with Montego Bay. Applauding the sunset from Rick's Cafe may still be the highlight of a day in Negril, yet increasingly the hours before and after have come to be filled with conventional recreation.

One thing that has not changed around this west coast center (whose only true claim to fame is a 7-mile beach) is the casual approach to life. As you wander from lunch in the sun to shopping in the sun to sports in the sun, you'll find that swimsuits are common attire. Want to dress for a special meal? Slip a caftan over your bathing suit.

Even though you may be staying at one of the charming smaller inns in Negril, you may enjoy spending a day at **Hedonism II,** a kind of love poem to health, Mother Nature, and good (mostly clean) fun. The owners love to publicize the occasional nude volleyball game in the pool at 3 AM, but most of the pampered campers are in clothes and in bed well before that hour. And what if Hedonism II is not the den of iniquity it likes to appear to be? What it is, and what your day pass ($50) gets you, is a taste of the spirit as well as the food and drink—and participation in water sports, tennis, squash, and daily activities.

Next to Hedonism II is a sister resort, the **Grand Lido,** that offers a "night pass" for nonguests that includes dinner at the Cafe Lido, live entertainment, and dusk-to-dawn dancing. The price is a hefty $80, and reservations are a must. Further information on Negril is available from the Negril JTB office (tel. 809/957–4243).

After sunset, activity centers on **West End Road,** Negril's main (and only) thoroughfare, which comes to life in the evening with bustling bistros and ear-splitting discos. West End Road may still be unpaved, yet it leads to the town's only building of historical significance, the **Lighthouse.** All anyone can tell you about it, however, is that it's been there for a while. Even historians find it hard to keep track of the days in Negril.

Negril today stretches along the coast north from the horse-shoe-shaped **Bloody Bay** (named during the period when it was a whale-processing center), along the calm waters of **Long Bay** to the Lighthouse section and the landmark **Rick's Cafe** (tel. 809/957–4335). Sunset at Rick's is a tradition, one not unlike the event observed at Mallory Square in Key West. Here there are jugglers and fire-eaters, 50-foot cliffs, and divers who go spiraling downward into the deep green depths.

In the 18th century Negril was where the English ships assembled in convoys for the dangerous ocean crossing. Not only were there pirates in the neighborhood, but the infamous Calico Jack and his crew were captured right here, while they guzzled the local rum. All but two of them were hanged on the spot; Mary Read and Anne Bonney were pregnant at the time, and their execution was delayed.

Mandeville More than a quarter of a century after Jamaica achieved its in-
⑩ dependence from Great Britain, **Mandeville** seems like a hilly tribute to all that is genteel and admirable in the British character. At 2,000 feet above sea level, 70 miles southeast of Montego Bay, Mandeville is considerably cooler than the coastal area 25 miles to the south. Its vegetation is more lush, thanks to the mists that drift through the mountains. The people of Mandeville live their lives around a village green, a Georgian courthouse, tidy cottages and gardens, even a parish church. The entire scene could be set down in Devonshire, were it not for the occasional poinciana blossom or citrus grove.

Mandeville is omitted from most tourist itineraries even though its residents are increasingly interested in showing visitors around. It is still much less expensive than any of the coastal resorts, and its diversions include horseback riding, cycling, croquet, hiking, tennis, golf, and people-meeting.

The town itself is characterized by its orderliness. You may stay here several days, or a glimpse of the lifestyle may satisfy you and you'll scurry back to the steamy coast. **Manchester Club** features tennis, nine holes of golf, and well-manicured greens; **Mrs. Stephenson's Gardens** are lovely, with orchids and fruit trees; the natural **Bird Sanctuary** at Marshalls Pen (tel. 809/962–2260) shows off 25 species indigenous to Jamaica; and **Marshall's Penn Great House** offers an array of walking tours. The cool, crisp air will make you feel up to any stroll in Mandeville. Further information on Mandeville is available from the Mandeville office of the JTB (tel. 809/962–1072), or through the visitors information center at the Hotel Astra (tel. 809/962–3265 or 809/962–3377).

Kingston The reaction of most visitors to the capital city, situated on the southeast coast of Jamaica, is anything but love at first sight. In fact, only a small percentage of visitors to Jamaica see it at all. ⑪ **Kingston,** for the tourist, may seem as remote from the resorts of Montego Bay as the loneliest peak in the Blue Mountains. Yet the islanders themselves can't seem to let it go. Everybody talks about Kingston, about their homes or relatives there, about their childhood memories. More than the sunny havens of the north coast, Kingston is a distillation of the true Jamaica. Parts of it may be dirty, crowded, often raucous, yet it is the ethnic cauldron that produces the cultural mix that is the nation's greatest natural resource (the Jamaican motto is "Out of many, one people"). Kingston is a cultural and commercial crossroads of international and local movers and shakers, art-show openings, theater (from Shakespeare to pantomime), and superb shopping. Here, too, the University of the West Indies explores Caribbean art and literature, as well as science. As one Jamaican put it, "You don't really know Jamaica until you know Kingston."

The best way to approach this city is from within, staying in one of the quiet residential sections and dining with the local inhabitants in restaurants that seem to have no names (people refer to them by their addresses, such as 73 or 64, and everyone knows where to meet). The first-time business or pleasure traveler may prefer to begin with New Kingston, a former racetrack property that now glistens with hotels, office towers, apartments, and boutiques. Newcomers may feel more comfortable settling in here and venturing forth from comfort they know will await their return.

Kingston's colonial past is very much alive away from the high rises of the new city. **Devon House** (tel. 809/929–6602), our first stop, is reached through the iron gates at 26 Hope Road. Built in 1881 and bought and restored by the government in the 1960s, the mansion has period furnishings. Shoppers will appreciate Devon House, for the firm Things Jamaican has converted portions of the space into some of the best crafts shops on the island. On the grounds you'll find one of the few mahogany trees to survive Kingston's ambitious but not always careful development. Further information on Kingston is available at the Kingston JTB Office (tel. 809/929–9200).

Time Out Bob Marley's former cook has opened her own restaurant, on two floors of a simple wooden rondel. **Minnie's Ethiopian Herbal-Health Food** (176 Old Hope Rd., tel. 809/927–9207) sells food and fresh juices (at last count, there were more than 15 fresh fruit juices), prepared Rasta-health style. From early in the AM, this is the place for a true Jamaican breakfast of *ackee* with festival (a vegetable with cornmeal bread), or *callaloo* with "food" (a spinach with ground tubers), then on to a lunch of vegetable run-down or gungo-pea stew. On Friday nights musicians drop by to jam and juice.

Among nearby residences, **Kings House,** farther along Hope Road, is the home of Jamaica's governor-general, and **Vale Royal** on Montrose Road is home to the prime minister. The latter structure, originally built as a plantation house in the 1700s, is one of the few still standing in the capital that has a lookout tower for keeping an eye on ships in the harbor. *Tel. 809/927–6424. King's House is only open weekdays, 10–5.*

Once you have accepted the fact that Kingston doesn't look like a travel poster—too much life goes on here for that—you may see your trip here for precisely what it is, the single best introduction to the people of Jamaica. Near the waterfront, the **Institute of Jamaica** (tel. 809/922–0620) is a museum and library that traces the island's history from the Arawaks to current events. The charts and almanacs here make fascinating browsing; one example, famed as the Shark Papers, is made up of damaging evidence tossed overboard by a guilty sea captain and later recovered from the belly of a shark.

From the Institute, push onward to the **University of the West Indies** (tel. 809/927–1660) in the city's Mona section. A cooperative venture begun after World War II by several West Indian governments, the campus is set in an eye-catching cradle of often misty mountains. In addition to a bar and a disco where you can meet the students (they pay dues, while tourists enter free), the place seems a monument to the conviction that education and commitment lead to a better life for the entire Caribbean.

Jamaica's rich cultural life is evoked at the **National Gallery** (12 Ocean Blvd., tel. 809/922–1561), which was once at Devon House and can now be found at Kingston Mall near the reborn waterfront section. The artists represented here may not be household words in other nations, yet the paintings of such intuitive masters as John Dunkley, David Miller, Sr., and David Miller, Jr., reveal a sensitivity to the life around them that transcends academic training. Among other highlights from the 1920s through the 1980s are works by Edna Manley and Mallica Reynolds, better known as Kapo. Reggae fans touring the National Gallery will want to look for Christopher Gonzalez's controversial statue of Bob Marley.

Reggae fans will also want to see **Tuff Gong International** (56 Hope Rd.). Painted in Rastafarian red, yellow, and green, this recording studio was built by Marley at the height of his career. The house has since become the **Bob Marley Museum** (tel. 809/ 927–9152), with impromptu tours given by just about anyone who may be around. Certainly there is much here to help the outsider understand Marley, reggae, and Jamaica itself. The Ethiopian flag is a reminder that Rastas consider the late Ethiopian emperor Haile Selassie to be the Messiah, a descendant of King Solomon and the Queen of Sheba. A striking mural by Everald Brown, *The Journey of Superstar Bob Marley*, depicts the hero's life from its beginnings in a womb shaped like a coconut to enshrinement in the hearts of the Jamaican people.

A distinct change of pace is offered by the **Royal Botanical Gardens at Hope** (tel. 809/927–1257), a cooling sanctuary donated to Jamaica by the Hope family following the abolition of slavery. Some 200 acres explode with tropical trees, plants, and flowers, each clearly labeled and lovingly discussed by qualified guides. Free concerts are given here on the first Sunday of each month.

Unless your visit must be very brief, you shouldn't leave Kingston without a glimpse of "the wickedest city in the world." **Port Royal** has hardly been that since an earthquake tumbled it into the sea in 1692, yet the spirits of Henry Morgan and other buccaneers add a great deal of energy to what remains. The proudest possession of **St. Peter's Church,** rebuilt in 1725 to replace Christ's Church, is a silver communion plate donated by Morgan himself.

You can no longer down rum in Port Royal's legendary 40 taverns, but you can take in a draft of the past at the **Archaeological and Historical Museum** (tel. 809/924–8706), located within the Police Training School building, and explore the impressive remains of Fort Charles, once the area's major garrison. On the grounds are a small **Maritime Museum** and a tipsy, angled structure known as **Giddy House.** Nearby is a graveyard in which rests a man who died twice. According to the tombstone, Lewis Goldy was swallowed up in the great earthquake of 1692, spewed into the sea, rescued, and lived another four decades in "Great Reputation." Port Royal attractions are open daily 9–5.

Jamaica for Free

Fifteen years ago Jamaica introduced the *Meet the People* concept that has become so popular in the Caribbean. One of the best free attractions anywhere, it allows visitors to get together with islanders who have compatible interests and expertise. The nearly 600 Jamaican families who participate in Meet the People on a voluntary basis offer their guests a spectrum of activities from time at a business or home to musical or theatrical performances. The program's theme is Forget Me Not, the name of a tiny blue flower that grows on Jamaican hillsides. Once you've met these people, you're not likely to forget them. It's important to arrange your occasion in advance of your trip through the Jamaica Tourist Board.

Off the Beaten Track

The Cockpit Country, 15 miles inland from Montego Bay and one of the most primitive areas in the West Indies, is a terrain of pitfalls and potholes carved by nature in limestone. For nearly a century after 1655 it was known as the Land of Look Behind because British soldiers rode their horses back to back in pairs, looking out for the savage freedom fighters known as Maroons. Fugitive slaves who refused to surrender to the invading English, the Maroons eventually won a treaty of independence and continue to live apart from the rest of Jamaica in the Cockpit Country. The government leaves them alone, untaxed and ungoverned by outside authorities. The Jamaica Tourist Board has information on minibus tours from Montego Bay to Maroon headquarters at Accompong.

Admirers of Jamaica's wonderful coffee may wish to tour the **Blue Mountains.** The best way to do so is in your own rental car, driving into the mountains from Kingston along Highway A3. Before departing, you should obtain directions either to **Pine Grove** or to the Jablum coffee plant at **Mavis Bank,** then follow the handlettered signs after you leave A3. It's an exciting excursion and a virtual pilgrimage for many coffee lovers. Pine Grove, a working coffee farm that doubles as an inn, has a restaurant that serves the owner Marcia Thwaites's Jamaican cuisine. Mavis Bank is delightfully primitive—considering the retail price of the beans it processes. There is no official tour; ask someone to show you around.

Spanish Town, 12 miles west of Kingston on A1, was the island's capital under Spanish rule. The town boasts the noblest Georgian square (Government Square) and the oldest cathedral (St. James) in the Western Hemisphere. Spanish Town's original name was Santiago de la Vega, which the English corrupted to St. Jago de la Vega, both meaning St. James of the Plains.

Beaches

Jamaica has some 200 miles of beaches, some of them still uncrowded. The beaches listed below are public places, and they are among the best Jamaica has to offer. In addition, nearly every resort has its own private beach, complete with towels and water sports. Some of the larger resorts sell day passes to nonguests. Generally, the farther west you travel, the lighter and finer the sand.

Doctor's Cave Beach at Montego Bay shows a tendency toward population explosion, attracting Jamaicans and tourists alike; at times it may resemble Fort Lauderdale at spring break. The 5-mile stretch of sugary sand has been spotlighted in so many travel articles and brochures over the years that it's no secret to anyone. On the bright side, Doctor's Cave is well fitted for all its admirers with changing rooms, colorful if overly insistent vendors, and a large selection of snacks.

Two other popular beaches in the Montego Bay area are **Cornwall Beach,** farther up the coast, which is smaller, also lively, with lots of food and drink available, and **Walter Fletcher Beach,** on the bay near the center of town. Fletcher offers protection from the surf on a windy day and therefore unusually fine swimming; the calm waters make it a good bet for children, too.

Ocho Rios appears to be just about as busy as MoBay these days, and the busiest beach is usually **Mallard's. The Jamaica Grande** hotel, formerly The Mallards Beach and Americana hotels, is here, spilling out its large convention groups at all hours of the day. Next door is **Turtle Beach,** which islanders consider the place for swimming in Ocho Rios.

In Port Antonio, head for **San San Beach** or **Boston Bay.** Any of the shacks spewing scented smoke along the beach at Boston Bay will sell you the famous peppery delicacy jerk pork.

Puerto Seco Beach at Discovery Bay is a sunny, sandy beach.

Kingston may seem an unlikely place for beach lovers, yet Kingstonians enjoy the water, too. **Gunboat Beach** is the most popular choice, and there are other options. **Fort Clarence,** a black-sand beach in the Hellshire Hills area southwest of the city, has changing facilities and entertainment. Sometimes Kingstonians are willing to drive 32 miles east to the lovely golden **Lyssons Beach** in Morant Bay or, for a small negotiable fee, to hire a boat at the Morgan's Harbor Marina at Port Royal to ferry them to **Lime Cay.** This island, just beyond Kingston Harbor, is perfect for picnicking, sunning, and swimming.

Not too long ago, the 7 miles of white sand at **Negril Beach** offered a beachcomber's vision of Eden. Today much of it is fenced off. The nude beach areas are sectioned off, and some new resorts are building accommodations overlooking their nude beaches, thereby adding a new dimension to the traditional notion of "ocean view."

Those who seek beaches off the main tourist routes will want to explore Jamaica's unexploited south coast. Nearest to "civilization" is **Bluefields Beach** near Savanna-la-Mar, south of Negril along the coast. **Crane Beach** at Black River is another great discovery. And the best of the south shore has to be **Treasure Beach,** 20 miles farther along the coast beyond Crane.

Sports and the Outdoors

The Tourist Board licenses all operators of recreational activities, which should ensure you of fair business practices as long as you deal with companies that display the decals.

Fishing Deep-sea fishing can be great around the island. Port Antonio gets the headlines with its annual Blue Marlin Tournament, and Montego Bay and Ocho Rios have devotees who talk of the sailfish, yellowfin tuna, wahoo, dolphin, and bonita. Licenses are not required. Boat charters can be arranged at your hotel.

Golf The best courses may be found at **Caymanas** (tel. 809/997–8026) and **Constant Spring** (tel. 809/924–1610) in Kingston; **Half Moon,** (tel. 809/953–2560), **Rose Hall,** (tel. 809/953–2650), **Tryall,** (tel. 809/952–5110), and **Ironshore** (tel. 809/953–2800) in Montego Bay; and **Runaway Bay** (tel. 809/973–2561) and **Upton** (tel. 809/974–2528) in Ocho Rios. A nine-hole course in the hills of Mandeville is called **Manchester Club** (tel. 809/962–2403), and Prospect Estate (tel. 809/974–2058) in Ocho Rios has an 18-hole mini-golf course.

Horseback Riding Jamaica is fortunate to have the best equestrian facility in the Caribbean, **Chukka Cove** (write Box 160, Ocho Rios, St. Ann, tel. 809/972–2506), near Ocho Rios. The resort, complete with stylishly outfitted villas, offers full instruction in riding, polo, and jumping, as well as hour-long trail rides, three-hour beach rides, and overnight rides to a Great House. Weekends, in-season, this is the place for hot polo action and equally hot social action. **Rocky Point Stables** (tel. 809/953–2286), at the Half Moon Club in Montego Bay and **Rhodes Hall Plantation Ltd.,** located between Green Island and Negril (tel. 809/957–4258), also offers rides.

Tennis Many hotels have tennis facilities that are free to their guests, but some will allow you to play for a fee. The sport is a highlight at **Tyrall** (tel. 809/952–5110), **Round Hill Hotel and Villas** (tel. 809/952–5150), and **Half Moon Club** (tel. 809/953–2211) in Montego Bay; **Swept Away** (tel. 809/957–4061) in Negril; and **Sans Souci Hotel & Spa** (tel. 809/974–2353) and **Ciboney** (tel. 809/974–5503) in Ocho Rios.

Water Sports The major areas for swimming, windsurfing, snorkeling, and scuba diving are Negril in the west and Port Antonio in the east. All the large resorts rent equipment for a deposit and/or a fee. Diving is perhaps the only option that requires training because you need to show a C-card in order to participate. However, some dive operators on the island are qualified to certify you. **Blue Whale Divers** (tel. 809/957–4438); **Sun Divers,** Poinciana Beach Hotel, Negril (tel. 809/957–4069), and Ambiance Hotel, Runaway Bay, tel. 809/973–2346); **Fantasea Divers** at the Beach Bar of the Sans Souci Hotel & Spa (Ocho Rios, tel. 809/975–4504); and **Seaworld Resorts Ltd.** (Montego Bay, tel. 809/953–2180, fax 809/952–5018) offer certification courses and dive trips. Some tour operators offer day trips that include an offshore excursion, snorkeling equipment, lunch, and cocktails. **Lady Godiva Ltd. at San-San Beach** (tel. 809/993–3318), in Port Antonio, has scuba diving, snorkeling, windsurfing, a glass-bottom boat, and sailing.

Shopping

Shopping in Jamaica goes two ways: things Jamaican and things imported. The former are made with style and skill; the latter are duty-free luxury finds. Jamaican crafts take the form of resortwear, hand-loomed fabrics, silk screening, wood carvings, paintings, and other fine arts.

Jamaican rum is a great take-home gift. So is Tia Maria, Jamaica's world-famous coffee liqueur. The same goes for the island's prized Blue Mountain and High Mountain coffees and its jams, jellies, and marmalades.

Some bargains, if you shop around, include Swiss watches, Irish crystal, jewelry, cameras, and china. The top-selling French perfumes are also available alongside Jamaica's own fragrances.

Shopping Areas A shopping tour of the Kingston area should begin at **Constant**
Kingston **Spring Road** or **King Street.** No matter where you begin, keep in mind that the trend these days is shopping malls, and in Jamaica it has caught on with a fever and an ever-growing roster: **Twin Gates Plaza, New Lane Plaza,** the **New Kingston Shopping Centre, Tropical Plaza, Manor Park Plaza, The Village, The Springs,** and the newest (and some say nicest), **The Sovereign Shopping Centre** (tel. 809/927–5955).

A day at **Devon House** (26 Hope Rd., Kingston, tel. 809/929–6602) should be high on your shopping list. This is the place to find old and new Jamaica. The great house is now a museum with antiques and furniture reproductions and the Lady Nugent's Coffee Terrace outside. There are boutiques in what were once the house's stables: a branch of Things Jamaican, Tanning and Turning for leather finds, first-rate furnishings and antique reproductions at Jacaranda, silver and pewter recreations (many from centuries-old patterns) at The Olde Port Royal, and some of the best tropical-fruit ice cream (mango, guava, pineapple, and passionfruit) at I-Scream.

Montego Bay and A must to avoid are the "crafts" stalls in MoBay and Ocho Rios
Ocho Rios that are literally filled with "higglers" desperate to sell touristy straw hats, T-shirts, and cheap jewelry. You may find yourself purchasing an unwanted straw something just to get out alive. If you're looking to spend money, head for **Overton Plaza, Miranda Ridge Plaza, St. James's Place,** and **Westgate Plaza** in Montego Bay; in Ocho Rios, the shopping plazas are **Pineapple Place, Ocean Village,** the **Taj Mahal, Coconut Grove,** and **Island Plaza.** It's also a good idea to chat with salespeople, who can enlighten you about the newer boutiques and their whereabouts.

Special Buys The **Gallery of West Indian Art** (1 Orange La., MoBay, tel. 809/
Arts and Crafts 952–4547 and at Round Hill, tel. 809/952–5150) is the place to find Jamaican and Haitian paintings. A corner of the gallery is devoted to hand-turned pottery (some painted) and beautifully carved birds and jungle animals.

Cheap sandals are good buys in shopping centers throughout Jamaica. While workmanship and leathers don't rival the craftsmanship of those found in Italy or Spain, neither do the prices (about $20 a pair). In Kingston there's **Lee's** (New Kingston Shopping Center, tel. 809/929–8614). In Ocho Rios, the **Pretty Feet Shoe Shop** (Ocean Village Shopping Centre, tel. 809/974–5040) is a good bet. In Montego Bay, try **Overton Plaza** or **Westgate Plaza.**

Things Jamaican (Devon House, Hope Rd., Kingston, tel. 809/929–6602; Fort St., MoBay, tel. 809/952–5650) has two outlets and two airport stalls that display and sell some of the best native crafts made in Jamaica. The Devon House branch offers items that range from carved wood bowls and trays to reproductions of silver and brass period pieces.

Records   Reggae tapes by world-famous Jamaican artists, such as Bob Marley, Ziggy Marley, Peter Tosh, and Third World, can be found easily in U.S. or European record stores, but a pilgrimage to **Randy's Record Mart** (17 N. Parade, Kingston, tel. 809/922–4859) should be high on the reggae lover's list. Also worth checking is the **Record Plaza** (Tropical Plaza, Kingston, tel. 809/926–7645), **Record City** (1 William St., Port Antonio, tel. 809/993–2836), and **Top Ranking Records** (Westgate Plaza, Montego Bay, tel. 809/952–1216). While Kingston is the undisputed place to make purchases, the determined somehow (usually with the help of a local) will find **Jimmy Cliff's Records** (Oneness Sq., MoBay, no phone), owned by reggae star Cliff.

Gift Ideas   Fine Macanudo handmade cigars make sensational gifts. They can be bought on departure at Montego Bay airport. Call 809/925–1082 for outlet information. Blue Mountain coffee can be found at **John R. Wong's Supermarket** (1 Tobago Ave., Kingston, tel. 809/926–4811) and the **Sovereign Supermarket** (Hope Rd., tel. 809/927–5955). If they're out of stock, you'll have to settle for High Mountain coffee, the natives' second preferred brand. If you're set on Blue Mountain, you may try **Magic Kitchen Ltd.** (Village Plaza, Kingston, tel. 809/926–8894).

Jamaican-brewed rums and Tia Maria can be bought at either the Kingston or MoBay airports before your departure. While the airport prices are no cheaper, there's no toting of heavy, breakable bottles from the hotel to the airport.

Specialty Shops   Belts, bangles, and beads are the name of the game at the factory of **Ital-Craft** (Shop 8, Upper Manor Park Shopping Plaza, 184C Spring Rd., Kingston, tel. 809/931–0477). Belts are the focus of this savvy operation, but it also produces some intriguing jewelry and purses (many made from reptile skins). While Ital-Craft's handmade treasures are sold in boutiques throughout Jamaica, we recommend a visit to the factory for the largest selection of these belts, made of spectacular shells, combined with leather, feathers, or fur. (The most ornate belts sell for about $75.) Go to **Patoo** (Upper Manor Park Plaza, Kingston, tel. 809/924–1552) for fine art, folk art, crafts, and collectibles.

L. A. Henriques (Upper Manor Park Plaza, tel. 809/942–2487) sells high-quality jewelry made to order.

Silk batiks, by the yard or made into chic designs, are at **Caribatik** (tel. 809/954–3314), the studio of the late Muriel Chandler, 2 miles east of Falmouth. Drawing on patterns in nature, Chandler has translated the birds, seascapes, flora, and fauna into works of art.

Teeny-weeny bikinis, which more than rival Rio's, are designed by **Sonia Vaz** and sold at her manufacturing outlet (77 East St., Kingston, tel. 809/922–9200) and at the Sandals and resorts (*see* Lodging, *below*).

Sprigs and Things (Miranda Ridge Plaza, Gloucester Ave., MoBay, tel. 809/952–4735) is where artist Janie Soren sells T-shirts featuring her hand-painted designs of birds and animals. She also paints canvas bags and tennis dresses.

Annabella Proudlock sells her unique wood Annabella Boxes, the covers depicting reproductions of Jamaican paintings, at a restored great house, Harmony Hall (an eight-minute drive from Ocho Rios, east on A1; tel. 809/975–4222). Reproductions of paintings, lithographs, and signed prints of Jamaican scenes are also for sale, along with hand-carved wood combs—all magnificently displayed. Harmony Hall is also well known for its year-round art shows by local artists.

Dining

Sampling the island's cuisine introduces you to virtually everything the Caribbean represents. Every ethnic group that has made significant contributions on another island has made them on Jamaica, too, adding to a Jamaican stockpot that is as rich as its melting pot. So many Americans have discovered the Caribbean through restaurants owned by Jamaicans that the very names of the island's dishes have come to represent the region as a whole.

Jamaican food represents a true cuisine, organized, interesting, and ultimately rewarding. It would be a terrible shame for anyone to travel to the heart of this complex culture without tasting several typically Jamaican dishes. Here are a few:

Rice and Peas. A traditional dish, known also as Coat of Arms and similar to the *moros y christianos* of Spanish-speaking islands: white rice cooked with red beans, coconut milk, scallions, and seasoning.

Pepperpot. The island's most famous soup—a peppery combination of salt pork, salt beef, okra, and the island green known as callaloo—is green, but at its best it tastes as though it ought to be red.

Curry Goat. Young goat is cooked with spices and is more tender and has a gentler flavor than the lamb for which it was a substitute for immigrants from India.

Ackee and Saltfish. Salted fish was once the best islanders could do between catches, so they invented this incredibly popular dish that joins saltfish (in Portuguese, *bacalao*) with ackee, a vegetable (introduced to the island by Captain Bligh of *Bounty* fame) that reminds most people of scrambled eggs.

Jerk Pork. Created by the Arawaks and perfected by the Maroons, jerk pork is the ultimate island barbecue. The pork (the purist cooks the whole pig) is covered with a paste of hot peppers, berries, and other herbs and cooked slowly over a coal fire. Many think that the "best of the best" jerk comes from Boston Beach in Port Antonio.

Patties are spicy meat pies that elevate street food to new heights. Although, in fact, they originated in Haiti, Jamaicans can give patty lessons to anybody.

Where restaurants are concerned, Kingston has the widest selection; its ethnic restaurants offer Italian, French, Rasta natural foods, Cantonese, German, Thai, Indian, Korean, and Continental fare. There are fine restaurants as well in all the resort areas, and the list includes many that are in large hotels.

Dress is casual chic (just plain casual at the local hangouts), except at the top resorts, some of which require semi-formal wear in the evening during high season.

Highly recommended restaurants are indicated by a star ★.

Category	Cost*
Very Expensive	over $40
Expensive	$30–$40
Moderate	$20–$30
Inexpensive	under $20

per person, excluding drinks and service charge (or tip)

Kingston

★ **Blue Mountain Inn.** The elegant Blue Mountain Inn is a 30-minute taxi ride from downtown and worth every penny of the fare. A former coffee-plantation great house built in 1754, the inn complements its atmosphere with Continental cuisine. All the classics of the beef and seafood repertoires are here, including steak Diane and lobster thermidor. *Gordon Town, tel. 809/927–1700. Reservations required. AE, MC, V. Expensive.*

Le Pavillon. Situated just off the Jamaica Pegasus lobby and noted for its afternoon teas, this is *the* place to go for lunch and dinner. The fare is international with a Jamaican flair. The wine list is excellent and costly. The seafood buffet lunch is served on Friday. *Jamaica Pegasus Hotel, tel. 809/926–3690. Reservations required. AE, DC, MC, V. Expensive.*

The Palm Court. Nestled on the mezzanine floor of the Wyndham Kingston, the elegant Palm Court is open for lunch and dinner (lunch is noon to 3 PM; dinner from 7 PM onward). The menu is Continental, with a heavy Italian accent: tagliatelle Alfredo, with ham and fresh mushrooms; tricolor pasta with shrimp, fish, and lobster; and a seafood kebab. *Wyndham Kingston, tel. 809/926–5430. Reservations recommended. AE, DC, MC, V. Moderate–Expensive.*

Temple Hall. Located in the hills, 30 minutes from New Kingston, this restaurant has the ambience of a 17th-century plantation house. The menu features home-grown vegetables, meats, and poultry effectively combining Caribbean nouvelle and Jamaican cuisine. *Stony Hill, tel. 809/942–2340. Reservations required. AE, MC, V. Moderate–Expensive.*

Hotel Four Seasons. The Four Seasons has been pleasing local residents for more than 25 years with its cuisine from the German and Swiss schools as well as local seafood. The setting tries to emulate Old World Europe without losing its casual island character. *18 Ruthven Rd., tel. 809/926–8805. Reservations recommended. AE, DC, MC, V. Moderate.*

Ivor Guest House. Serving international and Jamaican cuisines, this elegant yet cozy restaurant has an incredible view of Kingston, from 2,000 feet above sea level. Go for dinner, when the view is dramatically caught between the stars and the glittering brooch of Kingston's lights. Owner Hellen Aitken is an animated and cordial hostess. *Jack's Hill, tel. 809/977–0033. Reservations required. AE, MC, V. Moderate.*

★ **The Hot Pot.** Jamaicans love the Hot Pot for breakfast, lunch, and dinner. Fricassee chicken is the specialty, along with other local dishes, such as mackerel run-down (salted mackerel cooked down with coconut milk and spices) and ackee and salted cod. The restaurant's fresh juices "in season" are the best—tamarind, sorrel, coconut water, soursop, and cucumber. *2 Altamont Terr., tel. 809/929–3906. Reservations unnecessary. V. Inexpensive.*

Peppers. This casual outdoor bar is the "in" spot in Kingston, particularly on weekends. Sample the jerk pork and chicken

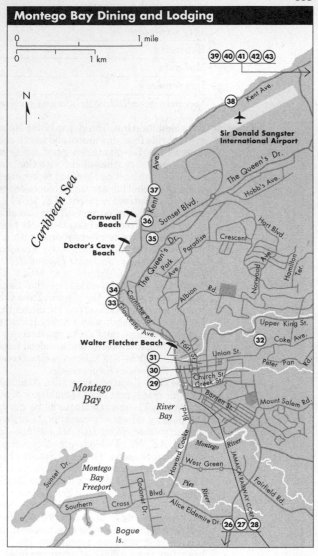

Montego Bay Dining and Lodging

with the local Red Stripe beer. *31 Upper Waterloo Rd., tel. 809/
925–2219. No credit cards. Inexpensive.*

Montego Bay　**Georgian House.** A landmark restaurant in the heart of town,
the Georgian House occupies two restored 18th-century build-
ings set in a shady garden courtyard. An extensive wine cellar
complements the Continental and Jamaican cuisines, the best
of which are the steaks and the dishes made with the local spiny
lobster. Free pickup from Montego Bay hotels. *Union and Orange Sts., tel. 809/952–0632. Reservations required. AE, DC,
MC, V. Expensive–Very Expensive.*

Pier 1. Despite the fact that it shares a name with the American
"import" store, Pier 1 writes the book daily on waterfront dining. After tropical drinks at the deck bar, you'll be ready to dig

into the international variations on fresh seafood, the best of which are the grilled lobster and any preparation of island snapper. *Just off Howard Cooke Blvd., tel. 809/952–2452. Reservations recommended. AE, MC, V. Expensive.*

★ **Sugar Mill.** The Sugar Mill (formerly the Club House) is where seafood is served with flair—on a terrace. Caribbean specialties, steak, and lobster are usually offered in a pungent sauce that blends Dijon mustard with Jamaica's own Pickapeppa. Other wise choices are the daily à la carte specials and anything flamed. *At Half Moon Golf Course, tel. 809/953–2228. Reservations required for dinner, recommended for lunch. AE, DC, MC, V. Expensive.*

Town House. Most of the rich and famous who have visited Jamaica over the decades have eaten at the Town House. You will find specials of the day and good versions of standard ideas (red snapper papillot is the specialty, with lobster, cheese, and wine sauce) in an 18-century Georgian house complete with shuttered windows. The restaurant offers free pickup service from your hotel. *16 Church St., tel. 809/952–2660. Reservations recommended. AE, DC, MC, V. Moderate–Expensive.*

Hemingway's Pub. Opened in 1990, this eatery has been a great success with the local business community, which enjoys the pub lunches and dinners. It's an air-conditioned casual bar/restaurant with satellite TV and the added bonus of a terrace for watching the sun go down. *At Miranda Ridge Plaza, Gloucester Ave., tel 809/952–8606. No credit cards. Inexpensive–Moderate.*

★ **Le Chalet.** Don't let the French name fool you. This Denny's lookalike, set in a nondescript shopping mall, serves heaping helpings of some of the best Chinese and Jamaican food in MoBay. Its staff will even pick you up from your hotel. *32 Gloucester Ave., tel. 809/952–5240. AE, MC, V. Inexpensive.*

★ **Pork Pit.** This open-air hangout three minutes from the airport must introduce more travelers to Jamaica's fiery jerk pork than any other place on the island. The Pork Pit is a local phenomenon down to the Red Stripe beer, yet it's accessible in both location and style. Plan to arrive around noon, when the jerk begins to be lifted from its bed of coals and pimento wood. *Adjacent to Fantasy Resort Hotel, tel. 809/952–1046. No reservations. No credit cards. Inexpensive.*

Negril **Rick's Cafe.** Here it is, the local landmark complete with cliffs, cliff divers, and powerful sunsets, all perfectly choreographed. It's a great place for a sunny brunch of omelets or eggs Benedict. In the sunset ritual, the crowd toasts Mother Nature with rum drinks, shouts and laughter, and ever-shifting meeting and greeting. When the sun slips below the horizon, there are more shouts, more cheers, and more rounds of rum. *Lighthouse Rd., tel. 809/957–4335. No credit cards. Moderate–Expensive.*

Cafe au Lait. The proprietors of Cafe au Lait are French and Jamaican, and so is the cuisine. Local seafood and produce are prepared with delicate touches and presented in a setting overlooking the sea. *Mirage Resort on Lighthouse Rd., tel. 809/957–4471. Reservations recommended. MC, V. Moderate.*

Tan-ya's. This alfresco restaurant is on the edge of the beach of its hotel, Seasplash. It features Jamaican delicacies with an international flavor for breakfast, lunch, and dinner. *Seasplash Hotel, Norman Manley Blvd., Negril, tel. 809/957–4041. AE, DC, MC, V. Moderate.*

★ **Cosmo's Seafood Restaurant and Bar.** Owner Cosmo Brown has made this seaside open-air bistro one of the best places in town to spend a lunch, an afternoon, and maybe stay on for dinner. (He's also open for breakfast. In fact, he only closes from 5 PM to 6:30 PM for a scrub-down.) The fresh fish is the featured attraction, and the conch soup that's the house specialty is a meal in itself. There's also lobster (grilled or curried), fish-and-chips, and a catch-of-the-morning. Customers often drop cover-ups to take a beach dip before coffee and dessert and return later to lounge in chairs scattered under almond and sea-grape trees. (There's an entrance fee for the beach alone, but it's less than $1.) *Norman Manley Blvd., tel. 809/957–4330. MC, V. Inexpensive.*

Paradise Yard. Locals enjoy this alfresco restaurant on the Savana-La-Mar side of the roundabout in Negril. Sit back and relax in the casual atmosphere while eating Jamaican dishes or the house special Rasta Pasta. Open for breakfast, lunch, and dinner. *Negril, tel. 809/957–4006. V. Inexpensive.*

Ocho Rios **Casanova.** The Sans Souci Hotel and Spa is imaginative enough
★ to serve homemade pastas in a comfortable open-air setting. All the Italian items are fine, and so are the smoked marlin, the "catch of the day," and light Jamaican cuisine. At lunch you must try chicken à la Deta, a spicy island version of barbecue; if it's not on the menu, ask for it. *Sans Souci Hotel, tel. 809/974–2353. Reservations recommended. AE, DC, MC, V. Expensive.*

★ **Almond Tree.** One of the most popular restaurants in Ocho Rios, the Almond Tree offers Jamaican dishes enlivened by a European culinary tradition. The swinging rope chairs of the terrace bar and the tables perched above a lovely Caribbean cove are great fun. You'll also find pumpkin and pepperpot soups, dramatic tableside preparations, and, among the entrées, wonderful family mementos. *83 Main St., Ocho Rios, tel. 809/974–2813. Reservations required. AE, DC, MC, V. Moderate–Expensive.*

The Ruins. A 40-foot waterfall dominates the open-air Ruins restaurant, and in a sense it dominates the food as well. Surrender to local preference and order the Lotus Lily Lobster, a stirfry of the freshest local shellfish, then settle back and enjoy the tree-shaded deck and the graceful footbridges that connect the dining patios. *DaCosta Dr., tel. 809/974–2442. Reservations recommended. AE, DC, MC, V. Moderate.*

★ **Evita's.** The setting here is a sensational, nearly 100-year-old gingerbread house high on a hill overlooking Ocho Rio's Bay (but also convenient from MoBay). More than 18 kinds of pasta are served here, ranging from lasagna Rastafari (vegetarian) to *rotelle alla Eva* (crabmeat with white sauce and noodles). There are also excellent fish dishes—sautéed fillet of red snapper with orange butter, red snapper stuffed with crabmeat—and several meat dishes, among them grilled sirloin with mushroom sauce and barbecued ribs glazed with honey-and-ginger sauce. *Mantalent Inn, Ocho Rios, tel. 809/974–2333. Reservations required. AE, MC, V. Inexpensive–Moderate.*

Lodging

The island has a variety of destinations to choose from, each of which offers its own unique expression of the Jamaican experience. **Montego Bay** has miles of hotels, villas, apartments, and duty-free shops set around Doctor's Cave Beach. Although lacking much cultural stimuli, MoBay presents a comfortable island backdrop for the many conventions and conferences it hosts.

Ocho Rios, on the northwest coast halfway between Port Antonio and Montego Bay, long enjoyed the reputation of being Jamaica's most favored out-of-the-way resort, but the late-blooming Negril has since stolen much of that distinction. Ocho Rios's hotels and villas are all situated within short driving distance of shops and one of Jamaica's most scenic attractions, Dunn's River Falls.

Port Antonio, described by poet Ella Wheeler Wilcox as "the most exquisite port on earth," is a seaside town nestled at the foot of verdant hills toward the east end of the north coast. The two best experiences to be had here are rafting the Rio Grande and a stop at the Trident, arguably the island's classiest resort.

Negril, some 50 miles west of Montego Bay, has become a by-word for the newest crop of all-inclusive resorts (the first, Hedonism II, the Grand Lido, Swept Away, and Sandals Negril). Negril itself is only a small village, so there isn't much of historical significance to seek out. Then again, that's not what brings the sybaritic singles and couples here. The crowd is young, hip, laid back, and open to alternative lifestyles.

Mandeville, 2,000 feet above the sea, is noted for its cool climate and proximity to secluded south coast beaches.

The smallest of the resort areas, **Runaway Bay** has a handful of modern hotels and an 18-hole golf course.

Kingston is the most culturally active place on Jamaica. Some of the island's finest hotels are located here, and those high towers are filled with rooftop restaurants, English pubs, serious theater and pantomime, dance presentations, art museums and galleries, jazz clubs, upscale supper clubs, and disco dives.

Jamaica was the birthplace of the Caribbean all-inclusive, the vacation concept that took the Club Med idea and gave it a lusty, excess-in-the-tropics spin. From Negril to Ocho Rios, resorts make their strongest statement by including everything, even drinks and cigarettes, in a single price of $175–$350 per person per night. (The only surcharges are usually for such luxuries as massages and PADI scuba certification–resort courses are free–for the more expensive tours.) At times they may feel a bit like Pleasure Island, where Pinocchio picks up long ears and a tail for doing everything bad he ever wanted to do. Yet their financial structure and their wealth of "free" recreation have a definite appeal. The allinclusives are now branching out, some of them courting families, others going after an upper crust that would not even have picked up a brochure two or three years ago.

If you're the exploring type who likes to get out and about, you may prefer an EP property. Many offer MAP or FAP packages that include extras like airport transfers and sightseeing tours. Even if you don't want to be tied down to a meal plan, it pays to inquire because the savings can be considerable.

Highly recommended lodgings are indicated by a star ★.

Category	Cost EP*	Cost AI**
Very Expensive	over $300	over $575
Expensive	$225–$300	$475–$575
Moderate	$150–$225	$350–$475
Inexpensive	under $150	under $350

*EP prices are for a standard double room for two, excluding 6% tax and any service charge.
**All-inclusive (AI) prices include tax, service, all meals, drinks, facilities, lessons, airport transfers.

Falmouth **Trelawny Beach Hotel.** The dependable Trelawny Beach resort offers seven stories of rooms overlooking 4 miles of beach. In recent years it has become semi–all-inclusive (lunch and liquor are excluded) with an emphasis on families. Children under 12 get free room and board during the off-season when they share accommodations with their parents. *Box 54, Falmouth, tel. 809/954–2450, fax 809/954–2173. 350 rooms. Facilities: 2 dining rooms, 4 lighted tennis courts, pool, complimentary use of water-sports equipment, shopping arcade, beauty salon, disco, nightly entertainment. AE, DC, MC, V. EP, MAP. Moderate.*

★ **Fisherman's Inn Dive Resort.** A charming red tile-and-stucco building fronts a phosphorescent lagoon at this welcoming, well-run hotel. At night the hotel restaurant offers a free boat ride to diners; dip your hand in the water and the bioluminescent microorganisms glow. It's really a treat. The bright breezy rooms all face the water, with air-conditioning, satellite TV, patio, and full bath. A great bargain, whether you dive (excellent packages are available) or not. *Falmouth P.O., tel. and fax 809/954–3427. 12 rooms. Facilities: restaurant, bar, pool, watersports (include PADI shop). AE, MC, V. EP, MAP. Inexpensive.*

Kingston **Jamaica Pegasus.** The Jamaica Pegasus is one of two fine business
★ ness hotels in the New Kingston area. The 17-story complex near downtown is virtually a convention center, with some good restaurants, handsome old-world decor, and at least a little pampering. The Polo Bar Lounge in the hotel lobby is a comfortable place to sit and have a drink. *Box 333, Kingston, tel. 809/926–3690, fax 809/929–4062. 350 rooms, 13 suites. Facilities: meeting rooms for 1,000, audiovisual services, restaurants, cocktail lounge, shops, Olympic-size pool, jogging track, health club, 2 lighted tennis courts. AE, DC, MC, V. EP, MAP. Moderate–Expensive.*

Wyndham Kingston. The main competition to Jamaica Pegasus on the Kingston business beat, the high-rise Wyndham Kingston also has 17 stories but adds seven cabana buildings, with additional apartment units planned for completion in 1994. A recent renovation upgraded the facilities; the pleasant modern rooms all include air-conditioning, satellite TV, direct dial phone, and hairdryer. *Box 112, Kingston, tel. 809/926–5430, fax 809/929–7439. 300 rooms, 14 1-bedroom suites. Facilities: Olympic-size pool, gardens, conference space for 800, meeting rooms, 2 lighted tennis courts, health club, 2 restaurants, 3 bars, disco. AE, DC, MC, V. EP, MAP. Moderate.*

Morgan's Harbour Hotel, Beach Club, and Yacht Marina. A favorite of the sail-into-Jamaica set, this small property boasts 22 acres of beachfront at the very entrance to the old pirate's town. Rooms are decorated in either a provincial or 18th century nautical style that the pirate Captain Morgan would have appreciated. *Port Royal, Kingston, tel. 809/924–8487, fax 809/924–8562. 46 rooms, 5 1-bedroom suites. Facilities: full-service marina, pier bar, restaurant, disco, access to Lime Cay and other cays. AE, MC, V. EP. Inexpensive–Moderate.*

Hotel Oceana. The high-rise Hotel Oceana property affords convenient access to the National Gallery, government offices, and the ferry to Port Royal. While it lacks the finesse of the Pegasus or Wyndham, the rooms are quieter and extremely comfortable, with floral decor, fine mountain or harbor views, and all the amenities. *Box 986, Kingston, tel. 809/922–0920, fax 809/922–3928. 250 rooms. Facilities: meeting space for 1,200, 2 restaurants, 2 bars, beauty salon, cocktail lounge, shopping arcade, pool. AE, DC, MC, V. EP, MAP. Inexpensive.*

Mandeville

Astra Hotel. A hotel with guest-house charm, the Astra is situated 2,000 feet up in the hills, providing an ideal getaway for nature lovers and outdoors enthusiasts. *Ward Ave., Box 60, Mandeville, tel. 809/962–3265, fax 809/962–1461. 22 rooms. Facilities: restaurant and bar, swimming pool, golf course and 1 tennis court nearby, horseback riding, bird-watching, fitness center, satellite TV. AE, V. EP. Inexpensive.*

★

Mandeville Hotel. The Victorian Mandeville Hotel, set in tropical gardens, has redecorated for the 1990s. There's now a flower-filled garden terrace for breakfast and lunch, and simple private rooms. *Box 78 Mandeville, tel. 809/962–2460, fax 809/962–0700. 60 rooms. Facilities: restaurant, cocktail lounge, golf privileges at nearby Manchester Club. AE, MC, V. EP. Inexpensive.*

Montego Bay

Half Moon Club. For four decades the 400-acre Half Moon Club resort has been a destination unto itself with a reputation for doing the little things right. Although it has mushroomed from 30 to over 200 units, it has maintained its intimate, luxurious feel. The rooms, suites, and villas, whether in modern or Queen Anne style, are decorated in exquisite taste, with marvelous touches like Oriental throw rugs and antique radios. *East of Montego Bay (7 mi), tel. 809/953–2211, fax 809/953–2731. 209 rooms. Facilities: golf course, 4 squash courts, 13 tennis courts (7 lighted), horseback riding, health spa, water-sports center, minigolf, 19 pools, children's pool, 3 restaurants, 3 bars. AE, DC, MC, V. EP, MAP, FAP, All-inclusive. Very Expensive.*

★

Round Hill. Eight miles west of town on a hilly peninsula, this peaceful resort is popular with the Hollywood set. The 27 villas are scattered over 98 acres, and each villa has a maid who cooks breakfast. There are also 36 hotel rooms in a two-story building overlooking the sea. The refined rooms all feature mahogany furnishings and terracotta floors. The privately owned villas vary in decor, but jungle motifs are a favorite. *Box 64, Montego Bay, tel. 809/952–5150, fax 809/952–2505. 36 rooms, 27 villas. Facilities: 2 lighted tennis courts, horseback riding, water-sports center, restaurant. AE, DC, MC, V. EP, MAP, FAP, All-inclusive. Very Expensive.*

★

Tryall Golf, Tennis, and Beach Club. Part of a posh residential development 12 miles west of Montego Bay, Tryall clings to a hilltop overlooking the golf course and the Caribbean. Here you choose between accommodations in the former great house of a 3,000-acre island plantation and one of the private villas dotting the landscape. *Sandy Bay, Hanover, Montego Bay, tel. 809/952–5110 or 800/336–4571, fax 809/952–0401. 53 rooms, 45 villas. Facilities: golf course, 9 tennis courts (5 lighted), pool* with swim-up bar, water sports, terrace restaurant. AE, DC, MC, V. EP, MAP, FAP, All-inclusive. Very Expensive.

Wyndham Rose Hall. The veteran Wyndham Rose Hall, a self-contained resort, built on the 400-acre Rose Hall Plantation, mixes recreation with a top-flight conference setup. A typical bustling business hotel, popular with groups, has all the amenities, but is somewhat lacking in charm. *Box 999, Montego Bay, tel. 809/953–2650, fax 809/953–2617. 489 rooms, 19 suites. Facilities: 3 pools, water sports, 6 tennis courts, golf course, 4 restaurants, coffee shop, nightclub, lounge, 8 meeting rooms, audiovisual equipment, fitness center, laundry service, shopping arcade. AE, DC, MC, V. EP. Moderate.*

Holiday Inn Rose Hall. Here the great equalizer of hotel chains has done much to raise a run-down campground to the level of a full-service property with activities day and night and many tour facilities. It's big and noisy, with drab hallways and public areas, though the rooms are cheerful enough. The quietest rooms are those farthest from the pool. *Box 480, Montego Bay, tel. 809/953–2485. 520 rooms. Facilities: pool, water-sports center, 3 restaurants, 4 bars, exercise room, shops. AE, DC, MC, V. EP. Moderate.*

Reading Reef Club. Four miles west of Montego Bay airport, this owner-operated resort is ideal for families and honeymooners. Another of Jamaica's fine small-hotel values, it offers simply but tastefully furnished rooms and an excellent pasta/seafood restaurant, the Safari. Golf and horseback riding can be arranged. *Box 225, Reading, Montego Bay, tel. 809/952–5909 or 800/223–6510, fax 809/952–7217. 26 rooms, 2 suites. Facilities: private beach, pool, dive shop, water sports, gourmet restaurant. AE, MC, V. EP, MAP. Inexpensive–Moderate.*

Fantasy Resort. After a brief stint as an all-inclusive resort, this property has gone back to normal hotel status. The resort sports high-rise design and a Mediterranean flair. All nine stories have terraces with ocean views. A small beach is across the street. Efficient and pleasant, Fantasy is a good buy, usually booked solid with tour groups. *Opposite Cornwall Beach, Box 161, Montego Bay, tel. 809/952–4150, fax 809/952–3637. 119 rooms. Facilities: open-air bar, dining room, pool, disco, shopping arcade. AE, DC, MC, V. EP. Inexpensive.*

★ **Richmond Hill Inn.** The hilltop Richmond Hill Inn, a quaint, daintily decorated 200-year-old great house originally owned by the Dewars clan, attracts repeat visitors by providing spectacular views of the Caribbean and a great deal of peace, compared with MoBay's hustle. *Union St., Box 362, Montego Bay, tel. 809/952–3859. 15 rooms, 5 suites. Facilities: pool, terrace dining room, coffee shop, bar, free beach shuttle. AE, MC, V. EP, MAP. FAP. Inexpensive.*

Sandals Montego Bay. The largest private beach in Montego Bay is the spark that lights Sandals, one of the most popular couples resorts in the Caribbean. The all-inclusive, seven-day format includes airport transfers, government taxes, sports equipment, aerobics classes, meals, theme parties, and other entertainment. It's a bit like a cruise ship that remains in port, with air-conditioned rooms overlooking the bay. The revelers don't seem to mind the zooming planes (the airport is next door) or booming music. *Box 100, Montego Bay, tel. 809/952–5510 or 800/SANDALS, fax 809/952–0816. 243 rooms. Facilities: 2 pools, 4 Jacuzzis, gym, body shop, water-sports center, 4 lighted tennis courts, 1 racquetball court, 3 restaurants, 4* *bars, nightclub, satellite TV. AE, DC, MC, V. All-inclusive. Moderate–Expensive.*

★ **Sandals Royal Caribbean.** An all-inclusive for couples only, the Royal Caribbean is enlivened by Jamaican-style architecture arranged in a semicircle around attractive gardens. It's a sister in both theme and quality to other Sandals resorts; the rooms are among the nicest, and the "play makers" are not quite as insistent. *Box 167, Montego Bay, tel. 809/953–2231 or 800/ SANDALS, fax 809/953–2788. 190 rooms. Facilities: 3 pools, 4 Jacuzzis, gym, body shop, 4 restaurants, 3 bars, disco, private beach, 2 lighted tennis courts, putting green, dining room, satellite TV. AE, DC, MC, V. All-inclusive. Moderate–Expensive.*

Sandals Inn. Now a part of the Sandals group, the cozy Sandals Inn operates as an all-inclusive for couples. Its charming rooms have balconies facing the sea, and it is convenient to shopping and tours in Montego Bay. It should offer the best of both worlds—privacy and plenty of activity—but there's no escaping the festivities at this intimate resort. The PA system may blast you out of your room. *Box 412, Montego Bay, tel. 809/952– 4140 or 800/SANDALS, fax 809/952–6913. 52 rooms. Facilities: beach privileges, pool, restaurants, pub, satellite TV, gift shop, 1 lighted tennis court, fitness center. AE, DC, MC, V. All-inclusive. Inexpensive.*

Negril   **Charela Inn.** Intimacy is special at the Charela Inn, each of the
★   quiet, elegantly appointed rooms offering a balcony or a covered patio. The owners' French-Jamaican roots find daily expression in the kitchen, and there's an excellent selection of wines. *Box 33, Negril, Westmoreland, tel. 809/957–4277. 26 air-conditioned rooms, 4 suites. Facilities: restaurant, beach. DC, MC, V. EP, MAP. Inexpensive–Moderate.*

Negril Cabins. The 12 timber cottages are nestled amid lush vegetation and towering royal palms. The rooms are unadorned but warm and snug, with a fresh, natural look. The gleaming beach is right across the road. A most convivial place, highly popular with young Europeans. *Negril, tel. 809/957–4350, fax 809/957–4381. 24 rooms. Facilities: restaurant, bar. AE, MC, V. EP. Inexpensive.*

Negril Gardens. A study in colonial pink and white, the new Negril Gardens bills itself as the "friendly alternative" to Negril's all-inclusive scene. It is attractive and offers a nice beach with water sports. *Negril, Westmoreland, tel. 809/957– 4408, fax 809/957–4374. 54 rooms. Facilities: terrace restaurant, tennis, beach, pool, water sports. AE, MC, V. EP. Inexpensive.*

★ **Grand Lido.** The opening of the SuperClubs' all-inclusive Grand Lido in 1989 broke new ground by extending this popular concept to the upper income bracket. The dramatic entrance of marble floors and columns sets a tone of striking elegance. The well-appointed oceanfront rooms (split-level and by far the most spacious and stylish of the all-inclusives), sports facilities, and 24-hour room service follow up in high style. For some, the pièce de résistance is a sunset cruise on the resort's 147-foot yacht, *Zien,* which was a wedding gift from Aristotle Onassis to Prince Rainier and Princess Grace of Monaco and is now captained by Wynn Jones. Grand Lido attracts a slightly more mature and settled crowd than does the usual Negril resort. The gourmet restaurant Piacere is one of Jamaica's best, and an atmosphere of cool elegance prevails throughout. *Box 88, Negril,* *tel. 809/957–4010 or 800/858–8009, fax 809/957–4317. 200 suites. Facilities: 3 specialty restaurants, satellite TV, 24-hour room service, valet, concierge, water-sports center, including scuba diving, pools, clothed and nude beaches, 4 tennis courts (2 lighted), gym, beauty salon. AE, DC, MC, V. All-inclusive. Expensive–Very Expensive.*

Sandals Negril. The opening in 1989 of Sandals, built from the best parts of the old Sundowner and Coconut Cove resorts, made this 7-mile beach available to a new category of popular traveler. Both rooms and staff are sunny and appealing. *Negril, tel. 809/957–4216; Unique Vacations, 7610 S.W. 61st St., Miami, FL 33143, tel. 800/SANDALS. 199 rooms. Facilities: 2 pools, swim-up bar, private island, water-sports center, Jacuzzis, saunas, fitness center, movies, satellite TV, disco, piano bar. AE, DC, MC, V. All-inclusive. Moderate–Expensive.*

★ **Hedonism II.** Here is the resort that introduced the Club Med-style all-inclusive to Jamaica a little over 15 years ago. Still wildly successful, Hedonism appeals most to vacationers who like a robust mix of physical activities, all listed daily on a chalkboard. A recent $2 million refurbishment spruced up the public areas; the rooms are modern and handsome, with a lot of blond woods. But the 60% single clientele spends little time in them. *Box 25, Negril, tel. 809/957–4200 or 800/858–8009, fax 809/957–4289. 280 rooms. Facilities: water-sports center, including scuba diving; fitness center and trapeze and trampoline clinics; open-air buffet dining room, disco and bar, horseback riding, 6 lighted tennis courts, shuffleboard, volleyball, squash. AE, MC, V. All-inclusive. Moderate.*

★ **Swept Away.** The newest all-inclusive in Jamaica, and one of the best, this couples resort opened in early 1990. There are 130 suites in 26 cottages (all with private inner-garden atrium), plus 4 two-bedroom villas spread out along a half-mile of "drop-dead" beach, and a "total" sports complex just across the road. Feathers Continental Restaurant, at the Sports Complex, is open to nonguests. The compound's chefs concentrate on healthful dishes with lots of fish, white meat, fresh fruits, and veggies. *Long Bay, Negril, tel. 809/957–4061 or 800/545–7937, fax 809/957–4060. Facilities: 10 lighted tennis courts, 2 squash courts, 2 racquetball courts, 2 restaurants, 2 bars, fitness center, steam rooms and saunas, Jacuzzis, pool with lap lines. Full water-sports center, including scuba diving. AE, MC, V. All-inclusive. Moderate.*

Negril Inn. One of the prettiest palm-speckled sandy beaches in Jamaica is the center of almost everything the all-inclusive Negril Inn does for its guests. *Negril, tel. 809/957–4209 or 800/634–7456, fax 809/957–4365. 46 rooms. Facilities: restaurant, dancing, entertainment, satellite TV, lounge, 2 tennis courts, disco, water-sports center. AE, MC, V. All-inclusive. Inexpensive–Moderate.*

Ocho Rios **Jamaica Inn.** This vintage property is a special favorite of the
★ privileged from both the United States and Europe, a clientele fascinated by the combination of class and quiet. There are weeks in season when every single guest is on at least his or her second visit. Each room has its own veranda (larger than most hotel rooms) on the powdery champagne-color beach. This is the kind of retreat that makes Americans yearn to be colonists again, happily discussing the royals' latest trials. The owning Morrow brothers are committed to making everything perfect;

they're not far off. *Box 1, Ocho Rios, tel. 800/243–9420 or 809/ 974–2514, fax 809/974–2449. 45 rooms. Facilities: restaurant, bar, pool, golf, tennis and horseback riding nearby. AE, MC, V. EP, MAP, FAP. Very Expensive.*

Plantation Inn. This plantation actually looks like one—the Deep South variety à la *Gone with the Wind*. The whole place serves up a veranda-soft existence. All the rooms come with private balconies, and each has a dramatic view down to the sea. *Box 2, Ocho Rios, tel. 809/974–5601, fax 809/974–5912. 77 rooms. Facilities: dining and dancing by candlelight, shops, 2 lighted tennis courts, health club, afternoon tea, entertainment twice weekly. No children under 12. AE, DC, MC, V. EP, MAP, FAP, All-inclusive (drinks not included). Very Expensive.*

Chukka Cove. The battle cry at Chukka Cove is "Saddle Up." Chukka Cove earns its horse feed by maintaining some of the best equestrian facilities in the Western Hemisphere. In addition to polo, experienced riders will want to investigate Chukka Cove's Jamaican Riding Holiday, an exploration of the north coast on horseback. Less dedicated riders have a choice of trail rides, mountain trail rides, beach rides, or an overnight escorted ride to the Lillyfield Great House. *Box 160, Ocho Rios, tel. 809/974–2593, fax 809/974–5568. 6 villas with 12 sets of private suites, with cook and maid. Facilities: stables, equestrian instruction (all levels), cooks to prepare meals in villas, swimming from rocks. No credit cards. EP, MAP, FAP. Expensive.*

★ **Sans Souci Hotel & Spa.** This pastel-pink cliffside fantasyland looks and feels like a dream, if indeed the dreamer had absolute taste and no need to fret over the bill (unlike the owners, who recently completed a $7 million renovation). Cuisine at the five-star Casanova Restaurant not only delights resort guests but attracts diners from other properties for breakfast, lunch, and dinner. A wonderfully pampering experience. *Ocho Rios, tel. 809/974–2353 or 800/237–3237, fax 809/974–2544. 13 rooms, 98 suites. Facilities: health spa and fitness center, freshwater and mineral pool, 3 lighted tennis courts, scuba diving, watersports center. AE, DC, MC, V. EP, MAP, FAP, All-inclusive. Expensive.*

Jamaica Grande. Ramada bought the Americana (Divi-Divi) and the Mallards Beach Resort and created Jamaica Grande, now the largest conference hotel in Jamaica. Under way are a major refurbishment program and the addition of a conference center, to be completed for summer 1993, at a cost of $20 million. This property's clientele is mostly families, couples, conference attendees, and incentive-travel winners, who enjoy the focal point—the fantasy pool with waterfall, swaying bridge, and swim-up bar. Accommodations in the south building are a bit roomier, whereas those in the north boast slightly better views. The staff is quite friendly for such a large, rather charmless property. *Box 100, Ocho Rios, tel. 809/974–2201, fax 809/974–5378. 691 rooms, 21 suites. Facilities: 5 restaurants, water-sports center, fitness center, disco, 4 tennis courts, children's day-care center, secretarial services, 3 swimming pools, gaming parlor, shopping arcade, beauty salon, 1 lighted tennis court. AE, DC, MC, V. EP. Moderate.*

Shaw Park Beach Hotel. Another popular property, Shaw Park offers a pleasant alternative to downtown high rises. The grounds are colorful and well tended, while the Silks disco is a favorite for late-night carousing. *Cutlass Bay, Box 17, Ocho Rios, tel. 809/974–2552 or 800/243–9420, fax 809/974–5042. 118*

*rooms. Facilities: restaurant, water sports, disco, pool, mas-
sage. AE, DC, MC, V. EP. Moderate.*

Jamel Continental. This spotless upscale tropical motel is set on
its own beach in a relatively undeveloped area close to all the
activities of Ocho Rios and Runaway Bay. The well-appointed
units are spacious and breezy; all feature a balcony with sea
view, full bath, phone, air-conditioning, and satellite TV. In
addition to the usual floral prints and pastel hues, there are unexpected touches, such as mahogany writing desks and Oriental throw rugs. The moderately priced restaurant serves fine
local dishes, and the staff is friendly and helpful. *2 Richmond
Estate, Priory, St. Ann, tel. 809/972–1031. 17 rooms, 3 suites.
Facilities: restaurant, bar, pool, gift shop. MC, V. EP, MAP,
FAP. Inexpensive.*

★ **Hibiscus Lodge.** This gleaming white building with a blue canopy sits amid beautifully manicured lawns laced with trellises,
overlooking its own tiny private beach. The impeccably neat,
cozy rooms all have at least a partial sea view, terrace, air-conditioning, and full bath. This German-run property may be
Jamaica's best bargain, attracting a discriminating (and jubi-
lant) crowd. *Box 52, Ocho Rios, tel. 809/974–2676, fax 809/974–
1874. 26 rooms. Facilities: pool, restaurant, piano bar, 1
lighted tennis court. AE, DC, MC, V. EP, MAP, FAP. Inexpensive.*

★ **Sandals Dunn's River.** This luxury all-inclusive, couples-only
resort in 23 acres of gardens opened its doors in winter 1991. A
complete architectural reconstruction transformed the former
Hilton/Eden II hotel into a Continental-Italian masterpiece.
The accommodations are unusually spacious. Sandals Dunn's
River is considered to be the best of the Sandals group. *Box 51,
Ocho Rios, tel. 809/972–1610 or 800/SANDALS, fax 809/972–
1611. 256 rooms. Facilities: beach, 2 swimming-pool bars, 3
whirlpools, water sports, 9-hole pitch-and-putt golf green, 4
tennis courts (2 lighted), gaming parlor, disco, air-conditioned night club, 4 restaurants, satellite TV in all rooms. AE,
MC, V. All-inclusive. Expensive.*

Ciboney, Ocho Rios. A Radisson Villa, Spa and Beach Resort,
this stately Mediterranean-style property opened its doors in
winter 1991. The $46 million project has 300 rooms and villa
suites on 45 lush hillside acres overlooking the Caribbean. It is
operated as an all-inclusive. Outstanding features are the European-style spa and its four signature restaurants, including
the Orchids restaurant, whose menu was developed by the Culinary Institute of America. *Box 728, Main St., Ocho Rios, tel.
809/974–5503 or 800/777–7800, fax 809/974–5838. 200 1-bed-
room suites, 85 studios and rooms. Facilities: pools, 6 tennis
courts, 4 restaurants, spa, 3 bars, 2 squash courts, water-
sports center, beach shuttle, disco, boutique, beauty salon,
conference facilities. All-inclusive. Moderate–Expensive.*

★ **Boscobel Beach.** Boscobel Beach is a parent's dream for a Jamaican vacation, an all-inclusive that makes families feel welcome. Everybody is kept busy all week for a single package
price, and everyone leaves happy. The cheery day-care centers, divided by age group, should be a model for the rest of the
Caribbean. Thoughtfully, there is an "adults only" section (for
when the kids want to get away). *Box 63, Ocho Rios, tel. 809/
974–3291 or 800/858–8009, fax 809/975–3270. 208 rooms, half
of them junior suites. Facilities: satellite TV, gym, Jacuzzi,
windsurfing, scuba diving, sailing, snorkeling, 3 restaurants,
5 bars, 2 pools, disco, day-care center, boutique, 4 lighted ten-*

nis courts, volleyball, golf at Jamaica-Jamaica/Runaway Bay. AE, DC, MC, V. All-inclusive. Moderate.

Couples. No singles, no children. The emphasis at Couples is on romantic adventure for just the two of you, and the all-inclusive concept eliminates the decision making that can intrude on social pleasure. Couples has the highest occupancy rate of any resort on the island—and perhaps the most suggestive logo as well. There may be a correlation. *Tower Isle, St. Mary, tel. 809/ 975-4271, fax 809/975-4439. 172 rooms, 12 suites. Facilities: pool, satellite TV, island for nude swimming, 3 lighted tennis courts, Nautilus gym, 2 air-conditioned squash courts, a water-sports center that includes scuba diving, horseback riding, nightly entertainment, golf at Runaway Bay, 3 Jacuzzis, 3 restaurants, 3 bars, shopping arcade. AE, DC, MC, V. All-inclusive. Moderate.*

The Enchanted Garden. Set on 20 acres in the former Carinosa Gardens, this all-inclusive resort opened its doors in the winter of 1991–1992. The gardens have been maintained and are stunning with tropical plants, flowers, and a dramatic series of streams and waterfalls. There is an aviary, and a seaquarium where you can enjoy a delicatessen lunch or tea surrounded by tanks of fish and hanging orchids. The futuristic pink cinderblock buildings regrettably seem incongruous amid the natural splendor, but the rooms are comfortable and you're never far from the soothing sound of rushing water. *Box 284, Ocho Rios, tel. 809/974-1400 or 800/654-1337, fax 809/974-5623. 60 rooms, 40 suites, some with private plunge pool. Facilities: spa, disco, gift shop, beauty parlor, satellite TV, aviary, 4 restaurants, hillside gardens, 2 lighted tennis courts, and golf and horseback riding nearby. Daily transportation and picnic to private beach. AE, MC, V. All-inclusive. Moderate.*

Sandals Ocho Rios. The Sandals concept follows its successful formula at this couples-only, all-inclusive nine-acre resort. The mix of white and sand colors contrasts nicely with the vegetation and the sea. The accommodations are airy and pleasant, with king-size beds, air-conditioning, satellite TV, direct-dial phones, hairdryers, and safety deposit boxes. Geared to the super couple, this Sandals seems to offer even more daily activities than do the other all-inclusives. *Ocho Rios, tel. 809/974- 5691 or 800/327-1991, fax 809/974-5700. 237 units. Facilities: 3 restaurants, 4 bars, gift shop, 3 pools, 2 lighted tennis courts, disco, fitness center, satellite TV, water-sports center. AE, DC, MC, V. All-inclusive. Moderate.*

Port Antonio
★
Trident Villas and Hotel. If a single hotel had to be voted the most likely for coverage by "Lifestyles of the Rich and Famous," this would have to be it. Peacocks strut the manicured lawns; colonnaded walkways wind through whimsically sculpted topiary; and the pool, buried in a rocky bit of land jutting out into crashing surf, is a memory unto itself. The luxurious Laura Ashley–style rooms, many with turrets and bay windows, are awash in mahogany and lace. The truly gracious living will transport you back to the days of Empire. *Box 119, Port Antonio, tel. 809/993-2602 or 800/237-3237; fax 809/993- 2590. 26 rooms, 13 suites. Facilities: water sports, boutique, tennis court, swimming pool, restaurant. AE, MC, V. EP, MAP, FAP, All-inclusive. Very Expensive.*

Goblin Hill. For a while this was known as the Jamaica Hill resort, but it is once again going by its original, evocative name. It's a lush 13-acre estate atop a hill overlooking San San cove.

Each attractively appointed villa comes with its own dramatic view, plus a housekeeper-cook. *Box 26, Port Antonio, tel. 809/ 993-3286, fax 809/925-6248. 28 villas. Facilities: pool, beach, 2 tennis courts. AE, MC, V. EP. Moderate-Expensive.*

Jamaica Palace. Errol Flynn might have loved this place for its sense of style and humor. Built to resemble an Edwardian mansion, this imposing five-year-old property rises in an expanse of white pillared marble, with the all-white theme continued on the interior, broken only by the black lacquer and gilded oversize furniture. Each room has a semicircular bed and original European objets d'art and Oriental rugs; some are more lavish than others. Although the hotel is not on the beach, there is a 114-foot swimming pool shaped like Jamaica. *Box 227, Port Antonio, tel. 809/993-2021. 54 rooms, 5 suites, 20 junior suites. Facilities: restaurant, 2 bars, swimming pool, baby-sitters on request, boutique. AE, MC, V. EP, MAP. Inexpensive-Moderate.*

Bonnie View Plantation Hotel. Though the main appeal of this property is to the budget, it does have a few nice rooms with private verandas overlooking spectacular scenery. Its restaurant atop a 600-foot hill offers the finest view of all. *Box 82, Port Antonio, tel. 809/993-2752, fax 809/993-2862. 20 rooms. Facilities: pool, sun deck. AE, DC, MC, V. EP. Inexpensive.*

DeMontevin Lodge. This historic place offers the ambience of a more genteel time. The rooms are basic and spotless, with circular fans overhead. Outsiders are welcome for very tasty home cooking at lunch or dinner, with prior reservations. *Fort George St. on Titchfield Hill, Port Antonio, tel. 809/993-2604. 15 rooms. Facilities: bar, restaurant. AE. EP. Inexpensive.*

Fern Hill Club. This is an all-inclusive hilltop property that's well run and usually full. The newest rooms are split-level suites shaped into steep cliffs, with TVs, videos on request, small refrigerators, and a whirlpool-spa surrounded by a minigarden. The views are predictably spectacular. *Box 100, Port Antonio, tel. 809/993-3222 or 416/620-4666, fax 809/993-2257. 15 rooms, 20 suites, 1 4-bedroom villa. Facilities: 4 swimming pools, 1 lighted tennis court, nightly entertainment, billiards, table tennis, shuffleboard, horseback riding (extra cost), transport to and from nearby San San Beach, where scuba diving (extra cost) can be arranged. AE, MC, V. All-inclusive. Expensive.*

Runaway Bay
★

H.E.A.R.T. Country Club. It's a shame more visitors don't know about this place, perched above Runaway Bay and brimming with Jamaica's true character. While providing training for young islanders interested in the tourism industry, it also provides a remarkably quiet and pleasant stay for guests. The employees make an effort to please. The tranquil restaurant serves delicious local and Continental specialties. *Box 98, St. Ann, tel. 809/973-2671, fax 809/973-2693. 20 rooms. Facilities: satellite TV, golf, beach shuttle, restaurant. AE, MC, V. EP, MAP. Inexpensive.*

FDR, Franklyn D. Resort. Jamaica's first all-suite, all-inclusive resort for families, the FDR opened in 1990. The sugary pink buildings of this casual resort are grouped in a horseshoe around the swimming pool and face the ocean. Girl-Fridays, as they are known here, are available to make your stay as comfortable as possible—not a difficult task, considering the light, roomy accommodations. *Runaway Bay, tel. 809/973-3067 or 800/654-1FDR, fax 809/973-3071. 67 suites. Facilities: pool,* *water sports, beach, gym, restaurant, satellite TV, lighted tennis court, golf, disco, piano bar, miniclub for children with supervised activities. AE, MC, V. All-inclusive. Moderate–Expensive.*

Jamaica, Jamaica. This all-inclusive was a pioneer in emphasizing the sheer Jamaican-ness of the island, rather than generic sensuality. The cooking is particularly first-rate. Lodgings are rather spartan, resembling tropical dorm rooms, but comfortable, with amenities that include hairdriers and safety deposit boxes. The happy campers don't mind; Germans, Italians, and Japanese flock here for the superb golf school (plans are afoot to make the already excellent course more challenging) and pyrotechnic reef surrounding the beach. *Box 58, Runaway Bay, tel. 809/973–2436, fax 809/973–2352. 238 rooms, 4 suites. Facilities: water-sports center, 2 lighted tennis courts, horseback riding, 2 restaurants, PADI 5-star dive center, 2 bars, gym, sundry shop, sightseeing tours, disco, nightly entertainment, 3 Jacuzzis, 18-hole golf course with golf school nearby. Guests must be over 16. AE, DC, MC, V. All-inclusive. Moderate.*

Club Caribbean. This resort reopened its doors in winter 1990 after a $3 million renovation. A series of 128 typically Caribbean cottages, 68 with kitchenette, line the long but narrow gray-sand beach. The rooms are simple but clean, with rattan furnishings and floral prints. Very popular with European families (children under 12 stay free and the 60 cottages with bunk rooms instead of kitchenettes are quite reasonable). *Box 65, Runaway Bay, tel. 809/973–3507, fax 809/973–3509. 128 rooms. Facilities: pool, shopping arcade, JAMAQUA PADI 5-star dive center, water-sports center, tennis courts, massage and exercise, day-care center with children's program, 2 restaurants. AE, MC, V. EP, MAP. All-inclusive. Inexpensive–Moderate.*

The Arts and Nightlife

Jamaica—especially Kingston—supports a lively community of musicians. For starters there is reggae, popularized by the late Bob Marley and the Wailers and performed today by son Ziggy Marley, Jimmy Tosh (the late Peter Tosh's son), Gregory Isaccs, the Third World, Jimmy Cliff, and many others. If your experience of Caribbean music has been limited to steel drums and Harry Belafonte, then the political, racial, and religious messages of reggae may set you on your ear; listen closely and you just might hear the heartbeat of the people. Those who already love reggae may want to plan a visit in mid-July to August for the Reggae Sunsplash. The four-night concert at the Bob Marley Performing Center (a field set up with a temporary stage), in the Freeport area of Montego Bay, showcases local talent and attracts such performers as Rick James, Gladys Knight and the Pips, Steel Pulse, Third World, and Ziggy Marley and the Melody Makers.

Nightlife and Bars For the most part, the liveliest late-night happenings throughout Jamaica are in the major resort hotels. Some of the best music will be found in Negril at **De Buss** (tel. 809/957–4405) and of course at the hot, hot spot, **Kaiser's Cafe** (tel. 809/957–4070), as well as at the **Disco** at Hedonism II (tel. 809/957–4200), and **Horselips** (no tel.). The most popular spots in Kingston today are **Mingles** at the Courtleigh (tel. 809/929–5321), **Illusions** in the New Lane Plaza (tel. 809/929–2125), and **Jonkanoo** in the Wyndham New Kingston (tel. 809/926–5430).

In Port Antonio, if you have but one night to disco, do it at **The Roof Club,** 11 West Street. On weekends, from eleven-ish on, this is where it's all happening. If you want to "do the town," check out **Blue Jays,** Centre Point (no phone). The principal clubs in Ocho Rios are **Acropolis** on Main Street (tel. 809/974–2633), **Silks** in the Shaw Park Beach Hotel (tel. 809/974–2552), and the **Little Pub on Main Street** (tel. 809/974–2324), which produces Caribbean revues. The hottest places in Montego Bay are the **Cave** disco at the Seawinds Beach Resort (tel. 809/952–4070), **Sir Winston's Reggae Club** on Gloucester Street (tel. 809/952–2084), and the **Witches Hideaway** at **Holiday Inn** (tel. 809/953–2485). Some of the all-inclusives offer a dinner and disco pass from about $50.

15 Martinique

Updated by
Nigel Fisher

Not for naught did the Arawaks name Martinique *Madinina*, which means "Island of Flowers." This is one of the most beautiful islands in the Caribbean, lush with exotic wild orchids, frangipani, anthurium, jade vines, flamingo flowers, and hundreds of vivid varieties of hibiscus. Trees bend under the weight of such tropical treats as mangoes, papayas, bright red West Indian cherries, lemons, limes, and bananas. Acres of banana plantations, pineapple fields, and waving green seas of sugarcane show the bounty of the island's fertile soil.

The towering mountains and verdant rain forest in the north lure hikers, while underwater sights and sunken treasures attract snorkelers and scuba divers. Martinique appeals as well to those whose idea of exercise is turning over every 10 or 15 minutes to get an even tan or whose adventuresome spirit is satisfied by finding booty in a duty-free shop. Francophiles in particular will find the island enchanting.

This 425-square-mile island, the largest of the Windward Islands, is 4,261 miles from Paris, but its spirit (and language) is French with more than a mere soupçon of West Indian spice. Tangible, edible evidence of that fact is the island's cuisine—a tempting blend of classic French and Creole dishes.

Columbus sailed near Martinique in 1493, but it was not until his fourth voyage in 1502 that he came ashore at Le Carbet. He paused long enough to remark, "My eyes would never tire of contemplating such vegetation," and to put ashore a number of goats to provide fresh meat for future visits. His eyes very quickly tired of the snakes he saw slithering about in his newfound Eden, so he weighed anchor and put water between him and them, never to return.

By the time Columbus made his way to Martinique, the cannibalistic Caribs had long since arrived on the island and eaten the Island of Flowers's Arawaks. Carib arrows kept outsiders at bay until 1635, when Pierre Belain d'Esnambuc, a Norman nobleman and adventurer, landed with a group of 100 settlers at the mouth of the Roxelane River. The French promised the Caribs the western half of the island, but instead polished them off and imported African slaves to work their sugarcane plantations.

By the mid-17th century, Martinique was an important sugar-producing island. Britain wanted to pluck the pearl away from the French, and the two nations fought over the island until the early 19th century. In 1815, the island was ceded by treaty to France, and French it has remained ever since.

Martinique became an overseas department of France in 1946 and a *région* in 1974, a status not unlike that of an American state vis-à-vis the federal government. The Martinicans vote in French national elections and have all the benefits of France's social and economic systems. The island is governed by a prefect who is appointed by the French minister of the interior. Martinique has one of the highest standards of living in the Caribbean.

Though the majority of tourists are from France, Martinique is encouraging North Americans to visit the island. Efforts are being made to teach taxi drivers a few important words in English; the tourist office has a number of free guide booklets written in English; and most hotels, restaurants, and shops have English-speaking staff.

Before You Go

Tourist Information For information contact the **French West Indies Tourist Board** by calling France-on-Call at 900/990–0040 (50¢ per minute) or write to the **French Government Tourist Office,** 610 5th Ave., New York, NY 10020; 9454 Wilshire Blvd., Beverly Hills, CA 90212, tel. 213/272–2661; 645 N. Michigan Ave., Chicago, IL 60611, tel. 312/337–6301; 2305 Cedar Spring Rd., Dallas TX 75201, tel. 214/720–4010. In Canada contact the French Government Tourist Office, 1981 McGill College Ave., Suite 490, Montreal, P.Q. H3A 2W9, tel. 514/288–4264; or 1 Dundas St. W, Suite 2405, Toronto, Ont. M5G 1Z3, tel. 416/593–4723 or 800/361–9099. In the United Kingdom the tourist office can be reached at 178 Piccadilly, London, United Kingdom W1V 0AL, tel. 071/499–6911.

Arriving and Departing **By Plane** The most frequent flights from the United States are on **American Airlines** (tel. 800/433–7300), which has year-round daily service from more than 100 U.S. cities to San Juan. From there, the airline's American Eagle flies on to Martinique with a stop first at Guadeloupe. **Minerve Airlines** (tel. 212/980–4546 or 800/765–6065), a French charter company, now flies Friday, Saturday, and Sunday nonstop from New York's JFK during the winter season (December through April). **Air France** (tel. 800/237–2747) flies direct from Miami and San Juan; **Air Canada** (tel. 800/422–6232) has service from Montreal and Toronto; **LIAT** (tel. 809/462–0700), with its extensive coverage of the Antilles, flies in from Antigua, St. Maarten, Guadeloupe, Dominica, St. Lucia, Barbados, Grenada, and Trinidad and Tobago. **Air Martinique** (tel. 596/51–09–90) has service to and from St. Martin, Dominica, and Guadeloupe.

From the Airport You'll arrive at Lamentin International Airport, which is about a 15-minute taxi ride from Fort-de-France and about 40 minutes from the Trois-Ilets peninsula, where most of the hotels are located.

Passports and Visas U.S. and Canadian citizens must have a passport (an expired passport may be used as long as the expiration date is no more than five years ago) or proof of citizenship, such as an original (not photocopied) birth certificate or a voter registration card accompanied by a government-authorized photo identification. British citizens are required to have a passport. In addition, all visitors must have a return or ongoing ticket.

Language Many Martinicans speak Creole, which is a mixture of Spanish and French. Try *sa ou fe* for hello. In major tourist areas you'll find someone who speaks English, but the courtesy of using a few French words, even if it is *Parlez-vous anglais,* is appreciated. The people of Martinique are extremely courteous and will help you through your French. Even if you do speak fluent French, you may have a problem understanding the accent of the country people. Most menus are written in French, so a dictionary is helpful.

Precautions Exercise the same safety precautions you would in any other big city: Leave valuables in the hotel safe-deposit vault and lock your car, with luggage and valuables stashed out of sight. Also, don't leave jewelry or money unattended on the beach.

Martinique

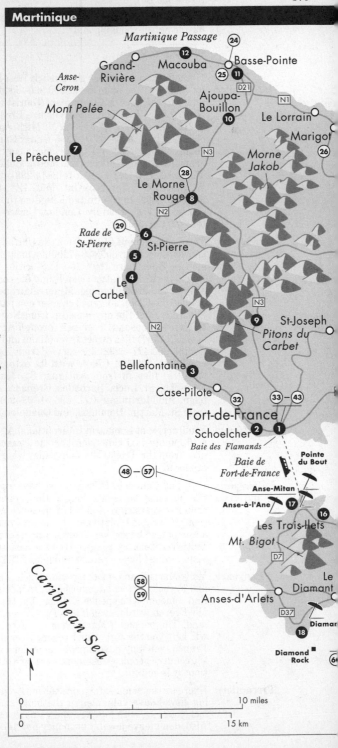

Exploring Sites ①

Hotels and Restaurants ㉔

Beware of the *mancenillie* (manchineel) trees. These pretty trees with little green fruits that look like apples are poisonous. Sap and even raindrops falling from the trees onto your skin can cause painful, scarring blisters. The trees have red warning signs posted by the Forestry Commission.

If you plan to ramble through the rain forest, be careful where you step. Poisonous snakes, cousins of the rattlesnake, slither through this lush tropical Eden.

Except for the area around Cap Chevalier, the Atlantic waters are rough and should be avoided by all but expert swimmers.

Staying in Martinique

Important Addresses
Tourist Information: The **Martinique Tourist Office** (Blvd. Alfassa, tel. 596/63–79–60) is open Monday–Thursday 7:30–12:30 PM and 2:30–5:30, Friday 7:30–12:30 and 2:30–5, Saturday 8–noon. The office's free booklet, *Martinique Info*, and maps are useful. The Tourist Information Booth at Lamentin Airport is open daily until the last flight has landed.

Emergencies
Police: Call 17. **Fire:** Call 18. **Ambulance:** Call 70–36–48 or 71–59–48. **Hospitals:** There is a 24-hour emergency room at **Hôpital La Meynard** (Châteauboeuf, just outside Fort-de-France, tel. 596/50–15–15). **Pharmacies:** Pharmacies in Fort-de-France include **Pharmacie de la Paix** (corner rue Victor Schoelcher and rue Perrinon, tel. 596/71–94–83) and **Pharmacie Cypria** (Blvd. de Gaulle, tel. 596/63–22–25). **Consulate:** The **United States Consulate** (14 rue Blénac, Fort-de-France, tel. 596/63–13–03).

Currency
The coin of the realm is the French franc, which consists of 100 *centimes* (for example, the cost of an airmail stamp is 4.40F: 4 francs, 40 centimes). At press time, the rate was 5.00F to U.S. $1, but check the current exchange rate before you leave home. U.S. dollars are accepted in some of the tourist hotels, but for convenience, it's better to convert your money into francs. Banks give a more favorable rate than do hotels. A currency exchange service, **Change Caraibes,** is located at the Arrivals Building at Lamentin Airport (tel. 596/51–57–91; open weekdays 8–7:30, Sat. 8:30–2) and at the Galerie des Flibustiers in Fort-de-France (tel. 596/60–28–40; open weekdays 8–5:30, Sat. 8:30–1, closed Sun.). Note: Prices quoted here are in U.S. dollars unless indicated otherwise.

Major credit cards are accepted in hotels and restaurants in Fort-de-France and the Pointe du Bout areas; few establishments in the countryside accept them. There is a 20% discount on luxury items paid for with traveler's checks or with certain credit cards.

Taxes and Service Charges
A resort tax varies from hotel to hotel; the maximum is $1.50 per person per day.

Rates quoted by hotels usually include a 10% service charge; some hotels add 10% to your bill. All restaurants include a 15% service charge in their menu prices.

Guided Tours
For a personalized tour of the island, ask the Tourist Office to arrange for a tour with an English-speaking taxi driver. There are set rates for tours to various points on the island, and if you share the ride with two or three other sightseers, the price will be whittled down.

Madinina Tours (tel. 596/61–49–49) offers half- and full-day jaunts, with lunch included in the all-day outings. Boat tours are also available, as are air excursions to the Grenadines and St. Lucia. Madinina has tour desks in most of the major hotels.

Hélicaraibes (tel. 596/73–30–03) provides charter tours by helicopter for a mere $700 or so per hour.

Parc Naturel Regional de la Martinique (Regional Nature Reserve, tel. 596/73–19–30) organizes inexpensive guided hiking tours year-round. Descriptive folders are available at the Tourist Office.

Getting Around Taxi stands are located at Lamentin Airport, in downtown
Taxis Fort-de-France, and at major hotels. They are expensive. Rates are regulated by the government, but local taxi drivers are an independent lot, and prices often turn out to be higher than the minimum "official" rate. The official rate is established at the beginning of each year and is listed in the tourist brochures, which you can get on your arrival at the tourist office at the airport. When taxi drivers overcharge, passengers have little recourse. You can either cause a fuss by contacting the police or show the driver the "officially quoted rate" in the brochure and hope that he accepts it. The cost from the airport to Fort-de-France is about 70F; from the airport to Pointe du Bout, about 150F. A 40% surcharge is in effect between 8 PM and 6 AM. This means that if you arrive at Lamentin at night, depending on where your hotel is, it may be cheaper to rent a car from the airport and keep it for 24 hours than to take a one-way taxi to your hotel.

Buses Public buses and eight-passenger minivans (license plates bear the letters TC) are an inexpensive means of getting from point to point around the island. Buses are always crowded and are not recommended for the timid traveler. In Fort-de-France, the main terminal for the minivans is at Pointe Simon on the waterfront. There are frequent departures from early morning until 8 PM; fares range from $1 to $5.

Ferries Weather permitting, *vedettes* (ferries) operate daily between Fort-de-France and the Marina Méridien in Pointe du Bout and between Fort-de-France and Anse-Mitan and Anse-à-l'Ane. The Quai d'Esnambuc is the arrival and departure point in Fort-de-France. At press time, the one-way fare was 12F; round-trip, 20F. The trip takes 20 minutes. Ferry schedules are listed in the visitors' guide, *Martinique Info*, available at the Tourist Office.

The **Caribbean Express** (tel. 590/60–12–38) offers daily, scheduled interisland service aboard a 128-foot, 227-passenger motorized catamaran, linking Martinique with Guadeloupe, and Dominica. Fares run approximately 25% below economy airfares.

Bicycles or Bikes and motorbikes can both be rented from **Vespa** (tel. 596/
Motorbikes 71–60–03), **Funny** (tel. 596/63–33–05), or **T. S. Autos** (tel. 596/63–42–82), all of which are located in Fort-de-France.

Rental Cars Having a car will make your stay in Martinique much more pleasurable. You will be limited to the environs of your hotel otherwise, and most of the better beaches are away from the hotel complexes. Martinique has about 175 miles of well-paved and well-marked roads (albeit with international signs). Streets in Fort-de-France are narrow and clogged with traffic;

country roads are mountainous with hairpin curves. The Martinicans drive with aggressive abandon, but are surprisingly courteous and will let you into the flow of traffic. When driving up-country, take along the free map supplied by the Tourist Office and you will have no trouble finding your way. If you want a detailed map, the *Carte Routière et Touristique* is available at bookstores. There are plenty of gas stations in the major towns, but a full tank of gas will get you all the way around the island with gallons to spare.

If you book a rental car from the United States at least 48 hours in advance, you can qualify for a hefty discount.

A valid driver's license is needed to rent a car for up to 20 days. After that, you'll need an International Driver's Permit. Major credit cards are accepted by most car-rental agents. Rates are about $60 per day (unlimited mileage). Lower daily rates with per-mile charges, which usually turn out to be higher over-all rates, are sometimes available. Question agents closely. Among the many agencies are **Avis** (tel. 596/70–11–60 or 800/331–1212), **Budget** (tel. 596/63–69–00 or 800/527–0700), **Hertz** (tel. 596/60–64–64 or 800/654–3131), and **Europcar/National Car Rental** (tel. 596/51–20–33 or 800/328–4567). Most hotels have a car rental desk. For Jeep rentals, try **Suncar** (tel. 596/76–25–36), with an office in the Diamant Novotel.

Telephones and Mail To call Martinique station-to-station from the United States, dial 011 plus 596 plus the local six-digit number.

It is not possible to make collect or credit calls from Martinique to the United States. There are few coin telephone booths on the island, and those are usually in hotels and restaurants. Most public telephones now use the *Telecarte*. Units are deducted from your card according to how long and far a phone call you make. Telecartes may be purchased from post offices, café-tabacs, and hotels. Long-distance calls made with *Telecartes* are less costly than are operator-assisted calls.

To place an interisland call, dial the local six-digit number. To call the United States from Martinique, dial 19–1, area code, and the local number. For Great Britain, dial 19–44, area code (without the first zero), and the number.

Airmail letters to the United States cost 4.40F for up to 20 grams; postcards, 3.80F. For Great Britain, the cost is 3.80F and 3.00F, respectively. Stamps may be purchased from post offices, café-tabacs, or hotel newsstands.

Opening and Closing Times Stores that cater to tourists are generally open weekdays 8:30–6; Saturday 8:30–1. Banking hours are weekdays 7:30–noon and 2:30–4.

Exploring Martinique

Numbers in the margin correspond to points of interest on the Martinique map.

The starting point of the tour is the capital city of Fort-de-France, where almost a third of the island's 320,000 people live. From here, we'll tour St-Pierre, Mont Pelée, and other points north; go along the Atlantic coast; and finish with a look at the sights in the south.

Fort-de-France
❶

Fort-de-France lies on the beautiful Baie des Flamands on the island's Caribbean (west) coast. With its narrow streets and pastel buildings with ornate wrought-iron balconies, the capital city is reminiscent of the French Quarter in New Orleans. However, where New Orleans is flat, Fort-de-France is hilly. Public and commercial buildings and residences cling to its hillsides behind downtown.

Stop first at the **Tourist Office,** which shares a building with Air France on the boulevard Alfassa, right on the bay near the ferry landing. English-speaking staffers provide excellent, free material, including detailed maps; a visitors' guide called *Martinique Info,* which lists events; and *Une Histoire d'Amour Entre Ciel et Mer,* an 18-page booklet in English, with a series of seven self-drive tours that are well worth your while.

Thus armed, walk across the street to **La Savane.** The 12½-acre landscaped park is filled with gardens, tropical trees, fountains, and benches. It's a popular gathering place and the scene of promenades, parades, and impromptu soccer matches. A statue of Pierre Belain d'Esnambuc, leader of the island's first settlers, is upstaged by Vital Dubray's flattering white Carrara marble statue of the Empress Josephine, Napoleon's first wife. Sculpted in a high-waisted Empire gown, Josephine gazes toward Trois-Ilets across the bay, where in 1763 she was born Marie-Joseph Tascher de la Pagerie. Near the harbor is a **marketplace** where high-quality local crafts are sold. On the edge of the Savane, you can catch the **ferry** for the beaches at Anse-Mitan and Anse-à-l'Ane and for the 20-minute run across the bay to the resort hotels of Pointe du Bout. The ferry is more convenient than a car for travel between Pointe du Bout and Fort-de-France.

Rue de la Liberté runs along the west side of La Savane. Look for the main post office (rue de la Liberté, between rue Blénac and rue Antoine Siger). Just across rue Blénac from the post office is the **Musée Departementale de Martinique,** which contains exhibits pertaining to the pre-Columbian Arawak and Carib periods. On display are pottery, beads, and part of a skeleton that turned up during excavations in 1972. One exhibit examines the history of slavery; costumes, documents, furniture, and handicrafts from the island's colonial period are on display. *9 rue de la Liberté, tel. 596/71–57–05. Admission: 5F. Open weekdays 9–1 and 2–5, Sat. 9–noon.*

Leave the museum and walk west (away from La Savane) on rue Blénac along the side of the post office to rue Victor Schoelcher. There you'll see the Romanesque **St-Louis Cathedral,** whose steeple rises high above the surrounding buildings. The cathedral has lovely stained-glass windows. A number of Martinique's former governors are interred beneath the choir loft.

Rue Schoelcher runs through the center of the capital's primary shopping district, which consists of a six-block area bounded by rue de la République, rue de la Liberté, rue de Victor Severe, and rue Victor Hugo. Stores feature Paris fashions (at Paris prices) and French perfume, china, crystal, and liqueurs, as well as local handicrafts.

Time Out

Drugstore de la Galerie (46 rue Ernest Duproge, tel. 596/73–90–85) is a combination restaurant, cafeteria, and tearoom, where you can rest your feet and get a light repast every day from 7 AM to midnight.

Three blocks north of the cathedral, make a right turn on rue Perrinon and go one block. At the corner of rue de la Liberté is the **Bibliothèque Schoelcher,** the wildly elaborate Byzantine-Egyptian-Romanesque–style public library. It's named after Victor Schoelcher, who led the fight to free the slaves in the French West Indies in the 19th century. The eye-popping structure was built for the 1889 Paris Exposition, after which it was dismantled, shipped to Martinique, and reassembled piece by ornate piece on its present location.

Follow rue Victor Severe five blocks west, just beyond the Hôtel de Ville, and you'll come to Place Jose-Marti. The **Parc Floral et Culturel** will acquaint you with the variety of exotic flora on this island. There's also an aquarium showing fish that can be found in these waters. *Place Jose-Marti, Sermac, tel. 596/71–66–25. Admission free. Open Mon.–Sat. 9–noon and 3–6.*

The Levassor River meanders through the park and joins the bay at **Pointe Simon,** where yachts can be chartered. The river divides the downtown area from the ritzy residential district of Didier in the hills.

If you have children with you, you may want to take them to the new **Martinique Aquarium,** which focuses primarily on marine animals from the surrounding waters but also features the exotic from the world's oceans. Special exhibits include a shark tank and a 59-foot-aquaterrarium, home to a school of piranhas. *3 blvd. de la Marne, tel. 596/73–02–29. Admission: 35F adults, 24F children. Open daily 9–7.*

The North   The tour of the north is divided into two sections: a short day's trip and a long day's (even overnight) excursion. Martinique's "must do" is the drive north along the coast from Fort-de-France to St-Pierre. The 40-mile round-trip to St-Pierre can be made in an afternoon, although there is enough to see to fill an entire day. The drive to the north coast will appeal primarily to nature lovers, hikers, and mountain climbers. If you are interested in climbing Mont Pelée or hiking, plan to spend at least a night on the road (*see* Sports and the Outdoors, *below,* for guided hikes). Bear in mind that a 20-mile mountain drive takes longer than driving 20 miles on the prairie.

Tour 1   Head west out of Fort-de-France on Route N2. You'll pass ❷ through the suburb of **Schoelcher,** home of the University of the French West Indies and Guyana. La Batelière Hotel, noted for its sports facilities, is also here.

Just north of Schoelcher is Fond-Lahaye, where the road begins to climb sharply. About 4½ miles farther along, you'll come to the fishing village of **Case-Pilote,** named after a Carib chief to whom the French took kindly and called Pilote.

Continuing along the coastal road, you'll see red-roof houses ❸ clinging to the green mountainside on the way to **Bellefontaine,** 4 miles north. This is another fishing village, with pastel houses on the hillsides and colorful gommier canoes (fishing boats made from the gum tree) bobbing in the water. One of the houses here is built in the shape of a boat.

❹ Continue north along the coast until you get to **Le Carbet.** Columbus is believed to have landed here on June 15, 1502. In

1635, Pierre Belain d'Esnambuc arrived here with the first French settlers.

Le Carbet is home to the **Zoo de Carbet,** also called the Amazona Zoo, which features animals from the Caribbean, Amazonas, and Africa, including rare birds, snakes, wildcats, and caimans. *Le Coin, Le Carbe t, tel. 596/78–00–64. Admission: 15F adults, 10F children. Open daily 9–6.*

Just north of Carbet is **Anse-Turin,** where Paul Gauguin lived for a short time in 1887 with his friend and fellow artist, Charles Laval. The **Musée Gauguin** traces the history of the artist's Martinique connection through documents, letters, and reproductions of some of the paintings he did while on the island. There is also a display of Martinican costumes and headdresses. *Anse-Turin, tel. 596/77–22–66. Admission: 10F. Open daily 10–5.*

Time Out   **La Guinguette** (coast road at Le Mouillage just as you enter St-Pierre, tel. 596/77–15–02) is a 20-table oceanside bistro where fishing boats bring fresh seafood to the kitchen doors and spicy Creole dishes are served on the wave-washed patio.

St-Pierre, the island's oldest city, now has a population of about 6,000. At the turn of this century, St-Pierre was a flourishing city of 30,000 and was called the Paris of the West Indies. In spring 1902, Mont Pelée began to rumble and spit out ash and steam. By the first week in May, all wildlife had wisely vacated the area. City officials, however, ignored the warnings, needing voters in town for an upcoming election. At 8 AM on May 8, 1902, the volcano erupted, belching forth a cloud of burning ash with temperatures over 3,600°F. In the space of three minutes, Mt. Pelée transformed the Paris of the West Indies into Martinique's Pompeii. The entire town was destroyed, and its inhabitants were instantly calcified. There was only one survivor, a prisoner named Siparis, who was saved by the thick walls of his underground cell. (He was later pardoned and for some years afterward was a sideshow attraction at the Barnum & Bailey Circus.) You can wander through the site to see the ruins of the island's first church, built in 1640; the theater; the toppled statues; and Siparis's cell. *For a guided tour of the area, contact Syndicat d'Initiative, La Guinguette Restaurant, tel. 596/77–15–02. Tours: 15F adults, 10F children. Open weekdays 9–noon.*

The **Musée Vulcanologique** was established in 1932 by American volcanologist Franck Perret. His collection includes photographs of the old town, documents, and a number of relics excavated from the ruins, including molten glass, melted iron, and contorted clocks stopped at 8 AM, the time of the disaster. *St-Pierre, tel. 596/78–15–16. Admission: 10F adults, 1F children. Open daily 9–noon and 3–5.*

Walk along St-Pierre's main street parallel to the sea, and drop in at La Vogue St-Pierre Hotel and restaurant (tel. 596/78–14–36). The barroom close to the street is a local hangout, but the dining room facing the sea offers reasonably priced Creole food. For anyone wishing to experience the Humphrey Bogart days of rumrunners, there are bedrooms on the second floor, bare except for a cot and a vibrating ceiling fan.

In St-Pierre, Route N2 turns inland toward Morne Rouge, but before going there, you may want to follow the coastal road 8 **7** miles north to **Le Prêcheur.** En route, you'll pass what is called the Tomb of the Carib Indians. The site is actually a formation of limestone hills from which the last of the Caribs are said to have flung themselves to avoid capture by the French. The village of Le Prêcheur was the childhood home of Françoise d'Aubigné, later to become the Marquise de Maintenon and the second wife of Louis XIV.

Return to St-Pierre and drive 4 miles east on Route N2 to reach **8** **Le Morne Rouge.** Lying on the southern slopes of Mont Pelée, the town of Morne Rouge, too, was destroyed by the volcano. It is now a popular resort spot, with spectacular mountain scenery. This is the starting point for a climb up the 4,600-foot mountain, but you must have a guide (*see* Sports and the Outdoors, *below*).

At this point, you have the option of returning to Fort-de-France or continuing on for a tour of the north and Atlantic coasts.

If you choose to return to the capital, take the Route de la Trace (Rte. N3) south from Le Morne Rouge. The winding, two-lane paved road is one of the island's great drives, snaking through dense tropical rain forests.

9 La Trace leads to **Balata,** where you can see the **Balata Church,** an exact replica of Sacré-Coeur Basilica in Paris, and the **Jardin de Balata** (Balata Gardens). Jean-Philippe Thoze, a professional landscaper and devoted horticulturalist, spent 20 years creating this collection of thousands of varieties of tropical flowers and plants. There are shaded benches where you can relax and take in the panoramic views of the mountains. *Rte. de Balata, tel. 596/72–58–82. Admission: 30F adults, 10F children. Open daily 9–5.*

From Balata, Route N3 continues 8 miles south to the capital city.

If you've opted to continue exploring the north and Atlantic coasts, take Route N3 north from Morne Rouge. You'll pass through Petite Savane and wind northeast to the flower-filled **10** village of **Ajoupa-Bouillon,** a 17th-century settlement in the midst of pineapple fields.

A mile and a half east of Ajoupa-Bouillon, Route N3 dead-ends at Route 1, which runs north–south. Turn left and drive 3 miles through sugarcane, pineapple, and banana fields to **Basse-Pointe,** which lies at sea level on the Atlantic coast. Just before reaching Basse-Pointe you'll pass a Hindu temple, one of the relics of the East Indians who settled in this area in the 19th century. The view of the eastern slope of Mont Pelée is lovely from here.

On the approach to Basse-Pointe, you'll see a small road (D21) **11** off to the left. This road leads to the estimable **Leyritz Plantation,** which has been a hotel for several years. Guests have the questionable pleasure of staying in the converted slave cabins. Recently, the property was acquired by new owners, who have expanded the tourist attractions to include a boutique, conference/seminar dining room, and spa-fitness center. When tour groups from the cruise ships are not swarming over the property, the rustic setting, complete with sugarcane factory and gardens, is delightful. Visit the plantation's **Musée de Poupées Végétales,** which contains a collection of exotic "doll sculptures," in which a local plant is shaped into a figurine. The creative results, which depict famous women of French history, are made entirely of plants and leaves. They are the work of local artisan Will Fenton. *Musée de Poupées Végétales, Leyritz Plantation, tel. 596/78–53–92. Admission: 15F. Open daily 7–5.*

⑫ Three miles along, you'll come to **Macouba** on the coast. From here, the island's most spectacular drive leads 6 miles to **Grand-Rivière,** on the northernmost point. Perched on high cliffs, this village affords magnificent views of the sea; the mountains; and, on clear days, the neighboring island of Dominica. From Grand-Rivière, you can trek 11 miles on a well-marked path that leads through lush tropical vegetation to the beach at Anse-Ceron on the northwest coast. The beach is lovely and the diving is excellent, but the currents are very strong and swimming is not advised.

Time Out Stop in at **Chez Vava** (Rte. 1 on the eastern edge of Grand-Rivière, tel. 596/55–72–72) for a rum punch and a lunch of seafood and Creole dishes including an excellent fish soup and a tasty fricassee of crayfish.

From Grand-Rivière, backtrack 13 miles to the junction of Routes N1 and N3.

⑬ From the junction, continue 10 miles on Route 1 along the Atlantic coast, driving through the villages of Le Lorrain and Marigot to **Ste-Marie,** a town of about 20,000 Martinicans and the commercial capital of the island's north. There is a lovely mid-19th-century church in the town and, on a more earthy note, a rum distillery.

The **Musée du Rhum,** operated by the St. James Rum Distillery, is housed in a graceful galleried Creole house. Guided tours of the museum take in displays of the tools of the trade and include a visit to the distillery. And, yes, you may sample the product. *Ste-Marie, tel. 596/69–30–02. Admission free. Open weekdays 9–5, weekends 9–1.*

⑭ **La Trinité,** a subprefecture in the north, is 6 miles to the south in a sheltered bay. From La Trinité, the **Caravelle Peninsula** thrusts 8 miles into the Atlantic Ocean. Much of the peninsula is under the auspices of the Regional Nature Reserve and offers places for trekking, swimming, and sailing. This is the home of the **Morne Pavilion,** an open-air sports and leisure center operated by the nature reserve (*see* Sports and the Outdoors, *below*). To reach it, turn right before Tartane on the Spoutourne Morne Pavilion road. Tartane has a popular beach with cool Atlantic breezes. Across the road from the brown-gold sand are numerous local restaurants—**Le Dubuc** (tel. 596/58–60–81) for good Creole food and the **Madras Hotel and Restaurant** (tel. 596/58–33–95) for air-conditioned comfort, good dining, and clean comfortable lodging.

⑮ At the eastern tip of the peninsula, you can root through the ruins of the **Dubuc Castle.** This was the home of the Dubuc de Rivery family, which owned the peninsula in the 18th century. According to legend, young Aimée Dubuc de Rivery was captured by Barbary pirates, sold to the Ottoman Empire, became a favorite of the sultan, and gave birth to Mahmoud II.

Return to La Trinité and take Route N4, which winds about 15 miles through lush tropical scenery to Lamentin. There you can pick up Route N1 to Fort-de-France or Route N5 to D7 and the southern resort areas.

Tour 2 The loop through the south is a round-trip of about 100 miles. This excursion will include the birthplace of the Empress Josephine, Pointe du Bout and its resort hotels, a few small museums, and many large beaches. You can spend an afternoon, a day, or a couple of weeks exploring this region, depending on the time at your disposal and your frame of mind.

From Fort-de-France, take Route N1 to Route N5, which leads south through Lamentin, where the airport is located. A 20-mile drive will bring you to Rivière-Salée, where you'll make a right turn on Route D7 and drive 4½ miles to the village of **Les Trois-Ilets.**

Time Out **Euromarche** (Lamentin) is one of the most complete supermarkets in the Western Hemisphere. For under $15, two of you can stagger out with hot French breads, pâtés, cheeses, and salmon flown in from Europe. Add some Creole boudin from the deli counter and a chilled bottle of wine or the local dark Rhum St. James, and have a gourmet picnic. *Closed Sun.*

Les Trois-Ilets, named after the three rocky islands nearby, is a lovely little village with a population of about 3,000. It's known for its pottery, straw, and wood works and as the birthplace of Napoleon's Empress Josephine. On the village square, you can visit the simple church where she was baptized Marie-Joseph Tascher de la Pagerie. To reach the museum and the old sugar plantation on which she was born, drive a mile west on Route D7 and turn left on Route D38.

A stone building that held the kitchen of the estate is now home to the **Musée de la Pagerie.** (The main house blew down in the hurricane of 1766, when Josephine was three.) It contains an assortment of memorabilia pertaining to Josephine's life and loves (she was married at 16 in an arranged marriage to Alexandre de Beauharnais). There are family portraits; documents, including a marriage certificate; a love letter written to her in 1796 by Napoleon; and various antique furnishings, including the bed she slept in as a child. *Trois-Ilets, tel. 596/68–34–55. Admission: 15F adults, 3F children. Open Tues.–Sun. 9–5.*

The **Maison de la Canne** will teach you everything you ever wanted to know about sugarcane. Exhibits take you through three centuries of sugarcane production, with displays of tools, scale models, engravings, and photographs. *Trois-Ilets, tel. 596/68–32–04. Admission: 15F. Open Tues.–Sun. 9–5:30.*

You can reach **Pointe du Bout** and the beach at **Anse-Mitan** by turning right on Route D38 west of Trois-Ilets and just past the **Golf de Impératrice Joséphine** (a golf course). This area is filled with resort hotels, among them the Bakoua and the Méridien. The Pointe du Bout marina is a colorful spot where a whole slew of boats are tied up. The ferry to Fort-de-France leaves from this marina. More than anywhere else on Martinique, Pointe du Bout caters to the vacationer. A cluster of boutiques, ice-cream parlors, and rental-car agencies forms the hub from which restaurants and hotels of varying caliber radiate. If you are looking for resort life and action, what little there is in Martinique will be found here.

When you return to Route D7, turn right and head west. Less than five miles down the road you will reach **Anse-à-l'Ane,** where there is a pretty white-sand beach complete with picnic tables. There are also numerous small restaurants and inexpensive guest-house hotels for the budget traveler.

South from Anse-à-l'Ane, Route D7 turns into a 10-mile roller coaster en route to **Anse-d'Arlets,** a quiet backwater fishing village. You'll see fishermen's nets strung up on the beach to dry and pleasure boats on the water. In recent years, the activity has focused around the restaurants and small shops lining the shore. The popular gathering spot for Sunday brunch is **Ti Sable** (tel. 596/68–62–44), a restaurant on the beach at the northern edge of the village that offers a fixed menu at 180F. Another good place, especially to view the sunsets, is **Bidjoul** in the center of the village (*see* Dining, *below*).

From the center of town, take Route D37 along the coast down to Morne Larcher and on to **Le Diamant.** The road—narrow, twisting, and hilly—offers some of the best shoreline views in Martinique. Be sure to pull to the side at a scenic spot from which you can stare out at **Diamond Rock,** a mile or two offshore.

In 1804, during the squabbles over possession of the island between the French and the English, the latter commandeered the rock, armed it with cannons, christened it HMS *Diamond Rock*, and proceeded to use it as a warship. For almost a year and a half, the British held the rock, bombarding any French ships that came along. The French got wind of the fact that the British were getting cabin fever on their isolated ship-island and arranged a supply of barrels of rum for those on the rock. The French easily overpowered the inebriated sailors, ending one of the most curious engagements in naval history.

Le Diamant is a small, friendly village with a little fruit-and-vegetable market on its town square. Next to the town square is **Longchamp** (tel. 596/76–25–47), an ice-cream/pizza restaurant (a more elaborate menu is offered in the second-floor dining room), but the adventurous will want to cross the street and enter a dark, wood-tabled bar called **Maully's** (no phone). You'll be the only tourist here, but on your second *'ti punch*, the locals will warm to you. This town also offers the reasonable and accommodating **Diamant Les Bains** hotel.

Just out of town, heading toward Rivière-Salée, you'll see on the right-hand side a small shop, **Atelier Ceramique** (tel. 596/76–42–65), that sells ceramics. The owners and talented artists, David and Jeannine England, have lived in the Caribbean for more than a decade and are members of the small British expatriate community on the island. Whether or not you like their products—ceramics, paintings, and miscellaneous souvenirs—it's a rare chance to brush up on your English.

A mile farther along the road to Rivière-Salée is the turnoff for the **Diamant-Novotel,** the **Diamant Marine** hotel, and the **Relais Caraibes** (tel. 596/76–44–65), one of Martinique's better dining establishments.

Back on the road (D7), it's about 5 miles to the junction of the island's main highway to the south (N5). If you go to the north, you'll be back in Fort-de-France within a half hour. Instead, go south along the coast.

Some 10 miles down the coastline lies **Ste-Luce,** another fishing village with a pretty white beach. From Ste-Luce, you can take Route D17 north 1 mile to the **Forêt de Montravail,** where arrows point the way to Carib rock drawings.

Time Out **La Vogue du Sud** (rue Schoelcher, Ste-Luce, tel. 596/62–44–96) is an unpretentious little eatery serving seafood.

The recent repaving and straightening of the highway can quickly take you through to Ste-Anne or you can say good-bye to Route D7 in Ste-Luce and hook up with Route D18, which will take you northeast 4 miles to **Rivière-Pilote,** a town of about 12,000 people. From there, Route D18A trickles down south to **Pointe Figuier,** where the scuba diving is excellent. Stay with Route D18A and curve around the beautiful Cul-de-Sac inlet through **Le Marin.** Just east of Le Marin, turn right on Route D9 and drive all the way down to the sea. En route you'll pass the turnoff to Buccaneer's Creek/Club Med and the pretty village of **Ste-Anne,** where a Roman Catholic church sits on the square facing a lovely white beach. Not far away, at the southernmost tip, is the island's best beach, **Les Salines.** It's 1½ miles of soft white sand, calm waters, and relative seclusion (except on weekends).

In sharp contrast to the north, this section of the island is dry. The soil does not hold moisture for long. A rutted track—suitable for vehicles but not for queasy stomachs—leads all the way to **Pointe des Salines** and slightly beyond. The gnarled, stubby trees have given the area the name **Petrified Forest,** in part because the sight is unexpected in a place known as the Island of Flowers.

Though there is a restaurant, **Aux Delices de la Mer** (tel. 596/76–73–75), near the point facing the channel that separates Martinique from St. Lucia, many people bring their own refreshments and picnic in the shade of the palms.

Backtrack 9 miles to Le Marin. The adventuresome should take a detour a mile before reaching town. Take the small road on your right that leads to **Cap Chevalier.** After less than 2 miles, the road forks. The road to the left dead-ends at a small community and does not justify the 4 miles of driving. The fork to the right, however, runs for about 4 miles to a tiny cove with five or six one-man fishing boats and racks where the fishermen dry their nets. The scene is definitely worth a photograph. Facing the cove is a small Creole restaurant, the **Gracieuse** (tel. 596/76–93–10). Choose the terrace and order the catch of the day or a grilled lobster. The cooking is quite good, and this remains one of the undiscovered bargains on Martinique.

If you retrace your steps for half a mile, you will come to a turnoff on the right. Less than a mile down this road there is a long, empty beach that rarely has more than four or five couples taking sun and a cool dip in the Atlantic waters.

To get out of Cap Chevalier, you must go back toward Le Marin. On the outskirts of Le Marin, Route N6 branches off to the right and goes north 7 miles to **Le Vauclin,** skirting the highest point in the south, **Mt. Vauclin** (1,654 feet). Le Vauclin is an important fishing port on the Atlantic coast, and the return of the fishermen shortly before noon each day is a big event.

㉓ Continue north 9 miles on Route N6 to **Le François**, a sizable city of some 16,000 Martinicans. This is a great place for snorkeling. Offshore are a number of shallow basins with white-sand bottoms between the reefs.

There is a lovely bay 6 miles farther along at **Le Robert.** You'll also come to the junction of Route N1, which will take you west to Fort-de-France, 12½ miles away.

Beaches

All Martinique's beaches are open to the public, but hotels charge a fee for nonguests to use changing rooms and facilities. There are no official nudist beaches, but topless bathing is prevalent at the large resort hotels. Unless you're an expert swimmer, steer clear of the Atlantic waters, except in the area of Cap Chevalier and the Caravelle Peninsula. The soft, white-sand beaches begin south of Fort-de-France and continue; to the north the beaches are made up of hard-packed gray volcanic sand.

The soft white beaches of **Pointe du Bout** are man-made, superb, and lined with luxury resorts, among them the Méridien and the Bakoua.

Anse-Mitan was created by Mother Nature, who placed it just to the south of Pointe du Bout and sprinkled it with white sand. The waters around this beach offer superb snorkeling opportunities. Small, family-owned bistros are half hidden in palm trees nearby.

On the beach at **Anse-à-l'Ane,** you can spread your lunch on a picnic table, browse through the nearby shell museum, and cool off in the bar of the Calalou Hotel.

Diamant, the island's longest beach (2½ miles), has a splendid view of Diamond Rock, but the waters are sometimes rough and the currents are strong. This area is home to the Diamant-Novotel, Diamant Les Bains, Diamant Marine, and Relais Caraibes hotels.

Anse-Trabaud is on the Atlantic side, across the southern tip of the island from Ste-Anne. There is nothing here but white sand and the sea.

Les Salines is a 1½-mile cove of soft white sand lined with coconut palms. A short drive south of Ste-Anne, Les Salines is awash with families and children during holidays and on weekends, but quiet and uncrowded during the week even at the height of the winter season. This beach, especially the far end, is the most peaceful and beautiful. Take along a picnic, including plenty of liquids; there is only one restaurant, Aux Delices de la Mer (tel. 596/76–73–71), close to Pointe des Salines.

Near Les Salines, **Pointe Marin** stretches north from Ste-Anne. A good windsurfing and waterskiing spot, it also has restaurants, campsites, sanitary facilities, and a 10F admission charge. Club Med occupies the northern edge, and Ste-Anne, with several good restaurants, is near at hand.

Sports and the Outdoors

Bicycling The *Parc Naturel Regional de la Martinique* (tel. 596/64–42–59) has designed biking itineraries off the beaten track. Bikes can be rented from **Funny** (tel. 596/63–33–05), **Discount** (tel. 596/66–33–05), and **T S Location Sarl** (tel. 596/63–42–82), all located in Fort-de-France. In Ste-Luce, try **Marquis Moto** (no phone). Mountain biking is popular in mainland France. Now it has reached Martinique. VTT (Vélo Tout Terrain) bikes specially designed with 18 speeds to handle all terrains may be rented from **VTTilt** (Anse-Mitan, tel. 596/66–01–01).

Boating For boat rentals and yacht charters, check with **Ship Shop** (6 rue Joseph-Compère, Fort-de-France, tel. 596/71–43–40), **Carib Charter** (Habitation Croix du Sud, Pointe de Jaham, Schoelcher, tel. 596/71–58–96 or 596/73–08–80), **Soleil et Voile** (Marina Pointe du Bout, tel. 596/66–07–74 or 596/66–07–87), **Voile et Vent aux Antilles** (Star Voyages, Marina Pointe du Bout, Trois-Ilets, tel. 596/66–00–72), **Dufour Antilles** (Marina Pointe du Bout, Trois-Ilets, tel. 596/66–05–35), **Caraibes Nautique** (Hotel Bakoua, Trois Ilets, tel. 596/66–06–06), **Captains Shop** (Marina Pointe du Bout, tel. 596/76–35–64), **Somatour** (14 rue Blénac, tel. 596/71–31–68), **Yachting Caraibe** (Cite Mansarde at Robert, tel. 596/65–18–18 or 8 Lotissement Bardinet, Fort-de-France, tel. 596/71–85–96), and **Agence Le Marin** (rue Osman Duquesnay, Le Marin, tel. 596/74–99–34).

Deep-Sea Fishing Fish cruising these waters include tuna, barracuda, dolphin, kingfish, and bonito. For a day's outing on the 37-foot *Egg Harbor*, with gear and breakfast included, contact **Bathy's Club** (Méridien, tel. 596/66–00–00). Charters of up to five days can be arranged on Captain Réné Alaric's 37-foot *Rayon Vert* (Auberge du Vare, Case-Pilote, tel. 596/78–80–56).

Golf At **Golf de l'Impératrice Joséphine** (tel. 596/68–32–81) there is an 18-hole Robert Trent Jones course with an English-speaking pro, fully equipped pro shop, a bar, and restaurant. Located at Trois-Ilets, a mile from the Pointe du Bout resort area and 18 miles from Fort-de-France, the club offers special greens fees for hotel guests and cruise-ship passengers.

Hiking Inexpensive guided excursions are organized year-round by the Parc Naturel Regional de la Martinique (Regional Nature Reserve, Caserne Bouille, Fort-de-France, tel. 596/73–19–30).

Horseback Riding Excursions and lessons are available at **Ranch Jack** (near Anse-d'Arlets, tel. 596/68–63–97), the **Black Horse Ranch** (near La Pagerie in Trois-Ilets, tel. 596/68–37–80), **La Cavale** (near Diamant on the road to the Novotel hotel, tel. 596/76–22–94), and **Ranch Val d'Or** (Quartier Val d'Or, Ste-Anne, tel. 596/76–70–58). Promenades of 1–3 hours cost $16–$46; two-day excursions run about $120.

Sailing Hobie Cats, Sunfish, and Sailfish can be rented by the hour from hotel beach shacks. If you're a member of a yacht club, show your club membership card and enjoy the facilities of **Club de la Voile de Fort-de-France** (Pointe Simon, tel. 596/70–26–63) and **Yacht Club de la Martinique** (blvd. Chevalier, Ste-Marthe, 596/63–26–76). Also check **Club Nautique du Marin** (tel. 596/74–92–48), **Cercle Nautique de Schoelcher** (Anse Madame, tel. 596/61–15–21), **Association Madiawind** (Madiana Plage, Schoelcher, tel. 595/73–55–07), **Windsurfing** (rue Martin Luther King, tel. 596/73–55–07), **Hotel Frantel** (tel. 596/66–04–

04), and **ATM Yachts** (Club Nautique du Marin, tel. 596/74–98–17; or in the U.S., tel. 714/678–2250 or 800/227–5317).

Scuba Diving To explore the old shipwrecks, coral gardens, and other undersea sites, you must have a medical certificate and insurance papers. Among the island's dive operators are **Tropicasub** (La Guinguette, St-Pierre, tel. 596/77–15–02), **CSCP** (Le Port, Case-Pilote, tel. 596/78–73–75), **Cressma** (Fort-de-France, tel. 596/61–34–36 or 596/58–04–48), **Bathy's Club** (Méridien, tel. 596/66–00–00), **Planete Bleue** (La Marina, Trois-Ilets, tel. 596/66–08–79), **Sub Diamant Rock** (Novotel, tel. 596/76–42–42), and **Oxygene Bleu** (Longpre, Lamentin, tel. 596/50–25–78).

Sea Excursions and Snorkeling The *Aquarium* (Fort-de-France, tel. 596/61–49–49) is a glass-bottom boat that does excursions. For information on other sailing, swimming, snorkeling, and beach picnic trips, contact **Affaires Maritimes** (tel. 596/71–90–05).

Sports Center The **Morne Pavilion** (tel. 596/73–19–30), on the Caravelle Peninsula, is an open-air sports and leisure center offering sailing, tennis, and other activities.

Tennis In addition to its links, the **Golf de l'Impératrice Joséphine** (Trois-Ilets, tel. 596/68–32–82) has three lighted tennis courts. There are also two courts at the **Bakoua Beach Hotel** (tel. 596/66–02–02); six courts at **La Batelière Hotel** (tel. 596/61–49–49); seven courts at **Buccaneer's Creek/Club Med** (tel. 596/76–74–52); two courts at **Diamant-Novotel** (tel. 596/76–42–42); one court at the **Leyritz Plantation** (tel. 596/78–53–92); and two courts at the **Méridien Hotel** (tel. 596/66–00–00). Other hotels with tennis courts are **Hotel PLM Azur Carayou** (tel. 596/66–04–04), **Le Calalou** (tel. 596/68–31–67), **Relais Caraibes** (tel. 596/74–44–65), **La Caravelle** (tel. 596/58–37–32), **Diamant Bleu** (tel. 596/76–42–15), **Rivage Hotel** (tel. 596/66–00–53), **La Margelle** (tel. 596/76–40–19), and **Brise Marine** (tel. 596/62–46–94). For additional information about tennis on the island, contact **La Ligue Regionale de Tennis** (Petit Manoir, Lamentin, tel. 596/51–08–00).

Shopping

French fragrances and designer scarves, fine china and crystal, leather goods, and liquors and liqueurs are all good buys in Fort-de-France. Purchases are further sweetened by the 20% discount on luxury items when paid for by traveler's checks and major credit cards. Among local items, look for Creole gold jewelry, such as loop earrings, heavy bead necklaces, and slave bracelets; white and dark rum; and handcrafted straw goods, pottery, and tapestries. In addition, U.S. Customs allows you to bring some of the local flora into the country.

Shopping Areas The area around the cathedral in Fort-de-France has a number of small shops carrying luxury items. Of particular note are the shops on **rue Victor Hugo, rue Moreau de Jones, rue Antoine Siger,** and **rue Lamartine.** There is also a duty-free shop at the airport. On the outskirts of Fort-de-France, shopping malls include **Centre Commercial de Cluny, Centre Commercial de Dillon, Centre Commercial de Bellevue,** and more than 60 boutiques at **La Galleria** in Le Lamentin.

Good Buys Look for Lalique, Limoges, and Baccarat at **Cadet Daniel** (72
China and Crystal rue Antoine Siger, Fort-de-France, tel. 596/71–41–48) and

Roger Albert (7 rue Victor Hugo, Fort-de-France, tel. 596/71–71–71).

Flowers Anthuriums, torch lilies, and lobster claws are packaged for shipment at **MacIntosh** (31 rue Victor Hugo, Fort-de-France, tel. 596/70–09–50, and at the airport, tel. 596/51–51–51) and **Les Petites Floralies** (75 rue Blénac, Fort-de-France, tel. 596/71–66–16).

Local Handicrafts A wide variety of dolls, straw goods, tapestries, pottery, and other items are available at the **Caribbean Art Center** (Centre de Metiers Arts, opposite the Tourist Office, blvd. Alfassa, Fort-de-France, tel. 596/70–32–16). The **Galerie d'Art** (89 rue Victor Hugo, tel. 596/63–10–62) has some unusual and excellent Haitian art—paintings, sculptures, ceramics, and intricate jewelry cases—at reasonable prices.

Perfumes Dior, Chanel, and Guerlain are among the popular scents at **Roger Albert** (7 rue Victor Hugo, Fort-de-France, tel. 596/71–71–71). Airport minishops sell the most popular scents at in-town prices, so there's no need to carry purchases around.

Rum Rum can be purchased at the various distilleries, including **Duquesnes** (Fort-de-France, tel. 596/71–91–68), **St. James** (Ste-Marie, tel. 596/69–30–02), and **Trois Rivières** (Ste-Luce, tel. 596/62–51–78).

Dining

It used to be argued that Martinique had the best food in all the Caribbean, but many believe this top-ranking position has been lost to some of the other islands of the French West Indies—Guadeloupe, St. Barts, even St. Martin. Nevertheless, Martinique remains an island of restaurants serving classic French cuisine and Creole dishes, its wine cellars filled with fine French wines. Some of the best restaurants are tucked away in the countryside, and therein lies a problem. The farther you venture from tourist hotels, the less likely you are to find English-speaking folk. But that shouldn't stop you from savoring the countryside cuisine. The local Creole specialties are *colombo* (curry), *accras* (cod or vegetable fritters), *crabes farcies* (stuffed land crab), *écrevisses* (freshwater crawfish), *boudin* (Creole blood sausage), *lambi* (conch), *langouste* (clawless Caribbean lobster), *soudons* (sweet clams), and *oursin* (sea urchin). The local favorite libation is *le 'ti punch*, a "little punch," concocted of four parts white rum, one part sugarcane syrup (some people like a little more syrup), and a squeeze of lime.

Like Guadeloupe, people dress for dinner in casual resort wear. Men don't wear a jacket, but do sport a new shirt bought for their vacation. Women wear dresses that show off their suntan, but fashion here is practical not Parisian.

Highly recommended restaurants are indicated by a star ★.

Category	Cost*
Expensive	over $50
Moderate	$30–$50
Inexpensive	under $30

per person, excluding drinks and service

Anse-d'Arlets **Tamarin Plage Restaurant.** The lobster *vivier* in the middle of the room gives you a clue to the specialty here, but there are other recommendable offerings as well. Fish soup or Creole boudin are good starters, then consider court bouillon, chicken fricassee, and curried mutton. The beachfront bar is a popular local hangout. *Anse-d'Arlets, tel. 596/68–67–88. Reservations accepted. No credit cards. Moderate.*

Bidjoul. The small side street off the main road is Anse-d'Arlets' main drag, with numerous modest restaurants on either side. The latest addition is the small Bidjoul, with tables on the sand under a canopy and across the road a tiny indoor dining room. The salads are huge and the grilled fish as fresh as could be. So, too, is the fish at the neighboring restaurants, but the enthusiasm of the owner makes this one stand out and become the popular gathering spot to watch the sun set into the Caribbean Sea. *Anse-d'Arlets, tel. 596/68–65–28. No reservations. No credit cards. Inexpensive.*

Anse-Mitan/ **La Matador.** Fresh flowers adorn each table in this simply fur-
Pte. du Bout nished terrace restaurant. Creole boudin, quiche, or sea urchins are good for openers. Main dishes include turtle steak, Creole bouillabaisse, lobster thermidor, and fillet of beef with port wine and mushrooms. This pretty restaurant with checkered tablecloths would be more enjoyable if it had a view of the sea instead of the road and the Bambou Hotel. *Anse-Mitan, tel. 596/68–05–36. Reservations suggested in high season. AE, DC, MC, V. Closed Wed. Moderate.*

L'Amphore. Dining is either on the front terrace, where there's a nice view of the bay, or in a gas-lit garden. Lobster, selected from a tank, is the menu's highlight, but there are Creole specialties and classic French dishes as well. During dinner, a guitarist strums and sings in several languages. *Anse-Mitan, tel. 596/66–03–09. Reservations accepted. No credit cards. Closed Mon., and Tues. lunch. Moderate.*

★ **La Villa Creole.** The steak béarnaise, curried dishes, conch, court bouillon, and other dishes are all superb. However, the real draw here is owner Guy Dawson, a popular singer and guitarist who entertains during dinner, either solo or en duo with Roland Manere or Guy Vadeleux. The setting is romantic, with oil lamps flickering in the lush back garden of this very popular place. *Anse-Mitan, tel. 596/66–05–53. Reservations essential. AE, DC, V. Dinner only. Closed Sun. Moderate.*

Bambou Restaurant. This casual place, right on the beach, serves omelets and salads, as well as lamb cutlets, curried chicken, steak au poivre, codfish pie, and sole meunière. For dessert there's coconut flan or banana or pineapple flambé. *Bambou Hotel, Anse-Mitan, tel. 596/66–01–39. Reservations accepted. AE, DC, MC, V. Inexpensive.*

Basse-Pointe **Leyritz Plantation.** The pride of Martinique is *the* place all the
★ cruise passengers head to as soon as they disembark. The restored 18th-century plantation has the ambience of a country inn and a dramatic view of Mont Pelée. The menu is mostly Creole, featuring boudin, chicken with coconut, and several curried dishes. *Basse-Pointe, tel. 596/78–53–92. Reservations essential. DC, MC. Moderate–Expensive.*

Restaurant Mally. Unpretentious and popular, Mally Edjam's home has a few tables inside and only four on the side porch under an awning. The lady is a legend on the island, and you'll be rewarded with the likes of papaya soufflé, spicy Creole concoctions such as curried pork and stuffed land crabs, and fresh local vegetables. Her exotic confitures of guava, pineapple, and cornichon top off the feast, along with a yogurt or light coconut cake. *Rte. de la Côte Atlantique, tel. 596/75–51–18. Reservations required. No credit cards. Inexpensive.*

Fort-de-France **La Belle Epoque.** The nine tables on the terrace of this turn-of-
★ the-century house are much in demand. You can feast on duck fillet in mango sauce, hot spinach mousse, lobster medallions with slices of leek, and a Creole swordfish fillet. Yves Coyac is the talented Martinican chef. This restaurant, along with La Fontane and Le Lafayette, is one of the best in Fort-de-France. *Km 2.5, Rte. de Didier, tel. 596/64–47–98. Reservations required for dinner. Jacket required for dinner. DC, MC, V. Closed Sun. and Mon. Expensive.*

★ **La Fontane.** In a pastoral setting on the road to Balata, this lovely gingerbread house with a wraparound veranda is shaded by mango trees. Inside you'll find Oriental rugs, fresh flowers, and a display of antiques that includes a handsome gramophone and a grandmother's clock. *Le Bambou de la Fontane* is a mixed salad with fish, tomato, corn, melon, and crawfish. Other dishes served here are cream soup with crabs, crayfish bisque, red snapper with lemon-lime sauce, *magret de canard* (breast of duck), and steak au poivre. *Km 4, Rte. de Balata, tel. 596/64–28–70. Reservations essential. Jacket and tie required. AE. Closed Sun. and Mon. Expensive.*

La Grand' Voile. Crisp white cloths, fine china and crystal, and lots of windows overlooking the harbor contribute to a lovely dining room. Starters include chilled chicken liver mousse and fresh steamed mussels. Main dishes include lobster in Creole sauce and fillet of beef Rossini (with artichoke hearts, foie gras, truffles, and Madeira sauce). The *menu dégustation* (a variety of sample-size portions) is a practical way to savor the restaurant's specialties. Service here is sometimes on the slow side. *Pte. Simon, tel. 596/70–29–29. Reservations suggested. Jacket suggested. AE, MC, V. Open daily for lunch and dinner. Expensive.*

Le Bristol. Selecting from a long list of rum drinks is the first order of business in this handsome terrace restaurant. The menu changes monthly, but you may find gazpacho or escargots in garlic butter for starters, and such main dishes as lobster fricassee and magret de canard, as well as a variety of beef and fish dishes. Hot apple tarts and feathery coconut soufflés are usually on the dessert list. *Km 0.2, rue Martin Luther King, tel. 596/63–66–76. Reservations required for dinner. Jacket required for dinner. AE. Expensive.*

★ **Le Lafayette.** This is a true "salon" on the second story of a renovated hotel of the same name. Clusters of indoor greenery combine with white latticework and rich Haitian paintings as the setting for what may be the finest dining room in Fort-de-France. Begin the day with a chocolate brioche for breakfast, continue to a light fondue and salad for lunch, and end with a perfectly grilled lobster in a spicy sauce or perhaps with imported sirloin in a black-pepper sauce. Dessert is something simple, such as banana flambé in 20-year-old rum. *Lafayette Hotel, 5 rue de la Liberté, tel. 596/63–24–09. Reservations required. AE, MC, V. Closed Sun. Expensive.*

Diamant Creole. Claudine Victoire's popular seven-table restaurant is on the second floor of a little red-and-white house. The old-fashioned Creole dishes served include tiny local clams in white wine or with chives and shallots, fish or conch brochette, Creole paella, and soups and local vegetables not offered on most island menus. *7 blvd. de Verdun, tel. 596/73–18–25. Reservations suggested. AE, MC, V. Closed Sun. Moderate.*

La Biguine. Downstairs is a cozy, casual café with red-and-white check cloths and upstairs, a more formal candlelit dining room. Local fish poached in Creole sauce, shark cooked in tomato sauce, and duck fillet with pineapple or orange sauce are among the à la carte offerings, with homemade tarts for dessert. It's a convenient place for lunch, and there is a special fixed-price businessmen's menu. *11 Rte. de la Folie, tel. 596/71–47–75. Reservations required for dinner. Jacket required for dinner. AE. No lunch Sat.; closed Sun. Moderate.*

★ **Le Coq Hardi.** Crowds flock here for the best steaks and grilled meats in town. You can pick out your own steak and feel confident that it will be cooked to perfection. Steak tartare is the house specialty, but there are tournedos Rossini (with artichoke hearts, foie gras, truffles, and Madeira sauce), entrecote Bordelaise, prime rib, and T-bone steaks among the wide selection of beef offerings. For dessert, there's a selection of sorbets, profiteroles, and pear Belle Hélène. *Km 0.6, rue Martin Luther King, tel. 596/71–59–64. Reservations suggested. AE, DC, MC, V. Closed Wed. and Sat. lunch. Moderate.*

Chez Gaston. Its cozy upstairs dining room, very popular with local residents, features a Creole menu that includes such items as ox-foot soup, conch kebabs, and simmered sea urchins. The brochettes are especially recommended. The kitchen stays open late, and there's a small dance floor. The downstairs section serves snacks all day. A French phrase book will be very helpful. *10 rue Felix Eboue, tel. 596/71–45–48. Reservations accepted. No credit cards. Inexpensive.*

Le Crew. The meals here are served family-style in rustic dining rooms, where the bill of fare features a few Creole dishes and lots of typical French bistro dishes: fish soup and stuffed mussels, snails, country pâté, frogs' legs, tripe, grilled chicken, and steak. The portions are ample, and there's a daily 60F three-course tourist menu that simplifies ordering. *42 rue Ernst Deproge, tel. 596/73–04–14. Reservations accepted. No credit cards. Closed Sat. evening and Sun. Inexpensive.*

Lamentin **Le Verger.** An orchard is the setting for this green-and-white
★ country house, not far from the airport. Pheasant and duck, as well as game, are on the extensive menu, which also includes classic French and Creole dishes. Follow the signs for La Trinité; the entrance to the restaurant is on the right immediately after the Esso and Shell stations. *Place d'Armes, tel. 596/51–43–02. Reservations suggested. AE, DC, MC, V. Closed Sat. afternoon and Sun. night. Moderate–Expensive.*

La Trinité **L'Ami Fritz.** Named after the popular Weinstub in Strasbourg,
★ this is where locals flock for Muenster cheese, game, sauerkraut, and fine wines. The cuisine is Alsatian, but the chef uses local produce to create an interesting repertoire of dishes, from grilled lobster with a gratin Creole to "Royal Sauerkraut." The lovely country mansion nestles in rolling hills, surrounded by flowers and greenery. *Brin d'Amour, tel. 596/58–20–81. Reservations suggested. Jacket and tie required. V. Closed Mon. Expensive.*

Le Diamant **Relais Caraibes.** Parisians M. and Mme. Senez have opened this
★ individual bungalow colony *avec* restaurant but still manage to

spend enough time in Paris to gather original objets d'art for decor and for sale. Dishes include chicken Antilloise, a half lobster in two sauces, fresh-caught fish in a basil sauce, and fricassee of country shrimp. The crisply decorated dining room, always awash in fresh flowers, commands an always-clear view of Diamond Rock. *La Cherry, Diamant, tel. 596/76–44–65. Open for lunch and dinner. AE, MC, V. Closed Mon. Expensive.*

Le Diam's. For an inexpensive meal that may consist of crisp and tasty pizzas or a grilled fish of the day, this casual, open-sided restaurant facing the village square is hard to beat. Checkered tablecloths and wicker furniture are the only decor; the overhead fan helps to keep a breeze going through the dining room. *Place de l'Eglise, tel. 596/76–23–28. No reservations. MC, V. Closed Tues. and Wed. lunch. Inexpensive.*

Le François **Club Nautique.** While this little place is not going to turn up in
★ *Architectural Digest*, the food that comes fresh daily out of the sea is exquisitely prepared. Have a couple of rum punches, then dig into turtle steak or charcoal-broiled lobster. The restaurant is right on the beach, and boat trips leave here for snorkeling in the nearby coral reefs. *Le François, tel. 596/54–31–00. Reservations accepted. AE, DC, MC, V. Open for lunch only. Inexpensive.*

Le Morne Rouge **Auberge de la Montagne Pelée.** This restaurant is open for dinner by reservation only, but the real treat is lunch on a clear day, when you can see Mont Pelée's summit from the terrace. Creole and French dishes are featured, including a Caribbean-style pot-au-feu, with whitefish, scallops, salmon, crayfish, and tiny vegetables. *Rte. de l'Aileron, tel. 596/52–32–09. Reservations essential. MC, V. Moderate.*

Morne-des-Esses **Le Colibri.** In the northwestern reaches of the island, this is the domain of Clotilde Palladino, who presides over the kitchen while her children serve. Choice seating is at one of the seven tables on the back terrace. For starters, try *buisson d'écrevisses*, six giant freshwater crayfish accompanied by a tangy tomato sauce flavored with thyme, scallions, and tiny bits of crayfish. Stuffed pigeon, lobster omelets, suckling pig, and coconut chicken are among the main dishes. *Morne-des-Esses, tel. 596/69–91–95. Reservations essential. AE, DC, MC, V. Closed Mon. Moderate–Expensive.*

Ste-Anne **Aux Filets Bleus.** This breezy open-air eatery is right on the beach, and you can go for a swim before or after dining. Turtle or fish soup, stuffed crab, and avocado vinaigrette are all good opening bids. In addition to an assortment of lobster entrées, there is grilled or steamed fish and octopus with red beans and rice. Prices are slightly above what you'd expect for basically straightforward cooking and beachfront ambience. *Pointe Marin, tel. 596/76–73–42. Reservations essential. No credit cards. Closed Mon. Expensive.*

Athanor. Replacing the L'Arbre à Pain, the new owners offer an ambitiously extensive menu that includes pizzas, grilled fish, creole dishes, and meats with French sauces. However, the grilled lobster is the real treat. Choose a table either in a plant-filled room or in the small garden at the back. *Rue de Bord de Mer, Ste-Anne, tel. 596/76–97–60. No credit cards. Inexpensive–Moderate.*

La Dunette. Located in the center of Ste-Anne with the sea washing its foundations, this restaurant in a small hotel has a terrace shaded by bright blue awnings. The wrought-iron chairs and tables are surrounded by hanging plants. Your choices for lunch or dinner include fish soup, grilled fish or lobster, poached sea urchins, pork en brochette with pineapple, and several curried dishes. *Ste-Anne, tel. 596/76–73–90. Reservations suggested in high season. MC, V. Closed Wed. Inexpensive.*

Ste-Luce **La Petite Auberge.** This country inn is hidden behind a profusion of tropical flowers, just across the main road from the beach. Fresh seafood is turned into such dishes as *filet de poisson aux champignons* (fish cooked with mushrooms), *crabe farci,* and fresh langouste in a Creole sauce. Or sample *canard à l'ananas* (duck with pineapple), *poulet Creole* (chicken Creole), or entrecote Creole. They're all winners. *Plage du Gros Raisins, Ste-Luce, tel. 596/62–47–26. No credit cards. Moderate.*

St-Pierre **La Factorérie.** Alongside the ruins of the Eglise du Fort is this open-air restaurant connected to the agricultural training school, where students raise the crops. The food is pleasant and the view is outstanding. Dishes include grilled langouste, grilled chicken in a piquant sauce, *fricassee de lambi* (conch), and the fresh catch of the day. This restaurant is convenient for lunch when visiting St-Pierre, but it is not worth a special trip. *Quartier Fort, St-Pierre, tel. 596/78–12–53. No credit cards. Closed Sat. and Sun. evenings. Inexpensive.*

Lodging

Martinique's range of accommodations runs from tiny French inns called *Relais Creoles* to splashy tourist resorts, with an 18th-century plantation to round things out. The majority of the hotels are clustered in Pointe du Bout and Anse-Mitan on the Trois-Ilets peninsula across the bay from Fort-de-France, but Le Diamant and Ste-Anne are becoming rival resort areas. You will also find other notable lodgings scattered around the island. Attractive packages are offered by many of the hotels during the year, and it's a good idea to ask what's available when you call to reserve. Martinique is not an island distinguished for its hotels. Expect functional accommodations and friendly but laid-back service. At press time, Martinique's most historic hotel, the Manoir de Beauregard in Ste-Anne, was faltering in its rebuilding program after a serious fire. The Manoir de Beauregard should not be confused (as some locals do) with the nearby, new Hameau de Beauregard (tel. 596/63–13–72), a complex of condominium-hotel accommodations for 600F for a double and located 2 miles from the beach. Most of the major hotels include a large buffet breakfast in their tariff or will arrange a MAP plan. Perhaps because there are so many good restaurants on the island, hotels have refrained from developing all-inclusive packages.

Highly recommended lodgings are indicated by a star ★.

Category	Cost*
Very Expensive	over $220
Expensive	$150–$220

Moderate	$85–$150

Inexpensive	under $85

All prices are for a standard double room for two with Continental breakfast, excluding $1.50 per person per night tax and a 10% service charge.

Hotels
Anse-Mitan/
Pte. du Bout
★

Le Bakoua. This hotel was thoroughly renovated in 1990. Now, under the stewardship of the Sofitel chain, Le Bakoua is the best of Martinique's resort hotels. Located in Pointe du Bout, the hotel has accommodations in three hillside buildings and a fourth on its man-made white-sand beach. The decor is cushy-cum-rustic, with wooden furnishings and tile floors. All rooms have a balcony or patio, TV, radio, king-size bed, direct-dial phone, and air-conditioning. The rooms are relatively small, given the $250-a-night tariff, and the price is higher if they face the sea rather than the garden. The beach is compact and adjoins that of the Méridien. The pool, referred to as a *piscine trompe de l'oeil,* is above the beach, and the water flows over one side, giving the impression that the pool is part of the ocean. Entertainment consists of live music and shows nightly, including dinner dancing, limbo, and Friday-night performances of Les Grands Ballets de la Martinique. Most of the staff speaks commendable English. Be sure to inquire about special package deals. *Box 589, Fort-de-France, tel. 596/66–02–02 or 800/221–4542, fax 596/66–00–41; in the United Kingdom, 071/730–7144. 140 rooms, including 2 1-bedroom suites. Facilities: 2 restaurants, bar, pool, 2 lighted tennis courts, boutique, beauty salon, water-sports center. AE, DC, MC, V. CP. Very Expensive.*

Le Méridien Trois-Ilets. There is a great deal of activity here, even in the low season, much of it revolving around the pool, the strip of white-sand beach, and the Air France flight crews who stay here. But the hotel has aged, and despite sporadic redecorations, the small rooms remain patchworked with repairs. New sand has been brought in to replace that lost to hurricanes, but the beach can become congested during peak season. All rooms are air-conditioned, with wall-to-wall carpeting, built-in hair dryers, and boat-size tubs; some have balconies with a splendid view of the bay and of Fort-de-France. Dinner at La Case Créole offers some of the better hotel dining on the island. English is spoken well here, and there's live entertainment nightly. *Trois-Ilets 97229, tel. 596/66–00–00 or 800/543–4300, fax 596/66–00–74; in NY, 212/245–2920. 303 rooms, 10 suites. Facilities: 2 restaurants, bar, casino, disco, pool, 2 lighted tennis courts, duty-free shops, marina, car-rental desk, tour desk, water-sports center. AE, DC, MC, V. BP. Very Expensive.*

PLM Azur-Carayou. The style here is definitely tropical. The reception area has rattan furniture and, overhead, quaint wood rafters. The rooms, built around the large swimming pool in the garden, are air-conditioned, equipped with TVs, direct-dial phones, and well-stocked minibars. There are lots of sporting options for daytime activity, and a popular disco, Le Vésou, for evening. Located on the other side of the marina to Le Bakoua, the hotel has its own small but pleasant beach. The hotel is well run, and the staff is helpful and friendly. *Pointe du Bout 97229, tel. 596/66–04–04 or 800/221–4542, fax 596/66–00–57. 200 double rooms. Facilities: 3 restaurants, 2 bars, 2 tennis courts, pool, archery, golf practice, scuba diving, fishing,* *waterskiing, sailing. AE, DC, MC, V. MAP. Moderate–Expensive.*

Bambou. The young and the hardy will enjoy this complex of rustic A-frame "chalets" with shingled roofs. The rooms are paneled in pink; they are tiny and Spartan, albeit with such modern conveniences as air-conditioning, phones, and shower baths. The hotel is open year-round, and during high season, entertainment is featured five nights a week. *Anse-Mitan 97229, tel. 596/66–01–39 or 800/224–4542, fax 596/66–05–05. 118 rooms. Facilities: restaurant and bar, pool, water-sports center. AE, DC, MC, V. CP, MAP. Moderate.*

★ **PLM Azur La Pagerie.** La Pagerie looks as if it were plucked out of southern Louisiana and planted near the marina in Pointe du Bout. Fully air-conditioned, the hotel has small rooms and studios, some with kitchenettes, all with private baths. Although the hotel has no beach or water-sports activities, it is within a short stroll of the resort hotels, restaurants, and activity. Lunch and dinner are served alfresco by the pool. On an island not known for the attractiveness of its hotels, this exception draws the local ex-patriate and sailing crowd for a round of evening cocktails. *Pointe du Bout 97229, tel. 596/66–05–30, fax 596/66–00–99. U.S. reservations, 800/221–4542; in NY, 212/ 757–6500. 98 rooms. Facilities: restaurant, bar, pool. AE, MC, V. EP. Inexpensive–Moderate.*

Auberge de l'Anse-Mitan. This beachfront hotel, established in 1930, is the island's oldest family-run inn. The rooms are spartan, but all are air-conditioned and have a shower bath. Views are either of the bay or the tropical garden at the back, and some rooms have balconies. Informal meals are served on the terrace for guests. At the end of the road along the beach front, things are peaceful and quiet here—even more so if you don't speak French. *Anse-Mitan 97229, tel. 596/66–01–12, fax 596/ 66–01–05; in Canada, 800/468–0023; in NY, 212/840–6636. 26 rooms. Facilities: restaurant, bar. AE, DC. CP. Inexpensive.*

Rivage Hotel. Maryelle and Jean Claude Riveti's garden studios have kitchenettes, air-conditioning, TVs, phones, and private baths. The hotel is right across the road from the beach. Breakfast and light meals are served in the friendly, informal snack bar. You get good value for your money, and you should have no difficulty communicating: English, Spanish, and French are spoken. *Anse-Mitan 97229, tel. 596/66–00–53, fax 596/66–06– 56. 17 rooms. Facilities: snack bar, pool, poolside barbecue pit. MC, V. EP. Inexpensive.*

Basse-Point **Leyritz Plantation.** Sleeping on a former sugar plantation in ei-
★ ther the old-fashioned furnished rooms at the manor house or in one of the restored former slave cabins is a novelty that may appeal to you. The place is authentic—and isolated in the northern part of the island on 16 acres of lush vegetation. Except for when tour buses carrying cruise-ship passengers pass through, it is very quiet here—a sharp contrast to the frenzied level of activity at the hotels in Pointe du Bout. The new owners are improving the property and have installed a health spa with a nutrition and fitness program, a swimming pool, a meeting room, and an enlarged boutique. Most people won't want to spend their entire vacation here, but it makes for an interesting overnight stay while visiting the northern part of the island. There's free transportation to the beach, which is about 30 minutes away. *Basse-Pointe 97218, tel. 596/78–53–92, fax 596/78–92–44. 53 rooms. Facilities: restaurant, bar, spa,*

health-and-fitness center, horseback riding, tennis courts, pool. DC, MC. CP. Moderate–Expensive.

Fort-de-France **Impératrice.** Overlooking La Savane park in the center of the city, the Impératrice's air-conditioned rooms are in a 1950s five-story building (with an elevator). The rooms in the front are either the best or the worst, depending upon your sensibilities: They are noisy, but they overlook the city's center of activity. All rooms have a TV and a private bath; 20 have balconies. Children under 8 stay free in the room with their parents, children 8–15 stay at 50% of the room rate. The hotel also has a popular sidewalk café. The owners recently opened **L'Impératrice Village** at Anse-Mitan. It is a cluster of small bungalows in a meadow off a rutted track and a good 10-minute hike from the nearest beach. It is not worth the $120-a-night tab. *Fort-de-France 97200, tel. 596/63–06–82 or 800/223–9815, fax 596/72–66–30; in Canada, 800/468–0023; in NY, 212/251–1800. 24 rooms. Facilities: restaurant, café, bar. AE, DC, MC, V. CP. Moderate.*

Lafayette. This hotel's claim to fame is its superb second-story dining room overlooking the Savane. For those who want to be right in the heart of town, this place is a real find. The choicest rooms are those with French windows. *5 rue de la Liberté, Fort-de-France, tel. 596/73–80–50 or 800/223–9815, fax 596/60–97–75. 24 rooms with TV, telephone, telex, and fax services. Facilities: restaurant, bar, complimentary use of Bakoua Hotel beach facilities. AE, DC, V. EP. Inexpensive.*

Lamentin **Martinique Cottages.** These garden bungalows in the countryside have kitchenettes, cable TVs, and phones. The restaurant here, La Plantation, is a gathering spot for gourmets. The beaches are about a 15-minute drive away. The cottages are difficult to find, and you should take advantage of the property's airport transfers. *Lamentin 97232, tel. 596/50–16–08, fax 596/50–26–83. 16 rooms. Facilities: restaurant, bar, pool, Jacuzzi. AE, MC, V. EP. Inexpensive.*

La Trinité **Saint Aubin.** This restored colonial house is in the countryside above the Atlantic coast. The rooms are modern, with air-conditioning, TVs, phones, and private baths. This is a peaceful retreat, and only 3 miles from La Trinité, 2 miles from the Spoutourne sports center and the beaches on the Caravelle Peninsula. The inn's restaurant is reserved for hotel guests and is closed during June and October. The new owner is trying to improve the property, but it still requires some refurbishing if it is to be more than a bed-and-breakfast guest house. *Box 52, La Trinité, 97220, tel. 596/69–34–77 or 800/223–9815; in Canada, 800/468–0023; in NY, 212/840–6636, fax 596/69–41–14. 15 double rooms. Facilities: restaurant, bar, pool. AE, DC, MC, V. CP. Moderate.*

Le Diamant **Diamant-Novotel.** This self-contained resort occupies half an island in an ideal windsurfing location. Just beyond the registration area, a footbridge spans a large pool on the way to the air-conditioned, spacious guest rooms, each of which has a small balcony facing either the sea or the pool. Furnishings are cane and wickerwork painted pastel peach and green, and the floors are tile. The four beaches on the 5-acre property are small. The dining room is large and unromantic, set up to accommodate groups, but there is a pleasant terrace bar where a local band plays on most nights. A smaller, more formal restaurant is open during peak season. Scuba packages are offered. The staff speaks English. *Le Diamant 97223, tel. 596/76–42–42 or 800/ 221–4542, fax 596/76–22–87. 180 rooms. Facilities: 2 restaurants, 3 bars, 2 tennis courts, pool, dive shop, car-rental desk, water-sports center. AE, DC, MC, V. CP, MAP. Expensive– Very Expensive.*

★ **Diamant Les Bains.** Although manager Hubert Andrieu and his family go all out to make their guests comfortable, you won't feel quite at home unless you speak at least a little French. A few of the rooms are in the main house, where the restaurant is located, but most are in bungalows, some just steps away from the sea. All rooms are air-conditioned, with private baths, TVs, and phones; eight have kitchenettes. *Le Diamant 97223, tel. 596/76–40–14 or 800/223–9815; in Canada, 800/468–0023; in NY, 212/251–1800, fax 596/76–27–00. 24 rooms. Facilities: restaurant, bar, car rental, pool, watersports center. DC, MC. CP, MAP. Closed Sept. Moderate.*

Diamant Marine. Here you'll find self-contained miniapartments (sleeping room with kitchenette and balcony) in a pristine stucco building, where the motel-style rooms are painted in pastel colors. The main part of the hotel is some 100 feet above the beach, and rows of dwelling units are tiered on the hillside down to the shore. The pool is just above the beach. Although this arrangement is visually attractive and the walk down is easy, the climb up the steps from the pool and beach to the main house and restaurant is strenuous. The hotel attracts French families. *Point de la Chery, near Diamant, tel. 596/76– 46–00 or 800/221–4542, fax 596/76–25–99. 149 rooms. Facilities: restaurant, 2 bars, 2 pools (1 for children), water sports, deep-sea fishing, 2 tennis courts. AE, V. CP. Moderate.*

★ **Relais Caraibes.** This is a colony of bungalows on manicured grounds, with Diamond Rock dominating the seascape. Each of the 12 bungalows has a bedroom, a small salon with a sofa bed, a kitchenette, and a bathroom. The decorations are objects the owner has brought from trips to her native Paris. There are also three standard rooms in the main house. The pool is perched at the edge of the cliff that drops to the sea—a very dramatic setting. Of all the hotels on Martinique, this one comes closest to having an individuality and the authenticity of a country inn with good food and attractive accommodations. *Point de la Chery, Diamant 97223, tel. 596/76–44–65 or 800/223–9815, fax 596/76–21–20. 15 rooms. Facilities: restaurant, bar, pool, private beach, boat, scuba instruction. AE, MC, V. CP. Moderate.*

Marigot **Habitation Lagrange.** This unexpected find, an 18th-century manor house, stands amid a rambling former sugar plantation scattered with crumbling stone buildings 1½ miles off the main road north of Marigot. High ceilings, austere furnishings, and polished wood floors set a degree of colonial formality that may not appeal to all, but Habitation Lagrange is Martinique's only hotel with a vestige of the island's cultivated past. The mood continues in the three master bedrooms, with high canopy beds on bare wood floors and ceiling fans. Bathrooms have modern fixtures but keep to the 18th-century style from the gold-plated taps to the bathtubs encased in wood. Two new two-story buildings house 12 rooms with gabled ceilings. Three more rooms are in an original stone building facing the pool and are decorated rather sparsely with little more than a canopy bed on white parquet floors. Dinner is served at polished tables in the dining room, followed by a brandy in the small library. The young owners are extremely enthusiastic, but you may need a little French to appreciate their hospitality. *97225 Marigot, tel. 596/53–60–60, fax 596/53–50–58. 18 rooms. Facilities: dining room, bar, library, pool, 2 tennis courts. MC, DC, V. BP. Very Expensive.*

Le Marin **The Last Resort.** John and Véronique Deschamps' bed-and-breakfast on rue Osman Duquesnay is in the former gendarmerie annex. Language will be no problem here, since the Deschampses once lived in Sausalito, but you'll have to be flexible enough to share a bathroom with the other guests on your floor. A small communal kitchen is available, and an excellent family-style dinner is served nightly. *Le Marin 97290, tel. 596/ 74–83–88, fax 596/74–76–41. 7 rooms. Facilities: restaurant. No credit cards. CP. Inexpensive.*

Le Morne Rouge **Auberge de la Montagne Pelée.** There are three rooms and six studios with kitchenettes in this hillside inn that faces the famed volcano. Accommodations are simple; the view from the restaurant terrace is spectacular. The inn was closed for repairs and renovations at press time, but should reopen for the 1993–94 season. *Le Morne Rouge 97260, tel. 596/52–32–09, fax 596/73–20–75. 12 rooms. Facilities: restaurant. No credit cards. EP. Inexpensive.*

Schoelcher **La Batelière Hotel.** This beachfront property boasts the island's largest rooms, and arguably the best tennis courts. But before you rush to stay here, consider the location—north of Fort-de-France and away from most of the island's resort activity (although, for some that would be a plus). The hotel overlooks the sea, and all rooms are air-conditioned, with direct-access phone, cable TV, radio, and private balcony or patio. The rooms have new furniture and marble-tiled bathrooms, and suites have canopy beds. Recent renovations have created a smart, if sober, reception area with a lounge facing the sea. One level below the lounge is the semicircular pool and pool bar and below that is a small beach sheltered from the waves by a breakwater. With these upgraded facilities and its proximity to Fort-de-France, the hotel should be attractive to businessmen. Ask about the scuba and honeymoon packages. *Schoelcher 97233, tel. 596/61–49–49 or 800/223–6510, fax 596/ 61–70–57. 192 rooms, 19 suites. Facilities: 2 restaurants, 2 bars, casino, pool, 6 lighted tennis courts, sauna, shopping arcade, conference rooms, water-sports center. AE, DC, MC, V. CP. Expensive–Very Expensive.*

Ste-Anne **Club Med/Buccaneer's Creek.** Occupying 48 landscaped acres, Martinique's Club Med is an all-inclusive village with plazas, cafés, restaurants, boutique, and a small marina. Air-conditioned pastel cottages contain twin beds and private shower bath. The only money you need spend here is for bar drinks, personal expenses, and excursions into Fort-de-France or the countryside. There's a white-sand beach, a plethora of water sports, and plenty of nightlife. *Pointe Marin 97180, tel. 596/76– 72–72 or 800/CLUBMED; in NY, 212/750–1670, fax 596/72– 76–02. 300 rooms. Facilities: 2 restaurants and bars, 6 tennis courts (4 lighted), fitness and water-sports center, nightclub, disco. AE, V. All-inclusive (drinks not included). Moderate–Expensive.*

St-François **Fregate Bleu.** The owner, Mme. De Lucie, left the management of Leyfritz Plantation because she wanted the quiet life. In

1991 she opened the Fregate Bleu, an eight-room glorified bed-and-breakfast. Five of the rooms are delightful—their spaciousness accentuated by off-white furnishings, patterned carpets, and the occasional antique. All of these five rooms have a balcony overlooking Les Islets de l'Impératrice. (The other three rooms do not have a balcony or this view.) All rooms have a small kitchenette and modern bathrooms with such niceties as bathrobes. Only *petit déjeuner* (breakfast) is served, so if you decline to use your kitchenette you must negotiate the rutted road to the highway and drive at least 20 minutes to a restaurant. Though the sea is a stone's throw away, there is no beach nearby and the Fregate Bleu's pool is small. You are paying the $200 a night for what Mme. De Lucie wanted—peace and quiet in very comfortable surroundings. *Le François 97240 (5 mi south of St-François on Vauclin Rd.), tel. 596/54–54–66 or 800/ 633–7411, fax 596/54–78–48. 8 rooms. Facilities: small pool. MC, V. BP. Expensive.*

Home and Villa Rentals The **Villa Rental Service** of the Martinique Tourist Office (tel. 596/63–79–60) can assist with rentals of homes, villas, and apartments. Most are in the south of the island near good beaches and can be rented on a weekly or monthly basis.

The Arts and Nightlife

The island is dotted with lively discos and nightclubs, but entertainment on Martinique is not confined to partying.

Be sure to catch a performance of **Les Grands Ballets de Martinique** (tel. 596/63–43–88). The troupe of young, exuberant dancers, singers, and musicians is one of the best folkloric groups in the Caribbean. They perform on alternate nights at the Bakoua, Méridien, La Batelière, and Carayou-PLM Azur.

Discos Your hotel or the Tourist Office can put you in touch with the current "in" places. It's also wise to check on opening and closing times and admission charges. For the most part, the discos draw a mixed crowd of locals and tourists, the young and the not so young. Some of the currently popular places are **Le New Hippo** (24 blvd. Allegre, Fort-de-France, tel. 596/71–74–60), **Le Sweety** (rue Capitaine Pierre Rose, Fort-de-France, no phone), **Le Must** (20 blvd. Allegre, Fort-de-France, tel. 596/60–36–06), **Le Vesou** (Carayou-PLM Azur, tel. 596/66–04–04), **VonVon** (Méridien, tel. 596/66–00–00), **La Cabane de Pêcheur** (Diamant-Novotel, tel. 596/76–42–42), **L'Oeil** (Petit Cocotte, Ducos, tel. 596/56–11–11), and **Zipp's Dupe Club** (Dumaine, Le François, tel. 596/54–47–06).

Zouk and Jazz Currently the most popular music is the zouk, which mixes the Caribbean rhythm and an Occidental tempo with Creole words. Jacob Devarieux (Kassav) is the leading exponent of this style and is occasionally on the island. More likely, though, you will hear zouk music played by one of his followers at the hotels and clubs. The **Neptune** (Diamant, tel. 596/76–34–23) is a current "in" place for the zouk. Jazz musicians, like the music, tend to be informal and independent. They rarely hold regular gigs. In season, you'll find one or two combos playing at clubs and hotels, but it is only at **Coco Lobo** (tel. 596/63–63–77, located next to the Tourist Office in Fort-de-France), that there are regular jazz sessions.

Casinos   The island's two casinos are open from 9 PM to 3 AM Monday to Saturday. You have to be at least 21 (with a picture ID); jacket and tie are not required. The **Casino Trois-Ilets** (Méridien, tel. 596/66–00–00) has American and French roulette, blackjack, and an admission charge of 70F. The other casino, at La Batelière, offers American roulette, blackjack, and craps with similar restrictions and a 60F admission.

16 Montserrat

*Updated by
Simon Worrall*

Christopher Columbus sailed by the leeward coast of this Caribbean island in 1493, and seeing the jagged mountains, he named it Montserrat, after the Santa Maria de Montserrate monastery near Barcelona, which is surrounded by similar terrain.

The Carib Indians who inhabited the island then were still there in 1632, when dissident Irish Catholics arrived from nearby St. Kitts, from which they were escaping persecution. These new settlers found an island whose topography strongly resembled that of their native Ireland, prompting Montserrat's nickname, The Emerald Isle of the Caribbean. Today the Irish influence is much diminished. Still, your passport is stamped with a shamrock upon arrival, the phone book is loaded with Irish places and surnames, and St. Patrick's Day is celebrated enthusiastically (albeit to commemorate a major 18th-century slave uprising).

Actually, the African influence is more pronounced, thanks to Montserrat's comparatively low profile. Newborns are still given "jumbie" nicknames to fool the evil spirits, and the related jumbie dances, designed to ward off or propitiate those spirits, are lusty and vibrant. The rollicking Carnival, held during the Christmas season, is a riot of color in traditional authentic costumes.

On the map Montserrat looks like a flint ax head, with the sharp end pointing north. The island is divided, along the center, by a range of switch-back hills, the highest of which is Chance's Peak in the south, rising to a height of 3,000 feet. Also in the southern hills is the volcano known as Galway's Soufrière. It is long extinct, but steam pouring from vents in the dramatic yellow-and-pink rock and the lush tropical vegetation circling the rim of the crater make this a powerful, evocative site.

Measuring only 11 miles by 8 miles, Montserrat is a small, friendly island that has escaped much of the large-scale development common in other parts of the Caribbean. It tends to attract independent travelers who want a low key, away-from-it-all vacation. If you want to pump iron, drink piña coladas, and boogie till dawn, you'll probably be bored. If you like seclusion, nature, and peace and quiet, you'll love it.

Most visitors arrive at Blackburn Airport on the Atlantic (east) coast of the island and then drive to the Caribbean (west) coast. Since there are no roads that traverse the island from east to west or circle it to the south, this will mean a trip around the northern tip. On the way, you will notice the landscape change considerably. The Atlantic coast is rockier, more windswept, and less fertile. Steep cliffs make most of the beaches on that side of the island inaccessible.

The best beaches, as well as the capital, Plymouth, and most of the villas and hotels are concentrated in a small area, measuring about five miles by two miles on the Caribbean coast. Here, too, Montserrat's lush vegetation is at its most luxuriant. Hibiscus and bougainvillea; giant philodendron and avocado trees; mango, flamboyance trees, christophines, and many others all thrive on the terracelike hills that slope down to the water. There are also spectacular views across the Caribbean to the mysterious island of Rodondo and St. Kitts, a sequence of indigo blue peaks on the horizon.

Nearly all Montserratians have harrowing tales of how they spent a night in September 1989 cowering in cellars or hiding in clothes cupboards as a wild vortex of wind and water ripped off roofs, defoliated trees and sent cars hurtling through the air like tin cans. Amazingly—and it is a tribute to the islanders' tenacity and courage—few traces of Hurricane Hugo remain today. The vegetation has grown back. The infrastructure has been repaired and, in many cases, upgraded. Thanks to Hugo, Montserrat will also soon have a brand-new port.

Before You Go

Tourist Information You can get information about Montserrat through **Pace Communications** (485 5th Ave., New York, NY 10017, tel. 212/818–0100).

Arriving and Departing
By Plane Antigua is not only the gateway, it's the best way to reach Montserrat. **American Airlines** (tel. 800/334–7200) and **BWIA** (tel. 800/JET–BWIA) fly here from New York; **BWIA** flies from Miami; **Air Canada** (tel. 800/422–6232) and BWIA from Toronto; **British Airways** (tel. 081/897–4000 in Britain, 800/247–9297 in the United States) from London; and **Lufthansa** transports visitors via Puerto Rico and Antigua (tel. 800/645–3880 in the United States).

From Antigua's **V.C. Bird International Airport,** you can make your connections with **LIAT** (tel. 809/491–2200) or **Montserrat Airways** (tel. 809/491–2713) for the 15-minute flight to Montserrat.

You will land on the 3,400-foot runway at **Blackburne Airport,** on the Atlantic coast, about 11 miles from Plymouth.

From the Airport Taxis meet every flight, and the government-regulated fare from the airport to Plymouth is E.C.$29 (U.S.$11). At press time, the rate was scheduled to increase.

Passports and Visas U.S. and Canadian citizens only need proof of citizenship, such as a passport, a notarized birth certificate, or a voter registration card. A driver's license is *not* sufficient. British citizens must have a passport; visas are not required. All visitors must hold an ongoing or return ticket.

Language It's English with more of a lilt than a brogue. You'll also hear a patois that's spoken on most of the islands.

Precautions Ask for permission before taking pictures. Some residents may be reluctant photographic subjects, and they will appreciate your courtesy.

Most Montserrattians frown at the sight of skimpily dressed tourists; do not risk offending them by strolling around in shorts and swimsuits.

Staying in Montserrat

Important Addresses **Tourist Information:** The **Montserrat Department of Tourism** (Church Rd., Plymouth, tel. 809/491–2230) is open weekdays 8–noon and 1–4 PM.

Emergencies **Police** (tel. 809/491–2555). **Hospitals:** There is a 24-hour emergency room at **Glendon Hospital** (Plymouth, tel. 809/491–2552). **Pharmacies: Lee's Pharmacy** (Evergreen Dr., Plymouth, tel.

408

Montserrat

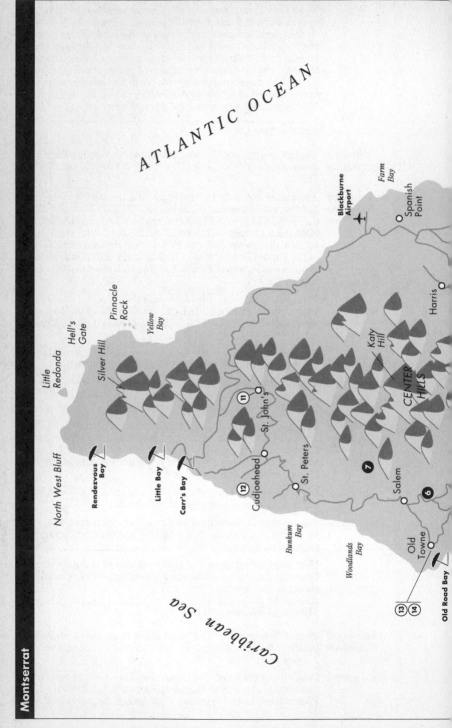

ATLANTIC OCEAN

Caribbean Sea

North West Bluff

Little Redonda

Hell's Gate

Pinnacle Rock

Silver Hill

Yellow Bay

Rendezvous Bay

Little Bay

Carr's Bay

⑪ St. John's

⑫ Cudjoehead

St. Peters

Katy Hill

CENTER HILLS

Harris

Blackburne Airport

Farm Bay

Spanish Point

Bunkum Bay

Woodlands Bay

⑦

Salem

⑥

Old Towne

⑬ ⑭ Old Road Bay

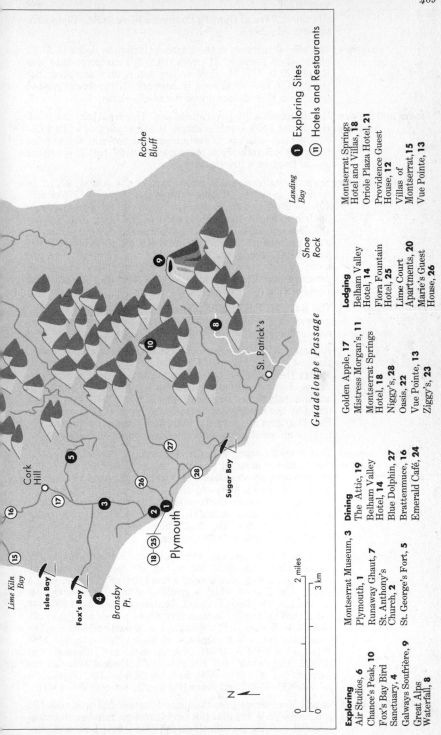

Exploring
Air Studios, **6**
Chance's Peak, **10**
Fox's Bay Bird
Sanctuary, **4**
Galways Soufrière, **9**
Great Alps
Waterfall, **8**

Montserrat Museum, **3**
Plymouth, **1**
Runaway Ghaut, **7**
St. Anthony's
Church, **2**
St. George's Fort, **5**

Dining
The Attic, **19**
Belham Valley
Hotel, **14**
Blue Dolphin, **27**
Brattenmuce, **16**
Emerald Café, **24**

Golden Apple, **17**
Mistress Morgan's, **11**
Montserrat Springs
Hotel, **18**
Niggy's, **28**
Oasis, **22**
Vue Pointe, **13**
Ziggy's, **23**

Lodging
Belham Valley
Hotel, **14**
Flora Fountain
Hotel, **25**
Lime Court
Apartments, **20**
Marie's Guest
House, **26**

Montserrat Springs
Hotel and Villas, **18**
Oriole Plaza Hotel, **21**
Providence Guest
House, **12**
Villas of
Montserrat, **15**
Vue Pointe, **13**

● Exploring Sites

⑪ Hotels and Restaurants

809/491–3274) and **Daniel's Pharmacy** (George St., Plymouth, tel. 809/491–2908).

Currency The official currency is the Eastern Caribbean dollar (E.C.$), often called beewee. At press time, the exchange rate was E.C.$2.70 to U.S.$1. U.S. dollars are readily accepted, but you'll often receive change in beewees. Note: Prices quoted here are in U.S. dollars unless noted otherwise.

Taxes and Service Charges Hotels collect a 7% government tax. The departure tax is $6. Hotels add a 10% service charge. Most restaurants add a 10%–15% service charge. If restaurants do not add the service charge, it's customary to leave a 10% or 15% tip. Taxi drivers should be given a 10% tip.

Guided Tours Several local companies offer tours of the island, either in minivans or sedans. **Runaway Tours** (tel. 809/491–2776 or 809/491–2800) offers a day tour of the island that includes Galway's Soufrière, St. George's Fort, and the Fox's Bay Bird Sanctuary. The price of $110 per person, reduced to $75 per person for a party of two or $58 for a party of three, includes refreshments and a meal, usually at the Emerald Cafe. The tour lasts five hours, and sturdy walking shoes are recommended. Other companies include **Carib World Tours** (tel. 809/491–2713) and **Best Foot Forward** (tel. 809/491–5872).

The Rotary Club of Montserrat (tel. 809/491–2240) conducts garden tours in high season. The cost is $30 per person and includes drinks at the Vue Point Inn.

A number of taxi drivers also do tours of the island. Of these, the best is run by Charles Frith, known to everyone simply as **Mango** (tel. 809/491–2134), an enormously likable Montserratian. Also recommended are **John Ryner** (tel. 809/491–2190) and the aptly named **Be-Beep Taylor** (tel. 809/491–3787). Prices (fixed by the Department of Tourism) are E.C.$30 per hour or E.C.$130 for a five-hour day tour. Refreshments are extra. For further information, contact the Department of Tourism.

Getting Around
Taxis Taxis, private vehicles, or the M11 (a play on the local registration numbers, meaning your own two legs) are the main means of transport on the island. A loosely organized network of minibuses travels between the villages and Plymouth, but schedules are erratic and unreliable. Taxis are always available at the airport, the main hotels, and the taxi stand in Plymouth (tel. 809/491–2261). The Department of Tourism publishes a list of taxi fares to most destinations.

Car Rentals The island has more than 150 miles of good roads. Unless you're uncomfortable about driving on the left, you won't have any trouble exploring. You'll need a valid driver's license, plus a Montserrat license, which is available at the airport or the police station. The fee is E.C.$30. Rental cars cost about $35–$40 per day. The smaller companies, whose prices are generally 10%–25% cheaper, will negotiate, particularly off-season. The local Avis outlet is **Pauline Car Rentals** (Plymouth, tel. 809/491–2345 or 800/331–1084). Other agencies are **Jefferson's Car Rental** (Dagenham, tel. 809/491–2126), **Budget** (Blackburne Airport, tel. 809/491–6065), **Reliable** (Marine Dr., Plymouth, tel. 809/491–6990), and **Fenco** (Plymouth, tel. 809/491–4901).

Telephones and Mail To call Montserrat from the United States, dial area code 809 and access code 491 plus the local four-digit number. International direct-dial is available on the island; both local and long-distance calls come through clearly. To call locally on the island, you need to dial only the local four-digit number.

Airmail letters and postcards to the United States and Canada cost E.C.$1.15 each. Montserrat is one of several Caribbean islands whose stamps are of interest to collectors. You can buy them at the main post office in Plymouth (open Mon. and Tues., Thurs. and Fri. 8:15–3:30; Wed. and Sat. 8:15–11:30 AM).

Opening and Most shops are open Monday to Saturday 8–5. Banking hours
Closing Times are Monday to Thursday 8–1, and Friday 3–5.

Exploring Montserrat

Numbers in the margin correspond to points of interest on the Montserrat map.

Plymouth About a third of the island's population of 12,500 live in
❶ **Plymouth,** the capital city that faces the Caribbean on the southwest coast. The town is neat and clean, its narrow streets lined with trim Georgian structures built mostly of stones that came from Dorset as ballast on old sailing vessels. Most of the town's sights are set right along the water. On the south side, a bridge over the Fort Ghaut ("gut," or ravine) leads to Wapping, where most of the restaurants are located.

We'll begin at **Government House** on the south side of town just above Sugar Bay. The frilly Victorian house, decorated with a shamrock, dates from the 18th century. Beautifully landscaped gardens surround the building, but unfortunately the house is no longer open to the public. The grounds, however, are open from 10 to noon and are worth a visit.

Follow Peebles Street north and cross the bridge. Just over the bridge at the junction of Harney, Strand, and Parliament streets you'll see the **Market,** where islanders bring their produce every Saturday—a very colorful scene.

From the market, walk along Strand Street for one block to the tall white **War Memorial** with a bell turret. The memorial is a tribute to the soldiers of both world wars. Next to the monument is the **Post Office and Treasury,** a galleried West Indian–style building by the water, where you can buy stamps that make handsome souvenirs.

Walk away from the water on George Street, which runs alongside the War Memorial. The town's main thoroughfare, Parliament Street, cuts diagonally north–south through the town. A left turn onto Parliament Street, at the corner of George Street, will take you to the Methodist Church and the Court House. If you continue straight on George Street, you'll come to the Roman Catholic Church. North of the church is the **American University of the Caribbean,** a medical school with many American students.

Elsewhere on From here on, you'll need wheels. Take Highway 2, the main
the Island road north out of Plymouth. On the outskirts of town there's a stone marker that commemorates the first colony in 1632.

Tour 1 **St. Anthony's Church,** which is just north of town, was conse-
❷ crated some time between 1623 and 1666. It was rebuilt in 1730 following one of the many clashes between the French and the English in the area. Two silver chalices displayed in the church

were donated by freed slaves after emancipation in 1834. An ancient tamarind tree stands near the church.

Richmond Hill rises northeast of town. Here you will find the ③ **Montserrat Museum** in a restored sugar mill. The museum contains maps, historical records, artifacts, and all sorts of memorabilia pertaining to the island's growth and development. *Richmond Hill, tel. 809/491–5443. Admission free (donations accepted). Open Sun. and Wed. 2:30–5 (but telephone to be sure).*

Take the first left turn past the museum to Grove Road; it will ④ take you to the **Fox's Bay Bird Sanctuary,** a 15-acre bog area. Marked trails lead into the interior, which is aflutter with egrets, herons, coots, and cuckoo birds.

The **Bransby Point Fortification** is also in this area and contains a collection of restored cannons.

Backtrack on Grove Road to Highway 2, drive north and turn ⑤ right on Highway 4 to **St. George's Fort.** It's overgrown and of little historical interest, but the view from the hilltop is well worth the trip.

Highway 2 continues north past the **Belham Valley Golf Course** to **Vue Pointe Hotel,** on the coast at Lime Kiln Bay. Head west to the green slopes of Centre Hills, almost in the center of the ⑥ island, for **Air Studios,** a recording studio founded in 1979 by former Beatles producer George Martin. Sting, Boy George, and Paul McCartney have all cut records here, but following Hugo, Martin closed up shop.

About 1½ miles farther north, a scenic drive takes you along ⑦ **Runaway Ghaut.** Two centuries ago, this peaceful green valley was the scene of bloody battles between the French and the English. Local legend has it that "those who drink its water clear they spellbound are, and the Montserrat they must obey." **Carr's Bay, Little Bay,** and **Rendezvous Bay,** the island's three most popular beaches, are along the northwest coast.

Tour 2 The next tour of the island will be considerably more arduous, taking in the mountains, rain forests, and *soufrières* (volcanic craters with sulfuric springs) to the south and east of Plymouth. To hire a knowledgeable guide, contact the Department of Tourism or ask at your hotel. The guide's fee will be about $6 per person to the waterfall. Wear rubber-soled shoes.

A 15-minute drive south of Plymouth on Old Fort Road will bring you to the village of **St. Patrick's.** From there, a scenic drive takes you to the starting point of the moderately strenu- ⑧ ous 30- to 45-minute hike through thick rain forests to **Great Alps Waterfall.** The falls cascade 70 feet down the side of a rock and splash into a shallow pool, where you can see a rainbow in the mist.

⑨ A rugged road leads eastward to **Galways Soufrière,** where another hike is involved, this one lasting about a half hour. Once there, you'll see volcanic rock, boiling water, and small vents of gurgling, molten sulfur. City people are fond of complaining in the summertime of streets so hot you could fry an egg on them. Here your guide will almost certainly fry an egg to demonstrate the intense heat of the rocks.

⑩ The island's highest point, **Chance's Peak,** pokes up 3,000 feet through the rain forests. The climb to the top is arduous—and you shouldn't attempt it without a guide—but if you do make it to the top, what little breath you may have left will be taken away by the view.

Also in this area is the old **Galways Estate,** a plantation built in the late 17th century by prosperous Irishmen John and Henry Blake, who came to Montserrat from Galway. All that now remains of the fine estate is the ruins of the house and factory and some rusted machinery. This is also the site of archaeological digs. It has been earmarked as an important archaeological site by the Smithsonian.

Off the Beaten Track

Head for the South Soufrière Hills at the southern tip of the island. It is the wildest and least spoiled part of Montserrat and includes, among its highlights, the **Bamboo Forest,** a large tract of semirainforest inhabited by birds, frogs, and plants. It is home to many of the 100 species of birds that visit Montserrat, among them the national emblem, *iaterus oberi,* or Monserrat oriole, also known locally as the Tannia Bird (don't expect to see one, though, because its habitat was severely damaged by Hurricane Hugo and is only now beginning to reestablish itself). What you will see are bromiades, tulip and breadfruit trees, and a plethora of other tropical plants. Because no roads lead into the area and there are no marked paths, you are advised to go with a guide. The most knowledgeable guide is **Joseph Peters,** a young man who will take you on a two- to three-hour tour and fill you in on the wildlife and botany. He can be reached at his home (tel. 809/491–6850) or via the Department of Tourism in Plymouth. James Daley, one of the forest rangers, can also provide you with helpful information. He can be reached at the Department of Agriculture (tel. 809/491–2546). Plans are afoot for some sort of low-impact, ecotourism development in the area, but things move very slowly on Montserrat.

Beaches

The sand on the beaches on Montserrat's south coast is of volcanic origin; usually referred to as black, it's actually light to dark gray. On the northwest coast, the sand is beige or white. The three most popular destinations for swimming and sunning are **Rendezvous Bay, Little Bay,** and **Carr's Bay,** all on the northwest coast. Though it is possible to drive to both Carr's Bay and Little Bay and to hike from Little Bay over the hill to Rendezvous Bay, it is certainly more relaxing to reach any of these beaches via the sailing and snorkeling excursions arranged by the **Vue Pointe Hotel** (tel. 809/491–5210).

Fox's Bay has a lovely strip of gray sand on the bay just north of the Bird Sanctuary. **Old Road Bay** and **Isles Bay** are on the coast north of Fox's Bay (4 miles north of Plymouth) and have stretches of gray-sand beaches.

Sugar Bay, to the south of Plymouth, is a beach of fine gray volcanic sand. The Yacht Club overlooks this beach.

Sports and the Outdoors

Boating   Boats are available through **Captain Martin,** who has a 46-foot trimaran and takes guests for a full-day sail to neighboring is-

lands from 10 AM to 5 PM for about $40 (tel. 809/491–5738), or
through **Vue Pointe Hotel** (tel. 809/491–5210).

Golf The Montserrat Golf Course, in the picturesque Belham Valley,
is "slope rated" by the USGA (in other words, it's incredibly
hilly) and must be one of the few golf courses in the world that
can list gopher holes and iguanas among its hazards. The number of holes (11) is also somewhat eccentric, though by playing
a number of them twice, you can get your 18. Four fairways run
along the ocean. The rest are uphill and down dale. Watch out
for the iguanas—they collect golf balls.

Mountain Biking Montserrat is perfect mountain-bike country: small, relatively
traffic-free roads with lots of challenging hills to try out all
those gears. An excellent addition to the island's facilities is the
fleet of cross-terrain and mountain bikes available from **Island
Bikes** (tel. 809/491–4686) in Harney Street, Plymouth. Rentals
run at $20 per day or $110 per week. Guided tours, which include refreshments and a support vehicle for the faint of heart,
are available.

Sailing, Snorkeling equipment is provided on the day cruises to the
Snorkeling, and white-sand coves on the west coast; boats usually have an open
Scuba Diving bar. Arrangements can be made through **Vue Pointe Hotel** (tel.
809/491–5210) or **Captain Martin** (tel. 809/491–5738).

Dive Montserrat (tel. 809/491–8812) operates from the Vue
Pointe Hotel, offering one- or two-tank dives, night dives, and
instruction from a PADI-certified teacher. Contact Chris Mason. Another outfit offering PADI courses and specialty
courses is the **Sea Wolf Diving School** (tel. 809/491–7807) in
Plymouth. Costs at both are about $40 for a one-tank dive and
$60 for a two-tank dive.

Danny Water Sports (tel. 809/491–5645), also operating out of
the Vue Point Inn, offers fishing, Sunfish sailing, and
waterskiing.

Tennis There are lighted tennis courts at the **Vue Pointe Hotel** (tel.
809/491–5210), **The Montserrat Golf Club** (tel. 809/491–5220),
and the **Montserrat Springs Hotel** (tel. 809/491–2481).

Windsurfing Contact the **Vue Pointe Hotel** (tel. 809/491–5210) to rent boards
(about $10 per hour).

Spectator Sports Cricket is the national passion. Cricket and soccer matches are
held from February through June in **Sturge Park. Shamrock
Car Park** is the venue for netball and basketball games. Contact
the Department of Tourism (tel. 809/491–2230) for schedules.

Shopping

Montserrat's sea-island cotton is famous for its high quality.
Unfortunately, only a limited amount could be grown, and that
was *before* Hurricane Hugo. Since then, the supply has been
even more limited. Several new boutiques have opened, however, and there are always good buys in hand-turned pottery,
straw goods, and jewelry bits made from shells and coral.
Montserratian stamps are prized by collectors; they can be purchased at the Post Office or at the Philatelic Bureau, just across
the bridge in Wapping. Two lip-smacking local food products
are Cassell's hot sauce, available at most supermarkets, and
Perk's Punch, an effervescent rum-based concoction manufactured by J.W.R. Perkins, Inc. (tel. 809/491–2596).

Good Buys **Jus' Looking** (George St., Plymouth, tel. 809/491–4076) is a
Clothes boutique that opened in 1989, featuring "sculpted," hand-
painted pillows from Antigua; painted and lacquered boxes
from Tortola; Sunny Caribbee's jams, jellies and packaged
spices from the British West Indies (including an Arawak love
potion and a hangover cure); special teas; and Caribelle Batik's
line of richly colored fabrics, shirts, skirts, pants, dresses, and
gowns for him and her. (These batiks originated in St. Kitts.)
The shop also has an excellent selection of local poetry and history books. **Montserrat Shirts** (Parliament St., tel. 809/491–
2892) has a good selection of T-shirts and sandals. **Etcetera**
(John St., tel. 809/491–3299) has American-imported dresses
and a small, but fine, selection of local crafts. If you're lucky,
you may see someone making a hat of coconut palm fronds).

The Lime Tree (Parliament St., tel. 809/491–3656) carries cotton clothing for men and boys, with some snappy styling. There
are also "I Am Part of Reconstruction" T-shirts for $13, de-
signed for owner Neville Bradshaw. **The Montserrat Sea Island
Cotton Co.** (corner of George and Strand Sts., Plymouth, tel.
809/491–7009) has long been famous for its cotton creations.
Should you really need to purchase a T-shirt, stop in at **Sea Isle
Style** (Parliament St., Plymouth, tel. 809/491–2892).

Crafts **The Tapestries of Montserrat** (Parliament St., tel. 809/491–
2520) provides a two-hour adventure wandering through this
second-floor gallery of hand-tufted creations—from wall hangings and pillow covers to tote bags and rugs—all with fanciful
yarn creations of flowers, carnival figures, animals, and birds.
Owners Gerald and Charlie Handley will even help you create
your own design for a small additional fee. **Carol's Corner** (Vue
Pointe Hotel, tel. 809/491–5210) has finds by Carol Osborne
that are first-rate: copper bookmarks and books, ranging from
the *Montserrat Cookbook* to Frane Lessac's books of prose and
paintings. Drop by **Dutcher's Studio** (Old Towne, tel. 809/491–
5823) to see hand-cut, hand-painted objects made from old bottles. If Paula Dutcher is there, ask about the morning iguana
feeding at her house. Anywhere from 5 to 50 reptiles converge
on her lawn, sunning themselves and eating hibiscus from your
hand. **Island House,** on John Street, stocks Haitian art, Caribbean prints, and clay pottery.

Dining

Restaurants tend to be expensive, and there are not as many
budget restaurants here as on some larger, more developed islands. What Montserrat does have are numerous rum-shops,
good places for a drink and a simple meal.

The national dish is goatwater stew, made with goat meat and
vegetables, similar to Irish stew. Goat meat is reminiscent of
mutton. Mountain chicken (actually enormous frogs) is also a
great favorite. Yam, breadfruit, christophine (a green vegetable), lime, mango, papaya, and a variety of seafood are served
in most restaurants.

Highly recommended restaurants are indicated by a star ★.

Category	Cost*
Expensive	over $30
Moderate	$20–$30
Inexpensive	under $20

Per person, excluding drinks and service. If the service charge is not added to the bill, leave a 10% to 15% tip.

Montserrat Springs Hotel. The split-level dining room, enclosed on three sides, faces a large pool and a sun deck, with views of the ocean. The menu features Caribbean cuisine that makes use of local fruits and vegetables; there are several chicken and seafood dishes. *Richmond Hill, Plymouth, tel. 809/491–2481. Reservations suggested in season. AE, MC, V. Expensive.*

★ **Vue Pointe.** Candlelit dining in the hotel's restaurant overlooking the sea makes this a very romantic place, and with the 60% roster of return guests, the atmosphere is that of a house party. The menu may include West Indian curried chicken; beef Wellington; red snapper with Creole sauce; and for dessert, a luscious lime pie or cheesecake. The Wednesday-night barbecue, accompanied by music from a steel band, is a popular island event. *Old Towne, tel. 809/491–5210. Reservations suggested for dinner. AE, MC, V. Expensive.*

★ **Belham Valley Hotel.** The best tables at this romantic candlelit restaurant are on the open-air terrace. Hung with ferns and croton plants, it looks down over picturesque Belham Valley and the lights of Isle Bay Hill opposite. The sound of tree frogs and the splash of the ocean mingle with the chink of glasses and the music of Stan Getz and Astrud Gilberto. Hibiscus tumbles over stone walls and sprouts from table vases; ceilings and floors are timbered—all this as you enjoy one of the best menus on the island. Appetizers include conch fritters and liver pâté. Main dishes include Seafood Delight (sautéed lobster, red snapper, and sea scallops in a vermouth sauce) and broiled baby lobster tails. Scrumptious desserts are mango or lime mousse, lemon cake, and a tropical fruit sundae with a ginger sauce. At lunchtime, the offerings are lighter: omelets, salads, and sandwiches. On Thursdays a good Chinese menu is offered. *Old Towne, tel. 809/491–5553. Reservations required for dinner. AE, MC, V. No lunch weekends; closed Mon. Moderate–Expensive.*

Emerald Café. Dining is relaxed at 10 tables inside and on the terrace, where there are white tables shaded by blue umbrellas. Burgers, sandwiches, salads and grilled-plate lunches are served at lunchtime. Dinner dishes feature tournedos sautéed in spicy butter; broiled or sautéed Caribbean lobster; T-bone steak; mountain chicken Diable; and kingfish, broiled or sautéed. The homemade pastries, such as Island Coconut Pie, are superb. There's also an ample list of liqueurs and wines, a full bar, and entertainment on weekends. *Wapping, Plymouth, tel. 809/491–3821. Dinner reservations suggested in season. No credit cards. Closed Sun. Moderate.*

Oasis. A 200-year-old stone building houses this restaurant, where you can dine outdoors on the patio. Entrées include mountain chicken, jumbo shrimp Provençale, and red snapper with lime butter. Owners Eric and Mandy Finnamore, well known for their fish-and-chips, will also cook to order with proper notice. *Wapping, Plymouth, tel. 809/491–2328. Reser-*

vations suggested in season. No credit cards. Closed Wed. Moderate.

The Attic. The story of the Attic (since Hugo) is the story of Montserrat itself. The (formerly) third-story Attic had a sister restaurant on the second story called The Pantry. Compliments of Hugo, the Attic ended up in the Pantry, where owners John and Jeanne Fagon decided it would stay! For breakfast, lunch, and dinner, 12 busy tables supply town folk with specialties of chicken, vegetable or shrimp quesadilla, ocean perch, pork chops with "pantry" sauce, breaded shrimp, and lobster tail. *Marine Dr., Plymouth, tel. 809/491–2008. No credit cards. Inexpensive.*

★ **Blue Dolphin.** It's short on ambience, the chairs are Naugahyde, and the menu's scrawled on a blackboard without prices or descriptions, but the seductive aromas wafting from the kitchen announce that the Blue Dolphin serves some of the best food on the island, including luscious pumpkin fritters, mouthwatering lobster, and meltingly tender mountain chicken. *Amersham, tel. 809/491–3263. No credit cards. Inexpensive.*

★ **Brattenmuce.** About 10 minutes by car above the road from Plymouth to Belham Valley, you can't miss the canary yellow facade and brightly colored croton bushes of this restaurant. The name is a play on the name of the owners, Matt Hawthorne and Bruce Munro, two Toronto exiles who have been in Montserrat since 1985. They serve no-frills, North American cuisine—meat loaf and creamed potatoes, curried pork chops, and chicken cordon bleu. On Wednesday nights they have a Games Night, which is popular with "the snow birds," retirees from the North. A three-course meal for E.C.$25 includes free use of the Scrabble boards and Trivial Pursuit. For those who want to stay over, Rogie's, above the restaurant, has simple rooms to let. In the off-season Brattenmuce is open on Wednesday, Friday, and Saturday in the evening. In season, it closes only on Mondays. *Belham Valley, tel. 809/419–7564. No credit cards. Reservations suggested. Inexpensive.*

Golden Apple. In this large, galleried stone building, you'll be served huge plates of good, local cooking: the restaurant's special goatwater stew (weekends only) cooked over an outside, open fire; souse; *pelau* (chicken-and-rice curry); conch, stewed or curried; and mountain chicken. Guests eat off cheerful red-and-white checked tablecloths and families will appreciate the relaxed atmosphere. There's also a grocery store attached. Fun and funky. *Cork Hill, tel. 809/491–2187. No credit cards. Inexpensive.*

Mistress Morgan's. Saturday is goatwater-stew day at Mistress Morgan's, and from 11:30 onward you can join the carloads of locals who make the trek up here to the north of the island to eat their fill for E.C.$20 at four picnic tables in a simple, unadorned room with sea-foam walls. The food is definitely downhome: souse, baked chicken, and the increasingly hard-to-find goatwater stew that's served just the way it should be—with the flesh falling off the bone, brimming with dumplings and innards. If you like that sort of thing, you'll find yourself coming back. *Airport Rd., St. John's, tel. 809/491–5419. No credit cards. Inexpensive.*

★ **Niggy's.** In his previous life, the owner was a British character actor in Hollywood for many years before he decided to trade the smell of greasepaint and the roar of the crowd for a place behind the bar in this simple, but attractive restaurant. When it opened in the fall of 1992, Niggy's immediately became one of the island's best kept secrets (the British governor eats here regularly). It doesn't look like much from the outside—a simple clapboard cottage with yellow bella flowers trailing over the gate—but the food, served at picnic-style benches under a trellis of flowering plants, is excellent and good value. Inside, the owner will regale you with tales of Hollywood at the bar, an ingeniously converted fishing-boat—and the whole place feels like a set for a Caribbean remake of *Casablanca*. For those who want to stay over, there are two simple, but clean rooms in the back. *Kinsale, tel. 809/491–7489. No credit cards. Inexpensive.*

Ziggy's. On top of a barrel at the entrance to their restaurant, John and Marcia Punter, Montserratians who returned home after 28 years in the United Kingdom, display all the fruits and vegetables that grow on the island, among them ginger, nutmeg, yams, plantain, christophine, and coconuts. They've turned what used to be a simple waterfront cafe and bar into one of the best bistro-style restaurants on the island. The furnishings are sparse, but the setting, right on the water, is very pleasant, and the varied menu, offering everything from chicken dishes to curried mutton and rice. Unfortunately, there is uncertainty about the lease from the Yacht Club. *Wapping, Plymouth, tel. 809/491–2237. Reservations recommended. No credit cards. Closed Wed. Inexpensive.*

Lodging

Villas are not only affordable here; given their comforts and conveniences, they're preferable to the hotels. You can even request the properties where your favorite rock stars—from Sting to Elton John—relaxed.

Most of Montserrat's hotels operate on the Modified American Plan (MAP: breakfast and dinner are included in the rate).

Highly recommended lodgings are indicated by a star ★.

Category	Cost*
Expensive	over $150
Moderate	$75–$150
Inexpensive	under $75

All prices are for a standard double room for two, excluding 7% tax and a 10% service charge.

Hotels **Montserrat Springs Hotel and Villas.** This hotel, even though it underwent substantial renovation after Hurricane Hugo, has lost some of its allure. The sweeping view—ocean in one direction, Chance's Peak in the other—from the terrace surrounding the beautiful outdoor swimming pool (at 70 feet, the largest in Montserrat) is still one of the island's highlights. The rooms, in a wing of the main building and in cottages along the steep hillside sloping down to the beach, are spacious and well appointed. All the rooms have private balconies, phones, hair dryers, and cable TV. There are two Astroturf tennis courts, and the beach-bar with a whirlpool filled with piping hot mineral water direct from the Soufrière is a special treat. But the breakfasts are overpriced and miserly, the staff is rather surly (and noisy at night), and the plumbing is below standard for a hotel of its class. *Box 259, Plymouth, tel. 809/491–2482 or 800/*

823–9815, fax 809/491–4070. 40 rooms and 6 suites. Facilities: restaurant, 2 bars, pool, hot/cold mineral-water Jacuzzi, beach, 2 lighted tennis courts, AE, MC, V. EP, MAP. Expensive.

★ **Villas of Montserrat.** If you've ever wanted to do an island in style, this is the way to do it. You'll be flown in on a private plane, chauffeured to your villa, and treated to a lobster dinner at Belham Valley on the night of your arrival. Each three-bedroom villa is decorated island-style, and each has a color TV, microwave oven, dishwasher, three bathrooms, and a Jacuzzi. The cluster of villas overlooks Isle Bay and the Caribbean. *Box 421, Plymouth, tel. 809/491–5513 or 408/685–3498. 3 villas. Facilities: pool. No credit cards. EP. Expensive.*

★ **Vue Pointe.** The moment you arrive here you feel as though both the staff and the owners, Cedric and Carol Osborne, really care about your well-being. The gracious Monday night cocktail parties that the Osbornes host at their house, with drinks, delicious homemade hors d'ouevres, and good conversation, is a perfect example. (Cedric Osborne comes from one of the island's first families and is a mine of information about local goings-on). Accommodations are in 12 rooms or 28 octagonal cottages that spill down to the gray-sand beach on Old Road Bay. Each cottage has a large bedroom, great view, cable TV, phone, and spacious bathroom. In the main building a large lounge and bar overlooks the pool and the Wednesday night barbecue, with steel bands and other entertainment, is a well-attended island event for locals and guests alike. In the adjacent sea-view restaurant, you can have a candlelight dinner of local and international specialties (the chef is one of the most skilled on the island). A 150-seat conference center serves as a theater and disco, and for water-sports enthusiasts, there is scuba diving, snorkeling, and fishing. What more could you want? *Box 65, Plymouth, tel. 809/491–5210, fax 809/491–4813. 12 rooms, 28 cottages. Facilities: restaurant, bar, gift shop, pool, 2 lighted tennis courts, water-sports center. AE, MC, V. EP, MAP. Expensive.*

★ **Providence Guest House.** On an island where it is almost impossible to find good bed-and-breakfast accommodations, this guest house, perched on a bluff high above the ocean, with spectacular views of St. Kitts and Redonda, stands out. Formerly a plantation house, this beautiful stone-and-wood building, with its spider-box balustrade, wrap-around verandah, and gleaming swimming pool edged with tiles from Trinidad, has been lovingly restored by its present owners. It now ranks as one of the finest examples of traditional Caribbean architecture on the island. In its day, it was home to such luminaries as Paul McCartney, Stevie Wonder, and Carl Perkins. The two guest rooms—one has a bath as well as a shower and is considerably larger—are on the ground floor and open directly onto the pool area. Both have the original timbered ceilings and massive stone walls, which keep them cool in the summer, and are decorated with red quarry tiles and attractive pastel fabrics. If there is any drawback to this idyll, it is the location. The nearest restaurant is three miles away in Belham Valley and the nearest beach is a hike down the hillside. But the owners have provided a kitchenette by the pool where guests can prepare their own meals and are willing to make evening meals on request. *Providence Estate House, Montserrat, tel. 809/491–6476. 2 rooms. Facilities: swimming pool, kitchenette, cable TV. No credit cards. CP. Moderate.*

Belham Valley Hotel. On a hillside overlooking Belham Valley and the Belham Valley River, this hotel has three self-catering units. There is a cottage and two apartments (a studio and a newer two-bedroom), all with stereo and phones. It's the restaurant here that's the big draw, with its lovely views and great food. *Box 409, Plymouth, tel. 809/491–5553. 3 units. Facilities: restaurant, maid service. AE, MC. EP. Inexpensive–Moderate.*

Flora Fountain Hotel. This is a hotel for people coming on business (only 35% of the clientele are tourists) or for those who appreciate an old, rambling hotel in the heart of town. The two-story hotel has been created around an enormous fountain that's sometimes lighted at night, with small tables scattered in the inner courtyard. There are 18 serviceable rooms, all with tile bath and air-conditioning. The restaurant has a chef from Bombay who serves simple sandwiches and fine Indian dishes, particularly on Friday night, which is Indian buffet night; several meat and fish dishes; at least two kinds of rice; *rathia* (yogurt and vegetable dishes with pork and spices); and *sambosa* (spicy meat patties). *Box 373, Church Rd., Plymouth, tel. 809/ 491–6092, fax 809/491–2568. 18 rooms with air-conditioning and phone, some with cable TV. Facilities: restaurant and bar. AE, D, MC, V. EP, CP, MAP, FAP. Inexpensive.*

Lime Court Apartments. This slightly run-down, large white colonial-style apartment building is right in the center of town, opposite the Parliament building. The downstairs apartments tend to be dark and airless, and with the sound of the generator and the puttering of the fridges, not that peaceful. But the large, well-equipped "penthouse," up a flight of steps at the top of the building, has a fine view from the balcony over the town's red corrugated rooftops to the sea beyond. It can sleep two couples and is reasonable at $45 per night. All apartments come with kitchenettes, including a stove and microwave, and have private bathrooms (showers only). *Box 250, Parliament St., Plymouth, tel. 809/491–3656. 8 apartments. Facilities: maid service, cable TV. AE, MC, V. EP. Inexpensive.*

Marie's Guest House. This well-kept modern bungalow, set on a half acre of garden, is half a mile from Plymouth on the main road north. Marie, a soft-spoken islander with a reserved manner, keeps the place neat and tidy, and the rooms, with their mosquito nets; tasteful fabrics; good solid furniture; and clean, tiled bathrooms are good value. At the front of the house there is a communal living-dining room area, where guests can make their own simple meals. *The Groves, Plymouth, tel. 809/419– 2745. 4 rooms. Facilities: maid service. No credit cards. EP. Inexpensive.*

Oriole Plaza Hotel. Right in the center of town, about five minutes' walk from the post office and from Wapping Beach, the town's only beach, this simple, but well-kept hotel was substantially refurbished after Hugo and now caters mostly to businesspeople. Rooms off a long corridor upstairs vary from suites, with two double beds and a balcony, to doubles. All rooms have ceiling fans, private bathrooms, cable TV, and phone. The three rooms at the back of the building are simpler—and cheaper—but have the advantage of opening onto a sunny wooden landing from which you can see Chance's Peak. BB's, the restaurant in the downstairs foyer, serves marlin, lobster, or mountain chicken at reasonable prices. *Box 250, Plymouth, tel. 809/491–6982, fax 809/491–6690. 12 rooms with* *ceiling fans. Facilities: restaurant and bar. AE, MC, V. EP. Inexpensive.*

Villas and Condominiums Villas at the top end of the market is a niche that Montserrat decided, back in the '80s, that it was going to fill. The result is a great range of accommodations catering to those who want to do it themselves on the island. All the villa developments are on the west coast of the island, within 20 minutes by car of Plymouth. The majority are in the districts of Old Towne, Olveston, and Woodlands. The latter, with its steep hillsides covered in luxuriant vegetation and magnificent views of the ocean, is especially noteworthy. Prices start at about $350 per week and spiral quickly up to $2,000 (for which you will get a veritable palace that can sleep 8 people). Off-season rates are as much as 50% lower (and usually negotiable), and some excellent bargains can be picked up by summer travelers. All come with maid service, and most come with pools.

D.R.V Edwards (Box 58, Marine Dr., Plymouth, tel. 809/491–2431, fax 809/491–4660) has 22 villas in Old Towne, Woodlands, and Isles Bay. **Neville Bradshaw Agencies** (Box 270, Plymouth, tel. 809/491–5270, fax 809/491–5069) has a wide range of villas, mostly in Old Towne and Isles Bay. **Isles Bay Plantation** (Box 64, Plymouth, tel. 809/491–5248, fax 890/491–5016; in London, tel. and fax 071/482–1071), known locally as the Beverly Hills of Montserrat, has the crème de la crème of Montserrat's villas. **Shamrock Villas** (Box 180, Plymouth, tel. 809/491–2974) are one- and two-bedroom apartments and town-house condominiums in a hillside development minutes from Plymouth.

Nightlife

The hotels offer regularly scheduled barbecues and steel bands, and the small restaurants feature live entertainment in the form of calypso, reggae, rock, rhythm and blues, and soul.

The **Yacht Club** (Wapping, tel. 809/491–2237) has live island music on Friday, while **The Plantation Club** (Wapping, upstairs over the Oasis, tel. 809/491–2892) is a lively late-night place with taped rhythm and blues, soul, and *soca* (Caribbean music). **La Cave** (Evergreen Dr., Plymouth, no phone), featuring West Indian–style disco with Caribbean and international music, is popular among the young locals. **Nepcoden** (Weekes, no phone), with its ultra-violet lights, peace signs, and black walls is a throw back to the '60s. In this cellar restaurant you can eat *rotis*, a large pancake filled with curried vegetables, or chicken for $6.

The Village Place. In its heyday this funky bar and disco on a hillside outside Plymouth was *the* hangout for rock glitterati like Eric Clapton, Sting, and Elton John while they recorded at Monserrat's legendary Air Studios, founded by George Martin of Beatles fame. Mick Jagger is even known to have eaten owner Andy Lawrence's secret chicken spiced with paprika and thyme. These days, though, Andy's allure is just a little faded—the local bands trying out are rarely that good; the drinking is heavy-duty; and on Saturdays, it is full and loud. A must for rock nostalgics; for others, a detour wouldn't hurt much. *Salem, tel. 809/491–5202. No credit cards. Open 6–midnight. Closed Tuesdays.*

17 Puerto Rico

Updated by
Karl Luntta

No city in the Caribbean is steeped in Spanish tradition as is Puerto Rico's Old San Juan. Originally built as a fortress enclave, the old city's myriad attractions include restored 16th-century buildings, museums, art galleries, bookstores, and 200-year-old houses with balustraded balconies of filigreed wrought iron overlooking narrow cobblestone streets. This Spanish tradition also spills over into the island's countryside, from its festivals celebrated in honor of various patron saints in the little towns to the *paradores*, those homey, inexpensive inns whose concept originated in Spain.

Puerto Rico has, in San Juan's sophisticated Condado and Isla Verde areas, glittering hotels; flashy, Las Vegas–style shows; casinos; and frenetic discos. It has the ambience of the Old World in the seven-square-block area of the old city and in its quiet colonial towns. Out in the countryside lie its natural attractions—the extraordinary, 28,000-acre Caribbean National Forest, more familiarly known as the El Yunque rain forest, with its 100-foot-high trees, more than 240 species of them, and its dramatic mountain ranges; there are forest reserves with trails to satisfy the most dedicated hiker, vast caves to tempt spelunkers, coffee plantations, old sugar mills, and hundreds of beaches.

Puerto Rico, 110 miles long and 35 miles wide (about the size of Connecticut), was populated by several tribes of Indians when Columbus landed on the island on his second voyage in 1493. In 1508, Juan Ponce de León, the frustrated seeker of the Fountain of Youth, established a settlement on the island and became its first governor, and in 1521, founded Old San Juan. For three centuries, the French, Dutch, and English tried unsuccessfully to wrest the island from Spain. In 1897, Spain granted the island dominion status. Two years later, Spain ceded the island to the United States, and in 1917, Puerto Ricans became U.S. citizens. In 1952, Puerto Rico became a semiautonomous commonwealth territory of the United States.

As such, if you're a U.S. citizen, you need neither passport nor visa when you land at the bustling Luis Muñoz Marín Airport, outside San Juan. You don't have to clear customs, and you don't have to explain yourself to an immigration official. English is widely spoken, though the official language is Spanish.

Puerto Rico also boasts hundreds of beaches with every imaginable water sport available, acres of golf courses and miles of tennis courts, and small colonial towns where you can quietly savor the Spanish flavor. Every town honors its individual patron saint with an annual festival, which is usually held in the central plaza and can last from one to 10 days. In San Juan, *LeLoLai* is a year-round festival celebrating Puerto Rican dance and folklore, with changing programs presented in major San Juan hotels. The high-energy carnival held in Ponce in early February is renowned for its elaborate costumes and masks. Having seen every sight on the island, you can then do further exploring on the islands of Culebra, Vieques, Icacos, and Mona, where more aquatic activities, such as snorkeling and scuba diving, prevail.

Before You Go

Tourist
Information

Contact the **Puerto Rico Tourism Company** (tel. 800/223–6530 or 800/866–STAR. Other branches: 575 5th Ave., 23rd floor,

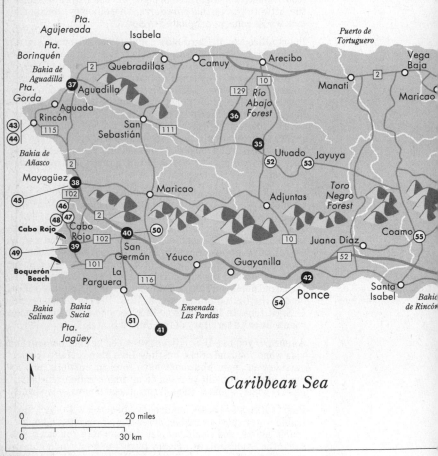

Caribbean Sea

N

| 0 | | 20 miles |
| 0 | | 30 km |

Exploring

Aguadilla, **37**

Barrilito Rum
Plant, **29**

Bayamón, **28**

Cabo Rojo, **39**

Caguana Indian
Ceremonial Park, **35**

Caparra Ruins, **27**

Caribbean
National Forest
(El Yunque), **30**

Culebra, **34**

Fajardo, **32**

Las Cabezas de San
Juan Nature
Reserve, **33**

Luquillo Beach, **31**

Mayagüez, **38**

Phosphorescent
Bay, **41**

Ponce, **42**

Río Camuy Cave
Park, **36**

San Germán, **40**

Dining

The Black Eagle, **44**

El Bohio, **47**

Horned Dorset
Primavera, **43**

La Casona de
Serafin, **46**

La Rotisserie, **45**

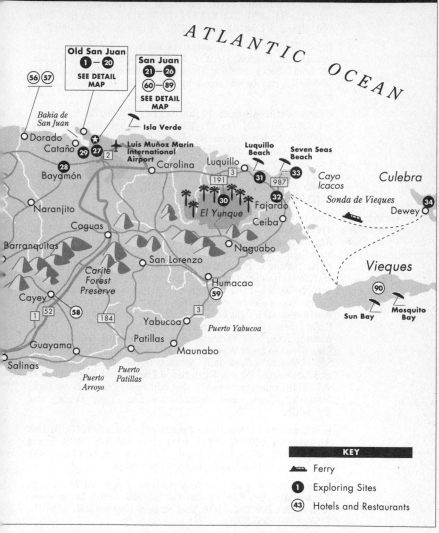

SEE DETAIL MAP

Restaurant El
Ancla, **54**
Sand and the Sea, **58**

Lodging
Hilton International
Mayagüez, **45**
Horned Dorset
Primavera, **43**
Hyatt Dorado
Beach, **57**
Hyatt Regency
Cerromar Beach, **56**

Palmas del Mar, **59**
Parador Baños de
Coamo, **55**
Parador Boquemar, **49**
Parador Casa
Grande, **52**
Parador Hacienda
Gripinas, **53**
Parador Oasis, **50**

Parador Perichi's, **48**
Parador Villa
Parguera, **51**
Sea Gate (Vieques), **90**

New York, NY 10017, tel. 212/599–6262, fax 212/818–1866; 3575 W. Cahuenga Blvd., Suite 560, Los Angeles, CA 90068, tel. 213/874–5991, fax 213/874–7257; 200 S.E. 1st St., Suite 700, Miami, FL 33131, tel. 305/381–8915, fax 305/381–8917.

In addition, sales representatives are located in Atlanta, Boston, Dallas, Detroit, Denver, Houston, Orlando, Philadelphia, St. Louis, San Francisco, Toronto, and Washington, DC. Their addresses can be obtained by calling the toll-free numbers above.

Overseas offices include 10 Rue de l'Isly, 75008, Paris, France, tel. 331/4293–0021, fax 331/4293–4729; Bahnhofstrasse 55–57, 6200 Wiesbaden, Germany, tel. 49–611/379–122, fax 49–611/303–801; Calle Capitan Haya, 23, 1–7–4 28020 Madrid, Spain, tel. 341/555–6811, fax 341/556–7286; Kammakargatan, 41 S-111 24 Stockholm, Sweden, tel. 468/115495, fax 468/206317; 67–69 Whitfield St., London W1P 5RL, United Kingdom, tel. 071/636–6558, fax 071/255–2131.

Arriving and Departing By Plane The Luis Muñoz Marín International Airport (tel. 809/462–3147), east of downtown San Juan, is the Caribbean hub for **American Airlines** (tel. 800/433–7300). American has daily nonstop flights from New York, Newark, Miami, Boston, Philadelphia, Chicago, Nashville, Los Angeles, Dallas, Baltimore, Hartford, Raleigh-Durham, Washington, DC, and Tampa. **Delta** (tel. 800/221–1212) has nonstop service from Atlanta and Orlando, as well as connecting service from major cities. **Northwest** (tel. 800/447–4747) has recently added nonstop flights from Detroit to San Juan. **TWA** (tel. 800/892–4141) flies nonstop from New York and Miami. **United** (tel. 800/241–6522) flies nonstop from Washington, DC, and Chicago. **USAir** (tel. 800/428–4322) offers daily nonstop flights from Philadelphia and Charlotte. Puerto Rico–based **Carnival Airlines** (tel. 800/437–2110) operates weekly nonstop flights from New York, Newark, Miami, and Orlando to San Juan, Ponce, and Aguadilla.

Foreign carriers include **Air France** (tel. 800/237–2747), **British Airways** (tel. 800/247–9297), **BWIA** (tel. 800/538–2942), **Iberia** (tel. 800/772–4642), **LACSA** (tel. 800/225–2272), **LIAT** (tel. 809/791–3838), and **Lufthansa** (tel. 800/645–3880).

Connections between Caribbean islands can be made through **Air Jamaica** (tel. 809/791–3870 or 800/523–5585), **Dominicana Airline** (tel. 809/724–7100), and **Sunaire Express** (tel. 809/791–4755 or 800/595–9501).

From the Airport **Airport Limousine Service** (tel. 809/791–4745) provides minibus service to hotels in the Isla Verde, Condado, and Old San Juan areas at basic fares of $2.50, $3.50, and $4.50, respectively; the fares, which are set by the Public Service Commission, can vary, depending on the time of day and number of passengers. Limousines of **Dorado Transport Service** (tel. 809/796–1214) serve hotels and villas in the Dorado area for $6 per person. Taxi fare from the airport to Isla Verde is about $6–$10; to the Condado area, $12–$15; and to Old San Juan, $15–$18. Be sure the taxi driver starts the meter.

Passports and Visas Puerto Rico is a commonwealth of the United States, and U.S. citizens do not need passports to visit the island. British citizens must have passports. Canadian citizens need proof of citizenship (preferably a passport).

Language Puerto Rico's official languages are Spanish and English. If you plan to rent a car and travel around the island, take along a Spanish phrase book.

Precautions San Juan, like any other big city and major tourist destination, has its share of crime, so guard your wallet or purse on the city streets. Puerto Rico's beaches are open to the public, and muggings occur at night even on the beaches of the posh Condado and Isla Verde tourist hotels. Don't leave anything unattended on the beach. Leave your valuables in the hotel safe, and stick to the fenced-in beach areas of your hotel. Always lock your car and stash valuables and luggage out of sight. Avoid deserted beaches day or night.

Staying in Puerto Rico

Important The government-sponsored **Puerto Rico Tourism Company**
Addresses (tel. 809/721–2400) is an excellent source for maps, brochures, and other printed tourist materials. Pick up a free copy of *¿Qué Pasa?*, the official visitors guide.

Information offices are located at **Luis Muñoz Marín International Airport,** Isla Verde (tel. 809/791–1014 or 809/791–2551); **301 Calle San Justo,** Old San Juan (tel. 809/723–3135 or 809/723–0017); and **La Casita,** near Pier 1 in Old San Juan (tel. 809/722–1709). Out on the island, information offices are located in **Ponce** (Casa Armstrong-Poventud, Plaza, Las Delicias, tel. 809/840–5695 or 809/844–8240); **Aguadilla** (Rafael Hernandez Airport, tel. 809/890–3315); and in each town's city hall on the main plaza, open weekdays from 8 AM to noon and 1 to 4:30 PM.

Emergencies **Police, Fire, and Medical emergencies:** Call 911. **Hospitals:** Hospitals in the Condado/Santurce area with 24-hour emergency rooms are **Ashford Community Hospital** (1451 Av. Ashford, tel. 809/721–2160) and **San Juan Health Centre** (200 Av. De Diego, tel. 809/725–0202). **Pharmacies:** In San Juan, **Walgreens** (1130 Av. Ashford, tel. 809/725–1510) operates a 24-hour pharmacy. In Old San Juan, try **Puerto Rico Drug Company** (157 Calle San Francisco, tel. 809/725–2202). Walgreens operates more than 20 pharmacies throughout the island.

Currency The U.S. dollar is the official currency of Puerto Rico.

Taxes and The government tax on room charges is 7% (9% in hotels with
Service Charges casinos). There is no departure tax.

Some hotels impose a 10%–15% service charge automatically added to your bill. In restaurants, a 15%–20% tip is expected.

Guided Tours Old San Juan can be seen either on a self-guided walking tour or on the free trolley. To explore the rest of the city and the island, consider renting a car. (We do, however, recommend a guided tour of the vast El Yunque rain forest.) If you'd rather not do your own driving, there are several tour companies you can call. Most San Juan hotels have a tour desk that can make arrangements for you. The standard half-day tours (at $10–$15) are of Old and New San Juan, Old San Juan and the Bacardi Rum Plant, Luquillo Beach and El Yunque rain forest. All-day tours ($15–$30) include a trip to Ponce, a day at El Comandante Racetrack, or a combined tour of the city and El Yunque rain forest.

Leading tour operators include **Borinquén Tours, Inc.** (tel. 809/725–4990), **Gray Line of Puerto Rico** (tel. 809/727–8080),

Normandie Tours, Inc. (tel. 809/725–6990 or 809/722–6308), **Rich Sunshine Tours** (tel. 809/729–2929), **Rico Suntours** (tel. 809/722–2080 or 809/722–6090), and **United Tour Guides** (tel. 809/725–7605 or 809/723–5578). **Cordero Caribbean Tours** (tel. 809/799–6002 or 809/780–2442; open 24 hours) does tours at hourly rates out on the island in air-conditioned limousines.

Getting Around   Roads in Puerto Rico are generally well marked; however, a good road map is helpful when traveling to more remote areas on the island. Some car rental agencies distribute free maps of the island when you pick up your car. Good maps are also found at **The Book Store** (255 Calle San José, Old San Juan, tel. 809/724–1815).

Taxis   Metered cabs authorized by the Public Service Commission (tel. 809/751–5050) start at $1 and charge 10¢ for every additional 1/10 mile, 50¢ for every suitcase, and $1 for home or business calls. Waiting time is 10¢ for each 45 seconds. Be sure the driver begins the meter.

Buses   The **Metropolitan Bus Authority** (tel. 809/767–7979) operates *guaguas* (buses) that thread through San Juan. The fare is 25¢, and the buses run in exclusive lanes, *against the traffic* on major thoroughfares, stopping at upright yellow posts marked *Parada* or *Parada de Guaguas*. The main terminals are Intermodal Terminal, Calles Marina and Harding, in Old San Juan, and Capetillo Terminal in Rio Piedras, next to the Central Business District.

Públicos   *Públicos* (public cars) with yellow license plates ending with "P" or "PD" scoot to towns throughout the island, stopping in each town's main plaza. The 17-passenger cars operate primarily during the day, with routes and fares fixed by the Public Service Commission. In San Juan, the main terminals are at the airport and at Plaza Colón on the waterfront in Old San Juan.

Trolleys   If your feet fail you in Old San Juan, climb aboard the free open-air trolleys that rumble and roller-coast through the narrow streets. Departures are from La Puntilla and from the marina, but you can board anywhere along the route.

Motor Coaches   The **Puerto Rico Motor Coach Co.** (tel. 809/725–2460) offers charter service and 50-passenger buses for conventions.

Ferries   The ferry between Old San Juan and Catano costs a mere 50¢ one-way. The ferry runs every half hour from 6:15 AM to 10 PM. The 400-passenger ferries of the **Fajardo Port Authority** (tel. 809/863–0705) make the 80-minute trip twice daily between Fajardo and Vieques (one-way $2 adults, $1 children under 12, free for children under 3), and the one-hour run between Fajardo and Culebra daily (one-way $2.25 adults, $1 children).

Rental Cars   U.S. driver's licenses are valid in Puerto Rico for three months. All major U.S. car-rental agencies are represented on the island, including **Avis** (tel. 809/721–4499 or 800/331–1212), **Hertz** (tel. 809/791–0840 or 800/654–3131), and **Budget** (tel. 809/791–3685 or 800/527–0700). Local rental companies, sometimes less expensive, include **Caribbean Rental** (tel. 809/724–3980) and **L & M Car Rental** (tel. 809/725–8416), fax 809/725–8307). Prices start at about $30 (plus insurance), with unlimited mileage. Discounts are offered for long-term rentals, and insurance can be waived for those who rent with American Express credit cards. Some discounts are offered for AAA or 72-hour advance bookings. Most car rentals have shuttle service to or from the airport and the pickup point. If you plan to drive across the island, arm yourself with a good map and be aware that there are many unmarked roads up in the mountains. Many service stations in the central mountains do not take credit cards. Speed limits are posted in miles, distances in kilometers, and gas prices in liters.

Planes **Vieques Air-Link** (tel. 809/722–3736) flies from the Isla Grande Airport to Vieques for about $28 one-way, and **Flamenco Airways** (tel. 809/725–7707) flies to Culebra for $25 one-way.

Telephones The area code for Puerto Rico is 809. Since Puerto Rico uses
and Mail U.S. postage stamps and has the same mail rates (19¢ for a postcard, 29¢ for a first-class letter), you can save time by bringing stamps with you. Post offices in major Puerto Rican cities offer Express Mail next-day service to the U.S. mainland and to Puerto Rican destinations.

Opening and Shops are open from 9 to 6 (from 9 to 9 during Christmas holi-
Closing Times days). Banks are open weekdays from 8:30 to 2:30 and Saturday from 9:45 to noon.

Exploring Puerto Rico

Numbers in the margin correspond to points of interest on the Old San Juan Exploring map.

Old San Juan Old San Juan, the original city founded in 1521, contains authentic and carefully preserved examples of 16th- and 17th-century Spanish colonial architecture, some of the best in the New World. More than 400 buildings have been beautifully restored in a continuing effort to preserve the city. Graceful wrought-iron balconies, decorated with lush green hanging plants, extend over narrow streets paved with blue-gray stones (*adequines*, originally used as ballast for Spanish ships). The old city is partially enclosed by the old walls, dating from 1633, that once completely surrounded it. Designated a U.S. National Historic Zone in 1950, Old San Juan is chockablock with shops, open-air cafés, private homes, tree-shaded squares, monuments, plaques, pigeons, and people. The traffic is awful. Get an overview of the inner city on a morning's stroll (bearing in mind that this "stroll" includes some steep climbs). However, if you plan to immerse yourself in history or to shop, you'll need two or three days.

El Morro and Fort San Cristóbal are described in our walking tour: You may want to set aside extra time to see them, especially if you're an aficionado of military history. UNESCO has designated each fortress a World Heritage Site; each is also a National Historic Site. Both are administered by the National Park Service; you can take one of its tours or wander around on your own.

Sitting on a rocky promontory on the northwestern tip of the ❶ old city is **Fuerte San Felipe del Morro** ("El Morro"), a fortress built by the Spaniards between 1540 and 1783. Rising 140 feet above the sea, the massive six-level fortress covers enough territory to accommodate a nine-hole golf course. It is a labyrinth of dungeons, ramps and barracks, turrets, towers, and tunnels. Built to protect the port, El Morro has a commanding view of the harbor. Its small, air-conditioned museum traces the history of the fortress. *Calle Norzagaray, tel. 809/729–6960. Admission free. Open daily 9:15–6.*

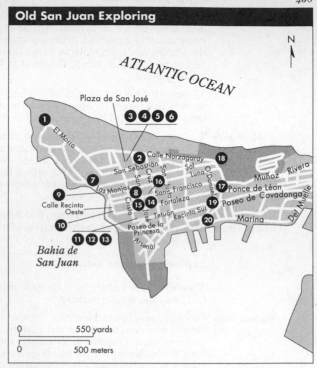

Old San Juan Exploring

ATLANTIC OCEAN

Plaza de San José

Bahia de San Juan

0   550 yards

0   500 meters

② San José Plaza is two short blocks from the entrance to El Morro, but for the moment we'll bypass it and head for the **San Juan Museum of Art and History,** which is a block east of the tour's path but a must. A bustling marketplace in 1855, this handsome building is now a modern cultural center that houses exhibits of Puerto Rican art. Multi-image audiovisual shows present the history of the island; concerts and other cultural events take place in the huge courtyard. The museum was closed for repairs at press time, but exhibitions are temporarily held 10 minutes away at the **Miensal Building** (tel. 809/722–1824), 200 Calle San Francisco, weekdays 8–noon and 1–4. *Calle Norzagaray, at the corner of Calle MacArthur, tel. 809/724–1875.*

③ Turn back west toward San José Plaza to **La Casa de los Contrafuertes,** on Calle San Sebastián. This building is also known as the Buttress House because wide exterior buttresses support the wall next to the plaza. The house is one of the oldest remaining private residences in Old San Juan. Inside is the Pharmacy Museum, a re-creation of an 18th-century apothecary shop. *101 Calle San Sebastián, Plaza de San José, tel. 809/724–5949. Admission free. Open Wed.–Sun. 9–4:30.*

④ The **Pablo Casals Museum,** a bit farther down the block, contains memorabilia of the famed cellist, who made his home in Puerto Rico for the last 16 years of his life. The museum holds manuscripts, photographs, and his favorite cellos, in addition to recordings and videotapes of Casals Festival concerts (the latter shown on request). *101 Calle San Sebastián, Plaza de*

San José, tel. 809/723-9185. Admission free. Open Tues.–Sat.
9:30–5:30; Sun. 1–5; closed Mon.

⑤ In the center of the plaza, next to the museum, is the **San José Church.** With its series of vaulted ceilings, it is a splendid example of 16th-century Spanish Gothic architecture. The church, which is one of the oldest Christian houses of worship in the Western Hemisphere, was built in 1532 under the supervision of the Dominican friars. The body of Ponce de León, the Spanish explorer who came to the New World seeking the Fountain of Youth, was buried here for almost three centuries before being removed in 1913 and placed in the cathedral. *Calle San Sebastián, tel. 809/725–7501. Admission free. Open Mon.–Sat. 8:30–4; Sun. 12:15 PM mass.*

⑥ Next door is the **Dominican Convent.** Built by Dominican friars in 1523, the convent in the past often served as a shelter during Carib Indian attacks and, more recently, as headquarters for the Antilles command of the U.S. Army. Now home to the Institute of Puerto Rican Culture, the beautifully restored building contains an ornate 18th-century altar, religious manuscripts, artifacts, and art. Classical concerts are occasionally held here. *98 Calle Norzagaray, tel. 809/724–0700. Admission free. Chapel museum open Wed.–Sun. 9–noon and 1–4:30.*

⑦ From San José Plaza, walk west on Calle Beneficencia to **Casa Blanca.** The original structure on this site, not far from the ramparts of El Morro, was a frame house built in 1521 as a home for Ponce de León. But Ponce de León died in Cuba, never having lived in it, and it was virtually destroyed by a hurricane in 1523, after which Ponce de León's son-in-law had the present masonry home built. His descendants occupied it for 250 years. From the end of the Spanish-American War in 1898 to 1966, it was the home of the U.S. Army commander in Puerto Rico. A museum devoted to archaeology is on the second floor. *1 Calle San Sebastián, tel. 809/724–4102. Admission free. Open Wed.–Sun. 9–noon and 1–4.*

⑧ Head east on Calle Sol and down Calle Cristo to **San Juan Cathedral.** This great Catholic shrine of Puerto Rico had humble beginnings in the early 1520s as a thatch-topped wood structure. Hurricane winds tore off the thatch and destroyed the church. It was reconstructed in 1540, when the graceful circular staircase and vaulted ceilings were added, but most of the work on the church was done in the 19th century. The remains of Ponce de León are in a marble tomb near the transept. *153 Calle Cristo, tel. 809/722–0861. Open daily 8:30–4. Masses: Sat. 7 PM, Sun. 9 AM and 11 AM, weekdays 12:15 PM.*

Time Out Stop in at **Kambalache, First House of Tea** (252 Calle Cristo, tel. 809/724–5654) for coffee and exotic teas from around the world; try vanilla rum, dragon well, cinnamon bark, or Taiwan broken leaf tea. Seating is inside or at the busy streetside cafe.

Across the street from the cathedral you'll see the Gran Hotel El Convento, which was a Carmelite convent more than 300 years ago. Go west alongside the hotel on Caleta de las Monjas
⑨ toward the city wall to the **Plazuela de la Rogativa.** In the little plaza, statues of a bishop and three women commemorate a legend, according to which the British, while laying siege to the city in 1797, mistook the flaming torches of a *rogativa* (religious

procession) for Spanish reinforcements and beat a hasty retreat. The monument was donated to the city in 1971 on its 450th anniversary.

⑩ One block south on Calle Recinto Oeste you'll come to **La Fortaleza,** which sits on a hill overlooking the harbor. La Fortaleza, the Western Hemisphere's oldest executive mansion in continual use, home of 170 governors and official residence of the present governor of Puerto Rico, was built as a fortress. The original primitive structure, built in 1540, has seen numerous changes over a period of three centuries, resulting in the present collection of marble and mahogany, medieval towers, and stained-glass galleries. Guided tours are conducted every hour on the hour in English, on the half hour in Spanish. Tours that include a visit to the mansion's second floor, a must-see, are held at 10 and 10:50 in English, 9:30 and 10:30 in Spanish. *Tel. 809/721-7000. Admission free. Open weekdays (except holidays) 9-4.*

⑪ At the southern end of Calle Cristo is **Cristo Chapel.** According to legend, in 1753 a young horseman, carried away during festivities in honor of the patron saint, raced down the street and plunged over the steep precipice. A witness to the tragedy promised to build a chapel if the young man's life could be saved. Historical records maintain the man died, though legend contends that he lived. Inside is a small silver altar, dedicated to the Christ of Miracles. *Open Tues. 10-4 and on most Catholic holidays.*

⑫ Across the street from the chapel, the 18th-century **Casa del Libro** has exhibits devoted to books and bookbinding. The museum's 5,000 books include rare volumes dating back 2,000 years; more than 200 of these books—40 of which were produced in Spain—were printed before the 16th century. *255 Calle Cristo, tel. 809/723-0354. Admission free. Open Tues. 11-4:30 and 7:30-10 PM, Wed.-Sat. (except holidays) 11-4:30.*

⑬ The **Fine Arts Museum** (253 Calle Cristo, tel. 809/723-2320), in a lovely colonial building next door, occasionally presents special exhibits. The museum usually holds the Institute of Puerto Rican Culture's collection of paintings and sculptures, but those pieces have been temporarily removed. The building was closed for restoration at press time.

⑭ Follow the wall east one block and head north on Calle San José two short blocks to **Plaza de Armas,** the original main square of Old San Juan. The plaza, bordered by Calles San Francisco, Fortaleza, San José, and Cruz, has a lovely fountain with 19th-century statues representing the four seasons.

⑮ West of the square stands **La Intendencia,** a handsome three-story neoclassical building. From 1851 to 1898, it was home to the Spanish Treasury. Recently restored, it is now the headquarters of Puerto Rico's State Department. *Calle San José, at the corner of Calle San Francisco, tel. 809/722-2121, ext. 230. Admission free. Tours at 2 and 3 in Spanish, 4 in English. Open weekdays 8-noon and 1-4:30.*

⑯ On the north side of the plaza is **City Hall,** called the *Alcaldía.* Built between 1604 and 1789, the alcaldía was fashioned after Madrid's city hall, with arcades, towers, balconies, and a lovely inner courtyard. A tourist information center and an art gallery are on the first floor. *Tel. 809/724–7171, ext. 2391. Open weekdays 8–noon and 1–4.*

Time Out   **La Bombonera** (259 Calle San Francisco, tel. 809/722–0658), established in 1903, is known for its strong Puerto Rican coffee and *Mallorca*—a Spanish pastry made of light dough, toasted, buttered, and sprinkled with powdered sugar. Breakfast, for under $5, is served until 11. It's a favorite Sunday-morning gathering place in Old San Juan.

⑰ Four blocks east on the pedestrian mall of Calle Fortaleza, you'll find **Plaza de Colón,** a bustling square with a statue of Christopher Columbus atop a high pedestal. Originally called St. James Square, it was renamed in honor of Columbus on the 400th anniversary of the discovery of Puerto Rico. Bronze plaques in the base of the statue relate various episodes in the life of the great explorer. On the north side of the plaza is a terminal for buses to and from San Juan.

⑱ Walk two blocks north from Plaza de Colón to Calle Sol and turn right. Another block will take you to **San Cristóbal,** the 18th-century fortress that guarded the city from land attacks. Even larger than El Morro, San Cristóbal was known as the Gibraltar of the West Indies. *Tel. 809/724–1974. Admission free. Open daily 9:15–6.*

⑲ South of Plaza de Colón is the magnificent **Tapia Theater** (Calle Fortaleza at Plaza de Colón, tel. 809/722–0407), named after the famed Puerto Rican playwright Alejandro Tapia y Rivera. Built in 1832, remodeled in 1949 and again in 1987, the municipal theater is the site of ballets, plays, and operettas. Stop by the box office to see what's showing and find out if you can get tickets.

⑳ Stroll from Plaza de Colón down to the **Port,** where the **Paseo de la Princesa** is spruced up with flowers, trees, and street lamps. Across from Pier 3, where the cruise ships dock, local artisans display their wares at the Plazoleta del Puerto. At the marina, pay 50¢ and board a ferry for a one-way ride to Catano.

San Juan   *Numbers in the margin correspond to points of interest on the San Juan Exploring, Dining, and Lodging map.*

You'll need to resort to taxis, buses, públicos, or a rental car to reach the points of interest in "new" San Juan.

Avenida Muñoz Rivera, Avenida Ponce de León, and Avenida Fernández Juncos are the main thoroughfares that cross Puerta de Tierra, just east of Old San Juan, to the business and tourist districts of Santurce, Condado, and Isla Verde.

㉑ In Puerta de Tierra is Puerto Rico's **Capitol,** a white marble building that dates from the 1920s. The grand rotunda, with mosaics and friezes, was completed a few years ago. The seat of the island's bicameral legislature, the Capitol contains Puerto Rico's constitution and is flanked by the modern buildings of the Senate and the House of Representatives. There are spectacular views from the observation plaza on the sea side of the Capitol. Pick up an informative booklet about the building from the House Secretariat on the second floor. Guided tours are by appointment only. *Av. Ponce de León, tel. 809/721–7305 or 809/ 721–7310. Admission free. Open weekdays 8:30–5.*

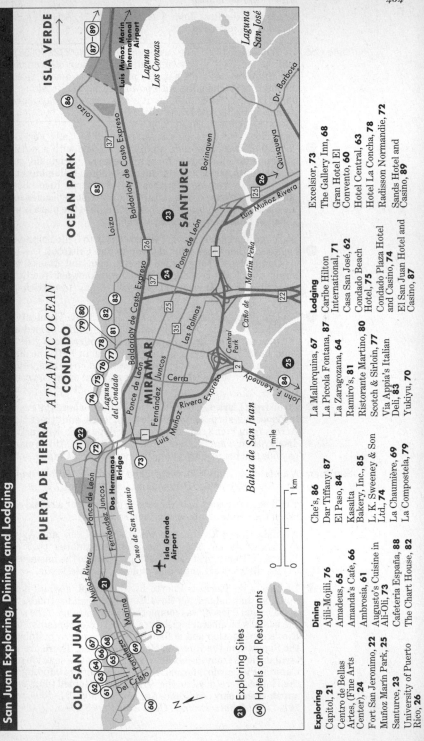

San Juan Exploring, Dining, and Lodging

ISLA VERDE

PUERTA DE TIERRA

OCEAN PARK

ATLANTIC OCEAN

CONDADO

Luis Muñoz Marín International Airport

Laguna Los Corozas

Laguna San José

SANTURCE

Boringuen

Quisqueya

Dr. Barbosa

OLD SAN JUAN

MIRAMAR

Laguna del Condado

Las Palmas

Central Park

Caño de Martín Peña

Bahía de San Juan

Isla Grande Airport

Dos Hermanos Bridge

Marina

Ponce de León

Muñoz Rivera

Fernández Juncos

Luis Muñoz Rivera Expreso

John F. Kennedy

Baldorioty de Costo Expreso

Ponce de León

Loiza

Cerra

Del Cristo

1 mile

1 km

21 Exploring Sites

60 Hotels and Restaurants

N

Exploring
Capitol, **21**
Centro de Bellas
Artes, (Fine Arts
Center), **24**
Fort San Jerónimo, **22**
Muñoz Marín Park, **25**
Santurce, **23**
University of Puerto
Rico, **26**

Dining
Ajili-Mojili, **76**
Amadeus, **65**
Amanda's Cafe, **66**
Ambrosia, **61**
Augusto's Cuisine in
Ali-Oli, **73**
Cafetería España, **88**
The Chart House, **82**

Che's, **86**
Dar Tiffany, **87**
El Paso, **84**
Kasalta
Bakery, Inc., **85**
L. K. Sweeney & Son
Ltd, **74**
La Chaumière, **69**
La Compostela, **79**

La Mallorquina, **67**
La Piccola Fontana, **87**
La Zaragozana, **64**
Ramiro's, **81**
Ristorante Martino, **80**
Scotch & Sirloin, **77**
Via Appia's Italian
Deli, **83**
Yukiyu, **70**

Lodging
Caribe Hilton
International, **71**
Casa San José, **62**
Condado Beach
Hotel, **75**
Condado Plaza Hotel
and Casino, **74**
El San Juan Hotel and
Casino, **87**

Excelsior, **73**
The Gallery Inn, **68**
Gran Hotel El
Convento, **60**
Hotel Central, **63**
Hotel La Concha, **78**
Radisson Normandie, **72**
Sands Hotel and
Casino, **89**

㉒ At the eastern tip of Puerta de Tierra, behind the splashy Caribe Hilton, the tiny **Fort San Jeronimo** is perched over the Atlantic like an afterthought. Added to San Juan's fortifications in the late 18th century, the structure barely survived the British attack of 1797. Restored in 1983 by the Institute of Puerto Rican Culture, it is now a military museum with displays of weapons, uniforms, and maps. *Tel. 809/724–5949. Admission free. Open Wed.–Sun. 9:30–noon and 1:30–4:30.*

Dos Hermanos Bridge connects Puerta de Tierra with Miramar, Condado, and Isla Grande. Isla Grande Airport, from which you can take short hops, is on the bay side of the bridge.

On the other side of the bridge, the Condado Lagoon is bordered by Avenida Ashford, which threads past the high-rise Condado hotels and El Centro Convention Center, and Av. Baldorioty de Castro Expreso, which barrels all the way east to the airport and beyond. Due south of the lagoon is Miramar, a primarily residential area with fashionable, turn-of-the-century homes and a cluster of hotels and restaurants.

㉓ **Santurce,** which lies between Miramar on the west and the Laguna San José on the east, is a busy mixture of shops, markets, and offices. The classically designed **Sacred Heart University** is the home of the **Museum of Contemporary Puerto Rican Art.** *Tel. 809/268–0049. Open Mon.–Fri. 9–4.*

㉔ Internationally acclaimed performers appear at the **Centro de Bellas Artes** (Fine Arts Center). This completely modern facility, the largest of its kind in the Caribbean, has a full schedule of concerts, plays, and operas. *Corner of Av. De Diego and Av. Ponce de León, tel. 809/724–4751.*

South of Santurce is the "Golden Mile"—Hato Rey, the city's bustling new financial hub. Isla Verde, with its glittering beachfront hotels, casinos, discos, and public beach, is to the east, near the airport.

Time Out | **Pescadería Atlántica** (81 Calle Loiza, tel. 809/726–6654) is a combination seafood restaurant and retail store. Stop in for a cool drink at the bar and a side dish of *calamares*, lightly breaded squid in a hot, spicy sauce.

Northeast of Isla Verde, Boca de Cangrejos sits between the Atlantic and Torrecilla Lagoon—a great spot for fishing and snorkeling. This is the point of embarkation for the 30-passenger launch *La Paseadora*, which tours the coast, the mangrove swamp, and the bird sanctuary at Torrecilla Lagoon.

Southeast of Miramar, Avenida Muñoz Rivera skirts along the northern side of **San Juan Central Park,** a convenient place for jogging, tennis, and calisthenics. The mangrove-bordered park was built for the 1979 Pan-American Games. *Cerra St. exit on Rte. 2, tel. 809/722–1646. Admission free. Open Tues.–Sat. 8–10, Mon. 2–10, Sun. 10–6.*

Las Américas Expressway, heading south, goes by Plaza Las Américas, the largest shopping mall in the Caribbean, and
㉕ takes you to the new **Muñoz Marín Park,** an idyllic tree-shaded spot dotted with gardens, lakes, playgrounds, and picnic areas. Cable cars connect the park with the parking area. *Next to Las Américas Expwy., west on Av. Piñero, tel. 809/763–*

0568 or 809/763–0787. Admission free; parking $1 per vehicle. Open Tues.–Sun. 9–5:30; closed Mon.

26 Río Piedras, a southern suburb of San Juan, is home to the **University of Puerto Rico,** located between Avenida Ponce de León and Avenida Barbosa. The university's campus is one of two sites for performances of the Puerto Rico Symphony Orchestra. Theatrical productions and other concerts are also scheduled here throughout the year. The University Museum has permanent archaeological and historical exhibits and occasionally mounts special art displays. *Next to the university's main entrance on Av. Ponce de León, tel. 809/764–0000, ext. 2452 or 2456. Open weekdays 9–9, Sat. 8–3:30; closed Sun. and holidays.*

The university's main attraction is the **Botanical Garden,** a lush garden with more than 200 species of tropical and subtropical vegetation. Footpaths through the thick forests lead to a graceful lotus lagoon, a bamboo promenade, an orchid garden, and a palm garden. *Intersection of Rtes. 1 and 847 at the entrance to Barrio Venezuela, tel. 809/763–4408. Admission free. Open Tues.–Sun. 9–5; when Mon. is a holiday, it is open Mon. and closed Tues.*

San Juan Environs *Numbers in the margin correspond to points of interest on the Puerto Rico map.*

From San Juan, follow Route 2 west toward Bayamón and **27** you'll spot the **Caparra Ruins,** where, in 1508, Ponce de León established the island's first settlement. The ruins are that of an ancient fort. Its small **Museum of the Conquest and Colonization of Puerto Rico** contains historical documents, exhibits, and excavated artifacts. (You can see the museum's contents in less time than it takes to say the name.) *Km 6.6 on Rte. 2, tel. 809/781–4795. Admission free. Open weekdays 9–5, weekends and holidays 10–6.*

28 Continue on Route 2 to **Bayamón.** In the Central Park, across from Bayamón's city hall, there are some historical buildings and a 1934 sugarcane train that runs through the park (open daily 8 AM–10 PM). On the plaza, in the city's historic district, stands the 18th-century Catholic church of Santa Cruz and the old neoclassical city hall, which now houses the **Francisco Oller Art and History Museum** (open weekdays 8–noon and 1–4).

29 Along Route 5 from Bayamón to Catano, you'll see the **Barrilito Rum Plant.** On the grounds is a 200-year-old plantation home and a 150-year-old windmill, which is listed in the National Register of Historic Places.

The **Bacardi Rum Plant,** along the bay, conducts 45-minute tours of the bottling plant, museum, and distillery, which has the capacity to produce 100,000 gallons of rum a day. (Yes, you'll be offered a sample.) *Km 2.6 on Rte. 888, tel. 809/788–1500. Admission free. Tours Mon.–Sat., except holidays, 9:30–3:30; closed Sun.*

Out on the Island Puerto Rico's 3,500 square miles is a lot of land to explore. While it is possible to get from town to town via público, we don't recommend traveling that way unless your Spanish is good and you know exactly where you're going. The public cars stop in each town's main square, leaving you on your own to reach the beaches, restaurants, paradores, and sightseeing attractions. You'll do much better if you rent a car. Most of the island's roads are excellent. However, there is a tangled web of roads through the mountains, and they are not always well marked. It helps to buy a good road map (*see* Getting Around, *above*).

East and South Our first excursion out on the island will take us east, down the coast to the south, and back up to San Juan. The first leg of the

30 trip—to Luquillo Beach and the nearby **Caribbean National Forest,** commonly known as **El Yunque,** can easily be done in a day. (There'll be heavy traffic and a crowded beach on weekends, when it seems as if the whole world heads for Luquillo.) The full itinerary will take two to three days, depending upon how long you loll on the beach and linger over the mountain scenery.

To take full advantage of the 28,000-acre El Yunque rain forest, go with a tour. Dozens of trails lead through the thick jungle (it sheltered the Carib Indians for 200 years), and the tour guides take you to the best observation points. Some of the trails are slippery, and there are occasional washouts.

However, if you'd like to drive there yourself, take Route 3 east from San Juan and turn right (south) on Route 191, about 25 miles from the city. The **Sierra Palm Visitor Center** is on Route 191, Km 11.6 (open daily 9:30–5). Nature talks and programs at the center are in Spanish and English and by appointment only—another good reason to go with a tour group.

El Yunque, named after the good Indian spirit Yuquiyu, is in the Luquillo Mountain Range. The rain forest is verdant with feathery ferns, thick ropelike vines, white tuberoses and ginger, miniature orchids, and some 240 different species of trees. More than 100 billion gallons of rainwater falls on it annually. Rain-battered, wind-ravaged dwarf vegetation clings to the top peaks. (El Toro, the highest peak in the forest, is 3,532 feet.) El Yunque is also a bird sanctuary and is the base of the rare Puerto Rican parrot. Millions of tiny, inch-long *coquis* (tree frogs) can be heard singing (or squawking, depending on your sensibilities). *For further information call the Catalina Field Office, tel. 809/887–2875 or 809/766–5335; or write Caribbean National Forest, Box B, Palmer, PR 00721.*

31 To reach **Luquillo Beach,** take Route 191 back to Route 3 and continue east 5 miles to Km 35.4. One of the island's best and most popular beaches, Luquillo was once a flourishing coconut plantation. Coral reefs protect its calm, pristine lagoon, making it an ideal place for a swim. The entrance fee is $1 per car, and there are lockers, showers, and changing rooms (*see* Beaches, *below*).

If you want to continue exploring, get back on Route 3 and

32 drive 5 miles to **Fajardo,** a major fishing and sailing center with thousands of boats tied and stacked in tiers at its three large marinas. Boats can be rented or chartered here, and the *Spread Eagle* catamaran can take you out for a full day of snorkeling, swimming, and sunning. Fajardo is also the embarkation point for ferries to the islands of Culebra (a $2.25 fare) and Vieques ($2).

North of Fajardo on Route 987, just past the Seven Seas Recre-

33 ational Area, is the entrance to **Las Cabezas de San Juan Nature Reserve.** Opened in 1991, the reserve contains mangrove swamps, coral reefs, beaches, a dry forest, and thalassia beds—all of Puerto Rico's natural habitats rolled into a micro-cosmic 316 acres. Nineteenth-century El Faro, one of the is-land's oldest lighthouses, is restored and still functioning; its first floor contains a small nature center that has an aquarium and other exhibits. The reserve is open, by reservation, to tours only, except from Friday to Sunday. *Rte. 987, tel. 809/ 722–5882, 809/722–5882 weekends. Admission: $4 adults, $1 children under 12. Open to the general public Fri.–Sun., ex-cept holidays; tours at 9:30, 10:30, and 1:30.*

34 **Culebra** has lovely white-sand beaches, coral reefs, and a wild-life refuge. In the sleepy town of Dewey, on Culebra's south-western side, check at the Visitor Information Center at city hall (tel. 809/742–3291) about boat rentals. On **Vieques,** Sun Bay public beach has picnic facilities; Blue Beach is superb for snorkeling; and Mosquito Bay is luminous even on moonless nights. You can stay overnight at the government-sponsored Parador Villa Esperanza (tel. 809/741–8675) on Vieques, which has, among other amenities, its own marina and fleet of sailing ships.

Resume your ramble on Route 3, heading south past the U.S. Naval Base, and ride through the sugarcane fields to Humacao. South of Humacao (take Route 906) is the 2,700-acre Palmas del Mar, the island's largest residential resort complex.

Stay on Route 3 through Yabucoa, tucked up in the hills, and Maunabo and Patillas, where you can pick up routes that will take you through the Cayey Mountains. Route 184 north skirts Lake Patillas and cuts smack through the Carite Forest Re-serve. Stay on Route 184 until it meets Route 1, where you'll shoot northward back to San Juan.

Western Island If you're short of time, drive the 64 miles from San Juan to Ponce in 90 minutes. Take the Las Américas Expressway, Route 52, which cuts through the splendid mountains of Cordil-lera Central.

If time is not a major problem, take a three- or four-day tour exploring the western regions of the island. This route covers Aguadilla, Rincón, Mayagüez, San Germán, and Ponce. There's much to see along the way—caves and coves, karst fields and coffee plantations, mountains, beaches, and even a zoo.

Start out going west on Route 2. In Arecibo pick up Route 10 and go south. Make a right on Route 111, and you'll find the **35** **Caguana Indian Ceremonial Park,** used 800 years ago by the Taino tribes for recreation and worship. Mountains surround a 13-acre site planted with royal palms and guava. According to Spanish historians, the Tainos played a game similar to soccer, and in this park there are 10 courts bordered by cobbled walk-ways. There are also stone monoliths, some with colorful petro-glyphs; a small museum; and a souvenir shop. *Rte. 111, Km 12.3, tel. 809/894–7325. Admission free. Open daily 8:30–4:30.*

Drive west on Route 111 and then north on Route 129 to Km **36** 18.9, where you'll find the **Río Camuy Cave Park,** a 268-acre re-serve that contains one of the world's largest cave networks. Guided tours take you on a tram down through dense tropical vegetation to the entrance of the cave, where you continue on foot over underground trails, ramps, and bridges. The caves, sinkholes, and subterranean streams are all spectacular (the world's second-largest underground river runs through here), but this trip is not for those with claustrophobia. Be sure to call ahead; the tours allow only a limited number of people. *Rte. 129, Km 18.9, tel. 809/898–3100 or 809/756–5555. Admission: $6 adults, $4 children. Parking $1. Open Wed.–Sun. and holidays 8–4. Last tour starts at 3:50.*

㊲ Backtrack to Route 111, which twists westward to **Aguadilla** on the northwest coast. In this area, somewhere between Aguadilla and Añasco, south of Rincón, Columbus dropped anchor on his second voyage in 1493. Both Aguadilla and **Aguada,** a few miles to the south, claim to be the spot where his foot first hit ground, and both towns have plaques to commemorate the occasion.

Route 115 from Aguadilla to **Rincón** is one of the island's most scenic drives, through rolling hills dotted with pastel-colored houses. Rincón, perched on a hill, overlooks its beach, which was the site of the World Surfing Championship in 1968. Skilled surfers flock to Rincón during the winter, when the water is rough and challenging.

㊳ Pick up Route 2 for the 6-mile drive to **Mayagüez,** Puerto Rico's third-largest city, with a population approaching 100,000. Mayagüez, known for its needlework, has plenty of shops to browse around in. (The Mayagüez Shopping Mall is one of the island's largest. The lounge of the hilltop Mayagüez Hilton is a popular gathering place for locals and tourists.)

North of town visit the **Mayagüez Zoo,** a 45-acre tropical compound that's home to about 500 animals. In addition to Bengal tigers, reptiles, and birds, including an Andean condor, there's a lake and a children's playground. *Rte. 108 at Barrio Miradero, tel. 809/834–8110. Admission: $1 adults, 50¢ children. Parking $1. Open Tues.–Sun. 9–4.*

㊴ Due south of Mayagüez, via the coastal Route 102, is **Cabo Rojo,** once a pirates' hangout and now a favorite resort area of Puerto Ricans. The area has long stretches of white-sand beaches on the clear, calm Caribbean Sea, as well as many seafood restaurants. There are also several paradores in the region. **Boquerón,** at the end of Route 101, has one of the best beaches on the island, as well as two-room cabins for rent. Parking is $1 per car.

㊵ From Cabo Rojo continue east on Route 102 to **San Germán,** a quiet Old World town that's home to the oldest intact church under the U.S. flag. Built in 1606, Porta Coeli (Gates of Heaven) overlooks one of the town's two plazas (where the townspeople continue the Spanish tradition of promenading at night). The church is now a museum of religious art, housing 18th- and 19th-century paintings and statues. *Tel. 809/892–5845. Admission free. Open Wed.–Sun. 8:30–noon and 1–4:30.*

The fishing village of **La Parguera,** an area of simple seafood restaurants, mangrove cays, and small islands, lies south of San Germán at the end of Route 304. This is an excellent scuba-**㊶** diving area, but the main attraction is **Phosphorescent Bay.** Boats tour the bay, where microscopic dinoflagellates (marine plankton) light up like Christmas trees when disturbed by any kind of movement. The phenomenon can be seen only on moonless nights. Boats leave for the hour-long trip nightly between 7:30 and 12:30, depending on demand, and the trip costs $6 per person. You can also rent or charter a small boat to explore the numerous cays.

From San Germán, Route 2 traverses splendid peaks and valleys; pastel houses cling to the sides of steep green hills. East of Yauco, the road dips and sweeps right along the Caribbean and **42** into **Ponce.**

Puerto Rico's second-largest city, with a population of 300,000, underwent a massive restoration in anticipation of both the 1992–93 quincentennial celebrating Columbus's discovery of the New World and the 300th anniversary of the city's first settlement. The town's 19th-century style was recaptured with pink marble-bordered sidewalks, gas lamps, and horse-drawn carriages. You have not seen a firehouse until you've seen the red and black **Parque de Bombas,** a structure first built in 1882 for an exposition and converted to a firehouse in 1883. The city hired architect Pablo Ojeda O'Neill to restore it, and it reopened as a museum in July 1990.

Ponce's charm stems from a combination of neoclassical, Ponce Creole, and art deco styles. Stop in and pick up information about this seaside city at the columned **Casa Armstrong-Poventud,** the home of the Institute of Puerto Rican Culture and Tourism Information Offices. Stroll around the **Plaza Las Delicias,** with its perfectly pruned India-laurel fig trees, graceful fountains, gardens, and park benches. View **Our Lady of Guadelupe Cathedral,** and walk down Calles Isabel and Christina to see turn-of-the-century wooden houses with wrought-iron balconies. Continue as far as Calles Mayor and Christina to the white stucco **La Perla Theater,** with its Corinthian columns. Be sure to allow time to visit the **Ponce Museum of Art.** The architecture alone is worth seeing: A two-story modern building designed by Edward Durell Stone (who designed New York's Museum of Modern Art) has seven interconnected hexagons, glass cupolas, and a pair of curved staircases. The collection includes late Renaissance and Baroque works from Italy, France, and Spain, as well as contemporary art by Puerto Ricans. *Av. Las Américas, tel. 809/840–0511 or 809/848–0505. Admission: $3 adults, $2 children under 12. Open Mon. and Wed.–Fri. 9–4, Sat. 10–4, Sun. 10–5.*

Off the Beaten Track

The **Blue Dolphin** is a hangout where you can rub elbows with some offbeat locals. Located behind the Empress Oceanfront Hotel at the northern tip of Isla Verde, the Blue Dolphin offers one of the best views on the island. While strolling along the Isla Verde beach, just look for the neon blue dolphin on the roof— you can't miss it. *2 Calle Amapola, Isla Verde, tel. 809/ 791–3083. Open weekends noon–4 AM, weeknights noon–2 AM.*

What to See and Do with Children

Beaches.
Botanical Garden, University of Puerto Rico, Rio Piedras.
Catano ferry.
El Morro and **San Cristóbal** forts.
El Yunque rain forest.
The **Hyatt Regency Cerromar Beach** and **Hyatt Dorado Beach**

offer chaperoned camps for children during the summer, as well as during Christmas and Easter holidays.

Las Cabezas de San Juan Nature Reserve, near Fajardo.

Mayagüez Zoo, Mayagüez.

Muñoz Marín Park, San Juan.

Río Camuy Caves, near Utuado.

Trolleys, Old San Juan.

Villa Coqui Wet N'Slide. A recreational park with pools, water slides, paddleboats, and canoes. *Rte. 763, Km 6, Caqua, tel. 809/747–4747. Open weekends and holidays 9–5.*

Beaches

By law, all Puerto Rico's beaches are open to the public (except for the Caribe Hilton's man-made beach in San Juan). The government runs 13 *balnearios* (public beaches), which have lockers, showers, picnic tables, and in some cases playgrounds and overnight facilities. Admission is free, parking $1. Most balnearios are open Tuesday through Sunday 9–6 in the winter, 8–5 in the summer. Listed below are some major balnearios.

Boquerón Beach is a broad beach of hard-packed sand, fringed with coconut palms. It has picnic tables, cabin rentals, bike rentals, basketball court, minimarket, scuba diving, and snorkeling. *On the southwest coast, south of Mayagüez, Rte. 101, Boquerón.*

A white sandy beach bordered by resort hotels, **Isla Verde** offers picnic tables and good snorkeling, with equipment rentals nearby. It's a lively beach popular with city folk. *Near metropolitan San Juan, Rte. 187, Km 3.9, Isla Verde.*

Crescent-shape **Luquillo Beach** comes complete with coconut palms, picnic tables, and tent sites. Coral reefs protect its crystal-clear lagoon from the Atlantic waters, making it ideal for swimming. Although it gets crowded on weekends, it's one of the largest and most well known. *30 mi east of San Juan, Rte. 3, Km 35.4.*

An elongated beach of hard-packed sand, **Seven Seas** is always popular with bathers. It has picnic tables and tent and trailer sites; snorkeling, scuba diving, and boat rentals are nearby. *Rte. 987, Fajardo.*

Sun Bay, a white-sand beach on the island of Vieques, has picnic tables, tent sites, and offers such water sports as snorkeling and scuba diving. Boat rentals are nearby. *Rte. 997, Vieques.*

Surfing The best surfing beaches are along the Atlantic coastline from Borinquén Point south to Rincón, where there are several surf shops; surfing is best from October through April. Aviones and La Concha beaches in San Juan and Casa de Pesca in Arecibo, are summer surfing spots; all have nearby surf shops.

Sports and the Outdoors

Bicycling The broad beach at Boquerón makes for easy wheeling. You can rent bikes at **Boquerón Balnearios** (Rte. 101, Boquerón, Dept. of Recreation and Sports, tel. 809/722–1551). In the Dorado area on the north coast, bikes can be rented at the **Hyatt Regency Cerromar Beach Hotel** (tel. 809/796–1234) or the **Hyatt Dorado Beach Hotel** (tel. 809/796–1234).

Boating   Virtually all the resort hotels on San Juan's Condado and Isla Verda strips rent paddleboats, Sunfish, Windsurfers, and the like. Contact **Condado Plaza Hotel Watersports Center** (tel. 809/721–1000, ext. 1361), **Caribbean School of Aquatics** (La Concha Hotel, Av. Ashford, Condado, tel. 809/723–4740), or **Castillo Watersports** (ESJ Towers, Isla Verde, tel. 809/791–6195). Sailing and boat rentals are also available at **Playita Boat Rental** (1010 Av. Ashford, Condado, tel. 809/722–1607).

Fishing   Half-day, full-day, split charters, and big- and small-game fishing can be arranged through **Benitez Deep-Sea Fishing** (Club Náutico de San Juan, Stop 9½, Av. Fernández Juncos, Miramar, tel. 809/723–2292 or 809/724–6265), **Castillo Watersports** (ESJ Towers, Isla Verde, tel. 809/791–6195 or evenings 809/726–5752), and **San Juan Fishing Charters** (Stop 10, Av. Fernández Juncos, Miramar, tel. 809/723–0415).

Golf   There are two 18-hole courses shared by the **Hyatt Dorado Beach Hotel** and the **Hyatt Regency Cerromar Beach Hotel** (Dorado, tel. 809/796–1234, ext. 3238 or 3013). You'll also find 18-hole courses at **Palmas del Mar Resort** (Humacao, tel. 809/852–6000, ext. 54), **Club Ríomar** (Río Grande, tel. 809/887–3964 or 809/887–3064), and **Punta Borinquén** (Aguadilla, tel. 809/890–2987).

Hiking   Dozens of trails lace **El Yunque** (information is available at the Sierra Palm Visitor Center, Rte. 191, Km 11.6). You can also hit the trails in **Río Abajo Forest** (south of Arecibo) and **Toro Negro Forest** (east of Adjuntas). Each reserve has a ranger station.

Horseback Riding   Beach-trail rides can be arranged at **Palmas del Mar Equestrian Center** (Palmas del Mar Resort, Humacao, tel. 809/852–6000, ext. 12721). Take to the rain-forest foothills trails, as well as the beaches, through **Hacienda Carabali** (tel. 809/889–5820 and 809/887–4954).

Sailing   Sailing instruction and trips are offered by **Palmas Sailing Center** (Palmas del Mar Resort, Humacao, tel. 809/852–6000, ext. 10310), **Calypso Watersports** (Sands Hotel, San Juan, tel. 809/791–6100), **Caribbean School of Aquatics** (La Concha Hotel, Av. Ashford, Condado, tel. 809/723–4740), **Caribe Aquatic Adventure** (Radisson Normandie Hotel, tel. 809/724–1882) and **Castillo Watersports** (ESJ Towers, Isla Verde, tel. 809/791–6195).

Snorkeling and Scuba Diving   Snorkeling and scuba-diving instruction and equipment rentals are available at **Caribbean School of Aquatics** and **Calypso Watersports** *(see* Sailing, *above)*, **Coral Head Divers** (Marina de Palmas, Palmas del Mar Resort, Humacao, tel. 809/850–7208 or 800/221–4874), **La Cueva Submarina Training Center** (Plaza Cooperativa, Isabela, tel. 809/872–3903 or evenings 809/872–1094), **Caribe Aquatic Adventure** *(see* Sailing, *above)*, **Castillo Watersports** *(see* Sailing, *above)*, and **Parguera Divers Training Center** (Road 304, MM3-2, Lajas, tel. 809/899–4171).

Caution: Puerto Rico's coral-reef waters and mangrove areas can be dangerous to novices. Unless you're an expert or have an experienced guide, avoid unsupervised areas and stick to the water-sports centers of major hotels.

Tennis   There are 17 lighted courts at **San Juan Central Park** (Calle Cerra exit on Rte. 2, tel. 809/722–1646); 6 lighted courts at the **Caribe Hilton Hotel** (Puerta de Tierra, tel. 809/721–0303, ext.

1730); 8 courts, 4 lighted, at **Carib Inn** (Isla Verde, tel. 809/791–3535, ext. 6); and 2 lighted courts at the **Condado Plaza Hotel** (Condado, tel. 809/721–1000, ext. 1775). Out on the island, there are 14 courts, 2 lighted, at **Hyatt Regency Cerromar Beach Hotel** (Dorado, tel. 809/796–1234, ext. 3040); 7 courts, 2 lighted, at the **Hyatt Dorado Beach Hotel** (Dorado, tel. 809/796–1234, ext. 3220); 20 courts, 4 lighted, at **Palmas del Mar Resort** (Humacao, tel. 809/852–6000, ext. 51); 3 lighted courts at the **Mayagüez Hilton Hotel** (Mayagüez, tel. 809/831–7575, ext. 2150); and 4 lighted courts at **Punta Borinquén** (Aguadilla, tel. 809/891–8778).

Windsurfing Windsurfing rentals are available at **Caribbean School of Aquatics, Castillo Watersports, Palmas Sailing Center, Playita Boat Rental** *(see* Boating, and Sailing, *above,* for all information) and at **Lisa Penfield Windsurfing Center** (El San Juan Hotel, tel. 809/726–7274).

Spectator Sports Thoroughbred races are run year-round at **El Comandante**
Horse Racing Racetrack. On race days the dining rooms open at 12:30 PM. *Rte. 3, Km 15.3, Canovanas, tel. 809/724–6060. Open Wed., Fri., Sun., and holidays.*

Baseball If you have a post–World Series letdown, you can fly down to the island, where the season runs October–April. Many major-league ballplayers in the United States got their start in Puerto Rico's baseball league, and some return in the off-season to hone their skills. Stadiums are in San Juan, Santurce, Ponce, Caguas, Arecibo, and Mayagüez. Contact the Tourist Office for details or call **Professional Baseball of Puerto Rico** (tel. 809/765–6285).

Shopping

San Juan is not a free port, and you won't find bargains on electronics and perfumes. You can, however, find excellent prices on china, crystal, fashions, and jewelry.

Shopping for local Caribbean crafts can be great fun. You'll run across a lot of tacky things you can live without, but you can also find some treasures, and in many cases you'll be able to watch the artisans at work. (For guidance, contact the Tourism Artisan Center, tel. 809/721–2400, ext. 248.)

The work of some Puerto Rican artists has brought them international acclaim: The paintings of Francisco Oller hang in the Louvre, and the portraits of Francisco Rodon are in the permanent collections of New York's Museum of Modern Art and Metropolitan Museum. Look for their works, and those of other native artists, in San Juan's stylish galleries.

Popular souvenirs and gifts include *santos* (small, hand-carved figures of saints or religious scenes), hand-rolled cigars, hand-made lace, carnival masks, and fancy men's shirts called *guayaberas.* Also, some folks swear that Puerto Rican rum is the best in the world.

Shopping Districts **Old San Juan** is full of shops, especially on Cristo, Fortaleza, and San Francisco streets. The **Las Américas Plaza** south of San Juan is one of the largest shopping malls in the Caribbean, with 200 shops, restaurants, and movie theaters. Other malls out on the island include **Plaza del Carmen** in Caguas and the **Mayagüez Mall.**

Good Buys You can get discounts on Hathaway shirts and Christian Dior
Clothing clothing at **Hathaway Factory Outlet** (203 Calle Cristo, tel. 809/
723–8946) and reductions on men's, women's, and children's
raincoats at the **London Fog Factory Outlet** (156 Calle Cristo,
tel. 809/722–4334).

Jewelry There is gold, gold, and more gold at **Reinhold** (201 Calle Cristo, tel. 809/725–6878) and brand-name watches at **The Watch
and Gem Palace** (204 Calle San José, Old San Juan, tel. 809/722–
2136).

Local Crafts For one-of-a-kind buys, head for **Puerto Rican Arts & Crafts**
(204 Calle Fortaleza, Old San Juan, tel. 809/725–5596), **Plazoleta del Puerto** (Calle Marina, Old San Juan, tel. 809/722–3053),
Don Roberto (205 Calle Cristo, tel. 809/724–0194), and **M. Rivera** (107 Calle Cristo, Old San Juan, tel. 809/724–1004).

Paintings and **Galería Palomas** (207 Calle Cristo, Old San Juan, tel. 809/724–
Sculptures 8904) is popular. **Galería Botello** (208 Calle Cristo, Old San
Juan, tel. 809/723–9987, and Plaza Las Américas, tel. 809/724–
7430) features a display of antique *santos* (religious sculptures).

Other galleries worth visiting are **Galería San Juan** (204–206
Calle Norzagaray, Old San Juan, tel. 809/722–1808 or 809/723–
6515) and **Corinne Timsit International Galleries** (104 Calle San
Jose, Old San Juan, tel. 809/724–1039 or 809/724–0994).

Dining

Over the past 10 years, phone book listings of restaurants in
Puerto Rico have grown fourfold. As a result, there are many
new places to try, many off the heavily beaten path. Whether
you're dining at a fine restaurant or picking up fast food in a
mall (be sure to visit the one in Plaza Las Américas to see the
action), you'll find that every place is extremely busy at lunchtime. Dinner is more relaxed and leisurely, with dress casual to
casually elegant; few establishments require a jacket.

On weekends it's common to see Puerto Rican families in their
cars sightseeing in the hilly interior of the island and stopping
for a late lunch on a beach or back up in the mountains. Visitors
should do as the locals do and go out on the island for at least
one meal. The drive is a curvy green adventure that is well
worth the trip.

One unique aspect of Puerto Rican cooking is its generous use
of local vegetables: Plantains are cooked a hundred different
ways—*tostones* (fried green), *amarillos* (baked ripe), and
chips. Rice and beans with tostones or amarillos are basic ac-
companiments to every dish. Locals cook white rice with
achiote (annatto seeds) or saffron, brown rice with *gandules*
(pigeon peas), and black rice with *frijoles* (black beans). *Gar-
banzos* (chickpeas) and white beans are served in many daily
specials. A wide assortment of yams is served baked, fried,
stuffed, boiled, smashed, and whole. *Sofrito*—a garlic, onion,
sweet pepper, coriander, oregano, and tomato puree—is used
as a base for practically everything.

Beef, chicken, pork, and seafood are all rubbed with *adobo*, a
garlic-oregano marinade, before cooking. *Arroz con pollo*
(chicken with rice), *sancocho* (beef and tuber soup), *asopao* (a
soupy rice with chicken or seafood), *empanada* (breaded cut-

let), and *encebollado* (steak smothered in onions) are all typical plates.

Fritters, also popular, are served in snack places along the highways as well as at cocktail parties. You may find *empanadillas* (stuffed fried turnovers), *surrullitos* (cheese-stuffed corn sticks), *alcapurias* (stuffed green banana croquettes), and *bacalaitos* (codfish fritters).

Local *pan de agua* is an excellent French loaf bread, best hot out of the oven. It is also good toasted and should be tried in the *Cubano* sandwich (made with roast pork, ham, Swiss cheese, pickles, and mustard).

Local desserts include flans, puddings, and fruit pastes served with native white cheese. Home-grown mangoes and papayas are sweet, and *pan de azucar* (sugar bread) pineapples make the best juice on the market. Fresh *parcha* (passion fruit) fruit, fresh *guarapo* (sugarcane) juice, and fresh *guanabana* juice (similar to papaya) are also sold cold from trucks along the highway. Puerto Rican coffee is excellent served espresso-black or generously cut *con leche* (with hot milk).

The best frozen piña coladas are served at the Caribe Hilton Hotel and Dorado Beach Hotel, although local legend has it that the birthplace of the piña colada is the Gran Hotel El Convento. Rum can be mixed with cola (known as a *cuba libre*), soda, tonic, juices, water, served on the rocks, or even up. Puerto Rican rums range from light white mixers to dark, aged sipping liqueurs. Look for Bacardi, Don Q, Ron Rico, Palo Viejo, and Barillito.

Highly recommended restaurants are indicated by a star ★.

Category	Cost*
Very Expensive	over $50
Expensive	$25–$50
Moderate	$15–$25
Inexpensive	under $15

per person, excluding drinks and service

Old San Juan
★
La Chaumière. Reminiscent of an inn in the French provinces, this intimate yet bright white restaurant serves a respected onion soup, oysters Rockefeller, rack of lamb, and veal Oscar in addition to daily specials. *367 Calle Tetuan, tel. 809/722–3330. Reservations advised. AE, DC, MC. Closed Sun. Very Expensive.*

La Zaragozana. One of the oldest restaurants around, this adobe hacienda re-creates an old Spanish atmosphere. The ambience is pleasant, with strolling musicians, murals, and vaulted archways. The menu offers black-bean soup, steaks, lobster, paella, and flan. *356 Calle San Francisco, tel. 809/723–5103 and 809/725–3262. Reservations advised. AE, DC, MC, V. Expensive.*

★ **Yukiyu.** This restaurant serves sushi, sashimi, and other Japanese-inspired specials. The soft-shell crab, shrimp and vegetable tempura, tuna teriyaki, and cod steamed with ginger-and-orange béarnaise are all recommended. *311 Recinto*

Sur., tel. 809/721-0653. Reservations advised for lunch. AE, MC, V. Closed Sun. and Mon. Expensive.

★ **Amadeus.** In an atmosphere of gentrified Old San Juan, this restaurant offers a nouvelle Caribbean menu. The roster of appetizers includes tostones with sour cream and caviar, marlin ceviche, and crabmeat tacos. Entrées range from grilled dolphin with coriander butter to chicken lasagna and tuna- or egg-salad sandwiches. *106 Calle San Sebastián, tel. 809/722-8635 or 809/721-6720. Reservations required. AE, MC, V. Closed Mon. Moderate.*

Amanda's Cafe. This airy cafe, on the north side of the city, offers seating inside or out, with a view toward the Atlantic and the old city wall. The cuisine is Mexican, French, and Caribbean, but the nachos and Margaritas are the best in town. *424 Calle Norzagaray, tel. 809/722-1682. AE, MC, V. Moderate.*

La Mallorquina. The Old World atmosphere and friendly service here are better than the food, which is good but basic Puerto Rican and Spanish fare, such as asopao and paella. *207 Calle San Justo, tel. 809/722-3261. AE, DC, MC, V. Inexpensive-Moderate.*

Ambrosia. At the bottom of Calle Cristo, this restaurant serves fresh, frozen fruit drinks at the bar, while the menu features pastas, veal, and chicken. The daily lunch specials usually include quiche and lasagna served with large mixed salads for good value. *205 Calle Cristo, tel. 809/722-5206. AE, MC, V. Inexpensive.*

San Juan **Dar Tiffany.** This restaurant, just off the lobby of the glittering
★ El San Juan Hotel, is a posh place with palm fronds etched in glass; voluptuous greenery; and, yes, Tiffany lamps. Knock back a two-fisted martini from the bar before tackling superb aged prime rib, Maine lobster, or fresh Norwegian salmon. *El San Juan Hotel Av., Isla Verde., tel. 809/791-7272. Reservations advised. Jacket suggested. AE, DC, MC, V. Very Expensive.*

★ **La Compostela.** Contemporary Spanish food and a serious 9,000-bottle wine cellar are the draws to La Compostela. Specialties include mushroom pâté and Port *pastelillo* (meat-filled pastries), grouper fillet with scallops in salsa verde, roast lamb, and paella. This is a favorite restaurant with the local dining elite, and it is honored yearly in local competitions. *106 Av. Condado, Santurce, tel. 809/724-6088. Reservations advised. AE, DC, MC, V. Very Expensive.*

★ **Ramiro's.** Step into a soft sea-green dining room serving imaginative Castilian cuisine. Chef-owner Jesus Ramiro has published a cookbook on Castillian cooking, and each of his dishes is artfully arranged and decorated. Specialties include flower-shape peppers filled with fish mousse; a seafood fantasy caught under a vegetable net; roast duckling with sugarcane honey; and, if you can stand more, a syrupy kiwi dessert arranged to resemble twin palms. *1106 Av. Magdalena, Condado, tel. 809/721-9049. Reservations advised. AE, DC, MC, V. Very Expensive.*

La Piccola Fontana. If intimate, elegant dining is your passion, this restaurant, tucked into a corner off the El San Juan Hotel lobby, is worth a visit. Succulent shrimp cocktail, Caesar salad, homemade pastas, and numerous veal dishes highlight the menu. *El San Juan Hotel. Av. Isla Verde, San Juan, tel. 809/791-1000. Reservations advised. AE, DC, MC, V. Expensive-Very Expensive.*

Ajili-Mojili. This place is recommended for its authentic Puerto Rican cuisine. House specialties include arroz con pollo and beef fillet marinated in island condiments and sautéed onions. *Hotel Condado Lagoon, tel. 809/725–9195. AE, MC, V. Closed Mon. and Sat. lunch. Expensive.*

Augusto's Cuisine in Ali-Oli. Chef-owner August Schriener and his wife, Claudia, run an elegantly comfortable restaurant featuring classic cooking. Menus change weekly. Specialties include salmon baked in filo, lamb tenderloin with pepper-vodka fettuccine, and veal medallions with smoked mozzarella. *Excelsior Hotel, Miramar, tel. 809/725–7700 or 809/721–7400. Reservations suggested. AE, MC, V. Expensive.*

The Chart House. Set in a restored Ashford mansion laced with graceful tropical verandas perfect for cocktails, the bar offers good drinks to a lively mix of people. Open-air dining rooms are upstairs, set at different levels. The menu includes prime rib, steak, shrimp teriyaki, Hawaiian chicken, and the signature dessert: mud pie. *1214 Av. Ashford, Condado, tel. 809/728–0110. Reservations required. AE, DC, MC, V. Expensive.*

L. K. Sweeney & Son Ltd. Brothers Larry and Tim Sweeney have opened a comfortable Continental restaurant that overlooks the lagoon lights at night. You'll have a choice of live Maine or Caribbean lobster, beluga caviar, Norwegian salmon, or Florida stone crab. *Condado Plaza Hotel and Casino, 999 Av. Ashford, Condado, tel. 809/723–5551. AE, DC, MC, V. Expensive.*

★ **Ristorante Martino.** Overlooking Condado from atop the Dutch Inn, this roof-garden restaurant's Northern Italian food and attentive service get rave reviews from the locals. Fresh pastas, a selection of veal dishes, and good wines make a moderate meal a pleasure. *Dutch Inn, 55 Av. Condado, Condado, tel. 809/722–5256. AE, MC, V. Expensive.*

Che's. The most established and casual of three Argentinian restaurants within a few blocks of one another, Che's features juicy *churrasco* (barbecue) steaks, lemon chicken, and grilled sweetbreads. The hamburgers are huge and the french fries are fresh. The Chilean and Argentinian wine list is also decent. *35 Calle Caoba, Punta Las Marias, tel. 809/726–7202. AE, DC, MC, V. Moderate.*

★ **Scotch & Sirloin.** Tucked back among the tropical overgrowth overlooking the lagoon, the Scotch & Sirloin has been San Juan's most consistently fine steakhouse. Aquariums light up the bar, and the fresh salad bar serves moist banana bread. Steaks are aged in-house and cooked precisely to order. *La Rada Hotel, 1020 Av. Ashford, Condado, tel. 809/722–3640. Reservations required. AE, DC, MC, V. Moderate.*

Cafeteria España. This is a busy Spanish cafeteria serving strong coffee, assorted croquettes, toasted sandwiches, soups, and a large selection of pastries. Spanish candies, canned goods, and other gourmet items for sale are packed into floor-to-ceiling shelves for a cozy, full feeling. *Centro Commercial Villamar, Baldorioty de Castro Marginal, Isla Verde, tel. 809/727–4517 and 809/727–3860. No credit cards. Inexpensive.*

El Paso. This family-run restaurant serves genuine Creole food seasoned for a local following. Specialties include asopao, pork chops, and breaded empanadas. There's always tripe on Saturday and arroz con pollo on Sunday. *405 Av. De Diego, Puerto Nuevo, tel. 809/781–3399. AE, DC, MC, V. Inexpensive.*

★ **Kasalta Bakery, Inc.** Walk up to the counter and order an assortment of sandwiches, cold drinks, strong café con leche, and

pastries. Try the Cubano sandwich. *1966 Calle McLeary, Ocean Park, tel. 809/727-7340. No credit cards. Inexpensive.*
Via Appia's Italian Deli. The only true sidewalk café in San Juan, this eatery serves pizzas, sandwiches, cold beer, and pitchers of sangria. It is a good place to people-watch. *1350 Av. Ashford, Condado, tel. 809/725-8711. AE, MC, V. Inexpensive.*

Out on the Island
★

Horned Dorset Primavera. Lunch, served in a comfortable wicker room, is casual and à la carte. A fixed-price gourmet dinner is served in the art deco dining room. No children under 12 are allowed. *Rte. 429, Km 3, Rincón, tel. 809/823-4030. Reservations required. AE, MC, V. Expensive.*
La Rotisserie. An institution in Mayagüez, this fine dining room offers the best value for the money in town with its lavish breakfast and lunch buffets. The restaurant is known for grilled steaks and fresh seafood. A different food festival is featured nightly: Italian, buffet, seafood, Latin night. *Hilton International Mayagüez, Hwy. 2, Km 152.5, Mayagüez, tel. 809/ 831-7575. Reservations suggested. AE, D, DC, MC, V. Moderate-Expensive.*
The Black Eagle. Literally on the water's edge, you dine outside on the restaurant's veranda listening to the lapping waves under the stars. Under new management, the restaurant has been upgraded and the menu improved. House specialties include breaded conch fritters, fresh fish of the day, lobster, and prime meats that are imported by the owner. *Hwy. 413, Km 1, Barrio Ensenada, Rincón, tel. 809/823-3510. AE, DC, MC, V. Moderate.*
La Casona de Serafin. This informal, ocean-side bistro, with blanched walls and mahogany furniture, specializes in steaks, seafood, and Puerto Rican *criolla* (Creole) dishes. Try sampling tostones, asopao, and surrullitos. *Hwy. 102, Km 9, Cabo Rojo, tel. 809/851-0066. AE, MC, V. Moderate.*
Restaurant El Ancla. This relaxed spot by the water serves seafood and Puerto Rican specialties with courteous service. Entrées are served with tostones, *papas fritas*, and garlic bread. The menu ranges from lobster and shrimp to chicken, beef, and asopao. The piña coladas, with or without rum, and the flan are especially good. *Av. Hostos Final 9, Playa-Ponce, tel. 809/840-2450. AE, DC, MC, V. Moderate.*
Sand and the Sea. Looking down onto Guayama and out across the sea, this mountain cottage is a retreat into Caribbean living. The menu leans toward steaks and barbecues with a good carrot vichyssoise and excellent baked beans. Bring a sweater—it cools down to 50°F at night. *Hwy. 715, Km 5.2, Cayey, tel. 809/745-6317. AE, DC, MC, V. Moderate.*
El Bohio. For fresh seafood in an informal setting overlooking the sea, a 10- to 15-minute drive south of Mayagüez, this restaurant reveals how the locals enjoy a meal. Selections range from red snapper to lobster and shrimp. *Hwy. 102, Playa Joyuda, Cabo Rojo, tel. 809/851-2755. AE, DC, MC, V. Inexpensive-Moderate.*

Lodging

Accommodations on Puerto Rico come in all shapes and sizes. Self-contained luxury resorts cover hundreds of acres. San Juan's high-rise beachfront hotels likewise cater to the epicurean; several target the business traveler. Out on the island, the government-sponsored paradores are country inns modeled after Spain's successful parador system. They are required to meet certain standards, such as proximity to a sightseeing attraction or beach and a kitchen serving native cuisine. (Parador prices range from $50 to $80 for a double room. Reservations for all paradores can be made by calling 800/443–0266 or 809/721–2884 in Puerto Rico.)

Most hotels in Puerto Rico operate on the European Plan. In some larger hotels, however, packages are available that include several or all meals, while others offer all-inclusive deals.

Highly recommended lodgings are indicated by a star ★.

Category	Cost*
Very Expensive	over $200
Expensive	$125–$200
Moderate	$50–$125
Inexpensive	under $50

All prices are for a standard double room for two, excluding 7% tax (9% for hotels with casinos) and a 10% service charge.

Old San Juan   **Casa San José.** Unassuming elegance defines the character of the newest Old San Juan hotel. Black-and-white marble floors decorate the foyer, and each of the 10 rooms, individually stylized with hand-picked Spanish, French, and English Colonial antiques, opens onto an interior patio filled with tropical plants. The second-floor salon is equipped with a small library and grand piano. Children under 12 are not accommodated. *159 Calle San José, 00901, tel. 809/723–1212, fax 809/723–7620. 4 1-bedroom suites, 1 2-bedroom suite, 4 doubles. Facilities: restaurant. AE, DC, MC, V. CP. Expensive–Very Expensive.*

★   **Gran Hotel El Convento.** This is one of Puerto Rico's most famous hotels. On Calle Cristo right across from the San Juan Cathedral, the light brown stucco building, with its dark wood paneling and arcades, was a Carmelite convent in the 17th century. All the rooms are air-conditioned, with twin beds and wall-to-wall carpeting. Fourteen rooms have balconies (ask for one with a view of the bay). *100 Calle Cristo, 00902, tel. 809/ 723–9020 or 800/468–2779, fax 809/721–2877. 99 rooms. Facilities: pool, 2 restaurants and bar, free transport to beach. AE, D, DC, MC, V. EP. Moderate–Expensive.*

The Gallery Inn. Owners Jan D'Esopo and Manuco Gandia restored one of the oldest private residences in the area and turned it into a rambling, classically Spanish guest house with winding, uneven stairs, private balconies, individually decorated rooms, and gardens hidden throughout. This small inn and art gallery (Galería San Juan) overlooks the Atlantic along the north wall of Old San Juan. With its views of El Morro and San Cristobal forts, the inn has a compelling and singular panorama that is one of the best in the old city. The gallery is also a working studio, and you may run into models posing in any of the suites in the house. The gallery features work by the likes of Jan D'Esopo, Bruno Lucchesi, and Burton Silverman. The inn even offers a package that combines a five-night stay with the creation of your portrait bust. *204–206 Calle Norzagaray, 00901, tel. 809/722–1808 or 809/725–3829, fax 809/724–7360. 3* *suites and 5 guest rooms. Facilities: self-service bar, restaurant for guests only. AE, MC, V. EP. Moderate–Expensive.*

Hotel Central. One of the older hotels in Old San Juan, this no-frills inn is also one of the city's better bargains. The dark-paneled main lobby, reminiscent of your grandmother's sitting room, is furnished with an eclectic array of musty furniture that has seen many, and better, days. But the rooms are clean and possess a travel-worn integrity. Located a stone's throw from the Plaza de Armas, the hotel is central to sights, shopping, and some of Puerto Rico's finest restaurants. *202 Calle San Jose, 00901, tel. 809/722–2751 or 809/721–9667. 62 rooms. Facilities: restaurant. No credit cards. EP. Inexpensive.*

San Juan **El San Juan Hotel and Casino.** An immense chandelier shines
★ over the hand-carved wood paneling and rose marble of the lobby in this sprawling 22-acre resort on the Isla Verde beach. You'll be hard pressed to decide if you want a spa suite in the main tower with whirlpool and wet bar; a garden lanai room, with private patio and spa; or a custom-designed casita with sunken Roman bath. (Some of the tower rooms have no view; your best bet is an oceanside lanai, with or without spa.) In any case, all rooms are air-conditioned, with three phones, remote-control TVs with VCRs, hair dryers, minibars, and many other amenities. *Av. Isla Verde, Box 2872, San Juan 00902, tel. 809/ 791–1000 or 800/468–2818, fax 809/791–0390. 392 rooms. Facilities: 2 pools, children's pool, 5 restaurants, 2 snack bars, 8 cocktail lounges, supper club, disco, casino, 3 lighted tennis courts with pro shop, activity center, water-sports center, shopping arcade, health club, nonsmoking floor, facilities for the disabled, complimentary shuttle bus to Condado Plaza Hotel, courtyard Jacuzzi, concierge, valet parking. AE, DC, MC, V. EP. Very Expensive.*

★ **Caribe Hilton International.** Built in 1949, this property occupies 17 acres on Puerta de Tierra and completed a $40 million renovation in early 1991. The spacious atrium lobby is decorated with rose marble, waterfalls, and lavish tropical plants. The hotel boasts San Juan's only private, palm-fringed swimming cove complete with a boardwalk and a bar to serve you as you swim by. The airy guest rooms have balconies with ocean or lagoon views. Three executive levels provide services and amenities for the business traveler. *Box 1872, San Juan 00902, tel. 809/721–0303 or 800/468–8585, fax 809/722–2910. 668 rooms and suites. Facilities: private beach, 2 pools, 6 lighted tennis courts, 5 restaurants, pastry shop, workout area, air-conditioned squash and racquetball courts, executive business center. AE, D, DC, MC, V. EP. Expensive–Very Expensive.*

Condado Plaza Hotel and Casino. Nestled between the Atlantic Ocean and the Condado Lagoon, this stunning resort is two hotels in one, with a Lagoon Wing and an Ocean Wing. Standard rooms have walk-in closets, separate dressing areas, and amenity packages. There is a variety of suites (including spa suites with whirlpools) and a fully equipped executive service center. If that isn't posh enough, you can check into the Plaza Club, which has 24-hour concierge service. *Box 1270, 999 Av. Ashford, Condado 00907, tel. 809/721–1000 or 800/468–8588, fax 809/721–4613. 580 rooms and suites. Facilities: 5 pools (1 saltwater); casino; disco; 2 lighted tennis courts; 6 restaurants; 7 bars and lounges; fitness, water-sports, and business centers. AE, D, DC, MC, V. EP. Expensive–Very Expensive.*

Radisson Normandie. Built in 1939 in the shape of the fabled ocean liner of the same name, this oceanfront hotel reopened in late 1988 under the Radisson banner. It's a national historic landmark, done up in art-deco style, and each room comes with sun room, minibar, and cable TV. Additional frills and pampering can be found at the seventh-floor executive club. *Corner of Av. Muñoz Rivera and Av. Rosales, Puerta Tierra, Box 50059, San Juan 00902, tel. 809/729-2929 or 800/333-3333, fax 809/729-3083. 180 air-conditioned rooms. Facilities: outdoor pool, 2 restaurants, lounge, business center, health club, watersports center. AE, D (for payment only), MC, V. EP, MAP. Expensive-Very Expensive.*

★ **Sands Hotel and Casino.** One of Puerto Rico's largest casinos glitters just off the lobby, and a huge free-form pool lies between the hotel and its beach. The air-conditioned hotel has rooms with private balconies (ask for one with an ocean view), minibars, and many frills. The exclusive Plaza Club section offers a masseuse, private spas, and other enticements. *Box 6676, Calle Isla Verde 187, Isla Verde 00913, tel. 809/791-6100 or 800/468-9076, fax 809/791-8525. 418 rooms. Facilities: pool, 5 restaurants, lounge, casino, concierge, 24-hr room service, facilities for the disabled, nightclub, water-sports center, business center, valet parking. AE, D, DC, MC, V. EP. Expensive-Very Expensive.*

★ **Condado Beach Hotel.** Built in 1919 by Cornelius Vanderbilt, the hotel has a pale-pink lobby adorned with bouquets of flowers, a sweeping double staircase, and Victorian furnishings. Guest rooms, each decorated in the Spanish colonial style of the 1920s, have either an ocean, lagoon, or city view. The Vanderbilt Club floors, reached by private elevator, provide all manner of pampering. *Box 41226, Minillas Station, Condado 00940, tel. 809/721-6090 or 800/468-2775, fax 809/722-5062. 245 rooms, including 18 junior suites, 2 1- and 2-bedroom suites, and a presidential suite. Facilities: cable TV, 3rd-level pool, 2 restaurants and lounges, facilities for the disabled. AE, D, DC, MC, V. EP. Expensive.*

Hotel La Concha. Looking like a large pink seashell, this hotel completed extensive renovations in 1992. Its individually air-conditioned rooms all face the ocean and are furnished in contemporary tropical decor. In the main building and the 12 poolside cabanas there are 18 junior suites and 17 one- or two-bedroom corner suites. The VIP suites are on the top three floors. The ritzy Club Mykonos disco is perched right over the water. *Box 4195, Condado 00905, tel. 809/721-6090 or 800/468-2822, fax 809/721-3200. 236 oceanfront rooms. Facilities: activity center, water-sports center, 2 lighted tennis courts, volleyball court on the beach, pool, poolside bar, 2 restaurants and lounges, disco, facilities for the disabled, shopping arcade. AE, D, DC, MC, V. EP. Expensive.*

★ **Excelsior.** Recently spruced up with English carpets in the corridors and new sculptures in the lobby, this hotel is home to the estimable restaurant Augusto's Cuisine in Ali-Oli. Each room has a private bath with phone and hair dryer. Although the decor is standard, this hotel is a very good value for its price range. Complimentary coffee, newspaper, and shoeshine are offered each morning. *801 Av. Ponce de León, Miramar 00907, tel. 809/721-7400 or 800/223-9815, fax 809/723-0068. 140 rooms, 60 with kitchenette. Facilities: pool, cocktail lounge, restaurants, fitness rooms, free parking and free transportation to the beach. AE, MC, V. EP. Moderate.*

Out on the Island
Cabo Rojo

Parador Boquemar. Located on Route 101 near the beach in a small, unpretentious fishing village, this parador has air-conditioned rooms, all with minifridges and private baths. *Box 133, 00622, tel. 809/851–2158 or 800/443–0266. 64 rooms. Facilities: pool, restaurant. AE, DC, MC, V. EP. Moderate.*

Parador Perichi's. On Route 102 along famous Joyuda Beach, the hotel offers access to fine beaches, including the Isla de Rationes. The basic rooms have air-conditioning, television, and private baths. *Rte. 102, Km 14.3, Playa Joyuda, Cabo Rojo, 00623, tel. 809/851–3131 or 800/443–0266. 25 rooms, 2 with ocean view. Facilities: game room, pool, restaurant, and lounge. AE, D, DC, MC, V. EP. Moderate.*

Coamo

Parador Baños de Coamo. On Route 546, Km 1, northeast of Ponce, this mountain inn is located at the hot sulfur springs that are said to be the Fountain of Youth of Ponce de León's dreams. *Box 540, 00640, tel. 809/825–2186 or 800/443–0266. 48 rooms. Facilities: pool, restaurant, lounge. AE, D, DC, MC, V. EP. Moderate.*

Dorado
★

Hyatt Dorado Beach. The ambience is a bit more subdued and family oriented at the Cerromar's sophisticated sister, where a variety of elegant accommodations are in low-rise buildings scattered over 1,000 lavishly landscaped acres. Most rooms have private patios or balconies, and all have polished terra-cotta floors, marble baths, air-conditioning, and many frills. Upper-level rooms in the Oceanview Houses have a view of the two half-moon beaches. *Rte. 693, Dorado 00646, tel. 809/796–1234 or 800/233–1234, fax 809/796–2022. 298 rooms. Facilities: 2 18-hole Robert Trent Jones golf courses, 7 tennis courts, horseback riding, hiking and jogging trails, 2 pools, wading pool, casino, 3 restaurants, 2 lounges, water-sports center. AE, D, DC, MC, V. EP. Expensive–Very Expensive.*

Hyatt Regency Cerromar Beach. Located 22 miles west of San Juan at Route 693, Km 11.8, smack on the Atlantic, the Cerromar not only has a lovely reef-protected beach, it also claims that its $3 million river pool—with 14 waterfalls, an underwater Jacuzzi, grottoes, and all manner of flumes—is the world's longest freshwater pool. The completely modern seven-story hotel, done up in tropical style, has tile floors, marble baths, air-conditioning, and rooms with a king-size or two double beds. (You'll find somewhat quieter rooms on the west side, away from the pool activity.) Guests at the Cerromar and its sister facility, the Hyatt Dorado Beach a mile down the road, have access to the facilities of both resorts, and colorful red trolleys (free, of course) make frequent runs between the two. *Dorado 00646, tel. 809/796–1234 or 800/ 233–1234, fax 809/796–4647. 504 rooms. Facilities: airport limo, casino, disco, 4 restaurants, 3 bars, 2 18-hole Robert Trent Jones golf courses, 14 tennis courts (2 lighted), pool, sauna, horseback riding, bike rentals, jogging and hiking trails. AE, D, DC, MC, V. EP. Expensive–Very Expensive.*

Humacao
★

Palmas del Mar. This is an already luxurious but still developing resort community, on 2,750 acres of a former coconut plantation on the sheltered southeast coast (about an hour's drive from San Juan). Two hotels, the elegant 23-suite Palmas Inn and 102-room Candelero Hotel, are the centerpieces of the complex. In addition, the resort is host to private homes and condominium villas. *Box 2020, Rte. 906, Humacao 00792, tel. 809/ 852–6000, 800/221–4874, or in NY, 212/983–0393, fax 212/949– 8084. 102 rooms; 85 villas; 1-, 2-, and 3-bedroom suites. Facilities: beach, 18-hole Gary Player golf course, 20 tennis courts (4 lighted), casino, equestrian center, 6 pools, 10 restaurants, bike rentals, fitness center, water-sports center, golf, tennis, and honeymoon packages. AE, DC, MC, V. EP. Expensive– Very Expensive.*

Jayuya **Parador Hacienda Gripinas.** This is a white hacienda with pol-
★   ished wood, beam ceilings, a spacious lounge with rocking chairs, and splendid gardens. The large airy rooms are decorated with native crafts—a very romantic hideaway. *Rte. 527, Km 2.5, Box 387, 00664, tel. 809/828–1717, 809/721–2884, or 800/443–0266. 19 rooms. Facilities: restaurant, lounge, pool, hiking and horseback-riding trails. AE, MC, V. EP. Moderate.*

La Parguera **Parador Villa Parguera.** This parador is a stylish hotel on Phosphorescent Bay, with large, colorfully decorated, air-conditioned rooms. A spacious dining room, overlooking the swimming pool and the bay beyond, serves excellent native and international dishes. *Rte. 304, Box 273, Lajas 00667, tel. 809/ 899–3975 or 800/443–0266. 50 rooms. Facilities: saltwater pool, restaurant, lounge, some facilities for disabled. AE, D, DC, MC. EP. Moderate.*

Mayagüez **Hilton International Mayagüez.** Built on 20 acres overlooking the Mayagüez Harbor, this resort on the island's west coast is about a 2½-hour drive from San Juan. The casino, one of the executive floors, and the Rotisserie restaurant were recently renovated, as was the pool. The hotel is 2 miles from the town of Mayagüez. Also close by are the Boquerón swimming beach, Punta Higuero surfing beach, the Mayagüez Marina for deep-sea fishing, seven excellent skin-diving spots, and two golf courses. *Rte. 2, Km 152.5, Box 3629, 00709, tel. 809/831 –7575, 800/445–8667, or 800/462–3954 in Puerto Rico, fax 809/834–3475. 141 air-conditioned rooms and suites. Facilities: Olympic-size pool, 3 lighted tennis courts, casino, disco, restaurant, lounge. AE, D, DC, MC, V. EP. Expensive– Very Expensive.*

Horned Dorset Primavera. Nestled amid lush landscaping with a dramatic view of the sea, this tranquil resort features 24 suites with private balconies. The architecture here is Spanish, and the location—on the west coast, north of Mayagüez— promises privacy. The resort's beach is long and secluded. *Rte. 429, Km 3, Box 1132, 00743, tel. 809/823–4030 or 809/823–4050, fax 809/823–5580. Facilities: pool, restaurant, lounge. AE, MC, V. EP. Expensive–Very Expensive.*

San Germán **Parador Oasis.** The Oasis, not far from the town's two plazas, was a family mansion 200 years ago. You'll get a better taste for its history in the older front rooms; rooms in the new section in the rear are small and somewhat motelish. *72 Calle Luna, Box 144, 00753, tel. 809/892–1175 or 800/443–0266. 50 rooms. Facilities: restaurant, pool, Jacuzzi, lounge, gym, sauna. AE, DC, MC, V. EP. Moderate.*

Utuado **Parador Casa Grande.** This restored hacienda is on 107 acres of a former coffee plantation, with wood walkways leading to cottages snuggled among the lush green hills. Each unit has four spacious balconied rooms (No. 9 is way in the back, quiet, with a lovely mountain view). There are trails for hikers, hammocks for loafers, and occasional music for romantics. *Box 616, 00761, tel. 809/894–3939 or 800/443–0266. 20 rooms. Facilities: pool, restaurant, lounge. AE, MC, V. EP. Moderate.*

Vieques **Sea Gate.** Occupying 2 acres of a hilltop on the island of Vieques, this whitewashed hotel is a family-run operation. Proprietors John, Ruthye, and Penny Miller will meet you at the airport or ferry, drive you to the beaches, arrange scuba-diving and snorkeling trips, and give you a complete rundown on their adopted home. Accommodations include three-room efficiencies with full kitchens and terraces. *Box 747, 00765, tel. 809/741–4661. 16 rooms. No credit cards. No restaurant. Inexpensive.*

The Arts and Nightlife

¿Qué Pasa?, the official visitors guide, has current listings of events in San Juan and out on the island. Also, pick up a copy of the *San Juan Star, Quick City Guide,* or *Sunspots,* and check with the local tourist offices and the concierge at your hotel to find out what's doing.

Music, Dance, and Theater **LeLoLai** is a year-round festival that celebrates Puerto Rico's Indian, Spanish, and African heritage. Performances take place each week, moving from hotel to hotel, showcasing the island's music, folklore, and culture. Because it is sponsored by the Puerto Rico Tourism Company and major San Juan hotels, passes to the festivities are included in some packages offered by participating hotels. Others can purchase tickets for $8 (adults) and $6 (children) for the series. *Contact the Condado Convention Center, tel. 809/723–3135. Reservations can be made by telephoning 809/722–1513.*

Casinos By law, all casinos are in hotels, primarily in San Juan. The government keeps a close eye on them. Dress for the larger casinos tends to be on the formal side, and the atmosphere is refined. The law permits casinos to operate noon–4 AM, but individual casinos set their own hours.

Casinos are located in the following San Juan hotels (*see* Lodging, *above*): **Condado Plaza Hotel, Caribe Hilton, Carib-Inn, Clarion Hotel, Ramada, Dutch Inn, Sands,** and **El San Juan.** Elsewhere on the island, there are casinos at the **Hyatt Regency Cerromar** and **Hyatt Dorado Beach hotels,** at **Palmas del Mar,** and at the **Hilton International Mayagüez.**

Discos In Old San Juan, young people flock to **Neon's** (203 Calle Tanca, tel. 809/725–7581) and **Lazers** (251 Calle Cruz, tel. 809/721–4479).

In Puerta de Tierra, Condado, and Isla Verde, the thirty-something crowd heads for **Juliana's** (Caribe Hilton Hotel, tel. 809/721–0303), **Isadora's** (Condado Plaza Hotel, tel. 809/721–1000), **Mykonos** (La Concha Hotel, tel. 809/721–6090), and **Amadeus** (El San Juan Hotel, tel. 809/791–1000).

Nightclubs The Sands Hotel's **Players Lounge** brings in such big names as Joan Rivers, Jay Leno, and Rita Moreno. El San Juan's **Tropicoro** presents international revues, occasional top-name entertainers, and a flamenco show four times a week. Try El San Juan's **El Chico** to dance to Latin music in a western saloon setting. The Condado Plaza Hotel has the **Copa Room,** and its **La**

Fiesta sizzles with steamy Latin shows. In Old San Juan, the Hotel El Convento's **Ponce de León Salon** (tel. 809/723–9020) puts on flamenco shows. Young professionals gather at **Peggy Sue** (1 Av. Roberto, tel. 809/722–4750), where the design is 1950s and the music includes oldies and current dance hits.

18 Saba

Updated by
Jordan Simon

This 5-square-mile fairy-tale isle is not for everybody. If you're looking for exciting nightlife or lots of shopping, forget Saba, or take the one-day trip from St. Maarten. There are only a handful of shops, even fewer inns and eateries, and only 1,200 friendly, but shy, inhabitants. Beach lovers should also take note that Saba is a beachless volcanic island, ringed with steep cliffs that plummet sharply to the sea.

So, why Saba? Saba is a perfect hideaway, a challenge for adventurous hikers (Mt. Scenery rises above it all to a height of 2,855 feet); a longtime haven for divers; and, for Sabans, heaven on water. It's no wonder that they call their island the Unspoiled Caribbean Queen.

The capital of Saba (pronounced *SAY*-ba) is The Bottom, which is at the top, not the bottom, of a hill. Meandering goats have the right of way on The Road (there's only one); chickens cross at their own risk. In tiny, toylike villages, narrow paths are bordered by flower-draped walls and neat picket fences. Tidy houses with red roofs and gingerbread trim are planted in the mountainside among the bromeliads, palms, hibiscus, orchids, and Norwegian pines. Saba may be the prettiest island in the Caribbean; it's certainly the most immaculate, with a "once upon a time" storybook enchantment.

Saba is part of the Netherlands Antilles Windward Islands, 28 miles—a 15-minute flight—from St. Maarten. The island is a volcano, extinct for 5,000 years (no one even knows where the crater was). Carib Indians may have hung out here around AD 800; Columbus spotted the little speck in 1493, but somehow Saba remained uninhabited until the first Dutch settlers arrived from Statia in 1640. Having established a foothold—no mean feat—they nestled into a bowl-shape valley and were soon joined by a handful of Scotch, English, and Irish settlers. *Botte* is Dutch for "bowl," but almost at the outset the word was Anglicized to "bottom."

In the 17th, 18th, and early 19th centuries the French, Dutch, English, and Spanish vied for control of the island. Saba changed hands 12 times before permanently raising the Dutch flag.

Sabans are a hardy lot. To get from Fort Bay to The Bottom, the early Sabans carved 900 steps out of the mountainside. Everything that arrived on the island, from a pin to a piano, had to be hauled up. Those rugged steps remained the only way to get about the island until The Road was built by Josephus Lambert Hassell (a carpenter who took correspondence courses in engineering) in the 1940s. An extraordinary feat of engineering, the handmade road took 20 years to build, and if you like roller coasters, you'll love it. The 6½-mile, white-knuckle route begins at sea level in Fort Bay, zigs up to 1,968 feet, and zags down to 131 feet above sea level at the airport.

After the success of the road venture, the Sabans, in 1963, constructed an airport on a flat point of land called (what else?) Flat Point. In 1965, the first television set arrived, and on Christmas Eve, 1970, Sabans received the gift of electricity 24 hours a day! In spite of these modern conveniences, the island's uncomplicated lifestyle has persevered: Saban ladies still hand-embroider the very special, delicate Saba lace—a reminder of Saban gentility that has continued to flourish since the 1870s—and brew the potent rum-based liquor, Saba Spice, sweetened

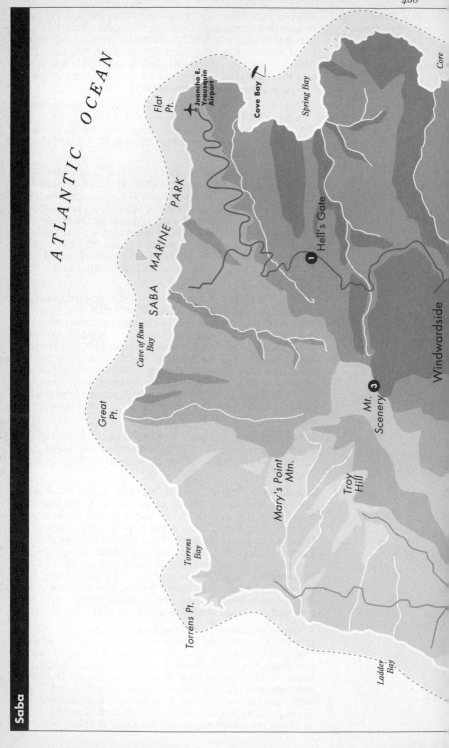

Saba

ATLANTIC OCEAN

Flat Pt.

Juancho E. Yrausquin Airport

Cove Bay

Spring Bay

Core

Great Pt.

Cave of Rum Bay

SABA MARINE PARK

Hell's Gate 1

Torrens Bay

Torrens Pt.

Mary's Point Mtn.

Mt. Scenery 3

Windwardside

Troy Hill

Ladder Bay

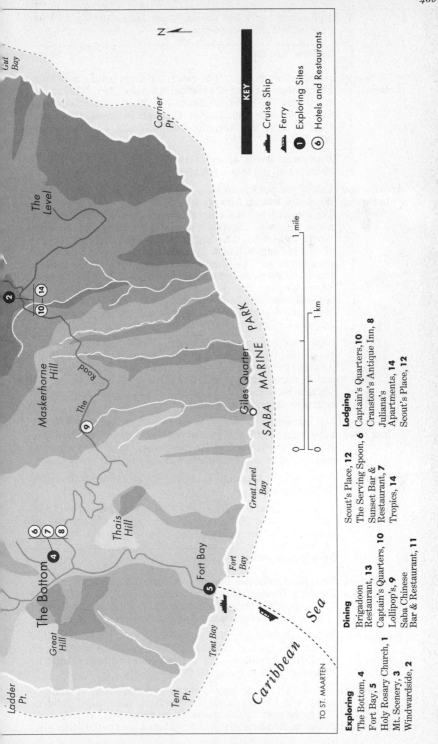

KEY

⛴ Cruise Ship

⛴ Ferry

1 Exploring Sites

⑥ Hotels and Restaurants

N

Gut Bay

Corner Pt.

The Level

2 **⑩** **⑭**

Maskerhorne Hill

The Road

⑨

Giles Quarter

SABA MARINE PARK

Great Level Bay

Thais Hill

⑥ **⑦** **⑧**

④

The Bottom

Great Hill

Ladder Pt.

⑤ *Fort Bay*

Fort Bay

Tent Bay

Tent Pt.

Caribbean Sea

TO ST. MAARTEN

0

0

1 km

1 mile

Exploring

The Bottom, **4**
Fort Bay, **5**
Holy Rosary Church, **1**
Mt. Scenery, **3**
Windwardside, **2**

Dining

Brigadoon
Restaurant, **13**
Captain's Quarters, **10**
Lollipop's, **9**
Saba Chinese
Bar & Restaurant, **11**

Scout's Place, **12**
The Serving Spoon, **6**
Sunset Bar &
Restaurant, **7**
Tropics, **14**

Lodging

Captain's Quarters, **10**
Cranston's Antique Inn, **8**
Juliana's
Apartments, **14**
Scout's Place, **12**

with secret herbs and spices. Older families still bury their dead in their neatly tended gardens.

Before You Go

Tourist Information For help planning your trip, contact the very helpful **Saba Tourist Information Office** (c/o **Medhurst & Assoc. Inc.**, 271 Main St., Northport, NY 11768, tel. 516/261–7474, 212/936–0050, or 800/344–4606) or, in Canada, **New Concepts in Travel** (410 Queens Quai W, Suite 303, Toronto, Ont. M5V 2Z3, Canada tel. 416/362–7707).

Book reservations through a travel agent or over the telephone because mail can take a week or two to reach the island.

Arriving and Departing
By Plane Unless you parachute in, you'll arrive from St. Maarten via **Windward Islands Airways** (tel. 599/5–42255 or 599/5–44237). The approach to Saba's tiny airstrip is the stuff of which nightmares are made. The strip is only 1,312 feet long, but the STOL (Short Takeoff and Landing) aircrafts are built for it, and the pilot needs only half of it. Try not to panic; remember that the pilot knows what he is doing and wants to live just as much as you do. (If you're nervous, don't sit on the right. The wing just misses grazing the cliffside on the approach.) Once you've touched down on the airstrip, the pilot taxis an inch or two, turns, and deposits you just outside a little shoebox called the Juancho E. Yrausquin Airport.

By Boat *Style*, an open-air vessel with an open bar, departs St. Maarten's Great Bay Marina, Phillipsburg, three times weekly at 9 AM and returns at 3 PM. The trip to Saba's Fort Bay takes an hour and the round-trip fare is $45 (tel. 599/5–22167 in St. Maarten). If you take the watery way, however, you'll have lost more than an hour of sightseeing time on Saba.

Passports and Visas U.S. citizens need proof of citizenship. A passport is preferred, but a birth certificate or voter registration card will do (a driver's license will *not* do). British citizens must have a British passport. All visitors must have an ongoing or return ticket.

Language Saba's official language is Dutch, but everyone on the island speaks English.

Precautions Everyone knows everyone else on the island, and crime is virtually nonexistent. Take along insect repellent, sunscreen, and sturdy, no-nonsense shoes that get a good grip on the ground.

Staying in Saba

Important Addresses **Tourist Information:** The amiable Glenn Holm is at the helm of the **Saba Tourist Office** (Windwardside, tel. 599/4–62231, fax 599/4–62350) weekdays 8–noon and 1–5. If needed, the tourist office will help secure accommodations in guest houses.

Emergencies **Police:** call 599/4–63237. **Hospitals:** The **A. M. Edwards Medical Center** (The Bottom, tel. 599/4–63288) is a 10-bed hospital with a full-time physician and various clinics. **Pharmacies:** The **Pharmacy** (The Bottom, tel. 599/4–63289).

Currency U.S. dollars are accepted everywhere, but Saba's official currency is the Netherlands Antilles florin (also called guilder). The exchange rate fluctuates but is around NAf1.80 to U.S.$1. Prices quoted here are in U.S. dollars unless noted otherwise.

Barclays Bank in Windwardside is the island's only major bank; it's open weekdays 8:30–2.

Taxes and Service Charges Hotels collect a 5% government tax. Most hotels and restaurants add a 10%–15% service charge to your bill. The departure tax is $2 from Saba to St. Maarten or St. Eustatius.

Guided Tours All 10 of the taxi drivers who meet the planes at Yrausquin Airport also conduct tours of the island. The cost for a full-day tour is $8 per person with a minimum of four people. If you're just in from St. Maarten for a day trip, have your driver make lunch reservations for you at **The Serving Spoon** or the **Captain's Quarters** (*see* Dining, *below*) before starting the tour. After a full morning of sightseeing, your driver will drop you off for lunch, complete the tour afterward, and return you to Yrausquin in time to make the last flight back to St. Maarten. Guides are available for hiking. Arrangements may be made through the tourist office.

Getting Around
Rental Cars Saba's one and only road—The Road—is a serpentine affair with many a hairpin (read hair-raising) curve. However, if you dare to make your way about by car, there are nine rental cars at **Doc's Car Rentals** (Windwardside, tel. 599/4–62271). Cars can also be rented at **Scout's Place** (Windwardside, tel. 599/4–62205) and at **Juliana's** (Windwardside, tel. 599/4–62269). A car rents for about $35 per day, with a full tank of gas and unlimited mileage. (If you run out of gas, call the island's only gas station, down at Fort Bay, tel. 599/4–63272. It closes at noon.) Scooters can be rented at **Steve's** (tel. 599/4–62507), next to Sandra's Salon & Boutique, for $30–$35 per day, less by the week.

Hitchhiking Carless Sabans get around the old-fashioned ways—walking and hitchhiking (very popular and safe). If you choose to get around by thumbing rides, you'll need to know the rules of The Road. To go from The Bottom (which actually is near the top of the island), sit on the wall opposite the Anglican Church; to go from Fort Bay, sit on the wall opposite Saba Deep dive center, where the road begins to twist upward.

Telephones and Mail To call Saba from the United States, dial 011/599/4 followed by the five-digit number, which always begins with a "6." On the island, it is only necessary to dial the five-digit number. Telephone communications are excellent on the island, and direct-dial long distance is in effect.

To airmail a letter to the United States costs NAf1.30; a postcard, NAf.60.

Opening and Closing Times Businesses and government offices on Saba are open weekdays 8–5.

Exploring Saba

Numbers in the margin correspond to points of interest on the Saba map.

Begin your driving tour with a trip from Flat Point, at the airport, up to Hell's Gate. Because there is only one road, we'll continue along its hairpin curves up to Windwardside, and then on to The Bottom and down to Fort Bay. This cross-island tour will give you a quick overview of tiny Saba, its limited cultural sights, and varied natural settings.

There are 20 sharp curves on The Road between the airport and Hell's Gate. On one of these curves, poised on Hell's Gate's hill, ❶ is the stone **Holy Rosary Church,** which looks medieval but was built in 1962. In the **Community Center** behind the church, village ladies sell blouses, handkerchiefs, tablecloths, and tea towels embellished with the very special and unique Saba lace. These same ladies also turn out innocent-sounding Saba Spice—each according to her old family recipe—a rum-based liqueur that will knock your proverbial socks off.

The Road spirals past banana plantations, oleander bushes, ❷ and stunning views of the ocean below. In **Windwardside,** the island's second-largest village, teetering at 1,968 feet, you'll see rambling lanes and narrow alleyways winding through the hills and a cluster of tiny, neat houses and shops.

On your right as you enter the village is the **Church of St. Paul's Conversion,** a colonial building with a red-and-white steeple. Your next stop should be the **Saba Tourist Office** (just down the road), where you can pick up brochures and books about Saba. You may then want to spend some time browsing through the **Square Nickel,** the **Breadfruit Gallery,** the **Weaver's Cottage, Saba Tropical Arts,** and the **Island Craft Shop** *(see* Shopping, *below).*

The **Saba Museum,** surrounded by lemongrass and clover, lies just behind the Captain's Quarters. There are small signs marking the way to the 150-year-old house that has been set up to look much as it did when it was a sea captain's home. Its furnishings include a handsome mahogany four-poster bed with pineapple design; an antique organ; and, in the kitchen, a rock oven and a hearth. Among the old documents on display is a letter a Saban wrote after the hurricane of 1772, in which he sadly says, "We have lost our little all." The first Sunday of each month, the museum holds croquet matches on its grounds; all-white attire is requested at this formal but fun social event. *Windwardside, no phone. Admission: $1 donation requested. Open weekdays 10–12:30 and 1–3.*

Near the museum are the stone and concrete steps—1,064 of ❸ them—that rise to **Mt. Scenery.** The steps lead past giant elephant ears, ferns, begonias, mangoes, palms, and orchids, up to a mahogany grove at the summit: six identifiable ecosystems in all. New, helpful signs have been posted naming the trees, plants, and shrubs. On a cloudless day the view is spectacular. For a breathtaking journey, have your hotel pack a picnic lunch, wear nonslip shoes, take along a jacket and a canteen of water, and hike away. The round-trip excursion will take about a half day and is best begun in the early morning.

Time Out   **The Corner Deli and Gourmet Shop,** opened by native New Yorker Alan Slatky, who spent 20 years as executive chef at four-star hotels before escaping the rat race, is *the* place to pick up picnic provisions and local gossip. It offers fresh salads, homemade breads, roast chicken, charcuterie, and a little bit of Soho in Saba.

You'll be zigzagging downhill, past the small settlement of St. ❹ John's, from Windwardside to **The Bottom,** which sits in its bowl-shape valley 820 feet above the sea. The Bottom is the seat of government and the home of the lieutenant-governor.

The large house next to Wilhelmina Park has fancy fretwork, a high-pitched roof, and wraparound double galleries.

On the other side of town is the **Wesleyan Holiness Church,** a small stone building, dating from 1919, with bright white fretwork. Stroll by the church, beyond a place called The Gap, and you'll come to a **lookout point** where you can see the roughhewn steps leading down to Ladder Bay. Ladder Bay, with 524 steps, and Fort Bay, with its 200 steps, were the two landing sites from which Saba's first settlers had to haul themselves and their possessions. Sabans sometimes walk down to Ladder Bay to picnic. Think long and hard before you do, bearing in mind that it's 524 steps back *up* to The Road. (Hitchhiking from down there will get you nowhere!)

5 The last stop on The Road is **Fort Bay,** which is the jumping-off place for two of the island's dive operations *(see* Scuba Diving and Snorkeling, *below)* and the St. Maarten ferry docks. There's also a gas station, a 277-foot deep-water pier that accommodates the tenders from ships that call here, and the information center for the **Saba Marine Park** *(see* Scuba Diving and Snorkeling, *below).* Recent hurricane damage has not only been repaired, but a new breakwater built to shelter small boats makes it easier for divers to clamber on board with all their gear. On the quay is a decompression chamber, one of the few in the Caribbean, and **Saba Deep's** dive shop, above which is its new snack bar, **In Two Deep.** It's a good place for getting your breath back over some refreshment while staring out to sea!

Off the Beaten Track

Well's Bay, Saba's famous wandering beach, hasn't reappeared since Hugo. **Cove Bay,** a 20-foot strip of rocks and pebbles laced with gray sand, is now the only place for sunning (and moonlit dips after a Saturday night out). The truly intrepid can then take The Road back to Lower Hell's Gate, where the Old Sulphur Mine Walk leads to bat caves (with typical sulphuric stench) that can—with caution—be explored.

Sports and the Outdoors

Boating   **Saba Deep** (tel. 599/4–63347 or 599/4–62201) conducts one-hour, round-island cruises that include cocktails, hors d'oeuvres, and a sunset you won't soon forget.

Deep-Sea Fishing   **Saba Deep** runs half- and full-day charters that include lunch, drinks, bait, and tackle.

Hiking   You can't avoid some hiking, even if you just go to mail a postcard. The big deal, of course, is Mt. Scenery, with 1,064 slippery steps leading up to the top *(see* Exploring Saba, *above).*

For information about Saba's 18 recommended botanical hiking trails, check with Glenn Holm at the Tourist Office *(see* Important Addresses, *above).* Botanical tours are available upon request. A guided strenuous full-day hike through the undeveloped backside of Mt. Scenery will cost about $50.

Scuba Diving and Snorkeling   The island's first settlers probably found the **Saba Bank** (a fertile fishing ground 3 miles southwest of Saba) a crucial point in their decision to set up house here. In more recent times, divers have enjoyed Saba's coral gardens and undersea mountains. As other islands become "dived out," Saba is dedicated to preserving its marine life, which more than 3,000 divers explore each year. **Saba Marine Park** was established in 1987 to preserve and manage Saba's marine resources. The park circles the entire island, dipping down to 200 feet, and is zoned for diving, swimming, fishing, boating, and anchorage. One of the unique features of Saba's diving is the submerged pinnacles (islands that never made it!) at about the 70-foot depth mark. Here all forms of sea creatures rendezvous. The park offers talks and slide shows for divers and snorkelers and provides brochures and literature on marine life. *Harbor Office, Fort Bay, tel. 599/ 4–63295. Open weekdays 8–5. Call first to see if anyone's around.*

Saba Deep (tel. 599/4–63347) and **Sea Saba** (tel. 599/4–62246) will take you to explore Saba's 25 dive spots. Both offer rental equipment and certified instructors, as well as hotel-dive packages. For inquiries from the United States, direct dial 599/4–63347. Sea Saba's Joan Bourque, whose accomplished photographs are displayed at island galleries, also offers underwater photography lessons.

Wilson's Diving (tel. 599/4–63410) in Fort Bay specializes in shorter dive trips for visitors over from St. Maarten for the day.

Shopping

Gift Ideas The island's most popular purchases are Saba lace and Saba Spice. The history of Saba lace (also called Spanish lace) goes back more than a century to Saban Gertrude Johnson, who attended a Caracas convent school where she learned the art of drawing and tying threads to adorn fine linens. When she returned home in the 1870s, she taught lacemaking to other Saban ladies, and the art has endured ever since. Every weekday Saban ladies display and sell their creations at the Community Center in Hell's Gate. Many also sell their wares from their houses; just follow the signs. Collars, tea towels, napkins, and other small items are relatively inexpensive, but larger items, such as tablecloths, can be pricey. You should also know that the fabric requires some care—it is not drip-dry.

Saba Spice may *sound* as delicate as Saba lace, and the aroma is as sweet as can be. However, the base for the liqueur is 151-proof rum, and all the rest is window dressing.

Shops Saba's famed souvenirs can be found in almost every shop. In Windwardside, stop in at **Saba Tropical Arts, The Square Nickel, Island Craft Shop, Piggy's Boutique, Lynn's Gallery,** and the **Breadfruit Gallery** downstairs from the Tourist Office. Ruth Buchanan's especially lovely clothing designs are available at local galleries and at her own **Weaver's Cottage.** In The Bottom, the **Saba Artisan Foundation** (tel. 599/4–63260) turns out handscreened fabrics that you can buy by the yard or already made into resort clothing for men, women, and children. Look also for the superlative *Saban Cottages: A Book of Watercolors*, sold at the Tourist Office and several stores.

Dining

In most of Saba's restaurants you pretty much have to take potluck. If you don't like what's cooking in one place, you can check out the other restaurants. However, it won't take you long to run out of options, and nowhere will you find gourmet-style cooking. It follows then, that dress here is quite casual wherever you go.

Highly recommended restaurants are indicated by a star ★.

Category	Cost*
Expensive	over $25
Moderate	$20–$25
Inexpensive	under $20

per person, excluding drinks and service

Captain's Quarters. Dining is comfortable on a cool porch surrounded by flowers and mango trees. Under new and enthusiastic ownership, the quality of food has considerably improved, thanks to the new chef, Manuela, whose cuisine artfully blends Dutch, Indonesian, French, and Creole influences. Her $18 three-course Saba menu and $20 chef's menu are wonderful bargains. *Windwardside, tel. 599/4–62201. Reservations required. AE, MC, V. Closed Sept. Moderate–Expensive.*

Brigadoon Restaurant. From the first floor of a colonial building, one can enjoy the street scene passing before this new, open-front restaurant. Fresh fish grilled and with a light Creole sauce is the specialty, but there are also chicken and steak dishes, lobster, and unusual creations like shrimp encrusted with salt and pepper. For light snacks, sandwiches are also offered. *Windwardside, tel. 599/4–62380. Closed lunch. AE, D, MC, V. Moderate.*

Lollipop's. Lollipop is the ironic if affectionate nickname of Carmen, the owner, celebrated for her "sweet" disposition. The outdoor terrace, with stonework and a charming aqua-and-white trellis, is a tranquil place to sample her fine land crab, goat, and fresh grilled fish. *St. John's, tel. 599/4–63330. No credit cards. Inexpensive–Moderate.*

Scout's Place. Here Diana Medero cooks up her version of chicken cordon bleu, braised steak with mushrooms, and curried goat. You can also opt simply to order a sandwich—the crab is best. Wednesday breakfast serves as the unofficial town meeting for expatriate locals, offering the visitor a slice of Saba life. *Windwardside, tel. 599/4–62295. Reservations required. Dinner is at 7:30. MC, V. Inexpensive–Moderate.*

Saba Chinese Bar & Restaurant. This restaurant is a plain house with plastic tablecloths where you can get, among other things, sweet-and-sour pork or chicken, cashew chicken, and some curried dishes. *Windwardside, tel. 599/4–62268. Reservations advised. No credit cards. Closed Mon. Inexpensive.*

The Serving Spoon. Queenie Simmons's house adjoins the sky-blue eight-table restaurant, where plates come heaped with huge portions. Stop by and ask her what she's preparing for the day: she'll start cooking to order. It might be meatballs with rice, baked onion chicken, or curried goat with butter. Eighteen dollars (you can haggle) buys all you can eat and then some. *The Bottom, tel. 599/4–63225. Reservations required. No credit cards. Inexpensive.*

Sunset Bar & Restaurant. Artificial flowers and colorful place mats enliven this humble, homey place, serving authentic Creole food, including heavenly johnnycakes, bread tart pudding, and lip-smacking ribs. *The Bottom, tel. 599/4–63332. No credit cards. Inexpensive.*

Tropics. This new, poolside café across the street from Juliana's offers great views of the Caribbean. This is a place for snacks— sandwiches and burgers—rather than full meals. *Windwardside, tel. 599/4–62469. No credit cards. Inexpensive.*

Lodging

Like everything else on Saba, the guest houses are tiny and tucked into tropical gardens. The selection is limited, and because most restaurants are located in the guest houses, you would do well to take advantage of meal plans. At press time a new hotel and a villa complex were under construction. Both are between Windwardside and The Bottom, off a newly constructed road up the shoulder of Mt. Scenery. The 20-room Queens Gardens Resort in eight acres of tropical gardens should be open for 1993 and will have a restaurant, bar, and swimming pool. An additional 30 units are planned. Saba Villas is planning some 50 luxury villas on 30 acres above the Queens Gardens Resort, which may be available for rental, but they are unlikely to be completed anytime soon.

Highly recommended lodgings are indicated by a star ★.

Category	Cost*
Expensive	over $125
Moderate	$75–$125
Inexpensive	under $74

All prices are for a standard double room for two with breakfast and dinner, excluding 5% tax and a 10%–15% service charge.

Hotels **Captain's Quarters.** All the rooms here are spacious and airy,
★ with antique Victorian furnishings (including four-poster beds) and views of the tiny pool that's perched 1,500 feet above the sea. Four choice bedrooms are in a small house that was built by a Saban sea captain in 1832. Adjacent to the main house is a long bungalow unit with six rooms—Nos. 9 and 10 are slightly larger than the others. Dining is in a shaded garden pavilion surrounded by hibiscus, poinsettia, and papaya trees. New owners, a local Saban family of Scots descent, have taken over and cheerfully renovated the property. Their love for the island is manifest throughout the hotel. *Windwardside, tel. 599/4–62201 or 800/468–0023. 10 rooms with bath. Facilities: pool, restaurant, gift shop, bar, and lounge. AE, MC, V. EP. MAP. Expensive.*

Juliana's Apartments. Near the Captain's Quarters, Mrs. Juliana Johnson offers eight comfortable, tidy studios and a 2½-room apartment with private bath, balcony, kitchenette, living/dining room, bedroom, and a large porch facing the sea. Across the street a pool has been added to the Juliana's complex, along with a café, Tropics, for breakfast and light meals. *Windwardside, tel. 599/4–62269; in the United States, 800/223–9815; in Canada, 800/468–0023. 8 rooms, 1 1-bedroom apartment. Facilities: pool, restaurant. AE, MC, V. EP. Moderate.*

★ **Scout's Place.** Billed as "Bed 'n Board, Cheap 'n Cheerful," Scout's Place, near the post office and within walking distance of Sea Saba Dive Center, was originally the Government Guest House. "Scout" is retired owner Scout Thirkield, who turned his place over to his longtime cook Diana Medero and who is still very much in evidence. Ten new rooms, all with four-poster beds, reproductions of antiques, private balconies, and private baths with hot water, have been added to the original four plain rooms, which have *no* hot water. There's a small breakfast room where you can have cheese omelets, bacon, and coffee. *Windwardside, tel. 599/4-62205. 14 rooms, 12 with private bath. Facilities: restaurant, pool, bar, and gift shop. D, MC, V. EP, MAP. Inexpensive–Moderate.*

Cranston's Antique Inn. There are six cozy rooms with elegant hardwood floors, most with four-poster beds, in this casual spot, is popular with the surfing set. The pool bar often rocks with live music on weekends. *The Bottom, tel. 599/4-63203. 6 rooms, 1 with private bath. Facilities: pool, bar, restaurant. No credit cards. EP. Inexpensive.*

Apartment Rentals Twenty apartments and wood cottages, all with hot water and modern conveniences, are available for weekly and monthly rentals. For information, check with Glenn Holm at the **Saba Tourist Office** *(see* Important Addresses, *above)* or with Medhurst Associates (tel. 516/261-7474 or 800/344-4606), both of which have a listing of all the rental properties.

The Arts and Nightlife

Guido's Pizzeria (Windwardside, tel. 599/4-62330) is transformed into the Mountain High Club and Disco, on Saturday night, and you can dance till 2 AM on Sunday. Do the nightclub scene at **The Lime Tree Bar & Restaurant** (The Bottom, tel. 599/4-63256) and the **Birds of Paradise, aka The Cozy Corner Club** (The Bottom, tel. 599/4-62240), or just hang out at **Scout's Place** or the **Captain's Quarters.** Consult the bulletin board in each village for a listing of the week's events.

19 St. Barthélemy

Updated by
Jordan Simon

Scale is a big part of St. Barthélemy's charm: a lilliputian harbor; red-roof bungalows dotting the hillsides; minimokes, really glorified golf carts, buzzing up narrow roads or through the neat-as-a-pin streets of Gustavia; and exquisite coves and beaches, most undeveloped, all with pristine stretches of white sand. Just 8 square miles, St. Barts is for people who like things small and perfectly done. It's for Francophiles, too. The French cuisine here is tops in the Caribbean, and gourmet lunches and dinners are rallying points of island life. A French *savoir vivre* pervades, and the island is definitely for the style conscious—casual but always chic. This is no place for the beach-bum set.

Rothschild owns property and Rockefeller built an estate here, and for a long time the island, 15 miles from St. Martin in the French West Indies, was the haunt of the well-heeled and well-informed. In the past decade, the tourist base has expanded, and last year more than 100,000 visitors stopped by, including day-trippers from nearby islands and passengers from the occasional cruise ships that now anchor just outside the harbor.

Longtime visitors speak wistfully of the old, quiet St. Barts. While development *has* quickened the pace, the island has not been overrun with prefab condos or glitzy resorts. The largest hotel has only 76 rooms, and the remaining 650 rooms are scattered in cottages and villas around the island; no high rises are allowed. The tiny airport accommodates nothing bigger than 19-passenger planes, and there aren't any casinos or flashy late-night attractions. Moreover, St. Barts is generally not a destination for the budget-minded. Development has largely been in luxury lodgings and gourmet restaurants, and, with the decline in the dollar, island-wide prices have increased sharply in recent years. Despite a couple of lean years for tourism, four new major hotels, the Carl Gustaf, Le Toiny, the Christophe Sofitel, and the Hotel Isle de France, as well as many rental villas, have opened in the past two years.

When Christopher Columbus "discovered" the island in 1493, he named it after his brother, Bartholomeo. A small group of French colonists arrived from nearby St. Kitts in 1656 but were wiped out by the fierce Carib Indians who dominated the area. A new group from Normandy and Brittany arrived in 1694. This time the settlers prospered—with the help of French buccaneers, who took full advantage of the island's strategic location and well-protected harbor. In 1784 the French traded the island to King Gustav III of Sweden in exchange for port rights in Göteborg. He dubbed the capital Gustavia, laid out and paved streets, built three forts, and turned the capital into a prosperous free port. The island thrived as a major shipping and commercial center until the 19th century, when earthquakes, fire, and hurricanes brought financial ruin. Many residents fled for newer lands of opportunity, and in 1878 France agreed to repurchase its beleaguered former colony.

Today the island is still a free port, and, as a dependency of Guadeloupe, is part of an overseas department of France. Dry, sunny, and stony, St. Barts was never one of the Caribbean's "sugar islands," and thus never developed an industrial slave base. Most natives are descendants of those tough Norman and Breton settlers of three centuries ago. They are feisty, industrious, and friendly but insular. However, you will find many

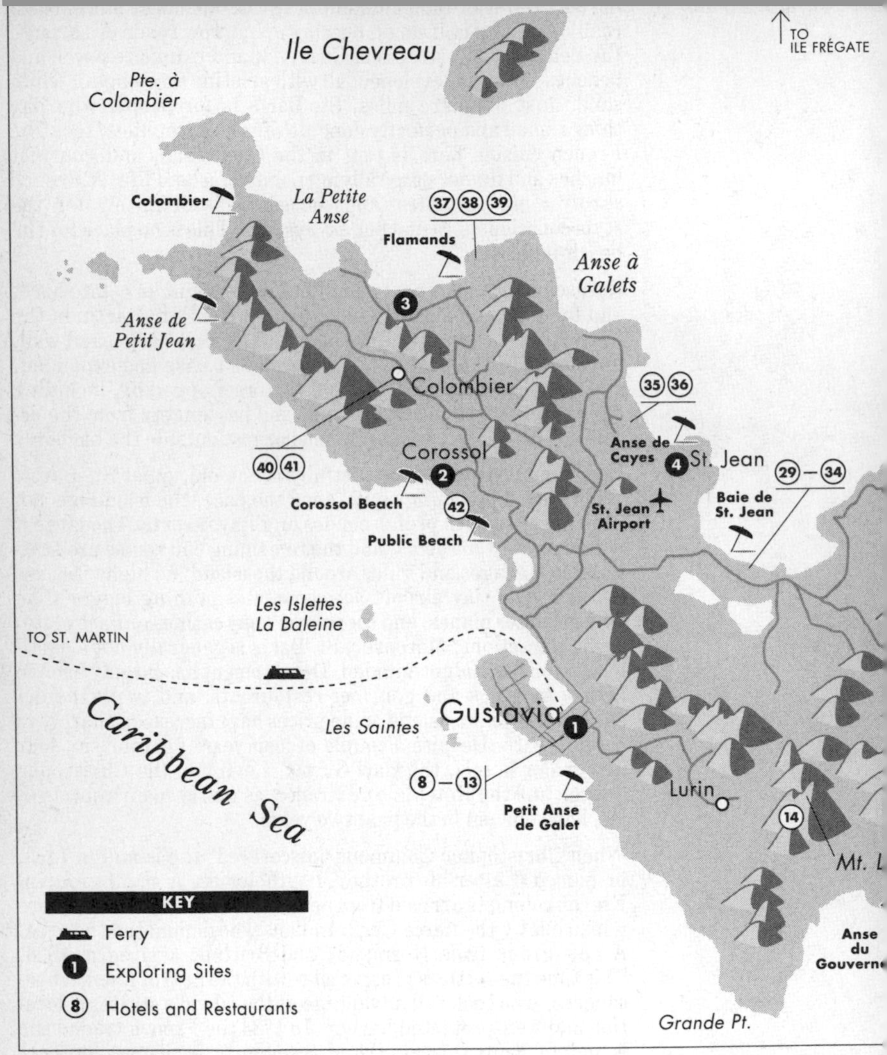
TO
ILE FRÉGATE
Ile Chevreau
Pte. à
Colombier
Colombier
La Petite
Anse
37 38 39
Flamands
Anse à
Galets
3
Anse de
Petit Jean
Colombier
35 36
Anse de
Cayes
4 St. Jean
Corossol
40 41
2
29 – 34
Baie de
St. Jean
Corossol Beach
42
St. Jean
Airport
Public Beach
Les Islettes
La Baleine
TO ST. MARTIN
Caribbean Sea
Gustavia
1
Les Saintes
8 – 13
Petit Anse
de Galet
Lurin
14
Mt. L
KEY
Ferry
Exploring Sites
Hotels and Restaurants
Anse
du
Gouvern
Grande Pt.

Exploring
Anse des Flamands, **3**
Corossol, **2**
Grande Saline, **7**
Gustavia, **1**
Lorient, **5**
St. Jean, **4**
Toiny coast, **6**

Dining
Bartolomeo, **22**
Carl Gustav, **12**
Chez Francine, **30**
Club Lafayette, **16**
Eddy's Ghetto, **11**
François Plantation, **40**
Gloriette, **17**
L'Escale, **8**
L'Hibiscus, **9**
La Fregate, **37**
La Marine, **10**
La Toque Lyonnaise, **19**
Le Flamboyant, **21**
Le Gaiac, **15**
Le Patio, **34**
Le Pelican, **29**
Le Rivage, **18**
Le Sapotillier, **13**
Marigot Bay Club, **23**
Maya's, **42**
New Born, **35**
Topolino, **31**

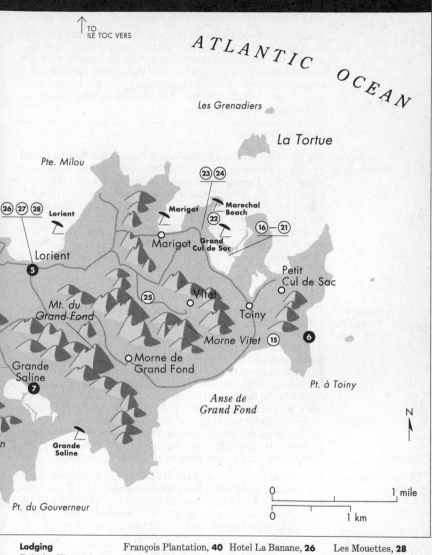

Lodging

Baie des Flamands, **37**
Carl Gustaf, **12**
Castelets, **14**
El Sereno Beach Hotel and Villas, **19**
Filao Beach, **32**

François Plantation, **40**
Grand Cul de Sac Beach Hotel and St. Barths Beach Hotel, **20**
Guanahani, **22**
Hostellerie des Trois Forces, **25**

Hotel La Banane, **26**
Hotel Manapany Cottages, **36**
Isle de France, **39**
La Normandie, **27**
Le P'tit Morne, **41**
Le Toiny, **15**

Les Mouettes, **28**
Marigot Bay Club, **23**
Sea Horse Club, **24**
Tropical Hotel, **33**
Village St. Jean, **34**
White Sand Beach Cottages, **38**

new, young French arrivals—predominantly from northwestern France—who speak English well.

You may hear some old-timers speak the old Norman patois of
their ancestors or see the older women dressed in the traditional garb of provincial France. They have prospered with the
tourist boom, but some are worried that the upward swing of
prices may threaten business, especially tour groups and families. So far, though, this gem of an island continues to draw an
ever-widening circle of fans.

Before You Go

Tourist
Information
For information contact the **French West Indies Tourist Board**
by calling France-on-Call at 900/990–0040 (50¢ per minute) or
write to the **French Government Tourist Office,** 610 5th Ave.,
New York, NY 10020; 9454 Wilshire Blvd., Beverly Hills, CA
90212; 645 N. Michigan Ave., Chicago, IL 60611; 2305 Cedar
Spring Rd., Dallas TX 75201. In Canada contact the French
Government Tourist Office, 1981 McGill College Ave., Suite
490, Montreal, P.Q. H3A 2W9, tel. 514/288–4264; or 1 Dundas
St. W, Suite 2405, Toronto, Ont. M5G 1Z3, tel. 416/593–4723 or
800/361–9099. In the United Kingdom the tourist office can be
reached at 178 Piccadilly, London W1V 0AL, tel. 071/499–
6911.

Arriving and
Departing
By Plane
The principal gateway from North America is St. Maarten's
Juliana Airport, where several times a day you can catch a 10-
minute flight to St. Barts on either **Windward Islands Airways**
(tel. 590/27–61–01) or **Air St. Barthélemy** (tel. 590/27–71–90).
Air Guadeloupe (tel. 590/27–61–90) and **Air St. Barthélemy** offer daily service from Espérance Airport in St. Martin, the
French side of the same island. Air Guadeloupe also has direct
flights to St. Barts from Guadeloupe, Antigua, and San Juan,
while **Virgin Air** (tel. 590/27–71–76) operates daily flights between St. Barts and both St. Thomas and San Juan. Reconfir-
mation on all return interisland flights, even during off-peak
seasons, is strongly recommended. Windward, Air St.
Barthélemy, and Virgin Air also offer charter service.

From the Airport
Airport taxi service costs $5 to $15 (to the farthest hotel). Since
the cabs are unmetered, you may be charged more if you make
stops on the way. Cabs meet all flights, and a taxi dispatcher
(tel. 590/37–66–31) operates from 8:30 AM until the last flight of
the day arrives. Many hotels offer free pick-up and drop-off.

By Boat
Catamarans leave Philipsburg in St. Maarten at 9 AM daily, arriving in Gustavia's harbor around 11 AM. These are one-day,
round-trip excursions (about $50, including open bar), with de-
partures from St. Barts at 3:30 PM. If there's room, one-way
passengers ($25) are often taken as well. Contact **Bobby's**
Marina in Philipsburg (tel. 599/5–23170) for reservations. *St.*
Barth Express, a 12-seat open powerboat, and *La Dame du*
Coeur leave Gustavia at 7:30 AM and 3:30 PM on a varying daily
schedule. The crossing to Marigot, St. Martin, takes one hour.
The boat departs from Marigot at 9 AM and 3:45 PM on the same
varying schedule and goes directly to St. Barts. One-way fare is
$30 and round-trip $60. The **Yacht Charter Agency** (tel. 590/27–
62–38) in Gustavia handles reservations. The *Princess* motorboat makes the same run every Wednesday and can be booked
through **La Marine Service** (tel. 590/27–70–34) in Gustavia. La

Marine also has boats for private charter, as does the Yacht Charter Agency.

Passports and Visas U.S. and Canadian citizens need either a passport (one that expired no more than five years ago will suffice) or other proof of citizenship, such as a notarized birth certificate with a raised seal or a voter registration card, both accompanied by photo identification. A visa is required for stays of more than three months. British citizens need a valid passport.

Language French is the official language, though a Norman dialect is spoken by some longtime islanders. Most hotel and restaurant employees speak English.

Precautions Roads are narrow and sometimes very steep, so check the brakes and gears of your rental car *before* you leave the lot. Some hillside restaurants and hotels require a bit of climbing, so if that's a problem, inquire ahead of time.

Staying in St. Barthélemy

Important Addresses **Tourist Information:** The **Office du Tourisme** (tel. 590/27–87–27) is in a white building on the Gustavia pier. Hours are weekdays 8:30–12:30 and 2–6. The office is closed on weekends and Wednesday afternoons.

Emergencies **Hospitals: Gustavia Clinic** (tel. 590/27–60–35 or 590/27–60–00) is on the corner of rue Jean Bart and rue Sadi Carnot. For the doctor on call, dial 590/27–76–03. **Pharmacies:** There is a pharmacy in Gustavia on rue de la République (tel. 590/27–61–82), and one in St. Jean (tel. 590/27–66–61).

Currency The French franc is legal tender. Figure about 5F to the U.S. dollar. U.S. dollars are accepted everywhere; credit cards are accepted at most shops, hotels, and restaurants. Note: Prices quoted here are in U.S. dollars unless indicated otherwise.

Taxes and Service Charges A 16F departure tax is charged regardless of where you're heading.

Some hotels add a 10%–15% service charge to bills; others include it in their tariffs. All restaurants are required to include a 15% service charge in their published prices. It is especially important to remember this when your credit-card receipt is presented to be signed with the tip space blank, or you could end up paying a 30% service charge.

Most taxi drivers own their vehicles and do not expect a tip.

Guided Tours Tours are by minibus or taxi. An hour-long tour costs about $40 for up to three people and $50 for up to eight people. A five-hour island tour costs about $100 per vehicle. Itineraries are negotiable; other officially recommended tours (of 45 and 90 minutes) are available. Tours can be arranged at hotel desks, through the Tourist Office, or by calling any of the island's taxi operators, including **Hugo Cagan** (tel. 590/27–61–28) and **Florian La Place** (Taxi Drivers Group, tel. 590/27–63–58).

Getting Around You may arrange cab service by calling 590/27–66–32, 590/27–*Taxis* 60–59, or 590/27–63–12. Note: Fares are 50% higher from 8 PM to 6 AM and on Sundays and holidays.

Rental Cars It's more fun to have your own car, and a virtual necessity, though the steep, curvy roads require careful driving. Check the rental car's brakes before you drive away. **Avis** (tel. 590/27–

71–43), **Budget** (tel. 590/27–67–43), and **Europcar** (tel. 590/27–73–33) are represented at the airport, among others. Check with several of the rental counters for the best price. **Mathew Aubin** (tel. 590/27–73–03) often has special discounts. All accept credit cards. You must have a valid driver's license, and in high season there may be a three-day minimum. Suzuki Jeeps, open-sided Gurgels (VW Jeep), and minimokes—all with stick shift only—rent in season for $40–$45 a day, with unlimited mileage and limited collision insurance. Jeeps, sturdier than the chic but rickety minimokes, are preferable. Car-rental reservations are advised, especially during February and around Christmas. Some hotels have their own car fleets, and a car should be rented at the time you make your room reservation. The choice of vehicles may be limited, but many hotels offer 24-hour emergency road service, which most rental companies do not.

Motorbikes Motorbike companies rent bikes for about $25 per day and require a $100 deposit. Call **Rent Some Fun** (tel. 590/27–70–59).

Telephones and Mail To phone St. Barts from the United States, dial 011–590 and the local number. To call the United States from St. Barts, dial 19–1, the area code, and the local number. For St. Martin, dial 3 and the number. For local information, dial 12. Public telephones do not accept coins; they accept Telecartes, a type of prepaid credit card that you can purchase from the post offices at Lorient and Gustavia as well as at the gas station next to the airport. Making an international call with a Telecarte is less expensive than making the call from your hotel.

Mail is slow. It can take up to three weeks for correspondence between the United States and the island. Post offices are in Gustavia and Lorient. It costs 3.10F to mail a postcard to the United States, 3.90F to mail a letter.

Opening and Closing Times Businesses and offices close from noon to 2 during the week and all day Sunday. Shops in Gustavia are open weekdays 8:30–noon and 2–5, and until noon on Saturday. Shops across from the airport and in St. Jean also open on Saturday afternoons and until 7 PM on weekdays. The banks are open weekdays 8–noon and 2–3:30.

Exploring St. Barthélemy

Numbers in the margin correspond to points of interest on the St. Barthélemy map.

Gustavia and the West With just a few streets on three sides of its tiny harbor, Gustavia is easily explored in a two-hour stroll, including time
❶ to browse through shops or visit a café. This will leave you the rest of the afternoon for a trip to the west coast to enjoy a picnic and a swim.

Park your car harborside on the rue de la République, where flashy catamarans, yachts, and sailboats are moored, then head to the **Tourist Office** right on the pier. Here you should pick up an island map and a free copy of *St. Barth Magazine*, a monthly publication on island happenings. Then settle in at either **Bar de l'Oubli** or **Gustavia's Le Select** (*see* Nightlife, *below*), two cafés at the corner of rue de la France and rue de la République, for coffee and croissants and a quick leaf through the listings of the week's events.

As you stroll through the little streets, you will notice that plaques sometimes spell out names in both French and Swedish, a reminder of the days when the island was a Swedish colony. Small shops along **rue du Roi Oscar II** and **rue du Général de Gaulle** sell French perfumes, resortwear, crystal, gold jewelry, and other luxury items. You might want to stop by **La Rotisserie** (rue du Lafayette and rue du Roi Oscar II) or **Taste Unlimited** (rue du Général de Gaulle) to pick up the makings for a picnic.

A **market** has been set up where ladies from Guadeloupe and Dominica have arranged colorful displays of tropical fruits and vegetables. And if you feel like a swim, drive around the end of the harbor to **Petit Anse de Galet.** This quiet little *plage* is also known as Shell Beach because of the tiny shells heaped ankledeep in some places.

On the other side of the harbor, at the point, locals are proud of the new **Municipal Museum,** detailing the island's history. *No phone. Admission: 10F. Open weekdays 8–noon and 1:30– 5:50, Sat. 8:30–noon, closed Sun.*

Head back the way you came and turn off at the sign for Lurin. The views up the winding road overlooking the harbor are spectacular. After about five minutes, look for a sign to Plage du Gouverneur. A small rocky route off to the right will take you bumping and grinding down a steep incline to **Anse du Gouverneur,** one of St. Barts's most beautiful beaches, where pirate's treasure is said to be buried. If the weather is clear, you will be able to see the islands of Saba, St. Eustatius, and St. Kitts.

Time Out The hilltop **Sante Fe Restaurant** (Morne Lorne, at the turnoff to Gouverneur's Beach, tel. 590/27–61–04) is a popular spot for sundowners, sunsets, and the island's best hamburgers. Sunday afternoons find it jammed with Americans and British cheering their favorite teams on the closed-circuit TV.

Corossol, Colombier, Flamands Starting at the intersection on the hilltop overlooking the airport (known as Tourmente), take the road to Public Beach and on to **Corossol,** a two-street fishing village with a little beach.
2 Corossol is where the island's French provincial origins are most evident. Residents speak an old Norman dialect, and some of the barefoot older women still wear traditional garb— ankle-length dresses and starched white sunbonnets called *quichenottes* (*kiss-me-not* hats). The women don't like to be photographed. However, they are not shy about selling you some of their handmade straw work—handbags, baskets, broad-brim hats, and delicate strings of birds—made from lantania palms. The palms were introduced to the island 100 years ago by foresighted Father Morvan, who planted a grove in Corossol and Flamands, thus providing the country folk with a living that is still pursued today. Here, too, is the **Inter Oceans Museum** (tel. 590/27–62–97), which features a small but excellent collection of marine shells from around the world. *Tel. 590/27–62–97. Admission: 20F. Open daily 10–5.*

3 From Corossol, head down the main road about a mile to **Anse des Flamands,** a wide beach with several small hotels, including the new Hotel Isle de France, and many rental villas. From here, take a brisk hike to the top of what is believed to be the now-extinct volcano that gave birth to St. Barts. From the peak you can take in the gorgeous view of the islands.

A drive to the end of Flamands Road brings you to a rocky footpath that leads to the island's most remote beach, **Anse de Colombier.** If you're not up to the 30-minute hike, take a 3 PM sail from Gustavia (*see* Sports and the Outdoors, *below*). You'll have time for a swim and refreshments before the sunset sail back to the harbor.

St. Jean, Grand Cul de Sac, Saline ❹ Brimming with bungalows, bistros, sunbathers, and windsurfing sails, the half-mile crescent of sand at **St. Jean** is the island's most famous beach. Lunch at a beachside bistro, such as **Le Pelican** or **Chez Francine** (*see* Dining, *below*), perhaps interrupted by a swim in the surf, is de rigueur, followed by a stroll through nearby boutiques.

❺ Leaving St. Jean, take the main road to **Lorient.** On your left are the royal palms and rolling waves of Lorient Beach. Lorient, site of the first French settlement, is one of the island's two parishes, and a newly restored church, historic headstones, a school, post office, and gas station mark the spot.

Turn right before the gleaming white Lorient cemetery. In a short while you'll reach a dusty cutoff to your right. The pretty little Creole house on your left is home to Ligne de Cosmetiques M (*see* Shopping, *below*). Behind it is one of St. Barthélemy's treasured secrets, **Le Manoir.** The 1610 Norman manor was painstakingly shipped and reconstructed in 1984 by the charming Jeanne Audy Rowland in tribute to the island's Viking forebears. The tranquil surrounding courtyard and garden contain a waterfall and a lily-strewn pool. Madame Rowland graciously allows visitors. The manor (and its cottage) are also available at a reasonable weekly rent, "but you must have an artist's soul," she requests sweetly and earnestly.

Retrace your route back to Lorient and continue along the coast. Turn left at the Mont Jean sign. Your route rolls around the island's pretty windward coves, past **Pointe Milou,** an elegant residential colony, and on to **Marigot,** where you can pick up a bottle of fine wine at **La Cave.** The bargain prices may surprise you (*see* Shopping, *below*).

The winding road passes through the mangroves, ponds, and beach of **Grand Cul de Sac,** where there are plenty of excellent beachside restaurants and water-sports concessions.

Time Out **Chez Pompi** (Petit Cul de Sac, tel. 590/27-75-67), on the road to Toiny, is a delightful cottage straight from a Cezanne painting. Pompi (aka Louis Ledee) is an artist of some repute, whose naive, slightly abstract artwork clutters the walls of his tiny studio. You can browse and chat with the amiable M. Pompi while enjoying his fine creole and country French cuisine.

❻ Over the hills beyond Grand Cul de Sac is the much photographed **Toiny coast.** Drystone fences crisscross the steep slopes of Morne Vitet along a rocky shoreline that resembles the rugged coast of Normandy. The road turns inland and up the slopes of Morne de Grand Fond. At the first fork (less than a mile), the road to the right leads back to Lorient. A left-hand turn at the next intersection will bring you within a few min-

❼ utes to a dead end at **Grande Saline.** Ten years ago the big salt ponds of Grande Saline were shut down after a half-century of operation. The place looks desolate, but climb the short hillock behind the ponds for a surprise—the long arc of **Anse de Grande Saline.**

Time Out Stop for lunch, dinner, or drinks at **Le Tamarin** (Saline, tel. 590/ 27–72–12), a delightful spot by a huge tamarind tree. Paco the peevish pet parrot greets guests. You may want to try your hand (if Paco doesn't get it first) at archery between sipping drinks and ordering from the imaginative specials listed on a blackboard.

Beaches

There are nearly 20 *plages* (beaches), each with a distinctive personality and all of them public. Topless sunbathing is common, but nudism is forbidden. Here are the main attractions:

St. Jean is like a mini Côte d'Azur—beachside bistros, bungalow hotels, bronze beauties, and lots of day-trippers. The reef-protected strip is divided by Eden Rock promontory, and there's good snorkeling west of the rock. **Lorient** is popular with St. Barts's families and surfers, who like its rolling waves. **Marigot** is a quiet fishing beach with good snorkeling along the rocky far end. Shallow, reef-protected **Grand Cul de Sac** is especially nice for small children and Windsurfers; it has excellent lunch spots and lots of pelicans. Around the point, next to the Guanahani Hotel, is tiny **Marechal Beach,** which offers some of the best snorkeling on the island. Secluded **Grande Saline,** with its sandy ocean bottom, is just about everyone's favorite beach and is great for swimmers. Despite the law, young and old alike go nude on this beach. It can get windy here, so go on a calm day. **Anse du Gouverneur** is even more secluded and equally beautiful, with good snorkeling and views of St. Kitts, Saba, and St. Eustatius.

A five-minute walk from Gustavia is **Petit Anse de Galet,** named after the tiny shells on its shore. Both **Public Beach** and **Corossol Beach** are best for boat- and sunset-watching. The beach at **Colombier** is the least accessible but the most private; you'll have to take either a rocky footpath from La Petite Anse or brave the 30-minute climb down a cacti-bordered trail from the top. **Flamands** is the most beautiful of the hotel beaches—a roomy strip of silken sand. Back toward the airport, the surf at **Anse de Cayes** is rough for swimming, but great for surfing.

Sports and the Outdoors

Boating St. Barts is a popular yachting and sailing center, thanks to its location midway between Antigua and St. Thomas. Gustavia's harbor, 13 to 16 feet deep, has mooring and docking facilities for 40 yachts, with good anchorages available at Public, Corossol, and Colombier. **Loulou's Marine** (tel. 590/27–62–74) is the place for yachting information and supplies. **Marine Service** (tel. 590/27–70–34), operated by Henri and Dominique Jouan, offers full-day outings on a 40-foot catamaran to the uninhabited Ile Fourchue for swimming, snorkeling, cocktails, and lunch at $90 per person. Marine Service also arranges deep-sea fishing trips, with a full-day charter of a 32-foot crewed cabin cruiser running $800. You can take an hour's cruise on the

glass-bottom boat *L'Aquascope* by contacting **Marine Service,**
and the **Yacht Charter Agency** (tel. 590/27–62–38) offers sunset
and half- and full-day sails. Marine and La Maison de la Mer
(tel. 590/27–81–00) also have unskippered motor rentals for
about $260 a day.

Diving and Deep-sea fishing can be arranged through **Yacht Charter Agen-**
Deep-Sea Fishing cy (tel. 590/27–62–38), **Marine Service** (tel. 590/27–70–34), or
with **Pierre Choisy** (tel. 590/27–61–22) on his *Bertram*. Marine
also operates a PADI diving center, with scuba-diving trips for
about $50 per person, gear included. **Club La Bulle** (tel. 590/27–
68–93) and PADI-certified **Dive with Dan** (tel. 590/27–64–78)
are other scuba options.

Horseback Riding Laure Nicolas leads two-hour excursions for $35 per person
from **Ranch des Flamands** (Anse des Flamands, tel. 590/27–
80–72).

Tennis There are two tennis courts at the **Guanahani** (tel. 590/27–66–
60), **Le Flamboyant Tennis Club** (tel. 590/27–69–82), and the
Sports Center of Colombier (tel. 590/27–61–07). The Manapany
(tel. 590/27–66–55), the **Taiwana** (tel. 590/27–65–01), the **Isle**
de France (tel. 590/27–61–81), which also has the island's only
squash court **Les Ilets de la Plage** (tel. 590/27–62–38), and the
St. Barths Beach Hotel (tel. 590/27–62–73) each have one court.

Windsurfing Windsurfing fever has definitely caught on here. Boards can be
rented for about $20 an hour at water-sports centers along St.
Jean and Grand Cul de Sac beaches. Lessons are offered for
about $40 an hour at **St. Barth Wind School** (St. Jean, tel. 590/
27–70–96), **Wind Wave Power** (St. Barths Beach Hotel, tel. 590/
27–62–73), and at **Grand Bay Watersports** (Guanahani, tel.
590/27–66–60). A new windsurfing school has opened at the **El**
Sereno Beach Hotel (tel. 590/27–64–80) on Grand Cul de Sac
Bay.

Shopping

St. Barts is a duty-free port, and there are especially good bargains in jewelry, porcelain, imported liquors, and French perfumes, cosmetics, and designer resortwear.

Shopping Areas Shops are clustered in **Gustavia, St. Jean's Commercial Center,**
and the **Villa Creole,** a cottage complex also in St. Jean. More
shops and a gourmet supermarket are located across from the
airport at **La Savane Commercial Center.**

Good Buys Stop in Corossol to pick up some of the intricate straw work
Island Crafts (wide-brim beach hats, mobiles, handbags) that the ladies of
Corossol create by hand (*see* Exploring St. Barthélemy,
above). For a very special kind of basket, visit **René Brin,** the
last practitioner of a dying art form. His beautiful and sturdy
fishermen's baskets each take three weeks to make and will last
30 years. For directions to his house/workshop in Lurin, contact Elise Magras at the Tourist Information Center (tel. 590/
27–87–27). In Gustavia, look for hand-turned pottery at **St.**
Barts Pottery (tel. 590/27–62–74) and exotic coral and shark's
tooth and shell jewelry at the **Shell Shop** (no phone). In
Colombier you'll find one of the best buys on the island, the ceramics of **Jean-Yves Froment. Superb local skin care products**
are available at Ligne de Cosmetiques M (tel. 590/27–82–63, *see*
Exploring St. Barthélemy, *above*).

Wine and Gourmet
Shops

Wine lovers will enjoy **La Cave** (Marigot, tel. 590/27–63–21), where an excellent collection of French vintages is stored in temperature-controlled cellars. Also check out **La Cave du Port Franc** (tel. 590/27–71–75), on the far side of the harbor, for vintage wines, contemporary paintings, and objets d'art. Look for the local Belon's P Punch, which packs a wallop.

For exotic groceries or picnic fixings, stop by St. Barts's fabulous gourmet delis—**La Rotisserie** (tel. 590/27–63–13) on rue du Roi Oscar II (branches in Villa Creole and Pointe Milou) and **Taste Unlimited** (tel. 590/27–70–42) on rue du Général de Gaulle. In Grand Fond, stop by **La Cuisine a Michel** (no tel.), a simple shack doling out delectable $10 take-out meals from the original chef at Castelets.

Dining

Dining out is a ritual on St. Barts, and since the ambience at the restaurants is tonier than on other islands so is the fashion. Anything goes as long as its tasteful. The quality of fare is generally high and so are the prices, which are among the steepest in the Caribbean. The island's culinary reputation and scarcity of fresh ingredients have kept the prices high. Many places offer prix-fixe menus, which usually offer superb value. Italian, Creole, and French/Creole restaurants tend to be less expensive. *Accras* (salt cod fritters) with Creole sauce (minced hot peppers in oil), spiced christophine (a kind of squash), *boudin Créole* (a very spicy blood sausage), and a lusty *soupe de poissons* (fish soup) are some of the delicious and ubiquitous Creole dishes.

Highly recommended restaurants are indicated by a star ★.

Category	Cost*
Very Expensive	over $60
Expensive	$45–$60
Moderate	$30–$45
Inexpensive	under $30

*per person, excluding drinks, service, and sales tax (4%)

Carl Gustav. Not even the sweeping views of the harbor can detract from the sublime creations of Patrick Gateau. M. Gateau, who trained at the Crillon in Paris, deftly weaves tropical influences into his classical cuisine. Among his standouts are fried crayfish and cabbage in honey and soy sauce and grilled salmon with leeks and a hint of vanilla. The $27 prix fixe lunch menu is an amazing bargain. *Rue des Normands, Gustavia, tel. 590/37–82–83. Reservations required. AE, D, MC, V. Very Expensive.*
Le Gaiac. Cool breezes waft through this refined open-air restaurant in the fabulous new Le Toiny. Jean Christophe Perrin studied with the Troisgros brothers, as well as with Michel Rostang. Their influence clearly shows in his elegant preparations, which are perhaps a tad rich for the climate. But who could complain after sampling his *farandole de canard* (five preparations of duck) or breast of chicken sliced with foie gras? The manager has promised to overhaul the outrageously expensive wine list. *Anse de Toiny, tel. 590/27–88–88. Reservations required. AE, MC, V. Expensive–Very Expensive.*

Bartolomeo. There's a small bar as you enter, and at the rear is a pretty dining room that seats 35. The eclectic menu includes such pleasant surprises as lobster-stuffed ravioli and chicken breasts with ratatouille. For dessert, don't miss the luscious crème brûlée. *Guanahani, Grand Cul de Sac, tel. 590/27–66–60. Reservations required. AE, MC, V. Dinner only. Expensive.*

Club Lafayette. This "in" beach bistro offers simple but tasty lunch fare to a casually chic crowd. The tourists pick up high tabs for small portions. Grilled ("barbecued" in local parlance) lobster or crispy duck, followed by a fruit sherbet or *tarte tatin*, is the way to go. *Grand Cul de Sac, tel. 590/27–62–51. Reservations suggested. No credit cards. Closed end of May–mid-Nov. Expensive.*

★ **François Plantation.** The approach to the dining room, through a flower-draped, lantern-hung arbor, is made for dramatic entrances. Young talented chef Christophe Picard's cuisine legere, concentrating on the food's natural flavors, is just as dramatic: warm sea-trout flan served with coriander-flavored crisp vegetable salad, paprika-scented cold codfish, white cheese soup, and red mullet steamed in vanilla bourbon dancing in pesto. You can also order the rare Coutancie beef: the cattle must drink three liters of beer and receive a 20-minute rubdown daily, among other strict guidelines, to qualify. *Colombier, tel. 590/27–61–26. Reservations essential. AE, V. Dinner only. Expensive.*

★ **Le Sapotillier.** Dining in this cozy boîte or in the courtyard under a grand old sapodilla tree will make you feel like guests in the owners' house—yet, their food is anything but down-home. Among the many marvelous selections are lamb perfumed with thyme and pumpkin, red snapper in ginger sauce with gnocchi, and young rabbit in puff pastry. At 195F and 250F, respectively, the three-course table d'hote and menu traditionnel are superb buys. *Rue de Centenaire, Gustavia, tel. 590/27–60–28. Reservations required. MC, V. Expensive.*

L'Hibiscus. This popular in-town spot has a romantic terrace overlooking the harbor and a jazz trio playing nightly until 11:30. Although the food has improved, this is really a place for a lively atmosphere from which to catch a great sunset. *Rue Thiers, Gustavia, tel. 590/27–64–82. Dinner reservations required. AE, MC, V. Expensive.*

★ **La Toque Lyonnaise.** In pleasant outdoor dining at El Sereno Beach Club, chef Michel Fredric, who apprenticed with the masters Bocuse, Troisgros, and Veras, creates a three-course *menu dégustation* for 240F. Courses vary, but a popular menu starts with a roquefort terrine with pears poached in Sauternes, followed by a salmon steak in its "passion" sabayon and a superb cinnamon apple tarte. À la carte choices may include foie gras encased in candied sweetbreads, croustillant of lobster perfumed with saffron, and rack of lamb in tapenade. M. Fredric learned quickly how to adapt classical recipes to the sultry surroundings; he may be St. Barthélemy's top hotel *chef de brigade. El Sereno Beach Hotel, Grand Cul de Sac, tel. 590/27–64–80. Reservations suggested. Dinner only. AE, DC, MC, V. Moderate–Expensive.*

Le Flamboyant. This restaurant features fine food on a charming, cozy terrace. Don't miss the tagliatelle St. Jacques for a starter. For dinner, the grilled lobster or fish, accompanied by a bottle of chilled Sancerre, is excellent. Be sure to get a table with a view. *Grand Cul de Sac, tel. 590/27-75-65. AE, V. Closed Mon. Dinner only. Moderate-Expensive.*

Le Pelican. Energetic Gilbert has one of the most deservedly popular seashore restaurants for lunch. At picnic tables under awnings, start with baby shrimp in avocado and follow it with the local grilled fish or a mammoth lobster, which you may choose from the tank. For those who like it hot and spicy, be sure to ask for Gilbert's chili sauce. At dinner inside, the menu is more elaborate and expensive, with a pianist and chanteuse accompanying your meal. Locals cluster around the piano bar for late-night desserts long after other restaurants have locked their doors. *St. Jean Bay, tel. 590/27-64-64. AE, MC, V. Moderate-Expensive.*

Maya's. Set dramatically on Public Beach, this is still one of the hippest eateries on the island. The fare is simple but freshly prepared, with only four or five choices per course, such as lobster brochettes or curried chicken. The scrumptious cakes and pies are baked on the premises. The schizophrenic service ranges from haughty to harried to helpful all in one evening. Yet somehow the atmosphere remains incomparably convivial. *Public Beach, tel. 590/27-73-61. Reservations suggested. AE, D, MC, V. Moderate-Expensive.*

★ **Eddy's Ghetto.** The combination of imaginatively prepared, modestly priced fare—crab salad, ragout of beef, crème caramel—served in a disarmingly fun-loving atmosphere turned Edward Stakelborough's restaurant into an instant success when it opened in 1989. The crowd is lively, the wine list impressive. *Gustavia, just off rue du Général de Gaulle. No phone. Reservations requested. No credit cards. Moderate.*

La Fregate. Solange Greaux is the charming hostess, Thierry and Jean-Pierre the inventive chefs at this casual restaurant. You may order something from the grill (selecting one of 11 sauces) or opt for the fine regular menu. There are also two reasonable set-priced Creole menus. *Anse des Flamands, tel. 590/27-64-85. Reservations suggested. MC, V. Moderate.*

★ **Le Patio.** Gourmet pizzas, salads, pastas, brochettes, and hamburgers are offered for lunch. In the evening there's all that, plus fancier Italian fare—all reasonably priced, especially the homemade pasta. You'll like the breezy outdoor and indoor dining rooms, the views of the bay, and the friendly family service. *St. Jean, tel. 590/27-61-39. MC, V. Closed Wed. Moderate.*

Marigot Bay Club. Generous portions and consistent quality help make this 16-table beachside place a favored lunch and dinner spot. Lightly spiced Creole dishes and simple fish and seafood entrées are featured, and the friendly owners are always on hand to explain the menu. *Marigot, tel. 590/27-75-45. Reservations required. AE, V. Closed Sun. and lunch Mon. Moderate.*

New Born. With the closing of the delightful La Santoise, this unadorned but pleasant restaurant offers the closest thing to authentic Creole cooking on St. Barth's. The fresh seafood is caught right at the beach steps away. Mouthwatering accras, turtle steak, salt cod salad, and coconut flan may make up one memorable dinner. *Anse des Cayes, tel. 590/27-67-07. Reservations suggested. MC, V. Moderate.*

Gloriette. This beachside bistro serves delicious local dishes such as crunchy accras and grilled red snapper with Creole sauce. Light salads and Creole dishes are served at lunch, and the house wine is always good. *Grand Cul de Sac, tel. 590/27-*

75–66. No credit cards. Closed Sun. evening. Inexpensive–Moderate.

La Marine. Mussels from France arrive on Thursday and in-the-know islanders are there to eat them at dockside picnic tables. The menu always includes fresh fish, hamburgers, and omelets. *Rue Jeanne d'Arc, Gustavia, tel. 590/27–70–13. No credit cards. Inexpensive–Moderate.*

★ **Le Rivage.** This popular and very casual Creole establishment on the beach at Grand Cul de Sac serves delicious lobster salad, accras, and fresh grilled fish. The relaxed atmosphere and surprisingly low prices make for a very enjoyable time. *Grand Cul de Sac. tel. 590/27–60–70. AE, MC, V. Open for lunch and dinner. Closed Thurs. Inexpensive–Moderate.*

★ **L'Escale.** This pretty, cheery, and very popular restaurant is located on the waterfront of the far side of Gustavia's harbor. Chef Eric Dugast cooks up the best pizza on the island, while Pierre Lebrech prepares first-rate filet Mignon, seafood, and pastas. With friendly service and low prices, it all adds up to a real winner! *Gustavia, tel. 590/27–81–06. MC, V. Closed Tues. Dinner only. Inexpensive–Moderate.*

Chez Francine. Swimsuit-clad patrons lunch on the terrace or at wood tables set in the sand. Fewer day trippers from St. Martin find their way here than they do to the Pelican, so it is quieter and has better prices. The lunch-only menu features grilled chicken, beef, and lobster, all served with crispy french fries for $15. *St. Jean Bay, tel. 590/27–60–49. MC, V. Inexpensive.*

Topolino. Popular with families, Topolino's offerings range from hearty Italian dishes to pizza. Trap your own lobster in the pond. *St. Jean, tel. 590/27–70–92. MC, V. Inexpensive.*

Lodging

Expect to be shocked at the prices that you must pay for accommodations. You pay for the privilege of staying on the island rather than for the hotel. Even at $500 a night, bedrooms tend to be small, but that does not deter the lure of St. Barts for those who can afford it. Away from the beaches are a number of small hotels and a multitude of rental bungalows that offer less expensive accommodations. Most hotels offer either CP or EP, though MAP is sometimes available.

Highly recommended lodgings are indicated by a star ★.

Category	Cost*
Very Expensive	over $400
Expensive	$300–$400
Moderate	$200–$300
Inexpensive	under $200

All prices are for a standard double room for two, excluding a 10%–15% service charge; there is no government room tax.

Hotels **Carl Gustaf.** At last the island has a hotel where the rooms are
★ large, spacious, and comfortable—all with spectacular views. All accommodations are either one- or two-bedroom suites, and each one looks out onto pretty Gustavia harbor. The bedrooms, with huge beds draped with large, cheerfully patterned cover-

lets, are cooled by an overhead fan and individually controlled air-conditioning. The bathroom, smacking a little of nouveau-riche taste with gold-plated faucets, does not have a tub—just a shower. On the patio are deck chairs and a table for morning croissants or dinner in the moonlight with the private (plunge) pool floodlit from beneath the surface. The breeze from the patio flows into a sitting room furnished with a couch, bamboo easy chairs, a table, and a television. (There is another television in the bedroom.) Off the sitting room is an adequate kitchenette, should you plan a small cocktail party. In the main building is a crisply laid-out dining room—again with an unparalleled view of Gustavia—and a piano bar lounge. *Box 700, rue des Normands, Gustavia 97133, tel. 590/27–82–83 or 800/645–6030, fax 590/27–82–37. 14 1- and 2-bedroom suites. Facilities: restaurant, pool, private plunge pools, fitness club, sauna. AE, DC, MC, V. CP. Very Expensive.*

Guanahani. This 7-acre resort adjoining the Rothschild estate is the island's largest. Gray-roof bungalows nestle in the hillside and some have lovely private pools. Oceanfront suites are the best—the bungalows farther up the hill are a hike away from the beach and the action. Thanks to a recent refurbishment, the resort now just meets the standards of the Leading Hotels of World, of which the hotel is a member. *Box 109, Grand Cul de Sac 97133, tel. 590/27–66–60, fax 590/27–70–70. 17 double rooms, some with ocean views; 33 deluxe doubles; 3 spa suites with Jacuzzis; 27 1-bedroom suites with private pool and kitchens. Facilities: 2 restaurants, 2 lighted tennis courts, 2 pools, 1 with Jacuzzi, 2 beaches, water-sports center, dive shop, beauty salon. AE, MC, V. CP. Very Expensive.*

Isle de France. This intimate luxury enclave re-creates gracious plantation living (on a scale no doubt unfamiliar to the original hardy Norman settlers). There are spacious garden and seaside rooms on lovely Flamands Beach, each individually decorated with mahogany furniture and island prints. All feature a private bath (with two sinks and a tub), a safe, a cable TV and a phone. Garden bungalows include kitchenettes. *Box 612, Baie des Flamands 97098, tel. 590/27–61–81, fax 590/27–86–83. 24 rooms, 5 1-bedroom suites. Facilities: pool, beach, bar, restaurant, tennis. AE, MC, V. CP. Very Expensive.*

Hotel Manapany Cottages. A ramshackle entry road ends at this luxury enclave, which is built around Anse des Cayes. Accommodations vary from St. Barts–style cottages and suites tucked into the hillside to much-in-demand beachfront suites with marble baths and four-poster beds. Bronze bodies line the pretty but small pool, and the most frequent guests are Italians arriving on packaged vacations (the manager is Italian). The small beach sometimes has a strong undercurrent, but the waves are great for surfing. *Box 114, Anse des Cayes 97133, tel. 590/27–66–59; in the U.S., 212/757–0225, fax 590/27–75–28. 20 cottages and 12 club suites. Facilities: 2 restaurants, 2 bars, pool, Jacuzzi, beach, bocce-ball court, exercise room, boutique, lighted tennis court, water-sports center. AE, MC, V. CP. Very Expensive.*

★ **Le Toiny.** This posh new villa resort is that rare St. Barth's property where the billeting lives up to its billing. The villas are staggered along the hillside to afford total privacy and spectacular views of the neighboring islands. The exquisitely appointed units, with mahogany furnishings and oriental-style Italian fabrics, achieve the perfect balance between modern and traditional, elegant and comfortable. Though it provides everything one needs—minibar, two TVs, VCR, hairdryer, fax, safety deposit, stereo, air-conditioning, three direct-dial telephones, private balcony, and plunge pool—the overall effect is welcoming, rather than overpowering. *Anse Toiny 97133, tel. 590/27–88–88, fax 590/27–89–30. 12 1-bedroom cottages. Facilities: bar, restaurant, beach, pool. AE, MC, V. EP. Very Expensive.*

Filao Beach. The smallish rooms in single-story units form a semicircle around the pool and terrace restaurant. All rooms are carpeted and have air-conditioning. Bathrooms are compact but neat and include toiletries. Rooms closer to the beach rise accordingly in price, but the "garden rooms" are still only steps away from the sands. Breakfast is served in the rooms, and only lunch is served at the poolside restaurant. *Box 167, St. Jean 97133, tel. 590/27–64–84, 800/742–4277 in the U.S., fax 590/27–62–24. 30 rooms. Facilities: pool, luncheon, restaurant/bar. CP. Expensive–Very Expensive.*

★ **El Sereno Beach Hotel and Villas.** A quiet, casually chic ambience pervades, and manager Marc Llepez is a perfect host. Small but tasteful rooms, all with air-conditioning, minifridge, satellite TV, and high-walled patio, surround a central garden. The beach is steps away. Nine new villas are on the nearby hillside. The restaurant food is outstanding, and the clientele includes many repeats. This is one of the better-value hotels on St. Barts. *Box 19, Grand Cul de Sac 97133, tel. 590/27–64–80, fax 590/27–75–47. 20 rooms (3 sea-view), 9 1-bedroom villas. Facilities: 2 restaurants, bar, pool, beach with water-sports center, boutique. AE, DC, MC, V. EP. Expensive.*

Hotel La Banane. Rustic luxury is the style of these romantic bungalows just off the beach. The rooms are tastefully decorated, combining antiques with contemporary design and lots of plants, and especially popular with owner Jean Marie Rivière's celebrity friends. By the pool is a delightful, small restaurant serving classic cuisine by chef Jean-Marc Fauchaux. *Quartier Lorient 97133, tel. 590/27–68–25, fax 590/27–68–44. 9 rooms. Facilities: restaurant, 2 pools, Jacuzzi. AE. CP. Expensive.*

François Plantation. A colonial-era graciousness pervades this elegant complex of hilltop bungalows managed by longtime island habitués Françoise and François Beret. Everything is designed to take full advantage of the terrain, vegetation, and location high above Flamands. Rooms are air-conditioned, furnished with antique queen-size four-poster beds, and decorated with paisley fabrics. They all have refrigerators and satellite TV. You'll need a car for the beach and reservations for its smart and gourmet restaurant. *Colombier 97133, tel. 590/27–78–82; in the U.S., 800/932–3222, fax 590/27–61–26. 4 garden and 8 sea-view rooms. Facilities: pool, restaurant. AE, V. CP. Moderate–Expensive.*

Baie des Flamands. Upper-level rooms have balconies, and lower-level ones have terrace kitchenette units in this newly refurbished motel-style hotel. One of the first hotels on the island, it is still run by a St. Barts family, with a gentle laid-back island ambience, and is popular with families and tour groups. It has a good restaurant and an outstanding beach location. *Box 68, Anse des Flamands 97133, tel. 590/27–64–85, fax 590/27–83–98. 24 rooms with baths. Facilities: restaurant, bar, beach, saltwater pool, TV/library room, rental cars. AE, MC, V. CP. Moderate.*

Grand Cul De Sac Beach Hotel and **St. Barths Beach Hotel.**

These side-by-side properties owned by Guy Turbé stretch out on a narrow peninsula between lagoon and sea. Both are comfortable, unpretentious, and popular with families and tour groups who take advantage of the full range of sports available on the hotels' beach. Upper-level rooms are best at the two-story St. Barths Beach Hotel; the best rooms at Grand Cul de Sac Beach Hotel, a group of small air-conditioned bungalow units with kitchenettes, are right on the beach. The windows are screenless and if they are left open, mosquitoes can be a problem. There's limited parking for cars not rented through Turbé's agency. *Box 81, Grand Cul de Sac 97133, tel. 590/27–60–70, fax 590/27–75–57. 35 rooms; 16 bungalows. Facilities: 2 restaurants, bar, saltwater pool, tennis court, windsurfing school and water-sports center, TV/library room, car rental, boutique. AE, MC, V. EP. Moderate.*

Marigot Bay Club. Jean Michel Ledee's pleasant apartments across from his popular seaside restaurant feature comfortable furniture, louvered doors and windows, air-conditioning, twin beds, kitchen/living areas, and large terraces with good views. *Marigot 97133, tel. 590/27–75–45, fax 590/27–70–70. 6 apartments. Facilities: restaurant, nearby beach. AE, V. EP. Moderate.*

Castelets. After a brief stint as Sapore di Mare, Mme. Jouany's hotel is back to it's former self. At this exclusive retreat the antiques-furnished rooms are in terraced chalets, with the exception of two in the main house, that are connected by steep paths. These rooms vary in size in direct relation to their price, and while the hotel is listed as "Moderate," the smaller rooms have an "Inexpensive" and the suites an "Expensive–Very Expensive" price tag. The pool is small, but the views from this property, situated atop Morne Lurin, are breathtaking. Since the hotel is inland and off by itself, you will need a car. The friendliest, most varied clientele on the island parks here. *Box 60, Morne Lurin 97133, tel. 590/27–61–73 or 800/322–VILLAS, fax 590/27–85–27. 10 rooms, 1 2-bedroom suite. Facilities: restaurant, small pool. AE, MC, V. CP. Moderate.*

Sea Horse Club. Next door to the Marigot Bay Club, this property has suites and a beautifully landscaped garden. All rooms have living room, kitchen, terrace, shower/bath. *Marigot 97133, tel. 590/27–75–36, fax 590/27–60–52. 11 suites. Facilities: restaurant and beach within walking distance. AE, MC, V. EP. Moderate.*

Tropical Hotel. Up the hill from St. Jean's Beach, this cozy gingerbread complex encircles a lush garden and small pool. Everything has been thoroughly renovated, and the ambience is friendly; accommodations are air-conditioned. *Box 147, St. Jean 97133, tel. 590/27–64–87, fax 590/27–81–74. 20 rooms. Facilities: restaurant, reception bungalow with bar and wide-screen video lounge, pool. AE, MC, V. CP. Moderate.*

★ **Village St. Jean.** This stone-and-redwood resort, up a short, steep hill from St. Jean's Beach, is now run by the second generation of the Charneau family. It has acquired a strong following over the years. The accent is on service, privacy, and wholesomeness. There are a variety of accommodations with air-conditioning and fine views of the sea. There is a patio restaurant serving pizza-type fare by the small new pool. This is a good value. *Box 23, St. Jean 97133, tel. 590/27–61–39, fax 590/27–77–96. 24 rooms. Facilities: restaurant, bar, pool, small grocery, boutique, games room, library. MC, V. EP. Moderate.*

White Sand Beach Cottages. The road in front of the place is a little ramshackle, but these tiny cottages are pleasant, air-conditioned, and well equipped. The cottage on the beach is the best. *Anse des Flamands 97133, tel. 590/27–63–66, fax 590/27–70–69. 4 cottages with kitchenettes. Facilities: beach, sun deck, MC, V. EP. Inexpensive–Moderate.*

★ **Hostellerie des Trois Forces.** This rustic mountaintop inn is an idiosyncratic delight, with rooms charmingly decorated according to astrological color schemes. All feature a minibar, a terrace with ocean view, and air-conditioning or a ceiling fan. Most have four-poster beds. The aroma of a wood-burning fireplace and the tinkle of wind chimes float through the pleasant restaurant. Hubert de la Motte (he's a Gemini, by the way) is the personable owner, who may even arrange a reading for you by one of his psychic friends. *Morne Vitet, tel. 590/27–61–25, fax 590/27–81–38. 12 rooms. Facilities: restaurant, bar, pool. AE, MC, V. CP. Inexpensive.*

La Normandie. This small inn offers reasonably priced rooms, a restaurant, and dancing in the evening on a glass floor set over the pool. Ask for one of the two air-conditioned rooms. *Lorient 97133, tel. 590/27–61–66, fax 590/27–68–64. 8 rooms. Facilities: pool, restaurant. V. EP. Inexpensive.*

★ **Le P'tit Morne.** There is good value in these mountainside studios, each with a private balcony, air-conditioning, and panoramic views of the coastline below. A snack bar serving breakfast and light lunches recently opened, but each room has a kitchenette that is small but adequate for creating light meals or making picnic lunches. *Box 14, Colombier 97133, tel. 590/27–62–64, fax 590/27–84–63. 14 rooms with kitchens. Facilities: pool, snack bar, reading room. AE, MC, V. CP. Inexpensive.*

★ **Les Mouettes.** Good family accommodations are provided in bungalows overlooking the island's best surfing beach. *Lorient 97133, tel. 590/27–60–74. 6 rooms. Each room has a shower, patio, and kitchenette. Facilities: car rental. No credit cards. EP. Inexpensive.*

Villas, Condos, Apartments For the price of an inexpensive hotel room, you can get your own little cottage, and for the price of a room at an expensive hotel, you'll get a villa with several bedrooms and your own swimming pool. On an island where the restaurants are so expensive, having a kitchen of your own makes sense. What you sacrifice in room service and the amenities of a hotel, you'll gain in privacy, more room, and money saved. Villas represent a tremendous bargain, but don't forget to factor in the almost necessary cost of a car rental.

Villas, apartments, and condos can be rented through **SIBARTH** (tel. 590/27–62–38), which handles about 200 properties. **WIMCO** (tel. 800/932–3222) is the agency's representative in the United States. Rents average $700–$1,000 per week for one-bedroom villas, $3,500 for three-bedroom villas, and more for houses with pools. **Villas St. Barts** (tel. 590/27–74–29) has about 100 properties. Manager Joe Ledee speaks English and meets his clients at the airport.

Nightlife

St. Barts is a mostly in-bed-by-midnight island. However, some of the hotels and restaurants provide late-night fun. Cocktail hour finds the barefoot boating set gathered in the garden of **Gustavia's Le Select** (tel. 590/27–86–87); the more sophisti-

cated up at **L'Hibiscus's** (tel. 590/27–64–82) jazz bar; the
French at **Bar de l'Oubli** (no tel.). **Carl Gustav** (tel. 590/27–82–
83) has supplanted L'Hibiscus as the choice of sunset-watchers.
Roger Parat holds forth in **Manapany's** piano bar (tel. 590/27–
66–59) nightly, and there's a talented pianist at the **Guanahani**
(tel. 590/27–66–60) till midnight. The young and the hip (and all
those who go by one name—Liza, Cher, Madonna, and so on)
gather after 10 at Gustavia's aptly named **Le Petit Club** (no
tel.). Locals also flock to **Le Pelican** (tel. 590/27–64–64) and the
retro hip **American Bar-Video** (tel. 590/27–86–07) next door to
L'Escale. **La Licorne,** (no tel.), a disco, can be lively on weekends, as can **Club Hurricane** (no tel.) in St. Jean. At 10 PM on
weekends the owner of Hotel La Banane (Jean Marie Riviere,
famed in France for his spectacular drag shows) hosts a Parisian-
style revue made up of the waiters and waitresses at his **Club La
Banane** (tel. 590/27–68–25). The audience participates, and—
frequently—by the end of the show most of the performers,
and some of the audience, wind up in the hotel swimming pool.

20 St. Eustatius

Updated by
Jordan Simon

The flight approach to the tiny Dutch island of St. Eustatius, commonly known as Statia (pronounced *STAY-sha)* in the Netherlands Antilles, is almost worth the visit itself. The plane circles The Quill, a 1,968-foot-high extinct volcano that encloses a stunning primeval rain forest within its crater. Here you'll find giant elephant ears, ferns, flowers, wild orchids, fruit trees, wildlife, and birds hiding in the trees. The entire island is alive with untended greenery—bougainvillea, oleander, hibiscus, and alemanda.

During the American Revolutionary War, when the British blockaded the North American coast, food, arms, and other supplies for the American revolutionaries were diverted through the West Indies, notably through neutral Statia. (Benjamin Franklin had his mail routed through Statia to ensure its safe arrival in Europe.) On November 16, 1776, the brig-of-war *Andrew Doria,* commanded by Captain Isaiah Robinson of the Continental Navy, sailed into Statia's port flying the Stars and Stripes and fired a 13-gun salute to the Royal Netherlands standard. Governor Johannes de Graaff ordered the cannons of Fort Oranje to return the salute, and that first official acknowledgment of the new American flag by a foreign power earned Statia the nickname "America's Childhood Friend." Each year on November 16, Statian dignitaries in colonial-style garb participate in a colorful reenactment of the occasion at Fort Oranje; the festivities include parades, bands, picnics, and speeches.

Little 12-square-mile Statia, past which Columbus sailed in 1493, had prospered almost from the day the Dutch Zeelanders colonized it in 1636. In the 1700s, a double row of warehouses crammed with goods stretched for a mile along the bay, and there were sometimes as many as 200 ships tied up at the duty-free port. The island was called the Emporium of the Western World and Golden Rock. There were almost 8,000 Statians on the island in the 1790s (today, there are about 1,700). Holland, England, and France fought one another for possession of the island, which changed hands 22 times. In 1816, it became a Dutch possession and has remained so to this day.

Four years after Statia's salute to the new American flag, Britain declared war on Holland, and on February 3, 1781, British Admiral George Rodney captured Oranjestad and proceeded to rob the island blind. Statia had aided, abetted, and acknowledged Britain's rebellious colony, and in revenge Rodney closed its shops, sealed its warehouses, auctioned off goods, and even confiscated the personal possessions of the islanders. For a month he kept the Dutch flag flying, thus luring and entrapping as many as 150 ships and confiscating their cargoes. Less than a year later, having fattened his personal purse with about £4 million, Rodney departed. Statia bounced back and flourished for another 10 years. Ironically, Statia's prosperity ended partly because of the success of the American Revolution. The island was no longer needed as a transshipment port, and its bustling economy gradually came to a stop.

Statia is in the Dutch Windward Triangle, 178 miles east of Puerto Rico and 35 miles south of St. Maarten. Oranjestad, the capital and only "city" (note quotes), is on the western side facing the Caribbean. The island is anchored at the north and the south by extinct volcanoes, like the Quill, that are separated by a central plain.

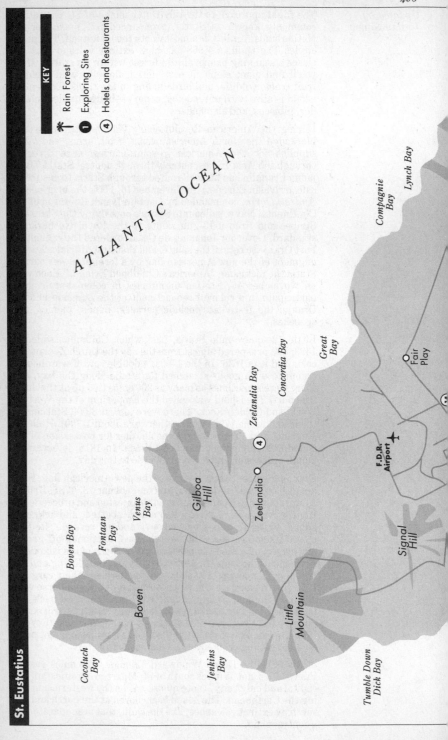

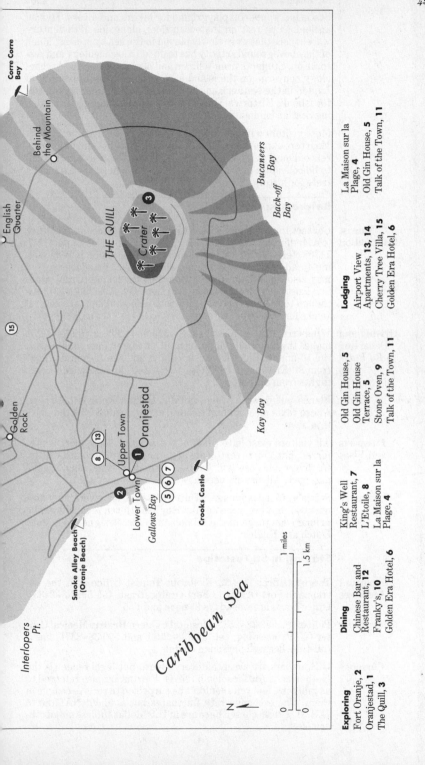

Exploring
Fort Oranje, **2**
Oranjestad, **1**
The Quill, **3**

Dining
Chinese Bar and
Restaurant, **12**
Franky's, **10**
Golden Era Hotel, **6**

King's Well
Restaurant, **7**
L'Etoile, **8**
La Maison sur la
Plage, **4**

Old Gin House, **5**
Old Gin House
Terrace, **5**
Stone Oven, **9**
Talk of the Town, **11**

Lodging
Airport View
Apartments, **13, 14**
Cherry Tree Villa, **15**
Golden Era Hotel, **6**

La Maison sur la
Plage, **4**
Old Gin House, **5**
Talk of the Town, **11**

Statia is a wonderful playground for hikers and divers. Myriad ancient ships rest on the ocean floor alongside 18th-century warehouses that were slowly buried in the sea by storms. Much of the aboveground activity has to do with archaeology and restoration. Students from William and Mary's College of Archaeology converge on the island each summer; the University of Leiden in the Netherlands has a pre-Columbian program; and the island's Historical Foundation is actively engaged in restoring Statian landmarks.

Most visitors will be content with a day visit from nearby St. Maarten, exploring some of the historical sights and enjoying a relaxed meal at the Old Gin House. Those who stay longer tend to be collectors of unspoiled islands with a need to relax and a taste for history.

Before You Go

Tourist Information Contact the **Saba and St. Eustatius Tourist Information Office** (c/o Medhurst & Associates, Inc., 271 Main St., Northport, NY 11768, tel. 516/261–7474 or 800/344–4606), which is very willing to advise and reserve guest-house accommodations. You may also contact the **Tourist Board** on the island (Oranjestad, St. Eustatius, Netherlands Antilles, tel. 599/38–2433). Although telephone communications are good, it can take several weeks for mail to get through.

Arriving and Departing *By Plane* **Windward Islands Airways** (tel. 599/5–44230 or 599/5–44237) makes the 20-minute flight from St. Maarten four times a day, the 10-minute flight from Saba daily, and the 15-minute flight from St. Kitts daily. **LIAT** (tel. 809/462–0700) has twice-weekly flights from St. Kitts.

From the Airport Planes put down at the **Franklin Delano Roosevelt Airport,** where taxis meet all flights and charge about $4 for the drive into town.

Passports and Visas All visitors must have proof of citizenship. A passport is preferred, but a birth certificate or voter registration card will do. (A driver's license will *not* do.) British citizens need a valid passport. All visitors need a return or ongoing ticket.

Language Statia's official language is Dutch (it's used on government documents), but everyone speaks English. Dutch is taught as the primary language in the schools, and street signs are in both Dutch and English.

Staying in St. Eustatius

Important Addresses **Tourist Office:** The **St. Eustatius Tourist Office** is at the entrance to Fort Oranje (3 Fort Oranjestraat, tel. 599/38–2433). Office hours are weekdays 8–noon and 1–5.

Emergencies **Police:** tel. 599/38–2333. **Hospitals: Queen Beatrix Medical Center** (25 Prinsesweg, tel. 599/38–2211 and 599/38–2371) has a full-time licensed physician on duty.

Currency U.S. dollars are accepted everywhere, but legal tender is the Netherlands Antilles florin (NAf). Florins are also referred to as guilders, and you shouldn't be surprised to receive change in them. The exchange rate fluctuates but is about NAf1.80 to U.S.$1. Prices quoted here are in U.S. dollars unless noted otherwise.

Taxes and   Hotels collect a 7% government tax and a 5% electricity tax.
Service Charges   The departure tax is $3 for flights to other islands of the Neth-
erlands Antilles and $5 to foreign destinations. In addition,
you'll probably be asked to contribute your leftover guilders to
the latest cause.

All hotels and restaurants add a 10%–15% service charge.

Guided Tours   All 10 of Statia's taxis are available for island tours. A full day's
outing costs $35 per vehicle, usually including airport pickup.

Getting Around   To explore the island (and there isn't very much), car rentals
are available through the **Avis** outlet at the airport (tel. 599/38–
2421 and 800/331–1084) at a cost of $40–$45 per day. **Rainbow
Car Rental** (tel. 599/38–2586) has several Hyundai for rent.
Brown's (tel. 599/38–2266) and **Lady Ama's Services** (tel. 599/
38–2451) rents cars and Jeeps; rentals are also available
through the island's taxi drivers. A taxi driver with a broad
knowledge of the island and its folklore is Mr. Daniel. Statia's
roads are pocked with potholes and the going is slow and
bumpy. Goats and cattle have the right of way.

Telephones   Statia has microwave telephone service to all parts of the
and Mail   world. To call Statia from the United States, dial 011–599/38 +
local number. When calling interisland, dial only the 4-digit
number. Direct dial is available. Airmail letters to the United
States are NAf1.30; postcards NAf.60.

Opening and   Most offices are open weekdays 8–noon and 1–4 or 5. **Barclays
Closing Times   Bank** (the only bank on the island) is open Monday–Thursday
8:30–1; Friday 8:30–1 and 4–5.

Exploring St. Eustatius

*Numbers in the margin correspond to points of interest on the
St. Eustatius map.*

Oranjestad   Statia's capital and only town, **Oranjestad** sits on the western
 ❶   coast facing the Caribbean. It's a split-level town: Upper Town
and Lower Town. History buffs will enjoy poking around the
ancient Dutch Colonial buildings, which are being restored by
the Historical Foundation, while hikers will want to head for
the hills of The Quill. Both Upper Town and Lower Town are
easily explored on foot.

The first stop is the **Tourist Office,** which is right at the entrance to Fort Oranje. You can pick up maps, brochures, and
friendly advice, as well as a listing of 12 marked hiking trails.
You can also arrange for guides and guided tours.

When you leave the Tourist Office, you will be at the entrance
 ❷   to **Fort Oranje.** With its three bastions, the fort has clutched
these cliffs since 1636. In 1976, Statia participated in the U.S.
Bicentennial celebration by restoring the old fort, and now
gleaming black cannons point out over the ramparts. In the parade grounds a plaque, presented in 1939 by Franklin D. Roosevelt, reads, "Here the sovereignty of the United States of
America was first formally acknowledged to a national vessel
by a foreign official." A few government offices are within the
fort, and restoration continues.

From the fort, cross over to Wilhelminaweg (Wilhelmina Way)
in the center of Upper Town. The **St. Eustatius Historical Foundation Museum** is in the Doncker/de Graaff house, a lovely

building with slim columns and a high gallery. British Admiral Rodney is believed to have lived here while he was stealing everything in sight. The house, acquired by the foundation in 1983 and completely restored, is Statia's most important intact 18th-century dwelling. Exhibits trace the island's history from the 6th century to the present. The most recent addition is a pre-Columbian annex across the street. Statia is the only island thus far where ruins and artifacts of the Saladoid, a newly discovered tribe, have been excavated. *12 Van Tonningenweg, tel. 599/38–2288. Admission: $1 adults, 50¢ children. Open weekdays 9–5, weekends 9–noon.*

Return to Fort Oranjestraat (Fort Orange St.) and turn left. Continue to 4 **Fort Oranjestraat,** at the corner of Kerkweg (Church Way). The big yellow house, with a stone foundation, shingled walls, and gingerbread trim, is typical of the houses built in the West Indies around the turn of the century. Just behind it is **Three Widows Corner,** a tropical courtyard where you'll see two more examples of Statian architecture in a town house and another gingerbread house.

Now head west down Kerkweg to the edge of the cliff, where you'll find the **Dutch Reformed Church,** built in 1775. Ancient tales can be read on the gravestones in the 18th-century cemetery adjacent to the church.

Continue on Kerkweg and take the next two left turns onto Synagogepad (Synagogue Path) to **Honen Dalim** ("She Who Is Charitable to the Poor"), one of the Caribbean's oldest synagogues. Dating from 1738, it is now in ruins but is slated for restoration.

❸ **The Quill,** the volcanic cone rising in the southern sector, is 3 miles south of Oranjestad on the main road *(see Hiking, below).*

Time Out   The **Cool Corner,** just up from the Tourist Office, is a cool spot to have a beer, a snack, and shoot the breeze if you want to catch up on island gossip. *Fort Oranjestraat, tel. 599/38–2523. Open Mon.–Sat. 7 AM–2 AM.*

Follow Prinsesweg back to the main square and zigzag down the cobblestone Fort Road to Lower Town. Warehouses and shops that in the 18th century were piled high with European imports are now either abandoned or simply used to store local fishermen's equipment, but the restoration of the 18th-century cotton mill, on the land side of Bay Road, now the **Old Gin House,** is impressive. The palms, flowering shrubs, and park benches along the water's edge are the work of the Historical Foundation members.

Off the Beaten Path

Local boys go up to the Quill by torchlight for delectable sand crabs. You can join them and ask your hotel to prepare your catch for dinner. The tourist board will make arrangements.

Beaches

Beachcombing is a sport for the intrepid: The beaches are pristine but unmaintained and occasionally rocky.

Smoke Alley Beach (also called **Oranje Beach**) is the nicest and most accessible. The beige-and-black-sand beach is on the Caribbean, off Lower Town, and is relatively deserted until late afternoon when the locals arrive.

A 30-minute hike down an easy marked trail behind the Mountain Road will bring you to **Corre Corre Bay** and its gold-sand cove. Two bends north, **Lynch Bay** is somewhat protected from the wild swells. On the Atlantic side, especially around Concordia Bay, the surf is rough and there is sometimes a dangerous undertow, making beaches in this area better for sunning than swimming.

A big deal on the beaches here is searching for Statia's famed blue glass beads. Manufactured in the 17th century by the Dutch West Indies Company, the blue glass beads were traded for rum, slaves, cotton, and tobacco. They were also awarded to faithful slaves or included as a part of the groom's settlement by the bride's father. Although they are found only on Statia, some researchers believe that it was beads like these that were traded for Manhattan. They're best unearthed after a heavy rain, but as the locals chuckle, "If you find one, it's a miracle, man."

Sports and the Outdoors

Fishing **Dive Statia** (tel. 599/38–2435) has a 31-foot Chris-Craft available for deep-sea fishing. It also rents fishing gear.

Hiking Trails range from the easy to the "Watch out!" The big thrill here is The Quill, the 1,968-foot extinct volcano with its crater full of rain forest. Give yourself two to three hours to make the climb and the return. The Tourist Office has a list of 12 marked trails and can put you in touch with a guide (whose fee will be about $20).

Scuba Diving If you've never gone to an undersea supermarket, here's your chance. The "supermarket" is actually two parallel shipwrecks less than 50 yards apart. It's but one of the many wrecks and 18th-century submerged seaports you can see. **Dive Statia** (tel. 599/38–2435), a fully equipped dive shop offering certification courses, is operated by Americans Mike and Judy Brown out of a warehouse just down the road from the Old Gin House. Most of the hotels offer dive packages with Dive Statia.

Snorkeling Crooks Castle has several stands of pillar coral, giant yellow sea fans, and sea whips. Jenkins Bay and Venus Bay are other favorites with snorkelers. For equipment rental, contact **Dive Statia** (*see* Scuba Diving, *above*).

Tennis There's a lone tennis court at the **Community Center** that's even lighted at night. It has changing rooms, but you'll have to bring your own racquets and balls. The cost is $2 (check with the Tourist Office for more information).

Shopping

Though shopping on Statia is duty-free, it is also somewhat limited. A handful of shops do offer unusual items, however. **The Old Gin House** (tel. 599/38–2319) features handicrafts from around the Caribbean, as well as cottons silk-screened with traditional Statian motifs, sold both by the yard and made up into attractive resortwear. Barbara Lane shows her own sophisticated ceramic pieces, together with paintings and woven sculptures by local artists at **The Park Place Gallery** (tel. 599/ 38–2452) across from the Cool Corner in the center of town. **Mazinga Gift Shop** on Fort Oranje Straat in Upper Town (tel. 599/38–2245) is a small department store of sorts. It has duty-free jewelry, cosmetics, and liquor, in addition to beachwear, sports gear, stationery, books, and magazines.

Dining

The variety of cuisines here is surprising, given the size of the island. Besides the traditional West Indian fare, you can find French and Chinese cuisine. Also, it's super-casual here; a beach wrap or a bathing suit will do.

Highly recommended restaurants are indicated by a star ★.

Category	Cost*
Expensive	over $25
Moderate	$15–$25
Inexpensive	under $15

per person, excluding drinks and service

★ **Old Gin House.** Here you'll find the most sophisticated dining on the island even though it's lost some of its past flair. Your four-course, fixed-price feast will probably begin with warm grapefruit soup or a salad of smoked red snapper. The main course could be chateaubriand Dijonnaise, roast duck with sweet-and-sour sauce, or lobster mousse with caviar and horse-radish. Two wines are included with the dinner. The poolside setting is elegantly rustic, with old-brick walls, candlelight, pewter, and gleaming crystal. *Old Gin House, Lower Town, Oranjestad, tel. 599/38–2319. Reservations suggested. AE, D, MC, V. Expensive.*

Golden Era Hotel. The restaurant and bar of this establishment are somewhat stark, but the Creole food is good and the setting is right on the water. Sunday-night buffets, a steal at $14.50, are popular, served outside by the pool and ocean, with a local band providing entertainment. *Golden Era Hotel, Lower Town, Oranjestad, tel. 599/38–2345. AE, D, MC, V. Moderate.*

King's Well Restaurant. "Good food, cold drinks and easy prices" reads the hand-painted sign at this breezy terrace eatery overlooking the sea, run by a fun-loving expatriate couple. Fine grilled chicken and fish and authentic rostbraten and schnitzels are featured. *Bay Rd., Lower Town, Oranjestad, tel. 599/38–2538. No credit cards. Moderate.*

La Maison sur la Plage. The view here is of the Atlantic, the cloths are crisp and white, and the fare is French. For dinner, openers include fish soup and quiche Lorraine. Among the entrées are duck breast with green-peppercorn sauce and *entrecôte forestière* (sirloin with mushrooms, cream, and red wine). Try the crepes à l'orange for dessert. *Zeelandia, tel. 599/38–2256. Reservations required. AE, MC, V. Moderate.*

★ **Old Gin House Terrace.** Dining is delightful on the oceanside terrace of this hotel. The menu may include peanut soup, fillet of orange roughy fish, lobster Antillean (lobster chunks stewed with onions, red wine, Pernod, and a dash of hot pepper), plain burgers and dillyburgers (with sour cream and dill sauce), lobster salad, and sandwiches. Lunch is more casual and offers lighter fare than dinner. *Old Gin House, Lower Town, Oranjestad, tel. 599/38–2319. Reservations suggested. AE, D, MC, V. Moderate.*

Talk of the Town. Breakfast, lunch, and dinner are served at this pleasant restaurant midway between the airport and town. Caribbean, Oriental, and American dishes are offered. *L. E. Sadler Weg, near Upper Town, tel. 599/38–2236. MC, V. Moderate.*

Chinese Bar and Restaurant. Owner Kim Cheng serves up tasty Oriental and Caribbean dishes—*Bamigoreng* (Indonesian chow mein), pork chops Creole—in hearty portions at his unpretentious establishment. Dining indoors can be slightly claustrophobic, but just ask your waitress if you may tote your Formica-top table out onto the terrace. She'll probably be happy to lend a hand and then serve you under the stars. *Prinsesweg, Upper Town, Oranjestad, tel. 599/38–2389. No credit cards. Inexpensive.*

★ **Franky's.** Come here for good local barbecue: ribs, chicken, lobster, and fish served later than at most other places on Statia. Try the bullfoot soup and goatwater stew. The less adventurous can get pizza on the weekend, when there is live music. The person often lending a hand is the director of tourism. *Ruyterweg, Upper Town, Oranjestad, tel. 599/38–2575. Inexpensive.*

L'Etoile. West Indian dishes, such as spicy stuffed land crab and goat meat, are prepared by Caren Henriquez in a simple snack bar/restaurant. You can also get hot dogs, hamburgers, and spareribs. *Heiligerweg, Upper Town, Oranjestad, tel. 599/38–2299. No credit cards. Inexpensive.*

Stone Oven. Such West Indian specialties as goatwater stew are featured here. You can eat either indoors in the little house or outside on the palm-fringed patio. *16A Feaschweb, Upper Town, Oranjestad, tel. 599/38–2247. Reservations required. No credit cards. Inexpensive.*

Lodging

Accommodations, already scarce, are even harder to find because of the influx of Dominicans and Jamaicans seeking work. You may also compete for a room with young Dutch on driving-license vacation packages, here to avoid the excessive length and cost of lessons back home. There are only three full-service hotels and a few apartment rentals on the island, usually on EP.

Highly recommended lodgings are indicated by a star ★.

Category	Cost*
Very Expensive	over $125
Expensive	$100–$125
Moderate	$75–$100
Inexpensive	under $75

All prices are for a standard double room for two, excluding 10% tax and a 15% service charge.

Hotels **Old Gin House.** This once-proud property, fashioned by American expatriate John May out of the ruins of an 18th-century cotton-gin factory and warehouse, is living off its faded glory. The cluster of buildings includes one that is two stories high, its bougainvillea-swathed double balconies overlooking a secluded tropical courtyard and pool; the highly acclaimed Old Gin House Restaurant; a terrace restaurant and bar by the sea; and an additional six rooms in a two-story building with high ceilings, custom-made furnishings, and balconies that jut out over the ocean. The comfortable rooms are relatively spacious with superb Haitian artwork and antiques for furnishings. Regrettably, over the last few years, enthusiasm and upkeep for the hotel's facilities have waned. *Box 172, Oranjestad, tel. 599/38–2319 or 800/223–5581 in U.S. 20 rooms with bath. Facilities: pool, 2 restaurants, bar, lounge, library, boutique. AE, DC, MC, V. EP, MAP. Very Expensive.*

Golden Era Hotel. This is a harborfront hotel whose rooms are neat, small, air-conditioned, and motel-modern. All have little terraces, but only half have a full or partial view of the sea. The other rooms look out over concrete or down onto the roof of the restaurant. There is little that is aesthetically attractive about this hotel, but at least it is central, by the water, and enjoys a cheerful clientele. *Box 109, Oranjestad, tel. 599/38–2345 or 800/223–6510. 19 rooms, 1 suite; all with private bath. Facilities: pool, restaurant, bar. AE, D, MC, V. EP. Moderate.*

La Maison sur la Plage. The *plage* is a 2-mile crescent of gray sand slapped by the wild waters of the Atlantic. The undertow here can be dangerous, so you should do your swimming in the pool. A cozy lobby has rattan furnishings, a checkerboard on the coffee table, and shelves filled with books. There's a stone-and-wood bar, and a *très* French dining room bordered by a trellis and greenery. French-born Michelle Greca's *maison* (house) is actually eight spartan cottages, where you have a choice of twin, double, or king-size beds. Each cottage has a bath and a private veranda, where a Continental breakfast is served. Repairs from recent hurricanes, however, have so far been makeshift rather than improvements. The most active thing in this isolated area is the Atlantic. *Box 157, Zeelandia, tel. 599/38–2256 or 800/845–9504. 10 rooms with bath. Facilities: pool, restaurant, bar, lounge. AE, MC, V. EP. Moderate.*

★ **Talk of the Town.** These bright and simply furnished rooms are for those who don't need a view. There is a deck with lounge chairs for guests' use and a restaurant downstairs. The hotel is on the road between the airport and town. *L. E. Saddlerweg, tel. 599/38–2236. 17 rooms with shower. Facilities: restaurant, bar. MC, V. EP. Inexpensive.*

Apartment Rentals Statia has only a handful of apartments, though a spate of small developments and guest houses have gone up recently to meet demand. As a general rule, figure $50 and under per night and don't expect much beyond a bathroom and kitchenette. The only luxury accommodation is **Cherry Tree Villa** (tel. 800/325–2222 or 813/787–2579), which sprawls over 17 lush acres. The moderately priced two-bedroom villa sleeps four, and its luxe touches include a Cuisinart, dishwasher, microwave oven, outdoor Jacuzzi facing the sea, and the use of a car. A Hobie Cat and a 32-foot skippered yacht are available for an extra charge.

★ The **Airport View Apartments** (tel. 599/38–2299), near the airport, are inexpensive studios with carpeted floors, small refrigerators, TVs, air-conditioning, coffee makers, private baths, and either two double or twin beds. There's an outdoor patio with a barbecue pit and a meeting room that can accommodate 12. The Airport View also has a vastly inferior in-town location.

Check with the Tourist Office for information about these and other apartment rentals in Oranjestad.

Nightlife

Statia's five local bands stay busy, dividing their time among gigs at the occasional Saturday-night dances at the **Community Center** *(see* Sports and the Outdoors, *above)*; alfresco soirees at the **Chinese Bar and Restaurant** *(see* Dining, *above)* and **Sonny's Place** in Oranjestad; and Saturday nights at the **Cool Corner** *(see* Exploring St. Eustatius, *above)*. Sunday nights find everyone at the **Golden Era Hotel** *(see* Lodging, *above)*. **Talk of the Town** *(see* Lodging, *above)* is the place to be for live music Friday nights; weekend nights at **Franky's** *(see* Dining, *above)* are also popular. The **Lago Heights Club and Disco** (no phone), known to all as Gerald's, at the shopping center in Chapelpiece, has dancing and a late-night barbecue.

21 St. Kitts and Nevis

Updated by
Harriet Edleson

Tour groups are not attracted to islands that have no nonstop flights from the United States, virtually no glittering nightlife or shopping, and no high-rise hotels. Visitors tend to be self-sufficient types who know how to amuse themselves and appreciate the warmth and character of country inns. The local population is one that truly enjoys playing host to those who seek low-key pleasures in a discreet manner.

Tiny though it is, St. Kitts, the first English settlement in the Leeward Islands, crams some stunning scenery into its 65 square miles. St. Kitts is fertile and lush with tropical flora and has some fascinating natural and historical attractions: a rain forest, replete with waterfalls, thick vines, and secret trails; a central mountain range, dominated by the 3,792-foot Mt. Liamuiga, whose crater has been long dormant; and Brimstone Hill, the Caribbean's most impressive fortress, which was known in the 17th century as the Gibraltar of the West Indies. The island is home to 35,000 people and hosts some 60,000 visitors annually. The shape of St. Kitts has been variously compared to a whale, a cricket bat, and a guitar. It's roughly oval, 19 miles long and 6 miles wide, with a narrow peninsula trailing off toward Nevis, 2 miles across the strait.

Until 1988, the island's official name was St. Christopher (Columbus named it after his patron saint), and its nickname was St. Kitts. Since everybody called it by its nickname anyway, the island officially changed its name to St. Kitts. The island is known as the Mother Colony of the West Indies because it was from here that the English settlers sailed to Antigua, Barbuda, Tortola, and Montserrat and the French dispatched colonizing parties to Martinique, Guadeloupe, St. Martin, St. Barts, La Désirade, and Les Saintes. The French, who inexplicably brought a bunch of monkeys with them, arrived on St. Kitts a few years after the British.

In 1493, when Columbus spied a cloud-crowned volcanic isle during his second voyage to the New World, he named it *Nieves*, the Spanish word for "snows." It reminded him of the snowcapped peaks of the Pyrenees. Nevis (pronounced *NEE-vis*) rises out of the water in an almost perfect cone, the tip of its 3,232-foot central mountain smothered in clouds. It's lusher and less developed than its sister island, St. Kitts.

Nevis is known for its natural beauty—long beaches with white and black sand, lush greenery—for a half-dozen mineral spa baths, and for the restored sugar plantations that now house some of the Caribbean's most elegant hostelries. In 1628, settlers from St. Kitts sailed across the 2-mile channel that separates the two islands. At first they grew tobacco, cotton, ginger, and indigo, but with the introduction of sugarcane in 1640, Nevis became the island equivalent of a boomtown. As the mineral baths were drawing crowds, the island was producing an abundance of sugar. Slaves were brought from Africa to work on the magnificent estates, many of them nestled high in the mountains amid lavish tropical gardens.

The restored plantation homes that now operate as inns are the island's most sybaritic lures for the leisurely life. There is plenty of activity for the energetic—mountain climbing, swimming, tennis, horseback riding, snorkeling. But the going is easy here, with hammocks for snoozing, lobster bakes on palm-lined beaches, and candlelit dinners in stately dining rooms and on romantic verandas.

As rich in history as it is fertile and lush with tropical flora, St. Kitts is just beginning to develop its tourism industry, and this quiet member of the Leeward group has that rare combination of natural and historic attractions and fine sailing, island hopping, and water-sports options offshore.

Nevis is linked with St. Kitts politically. The two islands, together with Anguilla, achieved self-government as an Associated State of Great Britain in 1967. In 1983, St. Kitts and Nevis became a fully independent nation. Nevis papers sometimes run fiery articles advocating independence from St. Kitts, and the sister islands may separate someday. However, it's not likely that a shot will be fired, let alone one that will be heard around the world.

Before You Go

Tourist Information
Contact the **St. Kitts & Nevis Tourist Board** (414 E. 75th St., New York, NY 10021, tel. 212/535–1234, fax 212/734–6511), **St. Kitts & Nevis Tourist Office** (11 Yorkville Ave., Suite 508, Toronto, Ont., Canada M4W 1L3, tel. 416/921–7717), **St. Kitts & Nevis Tourist Office** (10 Kensington Ct., London W8 5DL, tel. 071/376–0881, fax 071/937–3611), and **St. Kitts & Nevis Tourist Office** (3166 S. River Rd., Suite 33, Des Plaines, IL 60018, tel. 708/699–7583).

Arriving and Departing
By Plane
American (tel. 800/433–7300) and **Delta** (tel. 800/221–1212) fly from the United States to Antigua, St. Croix, St. Thomas, St. Maarten, and San Juan, Puerto Rico, where connections can be made on regional carriers such as **American Eagle,** part of the **American Airlines** system (tel. 800/433–7300); **LIAT** (tel. 809/465–2511); **Windward Island Airways** (tel. 809/465–0810); and **Air BVI** (tel. 800/468–2485). LIAT has two flights daily to and from Nevis, **British Airways** (tel. 800/247–9297) flies from London to Antigua, **Air Canada** (tel. 800/422–6232) flies from Toronto to Antigua, and American flies from Montreal to San Juan. **Air St. Kitts-Nevis** (tel. 809/465–8571) and **Carib Aviation** (tel. 809/465–3055, St. Kitts; 809/469–9295, Nevis; fax 809/469–9185) are reliable air-charter operations providing service from St. Kitts to other islands. Carib Aviation brings guests from Antigua to Nevis, which avoids a lot of hassle.

From the Airport
Taxis meet every flight at the airports on both islands. The taxis are unmetered, but fixed rates are posted at the airport and at the jetty. On St. Kitts the fare from the airport to the closest hotel in Basseterre is E.C.$16 (U.S.$6); to the farthest point, E.C.$52 (U.S.$20). On Nevis some sample fares are from the ferry slip to Nesbit Plantation, U.S. $11, and to Golden Rock, U.S. $10. Be sure to clarify whether the rate quoted is in E.C. or U.S. dollars.

By Boat
The 150-passenger government-operated ferry MV *Caribe Queen* makes the 45-minute crossing from Nevis to St. Kitts daily except Thursday, which is maintenance day, and Sunday. The schedule is a bit erratic, so confirm departure times with the tourist office. Round-trip fare is U.S.$8. A new, air-conditioned, 110-passenger ferry, MV *Spirit of Mount Nevis*, makes the run twice daily except Wednesday. The fare is U.S.$12 round-trip. Call **Nevis Cruise Lines** (tel. 809/469–9373)

for information and reservations. Sea-taxi service between the two islands is operated by dive master Kenneth Samuel (tel. 809/465–2670) and by Auston MacLeod of Pro-Divers (tel. 809/465–2754) for U.S. $20 (summer), $25 (winter).

Passports U.S. and Canadian citizens need only produce proof of citizen-
and Visas ship (voter registration card or birth certificate; a driver's license will not suffice). British citizens must have a passport;
visas are not required. All visitors must have a return or ongoing ticket.

Language English with a West Indian lilt is spoken here.

Precautions Visitors, especially women, are warned not to go jogging on
long, lonely roads.

St. Kitts

Staying in St. Kitts

Important **Tourist Information: St. Kitts/Nevis Department of Tourism**
Addresses (Pelican Mall, Bay Rd., Box 132, Basseterre, tel. 809/465–2620
and 809/465–4040, fax 809/465–8794) and the **St. Kitts-Nevis
Hotel Association** (Box 438, Basseterre, tel. and fax 809/465–
5304).

Emergencies **Police:** Call 911. **Hospitals:** There is a 24-hour emergency room
at the **Joseph N. France General Hospital** (Basseterre, tel. 809/
465–2551). **Pharmacies:** In Basseterre, **Skerritt's Drug Store**
(Fort St., tel. 809/465–2008) is open Monday–Wednesday 8–5,
Thursday 8–1, Friday 8–5:30, and Saturday 8–6; closed Sunday; **City Drug** (Fort St., Basseterre, tel. 809/465–2156) is open
Monday–Wednesday, Friday–Saturday 8–7; Thursday 8–5,
Sunday 8–10 AM; and **City Drug** (Sun 'n' Sand, Frigate Bay, tel.
809/465–1803) is open Monday–Saturday 8:30–8; Sunday 8:30–
10:30 AM and 4–6 PM.

Currency Legal tender is the Eastern Caribbean (E.C.) dollar. At press
time, the rate of exchange was E.C.$2.70 to U.S.$1. U.S. dollars are accepted practically everywhere, but you'll almost always get change in E.C.s. Prices quoted here are in U.S.
dollars unless noted otherwise. Most large hotels, restaurants,
and shops accept major credit cards, but small inns and shops
usually do not. It's always a good idea to check current credit-
card policies before you turn up with only plastic in your
pocket.

Taxes and Hotels collect a 7% government tax. The departure tax is $8.
Service Charges (There is no departure tax from St. Kitts to Nevis.)

All hotels add a 10% service charge to your bill. In restaurants,
a tip of 10%–15% is appropriate.

Guided Tours **Tropical Tours** (tel. 809/465–4167) can run you around the island and take you to the rain forest. **Delise Walwyn** (tel. 809/
465–2631) also offers a variety of island tours. **Kriss Tours** (tel.
809/465–4042) and **Greg Pereira** (tel. 809/465–4121) both specialize in rain-forest and volcano tours.

Getting Around Both **Little** and **Big Mac** (tel. 809/465–2016) are reliable, help-
Taxis ful drivers, as is **Jimmy Herbert** (tel. 809/465–4694). **Pat Riley**
(tel. 809/465–2444) is an experienced and knowledgeable driv-

er. Expect to pay approximately $50 for a 3½-hour island taxi tour.

Buses A privately owned minibus circles the island. Check with the tourist office about schedules.

Rental Cars and Scooters You'll need a local driver's license, which you can get by presenting yourself, your valid driver's license, and E.C.$30 (U.S.$12) at the police station, Cayon Street, Basseterre. Rentals are available at **Holiday** (tel. 809/465–6507) and **Caines** (tel. 809/465–2366). Delise Walwyn (tel. 809/465–8449) operates **Economy Car,** which also rents scooter bikes. **TDC Rentals** (tel. 809/465–2991) can put you in minimokes, as well as cars. Car rentals run about U.S.$35 per day. At press time, the price of gas was U.S.$1.70 per gallon. Remember to drive on the left!

Telephones and Mail To call St. Kitts from the United States, dial area code 809, then access code 465 and the local number. Telephone communications, both on the island and with the United States, are as clear as a bell, and you can make direct long-distance calls. To make an intraisland call, simply dial the seven-digit number.

Airmail letters to the United States and Canada cost E.C.$.80 per half ounce; postcards require E.C.$.50. Mail takes at least 7–10 days to reach the United States. St. Kitts and Nevis each issues its own stamps, but each also honors the other's. The beautiful stamps are collector's items, and you may have a hard time pasting them on postcards.

Opening and Closing Times Shops are open Monday–Saturday 8 AM–noon and 1–4 PM. Some shops close earlier on Thursday. Banking hours are Monday–Thursday 8 AM–1 PM; Friday 8 AM–1 PM and 3–5 PM. St. Kitts & Nevis National Bank is also open Saturday 8:30–11 AM.

Exploring St. Kitts

Numbers in the margin correspond to points of interest on the St. Kitts map.

Basseterre ❶ The capital city of **Basseterre,** set in the southern part of the island, was once held by the French, hence its French name. It's an easily walkable town, graced with tall palms and small, beautifully maintained houses and buildings of stone and pastel-colored wood.

You can see the main sights of the capital city in a half hour or so; allow three to four hours for an island tour.

Your first stop is at the **St. Kitts Tourist Board** (Tourism Complex, Bay Rd.) to pick up maps. Turn left when you leave there and walk past the handsome Treasury Building. It faces the octagonal **Circus,** which contains a fanciful memorial to Thomas Berkeley, a former president of the Legislative Assembly. Duty-free shops fill the streets and courtyards leading off from around the Circus. The **St. Kitts Philatelic Bureau** (open weekdays 8–4) is nearby on the second floor of the Social Security Building (Bay Rd.).

The colorful **Bay Road produce market** is open on weekends only. On the waterfront, next to the Treasury Building, is the air-conditioned **Shoreline Plaza,** with its tax-free shops, and nearby is the landing for the ferries to Nevis.

Time Out **Chef's Place** (Upper Church St., tel. 809/465–6176) is a lively place with an outdoor patio where local businesspeople go for spicy chicken platters and mutton curry. The Kittitian owner used to live in Brooklyn.

From the Circus, Bank Street leads to **Independence Square,** with lovely gardens on the site of a former slave market. The square is surrounded on three sides by Georgian buildings, including the popular **Georgian House** restaurant.

Walk up West Square Street, away from the bay, to Cayon Street, turn left, and walk one block to **St. George's Anglican Church.** This handsome stone building with crenellated tower was built by the French in 1670 and called Nôtre Dame. The British burned it down in 1706 and rebuilt it four years later, naming it after the patron saint of England. Since then, it has suffered fire, earthquake, and hurricanes and was once again rebuilt in 1859.

Elsewhere on Main Road traces the perimeter of the island, circling the cen-
the Island tral mountain ranges. Head west on it out of Basseterre to explore the rest of St. Kitts. For the first few miles, you'll be driving through gently rolling hills, past old sugar plantations and ancient stone fences covered with vines, and through tiny villages with tiny houses of stone and weathered wood.

You won't have any trouble identifying the villages as you come across them; small white welcome signs are posted outside each village, placed by members of the 4-H Club. Just outside Challengers is **Bloody Point,** where in 1629, French and British soldiers joined forces to repel a mass attack by the Caribs. The scenery on the drive into **Old Road Town** is spectacular.

❸ From Old Road Town, take the road through the rain forest to visit **Romney Manor,** where batik fabrics are printed at **Caribelle Batik** (*see* Shopping, *below*). The house is set in 6 acres of gardens, with exotic flowers, an old bell tower, and a 350-year-old saman tree (sometimes called a rain tree). Inside, you can watch artisans hand-printing fabrics by the 2,500-year-old Indonesian process known as *batik*.

❹ The village after Old Road Town is **Middle Island,** where Thomas Warner, the "gentleman of London" who brought the first settlers here, died in 1648 and is buried beneath a green gazebo in the churchyard of **St. Thomas Church.**

❺ The road continues through the village of Half-Way Tree to **Brimstone Hill,** the most important historic site on St. Kitts. From the parking area it's a long walk to the 38-acre fortress, but the exercise is well worth it if military history and/or spectacular views interest you. After routing the French in 1690, the English erected a battery on top of Brimstone Hill, and by 1736, there were 49 guns in the fortress. In 1782, the French lay siege to the fortress, which was defended by 350 militia and 600 regular troops of the Royal Scots and East Yorkshires. A plaque in the old stone wall marks the place where the fort was breached. When the English finally surrendered, the French allowed them to march from the fort in full formation out of respect for their bravery. (The English afforded the French the same honor when they surrendered the fort a mere year later.) A hurricane did extensive damage to the fortress in 1834, and in 1852 it was evacuated and dismantled.

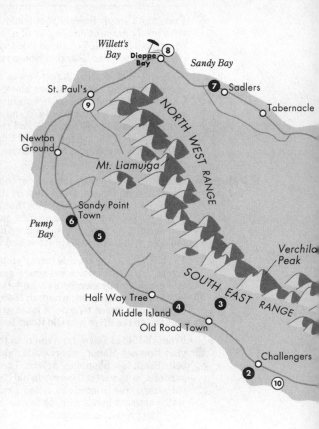

Exploring
Basseterre, **1**
Black Rocks, **7**
Bloody Point, **2**
Brimstone Hill, **5**
Middle Island, **4**
Romney Manor, **3**
Sandy Point Town, **6**

Dining
The Atlantic Club, **12**
Ballahoo, **15**
Blue Horizon, **19**
Chef's Place, **17**
Coconut Cafe, **23**
Fisherman's Wharf, **16**
The Golden Lemon, **8**
The Lighthouse Gourmet Restaurant, **20**
Ocean Terrace Inn, **16**
OTI Turtle Beach Bar and Grill, **27**
PJ's Pizza, **26**
The Patio, **22**
Rawlins Plantation, **9**
The Royal Palm, **11**
The White House, **14**

Lodging
Bird Rock Beach Resort, **20**
Colony's Timothy Beach Resort, **23**
Fairview Inn, **10**
Fort Thomas Hotel, **18**
Frigate Bay Beach Hotel, **21**
The Golden Lemon, **8**
Jack Tar Village Beach Resorts and Casino, **24**
The Lemon Court and Lemon Grove Condominiums, **8**
Morgan Heights Condominiums, **13**
Ocean Terrace Inn, **16**
Ottley's Plantation Inn, **11**
Rawlins Plantation, **9**
Sun 'n Sand Beach Village, **25**
The White House, **14**

St. Kitts

Willett's Bay
Dieppe Bay
Sandy Bay
St. Paul's
Sadlers
Tabernacle
Newton Ground
NORTH WEST RANGE
Mt. Liamuiga
Sandy Point Town
Pump Bay
Verchilo Peak
SOUTH EAST RANGE
Half Way Tree
Middle Island
Old Road Town
Challengers
Caribbean Sea

KEY

Ferry

1 Exploring Sites

8 Hotels and Restaurants

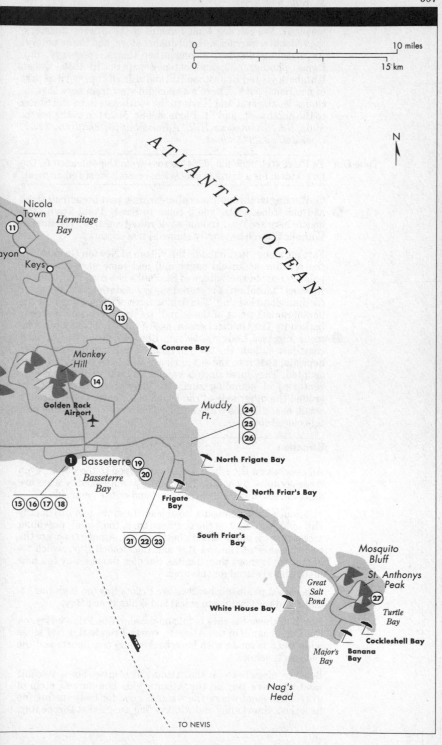

10 miles

15 km

N

ATLANTIC OCEAN

Nicola
Town

Hermitage
Bay

⑪

ayon

Keys

⑫
⑬

Conaree Bay

Monkey
Hill

⑭

Golden Rock
Airport

Muddy
Pt.

㉔
㉕
㉖

North Frigate Bay

① Basseterre ⑲
⑳

Basseterre
Bay

⑮⑯⑰⑱

㉑㉒㉓

North Friar's Bay

Frigate
Bay

South Friar's
Bay

Mosquito
Bluff

St. Anthonys
Peak

㉗

Turtle
Bay

Great
Salt
Pond

White House Bay

Cockleshell Bay

Major's
Bay

Banana
Bay

Nag's
Head

TO NEVIS

The citadel has been partially reconstructed and its guns remounted. You can see what remains of the officers' quarters, the redoubts, barracks, the ordnance store, and the cemetery. Its museums display, among other things, weaponry, uniforms, photographs, and old newspapers. In 1985, Queen Elizabeth visited Brimstone Hill and officially opened it as part of a national park. There's a splendid view from here that includes Montserrat and Nevis to the southeast, Saba and Statia to the northwest, and St. Barts and St. Maarten to the north. *Main Rd., Brimstone Hill. Admission: $5; children, $2.50. Open daily 9:30–5:30.*

Time Out **J's Place** (tel. 809/465–6264) across from the entrance to the fort is ideal for a drink, a sandwich, or a full West Indian meal.

❻ Continuing on through seas of sugarcane, past breadfruit trees and old stone walls, you'll come to **Sandy Point Town.** The houses here are West Indian–style raised cottages. The **Roman Catholic Church** has lovely stained-glass windows.

Farther along, just outside the village of **Newton Ground,** are the remains of an old sugar mill and some ancient coconut palms. Outside the village of **St. Paul's** is a road that leads to **Rawlins Plantation,** a restored sugar plantation that's popular for dining and lodging. The fishing town of **Dieppe Bay** is at the northernmost point of the island. Its tiny black-sand beach is backed by **The Golden Lemon,** one of the Caribbean's most fa-
❼ mous inns (*see* Lodging, *below*). **Black Rocks** on the Atlantic coast just outside the town of Sadlers, in Sandy Bay, are lava deposits, spat into the sea ages ago when the island's volcano erupted. They have since been molded into fanciful shapes by centuries of pounding surf. The drive back to Basseterre around the other side of the island is a pleasant one, through small, neat villages with centuries-old stone churches and pastel-colored cottages.

Beaches

All beaches on the island are free and open to the public, even those occupied by hotels. The powdery white-sand beaches are all at the southern end of the island and on the peninsula.

The South East Peninsula Road leads from the foot of Timothy Hill to Major's Bay on the southern tip of the island, providing access to some of the island's best beaches. Among them are the twin beaches of **Banana Bay** and **Cockleshell Bay,** which together cover more than 2 miles. Sandals Banana Bay is a new luxury hotel slated for this area.

Other good peninsula beaches are **Friar's Bay** (on both the Atlantic and the Caribbean sides) and **White House Bay.**

North of these beaches is talcum-powder-fine **Frigate Bay,** on the Caribbean. On the Atlantic, **North Frigate Bay** is 4 miles wide and a favorite with horseback riders (*see* Sports and the Outdoors, *below*).

Beaches elsewhere on the island are of gray-black volcanic sand. **Conaree Bay** on the Atlantic side is a narrow strip of gray-black sand where the water is good for body surfing (no facilities). Snorkeling and windsurfing are good at **Dieppe Bay,** a black-sand beach on the north coast, where the Golden Lemon Hotel is located.

Sports and the Outdoors

Boating   Sunfish can be rented at **Tropical Surf** in Turtle Bay (tel. 809/496–9086) and Hobie Cats at **R. G. Watersports** in Frigate Bay (tel. 809/465–8050).

Deep-Sea Fishing   Angle for yellowtail snapper, wahoo, mackerel, dolphin, and barracuda with **Tropical Tours** (tel. 809/465–4167) or **Pelican Cove Marina** (tel. 809/465–2754).

Golf   The **Royal St. Kitts Golf Club** (tel. 809/465–8339) is an 18-hole championship course in the Frigate Bay area. There is a 9-hole course at **Golden Rock** (tel. 809/465–8103).

Hiking   Trails in the central mountains vary from easy to don't-try-it-by-yourself. Monkey Hill and Verchild's Mountain are not difficult, although the Verchild's climb will take the better part of a day. Don't attempt Mt. Liamuiga without a guide. You'll start at Belmont Estates on horseback, then proceed on foot to the lip of the crater at 2,600 feet. You can go down into the crater, clinging to vines and roots. **Greg Pereira** (tel. 809/465–4121) takes groups on half-day trips into the rain forest and on full-day hikes up the volcano. **Kriss Tours** (tel. 809/465–4042) takes small groups into the crater and to Dos d'Anse Pond on Verchild's Mountain.

Horseback Riding   Frigate Bay and Conaree Beach are great for riding. Guides from **Trinity Stable** (tel. 809/465–3226) will lead you into the hills at a more leisurely gait. **Royal Stables** (tel. 809/465–2222) offers sunset beach rides and tours into the rain forest on horseback.

Scuba Diving and Snorkeling   Kenneth Samuel of **Kenneth's Dive Centre** (tel. 809/465–7043 or 809/465–2670) is a PADI-certified dive master who takes small groups of divers with C cards to nearby reefs. Auston MacLeod, a PADI-certified dive master/instructor and owner of **Pro-Divers** (tel. 809/465–3223 or 809/465–2754), offers resort and certification courses. He also has Nikonos camera equipment for rent.

Sea Excursions   **Leeward Island Charters** (tel. 809/465–7474) offers day and overnight charters on two catamarans—the 47-foot *Caona* or the 70-foot *Spirit of St. Kitts*. Day sails are from 9:30 to 4:30 and include barbecue, open bar, and snorkeling equipment. **Tropical Tours** (tel. 809/465–4167) offers moonlight cruises on the 52-foot catamaran *Cileca III* and glass-bottom-boat tours. *Tropical Dreamer* (tel. 809/465–8224) is another catamaran available for day and sunset cruises. For the ultimate underwater trip, call **Blue Frontier Ltd.** (tel. 809/465–4945); owner Lindsey Beck will take even nondivers for a half-hour ride off Frigate Bay in his two-man submarine. **Kantours** (tel. 809/465–2098) will take you on a Banana Bay Beach Safari for a day of snorkeling and swimming and an evening barbecue.

Tennis   There are two lighted courts at **Jack Tar Village/Royal St. Kitts** (tel. 809/465–2651) and a functional grass court at **Rawlins Plantation** (tel. 809/465–6221).

Waterskiing and Windsurfing   **Tropical Surf** (tel. 809/469–9086) at Turtle Bay rents Windsurfers, surfboards, and boogie boards. **R. G. Watersports** (tel. 809/465–8050) has windsurfing and waterskiing equipment.

Spectator Sports   **Cricket** matches are played in Warner Park from January to July, **soccer** from July to December, **softball** from January to August. Contact the Tourist Board (tel. 809/465–4040) for schedules.

Shopping

St. Kitts has limited shopping, but there are a few duty-free shops where you can find some good buys in jewelry, watches, perfume, china, and crystal. Among the island crafts, the best-known are the batik fabrics, scarves, caftans, and wall hangings of Caribelle Batik. There are also locally produced jams, jellies, herb teas, and handcrafts of local shell, straw, and coconut. And CSR (Cane Spirit Rothschild) is a "new cane spirit drink" that's distilled from fresh sugarcane right on St. Kitts.

Shopping Districts   Most shopping plazas are near The Circus in downtown Basseterre. Some shops have outlets in other areas, particularly in Dieppe Bay. The **Pelican Mall**, opened in 1991, has 26 stores, a restaurant, tourism offices, and a bandstand. This shopping arcade is designed to look like a traditional Caribbean street. **TDC Mall** is just off The Circus in downtown Basseterre. At press time, the Ballaho Building, right on The Circus, was being renovated; it will house Spencer Cameron Fabrics, Island Hopper, the Ballaho Restaurant, and more. **Shoreline Plaza** is next to the Treasury Building, right on the waterfront in Basseterre. **Palms Arcade** is on Fort Street, also near The Circus.

Good Buys   **TDC** (TDC Plaza, on Bank St., tel. 809/465–2511) carries fine china and crystal, along with cameras and other imports.

Slice of the Lemon (Palms Arcade, tel. 809/465–2889) carries fine perfumes, but is better known for its elegant jewelry. **Lemonaid** (Dieppe Bay, tel. 809/465–7359) has select Caribbean handicrafts, antiques, and clothing by John Warden.

Caribelle Batik (Romney Manor, tel. 809/465–6253), **The Kittitian Kitchen** (Palms Arcade, Basseterre, and at the Golden Lemon, Dieppe Bay, no phone), and **Palm Crafts** (also in Palms Arcade, tel. 809/465–2599) all sell that special something (island crafts, jams and jellies, batik) to take home as gifts and souvenirs. **Spencer Cameron Fabrics** (Ballaho Bldg., The Circus) has silk, cotton, and muslin fabrics hand-painted with clever, colorful designs that include monkeys and tropical flowers. **Spencer Cameron Art Gallery** (South Square St., tel. 809/465–4047) has historical reproductions of Caribbean island charts and prints, in addition to owner Rosey Cameron's popular Carnevale clown prints and other work by Caribbean artists. **Splash** (tel. 809/465–9279) in the Pelican Mall, carries colorful ceramics, including eye-catching work by local artist Paula Fiorel.

Dining

St. Kitts restaurants range from funky little beachfront bistros to elegant plantation dining rooms. Most restaurants offer the visitor a chance to try a variety of West Indian specialties that are popular on St. Kitts, such as curried mutton, arawak chicken (seasoned rice and almonds served on breadfruit leaf), pepperpot, and honey-glazed garlic spare ribs.

Highly recommended restaurants are indicated by a star ★.

Category	Cost*
Expensive	over $25
Moderate	$15–$25
Inexpensive	under $15

*per person, excluding drinks and service. There is no sales tax on St. Kitts.

The Patio Restaurant. Owner Peter Mallalieu and his daughter Helen, a graduate of the Culinary Institute of America, prepare a full à la carte menu with complimentary wine and liqueur, by reservation only, in his flower-filled home. Try the flame-broiled mahimahi with shrimp, or treat yourself to a sampling of traditional local dishes, including *conki* (a coconut side dish) and pepperpot. Piña colada gâteau and tropical fruit mousses are tempting desserts. *Frigate Bay Beach, tel. 809/ 465–8666. Reservations required. MC, V. Expensive.*

★ **Rawlins Plantation.** Elegant dinners are served in a lovely white room with high, vaulted ceilings. The fixed-price (U.S.$35 per person) meal may include callaloo or fresh tomato soup, smoked salmon salad, shrimp in orange butter, and chocolate terrin with passion-fruit sauce. This is also a popular lunch spot, where you may find breadfruit salad, flying fish fritters, or *bobote* (ground beef, eggplant, spices, curry, and homemade chutney). *Mt. Pleasant, tel. 809/465–6221. Reservations required. No credit cards, but personal checks are accepted. Expensive.*

★ **The Royal Palm.** Set beside the pool and the walls of the old sugar factory at Ottley's Plantation, this is a restaurant to experi- ·ence at night, under the latticed roof and among the palms. Start with baked brie or coconut shrimp and then have lobster with fruit and herb stuffing or veal medallions. For dessert, try banana fritters l'antillaise or mango mousse with raspberry sauce. *Ottley's Plantation Inn, tel. 809/645–7234. Reservations required. AE, D, MC, V. Expensive.*

The White House. Lunch and dinner are served in the antiques-filled dining room or on the terrace under a billowing tent filled with plants. The menu features Continental cuisine with a distinctive West Indian flavor. Afternoon tea is served here. *St. Peter's, tel. 809/465–8162. Reservations required. AE, MC, V. Expensive.*

The Golden Lemon. Owner Arthur Leaman creates the recipes himself for the West Indian, Continental, and American cuisines served in his hotel, and he never repeats them more than once in a two-week period. The patio, lush with bougainvillea and ferns, is a popular spot for Sunday brunch, which can include banana pancakes, rum beef stew, and spaghetti with white clam sauce. *Dieppe Bay, tel. 809/465–7260. Reservations required. Dress: casually elegant. AE. Moderate–Expensive.*

The Lighthouse Gourmet Restaurant. Overlooking the harbor of Basseterre and close to town, this restaurant offers panoramic views and both West Indian and Continental cuisines. *Deepwater Port Rd., tel. 809/465–8914. AE, MC, V. Closed Sun. and Mon. Moderate.*

Ocean Terrace Inn. This is a popular place with locals and visitors, where you can dine by candlelight inside or on a balcony overlooking the bay. Lobster is the specialty here—grilled, broiled, and thermidor. At the Friday-night buffet, steak barbecue alternates with West Indian specialties. Dinner is followed by entertainment and dancing. *Fortlands, Basseterre, tel. 809/465–2754. Reservations required. AE, MC, V. Moderate.*

★ **Ballahoo.** Curried conch, beef Stroganoff, salads, and sandwiches are served in a delightful upstairs gallery overlooking Pelican Gardens and The Circus in the heart of town. *Fort St., Basseterre, tel. 809/465–4197. AE, MC, V. Closed Sun. Inexpensive–Moderate.*

★ **Fisherman's Wharf.** At the Ocean Terrace Inn, this informal waterfront eatery serves the island's best conch chowder, grilled lobster, and fish. It's a lively spot on weekend nights. *Fortlands, Basseterre, tel. 809/465–2754. No credit cards. Inexpensive–Moderate.*

OTI Turtle Beach Bar and Grill. Located at the end of the new South East Peninsula Road, this informal restaurant is on a beautiful stretch of beach facing Nevis and is a great place for lunch or dinner. Better yet, spend the day. Try the conch salad with garlic, tandoori chicken, fresh fish, or lobster on the grill. *Turtle Bay, tel. 809/469–9086. AE, MC, V. Inexpensive–Moderate.*

The Atlantic Club. After a morning of exploring, stop at this oceanside eatery for a West Indian meal, seafood dishes, or club sandwiches and hamburgers, accompanied by divine piña coladas. Genford Gumbs, a Nevisian who worked at the Golden Lemon for 15 years, opened this restaurant and bar next to his Morgan Heights Condominiums in 1992. He aims to please patrons and knows how: The portions are hearty and the prices can't be beat. *Morgan Heights Condominiums, Main Rd. near Basseterre, tel. 809/465–8633. AE, D, MC, V. Closed Sun. Inexpensive.*

Blue Horizon. On the cliffs of Bird Rock, this restaurant and bar affords a panoramic view of Basseterre and Nevis. The rustic atmosphere features indoor and outdoor dining with a menu that is French, but uses all local ingredients. Parents welcome the supervised playground for children. *Basseterre, tel. 809/465–5863. Reservations advised. AE, MC, V. Inexpensive.*

Chef's Place. This is a great place to have an inexpensive West Indian meal and meet the local businesspeople. The best seats are on the outdoor, white veranda; try the local version of jerk chicken, moist rather than dry, or the goat stew. *Upper Church St., Basseterre, tel. 809/465–6176. No credit cards. Closed Sun. Inexpensive.*

Coconut Cafe. This restaurant offers casual beachfront dining—breakfast, lunch, and dinner—at the Colony's Timothy Beach Resort on Frigate Bay. Featuring fresh grilled seafood, this is a perfect place from which to watch the sunset. *Frigate Bay, tel. 809/465–3020. AE, D, MC, V. Inexpensive.*

PJ's Pizza. You'll find excellent pizza right next to the Island Paradise Condominiums. Other Italian dishes are served, as are sandwiches. *Frigate Bay, tel. 809/465–8373. No credit cards. Closed Sun. and Mon. Inexpensive.*

Lodging

Choices run from guest houses to full-service hotels to elegant inns in restored plantation homes. Some of the inns include

breakfast and dinner in their rates, which will be indicated in
the descriptions that follow.

Highly recommended lodgings are indicated by a star ★.

Category	Cost*
Very Expensive	over $275
Expensive	$200–$275
Moderate	$125–$200
Inexpensive	under $125

*All prices are for a standard double room for two, MAP, ex-
cluding 7% tax and a 10% service charge.

Hotels
★
The Golden Lemon. Arthur Leaman, a former editor of *House
and Garden,* has created a hotel that is internationally famous,
and with good reason. The four original rooms have high ceilings, hardwood floors, and galleries overlooking the black-sand
beach, palm trees, and the ocean. Each room in the hotel is different; there are wonderful white-iron four-posters, carved ar-
moires, chaise lounges, ceiling fans, mosquito nets, rocking
chairs, and a fine collection of Meissen china in a display case.
Solar-heated water guarantees that showers (there are no
tubs) are always hot. Rates include breakfast (served in your
room or on the veranda), afternoon tea, and an elegant dinner.
There's a staff of 38, and the maximum stay is two weeks. **The
Lemon Court** and **Lemon Grove Condominiums** are sleek, secluded studios and one- and two-bedroom, two-story units that
surround manicured gardens. Some have private Grecian
pools, and all are decorated with a collection of antiques and
Caribbean art. *Box 17, Dieppe Bay, tel. 809/465–7260 or 800/
633–7411, fax 809/465–4019. 27 rooms and suites. Facilities:
beach, pool, restaurant, duty-free shop, free laundry service, 1
tennis court. AE. MAP. Very Expensive.*
The White House. This secluded property, opened in January
1990, is located in the foothills above Basseterre. The restored
plantation great house and rebuilt stable and carriage house
are set on several acres with manicured gardens, a grass tennis
court, and a swimming pool. The bedrooms have hardwood
floors, antiques, wicker furniture, and Laura Ashley fabrics.
Owners Malcolm and Janice Barber's attention to detail is obvious throughout. Dinner is served by candlelight in the main
dining room or outside under a marquee tent. Rates include
breakfast, afternoon tea, and dinner. *Box 436, St. Peter's, tel.
809/465–8162, fax 809/465–8275. 10 rooms. Facilities: restaurant, bar, pool, tennis court, laundry service, shuttle to beach/
town. AE, MC, V. MAP. Very Expensive.*
Jack Tar Village Beach Resorts and Casino. An almost completed $2 million renovation has definitely improved this Jack
Tar Village. What was once worn and overworked is now able to
hold its own among the other resorts in the chain as a very lively, all-inclusive, action-filled vacation destination. Grounds
have been relandscaped and guest rooms updated with cheerful bedspreads, drapes, and bathrooms. One price covers all the
activities—of which there are many—including the greens
fees for the golf course. Two pools fit everyone's needs—those
who want splashing, aerobics, or volleyball head one way,
while the others can have a quiet, relaxing dip at the other.

Nightly live entertainment, a disco, and the island's only casino keeps the action going late into the night. *Box 406, Frigate Bay, tel. 809/465–8651 or 800/999–9182, fax 809/465–8651. 240 rooms, 2 suites. Facilities: casino, 2 pools, 2 restaurants, bars and lounges, 2 lighted tennis courts, facilities for the disabled, water-sports center, access to golf course. AE, MC, V. All-inclusive. Expensive.*

★ **Ottley's Plantation Inn.** Opened in early 1990, this former sugar plantation is composed of 35 acres in the rain forest below Mt. Liamuiga with views out to the Atlantic Ocean. Accommodations are in the restored Great House, with rooms opening onto the wraparound veranda, and in the cut-stone cottages on the beautifully landscaped grounds. The high-ceiling rooms are spacious and decorated in English colonial style with hooked rugs, rattan furniture, and floral chintz fabrics. The large spring-fed pool is set among the remaining walls of the sugar factory with a bar at one end and the Royal Palm restaurant adjoining. Take a stroll through the on-property rain-forest trail. Rates include breakfast and dinner. *Ottley's Plantation Inn, Box 345, Ottley's, tel. 809/465–7234 or 800/772–3039, fax 809/465–4760. 15 rooms. Facilities: pool, restaurant, bar, shuttle to beach/town. AE, D, MC, V. EP, MAP. Expensive.*

★ **Rawlins Plantation.** This lovely inn is set 350 feet above sea level in 12 acres of a once-flourishing sugar plantation. The view from the veranda is splendid, and there is a cozy parlor, done in stylish tropical decor, with bookshelves lining the walls. Guests take dinner in a formal dining room (breakfast, afternoon tea, and dinner are included in the rate). Accommodations (with double, queen-size, or king-size beds) are in cottages tucked into the hillside. All are individually decorated with delicate prints and come equipped with much-needed mosquito nets on four-poster beds. A 17th-century stone windmill contains the split-level honeymoon suite with sunken bathroom. This may be the best spot on the island to view the sunset. Paul and Claire Rawson became the new owners of Rawlins in 1989. *Box 340, Mt. Pleasant, tel. 809/465–6221 or 800/621–1270, fax 809/465–4954. 10 rooms. Facilities: pool, restaurant, tennis court, croquet, and complimentary laundry service. No credit cards, but personal checks are accepted. MAP. Expensive.*

★ **Colony's Timothy Beach Resort.** This is the only hotel in the Frigate Bay area that sits directly on the calm, Caribbean beach. The rooms and suites are decorated in modern style with island accents; larger units have kitchens and multiple bedrooms. The bathrooms in all the rooms are attractive and particularly well kept-up. The best units sit right over the beach. Guests can participate in a wide variety of water and land activities, including nearby golf. The hotel's Coconut Cafe (*see* Dining, *above*) is a local favorite. The management is attentive and friendly. For couples and families who don't mind trading some atmosphere for modern comfort at a good price, this could well be the ideal spot for a beach-oriented vacation. Rates here are based on EP, so guests can feel free to sample the cuisine around St. Kitts. *Box 81, Frigate Bay, tel. 809/465–8597 or 800/621–1270, fax 809/465–7723; Colony Reservations Worldwide, 800/777–1700. 60 rooms. Facilities: pool, restaurant, beach, water activities, nearby golf, shopping, and other conveniences. AE, MC, V. EP. Moderate–Expensive.*

Sun 'n Sand Beach Village. These studio and two-bedroom, self-catering cottages are immaculately clean and right by the beach and pool on the Atlantic side of the island. Furnishings are simple and tropical, with tile floors, terraces, twin or queen-size beds, and private baths (shower only). Studios are air-conditioned; apartments have window air conditioners in bedrooms and ceiling fans in living rooms. Bedroom apartments have convertible sofas in living rooms and fully equipped kitchens with microwave ovens and full-size refrigerators. *Box 341, Frigate Bay, tel. 809/465–8037, 800/621–1270, or 800/223–6510, fax 809/465–6745. 32 studios, 18 2-bedroom cottages. Facilities: beach, restaurant, pool, children's pool, 2 lighted tennis courts, grocery store, nearby drugstore, gift shop. AE, D, MC, V. CP. Moderate.*

Frigate Bay Beach Hotel. The third fairway of the island's golf course adjoins the property, and the nearby beach is reached by complimentary shuttle buses. The whitewashed, air-conditioned buildings contain standard rooms as well as condominium units with fully equipped kitchens. There are hillside and poolside units; the latter are preferable. Standard rooms are large but simply furnished, with tile floors and sliding glass doors leading to a terrace or balcony. There's a pool with swim-up bar and a friendly staff. *Box 137, Basseterre, tel. 809/465–8936, 809/465–8935, or 800/223–9815, fax 809/465–7050. 64 rooms. Facilities: pool, restaurant, bar. AE, D, MC, V. EP, MAP. Inexpensive–Moderate.*

★ **Ocean Terrace Inn.** Affectionately called OTI, this is one of the island's most luxurious hotels, offering an assortment of rooms, all of which are air-conditioned, with cable TVs and radios. There are rooms with kitchenettes and condominium units with private terraces overlooking one of the inn's two pools. In a section called Fisherman's Village, there are luxury one- and two-bedroom split-level suites overlooking Basseterre's harbor. Fisherman's Wharf restaurant is famed island-wide for its seafood, and the hotel's Pelican Cove Marina has its own fleet of boats. There is a shuttle daily to the hotel's beach at Turtle Bay, where you'll find a restaurant/bar and all water sports. *Box 65, Basseterre, tel. 809/465–2754, 800/223–5695, or 800/524–0512, fax 809/465–1057. 52 rooms. Facilities: beach, 2 pools, outdoor Jacuzzi, 2 restaurants, 2 bars, cable TV, fleet of boats, water-sports center. AE, MC, V. EP, MAP. Inexpensive–Moderate.*

Bird Rock Beach Resort. Perched on a bluff overlooking the Caribbean, this new hotel has two-story units containing air-conditioned rooms and suites with direct-dial telephone, cable TV, and balcony. The tile-floored rooms are simply furnished with rattan furniture and floral fabrics. The hotel has its own beach and pool with a swim-up bar. There is an informal dining room next to the pool and shuttle service to the Lighthouse Gourmet Restaurant. A new, all-weather tennis court has also been added. It's just five minutes from the airport, town, golf, and Frigate Bay beaches. *Box 227, Basseterre, tel. 809/465–8914 or 800/621–1270, fax 809/465–1675. 24 rooms. Facilities: 2 restaurants, bar, pool, beach, tennis court, shuttle service to golf. AE, MC, V. EP, MAP. Inexpensive.*

Fairview Inn. The main building of this hotel is an 18th-century great house, with graceful white verandas and Oriental rugs on hardwood floors. The rooms are in cottages sprinkled around the backyard, which happens to be a mountain of considerable size. The rooms have functional furnishings, with either twin or double beds, private patios, and radios. All have simple private baths with showers or bathtubs. Some have air-conditioning, some fans, some neither. The Fairview is well

known for its superb West Indian cuisine. *Box 212, Basseterre,
tel. 809/465-2472 or 800/223-9815, fax 809/465-1056. 30
rooms. Facilities: restaurant, 2 bars, pool. AE, D, MC, V. EP.
Inexpensive.*

Fort Thomas Hotel. This hotel is on the site of an old fort. Popular with tour groups, it's set on 8 acres on a hillside in the outskirts of Basseterre. The rooms are spacious and all have
private baths, air-conditioning, radios, and phones; TVs can be
rented. There's a free shuttle bus to the beach. *Box 407, Basse-
terre, tel. 809/465-2695, fax 809/465-7518. 64 rooms. Facilities: pool, games room, restaurant, bar. AE, D, MC, V. EP.
Inexpensive.*

Morgan Heights Condominiums. Glenford Gumbs left the Gold-
en Lemon after 15 years to build Morgan Heights along the Atlantic Coast 10 minutes from Basseterre. Built in 1992, these
rooms are clean and comfortable—perfect for someone who
wants a laid-back atmosphere and reasonable prices. The
rooms are simple but contemporary, with ceramic tile floors,
shell motifs, and white wicker furniture. All are air-conditioned and have direct-dial phones, fully equipped kitchens, cable TV, and baths. Their covered patios overlook the water.
Gumbs plans to add 10 units by winter 1994. *Box 536, Basse-
terre, tel. 809/465-8633 or 809/465-9210, fax 809/465-9272. 5
2-bedroom units that can be rented as 1-bedroom units. Facilities: restaurant, freshwater pool. AE, D, MC, V. EP. Inexpensive.*

**Condos and
Guest Houses** This little island has a number of condominiums and guest
houses available to visitors. For information, contact the St.
Kitts Tourist Board (Box 132, Basseterre, St. Kitts, tel. 809/
465-2620).

Nightlife

Most of the Kittitian nightlife revolves around the hotels,
which host such live entertainment as folkloric shows, calypso
music, and steel bands.

Casinos The only game in town is at the **Jack Tar Village Casino** (*see*
Lodging, *above*), where you'll find blackjack tables, roulette
wheels, craps tables, and one-armed bandits. Dress is casual,
and play continues till the last player leaves. Note: You do not
need to purchase Jack Tar passes to play, even though the casino entrance is in the hotel lobby.

Discos On Saturday night head for the **Turtle Beach Bar and Grill**
(Turtle Bay, tel. 809/496-9086), where there is a beach dance-
disco. Play volleyball into the evening, then dance under the
stars into the night. At **J's Place** (across from Brimstone Hill,
tel. 809/465-6264), you and the locals can dance the night away
on Friday and Saturday. **Reflections Night Club** (tel. 809/465-
7616), upstairs at Flex Fitness Center, is the newest Kittitian
night spot. It's open Tuesday through Sunday from 9 until well
past midnight. Cover charge is E.C.$10 Thursday, Friday, and
Saturday nights.

Nevis

Staying in Nevis

Important Addresses

Tourist Information: The Tourism Office (tel. 809/469–5521) is on Main Street in Charlestown. The office is open Monday and Tuesday 8–4:30 and Wednesday–Friday 8–4.

Emergencies

Police: Call 911. **Hospitals:** There is a 24-hour emergency room at **Alexandra Hospital** (Charlestown, tel. 809/469–5473). **Pharmacies: Evelyn's Drugstore** (Charlestown, tel. 809/469–5278) is open weekdays 8–5, Saturday 8–7:30, and Sunday 7 AM–8 PM; and the **Claxton Medical Centre** (Charlestown, tel. 809/469–5357) is open Monday–Wednesday and Friday 8–6, Thursday 8–4, Saturday 7:30–7, and Sunday 6–8 PM.

Currency

Legal tender is the Eastern Caribbean (E.C.) dollar. The rate of exchange fluctuates but hovers around E.C.$2.60 to U.S.$1. The U.S. dollar is accepted everywhere, but you'll almost always get change in E.C.s. Prices quoted here are in U.S. dollars unless noted otherwise. Credit cards are accepted at many hotels and restaurants on the island, though some of the inns will take only personal checks.

Taxes and Service Charges

Hotels collect a 7% government tax. The departure tax is $8. Most hotels add a 10% service charge to your bill. For a job well done, a 10%–15% gratuity should be left in addition. Taxi drivers should be given a 10% tip.

Guided Tours

The **taxi driver** who picks you up will offer to act as your guide to the island. Each driver is knowledgeable and does a 3½-hour tour for $75. He'll probably ask if you'd like him to make lunch reservations for you at one of the plantations. Say yes.

All Seasons Streamline Tours (tel. 809/469–5705 or 809/469–1138, fax 809/469–1139) has a fleet of air-conditioned vans and uniformed drivers to take you around the island for $75 per day. Licensed agents Nelson and Wendy Amory can also arrange any activities for you.

Another tour option is **Jan's Travel Agency** (Arcade, Charlestown, tel. 809/469–5578), which arranges half- and full-day tours of the island.

Getting Around
Rental Cars

Arrive in Nevis with a valid driver's license and your car-rental agency will help you obtain a local license at the police station. The cost is E.C.$30 (U.S.$12), and it is valid for one year.

Beware: The island's roads are pocked with crater-size potholes; driving is on the left; goats and cattle crop up out of nowhere to amble along the road; and if you deviate from Main Street, you're likely to have trouble finding your way around. For all these reasons, we recommend that you take a taxi from point to point. Having said that, we won't withhold from you the information that **Skeete's Car Rental** (Newcastle Village, at the airport, tel. 809/469–9458) has Toyota Corollas, Suzuki Jeeps, and Mitsubishi Lancers; **TDC Rentals, Ltd.** (Charlestown, tel. 809/469–5690) and **Striker's Car Rental** (Hermitage, tel. 809/469–2654) have minimokes and compacts; **Nisbett Rentals Ltd.** (tel. 809/469–1913 or 809/469–6211) rents cars, minimokes, and jeeps. None of them charges for mileage, and all of them accept major credit cards.

Taxis Taxi service is available at the airport. Some of the island's fleet includes **Kurtley Maynard** (tel. 809/469–1973), **Ralph Hutton** (tel. 809/469–1767), and **Luther Morton** (tel. 809/469–1858).

Telephones and Mail To call Nevis from the United States, dial area code 809, followed by 469 and the local number. Communications are excellent, both on the island and with the United States, and direct-dial long distance is in effect. Note: The Gingerland area has a new exchange; all numbers that previously began with 469–5 have been changed to 469–3.

Airmail letters to the United States and Canada require E.C.80¢ per half ounce; postcards, E.C.50¢. It'll take at least a week to 10 days for mail to reach home. Nevis and St. Kitts have separate stamp-issuing policies, but each honors the other's stamps.

Opening and Closing Times Shops are open Monday–Saturday 8–noon and 1–4 (until 5 on Saturday). Banking hours vary but are generally Monday–Thursday 8–3; Friday 8–5. **St. Kitts-Nevis-Anguilla National Bank** and the **Bank of Nevis** are open Saturday 8:30–11 AM.

Exploring Nevis

Numbers in the margin correspond to points of interest on the Nevis map.

Charlestown About 1,200 of the island's 9,300 inhabitants live in **Charlestown,** the capital of Nevis. It faces the Caribbean, about 12½ miles south of Basseterre in St. Kitts. If you arrive by ferry, as most people do, you'll walk smack onto Main Street from the pier. You can tour the capital city in a half hour or so, but you'll need three to four hours to explore the entire island.

Turn right on Main Street and look for the **Nevis Tourist Office** (on your right as you enter the main square). Pick up a copy of the Nevis Historical Society's self-guided tour of the island and stroll back onto Main Street.

While it is true that Charlestown has seen better days—it was founded in 1660—it's easy to imagine how it must have looked in its heyday. The buildings may be weathered and a bit worse for wear now, but there is still evidence of past glory in their fanciful galleries, elaborate gingerbread, wood shutters, and colorful hanging plants.

The stonework building with the clock tower at the corner of Main and Prince William streets houses the **courthouse** and **library.** A fire in 1873 severely damaged the building and destroyed valuable records. The current building dates from the turn of the century. You're welcome to poke around the second-floor library (open Mon.–Sat. 9–6), which is one of the coolest places on the island.

If you intend to rent a car, the **police station** across from the courthouse is the place to go to for your local driver's license.

The little park opposite the courthouse is **Memorial Square,** dedicated to the fallen of World Wars I and II.

Time Out Drop into **Caribbean Confections** (across the street from the Tourist Office, tel. 809/469–5685) for coffee and homemade pastries. There are also sandwiches, peanut-butter cookies, and popcorn.

When you return to Main Street from Prince William Street, turn right and go past the pier. Main Street curves and becomes Craddock Road, but keep going straight and you'll be on Low Street. The **Alexander Hamilton Birthplace,** which contains the **Museum of Nevis History,** is on the waterfront, covered in bougainvillea and hibiscus. This Georgian-style house is a reconstruction of the statesman's original home, which was built in 1680 and is thought to have been destroyed during an earthquake in the mid-19th century. Hamilton was born here in 1755. He left for the American colonies 17 years later to contrive his education; he became secretary to George Washington and died in a duel with political rival Aaron Burr. The **Nevis House of Assembly** sits on the second floor of this building, and the museum downstairs contains Hamilton memorabilia and documents pertaining to the island's history. *Low St., no phone. Admission free. Open weekdays 8–4, Sat. 10–noon. Closed Sun.*

Elsewhere on the Island You'll have to resort to wheels to see the other sights and sites. The main road makes a 20-mile circuit, with various offshoots bumping and winding into the mountains. Take the road south out of Charlestown, passing **Grove Park** along the way, where soccer and cricket matches are played.

② About ¼ mile from the park you'll come to the ruins of the **Bath Hotel** (built by John Huggins in 1778) and **Bath Springs.** The springs, some icy cold, others with temperatures of 108°F, emanate from the hillside and spill into the "great poole" that John Smith mentioned in 1607. Huggins's hotel was adjacent to the waters, with the Spring House built over the springs. The swanky hotel, which charged an outrageous price of sixpence, accommodated 50 guests. Eighteenth-century accounts reported that a stay of a few days, bathing in and imbibing the waters, resulted in miraculous cures. It would take a minor miracle to restore the decayed hotel to anything like grandeur—it closed down in the late-19th century—but the Spring House has been partially restored and some of the springs are still as hot as ever. *Bathing costs $2. Open weekdays 8–noon and 1–3:30, Sat. 8–noon. Closed Sun.*

③ On Bath Road is the **Nelson Museum,** worth a visit for the memorabilia it has from the life and times of Lord Nelson, including letters, documents, paintings, and even furniture from his flagship. Nelson was based in Antigua, but returned often to court, and eventually marry, Frances Nisbet, who lived on a 64-acre plantation here. *Bath Rd., tel. 809/469–0408. Admission: U.S.$2. Open Mon.–Wed. 8–4:30, Thurs.–Fri. 8–4, Sat. 8–noon; closed Sun.*

④ About 2 miles from Charlestown, in the village of Fig Tree, is **St. John's Church,** which dates from 1680. Among its records is a tattered, prominently displayed marriage certificate that reads: "Horatio Nelson, Esquire, to Frances Nisbet, Widow, on March 11, 1787."

⑤ At the island's east coast, you'll come to the government-owned **Eden Brown Estate,** built around 1740 and known as Nevis's haunted house, or, rather, haunted ruins. In 1822, apparently, a Miss Julia Huggins was to marry a fellow named Maynard.

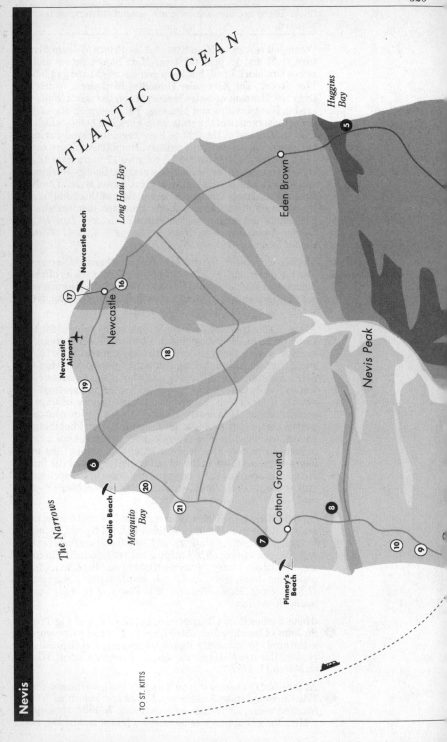

Nevis

ATLANTIC OCEAN

Huggins Bay

Eden Brown

Long Haul Bay

Newcastle Beach

Newcastle

Newcastle Airport

Nevis Peak

Cotton Ground

Oualie Beach

Mosquito Bay

The Narrows

Pinney's Beach

TO ST. KITTS

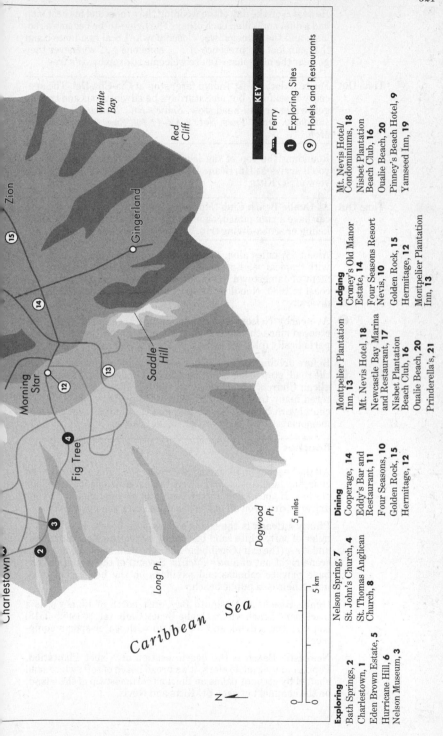

KEY

🚢 Ferry

1 Exploring Sites

9 Hotels and Restaurants

Exploring
Bath Springs, **2**
Charlestown, **1**
Eden Brown Estate, **5**
Hurricane Hill, **6**
Nelson Museum, **3**

Nelson Spring, **7**
St. John's Church, **4**
St. Thomas Anglican
Church, **8**

Dining
Cooperage, **14**
Eddy's Bar and
Restaurant, **11**
Four Seasons, **10**
Golden Rock, **15**
Hermitage, **12**

Montpelier Plantation
Inn, **13**
Mt. Nevis Hotel, **18**
Newcastle Bay Marina
and Restaurant, **17**
Nisbet Plantation
Beach Club, **16**
Oualie Beach, **20**
Prinderella's, **21**

Lodging
Croney's Old Manor
Estate, **14**
Four Seasons Resort
Nevis, **10**
Golden Rock, **15**
Hermitage, **12**
Montpelier Plantation
Inn, **13**

Mt. Nevis Hotel/
Condominiums, **18**
Nisbet Plantation
Beach Club, **16**
Oualie Beach, **20**
Pinney's Beach Hotel, **9**
Yamseed Inn, **19**

However, on the day of the wedding the groom and his best man had a duel and killed each other. The bride-to-be became a recluse, and the mansion was closed down. Local residents claim they can feel the presence of . . . someone . . . whenever they go near the old house. You're welcome to drop by. It's free.

Time Out For real, local West Indian fare, stop at **Cla-Cha-Del.** The specialty is seafood, but on Saturdays be adventurous and try the goatwater or bull-head stew. *Shaw's Rd., Newcastle, tel. 809/ 469–9640. Open Tues. Sat. 9 AM–11 PM, Sun. 6–11 PM, closed Mon.*

6 Rounding the top of the island, west of Newcastle Airport, you'll arrive at **Hurricane Hill,** from which there is a splendid view of St. Kitts.

Time Out At **Oualie Beach Club** (Mosquito Bay, tel. 809/469–9518), you can have a rum punch, swim in the sea, and sign up for a snorkeling or scuba-diving trip. Try the Sunday barbecue.

About 1½ miles along the Main Road, **Fort Ashby,** overgrown with tropical vegetation, overlooks the place where the settlement of Jamestown fell into the sea after a tidal wave hit the coast in 1680. Needless to say, this is a favored target of scuba divers.

7 At nearby **Nelson Spring,** the waters have considerably decreased since the 1780s, when young Captain Horatio Nelson periodically filled his ships with fresh water here.

8 Before driving back into Charlestown, a little over a mile down the road, stop to see the island's oldest church, **St. Thomas Anglican Church.** The church was built in 1643 and has been altered many times over the years. The gravestones in the old churchyard have stories to tell, and the church itself contains memorials to the early settlers of Nevis.

Beaches

All the beaches on the island are free to the public. There are no changing facilities, so you'll have to wear a swimsuit under your clothes. If you're doing a cab tour, you may arrange with your driver to drop you off at the beach and pick you up later.

Pinney's Beach is the island's showpiece beach. It's almost 4 miles of soft, white sand backed by a cyclorama of palm trees, and it's on the calm Caribbean Sea. The palm-shaded lagoon is a scene right out of *South Pacific.* Several of the mountain inns have private cabanas and pavilions on the beach, but it is, nevertheless, a public beach.

Oualie Beach, at Mosquito Bay, just north of Pinney's, is a black-sand beach where Oualie Beach Club (tel. 809/469–9518) can mix you a drink and fix you up with water-sports equipment.

Newcastle Beach is the beach location of Nisbet Plantation. Popular among snorkelers, it's a broad beach of soft, white sand shaded by coconut palms on the northernmost tip of the island, on the channel between St. Kitts and Nevis.

Sports and the Outdoors

Boating   Hobie Cats and Sunfish can be rented from **Oualie Beach Club** (tel. 809/469–9518). **Newcastle Bay Marina** (Newcastle, tel. 809/469–9373) has Phantom sailboats, a 23-foot KenCraft powerboat, and several inflatables with outboards available for rent. **Frank Morse** (Oualie Beach, tel. 809/469–9735) has a 65-foot aluminum sloop, *Never Say Never*, on which he takes guests for day sails.

Deep-Sea Fishing   The game here is kingfish, wahoo, grouper, and yellowtail snapper. If you want local knowledge, call **Captain Valentine Glasgow** (tel. 809/469–1989), who has a 31-foot Ocean Master, *Lady James*, to take you in search of the big ones. **Jans Travel Agency** (tel. 809/469–5578) arranges deep-sea fishing trips.

Hiking   The center of the island is Nevis peak, which soars up to 3,232 feet, flanked by Hurricane Hill on the north and Saddle Hill on the south. If you plan to scale Mt. Nevis, a daylong affair, it is highly recommended that you go with a guide. Your hotel can arrange it for you; you can also ask the hotel to pack a picnic lunch. The **Nevis Academy** (tel. 809/469–2091, fax 809/469–2113), headed by David Rollinson, offers ecorambles (slower tours) and hikes. Three-hour rambles or hikes are $20 per person.

Horseback Riding   You can arrange for mountain-trail and beach rides through **Cane Gardens** (tel. 809/469–5648) and Ira Dore at **Garner's Estate** (tel. 809/469–5528).

Tennis   There are 10 tennis courts at the **Four Seasons Resort Nevis** (tel. 809/469–1111), two at **Pinney's Beach Hotel** (tel. 809/469–5207), and one court each at **Nisbet** (tel. 809/469–9325), **Montpelier** (tel. 809/469–3462), and **Golden Rock** (tel. 809/469–3346).

Water Sports   The village of **Jamestown** was washed into the sea around Fort Ashby; the area is a popular spot for snorkeling and diving. Reef-protected **Pinney's Beach** offers especially good snorkeling.

Montpelier Plantation (tel. 809/469–5462) has a 17-foot Boston whaler for scuba, snorkeling, and waterskiing trips. Snorkeling and waterskiing trips can also be arranged through **Oualie Beach** (tel. 809/469–9518) and **Newcastle Bay Marina** (tel. 809/469–9373). Windsurfers can also be rented at both places. There is a full dive shop at Oualie Beach that offers resort and NAUI-certification courses. Dive packages are also available.

Windsurfing   For windsurfing, **Winston Crooke** (tel. 809/469–9615) rents equipment and teaches classes. A two-hour beginners class is $40 per person. If you rent equipment only, it's $12 an hour per person.

Spectator Sports   **Grove Park** is the venue for cricket (Jan.–July) and soccer
Cricket and Soccer   (July–Dec.). Your hotel or the Tourist Board can fill you in on dates, times, and grudge matches of particular interest between Kittitians and Nevisians.

Shopping

Rare is the traveler who heads for Nevis on a shopping spree. However, there are some surprises here, notably the island's stamps, batik and hand-embroidered clothing, and the artwork of Dame Eva Wilkins, who died in 1989.

For more than 50 years Wilkins painted island people, flowers, and landscapes. An Eva Wilkins mural hangs over the bar at the Golden Rock (*see* Dining, *below*). Her originals sell for $100 and up, and prints are available in some of the local shops.

For dolls and baskets handcrafted in Nevis, visit **The Sandbox Tree** (tel. 809/469–5662) in Evelyn's Villa, Charlestown. Among other items available here are handpainted chests. This is an appealing shop even if you are only browsing. The **Nevis Handicraft Co-op Society** (tel. 809/469–5509), next door to the Tourism Office, offers work by local artisans, including clothing, woven goods, and homemade jellies. Heading out of town, just past Alexander Hamilton's birthplace, you'll see the **Nevis Crafts Studio Cooperative.** Here Alvin Grante, a multitalented Nevisian artisan, displays his works and those of Ashley Phillips: hand-blocked prints and watercolors of the local landscape and architecture, hand-painted T-shirts, and baskets.

Stamp collectors should head for the **Philatelic Bureau,** just off Main Street opposite the Tourist Office. St. Kitts and Nevis are famous for their decorative, and sometimes lucrative, stamps. An early Kittitian stamp recently brought in $7,000.

Other local items of note are the batik caftans, scarves, and fabrics found in the Nevis branch of **Caribelle Batik** (in the Arcade of downtown Charlestown, tel. 809/469–1491). **Caribee Clothes** (off Main St., tel. 809/469–5217) has resort clothing with hand-embroidered designs that have been praised by *Vogue*.

Dining

All the plantation guest houses serve meals. Most of them have informal lobster bakes on the beach, as well as romantic candlelit dinners in elegant dining rooms. (For more detailed descriptions of the plantations, *see* Lodging, *below*). Meals in the plantations are mostly fixed price and run from about $25 to $45, including wine. In each case the menu changes daily.

Highly recommended restaurants are indicated by a star ★.

Category	Cost*
Expensive	$25–$45
Moderate	$15–$25
Inexpensive	under $15

**per person, excluding drinks and service*

Four Seasons. Each of the two restaurants has nouvelle cuisine with island touches. The more expensive dining room has handsome furnishings and dramatic lighting. The hotel also features a weekly Caribbean buffet with a full steel band. Especially good desserts are the coconut ice cream and rhubarb pie. *Reservations required. AE, D, MC, V. Expensive.*
Golden Rock. Dinner is in an opulent dining room with handsome tablecloths and soft candlelight. West Indian and Continental dishes are served. *Golden Rock, tel. 809/469–3346. Reservations required. AE, MC, V. Closed Sun. Expensive.*
Hermitage. The atmosphere here is subdued, with white

cloths, candlelight, and a backdrop of white latticework on the porch. Begin your meal with carrot-and-tarragon soup, then follow it with West Indian red snapper in ginger sauce, and finish off with a rum soufflé. The Hermitage is known for having the best rum punch on the island—no small accomplishment. *Hermitage Plantation, tel. 809/469–3477. Reservations required. AE, MC, V. Personal checks accepted. Expensive.*

Montpelier Plantation Inn. Dinner is by candlelight on the veranda. Your feast may include cream of avocado and coconut soup, lobster, red snapper, chicken calypso, sirloin steak Bordelaise, or even roast beef and Yorkshire pudding. Dessert could be grapefruit sorbet or rum and chocolate layer gâteau. *Montpelier Plantation, tel. 809/469–3462. Reservations required. No credit cards. Expensive.*

Mt. Nevis Hotel. The airy 60-seat dining room, where tables are set with fine china and silver, opens onto the terrace and pool, beyond which there is a splendid daytime view of St. Kitts in the distance. Starters include fish chowder and lobster bisque. Entrées may include red snapper, lobster, or sirloin steak embellished with mushrooms and onions. *Mt. Nevis Hotel/ Condominiums, Newcastle, tel. 809/469–9373. Reservations suggested. AE, D, MC, V. Expensive.*

Nisbet Plantation Beach Club. The antiques-filled dining room in the Great House at Nisbet has long been a popular place for lunch and dinner. There are also tables on the screened-in veranda, where there's a view down the palm-tree-lined fairway to the sea. Continental and Caribbean cuisines are served here and at the new beach and poolside restaurant Coconuts. *Nisbet Plantation, tel. 809/469–9325. Reservations required. AE, MC, V. Expensive.*

★ **Cooperage.** An old stone dining room provides an elegantly rustic setting. Among the specialties here are green-pepper soup, curried chicken breasts, coconut shrimp, and sorbets. An à la carte menu has been added; lobster for $19.50 is the most expensive item, making this a good bet. *Croney's Old Manor Estate, tel. 809/469–3445. Reservations required. AE, D, MC, V. Moderate–Expensive.*

Eddy's Bar and Restaurant. In the center of Charlestown, this place, owned by Nevisian Ed Williams and his Canadian wife, Shelia, may well become the most popular gathering spot in the town. You'll find fine local and stir-fried specialties; the conch chowder is especially good. Stop by between 5 and 8 on Wednesday for happy hour; drinks are half price, snacks are free. *Main St., Charlestown, tel. 809/469–5958. Reservations advised. AE, MC, V. Inexpensive–Moderate.*

Prinderella's. Although its perfect beachside setting made it a prime target for Hurricane Hugo, owners Ian and Charlie Mintrim have rebuilt and reopened their popular restaurant. On Tamarind Bay, with views across the channel to St. Kitts, it's a great spot for a sunset drink. Lunch features flying fish and chips, grilled lobster, and salmon. *Jones Bridge, tel. 809/ 469–9291. AE, MC, V. Open for lunch Mon.–Sun; dinner Tues.–Sat. Inexpensive–Moderate.*

Newcastle Bay Marina and Restaurant. The pizza here is excellent, but even non-pizza lovers will enjoy sitting back on the deck and looking out to sea. Try the conch chowder, a sandwich, or a salad. This complex, part of the Mt. Nevis Hotel, will soon include a fitness facility and live entertainment on certain evenings. Closed in low season. *Newcastle Bay Marina, tel. 809/469–9373. AE, D, MC, V. Inexpensive.*

Oualie Beach. This low-key, casual bar and restaurant on Oualie Bay is the perfect stop during a round-the-island tour or after a long day on the beach. Try the delicious homemade soups, including ground-nut or breadfruit vichyssoise. Then move on to Creole conch stew or lobster crepes. If you had something else in mind, the chef will cook to order with proper notice. *Oualie Beach, tel. 809/469-9735. MC, V. Inexpensive.*

Lodging

The island is filled with restored sugar plantations that are now guest houses and inns. Most of them operate on the MAP.

Highly recommended lodgings are indicated by a star ★.

Category	Cost*
Very Expensive	over $275
Expensive	$225–$275
Moderate	$150–$225
Inexpensive	under $150

All prices are for a standard double room for two, MAP, excluding 7% tax and a 10% service charge.

★ **Four Seasons Resort Nevis.** This prestigious Canadian company's first foray into the Caribbean is a real winner. The 196-room property manages to combine world-class elegance with a West Indian casual atmosphere and hospitality. Situated on a stunning stretch of Pinney's Beach, the hotel offers a complete range of water activities, along with clay and all-weather tennis courts, an attractive pool, and a challenging 18-hole golf course created by Robert Trent Jones II. Guest rooms feature luxurious marble double-sink baths, handsome furnishings with West Indian accents, private screened terraces, plus all the electronic gadgets you came here to escape, including multichannel cable TV. There are two outstanding restaurants; even the "formal" room is relaxed, with no jackets or ties required. Throw in a complete children's program, wonderful weekly cocktail parties, a (largely local) delightful staff, and a dramatic water-shuttle arrival from St. Kitts, and you've got a top-dollar vacation that's actually worth the price. Note: Four Seasons usually offers good-value sports and romantic packages even during the high season. *Box 565, Charlestown, tel. 809/469-1111; in the U.S., 800/332-3442; in Canada, 800/268-6288, fax 809/469-1112. 196 rooms. Facilities: 2 dining rooms, pub, casual outdoor dining, pool, beach, water sports, catamaran rentals, fitness center, free daily aerobics, 10 tennis courts, 18-hole golf course, children's program, baby-sitting, laundry service and free washer/dryers, 2 boutiques. AE, D, MC, V. EP, MAP, FAP. Very Expensive.*

★ **Hermitage.** This is a wonderful 250-year-old great house with modern facilities in the restored carriage house and cottages. Each cottage sleeps two, and most have a small kitchenette. There are verandas and hammocks for loafing and enjoying the tropical gardens, and an antiques-filled dining room for elegant dinners. *St. Johns, Fig Tree Parish, tel. 809/469-3477, fax 809/469-2481. 12 suites. Facilities: pool, restaurant. AE, MC, V. Personal checks accepted. EP, MAP. Very Expensive.*

Montpelier Plantation Inn. This old West Indian–style manor house is set on 100 beautifully landscaped acres. Neat brick paths lead through tropical gardens, and accommodations are in cottages, each with two patios and private shower. Transportation is provided to Pinney's Beach, where the estate has a cabana. The estate has a 17-foot Boston whaler for water-skiing, snorkeling, and fishing. *Box 474, Charlestown, tel. 809/469–3462 or 800/243–9420, fax 809/469–2932. 17 rooms. Facilities: restaurant, bar, pool, tennis court. No credit cards. BP, MAP. Very Expensive.*

★ **Nisbet Plantation Beach Club.** From the manor house of this 18th-century plantation you can see the beach at the end of a long avenue of coconut palms, and from the bar, you look out over an old sugar mill covered with hibiscus, cassia, frangipani, and flamboyants. Renovated and reopened in January 1990, Nisbet offers a range of accommodations, from plantation-style cottages to lanai suites, all simply but tastefully appointed in island style and situated along an avenue of palms that leads to the ocean. *Newcastle Beach, tel. 809/469–9325; in the U.S., 800/344–2049, fax 809/469–9864. 38 rooms. Facilities: beach, tennis court, 3 restaurants, 2 bars, free laundry, boutique, free snorkeling gear. AE, MC, V. EP, MAP. Very Expensive.*

Croney's Old Manor Estate. Vast tropical gardens surround this restored sugar plantation. Many guest rooms have high ceilings, king-size four-poster beds, and colonial reproductions, but some units are a bit gloomy and dark. The outbuildings, such as the smokehouse and jail, have been imaginatively restored, and the old cistern is now the pool. This is the home of The Cooperage, one of the island's best restaurants (*see* Dining, *above*). There's transportation to and from the beach. The hotel is not recommended for children under 12. *Box 70, Charlestown, tel. 809/469–3445; in the U.S., 800/223–9815 or 800/892–7093, fax 809/469–3388. 14 rooms. Facilities: pool, 2 restaurants, 2 bars. AE, MC, V. EP, MAP. Expensive.*

★ **Golden Rock.** Co-owner Pam Barry is a direct descendant of the original owner of this 200-year-old estate. She has decorated the five cottages in a style befitting a plantation. There are handsome four-poster beds of mahogany or bamboo, native grass rugs, rocking chairs, and island-made fabrics of floral prints. All rooms have private baths and a patio. The restored sugar mill is a two-level suite for honeymooners or families, and the old cistern is now a spring-fed swimming pool. The estate covers 150 mountainous acres and is surrounded by 25 acres of lavish tropical gardens, including a sunken garden. Enjoy the Atlantic view and cooling breeze from the bar. The Saturday night West Indian buffet is very popular, December through June. *Box 493, Gingerland, tel. 809/469–3346, fax 809/469–2113. 16 rooms. Facilities: 2 beaches, restaurant, bar, pool, tennis court, educational activities. AE, MC, V. Personal checks accepted. EP, MAP. Expensive.*

Mt. Nevis Hotel/Condominiums. Standard rooms and suites at this hotel are done up with handsome white wicker furnishings, glass-top tables, and colorful island prints. Suites have full, modern kitchens and dining areas; all units have a balcony, direct-dial phone, cable TV, and VCR. The main building houses the casual restaurant and bar, which open onto the terrace, with a view that overlooks the pool and, beyond, to St. Kitts. Shuttle service is provided to the water-sports center at Newcastle Beach, replete with a boutique and outdoor restaurant/bar. The hotel also has its own ferry, which is used for moonlight cruises when it's not ferrying passengers to and from St. Kitts. *Box 494, Newcastle, tel. 809/469–9373 (collect), fax 809/469–9375. 32 rooms. Facilities: pool, restaurant, bar, water sports, beach club. AE, D, MC, V. EP, MAP. Expensive.*

Oualie Beach. Six (more are being built) white West Indian cottages line the shore facing across the channel to St. Kitts—a great view. The rooms are bright, roomy, and simply furnished. There is a full dive shop here offering NAUI-certified instruction, and dive packages are available. Sunfish and Windsurfers may be rented. Breakfast, lunch, and dinner are served at an informal restaurant and bar. *Oualie Beach, tel. 809/469–9735, fax 809/469–9176. 6 rooms. Facilities: beach, restaurant, bar, water-sports center. MC, V. EP, MAP. Inexpensive.*

Pinney's Beach Hotel. Though these bungalows and rooms are smack on Pinney's Beach, don't expect more than just a basic room and you won't be disappointed. All rooms are air-conditioned, all have private baths, and some of the cottages are set around a garden. You'll be more comfortable in one that opens directly onto the beach. *Pinney's Beach, tel. 809/469–5207 or 312/699–7570 in the U.S. 48 rooms. Facilities: beach, 2 restaurants, 2 bars, 2 tennis courts, pool. AE, MC, V. EP. Inexpensive.*

Yamseed Inn. If you want a place with its own private beach, hidden away from resort and plantation hotels, stay at this pale yellow villa overlooking St. Kitts, a few minutes' drive from Newcastle Airport in the northernmost part of Nevis. Friendly innkeeper Sybil Siegfried officially opened Yamseed in January 1992 and operates it as a bed-and-breakfast. All four rooms are in her house right by the sea. *On the beach, Newcastle, tel. 809/469–9361. 4 rooms. 3-night minimum. No credit cards. BP. Inexpensive.*

Nightlife

The hotels usually bring in local calypso singers and steel or string bands one night a week. On Friday night the Shell All-Stars steel band entertains in the gardens at **Croney's Old Manor** (tel. 809/469–3445). The **Golden Rock** (tel. 809/469–3346) brings in the Honeybees String Band to jazz things up for the Saturday-night buffet. You can have dinner and a dance on Wednesday nights at **Pinney's Beach Hotel** (tel. 809/469–5207).

Apart from the hotel scene, there are a few places where young locals go on weekends for hi-fi calypso, reggae, and other island music: **Mariner's Pub & Bar** (tel. 809/469–1993) near Fort Ashby and **Dick's Bar** (no phone) in Brickiln are two such places.

22 · St. Lucia

Updated by
Nigel Fisher

Oval, lush St. Lucia, 27 miles long and 14 miles wide, sits at the southern end of the Windward Islands. It has two topographical features, apart from its beaches, that earn it a special place in the Caribbean tableaux of islands: the twin peaks of the Pitons (Petit and Gros), which rise to more than 2,400 feet, and the bubbling sulfur springs in the town of Soufrière, part of a low-lying volcano that erupted thousands of years ago and now attracts visitors for the springs' curative waters.

This is a ruggedly beautiful island, with towering mountains, lush green valleys, and acres of banana plantations. Yachtsmen put in at Marigot Bay, one of the Caribbean's most beautiful secluded bays. The diving is good, and so is the liming—the St. Lucian term for "hanging out."

Believing that Columbus came upon their island on December 13, 1502, St. Lucians celebrate that date as Discovery Day. But in recent years doubts have been cast on the theory. Some historians think St. Lucia (pronounced *LOO*-sha) was founded in 1499 by Juan de la Cosa, Columbus's navigator.

The first inhabitants were the Arawaks, who paddled up from South America sometime before AD 200. The ferocious Caribs followed them, killed them off, and were still living on the island when the first Europeans began to arrive.

In 1605, 67 English settlers bound for Guiana were blown off course and landed near Vieux Fort. Within a few weeks the cannibalistic Caribs had devoured all but 19, who escaped in a canoe. Another group of English settlers arrived 30 years later, but their attempt at colonization was also unsuccessful. It was the French who, in 1660, managed to sign a treaty with the Caribs and gain control of the island.

Thus began a 150-year period of battles between the French and the English for control of the 238-square-mile island. In the late 18th century, English Admiral George Rodney had his headquarters on St. Lucia. The island changed hands 14 times before the British took permanent possession in 1814.

During those battle-filled years, Europeans colonized the island. They developed sugar plantations, using slaves from West Africa to work the fields. Most of today's 140,000 St. Lucians are descendants of those West Africans. The coal industry was begun on the island in 1883, and by the turn of the century, Castries, the capital, had become the leading coal port in the West Indies. In 1960, banana plantations began to flourish, and bananas are now the island's leading export.

On February 22, 1979, St. Lucia became an independent state within the British Commonwealth of Nations, with a resident governor-general appointed by the queen. Still, there are many relics of French occupation, notably in the island patois, the Creole cuisine, and the names of the places and the people.

With the strengthening of Britain's economic ties with the European Economic Community, the export of bananas to Britain, once a major importer, has become less secure; tourism is now seen as an alternative source of income. St. Lucia, with its thickly forested mountains and sandy bays washed by the Caribbean, is gaining in appeal to those seeking an unspoiled island. The honeymoon set has already found out that St. Lucian law requires residence for only four days for couples to acquire a marriage license.

Before You Go

Tourist Information	Contact the **St. Lucia Tourist Board** (820 2nd Ave., 9th Floor, New York, NY 10017, tel. 212/867–2950 or 800/456–3984, fax 212/370–7867). In Canada: 151 Bloor St. W, Suite 425, Toronto, Ont., Canada M5S 1S4, tel. 416/867–2950, fax 416/961–4317. In the United Kingdom: 10 Kensington Court, London W8 5DL, tel. 071/937–1969, fax 071/937–3611).
Arriving and Departing *By Plane*	There are two airports on the island. Wide-body planes land at Hewanorra International Airport on the southern tip of the island. Vigie Airport, near Castries, handles interisland and charter flights. **BWIA** (tel. 800/327–7401) has direct service from Miami and New York. **American** (tel. 800/433–7300) has daily service from New York, Dallas, and other major U.S. cities, with a stopover in San Juan. (**American Eagle** flights from San Juan land at Vigie airport.) **Air Canada** (tel. 800/422–6232) flies from Toronto to Barbados and Antigua, connecting with flights to St. Lucia. **LIAT's** (tel. 809/462–0701) small island hoppers fly into Vigie Airport, linking St. Lucia with Barbados, Trinidad, Antigua, Martinique, Dominica, Guadeloupe, and other islands.
From the Airport	Taxis are unmetered, and although the government has issued a list of suggested fares, these are not regulated. You should negotiate with the driver *before* you get in the car, and be sure that you both understand whether the price you've agreed upon is in E.C. or U.S. dollars. The drive from Hewanorra to Castries takes about 75 minutes and should cost about U.S. $35.
Passports and Visas	U.S., Canadian, and British citizens must produce a valid passport. A driver's license alone will *not* do. In addition, all visitors must have a return or ongoing ticket.
Language	The official language is English, but you'll also hear some French and patois.
Precautions	Bring along industrial-strength insect repellent to ward off the mosquitoes and sand flies. Centipede bites, though rare and not lethal, can be painful and cause swelling. If you're bitten, you should see a doctor. If you happen to step on a sea urchin, its long black spines may lodge under the skin; don't try to pull them out because you could cause infection. Apply ammonia or an ammonia-based liquid as quickly as possible and the spine will retreat, allowing you to ease it out.
	Manchineel trees have poisonous fruit and leaves that can cause skin blisters on contact. Even raindrops falling off the trees can cause blisters, so you shouldn't sit beneath the trees.
	The waters on the Atlantic (east) coast can be rough, with dangerous undertows, so you shouldn't swim on that side of the island.
	Vendors and self-employed guides in places like Sulphur Springs (where your entrance fee includes a guided tour) can be tenacious. If you do hire a guide, be sure the fee is clearly fixed up front.
	As a courtesy rather than a precaution, you should always ask before taking an islander's picture and be prepared to part with a few coins.

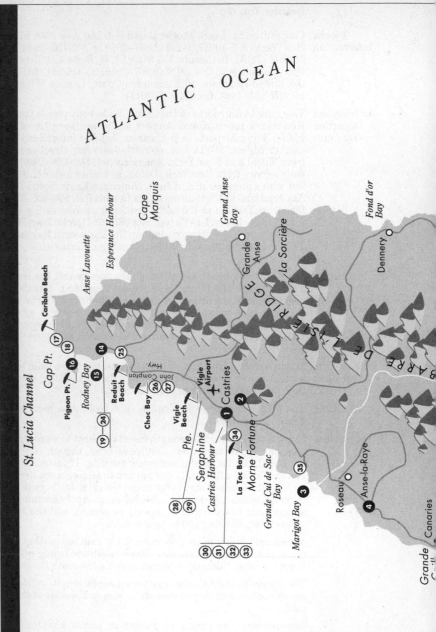

St. Lucia

ATLANTIC OCEAN

St. Lucia Channel

Cap Pt.
Cariblue Beach
(17)
(18)
Pigeon Pt. (16)
Rodney Bay (15)
(14) (25)
Reduit Beach (26)(27) John Compton Hwy.
(19)—(24)
Choc Bay
Vigie Beach
Vigie Pte.
Seraphine (34)
Castries Harbour
(28)(29)
(30)(31)(32)(33)

Anse Lavonette
Esperance Harbour
Cape Marquis
Grand Anse Bay
Fond d'or Bay

Grande Anse (o)
La Sorcière
Dennery (o)

Vigie Airport
✈ Castries
(1)
(2)

BARRE DE L'ISLE RIDGE

Morne Fortune
La Toc Bay
Grande Cul de Sac Bay
Marigot Bay (3)
(35)

Roseau (o)
Anse-la-Raye (4)

Grande
Canaries

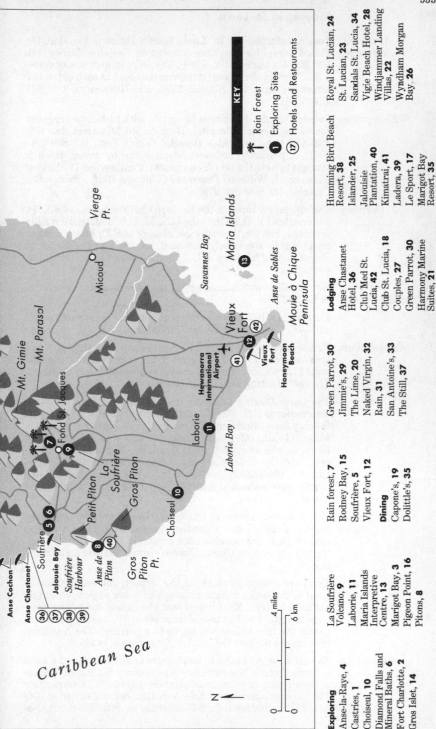

Caribbean Sea

N

0   4 miles

0   6 km

Exploring
Anse-la-Raye, **4**
Castries, **1**
Choiseul, **10**
Diamond Falls and
Mineral Baths, **6**
Fort Charlotte, **2**
Gros Islet, **14**

La Soufrière
Volcano, **9**
Laborie, **11**
Maria Islands
Interpretive
Centre, **13**
Marigot Bay, **3**
Pigeon Point, **16**
Pitons, **8**

Rain forest, **7**
Rodney Bay, **15**
Soufrière, **5**
Vieux Fort, **12**

Dining
Capone's, **19**
Dolittle's, **35**

Green Parrot, **30**
Jimmie's, **29**
The Lime, **20**
Naked Virgin, **32**
Rain, **31**
San Antoine's, **33**
The Still, **37**

Lodging
Anse Chastanet
Hotel, **36**
Club Med St.
Lucia, **42**
Club St. Lucia, **18**
Couples, **27**
Green Parrot, **30**
Harmony Marine
Suites, **21**

Humming Bird Beach
Resort, **38**
Islander, **25**
Jalouisie
Plantation, **40**
Kimatrai, **41**
Ladera, **39**
Le Sport, **17**
Marigot Bay
Resort, **35**

Royal St. Lucian, **24**
St. Lucian, **23**
Sandals St. Lucia, **34**
Vigie Beach Hotel, **28**
Windjammer Landing
Villas, **22**
Wyndham Morgan
Bay, **26**

KEY

 Rain Forest

* Exploring Sites

1 Hotels and Restaurants

Staying in St. Lucia

Important Addresses
Tourist Information: St. Lucia Tourist Board is based at the Pointe Seraphine duty-free complex on Castries Harbor (tel. 809/452–4094 or 809/452–5968). The office is open weekdays 8–4:30. There is also a tourist information desk at each of the two airports (**Vigie**, tel. 809/452–2596, and **Hewanorra**, tel. 809/454–6644).

Emergencies
Police: Call 999. **Hospitals:** Hospitals with 24-hour emergency rooms are **Victoria Hospital** (Hospital Rd., Castries, tel. 809/452–2421) and **St. Jude's Hospital** (Vieux Fort, tel. 809/454–6041), a privately endowed hospital run by nuns, which is thought to have the better equipment. **Pharmacies:** The largest pharmacy is **Williams Pharmacy** (Williams Bldg., Bridge St., Castries, tel. 809/452–2797).

Currency
The official currency is the Eastern Caribbean dollar (E.C.$). Figure about E.C.$2.70 to the U.S. $1. U.S. dollars are readily accepted, but you'll usually get change in E.C. dollars. Major credit cards are widely accepted, as are traveler's checks. Prices quoted here are in U.S. dollars unless indicated otherwise.

Taxes and Service Charges
Hotels collect an 8% government tax. The departure tax is $11 or E.C.$27.

Hotels add a 10% service charge to your bill; most restaurants add 10%. Taxi drivers expect a 10% tip.

Guided Tours
Taxi drivers take special guide courses and offer the most personalized way to see the island. A full tour around the island costs $120 not including tip, and takes approximately six hours. The cost of hiring a taxi by the hour is $20.

The **Carib Touring Company** (tel. 809/452–6791) and **Sunlink International** (tel. 809/452–8232) offer a variety of half- and full-day tours. **Barnard's Travel** (Bridge St., Castries, tel. 809/452–2214) also offers a full range of half- and full-day island tours, as well as excursions to Dominica, Martinique, St. Vincent, and the Grenadines. **St. Lucia Representative Services Ltd.** (tel. 809/452–3762) offers a full range of half- and full-day island tours, as well as excursions to a number of neighboring islands.

Getting Around
Buses
This is a cheap means of transportation. There's no organized service, but minivans cruise the island and, like taxis, will stop when hailed. You can also catch a minivan in Castries by hanging around outside Clarke Cinema (corner Micoud and Bridge Sts.).

Taxis
Taxis are always available at the airport, the harbor, and in front of the major hotels, although they are expensive and do not have meters. Most hotels post the names and phone numbers of drivers and a table of fares set by the taxi commission. Learn the fare before you agree to a journey. The cost from Hewanorra Airport to Castries, for example, is $45.

Rental Cars
To rent a car, you have to be 25 years or older and hold a valid driver's license. You must buy a temporary St. Lucian license at the airports or police headquarters (Bridge St., Castries) for $16. Rental agencies include **Avis** (tel. 809/452–2700 or 800/331–2112), **Budget** (tel. 809/452–0233 or 800/527–0700), **Na-**

tional (tel. 809/452–8028 or 800/328–4567), and **Dollar** (tel. 809/452–0994). Driving in St. Lucia is on the left.

Telephones and Mail To call St. Lucia from the United States, dial area code 809, access code 45, and the local five-digit number. You can make direct-dial long-distance calls from the island, and the connections are excellent. To place interisland calls, dial the local five-digit number.

Postage for airmail letters to the United States and Canada is E.C.$.95 and E.C.$1.10 to Great Britain up to one ounce; postcard postage is E.C.$.65 and E.C.$70, respectively.

Opening and Closing Times Shops are open weekdays 8–12:30 and 1:30–4, Saturday 8–noon. Banks are open Monday–Thursday 8–2, Friday 8–1 and 3–5.

Exploring St. Lucia

Numbers in the margin correspond to points of interest on the St. Lucia map.

Castries **Castries,** on the northwest coast, is a busy city with a popula-
❶ tion of about 60,000. It lies in a sheltered bay surrounded by green hills. Ships carrying bananas, coconut, cocoa, mace, nutmeg, and citrus fruits for export leave from **Castries Harbour,** one of the busiest ports in the Caribbean. Cruise ships dock here, too.

Take a cab or drive to **Pointe Seraphine,** the Spanish-style complex of 23 duty-free shops by Castries Harbour. Pick up maps, arrange tours, and find out anything you want to know about St. Lucia at the information desk of the **Tourist Board** just inside the main terminal. This is the starting point for many of the island tours.

The John Compton Highway connects the duty-free complex to downtown Castries. To reach the downtown center from Pointe Seraphine's transportation terminal, you can stroll for 20 minutes, drive, or take a cab.

Castries, with Morne Fortune (the Hill of Good Luck) rising behind it, has had more than its share of bad luck over the years, including two hurricanes and four fires. As a result, Castries lacks the colorful colonial buildings found in other island capitals. Most of Castries's buildings are modern, and the town has only a few sights of historical note.

Head first to **Columbus Square,** a green oasis ringed by Brazil, Laborie, Micoud, and Bourbon streets. At the corner of Laborie and Micoud streets there is a 400-year-old saman tree. A favorite local story is of the English botanist who came to St. Lucia many years ago to catalogue the flora. Awestruck by this huge old tree, she asked a passerby what it was. "Massav," he replied, and she gratefully jotted that down in her notebook, unaware that "massav" is patois for "I don't know."

Directly across the street is the Roman Catholic **Cathedral of the Immaculate Conception,** which was built in 1897.

Some of the 19th-century buildings that managed to survive fire, winds, and rains can be seen on Brazil Street, the southern border of the square.

Time Out   In the courtyard of the Victorian building that houses Rain Restaurant, the **Pizza Park** (Columbus Sq., tel. 809/452–3022) sells takeout or eat-in pizza all day.

Head north on Laborie Street and walk past the government buildings on your right. On the left, William Peter Boulevard is one of Castries's shopping areas. "The Boulevard" connects Laborie Street with Bridge Street, which is another shopping street.

Continue north for one more block on Laborie Street and you'll come to Jeremie Street. Turn right, and you'll see the **market** on the corner of Jeremie and Peynier streets. The market is a busy place, especially on Saturday mornings, when farmers bring their produce to town.

Elsewhere on   To reach **Morne Fortune,** head due east on Bridge Street. The
the Island   drive will take you past the **Government House,** the official resi-
Morne Fortune   dence of the governor-general of St. Lucia. If you want to take a picture of the house, ask the guard on duty before focusing your camera. You cannot take pictures when the governor-general is in residence.

Driving up the Hill of Good Fortune, you'll see some of the Caribbean's most beautiful tropical plants—frangipani, lilies, bougainvillea, hibiscus, and oleander—along the road.

Two hundred years ago the Vigie Peninsula had the island's heaviest concentration of fortifications. That former battleground and the area to the north of it now have the island's greatest concentration of resort playgrounds. The island rising on the horizon is Martinique. To the south you'll see the twin peaks of the Pitons.

② Fort Charlotte on the Morne was begun in 1764 by the French as the *Citadelle du Morne Fortune.* It was completed 20 years later, but during those years many battles were fought here, and the fortress changed hands a number of times. The Inniskilling Monument is a tribute to one of the most famous battles, fought in 1796, when the 27th Foot Royal Inniskilling Fusiliers wrested the Hill of Good Fortune from the French. Admission to Fort Charlotte is free, and you can wander at will to see the Four Apostles Battery; the Combermere Barracks, which are now part of an educational complex; and the redoubts, guard room, stables, and cells. Stop in the Military Cemetery. It was first used in 1782, and the faint inscriptions on the tombstones tell the tales of the French and English soldiers who died here. Six former governors of the island are buried here as well.

South of Castries   The road from Castries to Soufrière travels through beautiful country. Keep in mind, though, that the many hairpin curves make this road a difficult drive, although the road is currently being widened. Phase One from Castries to Anse-la-Raye is complete. Phase Two, which takes the road on to Soufrière, should be completed by the end of 1993. If it is not, then expect some delays during weekdays while construction crews are working. And remember, you'll also be handling a right-hand drive vehicle on the left side of a curving road.

③ In the area of Roseau, make a detour and drive to **Marigot Bay.** In 1778, British Admiral Samuel Barrington took his ships into this secluded bay within a bay and covered them with palm fronds to hide them from the French. The resort community today is a great favorite of yachtspeople. You can arrange to charter a yacht, swim, snorkel, or lime with the yachting crowd at one of the bars. A 24-hour water taxi connects the various points on the bay.

Time Out Stop for rum punch, lunch, and atmosphere at the **Rusty Anchor** (Hurricane Hotel, tel. 809/453–4230), a happy haunt of boaters.

If you continue south, you'll be in the vicinity of one of the island's two rum distilleries. Major production of sugar ceased here in about 1960, and distilleries now make rum with imported molasses. You're still in banana country, with acres of banana trees covering the hills and valleys. More than 127 different varieties of bananas are grown on the island.

In the mountainous region ahead you'll see **Mt. Parasol,** and if you look hard enough through the mists, you may be able to make out **Mt. Gimie,** St. Lucia's highest peak, rising to 3,117 feet.

4 The next village you'll come to is **Anse-la-Raye.** The beach here is a colorful sight, with fishing nets hanging on poles to dry and brightly painted fishing boats bobbing in the water. The fishermen of Anse-la-Raye still make canoes the old-fashioned way, by burning out the center of a log.

Soufrière As you approach the town of **Soufrière,** you'll be in the island's
5 breadbasket, where most of the mangoes, breadfruit, tomatoes, limes, and oranges are grown.

The town of Soufrière, which dates from the mid-18th century, was named after the nearby volcano and has a population of about 9,000 people. The Soufrière Harbour is the deepest harbor on the island, accommodating cruise ships that nose right up to the wharf. The nearby jetty contains an excellent small-crafts center. The **Soufrière Tourist Information Centre** (Bay St., tel. 809/454–7419) can provide information about the attractions in the area, which, in addition to the Pitons, include La Soufrière, billed as the world's only drive-in volcano, and sulfur springs; the Diamond Mineral Baths; and the rain forest. You can also ask at the Tourism Centre about Soufrière Estate, on the east side of town, replete with botanical gardens and minizoo.

6 Adjoining Soufrière Estate are the **Diamond Falls and Mineral Baths,** which are fed by an underground flow of water from the sulfur springs. Louis XVI provided funds for the construction of these baths for his troops to "fortify them against the St. Lucian climate." During the Brigand's War, just after the French Revolution, the baths were destroyed. They were restored in 1966, and you can see the waterfalls and the gardens before slipping into your swimsuit for a dip in the steaming curative waters. *Soufrière. Admission: E.C.$5. Open daily 10–5.*

7 The island's dense tropical **rain forest** is to the east of Soufrière on the road to Fond St. Jacques. The trek through the lush landscape takes three hours, and you'll need a guide. Mt. Gimie (St. Lucia's highest peak), Piton Canaries, Mt. Houlom, and Piton Tromasse are all part of this immense forest reserve. The views of the mountains and valleys are spectacular.

8 For the best land view of the **Pitons,** take the road south out of Soufrière. The road is awful and leads up a steep hill, but if you persevere, you'll be rewarded by the sight of the twin peaks. The perfectly shaped pyramidal cones, covered with tropical greenery, were formed of lava from a volcanic eruption 30 million to 40 million years ago. The tallest is Petit Piton (2,619 feet) and its twin, Gros Piton (2,461 feet). Gros Piton is so named because although it is shorter, it is fatter than its twin.

9 To the south of Soufrière, your nose will note the left turn that takes you to **La Soufrière,** the drive-in volcano, and its **sulfur springs.** There are more than 20 pools of black, belching, smelly sulfurous waters and yellow-green sulfur baking and steaming. Though the sign announces that this is the world's only drive-in volcano, it is not; moreover, it is not strictly a volcano, but a fault in the substratum rock. Take the guided tour offered by the Tourist Board. *La Soufrière. Admission: E.C.$3 (including guided tour). Open daily 9–5.*

10 Follow the road farther south and you'll come next to the coastal town of **Choiseul,** home to wood-carving and pottery shops. At the turn of the road past the Anglican Church, built in 1846, a bridge crosses the river Dorée, so named because the riverbed is blanketed with fool's gold. In La Fargue, just to the south, the **Choiseul Arts & Craft Centre** (tel. 809/452–3226) sells superb traditional Carib handicrafts, including pottery, wickerwork, and braided Khus-Khus grass mats and baskets.

11 The next stop is **Laborie,** a little fishing village, where you can buy cheese, bread, and fish.

12 Now drive along the southern coast of the island to **Vieux Fort,** St. Lucia's second-largest city and home of the Hewanorra International Airport. Drive out on the **Moule à Chique Peninsula,** the southernmost tip of the island. If you look to the north, you can see all of St. Lucia and, if the day is especially clear, you can spot the island of St. Vincent 21 miles to the south. Looking straight down, you can see where the waters of the Caribbean blend with the bluer Atlantic waters.

Time Out **Chak Chak** (Beanfield Rd., Vieux Fort, tel. 809/454–6260) is a casual, airy restaurant that serves Creole dishes.

13 At the **Maria Islands Interpretive Centre** you can find out all there is to know about the Maria Islands Nature Reserve. The reserve consists of two tiny islands in the Atlantic off the southeast coast of St. Lucia. The 25-acre Maria Major and its little sister, 4-acre Maria Minor, are inhabited by rare species of lizards and snakes that share their home with fregate birds, terns, doves, and other wildlife. *Moule à Chique, no phone. Admission: Wed.–Sat. E.C.$3, Sun. E.C.$.50. Open Wed.–Sun. 9:30–5.*

A good road leads from Vieux Fort through the towns on the Atlantic coast. The road will take you past **Honeymoon Beach,** a wide, grassy, flat Anse l'Islet peninsula jutting into the ocean. Drive through Micoud and, a few miles farther north, Dennery, both of which are residential towns overlooking the Atlantic. At Dennery the road turns west and climbs across the Barre de l'Isle Ridge through a tiny rain forest with dense vegetation. There are trails along the way that lead to lookout points where you can get a view of the National Forest Preserve. This bumpy road will take you all the way back to Castries.

The North End and Gros Islet For another tour up the coast north of Castries, take the John Compton Highway north out of town for about five minutes to the Vigie Airport. This whole northwest stretch of the Caribbean coast is of far more interest to the hedonist than to the historian. This area features some of the island's best beaches, and it's loaded with resort hotels.

⑭ **Gros Islet** to the north is a quiet little fishing village not unlike Anse-la-Raye to the south. But on Friday nights, Gros Islet hosts a street festival to which everyone is invited.

⑮ **Rodney Bay,** named after Admiral Rodney, is an 80-acre manmade lagoon that boasts a host of hotels and restaurants. The St. Lucian Hotel and Club St. Lucia are in this area, as are Capone's, Lime, and other popular restaurants.

Pigeon Point **Pigeon Point,** jutting out on the northwest coast, was Pigeon
⑯ Island until a causeway was built to connect it to the mainland. Tales are told of the pirate Jambe de Bois (Wooden Leg), who used to hide out here. This 40-acre area, a strategic point during the struggles for control of the island, is now a national park, with long sandy beaches, calm waters for swimming, and areas for picnicking.

The **Pigeon Point Museum** includes the ruins of barracks, batteries, and garrisons dating from the French and English battles. *Pigeon Point, no phone. Admission: E.C.$3. Open Mon.–Sat. 9–4.*

Off the Beaten Track

If you want a close-up of a working banana plantation and are willing to get a little wet and muddy in the process, you can tour the island's largest—the **Marquis Plantation. St. Lucia Plantation Tours** (tel. 809/542–8658) or **St. Lucia Representative Services Ltd.** (*see* Guided Tours, *above*) will pick you up at your hotel in an air-conditioned bus. Wear your most casual clothes, and be prepared to rough it.

Beaches

All of St. Lucia's beaches are public, and many are flanked by hotels where you can rent water-sports equipment and have a rum punch. There are also secluded beaches, accessible only by water, to which hotels can arrange boat trips. It is not advisable to swim along the windward (east) coast because the Atlantic waters are rough and sometimes dangerous.

Pigeon Point off the northern shore has secluded white-sand beaches, fine for picnicking and swimming.

Reduit Beach is a long stretch of beige sand between Choc Bay and Pigeon Point and is home to the St. Lucian Hotel, which offers numerous water sports.

Vigie Beach and **Choc Bay,** north of Castries Harbour, have fine beige sand and calm waters (*see* Lodging, *below*).

La Toc Bay is near Castries Harbour. The sand here is beige.

Anse Cochon, on the Caribbean coast, is a black-sand beach accessible only by boat. The waters are superb for swimming and snorkeling.

Anse Chastanet is a gray-sand beach just north of Soufrière with a backdrop of green hills and the island's best reefs for snorkeling and diving. The wooden gazebos of the Anse Chastanet Hotel are nestled among the palms, with a dive shop and bar on the beach (*see* Lodging, *below*).

Jalousie Bay, south of Soufrière, is a bay several miles deep between the Pitons. Accessible only by boat, it offers great snorkeling and diving.

Vieux Fort, at the southernmost tip, has a long secluded stretch of gray volcanic sand and waters protected by reefs. Honeymoon Beach is another sandy escape just west of Vieux Fort.

Sports and the Outdoors

Most hotels offer Sunfish, water skis, fins, masks, and other water-sports equipment free to guests and for a fee to nonguests.

Boating　Captain Mike's (tel. 809/452-0216) has a fleet of Bertram's charter boats for snorkeling and swimming cruises and private charter parties. Bare-boat or skippered yacht charters are available through Stevens Yachts (tel. 809/452-8648 or 800/638-7044), which has a fleet of 39- to 56-foot sailing yachts; Trade Wind Yacht Charters (Rodney Bay, tel. 809/452-8424 or 800/825-7245); and the Moorings Yacht Charter (Marigot Bay, tel. 809/453-4357 or 800/535-7289).

Deep-Sea Fishing　Among the sea creatures in these waters are dolphin, Spanish mackerel, barracuda, and white marlin. Contact Captain Mike's (tel. 809/452-0216) to steer you in the right direction.

Golf　At St. Lucia Sandals (tel. 809/452-3081), the former Cunard La Toc, there is a 9-hole course. There is also a 9-plus-9 course at Cap Estate Golf Club (tel. 809/452-8523). Greens fees at both are about E.C.$15, and clubs are available for rental.

Hiking　The island is laced with trails, but you should not attempt the challenging peaks on your own. Your hotel or the Tourist Board can provide you with a guide. The St. Lucia National Trust (tel. 809/452-5005), established to preserve the island's natural and cultural heritage, tours several sites, including Pigeon Island, the Maria Islands, and Fregate Island.

Horseback Riding　For trail rides on the beach, contact Trim's Riding Stables (Cas-En-Bas and Cap Estate, tel. 809/452-8273) and St. Lucia Riding Club (Choc Bay, tel. 809/452-3762).

Jogging　You can jog on the beach by yourself or team up with the Roadbusters (tel. Jimmie at 809/452-5142 or evenings at 809/452-4790).

Parasailing　Contact Jacob's Watersports (tel. 809/452-8281).

Scuba Diving　Scuba St. Lucia (tel. 809/454-7000) is a PADI five-star training facility that offers daily beach and boat dives, resort courses, underwater photography, and day trips. Marigot Bay Resort (tel. 809/453-4357) offers a full scuba program. Dive trips are also arranged through Buddies Scuba (tel. 809/452-5288) and through most of the hotels.

Sea and Snorkeling Excursions	The 140-foot square-rigger ***Brig Unicorn*** (tel. 809/452–6811) sails to Soufrière, with steel bands, a swim stop, rum punch, and soda. Its sister schooner, the ***Buccaneer,*** also does outings. **Captain Mike's** (tel. 809/452–0216) does swimming and snorkeling cruises; the ***Sailing Bus*** (tel. 809/452–8725) offers a full-day sail from Rodney Bay to Marigot; and **Jacob's Watersports** (tel. 809/452–8281) features speedboat and snorkeling cruises. Sea and snorkeling excursions can also be arranged through **Maho** (tel. 809/452–3762) and **The Surf Queen** (tel. 809/452–3762) or through your hotel.
Squash	There is one squash court at **Cap Estate Golf Course** (tel. 809/452–8523; open 8–4 and two at **Club St. Lucia** (tel. 809/452–0551) and **The St. Lucian Yacht Club** (Rodney Bay, tel. 809/452–8350).
Tennis	All the major hotels have their own tennis courts, but since so many of the hotels are all-inclusive and prohibit nonguests from playing, you will likely be limited to those at your own hotel. Failing that, **Club St. Lucia** (tel. 809/452–0551), with its seven lighted courts, offers temporary membership for nonguests.
Waterskiing	Contact **Jacob's Watersports** (tel. 809/452–8281). Rentals are also available at most of the hotels.
Windsurfing	The **St. Lucian Hotel** is the local agent for Mistral Windsurfers (tel. 809/452–8351). Also contact **Marigot Bay Resort** (tel. 809/453–4357) and **Jacob's Watersports** (tel. 809/452–8281). Most hotels rent Windsurfers to nonguests.
Spectator Sports	**Cricket** and **soccer,** the two national pastimes, are played at **Mindoo Philip Park** in Marchand, 2 miles east of Castries.
	Contact the Tourist Board (tel. 809/452–4094) for specific information regarding schedules.

Shopping

Shopping on St. Lucia is low-key, but the island's best-known products are the unique hand-silk-screened and hand-printed designs of Bagshaw Studios. Bagshaw products are designed, printed, and sold only on St. Lucia. The island is also home to Windjammer Clothing, which is sold on virtually every Caribbean island. Apart from those indigenous products, there are native-made wood carvings, pottery, and straw hats and baskets.

Shopping Areas	St. Lucia entered the duty-free market with the opening of **Pointe Seraphine,** a Spanish-style complex by the harbor, where 23 shops sell designer perfumes, china and crystal, jewelry, watches, leather goods, liquor, and cigarettes. Native crafts are also sold in the shopping center. Castries has a number of shops, mostly on **Bridge Street** and **William Peter Boulevard,** selling locally made souvenirs. There is also a shopping arcade at the **St. Lucian hotel.**
Good Buys *Duty-Free*	In Pointe Seraphine, look for designer perfumes at **Images** (tel. 809/452–6883). **J. Q. Charles** (tel. 809/452–2759) carries fine china and crystal. **A Touch of Class** (tel. 809/452–3817) is the place for Caribbean literature and local souvenirs. Leather handbags, jewelry, crystal, and perfumes can be found at **Meli** (tel. 809/452–7587). Be sure to bring your passport and airline ticket to get duty-free prices.

Fabrics and   Bagshaw's silk-screened fabrics and clothing can be found at
Clothing   Pointe Seraphine. **Windjammer Clothing Company** (tel. 809/
                452–1040) has its main store at Vigie Cove and an outlet at
                Pointe Seraphine. **Caribelle Batik** (Old Victoria Rd., The
                Morne, Castries, tel. 809/452–3785) creates batik clothing and
                wall hangings. Visitors are welcome to watch the craftspeople
                at work. **The Batik Studio** at Humming Bird Beach Resort
                (Soufrière, tel. 809/454–7232) offers superb sarongs, scarves,
                and wall panels.

Native Crafts Trays, masks, and figures are carved from mahogany, red ce-
                dar, and eucalyptus trees in the studio adjacent to **Eudovic's**
                (Morne Fortune, 15 min. south of Castries, tel. 809/452–2747).
                Hammocks, straw mats, baskets and hats, and carvings, as
                well as books and maps of St. Lucia, are at **Noah's Arkade**
                (Bridge St., Castries, and Pte. Seraphine, tel. 809/452–2523).
                Artsibit (corner Brazil and Mongiraud Sts., tel. 809/452–7865)
                features works by top St. Lucian artists.

Dining

If you stop by the Castries market (*see* Exploring St. Lucia,
above) on a Saturday, you'll see the riches produced in this
fertile volcanic soil. Mangoes, plantains, breadfruits, limes,
pumpkins, cucumbers, pawpaws (pronounced *poh-poh* here,
known as papaya elsewhere), yams, christophines (a green
vegetable), and coconuts are among the fruits and vegetables
that appear on menus throughout the island. Every menu lists
the catch of the day (especially flying fish), along with the ever-
popular lobster. Chicken, pork, and barbecues are also big-
time here. Most of the meats are imported—beef from Argentina and Iowa, lamb from New Zealand. The French influence is
strong in St. Lucian restaurants, and most chefs cook with a
Creole flair, pre–nouvelle cuisine. This is not an island for the
calorie- and cholesterol-conscious.

Highly recommended restaurants are indicated by a star ★.

Category	Cost*
Very Expensive	over $40
Expensive	$25–$40
Moderate	$15–$25
Inexpensive	under $15

**per person, excluding drinks and service*

★ **San Antoine's.** High on the Morne, with splendid views of
Castries below and Martinique in the distance, this restored
historic building was originally the great house of the San Antoine Hotel, built in the mid-1800s and destroyed by fire in
1970. This is one of the most elegantly appointed restaurants in
the Caribbean, although the food doesn't always match the
service and decor. The streamlined menu features such classic
standouts as *escargot en brioche* and *filet au poivre*. All in all, a
memorable experience. *Morne Fortune, tel. 809/452–4660.
Reservations suggested. Jacket recommended. AE, MC, V.
Closed Sun. Very Expensive.*
Green Parrot. The Green Parrot comes complete with somme-
lier and crisp napery. The Continental menu includes poached

fish fillet with mushroom cream and white-wine sauce glaze; *tournedos cordon rouge* (steak fillet topped with foie gras and Madeira sauce); and *escalope de volaille Viennese* (chicken breast grilled and served with mushrooms). There is lively entertainment on Wednesday and Saturday nights, with limbo and belly dancers, but the best reason for dining here is the view over Castries and the harbor. It rivals a similar view from the more expensive San Antoine's restaurant. *Red Tape La., Morne Fortune, tel. 809/452–3399. Reservations essential. Jacket recommended. AE, MC, V. Expensive.*

★ **Capone's.** The gang here does a skillful job of blending the tropics, the Jazz Age, and art deco touches. There are black-and-white tile floors, a polished wood bar, and a player piano. Waiters and waitresses dressed like gangsters serve rum drinks called Valentine's Day Massacre and Mafia Mai Tai and bring your check in a violin case. The pasta is fresh, and the meat dishes include *osso buco alla Milanese* (veal knuckle) and chicken rotisserie. The **Pizza Parlour** turns out burgers and sandwiches, as well as pizza. The management also runs **Sweet Dreams** across the street, with more than 150 tempting dessert options. *Rodney Bay, across from the St. Lucian Hotel, tel. 809/452–0284. Reservations suggested. AE, MC, V. No lunch; closed Mon. Moderate–Expensive.*

Dolittle's. Take the ferry across from the Hurricane Hotel to this waterside eatery, named after the Rex Harrison movie shot here. The views of Marigot harbor and the yachts makes this a great place for lunch. Callaloo soup is among the openers. Main dishes include marinated red snapper; ask about the daily specials. *Marigot de Roseau on Marigot Bay, tel. 809/453–4246. Reservations suggested. AE, MC, V. Moderate.*

★ **Jimmie's.** The bar here is a popular meeting place, and the restaurant is a romantic spot for dinner. Specialties include Madras fish, seafood risotto, and a lip-smacking saltfish and green fig (the national dish—and an acquired taste). There's also a wide choice of seafood, meat, chicken, and vegetable dishes. *Vigie Cove, Castries, tel. 809/452–5142. No reservations. AE, MC, V. Moderate.*

★ **The Lime.** Across the street from Capone's, the Lime is a favorite place for "liming," or hanging out. A casual place with lime-colored gingham curtains, straw hats decorating the ceiling, and hanging plants, it offers a businessman's three-course lunch. Starters may include homemade pâté or stuffed crab back. Entrée choices may be medallions of pork fillet with the chef's special orange-and-ginger sauce, stewed lamb, or fish fillet poached in white wine and mushroom sauce. The prices are more reasonable than neighboring Capone's, which is perhaps why the ex-patriates and locals gather here in the evenings. *Rodney Bay, tel. 809/452–0761. Reservations suggested for dinner. MC, V. Closed Tues. Moderate.*

Naked Virgin. Tucked away in the quiet Castries suburb of Marchand (just opposite a local post office—keep asking), this pleasant hangout offers terrific Creole cuisine. The owner, Mr. Paul John, has worked in many of the island's major hotels and his concoction, "the naked virgin," could be the best punch you've ever tasted. This tiny restaurant deserves to survive, but the trend of St. Lucia's hotels towards becoming all-inclusive makes the Naked Virgin's future precarious. *Marchand Rd., tel. 809/452–5594. Reservations advised. AE, MC, V. Moderate.*

Rain. This restaurant is in a Victorian building, and the balcony overlooking Columbus Square is a favored spot. It's usually crowded and the tables are a tad too close together, but you can still soak up the atmosphere, especially after a few Downpours—their knockout tropical punches and frozen concoctions. Lunchtime offerings include Creole soup, *crabe farcie*, rainburgers, quiches, and salads; Creole chicken is a specialty. At night, the "Champagne Buffet of 1885" is a lavish but moderately priced seven-course feast. For dessert there's old-fashioned, hand-cranked ice cream. You can browse in the chic downstairs boutique. *Columbus Sq., Castries, tel. 809/452–3022. Reservations advised. AE, MC, V. Moderate.*

The Still. Converted from an old rum distillery, this restaurant is on the grounds of a working plantation, which supplies most of the meats and produce served. The emphasis is on local foods—christophines, breadfruits, yams, and callaloo, as well as seafood, pork chops, and beef dishes. A popular Creole buffet is served at lunch. *Soufrière, tel. 809/454–7224. Reservations suggested. MC, V. No dinner. Moderate.*

Lodging

St. Lucia's Caribbean coast is splashed with hotels, most of them along the strip from Castries to Cap Estate. There are hotels with social directors who will have you doing calisthenics on the beach at dawn, and West Indian guest houses where hanging out is the day's only scheduled activity. You should reserve four months in advance for a room during the winter season. St. Lucia has become the island for all-inclusive resorts, the latest being Sandals, which took over Cunard La Toc. The few that are not all-inclusive offer EP or MAP.

Highly recommended lodgings are indicated by a star ★.

Category	Cost*
Very Expensive	over $350
Expensive	$200–$350
Moderate	$125–$200
Inexpensive	under $125

*All prices are for a standard double room for two, excluding 8% tax and a 10% service charge.

Hotels **Club St. Lucia.** A recent expansion has made this bustling friendly all-inclusive resort the island's largest. Everything is included in the price here, which means meals and unlimited drinks, two half-day boat cruises, and a supervised children's miniclub. The resort sits on 12 acres, with rooms and suites in bungalows scattered over the hillside, and has two beaches. The accommodations are spacious, with king-size beds (twins on request), tile floors, patios, baths with tubs and showers, and air-conditioning in all but the standard rooms, which have ceiling fans only. There are clock radios in all the rooms, but no phones. Live entertainment is scheduled nightly. Club St. Lucia is ideal for families and couples who want to be alone. *Box 915, Smugglers Village, Castries, tel. 809/452–0551 or 800/ 223–9815, fax 809/452–0281. 312 rooms and suites, not all air-conditioned. Facilities: restaurant, 2 bars, pool, 2 tennis courts, disco, minimart, boutique, Jacuzzi, water-sports cen-*

ter, transport to stables, golf club. AE, DC, MC, V. All-inclusive. Very Expensive.

Couples. Exactly as the name suggests, this all-inclusive resort is for couples only. Things tend to be quite active, with volleyball in the pool and on the beach, aerobics, and water exercises. The activities desk can arrange anything, including a wedding. Rooms and suites are somewhat chic, with king-size four-poster beds and marble baths. There is an oceanfront wing with 24 air-conditioned rooms. Other accommodations are in the three-story air-conditioned main building. There is nightly live music for dancing, and a piano bar that closes when the last couple leaves. Once you've paid the up-front fee, your hands need not touch money again during your stay. *Box 190, Malabar Beach, tel. 809/452–4211 or 800/221–1831, fax 809/452–7419. 100 rooms. Facilities: restaurant, 2 bars, pool, 2 lighted tennis courts, sauna, Jacuzzi, exercise room, bicycles, horseback riding, water-sports center, dive shop, catamaran. AE, MC, V. All-inclusive. Very Expensive.*

Jalousie Plantation. St. Lucia's five-star all-inclusive resort opened in late 1992. In a dramatic setting, situated between the Pitons, brown wood chalets tumble down the steep hillside to a small bay. Landscaped gardens lead down from the main buildings, with restaurants and lounges, to the rectangular pool, water-sports facilities, and gray-sand beach. People-movers transport guests from their chalets to the main building and beach. Unfortunately, the property's owner, an Iranian prince, hired an architect who seemingly has no feel for St. Lucia. Twin columns of coconut trees at measured distances apart from each other make the landscaped gardens stiff. The main reception area, lounges, and restaurants are designed with the formality of a palazzo. The chalets crowd together, and for these prices, you'd expect a greater feeling of spaciousness. Their private plunge pools are like vertical bathtubs, and the rooms are ordinary and uniform in design. The management is pretentious, organization is lacking, and the service leaves a lot to be desired. Perhaps it will improve. Jalousie is likely to appeal more to tour groups than to the discerning traveler. *Box 251, Soufrière, tel. 809/459–7566 or 800/877–3643, fax 809/459–7667. 115 cottages and junior suites. Facilities: 4 restaurants, 5 bars/lounges, tennis, squash, water sports and scuba diving (off-shore scuba diving is extra). AE, DC, MC, V. All-inclusive. Very Expensive.*

Le Sport. A $15 million investment transformed the Cariblue Hotel into this resort, which bills itself as the Body Holiday. If you've been dying to dip into thalassotherapy (seawater massages, thermal jet baths, and the like), this is the place in which to do it. In addition to the beauty treatments, eucalyptus inhalations, and seaweed nutrient wraps, the all-inclusive resort offers a daily program involving everything from aerobics to yoga. The architecture is a handsome variety of styles, from Moorish to Mediterranean, in every hue from mauve to mint. Cushy air-conditioned rooms are done in luscious pastels, all with queen-size beds, marble baths, hair dryers, phones, and fridges. A band plays nightly, and there's a piano bar. Although the location is unrivaled, guests who are not devotees would not be taking advantage of what Le Sport offers, including the Relaxation Temple to lounge in after seaweed treatments. *Box 437, Cariblue Beach, tel. 809/452–8551 or 800/544–2883, fax 809/450–0368. 102 rooms and suites. Facilities: restaurant, 2 bars, 2 pools, bicycles, 1 lighted tennis court, arch-*

ery, 9-hole golf course nearby (extra fee), water-sports center, thalassotherapy, laundry, beauty salon, beauty and rejuvenation treatments, Jacuzzi, Turkish baths, exercise rooms, health shop, boutique, bank, medical facilities. AE, DC, MC, V. All-inclusive. Very Expensive.

Marigot Bay Resort. Villas, an inn, and a hotel compose this village, which is located on a lovely bay, surrounded by green hills with lush tropical trees and flowers. A little trolley edges up the hill from Dolittle's Restaurant and the market to the one-, two-, and three-bedroom villas with wide-plank verandas and fully equipped kitchens. The West Indian–style Marigot Inn next to the restaurant has lanai studios, each with kitchenette and balcony overlooking the marina. Fan-cooled stone cottages, with wicker, bamboo, and rattan furnishings; king-size beds; and kitchenettes make up the harborside Hurricane Hole Hotel. A 24-hour water taxi connects the resort's facilities. *Box 101, Castries, tel. 809/453–4357 or 800/334–2435, fax 809/453–4353. 47 rooms. Facilities: 2 restaurants, 2 bars, market, dive shop, yacht charters, sailing, water-sports center. AE, DC, MC, V. EP, MAP. Very Expensive.*

Royal St. Lucian. This property caters to your every whim. The colonnaded reception area is stunning—a cathedralesque Italian palazzo with cool marble. However, the russet-roofed white buildings form an uninspired "U" in the pristine landscaped grounds. The large, rambling pool is laced with Japanese bridges and has a natural rock waterfall. The split-level oceanview suites are sumptuous, featuring a soothing pastel color scheme, cable TV, air-conditioning, direct-dial phone, jet shower, hair dryer, and safe. Guests may use the tennis and water-sports facilities at the adjacent sister property, the St. Lucian. *Box 977, Castries, tel. 809/452–0999 or 800/225–5859, fax 809/452–9639. 98 suites. Facilities: 2 restaurants, 2 bars, pool. AE, DC, MC, V. EP, MAP. Very Expensive.*

★ **Windjammer Landing Villas.** This sun-kissed resort, with sweeping prospects of one of St. Lucia's prettiest bays, fulfills anyone's beachcombing fantasies: White stucco villas crowned with tile alternate with a porticoed reception area and thatch-hut public rooms. Villas are huge and tastefully decorated in the ubiquitous island pastels and rattan furnishings. For example, Villa 144 has a fully equipped kitchen, lounge area, and patio dining room on the entry level; a bedroom and bathroom downstairs; and an upstairs roof sundeck. The ambience is rustic simplicity with painted natural wood timbers, tiled floors, wicker chairs, and straw mats. A people-mover transports guests up the steep hill from the main building and the shops. Truly an idyllic spot. *Box 1504, Labrelotte Bay, Castries, tel. 809/452–0913, fax 809/452–0907. 150 1-, 2-, and 3-bedroom villas. Facilities: 2 tennis courts, pool, market, satellite TV, boutique, water sports. AE, MC, V. EP, All-inclusive (drinks not included). Very Expensive.*

★ **Ladera.** This quiet, luxurious hideaway is nestled amid lush botanical gardens. The villas and suites, furnished with a harmonious blend of French colonial antiques and local crafts, feature a completely open western wall to afford dazzling unobstructed views of the Pitons. Most villas include plunge pools, and some have a Jacuzzi. Secluded and very special. *Box 255, Soufrière, tel. 809/454–7323. 7 villas, 8 suites. Facilities: restaurant, bar, pool, gift shop. AE, MC, V. MAP. Expensive–Very Expensive.*

St. Lucian. The lobby is broad and white, with potted plants and upholstered sofas, from which a corridor leads to the gardens, pool area, and beach. This was once two hotels, and the rooms are spread out over considerable acreage, some on Reduit Beach, some in gardens. All have air conditioners, two double beds, clock radios, direct-dial phones, and patios or terraces. Discounted package tours from Britain have taken their toll on this resort and the furnishings have that well-worn, drab look, but there is lots of action to distract you. This is the home of Splash, one of the island's hottest discos, and the local agent for Mistral Windsurfers. Water sports, including windsurfing lessons, are free to hotel guests. *Box 512, Castries, tel. 809/452–8351, fax 809/452–8331. 222 rooms. Facilities: 2 restaurants, 3 bars, disco, pool, laundry/dry cleaning, 2 lighted tennis courts, dive shop, boutiques, ice-cream parlor, beauty salon, minimarket, water-sports center. AE, DC, MC, V. EP, MAP. Expensive–Very Expensive.*

Sandals St. Lucia. This is St. Lucia's newest all-inclusive property. Previously, the hotel was the Cunard Hotel La Toc and La Toc Suites, a combination of high-rise hotel and luxury villa suites. But in the past few years the resort fell into disrepair, a shame since the secluded 100-acre valley is within a 10-minute drive of Castries and has a lovely beach, a nine-hole golf course, and four floodlit tennis courts. Sandals, a couples-only resort, has entirely renovated the property, keeping the best—from the private plunge pools and quarter-acre swimming pool to the four restaurants serving Oriental, Continental, and Caribbean cuisine. Added to the amenities are a fitness center and whirlpools scattered around the property. Guest rooms, done in mahogany furnishings with king-size four-poster beds, all have with air-conditioning, hair dryers, direct-dial telephones, and color TVs. *La Toc Rd., Castries, tel. 809/452–3081, fax 809/453–7089. 213 rooms, 60 suites. Facilities: 4 restaurants, 2 bars, 5 tennis courts, 9-hole golf course, water-sports center, fitness center. AE, DC, MC, V. All-inclusive. Expensive–Very Expensive.*

Anse Chastanet Hotel. Of all the hotels on St. Lucia, Anse Chastanet stands out as having the most dramatic interior designs in its guest rooms, which often have wide, sweeping views of the sea and the Pitons. Furnishings add to the sophistication with many items individually built by local craftsmen. The rooms are in a cluster of octagonal gazebos planted in a tropical hillside forest. In addition to the gazebos, there are 12 suites. All have ceiling fans and verandas. The hotel is on a 400-acre estate near Soufrière and the Pitons. From the main restaurant, 125 steps lead to a lovely black-sand crescent where there is another restaurant, a thatch-roof bar, and a dive shop. Sunfish and Windsurfers are gratis to guests. The restaurants serve fine West Indian fare. The hotel is quiet, peaceful, and secluded, reached by a rough, pot-holed road from Soufrière or an afternoon launch from Castries. *Box 7000, Soufrière, tel. 809/454–7355, fax 809/454–7067. 36 rooms and 12 suites. Facilities: 2 restaurants, 2 bars, tennis court, dive shop, water-sports center. AE, DC, MC, V. EP, MAP. Expensive.*

Club Med St. Lucia. This four-story air-conditioned hotel is on a 95-acre beachfront property on the southeast coast, where the Atlantic waters are rough. All the usual Club Med activities are here, including nightly entertainment. Hewanorra International Airport is five minutes away. *Vieux Fort, tel. 809/455–6001 or 800/CLUBMED, fax 809/452–0958. 256 rooms. Facilities: restaurant, bar, boutique, fitness center, 8 tennis courts,*

pool, horseback riding, water-sports center. AE, DC, MC, V.
All-inclusive (drinks not included). Expensive.

Wyndham Morgan Bay Resort. The expanding Wyndham Hotel
group took over this property from the Hotel Pullman in 1992,
to offer another all-inclusive property on St. Lucia. Despite Caribbean-style touches like open-air public areas and pastel colors, the architecture has a stark, new look that contrasts with
the luxuriant vegetation of the island. Most of the rooms, with
floral linens and peach wicker furniture, offer partial and angled sea views from each of the eight three-story buildings,
lined up on a small rise above the pool and restaurant area. All
have air-conditioning, cable TV, phone, and hair dryer. Party
goers are apt to be happiest here because drinks are generous
and free flowing and the guests seem to spend most of their
time at the bar/pool area. The beach—small, with cloudy water—is the biggest disappointment. *Box 2216, Gros Islet, tel.*
809/450–2511, fax 809/450–1050. 240 rooms. Facilities: 2 res-
taurants, 2 bars, beach grill, boutique, 4 tennis courts, pool,
games room, Jacuzzi, exercise room, sauna, satellite TV, wa-
ter-sports center. AE, D, MC, V. All-inclusive. Expensive.

Harmony Marine Suites. On Rodney Bay Marina, this two-story apartment hotel has one-bedroom apartments, four of which
have fully equipped electric kitchens. All have wall-to-wall carpeting, twin beds, showers, TVs with VCRs, balconies or patios, and token-operated air conditioners. Poolside rooms, away
from the marina, are quieter. Windsurfing is free; other water
sports are available. There's a manager's rum-punch party every Tuesday. The Mortar and Pestle restaurant features
"haute cuisine des Caraibes." *Box 155, Castries, tel. 809/452–*
8756 or 800/223–6510, fax 809/452–8677. 21 units. Facilities:
restaurant, minimarket, maid service, pool, water-sports cen-
ter, VCR library and books library. MC, V. EP. Moderate–
Expensive.

★ **Islander.** An upscale motel just 300 yards from Reduit Beach,
the Islander offers standard air-conditioned rooms with clock
radios, wall-to-wall carpeting, king-size beds, refrigerators,
balconies, cable TV, and phones. There are also suites with
kitchenettes. The Islander is in the Rodney Bay area. Supermarkets, restaurants, and nightlife are a few steps away. *Box*
907, Castries, tel. 809/452–8757 or 800/223–9815, fax 809/452–
0958. 60 units. Facilities: restaurant, bar, pool, movie room,
shuttle bus to beach. AE, D, MC, V. EP. Moderate–Expensive.

Vigie Beach Hotel. A glassed-in bar sits on the mile-long Vigie
Beach, and a path leads through gardens up to the hotel. Rooms
are spacious with modern decor, double beds, balconies with
garden or beach view, TV, phone, and air-conditioning. You'll
be sunning to the sound of small planes, since the hotel is located adjacent to Vigie Airport. The staff seems genuinely un-
concerned. *Box 395, Castries, tel. 809/452–5211, fax 809/452–*
5434. 47 rooms. Facilities: restaurant, 2 bars, pool, Jacuzzi.
AE, D, DC, MC, V. EP. Moderate–Expensive.

Green Parrot. There are green velvet chairs in the small reception room, in the first and lowest of three rows of buildings that
are stacked on the hillside high up in the Morne above Castries.
The large, motel-like rooms have a patio, phone, air-conditioning, and bath with tub/shower and vanity. Though there is a
restaurant for nonguests, hotel guests have a separate dining
room with a popular sunken bar. The hotel arranges boat trips
to Jambette Beach for barbecue and snorkeling for about $30
and a free bus scoots you to town and the beach. *Box 648,*

Castries, tel. 809/452-3399, fax 809/453-2272. 60 rooms. Facilities: 2 restaurants, bar, games room, pool, nightclub. AE, MC, V. EP, MAP. Moderate.

Humming Bird Beach Resort. A wide range of accommodations is available at this charming spot, with an abundance of ambience and an ideal location at the edge of Soufrière. Four-poster beds and African sculpture adorn the best rooms. It seems almost more appropriate to the South Seas, from the bar right out of Somerset Maugham to the flowing sarongs sold at the batik shop. The highly regarded restaurant is a favorite hangout of locals and expatriates. Joyce Alexander, the owner, is a marvelous, dynamic hostess who, when not making improvements to her small hotel, designs batiks for the adjoining boutique. *Box 280, Soufrière, tel. 809/454-7232. 10 units. Facilities: restaurant, bar, pool. MC, V. EP, MAP. Moderate.*

Kimatrai. This is a clean, family-owned and -operated hotel on the southeast coast, just above Vieux Fort. The Hewanorra International Airport is five minutes away. Accommodations include double rooms, self-contained apartments, and bungalows. All are air-conditioned with private showers. *Box 238, Vieux Fort, tel. 809/454-6328. 25 units. Facilities: restaurant, bar. No credit cards. EP. Inexpensive-Moderate.*

Home and Apartment Rentals For private-home rentals, contact **Caribbean Home Rentals** (Box 710, Palm Beach, FL 33480), **Happy Homes** (Box 12, Castries, St. Lucia), or **Tropical Villas** (Box 189, Castries, tel. 809/452-8240).

Nightlife

Most of the action is in the hotels, which feature entertainment of the island variety—limbo dancers, fire-eaters, calypso singers, and steel band jump-ups. Many offer entertainment packages, including dinner, to nonguests.

Splash (St. Lucian Hotel, tel. 809/452-8351) is a sophisticated place with a good dance floor and splashy lighting effects. Open Monday–Saturday from 9 PM. At the **Halcyon Wharf Disco** (Halcyon Beach Club, tel. 809/452-5331) you can dance on the jetty under the stars every night.

On weekends, locals usually hang out at **The Lime** (Rodney Bay, tel. 809/452-0761) or at **Capone's** (Rodney Bay, tel. 809/452-0284), an art deco place right out of the Roaring '20s, with a player piano and rum drinks. **The Charthouse** (Rodney Bay, tel. 809/452-8115) has a popular bar, jazz on stereo, and live music on Saturday. The **Rusty Anchor** (Marigot Bay, tel. 809/453-4357) is an informal hangout for the yachting crowd. Young boaters tie up at the **A-Frame** (Rodney Bay, tel. 809/452-8725) for drinks, chess, darts, and backgammon. (You can take the ferry across the bay for E.C.$2; it leaves every hour across the road from The Islander Hotel.) The **Green Parrot** (The Morne, tel. 809/452-3399) is in a class all by itself. Chef Harry Edwards hosts the floor show, which features limbo dancers. Harry has been known to shimmy under the pole himself. There are also belly dancers. Great fun; semiformal attire.

On Friday nights, sleepy Gros Islet becomes sin city, Bourbon Street during Mardi Gras, as the entire village is transformed into a street fair. At the far end of the street, mammoth stereos loudly beat out sounds as locals and strangers let their hair down. **Monroe's** (Grande Rivière, Gros Islet, tel. 809/452-8131) is probably the best spot for meeting locals. **The Banana Split** (St. Georges St., Gros Islet, tel. 809/452–8125) offers entertainment and special theme nights, with a perpetual "spring break" atmosphere. It can get rowdy, so it's best to travel in a group and keep your wits about you. But then Friday night is *the* night to hang, party, lime. Worried about crashing the party? Just roll down your window and ask: You'll know if you're invited. Another Friday night street scene and a popular alternate venue for liming can be found just before you enter Marigot Bay. The music is supplied by **J. J.'s Restaurant** (tel. 809/453–4076), and the popular fare is curried goat. More and more locals are choosing to come here instead of the more touristy Gros Islet happening.

23 St. Martin St. Maarten

*Updated by
Jordan Simon*

There are frequent nonstop flights from the United States to St. Maarten/St. Martin, so you don't have to spend half your vacation getting here—a critical advantage if you have only a few days to enjoy the sun. The 37-square-mile island is home to two sovereign nations, St. Maarten (Dutch) and St. Martin (French), so you can experience two cultures for the price of one. However, the Dutch side has lost much of its European flavor.

The island, particularly the Dutch side, is ideal for people who like to have lots of things to do. Whatever can be done in or on the water—snorkeling, windsurfing, waterskiing—is available here; and there is golf and tennis as well. Especially on the French side, there are enough good-quality restaurants for serious diners to try a different one each night, even on a two-week stay. The duty-free shopping is as good as anywhere in the Caribbean, except perhaps in the U.S. Virgin Islands. There's an active nightlife, with discos and casinos. Watersports enthusiasts will love Simpson Bay Lagoon, the largest inland body of water in the Caribbean. Day trips can be taken by ship or plane to the nearby islands of Anguilla, Saba, St. Eustatius, and St. Barthélemy. There are hotels for every taste and budget—from motel-type units for the package tour trade to some of the most exclusive resorts in the Caribbean. The standard of living is one of the highest in the Caribbean, so the islanders can afford to be honest and to treat visitors as welcome guests. Corruption and crime, which had been on the rise, have decreased dramatically in the '90s, thanks to an exemplary cooperative effort between the two governments.

On the negative side, St. Maarten/St. Martin has been thoroughly discovered and developed; unless you stay in an exclusive resort, you are likely to find yourself sharing beachfronts with tour groups or conventioneers. Yes, there is gambling, but the table limits are so low that hard-core gamblers will have a better time gamboling on the beach. It can be fun to shop, and there's an occasional bargain, but many goods, particularly electronics, are cheaper in the United States.

Perhaps what makes this island unique is the opportunity it affords the visitor to lead an active life one moment and to come to a complete halt the next. For all its bustle, St. Martin/St. Maarten is still a Caribbean island brushed by gentle trade winds. You can do nothing at all and enjoy yourself immensely.

Before You Go

**Tourist
Information** For information about the Dutch side, contact the **St. Maarten Tourist Office** (275 7th Ave., New York, NY 10001, tel. 212/989-0000) or the **St. Maarten Information Office** (243 Ellerslie Ave., Willowdale, Toronto, Ont., Canada M2N 1Y5, tel. 416/223-3501). Information about French St. Martin can be obtained through the **French West Indies Tourist Board** by calling France-on-Call at 900/990-0040 (50¢ per minute), or you can write to the **French Government Tourist Office**, 610 5th Ave., New York, NY 10020; 9454 Wilshire Blvd., Beverly Hills, CA 90212; 645 N. Michigan Ave., Chicago, IL 60611; 2305 Cedar Spring Rd., Dallas TX 75201. In Canada contact the French Government Tourist Office, 1981 McGill College Ave., Suite 490, Montreal. P.Q. H3A 2W9, tel. 514/288-4264; or 1 Dundas St. W, Suite 2405, Toronto, Ont. M5G 1Z3, tel. 416/593-4723 or

800/361-9099. In the United Kingdom the tourist office can be reached at 178 Piccadilly, London W1Z OAL, tel. 071/493-6594.

Arriving and Departing
By Plane

There are two airports on the island. L'Espérance on the French side is small and handles only island-hoppers. Bigger planes fly into Juliana International Airport on the Dutch side. The most convenient carrier from the United States is **American Airlines** (tel. 800/433-7300), with daily nonstop flights from New York and Miami, as well as connections from more than 100 U.S. cities via its San Juan hub. **Continental Airlines** (tel. 800/231-0856) has daily flights from Newark. **LIAT** (tel. 809/462-0701) flies from Antigua; **ALM** (tel. 800/327-7230) from Aruba, Bonaire, Curaçao, the Dominican Republic, and from Atlanta and Miami via Curaçao. ALM also offers a Visit Caribbean Air Pass, which offers savings for traveling to several Caribbean islands. **Air Martinique** (tel. 596/51-08-09) connects the island with Martinique twice a week. **Windward Islands Airways** (Winair, tel. 599/54-42-30), which is based on St. Maarten, has daily scheduled service to Saba, St. Eustatius, St. Barts, Anguilla, St. Thomas, and St. Kitts/Nevis. **Air Guadeloupe** (tel. 590/90-37-37) has several flights daily to St. Barts and Guadeloupe from both sides of the island. **Air St. Barthélemy** (tel. 590/27-71-90) has frequent service between Juliana and St. Barts. Tour and charter services are available from Winair and **St. Martin Helicopters** (Dutch side, tel. 599/5-4287).

By Boat

Motorboats zip several times a day from Anguilla to the French side at Marigot, three times a week from St. Barts. Catamaran service is available daily from the Dutch side to St. Barts. The 50-passenger *Style* (tel. 599/5-22167) slaps across from Saba three times a week.

Passports and Visas

U.S. citizens need proof of citizenship. A passport (valid or not expired more than five years) is preferred. An original birth certificate with raised seal (or a photocopy with notary seal), or a voter registration card is also acceptable. All visitors must have a confirmed room reservation and an ongoing or return ticket. British and Canadian citizens need valid passports.

Language

Dutch is the official language of St. Maarten and French is the official language of St. Martin, but almost everyone speaks English. If you hear a language you can't quite place, it's Papiamento, a Spanish-based Creole of the Netherlands Antilles.

Staying in St. Martin/St. Maarten

Important Addresses

Tourist Information: On the Dutch side, the **Tourist Information Bureau** is on Cyrus Wathey (pronounced *watty*) Square in the heart of Philipsburg, at the pier where the cruise ships send their tenders. The executive office is on Walter Nisbeth Road 23 (Imperial Building) on the third floor. *Tel. 599/5-22337. Open weekdays 8-noon and 1-5, except holidays.*

On the French side, there is the smart and very helpful **Tourist Information Office** on the Marigot pier. *Tel. 590/87-57-21. Open weekdays 8-12:30 and 2-5; Sat. 8-noon. Closed holidays and the afternoon preceding a holiday.*

Emergencies

Police: Dutch side (tel. 599/5-22222), French side (tel. 590/85-50-16); **Ambulance:** Dutch side (tel. 599/5-22111), French side (tel. 590/87-50-06); **Hospitals: St. Rose Hospital** (Front St., Philipsburg, tel. 599/5-22300) is a fully equipped 55-bed hospi-

Exploring

French Cul de Sac, **5**
Grand Case, **6**
Guana Bay Point, **2**
Marigot, **7**
Orléans, **4**
Oyster Pond, **3**
Philipsburg, **1**

Dining

Alizéa, **8**
Antoine's, **46**
Bistrot Nu, **23**
Captain Oliver's, **59**
Case Anny, **22**
Cha Cha Cha Caribbean Cafe, **13**
Chesterfield's, **47**
Chez Martine, **14**
Don Camillo da Enzo, **23**
Felix, **42**
Harbour Lights, **48**
L'Escargot, **49**
La Residence, **24**
La Rhumerie, **20**
La Samanna, **34**
La Vie En Rose, **25**
Le Bec Fin, **50**
Le Perroquet, **37**
Le Poisson d'Or, **26**
Le Santal, **30**
Le Tastevin, **15**
Maison sur le Port, **27**
Mark's Place, **11**
Mini Club, **28**
Oyster Pond Hotel, **58**
Rainbow, **16**
Shiv Sagar, **51**
Spartaco, **44**
Turtle Pier Bar and Restaurant, **38**
Wajang Doll, **52**
Yvette's, **60**

Lodging

Alizéa, **8**
Anse Margot, **31**
Captain Oliver's, **59**
Caribbean Hotel, **53**
Dawn Beach Hotel, **57**
Esmeralda Resort, **10**
Grand Case Beach Club, **17**
Great Bay Beach Hotel and Casino, **45**
Hevea, **18**
Holland House, **54**
Horny Toad Guest House, **39**
La Belle Creole, **33**

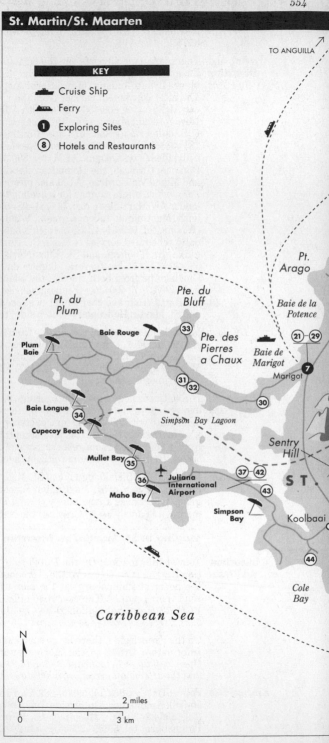

St. Martin/St. Maarten

KEY

🚢 Cruise Ship

⛴ Ferry

❶ Exploring Sites

⑧ Hotels and Restaurants

TO ANGUILLA

Pt. Arago

Pt. du Plum

Pte. du Bluff

Baie de la Potence

Baie Rouge

Plum Baie

Pte. des Pierres a Chaux

Baie de Marigot

Marigot

Baie Longue

Simpson Bay Lagoon

Cupecoy Beach

Mullet Bay

Sentry Hill

Juliana International Airport

S T

Maho Bay

Simpson Bay

Koolbaai

Cole Bay

Caribbean Sea

N

0 — 2 miles
0 — 3 km

tal. **Pharmacies:** Pharmacies are open Monday–Saturday 7–5. **Central Drug Store** (Philipsburg, tel. 599/5–22321), **Mullet Bay Drug Store** (tel. 599/5–42801, ext. 342), and **Pharmacie** (Marigot, tel. 590/87–50–79).

Currency Legal tender on the Dutch side is the Netherlands Antilles florin (guilder), written NAf; on the French side, the French franc (F). The exchange rate fluctuates, but in general it is about NAf 1.79 to U.S. $1 and 5F to U.S. $1. On the Dutch side, prices are usually given in both NAf and U.S. dollars, which are accepted all over the island, as are credit cards. Note: Prices quoted here are in U.S. dollars unless otherwise noted.

Taxes and Service Charges On the Dutch side, a 5% government tax is added to hostel bills. On the French side, a *taxe de séjour* (visitor's tax) is tacked onto hotel bills (the amount differs from hotel to hotel, but the maximum is $3 per day, per person). Departure tax from Juliana Airport is $5 to destinations within the Netherlands Antilles and $10 to all other destinations. It will cost you 15 French francs to depart by plane from l'Espérance Airport or by ferry to Anguilla from Marigot's pier.

In lieu of tipping, service charges are added to hotel bills all over the island, and, by law, are included in all menu prices on the French side. On the Dutch side, most restaurants add 10%–15% to the bill.

Hotels on the Dutch side add a 15% service/energy charge to the bill. Hotels on the French side add 10%–15% for service.

Taxi drivers expect a 10% tip.

Guided Tours A 2½-hour taxi tour of the island costs $35 for one or two people, $10 for each additional person. Your hotel or the Tourist Office can arrange it for you. Best bet is the 20-passenger vans of **St. Maarten Sightseeing Tours** (Philipsburg, tel. 599/5–22753), which offer, among other options, a 2½-hour island tour for $12 per person. You can tour in deluxe comfort with **St. Maarten Limousine Service** (tel. 599/5–24698 or 599/5–22698) for $40–$50 per hour with a three-hour minimum. Fully equipped Lincoln Continentals accommodate up to six people and are furnished with stereo, fully stocked bar, and air-conditioning. The limo service also offers transportation to and from Juliana Airport at rates ranging from $30 to $65 one-way. (This includes one hour of waiting time free of charge for late arrivals.) On the French side, **Societe Touristique de St. Martin** (tel. 590/87–56–20) also runs excellent islandwide tours.

Getting Around *Taxis* Taxi rates are government regulated, and authorized taxis display stickers of the St. Maarten Taxi Association. There is a taxi service, headed by Raymond Helligar, at the Marigot port near the Tourist Information Bureau. Fixed fares apply from Juliana Airport and the Marigot ferry to the various hotels and around the island. Fares are 25% higher between 10 PM and midnight, 50% higher between midnight and 6 AM.

Buses One of the island's best bargains at $.80 to $2.00, depending on your destination, buses operate frequently between 7 AM and 7 PM and run from Philipsburg through Cole Bay to Marigot.

Rental Cars You can book a car at Juliana Airport, where all major rental companies have booths, but to give taxi drivers work, you must collect the car at the rental offices located off the airport complex. (The Hertz office is closest to the airport, just a quarter of a mile away.) There are also rentals at every hotel area. Rental cars are inexpensive—approximately $35 a day for a subcompact car plus collision damage waiver. All foreign driver's licenses are honored, and major credit cards are accepted. **Avis** (tel. 800/331–1212), **Budget** (tel. 800/527–0700), **Dollar** (tel. 800/421–6868), **Hertz** (tel. 800/654–3131), and **National** (tel. 800/328–4567) all have offices on the island. Scooters rent for $20–25 a day at **Rent 2 Wheels** (Nettle Bay, tel. 590/87–20–59).

Telephones and Mail To call the Dutch side from the United States, dial 011–599 + local number; for the French side, 011–590 + local number. To phone from the Dutch side to the French, dial 06 + local number; from the French side to the Dutch, 3 + local number. Keep in mind that a call from one side to another is an overseas call, not a local call. Telephone communications, especially on the Dutch side, leave something to be desired. At the Landsradio in Philipsburg, there are facilities for overseas calls and an AT&T USADIRECT telephone, where you are directly in touch with an AT&T operator who will accept collect or credit-cards calls. On the French side, it is not possible to make collect calls to the United States, and there are no coin phones. If you need to use public phones, go to the special desk at Marigot's post office and buy a Telecarte (it looks like a credit card), which gives you 40 units for around 31F or 120 units for 93F. There is a small kiosk next to the tourist office in Marigot where you can make credit card phone calls. The operator will assign you a PIN (Personal Identification Number) number, valid for as long as you specify. Calls are $4 per minute to the United States.

Letters from the Dutch side to the United States and Canada cost NAf 1.30; postcards, NAf .60. From the French side, letters up to 20 grams, 4.10F; postcards, 3.50F.

Opening and Closing Times Shops on the Dutch side are open Monday–Saturday, 8–noon and 2–6; on the French side, Monday–Saturday 9–noon or 12:30, and 2–6. Some of the larger shops on both sides of the island open Sunday and holidays when the cruise ships are in port. Some of the small Dutch and French shops set their own capricious hours.

Banks on the Dutch side are open Monday–Thursday 8–1 and Friday 4–5. French banks open weekdays 8:30–1:30 and 2–3 and close afternoons preceding holidays.

Exploring St. Martin/St. Maarten

Numbers in the margin correspond to points of interest on the St. Martin/St. Maarten map.

Philipsburg ❶ The Dutch capital of **Philipsburg,** which stretches about a mile along an isthmus between Great Bay and the Salt Pond, has three more or less parallel streets: Front Street, Back Street, and Pond Fill. Front Street has been recently recobbled, cars discouraged from using it, and the pedestrian area widened. Shops, restaurants, and casinos vie for the hordes coming off the cruise boats. Head for **Wathey Square** and stroll out on the pier. **Great Bay** is rolled out before you, and the beach stretches alongside it for about a mile. The square bustles with vendors, souvenir shops, and tourists. There's a taxi stand where you can arrange for a driver to take you around if you'd rather not rent a car. Philipsburg should be explored on foot, but you'll need wheels to get around the island.

Directly across the street from Wathey Square, you'll see a striking white building with a cupola. It was built in 1793 and has since served as the commander's home, a fire station, and a jail. It now serves as the town hall, court house, and the post office.

The square is in the middle of the isthmus on which Philipsburg sits. To your right and left the streets are lined with hotels, duty-free shops, fine restaurants, and cafés, most of them in pastel-colored West Indian cottages gussied up with gingerbread trim. Narrow alleyways lead to arcades and flower-filled courtyards where there are yet more boutiques and eateries.

A half-block away across the street, Simart'n Museum, in a restored 19th-century West Indian house, hosts rotating cultural exhibits and the permanent historical display entitled "Forts of St. Maarten/St. Martin." (Open Mon.–Sat. 10–6, Sun. 9:30–noon. Admission: $1. 119 Front Street, Philipsburg, tel. 599/5–32125.) If you'd like to clamber through the ruins themselves, take the dirt path at the Great Bay Hotel parking lot to Fort Willem for a spectacular view of Philipsburg and the surrounding islands.

Little lanes called *steegjes* connect Front Street with Back Street, which is considerably less congested because it has fewer shops.

Our drive begins at the western end of Front Street. The road (it will become Sucker Garden Road) leads north along Salt Pond and begins to climb and curve just outside of town. Take
② the first right to **Guana Bay Point,** from which there is a splendid view of the island's east coast, tiny deserted islands, and small St. Barts, which is anything but deserted.

Sucker Garden Road continues north through spectacular scenery. Continue along a paved roller-coaster road down to **Dawn Beach,** one of the island's best snorkeling beaches.

③ **Oyster Pond** is the legendary point where two early settlers, a Frenchman and a Dutchman, allegedly began to pace in opposite directions around the island to divide it between their respective countries. (The official boundary marker is on the other side of the island.)

Elsewhere on From Oyster Pond, follow the road along the bay and around
the Island Etang aux Poissons (Fish Lake), all the way to **Orléans.** This
④ settlement, which is also known as the French Quarter, is the oldest on the island. Noted local artist and activist Roland Richardson makes his home here. He holds open studio on Thursdays from 10 to 6 to sell his art. He's a proud islander ready to share his wealth of knowledge about the island's cultural history.

A rough dirt road leads northeast to **Orient Beach,** the island's best-known nudist beach. There's even a pricey rustic resort catering to "naturists." Offshore, little **Ilet Pinel** is an uninhabited island that's fine for picnicking, sunning, and swimming.

⑤ Farther north you'll come to **French Cul de Sac,** where you'll see the French colonial mansion of St. Martin's mayor nestled in the hills. Little red-roof houses look like open umbrellas tumbling down the green hillside. The scenery here is glorious, and the area is great for hiking. There is a lot of construction, however, as the surroundings are slowly being developed. From the beach here, three shuttle boats make the five-minute trip ($5) to Ilet Pinel. The descent to L'Habitation, the elegant resort at Anse Marcel on the north coast, may turn your knuckles white.

The road swirls south through green hills and pastures, past flower-entwined stone fences. Past L'Espérance Airport is the ❻ town of **Grand Case.** Though it has only one mile-long main street, it's known as the "Restaurant Capital of the Caribbean": More than 20 restaurants serve French, Italian, Indonesian, and Vietnamese fare, as well as fresh seafood. The budget-minded will appreciate the "lolos"—savory barbecue stands along the waterfront. **Grand Case Beach Hotel** is at the end of this road and has two beaches to choose from for a short dip. Better yet, travel down the road about 5 miles toward Marigot and on the right is a turnoff to **Friar's Beach,** a small, picturesque cove that attracts a casual crowd of locals. A small snack bar, **Kali's,** owned by a welcoming gentleman wearing dreadlocks, serves refreshments. From here, you can turn inland and follow a bumpy tree-canopied road to Pic du Paradis, at 1,278 feet the highest point on the island, affording breathtaking vistas of the Caribbean.

❼ Just before entering the French capital of **Marigot,** you will notice a new shopping complex on the left. At the back of it is **Match** (tel. 590/87–92–36), now the largest supermarket on the French side, carrying a broad selection of tempting picnic makings—from country pâté to foie gras—and a vast selection of wines.

If you are a shopper, a gourmet, or just a Francophile, you'll want to tarry awhile in Marigot. Marina Port La Royale is the shopping complex at the port, but Rue de la République and Rue de la Liberté, which border the bay, are also filled with duty-free shops, boutiques, and bistros. The harbor area has stalls selling anything from fruits and vegetables to handmade crafts. Across from these stalls on pier road leading to the ferries for Anguilla is the helpful **French Tourist Office,** where you may collect an assortment of free maps and brochures.

Time Out   With a roguish glint in his eye, owner Roger Drovin proclaims the melt-in-your-mouth croissants at **Cafe Terrasse Mastedana** (Rue de la Liberté, no tel.) to be "zee best." This humble little establishment along the main road by Port La Royale, bedecked with pennants from around the world, is perfect for a light breakfast or snack.

You are likely to find more creative and fashionable buys in Marigot than in Philipsburg, and if you are not a shopper, there is less bustle and the open-air cafés are tempting places in which to stop for a rest. Also, unlike Philipsburg, Marigot does not die at night, so you may wish to return in the evening. **Le Bar de la Mer** (tel. 590/87–81–79) on the harbor is a popular gathering spot in the early evening, though the bar and restaurant are open all day.

The road due south of Marigot to Philipsburg passes the official boundary, where a simple border marker, erected by the Dutch and French citizenry to commemorate 300 years of peaceful coexistence, bears the dates "1648 to 1948." Straddling the border is a mammoth condominium hotel complex, the Port de

Plaisance, where Sheraton has constructed the extravagant Mont Fortune casino adjacent to the hotel.

At the airport, the road from Marigot to the north and Simpson Bay to the west join together and lead to Philipsburg, passing the cutoff to Divi Little Bay Beach Resort.

The other road from Marigot leads west and hugs the coastline to cross a small bridge to Sandy Ground and then along Baie Nettlé, with its many new, reasonably priced hotels. Soon thereafter, on the right, you'll come to the Mediterranean-style village resort of **La Belle Creole,** commanding Pointe du Bluff. Then you'll begin to see some of the island's best beaches—**Baie Rouge, Plum Baie,** and **Baie Longue**—clinging to its westernmost point. They are all accessible down bumpy but short dirt roads and perfect for swimming and picnicking.

At the end of Baie Longue and running eastward along the south coast is **La Samanna,** the fashionable jet-set resort. Just after this hotel you'll reenter Dutch territory at **Cupecoy Beach.** You'll have to endure the huge, garish vacation condo-hotel complexes of Mullet Bay and Maho Bay before you reach Juliana Airport and Philipsburg.

What to See and Do with Children

The St. Maarten Zoo and Botanical Garden. This ambitious development, the labor of love of a local policeman, features plants and animals indigenous to the Caribbean basin and South America, including coatimundis, ocelots, peccaries, and boa constrictors. The two large walk-through aviaries, petting zoo, and playground should delight children of all ages. *Madame Estate, tel. 599/5–32030. Admission: $4 adults, $2 children. Hours: weekdays 9–5, weekends 10–6.*

Off the Beaten Track

Ocean Explorers Sea Walk. Uniquely designed helmets enable you to breathe normally underwater as guides point out the profusion of riotously colored marine life in Simpson Bay. Swimming ability is not required, just curiosity and a bathing suit. The cost is $35 per person. *Simpson Bay, tel. 599/5–45252.*

Beaches

The island's 10 miles of beaches are all open to the public. Beaches occupied by resort properties charge a small fee (about $3) for changing facilities, and water-sports equipment can be rented in most of the hotels. You cannot, however, enter the beach via the hotel unless you are a paying guest. Some of the 37 beaches are secluded, some are located in the thick of things. Topless bathing is virtually de rigueur on the French side, where the beaches are generally better than on the Dutch side. If you take a cab to a remote beach, be sure to arrange a specific, clearly understood time for your driver to return to pick you up, and don't leave valuables unattended on the beach.

Hands down, **Baie Longue** is the best beach on the island. It's a beautiful, mile-long curve of white sand on the westernmost tip of the island. This is a good place for snorkeling and swimming, but beware of a strong undertow when the waters are rough.

You can sunbathe in the buff, though only a few do. Pack a lunch. There are no facilities.

Beyond Baie Longue is **Plum Baie,** where the beach arcs between two headlands and the occasional sunbather discloses all.

Baie Rouge is one of the most secluded beaches on the island. This little patch of sand is located at the base of high cliffs and is backed by private homes rather than by hotels. Some rate it the prettiest beach of the island, although it can have rough waves. A small snack/soda stand is located at the entrance.

Orient Beach is the island's best-known "clothes optional" beach—it's on the agenda for voyeurs from visiting cruise ships. You can enter from the parking area or through the **Club Orient** (tel. 590/87–33–85), which has chalet self-catering bungalows for rent, shops, and rental water-sports equipment.

You have to approach the **Dawn Beach–Oyster Pond** area through the Dawn Beach Hotel. This long white-sand beach is partly protected by reefs (good for snorkeling), but the waters are not always calm. When the waves come rolling in, this is the best spot on the island for bodysurfing.

Ilet Pinel is a little speck off the northeast coast, with about 500 yards of beach, where you can have picnics and privacy. There are no facilities. Putt putts are available to take you from Orient Beach.

Simpson Bay is a long half-moon of white sand near Simpson Bay Village, one of the last undiscovered hamlets on the island. In this small fishing village you'll find refreshments, the **Ocean Explorers** (*see* Sports and the Outdoors, *below*) for water-sports rentals, and neat little ultra-Caribbean town homes.

Ecru-color sand, palm and sea-grape trees, calm waters, and the roar of jets lowering to nearby Juliana Airport distinguish the beach at **Maho Bay.** Concession stand, beach chairs, and facilities are available.

At **Mullet Bay,** the powdery white-sand beach is crowded with guests of the Mullet Bay Resort.

Cupecoy Beach is a small shifting arc of white sand fringed with eroded limestone cliffs, just south of Baie Longue on the western side of the island, near the Dutch-French border. On the first part of the beach, swimwear is worn, but farther up, sun worshipers start shedding their attire. There are no facilities, but a truck is often parked at the entrance, with a vendor who sells cold sodas and beers.

Sports and the Outdoors

All the resort hotels have activities desks that can arrange virtually any type of water sport.

Boating Motorboats, speedboats, Dolphins, pedal boats, sailboats, and canoes can be rented at **Lagoon Cruises & Watersports** (tel. 599/5–52801, ext. 1873) and **Caribbean Watersports** (tel. 599/5–42801).

Sun Yacht-Charters (tel. 800/772–3500), based in Oyster Pond, has a fleet of 30 Centurion sailboats for hire. The cost of a week's bareboat charter for a 36-foot Centurion with six berths runs $2,590 in peak winter season. Also in Oyster Pond, **The**

Moorings (tel. 800/535–7289 or 590/87–32–55) has a fleet of Beneteau yachts, 38–50 feet in length. **Dynasty** (Marigot's Port La Royale Marina, tel. 590/87–85–21) offers an excellent fleet of Dynamique yachts.

Deep-Sea Fishing Angle for yellowtail, snapper, grouper, marlin, tuna, and wahoo on half-day deep-sea excursions, including bait and tackle, instruction for novices, and an open bar. Contact **Wampum** (Bobby's Marina, Philipsburg, tel. 599/5–22366) or **Sailfish Caraibes** (Port Lonvilliers, tel. 590/87–31–94).

Fitness **Le Privilege** (tel. 590/87–37–37), a sports complex at Anse Marcel above Meridien L'Habitation, features a full range of exercise equipment. **Fitness Caraibes** (tel. 590/87–97–04), a toning center run by Marc Bozzetto, is at Nettle Bay. On the Dutch side, **L'Aqualigne** at the Pelican Resort (tel. 599/5–54330) is a health spa with gym, sauna, and beauty and weight-loss treatments, among other things.

Golf **Mullet Bay Resort** (tel. 599/5–42081) has an 18-hole championship course.

Horseback Riding Contact **Crazy Acres Riding Center** (Wathey Estate, Cole Bay, tel. 599/5–42793), **Bayside Riding Club** (Orient Bay, 590/87–33–85) or **O.K. Corral** (Oyster Pond, tel. 590/87–40–72).

Jet- and Waterskiing Rent equipment through **Caribbean Watersports** (tel. 599/5–42801 or 599/5–44363) and **Maho Watersports** (tel. 599/5–44387). On the French side, try **Orient Watersports** (tel. 590/87–33–85).

Parasailing A great high can be arranged through **Lagoon Cruises & Watersports** (tel. 599/5–52898).

Running The **Road Runners Club** (Pelican Resort Activities Desk, tel. 599/5–42503) meets weekly for its 5K or 10K run.

Scuba Diving On the Dutch side is Proselyte Reef, named for the British frigate H.M.S. *Proselyte,* which sank south of Great Bay in 1802. In addition to wreck dives, reef, night, cave, and drift dives are popular. Off the northeast coast of the French side, dive sites include Ilet Pinel, for good shallow diving; Green Key, a prolific barrier reef; and Flat Island (also known as Ile Tintamarre) for sheltered coves and subsea geologic faults. NAUI- and PADI-certified dive centers offer instruction, rentals, and trips at **Tradewinds Dive Center/Maho Watersports** (tel. 599/5–54387), **St. Maarten Divers** (tel. 599/5–22446), and **Ocean Explorers Dive Shop** (599/5–45252). On the French side, PADI-certified **Lou Scuba** (tel. 590/87–28–58) has opened at the Laguna Beach Hotel at Nettle Bay. **Blue Ocean** (tel. 590/87–89–73) is PADI and CMAS certified.

Sea Excursions You can take a day-long picnic sail to nearby islands or secluded coves aboard the 45-foot ketch *Gabrielle* (tel. 599/5–23170), the 41-foot ketch *Pretty Penny* (tel. 599/5–2167), or the 60-foot schooner *Gandalf.* The catamaran *Bluebeard II* (tel. 599/5–42801 or 599/5–42898), moored in Marigot, sails around Anguilla's south and northwest coasts to Prickley Pear, where there are excellent coral reefs for snorkeling and powdery white sands for sunning.

The luxurious 75-foot motor catamaran *White Octopus* (tel. 599/5–23170) does full-moon and cocktail cruises, complete with calypso music. During the day the *White Octopus* makes the run to St. Barts, departing at 9 AM from Bobby's Marina and returning at 5 PM. In St. Martin, sailing, snorkeling, and picnic excursions to nearby islands can be arranged through **Orient Watersports** (Club Orient, tel. 590/87–33–85), **L'Habitation** (tel. 590/87–33–33), **La Belle Creole** (tel. 590/87–58–66), and **La Samanna** (tel. 590/87–51–22).

Snorkeling Coral reefs teem with marine life, and clear water allows visibility of up to 200 feet. Some of the best snorkeling on the Dutch side can be had around the rocks below Fort Amsterdam off Little Bay Beach, the west end of Maho Bay, Pelican Key and the rocks near the Caravanserai Hotel, and the reefs off Dawn Beach and Oyster Pond. On the French side, the area around Orient Bay, Green Key, Ilet Pinel, and Flat Island (or Tintamarre) is especially lovely for snorkeling, and has been officially classified a regional underwater nature reserve. Arrange rentals and trips through **Watersports Unlimited** (tel. 599/5–23434), **Red Ensign Watersports** (tel. 599/5–22929), **Ocean Explorers** (tel. 599/5–45252), and **Orient Watersports** (tel. 590/87–89–73).

Tennis There are four lighted courts at **Dawn Beach Hotel** (tel. 599/5–22944); four lighted courts at **Pelican Resort** (tel. 599/5–42503); three asphalt courts at **Little Bay and Belair Beach Resorts** (tel. 599/5–22333 or 599/5–23362); four courts at **Maho Reef & Beach** (tel. 599/5–42115); six lighted courts at **Le Privilege** (Anse Marcel, tel. 590/87–59–28), which also has squash and racquetball courts; 14 lighted courts at **Port de Plaisance** (tel. 599/5–45222); four lighted Omni courts at **La Belle Creole** (tel. 590/87–58–66); three lighted courts at **Nettle Bay Beach Club** (tel. 590/87–97–04); two lighted courts at **Mont Vernon Hotel** (tel. 590/87–62–00) and at **Simson Beach Marine Hotel** (tel. 590/87–54–54); and 16 all-weather courts at **Mullet Bay Resort** (tel. 599/5–42081).

Windsurfing Rental and instruction are available at **Little Bay Beach Hotel** (tel. 599/5–22333, ext. 186), **Maho Watersports** (tel. 599/5–44387), **Orient Watersports** (590/87–33–85), and **Red Ensign Watersports** (tel. 599/5–22929).

Shopping

About 180 cruise ships call at St. Maarten each year, and they do so for about 500 reasons. That's roughly the number of duty-free shops on the island.

Prices can be 25%–50% below those in the United States and Canada on French perfumes, liquor, cognac and fine liqueurs, cigarettes and cigars, Swedish crystal and Finnish stoneware, Irish linen, Italian leather, German cameras, European designer fashions, plus thousands of other things you never knew you wanted. But check prices before you leave home, especially if you live in the New York City area—Manhattan's prices for cameras and electronic equipment are hard to beat anywhere. In general, you will find more fashion on the French side in Marigot.

St. Maarten's best-known "craft" is its guavaberry liqueur, made from rum and the wild local berries (not to be confused with guavas) that grow only on this island's central mountains.

Prices are quoted in florins, francs, and dollars; shops take credit cards and traveler's checks. Most shopkeepers, especially on the Dutch side, speak English. (If more than one cruise ship is in port, avoid Front Street. It's so crowded you won't be able to move.) Although most merchants are reputable, there are occasional reports of inferior or fake merchandise passed off as the real thing. As a rule of thumb, if you can bargain excessively, it's probably not worth it.

Shopping Areas In St. Maarten: **Front Street,** Philipsburg, is one long strip lined with sleek boutiques and cozy shops gift wrapped in gingerbread. **Old Street,** near the end of Front Street, has 22 stores, boutiques, and open-air cafés. There are almost 100 boutiques in **Mullet** and **Maho** shopping plazas, as well as at the Simpson Bay Yacht Club complex.

In St. Martin: Wrought-iron balconies, colorful awnings, and gingerbread trim decorate Marigot's smart shops, tiny boutiques, and bistros in the **Marina Port La Royale; Galerie Perigourdine;** and on the main streets, **Rue de la Liberté** and **Rue de la République.**

Good Buys **Little Switzerland** (Marigot and Philipsburg, tel. 590/52–25–23) and **Spritzer and Fuhrmann** (Marigot, tel. 590/87–59–62; Philipsburg, tel. 599/5–44381) handle the finest in crystal and china.

Jewelry and watches can be found at **Oro del Sol** (Marigot, tel. 590/87–56–51), **Carat** (Marigot, tel. 590/87–73–40; Philipsburg, tel. 599/5–22180), **Little Europe** (Philipsburg, tel. 599/5–23062), and **H. Stern** (Philipsburg, tel. 599/5–23328).

Pick up a bottle of wine for your picnic at **La Cave du Savour Club** (Marigot, tel. 590/87–58–51).

Lipstick (Marigot, tel. 590/87–73–24) and **Oro del Sol** (Marigot, tel. 590/87–57–02) carry perfumes and cosmetics.

For designer fashions head to **La Romana** (2 locations on Front St., tel. 599/5–22181) and **Havane** (Marigot, tel. 590/87–70–39).

New Amsterdam Store (Philipsburg, tel. 599/5–22787) and **The Yellow House** (Philipsburg, tel. 599/5–23438) handle fine linens and porcelain.

The Lil' Shoppe (Philipsburg, tel. 599/5–2177) carries eel-skin wallets, handbags, perfumes, and a large selection of swimwear. Shoes, belts, and handbags are also sold at **Maximoflorence** (Philipsburg, tel. 599/5–23735).

Island Specialties Caribelle batik, hammocks, handmade jewelry, the local guavaberry liqueur, and herbs and spices are stashed at **The Shipwreck Shop** (Philipsburg, tel. 599/5–22962). T-shirts, beach towels, native dolls, Indian glass bangles, and hand-painted Delft souvenirs can all be found at **Sasha's** (Philipsburg, tel. 599/5–24331). Excellent galleries showcasing local artists include **Le Poisson D'Or** (Marigot, tel. 590/87–72–45), **ABC Art Gallery** (Marigot, tel. 590/87–96–00), **Galerie Lynn** (Grand Case, no tel.), **Minguet** (Rambaud Hill, 590/87–76–06), **Greenwith Galleries** (Phillipsburg, tel. 599/5–23842), and **Calabash** (Phillipsburg, tel. 599/5–25221).

Dining

It may seem that this island has no monuments. Au contraire, there are many of them, all dedicated to gastronomy. You'll scarcely find a touch of Dutch; the major influences are French and Italian. This season's "in" eatery may be next season's remembrance of things past, as things do have a way of changing rapidly. The generally steep prices reflect both the island's high culinary reputation and the difficulty of obtaining fresh ingredients. Not surprisingly, the hotel restaurants on the French side are usually more sophisticated, but at prices that would make almost anyone but a Rockefeller go Dutch. There's a big range of attire on this island, although, a sports jacket or cocktail dress is de riguer in fancier restaurants. In high season, unless otherwise noted in our text, be sure to make reservations, and call to cancel if you can't make it. Many restaurants close during August and/or September.

Highly recommended restaurants are indicated by a star ★.

Category	Cost*
Very Expensive	over $50
Expensive	$40–$50
Moderate	$30–$40
Inexpensive	under $30

per person, excluding drinks and service

Dutch Side **Antoine's.** This is an elegant, airy terrace overlooking Great Bay. You might start your meal, which is served by candlelight, with French onion soup, then move on to steak au poivre, veal sweetbreads in vermouth sauce, or lobster Thermidor. For dessert, try cheesecake with raspberry melba sauce. *Front St., Philipsburg, tel. 599/5–22964. AE, MC, V. Expensive.*

Felix. This classy little beachside eatery serves dinner by candlelight. At lunchtime, take a dip before feasting on salad Felix (an imaginative concoction of bananas, sweet potatoes, and avocado), rack of lamb Provençal, or steak au poivre. The restaurant is on the road to Pelican Resort. *Pelican Key, tel. 599/5–45237. AE. Closed Tues. Expensive.*

Le Bec Fin. To reach the well-known upstairs restaurant, you stroll through a flowery courtyard where La Coupole's croissants and cakes are baked daily (a nice thing to bear in mind come breakfast time). Despite the rotation of chefs, the classical French cuisine remains professional if inconsistent. Starters include vol-au-vent (pastry) bursting with snails in fennel cream sauce and tagliatelle with shrimp in ginger. Fish, such as red snapper filet in rum butter sauce, is your best bet for a main course. The meringue swan with mint ice cream is as delightful to the eye as to the palate. *119 Front St., Philipsburg, tel. 599/5–22976. AE. Expensive.*

Le Perroquet. In a cool green-and-white West Indian–style house on the peaceful lagoon, chef Pierre Castagna turns out such exotic specialties as breast of ostrich. *Airport Rd., Simpson Bay, tel. 599/5–44339. AE, V. Closed Mon. Expensive.*

★ **Oyster Pond Hotel.** A more genteel evening on St. Maarten is hard to find. You'll enjoy fine linens and china, fresh flowers, and a delightful terrace with wonderful sea views. Specialties include lobster medallions dancing in a truffle, tomato, and basil sauce; fillet of red snapper in sauce piquante; and sweet, billowy soufflés for dessert. The hotel's guests have priority in this romantic dining room, so you should reserve well in advance. *Oyster Pond, tel. 599/5–22206 or 599/5–23206. Reservations advised. AE, MC, V. Expensive.*

Spartaco. Northern Italian cuisine is served in this 200-year-old stone plantation house. Everything here is either home-made or imported from Italy. Some of the specialties are black angel-hair pasta with shrimp and garlic; tagliata of swordfish baked with pink pepper and rosemary; and veal Vesuviana, with mozzarella, oregano, and tomato sauce. *Almond Grove, Cole Bay, tel. 599/5–45379. No lunch. MC, V. Expensive.*

Captain Oliver's. A glorious cockatoo presides over the entrance to this engaging bistro, perched over the marina. Although the staff and cuisine are French, the restaurant is just over the Dutch border. Seafood is the thing here, such as lobster flambéed in cognac or tuna in a rollicking pink pepper sauce. You can catch your own lobster in the pool. *Oyster Pond, tel. 590/87–30–00. AE, MC, V. Moderate.*

L'Escargot. A lovely 19th-century house wrapped in verandas is home to one of St. Maarten's oldest French restaurants. Starters include baked brie en croûte in kiwi sauce. There is also, of course, a variety of snail dishes. For an entrée, try red snapper grilled on a bed of red beets. There's a fun cabaret Sunday nights; no cover charge with dinner. *76 Front St., Philipsburg, tel. 599/5–22483. AE, MC, V. Moderate.*

Wajang Doll. Indonesian dishes are served in the garden of this West Indian–style house. The specialty is *rijsttafel*—the Indonesian rice table that offers 14 or 19 dishes in a complete dinner. *137 Front St., Philipsburg, tel. 599/5–22687. AE, MC, V. Inexpensive–Moderate.*

Chesterfield's. Burgers and salads are served at lunch, but menus are more elaborate for dinner on this indoor/outdoor terrace overlooking the marina. Menu offerings include French onion soup, roast duckling with fresh pineapple and banana sauce, and chicken cordon bleu. The Mermaid Bar is a popular spot with yachtsmen. *Great Bay Marina, Philipsburg, tel. 599/5–23484. AE, MC, V. Inexpensive.*

Harbour Lights. This modest family-run spot is in a historic building built in 1870. The decor is warm, with peach and coral walls and native-print tablecloths. Choose among excellent rotis and pilaus and even better stewed or curried chicken, meats, and seafood. Try one of the knockout cocktails, all made with the local guavaberry liqueur. *30 Back St., Philipsburg, tel. 599/5–23504. AE, MC, V. Inexpensive.*

Shiv Sagar. Authentic East Indian cuisine, emphasizing Kashmiri and Mughlai specialties, is served in this small mirrored room fragrant with cumin and coriander. Marvelous tandooris and curries are offered, but try one of the less-familiar preparations like Amritsari fish. There's also a large selection of vegetarian dishes. *3 Front St., Philipsburg, tel. 599/5–22299. AE, D, MC, V. Inexpensive.*

★ **Turtle Pier Bar & Restaurant.** Chattering monkeys and squawking parrots greet you at the entrance to this classic Caribbean hangout, teetering over the lagoon and festooned with creeping vines. There are 200 animals in this informal zoo, but that's nothing compared to the menagerie hanging out at the bar during happy hour. The genial owner Sid Wathey, whose family is one of the island's oldest, leaves most of the business details to his American wife Lorraine. They've fashioned one of the funkiest, most endearing places in the Caribbean, with cheap beer on draft, huge American breakfasts, all-you-can-eat ribs dinners for $9.95, and eclectic live music several nights a week. *Airport Rd., tel. 599/5–52230. No credit cards. Inexpensive.*

French Side **Alizéa.** Many who have tried this terrace restaurant have come
★ away claiming that the cuisine is the best on the island. The refined contemporary cuisine respects tradition. The menu
changes constantly, but some outstanding dishes have been
scrambled eggs and seaweed blinis, lobster savarin with cara-
way, and breast of quail stuffed with pistachios in black-cur-
rant sauce. Try an iced soufflé for dessert. *Alizéa Hotel, Mont
Vernon 25, tel. 590/87-33-42. Reservations suggested. AE,
MC, V. Very Expensive.*

Chez Martine. A French couple, Eliane and Jean-Pierre
Bertheau, who have recently come to St. Martin after spending
a decade in Morocco, have made this small hotel into a personable hostelry with a gastronomic restaurant. Dine by the water's edge in an intimate room with polished silverware and
sparkling glasses. The chef, Thierry de Launay, studied under
Joel Robuchon, whom many consider the world's greatest chef.
You might begin with a superb velvety lobster velouté, then
segue into roast lamb on a bed of eggplant and spinach in corn
sauce or lobster in puff pastry. The wine list is well selected
even if a bit overpriced, but for 150F you can select a drinkable
wine. *140 blvd. Grand Case, Grand Case 97150, tel. 590/87-51-
59, fax 590/87-87-30. Dinner only. Reservations suggested.
AE, MC, V. Very Expensive.*

La Samanna. This restaurant has an exquisite setting in the
celebrated hotel; you'll dine by candlelight on a tented terrace
surrounded by bougainvillea. The clientele is chic, international, and often famous. Rosewood Hotels, the new management,
spirited away innovative chef Mark Ehrler from Barbuda's
tony K Club. Standouts include air-dried Creole squab in fig
sauce and polenta of grilled foie gras. The kitchen is still feeling its "hautes," and dinner for two (with wine) can happily set
you back $250. The superb wine cellar boasts over 25,000 bot-
tles. *Baie Longue, tel. 590/87-51-22. Jacket suggested. Reservations required. AE, DC, MC, V. Very Expensive.*

Le Santal. The approach to this dazzler, through a working-
class suburb of Marigot, is forbidding. The exterior appears
ramshackle, but the interior is transformed by soft lighting,
china, and crystal. Dine on lobster soufflé on a bed of eggplant
and spinach, foie gras sauteed in cassis, or lacquered duck. The
owners also run the excellent Jean Dupont and Asia, but this is
their showplace. *Sandy Ground, tel. 590/87-53-48. Reservations suggested. AE, MC, V. Very Expensive.*

★ **Le Poisson d'Or.** Posh and popular, this restaurant is in a restored stone house with a 20-table terrace. You can feast on a
hot foie gras salad in raspberry vinaigrette, house-smoked lobster in fine tea in parsley cream sauce; salmon trout in orange
sabayon; or veal in Roquefort, hazelnut, and tarragon sauce.
The young chef, François Julien, cooks with enthusiasm, but
his cuisine has stiff competition from the setting—the waters
of the bay lapping the terrace. The space also doubles as a gallery exhibiting top-notch Caribbean artists. Closed for lunch
during off-season. *Off rue d'Anguille on the sea, Marigot, tel.
590/87-72-45. AE, MC, V. Closed Tues. for lunch in high season. Reservations suggested. Expensive-Very Expensive.*

★ **Rainbow.** This split-level eatery is strikingly simple in cobalt
blue and white and highly romantic, thanks to lapping waves
and murmuring guests. Fleur and David are the stylish, energetic hosts, and chef Mario Tardif is from one of the world's gastronomic capitals, Quebec City. Don't miss his fettucine with
smoked salmon and capers; sweetbreads galette with port,

pine nuts, and rosemary; or duck magret in cashew curry sauce. Dishes are dressed with fanciful touches like red cabbage crisps. Finish the meal off with the sublime orange, honey, and ginger soufflé. One of the first and still one of the best restaurants in this town of splendid seaside boîtes. *Grand Case, tel. 590/87–55–80. Reservations suggested. MC, V. Expensive–Very Expensive.*

La Rhumerie. The chef turns out Creole and traditional French fare, with specialties including crab farci, curried goat, herbed conch, boudin, frogs' legs, snails, and duck à l'orange. *Colombier, tel. 590/87–56–98. AE, MC, V. Expensive.*

La Vie En Rose. Prices here have escalated based as much on the restaurant's past fame as on its present culinary art. The menu rewards adventurous eaters with mint-flavored vichyssoise with mussels, lobster salad with celery and truffles, breaded sautéed foie gras with pears, and sliced breast of duck in lemon-ginger sauce. Save room for chocolate mousse cake topped with vanilla sauce. The ground-floor tearoom and pastry shop serve an excellent luncheon with wine for $20. *Blvd. de France, Marigot, tel. 590/87–54–42. AE, MC, V. Expensive.*

Le Tastevin. The setting at this terrace restaurant is elegant: A chic pavilion, with tropical plants and ceiling fans, overlooks the water. Chef Daniel Passeri, a native of Burgundy, is also in charge of the homey Auberge Gourmande across the street. The menu here is more ambitious, including foie gras scaloppini in Lillet sauce, duck breast in banana-lime sauce, and red snapper poached in vanilla. *Grand Case, tel. 590/87–55–45. MC, V. Expensive.*

Case Anny. Creole cooking is the specialty of Anne-Marie Boissard's seaside terrace restaurant. She turns out Creole boudin, crab farci, and lambi (conch) Provençal. *Rue d'Anguille, tel. 599/87–53–38. AE, MC, V. Moderate.*

★ **Cha Cha Cha Caribbean Cafe.** Pascal and Christina Chevillot's culinary pedigree is impeccable: His uncle Charles owns New York's La Petite Ferme. So what do they do? They create a chichi dive with Japanese gardens, gaudy colors, and a gaudier clientele who have made this the island's hot spot. Everyone eventually seems to end up here. (The mouth-watering haute Caraibes cuisine and reasonable prices don't hurt.) Try the giant prawns in passion-fruit butter or the grilled snapper with avocado, then wash it down with a "Grand Case Sunset." *Grand Case, tel. 590/87–53–63. MC, V. Moderate.*

Don Camillo da Enzo. Country-style decor and excellent service distinguish this small eatery. Both northern and southern Italian specialties are featured. Some favorites are the carpaccio, green gnocchi in Gorgonzola cream sauce, and veal medallions in marsala sauce. *Port La Royale, Marigot, tel. 590/87–52–88. AE, MC, V. Moderate.*

La Residence. An intimate setting with soft lighting and a tinkling fountain, this restaurant offers such specialties as fresh snapper baked in foil with olive oil and spices, bouillabaisse, and fresh lobster in a cognac sauce. The soufflés are sensational, as is the $28 three-course prix fixe menu gastronomique. *Marigot, tel. 590/87–70–37. AE, MC, V. Expensive.*

Maison sur le Port. Watching the sunset from the palm-fringed terrace is not the least of the pleasures in this old West Indian house. Try the sautéed duck filet in mango sauce or red snapper steamed with leeks and champagne. There is also a tempting three-course prix fixe menu. Chef Jean-Paul Fahrner's imaginative salads are lunchtime treats. *On the port, Marigot, tel. 590/87–56–38. AE. Moderate.*

Mini Club. The popular upstairs terrace is virtually a treehouse nestled in the coconut palms. A pleasant eatery anytime, but especially Wednesday and Saturday, when there is a sumptuous buffet of almost 35 dishes—salads, roast pork, suckling pig, beef, fish, lobster—all for $45 per person, with wine. *Rue d'Anguille, Marigot, tel. 590/87–50–69. AE. Moderate.*

★ **Bistrot Nu.** This friendly and enormously popular late-night spot serves traditional brasserie-style food, from coq au vin to fish soup, snails, pizza, and seafood, until 2 AM. For simple, unadorned fare at a reasonable price, this may be the best spot on the island. *Rue de Hollande, Marigot, tel. 590/87–77–39. MC, V. Inexpensive–Moderate.*

Mark's Place. This barnlike restaurant is an institution on Sundays. You may start with pumpkin soup or stuffed crab, then follow with linguine bolognese or curried goat. Daily specials are posted on a blackboard and the homemade pies and pastries, and are scrumptious. Groups of 6–12 can eat a five-course meal in the snug wine cellar with their own chef and staff for $50 per person. All Mark needs to whip up a gourmet repast just for you is 24 hours' notice. *French Cul de Sac, tel. 590/87–34–50. AE, MC, V. Inexpensive.*

★ **Yvette's.** The attempts at romance couldn't be more endearing: Classical music plays softly, and the room is a symphony in Valentine red, from curtains and tablecloths and roses to hot pepper sauce. But kindly Yvette herself couldn't be more downhome nor her food more delicious. Plates are piled high with smashing lip-smacking Creole specialties like accras, stewed chicken with rice and beans, or conch and dumplings. This is the kind of place that is so good you're surprised to see other tourists—but word gets around. *Orleans, tel. 590/87–32–03. AE (5% surcharge). Inexpensive.*

Lodging

Until recently, the Dutch side commanded all the big, splashy resorts. The casinos are still to be found exclusively on the Dutch side—gambling is illegal on the French side. However, St. Martin is having something of a building boom, especially in the area around Nettle and Orient bays. All the hotels on the French side have an English-speaking staff. There are also small inns and Mediterranean-style facilities on both sides of the island. Many of the hotels offer enticing packages that are worth investigating. You'll also save substantially if you travel off-season; the downside of this is that many hotels and restaurants are closed for refurbishing or just plain recovering from the winter onslaught. In general, the French resorts are more intimate and romantic, but what the Dutch properties lack in ambience, they compensate for in clean, functional, comfortable rooms with all the "extras." Most of the larger Dutch resorts feature time-share annexes; the units are often available for rental for those who prefer the condo lifestyle at comparable rates.

As a rule, rooms on the beach command the highest prices. Most properties are EP or CP (the latter usually only in season), though meal plans are sometimes available.

Highly recommended lodgings are indicated by a star ★.

Category	Cost*
Very Expensive	over $300
Expensive	$225–$300
Moderate	$150–$225
Inexpensive	under $150

All prices are for a standard double room for two, excluding 5% tax (Dutch side), a taxe de séjour (set by individual hotels on the French side), and a 10%–15% service charge.

Hotels
Dutch Side

Port de Plaisance. If you're going to build a huge complex, this is the way to do it. Situated on its own island, this resort complex has 88 luxurious studios and 1- and 2-bedroom apartments, with a 550-room Sheraton scheduled to open by 1994. Nothing is left to chance or the imagination. All the units are fully equipped with air-conditioning, kitchen (including dishwasher and microwave), safe, satellite TV, direct dial phones, and even a trouser press. The decor is in soft soothing seashell hues; the views are of either the lagoon or the marina. One pool is carved out of rock with a majestic waterfall. The polished marble entrance to the gleaming casino is dominated by a 25-foot bronze mermaid astride four dolphins. You receive one free ride in a stretch limo during your stay. The gourmet restaurant La Terrasse has obtained the services of chef Nicolas Maire, who apprenticed with the three-star Michelin chefs Paul Bocuse, Alain Senderens, and Michel Guerard. *Box 2089, Simpson Bay, tel. 599/5–45222 or 800/732–9480, fax 599/5–42428. 88 apartments. Facilities: casino, fitness center, health bar, 2 pools, marina, water-sports center, 14 lighted tennis courts, 2 shopping arcades, 2 boats, 2 restaurants, 4 bars, car rental, disco. AE, D, MC, V. EP. Very Expensive.*

Maho Beach Hotel & Casino. A variety of accommodations are available at this facility. All have two double beds or a king-size bed and a private balcony. The Casino Royale is the island's largest casino, and Studio 7, atop the casino, is currently the rage. The trick here is to get a room far enough away from the airport's landing strip (those behind the main lobby are the quietest). Built in 1992, a new tower has added 433 rooms, 33 shops, five restaurants, and several banquet rooms. The complex may be likened to a minicity in an already congested hotel area near the airport. *Maho Bay, tel. 599/5–52115 or 800/835–6246, fax 599/5–53180. 688 rooms. Facilities: beach, casino, 10 restaurants, 3 bars, disco, pool, boutiques, 4 lighted tennis courts, 75 shops, all water sports. AE, DC, MC, V. EP. Expensive–Very Expensive.*

Mullet Bay Resort and Casino. Of the self-contained mega-resorts, this is probably the least intrusive and most private, because it's spread out over a large area (easily negotiable by the ubiquitous golf carts), rather than condensed in high rises. There are an excellent championship 18-hole golf course; a gleaming crescent of sand; and water sports galore; and comfortable, well-maintained accommodations. For those who like constant activity and variety, Mullet Bay is the place. *Box 309, Mullet Bay, tel. 599/5–52801 or 800/642–6401, fax 599/5–54281. 300 rooms and 300 1-bedroom suites. Facilities: beach, 2 pools, 14 lighted tennis courts, 18-hole championship golf course, water-sports center, 6 restaurants, disco, 2 bars, shop-*

ping arcade, medical center, bank, food mart. AE, D, MC, V. EP. Expensive–Very Expensive.

Pelican Resort & Casino. Walk into the reception area and one-armed bandits and gaming tables greet you. On the lower level is a sales office enticing guests to buy into this hotel-condo complex. An assortment of white stucco buildings house the resort's air-conditioned apartments, suites, and deluxe studios, all of which have a sweeping view of the Caribbean. Each has a fully equipped kitchen (including hibatchi and microwave), satellite TV, king-size beds, rattan furniture, and many frills (some have hot tubs). The resort has 1,400 feet of ocean frontage, though not good for bathing, and its own 60-foot catamaran, *El Tigre*, which is available for charters. *Simpson Bay, tel. 599/5–42503 or 800/327–3286, fax 599/5–42133. 660 suites and studios. Facilities: casino, 2 restaurants, 6 bars, 8 pools, health spa, Jacuzzi, 6 lighted tennis courts, car rental, medical center, children's playground, grocery store and shopping area, water-sports center. AE, DC, MC, V. EP. Expensive–Very Expensive.*

Dawn Beach Hotel. The rooms are air-conditioned and are located on the hillside or on the beach. All are spacious, with handsome rattan furnishings, combination living room/bedroom with king-size bed, kitchenette, closed-circuit color TV, radio, and private patio. (If you prefer tubs to showers, opt for the hillside villa.) The pool has a waterfall and the white-sand beach is one of the island's best for snorkeling, but the breeze is often strong and can whip up the waves. Since the hotel is off by itself, there's bus service to town twice daily. *Box 389, Philipsburg, tel. 599/5–22929; in the U.S., 800/223–9815; in Canada, 800/468–0023, fax 599/5–24421. 155 rooms. Facilities: restaurant, 2 beach bars, pool, 2 lighted tennis courts, car-rental desk, water-sports center. AE, DC, MC, V. EP. Expensive.*

Great Bay Beach Hotel and Casino. One of the island's few all-inclusive properties, this resort, just outside Philipsburg, has terrific views of the bay. The white stucco and black tile lobby is more striking than the rooms, which are furnished in typical muted pastels and feature the usual amenities, including terrace, satellite TV, and direct-dial phones. *Box 310, Great Bay, tel. 599/5–22446, fax 599/5–23859. 285 rooms, 5 1-bedroom suites. Facilities: beach, 2 pools, 2 restaurants, bar, casino, nightclub, disco, water-sports center, 1 lighted tennis court, car rental. AE, DC, MC, V. EP, All-inclusive. Expensive.*

★ **Horny Toad Guesthouse.** This is one of the most charming properties on the island, thanks to the caring touch of owners Bette and Earle Vaughn, who keep things as immaculate as if it were their own home (which it is most of the year). Each of the eight apartments on the beach is individually and thoughtfully decorated and fully equipped. (The many repeat guests usually request the same room.) The blue-and-white sun terrace duplicates the patterns of Delft china, chirping birds and fresh flowers greet you every morning, and Bette and Earle always treat you like family. *Simpson Bay, tel. 599/5–54323, fax 599/5–53316. 2 studios, 6 1-bedroom apartments. Facilities: beach, library, barbecue. No credit cards. EP. Moderate–Expensive.*

★ **Oyster Pond Hotel.** The refined, low-key quality of this hotel is quite out of character with the rest of St. Maarten. Built around a courtyard, each of the two towers has two split-level suites and individually decorated rooms with terra-cotta floors, white wicker furnishings, ceiling fans, and pastel French cottons. All these rooms have a secluded balcony or terrace and a view of the ocean, the courtyard, or the yacht basin. The rooms have screened louvers for those who prefer sea breezes to air-conditioning. The new, adjacent building offers larger rooms with subdued furnishings and balconies facing the sea. The hotel is on a mile-long beach that's excellent for snorkeling though not for sunbathing or lazy swimming. The dining room opens onto the Atlantic Ocean; the pool is perched right on the ocean's edge. You'll find hammocks instead of TVs, and the hotel's only phone is manned by a staff member at the front desk. *Box 239, Philipsburg, tel. 599/5–22206, 599/5–23206, or 800/374–1323, fax 599/5–25695. 40 rooms. Facilities: restaurant, bar, saltwater pool, 2 tennis courts, water-sports center. AE, MC, V. EP. Moderate–Expensive.*

Holland House. This is a centrally situated hotel, with the shops of Front Street at its doorstep and a mile-long backyard called Great Bay Beach, which, unfortunately, is slightly polluted from the cruise ships and freighters anchored in the bay. (Rooms 104 through 107 open directly onto the beach.) Each room has contemporary tropical furnishings, balcony, kitchenette, satellite cable TV, and air-conditioning. Its delightful open-air restaurant overlooking the water serves reasonably priced dinners. *Box 393, Philipsburg, tel. 599/5–22572 or 800/223–9815; in NY, 212/840–6636, fax 599/5–24673. 52 rooms, 2 suites. Facilities: beach, restaurant, lounge, gift shop. AE, DC, MC, V. EP. Moderate.*

La Vista. All the accommodations are air-conditioned suites with cable TVs, direct-dial phones, balconies, and lovely white iron queen-size beds. Guests have the use of the facilities at the adjacent Pelican Resort. The service is personalized at this intimate property of quaint Antillean buildings connected by brick walkways lined with just barely contained hibiscus and bougainvillea. *Box 40, Pelican Key, tel. 599/5–43005 or 800/365–8484, fax 599/5–43010. 24 suites. Facilities: horseback riding, pool, restaurant, tennis. AE, MC, V. EP. Moderate.*

Mary's Boon. This informal inn has enormous rooms with kitchenettes, seaside patios, and ceiling fans. Meals are served family-ly style, and there is an honor bar. Pets are welcome. The inn is on Simpson Bay's big beach. The many repeat guests don't seem fazed by the roar of the jets landing at the nearby airport. *Box 2078, Philipsburg, tel. 599/5–44235; in the U.S., 212/986–4373. 12 studios. Facilities: beach, restaurant, bar. No credit cards. EP. Moderate.*

★ **Passangrahan Royal Guest House.** It's entirely appropriate that the bar here is named Sidney Greenstreet. This is the island's oldest inn, and it looks like a set for an old Bogie–Greenstreet film. The building was once Queen Wilhelmina's residence (there's a picture of her in the lobby) and the government guest house. Wicker peacock chairs, slowly revolving ceiling fans, balconies shaded by tropical greenery, king-size mahogany four-poster beds, and a broad tile veranda are some of the hallmarks of this guest house. Afternoon tea is served. There are no TVs or phones in the guest house. *Box 151, Philipsburg, tel. 599/5–23588, fax 599/5–22885. 30 rooms and suites. Facilities: Great Bay Beach, rental bikes, bar, restaurant. AE, MC, V. EP. Inexpensive–Moderate.*

Caribbean Hotel. You expect Sadie Thompson to vamp through those beaded glass curtains any minute. Frankly, this hotel is recommended more for its atmosphere, which is funky, almost campy, than for its facilities, which are passable and clean. It's on a second floor above Front Street, across the street from the beach. The rooms have tile floors, air-conditioning, TVs, and private baths. Those in the back are quieter, and a renovation is planned. *Box 236, Philipsburg, tel. 599/5–22028. 50 rooms. Facilities: restaurant, bar. AE, MC, V. EP. Inexpensive.*

Seaview Hotel & Casino. This is another good buy on Front Street and Great Bay Beach. The air-conditioned, twin-bed rooms are modest, cheerful, and clean. All rooms have baths (some with showers only), satellite TV, and phones. The four rooms above the sea have the best views. *Box 65, Philipsburg, tel. 599/5–22323 or 800/223–9815; in NY, 212/545–8469; in Canada, 800/468–0023, fax 599/5–24356. 45 rooms. Facilities: beach, breakfast room, casino. AE, MC, V. EP. Inexpensive.*

French Side **Esmeralda Resort.** It looks like a housing development in the Sun Belt, but the interiors of these deluxe villas are tastefully decorated. The 54 rooms and suites in 15 villas can be combined any way you like, from studio to 5-bedroom palatial digs. All feature satellite TV, fully equipped kitchenette, direct-dial phone, and private terrace. *Box 541, Orient Bay, tel. 590/87–36–36 or 800/622–7836, fax 590/87–35–18. 15 villas. Facilities: beach, pool, 5 restaurants, water-sports center, lighted tennis court, Jacuzzi. AE, MC, V. CP. Very Expensive.*

★ **La Belle Creole.** This 25-acre re-creation of an old Mediterranean village is replete with a stone central plaza. The enormous rooms and suites have every modern convenience, including air-conditioning, direct-dial phones, cable TVs, marble and tile bathrooms, and minibars. Accommodations (king-size or two double beds) are in 27 one- to three-story villas linked by stone-paved streets and graceful courtyards. Most villas have private balconies with a view of the ocean, the island, or Marigot Bay. Grand as it is, La Belle Creole has a casual, relaxed atmosphere even when it's crowded. A new water-sports complex has been added, and there are plans to extend the beach area. Though it is on its own estate, the hotel has the advantage of quick and easy access to Marigot and the island's best beaches. La Provence is a fine gourmet restaurant, with especially popular weekly seafood and barbecue buffets. *Box 118, Marigot 97150, tel. 590/87–58–66 or 800–HILTONS, fax 590/87–56–66. 138 rooms and 18 1-bedroom suites. Facilities: 3 beaches, activities desk, shopping arcade, free-form pool, 4 lighted tennis courts, fitness/beauty center, restaurant, 2 bars, 5 rooms with facilities for the disabled, water-sports center. AE, DC, MC, V. CP. Very Expensive.*

Le Meridien L'Habitation. A white-knuckle road leads down to this huge, sleek, everything-you-could-ask-for enclave that sits amid beautifully landscaped gardens on enchanting Marcel Cove, with 1,600 feet of white-sand beach. The two-story main building is a white-column structure with red-tile roof and graceful galleries. All the air-conditioned rooms, suites, and apartments have spacious baths, balconies, wall safes, TVs, direct-dial phones, and fridges. One-bedroom apartments on the marina have fully equipped kitchens and private patios. Guests have complimentary access to the facilities of Le Privilege, a sports and entertainment complex on the hill (a minibus makes frequent trips to it). La Belle France is a typically solid and tres cher gourmet restaurant. Another two-story building, called "Le Domaine," were added in 1992 to provide an additional 125 rooms, 20 suites, and an Italian restaurant. The rooms in Le Domaine are smaller and pricier, yet brighter and more tropical. But wherever you stay on the compound, few units boast an ocean view, the ambience is lacking, the service is polite but impersonal, and French muzak blares throughout. There are better—or at least chicer—bargains on the island, yet this bustling resort remains wildly popular with tour groups and families seeking a "safe" vacation. *Box 581, Marcel Cove 97150, tel. 590/87–33–33 or 590/87–78–80; in the U.S., 800/543–4300, fax 590/87–30–38. 314 rooms, 82 suites. Facilities (including Le Privilege): beach, boutiques, aerobics, car rental, disco, 4 restaurants, 4 bars, 6 lighted tennis courts, minigolf, 2 pools, 2 squash courts, 1 racquetball court, 100-slip marina, water-sports center. AE, DC, MC, V. EP. Very Expensive.*

★ **La Samanna.** This luxurious, secluded hotel, now under the management of Dallas-based Rosewood Hotels, looks as if it were transported to St. Martin from Morocco. The hotel is set in a tropical garden on a slope overlooking Baie Longue. Red hibiscus is everywhere. There is a rich (the word is used advisedly) variety of accommodations from which to choose. Studios and one- and two-bedroom villas all feature private patio, minibar, full bath, and such thoughtful touches as potpourri and fresh flowers daily. The new, distinctive decor is stunning: cool mint, apricot, and teal fabrics; unusual ceramic work; painted tiles; and clever variations on traditional Caribbean wicker and rattan. It is a model of how to refurbish a classic property. *Box 159, Marigot 97150, tel. 590/87–51–22 or 800/854–2252, fax 590/87–87–86. 25 rooms, 30 1-bedroom suites and 30 2-bedroom suites. Facilities: restaurant, lounge, pool, fitness center, 3 tennis courts, library, TV room, boutique, water-sports center. AE. CP. Very Expensive.*

Grand Case Beach Club. This informal condo complex is situated on Grand Case's crescent-shape beach. Air-conditioned studios and one- and two-bedroom apartments all have balconies or patios and kitchenettes. The 62 oceanfront units are much in demand. There are lots of repeat guests, so reserve well in advance. Attractive packages are offered. *Box 339, Grand Case 97150, tel. 590/87–51–87 or 800/223–1588, fax 590/87–59–93. 40 studios and 33 1- and 2-bedroom apartments. Facilities: 2 beaches, restaurant, lounge, 1 lighted tennis court, billiards, car rental, catamaran. AE, MC, V. CP. Expensive.*

Mont Vernon. This rambling hotel has a gingerbread, almost lacelike architecture and sits on a bluff overlooking Orient Bay, usually swept by a cooling sea breeze. The light, airy quality is maintained as you enter the large, open reception area. Each room has either a king-size bed or twin beds and a private balcony. The bathrooms are equipped with hair dryers, the sitting area with satellite TV. The rooms in the buildings on the crest facing the ocean have the best views and are slightly larger than the others. The other choice rooms are in the buildings down by the pools and beach. This is a big resort that lures package-tour groups as well as business seminars to its 20 15-people boardrooms and large parties to fill a 250-person banquet room. *Chevrise Baie Orientale, BP 1174, 97150, tel. 599/87–42–00 or 800/543–4300, fax 590/87–37–27. 370 rooms, 28 2-bedroom suites. Facilities: pool, 2 tennis courts, beach, 2 restaurants, 2 bars, water sports. Free minibus to Marigot, Philipsburg, and casinos. AE, DC, MC, V. CP. Expensive.*

Anse Margot. The stretch divided by the sea and Simpson's Bay, known as Baie Nettlé, has become a row of hotels. While next door Le Flamboyant Bounty offers the all-inclusive packages, Anse Margot offers very reasonable room-only (EP) rates for attractive accommodations. The rooms are in eight three-story town-house buildings. Each room has a balcony, some with garden view and some with sea view, bathroom, and separate toilet. The furnishings are in light floral patterns. There are two pools, and the beach is on Simpson Bay. Entre Deux Mers is one of the better hotel restaurants. *Baie Nettlé 97150, tel. 590/87–92–01, fax 590/87–92–13; in the U.S., 800/333–1970, fax 590/87–92–13. 96 rooms, 35 1-bedroom suites. Facilities: restaurant, bar with nightly entertainment, 2 pools, meeting rooms. AE, MC, V. EP. Moderate–Expensive.*

★ **Captain Oliver's.** At Oyster Pond facing a beautiful horseshoe-shape bay, this small hotel, with bungalows featuring a view of the bay or garden, is for those who want to be away from the hustle of St. Maarten. The exceptionally clean, fresh air-conditioned rooms—those facing the bay are the choicest—have their own patio decks, satellite TVs, minibars, direct-dial phones and kitchenettes. The property straddles the border: Stay in France, dine in the Netherlands. Sail-and-stay packages can be arranged by the friendly helpful staff. A great bargain. *Oyster Pond, 97150, tel. 590/87–40–26 or 800/223–9862, fax 590/87–40–84. 50 rooms. Facilities: restaurant, snack bar. AE, DC, MC, V. CP. Moderate–Expensive.*

Pavillon Beach Hotel. Every room of this small, new (1991) hotel faces the sea and comes with a private balcony. The spacious rooms with tile floors and warm colored fabrics have clean bathrooms that come with a hair dryer and fixed-head shower (no tubs). On the balcony is a small but fully equipped kitchenette. The rooms on the ground level allow you to walk right onto the beach but do require that you close yourself in at night with sliding shutters: You may prefer the upper-story rooms, where you are not as exposed. The managers, Paul and Marie-Florence, are wonderfully warm-hearted and helpful. *Plage de Grand Case, RN 7, Grand Case 97150, tel. 590/87–96–46, fax 590/87–71–04; in the U.S., tel. 800/223–9815. 17 rooms. Facilities: kitchenettes, in-room safes. MC, V. EP. Moderate–Expensive.*

Alizéa. The Alizéa is on Mont Vernon hill and offers splendid views over Orient Bay. Though there is a path for a 10-minute walk to the beach on Orient Bay, you will need a car to go elsewhere on the island. An open-air feeling pervades the hotel from its terrace restaurant, where the food is superb, to the 26 guest apartments done up with contemporary wood furnishings and pastel fabrics. Rooms vary in style and design, but all are tasteful and each has a large private patio balcony that makes breakfast a special treat. *Mont Vernon 25, 97150, tel. 590/87–33–42, fax 590/87–41–15. 8 1-bedroom bungalows, 18 studios. Facilities: pool, restaurant. AE, MC, V. CP. Moderate.*

★ **Marine Hotel Simson Beach.** This may be the best buy on the hotel "strip" known as Nettle Bay. Rooms and duplex suites are cheerfully decorated, most with a view of the water, all with kitchenette, balcony, safe, cable TV, and direct-dial phone. The youthful fun-loving clientele make sure there's never a dull moment. Budget-conscious Europeans love this place because of the many extras, like a huge breakfast buffet and nightly local entertainment. *Box 172, Nettle Bay, tel. 590/87–54–54, fax 590/87–92–11. 120 studios, 45 1-bedroom duplexes. Facilities: beach, pool, water-sports center, restaurant, bar, car and bike rental, mini mart, laundromat, dive shop. AE, MC, V. BP. Inexpensive–Moderate.*

★ **Hevea.** This is a small, white guest house with smart awnings in the heart of Grand Case. The rooms are dollhouse small but will appeal to romantics. There are beam ceilings, washstands, and carved wood beds with lovely white coverlets and mosquito nets. The air-conditioned rooms, studios, and apartment are on the terrace level; fan-cooled studios and apartments are on the garden level. *Grand Case 97150, tel. 590/87–56–85 or 800/423–4433, fax 590/87–83–88. 8 units. Facilities: restaurant. MC, V. EP. Inexpensive.*

★ **La Residence.** Located in Marigot and popular with business travelers, this soundproof hotel is an excellent choice. All the accommodations have baths (with showers only), phones, safes, cable TVs, minibars and air-conditioning. You've a choice among double rooms, studios, mezzanine loft beds, and apartments with or without kitchenettes. You'll have to take a cab to get to the beach. *Rue du Général de Gaulle, Marigot 97150, tel. 590/87–70–37, fax 590/87–90–44. 20 rooms. Facilities: restaurant, lounge, sundry shop. AE, MC, V. CP. Inexpensive.*

La Royale Louisiana. Located in downtown Marigot in the boutique shopping area, this upstairs hotel is pleasant and pretty. White and pale green galleries overlook the flower-filled courtyard. There's a selection of twin, double, and triple air-conditioned duplexes, all with private baths (tubs and showers), TVs, VCRs, and phones. *Rue du Général de Gaulle, Marigot 97150, tel. 590/87–86–51, fax 590/87–86–51. 68 rooms. Facilities: restaurant, snack bar, beauty salon. AE, DC, MC, V. CP. Inexpensive.*

Home and Apartment Rentals
Both sides of the island offer a wide variety of homes, villas, condominiums, and housekeeping apartments. Information in the United States can be obtained through **Caribbean Home Rentals** (Box 710, Palm Beach, FL 33480, tel. 407/833–4454), **Jane Condon Corp.** (211 E. 43rd St., New York, NY 10017, tel. 212/986–4373), or **St. Maarten Villas** (707 Broad Hollow Rd., Farmingdale, NY 11735, tel. 516/249–4940). On the island, contact **Carimo** (tel. 590/87–57–58), **Ausar** (tel. 590/87–51–07), or **St. Maarten Rentals** (tel. 599/5–44330). **WIMCO** (Box 1461, Newport, RI 02840, tel. 800/932–3222) represents several higher-end properties, primarily on St. Martin.

Nightlife

To find out what's doing on the island, pick up any of the following publications: *St. Maarten Nights, What to Do in St. Maarten, St. Maarten Events,* or *St. Maarten Holiday*—all distributed free in the tourist office and hotels. *Discover St. Martin/St. Maarten,* also free, is a glossy magazine that includes articles about the island's history and the latest on shops, discos, restaurants, and even archaeological digs.

Each of the resort hotels has a Caribbean spectacular one night a week, replete with limbo and fire dancers and steel bands.

Casinos are the main focus on the Dutch side, but there are discos that usually start late and keep on till the fat lady sings.

Casinos
All 10 of the casinos have craps, blackjack, roulette, and slot machines. You must be 18 years old to gamble. The casinos are located at the **Great Bay Beach Hotel, Divi Little Bay Beach Hotel, Pelican Resort, Mullet Bay Hotel, Seaview Hotel** and the **Coliseum** in Philipsburg, **St. Maarten Beach Club, Port de Plaisance,** and **Casino Royal at Maho Beach.**

Discos Last Stop (A. T. Illidge Road, no tel.) and **The Tropics** (by Madame Estate in the Royal Inn Motel, no tel.) are hot, somewhat rowdy discos frequented by locals. There have been reports of drug activity at the latter. **Studio 7** (tel. 599/5–42115) attracts a young crowd in its ultramodern digs atop Casino Royale across from Maho Beach Resort. Casino Royale also produces the splashy "Paris Revue Show." **Le Club** (Mullet Bay, tel. 599/5–42801) draws a mixed crowd of locals and tourists. French nationals and locals flock to **L'Atmosphere** (no phone) on the second floor of L'Auberge de Mer in Marigot for the best in salsa and soca. **Night Fever** (Colombier, outside Marigot, no phone) attracts a young crowd of locals who gyrate to the latest Eurodisco beat.

Bars and Nightclubs **Cheri's Cafe** (by the Maho Beach Hotel, tel. 599/5–53361) is a local institution, with cheap food and great live bands. **Turtle Pier Bar & Restaurant** (Airport Road, tel. 599/5–52230) always hops with a lively crowd. **David's** (Rue de la Liberté, Marigot, tel. 590/87–51–58) is run by an expatriate Brit; its raucous Tuesday and Friday trivia nights are legendary. **La Fiesta** (Rue de la Liberté, Marigot, tel. 590/87–99–41) pulsates to Brazilian rhythms, with occasional live magic and cabaret acts between sambas. In Grand Case, happy hours rock at the **Surf Club South** (no phone). **Jimbo Lolo** (no phone) stays open until midnight for French punks and American wannabes who then head over for a nightcap at **Cha Cha Cha Caribbean Cafe** (tel. 590/87–53–63).

24 St. Vincent and the Grenadines

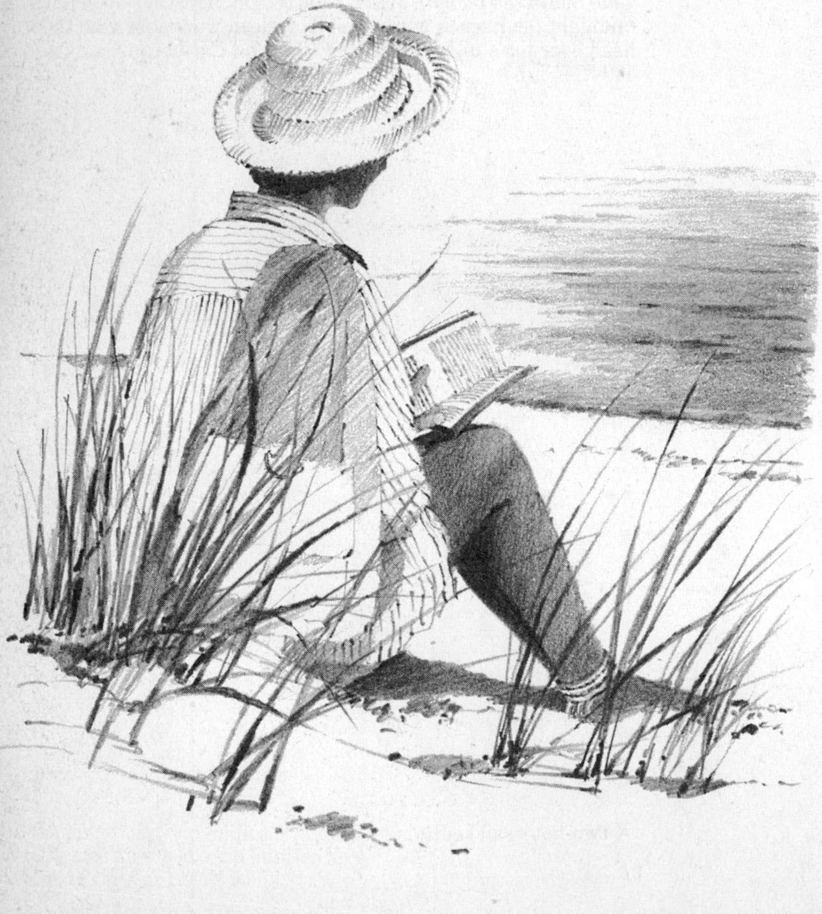

Updated by
Joan Iaconetti

St. Vincent and the Grenadines form a necklace of lush, mountainous islands that beckon the traveler, sailor, and day-tripper who are more intrigued by blooming flowers than by Bloomingdale's. The fertile volcanic soil has helped to create the oldest botanical gardens in the Western Hemisphere, and rich aromatic valleys of bananas, coconuts, and arrowroot cover these relatively undeveloped islands.

St. Vincent, with a population of about 99,000, is only 16 miles long and 9 miles wide, but it delights those who have discovered its stunning natural beauty, both below and above its crystal seas. Equipped with little more than a snorkel and a sense of adventure, visitors can discover unrivaled underwater landscapes; a pair of comfortable shoes and a little stamina are enough to hike mountains that are as verdant as Hawaii's.

The Grenadines appeal to adventurous singles and couples who prefer active sports to glitz and gambling. Those looking for five-star amenities or designer shopping should go elsewhere. Hotels are small, the food is simple, and the residents' hospitality provides a peaceful, laid-back atmosphere. In contrast to St. Vincent's beaches of black volcanic sand, the Grenadines offer numerous powdery white bays and coves on both the calm leeward and surfy windward shores.

While the islands have their share of the poor and unemployed, the superfertile soil allows everyone to grow enough food to eat and trade for necessities. Since the locals haven't come to regard tourists as meal tickets, beggars are few. Recent progress (improved roads, Bequia's new airport), however, has its price; it is no longer entirely safe to hike alone along forest trails, and petty theft has become a reality.

Historians believe that in 4300 BC, long before King Tut ruled Egypt, the Ciboney Indians first inhabited St. Vincent. Unhampered by passports and political unrest, the Ciboney made their way to Cuba and Haiti, leaving St. Vincent to the Arawaks. Columbus sailed by in 1492, while the Arawaks were involved in intermittent skirmishes with the bellicose Caribs; though Columbus never actually stopped on St. Vincent, Discovery Day (or St. Vincent and the Grenadine's Day) is still commemorated on January 22.

Declared a neutral island by French and British agreement in 1748, St. Vincent became something of a political football in the years that followed. Ceded to the British in 1763, it was captured by the French in 1779 and restored to the British by the Treaty of Versailles in 1783. By the 19th century, St. Vincent was quite sure it was more British than French, and on October 27, 1979, it gained independence from Great Britain.

In contrast to their colorful history, the 32 islands and cays that make up the Grenadines seem timeless, as free from politics as the beaches are free from debris and crowds. Nine miles south of St. Vincent is Bequia, the second-largest Grenadine. Admiralty Bay is one of the finest anchorages in the Caribbean. With superb views, snorkeling, hiking, and swimming, the island has much to offer the international mix of backpackers and luxury yacht owners who frequent its shores.

A two-hour sail south is Mustique, equipped with a small airstrip. More arid than Bequia, Mustique does not seek tourists, least of all those hoping for a glimpse of the rich and famous

(Princess Margaret, Mick Jagger) who own houses here. The appeal of Mustique is seclusion and privacy.

Just over 3 square miles, Canouan is an unspoiled island that offers travelers an opportunity to relax, snorkel, and hike.

Numerous yachts and catamarans can be chartered for day sails from any of the Grenadines to the tiny uninhabited Tobago Cays. Avid snorkelers claim that the Cays have some of the best hard and soft coral formations found outside the Pacific Ocean. The beaches here are perfect for secluded picnics.

The tiny island of Mayreau has 182 residents, no phones, and one of the area's most beautiful beaches. The Caribbean is often mirror-calm, yet just yards away on the southern end of this narrow island is the rolling Atlantic surf.

John Caldwell has spent 20 years turning Palm Island from a mosquito-infested mangrove swamp into a small island paradise for couples and families. The Caldwell family also hosts day-tripping cruise passengers who come to lounge on the wide white beaches, which are dotted and fringed with palm trees.

Union Island isn't really a place for landlubbers: The island caters almost completely to French sailors, who keep very much to themselves. Surface transport is limited, and to see the island you need a boat. You won't find the laid-back friendliness of the other Grenadines here.

Petit St. Vincent is another private luxury resort island, reclaimed from the jungle by manager Haze Richardson. It's actually possible to spend your entire vacation in one of the resort's widely spaced stone houses without ever seeing another human being.

Before You Go

Tourist Information   The **St. Vincent and the Grenadines Tourist Office** (801 2nd Ave., 21st floor, New York, NY 10017, tel. 212/687–4981 or 800/729–1726, fax 212/949–5946; or 6505 Cove Creek Pl., Dallas, TX 75240, tel. 214/239–6451, fax 214/239–1002; in Canada: 100 University Ave., Suite 504, Toronto, Ont. M5J 1V6, tel. 416/971–9666, fax 416/971–9667; in the United Kingdom: 10 Kensington Court, London W8 5DL, tel. 071/937–6570, fax 071/937–3611). Write for a visitors guide, filled with useful, up-to-date information.

Arriving and Departing
By Plane   Most U.S. visitors fly via **American** (tel. 800/433–7300) into Barbados or St. Lucia, then take a small plane to St. Vincent's E.T. Joshua Airport or to Bequia, Mustique, Canouan, Union, or Palm. (Other destinations require a boat ride on either a scheduled ferry, a chartered boat, or your hotel's launch.) Other airlines that connect with interisland flights are **BWIA** (tel. 800/JET–BWIA), **British Airways** (tel. 800/247–9297), **Air Canada** (tel. 800/776–3000), and **Air France** (tel. 800/237–2747).

LIAT (Leeward Islands Air Transport, tel. 809/462–0700; in NY, 212/251–1717; in the U.S., 800/253–5011), **Air Martinique** (tel. 809/458–4528), and **SVGAIR** (tel. 809/456–9246; in the U.S., 800/677–3195; in FL, 813/799–1858) fly interisland. Delays are common but usually not outrageous. A surer way to go is with **Mustique Airways** (tel. 809/458–4380 or 809/458–4818. In the U.S., contact Anchor Travel at tel. 800/526–4789 or in New Jersey, 201/891–1111). Its six- or eight-seat charter flights meet and wait for your major carrier's arrival even if it's delayed (bring earplugs if you're supersensitive to noise).

From the Airport Taxis and/or buses are readily available at the airport on every island. A taxi from the airport to Kingstown will cost $5–$7 (E.C.$15–$20); bus fare is less than 75¢. If you have a lot of luggage, it might be best to take a taxi—buses (actually minivans) are very short on space.

Passports and Visas U.S. and Canadian citizens must have a passport; all visitors must hold return or ongoing tickets. Visas are not required.

Language English is spoken everywhere in the Grenadines, often with a Vincentian patois or dialect.

Precautions Insects are a minor problem on the beach during the day, but when hiking and sitting outdoors in the evening, you'll be glad you brought industrial-strength mosquito repellent.

Beware of the manchineel tree, whose little green apples look tempting but are toxic. Even touching the sap of the leaves will cause an uncomfortable rash. Most trees on hotel grounds are marked with signs; on more remote islands, the bark may be painted red. Hikers should watch for Brazil wood trees/bushes, which look and act similar to poison ivy.

When taking photos of market vendors, private citizens, or homes, be sure to ask permission first and expect to give a gratuity for the favor.

There's relatively little crime here, but don't tempt fate by leaving your valuables lying around or your room or car unlocked.

Staying in St. Vincent and the Grenadines

Important Addresses **Tourist Information:** The **St. Vincent Board of Tourism** (tel. 809/457–1502) is located in a marked building on Egmont Street, on the second floor.

Emergencies **Police:** (tel. 809/457–1211). **Hospitals:** (tel. 809/456–1185). **Pharmacies: Deane's** (tel. 809/457–1522), **Reliance** (tel. 809/456–1734), both in Kingstown; on Bequia: **Bequia Pharmacy** (tel. 809/458–3296).

Currency Although U.S. and Canadian dollars are taken at all but the smallest shops, Eastern Caribbean currency (E.C.$) is accepted and preferred everywhere. At press time, the exchange rate was U.S.$1 to E.C.$2.67; banks give a slightly better rate of exchange.

Price quotes are normally given in E.C. dollars; however, when you negotiate taxi fares and such, be sure you know which type of dollar you're agreeing on. Note: Prices quoted here are in U.S. dollars unless indicated otherwise.

Taxes and Service Charges The departure tax from St. Vincent and the Grenadines is $6 (E.C.$15). Restaurants and hotels charge a 5% government tax, and if a 10% service charge is included in your bill, no additional tip is necessary.

Guided Tours Tours can be informally arranged through taxi drivers who double as informal but knowledgeable guides. Your hotel or the Tourism Board will recommend a driver. When choosing a driver/guide, look for the Taxi Driver's Association decal on the windshield and talk with the driver long enough to be sure you'll be able to understand his patois over the noise of the engine. Settle the fare first ($30–$40 is normal for a two- or three-hour tour). To prearrange a taxi tour, contact the Taxi Driver's Association (tel. 809/457–1807).

Grenadine Tours (St. Vincent, tel. 809/458–4818) arranges air, sea, and land excursions throughout the islands, as does **Barefoot Holidays** (tel. 809/456–9334; in the U.S., 800/677–3195).

Getting Around Many of the roads in the Grenadines are not in the best condi-
Taxis tion, so you may prefer taxis to a rented car.

Minivans Public buses come in the form of brightly painted minivans with names like "Struggling Man" and "Who to Blame." Bus fares run E.C.$1–$5 in St. Vincent, with the route direction indicated on a sign in the windshield. Just wave from the road, and the driver will stop for you.

Smaller islands also have taxi-vans and pickup trucks with benches in the back and canvas covers for when it rains.

Rental Cars Rental cars cost an average of $45–$50 per day; driving is on the left. Although major improvements are being made, many roads are not well marked or maintained.

To rent a car you'll need a temporary Vincentian license (unless you already have an International Driver's License), which costs E.C.$20. Among the rental firms are **Johnson's U-Drive** (tel. 809/458–4864) at the airport and **Kim's Auto Rentals** (tel. 809/456–1884), which has a larger selection of slightly more expensive rental cars that must be rented by the week.

Telephones The area code for St. Vincent and the Grenadines is 809. If you
and Mail use Sprint or MCI in the United States, you may need to access an AT&T line to dial direct to St. Vincent and the Grenadines. From St. Vincent, you can direct-dial to other countries; ask the hotel operator for the proper country code and the probable charge, surcharge, and government tax on the call. Local information is 118; international is 115.

When you dial a local number from your hotel in the Grenadines, you can drop the 45-prefix. Few hotels have phones in the rooms. Pay phones are E.C.$.25.

Mail between St. Vincent and the United States takes two to three weeks. Airmail postcards cost 45¢; airmail letters cost 65¢ an ounce.

Federal Express is located on Bay Street in Kingstown (tel. 809/456–1649) and at Solana's Boutique in Bequia (tel. 809/458–3554).

Opening and Stores and shops in Kingstown are open weekdays 8–4. Many
Closing Times close for lunch from noon to 1 or so. Saturday hours are 8–noon. Banks are open weekdays 8–noon, Fridays from 2 or 3 to 5. The post office is open weekdays 8:30–3, Saturdays 8:30–11:30.

St. Vincent

Exploring St. Vincent

Numbers in the margin correspond to points of interest on the St. Vincent map.

Kingstown's shopping/business district, cathedrals, and sights can easily be seen in a half-day tour. Outlying areas, botanical gardens, and the Falls of Baleine will each require a full day of touring. City maps are in the "Discover SVG" booklet, available everywhere.

Kingstown The capital and port of St. Vincent, **Kingstown** is at the
❶ southeastern end of the island. Begin your tour on Bay Street, near Egmont Street. Kingstown's boutiques feature such local crafts as cotton batik hangings and clothing, floor mats, baskets, and black coral jewelry.

The **fish/vegetable market** on Bay Street is a hectic, lively place, especially on Saturday before 11 AM. Note: Keep a tight grip on your valuables in the market.

Unusual gifts for stamp collectors are at the **post office** on Granby Street east of Egmont. St. Vincent is known worldwide for its particularly beautiful and colorful issues, which commemorate flowers, undersea creatures, and architecture.

Follow Back Street (also called Granby Street) west past the Methodist Church to **St. George's Cathedral,** a yellow Anglican church built in the early 19th century. The dignified Georgian architecture includes simple wood pews, an ornate hanging candelabra, and stained-glass windows. The gravestones tell the history of the island.

Across the street is **St. Mary's Roman Catholic Cathedral,** built in 1823 and renovated in the 1930s. The renovations resulted in a strangely appealing blend of Moorish, Georgian, and Romanesque styles in black brick.

A few minutes away by taxi or bus is St. Vincent's famous **Botanical Gardens.** Founded in 1765, it is the oldest botanical garden in the Western Hemisphere. Captain Bligh brought the first breadfruit tree to this island, a direct descendant of which is in the gardens. St. Vincent parrots and green monkeys are housed in cages, and unusual trees and bushes cover the well-kept grounds. Local guides offer their services for $2–$4 an hour. *Information: c/o Minister of Agriculture, Kingstown, tel. 809/457–1003. Open weekdays 7–4, Sat. 7–11 AM, Sun. 7–6.*

The tiny **National Museum** houses ancient Indian clay pottery found by Dr. Earle Kirby, St. Vincent's resident archaeologist. Dr. Kirby's historical knowledge is as entertaining as it is extensive. Contact him for a guided tour, since the labels in the museum offer little information. *Tel. 809/456–1787. Open Wed. 9–noon, Sat. 3–6.*

❷ Flag another taxi for the 10-minute ride to **Fort Charlotte,** built in 1806 to keep Napoleon at bay. The fort sits 636 feet above sea level, with cannons and battlements perched on a dramatic promontory overlooking the city and the Grenadines to the south, Lowman's Beach and the calm east coast to the north. The fort saw little military action; it was used mainly to house paupers and lepers.

Outside Kingstown The coastal roads of St. Vincent offer panoramic views and insights into the island way of life. Life in the tiny villages has changed little in centuries. This full-day driving tour includes Layou, Montreal Gardens, Mesopotamia Valley, and the Windward coast. Be sure to drive on the left, and honk your horn before you enter the blind curves.

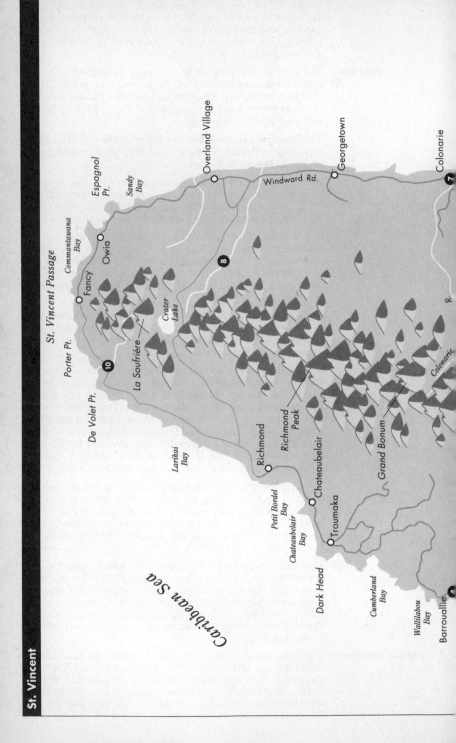

585

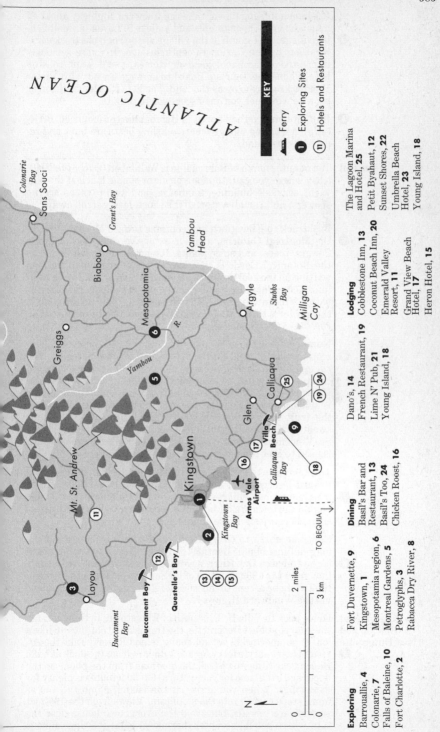

KEY

Ferry

① Exploring Sites

⑪ Hotels and Restaurants

Exploring

Barrouallie, 4
Colonarie, 7
Falls of Baleine, 10
Fort Charlotte, 2
Fort Duvernette, 9
Kingstown, 1
Mesopotamia region, 6
Montreal Gardens, 5
Petroglyphs, 3
Rabacca Dry River, 8

Dining

Basil's Bar and
  Restaurant, 13
Basil's Too, 24
Chicken Roost, 16
Dano's, 14
French Restaurant, 19
Lime N' Pub, 21
Young Island, 18

Lodging

Cobblestone Inn, 13
Coconut Beach Inn, 20
Emerald Valley
  Resort, 11
Grand View Beach
  Hotel, 17
Heron Hotel, 15
The Lagoon Marina
  and Hotel, 25
Petit Byahaut, 12
Sunset Shores, 22
Umbrella Beach
  Hotel, 23
Young Island, 18

ATLANTIC OCEAN

③ Beginning in Kingstown, take the Leeward Highway about 45 minutes north through hills and valleys to **Layou,** a small fishing village. Just north of the village are **petroglyphs** (rock carvings) left by the Caribs 13 centuries ago. If you're seriously interested in archaeological mysteries, you'll want to stop here. Phone the Tourism Board to arrange a visit with Victor Hendrickson, who owns the land. For E.C.$5, Hendrickson or his wife will meet you and escort you to the site.

④ Half an hour farther north is **Barrouallie** (pronounced *BAR-relly*), a whaling village where whaling boats are built and repaired year-round.

Time Out Ten minutes north of Barrouallie is **Wallilabou** (*wally-la-BOO*), a bay where you can stop for a picnic or simple lunch at the new yacht services building, sunbathe, and swim (there are no showers, but a small waterfall is a short, lovely stroll away).

⑤ Backtrack to Kingstown and continue toward Mesopotamia to the **Montreal Gardens,** another extensive collection of exotic flowers, trees, and spice plants. It's not as well maintained as the Botanical Gardens, but the aroma of cocoa and nutmeg wafting on the cool breeze is enticing. Spend an hour with well-informed guides or wander on your own along the narrow paths. Vincentian newlyweds often spend their honeymoon in the garden's tiny cottage, appropriately named Romance. *Tel. 809/458–5452. Open daily.*

⑥ Now drive southeast (roads and signs aren't the best, so ask directions at Montreal Gardens) to the **Mesopotamia region.** The rugged, ocean-lashed scenery along St. Vincent's windward coast is the perfect counterpoint to the lush, calm west coast. Mesopotamia is full of dense forests, streams, and bananas, the island's major export. The blue plastic bags on the trees protect the fruit from damage in high winds. Coconut, breadfruit, sweet corn, peanuts, and arrowroot grow in the rich soil here. St. Vincent is the world's largest supplier of arrowroot, which is used to coat computer paper.

⑦ Turn north on the Windward Highway up the jagged coast road toward Georgetown, St. Vincent's second-largest city. You'll pass many small villages and the town of **Colonarie.** In the hills behind the town are hiking trails. Locals are helpful with directions, because signs are limited.

⑧ Continue north to **Georgetown,** amid coconut groves and the long-defunct Mount Bentinck Sugar factory. A few miles north is the **Rabacca Dry River,** a rocky gulch carved out by the lava flow from the 1902 eruption of La Soufrière. Here hikers begin the two-hour ascent to the volcano. Return south to Kingstown via the Windward Highway.

The Falls of Baleine and Fort Duvernette **⑨** Drive back to Villa Beach, south of Kingstown, in time to catch the sunset at **Fort Duvernette,** the tiny island that juts up like a loaf of pumpernickel behind Young Island Resort. Take the *African Queen*–style ferry for a few dollars from the dock at Villa Beach near Kingstown (call the boatman from the phone on the dock) and set a time for your return (60–90 minutes is plenty for exploring). When you arrive at the island, climb the 100 or more steps carved into the mountain. Views from the 195-foot summit are terrific, but avoid the overgrown house near the top, where you'll encounter (harmless) bats. Rusting cannons from the early 1800s are still here, aimed not at seagoing invaders but at the marauding Caribs.

⑩ Nearly impossible to get to by car, the **Falls of Baleine** are an absolute must to see on an escorted all-day boat trip or by chartered boat from Villa Beach (*see* Sports and the Outdoors, *below*). The ride offers scenic island views. When you arrive, be prepared to climb from the boat into shallow water to get to the beach. Local guides help visitors make the 15-minute sneakers-and-swimsuit trek over the boulders in the stream leading to the falls; a walkway allows the less adventurous to enjoy them as well. Swim in the freshwater pool, climb under the 63-foot falls (they're chilly), and relax in this bit of utterly untouched Eden.

Beaches

Most of the hotels and white-sand beaches are near Kingstown; black-sand beaches ring the rest of the island. The placid west coast, site of **Villa Beach** (white sand), **Questelle's Bay** (black sand), and **Buccament Bay** (black sand), is good for swimming; the beaches at Villa and the CSY Yacht Club are small but safe, with dive shops nearby. The exposed Atlantic coast is dramatic, but the water is rough and unpredictable. No beach has lifeguards, so even experienced swimmers are taking a risk. The windward side of the island has no beachfront facilities.

Sports and the Outdoors

Water Sports The constant trade winds are perfect for windsurfing, and 80-foot visibility on numerous reefs means superior diving. Many experienced divers find St. Vincent and Bequia far less crowded and nearly as rich in marine life as Bonaire and the Caymans; snorkeling in the Tobago Cays is among the world's best.

Dive operations are small and often less luxurious than on other islands, but competent and professional. Many offer three-hour beginner "resort" courses, full certification courses, and excursions to nearby reefs, walls, and wrecks. Dive shops are on St. Vincent, Bequia, Mustique, Union, and Palm islands; individual island listings have full information. Most dive shops and larger hotels also rent Sunfish, Windsurfers, and snorkel gear.

Dive St. Vincent (tel. 809/457–4714), on Villa Beach, just across from Young Island, is where NAUI instructor Bill Tewes and his staff offer beginner and certification courses, and trips to the Falls of Baleine. A single-tank dive is about $50. Attractive hotel and dive packages throughout the Grenadines are available here.

Depending on the weather, Young Island has some of the area's most colorful snorkeling. If you're not a guest on this private island, phone the resort for permission to take the ferry and rent equipment from the resort's water-sports center (*see* Lodging, *below*).

Hiking Dorsetshire Hill, about 3 miles from Kingstown, rewards you with a sweeping view of city and harbor; picturesque Queen's Drive is nearby. Mt. St. Andrew, on the outskirts of the city, is a pleasant climb through a rain forest on a well-marked trail.

But the queen of climbs is La Soufrière, St. Vincent's active volcano (which last erupted, appropriately enough, on Friday the 13th in 1979). Approachable from both windward and leeward coasts, this is *not* a casual excursion for inexperienced walkers; you'll need stamina and sturdy shoes for this climb of just over 4,000 feet. Be sure to check the weather before you leave; hikers have been sorely disappointed to reach the top only to find the view completely obscured by enveloping clouds.

Climbs are all-day affairs; a LandRover and guide can be arranged through your hotel or a knowledgeable taxi driver. The four-wheel-drive vehicle takes you past Rabacca Dry River through the Bamboo Forest. From there it's a two-hour hike to the summit, and you can arrange in advance to come down the other side of the mountain to the Chateaubelair area.

Sailing and Charter Yachting Unless you're plagued with motion sickness, the Grenadines are the perfect place to charter a sailboat or catamaran (bareboat or complete with captain, crew, and cook) to weave you around the islands for a day or a week. Boats of all sizes and degrees of luxury are available; the Lagoon Marina and Hotel (tel. 809/458–4308) in the Blue Lagoon area of St. Vincent has 44-foot crewed sloops. Hotels can also recommend charter yachts.

Shopping

St. Vincent isn't a duty-free port, but appealing local crafts (batik, baskets) and resort wear can be found at **Noah's Arkade** (tel. 809/457–1513) on Bay Street. The best batiks are at **Batik Carib** (tel. 809/456–1666) and **Sprotties** (tel. 809/458–4749), also on Bay Street. The **St. Vincent Craftsmen Center** (tel. 809/457–1288), in the northwest end of Kingstown on James Street above Granby Street, sells grass floor mats and other woven items. Swiss watches, crystal, china, and jewelry can be found at **Stecher's** (tel. 809/457–1142) on Bay Street in the Cobblestone Arcade (a branch is at the airport).

Dining

West Indian food is the way to go in St. Vincent. You'll enjoy interesting local fare that is reasonably priced at all but the expensive hotels. Dishes include callaloo (a spinachlike vegetable) soup, goat stew, *rotis* (burritos filled with curried potatoes and meat or conch), and unusual fruits like soursop, cristophenes, and eddoes. Fried chicken and burgers are available everywhere. Avoid choosing beef or steak at hotel buffets; shoe leather comes to mind.

Highly recommended restaurants are indicated by a star ★.

Category	Cost*
Expensive	over $20
Moderate	$10–$20
Inexpensive	under $10

per person, excluding drinks and sales tax (5% on credit-card purchases only)

★ **Basil's Bar and Restaurant.** This air-conditioned restaurant, downstairs in the Cobblestone Inn, opens at 8 AM for Kingstown's version of the power breakfast. Basil's also serves a buffet lunch with hearty callaloo soup, lobster, and barbecued conch, plus seafood pasta and chicken in fresh ginger and coconut milk. *Bay St., Kingstown, tel. 809/457-2713. Reservations recommended. AE, MC, V. Expensive.*

★ **French Restaurant.** Referred to as "The French," this open-air place has some of the best food in the Grenadines. A nearby lobster pool assures freshness, and the chef cooks with locally available ingredients (garlic soup instead of onion soup, for example). Choose from crepes, lobster bisque, and grilled lamb chops; the lunch menu includes quiche and sandwiches. There's also a varied wine list and a bar inside. *Villa Beach, tel. 809/458-4972. Dinner reservations recommended. AE, V. Expensive.*

Young Island. Five-course chef's-choice dinners of seafood, roast pig, beef, and chicken tend to be heavy and old-fashioned; lunches are better, with fresh breads, fruits, and cold cuts. The open-air dining room has a rustic tropical appeal with a rough stone floor, heavy wooden tables, and walls hung with fishnet. A barbecue with a steel band is featured on Saturday night. *Young Island, tel. 809/458-4826. Reservations required. AE, MC, V. Expensive.*

Basil's Too. Burgers and good West Indian dishes are offered in a beautiful, airy complex on the water at Villa Beach. The main dining room is awash in white with pastel-flower linens. Colorful and creative murals cover the walls at the back. *Opposite Young Island, tel. 809/758-4025. AE, MC, V. Moderate–Expensive.*

Chicken Roost. This eatery is handy if you're waiting at the airport. The *rotis* (Caribbean burritos), sandwiches (including shark), pizzas, and ice cream can't be beat. Open daily till midnight. *Opposite airport, tel. 809/456-4939. No credit cards. Inexpensive.*

Dano's. Stop in while you're strolling around Kingstown for good, cheap Caribbean rotis and lots of local color. *Middle St., Kingstown, tel. 809/457-2020. No credit cards. Inexpensive.*

Lime N' Pub. Locals and sailors enjoy drinks, burgers, and West Indian cooking at this relaxed spot on Villa Beach. *Opposite Young Island, tel. 809/458-4227. Inexpensive.*

Lodging

Luxury resorts require booking about six months in advance, but most St. Vincent hotels can squeeze you in with far less notice. There's a bit of a lull in January, between Christmas week and the February rush, when rooms are sometimes available on a day's notice. Many hotels offer MAP (Modified American Plan, with breakfast and dinner included).

Highly recommended lodgings are indicated by a star ★.

Category	Cost*
Very Expensive	over $200
Expensive	$130–$200

Moderate	$80–$130

Inexpensive	under $80

All prices are for a standard double room for two, excluding 5% tax and a 10% service charge.

Young Island **Young Island.** A 36-acre privately owned island just 200 yards
★ off the Villa Beach dock in St. Vincent, Young Island is an upscale resort that attracts mostly over-35 couples who prefer casual elegance to the glitzy atmosphere of traditional luxury
resorts. Airy rooms are set in the hills amid flowering almond
and hibiscus trees. Each room has lovely views, though Cottages 30 and 17 near the summit have the most dramatic vistas
(also the longest walk uphill). Sail-hotel packages and day sails
are available on Young Island's two yachts, and snorkeling in
the area is superior. Dive St. Vincent is just across the channel.
*Box 211, Young Island, tel. 809/458–4826; U.S. agent: Ralph
Locke Islands, Box 800, Waccabuc, NY 10597, tel. 914/763–
5526 or 800/223–1108. 29 rooms. Facilities: scuba diving, saltwater pool, water-sports center, lighted tennis court. AE, D,
MC, V. MAP. Very Expensive.*

Emerald Valley **Emerald Valley Resort.** About 30 minutes from Kingstown, up
in the hills, Emerald Valley is the one place in the Grenadines
where you can gamble—but don't expect Las Vegas glitz. New
management is downplaying gaming in favor of family activities that take advantage of the natural beauty of the site. Hikers will enjoy the nature trail in the surrounding hills. Simple
accommodations are in chalets with kitchens. *Penniston Valley, Box 1081, St. Vincent, tel. 809/456–7140, fax 809/456–
7145. 12 chalets. Facilities: casino, restaurant, 2 tennis courts,
grass volleyball court, croquet, pool. No credit cards. EP, CP.
Moderate–Expensive.*

Villa Beach **Grand View Beach Hotel.** The original plantation house of the
★ Sardine family, this hotel is still run by managers Tony and
Heather Sardine. A charmingly homey hotel with fantastic
views, it sits on eight secluded acres about five minutes from
the airport. There's a trail down to the beach, good snorkeling,
and the picture-perfect pool sits atop Villa Point. *Box 173, St.
Vincent, tel. 809/458–4811, fax 809/457–4174; U.S. agent:
Charms Caribbean Vacations, tel. 800/742–4276. 19 rooms. Facilities: tennis and squash courts, fitness center, pool, reading
room, restaurant, water-sports center nearby. AE, MC, V.
CP. Expensive.*

Sunset Shores. Everything in this very simple but livable hotel
is arranged around the pool. Business travelers appreciate the
clipboard in the central sitting area that carries daily Caribbean, financial, sports, and international news from the wire services. The better rooms have patios. *Box 849, across from
Young Island on Villa Beach, St. Vincent, tel. 809/458–4411,
fax 809/457–4800. 31 air-conditioned rooms. Facilities: restaurant, pool, watersports center nearby. AE, D, MC, V. EP.
Moderate–Expensive.*

Coconut Beach Inn. New management, which thankfully pre-
fers "the music of the wind and waves" to taped reggae, has
transformed this inn into a charming, lively place for families
and singles. If Cleo is still cooking, be sure to have dinner here.
*Indian Bay, Box 355, St. Vincent, tel. 809/458–4231. 8 rooms.
Facilities: bar, restaurant, water-sports center nearby. AE, V.
CP. Inexpensive–Moderate.*

Umbrella Beach Hotel. The hotel's small and simple rooms with kitchenettes are set in a garden on Villa Beach. The three best rooms face the water. Breakfast is served outdoors in a garden. Here you'll find superior value and location for the price. Next door is The French, St. Vincent's best restaurant. *Box 530, St. Vincent, tel. 809/458–4651, fax 809/457–4930. 9 rooms. Facilities: bar, restaurant. MC, V. EP. Inexpensive.*

Petit Byahaut **Petit Byahaut.** The truly adventurous will enjoy staying in private room-size screened tents that sit on platforms (cabins are being built) in this secluded valley 2 miles north of Kingstown. Accessible only by boat, Petit Byahaut is a haven for divers, snorkelers, hikers, and anyone tired of civilization. The 3-resort 2-island packages, transportation included, are a good value. *Petit Byahaut Bay, St. Vincent, tel. and fax 809/457–7008. 5 tents. Facilities: restaurant, bar, gardens, solar-heated showers, water sports. No credit cards. FAP. Moderate–Expensive.*

Blue Lagoon **The Lagoon Marina and Hotel.** About 15 minutes from the airport, this is the place for chartering a crewed, 44-foot sailboat or trading stories with yacht owners. The spacious, modern rooms have cathedral ceilings and private patios. The long shallow-water beach that curves around Blue Lagoon offers a view of anchored sailboats. A beach bar has music and dancing on weekends. The secluded swimming pool is up a circuitous stone walk, set among flowering bushes. *Box 133, St. Vincent, tel. 809/458–4308; U.S. agent: Charms Caribbean Vacations, tel. 800/742–4276. 19 rooms (10 with air-conditioning, 9 with fans). Facilities: pool, bar, restaurant, conference room. AE, V. EP. Moderate–Expensive.*

Kingstown **Cobblestone Inn.** This pre-1814 stone building used to be a sugar warehouse; wicker furniture now fills its large, airy rooms. Room No. 5 overlooks the street and is sunny but a bit noisy. The nearest beach is 3 miles away. The plant-filled courtyard leads to a rooftop bar that's popular for breakfast and lunch. *Box 867, St. Vincent, tel. 809/456–1937. 19 rooms. Facilities: bar, restaurant. AE, V. CP. Inexpensive–Moderate.*

Heron Hotel. Right out of a Somerset Maugham novel, this Kingstown inn is on the second floor of a converted Georgian plantation's warehouse. Pleasantly eccentric travelers, young and old, stay here to be near the dock for the early boat. Rooms are faded but atmospheric, and No. 15 is large and has a sitting area. *Box 226, St. Vincent, tel. 809/457–1631. 12 air-conditioned rooms. Facilities: courtyard, dining room. AE, MC, V. CP. Inexpensive.*

Nightlife

Don't look for fire-eaters and limbo demonstrations on St. Vincent. Nightlife here consists mostly of hotel barbecue buffets and jump-ups, so called because the lively steel-band music makes listeners jump up and dance.

The Attic (on Grenville St., above the Kentucky Fried Chicken, tel. 809/457–2558), a jazz club with modern decor, features international artists and steel bands. There is a small cover charge; call ahead for hours and performers.

Vidal Browne, manager of **Young Island** (tel. 809/458–4826), hosts sunset cocktail parties with hors d'oeuvres once a week on Fort Duvernette, the tiny island behind the resort. On that night 100 steps up the hill are lit by flaming torches and a string band plays. Reservations are necessary for nonguests.

Basil's Too (tel. 809/458–4205) opened in late 1989, and this newest addition offers lunch, dinner and dancing amid painted murals, all set on Villa Beach overlooking Young Island.

The Grenadines

The Grenadines are wonderful islands to visit for fine diving and snorkeling opportunities, good beaches, and unlimited chances to laze on the beach with a picnic, waiting for the sun to set so you can go to dinner. For travelers seeking privacy, peace and quiet or active water sports and informal socializing, these are the islands of choice.

Bequia

Arriving and Departing
By Plane Mustique Airways (tel. 809/458–4380 or 809/458–4818) now flies into Bequia's new airport daily from Barbados. Flights from St. Vincent cost E.C.$45 one way. There are three flights daily.

By Ferry The SS *Admiral I* and the SS *Admiral II* motor ferries leave Kingstown for Bequia Monday through Friday at 9 AM, 10:30 AM, 4:30 PM, and, depending on availability, 7 PM. Saturday departures are at 12:30 PM and 7 PM; Sunday, 9 AM and 5:15 PM. Schedules are subject to change, so be sure to check times upon your arrival. All scheduled ferries leave from the main dock in Kingstown. The trip takes 70–90 minutes and costs $4.

The SS *Snapper* mail boat travels south on Mondays and Thursdays at about 10 AM, stopping at Bequia, Canouan, Mayreau, and Union, and returns north on Tuesdays and Fridays. The cost is under $10.

Weekday service between St. Vincent and Bequia is also available on the island schooner *Friendship Rose*, which leaves St. Vincent at about 12:30 PM. The *St. Vincent and the Grenadines Visitor's Guide*, available in hotels and at the airport, has complete interisland schedules.

Important Addresses **Tourist Information:** The **Bequia Tourism Board** (tel. 809/458–3286) is located on the main dock.

Emergencies **Police:** (tel. 809/456–1955). **Medical Emergencies** (tel. 999). **Hospital** (tel. 809/458–3294).

Guided Tours To see the views, villages, and boat-building around the island, hire a taxi (Gideon and Curtis are recommended) and negotiate the fare in advance. Water taxis, available from any dock, will also take you by Moonhole, a private community of stone homes with glassless windows, some decorated with bleached whale bones. The fare is about $11.

For those who prefer sailboats to motorboats, Arne Hansen and his catamaran *Toien* can be booked through the **Frangipani Hotel** (tel. 809/458–3255). Day sails to Mustique run $35–$40 per person, including drinks. An overnight snorkel/sail trip to the Tobago Cays costs about $150 for two people, including breakfast and drinks.

Beaches A half-hour walk from the Plantation House Hotel will lead you over rocky bluffs to **Princess Margaret Beach,** which is quiet and wide, with a natural stone arch at one end. Though it has no facilities, this is a popular spot for swimming, snorkeling, or simply relaxing under palms and sea-grape trees. Snorkeling and swimming are also excellent at **Lower Bay,** a wide, palm-fringed beach that can be reached by taxi or by hiking beyond Princess Margaret Beach; wear sneakers, not flip-flops. Facilities for windsurfing and snorkeling are here, and the **De Reef** restaurant features waiters who will eventually find you on the sand when your lunch is ready.

Friendship Bay can be reached by land taxi and is well equipped with windsurfing and snorkeling, rentals and an outdoor bar.

Hope Beach, on the rougher Atlantic side, is accessible by a long taxi ride (about E.C.$20—every driver knows how to get there) and a mile-long walk downhill on a semipaved path. Your reward is a magnificent beach and total seclusion, and—if you prefer—nude bathing. Be sure to ask your taxi driver to return at a prearranged time. Bring your own lunch and drinks; there are no facilities, and swimming can be dangerous.

Industry Bay boasts towering palm groves, a nearly secluded beach, and a memorable view of several uninhabited islands. The tiny, three-room Crescent Bay Lodge is here; its huge bar offers drinks and late lunches (tel. 809/458–3400).

Sports and the Outdoors
Water Sports Of Bequia's two dozen dive sites, the best are Devil's Table, a shallow dive rich in fish and coral; a sailboat wreck nearby at 90 feet; the 90-foot drop at The Wall, off West Cay; the Bullet, off Bequia's north point for rays, barracuda, and the occasional nurse shark; the Boulders for soft corals, tunnel-forming rocks, thousands of fish; and Moonhole, shallow enough in places for snorkelers to enjoy.

Dive Bequia (tel. 809/458–3504, fax 809/458–3886) and **Sunsports** (tel. 809/458–3577, fax 809/458–3907) offer one- and two-tank dives, night dives, and certified instruction, plus snorkel excursions and equipment rental.

For snorkeling on your own, take a water taxi to the bay at Moonhole and arrange a pickup time.

Shopping All Bequia's shops are along the beach and are open weekdays 10:30–5 or 6, Saturdays 10:30–noon.

Best Buys Handmade model boats (you can special order a replica of your own yacht) are at **Mauvin's** (¼ mile down the road to the left of the main dock, no phone). Along Admiralty Bay, hand-printed and batik fabric, clothing, and household items are sold at the **Crab Hole** (tel. 809/458–3290). You can watch the fabrics being made in the workshop out back. **Solana's** (tel. 809/458–3554) offers attractive beachwear, saronglike pareos, and handy plastic beach shoes. **Local Color** (tel. 809/458–3202), above the Porthole restaurant in town, has an excellent and unusual selection of handmade jewelry, wood carvings, and resort clothing. Next door is **Melinda's By Hand** (tel. 809/458–3409), with hand-painted cotton and silk clothing and accessories.

Dining Dining on Bequia ranges from West Indian to gourmet cuisine, and it's consistently good. Barbecues at Bequia's hotels mean spicy West Indian seafood, chicken, or beef (although it is usually tougher than Hulk Hogan), plus a buffet of spicy side

The Grenadines

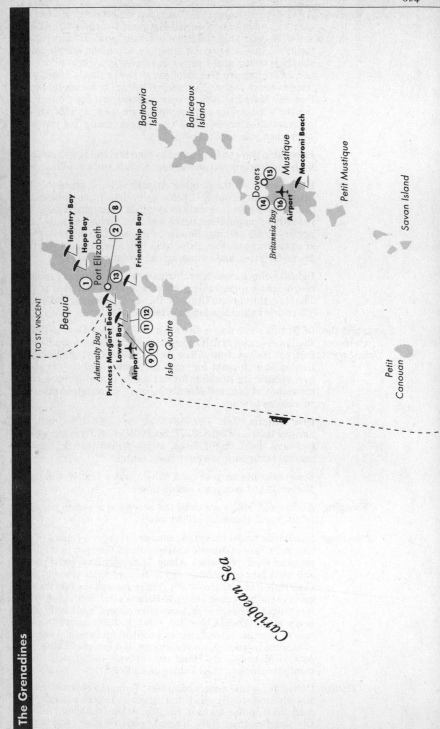

TO ST. VINCENT

Bequia

Industry Bay

Hope Bay

Port Elizabeth

① ②—⑧

⑬

Friendship Bay

Admiralty Bay

Princess Margaret Beach

Lower Bay

Airport

⑨⑩ ⑪⑫

Isle a Quatre

Battowia Island

Baliceaux Island

Mustique

Macaroni Beach

Dovers

⑮

⑭ ⑯

Britannia Bay

Airport

Petit Mustique

Savan Island

Petit Canouan

Caribbean Sea

595

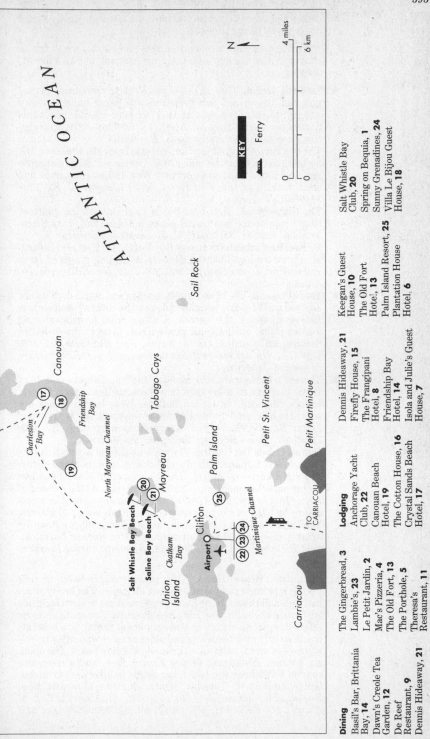

ATLANTIC OCEAN

Sail Rock

Canouan

Friendship Bay

Charleston Bay

Tobago Cays

North Mayreau Channel

Mayreau

Salt Whistle Bay Beach

Saline Bay Beach

Chatham Bay

Union Island

Clifton

Airport

Palm Island

Martinique Channel

Petit St. Vincent

Petit Martinique

TO CARRIACOU

Carriacou

N

KEY

Ferry

0   4 miles

0   6 km

Dining

Basil's Bar, Brittania Bay, **14**
Dawn's Creole Tea Garden, **12**
De Reef Restaurant, **9**
Dennis Hideaway, **21**

The Gingerbread, **3**
Lambie's, **23**
Le Petit Jardin, **2**
Mac's Pizzeria, **4**
The Old Fort, **13**
The Porthole, **5**
Theresa's Restaurant, **11**

Lodging

Anchorage Yacht Club, **22**
Canouan Beach Hotel, **19**
The Cotton House, **16**
Crystal Sands Beach Hotel, **17**

Dennis Hideaway, **21**
Firefly House, **15**
The Frangipani Hotel, **8**
Friendship Bay Hotel, **14**
Isola and Julie's Guest House, **7**

Keegan's Guest House, **10**
The Old Fort Hotel, **13**
Palm Island Resort, **25**
Plantation House Hotel, **6**

Salt Whistle Bay Club, **20**
Spring on Bequia, **1**
Sunny Grenadines, **24**
Villa Le Bijou Guest House, **18**

dishes and sweet desserts. Restaurants are occasionally closed on Sundays; phone to check.

For price information on restaurants and hotels, see the price charts in the Dining and Lodging sections of St. Vincent, above.

★ **Le Petit Jardin.** This chalet-style French restaurant serves gourmet lobster and fish prepared with West Indian touches and ingredients. The style and service here are welcome in this part of the world. *Port Elizabeth, tel. 809/458-3318. Reservations necessary. No credit cards. Expensive.*

The Old Fort. Overlooking the Atlantic from Mt. Pleasant, the building dates from the mid-1700s. Otmar and Sonja Schaedle restored it and created a gourmet West Indian restaurant and small hotel. *The Old Fort Hotel, Mt. Pleasant, tel. 809/458-3440. MC, V. Expensive.*

The Gingerbread. Your best bet is to stick with the gourmet shop's cappuccino and baked goods for breakfast. *Port Elizabeth, tel. 809/458-3577. MC, V. Moderate-Expensive.*

De Reef Restaurant. On Lower Bay Beach, De Reef serves casual lunches and exceptional dinners, including gingered lamb and seafood. *Lower Bay, tel. 809/458-3447. No credit cards. Inexpensive-Moderate.*

★ **Mac's Pizzeria.** The island's best lunches and casual dinners are enjoyed amid fuschia bougainvillea on the covered outdoor terrace overlooking the harbor. Choose from mouth-watering lobster pizza, quiche, pita sandwiches, lasagna, home-baked cookies, and muffins. *On the beach, Port Elizabeth, tel. 809/458-3474. Dinner reservations necessary. No credit cards. Inexpensive-Moderate.*

★ **Theresa's Restaurant.** On Monday nights, Theresa and John Bennett offer a rotating selection of enormous and tasty Greek, Indian, Mexican, or Italian buffets. West Indian dishes are served at lunch and dinner the rest of the week. *At the far end of Lower Bay beach. Dinner reservations necessary. Tel. 809/458-3802. No credit cards. Inexpensive-Moderate.*

Dawn's Creole Tea Garden. The walk up the hill is worth the delicious West Indian lunches and dinners, especially the Saturday night barbecue buffet. There's a wonderful view and live guitar entertainment most Saturday nights. *At the far end of Lower Bay beach, tel. 809/458-3154. Dinner reservations necessary by VHF radio. No credit cards. Inexpensive-Moderate.*

The Porthole. Located in town, this is where sailors gather for drinks, chicken and rice, or *rotis* (goat or chicken burritos). *Port Elizabeth, tel. 809/458-3458. No credit cards. Inexpensive.*

Lodging **Plantation House Hotel.** This peach-colored hotel is now Bequia's prime example of barefoot elegance. The lovely small cottages and rooms in the main house combine modern facilities with colonial charm. The Dive Bequia scuba shop on its grounds offers complete instruction and equipment rental. The hotel attracts mostly upscale divers and older couples who enjoy its relatively secluded, palm-filled grounds and tiny beach. The open-air veranda restaurant serves French food, and a room-size cage of birds near the beach bar keeps imbibers entertained. Great jump-up on Tuesday nights. *Box 16, Admiralty Bay, Bequia, St. Vincent, tel. 809/458-3425. U.S. agent: E & M Assoc., 211 E. 43 St., NY 10017, tel. 212/599-8280, fax 212/*

*599–1755. 25 cottages. Facilities: diving, pool, bar, restaurant.
AE, MC, V. MAP. Very Expensive.*

Spring on Bequia. Spring is nestled in green hills overlooking groves of tall palms and grazing goats. The hotel is about a mile above town (a pretty walk, though you may want to take a taxi back uphill), and the nearest beach, lovely but too shallow and occasionally seaweedy for serious swimming, is a 10-minute stroll away. The large wood and stone rooms attract upscale travelers who want serenity and seclusion. The airy veranda bar is the site of manager Candy Leslie's deservedly famous Sunday curry lunch (reservations necessary). *Bequia, St. Vincent, tel. 809/458–3414; U.S. agent: Spring on Bequia, Box 19251, Minneapolis, MN 55419, tel. 612/823–1202 or 612/823–9925. 11 rooms. Facilities: pool, bar, restaurant, tennis. AE, D, MC, V. EP. Expensive.*

Friendship Bay Hotel. This sprawling white house on a hill with large terraces and sweeping views overlooks another group of pretty, coral stone accommodations close to the beach. Because of the new management, service may be uneven, but Friendship offers a beautiful curve of white-sand beach and tropical plant-filled grounds. The liveliest barbecue/jump-up in the Caribbean happens Saturday nights around the Mau Mau Beach Bar, whose seats around the bar are swings, cleverly built to keep you upright even after potent rum punches. *Box 9, Bequia, St. Vincent, tel. 809/458–3222, fax 809/458–3840. 27 rooms. Facilities: water-sports center, restaurant, 2 bars, boutique. AE, MC, V. CP. Moderate–Expensive.*

The Old Fort Hotel. A stunning setting on a cliff above the Atlantic, with dining in a trellised garden and rooms imaginatively decorated. The Old Fort dates from the 1700s and is eons from the noise (except for a few goats) and cares of the world. Here you'll find excellent food and a welcoming staff—a true hideaway. *Mt. Pleasant, Bequia, St. Vincent, tel. 809/458–3440, fax 809/458–3824. 5 rooms. Facilities: restaurant, hiking. MC, V. EP, MAP. Moderate–Expensive.*

★ **The Frangipani Hotel.** The Frangipani, which has gained the status of venerable institution, is a local guest house and gossip center for international yachties and tourists. Surrounded by flowering bushes, the garden units are built of stone, with private verandas and baths. Four simple, less expensive rooms are in the main house; only one has a private bath. A two-bedroom house with a patio and another apartment with a large bedroom and kitchen are nearby. Several more garden units and two-bedroom dwellings are planned. String bands appear on Mondays, with folk singers on Friday nights during tourist season. The Thursday-night steel-band jump-up is a must. *Box 1, Bequia, St. Vincent, tel. 809/458–3255. 14 rooms. Facilities: tennis, bar, restaurant, water-sports center, yacht services. MC, V. EP. Inexpensive–Moderate.*

Isola and Julie's Guest House. Right on the water in Port Elizabeth, these two separate buildings share a small restaurant and bar. Furnishings (which are few) run to early Salvation Army, but the food is great and the rooms are airy and light, with private baths; some have hot water. *Box 12, Isola and Julie's Guest House, Bequia, St. Vincent, tel. 809/458–3304, 809/458–3323, or 809/458–3220. 25 rooms. Facilities: bar, restaurant. No credit cards. MAP. Inexpensive.*

Keegan's Guest House. This is the place for budget-minded beach lovers who want quiet, friendly surroundings. Located on Lower Bay, this *very* simple place offers family-style West

Indian breakfasts and dinners for its guests. Rooms 3, 4, and 5 have a shared bath and are cheaper, although there is no hot water to be found (you really do get used to it). *Bequia, St. Vincent, tel. 809/458-3254 or 809/458-3530. 11 rooms. Facilities: dining room. No credit cards. MAP. Inexpensive.*

Canouan

Goat-herding is still a career option here, and organized activities are nil. Walk, loaf, swim, or snorkel; Canouan still lives in the 18th century. Unfortunately, the 18th-century hotels don't live up to their 21st-century prices.

Dining and Lodging
Canouan Beach Hotel. This hotel, the only modern one on the island, caters to French people and French people only—even if all you want is a dinner reservation. You won't find laid-back island friendliness here. Simple white cottages, catamaran day-sails weekdays, and live music twice a week are what's offered here. *Canouan, St. Vincent, tel. 809/458-8888. 43 rooms. Facilities: air-conditioning, bar, restaurant, marina, windsurfing, snorkeling. AE, MC, V. MAP. Very Expensive.*

Crystal Sands Beach Hotel. Locally run and extremely simple, Crystal Sands is located on Charleston Bay and has a veranda bar and dining area. Cottages share a connecting door for larger groups and have private baths and patios. Fishing, sailing, and great snorkeling can be found off the fine beach. Phone the managers to arrange for air pickup in St. Vincent. If you take the mail boat from Kingstown (*see* Arriving and Departing in Bequia, *above*), pack light and be prepared to climb from the large ferry into a small rowboat to get to shore. *Canouan, St. Vincent, tel. 809/458-8015. 10 rooms. Facilities: bar, dining area, snorkeling, fishing. No credit cards. EP. Moderate–Expensive.*

Villa Le Bijou Guest House. Up the hill and only a 10-minute walk from Friendship Bay (15 minutes from the airstrip; pack light—taxis are rarely available). Accommodations border on the primitive, and the electricity is often on vacation, but the view is stunning. *M. de Roche, Villa La Bijou, Canouan, St. Vincent, tel. 809/458-8025. 6 rooms. No hot water in the shared baths. Facilities: snorkeling, Sunfish, windsurfing, dining area. No credit cards. MAP. Moderate–Expensive.*

Nightlife Surprise: There's a bar/disco on weekends at **Le Bijou.**

Mayreau

Farm animals outnumber citizens on tiny Mayreau. Except for water sports and hiking, there's nothing to do, and visitors like it that way. This is the perfect place for a meditative or vegetative vacation.

Guided Tours You can swim and snorkel in the Cays or nearby islands on day trips with charter yachts arranged by the hotel. Contact **Undine Potter** at the Salt Whistle Bay Resort (from the U.S., tel. 800/263-2780; in the Grenadines, marine radio VHF channel 68 or 16). Note that the Salt Whistle Bay's snorkel equipment has seen better days. Buy or rent your own before you arrive.

Beaches Top honors go to **Salt Whistle Bay Beach**—the Caribbean's prettiest. The beach is an exquisite half-moon of powdery white sand, shaded by perfectly spaced palms and flowering bushes, with the rolling Atlantic a stroll away. Hike 25 minutes over

Mayreau's mountain (wear shoes; bare feet or flip-flops are a big mistake) to a good photo opportunity at the stone church atop the hill and stunning views of the Cays. Then have a drink at Dennis Hideaway and enjoy a swim at beautiful **Saline Bay Beach.** No facilities; the mail boat's tender stops at the dock here.

Sports and the Outdoors Scuba diving can be arranged through **Grenadines Dive** (tel. 809/458–8138 or 809/458–8122; *see* Sports and the Outdoors, Union Island, *below.*)

Dining and Lodging **Salt Whistle Bay Club.** Set far back from the water, the roomy stone cottages at Mayreau's only hotel are so cleverly hidden that sailors need binoculars to be sure a hotel is there at all. With names like "Oleander" and "Ivora," the cottages sport round-stone, hot-water showers that look like large, medieval telephone booths. You can dry your hair on the breezy, shared second-story veranda atop each two-room building. The outdoor dining area has stone tables covered by thatched palms where guests enjoy turtle steak, duckling, lobster, and à la carte lunches. Music is on CD if you like; there used to be a jump-up, but guests preferred peace and quiet. *Salt Whistle Bay Club, 1020 Bayridge Dr., Kingston, Ontario, Canada K7P 2S2, tel. 800/263–2780, in the U.S.; call collect 613/634–1963 from anywhere else. Fax 613/384–6300; in the U.S., 800/263–2780; in the Caribbean, marine radio channel 16 or 68. 10 cottages, 4 refurbished suites. Facilities: windsurfing, snorkeling, catamaran charter, bar, restaurant. No credit cards. FAP. Very Expensive.*

Dennis Hideaway. It would still be *the* place to go, even if it weren't practically the only place on the island. Dennis (who plays the guitar two nights a week) is a charmer, the food is great, the drinks are strong, and the view is heaven. The rooms are clean, but very simple: a bed, nightstand, chair, and a place to hang some clothes. *Saline Bay, tel. 809/458–8594. 3 rooms. Facilities: restaurant. Reservations recommended. No credit cards. Restaurant: Moderate–Expensive. Lodging: EP. Inexpensive–Moderate.*

Mustique

This island has no town, and activities are limited to horseback riding and motorbiking, both of which can be arranged by **TechServe** (tel. 809/458–4621). If you're not a hotel or villa guest, it's easiest to arrange for these via marine radio from Basil's Bar when you arrive.

Beaches **Macaroni Beach** is Mustique's most famous stretch of sand, offering surfy swimming (no lifeguards, so be careful) with trees and mountains rising behind you. There's not much shade, and no facilities, which also describes Mustique's smaller, nameless beaches. Day-trippers can swim near **Basil's Bar,** and snorkeling is good near the Cotton House Hotel.

Dining **Basil's Bar, Britannia Bay.** Day sailors are welcome for lunch at the famous if exorbitantly priced Basil's, another Grenadines institution. Homemade ice cream, lobster, and occasional glimpses of the rich and famous provide gastronomic and visual distractions. Wednesday features a jump-up and barbecue; Monday night, live music. *Tel. 809/458–4621. Reservations suggested. AE, MC, V. Moderate–Expensive.*

Lodging **The Cotton House.** This lovingly restored 18th-century water house is built of stone and coral. It has guest rooms, a dining room, an elegant bar and sitting room, and a pool. Three additional buildings house cedar-louvered, pastel guest rooms with private balconies or patios and views to die for. The Cotton House continues its tradition of superb cuisine (meals are included in rates) and faultless service. Water sports, tennis, and horseback riding are pastimes. *Mustique, St. Vincent, tel. 809/ 456–4777. U.S. agent: Ralph Locke Islands, tel. 800/223–1108; in NY, 914/763–5526. 24 rooms. Facilities: pool, bar, restaurant, boutique, diving, windsurfing, tennis, horseback riding. AE, D, MC, V. FAP. Very Expensive.*

Firefly House. Tiny and charming with just five rooms, this is possibly the most unpretentious place on the island. Breakfast is included. *Mustique, Box 349, tel. 809/458–4621 and 809/456– 3414. 4 rooms. No credit cards. CP. Moderate.*

Villa Rentals Leasing an elegant villa of your own (complete with maid and cook) can be expensive, but sharing the cost with another couple makes the price more reasonable. Contact the manager of the Mustique Company (Mustique, St. Vincent, tel. 809/458– 4621; U.S. agent, Wegner Assoc. Inc., tel. 212/758–8800) for listings and information.

Palm Island

Palm Island Resort, one of the Caribbean's most beautiful and secluded private isles for 26 years, now has a "yacht club" restaurant for small-cruise-ship visitors and yacht sailors; active guests enjoy the fitness walk that circles past private homes, hills, and secluded Atlantic beaches. The 12 stone cottages (most with outdoor hot-water showers) all have beach views, verandas, and pastel and rattan interiors. Tea is served on your terrace each day at 4; dinners include Creole and seafood dishes, with barbecues Wednesday and Saturday nights. Snorkel and dive off the beach in water as clear as air. *Palm Island, St. Vincent, tel. 809/458–4804. US agent: Paradise Found, 800/ 776–PALM; in Canada, tel. 301/309–1698, fax 301/762–7283. 24 rooms. Facilities: minifridge, ceiling fans, open-air bar/restaurant, fitness course, water sports (diving at extra charge), catered charter yacht sails, yacht provisioning. AE, MC, V. FAP. Very Expensive.*

Petit St. Vincent

Many upscale travelers consider Petit St. Vincent the finest private island in the Caribbean. The privacy is as perfect as the food—worthy of any four-star Manhattan restaurant—the ideal place to pretend you own an uninhabited (yet elegantly serviced) island. Hoisting a yellow flag outside your spacious, secluded stone and wood house means you want room service; after the staff takes your order, don't confuse them by hoisting the red "leave me alone" flag.

Meals are also served in the expanded Pavilion, where you can play table tennis and listen to occasional live piano music in the outdoor bar.

Beaches Small, secluded beaches surround the island, now hidden from the jogging/fitness trail by skillful new landscaping. The hotel will drop you for the day at Mopion (also known as Petit St.

Richardson), a tiny sandbar with one thatch-roof shelter for shade. There is good swimming all over.

Sports and the Outdoors Activities include tennis, croquet, windsurfing, waterskiing (small extra charge), snorkeling, sailing trips, and jogging on a new 20-stop, 32-exercise fitness trail that runs along the beaches and around a wooded area. Shaded hammocks are strung up every 100 feet along the trail. *PSV, Box 12506, Cincinnati, OH 45212, tel. 513/242–1333, 800/654–9326, or 809/458–8801. 22 houses. No credit cards. Closed Sept. and Oct. FAP. Very Expensive.*

Union

Union's airstrip is right behind the Anchorage Yacht Club. Gorgeous from a distance, Union doesn't offer the charm or friendliness of other Grenadines.

Beaches The beach around Clifton Harbour is narrow, unattractive, rocky, and shadeless. Other beaches have no facilities and are virtually inaccessible without a boat; the desolate but lovely Chatham Bay offers good swimming.

Sports and the Outdoors **Grenadines Dive,** run by NAUI instructor Glenroy Adams and his brother Rick at the Sunny Grenadines Hotel, offers reef dives at Mayreau and in the Tobago Cays and wreck dives at the *Purina,* a sunken World War I English gunship. Resort courses, certification courses, glass-bottom boat trips, and snorkel trips are offered. *Tel. 809/458–8138 or 809/458–8122. Single tank dive: U.S.$45; double tank, U.S.$80. No credit cards.*

Dining **Lambie's.** On the main street in Clifton, Lambie's offers good conch Creole and walls made from their shells. *No phone. No credit cards. Moderate.*

Lodging **Anchorage Yacht Club.** Between the airstrip and what little beach there is are rooms and bungalows with concealed outdoor showers and terraces facing the water, all comfortably refurbished. Scuba, fishing, windsurfing, and Hobie Cats are available, plus charter yachts to nearby islands and provisioning for visiting boats. The enormous bar area is fronted by a pool inhabited by dozens of nurse sharks so docile that a sign warns, PLEASE DO NOT TOUCH THE SHARKS. *Union, St. Vincent, tel. 809/458–8221. 10 rooms, 6 bungalows. Facilities: water-sports center, restaurant, bar, boutique, air-conditioning, yacht provisioning and charters. AE, MC, V. CP. Moderate–Expensive.*

Sunny Grenadines. Simply furnished and airy, the dozen rooms are in several two-story stone buildings arranged around a garden with harbor view. A few rooms have kitchens, some are big enough for four or five people, and all have small porches and twin beds. Manager Augustus Mitchell arranges boat trips to the Cays. *Union, St. Vincent, tel. 809/458–8327, fax 809/458–8398. 19 rooms, some with kitchen. Facilities: bar, restaurant, dive shop. MC, V. CP. Inexpensive–Moderate.*

25 Trinidad and Tobago

Updated by
Nigel Fisher

Trinidad and Tobago, the southernmost islands in the West Indies chain, could not be more dissimilar. Trinidad's cosmopolitan capital, Port-of-Spain, bustles with shopping centers, modern hotels, sophisticated restaurants, and an active night life. It is also home to a riotous Carnival, the birthplace of steel-band music, and a busy port. The 1.3 million Trinidadians know prosperity from oil (Trinidad is one of the biggest producers in the Western Hemisphere), a steel plant, natural gas, and a multiplicity of small businesses. More than half of them—Indians, Africans, Europeans, Asians, and Americans, each with their own language and customs—live in Port-of-Spain. The Trinidadians are heavy on cricket and horse racing. But you have to leave the capital to find a good beach. And because it is one of the most active commercial cities in the West Indies, most visitors are business travelers.

Tobago, 22 miles away, offers the lazier life most tourists seek. The Robinson Crusoe island is more laid-back; the pace is slower, with beautiful, near-deserted beaches, secluded bays, small hotels, and little fishing villages. Goats outnumber cars. Tobago is popular with snorkelers and divers; its Buccoo and Speyside reefs are underwater wonderlands.

Columbus reached these islands on his third voyage in 1498. Three prominent peaks around the southern bay where he anchored prompted him to name the land La Trinidad, after the Holy Trinity. Trinidad was formally ceded to England in 1802, ending 300 years of Spanish rule.

Tobago's history was more complicated. It was "discovered" by the British in 1508. The Spanish, Dutch, French, and British all fought for it until it was ceded to England under the Treaty of Paris in 1814. In 1962, both islands—T & T, as they're commonly called—gained their independence within the British Commonwealth, finally becoming a republic in 1976.

In 1986, the National Alliance for Reconstruction (NAR) won a landslide victory, toppling the People's National Movement (PNM), which had been in power for 30 years but had brought the country to the brink of economic ruin. Then, in the 1991 elections, the electorate presumably were not impressed by the NAR and returned power back to the PNM. The new government, especially because of the decline in oil prices, is now looking for ways to encourage tourist development.

Trinidad's capital may be noisy and its way of life somewhat frenetic, but its countryside is rich in flora and fauna, home to more than 400 species of birds and 700 varieties of orchids.

Before You Go

Tourist Information

Contact the **Trinidad and Tobago Tourism Development Authority.** In the United States: 25 W. 43rd St., Suite 1508, New York, NY 10036, tel. 212/719–0540 or 800/232–0082, fax 212/719–0988. In the United Kingdom: 8a Hammersmith Broadway, London W6 7AL, tel. 081/741–4466, fax 081/741–1013. In Canada: 40 Holly St., Suite 102, Toronto, Ont. M4S 3C3, tel. 416/486–4470 or 800/268–8986, fax 416/440–1899.

Arriving and Departing
By Plane

There are daily direct flights to Piarco Airport, about 30 miles east of Port-of-Spain, from New York, Miami, and Toronto on **BWIA** (tel. 800/JET–BWIA), Trinidad and Tobago's national airline. You can also fly from one or more of these cities on

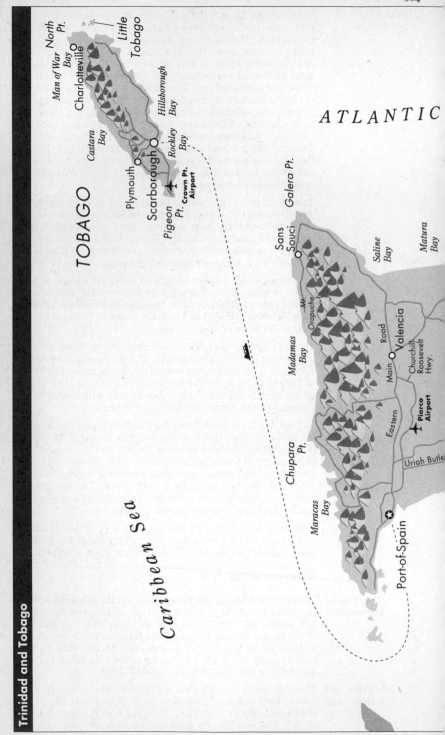

Trinidad and Tobago

ATLANTIC

Caribbean Sea

TOBAGO

North Pt.
Man of War Bay
Little Tobago
Charlotteville
Castara Bay
Hillsborough
Rockley Bay
Plymouth
Scarborough
Pigeon Pt. **Crown Pt. Airport**

Galera Pt.
Sans Souci
Saline Bay
Matura Bay
Mt. Oropuche
Valencia
Main Road
Churchill Roosevelt Hwy.
Madamas Bay
Piarco Airport
Eastern
Chupara Pt.
Uriah Butle
Maracas Bay
Port-of-Spain

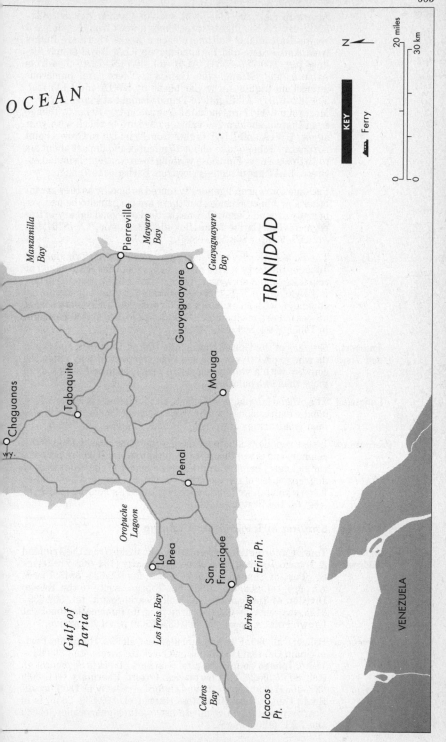

American (tel. 800/433–7300) and **Air Canada** (tel. 800/422–6232). BWIA has flights three times a week from London and serves Boston and Baltimore once a week. There are flights from Amsterdam and Paramaribo via **KLM Royal Dutch Airlines** (tel. 800/777–5553). **ALM** (tel. 800/327–7230) flies from Atlanta and Miami via Curaçao. There are numerous interisland flights in the Caribbean by BWIA and **LIAT** (tel. 809/462–0701). All flights to Trinidad alight at Piarco Airport. Most round-trip fares include a free round-trip ticket to Tobago from Piarco, about a $50 value, so be sure to check with your agent. BWIA and LIAT flights from Trinidad to Crown Point Airport in Tobago take about 15 minutes and depart about six to 10 times a day. For those wishing to circumvent Trinidad entirely, LIAT has direct service from Barbados to Tobago.

Package tours aren't generally touted as heavily as they are for other Caribbean islands, but there are bargains to be had, especially around Carnival. One particularly good agency in this regard is **Pan Caribe Tours** (Box 46 3223, Austin, TX 78764, tel. 512/267–9209 or 800/525–6896).

By Boat The Port Authority runs a ferry service between Trinidad and Tobago; the ferry leaves once a day, except for Saturday. The trip takes about six hours (flying is preferable); round-trip fare is TT$60, about U.S.$12; cabin fare is $22 (one-way double occupancy), with an extra charge for vehicles. Tickets are sold at offices in Port-of-Spain (tel. 809/625–4906) and at Scarborough, in Tobago (tel. 809/639–2181).

Passports and Visas Citizens of the United States, the United Kingdom, and Canada who expect to stay for less than two months may enter the country with a valid passport. A visa is required for a stay of more than two months.

Language The official language is English, although there is no end of idiomatic expressions used by the loquacious Trinis. You will also hear smatterings of French, Spanish, Chinese, and Hindi.

Precautions Insect repellent is a must during the rainy season (June–December) and is worth having around anytime. If you're prone to car sickness, bring your preferred remedy. Trinidad is only 11 degrees north of the equator, and the sun here can be intense. Even if you tan well, it's a good idea to use a strong sun block, at least for the first few days.

Staying in Trinidad and Tobago

Important Addresses **Tourist Information:** Information is available from the **Trinidad & Tobago Tourism Development Authority** (134–138 Frederick St., Port-of-Spain, tel. 809/623–1932, fax 809/623–3848; Piarco Airport, tel. 809/664–5196). For Tobago, write to the **Tobago Division of Tourism** (N.I.B. Mall, Scarborough, tel. 809/639–2125, fax 809/639–0509) or drop in at its information booth at Crown Point Airport (tel. 809/639–0509) when you arrive.

Emergencies **Police:** Call 999. **Fire and Ambulance:** Call 990. **Hospitals: Port-of-Spain General Hospital** is on Charlotte Street (tel. 809/625–7869). **Tobago County Hospital** is on Fort Street in Scarborough (tel. 809/639–2551). **Pharmacies: Oxford Pharmacy** (tel. 809/627–4657) is at Charlotte and Oxford streets near the Port-of-Spain General Hospital. **Ross Drugs** (tel. 809/639–2658) is in Scarborough. For a complete list of other pharmacies, check the T&T Yellow Pages.

Currency   The Trinidadian dollar (TT$) has been devalued twice in recent years. The current exchange rate is about U.S.$1 to TT$4.25. The major hotels in Port-of-Spain have exchange facilities whose rates are comparable to official bank rates. Most businesses on the island will accept U.S. currency if you're in a pinch. Note: Prices quoted here are in U.S. dollars unless indicated otherwise.

Taxes and   Restaurants and hotels add a 15% Value Added Tax (VAT). The
Service Charges   airport departure tax is TT$50, or about U.S. $12.

Many hotels and restaurants add a 10% service charge to your bill. If the service charge is not added, you should tip 10%–15% of the bill for a job well done.

Guided Tours   **Trinidad and Tobago Sightseeing Tours** (Galleria Shopping Centre, Western Main Rd., St. James, Port-of-Spain, tel. 809/628–1051) has a variety of sightseeing packages, from a tour of the city to an all-day drive to the other side of the island. Another reputable agency is **Hub Travel Limited** (Hilton Hotel lobby, tel. 809/625–3155; Piarco Airport, tel. 809/664–4359). Almost any **taxi driver** in Port-of-Spain will be willing to take you around the town and to the beaches on the north coast, and you can haggle for a cheaper rate. For a complete list of tour operators and sea cruises, contact the Tourism Office. For nature guides, *see* Sports and the Outdoors, *below*.

Getting Around   Taxis in Trinidad are easily identified by their license plates,
Taxis   which begin with the letter *H*. Passenger cars and vans, called Maxi Taxis, pick up and drop off passengers as they travel. They are easily hailed day or night along most of the main roads near Port-of-Spain. For longer trips you will need to hire a private taxi. There are set rates, though they are not always observed, particularly at Carnival. To be sure, pick up a rate sheet from the Tourism Office. On the whole, the drivers are honest, friendly, and informative, and the experience of riding in a Maxi Taxi with a souped-up sound system during Carnival is worth whatever fare you pay.

Buses   Buses cover the island and are inexpensive, but they are very old and very crowded.

Rental Cars/   If you are a first-time visitor to Port-of-Spain, where the
Scooters   streets are often jammed with traffic and drivers who routinely play "chicken" with one another, taxis are your best bet. But if you're set on wheels and not prone to headaches, you can call on several car-rental services around town. **Auto Rentals** (tel. 809/675–2258) has eight locations or, perhaps, try **Bacchus Taxi Service** (37 Tragerete Rd., Port-of-Spain, tel. 809/622–5588). All agencies require a large deposit, and you must make reservations well in advance of your arrival. Figure on paying about $30–$45 per day.

In Tobago you will be better off renting a car or Jeep than relying on taxi service, which is less frequent and ultimately much more expensive. Try **Sweet Jeeps** (Sandy Point, tel. 809/639–8533) or **Tobago Travel** (Box 163, Tobago, tel. 809/639–8778). You can also rent **motor scooters** from **Banana Rentals** (c/o Kariwak Village, Crown Point, tel. 809/639–8441). Rentals average $25–$35 a day.

As befits one of the world's largest exporters of asphalt, Trinidad's roads are fairly well paved. In the outback, however, they are often narrow, twisting, and prone to washouts in the rainy season. Inquire about conditions before you take off, particularly if you're heading toward the north coast. Never drive into downtown Port-of-Spain during afternoon rush hour. Don't forget to drive on the left.

Telephones and Mail The area code throughout the two islands is 809. For telegraph, telefax, teletype, and telex, contact **Textel** (1 Edward St., Port-of-Spain, tel. 809/625–4431). Cables can be sent from the Tourism office and major hotels.

To place an intraisland call, dial the local seven-digit number. To reach the United States by phone, dial 1, the appropriate area code, and the local number.

Postage for first-class letters to the United States is TT$2.25; postcards, TT$2.00.

Opening and Closing Times Most shops open weekdays 8–6:30 and Saturday 8–noon. Banking hours are Monday–Thursday 9–2 and Friday 9–1 and 3–5.

Carnival

Trinidad always seems to be either anticipating, celebrating, or recovering from a festival, the biggest of which is **Carnival.** Carnival occurs each year between February and early March. Trinidad's version of the pre-Lenten bacchanal is reputedly the oldest in the Western Hemisphere; there are festivities all over the country, but the most lavish is in Port-of-Spain.

Carnival officially lasts only two days (from *J'ouvert* [sunrise] on Monday to midnight the following day). If you're planning to go, it's a good idea to arrive in Trinidad a week or two early to enjoy the events leading up to Carnival. Not as overwhelming as its rival in Rio or as debauched as Mardi Gras in New Orleans, Trinidad's fest has the warmth and character of a massive family reunion.

Carnival is about extravagant costumes: Individuals prance around in imaginative outfits. Colorfully attired troupes—called *mas*—that sometimes number in the thousands march to the beat set by the steel bands. You can visit the various mas "camps" around the city where these elaborate costumes are put together—the addresses are listed in the newspapers—and perhaps join one that strikes your fancy. Fees run anywhere from $35 to $100; you get to keep the costume. Children can also parade in a Kiddie Carnival that takes place on Saturday morning a few days before the real thing.

Throwing a party is not the only purpose of Carnival; it's also a showcase for calypso performers. Calypso is music that mixes dance rhythms with social commentary, sung by characters with such evocative names as Shadow, the Mighty Sparrow, and Black Stalin. As Carnival approaches, many of these singers perform nightly in calypso tents, which are scattered around the city. You can also visit the pan yards of Port-of-Spain, where steel orchestras, such as the Renegades, Desperadoes, Catelli All-Stars, Invaders, and Phase II, rehearse their arrangements of calypso.

For several nights before Carnival, costume makers display their talents, and the steel bands and calypso singers perform in spirited competitions in the grandstands of the racetrack in Queen's Park, where the Calypso Monarch is crowned. At sunrise, or J'ouvert, the city starts filling up with metal-frame carts carrying steel bands, flatbed trucks hauling sound systems, and thousands of revelers who squeeze into the narrow streets. Finally, at the stroke of midnight on "Mas Tuesday," Port-of-Spain's exhausted merrymakers go to bed. The next day everybody settles back to business.

Exploring Trinidad

Numbers in the margin correspond to points of interest on the Trinidad map.

Port-of-Spain It is not really surprising that a sightseeing tour of **Port-of-**
❶ **Spain** begins at the port. (If you're planning to explore by foot, which will take two to four hours, start early in the day; by midafternoon Port-of-Spain can be hot.) Though it is no longer as frenetic as it was during the oil boom of the 1970s, **King's Wharf** entertains a steady parade of cruise and cargo ships, a reminder that the city started from this strategic harbor. Across Wrightson Road is **Independence Square,** which is not a square at all: It's a wide, dusty thoroughfare crammed with pedestrians, car traffic, taxi stands, and peddlers of everything from shoes to coconuts. Flanked by government buildings and the familiar twin towers of the Financial Complex (familiar because its facade also adorns one side of all TT dollar bills), the square is representative of this city's chaotic charm.

Near the east end of Wrightson Road stands the Roman Catholic **Cathedral of the Immaculate Conception,** built in 1832 under the aegis of an Anglican governor, Sir Ralph Woodford. Its treasures consist of a Florentine-marble altar, iron framework from England, and stained glass from Ireland.

Up Picton Road are **Fort Chacon** and **Fort Picton,** erected to ward off invaders by the Spanish and British regimes, respectively. The latter is a martello tower with a fine view of the gulf.

At the corner of Prince and Frederick streets, look across **Woodford Square** toward the magnificent **Red House,** a Renaissance-style building that takes up an entire city block. Trinidad's House of Parliament takes its name from a paint job done in anticipation of Queen Victoria's Diamond Jubilee in 1897. Woodford Square has served as the site of political meetings, speeches, public protests, and occasional violence. The original Red House, in fact, was burned to the ground in a 1903 riot. The present structure was built four years later. The chambers are open to the public.

The view of the south side of the square is framed by the Gothic spires of **Trinity,** the city's other cathedral, and by the impressive **public library** building. *Tel. 809/623–6142. Open weekdays 7–3.*

Continue north along Pembroke Street and note the odd mix of modern and colonial architecture, gingerbread and graceful estate houses, and stucco storefronts. Pembroke crosses Keate Street at **Memorial Park.** A short walk north leads to the greater green expanse of **Queen's Park,** more popularly called the **Savannah.**

Time Out Buy a cool coconut drink—called "iced nut"—from any of the vendors operating out of flatbed trucks along the Savannah. For about 50¢, he'll lop off a green coconut with a deft swing of

Trinidad

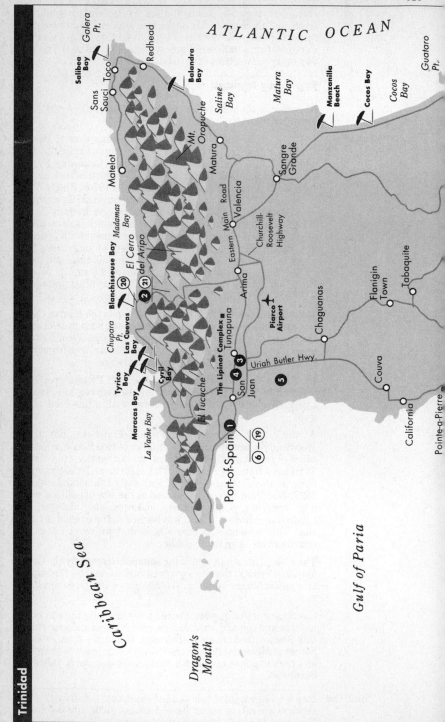

ATLANTIC OCEAN

Caribbean Sea

Galera Pt.

Salibea Bay

Sans Souci

Toco

Redhead

Balandra Bay

Saline Bay

Matura Bay

Manzanilla Beach

Cocos Bay

Guataro Pt.

Oropuche

Mt. Oropuche

Matura

Matelot

Sangre Grande

Madamas Bay

El Cerro del Aripo

Eastern Main Road

Valencia

Blanchisseuse Bay

Churchill Roosevelt Highway

Chupara Pt.

Las Cuevas Bay

Arima

Flanigin Town

Tabaquite

20

2 21

Tyrico Bay

Cyril Bay

El Tucuche

The Lipinot Complex

Tunapuna

Piarco Airport

Chaguanas

Maracas Bay

4 3

San Juan

Uriah Butler Hwy.

5

Couva

La Vache Bay

1

6 — 19

Port-of-Spain

Dragon's Mouth

Gulf of Paria

California

Pointe-à-Pierre

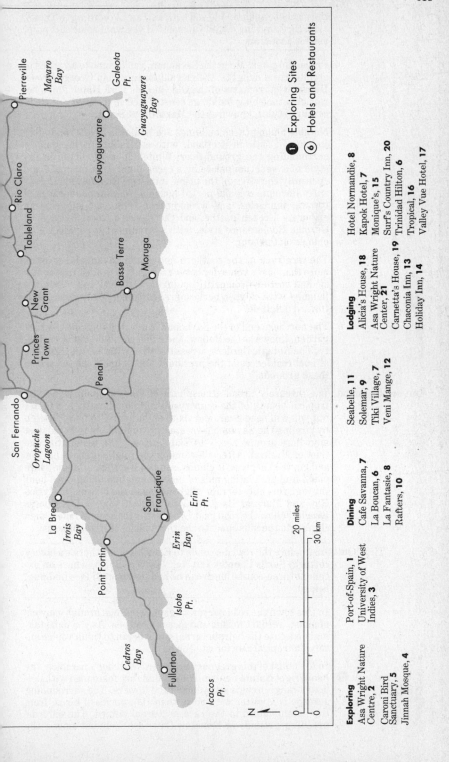

Pierreville

Mayaro Bay

Galeota Pt.

Guayaguayare

Guayaguayare Bay

Rio Claro

Tableland

Basse Terre

Moruga

San Fernando

New Grant

Princes Town

Penal

Oropuche Lagoon

San Francique

Erin Pt.

La Brea

Irois Bay

Erin Bay

Point Fortin

Islote Pt.

Cedros Bay

Fullarton

Icacos Pt.

N

0   20 miles

0   30 km

● Exploring Sites

⑥ Hotels and Restaurants

Exploring
Asa Wright Nature Centre, **2**
Caroni Bird Sanctuary, **5**
Jinnah Mosque, **4**
Port-of-Spain, **1**
University of West Indies, **3**

Dining
Cafe Savanna, **7**
La Boucan, **6**
La Fantasie, **8**
Rafters, **10**
Seabelle, **11**
Solemar, **9**
Tiki Village, **7**
Veni Mange, **12**

Lodging
Alicia's House, **18**
Asa Wright Nature Center, **21**
Carnetta's House, **19**
Chaconia Inn, **13**
Holiday Inn, **14**
Hotel Normandie, **8**
Kapok Hotel, **7**
Monique's, **15**
Surf's Country Inn, **20**
Trinidad Hilton, **6**
Tropical, **16**
Valley Vue Hotel, **17**

the machete and provide you with a straw. According to Trinis, "It'll cure anyt'ing dat ail ya, mon." If you want some soft pulp, ask for a medium.

Proceeding west along the Savannah, you'll come to a garden of architectural delights: the elegant lantern-roof **George Brown House;** what remains of the **Old Queen's Park Hotel;** and a series of astonishing buildings constructed in a variety of 19th-century styles, known as the **Magnificent Seven.**

Notable among these buildings are **Killarney,** patterned after Balmoral Castle in Scotland, with an Italian-marble gallery surrounding the ground floor; **Whitehall,** constructed in the style of a Venetian palace by a cacao-plantation magnate and currently the office of the prime minister; **Roomor,** a flamboyantly Baroque colonial-period house with a preponderance of towers, pinnacles, and wrought-iron trim that suggests an elaborate French pastry; and the **Queen's Royal College,** in German Renaissance style, with a prominent tower clock that chimes on the hour.

The **racetrack** at the southern end of the Savannah serves as more than just a venue for horse racing. It is the setting for music and costume competitions during Carnival and, when not jammed with calypso performers, costumes, or horses, tends toward quietude.

The northern end of the Savannah is devoted to plants. A rock garden, known as the **Hollow,** and a fish pond add to the rusticity. The **Botanic Gardens,** across the street, date from 1820. The official residences of the president and prime minister are on these grounds.

Out on the Island   The intensely urban atmosphere of Port-of-Spain belies the tropical beauty of the countryside surrounding it. It's there, but you will need a car, and six to eight hours, to find it. Begin by circling the Savannah—seemingly obligatory to get almost anywhere around here—to Saddle Road, the residential district of **Maraval.** After a few miles the road begins to narrow and curve sharply as it climbs into the Northern Range. Here you'll find undulating hills of lush, junglelike foliage. An hour through this hilly terrain will lead you to the beaches at **Tyrico Bay** and **Maracas Bay;** a few miles past that is **Las Cuevas Beach.** Follow the road past Las Cuevas for several miles, then climb into the hills again to the tiny village of **Blanchisseuse.**

Time Out   Just before the road descends to Blanchisseuse there's a homey cottage, **Surf's Country Inn** (tel. 809/669–2475), where an excellent three-course lunch can be had for about $7 (*see* Lodging, *below*).

In this town the road narrows again, winding through canyons of moist, verdant foliage and mossy grottoes. As you painstakingly execute the hairpin turns, you'll begin to think you've entered a tropical rain forest. You have.

In the midst of this greenery lies a bird-watcher's paradise, the ❷ **Asa Wright Nature Centre.** The grounds are festooned with delicate orange orchids and yellow tube flowers. The surrounding acreage is atwitter with more than 100 species of birds, from the hummingbird to the rare nocturnal oilbird. The oilbirds' breeding grounds in Dunston Cave are included among the sights along the center's guided hiking trails. If you're not feeling too energetic, lounge on the veranda of the handsome estate house, which offers a panorama of the Arima Valley. You can also make reservations for lunch (call one day in advance). *Tel. 809/667–4655. Admission: $6 adults, $3 children. Open daily 9–5.*

The descent to **Arima,** about 7 miles, is equally pastoral. The Eastern Main Road connecting Arima to Port-of-Spain is anything but: It's a busy, bumpy, and densely populated corridor full of roadside stands and businesses. Along the way you'll pass the **University of West Indies** campus in Curepe and the majestic turrets and arches of the **Jinnah Mosque** in St. Joseph.

Proceed west from Arima along the Churchill-Roosevelt Highway, a limited-access freeway that runs parallel to the Eastern Main Road a few miles to the south. Both avenues cross the Uriah Butler Highway just outside Port-of-Spain in San Juan; a few miles south on Butler Highway, take the turnoff for the **Caroni Bird Sanctuary.** Across from the sanctuary's parking lot is a sleepy canal with several boats and guides for hire; the smaller boats are best.

The Caroni is a large swamp with mazelike waterways bordered by mangrove trees, some plumed with huge termite nests. In the middle of the sanctuary are several islets that are home to Trinidad's national bird, the scarlet ibis. Just before sunset the ibis arrive by the thousands, their richly colored feathers brilliant in the gathering dusk, and, as more flocks alight, they turn their little tufts of land into bright Christmas trees. It's not something you see every day. Bring a sweater and insect repellent for your return trip. The boat fee is usually about $6–$15. Advance reservations can be made with boat operators Winston Nanan (tel. 809/645–1305) or David Ramsahai (tel. 809/663–2207). Nanan also arranges highly recommended bird-watching tours to Guyana and Venezuela.

What to See and Do with Children

Emperor Valley Zoo and the **Botanical Gardens** are a cultivated expanse of parkland just north of the Savannah, the site of the president's official residence. A meticulous lattice of walkways and local flora, the parkland was first laid out in 1820 and is a model of what a tropical garden should be. In the midst of this serene wonderland is the zoo, leisurely apportioned on eight acres and largely featuring birds and animals of the region— from the brilliantly plumed scarlet ibis to slithering anacondas and pythons; wild parrots breed in the area and can be seen (and heard) in the surrounding foliage. The zoo draws a quarter of a million visitors a year and more than half of them are children, so admission is priced accordingly—a mere TT$1. *80 Independence Sq., Port-of-Spain, tel. 809/625–2264. Open daily 9:31–6.*

Junior Carnival (*see* Carnival, *above*)

Off the Beaten Track

The Lopinot Complex is a French settlement founded in the 19th century; there's a well-preserved estate house from a once-prosperous colonial coffee and cocoa plantation that displays various memorabilia of that era. (A guide is available from 10 to 6.) The surrounding grounds and gardens are a popular picnic spot, with a children's playground and a river to cool your feet. The area also abounds with practitioners of Parang, a beautiful string-based folk music featuring guitar, mandolin, violin, quatro (a small, ukelelelike instrument) and a chorus of vocal harmonies sung in Spanish. Parang tunes have become Trinidad's more or less official Christmas carols. To get there, take the Eastern Main Road from Port-of-Spain to Arouca and look for the sign that points north. The drive from there offers thrilling and hair-raising twists as it rises into the hills and decends into the lush Lopinot Valley—an adventure in itself.

Exploring Tobago

Numbers in the margin correspond to points of interest on the Tobago map.

A driving tour of Tobago, from Scarborough to Charlotteville and back, can be done in about four hours.

❶ **Scarborough** is nestled around **Rockley Bay,** and it gives the feeling that not much here has changed since the area was settled two centuries ago. This is its charm.

The road east from Scarborough soon narrows as it twists **❷** through **Mt. St. George,** a village that clings to a cliff high above the ocean. Fort King George is a lovely, tranquil spot commanding sweeping views of the bay, with a restored 18th-century English fort and barracks, a Fine Arts Centre, and lush landscaped gardens.

The sea dips in and out of view as you pass through a series of small settlements and the town of Roxborough. About an hour's **❸** drive will bring you to **King's Bay,** an attractive crescent-shape beach. Just before you reach the bay there is a bridge with an unmarked turnoff that leads to a gravel parking lot; beyond that, a landscaped path leads to a waterfall with a rocky pool where you can refresh yourself. You may meet enterprising locals who'll offer to guide you to the top of the falls, a climb that you may find not worth the effort.

After King's Bay the road rises dramatically; just before it dips **❹** again there's a marked lookout with a vista of **Speyside,** a small fishing village, and several offshore islands.

Time Out **Jemma's Sea View Kitchen** (tel. 809/660–4066), along the main road in Speyside, offers tasty West Indian meals served in a house on stilts by the ocean. You'll find nothing fancy here, just delicious Tobagonian home cooking, including a wondrous baked chicken, and great views.

Past Speyside the road cuts across a ridge of mountains that separates the Atlantic side of Tobago from the Caribbean. On **❺** the far side is **Charlotteville,** a remote fishing community, albeit the largest village on the island. Fishermen here announce the day's catch (usually flying fish, red fish, or bonito) by sounding their conch shells.

The paved road ends a few miles outside Charlotteville, in Camberton. Returning to Speyside, take a right at the sign for **❻** **Flagstaff Hill.** Follow a well-traveled dirt road for about 1½ miles to a radio tower. It's one of the highest points in Tobago, surrounded by ocean on three sides and with a view of the hills, Charlotteville, and Bird of Paradise Island in the bay.

Beaches

Trinidad Contrary to popular notion, Trinidad has far more beaches than Tobago; the catch is that Tobago's beaches are close to hotels, and Trinidad's are not. There are, however, some worthy sites within an hour's drive of Port-of-Spain, spread out along the north-coast road.

Maracas Bay is a long stretch of sand with a cove and a fishing village at one end. It's a local favorite, so it can get crowded on weekends. Parking sites are ample, and there's a snack bar and rest facilities. **Cyril Bay,** a pebble-and-sand cove reachable only by foot, is laced with small waterfalls and is an idyllic picnic spot. **Tyrico Bay** is a small beach lively with surfers who flock here to enjoy the excellent surfing. The strong undertow may be too much for some swimmers.

A few miles farther along the north-coast road is **Las Cuevas Bay,** a narrow, picturesque strip of sand named for the series of partially submerged and explorable caves that ring the beach. A food stand offers tasty snacks, and vendors hawk fresh fruit across the road. It's less crowded here, and seemingly serene, although, as at Maracas, the current can be treacherous. About 8 miles east, along the north-coast road, is another narrow beach. **Blanchisseuse Bay** is palm-fringed and the most deserted of the lot. Facilities are nonexistent, but the beach is ideal for a romantic picnic. You can haggle with local fishermen to take you out in their boats to explore the coast.

The drive to the northeast coast takes several hours. To get there you must take the detour road to Arima, but "goin' behind God's back," as the Trinis say, does reward the persistent traveler with gorgeous vistas and secluded beaches. **Balandra Bay,** sheltered by a rocky outcropping, is popular among bodysurfers. **Salibea Bay,** just past Galera Point, which juts toward Tobago, is a gentle beach with shallows and plenty of shade—perfect for swimming. Snack vendors abound in the vicinity. The road to **Manzanilla Beach** and **Cocos Bay** to the south, nicknamed the Cocal, is lined with stately palms whose fronds vault like the arches at Chartres. Manzanilla has picnic facilities and a postcard-pretty view of the Atlantic, though its water is occasionally muddied by the Orinoco River, which flows in from South America.

Tobago Traveling to Tobago without sampling the beaches is like touring Burgundy in France without drinking the wine. So, starting from the town of Plymouth and gravitating—slowly—counterclockwise, we'll explore a dozen of the island's more memorable sand spots.

Great Courland Bay, near Fort Bennett, is a long stretch of clear, tranquil water, bordered on one end by **Turtle Beach,** so named for the turtles that lay their eggs here at night between April and May. (You can watch; the turtles don't seem to mind.) A short distance west, there's a side road that runs along **Stone Haven Bay,** a gorgeous beach that's across the street from Grafton Beach Resorts, a luxury hotel complex.

Mt. Irvine Beach, across the street from the Mt. Irvine Beach Hotel, is an unremarkable setting that has the best surfing in

Tobago

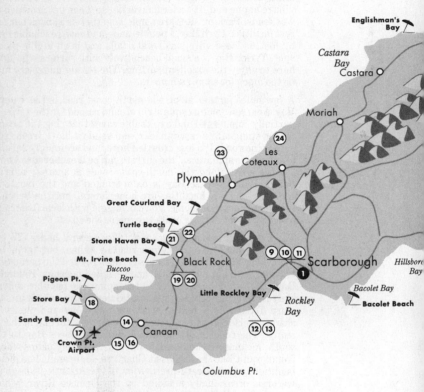

Caribbean Sea

Englishman's Bay

Castara Bay

Castara

Moriah

24

23 Les Coteaux

Plymouth

Great Courland Bay

Turtle Beach

Stone Haven Bay 21 22

Mt. Irvine Beach

Black Rock

9 10 11 Scarborough

Buccoo Bay

Hillsboro

Pigeon Pt.

19 20

1

Store Bay 18

Little Rockley Bay

Bacolet Bay

Sandy Beach

14 Canaan

Rockley Bay

Bacolet Beach

17 Crown Pt. Airport

15 16

12 13

Columbus Pt.

Exploring
Charlotteville, **5**
Flagstaff Hill, **6**
King's Bay, **3**
Mt. St. George, **2**
Scarborough, **1**
Speyside, **4**

Dining
Blue Crab, **9**
Cocrico Inn, **23**
Dillon's, **14**
The Old Donkey Cart
House, **10**
Papillon, **20**
Rouselles, **11**

Teaside, **13**
The Village, **15**

Lodging
Arnos Vale Hotel, **26**
Blue Waters Inn, **7**
Cocrico Inn, **23**
The Golden Thistle
Hotel, **16**
Grafton Beach
Resorts, **21**

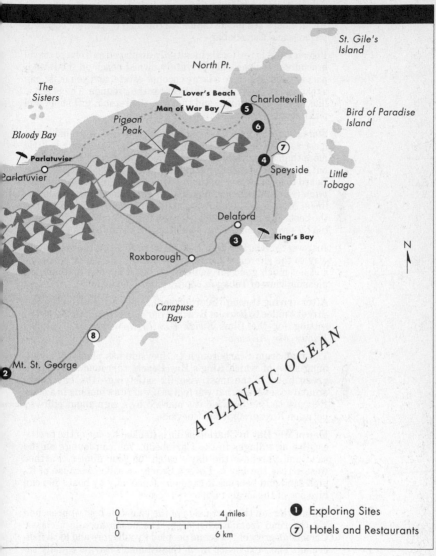

The Sisters

North Pt.

St. Gile's Island

Lover's Beach

Man of War Bay

Charlotteville

⑤

⑥

Bird of Paradise Island

Pigeon Peak

Bloody Bay

④

⑦

Speyside

Little Tobago

Parlatuvier

Parlatuvier

Delaford

King's Bay

③

N

Roxborough

Carapuse Bay

⑧

ATLANTIC OCEAN

Mt. St. George

②

0		4 miles
0	6 km	

❶ Exploring Sites

⑦ Hotels and Restaurants

July and August. It's also ideal for windsurfing in January and April. There are picnic tables surrounded by painted concrete pagodas and a snack bar.

Pigeon Point is the locale inevitably displayed on Tobago travel brochures. It's the only privately owned beach on the island, part of what was once a large coconut estate, and you must pay a token admission (about $2) to enter the grounds. The beach is lined with royal palms, and there's a food stand, gift shop, and paddleboats for rent. The waters are calm.

Store Bay, where boats depart for Buccoo Reef, is probably the most socially convivial setting in the area. The beach is little more than a small sandy cove between two rocky breakwaters, but, ah, the food stands here: six shacks licensed by the Tourist Board to local ladies, featuring *roti* (an East Indian sandwich), *pilau* (rice and peas), and messy but marvelous crab and dumplings. Miss Jean's (tel. 809/639–0563) is generally considered the best. Farther west along Crown Point, **Sandy Beach** is abutted by several hotels. You won't lack for amenities around here.

Just west of Scarborough, take Milford Road off the main highway to the shores of **Little Rockley Bay.** The beach is craggy and not much good for swimming, but it is quiet and offers a pleasing view of Tobago's capital across the water.

After driving through Scarborough, continue south on Bacolet Street 4 miles to **Bacolet Beach,** a dark-sand beach that was the setting for the films *Swiss Family Robinson* and *Heaven Knows, Mr. Allison.*

The road from Scarborough to Speyside has plenty of swimming sites of which **King's Bay Beach,** surrounded by steep green hills, is the most visually satisfying—the bay hooks around so severely that you feel as if you're swimming in a lake. It's easy to find because it's marked by a sign about halfway between Roxborough and Speyside.

Man of War Bay in Charlotteville is flanked by one of the prettiest fishing villages in the Caribbean. You can lounge on the sand and purchase the day's catch for your dinner. Farther west across the bay is **Lover's Beach,** so called because of its pink sand and because it can be reached only by boat. You can hire one of the locals to take you across.

Parlatuvier, on the north side of the island, is best approached via the road from Roxborough. The beach here is a classic Caribbean crescent, a scene peopled by villagers and local fishermen. The next beach over, **Englishman's Bay,** is equally seductive and completely deserted.

Sports and the Outdoors

Bird-watching   Bird-watchers can fill up their books with notes on the variety of species to be found in Trinidad at the **Asa Wright Nature Center,** the **Caroni Bird Sanctuary** *(see* Exploring Trinidad, *above),* and the **Pointe-à-Pierre Wild Fowl Trust,** which is located within the confines of a petrochemical complex (42 Sandown Rd., Pt. Cumana, tel. 809/637–5145). In Tobago, naturalist **David Rooks** offers walks inland and trips to offshore bird colonies (tel. 809/639–4276).

Deep-Sea Fishing   The islands off the northwest coast of Trinidad offer excellent waters for deep-sea fishing; the ocean here was a favorite angling spot of Franklin D. Roosevelt. Members of the **Trinidad and Tobago Yacht Club** (Bayshore, tel. 809/637–4260) may be willing to arrange a tour. Contact Riad Shakeer. The Tourism Office also recommends **Mr. Pouchet** (tel. 809/622–8974).

In Tobago, contact **Dillon Tours and Charters** (tel. 809/639–8765). Dillon is the most expensive, about $350 per day.

Golf There are nine golf courses in the country, the best of which are the **Mt. Irvine Golf Club** (tel. 809/639–8871) in Tobago and **Moka Golf Course** in Maraval (tel. 809/629–2314), just outside Port-of-Spain.

Horseback Riding Try **Palm Tree Village** (Tobago, tel. 809/639–4347) or **Park Stables** (Tobago, tel. 809/639–2154) for rides along the beach.

Scuba Diving Tobago draws scuba-diving aficionados from around the world. You can get information, supplies, and instruction at **Dive Tobago** (tel. 809/639–3695), **Sean Robinson** (tel. 809/639–1279), **Tobago Marine Sports Ltd.** (tel. 809/639–0291), **Tobago Scuba** (tel. 809/660–4327), and **Tobago Dive Experience** (Grafton Beach, tel. 809/639–0191; in Trinidad, tel. 809/639–1263). Also in Trinidad is **Scuba Shop Ltd.** (Mirabella, tel. 809/658–2183).

Snorkeling The best spots for snorkeling are on Tobago, of which **Buccoo Reef** is easily the most popular—perhaps too popular. Over the years the reef has been damaged by the ceaseless boat traffic and by the thoughtless visitors who take pieces of coral for souvenirs. Even so, it's still a trip worth experiencing, particularly if you have children. For $8 (tickets are available in almost any hotel), you board a Plexiglas-bottom boat at either Store Bay or Buccoo Beach; the 15-minute trip to the reef, 2 miles offshore, is made only at low tide. Operators provide rubber shoes, masks, and snorkels but not fins, which are helpful in the moderate current.

There is also good snorkeling by the beach near the **Arnos Vale Hotel** and at **Blue Waters,** and the government is slowly developing reefs around Speyside that rival if not surpass Buccoo.

Tennis The following hotels have tennis courts: **The Trinidad Hilton** (tel. 809/624–3211), **Arnos Vale** (tel. 809/639–2881), **Turtle Beach** (tel. 809/639–2851), **Mt. Irvine** (tel. 809/639–8817), **Blue Waters Inn** (tel. 809/660–4341); so do the **Trinidad Country Club** (tel. 809/622–3470) and **Tranquility Lawn Tennis Club** (Victoria Ave., Port of Spain, tel. 809/625–4182).

Shopping

Thanks in large part to Carnival costumery, there's no shortage of fabric shops on the islands. The best bargains for Oriental and East Indian silks and cottons can be found in downtown Port-of-Spain, on **Frederick Street** and around **Independence Square.** Other good buys are such duty-free items as Angostura Bitters and Old Oak or Vat 19 rum, all widely available throughout the country.

Good Buys Upscale boutiques at the **Hilton** and in the **Long Circular Mall**
Boutiques make for more relaxed browsing. Luxury items are available at **Y. de Lima,** with branches on High Street and at the West Mall, and at **Stecher's** at the Hilton Hotel—on Lady Young Street, in the Long Circular Mall, and in the Cruise Ship Complex (Number ID Wrightson Rd.), all in Port-of-Spain. There are no real bargains, though.

Local Crafts The Tourism Office can provide an extensive list of local artisans who specialize in everything from straw and cane work to miniature steel pans. **The Village** (Nook Ave. by the Hotel Normandie) has several shops that specialize in indigenous fashions. Around the corner is **Art Creators** (7 St. Ann's Rd., tel. 809/624–4369), a top-notch gallery. On Tobago, **The Hangover Cafe and Art Gallery** (Pigeon Point Gate, tel. 809/639–7940) sells watercolors, handicrafts, and T-shirts. **The Cotton House** (Bacolet and Windward Rds., tel. 809/639–3695) is a good bet for jewelry and imaginative batik work. Paula Young runs her shop like an art school. You can visit the upstairs studio; if it's not too busy, you can even try batiking at no charge.

Records For the best selection of calypso and soca music, check out **Rhyner's Record Shop** (54 Prince St., 809/623–5673, and at the Cruise Ship Complex, tel. 809/627–8717) or **Metronome** (83 Western Main Rd., tel. 809/622–4157), both in Port-of-Spain.

Dining

Trinidad Port-of-Spain doesn't lack for variety when it comes to eateries, highlighting imaginative hybrids of European, Oriental, East Indian, and Caribbean influences. In addition to the establishments listed below, there is also no shortage of East Indian and Chinese restaurants and pizzerias (but don't expect New York–style pizza).

Trinidadians are particularly fond of *callaloo*, a soup or stew of dasheen leaves (similar to spinach) and okra, flavored with anything from pork to coconut, pureed and served at every restaurant on the island. It's hard to believe anything this green and swampy-looking can taste so delicious. Other items in a Trinidadian menu worth sampling are *coocoo*, a dumpling of cornmeal and coconut (similar to polenta); *roti*, a sandwich of East Indian origin, on flat bread or in a pocket pita, usually filled with curried chicken and potatoes; *pilau*, a rice-and-peas dish inspired by Chinese cuisine; tamarind ball, a dessert made from the sweet-sour tamarind; and peanut shake, a peanut butter–flavored milk shake that really does taste better than it sounds.

No Trinidadian dining experience can be complete, of course, without a rum punch with fresh fruit and the legendary Angostura Bitters, made by the same company that produces the excellent Old Oak rum. Carib beer and Stag are recommended for washing down the spicier concoctions. Dark-beer aficionados can try Royal Extra Stout (R.E.), which is even sweeter than Guinness.

Tobago With few exceptions, the restaurants in Tobago are located in hotels and guest houses; several of the large resort complexes also feature some form of nightly entertainment. The food isn't as eclectic as on Trinidad, generally favoring local styles, but in terms of quality and service Tobagonian "home cooking" more than holds its own.

Highly recommended restaurants are indicated by a star ★.

Category	Cost*
Expensive	over $25
Moderate	$15–$25
Inexpensive	under $15

per person, excluding drinks, service, and sales tax (15%)

Trinidad **Cafe Savanna.** Caribbean style, with bare wood walls and Sade
★ on the sound system, this cozy den consistently serves the best
fare on the island. The menu specializes in Trinidadian dishes
with a distinctive flair, such as Bacchannal Woman—fillets of
red snapper dipped in cinnamon and baked. The callaloo soup
here sets the standard for other island delicacies. A 3-course
lunch menu gives you choices for TT$40. *Kapok Hotel, 16–18
Cotton Hill, Port-of-Spain, tel. 809/622–6441. Closed Sunday.
AE, DC, MC, V. Expensive.*
La Boucan. Geoffrey Holder's large mural of a social idyll in the
Savannah dominates one wall of the room. The restaurant
strives for elegance: silver service, uniformed waiters, candle-
light, pink tablecloths, and the soft tinkling of a grand piano.
The chef is less inventive than in the past, and meals here tend
toward good-but-not-really-gourmet, suggesting an Angli-
cized French restaurant. *Trinidad Hilton, Lady Young Rd.,
Port-of-Spain, tel. 809/624–3211. Reservations recommended.
Jacket recommended. AE, DC, MC, V. Expensive.*
La Fantasie. In this restaurant a pastel dining room with high
ceilings seeks to mix postmodern design with a sense of fun.
The menu calls itself Cuisine Créole Nouvelle and tends toward
Trinidadian dishes of fresh fish and poultry, seasoned and presented in the French manner. Customers are invited to name
dishes. The selections change often; if you happen to dine here
on a night when fresh homemade ice cream is offered, you're in
luck. *Hotel Normandie, 10 Nook Ave., St. Ann's, Port-of-
Spain, tel. 809/624–1181. AE, DC, MC, V. Expensive.*
Solemar. Joe Brown, the former chef from the Trinidad Hilton,
has won a strong following for dinner with his sophisticated
menu. Using local fresh fish and imported meats, Brown has
put a French twist on many of his dishes. The setting resembles
a greenhouse; potted plants of all varieties flow over the sides
of shelves, and trellises support orchids. *6 Nook Ave., St.
Ann's, Port-of-Spain, tel. 809/624–1459. AE, DC, MC, V.
Moderate–Expensive.*
Rafters. Behind a stone facade with green rafters is a pub that
has become an urban institution. Once it was a rum shop; currently under the proprietorship of Paul Mowser, it's a bar and a
restaurant. The pub is the center of activity, especially Friday
night. In late afternoons the place begins to swell with Port-of-
Spainers ordering from the tasty selection of burgers and barbecue and generally loosening up. *6A Warner St., Port-of-
Spain, tel. 809/628–9258. AE, DC, MC, V. Moderate.*
Seabelle. This restaurant is hard to find—there's no sign or
street number. The entrance looks like the door to a private
home—which is part of its charm. The ambience is beatnik—
with 1950s jazz on the stereo, a pool in the back, and a darkened
bar where time almost stands still. The accent is on seafood.
There are only seven tables, so you must call for reservations—
and directions. *27 Mucurapo Rd., St. James, Port-of-Spain,
tel. 809/622–3594. No credit cards. Moderate.*
Tiki Village. Cosmopolitan Port-of-Spainers are as passionate

about their Oriental food as New Yorkers and San Franciscans are. Everyone touts their favorite, but this eatery, a serious version of Trader Vic's, is the most reliable: What it lacks in kitsch, it compensates for in fine Oriental food. *Kapok Hotel, 16–18 Cotton Hill, Port-of-Spain, tel. 809/622–6441. AE, D, DC, MC, V. Moderate.*

★ **Veni Mange.** The best lunches in town are served inside this small stucco house. Credit Allyson Hennessy, a Cordon Bleu-trained cook who has become a celebrity of sorts because of a TV talk show she hosts, and her sister-partner Rosemary Hezekiah. The cuisine here is Creole. The restaurant has become so popular that they have decided to stay open for dinner. The Wednesday evening buffet is a good way to sample the regional cuisine. *13 Lucknow St., St. James, Port-of-Spain, no phone. No credit cards. No dinner. Moderate.*

Tobago **Blue Crab.** Perched on a wide porch above a busy corner of
★ downtown Scarborough, this is the spot for lunch. Best bets here are the fish chowder or flying fish with callaloo and vegetables, prepared with élan by cook Ken Sardinha. His wife, Alison, is one of Tobago's most gracious hostesses. Dinner is officially served only on Wednesday and Friday nights, but the proprietors will open the restaurant for a supper upon the request of even one couple. *Corner of Main and Fort Sts., Scarborough, tel. 809/639–2737. AE, MC, V. Moderate.*

Cocrico Inn. A café with a bar against one wall, the Cocrico offers delectable home cooking. The three rotating chefs frequently use fresh fruits and vegetables grown in the neighborhood. They zealously guard their recipes, including a marvelous coocoo and lightly breaded, subtly spiced grouper. There is nothing fancy here, just warm and delicious food. *Corner of North and Commissioner Sts., Plymouth, tel. 809/639–2661. AE, V. Moderate.*

Dillon's. This cozy recent arrival, with checked tablecloths and local artwork adorning the walls, offers friendly service, imaginatively prepared seafood, and delicate garlic bread. *Airport Rd. near Crown Point, tel. 809/639–8765. AE, MC, V. Moderate.*

The Old Donkey Cart House. The name is something of a curiosity, since this attractive restaurant is set in and around a green-and-white colonial house, about a 2-mile drive south of Scarborough. There's outdoor dining in a garden with twinkling lights. The cuisine is standard Caribbean, nothing special, but German side dishes and an extensive selection of Rhine and Moselle wines set it apart. *Bacolet St., Scarborough, tel. 809/639–3551. AE, V. Moderate.*

Papillon. Named after one of the proprietor's favorite books, this seafood restaurant is a homey room with an adjoining patio. What was once reckoned to be Tobago's most adventurous menu now offers more conventional, well-prepared Caribbean fare with a few fanciful touches. *Buccoo Bay Rd., Mt. Irvine, tel. 809/639–0275. AE, DC, MC, V. Moderate.*

★ **Rouselles.** A charming setting, attentive service, and a rotating menu make this one a winner. Featured are pork chops in ginger, calypso chicken, grouper in a true tangy Creole sauce, and beet or christophine pie. The $15 tasting menu is an amazing bargain—altogether a popular place for liming. *Old Windward Rd., Bacolet, tel. 809/639–4738. Lunch only by reservation. AE, MC, V. Moderate.*

★ **The Village.** Steel-band music plays gently in the background at this romantic candlelit spot. Under a thatched roof, waitresses clad in colorful island prints recite the prix-fixe, four-course menu. Changing daily, it may include christophine soup, green fig salad, and shrimp with two sauces (sweet and sour, and Creole). Co-owner Cynthia Clovis creates sophisticated variations on Caribbean cuisine; everything she prepares is fresh and bursting with flavor. *Kariwak Village, Crown Point, tel. 809/639-8442. AE, DC, MC, V. Moderate.*

Teaside. This peaceful teahouse is an oasis of civility, the ideal place to watch the sun disappear behind Trinidad on the horizon. The pastel structure looks Japanese, but the service is *terribly* British. Pizzas, tasty cakes, and more than 25 selections of tea are offered. *Lambeau Rd., tel. 809/639-4306. No credit cards. Inexpensive.*

Lodging

On Trinidad most lodging establishments are within the vicinity of Port-of-Spain, far from any beach. On Tobago, it's the opposite; every establishment listed here, with one exception, is either on or within walking distance of the ocean. Carnival week is one of two times in the year (the other is Christmas) that you should book reservations far in advance; expect to pay twice the price charged during the rest of the year.

Most places do offer breakfast and dinner for an additional flat rate (MAP), but on the whole these offer less variety than you'll get if you strike out for meals on your own. If you're lodging on the east side of Tobago, however, MAP is almost essential because of the dearth of restaurants.

Highly recommended lodgings are indicated by a star ★.

Category	Cost*
Very Expensive	over $175
Expensive	$100–$175
Moderate	$60–$100
Inexpensive	under $60

*All prices are for a standard double room for two, excluding 15% tax and a 10% service charge.

Trinidad
★
Trinidad Hilton. Perched above Port-of-Spain, the Hilton radiates the feeling of comfort and competence. Each room either has a balcony, which opens to a fine view of Savannah Park, the city, and the sea beyond, or overlooks the equally inviting Olympic-size pool, shaded by trees harboring brightly crested cornbirds. This is Port-of-Spain's most stylish hotel, with prices to match. It frequently bustles with conventioneers, which may be its only drawback. The good news is that it's usually available for last-minute Carnival bookings. The rooms are comfortably uniform and those on the Executive Floors have good working desks and a small sitting area. The rooms have no clocks, but if you're on "island time," perhaps it won't matter. *Lady Young Rd., Box 442, Port-of-Spain, tel. 809/624-3211, fax 624-4485. 394 rooms. Facilities: 2 restaurants, bar, conference rooms, satellite TV, pool, health club, tennis courts, drugstore, gift shops, car rental, taxi service. AE, DC, MC, V. EP. Expensive–Very Expensive.*

Holiday Inn. This hotel is at the port and close to Independence Square, which affords lodgers a pastel view of the old town and of ships idling in the Gulf of Paria. There's not a whole lot to do within walking distance, and traffic during rush hour is not a pretty sight (although during Carnival, you're in the middle of all the festivities). The rooms are due for a refurbishing, but hair dryers have been added, making this the only hotel in Trinidad to have them. The hotel's rooftop restaurant, **La Ronde,** is a revolving bistro that offers a striking panorama of the city at night. This is a more moderate alternative to the swankier but similar Hilton. *Wrightson Rd., Box 1017, Port-of-Spain, tel. 809/625–3361, fax 809/625–4166. 235 rooms. Facilities: satellite TV, pool, health spa, conference rooms, beauty salon, taxi service. AE, DC, MC, V. BP. Expensive.*

Hotel Normandie. Built in the 1930s by French Creoles on the ruins of an old coconut plantation, the Normandie has touches of Spanish, English colonial, and even postmodern architecture, giving the place an agreeably artsy patina that offsets the drab lighting and slightly tatty decor. The standard rooms are fairly dark and uninspired, with the exception of the 13 loft rooms furnished in natural wood. The loft rooms also have the advantage of an upstairs room that serves as a lounge or extra sleeping area and large bathrooms. Fittingly, it has become the linchpin of a complex in St. Ann's that includes a gallery, a café, and an array of shops. *10 Nook Ave., St. Ann's Village, Port-of-Spain, tel. and fax 809/624–1181. 61 rooms. Facilities: restaurant and bar, pool, meeting rooms, gallery, café, shops, car rental, taxi service. AE, DC, MC, V. EP. Moderate–Expensive.*

★ **Kapok Hotel.** Although now part of the Golden Tulip hotel chain, this hotel has been run by the Chan family for years and all but gleams with cheerful efficiency. It's a great location, just off the north end of the park, near the zoo and Presidential Palace, and away from the worst traffic. Its two distinctive restaurants, Cafe Savanna, for local seafood and grills, and Tiki Village, for Chinese and Polynesian specialties, are among the best in town. The rooms are comfortably furnished in a wicker motif and command a pleasing view on the park side. The Kapok is a good bargain for your buck. *16–18 Cotton Hill, Port-of-Spain, tel. 809/622–6441, fax 809/622–9677. 71 rooms. Facilities: TV, pool, 2 restaurants, taxi service. AE, DC, MC, V. EP. Moderate–Expensive.*

Valley Vue Hotel. This modern, fairly charmless hotel, sandwiched in a narrow valley 15 minutes from downtown Port of Spain, caters primarily to the business traveler. The rooms have contemporary furnishings and balconies that face the steep mountainside. The hotel recently completed a restaurant and adjoining nightclub with a glass dome that has you literally dancing under the stars. Besides business people, the hotel attracts a fair number of families from Trinidad and elsewhere, who come for the hotel's water-slide park, the largest in the West Indies. *Ariapita Rd., St. Ann's, Port-of-Spain, tel. 809/624–0940, fax 809/627–8046. 68 rooms and suites. Facilities: pool, 2 squash courts, lighted tennis court, gym, sauna, water slides, satellite TV, restaurant, nightclub, boutique, gift shop, beauty parlor. AE, MC, V. CP. Moderate–Expensive.*

Asa Wright Nature Center. Set in a lush rain forest about 90 minutes east of Port-of-Spain, this handsome lodge, constructed in 1908 by a tycoon for his young bride, attracts international legions of bird-watchers and nature photographers. There are impressive views of the verdant Arima Valley and the Northern Range from the veranda, where tea is served each afternoon. The rooms are uncomplicated and comfortably furnished; some of the beds have hand-carved frames cut from trees from the surrounding forest, which is now protected by a private trust. Three meals a day and an evening rum punch are included in the rates. Reservations at least six months in advance are recommended. (For more information about the center, *see* Exploring, *above.*) *Bag 10, Port-of-Spain; write Caligo Ventures, Box 21, Armonk, NY 10504, tel. 914/273–6333 or 800/426–7781. 23 rooms. No credit cards. MAP. Moderate.*

Chaconia Inn. This upscale motel has a cheerful decor, a good restaurant, and great entertainment on weekends (soca queen Denyse). All rooms have TV, phone, and private bath. *106 Saddle Rd., Maraval, Port-of-Spain, tel. 809/628–8603, fax 809/ 628–3214. 35 rooms and apartments. Facilities: pool, restaurant, nightclub. AE, DC, MC, V. EP. Moderate.*

Alicia's House. This private home, only a 10-minute walk from the Savannah, was converted into a 15-room inn but retained its family atmosphere. The Govias named the house after their daughter, who lives in Texas, and treat their guests like long lost cousins. The rooms range from spacious with four beds (convenient for a family) to closet size with a single bed, but each has air-conditioning and a private shower or bath. The pool is large enough for a quick dip while relaxing on the patio. A lounge area has a TV and piano for guests to play. Lunch and dinners are available on request; the food is home-style cooking served family style, and the pervading culinary odor through the public rooms is curry. *7 Coblentz Gardens, St. Ann's, Port-of-Spain, tel. 809/623–2802, fax 809/622–8560. 15 rooms. Facilities: breakfast room, pool, Jacuzzi. MC, V. EP, CP, MAP. Inexpensive–Moderate.*

★ **Monique's.** This homey lodging is a nest of congeniality only minutes from downtown. Mike and Monique Charbonne have been running their home as a guest house for 10 years. Of the 11 rooms, one is specifically designed for the disabled. All rooms have private baths. Their philosophy is to make their house your own, and it's not unusual for hosts and lodgers to be found fraternizing in the living room. Meals are available on request, and Mike will occasionally organize a picnic to the couple's 100-acre plantation near Blanchisseuse. *114 Saddle Rd., Maraval, Port-of-Spain, tel. 809/628–3334, fax 809/622–3232. 11 rooms. Facilities: common-room area with TV. AE. EP, CP, MAP. Inexpensive–Moderate.*

Carnetta's House. When Winston Borell retired as director of tourism for Trinidad and Tobago, he and his wife, Carnetta, opened up their suburban two-story house to guests. One guest room is on the upper floor of the two-story house and on the same level as the lounge and terrace dining room. The other four are on the ground floor, with the choice room, Le Flamboyant, opening on to the garden's patio. All rooms have a private bathroom with shower, telephones, radio and TV. And, although there is air-conditioning, cool breezes usually do the trick. Unfortunately, at night time, the doors need to be shuttered for security reasons. Winston is a keen gardener, and his garden has a sampling of plants that are a fascinating introduction to tropical flowers and herbs. Carnetta uses the herbs in her cooking, and she can prepare some of the best dinners that you may find in Port of Spain. Equally important is the fund of information that both Carnetta and Winston can offer on what to see and do in Trinidad and the necessary arrangements they can make to do it. *28 Scotland Terrace, Andalusia, Maraval, Port of Spain, tel. 809/628–2732, fax 809/628–7717. 5 rooms. Facilities: lounge, dining room, laundry facilities, car-rental arrangements, airport transfers. AE, DC, MC, V. EP, BP, MAP. Inexpensive.*

Surf's Country Inn. Six new guest rooms have been added in buildings adjoining this popular fish restaurant. On a hillside overlooking the sea, these new accommodations will offer the traveler the chance to stay comfortably on the north coast instead of returning to Port of Spain after a day of swimming, surfing, and exploring the mountains of the interior. *Blanchisseuse, tel. 809/669–2475. 6 rooms. Facilities: restaurant, bar. No credit cards. EP, BP. Inexpensive.*

Tropical. Here you'll find bare but cozy rooms in wild "tropical" colors, all with air-conditioning and phone. The friendly service and fine restaurant make this a good budget bet. *6 Rookery Nook, Maraval, Port-of-Spain, tel. 809/622–5815, fax 809/622–4249. 16 rooms. Facilities: pool, restaurant. AE. EP. Inexpensive.*

Bed-and-Breakfasts The number of private homes in Trinidad and Tobago offering bed-and-breakfast accommodations is growing each year. This is an excellent, inexpensive option and a wonderful way to meet the friendly locals. Contact the **Trinidad and Tobago Bed and Breakfast Association** (Box 3231, Diego Martin, or Park Lane Court, Amethyst Dr., El Dorado, Tunapuna, tel. 809/663–5265). All members conform to the association's rigorous standards.

Tobago **Arnos Vale Hotel.** The most romantic spot on Tobago, this hotel
★ is an attractive hideaway that crosses Tobago horticulture with Mediterranean design. White stucco cottages are set on a hill that descends through a series of winding paths to a secluded beach, pool, and handy bar. Suite 20 down on the beach is a favorite, though others may prefer the more isolated suites on top of the hill. Standard rooms, at the base of the hill, face the pool and are near the beach. The elegant hilltop restaurant, with iron lattice tables, a chandelier, and a hand-painted piano, leads to a crescent-shape patio that offers a sweeping view of the sea. One drawback: Most, if not all, the rooms are often fully taken with tour groups. *Arnos Vale, Box 208, Scarborough, tel. 809/639–2881. 32 rooms. Facilities: pool, bar, restaurant, tennis, beach, snorkeling dive shop, disco, gift shop. AE, DC, MC, V. EP. Very Expensive.*

★ **Grafton Beach Resorts.** This new luxury complex overlooks one of the finest—formerly secluded—beaches on the island. Most rooms have king-size or double beds, a minibar, quiet air-conditioning, a ceiling fan, and a private balcony facing the beach. For a casual meal, the Neptune, perched over the pool, serves seafood. The main restaurant looks out to sea and offers an elaborate menu and theme-buffet dinners. On the beach, there is a rustic bar for drinks and snacks during the day. *Black Rock, Tobago. tel. 809/639–0191, fax 809/639–0030. 108 rooms. Facilities: beach, pool and beach bar, 2 restaurants, beauty shop, night lounge, satellite TV, shopping arcade, 2 squash courts, gym with sauna. AE, DC, MC, V. EP, MAP. Very Expensive.*

Mt. Irvine Bay Hotel. Prices are the highest on the island at this

two-story complex on the site of a 17th-century sugar plantation overlooking a magnificent pool, a cabana bar, and the quiet
waters of the Caribbean. The rooms in the main building are
reasonably large, with king-size or double beds, a private balcony, and a satellite TV. On the hill leading to the beach are the
newer and better-maintained cottage suites, although they are
double the price of the standard rooms. The sea is a five-minute
walk down the small hill, where a rather shabby beach bar offers basic refreshments. The old mill has been deftly converted
into a restaurant, with open-air dining on the surrounding patio and similar views. Adjacent is Mt. Irvine golf course, considered among the finest in the world. There is also a highly
regarded gourmet French restaurant in the old clubhouse. *Mt.
Irvine Bay, Box 222, Tobago, tel. 809/639–8871. 64 rooms, 23
cottages. Facilities: pool, 2 bars, 2 restaurants (1 formal), tennis courts, convention facilities, beach across the street, beauty
parlor, shops, taxi service, sauna, health spa, golf. AE, DC,
MC, V. EP. Very Expensive.*

Turtle Beach Hotel. The ranch-style lobby of this sprawling hotel leads to a lengthy bar, which in turn empties onto a wide
beach peppered with thatch umbrellas. The rooms have easy
access to the beach, which may be their greatest charm at the
inflated price. The restaurant boasts a reputable Creole buffet
on Sundays and lively entertainment. There are two bars (one
on the beach) and a tiny pool that is a good place from which to
watch the sunset. It's very popular with British and German
tour groups. *Great Courland Bay, tel. 809/639–2851; write Box
201, Scarborough, Tobago, fax 809/639–1495. U.S. reservations 305/225–1740. 125 rooms. Facilities: restaurant, 2 bars,
beach, pool, 2 tennis courts, water-sports center, bike rentals,
gift shop. AE, DC, MC, V. EP, MAP. Expensive–Very Expensive.*

Palm Tree Village. This is a graceful complex of fully equipped
villas—all with air-conditioning, satellite TV, minisafe, phone,
and kitchen—clustered around a small hotel, with another 20
rooms at half the price of the cottages. The drawbacks are unattractive grounds and a rough, skimpy beach. It's very popular with families. *Box 327, Little Rockley Bay, Scarborough,
tel. 809/639–4367, fax 809/639–4180. 18 villas, 20 rooms. Facilities: beach, pool, restaurant, bar, disco, piano room, conference center, tennis court, horseback riding, water sports. AE,
DC, MC, V. EP, MAP. Expensive.*

★ **Blue Waters Inn.** It's easy to miss the sign for this gem of a hotel, nestled on the shore of Batteaux Bay, 24 miles from the airport and cooled by the northeast trade winds. The entrance
road appears to drop over a cliff. It's all part of the charm of this
rustic retreat, where birds fly through a dining room orna-
mented with driftwood. A variety of beamed rooms and cabins
include new apartments with kitchenettes. The beach here is
free of currents; nature walks are popular along the 48 acres of
grounds. Anyone craving peace and quiet will welcome the
news that the place doesn't have a pool, or air-conditioning in
most of the rooms and only a satellite TV in the lounge. Instead, enjoy the sincere hospitality of the owner, Mrs.
McClean. *Batteaux Bay, Speyside, Tobago, tel. 809/660–4341,
fax 809/639–4180. 29 rooms. Facilities: tennis, beach, dive instruction, gift shop, restaurant, bar. AE, DC, MC, V. EP,
MAP. Moderate–Expensive.*

Cocrico Inn. Named after the national bird of Tobago, this inn
is set on a quiet side street in the village of Plymouth, a 10-min-

ute walk from the beach. Nick and Bev Sanford, a delightful Connecticut couple who left it all to pursue their retirement dream, have created this inn, built around a courtyard and a small pool, giving it the appearance of a motel. The rooms are sizable but rather drab, with stained carpets and little by way of furnishings. Still, it's a reasonably priced option with a family atmosphere. *North and Commissioner Sts., Box 287, Plymouth, Tobago, tel. 809/639–2961, fax 809/639–6565. 16 rooms. Facilities: restaurant, bar, pool, gift shop. AE, MC, V. EP, MAP. Moderate.*

★ **Kariwak Village.** The resort's motif recaptures the spirit of the Carib and Arawak Indians, without diminishing the creature comforts. There's a suitably tropical bar, highly praised Caribbean cooking, and open-air dining. The gift shop features a thoughtful selection of local crafts and books; there are often shows on the premises by Tobago artists. Nine cabanas, which resemble equatorial igloos, have been divided into 18 cozy apartments, all of which look onto the pool. (The beach is a five-minute walk away.) The owners, Cynthia and Allan Clovis, create a warm and congenial atmosphere with an emphasis on personal attention. *Crown Point, tel. 809/639–8442; fax 809/639–8441, Scarborough, Tobago; write Box 27. 18 rooms. Facilities: shuttle service to beach, pool, restaurant, bar, scooter rentals. AE, DC, MC, V. EP, MAP. Moderate.*

Richmond Great House. This is a restored late 18th-century plantation house with high-beamed ceilings on a 1,500-acre citrus estate. The common rooms have a great view, but what holds your gaze are the African sculptures and furniture collected by the professor who owns the place. You can also stop by for lunch; just call in the morning. Visitors can choose either one of the two rooms in the main house or one of the four guest cottages. *Belle Garden, Tobago, tel. 809/660–4467. 6 rooms. Facilities: 10-minute drive to beach, dining room, pool, TV, and music. MC, V. MAP. Moderate.*

★ **Sandy Point Beach Club.** If you can't do without the comforts of home but want an unbeatable price, this is the place. Spacious, modern, charmingly furnished villas have all the amenities, including satellite TV. *Crown Point, Tobago, tel. 809/639–8533 or 800/223–6510, fax 809/639–8495. 36 rooms, 6 apartments. Facilities: 2 pools, restaurant, 2 bars, car rentals, dive shop, boutique, laundry. DC, MC, V. EP. Moderate.*

Tropikist. This amiable, gleaming-white little beach hotel spread out across Store Bay attracts a fun, youngish crowd who appreciate a bargain. *Store Bay, tel. 809/639–8512, fax 809/638–1110. 30 rooms. Facilities: beach, pool, restaurant, bar, disco, volleyball. AE, DC, MC, V. EP. Inexpensive.*

The Golden Thistle Hotel. The look here is that of a respectable 1950s motel. All rooms include kitchenettes, making this spot particularly attractive to travelers on a budget. *Store Bay Rd., Crown Point, Tobago, tel. and fax 809/639–8521. 36 rooms. Facilities: pool, bar, TV room, restaurant, kitchenette. DC, V. EP. Inexpensive.*

The Arts and Nightlife

Trinidad Trinidadian culture doesn't end with music, but it definitely begins with it. While both calypso and steel bands are best displayed during Carnival, the steel bands play at clubs, dances, and fetes throughout the year. There's no lack of nightlife in Port-of-Spain. Music that's popular right now is "sweet parang," a mixture of Spanish patois and calypso sung to tunes played on a string instrument much like a mandolin.

Mas Camp Pub (corner of Ariapata and French Sts., Woodbrook, tel. 809/627–8449) is Port-of-Spain's most comfortable and dependable night spot. There are tables, a bar, an ample stage in one room, and an open-air patio with more tables and a bar with a TV. There's a kitchen if you're hungry, and **Hush,** which makes delicious fruit-flavored ice cream, is right next door. **Cricket Wicket** (149 Tragarete Rd., tel. 809/622–1808), a popular watering hole with a cupola-shape bar in the center, is a fine place to hear top bands, dance, or just sit and enjoy the nocturnal scenery. Currently the favorite hangout is **Swanky's** (69 Western Main Rd., tel. 809/622–0569), which you'll easily recognize by the large number of people gathered outside drinking beer on the sidewalk.

In the late afternoons the locals come to **Rafters** (6A Warner St., tel. 809/628–9258) to wind down and wind up. Later in the evening, it's mainly tourists and resembles a college frat party.

There are several excellent theaters in Port-of-Spain. Consult local newspapers for listings.

Tobago   Nightlife on Tobago is generally confined to hotel-sponsored entertainment, which runs the gamut from steel-band performances to limbo dancers. Turtle Beach produces the most extravagant—and touristy—spectacles Wednesday and Sunday. In addition, **Kariwak Village** (tel. 809/639–8442) features a mélange of calypso and jazz. La Tropicale at the **Della Mira Guest House** (tel. 809/639–3531) in Scarborough features dancing on weekends and occasional live performances, usually during Carnival season. The **Foundation for the Arts** occasionally sponsors authentic calypso concerts, usually at Signal Hill High School. For information contact the Tourist Office at 809/639–2125.

Locals head for the discos—John Grant near Store Bay and the rambunctious Christie's in Scarborough—the Tobagan equivalent of a singles bar. The Starting Gate, an unlikely but ingratiating cross between an English pub and a community social hall, rocks with a DJ on weekends. The **Drifter** is another popular hangout.

Sunday nights at Buccoo, there is an informal hop, affectionately dubbed Sunday School, that takes place in the village at Henderson's disco. It's great fun. "Blockos" (spontaneous block parties) spring up all over the island; look for the hand-painted signs. Tobago also has Harvest parties on Sundays, when a particular village opens its doors to visitors for hospitality. These occur throughout the year and are a great way to meet the locals.

2 Turks and Caicos Islands

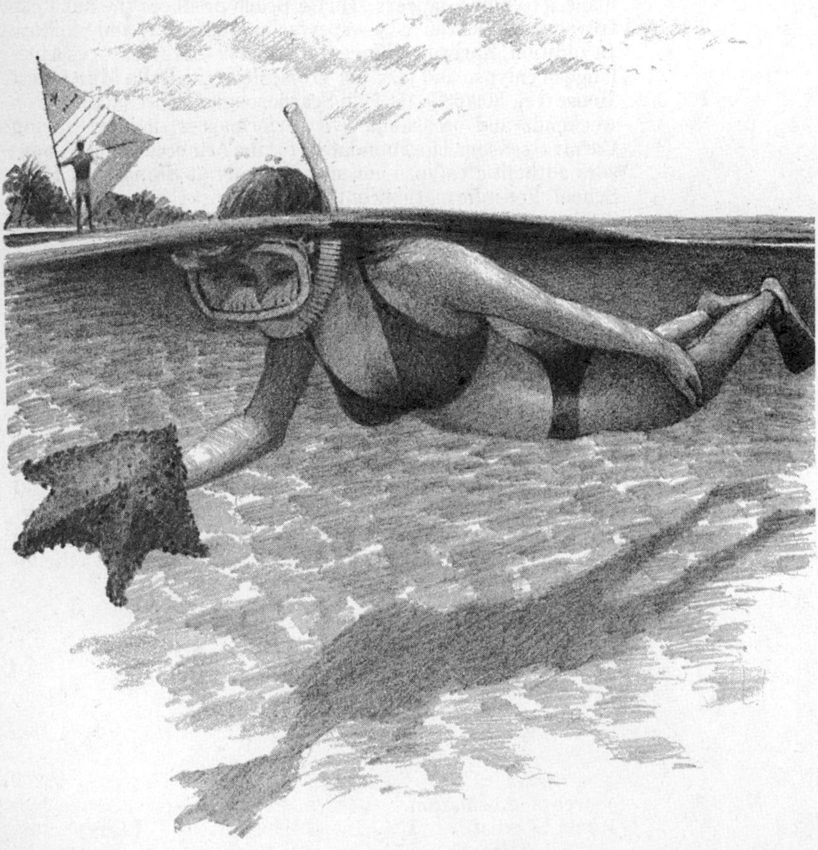

Updated by
Laurie Senz

The Turks and Caicos Islands are relatively unknown except to collectors of beautiful beaches and scuba divers, who religiously return to these waters year after year. The islands have officially adopted the designation "Beautiful by Nature" to reflect their tranquility and natural wonders.

It is claimed that Columbus's first landfall was on Grand Turk. First settled by the English more than 200 years ago, the British Crown Colony of Turks and Caicos is renowned in two respects: Its booming banking and insurance institutions lure investors from the United States and elsewhere; and its offshore reef formation entices divers to a world of colorful marine life surrounding its 40 islands, only eight of which are inhabited.

The Turks and Caicos are two groups of islands in an archipelago lying 575 miles southeast of Miami and about 90 miles north of Haiti. Some 15,000 people live on the eight large islands and more than 40 small cays that have a total landmass of 193 square miles. The Turks Islands include Grand Turk, which is the capital and seat of government, and Salt Cay, with a population of about 200. According to local legend, these islands were named by early settlers who thought the scarlet blossoms on the local cactus resembled the Turkish fez.

Some 22 miles west of Grand Turk, across the 7,000-foot-deep Christopher Columbus Passage, is the Caicos group, which includes South, East, West, Middle, and North Caicos and Providenciales. South Caicos, Middle Caicos, North Caicos, and Providenciales (nicknamed Provo) are the only inhabited islands in this group; Pine Cay, Parrot Cay and Salt Cay are the only inhabited cays. "Caicos" is derived from *cayos*, the Spanish word for cay, and is believed to mean "string of islands."

In the years following Ponce de León's landing in 1515, a band of pirates also established communities in the archipelago. Around 1678, Bermudians, lured by the wealth of salt in these islands, began raking salt from the flats and returning to Bermuda to sell their crop. Despite French and Spanish attacks and pirate raids, the Bermudians persisted and established a trade that became the bedrock of the Bermudian economy. In 1766, Andrew Symmers settled here to hold the islands for England. Later, Loyalists from Georgia obtained land grants in the Caicos Islands, imported slaves, and continued the lifestyle of the pre–Civil War American South.

With an eye toward tourism dollars to create jobs and increase the standard of living, the government has devised a long-term development plan to improve the Turks' and Caicos' visibility in the Caribbean tourism market. Providenciales, in particular, is slated not only for tourism development, but also for the development of banking, registration of business companies, and offshore insurance.

Before You Go

Tourist Contact the **Turks and Caicos Islands Tourist Board** (tel. 800/
Information 241–0824). **The Caribbean Tourist Organization** (20 E. 46th St.,
New York, NY 10017, tel. 212/682–0435) is another reliable
source of information. In the United Kingdom, contact **Morris-
Kevan International Ltd.** (International House, 47 Chase Side,
Enfiled Middlesex EN2 6NB, tel. 081/367–5175). For hotel in-

Turks and Caicos Islands

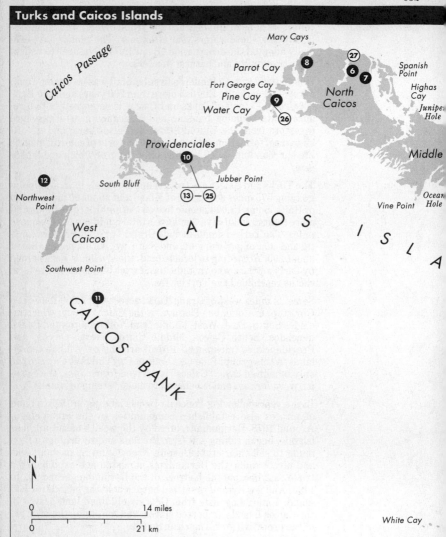

Mary Cays

Caicos Passage

Parrot Cay

Fort George Cay
Pine Cay
Water Cay

Providenciales

South Bluff

Northwest
Point

West
Caicos

Southwest Point

CAICOS BANK

N

Jubber Point

Spanish
Point

North
Caicos

Highas
Cay

Junipe
Hole

Middle

Vine Point

Ocean
Hole

CAICOS   ISLA

0   14 miles
0   21 km

White Cay

Exploring
Balfour Town, **2**
Cockburn Harbour, **3**
Cockburn Town, **1**
Conch Bar Caves, **5**
East Caicos, **4**

Flamingo Pond, **6**
Kew, **7**
Molasses Reef, **11**
Northwest Reef, **12**
Pine Cay, **9**
Providenciales, **10**
Sandy Point, **8**

Dining
Alfred's Place, **13**
Dora's, **14**
Hey, José, **16**
Hong Kong
Restaurant, **17**
Regal Begal, **32**

Salt Raker Inn, **30**
Sandpiper, **31**
Sharney's Restaurant
and Bar, **15**
Top O' The Cove
Gourmet
Delicatessen, **18**
Yum Yum's, **19**

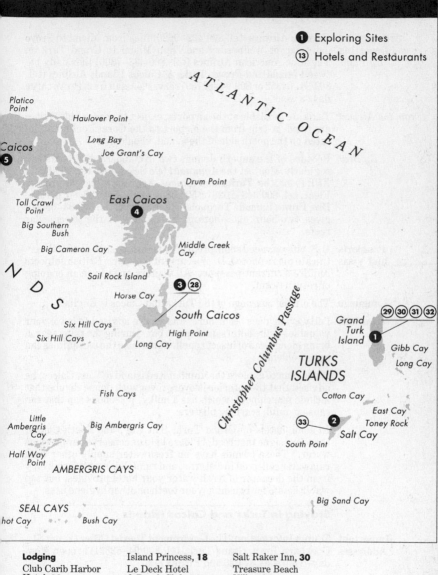

ATLANTIC OCEAN

Platico
Point

Haulover Point

Long Bay
Joe Grant's Cay

Caicos
5

Drum Point

Toll Crawl
Point

East Caicos
4

Big Southern
Bush

Big Cameron Cay

Middle Creek
Cay

N D S

Sail Rock Island

Horse Cay

3 **28**

South Caicos

Six Hill Cays

Six Hill Cays

High Point

Long Cay

Christopher Columbus Passage

Grand
Turk
Island **1**

29 **30** **31** **32**

Gibb Cay

Long Cay

**TURKS
ISLANDS**

Fish Cays

Cotton Cay

East Cay

Little
Ambergris
Cay

Big Ambergris Cay

Toney Rock

33 **2**
Salt Cay

Half Way
Point

South Point

AMBERGRIS CAYS

SEAL CAYS

Big Sand Cay

hot Cay   Bush Cay

● Exploring Sites
⑬ Hotels and Restaurants

Lodging

Club Carib Harbor
Hotel, **28**

Club Med Turkoise, **22**

Coral Reef Resort, **29**

Erebus Inn, **15**

Grace Bay Club, **23**

Hotel Kittina, **31**

Island Princess, **18**

Le Deck Hotel
& Beach Club, **20**

The Meridian Club, **26**

Prospect of Whitby
Hotel, **27**

Ramada Turquoise Reef
Resort & Casino, **21**

Salt Raker Inn, **30**

Treasure Beach
Villas, **24**

Turtle Cove Inn, **25**

Windmill's Plantation, **33**

formation, contact **The Turks & Caicos Resort Association** (tel. 800/2TC–ISLES).

Arriving and Departing By Plane **Cayman Airways** (tel. 800/422–9626) flies from Miami to Provo daily except Wednesday and from Miami to Grand Turk on Tuesday. **American Airlines** (tel. 800/433–7300) flies daily between Miami and Provo. **Turks & Caicos Islands Airlines** (tel. 809/94–64352 or 809/94–62709) serves Nassau from Provo three days a week.

From the Airport Taxis are available at the airports; expect to share a ride. Rates are fixed. A trip from the airport to the Coral Reef hotel, located on the north side of the island, should be $15.

By Boat Because of the superb diving, two live-aboard dive boats call regularly. Contact the ***Aquanaut*** (c/o See & Sea, tel. 800/DIV–XPRT) or the ***Turks and Caicos Aggressor*** (c/o Aggressor Fleet, tel. 800/348–2628 or 504/385–2416). For $20 per person, **Dive Provo** (Ramada Turquoise Reef Resort, tel. 809/94–65040) gives two-hour glass-bottom boat tours of the spectacular reefs.

Passports and Visas U.S. citizens need some proof of citizenship, such as a birth certificate plus a photo I.D. or a current passport. British subjects require a current passport. All visitors must have an ongoing or return ticket.

Language The official language of the Turks and Caicos is English.

Precautions Petty crime does occur here, and you're advised to leave your valuables in the hotel safe-deposit box. During the rainy season bring along a can of insect repellent because the mosquitoes can be a problem.

If you plan to explore the uninhabited island of West Caicos, be advised that the interior is overgrown with dense shrubs that include manchineel, which has a milky, poisonous sap that can cause painful, scarring blisters.

In some hotels on Grand Turk, Salt Cay, and South Caicos, there are signs that read, "Please help us conserve our precious water." These islands have no freshwater supply other than rainwater collected in cisterns, and rainfall is scant. Drink only from the decanter of fresh water your hotel provides, but tap water is safe for brushing your teeth or other hygiene uses.

Staying in Turks and Caicos Islands

Important Addresses **Tourist Information:** The **Government Tourist Office** (Front St., Cockburn Town, Grand Turk, tel. 809/94–62321) is open Monday–Thursday 8–4:30 and Friday 8–5.

Emergencies **Police:** Grand Turk, tel. 809/94–62299; Providenciales, tel. 809/94–64259; South Caicos, tel. 809/94–63299. **Hospitals:** There is a 24-hour emergency room at **Grand Turk Hospital** (Hospital Rd., tel. 809/94–62333) and the **Providenciales Health-Medical Center** (Leeward Hwy. and Airport Rd., tel. 809/94–64910). **Pharmacies:** Prescriptions can be filled at the **Government Clinic** (Grand Turk Hospital, tel. 809/94–62040) and in Provo, at the **Providenciales Health-Medical Center** (Leeward Hwy. and Airport Rd., tel. 809/94–64910).

Currency The unit of currency is U.S. dollars.

Taxes and Hotels collect a 7% government tax. The departure tax is $15.
Service Charges Hotels add a 10%–15% service charge to your bill. In restaurants, a tip of 10%–15% is appropriate and sometimes already added to your bill. Taxi drivers expect a token tip.

Guided Tours A taxi tour of any one of the islands costs $25 an hour. On Provo, contact **Nell's Taxi** (tel. 809/94–65585, 809/94–64595 or 809/94–64393). The drivers are friendly and know everything and everybody. **Executive Tours** (tel. 809/94–64524 or 809/94–67310 from North Caicos) offers a guided tour in an air-conditioned bus for $10 per person, for a minimum of eight people and a maximum of 22. **Turtle Tours** (tel. 809/94–65585) offers a variety of bus and small-plane tours. A bus tour takes in all of Provo, including the conch farm, and stops for drinks at Hey Jose. You can also fly to Middle Caicos, the largest of the islands, for a visit to its mysterious caves or to North Caicos to see the ruins of a former slave plantation. If you want to island-hop on your own schedule, air charters are available through **Turks & Caicos Islands Airlines** (tel. 809/94–64352 or 809/94–62709), **Blue Hills Aviation** (tel. 809/94–64388), and **Flamingo Air Services** (tel. 809/94–62109).

Getting Around Taxis are unmetered, and rates, posted in the taxis, are regu-
Taxis lated by the government.

Ferries **Caicos Express** (tel. 809/94–67111 or 809/94–67258) offers two scheduled interisland ferries between Provo, Pine Cay, Middle Caicos, Parrot Cay, and North Caicos daily except Sunday. Tickets cost $15 each way.

Rental Cars Local rental agencies on Provo are **Budget** (tel. 809/94–64079) and **Provo Rent-A-Car** (tel. 809/94–64404); on Grand Turk, **Dutchie's Car Rental** (tel. 809/94–62244). Rates average $33 to $64 per day. To rent cars on South Caicos, check with your hotel manager for rates and information.

Scooters You can scoot around Provo by contacting **Holiday Scooter Rentals** (tel. 809/94–64422), **The Honda Shop** (tel. 809/94–65555, ext. 81), or **Scooter** (tel. 809/94–64684). Rates generally start at $25 per day.

Telephones You can call the islands direct from the United States by dialing
and Mail 809 and the number. Calling home from Turks and Caicos, dial direct from most hotels, from some pay phones, and from **Cable and Wireless,** which has offices in Provo (tel. 809/94–64499) and Grand Turk (tel. 809/94–62200) that are open Monday–Thursday 8–4:30 and Friday 8–4. You must dial 0, followed by the country code (1 for U.S. and Canada; 44 for U.K.), area code, and local number.

Postal rates for letters to the United States, Bahamas, and Caribbean are 50¢ per half ounce; postcards, 35¢. Letters to the United Kingdom and Europe, 65¢ per half ounce; postcards, 45¢. Letters to Canada, Puerto Rico, and South America, 65¢; postcards, 45¢.

Opening and Most offices are open weekdays from 8 or 8:30 till 4 or 4:30.
Closing Times Banks are open Monday–Thursday 8:30–2:30, Friday 8:30–12:30 and 2:30–4:30.

Exploring Turks and Caicos Islands

Numbers in the margin correspond to points of interest on the Turks and Caicos Islands map.

Grand Turk Horses and cattle wander around as if they owned the place,
and the occasional donkey cart clatters by, carrying a load of
water or freight. Front Street, the main drag, lazes along the
❶ western side of the island and eases through **Cockburn Town,**
the colony's capital and seat of government. Buildings in the
capital reflect the 19th-century Bermudian style of architecture, and the narrow streets are lined with low stone walls and
old street lamps, now powered by electricity.

The **Turks & Caicos National Museum** opened last year in the
restored Guinep House. One of the oldest native stone buildings in the islands, the museum now houses the Molasses Reef
wreck of 1513, the earliest shipwreck discovered in the
Americas, and natural history exhibits that include artifacts
left by African, North American, Bermudian, French, Hispanic, and Taino settlers. *Tel. 809/94–62160. Admission: $5. Open
weekdays 10–4, Sat. 10–1.*

Time Out The **Pepper Pot** (tel. 809/94–62389) is a little blue shack at the
end of Front Street, where Peanuts Butterfield is famous for
conch fritters.

Fewer than 4,000 people live on this 7½-square-mile island.
Diving is definitely the big deal here. Grand Turk's Wall, with a
sheer drop to 7,000 feet, is well known to divers.

Salt Cay This tiny 2½-square-mile dot in the water is home to about 200
people. The island boasts the new Windmills Plantation hotel, a
❷ few stores in **Balfour Town,** and splendid beaches on the north
coast. Old windmills, salt sheds, and salt ponds are silent re-
minders of the days when the island was a leading producer of
salt.

South Caicos **Cockburn Harbour,** the best natural harbor in the Caicos chain,
❸ is home to the South Caicos Regatta, held each year in May.
This 8½-square-mile island was once an important salt producer; today it's the heart of the fishing industry. Spiny lobster
and Queen Conch may be found in the shallow Caicos bank to
the west and are harvested for export by local processing
plants. Bonefishing here is some of the best in the West Indies.

At the northern end of the island there are fine, white-sand
beaches; the south coast is great for scuba diving along the
drop-off; and the windward (east) side is excellent for snorkeling, where large stands of elkhorn and staghorn coral shelter a
variety of small tropical fish.

East Caicos Uninhabited and accessible only by boat, **East Caicos** has on its
❹ north coast a magnificent 17-mile beach. It was once a cattle
range and the site of a major sisal-growing industry.

Middle Caicos The largest (48 square miles) and least-developed of the inhabited Turks and Caicos Islands, Middle Caicos is home to lime-
❺ stone **Conch Bar Caves,** with their eerie underground salt lakes
and milky-white stalactites and stalagmites. Archaeologists
have discovered Arawak and Lucayan Indian artifacts in the
caves and the surrounding area. Since telephones are a rare
commodity here, the boats that dock here and the planes that
land on the little airstrip provide the island's 270 residents with
their main connection to the outside world. **Executive Tours** can
fly you over and take you through the mysterious caves (*see*
Guided Tours, *above*).

North Caicos The **Prospect of Whitby Hotel** is on the north end of this 41-
6 square-mile island. To the south of Whitby is **Flamingo Pond,** a
nesting place for the beautiful pink birds. If you take a taxi tour
of the island, you'll see the ruins of the old plantations and, in
7 8 the little settlements of **Kew** and **Sandy Point,** a profusion of
tropical trees bearing limes, papayas, and custard apples. The
beaches here are superb for shelling and lolling, and the waters
offshore offer excellent snorkeling, scuba diving, and fishing.

Pine Cay One of a chain of small cays connecting North Caicos and Provo,
9 800-acre **Pine Cay** is privately owned and under development as
a planned community. It's home to the exclusive **Meridian Club**
resort, playground of jet-setters, and its 2½-mile beach is the
most beautiful in the archipelago. The island has a 3,800-foot
airstrip and electric carts for getting around.

Providenciales In the mid-18th century, so the story goes, a French ship was
wrecked near here and the survivors were washed ashore on an
island they gratefully christened La Providentielle. Under the
10 Spanish, the name was changed to **Providenciales.**

Provo's 44 square miles are by far the most developed in the
Turks and Caicos. With its rolling ridges and 12-mile beach, the
island is a prime target for developers. More than 17 years ago a
group of U.S. investors, including the DuPonts, Ludingtons,
and Roosevelts, opened up this island for visitors and those
seeking homesites in the Caribbean. In 1990 the island's first
luxury resort, the **Ramada Turquoise Reef Resort & Casino,** o-
pened, and with it, the island's first gourmet Italian restaurant. The luxurious **Ocean Club,** a condominium resort at Grace
Bay, was also completed in 1990. A new Sheraton is now being
built. Provo is also the home of Club Mediteranée's showpiece,
Club Med Turkoise, which was built in 1984.

Downtown Provo, near Providenciales International Airport, is
a cluster of stone and stucco buildings that house car-rental
agencies, law offices, boutiques, banks, and other businesses.

Time Out Stop in at **Fast Eddie's** (Airport Rd., tel. 809/94–64075), a casual eatery, for a relaxing drink and a platter of seafood.

Provo is home to the **Island Sea Center** (on the northeast coast
tel. 809/94–65330), where tourists can learn about the sea and
its inhabitants. Here you'll find the **Caicos Conch Farm,** (tel.
809/94–65849), a major mariculture operation where the mol-
lusks are farmed commercially. You can tour the farm's facilities and geodesic dome, watch a video show, and take photos at
the "hands-on" tank. Established by the PRIDE Foundation
(Protection of Reefs and Islands from Degradation and Exploi-
tation) and now funded by Into the Blue, the **JoJo Dolphin Project,** named after a 7-foot male bottle-nose dolphin who cruises
these waters and enjoys playing with local divers, is also here.
You can watch a video on JoJo and learn how to interact with
him safely if you see him on one of your dives.

About 8,000 people live on Provo, a considerable number of
whom are expatriate U.S. and Canadian businesspeople and
retirees.

West Caicos Over the past few centuries numerous wrecks have occurred in
the area between West Caicos and Provo, and author Peter
Benchley is among the treasure-seekers who have been lured to
11 this island. **Molasses Reef** is rumored to be the last resting site

of the *Pinta*, which is thought to have been wrecked here in the early 1500s.

12 Accessible only by boat, this island is uninhabited and untamed, and there are no facilities whatsoever. A glorious white beach stretches for a mile along the northwest point, and offshore diving is among the most exotic in the islands. A wall inhabited by every kind of large marine life begins a quarter-mile offshore, and the **Northwest Reef** offers great stands of elkhorn coral and acres of staghorn brambles. But this area is only for experienced divers. The wall starts deep, the currents are strong—and there are sharks in the waters.

If you do tour West Caicos, take along several vats of insect repellent. It won't help much with the sharks, but it should fend off the mosquitoes and sand flies. Be advised, too, that the interior is overgrown with dense shrubs, including manchineel.

Beaches

There are more than 230 miles of beaches in the Turks and Caicos Islands, ranging from secluded coves to miles-long stretches. Most beaches are soft coralline sand. Tiny uninhabited cays offer complete isolation for nude sunbathing and skinny-dipping. Many are accessible only by boat.

Big Ambergris Cay, an uninhabited cay about 14 miles beyond the Fish Cays, has a magnificent beach at **Long Bay.**

East Caicos, an uninhabited island accessible only by boat, boasts a magnificent 17-mile beach along its north coast.

Governor's Beach, a long white strip on the west coast of **Grand Turk,** is one of the nicest beaches on this island.

The north and east coasts of **North Caicos** are bordered by great beaches for swimming, scuba diving, snorkeling, and fishing.

Pine Cay, a private upscale retreat, has a 2½-mile strip of beach—the most beautiful in the archipelago.

A fine white-sand beach stretches 12 miles along the northeast coast of **Providenciales.** Other splendid beaches are at **Sapodilla Bay** and rounding the tip of the northwest point of the island.

There are superb beaches on the north coast of **Salt Cay,** as well as at **Big Sand Cay** 7 miles to the south.

Only in South Caicos are the beaches small and unremarkable, but the vibrant reef makes it a popular destination for divers.

Sports and the Outdoors

Bicycling Provo has a few steep grades to conquer, but very little traffic. Bikes can be rented at **Island Princess Hotel** at The Bight (tel. 809/94–64260) for $8 per day. **Ramada Turquoise Reef Resort & Casino** (tel. 809/94–65555), in Grace Bay, lends bikes to guests. In Grand Turk on Duke Street, **Salt Raker Inn** (tel. 809/94–62260) rents bikes to guests for $10 per day, $40 per week; **Hotel Kittina** (tel. 809/94–62232) also rents bikes to the public.

Boat Rentals You can rent a boat with private pilot for a half or full day of sportsfishing through **Black Diamond Tours** (Provo, tel. 809/94–64451) for $300 per day or **Porpoise** (Salt Cay tel. 809/94–

66927). **Dive Provo** (Ramada Turquoise Reef Resort, Provo, tel. 809/94–65040) rents small sailboats for $20 per hour and provides beginning instruction for $40 for up to two hours. Sailing not your bent? Try open-cockpit ocean kayaking, available at Dive Provo for $10 per hour for one and $15 per hour for two.

Fishing **Black Diamond Tours** (Provo, tel. 809/94–64451) will take a maximum of three people out for half- or full-day bone or bottom fishing expeditions, bait and tackle included, for $150 per half day. The same outfit will arrange half- or full-day deep-sea fishing trips in search of shark, marlin, kingfish, sawfish, wahoo, and tuna, with all equipment furnished. Deep-sea, bonefishing, and bottom fishing are also available aboard the *Sakitumi* (tel. 809/94–64203).

Golf This arid archipelago introduced a 6,529-yard golf course on Providenciales in November. **Provo Golf Club** (tel. 809/94–695991) is an 18-hole par 72 championship course, designed by Karl Litten, that is sustained by a desalination plant producing 250,000 gallons of water a day. The turf is sprinkled in green islands over 12 acres of natural limestone outcroppings, creating a desert-style design of narrow "target areas" and sandy waste areas—a formidable challenge to anyone playing from the championship tees. Fees are $65 plus $15 for a mandatory electric cart.

Horseback Riding Horses roam lazily around the main roads on Grand Turk. There is no organized riding program; however, rates can be negotiated with individual owners.

Parasailing A 15-minute flight is available for $45 at **Dive Provo** (Ramada Turquoise Reef Resort, Provo, tel. 809/94–65040).

Scuba Diving Diving is the top attraction here. (All divers must carry and present a valid certificate card before they'll be allowed to dive.) These islands are surrounded by a reef system of more than 200 square miles—much of it unexplored. Grand Turk's famed wall drops more than 7,000 feet and is one side of a 22-mile-wide channel called the Christopher Columbus Passage. From January through March, an estimated 6,000 eastern Atlantic humpback whales swim through this passage en route to their winter breeding grounds. There are undersea cathedrals, coral gardens, and countless tunnels. Among the operations that provide instruction, equipment rentals, underwater video equipment, and trips are **Omega Divers** (Hotel Kittina, Grand Turk, tel. 809/94–62232 or 800/255–1966), **Blue Water Divers** (Salt Raker Inn, Grand Turk, tel. 809/94–62432), **Off the Wall Divers** (Grand Turk, tel. 809/94–62159 or 809/94–62517), **Barracuda Divers** (South Caicos, tel. 809/94–63360), **Dive Provo** (Ramada Turquoise Reef Resort, Provo, tel. 809/94–65040), **Flamingo Divers** (Provo, tel. 809/94–64193), **Provo Turtle Divers** (Provo, tel. 809/94–64232 or 800/328–5285), and **Porpoise Divers** (Salt Cay, tel. 809/94–66927).

Note: A modern hyperbaric/recompression chamber is located on Provo (tel. 809/94–64242) on the grounds of the Erebus Inn compound. Divers in need on Grand Turk are airlifted to Provo—a 30-minute flight.

Sea Excursions The *Island Diver* (tel. 809/94–64393), a 70-foot motor cruiser, does BBQ and snorkel cruises to uninhabited islands. Both the 37-foot catamaran *Beluga* (tel. 809/94–65040), $39 per half day) and the 56-foot trimaran *Tao* (tel. 809/94–64393) run sunset cruises, as well as sailing and snorkeling outings. A full-day outing on the Tao is $59 per person, including snorkel rental and lunch. The Provo Turtle Divers' 20-foot glass-bottom *Grouper Snooper* (Provo, tel. 809/94–64232) offers sightseeing and snorkeling excursions. *The Aggressor* (tel. 809/348–2628, fax 809/946–5390) offers luxury six-day dive cruises with full accommodations.

Snorkeling **Dive Provo** (Provo, tel. 809/94–65040), **Blue Water Divers** (tel. 809/94–62432), and **Provo Turtle Divers** (Provo, tel. 809/94–64232) all provide rentals for about $5 and trips for $20. **Omega Diving International** (tel. 809/94–62978 or 800/255–1966) offers equipment and transportation, as well as diving packages and instruction.

Tennis There are two lighted courts at **Turtle Cove Inn** (Provo, tel. 809/94–64203), eight courts (four lighted) at **Club Med Turkoise** (Provo, tel. 809/94–64491), one court at the **Meridian Club** (Pine Cay, tel. 800/225–4255), two courts at the **Erebus Inn** (Grand Turk, tel. 809/94–64240), and two courts at the **Ramada Turquoise Reef Resort** (Provo, tel. 809/94–65555).

Waterskiing Waterskiers will find the calm turquoise water ideal for long-distance runs. **Dive Provo** (Ramada Turquoise Reef Resort, Provo, tel. 809/94–65040) will take you at $35 for a 15-minute run.

Windsurfing Rental and instruction are available at **Prospect of Whitby Hotel** (North Caicos, tel. 800/346–67119) and **Dive Provo** (Ramada Turquoise Reef Resort, Provo, tel. 809/94–65040).

Spectator Sports Cricket is the most popular game in town. The season runs from July through August. Tennis, basketball, softball, and darts are also well cheered by locals. You're welcome to join in. Inquire at the Tourist Board (tel. 800/441–4419) for a list of events.

Shopping

Delicate baskets woven from the local top grasses are the only craft native to the Turks and Caicos, and they are sold at the airport. Crafts from other islands are available at Turtle Cove's shopping district.

Greensleeves (MarketPlace, Provo, tel. 809/94–64147) is the place to go for paintings by local artists, island-made rag rugs, baskets, jewelry, and sisal mats and bags.

Local Color (MarketPlace, and at Le Deck Hotel, Provo, tel. 809/94–65547) sells art and sculpture made by local artists as well as native basketry, hand-painted tropical clothing, tie-dyed pareos, and silk-screened T-shirts.

Tropical Fashions (Turtle Cove, Provo, tel. 809/94–64343) is where you'll find resortwear, sandals, Provo T-shirts, perfumes, and gold jewelry.

Dining

Like everything else on these islands, dining out is a very laid-back affair, which is not to say that it is cheap. Because of the high cost of importing all edibles, the cost of a meal is usually higher than that of a comparable meal in the United States, and all the menus are à la carte. A 7% government tax and a 10%–15% service charge are added to your check. Reservations are not required, and dress is casual.

Highly recommended restaurants are indicated by a star ★.

Category	Cost*
Expensive	over $25
Moderate	$15–$25
Inexpensive	under $15

per person, excluding drinks, service, and sales tax (7%)

Grand Turk   **Salt Raker Inn.** In this rustic, informal patio restaurant you may start with tomato and mozzarella salad or melon and ginger. Popular entrées include lobster in cream and sherry sauce, barbecued steak, and seafood curry. For dessert, try apple pie. The Sunday dinner and sing-along is a fun way to end the week. *Salt Raker Inn, tel. 809/94–62260. AE, D, MC, V. Moderate.*

Sandpiper. Candles flicker on the Sandpiper's terrace beside a flower-filled courtyard. The restaurant's blackboard specialties may include pork chops with applesauce, lobster, filet Mignon, or seafood platter. *Hotel Kittina, tel. 809/94–62232. AE, D, MC, V. Moderate.*

Regal Begal. This popular local eatery is the place to get native specialties, such as cracked conch, minced lobster, and fish-and-chips. The atmosphere is casual, the portions large, and the prices easy on your wallet. *Hospital Rd., tel. 809/94–62274. No credit cards. Inexpensive.*

Providenciales   **Alfred's Place.** Austrian owner Alfred Holzfeind caters to an
★   American palate on his extensive menu with everything from prime rib to chicken salad. The alfresco lounge is a popular watering hole for locals and tourists alike. *Turtle Cove, tel. 809/94–64679. AE, D, MC, V. Closed Mon. July–Oct. Moderate–Expensive.*

Sharney's Restaurant and Bar. The new local owner has revamped this well-known restaurant at the Erebus Inn and the menu now reflects the English roots of this crown colony. Starters include hearty leek and potato soup or smoked trout with creamy horseradish sauce, while entrées include fresh seafood and English favorites prepared to order. Located on a hilltop, the bar is one of the best places from which to watch the sun slip into the sea. A band provides music on Thursday and Friday nights. *Erebus Inn, tel. 809/94–64120. AE, D, MC, V. Moderate–Expensive.*

Hong Kong Restaurant. A no-frills place with plain wood tables and chairs, the Hong Kong offers dine in, delivery, or take out, and a menu that ranges from lobster with ginger and green onions, chicken with black-bean sauce, sliced duck with salted mustard greens, to sweet-and-sour chicken. *Leeward Hwy., tel. 809/94–65678. AE, MC, V. Inexpensive–Moderate.*

Dora's. Small vases of hibiscus sit on blue plastic cloths in this restaurant's cheerful white room. Appetizers include conch fritters and fish chowder, and among the main dishes are pork chops, fish-and-chips, lobster salad, and turtle steak. Be sure to come early for the packed Monday-night and Thursday-night all-you-can-eat $20 seafood buffet. *Leeward Hwy., tel. 809/94–64558. No credit cards. Inexpensive.*

★ **Hey, José.** This restaurant with an atrium is popular for such Tex-Mex treats as tacos, tostados, nachos, burritos, fajitas, and margaritas. You can build your own pizza. *Leeward Hwy., tel. 809/94–64812. AE, MC, V. Closed Sun. Inexpensive.*

Top O' the Cove Gourmet Delicatessen. On Leeward Highway, this tiny cafe is a convenient walk from the Turtle Cove and Erebus Inns and offers a rare cup of potable coffee, as well as genuine espresso and frothy cappuccino. Open every day but Christmas and New Year's from 7 AM to 3:30 PM, the cafe, owned by Angela Belvin, serves breakfast, deli subs, sandwiches, and salads to go or to eat at bistro tables topped with colorful tropical cloths that belie its location in the Napa Auto Parts plaza. *Leeward Hwy., tel. 809/94–64694. No credit cards. Inexpensive.*

Yum Yum's. One of the newer eateries in town, this restaurant features native dishes, deli sandwiches, ice cream, yogurt, and fresh pastries served in a modern, air-conditioned setting. *Town Centre Mall, Butterfield Sq., tel. 809/94–64480. No credit cards. Inexpensive.*

Lodging

Hotel accommodations are available on Grand Turk, North Caicos, South Caicos, Pine Cay, and Provo. There are also some small, un-air-conditioned guest houses on Salt Cay and Middle Caicos. Accommodations range from small island inns to the splashy Club Med Turkoise to the new luxury Grace Bay Club in Providenciales. Because of the popularity of scuba diving here, virtually all the hotels have dive shops and offer very attractive dive packages. Most of the medium and large hotels offer a choice of EP and MAP. People generally tend to eat at their hotels, so MAP may be the better option.

Highly recommended lodgings are indicated by a star ★.

Category	Cost*
Expensive	over $140
Moderate	$100–$140
Inexpensive	under $100

All prices are for a standard double room for two, excluding 7% tax and a 10% service charge.

Grand Turk **Coral Reef Resort.** These modern, air-conditioned efficiency, ★ one- and two-bedroom units sit on a ridge on the eastern coast, where you can stroll out of your room and onto the beach. It's a combination apartment/hotel, with each unit boasting contemporary furnishings and a complete electric kitchen. *Box 10, tel. 809/94–62055 or 800/243–4954, fax 809/94–62911. 21 rooms. Facilities: restaurant, bar, tennis, pool, boutique, mini-fitness center, water sports arranged with dive operations. AE, MC, V. EP, MAP. Moderate.*

★ **Hotel Kittina.** This family-owned hostelry is the largest hotel on Grand Turk. Choose between the sleek, balconied, air-conditioned suites with kitchens, which sit on a gleaming white-sand beach, or the older main house across the street, which oozes island atmosphere. Rooms in the latter are simple; strong winds blow through the rooms and keep things so cool you don't need the ceiling fans. Be sure to catch the hotel's occasional Friday-night poolside barbecue. *Duke St., Box 42, tel. 809/94–62232 or 800/548–8462, fax 809/94–62877. 43 rooms and suites. Facilities: restaurant, 2 bars, pool, boutique, Omega Dive Shop, T&C Travel Agency, scooter rentals, windsurfing, babysitting, room service, boat rentals, ice-cream parlor. AE, MC, V. EP, MAP. Moderate.*

Salt Raker Inn. Across the street from the beach, this galleried house was the home of a Bermudian shipwright 180 years ago. The rooms and suites are not elegant, but are individually decorated and have a homelike atmosphere. Accommodations include a garden house with screened porches and three one-bedroom suites, all with air-conditioning, TV, telephone, and minifridge. *Duke St., Box 1, tel. 809/94–62260, fax 809/94–62432. In U.K., 44 Birchington Rd., London NW6 4LJ, tel. 071/328–6474. 12 rooms and suites. Facilities: restaurant, bar, dive packages with Blue Water Diving. AE, D, MC, V. EP. Moderate.*

Pine Cay **The Meridian Club.** High rollers get away from it all in high
★ style on this privately owned 800-acre island. Club guests enjoy, among other things, an unspoiled cay with 2½ miles of soft white sand and a 500-acre nature reserve, with tropical landscaping, freshwater ponds, and nature trails that lure bird-watchers and botanists. There are seaside cottages with king-size beds (or twin beds on request), a patio fronting on the beach, and a newly renovated "round room" with two ocean-view atrium units. *Pine Cay, tel. 800/331–9154, fax 809/94–65128. RMI Marketing, 201½ E. 29th St., New York, NY 10016. 12 rooms and 14 cottages. Facilities: restaurant, bar, pool, tennis court, bicycles, windsurfing, sailing. No credit cards. FAP. Expensive.*

Salt Cay **Windmills Plantation.** The attraction here is the lack of distrac-
★ tion: no nightlife, no cruise ships, no crowds, and no shopping. Owner-manager-architect Guy Lovelace and his interior designer wife, Patricia, built the hotel as their version of a colonial-era plantation. The Great House has four suites, each with a sitting area, four-poster bed, ceiling fans, and a veranda or balcony with a view of the sea. All are furnished in a mix of antique English and wicker furniture. Four other rooms are housed in two adjacent buildings. Room rates include snorkeling equipment, three meals, and unlimited bar drinks, wine, and beer. *Salt Cay, tel. 809/94–66962 or 800/822–7715. 8 rooms. Facilities: pool, library, nearby diving, fishing, horseback riding, snorkeling, beach, restaurant, bar. AE, MC, V. FAP. Expensive.*

Providenciales **Club Med Turkoise.** This lavish $23 million resort is one of the most sumptuous of all Club Med's villages. One-, two-, and three-story bungalows line a mile-long beach, and all the usual sybaritic pleasures are here. This club is especially geared toward couples, older singles, and divers. The one-price-covers-all-except-drinks package includes all the diving you can handle. *Providenciales, tel. 809/94–65500 or 800-CLUBMED; in NY, 212/750–1684 or 212/750–1685; fax 809/94–65501. 298 rooms. Facilities: restaurant, 2 snack bars, bar, disco, boutique, 8 tennis courts (4 lighted), bicycles, TV/video room, library, beach, pool, dive center, deep-sea-fishing excursions, water-sports center. AE, MC, V. All-inclusive (except for drinks). Expensive.*

Grace Bay Club. Managed by the Ricketts Group, Grace Bay, which opened in 1992, is the epitome of comfort and elegance. At the touch of your fingers, you can order in a chef, who supplies the ingredients, whips up a gourmet meal, and then serves it to you in your own dining room. You can also request a nanny or a massage therapist. The rooms are furnished with rattan and pickled wood, and the Mexican-tile floors are elegantly appointed with throw rugs from Turkey and India. Kitchens are furnished with a full-sized refrigerator, microwave, and all utensils, plus a full-size washer and dryer. Though the rooms are pricey, the smallest one-bedroom, two-bath luxury suite easily sleeps a family of four. Complimentary amenities include windsurfing, Hobie Cat, sunfish day sailors, snorkeling gear, and a video and book library. At press time, only 30 rooms and the restaurant were open at this planned large condominium resort, with construction expected to be completed by the end of 1993. *Box 128, Provo, tel. 809/94–65050 or 800/677–9609, fax 809/94–65758. Facilities: pool, beach, Jacuzzi, water sports. AE, MC, V. EP, MAP. Expensive.*

★ **Ramada Turquoise Reef Resort & Casino.** This new beachfront hotel is the island's first full-service luxury resort. Oversized oceanfront rooms have rattan furniture and an aqua, deep-green, gold, and mauve color scheme. Furnished with a king or two double beds, all rooms are air-conditioned and have a color TV and ceiling fan and either a terrace or a patio. The island's first gourmet Italian restaurant is located here, as is the island's only casino. Guests enjoy a free daily activities program that includes pool volleyball, and children's treasure hunts. *Box 205, Provo, tel. 809/94–65555 or 800/228–9898, fax 809/94–65522. 228 rooms. Facilities: beach, free-form pool, Jacuzzi, 2 restaurants, snack bar, 3 bars, water-sports facility, 2 tennis courts, dive shop, boutiques, exercise/fitness room, room service, live nightly entertainment/disco, casino, tour desk, babysitting, daily activities program. AE, MC, V. EP, MAP. Expensive.*

★ **Erebus Inn Resort.** All units in this stylish resort have two double beds and modern wicker furnishings. Some rooms are in the older chalet; units in the newer section are air-conditioned, with 13-channel cable TV and phones. Recently face-lifted and expanded, the hotel sits on a cliff overlooking Turtle Cove, which affords a wonderful view of the marina and the Caribbean beyond. A frequent shuttle service ferries guests by bus to a nearby beach. The casual restaurant and lively bar make this a popular gathering spot. *Turtle Cove, Box 238, Providenciales, tel. 809/94–64240, fax 809/94–64704. 30 rooms. Facilities: restaurant, bar, 2 pools (1 saltwater), fitness center, aqua aerobics, 2 lighted tennis courts. AE, MC, V. EP, MAP. Moderate–Expensive.*

★ **Le Deck Hotel & Beach Club.** This 27-room pink hostelry was built in classic Bermudian style around a tropical courtyard that opens onto a tiki hut- and palm tree-dotted beach on Grace Bay. Popular with divers, it offers clean rooms with a tile floor, color TV, and air-conditioning. The atmosphere is informal and lively with a mostly thirtysomething-and-over crowd. *Box 144, Grace Bay, Provo, tel. 809/94–65547 or 800/528–1905, fax 809/94–65770. 27 rooms, including 2 honeymoon suites. Facilities: restaurant, bar, pool, boutique, water sports, beach. AE, D, MC, V. CP, MAP. Moderate–Expensive.*

Island Princess. Wood walkways at the hotel lead up to and around the rooms, which are situated in two wings. All rooms have cable TV and private balcony. This is a great little hotel for families. It's on the beach, the restaurant serves excellent food, and there's nightly entertainment. *The Bight, tel. 809/94–64260, fax 809/946–4666. 80 rooms. Facilities: restaurant, bar, 2 pools, games room, children's playground, boat rentals, water-sports center. AE, D, MC, V. MAP. Moderate.*

Treasure Beach Villas. These one- and two-bedroom modern self-catering apartments have fully equipped kitchens, fans, and Provo's 12 miles of white sandy beach for beachcombing and snorkeling. *The Bight, tel. 809/94–64325, fax 809/94–64108. Box 8409, Hialeah, FL 33012. 8 single, 10 double rooms. Facilities: pool, tennis court. AE, D, MC, V. EP. Moderate.*

Turtle Cove Inn. Occupying 1½ acres, this two-story recreational facility has rooms facing either the marina or the free-form pool and sundeck. This quiet inn, geared toward tennis players, divers, and boaters, offers free boat shuttles to a nearby beach and snorkeling reef. All rooms have a TV, phone, and air-conditioning and eight also have minifridges. A handful of good restaurants are within walking distance. *Providenciales, tel. 809/94–64203 or 800/633–7411, fax 809/94–64040. Facilities: 2 restaurants, 2 bars, lounge, game room, 2 lighted tennis courts, pool, marina, 3 dive shops nearby. AE, D, MC, V. EP. Moderate.*

South Caicos **Club Carib Harbor Hotel.** Within walking distance of the township, this small resort overlooking Cockburn Harbour and the fishing district has simple, functional rooms with air-conditioning and color TV in the six waterfront suites. *Box 1, South Caicos, tel. 809/94–63360. 12 rooms and 6 suites. Facilities: restaurant, bar. AE, D, MC, V. EP, MAP. Moderate–Inexpensive.*

North Caicos **Prospect of Whitby Hotel.** This secluded retreat is a quiet get-
★ away located on a 7-mile-long beach. If you want them, diversions can include windsurfing, snorkeling, and bonefishing. The spacious rooms are tasteful island basic with air-conditioning. Both the service and the food are superb. *Kew Post Office, North Caicos, tel. 809/94–67119, fax 809/94–67114. 28 rooms and 4 suites. Facilities: restaurant, bar, pool, bicycles, tennis, windsurfing, tour desk. AE, MC, V. EP, MAP. Moderate–Expensive.*

Nightlife

On Provo, a full band plays native, Reggae, and contemporary music on Tuesday and Thursday nights at the **Erebus Inn** (tel. 809/94–64240). **Le Deck** (tel. 809/94–65547) offers one-armed bandits every night. The island's liveliest lounge can be found at the **Ramada Turquoise Reef Resort** (tel. 809/94–65555) disco, where a musician plays to the mostly tourist crowd. The Ramada is also the location of **Port Royale** (tel. 809/94–65508), the island's only gambling casino. **Disco Elite** (Airport Rd., no phone) sports strobe lights and an elevated dance floor.

27 The U.S. Virgin Islands

St. Thomas, St. Croix,
St. John

Updated by Heidi Waldrop and Denise Nolty

It is the combination of the familiar and the exotic found in the United States Virgin Islands that defines this "American Paradise" and explains much of its appeal. The effort to be all things to all people—while remaining true to the best of itself—has created a sometimes paradoxical blend of island serenity and American practicality in this U.S. territory 1,000 miles from the southern tip of the U.S. mainland.

The postcard images you'd expect from a tropical paradise are here: Stretches of beach arc into the distance, and white sails skim across water so blue and clear it stuns the senses; red-roof houses add their spot of color to the green hillsides' mosaic, along with the orange of the flamboyant tree, the red of the hibiscus, the magenta of the bougainvillea, and the blue stone ruins of old sugar mills, and towns of pastel-tone European-style villas, decorated by filigree wrought-iron terraces, line narrow streets climbing up from a harbor.

The other part of the equation are all those things that make it so easy and appealing to visit this cluster of islands. The official language is English, the money is the dollar, and the U.S. government runs things. There's cable TV, Pizza Hut, and McDonald's. There's unfettered immigration to and from the mainland, and investments are protected by the American flag. Visitors to the U.S.V.I. have the opportunity to delve into a "foreign" culture, while anchored by familiar language and landmarks.

Your destination here will be St. Thomas (13 miles long); its neighbor St. John (9 miles long); or, 40 miles to the south, St. Croix (23 miles long). A pro/con thumbnail sketch of these three might have it that St. Thomas is bustling (hustling) and the place for shopping and discos (commercial glitz and overdevelopment); St. Croix is more Danish, picturesque, and rural (more provincial and duller, particularly after dark); and St. John is matchless in the beauty of its National Park Service–protected land and beaches (a one-village island mostly for the rich or for campers). Surely not everything will suit your fancy, but chances are that between the three islands you'll find your own idea of paradise among the choices.

Before You Go

Tourist Information

Information about the United States Virgin Islands is available through the following **U.S.V.I. Government Tourist Offices:** 225 Peachtree St., Suite 760, Atlanta, GA 30303, tel. 404/688–0906, fax 404/525–1102; 122 S. Michigan Ave., Suite 1270, Chicago, IL 60603, tel. 312/461–0180, fax 312/461–0765; 3460 Wilshire Blvd., Suite 412, Los Angeles, CA 90010, tel. 213/739–0138, fax 213/739–2005; 2655 Le Jeune Rd., Suite 907, Coral Gables, FL 33134, tel. 305/442–7200, fax 305/445–9044; 1270 6th Ave., New York, NY 10020, tel. 212/582–4520, fax 212/581–3405; 900 17th Ave. NW, Suite 500, Washington, DC 20006, tel. 202/293–3707, fax 202/785–2542; 1300 Ashford St., Condado, Santurce, Puerto Rico 00907, tel. 809/724–3816, fax 809/724–7223; and 2 Cinnamon Row, Plantation Wharf, York Place, London, Eng. SW11 3TW, tel. 071/978–5262, telex 27231, fax 071/924–3171.

You can also call the Division of Tourism's toll-free number (tel. 800/USVI–INFO).

The U. S. Virgin Islands

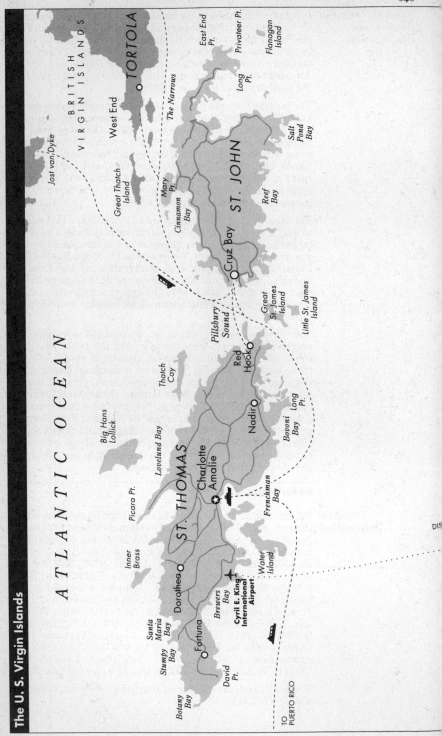

ATLANTIC OCEAN

BRITISH VIRGIN ISLANDS

TORTOLA

West End

Jost van Dyke

Great Thatch Island

The Narrows

Mary Pt.

Cinnamon Bay

ST. JOHN

East End Pt.

Privateer Pt.

Flanagan Island

Long Pt.

Salt Pond Bay

Reef Bay

Cruz Bay

Pillsbury Sound

Great St. James Island

Little St. James Island

Red Hook

Thatch Cay

Big Hans Lollick

Loveland Bay

Nadir

Long Pt.

Bovoni Bay

Picara Pt.

ST. THOMAS

Charlotte Amalie

Frenchman Bay

Inner Brass

Dorothea

Santa Maria Bay

Stumpy Bay

Fortuna

Brewers Bay

Cyril E. King International Airport

Water Island

David Pt.

Botany Bay

TO PUERTO RICO

DIS

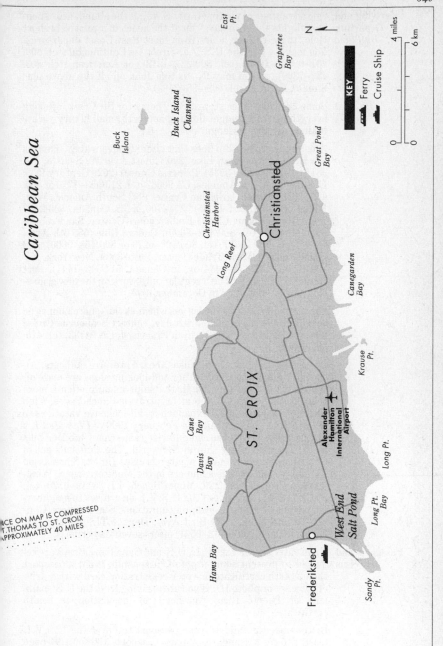

Caribbean Sea

East Pt.

Grapetree Bay

Buck Island Channel

Buck Island

Christiansted Harbor

Long Reef

Great Pond Bay

Christiansted

Canegarden Bay

Krause Pt.

ST. CROIX

Alexander Hamilton International Airport

Cane Bay

Davis Bay

Long Pt.

Long Pt. Bay

Hams Bay

West End Salt Pond

Frederiksted

Sandy Pt.

NCE ON MAP IS COMPRESSED
T.THOMAS TO ST. CROIX
PPROXIMATELY 40 MILES

N

KEY

Ferry

Cruise Ship

4 miles

6 km

0   0

Arriving and Departing

By Plane One advantage of visiting the U.S.V.I. is the abundance of non-stop flights that can have you at the beach in a relatively short time, three to four hours from most East Coast departures. You may fly into the U.S.V.I. direct via **Continental** (tel. 800/231–0856), **Delta** (tel. 800/221–1212), or **American** (tel. 800/433–7300), or you may fly via San Juan on all the above plus **Sunaire Express** (tel. 809/495–2480).

By Boat Some 20 cruise lines stop at St. Thomas or St. Croix, offering everything from budget floating hotels to small luxury yachts taking only 100 passengers.

Among the cruise-ship lines that offer stopovers at St. Thomas are **Holland American Line** (300 Elliott Ave. W, Seattle, WA 98119, tel. 206/281–3535), **Princess Cruises** (2029 Century Park E, Suite 3000, Los Angeles, CA 90067, tel. 213/553–1770 or 800/421–0522), **Royal Caribbean Cruises** (903 South America Way, Miami, FL 33132, tel. 800/327–6700 or, in Canada, 800/245–7225), **Royal Viking Line** (1 Embarcadero Center, San Francisco, CA 94111, tel. 800/422–8000), **Cunard Line** (555 5th Ave., New York, NY 10017, tel. 800/528–6273 or 800/458–9000), and **Home Lines** (1 World Trade Center, Suite 3939, New York, NY 10048, tel. 212/432–1414 or, in Canada, 514/842–1441). Port calls to St. Croix will be irregular until work on the new cruise-ship pier is completed in December 1993.

For a smaller luxury cruise on which caviar and champagne service is the norm 24 hours a day, contact **Seabourne Cruise Line** (55 San Francisco St., San Francisco, CA 94133, tel. 415/391–7444).

Increasingly popular are cruises aboard oversize sailboats. Although the sails on these rather odd-looking ships are more often cosmetic than functional, the ships usually offer a more relaxed itinerary and stop at less traveled anchorages. **Club Med** (tel. 800/258–2633) expanded its all-inclusive vacations to the sea with the launching in February 1990 of *Club Med I,* a 614-foot ship with seven computerized sails that Club Med bills as the largest sailing ship in the world. The ship sails out of Guadaloupe on seven-day winter cruises (in St. Thomas on Thursday) and spends summers in the Mediterranean. **Windjammer Cruises** (Box 120, Miami Beach, FL 33119–0120, tel. 800/327–2601) sails out of the U.S.V.I. on cruises to neighboring islands for two- to seven-day durations. **Star Clippers** (Clipper Ship Cruises, 2833 Bird Ave., Dept. ETLF, Miami, FL 33133–4604, tel. 800/442–0551) offers seven-day cruises.

Passports and Visas Upon entering the U.S.V.I., U.S. and Canadian citizens are required to present some proof of citizenship, if not a passport then a birth certificate or voter-registration card with a driver's license or photo ID. If you are arriving from the U.S. mainland or Puerto Rico, you need no inoculation or health certificate.

Britons need a valid 10-year passport to enter the U.S.V.I. (cost: £15 for a standard 32-page passport, £30 for a 94-page passport). You do not need a visa for the U.S.V.I. if you are visiting either on business or pleasure, are staying fewer than 90 days, have a return ticket or onward ticket, are traveling with a major airline (in effect, any airline that flies from the United Kingdom to the United States), and complete visa waiver I-94W, which is supplied either at the airport of departure or on the plane.

Language English, often with a Creole or West Indian lilt, is the medium of communication in these islands.

Precautions Crime exists here, but not to the same degree that it does in larger cities on the U.S. mainland. Still, it's best to stick to well-lit streets at night and use the same kind of street sense (don't wander the back alleys of Charlotte Amalie after five rum punches, for example) that you would in any unfamiliar territory. If you plan on carrying things around, rent a car, not a jeep, and lock possessions in the trunk. Keep your rental car locked wherever you park. Don't leave cameras, purses, and other valuables lying on the beach while you're off on an hour-long snorkel, whether at the deserted beaches of St. John or the more crowded Magens and Coki beaches on St. Thomas.

Staying in the U.S. Virgin Islands

Important Addresses **Tourist Information:** The **U.S. Virgin Islands Division of Tourism** has an office in St. Thomas (Box 6400, Charlotte Amalie, U.S. Virgin Islands 00804, tel. 809/774–8784, fax 809/774–4390), St. Croix (Box 4538, Christiansted, U.S. Virgin Islands 00822, tel. 809/773–0495, and on the pier, Strand St., Frederiksted, U.S. Virgin Islands 00840, tel. 809/772–0357), and St. John (Box 200, Cruz Bay, U.S. Virgin Islands 00830, tel. 809/776–6450).

There are two **Visitor Centers** in Charlotte Amalie: one across from Emancipation Square and one at Havensight Mall. In St. Croix, go to the Old Scale House at the waterfront in Christiansted, across from Fort Christiansvaern. The **National Park Service** also has visitor centers at the ferry areas on St. Thomas (Red Hook) and St. John (Cruz Bay).

Emergencies **Police:** To reach the police dial 915.

Hospitals: The emergency room of **St. Thomas Hospital** (tel. 809/776–8311) in Sugar Estate, Charlotte Amalie, is open 24 hours a day. In Christiansted there is the **St. Croix Hospital and Community Health Center** (6 Diamond Bay, north of Sunny Isle Shopping Center, on Route 79, tel. 809/778–6311 or 809/778–5895), and in Frederiksted, the **Frederiksted Health Center** (tel. 809/772–1992 or 809/772–0750). On St. John contact the **Morris F. DeCastro Clinic** (Cruz Bay, tel. 809/776–6400) or call an **emergency medical technician** directly (tel. 809/776–6222).

Air Ambulance: Bohlke International Airways (tel. 809/778–9177) operates out of the airport in St. Croix. **Air Medical Services** (tel. 800/443–0013) and **Air Ambulance Network** (tel. 800/327–1966) also service the area from Florida.

Coast Guard: For emergencies on St. Thomas or St. John, call the **Marine Safety Detachment** (tel. 809/776–3497) from 7 to 3:30 weekdays; on St. Croix, call 809/773–7614. If there is no answer, call the **Rescue Coordination Center** (tel. 809/722–2943) in San Juan, open 24 hours a day.

Pharmacies: Sunrise Pharmacy has two branches on St. Thomas: one in Red Hook (tel. 809/775–6600) and another in the Wheatley Center (tel. 809/774–5333). **Drug Farm Pharmacy's** main store (tel. 809/776–7098) is located across from the General Post Office; another branch (tel. 809/776–1880) is located next to St. Thomas Hospital. On St. Croix, try **People's Drug Store, Inc.** (tel. 809/778–7355) in Christiansted or **D & D Apoth-**

ecary Hall (tel. 809/772–1890) in Frederiksted. On St. John, contact the **St. John Drug Center** (tel. 809/776–6353) in Cruz Bay.

Currency   The U.S. dollar is the medium of exchange here.

Taxes and Service   A 7.5% tax is added to hotel rates. Departure tax for the
Charges   U.S.V.I. is included in the cost of your airplane ticket. Some hotels and restaurants add a 10% or 15% service charge to your bill, generally only if you are part of a group of 15 or more. There is no sales tax in the U.S.V.I.

Guided Tours   On St. Thomas, the **V.I. Taxi Association City-Island Tour** (tel. 809/774–4550) gives a two-hour tour aimed at cruise-ship passengers that includes stops at Drake's Seat and Mountain Top. **Tropic Tours** (tel. 809/774–1855) offers one half-day shopping and sightseeing tours of St. Thomas by bus on Mondays, Wednesdays, Fridays, and Saturdays for $18 per person and full-day snorkeling tours to St. John every day for $40 per person (including lunch). It picks up at all the major hotels. Bird-watching, whale-watching, and a chance to wait hidden on a beach while the magnificent hawksbill turtles come ashore to lay their eggs are all open to visitors. Write the **Virgin Islands Conservation Society** (Box 3839, St. Croix 00822, tel. 809/773–1989) for more information on hikes and special programs, or check the community calendar in the *Daily News* for up-to-date information.

Van tours of St. Croix are offered by **St. Croix Safari Tours** (tel. 809/773–6700) and **Smitty's** (tel. 809/773–9188). The tours, which depart from Christiansted and last about three hours, cost from $20 per person. One of the best ways to see the rain forest and hills of the west end may be a tour by horseback with **Paul and Jill's Equestrian Stable** (tel. 809/772–2880 or tel. 809/772–2627).

On St. John, the park service gives a variety of guided tours on-and off-shore. For more information or to arrange a tour contact the **St. John National Park Visitor Center** (Cruz Bay, tel. 809/776–6201).

Getting Around   Any U.S. driver's license is good for 90 days here; the minimum
Car   age for drivers is 18, although many agencies won't rent to anyone under the age of 25. Driving is on the left side of the road (although your steering wheel will be on the left side of the car). Many of the roads are narrow and the islands are dotted with hills, so there is ample reason to drive carefully. Jeeps are particularly recommended on St. John, where dirt roads prevail.

On St. Thomas, you can rent a car from **ABC Rentals** (tel. 809/776–1222 or 800/524–2080), **Anchorage E-Z Car** (tel. 809/775–6255), **Avis** (tel. 809/774–1468), **Budget** (tel. 809/776–7575), **Cowpet Car Rental** (tel. 809/775–7376 or 800/524–2072), **Dependable** (tel. 809/774–2253 or 800/522–3076), **Discount** (tel. 809/776–4858), **Hertz** (tel. 809/774–1879), **Sea Breeze** (tel. 809/774–7200), **Sun Island** (tel. 809/774–3333), or **Thrifty** (tel. 809/776–8600).

On St. Croix, call **Atlas** (tel. 809/773–2886), **Avis** (tel. 809/778–9355), **Budget** (tel. 809/778–9636), **Caribbean Jeep & Car** (tel. 809/773–4399), **Hertz** (tel. 809/778–1402), **Olympic** (tel. 809/773–9588 or 722–1617), and **Thrifty** (tel. 809/773–7200).

On St. John, call **Avis** (tel. 809/776–6374), **Budget** (tel. 809/776–7575), **Cool Breeze** (tel. 809/776–6588), **Delbert Hill Taxi and Jeep** (tel. 809/776–6637), **Hertz** (tel. 809/776–6695), **O'Connor Jeep** (tel. 809/776–6343), **St. John Car Rental** (tel. 809/776–6103), or **Spencer's Jeep** (tel. 809/776–7784).

Taxis Taxis of all shapes and sizes are available at various ferry, shopping, resort, and airport areas on St. Thomas and St. Croix and respond quickly to a call.

In Charlotte Amalie, taxi stands are located across from **Emancipation Gardens** (in front of Little Switzerland behind the post office) and along the waterfront. Away from Charlotte Amalie, you'll find taxis available at all major hotels and at such public beaches as Magens Bay and Coki Point. Calling taxis will work, too, but allow plenty of time.

Taxis on St. Croix, generally station wagons or minivans, are a phone call away from most hotels and are available in downtown Christiansted, at the Alexander Hamilton Airport, and at the Frederiksted pier during cruise-ship arrivals. Rates, set by law, are prominently displayed at the airport. Try the **St. Croix Taxi Association** (tel. 809/778–1088) at the airport and **Antilles Taxi Service** (tel. 809/773–5020) or **Cruzan Taxi Association** (tel. 809/773–6388) in Christiansted.

On St. John buses and taxis are the same thing: open-air safari buses. Technically the safari buses are private taxis, but everyone uses them as an informal bus system. You'll find them congregated at the Cruz Bay Dock, ready to take you to any of the beaches or other island destinations, but you can also pick them up anywhere on the road by signaling.

Buses Public buses are not the quickest way to get around on the islands because service is minimal, but the deluxe mainland-size buses on St. Thomas make public transportation a very reasonable and comfortable way to get from east and west to town and back (there is no service North, however). Fares are $1 between outlying areas and town and 75¢ in town. St. Croix and St. John have no public bus system, and residents rely on the kindness of taxi vans and safari buses for mass transportation.

Ferries Ferries ply two routes between St. Thomas and St. John—either between the Charlotte Amalie waterfront and Cruz Bay or between Red Hook and Cruz Bay. The schedules for daily service between Red Hook, St. Thomas, and Cruz Bay, St. John: Ferries leave Red Hook weekdays 6:30 and 7:30 AM, and all week long hourly 8 AM to midnight. They leave Cruz Bay for Red Hook hourly 6 AM to 10 PM and at 11:15 PM. The 15–20 minute ferry ride is $3 one way for adults, $1.50 for children under 12.

Telephones and Mail The area code for all the U.S.V.I. is 809, and there is direct dialing to the mainland. Local calls from a public phone cost 25¢ for each five minutes. On St. John the place to go for any telephone or message needs is **Connections** (tel. 809/776–6922). On St. Thomas, it's **Islander Services** (tel. 809/774–8128) behind the Greenhouse Restaurant in Charlotte Amalie or **East End Secretarial Services** (tel. 809/775–5262, fax 809/775–3590), upstairs at the Red Hook Plaza. On St. Croix, visit the **Business Bureau** (42–43 Strand St., Christiansted, tel. 809/773–7601) or **St. Croix Communications Centre** (61 King St., Frederiksted, tel. 809/772–5800).

By 1994 the telephone exchange throughout St. John will be switched to **693**. However, at press time the change had not been integrated. When you dial the current listing, a recording will redirect you if necessary.

The main **U.S. Post Office** on St. Thomas is near the hospital, with branches in Charlotte Amalie and Frenchtown; there's a post office at Christiansted and Fredriksted on St. Croix and at Cruz Bay on St. John. Postal rates are the same as elsewhere in the United States: 29¢ for a letter, 19¢ for a postcard to anywhere in the United States, 45¢ for a ½-oz letter mailed to a foreign country.

Opening and Closing Times   On **St. Thomas,** Charlotte Amalie's Main Street–area shops are open weekdays and Saturday 9–5. Havensight Mall shops (next to the cruise-ships dock) hours are the same, though some shops sometimes stay open until 9 on Friday, depending on how many cruise ships are staying late at the dock. You may also find some shops open on Sunday if a lot of cruise ships are in port. **St. Croix** store hours are usually weekdays 9 to 5, but you will definitely find some shops in Christiansted open in the evening. On **St. John,** store hours are reliably similar to those on the other two islands, and Wharfside Village shops in Cruz Bay are often open into the evening.

Exploring St. Thomas

Numbers in the margin correspond to points of interest on the St. Thomas map.

Charlotte Amalie   This tour of historic (and sometimes hilly) **Charlotte Amalie** and environs is on foot, so wear comfortable shoes, start early, and stop often to refresh. A note about the street names: In deference to the island's heritage, the streets downtown are labeled by their Danish names. Locals will use both the Danish name and the English name (such as Dronnigen's Gade and Main Street).

Begin at the waterfront. Waterfront and Main streets are connected by cobblestone-paved alleys kept cool by overhanging green plants and the thick stone walls of the warehouses on either side. The alleys (particularly Royal Dane Mall and Palm Passage, Main Street between the post office and Market Square, and Bakery Square on Back Street) are where you'll find the unique and glamorous—and duty-free—shops for which Charlotte Amalie is famous (*see* Shopping, below).

At the end of Kronprindsens Alley north of the waterfront is the pale-pink Roman Catholic **Cathedral of St. Peter and St. Paul,** consecrated as a parish church in 1848. The ceiling and walls of the church are covered in the soft tones of murals painted in 1899 by two Belgian artists, Father Leo Servais and Brother Ildephonsus. The San Juan-marble altar and side walls were added in the 1960s. *Tel. 809/774–0201. Open Mon.–Sat. 8–5.*

At **Market Square,** east of the church on Main Street, try to block out the signs advertising cameras and electronics and imagine this place as it was in the early 1800s, when plantation owners stood on the delicately draped wrought-iron balconies and chose from the human merchandise below, where the slaves for sale were displayed. Today in the square, a cadre of old-timers sell papaya, taina roots, and herbs, and sidewalk vendors offer a variety of African fabrics and artifacts, tie-dye cotton clothes at good prices, and fresh-squeezed fruit juices. Go east on Back Street, then turn left on Store Tvaer Gade; walk a short block, and take a left on Bjerge Gade.

As you walk up Bjerge Gade you'll end up facing a weather-beaten but imposing two-story red house known as the **Crystal Palace,** so-named because it was the first building on the island to have glass windows. The Crystal Palace anchors the corner of Bjerge and Crystal Gade. Here the street becomes stairs, which you can climb to Denmark Hill and the old Greek Revival **Danish Consulate building** (1830)—look for the red-and-white flag.

Descend to Crystal Gade and go east. At Number 15 you'll come to the **St. Thomas Synagogue.** Its Hebrew name translates as the Congregation of Blessing, Peace, and Loving Deeds. Since the synagogue first opened its doors in 1833, it has held a week-ly Sabbath service, making it the oldest synagogue building in continuous use under the American flag and the second oldest (after the one on Curaçao) in the western hemisphere. *15 Crystal Gade, tel. 809/774–4312. Open Mon.–Fri. 9–4.*

One block east, down the hill, you'll come to the corner of Nye Gade. On the right corner is the St. Thomas **Dutch Reformed Church,** founded in 1744, burned in 1804, and rebuilt to its aus-tere loveliness in 1844. The unembellished cream-color hall ex-udes peace—albeit monochromatically. The only touches of another color are the forest green shutters and carpet. *Tel. 809/776–8255. Open Mon.–Fri. 9–5.*

Continue on Crystal Gade one block east and turn left (north) on Garden Street. The **All Saints Anglican Church** was built in 1848 from stone quarried on the island. Its thick, arched win-dow frames are lined with the yellow brick that came to the is-lands as ballast aboard merchant ships. The church was built in celebration of the end of slavery in the Virgin Islands in 1848. *Tel. 809/774–0214. Open Mon.–Sat. 6 AM–3 PM.*

Return down Garden Street and go east on Kongen's Gade. Keep walking up the hill to the east and you'll find yourself at the foot of the **99 Steps,** a staircase "street" built by the Danes in the 1700s. (If you count the stairs as you go up, you'll discov-er, like thousands before you, that there are more than 99.)

Up the steps you'll find the neighborhood of **Queen's Street.** The homes are privately owned except for one guest house—Blackbeard's Castle. The tower of **Blackbeard's Castle** was built in 1679 and is believed to have been used by the notorious pirate Edward Teach. The castle is now the site of a charming guest house, a good restaurant, and a swimming pool open to customers. Here you can lunch and sit by the pool, taking in the view from the terrace.

Go back down the steps and continue east to **Government House.** This elegant home was built in 1867 and is the official residence of the governor of the U.S.V.I. The first floor is open to the public. The staircases are of native mahogany, as are the plaques hand-lettered in gold with the names of the governors appointed and, since 1970, elected. The three murals at the back of the lobby were painted by Pepino Mangravatti in the 1930s as part of the U.S. government's Works Projects Admin-istration (WPA). The murals depict Columbus's landing on St.

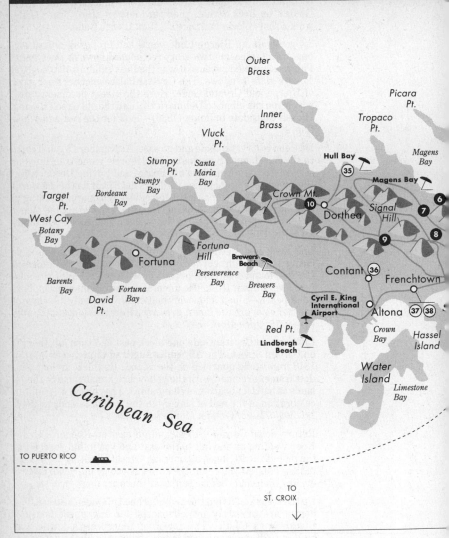

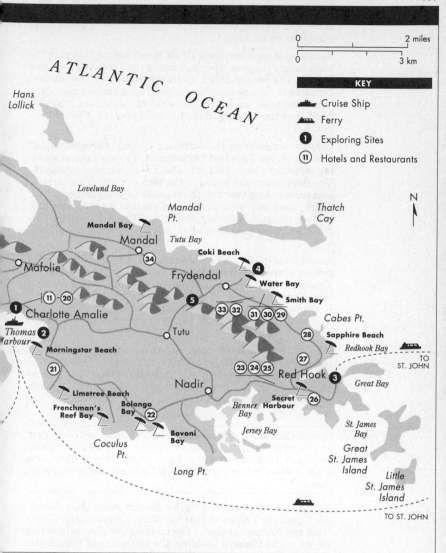

KEY

- Cruise Ship
- Ferry
- ① Exploring Sites
- ⑪ Hotels and Restaurants

ATLANTIC OCEAN

Hans Lollick

Lovelund Bay

Mandal Bay

Mandal Pt.

Thatch Cay

Mandal ③④

Tutu Bay

Coki Beach

Mafolie

Frydendal ④

Water Bay

⑪-⑳

⑤

Smith Bay

Charlotte Amalie

③③ ③② ③① ③⓪ ②⑨

Cabes Pt.

Thomas Harbour

②

Tutu

②⑧

Sapphire Beach

Morningstar Beach

Redhook Bay

TO ST. JOHN

②①

②⑦

②③ ②④ ②⑤

Red Hook ③

Great Bay

Limetree Beach

Nadir

②⑥

Frenchman's Reef Bay

Bolongo Bay

Secret Harbour

②②

Benner Bay

St. James Bay

Bovoni Bay

Jersey Bay

Great St. James Island

Coculus Pt.

Long Pt.

Little St. James Island

TO ST. JOHN

N

0 — 2 miles
0 — 3 km

Bolongo Inclusive Beach Resort, **22**
Bunker Hill Hotel, **19**
Heritage Manor, **18**
Hotel 1829, **12**
Island View Guesthouse, **36**
Marriott's Frenchman's Reef and Morning Star Beach Resorts, **21**

Pavilions & Pools, **27**
Point Pleasant Resort, **29**
Sapphire Beach Resort and Marina, **28**
Sign of the Griffin, **34**
Stouffer Grand Beach Resort, **31**
Sugar Bay Plantation, **30**
Villa Blanca Hotel, **20**

Croix during his second voyage in 1493; the transfer of the islands from Denmark to the United States in 1917, and a sugar plantation on St. John.

Return west on Norre Gade (Main Street) toward town. In the block before the post office you'll pass the **Frederick Lutheran Church,** the second-oldest Lutheran church in the western hemisphere. The inside is highlighted by a massive mahogany altar. The pews, each with its own door, were once rented to families of the congregation. *Tel. 809/776–1315. Open Mon.– Sat. 9–4.*

Directly across from the Lutheran Church, through a small side street, you'll see **Fort Christian,** St. Thomas's oldest standing structure, built 1672–87, and a U.S. national landmark. The clock tower was added in the 19th century. This remarkable redoubt has, over time, been used as a jail, governor's residence, town hall, courthouse, and church. Its dungeons now house a museum featuring artifacts of U.S.V.I. history. *Tel. 809/776–4566. Open Mon.–Fri. 8:30–4:30; Sat. 9:30–4; Sun. noon–4.*

Across from the fort is **Emancipation Garden,** which honors the freeing of slaves in 1848. On the other side of the garden is the **legislature building,** its pastoral-looking lime green exterior concealing the vociferous political wrangling going on inside. Built originally by the Danish as a police barracks, the building was later used to billet U.S. Marines, and much later it housed a public school.

Stop in the **post office** to contemplate the murals of waterfront scenes by *Saturday Evening Post* artist Stephen Dohanos. His art was commissioned as part of the WPA in the 1930s. Behind the post office, on the waterfront side of Little Switzerland, are the hospitality lounge and **V.I. Visitor's Information Center.**

Time Out Stop at **Rasheda's Long Look Vegetarian Restaurant** (75 Corner and General Gade). Try a glass of seamoss ($2), a foamy concoction made from seaweed that has a slightly sweet taste, or a glass of West Indian Style Punch ($1.50), a blend of local fruit juices.

As you head back toward Market Square along Main Street, you'll pass the Tropicana Perfume Shop, between Store Tvaer Gade and Trompeter Gade. The building the shop is in is also known as the **Pissarro Building,** the birthplace of French Impressionist painter Camille Pissarro.

The South Shore and East End Leaving Charlotte Amalie, take Veterans Drive (Route 30) east along the waterfront. Once you bear to the right at **Nelson Mandela Circle** (Yacht Haven is on your right), you'll make ② quicker progress. You may want to stop at **Havensight Mall,** across from the dock. This shopping center is a less crowded (and less charming) version of the duty-free shopping district along Main Street in town.

Route 30 is narrow and winds up and down. It also changes names several times along the way; it is called Frenchman's Bay Road just outside town (sharp left turn), then becomes Bovoni Road around Bolongo Bay. Whatever it is called, you will be treated to some southerly vistas of the Caribbean Sea (and, on clear days, St. Croix, 40 miles away) as you drive past

Frenchman's Reef Hotel and its luxurious companion, Morningstar Beach Resort.

Route 30 becomes Route 32 and then is called Red Hook Road as it passes by **Benner Bay.** Staying on Route 32 brings you into **Red Hook,** where you can catch the ferry to St. John (parking available for $5 a day). Red Hook has grown from a sleepy little town connected to the rest of the island only by dirt roads (or by boat) to an increasingly self-sustaining village. There's shopping and a deli at American Yacht Harbor, and you can stop in at The Big Chill for a frozen yogurt or croissant sandwich. Or walk along the docks and visit with sailors and fishermen and stop for a beer at Piccola Marina Cafe or the Warehouse bar.

Above Red Hook the main road swings toward the north shore and becomes Route 38, or Smith Bay Road, taking you past Sapphire Beach, a resort and restaurant with water-sports rentals and a popular snorkeling and windsurfing spot. As you come to Smith Bay, you'll pass the lush green landscaping of Stouffer Grand Beach Resort, and then you'll see a turn-off to the right for Coki Point Beach and **Coral World,** with its three-level underwater observatory, the world's largest reef tank, and an aquarium with more than 20 TV-size tanks providing capsulized views of sea life. A new semisubmarine (a craft that is half-submarine, half-boat, allowing passengers to come up on deck) offers 20-minute undersea tours for $12 per person. Coral World's staff will answer your questions about the turtles, iguanas, parrots, and flamingos that inhabit the park, and there's a restaurant, souvenir shop, and the world's only underwater mailbox, from which you can send postcards home. *Tel. 809/775–1555. Admission: $14 adults, $9 children. Open daily 9–6.*

Continue west on Route 38 and you'll come to **Tillet's Gardens,** where local artisans craft stained glass, pottery, and ceramics. Tillet's paintings and fabrics are also on display.

North Shore, Center Islands, and West The north shore is home to many inviting attractions, not to mention much lusher vegetation than is found on the rest of the island. The most direct route from Charlotte Amalie is Mafolie Road (Route 35), which can be picked up east of Government Hill.

In the heights above Charlotte Amalie is **Drake's Seat,** the mountain lookout from which Sir Francis Drake was supposed to have kept watch over his fleet and looked for enemy ships of the Spanish fleet. Magens Bay and Mahogany Run are to the north, with the British Virgin Islands and Drake's Passage to the east. Off to the left, or west, are Fairchild Park, Mountain Top, Hull Bay, and such smaller islands as the Inner and Outer Brass islands. The panoramic vista is especially breathtaking (and romantic) at dusk, and if you arrive late in the day you'll miss the hordes of day trippers on taxi tours who stop at Drake's Seat to take a picture and buy a T-shirt from one of the vendors there. The vendors are gone by the afternoon.

West from Drake's Seat is **Mountain Top,** not only a mecca for souvenir shopping, but also the location of the establishment that claims to have invented the banana daiquiri. There is a restaurant here, and, because you are more than 1,500 feet above sea level, there are some spectacular views as well.

8 Below Mountain Top is **Fairchild Park,** a gift to the people of the U.S.V.I. from the philanthropist Arthur Fairchild.

If you head west from Mountain Top, on Crown Mountain Road **9** (Route 33) you'll come to **Four Corners.** Take the extreme right turn and drive along the northwestern ridge of the mountain through **Estate Pearl, Sorgenfri,** and **Caret Bay.** There's not much here except peace and quiet, junglelike foliage, and breathtaking vistas. You may want to stop at one of the inviting plant stores run by the talkative French. Near Bryan's Plants **10** you'll pass the **U.S. Department of Agriculture Inspection Station.** If you buy a plant, be sure to stop here to get the plant's roots sprayed for diseases and to get a certificate to present to U.S. customs when you leave the territory. Continue west to Brewer's Bay, then follow Route 30 east back to Frenchtown and Charlotte Amalie.

Time Out Pull into Frenchtown and reward yourself for a long day's travels with a stop at **Epernay,** a Frenchtown champagne bar tucked behind Alexander's Cafe. You'll find wines and champagnes by the glass and hors d'oeuvres to linger over while you contemplate life in the islands. *Open Mon.–Sat. 4:30 PM–1 AM (often until later Fri. and Sat.). Food served 5 PM–midnight. AE, MC, V.*

Exploring St. Croix

Numbers in the margin correspond to points of interest on the St. Croix map.

1 This tour starts in the historic, Danish-style town of **Christiansted,** St. Croix's commercial center. Many of the structures, which are built from the harbor up into the gentle hillsides, date from the 18th century. An easy-to-follow walking tour begins at the **visitor's bureau,** set at the harbor. The building was constructed in 1856, and once served as a scale house, where goods passing through the port were weighed and inspected. Directly across the parking lot, at the edge of D. Hamilton Jackson Park (the park is named for a famed labor leader, journalist, and judge), is the **Old Customs House.** Completed in 1829, this building now houses the island's national park offices. To the east stands yellow **Fort Christiansvaern.** Built by the Danish from 1738 to 1749 to protect the harbor against attacks on commercial shipping, the fort was repeatedly damaged by hurricane-force winds and was partially rebuilt in 1772. It is now part of the National Historic Site and the best-preserved of the remaining Danish-built forts in the Virgin Islands. Five rooms, including military barracks and a dungeon, have been restored to demonstrate how the fort looked in the 1840s, when it was at its height as a military establishment. There is also an exhibit that documents the Danish military's 150-year presence in Christiansted. *Box 160, Christiansted 00822, tel. 809/773–1460. Admission: $2 (includes admission to Steeple Building); free to children under 16 and senior citizens. Open weekdays 8–5, weekends and holidays 9–5. Closed Christmas.*

Cross Hospital Street from the customs house to reach the **post office building.** Built in 1749, it once housed the Danish West India & Guinea Company warehouse. To the south of the post office, across Company Street, stands the maroon-and-white **Steeple Building.** Built by the Danes in 1754, the building once housed the first Danish Lutheran church on St. Croix. It is now a national-park museum and contains exhibits documenting the island's habitation by Native Americans through an extensive array of archaeological artifacts. There are also displays on the architectural development of Christiansted and the African American experience in the town during the Danish colonial rule. *Box 160, Christiansted 00822, tel. 809/773–1460. Admission: $1 (includes admission to fort). Open Wed. and weekends 9–4.*

One of the town's most elegant buildings is **Government House,** on King Street. Built as a home for a Danish merchant in 1747, the building today houses U.S.V.I. government offices and the U.S. district court. Slip into the peaceful inner courtyard to admire the still pools and gardens. A sweeping staircase leads visitors to a second-story ballroom, still the site of official government functions.

To leave Christiansted, drive up Hospital Street from the tourist office and turn right onto Company Street. Follow Company Street for several blocks and turn right with the flow of traffic past the police station. Make a quick left onto King Street, and follow it out of town. At the second traffic light, make a right onto Route 75, Northside Road. A few miles up the road, you can make a side trip by turning right, just past the St. Croix Avis building, onto Route 751, which leads you past the **St. Croix by the Sea** hotel to **Judith's Fancy,** where you can see the ruins of an old great house and the tower left from a 17th-century château that was once home to the governor of the Knights of Malta. The "Judith" comes from the first name of a woman buried on the property. From the guardhouse at the entrance to the neighborhood, follow Hamilton Drive to its end for a view of Salt River Bay, where Christopher Columbus anchored in 1493.

After driving back to Route 75, continue west for 2 miles and turn right at Tradewinds Road onto Route 80, which quickly returns to the grassy coastline and **Cane Bay.** This is one of St. Croix's best beaches for scuba diving, and near the small stone jetty you may see a few wet-suited, tank-backed figures making their way out to the drop-off (a bit farther out there is a steeper drop-off to 12,000 feet). Rising behind you is Mt. Eagle, St. Croix's highest peak, at 1,165 feet. Leaving Cane Bay and passing North Star beach, follow the beautiful coastal road as it dips briefly into the forest, then turn left. There is no street sign, but you'll know the turn: The pavement is marked with the words "The Beast" and a set of giant paw prints—the hill you are about to climb is the infamous Beast of the America's Paradise Triathalon, an annual St. Croix event in which participants must bike up this intimidating slope.

Follow this road, Route 69, as it twists and climbs up the hill and south across the island. The golf course you pass on the right is a Robert Trent Jones course, part of the Carambola resort complex. You will eventually bear right to join Route 76, **Mahogany Road.** Follow Mahogany Road through the heart of the rain forest until you reach the end of the road at Ham's Bluff Road (Route 63), running along the west coast of the island. Turn right and, after a few miles, look to the right side of the road for the **Estate Mount Washington Plantation** (tel. 809/772–

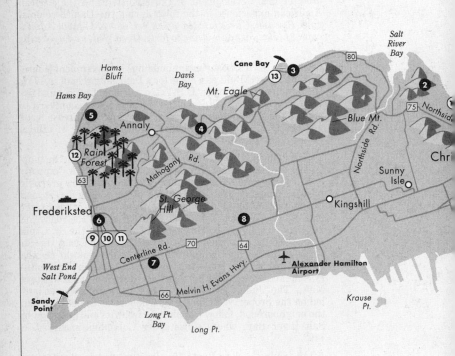

↑
TO
ST. THOMAS

Salt
River
Bay

Hams
Bluff

Davis
Bay

Cane Bay 13 3

80

Hams Bay

Mt. Eagle

2

5

Annaly

4

Blue Mt.

75 Northside

12 Rain
Forest

Mahogany Rd.

Northside Rd.

Chr

63

Sunny
Isle

Kingshill

Frederiksted

St. George
Hill

8

6

9 10 11

Centerline Rd.

70

64

West End
Salt Pond

7

Alexander Hamilton
Airport

Sandy
Point

66

Melvin H. Evans Hwy.

Krause
Pt.

Long Pt.
Bay

Long Pt.

KEY

Cruise Ship

1 Exploring Sites

9 Hotels and Restaurants

Caribbean Sea

Exploring
Cane Bay, **3**
Christiansted, **1**
Estate Mount
Washington
Plantation, **5**

Estate Whim
Plantation Museum, **7**
Frederiksted, **6**
Judith's Fancy, **2**
Mahogany Road, **4**
St. George Village
Botanical Gardens, **8**

Dining
Blue Moon, **9**
Cafe Madeleine, **26**
Camille's, **19**
Cormorant Beach
Club, **15**

Dino's, **18**
Kendricks, **23**
La Guitarra, **24**
Le Tropez, **11**
Top Hat, **20**

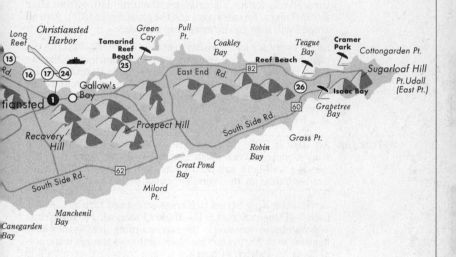

Buck Island

Buck Island Beach

Long Reef

Christiansted Harbor

Green Cay

Pull Pt.

Tamarind Reef Beach 25

Coakley Bay

Teague Bay

Cramer Park

Cottongarden Pt.

15 Rd.

16 17 24

Gallow's Bay

East End Rd. 82

Reef Beach

Sugarloaf Hill

Pt. Udall (East Pt.)

...tiansted 1

26

Isaac Bay

Recovery Hill

Prospect Hill

South Side Rd.

60

Grapetree Bay

Grass Pt.

Robin Bay

62

South Side Rd.

Great Pond Bay

Milord Pt.

Manchenil Bay

Canegarden Bay

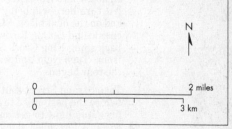

N

| 0 | | 2 miles |
| 0 | | 3 km |

Lodging

The Buccaneer, **25**
Club St. Croix, **16**
Cormorant Beach Club, **15**
The Frederiksted, **10**
Hibiscus Beach Hotel, **14**

Hotel Caravelle, **17**
Hotel on the Cay, **21**
The Pink Fancy, **22**
Sprat Hall, **12**
Villa Madeleine, **26**
Waves at Cane Bay, **13**

1026). Several years ago, while surveying the property, the owners discovered the ruins of a historic sugar plantation buried beneath the rain forest brush. The grounds have since been cleared and opened to the public. A free, self-guided walking tour of the animal-powered mill, rum factory, and other ruins is available daily, and the antique shop located in the old stables is open on Saturdays.

6 Double back along Ham's Bluff Road to reach **Frederiksted,** founded in 1751. A single long cruise-ship pier juts into the sparkling sea from this historic coastal town, noted less for its Danish than for its Victorian architecture (dating from after the uprising of former slaves and the great fire of 1878). A stroll around will take you no more than an hour.

Begin your tour at the **visitor center** (tel. 809/772–0357) on the pier. From here, it's a short walk across Emancipation Park to **Fort Frederik** where, in 1848, the slaves of the Danish West Indies were freed by Governor General Peter van Scholten. The fort, completed in 1760, houses a number of interesting historical exhibits as well as an art gallery. *Tel. 809/772–2021. Admission free. Open Mon.–Fri. 8:30–4:30.*

Time Out Set back in a hidden courtyard on the corner of Market and King streets is **Tradewinds Bar and Deli** (tel. 809/772–0718). Serving well-built sandwiches and well-priced daily specials, Tradewinds is an ideal spot for casual lunches on the west end.

Stroll along King Street to Market Street and turn left. At the corner of Queen Street is the **Market Place,** where fresh fruits and vegetables are sold in the early morning, just as they have been for over 200 years. One block farther on the left is the coral-stone **St. Patrick's Church,** a Roman Catholic church built in 1842.

Head back to King Street and follow it to King Cross Street. A left turn here will bring you to **Apothecary Hall,** built in 1839, and on the next block, **St. Paul's Episcopal Church,** a mixture of classic and Gothic Revival architecture, built in 1812. Double back along King Cross Street to Strand Street and the waterfront. Turn right and walk along the water to the pier, where the tour began.

Take Strand Street south to its end, turn left, then bear right before the post office to leave Frederiksted. Make a left at the first stop light to get on Centerline Road (Queen Mary Highway). A few miles along this road, on the right, is the **Estate**
7 **Whim Plantation Museum.** The lovingly restored estate, with a windmill, cook house, and other buildings, will give you a true sense of what life was like on St. Croix's sugar plantations in the 1800s. The oval-shaped, high-ceilinged great house has antique furniture, decor, and utensils well worth seeing. Notice that it has a fresh and airy atmosphere. (The waterless moat around the great house was used not for defense but for gathering cooling air.) It is built of stone, coral, and lime. Its apothecary exhibit is the largest in all the West Indies. You will also find a museum gift shop. *Box 2855, Frederiksted 00841, tel. 809/772–0598. Admission: $5 adults, $1 children. Open Tues.–Sat. 10–4.*

Continue along Centerline Road to the St. George Estate. Turn
8 left here to reach the **St. George Village Botanical Gardens,** 17

acres of lush and fragrant flora amid the ruins of a 19th-century sugarcane plantation village. *Box 3011, Kingshill 00851–3011, tel. 809/772–3874. Admission: $3 adults, $1 children. Open Tues.–Sat. 10–3. Closed federal holidays.*

Continue east along Centerline Road all the way back to Christiansted.

Exploring St. John

Numbers in the margin correspond to points of interest on the St. John map.

St. John may be small, but the roads are narrow and wind up and down steep hills, so don't expect to get anywhere in a hurry. Bring along your swimsuit for stops at some of the most beautiful beaches in the world.

❶ Cruz Bay town dock is the starting point for just about everything on St. John. Take a leisurely stroll through the streets of this colorful, compact town: There are plenty of shops through which to browse, along with a number of watering holes where you can stop to take a breather.

Follow the waterfront out of town (about 100 yards) to another dock at the edge of a parking lot. At the far side of the lagoon here you'll find the **National Park Service Visitors Center** (tel. 809/776–6201), where you can pick up a handy guide to St. John's hiking trails or see various large maps of the island.

Begin your tour traveling north out of Cruz Bay. You'll pass **Mongoose Junction,** recently expanded to include Mongoose Junction II, one of the prettiest shopping areas to be found. At the ½-mile mark you'll come to the well-groomed gardens and beaches of **Caneel Bay,** purchased from the Danish West India Company and developed by Laurance Rockefeller in the 1950s, who then turned over much of the island to the U.S. government as parkland. Caneel Bay Beach (home of two friendly stingrays) is reached by parking in the Caneel parking lot and walking through the grounds (ask for directions). Visitors are welcome at the three restaurants and other designated areas.

Continue east on North Shore Road, with all the sense of anticipation that you can muster; you are about to see, one after another, four of the most beautiful beaches in all of the Caribbean. The road is narrow and hilly (it was actually just expanded, believe it or not) with switchbacks and steep curves that make driving a challenge. **Hawksnest,** the first beach you will come to, is where Alan Alda shot scenes for his film *The Four Seasons.* Just past Hawksnest Hill swing left to Peace **❷** Hill, sometimes called Sugarloaf Hill, to the *Christ of the Caribbean* **statue** and an old sugar-mill tower. Park in the small unmarked parking lot and walk about 100 yards up a rocky path. The area is grassy, and views do not get much better than this. *Christ of the Caribbean* was erected in 1953 by Colonel Julius Wadsworth and donated, along with 9 acres of land, to the national park in 1975.

Your next stop, and that of quite a few tourist-filled safari buses, is **Trunk Bay,** a beautiful beach with an underwater trail that's good for beginner snorkelers.

Continuing on the beach hunt, you'll come to wide **Cinnamon Bay.** The snorkeling around the point to the right is good—look

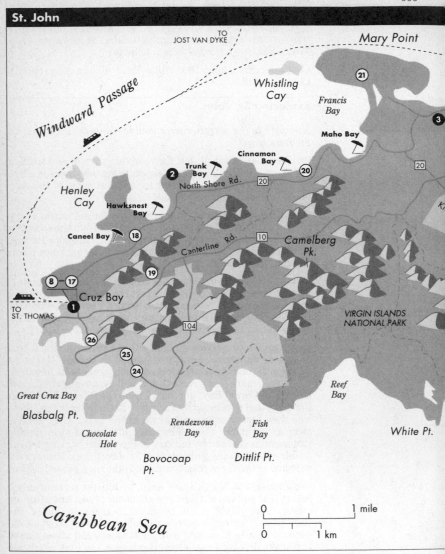

TO JOST VAN DYKE

Mary Point

Windward Passage

Whistling Cay

Francis Bay

21

3

Maho Bay

Cinnamon Bay

Trunk Bay

2

North Shore Rd.

20

20

20

Henley Cay

Hawksnest Bay

Caneel Bay

18

Centerline Rd.

10

Camelberg Pk.

19

8 17

Cruz Bay

1

TO ST. THOMAS

104

VIRGIN ISLANDS NATIONAL PARK

26

25

24

Reef Bay

Great Cruz Bay

Blasbalg Pt.

White Pt.

Chocolate Hole

Rendezvous Bay

Fish Bay

Bovocoap Pt.

Dittlif Pt.

Caribbean Sea

0   1 mile

0   1 km

Exploring
Annaberg Plantation, **3**
Bordeaux Mountain, **7**
Christ of the Caribbean
Statue, **2**
Coral Bay, **4**
Cruz Bay, **1**
East End, **5**
Salt Pond, **6**

Dining
Caneel Bay Resort, **18**
Chow Bella, **24**
Ellington's, **10**
The Fish Trap, **8**
Le Chateau de
Bordeaux, **23**
Lime Inn, **9**
Shipwreck Landing, **22**

Lodging
Battery Hill, **16**
Caneel Bay Resort, **18**
Cinnamon Bay
Campground, **20**
Cruz Bay Villas, **12**
Cruz Views, **17**
Gallows Point Suite
Resort, **14**

Hyatt Regency
St. John, **24**
The Inn at Tamarind
Court, **13**
Lavender Hill
Estates, **15**
Maho Bay Camp, **21**
Pastory Estates, **19**
Raintree Inn, **11**
Serendip, **26**
Virgin Grand Villas, **25**

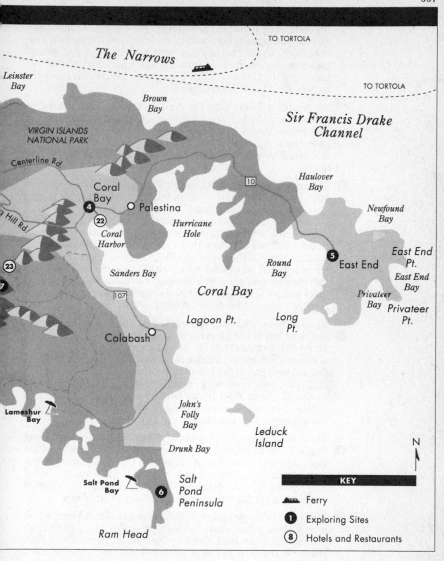

The Narrows

TO TORTOLA

TO TORTOLA

Leinster
Bay

Brown
Bay

VIRGIN ISLANDS
NATIONAL PARK

Sir Francis Drake
Channel

Centerline Rd

Coral
Bay

○ Palestina

10

Haulover
Bay

Hill Rd

4

22

Coral
Harbor

Hurricane
Hole

Newfound
Bay

23

Sanders Bay

107

Round
Bay

5 East End

East End
Pt.

East End
Bay

7

Coral Bay

Lagoon Pt.

Long
Pt.

Privateer
Bay

Privateer
Pt.

Calabash ○

John's
Folly
Bay

Leduck
Island

N

Lameshur
Bay

Drunk Bay

Salt Pond
Bay

6

Salt
Pond
Peninsula

KEY

⛴ Ferry

1 Exploring Sites

8 Hotels and Restaurants

Ram Head

for the big angelfish and the swarms of purple triggerfish that live here. The national-park campground is at Cinnamon Bay and includes a snackbar, bathhouse, boutique, restaurant, general store, water-sports equipment rental, and a self-guided museum. Across the road from the beach parking lot is the beginning of the Cinnamon Bay hiking trail: look for the ruins of a sugar mill to mark the trailhead.

As you leave Cinnamon, the road flattens out and you'll find yourself on a shaded lane running under flowering trees. **Maho Bay** comes almost to the road here, and you may want to stop and take a dip. The Maho Bay Campground is here, too—a wonderful mélange of open-air cottages nestled in the hillside above.

❸ The partially restored **Annaberg Plantation** at Leinster Bay, built in the 1780s and once an important sugar mill, is just ahead on North Shore Road. As you stroll around, look up at the steep hillsides and imagine cutting sugarcane against that grade in the hot sun. Slaves, Danes, and Dutchmen toiled here to harvest the sugarcane that produced sugar, molasses, and rum for export. There are no official visiting hours, no charge for entry, and no official tours, although some well-informed taxi drivers will show you around. *For more information on talks and cultural demonstrations, contact the National Park Service Visitors Center, tel. 809/776–6201.*

❹ From Annaberg keep to the left and go south, then head uphill and bear left at the junction to Route 10, to **Coral Bay,** named for its shape rather than for its underwater life. The word *Coral* comes from *krawl*, Danish for *corral*. The community at the dry, eastern end of the island is the ultimate in laid-back style. It's quiet, neighborhoody, local, and independent. The small wood-and-stucco West Indian homes here house everyone from families born here to newer residents who offer palm readings and massage. This is a place to get away from it all.

❺ The road forms a loop around Coral Bay. Head northeast along Route 10 to Hurricane Hole at the remote and pristine **East End,** only a 15- to 20-minute ride from Coral Bay, where Arawak Indians are believed to have first settled on the island 2,000 years ago. At **Haulover Bay** only a couple of hundred yards separate the Atlantic Ocean from the Caribbean.

❻ Route 107 takes you south to the peninsula of **Salt Pond,** which is only about 1 foot above sea level. If you're weary of driving, you can hike the trail south to the spectacular cliffs of **Ram Head.** In any case you or your rented car can't proceed much farther on 107 without venturing onto a truly rocky road that heads west. Be sure at least to get a view of **Lameshur Bay,** one of the best snorkeling places on St. John and an area used for underwater training by the U.S. Navy.

❼ Once you've run out of road on Route 107, retrace your steps to Coral Bay and go west (left) on Route 10 again, which takes you over the heights of the island toward Cruz Bay. On your left is the turnoff for **Bordeaux Mountain,** at 1,277 feet St. John's highest peak. This is also an area of rain forest. Stop for a moment hereabouts and you'll find bay trees. Crackle a leaf from one, and you'll get a whiff of the spicey aroma that you may recognize from the bay rum for which St. John is famous. To appreciate the Bordeaux Mountain region fully, save some time during your stay to hike the **Reef Bay Trail.** Join a hike led by a

National Park Service ranger, who can identify the trees and plants on the hike down, fill you in on the history of the Reef Bay Plantation, and tell you about the carvings you'll find in the rocks at the bottom of the trail. You can continue straight back into Cruz Bay on Route 10.

Beaches

All beaches on these islands are open to the public, but often you will have to walk through a resort to reach them. Once there, you'll find that resort guests will often have access to lounge chairs and beach bars that are off limits to you; for this reason, you may feel more comfortable at one of the beaches not associated with a resort. Whichever one you choose, remember to remove your valuables from the car.

St. Thomas **Coki Beach,** next to Coral World, is a popular snorkeling spot for cruise ship passengers; it's common to find a group of them among the reefs on the east and west ends of the beach. If you are visiting Coral World, you can use its lockers and changing rooms. **Magens Bay** is usually lively because of its spectacular arc of white sand, more than a half-mile long, and its calm waters—two peninsulas protect it. The bottom is flat and sandy, so this is a place for sunning and swimming rather than snorkeling. The condo resort at **Secret Harbour** doesn't at all detract from the attractiveness of this covelike East End beach. Not only is it pretty, it is also superb for snorkeling—go out to the left, near the rocks. At **Morningstar Beach,** close to Charlotte Amalie, many young residents show up for body surfing or volleyball. The sandy-bottom water is in the shadow of the huge, cliffside Frenchman's Reef Hotel. Snorkeling is good here when the current doesn't affect visibility. From **Sapphire Beach** there is a fine view of St. John and other islands. Snorkeling is excellent at the reef to the right or east, near Pettyklip Point. All kinds of water-sports gear are for rent. **Hull Bay,** on the north shore, has a rugged beach that faces Inner and Outer Brass cays and attracts fishermen and beachcombers. Snorkeling is good here; it's also the only place to surf on the island.

St. Croix **Buck Island** and its reef, which is under environmental protection, can be reached only by boat; nonetheless, it is a must outing on any visit to St. Croix. Its beach is beautiful, but its finest treasures are those you can see when you plop off the boat and adjust your face mask, snorkel, and flippers. The waters are not always gentle at **Cane Bay,** a breezy northshore beach, but the scuba diving and snorkeling are wondrous, and there are never many people around. Just swim straight out to see elkhorn and brain corals. Less than 200 yards out is the drop-off or so-called Cane Bay Wall. **Tamarind Reef Beach** is a small but attractive beach east of Christiansted. Both Green Cay and Buck Island seem smack in front of you and make the view arresting. Snorkeling is good. There are several popular West End beaches along the coast north of Frederiksted. Tiny **La-Grange Beach** is connected to a casual restaurant/bar of the same name, and the beach at the **West End Beach Club** features a bar, water sports, and volleyball. South of Frederiksted, try the beach at the **King Frederik Hotel,** where palm trees can provide plenty of shade for those who need it, and there is a fine beachside restaurant (*see* Dining, *below*) for a casual lunch on weekends.

St. John **Caneel Bay.** This is actually seven white-sand beaches on the north shore, six of which can be reached only by water if you are not a hotel guest. The main beach (ask for directions) provides easy access to the public. **Hawksnest Beach** is becoming more popular every day; it's narrow and lined with sea-grape trees. There are rest rooms, cooking grills, and a covered shed for picnicking. It's popular for group outings, but most of the time it's quiet. **Trunk Bay** is probably St. John's most-photographed beach and the most popular spot for beginning snorkelers because of its underwater trail. It's the St. John stop for cruise-ship passengers who choose a snorkeling tour for the day, so if you're looking for seclusion, check cruise-ship listings in *St. Thomas This Week* to find out what days the highest number are in port. There are changing rooms, a snack bar, picnic tables, and snorkeling equipment for rent. **Cinnamon Bay,** a long, sandy beach facing beautiful cays, serves the adjoining national-park campground. Facilities (showers, toilets, commissary, restaurant, beach shop) are open to all. There's good snorkeling off the point to the right, and rental equipment is available. **Salt Pond Bay,** on the southeastern coast of St. John, is a scenic area to explore, next to Coral Bay and rugged Drunk Bay. This beach is for the adventurous. It's a short hike down a hill from the parking lot, and the only facility is an outhouse. The beach is a little rockier here, but there are interesting tide pools and the snorkeling is good. Take special care to leave nothing valuable in the car, because reports of thefts are numerous here.

Sports and the Outdoors

Fishing In the past quarter-century, some 20 world records, many for blue marlin, have been set in the waters surrounding the Virgin Islands, most notably at St. Thomas's famed North Drop. To book a boat from St. Thomas or St. John, call **St. Thomas Sportfishing Center** (tel. 809/775–7990) or **American Yacht Harbor** (tel. 809/775–0685). On St. Croix, contact **Cruzan Divers** (tel. 809/772–3701), **Mile Mark** (tel. 809/773–2628), or **Ruffian Enterprises** (St. Croix Marina, tel. 809/773–6011 day, 809/773–0917 night).

Golf On St. Thomas, scenic *Mahogany Run* (tel. 809/775–5000), with a par-70, 18-hole course and a view of the B.V.I., lies to the north of Charlotte Amalie and has the especially tricky "Devil's Triangle" trio of holes. On St. Croix, **The Buccaneer's** (tel. 809/773–2100) 18-hole course is conveniently close to (east of) Christiansted. Yet more spectacular is **Carambola** (tel. 809/778–5638), in the valleyed northwestern part of the island, designed by Robert Trent Jones. **The Reef Club** (tel. 809/773–8844), at the northeastern part of the island, has nine holes.

Horseback Riding At Sprat Hall on St. Croix, near Frederiksted, Jill Hurd runs **Paul and Jill's Equestrian Stables** (tel. 809/772–2880 or 809/772–2627) and will take you clip-clopping through the rain forest, along the coast, or on moonlit rides. Costs range from $50 to $75 for the three-hour rides. On St. John, join a trail ride with **Pony Express** (tel. 809/776–6494). A one-hour ride costs $40; the two- and three-hour tours ($75 and $100) can take you both along the beach and through the rainforest. There is also a Moonlight Ride, offered the three days before and after a full moon. All rides are by appointment only.

Sailing/Boating The U.S.V.I. constitutes the biggest charter-boat fleet base in the Western Hemisphere. You can go through a broker to book a private sailing vessel with crew or contact a charter-boat company directly. Among brokers for the U.S.V.I., **Blue Water Cruises** (Box 292, Islisboro, MA 04848, tel. 800/524–2020) has an excellent worldwide reputation. Charter-boat companies on St. Thomas include **Avery's Marine, Inc.** (Box 5248, St. Thomas 00803, tel. 809/776–0113), at Charlotte Amalie, or **Island Yachts** (6100 Red Hook, Suite 4, Red Hook 00802, tel. 809/775–6666 or 800/524–2019), in Red Hook. On St. Croix, the **Annapolis Sailing School** (Box 3334, 601 6th St., Annapolis, MD 21403, tel. 410/267–7205 or 800/638–9192) offers one-week live-aboard cruises leaving from Christiansted. On St. John, **Hinckley Charters Caribbean** (Box 70, Cruz Bay 00830, tel. 809/776–6256) is a small operation based out of Caneel Bay.

Small Powerboat Rentals This is an interesting—and surprisingly, affordable—way to see the islands. **Club Nautico** (American Yacht Harbor, 00802, tel. 809/779–2555) and **Nauti Nymph** (American Yacht Harbor, 00802, tel. 809/779–5066) both have a variety of 21- to 27-foot boats.

Day Sail Charter Companies The following businesses can effortlessly book you on a submarine ride, a parasail boat, a kayak trip, a jet ski ride, a Hobie Cat sail, or a ½ day inshore light-tackle fishing excursion. They get customer feedback on a daily basis and know exactly what type of boats and crew they are booking. They will be happy to answer any questions.

On St. Thomas, call the **Red Hook Charter office** (Box 57, 00802, tel. 809/775–9333). **Coconut Charters** (Suite 202, Red Hook Plaza, 00802, tel. 809/775–5959) usually has a number of multihull vessels doing daysails.

On St. Croix, try **Mile-Mark Charters** (Box 3045, 59 King's Wharf, Christiansted 00822, tel. 809/773–2628 or 800/524–2012; fax 809/773–9411). **Big Beard's Adventure Tours** (Box 4534, Pan Am Pavilion, Christiansted 00822, tel. 809/773–4482) runs trips to Buck Island and beach barbecues using two catamarans, one with a glass bottom. **Buck Island Charters**, with Captain Heinz's trimaran, the *Teroro II* (Box 2881, Christiansted, tel. 809/773–3161) departs for full or half day Buck Island trips from Green Cay Marina.

On St. John, **Connections** (Box 37, 00831, tel. 809/776–6922) represents a dozen of the finest local boats; many of its employees have actually worked on the boats they book.

Scuba Diving/Snorkeling There are numerous dive operators on the three islands, and some of the hotels offer dive packages. Many of the operators listed below also offer snorkeling trips; call individual operators for details.

St. Thomas **Aqua Action Watersports** (Box 15, Red Hook 00802, tel. 809/775–6285) is a full service, PADI five-star shop with all levels of instruction. They also rent sea kayaks and Windsurfers.
Joe Vogel Diving Co. (Box 7322, 00801, tel. 809/775–7610 for the shop), the oldest certified diving operation in the U.S.V.I., leaves from the West Indies Inn for day or night, reef or wreck dives. It has both PADI and NAUI instructors and will dive even if only one person shows up.
Seahorse Dive Boats (Crown Bay Marina, Suite 505, St. Thomas, U.S.V.I. 00802, tel. 809/774–2001) now has two locations

and an expanding teaching facility at Emerald Beach. It is a
PADI five-star operation and does both day and night dives on
local wrecks and reefs.

Underwater Safaris (Box 8469, St. Thomas, U.S.V.I. 00801, tel.
809/774–1350) is conveniently located in Long Bay at the
Ramada Yacht Haven Marina—which is also home to the
U.S.V.I. charterboat fleet. It is a PADI five-star dive operation
that specializes in Buck Island dives to the wreck of the WWI
cargo ship *Cartenser Sr.*

St. Croix   **Anchor Dive** (Box 5588, Salt River Marina, Sunny Isle 00823,
tel. 809/778–1522).

Dive Experience, Inc. (Box 4254, Strand St., Christiansted
00822–4254, tel. 809/773–3307 or 800/235–9047) is a PADI five-
star training facility providing the range from certification to
introductory dives.

Dive St. Croix (59 King's Wharf, Box 3045, Christiansted 00820,
tel. 809/773–3434 or 800/523–3483, fax 809/773–9411), takes
divers to walls and wrecks—over 50 sites—and offers introductory, certification, and PADI, NAUI, and SSI C-card completion courses. It has custom packages with five hotels. Dive St.
Croix is the only dive operation on the island allowed to run
dives to Buck Island.

V.I. Divers, Ltd. (Pan Am Pavilion, Christiansted 00820, tel.
809/773–6045 or 800/544–5911) is a PADI five-star training facility with a 35-foot dive boat and hotel packages.

St. John   **Cruz Bay Watersports Co., Inc.** (Box 252, 00830, tel. 809/776–
6234 or 800/835–7730; fax 809/776–8303) is a PADI five-star diving center with two locations in Cruz Bay. Owner/operators
Patty and Marcus Johnson offer regular reef, wreck, and night
dives aboard three custom dive vessels.

Low Key Water Sports (Box 431, 00831, tel. 809/776–7048), located at the Wharfside Village, offers PADI certification and
resort courses, one- and two-tank dives, wreck dives, and specialty courses.

St. John Watersports (Box 70, 00830, tel. 809/776–6256) is a five-
star PADI center located in the Mongoose Junction shopping
mall.

Tennis   Most hotels rent time to nonguests. For reservations call
St. Thomas   **Bluebeard's Castle Hotel** (tel. 809/774–1600, ext. 195 or 196),
Bolongo Bay (tel. 809/775–1800, ext. 486), **Limetree Tennis
Center** (tel. 809/774–8990), **Mahogany Run Tennis Club** (tel.
809/775–5000), **Sapphire Beach Resort** (tel. 809/775–6100), or
Stouffer Grand Beach Resort (tel. 809/775–1510). All the above
courts have lights and are open into the evening. **Frenchman's
Reef Tennis Courts** (tel. 809/776–8500) has four courts for the
use of guests only. There are two public courts at **Sub Base**
(next to the Water and Power Authority), open on a first-come,
first-served basis.

St. Croix   There are courts at **The Buccaneer, Chenay Bay Beach Resort,
St. Croix by the Sea, Cormorant Beach Club, The Reef, Villa
Madeleine,** and **Club St. Croix** hotels. Public courts can be found
at Conegata Park (two) and Fort Frederik (two), though they
may not be in the best condition.

St. John   **Caneel Bay** (tel. 809/776–6111) has 11 courts (none lighted) and
a pro shop. The **Hyatt Regency** (tel. 809/776–7171) has six
lighted courts and a pro shop.

Shopping

St. Thomas   Most people would agree that St. Thomas lives up to its self-described billing as a shopper's paradise. Even if shopping isn't your idea of paradise, you still may want to slip in on a quiet day (check the cruise-ship listings—Monday and Saturday are usually the least crowded) to check out the prices. Among the best buys are liquor, linens, imported china, crystal (most stores ship), and jewelry. The sheer volume of jewelry available makes this one of the few items for which comparison shopping is worth the effort.

Most stores take major credit cards. There is no sales tax in the U.S.V.I., and shoppers can take advantage of the $1,200 duty-free allowance per family member and the additional 10% discount on the next $1,000 worth of goods, but remember to save your receipts.

Shopping Districts   The prime shopping area in **Charlotte Amalie** is between Post Office and Market squares and consists of three parallel streets running east to west (Waterfront, Main Street, and Back Street) and the alleyways connecting them. A new addition is **Vendors Plaza.** Located on the waterfront at Emancipation Gardens, this is a centralized location for all the vendors who used to clog the sidewalks with their merchandise.

Havensight Mall, next to the cruise-ship dock, though not as charming as Charlotte Amalie, has parking and many of the same stores. West of town, the pink-stucco **Nisky Center** is more of a hometown shopping center than a tourist area, but there's an excellent bookstore (next to a bakery and yogurt shop), as well as a bank, gift shops, and clothing stores.

Out east, you can buy beachwear and accessories at **Red Hook Shopping Center** and **The Store Room.**

Art Galleries   **A.H. Riise Caribbean Art Print Gallery** (Riise's Alley off Main St., tel. 809/776–2303). Haitian and Virgin Islands art are displayed and sold here, along with art books and the exquisite botanical prints and note cards from Mapes de Monde.

The Gallery (Veteran's Dr., tel. 809/776–4641). The Gallery carries Haitian art, along with works by a number of Virgin Islands artists.

Books and Magazines   **Dockside Bookshop** (Havensight Mall, Bldg. IV, tel. 809/774–4937). There's a selection of books written in and about the Caribbean and the Virgin Islands, from literature to chartering guides to books on seashells and tropical flowers.

Cameras and Electronics   **Boolchand's** (31 Main St., tel. 809/776–0794, and Havensight Mall, tel. 809/776–0302). A variety of brand-name cameras as well as audio and video equipment are featured here.

Royal Caribbean (two locations on Main St., tel. 809/776–4110, and Havensight Mall, tel. 809/776–8890). This store has attractive prices on some cameras and accessories; portable cassette players are usually good buys here.

China and Crystal   **A.H. Riise Gift Shops** (Main St. and Riise's Alley and Havensight Mall; tel. 809/776–2303). A.H. Riise carries Waterford, Wedgwood, Royal Crown, and Royal Doulton at good prices.

The English Shop (Waterfront, tel. 809/776–5399, and Havensight Mall, tel. 809/776–3776). This store offers china and crystal from major European and Japanese manufacturers.

Little Switzerland (two locations—5 and 38—on Main St., one behind the post office, and one at Havensight Mall; tel. 809/776–2010). All of this establishment's shops carry crystal from Lalique, Baccarat, Waterford, Riedel, and Orrefors, and china from Villeroy & Boch and Wedgwood, among others.

Clothing **G'Day** (waterfront at Royal Dane Mall, tel. 809/774–8855). Everything in this tiny shop—from umbrellas to silk scarves to reasonably priced sportswear—is drenched in the bright colors of Australian artist Ken Done.

Janine's Boutique (8A-2 Palm Passage, tel. 809/774–8243) and **Luisa's Boutique** (located in Brumney's jewelry and gift shop, Main St., tel. 809/775–2703). These two related-by-ownership shops sit side by side in this elegant arcade. At Janine's you'll find women's and men's dressy and casual apparel from European designers and manufacturers, including the Louis Feraud collection, and select finds from Valentino, Christian Dior, and Pierre Cardin. Luisa's features Italian designer fashions and leather accessories, including shoes.

Java Wraps (24 Palm Passage, tel. 809/774–3700). Indonesian batik creations are the specialty here. This store offers a complete line of beach cover-ups, swimwear, and leisure wear for women, men, and children.

Lion in the Sun (Riise's Alley, tel. 809/776–4203). A feast of luscious fabrics labeled Go Silk, Donna Karan, Sonya Rykiel, Giorgio Armani, and Hugo Bass, just to name a few.

Local Color (Garden St., tel. 809/774–3727). St. Thomas artist Kerry Topper exhibits her island designs on cool cotton clothing. Also on display are wearable art by other local artists, unique jewelry, wall hangings, wood sculptures, and big-brim straw hats dipped in fuchsia, turquoise, and other tropical colors.

Thriving Tots Boutique (Garden St., tel. 809/776–0009). You'll find Caribbean clothing for children (infants to size 16), including locally made shorts sets and sundresses.

Crafts and Gifts **The Caribbean Marketplace** (Havensight Mall, Bldg. III, tel. 809/776–5400). This is the place to look for Caribbean handicrafts, including Caribelle batiks from St. Lucia; bikinis from the Cayman Islands; and Sunny Caribee spices, soaps, teas, and coffees from Tortola.

The Cloth Horse (Fort Mylner Shopping Center, tel. 809/774–4761). Here you'll find signed pottery from the Dominican Republic; wicker and rattan furniture and household goods from the island of Hispaniola; and pottery, rugs, and bedspreads from all over the world.

Down Island Traders (Bakery Sq., Veteran's Dr., and Frenchman's Reef, tel. 809/774–3419). These traders deal in hand-painted calabash bowls ($10); finely printed Caribbean note cards; jams, jellies, spices, and herbs; herbal teas made of rum, passion fruit, and mango; high-mountain coffee from Jamaica; and a variety of handicrafts from throughout the Caribbean.

Food   If you're cooking and want to get creative or to make up a special picnic for the trip to St. John, there's now a bounty of delis on St. Thomas. **I'll Take Manhattan** (Weymouth Rhymer Hwy. and Red Hook) is a New York–style deli featuring high-quality meats and a good selection of cheeses and sausages, and at **Gourmet Gallery**, at Yacht Haven, you'll find an excellent and reasonably priced wine selection, as well as condiments, cheeses, and specialty ingredients for everything from tacos to curries to chow mein. For fruits and vegetables, go to the **Fruit Bowl**, at Wheatley Center.

Jewelry   **A.H. Riise Gift Shops** (Main St. and Riise's Alley and Havensight Mall, tel. 809/776–2303). St. Thomas's oldest and largest shop for luxury items, with jewelry, pearls, ceramics, china, crystal, flatwear, perfumes, and watches.

Amsterdam Sauer (14 Main St., tel. 809/774–2222). Many fine one-of-a-kind designs are displayed here.

Aperiton (3A Main St., tel. 809/776–0780). A good spot for lovely jewelry made by Greek and Italian designers.

Blue Diamond (25A Main St., tel. 809/776–4340). Favored by many locals, this store shows its own 14- and 18-karat designs crafted by European goldsmiths.

Cardow's (three stores on Main St., tel. 809/776–1140; two on the waterfront, one at Frenchman's Reef Hotel, three at Havensight, tel. 809/776–1140). Cardows offers an enormous "chain bar" more than 100 feet long, where you're guaranteed 30%–50% savings off U.S. retail prices or your money will be refunded (within 30 days of purchase.)

Carson Co. Antiques (Royal Dane Mall, tel. 809/774–6175). This is a great place for finds. Browse through a selection that includes rare ancient treasures in pottery and porcelain, as well as a collection of vintage costume jewelry.

Cartier (30 Trompeter Gade, tel. 809/774–1590). In addition to the fantastically beautiful and fantastically priced items, there are a surprising number of affordable ones as well.

Colombian Emeralds (one on Main St., two on the waterfront, and one at Havensight Mall; tel. 809/774–0581). Well known in the Caribbean, this store offers set and unset gems of every description, including high-quality emeralds.

H. Stern (two on Main St., Havensight Mall, Frenchman's Reef, Stouffer Grand Beach Resort, and Bluebeards; tel. 809/776–1939). One of the most respected names in gems.

Irmela's Jewel Studio (Tolbod Gade, tel. 809/774–5875). For 22 years Irmela has been offering some of the Caribbean's most exquisite jewelry designs inside the historic stone walls of the Grand Hotel.

Little Switzerland (two locations—5 and 38—on Main St., one behind the post office and one at Havensight Mall, tel. 809/776–2010). The sole U.S.V.I. distributor for Rolex watches, the store also does a booming mail-order business.

Leather Goods   **Gucci** (Riise's Alley off Main St., tel. 809/774–7841, and at Havensight Mall, tel. 809/774–4090). Traditional Gucci-insignia designs for men and women are offered here.

The Leather Shop (Main St., tel. 809/776–3995, and Havensight Mall, Bldg. II, tel. 809/776–0040). You'll find big names at big prices here: Fendi and Bottega Veneta are prevalent.

Louis Vuitton (24 Main St. at Palm Passage, tel. 809/774–3633). Here is an example of St. Thomas shopping at its most elegant.

Traveler's Haven (Havensight Mall, tel. 809/775–1798). This store features leather bags, backpacks, vests, and money belts.

Zora's (Norre Gade across from Roosevelt Park, tel. 809/774–2559). Fine leather sandals made to order are the specialty here.

Linens **Shanghai Silk and Handicrafts** (Royal Dane Mall, tel. 809/776–8118) and **Shanghai Linen** (Waterfront, tel. 809/776–2828). These two stores do a brisk trade in linens and silks.

Mr. Tablecloth (Main St., tel. 809/774–4343). The friendly staff here will help you choose from their floor-to-ceiling array of linens.

Liquor and Wine **A.H. Riise Liquors** (Main St. and Riise's Alley and Havensight Mall; tel. 809/774–6900). This Riise venture offers a large selection of liquors, cordials, wines, and tobacco, including rare vintage cognacs, Armagnacs, ports, and Madeiras. They also stock imported cigars, fruits in brandy, and barware from England.

Al Cohen's Discount Liquor (across from Havensight Mall, Long Bay Rd., tel. 809/774–3690). A warehouse-style store with a large wine department.

Music **Parrot Fish Records and Tapes** (Back St., tel. 809/776–4514). Standard stateside tapes and compact discs are stocked here, plus a good selection of Caribbean artists, including local groups. For a catalogue of calypso, soca, steel band, and reggae music, write to Parrot Fish, Box 9206, St. Thomas 00801.

Third World Electronics (Four Winds Shopping Plaza, tel. 809/775–5510). This is where you'll find the latest cuts by Caribbean artists, including many underground tapes from "down island."

Perfumes **Sparky's** (Main St., tel. 809/776–7510). The impeccably turned-out salesclerks can give you a facial and makeup lesson.

Tropicana Perfume Shoppes (2 Main St., tel. 809/774–0010, and 14 Main St., tel. 809/774–1834). Tropicana has the largest selection of fragrances for men and women in all of the Virgin Islands; both shops give small free samples to customers.

Toys **Animal Crackers Fun Factory** (Inside Sparky's, off Royal Dane Mall, tel. 809/774–4939). This place is a must-visit, whether the children are with you or back home anticipating their gifts. It's a playland jungle aswarm with parrots and pirates, teddy bears and penguins.

Land of Oz (Royal Dane Mall, tel. 809/776–7888). This Oz has a huge selection of toys fashioned by European craftsmen that include Royal Doulton collector dolls, Brio wood trains, German nutcrackers, and English wood sailboats.

St. Croix Although St. Croix doesn't offer as many shopping opportunities as St. Thomas, the island does provide an array of smaller stores with unique merchandise. In Christiansted, the best shopping areas are the Pan Am Pavilion and Caravelle Arcade off Strand Street and along King and Company streets.

Books **The Writer's Block** (36C Strand St., Christiansted, tel. 809/773–5101) carries a full line of fiction and nonfiction, as well as travel guides and other books about St. Croix.

China and Crystal **The Royal English Shop** (5 Strand St., Frederiksted, tel. 809/772–2040). Saint-Louis and Beyer crystal and Wedgwood china are carried here at prices significantly lower than those on the mainland. Store hours vary, depending on the cruise-ship schedule, so check ahead.

Little Switzerland (Hamilton House, 56 King St., Christiansted, tel. 809/773–1976). The St. Croix branch of this Virgin Islands institution features a variety of Rosenthal flatware, Lladro figurines, Waterford and Baccarat crystal, Lalique figurines, and Wedgwood and Royal Doulton china.

Clothing **Caribbean Clothing Company** (55 Company St., Christiansted, tel. 809/773–5012). This fashionable store features contemporary sportswear by top American designers.

Java Wraps (Pan Am Pavilion, 42–43 Strand St., Christiansted, tel. 809/773–3770). Indonesian batik cover-ups and resort wear for men, women, and children are featured here.

Polo/Ralph Lauren Factory Store (52 C Company St., Christiansted, tel. 809/773–4388). The factory outlet for this popular, upscale clothing line presents men's and women's clothes at huge discounts.

Crafts and Gifts **American West India Company** (1 Strand St., Christiansted, tel. 809/773–7325). In the market for some Jamaican allspice or perhaps a piece of Haitian metalwork? Goods from around the Caribbean, including St. Croix, are available here.

Designworks (3 Queen Cross St., Christiansted, tel. 809/773–5355). This store features "everything for the home," from Danish candles and hand-woven palm baskets to heavy Mexican glassware and Marimekko fabrics imported from Finland.

Folk Art Traders (1B Queen Cross St. at Strand St., Christiansted, tel. 809/773–1900). The owners travel to Haiti, Jamaica, Guayana, and elsewhere in the Caribbean to find the treasures sold in this shop, including baskets, masks, pottery, and ceramics.

The Royal Ponciana (38 Strand St., Christiansted, tel. 809/773–9892). This attractively designed store carries island seasonings and hot sauces, West Indian crafts, bath gels, and herbal teas.

Jewelry **Colombian Emeralds** (43 Queen Cross St., Christiansted, tel. 809/773–1928 or 809/773–9189). Specializing—of course—in emeralds, including some that are under $100, this store also carries diamonds, rubies, sapphires, and gold.

Crucian Gold (57A Company St., Christiansted, tel. 809/773–5241). Located in a small courtyard in a West Indian–style cottage, this store carries the unique gold creations of St. Croix native Brian Bishop.

Sonya's (1 Company St., Christiansted, tel. 809/778–8605). This is the home of the island's signature hook bracelet, which was designed by owner Sonya Hough.

Liquor **Grog and Spirits** (59 Kings Wharf, Christiansted, tel. 809/778–8400 and Chandlers Wharf, Gallows Bay, tel. 809/773–8485). A good selection of liquor is available at these conveniently located shops.

Tradewind's Liquor Store (King St., Frederiksted, tel. 809/772–0718). Duty-free liquor is available at this popular combination bar/deli/liquor store.

Woolworth's (Sunny Isle Shopping Center, Centerline Rd., tel. 809/778–5466). This department store carries a huge line of discount, duty-free liquor.

Perfumes **St. Croix Shoppes** (53AB Company St., Christiansted tel. 809/773–2727). One of these side-by-side shops specializes solely in Estee Lauder and Clinique products, while the other carries a full line of fragrances.

St. Croix Perfume Center (1114 King St., Christiansted, tel. 809/773–7604). An extensive array of fragrances, including all the major brands, is available here.

St. John With so much natural beauty to offer, the pleasures of shopping on St. John are all but overlooked in travel literature, but the blend of luxury items and handicrafts found in the shops on St. John offers excellent opportunities. Two new shopping areas have widened the choices. Two levels of cool, stone-wall shops, set off by colorfully planted terraces and courtyards, make **Mongoose Junction** one of the prettiest shopping malls in the Caribbean. **Wharfside Village,** on the other side of Cruz Bay, is a painted-clapboard village with shops and restaurants.

Dining

Just about every kind of cuisine you can imagine is available in the U.S.V.I. The beauty and freedom of the islands has attracted a cadre of professionally trained chefs who know their way around fresh fish and local fruits. If you are staying in a large hotel, you will pay prices similar to those in New York City or Paris—in other words, dining out is usually expensive.

St. Thomas is the most cosmopolitan of the islands and has the most visitors, so it is not surprising that the island also has the largest number and greatest variety of restaurants. St. Croix restaurants are both more relaxed and, in some ways, more elegant. Dining on St. John is, in general, more casual; the emphasis is on simple food prepared to order in an informal setting at reasonable prices.

Highly recommended restaurants are indicated by a star ★.

Category*	Cost*
Very Expensive	over $35
Expensive	$25–$35
Moderate	$15–$25
Inexpensive	under $15

*average cost of a three-course dinner, per person, excluding drinks and service.

St. Thomas **Entre Nous.** The view here, from the terrace of Bluebeard's Castle high over Charlotte Amalie's harbor, is as exhilarating as the dining is elegant. In the evening, you can watch the light-bedecked cruise ships pull slowly out of the harbor, while deciding between such main courses as rack of lamb, Caribbean lobster, veal, and chateaubriand. *Bluebeard's Castle, Charlotte Amalie, tel. 809/774–4050. Reservations required. AE, MC, V. No lunch. Very Expensive.*

Fiddle Leaf. Patricia LaCorte's coral-and-blue restaurant, accented with vibrant art, is on a covered pavilion overlooking town. LaCorte's insistence on the freshest ingredients puts this restaurant a notch above most others. The Caesar salad prepared tableside is excellent. *Government Hill, near Main St., Charlotte Amalie, tel. 809/775–2810. Reservations advised. AE, MC, V. Very Expensive.*

Hotel 1829. You'll dine by candlelight flickering over stone walls and pink table linens at this restaurant on the gallery of the hotel. The menu and wine list are extensive, from Caribbean rock lobster to rack of lamb. Many items, including a warm spinach salad, are prepared tableside, and the restaurant is justly famous for its dessert soufflés, made of chocolate, Grand Marnier, raspberry, or coconut, to name a few. *Government Hill, near Main St., Charlotte Amalie, tel. 809/776–1829. Reservations required. AE, MC, V. Very Expensive.*

★ **Romanos.** Inside this huge old stucco house in Smith Bay is a delightful surprise: a spare, elegant setting and superb northern Italian cuisine. Owner Tony hasn't advertised since the restaurant opened five years ago, and it is always packed. Try the pastas, either with a classic sauce or one of the unique combinations created by Tony, such as a cream sauce with mushrooms, prosciutto, pine nuts, and Parmesan. *97 Smith Bay, tel. 809/775–0045. Reservations advised. Closed Sun. Very Expensive.*

Virgilio's. This is a romantic hideaway with excellent food and service. Its owner moved to the islands from Beverly Hills in 1987, and this corner café has been booming ever since. Its dark, air-conditioned interior is highlighted by dramatic, backlit, stained-glass partitions, and the Italian specialties are reasonably priced and delicious. Don't leave without having a Virgilio's cappuccino, a chocolate-and-coffee drink so rich it's dessert. *Back St., Charlotte Amalie, tel. 809/776–4920. Reservations advised. AE, MC, V. Very Expensive.*

Piccola Marina Cafe. Dockside dining at its friendliest is the trademark of this open-air restaurant close to the St. John ferry dock at Red Hook. The clientele is a mix of sailors and fishermen who work on the docks that your table overlooks. Specialties are fresh fish—you can watch your dinner being unloaded from the boat and carried to the kitchen during happy hour—and homemade pasta dishes. There are also good lunch specials and a Sunday brunch. *Red Hook, tel. 809/775–6350. Reservations advised. AE, MC, V. Expensive.*

★ **Alexander's Cafe.** This charming restaurant is a favorite with the people in the restaurant business on St. Thomas—always a sign of quality. Local media types, wine aficionados (the always-changing wine list offers the best value on the island), and people just out to relax pack this place seven nights a week. Alexander is Austrian, and the schnitzels are delicious and reasonably priced; the baked-brie-and-fruit plate and pasta specials are fresh and tasty. Save room for strudel. *24A Honduras, Frenchtown, tel. 809/776–4211. Reservations advised. AE, MC, V. Moderate–Expensive.*

The Chart House. Located in an old great house on the tip of the Frenchtown peninsula, this restaurant features kebab and teriyaki dishes, lobster, Hawaiian chicken, and a large salad bar. *Villa Olga, Frenchtown, tel. 809/774-4262. Reservations accepted for 10 or more. AE, DC, MC, V. Moderate-Expensive.*

For the Birds. The beer is served in Mason jars, and margaritas are available in 46-ounce servings at this beach restaurant with a disco floor (Sunday is ladies' night). You can have sizzling fajitas, barbecued baby-back ribs, seafood, or steak. For children there are coloring place mats and crayons. *Scott Beach, near Compass Point, East End, tel. 809/775-6431. Reservations required for 6 or more. AE, MC, V. Moderate-Expensive.*

★ **Little Bopeep.** Inside this unpretentious restaurant tucked behind the shops of Main Street is some of the best West Indian food on the island. Try the Conch in Creole Sauce, sweet potato stuffing, and fried plantains. *Back St., Charlotte Amalie, tel. 809/776-9292. AE, MC, V. Moderate.*

Zorba's Cafe. Tired of shopping? Summon up one last ounce of energy and head up Government Hill to Zorba's. Sit and have a cold beer or bracing iced tea in the 19th-century stone-paved courtyard surrounded by banana trees. Greek salads and appetizers, moussaka, and an excellent vegetarian plate top the menu. *Government Hill, Charlotte Amalie, tel. 809/776-0444. AE, MC, V. Moderate.*

Bryan's Bar and Restaurant. Located high on the cool north side of the island, overlooking Hull Bay, this surfer's bar offers some of the best food on the island. Dining is by lantern light at wood booths inside or at picnic tables outside. The chefs surf by day and cook by night, serving up gargantuan portions of grilled fish, steaks, and a great teriyaki-chicken sandwich. A local hangout complete with pool table, it's casual and cheap. *Hull Bay, tel. 809/774-3522. No credit cards. No lunch. Inexpensive-Moderate.*

Eunice's Terrace. Repeat visitors to Eunice's will find that this excellent West Indian cook has gone up in the world—literally. She's built a two-story restaurant behind the former one-room-with-porch affair that made her famous. The new restaurant is roomy and has a spacious bar, but much the same menu of native dishes, including conch fritters, fried fish, local sweet potato, fungi, and green banana. *Rte. 38, near Stouffer's Grand Beach Resort and Coral World, Smith Bay, tel. 809/775-3975. AE, MC, V. Inexpensive-Moderate.*

Wok & Roll. Tucked in a corner just below the Warehouse bar in Red Hook, this unpretentious nook is finally bringing tasty take-out Chinese to the East End. You'll find all the classics, from fried rice and chow mein to sweet and sour pork, at good prices. *Red Hook, across from the ferry dock, tel. 809/775-6246. Inexpensive.*

St. Croix   **Cafe Madeleine.** This elegant restaurant, part of the Villa Madeleine resort nestled in the hills on St. Croix's East End, features such diverse cuisine as lamb and polenta soup, swordfish medallions sautéed with green tomato and asparagus, and a number of fine beef dishes. The wine list is extensive. *Teague Bay (take Rte. 82 out of Christiansted and turn right at the Reef Condominiums), tel. 809/778-7377. Reservations advised. AE, DC, MC, V. Closed Mon. and Tues. Very Expensive.*

Kendricks. This restaurant is a tranquil oasis of civility in the heart of Christiansted. Waiters dote on diners seated at tables laid with crisp linens and fine china, serving such dishes as artichoke hearts filled with scallops on a bed of lemon cream sauce or roasted pecan crusted pork loin with ginger mayonaisse. *Queen Cross St., Christiansted, tel. 809/773–9199. Reservations advised. AE. No lunch; closed Sun. and Mon. Very Expensive.*

★ **Cormorant Beach Club.** Candlelight and the sounds of the night surf create the atmosphere here, where a California chef brings her own touch to Continental and Crucian dishes. The boneless breast of chicken is blackened with Creole spices and served with black beans and avocado salsa. Among the appetizers are conch fritters and carrot-orange soup. Don't miss the West Indian Buffet held here on Thursday nights. *La Grande Princesse, west of Christiansted, tel. 809/778–8920. Reservations advised. AE, MC, V. Expensive.*

★ **Dino's.** Homemade Italian food, often with a West Indian twist, is found at this cozy restaurant, one of the island's best. Pasta is made fresh daily by chefs/owners Dwight DeLude and Dino Natale. The hot antipasto appetizer features bacon-wrapped and grilled shrimp; broiled tomato with a veil of fresh pesto; fried eggplant in a tomato-butter sauce; and grilled, succulent scallops. *4-C Hospital St., Christiansted, tel. 809/778–8005. Reservations advised. No credit cards. Closed Sept. Closed Sun. and Thurs. Expensive.*

★ **Top Hat.** Many locals consider this restaurant to be the best on the island. It's been in business for 20 years, serving international cuisine with an emphasis on Danish specialties—roast duck, crepes with shrimp, and smoked eel. The old West Indian structure, complete with gingerbread trim, is nicely accented in gray, white, and pink. The photographs on the walls are the work of owner and European-trained chef Hans Rasmussen. *52 Company St., Christiansted, tel. 809/773–2346. Reservations advised. AE, MC, V. Closed May–Oct.; closed Sun. and lunch. Expensive.*

Blue Moon. This terrific little bistro, popular for its live jazz on Friday nights, has an eclectic, often changing menu that draws heavily on Cajun and French influences. Try the seafood chowder as an appetizer and leave room for the bittersweet chocolate torte for dessert. *17 Strand St., Frederiksted, tel. 809/ 772–2222. AE. Closed July–Sept. Closed Mon. and lunch. Moderate.*

Le Tropez. A dark-wood bar and soft lighting add to the Mediterranean atmosphere at this pleasant bistro, tucked into a courtyard off Frederiksted's main thoroughfare. Diners, seated either inside or on the adjoining patio, enjoy light French fare, such as quiches, salads, brochettes, and crepes. Daily specials often take advantage of fresh local seafood. *67 King St., Frederiksted, tel. 809/772–3000. Reservations accepted. AE, MC, V. Closed Sun. Moderate.*

★ **Camille's.** This tiny, lively spot is perfect for lunch or a light supper. Sandwiches and burgers are the big draw here, though the daily seafood special, often wahoo or mahi-mahi, is also popular. *Queen Cross St., Christiansted, tel. 809/773–2985. No credit cards. Closed Sun. Inexpensive.*

La Guitarra. If you'd like to try some authentic West Indian/Latin cooking, head for this small restaurant for dishes, such as stew beef, conch stew, or fried porkchops, all served with rice, beans, and salad. *39–40 Queen Cross St., Market Square,*

Christiansted, tel. 809/773–8448. No credit cards. Closed Sun. Inexpensive.

St. John **Caneel Bay Resort.** Three restaurants, all within the resort's 170-acre complex, offer good food and good service in a beautiful setting. From the more informal Sugar Mill to the elegant Turtle Bay (good wine list), you'll feel pampered. No air-conditioning, but cool breezes abound. *Northshore Rd., tel. 809/776–6111. Reservations advised. Jacket at the Beach Terrace and Turtle Bay for dinner during winter season. AE, MC, V. Expensive–Very Expensive.*

Chow Bella. This place is taking the Hyatt's on-site restaurant in a new direction. The menu here, says the maître d', is "transcultural"—Chinese and Italian, as you might have surmised from the name. Order from one side of the menu and you'll have pot stickers; from the other side you'll have pasta. *Hyatt Regency Beach Hotel, tel. 809/776–7171. Reservations advised. Dress: No shorts or collarless shirts. AE, MC, V. No lunch. Closed Mon. Expensive–Very Expensive.*

★ **Ellington's.** Extending onto the second-story veranda of the Gallows Point Suite Resort's central building, Ellington's is a pleasant surprise, informal yet a cut above Cruz Bay's typical ultracasual fish-fry joint. The menu leans heavily toward fish nevertheless: Start with the jumbo shrimp cooked in sweet coconut and served with a mango sauce or the seafood chowder. Entrées include flawlessly presented sea scallops and pesto, swordfish scampi, or filet mignon. Save room for dessert, perhaps the banana chocolate chip cake or the white chocolate brownie. *Gallows Point Suite Resort, tel. 809/776–7166. Reservations accepted. AE, MC, V. Expensive.*

★ **Le Chateau de Bordeaux.** The best view you're going to find to dine by is on the terrace here or in the air-conditioned dining room (go at sunset). The menu is a combination of French and West Indian cuisine and specializes in fresh seafood—Caribbean lobster, yellowtail, and sea snails. *Rte. 10, just east of Centerline Rd., tel. 809/776–6611. AE, MC, V. Expensive.*

★ **The Fish Trap.** Resting on a series of open-air wooden balconies among banana trees and coconut palms, this favorite of locals serves up six kinds of fresh fish nightly, along with tasty appetizers, such as conch fritters and Fish Trap chowder. The menu also includes steak, pasta, and chicken. *Downtown, Cruz Bay, tel. 809/776–9817. AE, D, MC, V. No lunch. Closed Mon. Moderate–Expensive.*

★ **Lime Inn.** This busy, roofed, open-air restaurant has an ornamental garden and beach-furniture chairs. There are several shrimp and steak dishes and such specials as sautéed chicken with artichoke hearts in lemon sauce. On Wednesday night there's an all-you-can-eat shrimp feast. *Downtown, Cruz Bay, tel. 809/776–6425. Reservations advised. AE, MC, V. Moderate.*

Shipwreck Landing. Start with a house drink, perhaps a fresh-squeezed concoction of lime, coconut, and rum, then move on to hearty taco salads, fried shrimp, teriyaki chicken, and conch fritters. The birds keep up a lively chatter in the bougainvillea that surround the open-air restaurant, and there's live music on Sunday nights in season. *Coral Bay, tel. 809/776–8640. MC, V. Inexpensive.*

Lodging

The U.S.V.I. has a myriad of lodging options to suit any style, from luxury five-star resorts to casual condominiums and national campgrounds.

On St. Thomas, guest houses and smaller hotels are not typically on the beach, but they offer pools and shuttle service to nearby beaches (St. Thomas is not a walking island), and the several historic inns above town offer a pleasing island ambience. In keeping with its small-town atmosphere and more relaxed pace, St. Croix offers a good variety of more moderately priced small hotels and guest houses, which are either on the beach or in a rural setting where a walk to the beach is easy. Accommodations on St. John defy easy categorization. The national-park campground offerings start with bare campsites and progress through standing tents, tent cabins, and small cottages. At the other end of the spectrum are luxury retreats of understated elegance that offer rest and relaxation of a high—and pricey—order.

The prices below reflect rates during high season, which generally runs from December 15 to April 15. Rates are from 25% to 50% lower the rest of the year.

Category	Cost*
Very Expensive	over $200
Expensive	$150–$200
Moderate	$100–$150
Inexpensive	under $100

All prices are for a standard double room, excluding 7.5% accommodations tax.

The most highly recommended lodgings are indicated by a star ★.

St. Thomas **Bolongo Elysian Beach Resort.** At this East End property, coral-color villas are stepped down the hillside to the edge of Cowpet Bay. Rooms are decorated in muted tropical floral print. Activity is centered on a kidney-shape pool complete with waterfall and thatched-roof pool bar. The Palm Court restaurant has gained a strong local following, a sure sign of success. All rooms have air-conditioning, terraces, ceiling fans, cable TV, telephone, and honor bar, and some have kitchenettes. *Box 51, Red Hook, 00802, tel. 809/775–1000 or 800/343–4079, fax 809/776–0910. 175 rooms. Facilities: 3 restaurants, 2 bars, freshwater pool, lighted tennis court. AE, MC, V. CP. Very Expensive.*

Marriott's Frenchman's Reef and Morning Star Beach Resorts. Sprawling, luxurious, and situated on a prime harbor promontory east of Charlotte Amalie like a permanently anchored cruise ship, Frenchman's Reef is St. Thomas's American superhotel. There are cavernous restaurants and ballrooms, 23 duty-free shops, a helicopter pad, and an elevator to the beach. Most rooms have sea views, but some have views of the parking lot; the luxury-class rooms are located at Morning Star, right next to the surf. There are guest activities and live entertainment galore, plus a ferry between the hotel and town. Baby-sitting can be arranged at $5 an hour, but there are no organized activities for children. G-rated and PG-rated movies are shown on Sunday and Monday nights. *Box 7100, 00801, tel. 809/776–8500 or 800/524–7100, fax 809/777–8820. 518 rooms. Facilities: 7 restaurants, 6 bars, 2 Olympic-size pools, 4 tennis courts, beach, water sports, helicopter tours. AE, DC, MC, V. EP, MAP. Very Expensive.*

★ **Sapphire Beach Resort and Marina.** This resort sits right on Sapphire Beach, one of St. Thomas's prettiest, where on a clear day the lush green mountains of the neighboring B.V.I. seem close enough to touch. There's excellent snorkeling on the reefs to each side of the beach. This is a quiet retreat where you can nap while swinging in one of the hammocks strung between the palm trees in your front yard, but on Sunday the place rocks with a beach party. All units have fully equipped kitchens, airconditioning, telephones, and cable TV. Children are welcome and may join the Little Gems Kids Klub. Children under age 12 eat free at the resort's restaurant. *Box 8088, Red Hook, 00801, tel. 809/775–6100 or 800/524–2090, fax 809/775–4024. 141 rooms. Facilities: restaurant, bar, beach, marina, 4 tennis courts, water sports. AE, MC, V. EP, MAP. Very Expensive.*

Stouffer Grand Beach Resort. This resort's zigzag architectural angles spell luxury, from the marble atrium lobby to the onebedroom suites with private whirlpool baths. The beach is excellent, and there's a fitness center with Nautilus machines. The lobby is often populated by those lucky business types whose companies favor the resort as a convention-and-conference center. Daily organized activities for children include iguana hunts, T-shirt painting, and sand-castle building. *Smith Bay Rd., Box 8267, 00801, tel. 809/775–1510 or 800/468–3571, fax 809/775–2185. 297 rooms. Facilities: 2 restaurants, beach, 6 lighted tennis courts, 2 pools, water sports. AE, DC, MC, V. EP. Very Expensive.*

Pavilions & Pools. Simple, tropical-cool decor and privacy set the mood here, where each island-style room has its own 20-by-14-foot or 18-by-16-foot pool. The unpretentious accommodations include air-conditioning, telephones, full kitchens, and VCRs. Water sports are available at Sapphire Beach on the adjacent property. The management is particularly attentive and does everything to preserve the general quiet. *Rte. 6, East End, 00802, tel. 809/775–6110 or 800/524–2001; fax 809/775–6110. 25 rooms. AE, MC, V. CP. Very Expensive.*

★ **Point Pleasant Resort.** Perched high over Smith Bay, affording a great view of St. John and Drake Passage to the east and north, this resort offers a range of accommodations, from simple bedrooms to multiroom suites scattered throughout several hillside units. The air-conditioned rooms have balconies, and all rooms have kitchens. Every guest gets four hours' free use of a car daily. There are monthly full-moon jazz concerts at the main pool. You can sign up for daily guided walks over the hilly property, which offers spectacular views of the B.V.I. and St. John. *Estate Smith Bay, 00802, tel. 809/775–7200, 800/524–2300, or 800/645–5306; fax 809/776–5694. 135 rooms. Facilities: restaurant, bar, 2 beaches, 3 pools, lighted tennis court, water sports. AE, MC, V. EP, MAP. Very Expensive.*

Bolongo Inclusive Beach Resort. Neighboring resorts Bolongo Bay Beach and Tennis Club and Limetree Beach Resort have combined into one megaresort. Oceanfront and garden-view rooms and villas all have air-conditioning, cable TV, VCR, phone, and an electronic safe. All villas have full kitchens, and many rooms have kitchenettes. All guests are part of Club Everything; the room rates include full breakfast, airport transfers, shuttle to town, use of tennis courts, snorkel gear, canoes, Sunfish sailboats, windsurfing and paddleboats, a scuba lesson, and vouchers for an all-day sail, a cocktail cruise, and a half-day snorkel tour on one of the resort's yachts. Guests can also choose the All-Inclusive Club Everything rate (3-night minimum), which includes lunch, dinner, and some drinks. The complimentary Kids Corner entertains the young ones all day. *50 Estate Bolongo, 00802, tel. 809/779–2844 or 800/524–4746; fax 809/775–3208. 225 units, from hotel rooms to 1–3-bedroom villas. Facilities: 5 restaurants, 3 pools, 2 beaches, 6 tennis courts, extensive health club, water sports, 2 night clubs, volleyball, shuffleboard. AE, DC, MC, V. BP, All-inclusive. Expensive–Very Expensive.*

Sugar Bay Plantation Resort. Sitting in the genteel lobby at this old plantation house-styled resort, with its white columns, potted palms, and soft breezes wafting down from the ceiling fans, it is hard to believe you are in a Holiday Inn Crown Plaza. Yet the guest rooms have the familiar Holiday Inn conveniences: TV with remote control, hair dryer, minirefrigerator, and a coffee maker with complimentary coffee. All rooms have a balcony, most with a view of the ocean. Children under 19 stay free when sharing a room with their parents. *Estate Smith Bay, 00802, tel. 809/777–7100 or 800/HOLIDAY; fax 809/777–7200. 300 rooms. Facilities: 3 pools, health club, beach, 2 restaurants, 4 bars, 5 tennis courts, snorkeling equipment. AE, MC, V. DC, Discover. BP, MAP. Very Expensive.*

Blackbeard's Castle. This small inn is laid out around a tower from which, it's said, Blackbeard kept watch on the horizon for invaders. A premier sunset-watching spot, it's an elegantly informal kind of place, where guests while away Sunday morning with the *New York Times*, crossword puzzles, and backgammon in the comfortable parlor. There's a freshwater pool overlooking the harbor. Charlotte Amalie is a short walk down the hill and beaches are close by. *Box 6041, Charlotte Amalie, 00801, tel. 809/776–1234; fax 809/776–4321. 20 rooms. Facilities: restaurant, bar, freshwater pool. AE, DC, MC, V. CP. Expensive.*

★ **Heritage Manor.** The four rooms in the vintage 1830 main structure of this European-style guest house have gleaming tiles, brass beds, and 12-foot ceilings with equally expansive windows. These rooms, along with the other four that cluster around a tiny gem of a pool and a courtyard, are all decorated with city theme prints (the "Tokyo Room" is coziness incarnate). Suites have refrigerators, and two rooms have kitchens. Guests should be cautious about wandering around after dark because the hotel is somewhat secluded. This is a place for those as interested in history as in the beach. Continental breakfast is complimentary during the winter season. *1A Snegle Gade, Charlotte Amalie, Box 90, 00804, tel. 809/774–3003 or 800/828–0757; fax 809/776–9585. 8 air-conditioned rooms, 4 with bath (another 4 rooms share 2 baths). Facilities: pool. AE, MC, V. CP. Moderate.*

Sign of the Griffin. If it's a house party you have in mind, you might want to consider these privately owned, furnished, one- and two-bedroom homes with great views on a hillside 500 feet above Tutu Bay. Each house has a fully equipped kitchen, telephone, private garden, and covered terrace. You'll need a car to get around from here. Maid service is provided on weekdays, and for stays of three weeks or more you'll receive a 10% discount. *Box 11668, 00801, tel. 809/775-1715. MC, V. EP. Moderate.*

Villa Blanca Hotel. Located above Charlotte Amalie on Raphune Hill, the hotel is surrounded by an attractive garden and has modern, balconied rooms with rattan furniture, kitchenettes, cable TVs, and ceiling fans. The eastern rooms face the Charlotte Amalie harbor; the western ones look out on rolling hills and a partial view of Drake's Channel and the B.V.I. *Box 7505, Charlotte Amalie, 00801, tel. 809/776-0749; fax 809/779-2661. 12 rooms. Facilities: pool. AE, MC, V. EP. Moderate.*

Hotel 1829. This historic Spanish-style hillside inn is popular with visiting government officials and people with business at Government House down the street. It's located on Government Hill, and has the pink-and-green facade you might expect from a hotel in the tropics. It is said author Graham Greene stayed here, and it's easy to imagine him musing over a drink in the small, dark bar. The restaurant is one of the most popular (and expensive) on the island. The rooms have a wet bar, TV, and air-conditioning. There's a small pool for cooling off after climbing the hill from town, and the bar offers five types of caviar (for a price) at happy hour. *Box 1567, Charlotte Amalie, 00801, tel. 809/776-1828 or 800/524-2002. 15 rooms. Facilities: restaurant, pool. AE, DC, MC, V. EP. Inexpensive–Very Expensive.*

Bunker Hill Hotel. The clean, air-conditioned rooms at this modestly furnished hotel are at different levels above the rooftops of the historic district and centered around a pool and terrace. All rooms have baths, and some have small balconies. The two suites have kitchens and broad porches. Because it is tucked in the quaint back streets of town (often deserted at night), be sure to take a taxi when returning after dark. Rates include complimentary breakfast. *9 Commandant Gade, Charlotte Amalie, 00802, tel. 809/774-8056; fax 809/774-3172. 15 rooms. Facilities: pool, restaurant, kitchenettes, TV. MC, V. BP. Inexpensive.*

Island View Guest House. This clean, simply furnished guest house rests amid tropical foliage on the southern face of 1500-foot Crown Mountain, the highest point on St. Thomas. As a result, its pool and shaded terrace, where complimentary breakfast is served, have one of the most sweeping views of Charlotte Amalie harbor around. All rooms have some view of the harbor, but on the balconies of the six newer rooms (all of which have air-conditioning and ceiling fans) that are perched on the very edge of the hill, you feel suspended in midair. *Box 1903, 00801, tel. 809/774-4270 or 800/524-2023; fax 809/774-6167. 12 rooms with bath (the other two share a bath) and 3 rooms with kitchenettes. Facilities: pool. AE, MC, V. CP. Inexpensive.*

St. Croix
★ **Cormorant Beach Club.** Breeze-bent palm trees, hammocks, the thrum of North Shore waves, and a blissful sense of respected privacy rule here. The open-air public spaces are filled with tropical plants and comfy wicker furniture in cool peach and mint-green shades. Ceiling fans and tile floors add to the atmosphere at this top-shelf resort. The beachfront villa rooms are lovely, with dark wicker furniture, pale-peach walls, white-tile floors, and floral-print spreads and curtains; all rooms have a patio or balcony and telephone. Bathrooms stand out for their coral-rock–wall showers, marble-top double sinks,

and brass fixtures. Coffee is set out daily in the building breezeways, and you'll receive a "CBC" terry robe to wear when you walk to the beautifully ledged polygonal pool. The airy, high-ceiling restaurant is one of St. Croix's best. *4126 La Grande Princesse, Christiansted 00820, tel. 809/778–8920 or 800/548–4460; fax 809/778–9218. 34 rooms, 4 suites. Facilities: restaurant, bar, beach, pool, snorkeling, 2 tennis courts, library with TV and VCR, croquet lawns. AE, DC, MC, V. EP, FAP. Very Expensive.*

★ **Villa Madeleine.** This exquisite hotel on the East End opened in 1990 and has quickly earned a reputation as one of St. Croix's best. The main building was patterned after a turn-of-the-century West Indian plantation great house. Richly upholstered furniture, Oriental rugs, and fine architectural detail set the mood in the billiards room, in the austere library and sitting room, and at Cafe Madeleine, the resort's highly praised Continental restaurant. The great house sits atop a hill, on which private guest villas are scattered in both directions, affording views of the north and south shores. The villas' decor is modern tropical, with rattan and plush cushions, and many bedrooms have bamboo four-poster beds. Each villa has a full kitchen and a private swimming pool. Special touches in the rooms include 5-foot-square pink-marble showers and, in many cottages, hand-painted floral borders along the walls, done in splashy tropical colors. *Box 3109, Christiansted 00822, tel. 809/778–7377 or 800/548–4461; fax 809/773–7518. 43 villas. Facilities: restaurant, bar, private pools, billiards room, library, tennis court, concierge, nearby golf course. EP. Very Expensive.*

The Buccaneer. If you want a self-contained tropical beach resort offering golf, all water sports, tennis, a nature/jogging trail, shopping arcade, health spa, and several restaurants, this 300-acre property on the East End of the island is the place for you. A palm-tree–lined main drive leads to the large pink hotel at the top of a hill, and a number of smaller guest cottages, shops, and restaurants are scattered throughout the property's rolling, manicured lawns. Stroll through the elegant lobby, with its green-and-white marble checkerboard floor, into the open-air terrace, where guests can relax and take in the view. Most of the guest rooms in this former sugar plantation have been renovated to incorporate eye-catching marble or colorful tile floors; they also feature four-poster beds and massive wardrobes of pale wood, along with pastel fabrics and locally produced artworks. Spacious bathrooms are noteworthy for their marble bench showers and double sinks. All rooms have refrigerators and TVs. The hotel's newsletter informs guests of island tours, pig roasts, and musical performances on the terrace. *Box 218, Christiansted 00821–0218, tel. 809/773–2100 or 800/223–1108; fax 809/778–8215. 150 rooms. Facilities: 4 restaurants, beach, golf, health spa, 2 pools, 8 tennis courts (2 lighted), jogging trail, water sports, shopping arcade, in-room safes, holiday activities for children. AE, DC, MC, V. EP. Expensive–Very Expensive.*

Hotel on the Cay. This resort, situated on a tiny island off Christiansted, is the visual centerpiece of the town's harbor and has a fine beach that guests at other hotels visit by boat. Canals and ponds are set in landscaped gardens around the hotel. Guest rooms are unspectacular but comfortable and have telephones, small refrigerators, toasters, and coffee pots. Ferry service is frequent, and the sheltered beach is especially suitable for children. *Box 4020, Christiansted, 00820, tel. 809/*

773–2035 or 800/524–2035; fax 809/773–7046. 55 rooms. Facilities: 2 restaurants, 2 bars, pool, tennis court, water sports. AE, MC, V. EP. Expensive.

Sprat Hall. This 20-acre seaside Frederiksted property is a restored plantation estate, the oldest in the U.S.V.I. The homey, antiques-filled great house (no smoking, please) has guest rooms that harken back to more genteel days, with high-standing four-poster beds, antique furniture, and no air-conditioning. There are also family cottages on the grounds, but these are rather dingy and not in the same class as the great house rooms. The Hurd family also operates extensive horseback riding facilities here. A short walk from the grounds brings you to a sunny beachfront restaurant. *Box 695, Frederiksted 00841, tel. 809/772–0305 or 800/843–3584. 9 rooms, 8 suites. Facilities: restaurant, beach, horseback riding, water sports. AE. EP. Moderate–Expensive.*

Waves at Cane Bay. Owners Kevin and Suzanne Ryan have done wonders with this 25-year-old property since purchasing it in 1989. The two peach-and-mint-green buildings house simple, balconied guest rooms done in pastel tropical prints. Bathrooms are clean and spacious, and all rooms have kitchens or kitchenettes. The small inn caters to divers, who take advantage of the fine reef located just offshore, as well as couples. The hotel is rather isolated—you'll need a car to get to the nearest restaurant—but Cane Bay Beach is next door. The hotel's beachfront is rocky, though there is a small patch of sand at poolside for sunbathing. The pool itself is unusual, having been carved from the coral along the shore: The floor and one wall are concrete, but the seaside wall is made of natural coral, and the pool water is circulated as the waves crash over the side. *Box 1749, Kings Hill, 00851, tel. 809/778–1805 or 800/545–0603. 12 rooms, 1 suite, 8 with air-conditioning. Facilities: bar, pool, complimentary snorkeling gear, Tues. night all-you-can-eat BBQ, in-room safes. AE, MC, V. EP. Moderate–Expensive.*

★ **Club St. Croix.** Popular with honeymooners, this condominium resort north of Christiansted made a strong comeback from Hurricane Hugo: Newly refurbished inside and out, the studio, one-, and two-bedroom apartments are spacious and bright. Indian-print throw rugs and cushions complement the bamboo furniture and rough, white-tile floors; the modern decor is further highlighted by glass-top tables and mirrored closet doors. Penthouses have loft bedrooms reached by spiral staircases, and studios enlist Murphy beds in the sitting rooms. Every room has a full kitchen and a sun deck, with waterfront views of Christiansted and Buck Island. On the beach you'll find a poolside restaurant and bar and a dock. Guests can take a sunset sail or go snorkling with the hotel's 42-foot catamaran, the *Cruzan Cat. Estate Golden Rock, Christiansted 00820, tel. 809/773–4800 or 800/635–1533; fax 809/773–4805. 54 suites. Facilities: restaurant, bar, 3 tennis courts, conference room, dock, pool, whirlpool, laundry room, water sports. AE, MC, V. EP. Moderate.*

Hibiscus Beach Hotel. Found on the same stretch of palm tree–lined beach as its sister hotel, the Cormorant, Hibiscus Beach is the island's newest addition. Guest rooms are divided among five two-story pink buildings, each named for a tropical flower. All have views of the oceanfront, but request a room in the Hibiscus building—it's closest to the water. The rooms are tastefully furnished: white-tile floors and white walls are brightened with pink-striped curtains; bright, flowered bed spreads; and fresh-cut hibiscus blossoms. The bathrooms are nondescript but clean—both the shower stalls and the vanity mirrors are on the small side. Every room has a spacious balcony facing the sea. The staff is friendly and helpful, and the Tuesday night manager's party in the open-air bar/restaurant is a pleasant gathering. *Box 4131, La Grande Princesse 00820–4441, tel. 809/773–4042; fax 809/773–7668. 38 rooms with bath. Facilities: 2 rooms for the handicapped, 1 kitchenette-equipped room, bar, restaurant, pool, complimentary snorkel equipment, minibar, room safes. EP. Moderate.*

★ **Hotel Caravelle.** The lovely three-story Caravelle is your best bet for moderately priced lodging in Christiansted. All rooms have refrigerators and were recently redone in tasteful dusky blues and whites, with floral-print bedspreads and curtains and vaulted ceilings. Baths are clean and new, though the unique tile in the showers is a holdover from when the hotel was built, 22 years ago. Superior rooms overlook the harbor, but most rooms do have some sort of ocean view. Owners Sid and Amy Kalmans are friendly and helpful. *44A Queen Cross St., Christiansted, 00820, tel. 809/773–0687 or 800/524–0410; fax 809/778–7004. 43 rooms. Facilities: restaurant, bar, pool, water sports, conference room, gift shops, guest parking. AE, D, DC, MC, V. EP. Moderate.*

The Frederiksted. You can't miss by staying at this modern four-story inn. In the outdoor tile courtyard, the glass tables and yellow chairs of the hotel's bar and restaurant crowd around a small freshwater swimming pool where live music can be enjoyed Friday and Saturday nights. Yellow-stripe awnings and tropical greenery create a sunny, welcoming atmosphere. Steps at one side of the courtyard lead to the second floor's main desk and sun deck. The bright, pleasant guest rooms are outfitted with tiny balconies, bar refrigerators, and sinks and are decorated with light-color rattan furniture and print bedspreads. Bathrooms are on the small side but are bright and clean. The nicest rooms are those with an ocean view; these are also the only rooms that have a bathtub in addition to a shower. *20 Strand St., Frederiksted, 00840, tel. 809/773–9150 or 800/524–2025; fax 809/778–4009. 40 rooms. Facilities: restaurant, bar, outdoor pool, sun deck, live entertainment. AE, DC, MC, V. EP. Inexpensive.*

The Pink Fancy. This homey, restful place is located a few blocks west of the center of town in a much-less-touristy neighborhood. The oldest of the four buildings here is a 1780 Danish town house, and old stone walls and foundations enhance the setting. The inn's efficiency rooms are some of the loveliest guest rooms in town. Clean and well tended, all feature hardwood floors, tropical-print fabrics, wicker furniture, and air-conditioning. The hotel is laid out around the pool, where pink-and-white awnings throw shade over the patio and small bar. Complimentary breakfast and cocktails are included in room rates. *27 Prince St., Christiansted, 00820, tel. 809/773–8460 or 800/524–2045; fax 809/773–6448. 13 rooms. Facilities: bar, pool. MC, V. CP. Inexpensive.*

St. John
Hotels and Inns
★ **Caneel Bay Resort.** This 170-acre peninsula resort was originally part of the Durloo plantation owned by the Danish West India Company and at one time extended as far as Cinnamon Bay (*Caneel* is Danish for cinnamon). It was opened as a resort in 1936 and was bought by Laurance Rockefeller in the 1950s.

Attention is paid to every detail, and the grounds are immaculately maintained. The flamboyant trees here even seem to shed their blossoms neatly. There are seven beaches, three restaurants, and an 18th-century sugar mill. The spacious rooms have simple interiors and no telephone or TV. Jackets are requested for men (during winter season) in restaurants after 6 PM. Formerly an all-inclusive resort, Caneel Bay now offers a choice of rooms with all meals or none. *Box 720, Cruz Bay, 00830, tel. 809/776–6111 or 800/223–7637; fax 809/776–2030. 171 rooms. Facilities: 7 beaches, 3 restaurants, 11 tennis courts, water sports. AE, MC, V. EP, MAP. Very Expensive.*

Hyatt Regency St. John. This 34-acre property at Great Cruz Bay shuns the weathered, old-money elegance of Caneel and lays on the gloss and glitz to the point that even the landscaping looks freshly polished. It's a beautiful place: The grounds are positively irridescent, and the pool area is a sybarite's delight, with waterfalls and islands and a poolside bar. Spacious, well-appointed guest rooms line the beach and encircle the pool, while some suites and luxurious town houses are set back slightly from the water. Try the on-site Chow Bella restaurant's "transcultural" menu of Italian and Chinese specialties. There are morning, afternoon, and evening children's programs that include beach olympics, stargazing, island tours, and arts and crafts. *Box 8310, Great Cruz Bay, 00830, tel. 809/776–7171 or 800/323–7249; fax 809/779–4985. 285 rooms. Facilities: beach, marina, 3 restaurants, pool, water sports, fitness room, tennis. AE, DC, MC, V. EP, MAP. Very Expensive.*

★ **Gallows Point Suite Resort.** These soft-gray buildings with peaked roofs and shuttered windows grace the peninsula south of the Cruz Bay ferry dock. The garden apartments have skylit, plant-filled showers big enough to frolic in. The upper-level apartments have loft bedrooms. Daily maid service is included. The entranceway is bridged by Ellington's restaurant. *Box 58, Cruz Bay, 00831, tel. 809/776–6434 or 800/323–7229; fax 809/776–6520. 60 rooms. Facilities: beach, pool, snorkeling. AE, DC, MC, V. EP. Expensive.*

Raintree Inn. If you want to be right in the center of the action in town and bunk at an affordable, island–style place, go no farther. The dark-wood rooms, some with air-conditioning, have a nicely simple, tropical-cabin decor. Three efficiencies here have kitchens and—if you don't mind climbing an indoor ladder—a comfortable sleeping loft. The Fish Trap restaurant is next door. *Box 566, Cruz Bay, 00831, tel. and fax 809/776–7449 or 800/666–7449. 11 rooms. AE, DC, MC, V. EP. Moderate–Inexpensive.*

The Inn at Tamarind Court. If you can just barely afford a vacation on St. John, try this inexpensive hostelry located on the east side of town. It's especially suited to singles. Its mismatched furnishing and somewhat shabby decor reflect the prices, but if saving money outweighs appearances, this is a good choice. Choose among traditional hotel rooms (some with shared bath), suites, or a one-bedroom apartment. The front-courtyard bar is a friendly hangout, as well as home to one of Cruz Bay's best West Indian restaurants. Continental breakfast is included. *Box 350, Cruz Bay, 00831, tel. 809/776–6378. 20 rooms, some with shared bath. Facilities: restaurant and bar. AE, D, MC, V. CP. Inexpensive.*

Homes and Villas **Caribbean Villas and Resorts** (Box 458, Cruz Bay 00830, tel. 809/776–6152 or 800/338–0987, fax 809/779–4044) is the island's largest short-term villa rental agent, with some 60 homes available on St. John. Its luxury properties are usually within a mile or two of Cruz Bay and are often right on the beach. **Vacation Vistas** (Box 476, Cruz Bay 00831, tel. 809/776–6462) has a smaller roster of select waterview properties, ranging from the extravagant (an indoor swimming pool and retractable living room walls that draw back to bring the indoors outside) to the merely lovely. **Destination St. John** (Box 37, Cruz Bay 00831, tel. 809/774–3843 or 800/562–1901) represents a number of properties, all perched high on hills overlooking fine views. **Catered To, Inc.** (Box 704, Cruz Bay 00831, tel. 809/776–6641, fax 809/779–6191) represents a number of luxury homes, many of which have pools and beach access. Other home-rental agents on the island include **Private Homes for Private Vacations** (Mamey Peak 00830, tel. 809/776–6876), **Paradise Hideaways** (Box 149, Cruz Bay 00831, tel. 809/776–6518), and **Vacation Homes** (Box 272, Cruz Bay 00831, tel. 809/776–6094).

Condominiums Among the condominiums controlled by Caribbean Villas and Resorts (see *above*) are **Cruz Views, Battery Hill, Pastory Estates,** and **Cruz Bay Villas,** all of which have dynamite ocean views from their one- and two-bedroom units. The 12 units at **Lavender Hill Estates** (Box 3606, Cruz Bay 00831, tel. 809/776–6969) are just a few minutes' walk into the center of town. Affordable **Serendip** (Box 273, Cruz Bay 00831, tel. 809/776–6646), just a short drive outside town, is a bit shabby but is certainly a good budget option. The luxurious **Virgin Grand Villas** (Great Cruz Bay 00830, tel. 809/775–3856, fax 809/779–4760) are somewhat removed from the Virgin Grand Resort, though guests at these 1-, 2-, and 3-bedroom town houses and villas have full use of the facilities at the Hyatt.

Campgrounds **Maho Bay Camp.** Eight miles from Cruz Bay, this private
★ campground is a lush hillside community of three-room tent cottages (canvas and screens) linked by boardwalks, stairs, and ramps that also lead down to the beach. The 16-by-16-foot shelters have beds, dining table and chairs, electric lamps (and outlets), propane stove, ice cooler, kitchenware, and cutlery. The camp has the chummy feel of a retreat and is very popular, so book well in advance. *Cruz Bay, 00830, tel. 212/472–9453, or 800/392–9004. 113 tent cottages. Facilities: beach, restaurant, commissary, barbecue areas, bathhouses (showers, sinks, and toilets), water sports. No credit cards. Moderate.*

Cinnamon Bay Campground. Tents, cottages with four one-room units in each cottage, and bare sites are available at this National Park Service location surrounded by jungle and set at the edge of big, beautiful Cinnamon Bay Beach. The tents are 10 feet by 14 feet, with flooring, and come with living, eating, and sleeping furnishings and necessities; the 15-by-15-foot cottages have twin beds. Bare sites, which come with a picnic table and a charcoal grill, must be reserved no earlier than eight months prior to arrival. You can reserve by phone with a credit card. The bare sites are cheap—at press time just $14 a site—but, if you're thinking of this option for budgetary reasons alone, be warned: the tent sites and cottages range from around $62 to $79 for two people per night. *Cruz Bay, 00830–0720, tel. 809/776–6330 or 800/223–7637. 44 tents, 40 cottages, 26 bare sites. Facilities: beach, commissary, bathhouses (showers and toilets), cafeteria, water sports. AE, MC, V. Inexpensive–Moderate.*

Nightlife

Nightlife in the U.S.V.I. is a spontaneous affair. Although there are many tourist-oriented cultural shows that can make for a fun night out—including Calypso Carnival at the Reef and some broken-bottle dancing at various hotels—socializing is what nightlife is about. Most of the music scene takes place in small clubs with dance floors.

St. Thomas
Nightspots

The **Atrium** at the Windward Passage Hotel (tel. 809/774–5200). Call the hotel to find out who is playing in the courtyard.

At **Barnacle Bill's** (tel. 809/774–7444), Bill Grogan has turned this Crown Bay landmark with the bright-red lobster on its roof into a musicians' home away from home.

Castaways (tel. 809/776–8410) is the watering hole and dance floor for the crews, owners, and those chartering the fleet of boats anchored at Yacht Haven.

Club 2 (tel. 809/776–4655) is a disco-style club located on Contant Hill, with a spectacular view of glittering harbor lights to enjoy on the terrace between dances.

The Old Mill (tel. 809/776–3004) located in—you guessed it—an old mill, is a lively spot with a small dance floor and a good sound system.

At **Walter's Living Room** (tel. 809/776–3880) on Back Street, you may find a late-night jam going on. Back Street can be a little dicey late at night, so keep your wits about you.

Piano Bars

The Mark (tel. 809/774–5511) and **Blackbeard's Castle** (tel. 809/776–1234), both atop Blackbeard's Hill; **Fiddle Leaf** (tel. 809/775–2810), on Government Hill; and **Raffles** (tel. 809/775–6004), on the East End, offer piano bars, each with its own flavor. The player at Raffles has been entertaining with his show "Gray, Gray, Gray" for many years and shouldn't be missed.

Point Pleasant (Smith Bay, tel. 809/775–7200). From its perch atop a cliff looking out across the Pillsbury Sound at Tortola, Point Pleasant's view is stupendous. When the moon is full Point Pleasant offers Full Moon Jazz, usually with top-name talent.

St. Croix

Christiansted has a lively and eminently casual club scene near the waterfront. At **Hondo's Backyard** (53 King St., tel. 809/778–8103) you'll hear live guitar and vocals in an open-air courtyard with a bar and Cinzano umbrella-covered tables. The upstairs **Moonraker Lounge** (43A Queen Cross St., tel. 809/773–1535) presents a constant calendar of live music, usually a singer with an acoustic guitar playing all your favorites, from Jimmy Buffet to Bob Dylan. Milder piano music can be heard on the broad veranda of **Club Comanche** (1 Strand St., tel. 809/773–0210). To party under the stars, head to the **Wreck Bar** (tel. 809/773–6092), on Christiansted's Hospital Street, for crab races as well as rock and roll. At **Calabash** (Strand St., tel. 809/778–0001) you'll find steel band music from Wednesday through Saturday, and on Friday there's a broken bottle dancer. **Hotel on the Cay** (Protestant Cay, tel. 809/773–2035) has a West Indian Buffet on Tuesday nights that features a broken bottle dancer and Mocko Jumbie. On Thursday nights, the **Cormorant** (La Grande Princess, tel. 809/778–8920) throws a similar event.

Although less hopping than Christiansted, Frederiksted restaurants and clubs have a variety of weekend entertainment. **Blue Moon** (17 Strand St., tel. 809/772–2222), a waterfront restaurant, is the place to be for live jazz on Friday 9 PM–1 AM. The island's premiere calypso band, Blinky and the Roadmasters, performs every Sunday night at **Stars of the West** (14 Strand St., tel. 809/772–9039). The **Lost Dog Pub** (King St., tel. 809/772–3526) is a favorite spot for a casual drink, a game of darts, and occasional live rock and roll on Sunday nights. Head north of town to the **Sand Bar** (Estate La Grange, no phone) on Sunday night to hear Green Flash play rock and roll. For another outdoor lime, head up to Mahogany Road to the **Mt. Pellier Hut Domino Club** (50 Mt. Pellier, tel. 809/772–9914). Piro, the one-man band, plays on Sunday.

St. John   Some friendly hubbub can be found at the rough-and-ready **Backyard** (tel. 809/776–8553), *the* place for sports watching as well as grooving to Bonnie Raitt et al. There's calypso and reggae on Wednesday and Friday at **Fred's** (tel. 809/776–6363). The **Courtyard Bar and Grill** at the Inn at Tamarind Court (tel. 809/776–6378) serves up a blend of jazz and rock on Friday and reggae on Saturday.

Notices on the bulletin bar across from the **U.S. Post Office** and at **Connections** (and on telephone poles) will keep you posted on special events: comedy nights, movies, and the like.

Index

Personal Itinerary

Departure *Date*

Time

Transportation

Arrival *Date*   *Time*

Departure *Date*   *Time*

Transportation

Accommodations

Arrival *Date*   *Time*

Departure *Date*   *Time*

Transportation

Accommodations

Arrival *Date*   *Time*

Departure *Date*   *Time*

Transportation

Accommodations

Personal Itinerary

Arrival *Date*   *Time*

Departure *Date*   *Time*

Transportation

Accommodations

Arrival *Date*   *Time*

Departure *Date*   *Time*

Transportation

Accommodations

Arrival *Date*   *Time*

Departure *Date*   *Time*

Transportation

Accommodations

Arrival *Date*   *Time*

Departure *Date*   *Time*

Transportation

Accommodations

Addresses

Name	*Name*
Address	*Address*
Telephone	*Telephone*
Name	*Name*
Address	*Address*
Telephone	*Telephone*
Name	*Name*
Address	*Address*
Telephone	*Telephone*
Name	*Name*
Address	*Address*
Telephone	*Telephone*
Name	*Name*
Address	*Address*
Telephone	*Telephone*
Name	*Name*
Address	*Address*
Telephone	*Telephone*
Name	*Name*
Address	*Address*
Telephone	*Telephone*
Name	*Name*
Address	*Address*
Telephone	*Telephone*

Escape to ancient cities and exotic

islands  *with CNN Travel Guide, a*

wealth of valuable advice. Host Valerie Voss will take you

to all of your favorite destinations,

including those off the beaten path.

Tune into your passport to the world.

CNN TRAVEL GUIDE
SATURDAY 10:00 PMᴘᴛ   SUNDAY 8:30 AMᴇᴛ

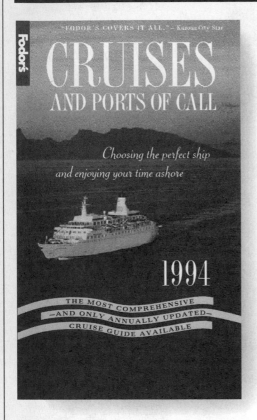

Announcing the only guide to explore a Disney World you've never seen before:

The one for grown-ups.

This terrific new guide is the only one written specifically for the millions of adults who visit Walt Disney World each year <u>without</u> kids. Upscale, sophisticated, packed full of facts and maps, *Walt Disney World for Adults* provides up-to-date information on hotels, restaurants, sports facilities, and health clubs, as well as unique itineraries for adults, including: a Sporting Life Vacation, Day-and-Night Romantic Fantasy, Singles Safari, and Gardens and Natural Wonders Tour. Get essential tips and everything you need to know about reservations, packages, annual events, banking service, rest stops, and much more. With *Walt Disney World for Adults* in hand, you'll get the most out of one of the world's most fascinating, most complex playgrounds.

At bookstores everywhere, or call 1-800-533-6478

Fodor's

Fodor's Travel Guides

Available at bookstores everywhere, or call 1–800–533–6478, 24 hours a day.

U.S. Guides

Alaska

Arizona

Boston

California

Cape Cod, Martha's Vineyard, Nantucket

The Carolinas & the Georgia Coast

Chicago

Colorado

Florida

Hawaii

Las Vegas, Reno, Tahoe

Los Angeles

Maine, Vermont, New Hampshire

Maui

Miami & the Keys

New England

New Orleans

New York City

Pacific North Coast

Philadelphia & the Pennsylvania Dutch Country

The Rockies

San Diego

San Francisco

Santa Fe, Taos, Albuquerque

Seattle & Vancouver

The South

The U.S. & British Virgin Islands

The Upper Great Lakes Region

USA

Vacations in New York State

Vacations on the Jersey Shore

Virginia & Maryland

Waikiki

Walt Disney World and the Orlando Area

Washington, D.C.

Foreign Guides

Acapulco, Ixtapa, Zihuatanejo

Australia & New Zealand

Austria

The Bahamas

Baja & Mexico's Pacific Coast Resorts

Barbados

Berlin

Bermuda

Brazil

Brittany & Normandy

Budapest

Canada

Cancun, Cozumel, Yucatan Peninsula

Caribbean

China

Costa Rica, Belize, Guatemala

The Czech Republic & Slovakia

Eastern Europe

Egypt

Euro Disney

Europe

Europe's Great Cities

Florence & Tuscany

France

Germany

Great Britain

Greece

The Himalayan Countries

Hong Kong

India

Ireland

Israel

Italy

Japan

Kenya & Tanzania

Korea

London

Madrid & Barcelona

Mexico

Montreal & Quebec City

Morocco

Moscow & St. Petersburg

The Netherlands, Belgium & Luxembourg

New Zealand

Norway

Nova Scotia, Prince Edward Island & New Brunswick

Paris

Portugal

Provence & the Riviera

Rome

Russia & the Baltic Countries

Scandinavia

Scotland

Singapore

South America

Southeast Asia

Spain

Sweden

Switzerland

Thailand

Tokyo

Toronto

Turkey

Vienna & the Danube Valley

Yugoslavia

Fodor's Travel Guides

Available at bookstores everywhere, or call 1–800–533–6478, 24 hours a day.

Special Series

Fodor's Affordables

Caribbean

Europe

Florida

France

Germany

Great Britain

London

Italy

Paris

Fodor's Bed & Breakfast and Country Inns Guides

Canada's Great Country Inns

California

Cottages, B&Bs and Country Inns of England and Wales

Mid-Atlantic Region

New England

The Pacific Northwest

The South

The Southwest

The Upper Great Lakes Region

The West Coast

The Berkeley Guides

California

Central America

Eastern Europe

France

Germany

Great Britain & Ireland

Mexico

Pacific Northwest & Alaska

San Francisco

Fodor's Exploring Guides

Australia

Britain

California

The Caribbean

Florida

France

Germany

Ireland

Italy

London

New York City

Paris

Rome

Singapore & Malaysia

Spain

Thailand

Fodor's Flashmaps

New York

Washington, D.C.

Fodor's Pocket Guides

Bahamas

Barbados

Jamaica

London

New York City

Paris

Puerto Rico

San Francisco

Washington, D.C.

Fodor's Sports

Cycling

Hiking

Running

Sailing

The Insider's Guide to the Best Canadian Skiing

Skiing in the USA & Canada

Fodor's Three-In-Ones (guidebook, language cassette, and phrase book)

France

Germany

Italy

Mexico

Spain

Fodor's Special-Interest Guides

Accessible USA

Cruises and Ports of Call

Euro Disney

Halliday's New England Food Explorer

Healthy Escapes

London Companion

Shadow Traffic's New York Shortcuts and Traffic Tips

Sunday in New York

Walt Disney World and the Orlando Area

Walt Disney World for Adults

Fodor's Touring Guides

Touring Europe

Touring USA: Eastern Edition

Fodor's Vacation Planners

Great American Vacations

National Parks of the East

National Parks of the West

The Wall Street Journal Guides to Business Travel

Europe

International Cities

Pacific Rim

USA & Canada

WHEREVER YOU TRAVEL, $\mathscr{H}$ELP IS NEVER FAR AWAY.

From planning your trip to providing travel assistance along the way, American Express® Travel Service Offices* are always there to help.

ANTIGUA
Antours, St. John's
BWIA Sunjet House
Long & Thames Streets
809-462-4788

ARUBA
S.E.L. Maduro & Sons
Oranjestad
Rockefellerstraat 1
297-823-888

BARBADOS
Barbados International Travel
Bridgetown
McGregor Street
809-431-2423

CAYMAN ISLANDS
Cayman Travel Services
Shedden Road
Elizabethan Square
809-949-8755

CURAÇAO
S.E.L. Maduro & Sons
Willemstad
Breedes Straat
599-961-6212

DOMINICAN REPUBLIC
American Express, Santo Domingo
Avda. J.F. Kennedy #3
809-563-3233

GUADELOUPE
Petrelluzzi Travel, Pointe-à-Pitre
2 Rue Henry IV
590-830-399

JAMAICA
Stuart's Travel, Montego Bay
32 Market Street
809-952-4350

MARTINIQUE
Roger Albert Voyages, Fort-de-France
7 Rue Victor Hugo
596-715-555

PUERTO RICO
Travel Network, San Juan
1035 Ashford Ave.
809-725-0950

TRINIDAD & TOBAGO
The Travel Centre, Port-of-Spain
Uptown Mall, Level 2, Edward Street
809-625-4266

American Express Travel Service Offices* are also found in the following locations:

DOMINICA	HAITI	ST. LUCIA	TURKS & CAICOS
GRENADA	MONTSERRAT	ST. MAARTEN	VIRGIN ISLANDS
	ST. KITTS	ST. VINCENT	

INTRODUCING

At last, your own personalized list of what's going on in the cities you're visiting.

Keyed to the days when you're there, customized for your interests, and sent to you before you leave home.

Exclusive for purchasers of Fodor's Guides...

Introducing a revolutionary way to get customized, time-sensitive travel information just before your trip.

Now you can obtain detailed information about what's going on in each city you'll be visiting <u>before</u> you leave home—up-to-the-minute, objective information about the events and activities that interest you most.

Your Itinerary:
Customized reports available for 160 destinations

This is a special offer for purchasers of Fodor's guides – a customized Travel Update to fit your specific interests and your itinerary.

Travel Updates contain the kind of time-sensitive insider information you can get only from local contacts – or from city magazines and newspapers once you arrive. But now you can have the same information before you leave for your trip.

The choice is yours: current art exhibits, theater, music festivals and special concerts, sporting events, antiques and flower shows, shopping, fitness, and more.

The information comes from hundreds of correspondents and thousands of sources worldwide. Updated continuously, it's like having your own personal concierge or friend in the city.

You specify the cities and when you'll be there. We'll do the rest — personalizing the information for you the way no guidebook can.

It's the perfect extension to your Fodor's guide and the best way to make the most of your valuable travel time.

t
99
Rege
The a
in this
domain o
tion as Joe
worthwhile.
the performan
Tickets are usu
venue. Alternat
mances are cancel
given. For more info
Open-Air Theatre, Inn
NW1 4NP Open Air T
Tel: 935-5756. Ends: 9-11-
International Air Tattoo
Held biennially, the world'
military air display i
demostra-
tions, milit
bands

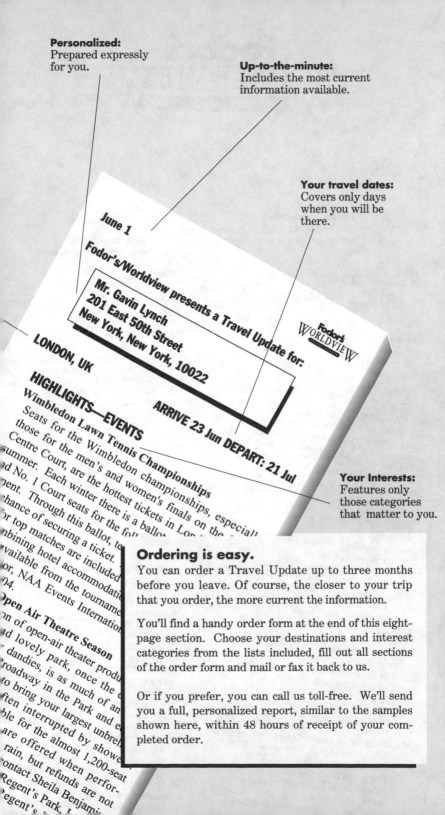

Personalized:
Prepared expressly
for you.

Up-to-the-minute:
Includes the most current
information available.

Your travel dates:
Covers only days
when you will be
there.

June 1

Fodor's/Worldview presents a Travel Update for:

Mr. Gavin Lynch
201 East 50th Street
New York, New York, 10022

Fodor's
WORLDVIEW

LONDON, UK

ARRIVE 23 Jun DEPART: 21 Jul

Your Interests:
Features only
those categories
that matter to you.

HIGHLIGHTS—EVENTS

Wimbledon Lawn Tennis Championships
Seats for the Wimbledon championships, especiall...
those for the men's and women's finals on the ...
Centre Court, are the hottest tickets in Lon...
summer. Each winter there is a ballo...
d No. 1 Court seats for the fol...
ent. Through this ballot, te...
hance of securing a ticket.
or top matches are included
nbining hotel accommodati...
vailable from the tournam...
or, NAA Events Internatio...
04.

Open Air Theatre Season
on of open-air theater produ...
d lovely park, once the ...
, dandies, is as much of an ...
roadway in the Park and ...
to bring your largest umbre...
ften interrupted by show...
ble for the almost 1,200-sea...
are offered when perfor...
rain, but refunds are not ...
ontact Sheila Benjami...
Regent's Park, ...
egent's ...

Ordering is easy.

You can order a Travel Update up to three months
before you leave. Of course, the closer to your trip
that you order, the more current the information.

You'll find a handy order form at the end of this eight-
page section. Choose your destinations and interest
categories from the lists included, fill out all sections
of the order form and mail or fax it back to us.

Or if you prefer, you can call us toll-free. We'll send
you a full, personalized report, similar to the samples
shown here, within 48 hours of receipt of your completed order.

**Special concerts—
who's performing
what and where**

**One-of-a-kind,
one-time-only events**

**Special interest,
in-depth listings**

Children — Events

Angel Canal Festival
The festivities include a children's funfair, entertainers, a boat rally and displays on the water. Regent's Canal. Islington. N1. Tube: Angel. Tel: 267 9100. 11:30am-5:30pm. 7/04.

Blackheath Summer Kite Festival
Stunt kite displays with parachuting teddy bears and trade stands. Free admission. SE3. BR: Blackheath. 10am. 6/27.

Megabugs
Children will delight in this infestation of giant robotic insects, including a praying mantic 60 times life size. Mon-Sat 10am-6pm; Sun 11am-6pm. Admission 4.50 pounds. Natural History Museum, Cromwell Road. SW7. Tube: South Kensington. Tel: 938 9123. Ends 10/01.

Childminders
This establishment employs only women, providing nurses and qualified nannies to

Music — Jazz & Blues

Tito Puente's Golden Men of Latin Jazz
The father of mambo and Cuban rumba king comes to town. Royal Festival Hall. South Bank. SE1. Tube: Waterloo. Tel: 928 8800. 8pm. 7/15.

Georgie Fame and The New York Band
Riding a popular tide with his latest album, the smoky-voiced Fame and his keyboard are on a tour yet again. The Grand. Clapham Junction. SW11. BR: Clapham Junction. Tel: 738 9000. 7:30pm. 7/07.

Jacques Loussier Play Bach Trio
The French jazz classicist and colleagues. Kenwood Lakeside. Hampstead Lane. Kenwood. NW3. Tube: Golders Green, then bus 210. Tel: 413 1443. 7pm. 7/10.

Tony Bennett and Ronnie Scott
Royal Festival Hall. South Bank. SE1. Tube: Waterloo. Tel: 928 8800. 8pm. 7/11.

Santana
Royal Festival Hall. South Bank. SE1. Tube: Waterloo. Tel: 928 8800. 8pm. 7/12.

Count Basie Orchestra and Nancy Wilson Trio
Royal Festival Hall. South Bank. SE1. Tube: Waterloo. Tel: 928 8800. 8pm. 7/14.

King Pleasure and the Biscuit Boys
Royal Festival Hall. South Bank. SE1. Tube: Waterloo. Tel: 928 8800. 6:30 and 9pm. 7/16.

Al Green and the London Community Gospel Choir
Royal Festival Hall. South Bank. SE1. Tube: Waterloo. Tel: 928 8800. 8pm. 7/13.

BB King and Linda Hopkins
Mother of the blues and successor to Bessi Smith, Hopkins meets up with "Blues Boy" King. Royal Festival Hall. South Bank. SE...

Music — Classical

Marylebone Sinfonia
Kenneth Gowen conducts music by Pucc... and Rossini. Queen Elizabeth Hall. So... Bank. SE1. Tube: Waterloo. Tel: 928 88... 7:45pm. 7/16.

London Philharmonic
Franz Welser-Moest and George Benjam... conduct selections by Alexander Goe... Messiaen, and some of Benjamin's own c... positions. Queen Elizabeth Hall. South B... SE1. Tube: Waterloo. Tel: 928 8800. 8pm...

London Pro Arte Orchestra and Forest Ch...
Murray Stewart conducts selection... Rossini, Haydn and Jonathan Willcocks. Queen Elizabeth Hall. South Bank. S... Tube: Waterloo. Tel: 928 8800. 7:45pm. ...

Kensington Symphony Orchestra
Russell Keable conducts Dvorak's Dr...

Here's what you get . . .

Detailed information about what's going on — precisely when you'll be there.

Show openings
during your visit

Reviews by
local critics

Exhibitions & Shows—Antique & Flower
Westminster Antiques Fair
  Over 50 stands with pre-1830 furniture and other Victorian and earlier items. Thu-Fri 11am-8pm; Sat-Sun 11am-6pm. Admission 4 pounds, children free. Old Royal Horticultural Hall. Vincent Square. SW1. Tel: 0444/48 25 14. 6-24 thru 6/27.

Royal Horticultural Society Flower Show
  The show includes displays of carnations, summer fruit and vegetables. Tue 11am-7pm; Wed 10am-5pm. Admission Tue 4 pounds, Wed 2 pounds. Royal Horticultural Halls. Greycoat Street and Vincent Square. SW1. Tube: Victoria. 7/20 thru 7/21.

ᴴᵃmpton Court Palace International Flower Show
  Major international garden and flower show ᵗᵃking place in conjunction with the British

Theater — Musical
Sunset Boulevard
  In June, the four Andrew Lloyd Webber musicals which dominated London's stages in the 1980s (Cats, Starlight Express, Phantom of the Opera and Aspects of Love) are joined by the composer's latest work, a show rumored to have his best music to date. The 1950 Billy Wilder film about a helpless young writer who is drawn into the world of a possessive, aging silent screen star offers rich opportunities for Webber's evolving style. Soaring, aching melodies, lush technical effects and psychological thrills are all expected. Patti Lupone stars. Mon-Sat at 8pm; matinee Thu-Sat at 3pm. In-person sales only at the box office; credit card bookings, Tel: 344 0055. Admission 15-32.50 pounds. Adelphi Theatre. The Strand. WC2. Tube: Charing Cross. Tel: 836 7611. Starts: 6/21

Leonardo A Portrait of Love
  A new musical about the great Renaissance artiˢ and inventor comes in for a London premierᵉ tested by a brief run at Oxford's Old Fire Statiᵒ autumn. The work explores the relationˢ Vinci and the woman '

Albercquerque • Atlanta • Atlantic City • N
Baltimore • Boston • Chicago • Cincinnati
Cleveland • Dallas/Ft.Worth • Denver • De
• Houston • Kansas City • Las Vegas • Los
Angeles • Memphis • Miami • Milwaukee •
New Orleans • New York City • Orlando •
Springs • Philadelphia • Phoenix • Pittsburg
Portland • Salt Lake • San Antonio • San Di
• San Franc
Oslo • Wash
Hawaii • Kauai • Maui • Abacos • Bimini
Ber
Antigua & B

Fodor's
WORLDVIEW
TRAVEL UPDATE

Spectator Sports — Other Sports
Greyhound Racing: Wembley Stadium
  This dog track offers good views of greyhound racing held on Mon, Wed and Fri. No credit cards. Stadium Way. Wembley. HA9. Tube: Wembley Park. Tel: 902 8833.

Benson & Hedges Cricket Cup Final
  Lord's Cricket Ground. St. John's Wood Road. NW8. Tube: St. John's Wood. Tel: 289 1611. 11am. 7/10.

Business-Fax & Overnight Mail
Post Office, Trafalgar Square Branch
  Offers a network of fax services, the Intelpost system, throughout the country and abroad. Mon-Sat 8am-8pm, Sun 9am-5pm. William IV Street. WC2. Tube: Charing
Cross. Tel: 930 0580.

Gorda • Barbados • Dominica • Grer
ᵃcia • St. Vincent • Trinidad &Tobago
ᵧmans • Puerto Plata • Santo Doming
Aruba • Bonaire • Curacao • St. Maᵃ
ᵉc City • Montreal • Ottawa • Torot
Vancouver • Guadeloupe • Martiniqu
ᵉlemy • St. Martin • Kingston • Ixta
ᵗᵒ Bay • Negril • Ocho Rios • Ponce
ⁿ • Grand Turk • Providenciales • S
St. John • St. Thomas • Acapulco •
& Isla Mujeres • Cozumel • Guadal
ᵃ • Los Cabos • Manzinillo • Mazatl
City • Monterrey • Oaxaca • Puerto
ᵈᵒ • Puerto Vallarta • Veracruz • Ix
ᵈam • Athens • Barcelona •

Interest Categories

For your personalized Travel Update, choose the categories you're most interested in from this list. Every Travel Update automatically provides you with *Event Highlights* – the best of what's happening during the dates of your trip.

1.	**Business Services**	Fax & Overnight Mail, Computer Rentals, Photocopying, Secretarial , Messenger, Translation Services

Dining

2.	**All Day Dining**	Breakfast & Brunch, Cafes & Tea Rooms, Late-Night Dining
3.	**Local Cuisine**	In Every Price Range—from Budget Restaurants to the Special Splurge
4.	**European Cuisine**	Continental, French, Italian
5.	**Asian Cuisine**	Chinese, Far Eastern, Japanese, Indian
6.	**Americas Cuisine**	American, Mexican & Latin
7.	**Nightlife**	Bars, Dance Clubs, Comedy Clubs, Pubs & Beer Halls
8.	**Entertainment**	Theater—Drama, Musicals, Dance, Ticket Agencies
9.	**Music**	Classical, Traditional & Ethnic, Jazz & Blues, Pop, Rock
10.	**Children's Activities**	Events, Attractions
11.	**Tours**	Local Tours, Day Trips, Overnight Excursions, Cruises
12.	**Exhibitions, Festivals & Shows**	Antiques & Flower, History & Cultural, Art Exhibitions, Fairs & Craft Shows, Music & Art Festivals
13.	**Shopping**	Districts & Malls, Markets, Regional Specialities
14.	**Fitness**	Bicycling, Health Clubs, Hiking, Jogging
15.	**Recreational Sports**	Boating/Sailing, Fishing, Ice Skating, Skiing, Snorkeling/Scuba, Swimming
16.	**Spectator Sports**	Auto Racing, Baseball, Basketball, Football, Horse Racing, Ice Hockey, Soccer

Please note that interest category content will vary by season, destination, and length of stay.

Destinations

The Fodor's/Worldview Travel Update covers more than 160 destinations worldwide. Choose the destinations that match your itinerary from this list. (Choose bulleted destinations only.)

United States (Mainland)
- Albuquerque
- Atlanta
- Atlantic City
- Baltimore
- Boston
- Chicago
- Cincinnati
- Cleveland
- Dallas/Ft. Worth
- Denver
- Detroit
- Houston
- Kansas City
- Las Vegas
- Los Angeles
- Memphis
- Miami
- Milwaukee
- Minneapolis/ St. Paul
- New Orleans
- New York City
- Orlando
- Palm Springs
- Philadelphia
- Phoenix
- Pittsburgh
- Portland
- St. Louis
- Salt Lake City
- San Antonio
- San Diego
- San Francisco
- Seattle
- Tampa
- Washington, DC

Alaska
- Anchorage/Fairbanks/Juneau

Hawaii
- Honolulu
- Island of Hawaii
- Kauai
- Maui

Canada
- Quebec City
- Montreal
- Ottawa
- Toronto
- Vancouver

Bahamas
- Abacos
- Eleuthera/ Harbour Island
- Exumas
- Freeport
- Nassau & Paradise Island

Bermuda
- Bermuda Countryside
- Hamilton

British Leeward Islands
- Anguilla
- Antigua & Barbuda
- Montserrat
- St. Kitts & Nevis

British Virgin Islands
- Tortola & Virgin Gorda

British Windward Islands
- Barbados
- Dominica
- Grenada
- St. Lucia
- St. Vincent
- Trinidad & Tobago

Cayman Islands
- The Caymans

Dominican Republic
- Puerto Plata
- Santo Domingo

Dutch Leeward Islands
- Aruba
- Bonaire
- Curacao

Dutch Windward Islands
- St. Maarten

French West Indies
- Guadeloupe
- Martinique
- St. Barthelemy
- St. Martin

Jamaica
- Kingston
- Montego Bay
- Negril
- Ocho Rios

Puerto Rico
- Ponce
- San Juan

Turks & Caicos
- Grand Turk
- Providenciales

U.S. Virgin Islands
- St. Croix
- St. John
- St. Thomas

Mexico
- Acapulco
- Cancun & Isla Mujeres
- Cozumel
- Guadalajara
- Ixtapa & Zihuatanejo
- Los Cabos
- Manzanillo
- Mazatlan
- Mexico City
- Monterrey
- Oaxaca
- Puerto Escondido
- Puerto Vallarta
- Veracruz

Europe
- Amsterdam
- Athens
- Barcelona
- Berlin
- Brussels
- Budapest
- Copenhagen
- Dublin
- Edinburgh
- Florence
- Frankfurt
- French Riviera
- Geneva
- Glasgow
- Interlaken
- Istanbul
- Lausanne
- Lisbon
- London
- Madrid
- Milan
- Moscow
- Munich
- Oslo
- Paris
- Prague
- Provence
- Rome
- Salzburg
- St. Petersburg
- Stockholm
- Venice
- Vienna
- Zurich

Pacific Rim Australia & New Zealand
- Auckland
- Melbourne
- Sydney

China
- Beijing
- Guangzhou
- Shanghai

Japan
- Kyoto
- Nagoya
- Osaka
- Tokyo
- Yokohama

Other
- Bangkok
- Hong Kong & Macau
- Manila
- Seoul
- Singapore
- Taipei

Fodor's WORLDVIEW Order Form

THIS TRAVEL UPDATE IS FOR (Please print):

Name

Address

City	State	ZIP

Country	Tel # ( ) -

Title of this Fodor's guide:

Store and location where guide was purchased:

INDICATE YOUR DESTINATIONS/DATES: Write in below the destinations you want to order. Then fill in your arrival and departure dates for each destination.

		Month	Day		Month	Day
(Sample) LONDON	From:	6 /	21	To:	6 /	30
1	From:	/		To:	/	
2	From:	/		To:	/	
3	From:	/		To:	/	

You can order up to three destinations per Travel Update. Only destinations listed on the previous page are applicable. Maximum amount of time covered by a Travel Update cannot exceed 30 days.

CHOOSE YOUR INTERESTS: Select up to eight categories from the list of interest categories shown on the previous page and circle the numbers below:

1   2   3   4   5   6   7   8   9   10   11   12   13   14   15   16

CHOOSE HOW YOU WANT YOUR TRAVEL UPDATE DELIVERED (Check one):

❏ Please mail my Travel Update to the address above **OR**

❏ Fax it to me at **Fax #** ( ) -

DELIVERY CHARGE (Check one)

	Within U.S. & Canada	Outside U.S. & Canada
First Class Mail	❏ $2.50	❏ $5.00
Fax	❏ $5.00	❏ $10.00
Priority Delivery	❏ $15.00	❏ $27.00

All orders will be sent within 48 hours of receipt of a completed order form.

ADD UP YOUR ORDER HERE. *SPECIAL OFFER FOR FODOR'S PURCHASERS ONLY!*

	Suggested Retail Price	Your Price	This Order
First destination ordered	$13.95	$ 7.95	$ 7.95
Second destination (if applicable)	$ 9.95	$ 4.95	+
Third destination (if applicable)	$ 9.95	$ 4.95	+
Plus delivery charge from above			+
		TOTAL:	$

METHOD OF PAYMENT (Check one):   ❏ AmEx   ❏ MC   ❏ Visa   ❏ Discover
❏ Personal Check   ❏ Money Order

Make check or money order payable to: Fodor's Worldview Travel Update

Credit Card #   **Expiration Date:**

Authorized Signature

SEND THIS COMPLETED FORM TO:
Fodor's Worldview Travel Update, 114 Sansome Street, Suite 700, San Francisco, CA 94104

OR CALL OR FAX US 24-HOURS A DAY
Telephone **1-800-799-9609** • Fax **1-800-799-9619** (From within the U.S. & Canada)
(Outside the U.S. & Canada: Telephone 415-616-9988 • Fax 415-616-9989)

(Please have this guide in front of you when you call so we can verify purchase.)

Offer valid until 12/31/94.